A COMMENTARY ON
THE PSALMS

KREGEL EXEGETICAL LIBRARY

A COMMENTARY ON
THE PSALMS

Volume 3 (90–150)

Allen P. Ross

A Commentary on the Psalms: Volume 3 (90–150)

© 2016 by Allen P. Ross

Published by Kregel Publications, a division of Kregel, Inc., 2450 Oak Industrial Dr. NE, Grand Rapids, MI 49505-6020.

All rights reserved. No part of this book may be reproduced, stored in a retrieval system, or transmitted in any form or by any means—electronic, mechanical, photocopy, recording, or otherwise—without permission of the publisher, except for brief quotations in printed reviews.

The English translations of the original Greek or Hebrew texts of the Bible are the author's own. The traditional renderings have been retained as much as possible because of the use of the psalms in churches, but the English has been modernized where appropriate.

The Hebrew font used in this book is NewJerusalemU and the Greek font is TeubnerLSCU; both are available from www.linguisticsoftware.com/lgku.htm, +1-425-775-1130.

Library of Congress Cataloging-in-Publication Data
Ross, Allen P.
    Commentary on the Psalms / Allen P. Ross.
        p. cm.
    1.Bible. O.T. Psalms—Commentaries. I. Bible. O.T. Psalms. English. New International. 2011. II. Title.
      BS1430.53.R67 2011
      223'.2077—dc22

2010028703

ISBN 978–0–8254–2666–7

Printed in the United States of America
16 17 18 19 20 / 5 4 3 2 1

To my aunt and uncle,
The Reverend Leonard and Beatrice Sukut,
for a lifetime given to ministering the Word of God
in exposition and music

CONTENTS

Preface for Volume 3 / 11

Abbreviations / 13

Psalm 90   Learning To Live Wisely / 19

Psalm 91   Secure in the Shadow of the Almighty / 43

Psalm 92   Confidence in the Goodness of the LORD / 61

Psalm 93   The Everlasting Reign of the LORD / 75

Psalm 94   Vindication through Divine Retribution / 91

Psalm 95   Unbelief or Rest / 111

Psalm 96   The Exalted King / 129

Psalm 97   Preparing for the Coming of the LORD / 145

Psalm 98   Celebration of the LORD's Reign / 161

Psalm 99   Exalt the Holy One of Israel / 173

Psalm 100   Jubilant Praise to the LORD Our Maker / 185

Psalm 101   The King's Righteous Reign / 195

Psalm 102   An Urgent Plea to the Eternal God of Heaven / 205

Psalm 103   God's Gracious Benefits for Frail and Sinful Believers / 225

Psalm 104	The Wisdom of the LORD's Manifold Creation	/ 241
Psalm 105	Praise for the Fulfillment of the Promises of the Covenant	/ 257
Psalm 106	God's Great and Gracious Acts for His Rebellious People	/ 275
Psalm 107	Praise from the Redeemed of the LORD for His Loving Care	/ 295
Psalm 108	Victory through God's Faithful Love	/ 311
Psalm 109	Divine Vengeance and Vindication	/ 321
Psalm 110	The Exaltation and Glorious Victory of the Coming King	/ 337
Psalm 111	Adoration and Praise for the LORD's Great and Gracious Works	/ 361
Psalm 112	The Blessings for the Righteous	/ 373
Psalm 113	God's Greatness Displayed in His Grace	/ 385
Psalm 114	The Supernatural Formation of the Nation	/ 397
Psalm 115	The Trustworthiness of the LORD Versus the Futility of Idols	/ 409
Psalm 116	Precious to the LORD is the Death of His Saints	/ 421
Psalm 117	Universal Praise for God's Faithful Love	/ 433
Psalm 118	Jubilant Praise for Deliverance and a New Beginning	/ 439
Psalm 119	The Word of the LORD and the Life of Faith	/ 459
Psalm 120	Longing to Dwell in Peace	/ 597
Psalm 121	Protection on the Pilgrim Way	/ 609
Psalm 122	The Joyful Journey to the City of God	/ 623
Psalm 123	Earnestly Expecting Divine Favor	/ 635
Psalm 124	The LORD Is On Our Side	/ 641

Psalm 125 The Security of the Believer / 649

Psalm 126 The Great Joy and Chief Concern of the Redeemed / 661

Psalm 127 Living under Divine Providence / 675

Psalm 128 The Blessed Life / 691

Psalm 129 Faith that Overcomes Affliction / 699

Psalm 130 There Is Forgiveness with God / 707

Psalm 131 Humility and Trust / 719

Psalm 132 The Glorious Future of God's Program / 725

Psalm 133 The Blessing of Unity / 745

Psalm 134 Blessing the LORD and Blessing His People / 753

Psalm 135 Praise for the LORD of Creation and History / 761

Psalm 136 Praise for the LORD's Enduring Love / 773

Psalm 137 By the Rivers of Babylon / 785

Psalm 138 The Demonstration of the LORD's Glory in His Care for the Lowly / 799

Psalm 139 The Perceiving, Pursuing, Planning God / 811

Psalm 140 An Imprecation against the Ungodly / 837

Psalm 141 A Righteous Prayer for Protection from a Sanctified Believer / 851

Psalm 142 No One Cares, except the LORD / 865

Psalm 143 Deliverance and Guidance / 877

Psalm 144 A Prayer for Peace and Prosperity / 889

Psalm 145 Praise for the Kingdom of the LORD, Its Greatness and Its Grace / 907

Psalm 146 Praise for the Faithfulness of the Sovereign Creator / 919

Psalm 147 God's Gracious Restoration, Sovereign Rule, and Powerful Word / 929

Psalm 148 Praise in the Heavens and on Earth / 941

Psalm 149 A Hymn of Triumph for the Final Victory / 951

Psalm 150 Let Everything Praise the LORD / 961

Index of Hebrew Word Studies / 971

Selected Bibliography for the Exposition of the Psalms / 977

PREFACE FOR VOLUME 3

Although this volume completes my commentary on the Book of Psalms, no work on the Psalter can be said to be complete. There still remain questions about difficult words and constructions, uncertainties about the translation of the tenses, and different proposals about the structure and setting of the psalms. And so there must be periodic updates with corrections and clarifications as research on this material continues. The expositor can be confident nonetheless that the messages of the psalms are clear and understandable, but must be cautious in some of the details where there are unresolved difficulties.

As I said in the preface to the first volume, I have written this commentary with pastors, teachers and serious students of the Bible in mind. That has guided my choices in how to present the material and how much detail to include, knowing that not all who use this commentary will have expertise in the biblical languages or foreign language resources. The selections made for the bibliography included in this third volume were made with that same idea in mind—what resources will be helpful and practical for biblical expositors to use in their study of the psalms. There were many resources that were popularly written, and many that were very technical; my selections for the most part lie between these two descriptions, sometimes popular and sometime technical, but mostly what I considered most helpful for anyone studying the Psalter seriously.

I grew up reading and studying the Bible. But it was in my second year in seminary that my approach was changed. I took a course called Hymnic Literature, basically on the psalms, taught by Dr. Bruce Waltke with the assistance of Dr. Haddon Robinson. There were six of us in the class and each of us was assigned four psalms for the semester. In turn we would write an exegetical paper and then preach an expository sermon on on each of those four psalms. After each exposition, Professor Waltke would evaluate the exegesis and Professor Robinson the exposition. We worked through 24 psalms that semester in that way. In a later discussion Professor Waltke said he did not think that was a very good class. But for me it transformed my reading of the psalms, my exegesis, and my expository preaching forever. And so in writing this commentary the influence of these two professors was constantly present in my mind; my goal has been not simply to interpret the passage, but to demonstrate a method that has proven to be effective, not just to me but to countless others who preach the word.

ABBREVIATIONS

Symbols
//	parallel lines of poetry; the point of division between them
=	the equivalent of
<	derived from

A
AJBL	*Annual of the Japanese Biblical Institute*
AJSL	*American Journal of Semitic Languages and Literature*
ANET	*Ancient Near Eastern Texts (J. B. Pritchard)*
AnOr	*Analecta orientalia*
AO	*Archiv orientalni*
Aquila	Greek version made about 130 A.D.
ASTI	*Annual of the Swedish Theological Institute*
ASV	American Standard Version, 1901
ATR	*Anglican Theological Review*
AUSS	*Andrews University Seminary Studies*
AV	Authorized Version

B
BArch	*Biblical Archaeologist*
BASOR	*Bulletin of American Schools of Oriental Research*
BBR	*Bulletin for Biblical Research*

ABBREVIATIONS

BDB	*A Hebrew and English Lexicon of the Old Testament* (F. Brown, S. R. Driver and C. A. Briggs; Oxford University Press. 1907)
BH3	Biblia Hebraica (ed. by Kittel)
BHS	Biblia Hebraica Stuttgartensia
Bib	*Biblica*
BibSac	*Bibliotheca Sacra*
BibV	*Biblical Viewpoint*
Bijdr	*Bijdragen Tijdschrit voor filosophie en theologie*
BiTod	*Bible Today*
BJRL	*Bulletin of the John Rylands Library*
BR	*Bible Review*
BSOAS	*Bulletin of the School of Oriental and African Studies*
BT	*Bible Translator*
BTB	*Biblical Theological Bulletin*
BZ	*Biblische Zeitschrift*
BZAW	*Beihefte zur ZAW*

C

CBQ	*Catholic Biblical Quarterly*
CJT	*Canadian Journal of Theology*
CTJ	*Calvin Theological Journal*
CTM	*Concordia Theological Monthly*

E

e.g.	for example
EncBib	*Encyclopedia Biblica*
EncJud	*Encyclopedia Judaica*
ESV	English Standard Version
EvQ	*Evangelical Quarterly*
EvTh	*Evangelische Theologie*
ExT	*Expository Times*

F

FS	*Festschrift*, a collection of articles in honor of someone

G

GKC	*Gesenius' Hebrew Grammar* (ed. by E. Kautzsch, trans. by A. E. Cowley, Oxford: Clarendon, 1910)

ABBREVIATIONS

Greek	The Old Greek version, Septuagint (LXX)
Greek[A]	Greek, Alexandrinus
Greek[B]	Greek, Vaticanus
Greek[S]	Greek, Sinaiticus
Greek[L]	Greek, Luciant
GTJ	Grace Theological Journal

H

HALOT	The Hebrew and Aramaic Lexicon of the Old Testament (ed. by Ludwig Koehler, Walter Baumgartner, et al, Leiden: Brill, 2001)
HAR	Hebrew Annual Review
HBT	Horizons in Biblical Theology
HeyJ	Heythrop Journal
HTR	Harvard Theological Review
HTS	Harvard Theological Studies
HUCA	Hebrew Union College Annual

I

IB	Interpreter's Bible
ICC	International Critical Commentary
IDB	Interpreter's Dictionary of the Bible
i.e.	that is
IEJ	Israel Exploration Journal
Int	Interpretation
ITQ	Irish Theological Journal

J

JANES	Journal of Ancient Near Eastern Studies
JAOS	Journal of the American Oriental Society
JBL	Journal of Biblical Literature
JBQ	Jewish Bible Quarterly
JBR	Journal of the Bible and Religion
JEOL	Jaarsberichte v. h. Vooraziatische-Egyptisch Genootschop 'Ex Oriente Lux'
JETS	Journal of the Evangelical Theological Society
JJS	Journal of Jewish Studies
JNES	Journal of Near Eastern Studies
JNSL	Journal of Northwest Semitic Languages

ABBREVIATIONS

JPS	*Jewish Publication Society*
JQR	*Jewish Quarterly Review*
JRel	*Journal of Religion*
JSNT	*Journal for the Study of the New Testament*
JSOT	*Journal of the Study of the Old Testament*
JSS	*Journal of Semitic Studies*
JTS	*Journal of Theological Studies*
Jud	*Judaica*

K

k^{e}thîv	what is written, the letters in the manuscript for words where the vowels are from the oral tradition (see also *q^{e}rê*)
KBL³	*Lexicon in Veteris Testamenti Libros* (3rd edition, ed. by Ludwig Koehler and Walter Baumgartner, Lieden: Brill, 1997)
KJV	King James Version

L

LSJ	*A Greek-English Lexicon* (ed. by Liddell, Scott, and Jones, Oxford: Clarendon, 1925–40; addenda and corrigenda, 1968; supplement, 1996)

M

ms(s)	manuscript(s)
MT	Masoretic Text, the received Hebrew text printed in BHS

N

NASB	New American Standard Version of the Bible
NBD	*New Bible Dictionary*
nd	no date
NEB	New English Bible
NIDOTTE	*New International Dictionary of Old Testament Theology and Exegesis* (ed. by Willem A. VanGemeren, Grand Rapids: Zondervan, 1997)
NIV	New International Version
NJPS	*New Jewish Publication Society*
NJV	New Jewish Publication Society Version

ABBREVIATIONS

NLT	New Living Translation
NovT	*Novum Testamentum*
NRSV	New Revised Standard Version
ns	new series
NT	New Testament
NTS	*New Testament Studies*

O
Or	*Orientalia*
OT	Old Testament
OTS	*Oudtestamentische Studien*
OTSt	*Old Testament Studies*

P
PIH	*Psalterium iuxta hebraeos* (Jerome's translation from the Hebrew)
PTR	*Princeton Theological Review*

Q
Q	Qumran, as in 11QPs^a (the Psalm a scroll found in Qumran, cave 11)
q^{e}rê	what is read, the oral tradition of a word written with the letters in the text; the vowels under the letters go with the word to be read

R
RB	*Revue biblique*
ResQ	*Restoration Quarterly*
RevExp	*Review and Expositor*
RSV	Revised Standard Version
RTR	*Reformed Theological Review*

S
SBL	Society of Biblical Literature
SBTh	*Studia Biblica et Theologica*
Sem	*Semeia*
SJOT	*Scandanavian Journal of Theology*
SJT	*Scottish Journal of Theology*
SP	Samaritan Pentateuch

StTh	*Studia Theologica*
s.v.	under the word, meaning see under
Symmachus	Greek version made near the end of second century A.D.
Syriac	the Bible of the ancient Syriac Church

T

Targum	ancient Aramaic paraphrases of the Hebrew Bible
TDOT	*Theological Dictionary of the Old Testament* (ed. by G. J. Botterweck and H. Ringgren, Grand Rapids: Eerdmans, 2003)
Theodotion	Greek version made in the early second century A.D.
ThL	*Theologische Literaturzeitung*
ThT	*Theology Today*
ThZ	*Theologische Zeitschrift*
TLOT	*Theological Lexicon of the Old Testament* (ed. by Ernst Jenni and Claus Westermann, Peabody: Hendrickson, 1997)
TynB	*Tyndale Bulletin*

U

UF	*Ugaritische Forschungen*

V

Vaticanus	Codex Vaticanus (B), Greek uncial manuscript of the Bible, 325–350 A.D.
VT	*Vetus Testamentum*
Vulgate	ancient Latin Bible, traced to Jerome

W

WTJ	*Westminster Theological Journal*
WW	*Word and World*

Z

ZAW	*Zeitschrift für die alttestamentliche Wissenschaft*
ZNW	*Zeitschrift für die neutestamentliche Wissenschaft*

PSALM 90
Learning To Live Wisely

INTRODUCTION

Text and Textual Variants

A Prayer of Moses, the Man of God.

1 Lord, you have been our dwelling place[1]
    throughout all generations.[2]
2 Before the mountains were brought forth,[3]

---

1. מָעוֹן has the sense of a dwelling place that is a refuge— a safe place. A few manuscripts have מָעוֹז, which is more of a stronghold or place of refuge; there is little difference in the general meaning of the line. The Greek version (and Vulgate) has "refuge," καταφυγή. Dahood connects the word to an Arabic cognate "give aid, help"; his translation is "mainstay" (*Psalms*, II:322, 172). Tate chooses the translation "help" (Psalms 51–100, p. 431).
2. Literally, "in generation and generation." Many manuscripts and the Syriac have "to generation and generation."
3. For the passive in the MT, יֻלָּדוּ the Greek translation uses γενηθῆναι, "existed, came to be." But the parallelism favors the MT.

19

or you gave birth to[4] the earth and the world,
and[5] from everlasting to[6] everlasting you are God.[7]
3 You turn[8] people[9] back to dust,
and you said,[10] "Return, you mortals."[11]
4 For a thousand years in your sight
are like a day, yesterday[12] when it passes,[13]
and like[14] a watch in the night.

---

4. The MT has the active וַתְּחוֹלֵל, "and/or you brought forth." The Greek version has the passive, πλασθῆναι, "were formed," which would reflect תְּחוֹלַל (so also Aquila, Symmachus, Jerome, and others). The passive makes a closer parallelism to the first line, which may be why it was assumed to be the reading. Some commentators prefer the passive rather than having the colon change to make the LORD the subject; A. A. Anderson acknowledges that ultimately it is the LORD who created everything, even in texts that use birth imagery, but concludes that in this passage the agent is the earth itself (*Psalms 73–150*, p. 650).
5. Many manuscripts and some versions omit the conjunction.
6. Many manuscripts, the Syriac and Vulgate have "and unto."
7. The word "God" in the text is אֵל. The Greek version took it to be the negative אַל, and translated it μή but joined it to the next line. That left simply "you are," σὺ εἶ
8. The MT has the *hiphil* תָּשֵׁב, "you turn (people/man)," a jussive form used for an imperfect; but the Greek version joins the negative and reads μὴ ἀποστρέψῃς "do not turn (people/man) away."
9. The word in the text is אֱנוֹשׁ, "man."
10. The form in the MT is the preterite with *waw* consecutive: וַתֹּאמֶר. The BHS editors propose reading it as a regular imperfect, וְתֹאמַר, "and you say" (with Aquila and Jerome). The change is not necessary since the form in the text could be translated as an English present tense as well.
11. The text has בְּנֵי־אָדָם, "sons/descendants of man."
12. The text has "a day formerly," meaning "yesterday."
13. The MT has an imperfect tense; the Greek and Syriac have a past tense—the Greek is διῆλθεν, "(that) passed," which might reflect a past form of עָבַר. See further C. Westermann, "Psalm 90: A Thousand Years Are But As Yesterday," in *The Living Psalms*, translated by J. R. Porter (Grand Rapids: Eerdmans, 1989), pp. 156–65.
14. Symmachus, the Syriac and Targum have "like"; in the MT and Greek it is implied.

5 You sweep them away,[15] they are *as* a sleep;[16]
   in the morning *they are* like grass *that* springs forth—[17]
6 *though* in the morning it flourishes and springs forth,[18]
   at the evening[19] it is cut down and withered.[20]

7 We are consumed by your anger
   and terrified by your indignation.

---

15. The translation of verses 5 and 6 have received a good deal of attention because at first reading they do not seem to flow naturally. As translated, the first colon says that God sweeps (people) away, meaning that they die, so that they are (as a) sleep. Then the second colon reiterates that they may flourish for a time, but quickly pass away. The verb זָרַם, translated here as "sweep away," has the idea of pouring out or flooding, as of water that rushes along (but an apparent Arabic cognate means "cut [them] off"). The idea of pouring out has been interpreted here as "sweep away." Tate suggests translating it as a temporal clause, with the meaning "pour" and the object "sleep": "when you pour sleep on them" (p. 433). The verb "they are" is then taken with the second colon. The relation between the ideas would then be that when God brings death (i.e., sleep) on people, they quickly fade away. This reading may be a little smoother but does not change the meaning of the verse that much. Other views vary significantly. One takes the line to read "their issue (progeny) will be a sleep" (T. Booj, "Psalm 90, 5–6: Junction of Two Traditional Motifs," *Bib* 68 [1987]:393–96); another suggests "emission of the bladder are they" (D. W. Thomas, "A Note on זְרַמְתָּם שֵׁנָה יִהְיוּ in Psalm XC 5," *VT* 18 [1986]:267, 8). Another changes "sleep" to "change" to get "their offspring changes, as grass" (C. Whitley, "The Text of Psalm 90, 5," *Bib* 63 [1982]:555–57). And another has, "You pour sleep on them, and they are like grass which fades away. In the morning it sprouts and grows, in the evening it withers and is parched" (Matitiahu Tsevat, "Psalm XC 5–6," *VT* 35 [1985]:115–17).
16. The text is very cryptic here; it simply has שֵׁנָה יִהְיוּ, "sleep are they," or "they are *as a* sleep." The Greek version took שֵׁנָה to mean "years," and rendered the colon as τὰ ἐξουδενώματα αὐτῶν ἔτη ἔσονται, "years shall be their rejection" or "the object of their scorn." The editors of BHS propose שָׁנָה שָׁנָה, "year by year."
17. The MT has יַחֲלֹף; the verb means "pass on, disappear, wither." The Greek translation reads τὸ πρωὶ ἀνθήσαι καὶ παρέλθοι, "in the morning may it pass like young growth." In the context "pass on" may have the sense of proceeding or springing forth.
18. The Greek version has ἀνθήσαι "may it flourish (and pass)."
19. Several manuscripts and the Syriac have "and at the evening."
20. The Greek version adds a verb to the verse: "may it fall (ἀποπέσοι = יִבּוֹל, "shrink, drop"), wither and shrivel."

PSALM 90

8 You have set our iniquities before you,
     our secret *sins*[21] in the light of your presence.
9 All our days pass away under your wrath;
     we finish[22] our years with a sigh.[23]
10 The length of our days is seventy years—
     or eighty, if we have the strength;
   yet their span[24] is but trouble and sorrow,
     for they pass quickly[25] and we fly away.

11 Who knows the power of your anger?
     For your wrath is as great as the fear that is due you.
12 Teach *us* to number our days aright,
     that we may gain a heart of wisdom.[26]

---

21. The text simply has "our secrets" (עֲלֻמֵנוּ), but the context indicates it is referring to sins. Dahood, following Briggs, interprets the line to read "sins of our youth" (II:321). The Greek version has ὁ αἰὼν ἡμῶν, "our age/lifetime"; it then reads the rest as "became lit up by your countenance." All these readings are from different roots with the same letters עָלַם.
22. The form in the MT is the *piel* כִּלִּינוּ with a direct object: "we finish our years." The Greek version reads the verse as "For all our days expired (ἐξέλιπον), and in your wrath we expired (ἐξελίπομεν)." The rest of the verse ("our years with a sigh") was joined to the next colon (fn 23).
23. Instead of "with a sigh" (הֶגֶה), the Greek version read a verb "ponder"; "our years" became its object; and a prepositional phrase was added for clarification: ὡς ἀράχνην ἐμελέτων "(our years) as a spider I would ponder (spin out like a cobweb)."
24. The MT has וְרָהְבָּם, meaning "and their pride." The versions have the idea of "and their width" or "span," which would reflect a Hebrew form וְרָחְבָּם, which may make a smoother reading, although "their pride" is not impossible. The Greek version has πλεῖον "greater part," perhaps thinking the form to be from רבב, "to be many."
25. The Hebrew text has כִּי־גָז חִישׁ וַנָּעֻפָה. The verb גוז means "pass along, disappear." Here the form is either the perfect tense or the participle; it would refer to "days," a plural form. The word could be taken collectively, or it could be adverbial, and the line translated: "indeed, declining rapidly, we fly away." The Greek version has this last line as "because meekness came upon us, and we shall become disciplined" (ὅτι ἐπῆλθεν πραΰτης ἐφ' ἡμᾶς καὶ παιδευθησόμεθα).
26. The translation of the verse in the Greek version reads: "Make us know how to reckon up your right hand and those fettered in heart by wisdom." The Hebrew verb (הוֹדַע) "cause to know" (i.e., "teach") was simply taken to mean "make known." But "our days" (יָמֵינוּ) was read as "your right hand"

13 Turn back,[27] O LORD! How long *will it be*?
   Have compassion on your servants.
14 Satisfy us[28] in the morning with your loyal love,
   that we may sing for joy and be glad all our days.[29]
15 Make us glad[30] for as many days as you have afflicted us,
   for as many years as we have seen trouble.
16 May your deeds appear[31] to your servants,
   your splendor[32] to their children.
17 May the beauty[33] of the LORD our God *be* upon us;

(יְמִינֶךָ). And "that we may gain" (וְנָבִא, the *hiphil*, "bring back, bring in") was translated "fettered." The editors of BHS propose reading with Aquila, Symmachus, Quinta, Jerome and the Syriac וְנָבִא בְלֵב, "and we will come with a heart . . . ." Others suggest, "we will bring wisdom into the heart." See Harold-Martin Wahl, "Psalm 90,12," *ZAW* 106 (1994):116–23.

27. שׁוּבָה is the imperative, "turn back" meaning "relent." The Greek version translated the word with ἐπίστρεψον, "bring back." But this idea is not completed with an object. See D. N. Freedman, "Who Asks (or Tells) God to Repent?" *Bible Review* 1 (1985):56–59.

28. For the imperative and the suffix, שַׂבְּעֵנוּ, "satisfy us," the Greek version assumed a perfect tense, 1cpl, and rendered it ἐνεπλήσθημεν, "we were filled." While it is easy to see how this choice occurred with an unpointed text, the resulting meaning does not harmonize with the meaning of the passage which is a prayer to be satisfied.

29. In harmony with its translation of the first verb of the verse, the Greek version has this colon read, "we rejoiced and were glad."

30. Here too the Greek translation took the form to be a perfect tense: εὐφράνθημεν, "we were glad" (assuming שָׂמַחְנוּ instead of MT's שַׂמְּחֵנוּ).

31. The form in the MT is יֵרָאֶה, the *niphal* imperfect form, 3msg. The meaning is "appear, be seen," "appear" working better with the following preposition "unto." And the singular verb is probably used collectively for the plural subject, "your deeds": "May your deeds appear/be shown to your servants." The Syriac version made the verb plural. The Greek translation has an imperative, καὶ ἰδὲ (= וּרְאֵה). Accordingly, the Greek translation has two objects for this verb: "and look upon your slaves and upon your works."

32. The MT has וַהֲדָרְךָ, "and your splendor." The Greek translation has καὶ ὁδήγησον, "and guide." It seems to have taken the word to be the *hiphil* imperative וְהַדְרֵךְ. In the MT the word "splendor" may have the meaning of a majestic vision, an appearance of the LORD in holiness (see Ps. 96:9 and 29:2). See J. D. Levenson, "A Technical Meaning for N'M in the Hebrew Bible," *VT* 35 (1985):61–67, esp. 3–4.

33. The word "beauty" is interpreted by Levenson (see above) to mean an affirmative, visible sign from God, i.e., meaning "approval."

establish[34] the work of our hands for us—
yes, establish the work of our hands.

Composition and Context

Psalm 90 is best taken as a communal lament, even though it has some characteristics of wisdom literature. The lament is written from the intense awareness of mortality and sin; apparently the nation had been enduring prolonged affliction from God because of sin, and so they cried out for God to put an end to it and instead give them a joyful and productive life. In spite of their terrifying awareness of human frailty, they hold fast to their faith in the everlasting God.

The psalm begins with an affirmation of their faith in a short hymn-like acknowledgment of the eternality of God. But the lament in verses 3–10 forms a contrast to this with a description of their fragile and fleeting life; the psalmist uniquely describes how the wrath of God for sin has brought trouble and sorrow to their lives. Verses 10 and 11 form a transition to the petition section: since they do not know the power of God's wrath and its relation to their morality, they ask God to teach them so that they will gain a heart of wisdom (v. 12). Here and throughout the psalm there is a clear influence of wisdom literature. In verses 13–17 they petition God to turn from his course of wrath, have compassion on them, and bless them with a joyful and productive life.

The psalm has been traditionally ascribed to Moses, the man of God (Deut. 31:1; Josh. 14:6). And yet, most commentators would place the writing of the psalm in the post-exilic period.[35] For example, Kirkpatrick took a later date for the composition; he based his conclusion on (1) the sense that it is hard to imagine Moses on the verge of entering the promised land saying verses 13–17, (2) that the psalm uses Deuteronomic language, and (3)

---

34. MT's כּוֹנְנָה, "establish," is a *polel* form from כּוּן. Levenson suggests that it could be translated "approve" (p. 64). The Greek translation interpreted it with κατεύθυνον, "prosper." It did not then repeat the verb, but ended the psalm with the second colon of the verse.
35. See further B. Vawter, "Post-exilic Prayer and Hope," *CBQ* 37 (1975):460–70.

that the psalm is in the last part of the collection.[36] Tate also concludes that the origin of the psalm was in the post-exilic communities who had suffered great affliction in exile for their sin and now prayed for God to change from wrath to favor.[37] And Von Rad, focusing on the wisdom elements, concludes that the psalm had links with post-exilic wisdom (like *Wisdom* 9:1–18; 15:1–3).[38]

Other commentators only tentatively suggest that the psalm is from a later period and not from Moses. Pointing to links with Deuteronomy 32 and 33, Goldingay says that the background of this psalm is from a later period of suffering, e.g., the exile, that was reckoned to be similar to the situation in Moses' time. The psalm then was written to indicate how Moses might pray for people in their present circumstances in the light of Exodus 32 and Deuteronomy 32–33; it is as if Moses himself had taken up the plea of Psalm 89.[39] VanGemeren too leans in this direction, saying that "the spirit of Moses' concern is certainly present in the psalm's deep sense of life's furtive passing, the connection between sin, suffering, and the wrath of God; and the submission of humanity in prayer for God's favor."[40] A. A. Anderson is much more cautious, saying that the ascription of the psalm to Moses may be (at least partly) an appreciation of the poem by a later generation.[41]

So the conclusion is that the psalm was written in the post-exilic period concerning the suffering in the exile; it was not simply attributed to Moses, but was written in the style that Moses would have used in the similar situation he had to experience in the wilderness wanderings.

The arguments given are plausible, of course, but none of them are convincing. The wisdom motifs do not demand a later

---

36. Kirkpatrick, *Psalms*, p. 548.
37. Tate, *Psalms* 51–100, p. 438. The connection to the exile does not completely satisfy the language of this psalm that laments the steady deaths over time because of sin and the need for divine compassion to change their lot in life. The communities of the returned exiles do not make a better fit for verses 13–17 than the Israelites in the wilderness.
38. Gerhard von Rad, "Psalm 90," pp. 210–23.
39. Goldingay, *Psalms* 90–150, pp. 23, 4.
40. *Psalms,* p. 689.
41. *Psalms 73–150*, p. 649.

II. Acknowledging that no one can understand the power of God's wrath, Moses appeals to God for instruction in planning a life that would reflect a heart of wisdom (11–12).
   A. He acknowledges that no one can understand the terrifying power of God (11).
   B. He asks God to teach him to number his days so that he will live wisely (12).
III. Moses prays for God's compassionate dealings with his servants so that joy will replace sorrow and human labor will meet with success (13–17).
   A. He calls for the LORD to turn in compassion to His servants (13).
   B. He specifies that the LORD should turn their sorrow into joy (14–15).
      1. If God would satisfy people with loyal love, they should rejoice all their days (14).
      2. God should make them glad according to their days of affliction (15).
   C. He also specifies that God should give them success in their labors (16–17).
      1. God's glorious work should be to his servants (16).
      2. God should establish the work of their hands (17).

COMMENTARY IN EXPOSITORY FORM

I. In contrast to the everlasting God, human life is brief because of God's anger over sin (1–10).

A. Human life is fragile and fleeting in contrast to the eternality of God (1–2).

The psalmist will lament the brevity and suffering of this life and then pray for relief and some time of blessing before it is over. But to lay the foundation for all of this, the writer begins with a short hymn addressed to God that focuses on the everlasting presence and provision of God—a striking contrast with fragile and fleeting human life. The beginning of the hymn is in fact an affirmation of faith: "Lord, you have been our dwelling place (מָעוֹן) throughout all generations." He addresses God as "Lord," emphasizing the sovereignty and majesty of God. And he identifies him as their dwelling place. This metaphor for a place of protection (see Deut. 33:27; Ps. 91:9) would have been most meaningful in the earlier setting when the newly formed nation of Israel had no home and no refuge apart from God. But this was no empty platitude, for God had proven himself to be both from generation to generation.[43]

God's constant presence with his people to protect and provide for them is consistent with his eternality. And so in the second verse the psalmist declares that the LORD is the everlasting God; the implication of this for the affirmation of verse 1 is that God's loving care for Israel is eternal. To stress the eternal nature of God the psalmist uses creation as a point of reference: before creation God was always the everlasting God. For his reflection on creation he uses birth imagery to stress that the LORD alone is the creator. The first colon uses the passive voice: "Before the mountains were brought forth" (יֻלָּדוּ; compare Prov. 8:25 where the earth is the subject). But the second colon uses the active voice and is more direct: "or you gave birth to (וַתְּחוֹלֵל) the earth and the world." It is unusual to say that God gave birth to the world, but in poetry it is not impossible to use such language to describe God as the source of all life (see Deut. 32:18). The two objects, "earth" (the general term אֶרֶץ) and "world" (the fruitful, inhabited world, תֵּבֵל), signify that God produced this planet and everything on it. So while the verse stresses the sovereignty of the LORD as creator, in this psalm the underlying point is that the eternal God precedes creation. And so the final affirmation of this little hymnic section keeps our attention on his eternality: "from everlasting to everlasting you are God." The doctrine of God in Scripture asserts that God has no beginning and no end—he is eternally present. Interestingly, although the Greek version incorrectly read the word "God" (אֵל) as the negative (אַל) and joined it to the next verse, it made perfectly good sense to the translator to read the remaining words as "from everlasting to everlasting you are." There is no other god who can compare. There is no other god.

---

43. Perowne, *Psalms,* II:164–5.

So while the faithful know all too well that human life is fragile and fleeting, they find comfort in the fact that God is always present. Their comfort is not simply in the fact that God is everlasting, but in the fact that this means he is their perpetual dwelling place.

B. The eternal God brings human life quickly to an end (3–6).

The tone of the psalm changes now to describe the lamentable frailty of humankind—people are but dust. Here is the contrast that clearly reveals God's sovereign authority: God outlasts the most enduring things in creation (v. 2), but humans return to dust (v. 3). God is the everlasting God, but he brings human life quickly to an end. Verse 3 states, "You turn (תָּשֵׁב; s.v. Ps. 126:1) people (אֱנוֹשׁ) back to dust." The verb has the jussive form (and has been taken as a jussive by some, a negated jussive in the Greek version to say "do not turn away"). But it is more appropriate in this lament section to interpret it as an indicative, a reference to the punishment of death. When sin entered the world and mankind's dream of divinity died, God announced that people were dust and would return to dust—they are not like God after all (Gen. 3:19). So creation out of the dust was reversed with the return to the dust. Here, however, the word for "dust" is stronger; the text (דַּכָּא) signifies the state of one crushed, and not merely returning to dust (עָפָר).

The second colon explains this action with the recording of a divine decree. It begins with the verb "you said" (וַתֹּאמֶר), which could be translated as an English present tense if it was interpreted to be a general reference to God's control over the extent of life. But it is probably better to take the form as a past tense (the preterite with the *waw* consecutive), for that would show that this act is subsequent to the first colon of the verse. The decree says, "Return (שׁוּבוּ), you mortals (בְּנֵי־אָדָם)." The decree is difficult and so open to various suggestions. Some commentators have chosen to give the decree a positive twist, making it either a call to repentance, or a call for a new generation to arise to life (the poetry in these cases would be antithetical parallelism). Anderson rejects these kinds of interpretations as unlikely, and takes the more natural interpretation that it is another reference to Genesis 3:19 and the divine decree that human beings will return to the dust. In this case the lines would form a more synonymous parallelism.[44] People may not think of the brevity of life when all is going well; but death comes quickly and they are quickly gone.

But for God the passing of time is different (v. 4). To him a thousand years is nothing. Two similes are used to attempt to explain this. The first is that to God a thousand years is like "a day formerly (yesterday) when it passes." It passes so quickly it is over before it is realized—to someone who is eternal it is nothing. The second simile compares a thousand years to a watch in the night. A watch is not the whole night; it lasts four hours. It may seem to go on and on, but is soon over (2 Pet. 3:8). If people lived to be a thousand, in God's sight it would be as a day, or less, a few hours. In the eternal plan, human life is so brief that it is almost insignificant.

And so in verse 5 we read, "You [God] sweep them away (זְרַמְתָּם), they are *as a* sleep." The verb suggests that people are so frail that they are easily swept away, as with a downpour, or with a flood (as the verb might indicate). But the verb is figurative for death in general: "You sweep them away, they are *as a* sleep." The relationship between the two clauses is not clearly stated, and so several suggested reconstructions of the line have been presented, some of which seem a little far-fetched. The idea seems to be that as soon as God sweeps people away, i.e., when they leave this life, they become sleep. "Sleep" is often figurative in the Bible for death (and so an implied comparison is in use here; see Dan. 12:2; Ps. 17:15 perhaps; Luke 8:52; John 11:11–14; Acts 7:60, and 1 Cor. 15:51). The point is that they pass over into the sleep of death—they become death.[45]

The rest of this verse and the next are problematic. In verse 5a we read that God sweeps people away into death, but in 5b we read that in the morning they are like grass that springs forth. The second half of the verse begins an illustrative restatement

---

44. *Psalms 73–150*, p. 651.
45. Tate takes this to mean a sleep that leads to death (*Psalms 51–100*, p. 441).

sentence for sin, which is both a curse and a blessing (that a cursed life will end). This psalm reminds us that as we live out this fragile and fleeting time on earth God is daily confronted by our sins. What we need, of course, is forgiveness for the sins and divine compassion for a longer and better life. But in this passage the focus is entirely on the sequence of sin, wrath, and judgment.[50]

Just how long, then, do people have before life slips away? Verse 10 says that the normal life expectancy is seventy years,[51] or eighty if by extraordinary strength (the plural גְּבוּרֹת being intensive; s.v. Ps. 45:3 for the word). This number fits the Israelite experience in the wilderness as Moses would be focusing on the general lifetime of the people. The adult population was condemned to wander for forty more years until they had passed off the scene, and the younger generation replaced them. As for Moses himself, he was extraordinary in that he lived much longer, which is why it is noted in Scripture.

So given this life expectancy, the psalmist then explains what those years are like: "yet their span is but trouble and sorrow." The form in the Hebrew Bible (וְרָהְבָּם) is "and their pride"; it would mean the pride of their years—all that they can boast of for those years. The variant reading (וְרָחְבָּם) is "their width," often rendered "their span." It would mean what all those years include. This is the proposed reading based on the versions. Although the meaning would be essentially the same with either word, the first word, "their pride," should not be quickly cast aside; it would say that even the best years they could boast were filled with trouble (עָמָל) and sorrow (אָוֶן; s.v. Ps. 28:3). But this troubled life is at least brief, for the time passes quickly (the participle גָּז [from גּוּז] meaning "to pass along, disappear," with the adverb חִישׁ, "quickly") and then we fly away (וַנָּעֻפָה). The implied comparison of death with flying away captures the idea of the fleeting life and the finality of death.

---

50. VanGemeren recalls how this is prominent in Moses' teaching (*Psalms*, p. 692; see Deut. 4:25–28; 5:9–11; 7:10; 9:19–26; 11:16–17; 17:2–5, 12; 18:19; 21:18–21; 27:15–26; 28:15–68).
51. Clifford suggests that this number is a reference to the time spent in the exile (*Psalms*, p. 96).

The detailed emphasis on sin, wrath and judgment in this psalm most likely arose out of a specific setting such as the wandering in the wilderness that was a time characterized by sorrow and unending deaths. But since the writer has not specified the occasion, it serves as a prayer that would be useful at any time of adversity when sorrow and death point so clearly to human sinfulness. The psalm is a reminder of God's rightful indignation over sins, that all are sinners and deserve divine wrath.[52] But when the collective sinfulness of the people is the focus, then the emphasis on wrath and judgment is compelling.

II. In view of the incomprehensible power of God's anger, people need God's instruction to use their time wisely (11–12).

A. People have to know the relationship between God's anger and the fear of God (11).

Verse 11 provides a transition to the petition section. It uses a rhetorical question (מִי־יוֹדֵעַ; for the verb, s.v. Ps. 67:2) to assert that no one knows the power of God's wrath. And this wrath is related to the fear that is due God (literally, "according to the fear of/due you *is* your wrath"). If more fear is due then more wrath comes, because it comes on disobedience that is evidence of a lack of fear of God. Anderson explains the verse to say, "(Who considers) according to his reverence for God, the (reasons) for divine wrath?" In other words, people seldom connect sin and mortality, and so they keep sinning.[53] But they should understand God's wrath as those who truly fear him do. VanGemeren observes that God's wrath is often ignored or explained away in times of trouble because the focus is usually on the suffering; but this prayer calls for a proper response to it all—we do not know the power of God's wrath, so God should enable us to know wisdom.[54]

---

52. VanGemeren, *Psalms*, p. 693.
53. *Psalms 73–150*, p. 654.
54. VanGemeren, *Psalms*, p. 693.

B. People can only pray for God to show them how to live their lives wisely (12).

When devout people measure God's anger for sin against their reverence (or lack of reverence) for God, they understand the reason for the anger. They also realize this is beyond their knowledge, for they have been ignorant of God's ways and unaware of their own sins. And so they must pray for divine instruction: "Teach us to number our days aright, that we may gain a heart of wisdom" (v. 12). Because people do not know the full power of God's wrath, they need to know how to live a life pleasing to God. And since wisdom begins with divine revelation, the appeal is for God to teach them (הוֹדַע, literally, "cause [us] to know"). How would God cause them to know? Certainly it would be through his word, but the communication of the truth of the word often came through priests and prophets who were charged with teaching Israel God's laws (e.g., the Levites according to Deut. 33:9–10). The object of this teaching is "to number (לִמְנוֹת) our days" (which is put first in the line for emphatic positioning). The word "days" means the events or activities on the days (so a metonymy of subject). And the infinitive "to number" means more than simply counting days; it includes planning, carrying out, and evaluating those activities in that period of time—70 or 80 years.[55] By teaching them to number their days, God would be making them realize how short, how fleeting, life actually is, and how important it is to plan out how to use that time.

And the result of this teaching would be the gaining of a heart of wisdom. The verb rendered "gain" is literally "that we may bring in" (וְנָבִא). The word "wisdom" (חָכְמָה; s.v. Ps. 19:7) has the sense of "skill"; in wisdom literature it describes a life that is disciplined, devout, and productive. People who live their lives with moral and ethical skill produce things that are honoring to God and beneficial to the community. A heart (s.v. Ps. 111:1) characterized by wisdom signifies a person who has the right affections and makes the proper choices—it is a life of faith. Anderson suggests that the colon may be understood to mean "that we may bring wisdom into our heart".[56] The prayer, then,

---
55. See Tate, p. 442; see also 1 Kings 20:25; Isaiah 53:12; and Psalm 147:4.
56. Tate. p. 654.

is that in view of the brevity of life, people need to learn how to use what God has given them to live a righteous and productive life. This is the essence of wisdom that is from above, a wisdom that will enable sinful people to live above the effects of the curse and produce a life that is pleasing to God. On the other hand, the wisdom of the world cannot please God.

III. In view of this transitory and troubled life, people also need God's compassion to give them a joyful and productive life (13–17).

A. They can only pray for God to turn and have compassion on them (13).

Now the psalmist prays for God to "return" or "turn back" from his course of judging his people in anger over their sins. The intensity of his prayer is developed in verses 13 and 14 with three imperatives followed by cohortatives: turn back, have compassion, satisfy us . . . that we may sing. The initial petition for God to "turn back" (שׁוּבָה) is a prayer for God's favor. The word was used earlier in the psalm for God's turning people back into dust in his anger; now it is used for God to turn back from that way (for a similar turn in meanings, see Jon. 3). The second half of the colon uses a familiar rhetorical question to stress the urgency of the appeal: "How long?"—"Turn back, O LORD; how long . . . ?" It expresses the lament that this affliction has been going on far too long. They want to know when the anger will cease.

How God should change or relent from this course of action is expressed by the second colon of the verse, an appeal for God to have compassion (וְהִנָּחֵם; s.v. Ps. 119:76) on his servants. This verb (נָחַם) in this (*niphal*) system, followed by the preposition "on" (עַל), usually means "to change one's mind." In another verbal system (*piel*) it means "to comfort." The meanings overlap somewhat; here the only way that God will turn from righteous judgment will be by a favorable compassion towards the people. And in this passage that change will be shown to people who although sinners are his servants—believers who are trying to please him.

life. Here is the dramatic reversal, for to live in the pleasure of God means that their labor is not in vain (1 Cor. 15:58).[58]

God's deeds of deliverance will endure as long as people call to him for compassion; and with his blessing the work of their hands will also be established.

MESSAGE AND APPLICATION

At first reading this psalm seems to be overwhelmingly depressing; but on closer analysis it is filled with confidence and hope. The psalm provides instruction for the righteous as they come face to face with their mortality, as they become aware of death all around them. The message of the psalm would be useful under the regular experiences of life and death, for in one sense all death is a result of the presence of sin in the world. But the focus of this psalm is on a situation that is far more serious. The nation had sinned grievously against the LORD, and as a result they were being consumed under his wrath. Accordingly, commentators are divided over the occasion, either the wilderness experience of Israel or the Babylonian exile, both of which would fit the intensity of God's anger and the increase in suffering and death. But in the midst of such suffering and death for sin, the faithful cling to their covenant relationship with the LORD and pray for him to turn their sad days into joyful and profitable days once again. So the words of the psalm imply an acknowledgment of sin and a genuine repentance. Their hope is not in themselves, but in the eternal God who has made a covenant with them. Their appeal challenges God in a sense: how can God let them perish when they are the people of his covenant, and he is their God?[59]

So a summary expository statement would be: *Because human life is so brief in contrast to the everlasting God, especially when people die prematurely because of God's anger for sin, the righteous can only pray to God to be compassionate and show them how to use their time wisely and thereby find joy and a productive life.*

---

58. Kidner, *Psalms* 73–150, p. 331.
59. Clifford, *Psalms*, p. 101.

In the final analysis, then, the psalm points us to the wonder of God's love: God can transform the weak and afflicted, here the guilty and fearful sinners, into joyful and productive servants. In other places the affliction will be a test and not the wrath of God for sin—there too God can change the circumstances by his compassion and love (see Ps. 44). But a prayer like this for God's compassion on all who have short and troubled lives requires an acknowledgment of sin and a desire to learn God's ways. And God will show his people how to fill their days with righteousness so that they enjoy his full blessing.

These themes are carried forward into the New Testament as well. Paul reminds the believers in Corinth that all these things were written to warn us not to sin as they did and perished in the wilderness (1 Cor. 10:5, 6 and 11). And in the book of Revelation, the letters to the churches are filled with warnings of God's dealings with collective disobedience (2:22 [suffering], 2:16 [decree of destruction], 2:23 [repay according to deeds], 3:5 [remove the witness], or 3:16 [spew out of his mouth]). While these warnings are concerned with collective disobedience as the psalm envisions, the warning would apply as well to individuals.

Likewise, Paul adapts the desire of this psalm to form an instruction: "Be very careful, then, how you live—not as unwise but as wise, making the most of every opportunity, because the days are evil. Therefore, do not be foolish, but understand what the Lord's will is" (Eph. 5:15–17 [NIV]).

PSALM 91

Secure in the Shadow of the Almighty

INTRODUCTION

***Text and Textual Variants*[1]**

1 He who dwells in the secret place[2] of the Most High
 will lodge in the shadow of the Almighty.[3]

---

1. The Greek version has a superscription: Αἶνος ᾠδῆς τῷ Δαυιδ, "A Praise, Of an Ode. Of David."
2. For MT's סֵתֶר, "hidden/secret place," the Greek translation has βοηθείᾳ, "help," perhaps an interpretation of the figure of speech—"who lives by the help of the Most High."
3. The Greek version interprets שַׁדַּי, "the Almighty," in this colon with ἐν σκέπῃ τοῦ θεοῦ τοῦ οὐρανοῦ, "(will lodge) in the shelter of the God of heaven."

14 "Because he loves me[20]
    I will rescue him;
   I will protect him,
     because he knows my name.
15 He will call upon me and I will answer him;
    I *will be* with him in trouble,
    I will deliver him and honor him.
16 With long life will I satisfy him
    and show him my salvation."

Composition and Context

In times of danger that far exceeds ordinary threats to life and represents the power of evil in the world, even believers can be shaken and live in fear. This psalm was written to provide the people of God with assurance that they would be kept safe and secure if they put their trust in the LORD and remained faithful to the covenant.[21] But the variety of images that are used in the psalm represent so many kinds of things that can happen to people it is difficult for everyone to accept these promises, especially if people have endured great suffering already—the psalm seems to them to be unconvincing or naive in its promises. And yet the psalmist does not diminish the promises of God, for that would call into question not only the word of the LORD but his nature as well. What is required is a precise analysis of the passage so that its message will not misapplied.

The psalm is probably anonymous, even though the Greek version attributes it to David (but there is nothing here that convincingly links it to David or his time). The passage therefore remains timeless—and with the variety of images for the threats its message is more applicable. Many commentators, however, would place it in the post-exilic period. Kirkpatrick said that since Psalm 90 was probably the plea of Israel in exile, and since

---

20. The word חָשַׁק means "cling to, be attached to, desire, love." The Greek version interpreted with "he hoped (in me)," ἤλπισεν. For this verse some translations supply "says the LORD" at the end of the first colon to clarify who the speaker is. But it seems clear enough without that addition.
21. Mowinckel suggests that the psalm is a divine answer to the petition of an afflicted person (*The Psalms in Israel's Worship*, II:102–3).

Psalm 92 is the praise deliverance from the exile, then Psalm 91 is the voice of faith ensuring safety for Israel as Babylon crumbles all around them.[22] But it would be possible as well to see the psalm in a pre-exilic setting when the nation experienced military or natural disasters. The psalmist draws on the experience of the ancestors in Egypt and in the wilderness to encourage them in their faith now (which is why the psalm was placed next to Psalm 90). God was fully able to protect his people from oppression, plagues and military attacks; but if Israel did not the trust him and obey his word, they would not be protected. Since the psalmist is speaking to and about faithful believers, his composition celebrates God's watchful and loving care for his people, who can therefore anticipate a peaceful and secure life. The psalm could come from almost any time when Israel was in need of God's protection and provision.

The first half of the psalm has similarities to wisdom literature; but the last half is more of an oracle from God, reiterating divine promises. The first half may be divided into three sections, verses 1–2 that express confidence, verses 3–8 that record the threats for which there is deliverance, and verses 9–13 that explain the deliverance as angelic. There are then three emphases: an expression of faith, the dangerous threats, and the promise of security. The second half of the psalm is a prophetic oracle in which God declares his presence with and protection of the people (14–16).

There may be a connection here with liturgies at the gate, for the psalm opens with the theme of dwelling securely in the presence of the LORD, and then includes instruction and promise. The dwelling of the LORD, the temple, is presented as the place to find true sanctuary, a place to which the psalmist and others could flee for refuge.[23] And perhaps some of the fears might have come from the anticipation of the pilgrimage to the holy city. But since there is no indication of the original occasion

---

22. *Psalms,* Books IV & V, p. 90. See also Andrew J. Schmutzer, "Psalm 91, Refuge, Protection and their Use in the New Testament," in *The Psalms, Language for All Seasons of the Soul*, ed. by A. J. Schmutzer and David Howard (Chicago: Moody, 2013), pp. 85–108.
23. Briggs says that the psalm is didactic, assuring safety for those who made the temple their regular dwelling place (*Psalms*, II:278).

of the psalm, the expositor must be careful about seeing too many references and allusions to the temple in ths psalm (such as the imagery of protection under the wings of a bird linked with the cherubim).

Exegetical Analysis

Summary

Declaring the truth that there is security in taking refuge in God, the psalmist encourages his own soul that he will be delivered from the various and fearful attacks of the wicked because the LORD has given his angels charge over him and vowed to deliver him because he believed.

Outline

I. Confidence: The psalmist declares that there is security in God (1–2).
  A. Whoever dwells in the secret place of the Most High shall have protection from the Almighty (1).
  B. The LORD, the God in whom he trusts, is his protection (2).
II. Encouragement: The psalmist encourages himself by expanding the truth that the LORD delivers him by angelic hosts (3–13).
  A. The LORD delivers him from the various and fearful attacks of the wicked (3–8).
    1. God delivers from the snare of the fouler (3a).
    2. God delivers from the deadly pestilence (3b).
    3. God faithfully provides caring protection (4).
    5. He will not fear terror by night, attack by day, pestilence or destruction (5–6).
    6. He will be preserved amidst the destruction of thousands (7–8).
  B. The LORD who is his refuge has given his angels charge to protect him from all calamity (9–13).
    1. Because he has made the LORD his refuge, he is convinced no calamity will come upon him (9–10).

2. The LORD will give his angels charge over him to bear him up (11–12).
  3. He shall overcome all serious danger (13).
III. Oracle: The LORD promises to requite the psalmist's faith with loving protection and concern for his needs (14–16).
  A. The LORD vows to deliver him because he believes (14).
  B. The LORD vows to answer his prayer in time of need (15).
  C. The LORD vows to bless him with long life and salvation (16).

COMMENTARY IN EXPOSITORY FORM

I. There is safety and security in the presence of the LORD God Almighty (1–2).

In the first two verses the psalmist declares with confidence that in God's presence there is safety and security. In these two verses he uses four different designations for God: the Most High (עֶלְיוֹן), the Almighty (שַׁדַּי), the covenant name Yahweh, and finally God. But the words that need explanation are those that describe the place of safety and the faith. The psalm opens with a description of the devout believer as the one who "dwells" (יֹשֵׁב) in the "secret place" (סֵתֶר) of the Most High. The secret place must be a reference to the sanctuary, the temple proper (and so the figure would be a metonymy of adjunct). Since believers did not live there, the image of dwelling signifies remaining in the presence of God. It is a description of the devout believer who comes to the sanctuary in need and remains to enjoy the sense of security and rest. The verb was used in the liturgies at the gate (Pss. 15 and 24) to refer to the devout worshiper who feels at home in this holy place. It is a secret place because it is set off from the world with all its chaos and danger; and it is a secret place because it is made known to the believer. This was as close as anyone could get to the presence of the Most High God.

And the promise for such a devout worshiper is that "he will lodge" (יִתְלוֹנָן) in the shadow of the Almighty. The verb "to lodge" signifies a temporary dwelling—but for the one who spiritually abides in God's presence, there is protection. And the image of that protection is the word "shadow" (an implied comparison between shade and a place of protection). Outside the sanctuary there is danger; but in the presence of God Almighty there is safety.[24]

The second verse continues the theme of confidence but returns to more familiar figures, "my refuge" and "my fortress." But the verse does not flow naturally from verse 1 for it begins with "I will say" (אֹמַר). In order to harmonize the two verses, many commentators suggest changing the form to the 3rd masculine singular (יֹאמַר); its subject would then be "he who dwells": "he will say of the LORD . . . ."[25] Apart from changing the text, one way around this difficulty is to say that there are different speakers here, a choir for verse 1 and the psalmist for verse 2. But even though there is an abrupt change in the grammar, there is no reason that there must be different speakers. The psalmist announces the principle (v. 1), and then declares his own trust (אֶבְטַח, s.v. Ps. 4:5) in God (v. 2). Two implied metaphors are here supplied to present God as a place of safety and security—"my refuge" (מַחְסִי, s.v. Ps. 7:1) and "my fortress" (מְצוּדָתִי). Even though "secret place," "shadow," "refuge" and "fortress" describe places of safety, the psalmist clearly means that it is the LORD who protects and delivers. And so the second verse complements the first with its initial idea of dwelling in the secret place. A solid faith in the LORD is like dwelling in a completely secure place; however, it is better because it means living life under divine protection.

II. Those who make the LORD their refuge need not fear any danger because the LORD has entrusted them to his angels (3–13).

A. *The LORD protects the faithful from every terrifying danger (3–8).*

In order to make it very clear that those who trust in the

---

24. In the ancient world the image was used for a king's protection of his people. Here it is not an earthly king, but the LORD—even an earthly king would have to come under his protection (see K. Luke, "Under the Shadow of the Almighty," *ITQ* 3 [1972]:187–93).
25. Perowne, *Psalms*, II:176.

LORD are safe and secure, the psalmist provides a list of the dangers and troubles of this life that might normally be terrifying and destructive. As Kidner notes, most of these are types that strike unseen, so that both the strong and the weak are helpless before them.[26] Verse 3 has two dangers, the trap of the hunter and the devouring pestilence. First, he declares that the LORD will deliver ("he will deliver you," יַצִּילְךָ; s.v. Ps. 22:20) the one who takes refuge in him from the hunter's trap. The line does not say the believer will never be caught in the trap, but that the LORD would deliver him from it. Anderson notes that the psalmist is not thinking literally and only of such a trap; he uses the image to represent any man-made threat, so the line promises deliverance from any attempt against his life.[27]

The second colon is difficult. Traditionally, the reading in the Hebrew Bible has been accepted with the main word being "pestilence" (דֶּבֶר), and the modifying word "devouring" (הַוּוֹת). The reading in the text is not impossible; it does not however form a close parallelism with the first colon. The Greek translation (and other versions) assumed the word in the text was "word, thing, matter" (דָּבָר), and came up with the reading "from a troublesome matter/word." Most commentators follow this variant and interpret the line to mean "a destroying word"—Anderson suggests slander or some plot (p. 656). In this way it is a little closer to the first half of the verse, perhaps offering the intent behind the man-made trap. But this assumes the two cola have to be referring to the same thing.

The next verse looks at the LORD's protective care of his people and not the danger that is lurking. In the first colon the psalmist focuses on God—he will cover you; and in the second on the believer—you shall find refuge. But the main figure used in the two cola compares the LORD's protective care to that of birds (so zoomorphism). The first is that God will cover (יָסֶךְ) the believer with his feathers (see Deut. 32:11; Ps. 17:8; and 63:7); and the second is that the believer shall find refuge (תֶּחְסֶה; s.v. Ps. 7:1) under his wings. Some have taken this to be a reference

---

26. *Psalms 73–150*, p. 332.
27. *Psalms 73–150*, p. 656.

metaphor "refuge" (מַחְסִי) signifies that the psalmist has come to trust in the LORD for all his safety and security. The line is unusual because it marks a shift in the focus to "my refuge." Some commentators suggest this one line is a parenthesis, because in the second colon of the verse the psalmist shifts back again to the style of addressing the one who trusts in the LORD: "You have made the Most High your habitation."

Verses 10–13 follow this arrangement. And so the promise of God is declared by the psalmist to the believer. The first declaration is that no evil shall come near the dwelling place of the righteous. "Evil" is used in the first colon and is paralleled with "plague" in the second. The allusion seems to be to Israel in Egypt (see Exod. 12:23). The houses of the Egyptians and others who did not believe the word of the LORD were struck with the plague, an unparalleled terror at night. Those who believed the LORD found protection from death.

The reason that such evil does not come near the tents of the righteous now is stated in verse 11: "For he will give his angels[32] charge over you, to keep you in all your ways." God has appointed angels to various tasks: they are God's guardians of the government of the world (34:7); they prosper the righteous in their journeys (see Exod. 23:20; Gen. 24:7, 40), and they watch over the faithful (Heb. 1:14). So here we read that God appointed or charged them (יְצַוֶּה; s.v. Ps. 119:6) to protect the righteous (לִשְׁמָרְךָ; s.v. Ps. 12:7) in all their ways—where they go, what they do, how they live. Angels are sent where they are needed (Matt. 4:11); but they are not there to serve some selfish advantage (Matt. 26:53).

This verse opens our minds to a great mystery, for we are normally unaware of the presence of angels, and have no idea what might have happened without their ministration (see 2 Kings 6 where the young man was allowed to see all the angels who were fighting for him). This protection is vividly illustrated

---

32. Goldingay chooses to translate the term מַלְאָכָיו, "his angels," as "his aides," even though he states clearly that angels are meant in this line, and that the meaning is that believers are so surrounded by supernatural support that no demon can overcome (if demons are implied in the dangers). There is little reason to change the common translation and obscure the idea (*Psalms 90–150*, pp. 46–7).

in verse 12. The angels bear up the believers on their hands (palms) lest they dash their feet against a stone. The idea of lifting up someone is a figurative expression (an implied comparison) for protective care (compare Exod. 19:4). Other places will use the everlasting hands of the LORD supporting people, but here it is the angels. And dashing a foot against a stone is one specific misfortune; it is meant to signify all types of harmful and painful accidents. God has made provision for the protection of his people; and because we do not see it clearly, we tend to forget about it and to attempt to guide and protect our own ways. Many believers are like Jacob, who thought he had outwitted his father-in-law and his brother—until the angels of God met him (Gen. 32:1–2; recalling another revelation of angels to him as he left the land [Gen. 28:10–22]).[33]

And so verse 13 provides an extension of the idea of divine protection: if God's angels protect people so they do not stumble and hurt their foot along the way, then God's people will trample underfoot all hostile forces, especially in nature. The verse raises a number of questions. Why does he focus on lions and serpents? Why would the righteous trample them under foot? And does not this kind of activity put God's protective care to the test? The animals listed here, a lion and a cobra, a great lion and a serpent, are symbolic of all dangerous forces, as confrontational as a lion, or as subtle as a serpent (so if they are referring to all animals of this nature, they are synecdoches; but if they symbolize every danger including humans who are like lions and serpents, then the figure would be an implied comparison).[34] The line might also symbolize the final victory of the righteous over forces of danger and destruction: not only will they see the reward of the wicked, they will trample all opposition under foot. Kidner comments that the righteous are not survivors, but victors.[35]

---

33. It is easy for a passage such as this to be misapplied, as in the case of the tempter (Matt. 4:6). A promise of divine protection does not give someone liberty to force the fulfillment by some reckless act (see further, Frederick J. Gaiser, "It Shall Not Reach You," *WW* 25 [2005]:191–202).
34. As symbols of evil men, see the use in Ps. 58:3–6 and Deut. 32:33.
35. *Psalms 73–150*, p. 333.

III. The LORD promises to meet the needs of believers and bless them with long life through salvation (14–16).

A. He will deliver believers (14).

In the last few verses of the psalm the LORD is the speaker. They record divine promises to believers, but these promises are more general than those declared earlier in the psalm. But on the other hand, they provide more information about the faith and conduct of the righteous.

In verse 14 God promises to deliver (וַאֲפַלְּטֵהוּ; s.v. Ps. 37:20) the faithful believer and set him on high (אֲשַׂגְּבֵהוּ). This second verb is figurative (an implied comparison) for making the believer safe and secure, setting him inaccessibly high above the danger of the enemies. But the construction of the verse emphasizes the faith of the recipient of this deliverance.[36] Two things are said about the true believer here. First, he has set his love (חָשַׁק) on the LORD. This is no simple faith; it is sincere love for and devotion to the LORD. It reminds the reader that love is the fundamental requirement in the covenant for believers (see Deut. 21:11; and of course, 6:4). The second description of the faithful believer is that he knows (s.v Ps. 67:2) the name of the LORD (for name, s.v. Ps. 20:1). The "name of the LORD" is a summary reference to his nature and his works. And to know the name of the LORD is to have experience it all by faith. This kind of intimate, personal experience is characteristic of faithful believers, people who are walking with the LORD.

B. He will answer their prayers (15).

One result of the LORD's protection is answered prayer. And so verse 15 emphasizes prayer as the means of deliverance. The first colon is the main point: "He will call upon me and I will answer him." The second half of the verse has two ideas: the first colon states "I will be with him in trouble," and the

---

36. The verse uses a chiasm: causal clause, promise of deliverance // promise of deliverance, causal clause. The two causal clauses bracket the promise, focusing our attention on the nature of the true believer.

second, "I will deliver him (אֲחַלְּצֵהוּ)[37] and honor him (וַאֲכַבְּדֵהוּ; s.v. Ps. 19:1)." When believers are in trouble, they naturally cry out to the LORD for help, knowing that he is a God who answers prayer. But what strengthens their faith to pray is the knowledge that he is with them, even in the times of trouble. He has not forsaken them; he is not unaware of their trouble; he stands ready to deliver those who trust in him. And that deliverance will be with honor.

C. He will bless them with long life through salvation (16).

Finally, the LORD promises to satisfy him with a long life ("length of days") and show him his salvation. To satisfy him (אַשְׂבִּיעֵהוּ; s.v. Ps. 90:14) means to give him life to the full, a long and prosperous life. The promise is reminiscent of the promises in wisdom literature: they are general, and not absolute promises, for there may be exceptions. But in general, the believer who is faithful and devout can expect God's provision of a blessed life.

And God will show him divine salvation. The verb "show" is the causative form of the common verb "to see" (וְאַרְאֵהוּ). However, some commentators suggest that this form is from another verb meaning "to drink deeply, be sated," making a better parallelism with the first colon.[38]

But the change is not necessary; earlier in the psalm the promise was made that the righteous would see the punishment of the wicked with their own eyes (v. 8); here it makes very good sense that they will see salvation.

The salvation that they will witness is most likely a temporal blessing in the mind of the psalmist, but it is open to a wider use than only military.[39] Perowne allows that the psalmist might have attached a deeper meaning than the average person

---

37. The verb חָלַץ may be related to a verb meaning "to draw out, off," with a noun "plunder"; or from a verb "to equip for war." In usage, the *piel* form clearly has the active meaning "to deliver" (see Ps. 6:5; 116:8; and 18:20).
38. Anderson, *Psalms 73–150*, pp. 659–60. He is following D. Winton Thomas, *The Text of the Revised Psalter*, p. 23
39. Leonard C. Knight, "I Will Show Him My Salvation," *ResQ* 43 (2001):280–92.

PSALM 92

Confidence in the Goodness of the LORD

INTRODUCTION

Text and Textual Variants

A Psalm. A Song. For the Sabbath Day.

1 It is good to give thanks to[1] the LORD
    and to sing praises to your name, O Most High,
2 to declare your loyal love in the morning
    and your faithfulness every night,[2]
3 set to a ten-stringed instrument and to[3] a lute,
    and to the melody on a harp.

---

1. The infinitive (לְהֹדוֹת) could also be translated "to give praise to" or better, "to acknowledge."
2. The form in the text is simply the plural, "in the nights."
3. The MT repeats "and set to" (וַעֲלֵי) here; it is represented in the Greek only with the preposition ἐν, "on/with" (Syriac). The MT uses it a third time to begin the final colon.

4 For you have made me glad[4] by your work,[5] O LORD;
    because[6] of the deeds of your hands[7] I will sing for joy.
5 How great are your deeds, O LORD,
    your thoughts are very deep.[8]
6 A senseless man does not know,
    and a fool does not understand this:[9]
7 although[10] ungodly people spring up like grass
    and all who do lawlessness flourish,
        they will be destroyed forever.[11]

8 But you are Most High[12] forever, O LORD!

9 For surely your enemies, O LORD,
    for surely your enemies will perish;
        all[13] who do lawlessness will be scattered.

---

4. The verb is the perfect tense שִׂמַּחְתַּנִי, which could also be rendered with an English present tense, a characteristic perfect nuance: "you make me glad."
5. The MT and the Greek version have the singular, "your work." A number of manuscripts and versions have the word in the plural.
6. The Greek and Syriac have "and" to begin the second colon.
7. Now the MT and the Greek version have the plural form of the noun, whereas many Hebrew manuscripts, the Syriac and Qumran have the singular.
8. The verb in the first colon is simply גָּדְלוּ, "(How) great are (your deeds)." The Greek version translated this as: "(How) were (your deeds) extolled," ἐμεγαλύνθη

   Then, in the MT the second colon reads "your thoughts are very deep" (עָמְקוּ), which some translations paraphrase to say, "how profound [deep] are your thoughts." The Greek version rendered this colon fairly closely: "(your thoughts) reached great depths," σφόδρα ἐβαθύνθησαν.
9. The Greek translation has interpreted "this," זֹאת, collectively with the plural ταῦτα, "these things."
10. The MT uses the preposition בְּ, "in the springing up of the ungodly." The adverbial clause may be interpreted in different ways: "when," "although," or "how."
11. The Hebrew text is a little difficult: לְהִשָּׁמְדָם עֲדֵי־עַד, "for their being destroyed forever." The Greek version has "so that they may be destroyed."
12. For MT's מָרוֹם the editors of BHS want to read it as מְרֹמָם, "(you are) exalted." The Greek translation uses ὕψιστος, "Most High."
13. A few manuscripts and the versions have the conjunction.

Confidence in the Goodness of the LORD

10 But you have exalted[14] my horn like a wild ox;
   fine oils have been poured upon me.[15]
11 My eyes have seen[16] the defeat of my adversaries;
   my ears have heard the rout of my wicked foes.

12 The righteous will flourish like a palm tree,
   they will increase like the cedar of Lebanon;
13 planted in the house of the LORD,
   they will flourish[17] in the courts of our God.[18]
14 They will still bear fruit[19] in old age,
   they will stay fresh and green,[20]
15 to declare that "The LORD is upright;
   he is my rock,[21] and there is no injustice in him.

---

14. MT has וַתָּרֶם, "and/but you have exalted." If the sense of the verse is future certainty, then this form would be treated the same as a prophetic perfect. The Greek version reads, "And my horn will be exalted," καὶ ὑψωθήσεται.
15. The Greek version took בַּלֹּתִי as "and my old age (with thick oil)," καὶ τὸ γῆράς. Symmachus has ἡ παλαίωσις. See further T. Booij, "The Hebrew Text of Psalm XCII 11," *VT* 38 (1988):210–13; S. E. Loewenstamm, "Balloti beshemen ra'anān," *UF* 10 (1978):211–13; and D. Winton Thomas, "Some Observations on the Hebrew Word רַעֲנָן," in *Hebraische Wortforschung*, FS Walter Baumgartner, VT Supp 16 (Leiden: E. J. Brill, 1967):387–97.
16. The first verb in the verse is the preterite with the *waw*, וַתַּבֵּט, and the second is the regular imperfect, תִּשְׁמַעְנָה. If the sense of the passage is future certainty, then the first verb could be interpreted as the equivalent of a prophetic perfect, and the second as a future. If the psalmist is referring to something that has already happened, then the first verb would be simply a past tense, or a present perfect, and the second a preterite without a *waw* consecutive.
17. MT has the *hiphil* form יַפְרִיחוּ, but Qumran has יפרחו.
18. A few manuscripts, and a few versions add "house of"—"in the courts of the house of God."
19. MT has יְנוּבוּן, "they will bear fruit." The Greek has "they will still increase," ἔτι πληθυνθήσονται.
20. Hebrew has דְּשֵׁנִים וְרַעֲנַנִּים יִהְיוּ; the Greek translation is "and they will continue to live in comfort," καὶ εὐπαθοῦντες ἔσονται.
21. The Greek version translates "rock" as "God": "to declare that the Lord my God is upright, and there is no unrighteousness in him."

Composition and Context

The psalm combines elements of descriptive praise with the individual praise. There is a short hymnic introduction (vv. 1–3) which serves as both a decision and call to praise. This is followed by the cause for the praise (vv. 4–15). There is only a slight hint of adversity as the psalm reports how the wicked flourish without giving divine judgment any consideration. So the psalm celebrates the mighty works of God, especially his just administration of the world including the destruction of the wicked in the final triumph.[22] The motif of the folly of the wicked, who flourish for a time but do not understand that God will judge them, occurs with slight variations in Psalms 1, 37, 49, and 73. In contrast to their impending doom, the righteous find themselves exalted and blessed. The message will prompt the true believer to praise the LORD for all his works, including the judgment on the wicked and the blessing on the righteous; and this should remind them that their praise must declare that the LORD is righteous and just.

The superscription indicates that this psalm was to be used for the Sabbath day, a tradition recorded in the Mishnah, *Tamid* 7:4.[23] The use of this psalm for the Sabbath reflects a post-exilic arrangement for the use of the psalms in worship. The general understanding is that the psalm is possibly post-exilic;[24] but without any evidence for its setting or authorship it is impossible to say when it was composed. Its use for Sabbath day worship has no bearing on when the psalm was actually written.

The psalm can be divided easily into two parts in order to facilitate the exposition. The first seven verses affirm the (vv. 1–3) value (vv. 1–3) and reason for (vv. 4–7) the faithful to praise the LORD. The last seven verses continue the reason with the preview of the destruction of the enemies (vv. 9–11) and the blessing of the righteous (vv. 12–15). Verse 8 is a single line; it separates the two parts and could be expounded separately. I have joined

---

22. Perowne, *Psalms*, II:178.
23. The Targum records an additional tradition that the psalm was created by Adam on the eve of the Sabbath and then uttered when he awoke on the Sabbath. For a general study of the passage, see N. M. Sarna, "The Psalm for the Sabbath Day (Ps. 92)," *JBL* 81 (1962):155–68.
24. See Anderson, *Psalms 73–150*, p. 660.

Confidence in the Goodness of the LORD

it to the second part as a foundational affirmation of faith (even though by doing so the pattern of seven verses in two sections is not maintained).

Exegetical Analysis

Summary

Recognizing that it is good to praise the Most High because of His goodness to the righteous, the psalmist anticipates the scattering of the wicked and the exaltation and blessing of the righteous because the LORD is on High forever.

Outline

I. The psalmist affirms that it is good to praise the LORD, the Most High, because he has done great things in triumph over the wicked (1–7).
   A. Affirmation of Praise: It is good to praise God (1–3).
      1. It is good to sing praise to the LORD, the Most High (1).
      2. It is good to declare his loyal love and faithfulness all the time (2).
      3. It is good to praise with music (3).
   B. Reason for Praise: The LORD has made the righteous glad with his mighty works which will culminate in judgment on the wicked (4–7).
      1. The LORD has made the righteous glad by his great and profound works (4–5).
      2. The LORD will destroy the wicked, even though in their prosperity they do not understand this (6–7).
II. The psalmist anticipates that God will destroy the wicked, but will exalt and bless those who trust in the LORD, the Most High, so that they will declare his righteousness (8–15).
   A. The righteous affirm the LORD is the Most High forever (8).
   B. The LORD exalts the righteous to look on the destruction of the wicked in triumph (9–11).

1. All those who do wickedly will be destroyed (9).
  2. God exalts the righteous to witness their destruction (10–11).
 C. The LORD blesses the righteous with a fruitful, long life in his presence, so that they will declare his righteousness (12–15).
  1. God blesses the righteous with a fruitful, long life in his presence (12–14).
  2. The righteous will declare that God is just (15).

COMMENTARY IN EXPOSITORY FORM

I. It is good to praise the LORD Most High continually for his loyal love and faithfulness demonstrated in his mighty works which include the destruction of the wicked (1–7).

A. *It is good to praise the LORD, the Most High, continually for his loyal love and faithfulness (1–3).*

1. It is good to praise the name of the LORD Most High (1).

The first verse of the psalm is an affirmation of the value of praise; as such it serves to express his decision to praise and to inspire all believers to praise. The affirmation is that it is good (טוֹב; s.v. Ps. 34:8) to praise the LORD. By this he means that praise harmonizes with the nature and plan of God; therefore it is fitting and right. This adjective will serve for all the statements of verses 1–3. It is all good. In this first verses there are two infinitives. The first is "to acknowledge/give thanks to" (לְהֹדוֹת, from יָדָה; s.v. Ps. 6:5). This verb indicates that the praise will be a public acknowledgment of the person and works of the LORD. In other words, it is praise that will edify others and not merely be a private thanksgiving. Parallel to this is the infinitive "and to sing praises" (וּלְזַמֵּר; s.v. Ps. 33:2). The verb means "to sing praises," usually with musical accompaniment. The form is related to the standard word in the collection for "psalm."

The LORD is clearly the subject of the praise; but the expression "your name" indicates that the praise will focus on God's nature demonstrated in his works (for "name," s.v. Ps. 20:1). But of all the wonderful attributes of the LORD, the psalmist stresses "Most High" (עֶלְיוֹן). It is an epithet first introduced in Abram's encounter with Melchizedek of Jerusalem (Gen. 14:17–24). It affirms the fundamental article of the faith, namely that there is no god greater or higher than the LORD; and it links the present beliefs to the historic Jerusalem ideology.

2. It is good to declare his loyal love and faithfulness continually (2).

The specific attributes of God communicated through this praise are his loyal love (חֶסֶד; s.v. Ps. 23:6) and faithfulness (אֱמוּנָה; s.v. Ps. 15:2). It is good to declare these, i.e., these are to be declared (לְהַגִּיד; s.v. Ps. 75:9) continually—the merism using "in the morning" and "every night" means all the time, whenever there is motivation and opportunity to do so. "Loyal love" and "faithfulness" are often placed together as the main themes of God's works on behalf of his people. These may be interpreted as one idea (by hendiadys), "faithfulness" modifying the word "love": "faithful covenant love." The attributes stand for what they produce (so they are metonymies of cause, the effect intended). In the final analysis, God's love delivers, defends, and blesses his covenant people. The recipients of God's faithful love should never tire of declaring it—it is good to do so, it is part of God's plan to do so.

3. It is good to praise him with musical accompaniment (3).

The praise will be a declaration of the person and works of God—there will be verbal communication. But it is also good that it be accompanied with musical instruments. These instruments would produce a sound of music, although it is unclear whether the word used (הִגָּיוֹן) indicates if there was a melody or just a loud sound of music. But lutes and harps and instruments of ten-strings required that the praise be more carefully prepared and presented; and it would ensure that the content of the praise would be much more memorable. In the Psalter we learn that God clearly has an ear for beauty.

B. Praise is fitting because of the LORD's mighty works which include his judgment on the wicked (4–7).

1. God has given his people every reason to rejoice (4–5).

Beginning with verse 4 the psalmist will give the reasons for praising. He begins with a personal affirmation: "For you, O LORD, have made me glad" (שִׂמַּחְתַּנִי; s.v. Ps. 48:11). He means, of course, that what God has done has made him glad (so a metonymy of effect, the cause intended). He has witnessed, perhaps experienced, the manifestation and triumph of God's righteousness in his mighty deeds. These are emphasized by the (chiastic) arrangement of the cola of verse 4:

For you, O LORD, have made me glad
    because of/by your work;
    because of/by the deeds of your hands
I will sing for joy.

God has made him glad; and that means he will sing for joy (אֲרַנֵּן; s.v. Ps. 33:1). The works of God are not specified in this passage; the wording of the text is all inclusive.

Without further identification the psalmist declares God's works to be great (v. 5a). The exclamation "How great" is intended to say that God's deeds are truly incomparable. His works are great because he is the Most High. But they are also great because his plans are immeasurable: "your thoughts (מַחְשְׁבֹתֶיךָ; s.v. Ps. 32:2) are very deep." The word for thoughts has the connotations of designs and intentions: every thought of God is a planned action. And to say that God's plans are deep is simply to say that they are too profound for our understanding (cf. Rom. 11:33).

2. The LORD will destroy the wicked even though they are ignorant of the fact (6–7).

Among the plans and intentions of God is the judgment of the wicked who are spiritually ignorant. They are described here as "brutish" ("a brute man," אִישׁ-בַּעַר) and "foolish" ("a fool," כְּסִיל). The first description means that they are dull; elsewhere it is used of beasts or cattle that are insensitive to the right things.

The second word is a common word for the fool in wisdom literature; he is stubborn and spiritually senseless, even though he may intelligent. These are unbelievers who willfully or ignorantly do not embrace divine truth. Their thoughts on the nature and work of God are but folly. In this context the point is that they refuse to believer there is a Most High God who will destroy all evil and all who practice lawlessness.[25]

Their folly, and hence their description as beastly, comes from the fact that they live for the moment—they flourish, and they do not consider the end of life. They spring up like the green herb, and they flourish in their self-indulgent and ungodly ways. But the point of the section is that they will be destroyed forever, even though they do not know (יֵדַע; s.v. Ps. 67:2) nor understand (יָבִין; s.v. Ps. 49:3). There is no spiritual understanding for they are ignorant of the works of God, especially the judgment that is coming.

II. Those who believe in the LORD, the Most High, will be exalted over the wicked and blessed abundantly in order to declare the righteousness of the LORD, their Rock (8–15).

A. God's people acknowledge that the LORD is the Most High (8).

Verse 8 stands out not only because it is one simple line of text, but also because it is a statement of faith in the middle of the verses that anticipate the destruction of the wicked. The psalmist acknowledges, "And you are the Most High forever, O LORD." This is the central fact on which all the psalm's doctrines rest.[26] The word "Most High" (מָרוֹם; s.v. Ps. 46:10) is literally "height" or "highest"; this is the second time the word is used in the psalm (see v. 1). The verse is a statement of faith that Yahweh is the Most High God—forever! There are no gods greater than Yahweh, not now and never. He is the supreme, sovereign God over all.

---

25. Anderson, *Psalms 73–150*, p. 662
26. Perowne, *Psalms*, II:179

B. God's people will be exalted over the wicked in the day of judgment (7–11).

Having affirmed the sovereignty of Yahweh, the psalmist now states one natural consequence of this—the enemies of God shall perish (יֹאבֵדוּ). After all, if Yahweh is the supreme and sovereign God, those who oppose him cannot hope to survive. These "enemies" are not just people who oppose the LORD, though; they are "doers of lawlessness" (אָוֶן; s.v. Ps. 28:3). Those who are characterized by lawlessness (as the participle פֹּעֲלֵי stresses) are God's enemies; and because he will judge with righteousness, they will pay for their sins. The verb (יִתְפָּרְדוּ) means they will be scattered, dispersed, but because it is parallel to "they shall perish," the image of being scattered is one of complete defeat and destruction. The words may be referring to a dramatic judgment at the end of the age; but they may also refer to a victory that God would accomplish in and through Israel.

Verses 10 and 11 provide a contrast to the lot of the wicked for the purpose of emphasizing the triumph of the righteous over the wicked. The first and contrasting statement is that God has exalted the psalmist: "You have exalted my horn like that of a wild ox." The verb "you have exalted" (וַתָּרֶם) is from the same root as "Most High" and forms an appropriate word play: those who acknowledge that the LORD is the Most High will find themselves exalted by his faithful covenant love. Here what is exalted is "my horn." The horn was a symbol of power in the biblical texts, and so it was used frequently for kings. It is possible that the psalm was written by a king who anticipated seeing his dominion exalted when God destroyed the wicked enemies. The parallelism of being anointed would support this idea—but it would be more compelling if a different word for anointing had been used. Neither is the variant reading, "You have exalted my old age," very compelling either. The psalmist most likely is saying that God has raised him up with power. The simile of a wild ox simply makes the picture of power more vivid. As Kirkpatrick says, the poet, speaking on behalf of the nation, draws the image from animals tossing their heads in the consciousness of vigor. So God has restored his people to a buoyant sense of power to repel the enemies.[27] The image of anointing in the second half of the verse is a little more difficult. If the reading stands it would be an anointing to restoration to health. Others follow the Greek version with a different reading of the letters to obtain a noun in place of the verb with the idea of "my old age" meaning "my failing strength." Israel would be pictured as aging and weak, but revitalized by God.

Finally, in verse 11 the psalmist announces that he has seen the defeat of his enemies. The first verb in the verse is a preterite, "has seen" (וַתַּבֵּט), but the parallel verb is the imperfect (תִּשְׁמַעְנָה), which could be translated in the past tense to parallel the first (as a preterite without the *waw* consecutive). In this way the psalmist would be referring to something he has witnessed. But given the fact that the passage is looking ahead to the defeat of the enemies, this verse anticipates triumph over the wicked enemies. The verse does not say that the psalmist is rejoicing over their defeat—that interpretation is assumed within the verb "has seen." It is essentially a report that he has witnessed (or affirming he will witness) the defeat of his enemies that will be both a triumph and a relief.

C. God's people will be blessed abundantly that they might declare his righteousness (12–15).

In the last four verses the psalmist focuses more on the blessings that the righteous can expect from God. The first is that they will increase in vigor. Verse 12 says that the righteous shall flourish like the palm, and will grow like the cedar of Lebanon. These figures (similes) stress an increase in life and vigor; but the ideas of perpetuity and uprightness are probably intended as well. This is a promise to all believers: they may experience a portion of it in this life under God's blessing, but the promise of life is not limited to this physical world.

The image of trees is carried on to verse 13 which states that they will be planted in the house of the LORD, flourishing in the courts of God. It is possible that trees were planted and well cared for in the sanctuary, and this would provide a picture of

---

27. *Psalms*, p. 561.

the life of the righteous protected and cared for in the presence of the LORD. But the meaning is more general than the location of the sanctuary. The people of God living in the land will thrive because they will be living a life in the presence of the LORD without fear of the wicked (Jer. 32:41; Isa. 61:3). In fact the life that they live will be fruitful even in their old age (like a tree with its longevity); like a tree they will stay fresh and green (an implied comparison with the tree).

So the practitioners of lawlessness, the wicked enemies of God, will be removed in God's judgment. But the righteous, those who believe in the sovereignty of the LORD, the Most High God, will not only survive the judgment, but will triumph on the victory of the LORD over evil and will enjoy his blessing of a long fruitful and vigorous life in his presence.

But there is a purpose in God's delivering his people from the wicked. It has been true in the past, and it will be true in the future. It is so that the righteous will declare that the LORD, their rock, is upright, and that there is no injustice in him. His judgment is right; his salvation is right. Therefore believers will enjoy God's blessings so that they might demonstrate by those blessings the righteousness and faithfulness of their covenant God.

MESSAGE AND APPLICATION

There is a fundamental reason why God preserves and blesses the lives of his people in this world. It is so that they will proclaim his righteousness to the world. And Psalm 92 shows us how to do that through praise. Unfortunately, believers today have all but abandoned individual or corporate praise of this kind. When this happens, the basic witness of the church is seriously weakened.

Psalm 92 is filled with praise for the mighty works of God, which the world in its foolishness fails to understand. The goodness of God preserves and blesses the lives of believers in many amazing ways. Unbelievers may flourish for a while, but it is not the same. Ultimately the righteousness of God will judge them and give eternal victory to his faithful people. The exposition of the psalm could be summarized in different ways, but this wording captures the theology: *Almighty God blesses and preserves the righteous so that they will praise him for his powerful and righteous works, which include the destruction of the wicked and the exaltation of the righteous.* We find this same emphasis in the New Testament. Paul tells us that God has redeemed us in order that we might be for the praise of his glory (Eph. 1:12). Specifically, he has extended saving grace to us in Christ Jesus in order to show the riches of his grace (Eph. 2:7). The exhibition of the grace of God necessarily includes the reason for the grace —sin. Without the grace of God, we all would stand condemned awaiting the justice of God.

The obvious application of the Psalm, then, would be to praise and acknowledge the Lord for his mighty works so that the world will hear. In praising God's glory and grace, as Paul would phrase it, we would be proclaiming the goodness of God to a world that is unwittingly facing the judgment of the righteous God. The good news is that they can enter into the blessing of God as we have done, and enjoy his eternal blessings.

PSALM 93

The Everlasting Reign of the LORD

INTRODUCTION

Text and Textual Variants[1]

1 The LORD reigns; he is clothed with majesty;
    the LORD is clothed, he[2] is girded with strength;

---

1. There is a superscription for this psalm in the Greek (B) version: "For the day before the Sabbath, when the land was inhabited. A Praise. A Song of David." Most commentators consider the reference to David as unreliable; but they use the first part of the superscription as a clarification of how the psalm was used later. The reference to filling or inhabiting the land could mean the psalm came to be used to celebrate the increased population at the return from the exile, even though the original composition could have been earlier (Anderson, *Psalms 73–150*, pp. 665–6). Or, it could refer to creation when God populated the world. According to the Mishnah, this is a "Friday Psalm" (*Tamid* 7:4); in the Talmud (*Rosh Ha-Shanah* 31a) it is linked to creation: God created in six days, and then began to reign over his creation.
2. There is a conjunction in the versions; the Greek has " . . . clothed with power and girded himself." The MT does not have a conjunction.

indeed, the world is established;[3]
   it cannot be moved.[4]
2 Your throne was established long ago;[5]
   you are from everlasting.
3 The seas[6] have lifted up, O LORD,
   the seas have lifted up their voice;[7]
   the seas lift up[8] their roaring.[9]

4 Mightier[10] than the sounds of many waters,
   the mighty[11] *waters,* breakers of the sea,
      is the LORD on high.

---

3. The form in the MT is the *niphal* תִּכּוֹן; the Greek (with the other versions) has an active verb, ἐστερέωσεν, "he has established," probably to harmonize with the idea of the LORD as the subject. This rendering may (or may not) reflect a verb תָּךְ , a *piel perfect* from another root, תָּכַן, "to measure," and hence "establish" (see also Pss. 75:4 and 96:10).
4. The Greek version subordinates the second colon: "Indeed, he established the world, that it shall not be shaken."
5. The text has "from then," meaning from long ago, or from remote time.
6. The Hebrew word is נְהָרוֹת, "rivers"; it probably refers to the currents or flow of the seas.
7. Greek has φωνὰς αὐτῶν, "their voices."
8. The verb in the first two cola is the perfect tense נָשְׂאוּ, but in the third it changes to the imperfect tense יִשְׂאוּ. The first two may be taken as characteristic perfects, stressing present continuing action, and the third as a progressive imperfect, also showing that the action is ongoing or not completed. On the other hand, Dahood notes that the sequence of perfect + perfect + imperfect is common in Ugaritic poetry as well as in Hebrew, and the imperfect tense may be taken in the same way as the preceding perfect tenses (*Psalms,* II:341).
9. This third colon is not found in some Greek texts.
10. The word order in the text begins with "More than the sounds" and expresses the main idea in the third colon—"the LORD on high is mighty." For clarification I have followed several translations that have moved the comparative to the beginning. The Greek version interprets the line a little differently, taking the preposition as causal and not comparative: "Because of the noises of many waters, wondrous are the billows of the sea, wondrous *is the Lord on high.*"
11. For "mighty" the MT has the plural form, אַדִּירִים (and here "waters" has been added from the context). But the syntax is difficult and therefore there are a number of explanations. If the adjective "mighty" or "majestic" stands as a plural form, the word may be functioning in the sentence as an attributive and not a predicate adjective. Perowne (*Psalms,* II:184)

5 Your statutes are very faithful.
    Holiness[12] adorns[13] your house,
       O LORD, for ever.[14]

Composition and Context

Psalm 93 is a brief hymn, a descriptive praise psalm, acclaiming the power and majesty of the LORD seen in his creation of the world. A. A. Anderson rightly notes that the main point is the everlasting kingship of the LORD; and since no power on earth can be compared with his majesty and might, he is sovereign and his word is sure and trustworthy.[15] This majestic LORD is, after all, the ruler of the universe.

While we cannot be sure of the original intended use of a psalm like this, the theological message is clear and must be our main interest. Nevertheless, this and similar psalms will also have to be analyzed with regard to their possible use in Israel's festival worship.

---

    suggests two ways the line can be interpreted: (1) the preposition may be expressing comparison: "more than the voice of many mighty waters, (even) the breakers ... ," (2) or the preposition may be taken as causal: "because of the voices of many waters, mighty are the breakers of the sea, the LORD on high is mighty" (as in the Greek). The Greek version arranges the lines this way: "Because of the noises of many waters, the billows of the sea are wondrous; wondrous on high is the LORD."

    But some commentators suggest that the ending מ on "mighty" should be attached to the next word, giving the meaning "mightier than the breakers of the sea"; but Tate suggests that the מ may simply be enclitic, leaving "mighty" as a construct form: "mighty ones of the breakers of the sea," meaning, "mighty breakers of the sea" (*Psalms 51–100*, p. 473).

12. The Hebrew word order is "to your house / is fitting / holiness," meaning, "your house has the adornment of holiness." A few manuscripts and the Syriac have the conjunction: "and to your house."
13. MT has נַאֲוָה, "becomes/is fitting." Tate accepts that the Greek text's πρέπει, "clearly seen, conspicuous, befits," works with the idea of "fitting, suits" (p. 473). Other commentators suggest reading the word as the Dead Sea scroll has it, "at your house, a holy abode" (*4QPs^b* has נוה; see further D. M. Howard, Jr., *The Structure of Psalms 93–100*, p. 48).
14. The text has "for the length of days" (which is rendered literally in the Greek version).
15. *Psalms 73–150*, pp. 666.

The date of the composition of Psalm 93 is almost impossible to determine as well. But a fairly strong case can be made for a very early date: Howard concluded that the psalm could have been written in the 10th century, or as early as the 12th century for a number of stylistic and literary reasons.[16] The fact that the psalm has several allusions to Canaanitish themes lends support to this date; Dahood says that because of the allusions to Canaanite ideas Psalm 93 is close to Psalm 29. So the superscription in the Greek manuscript linking the psalm to David's time is not without reasonable support.

Psalm 93 is a psalm of praise for the LORD's eternal sovereignty over all creation. It could have been written to celebrate a great victory. But when it was deposited in the sanctuary it became part of a group of psalms with similar motifs that were used at the great festivals to celebrate the reign of the LORD. Whenever the psalm was written, it found its way into Book IV of the final collection and was used in conjunction with the themes of other psalms in that book. It would have been particularly valued at the restoration from the exile, both for the proclamation of the LORD's sovereignty over the nations and for the hope of final victory that was yet to come.

The group of psalms that this psalm is linked with is called "enthronement psalms." They are Psalms 47 and 96–99; but Psalm 93 opens the section of Psalms 93–100. Within this section, Psalms 95 and 100 bracket Psalms 96–99.[17] As with many classifications of psalms, the label "enthronement psalms" can be used narrowly or widely. Tate lists the common features of these as a focus on all the nations, references to other gods, signs accompanying the exaltation of the king, references to the mighty acts of the LORD, and praise for him as the heavenly

---

16. His reasons include the following: there is an absence of prose particles (definite article, sign of the accusative, or relative pronoun) which were common later; there is an absence of conjunctions whereas later Hebrew poetry has them; more use of tricolons; the alternation of perfect and imperfect tenses; and the absence of "God" and use of "Yahweh" (D. M. Howard, Jr., *The Structure of Psalms 93–100*, pp. 38–57).
17. For a good survey of the discussion concerning the links between Psalms 92 and 93, as well as 93 and 94, see Tate, *Psalms 51–100*, p. 476.

king.[18] Psalms 96 and 97 have all these features, Psalms 98 and 99 have all but the second, and Psalm 93 has the 3rd and 4th features.[19]

The classification of "enthronement psalms" has been generally used but greatly modified since the formulation by Mowinckel. And the study of the psalms in this group has become more complex, witnessed by the variation of proposals that have been put forward.[20] Critical to these psalms is the interpretation of the expression "the LORD reigns" (יְהוָה מָלָךְ; see Pss. 47:8; 93:1; 96:10; 97:1; 98:6; and 99:1). Mowinckel's view was that this was an acclamation in an annual festival in Israel that celebrated the LORD's renewed kingship over the earth, the festival taking as its central feature the ritual enthronement of the LORD (perhaps represented by the ark). Accordingly, he translated the clause as "Yahweh has become king" (an ingressive perfect), as opposed to the present tense translation "reigns," which is the way most translations and commentators render it. As mentioned in the Introduction, much of Mowinckel's support came from parallel material from other nations, notably the Canaanites and Babylonians.[21] In Canaan Baal was said to have acquired kingship by vanquishing the Sea (a deity); and for this he was enthroned in a palace especially built for him on the sacred mountain. Some of the expressions in the Psalter indicate that the God of the Hebrews was also thought to have ensured world order and supremacy by a primeval combat through which he established his kingship. Whether this is described as borrowing or polemical depends on the presuppositions of the commentators.

---

18. See also J. D. W. Watts, "Yahweh Malak Psalms," *ThZ* 21 (1965):341–48.
19. Dahood, *Psalms,* II:474.
20. In addition to the general discussion by L. Sabourin, *The Psalms* (pp. 117–144), the work of Sigmund Mowinckel, *The Psalms in Israel's Worship,* and other references listed in the my Introduction in volume 1, such as P. A. H. DeBoer, "Vive le roi!" *VT* 5 (1955):225–231; J. Ridderbos, "Jahwah Malak," *VT* 4 (1954):87–89; W. Brueggemann, *Israel's Praise: Doxology against Idolatry and Ideology* (Philadelphia: Fortress Press, 1988), pp. 4–6; and D. M. Howard, Jr., *The Structure of Psalms* 93–100.
21 For the theory that this psalm was originally an old Canaanite song, see Helen G. Jefferson, "Psalm 93," *JBL* 71 (1952):155–60.

There is very little concrete evidence to support Mowinckel's full reconstruction. Moreover, the disagreement among scholars over the nature of such a festival argues against its being such an important part of Israel's worship—if it was so important, one would have expected some reference to it in the Bible if not a description. We do know that in the fall the Israelites gathered for the feast of tabernacles. But very little ceremony is connected with this feast, as far as we know (cf. Lev. 23:23–25 and Neh. 8:1–12). Tabernacles was essentially a time of rejoicing at the ingathering of the harvest, praying for the next harvest, and recalling the end of the wilderness wandering.

Mowinckel built on the theme that God's sovereignty was established at creation, explaining why the entire world is the focus of these psalms. He included the primeval conflict in his reconstruction because he assumed the biblical material to be comparable to the mythic accounts of gods like Baal or Marduk. Psalm 93:3 is used as evidence of this. Mowinckel did allow for the possibility that it was at the exodus that God established his sovereignty over the world as he became Israel's king, and so the "waters" mentioned in this psalm may refer to the victory at the crossing of the sea (Exod. 14).

Even though this theory has remained at least in the background, there is no convincing evidence in the psalms that the expressions and ideas that Mowinckel used in the working out of the details refer to such a festival, or can only be specifically associated with it. For example, Ollenburger accepts that there was a celebration of the LORD's kingship, established by his victory over chaos and exercised from Zion, especially in the time of the fall festival; but he says there is not enough evidence to reconstruct the festival in such details as Mowinckel and others have done, or to assign a group of psalms to a part of a festival.[22] Weiser and others suggested that there was an autumnal celebration of the LORD's kingship, but that it was more of a covenant renewal ceremony than an enthronement.

The psalm may have been designated for use in the fall feast of tabernacles, which is also referred to by commentators as the

---

22. B. C. Ollenburger, *Zion the City of the Great King, JSOT* Supplement 41 (Sheffield: *JSOT*, 1987), pp. 25–33.

The Everlasting Reign of the LORD

time of the fall enthronement festival (see the comments in the Introduction, Volume 1, on the enthronement psalms). Psalm 93 may have served as part of an acclamation of the LORD's sovereignty in such a formal worship service, even though it could have originally been written to celebrate some specific historic event. Additionally it has also taken on an eschatological sense: any use of this psalm would anticipate its application to the end of the age when the language would become historically realized. The LORD demonstrated his sovereignty in the past, and continues to do so in the present; but he will reign in the future with absolute power and authority.

Exegetical Analysis

Summary

The psalmist proclaims the LORD's reign from his eternal, holy throne with majesty, power, and faithfulness over the world he established.

Outline

I. The psalmist exults in the fact that the LORD reigns in majesty and strength from his eternal throne over the world he established (1–2).
   A. The LORD reigns in majesty and strength (1a).
   B. The LORD established the earth and it cannot be moved (1b).
   C. The LORD established his throne from everlasting (2).
II. The psalmist praises the LORD because he is mightier than the great sea (3–4).
   A. The seas with their mighty breakers have lifted up their sounds (3).
   B. (But) the LORD on high is mightier than these (4).
III. The psalmist declares that the testimonies of the LORD are faithful and his temple is adorned with holiness (5).
   A. The testimonies of the LORD are always faithful (5a).
   B. The house of the LORD is eternally holy (5b).

COMMENTARY IN EXPOSITORY FORM

I. The everlasting LORD reigns over his creation, adorned with majesty and might (1–2).

The psalm places the holy name "Yahweh" first to give it prominence. The full clause declares, "Yahweh reigns," a decisive expression that Kidner says calls for an exclamation mark.[23] He adds that this proclamation points to a future reality when the LORD will reign over the whole world.

Most translations use the present tense "reigns" for the perfect tense (מָלָךְ), which is a serviceable translation in this context. At a time of worship this acclamation of the sovereignty of God may have been understood as a universal truth (a gnomic perfect): "the LORD [always] reigns." But if the psalm was reporting a recent event in which the LORD established or demonstrated his sovereignty, or was a shout of victory for it, then the verb could be interpreted in a more restricted sense, perhaps as "the LORD reigns" (here and now—an instantaneous perfect), or "the LORD has become king" (as a present perfect). Mowinckel preferred "has become king" to fit the annual acclamation at the festival; he clarified that this did not nullify the fact that the LORD always was king.[24]

Whether the expression was general or had a specific event in mind, it has an eschatological meaning as well, anticipating the time when the LORD will reign over the whole earth in righteousness and power. This future emphasis is part of the meaning of the enthronement psalms as a whole. In this light the verb could also be understood as a prophetic perfect. The above translations would allow for this additional meaning, because future fulfillment is often presented in terms of a completed action or a present reality. So, the declaration of the LORD's reign, indeed, the message of the whole psalm, was probably made first at the celebration of an event in which the LORD displayed his sovereignty over his adversaries (whether that event was creation, the deliverance from Egypt, or some other event such as the restoration from the exile in Babylon), but any display of his

---

23. *Psalms 73–150*, p. 338.
24. *The Psalms in Israel's Worship*, II:223.

The Everlasting Reign of the LORD

sovereignty was typological of the future—the LORD's reign will be fully realized in the future when he comes to judge the world. Then, everyone will proclaim "Yahweh reigns" in fact.[25]

The sovereignty of the LORD is then described as fully magnificent and armed for battle. The first statement is that he is clothed with majesty. The language is figurative (an implied comparison): just as clothing covers a person and is what catches one's attention directly, so is the divine majesty (גֵּאוּת)[26] that is seen in this king. The imagery of clothing indicates that his entire nature is majestic (see also Isa. 59:17; 63:1; Dan. 7:9). Broyles adds that the clothing does not merely represent pomp, but the power to execute majestic things.[27] Then, the second line repeats the affirmation that the LORD is clothed, and some translations add "with majesty" from the first expression. But it is more likely the two verbs, "clothed" and "girded," both refer to "strength" (as the Greek version has it): "the LORD is clothed, girded with strength" (or "the LORD is clothed *and* girded with strength"). The images of clothing and being girded now focus on the LORD's being equipped with strength, i.e., he is by nature strong. This word "strength" (עֹז; s.v. Ps. 29:1) refers to the power of God that informs all of his mighty acts in nature and history. So the imagery calls attention to the majesty and strength of the LORD, which the psalm reminds us were revealed in his conquest and kingship. "Majesty" and "strength" then are figures (metonymies) because they imply the effect, what the majesty and strength actually do.

The second half of the verse immediately indicates the effect by applying these attributes to creation: "Indeed (אַף), the

---

25. Delitzsch classified these psalms (later to be called "enthronement psalms" in a cultic interpretation) as eschatological Yahwistic psalms (*Psalms,* I:70).
26. The basic verb גָּאָה means "rise up"; it can mean literally "rise up," or figuratively "be exalted." The verb is used in Exodus 15:1 and 21 to celebrate the LORD's triumph over the enemies at the crossing of the sea.

    One related noun (גַּאֲוָה) means "pride"; a second (גַּאֲוָה) means "majesty" and "pride," and a third noun גָּאוֹן means "exaltation" or "excellency." The word used here (גֵּאוּת), "majesty," is used for the swelling of the sea (Ps. 89:10), or majestic things God has done ((Isa. 12:5), or pride (Ps. 17:10).
27. *Psalms,* p. 368.

world is established and it cannot be moved." The "world" (תֵּבֵל) is the inhabited world, and so the reference is probably to the moral governing of the world order as well as physical creation. Although the verse is a simple declaration that the world is established (תִּכּוֹן),[28] the understanding is that the LORD established it. Some commentators follow the versions and use an active verb from a different root to get "he established." But if that were the original reading, it is difficult to explain why a scribe would change it to the passive form. It is more likely that another scribe changed the original passive to the active for clarification. In any case, the sense is clear: the LORD established the world, and it cannot be moved (בַּל־תִּמּוֹט; s.v. Ps. 62:2). Certainly at creation God set the world on its course, and nothing can alter the plan of God.

Verse 2 next connects God's establishment of the world with the fact that his throne was established long ago. The subject

---

28. The verb used in the text is כּוּן. In almost all the Semitic languages the meaning has to do with firmness, verity, correctness and existence. In the Old Testament usage is divided between the active stems *polel* (29x) and hiphil (110x), and the more stative than passive niphal (66x). The polel means "establish, found, assure," the hiphil "equip, care for, prepare, arrange," and the niphal "be firm, true, certain."

The verb in the niphal has the concrete meanings of "to be firm, firmly grounded, anchored." It is used for roofs or walls resting on columns (Judg. 16:26, 29) or mountains and the earth (Ps. 93:1). Abstract usages can have the meanings "fortified, lasting, dependable," such as royal dominion (1 Sam. 20:31) or a dream message (Gen. 41:32). In many cases the concern is whether something that seems uncertain will be established.

The *polel* expresses the idea that someone produces the firmness. E.g., the LORD establishes a person's steps (Ps. 40:3). The meaning of the hiphil is broader; it can be used for the preparation of things, such as materials for the temple (1 Kings 5:32), or sacrificial animals (Num. 23:1). It can also be used for the completion of a project, such as the altar (Ezra 3:3). It can have figurative meanings such as "arrange, determine, stabilize."

In passages about creation, this verb in its active stems is used synonymously for words of creation (see Ps. 24:2). Because the Bible links the creation of the world with the formation of Israel, this word is also used in contexts about the origin of Israel (Deut. 32:6). And on the personal level, setting one's heart on the LORD is the formula used for having the right attitude toward God (1 Sam. 7:3). See further E. Gerstenberger, "כּוּן, *kûn* ni. to stand firm*,*" in *Theological Lexicon of the Old Testament*, ed. by Jenni and Westermann, II:602–606.

"your throne" is a figure (implied comparison) for God's kingship or sovereign authority over all things. It "is established (נָכוֹן) from old" (the text says "from then," but it refers to the time when he set the world in order by his victory over the seas, or chaos; v. 3). The reference is to remote time when his sovereignty was first displayed. And so the psalmist simply adds, "You are from everlasting." The meaning of the word "everlasting" (for עוֹלָם; s.v., Ps. 61:4) must be derived from the context in which it is used. Here it refers to the distant past, certainly at least to creation when the LORD established his sovereign reign over his creation; but it could also mean eternity past, even though that may not have been understood by the psalmist. The verse then affirms that God established the world because his sovereignty was from old.

Kidner reminds us of the eschatological significance of this acclamation; he states that although kingship, glory and might are ever-present facts, this acclamation of them may well be a leap into the future, anticipating the great "day of the LORD" when these truths will be fully realized. In this way the acclamation displays the assurance of things hoped for.[29]

II. The sovereign LORD is more majestic than the mighty forces of nature (3–4).

The psalmist suddenly shifts his focus to mighty waters in a contrast with the power of the LORD. The imagery used here seems to reflect the Canaanite (Baal) and Babylonian (Marduk) themes of the god's battle for kingship.[30] If this is so, then the language is most likely polemical since the biblical account of creation reveals God as the absolute sovereign making decrees. There is no evidence that the LORD fought such a battle with any gods or even forces of nature later deified—the text states that it is Yahweh (not Baal) who is lord of all creation because

---

29. *Psalms 73–150,* p. 338.
30. See further John Day, *God's Conflict with the Dragon and the Sea: Echoes of a Canaanite Myth in the Old Testament* (Cambridge: Cambridge University Press, 1985), pp. 35–37.

he established it and controls it.[31] What the LORD created he controls, even those elements of nature that may have been deified by the pagans.

Verse 3 presents a hostile scene with the mighty and chaotic forces of nature rising up with their crashing sound: "The seas have lifted up, O LORD, the seas have lifted up their sound; the seas lift up their roaring." The word translated "seas" is literally "rivers" (נְהָרוֹת); but in this context it is used for the seas, perhaps the currents of the seas (see also Jon. 2:3). The "sound" ("voice") is that of the surging and roaring of the seas; and the parallel word "roaring" or "crashing" of the serf (דָּכְיָם, "their roaring," related to דָּכָה, "to crush") emphasizes the mighty and noisy power of the sea as a force to be reckoned with. In the syntax the first two verbs may be rendered as present perfects, and the third verb, an imperfect tense, may carry the same nuance in the context, or it may emphasize more the ongoing raging of the seas. The verse is a dramatic description of the majestic and frightening force of the seas mounting up with roaring and crashing in waves on the shore.

The reference of these lines certainly may be to the time of creation when the LORD by his word controlled the powerful and chaotic waters of the earth to form the seas (Job 38:8–11; Gen. 1:9, 10). If that is the case, then the psalm is also a polemic against the myths of the pagans in which the battle for kingship was between Baal and the deified Sea (*Yam*) and River (*Nahar*), or in the Babylonian material, Marduk's victory over Tiamat, the Seawater. In Israel the sea and the river were not gods or goddesses, just powerful and at times chaotic forces of nature; but the LORD's dominion was made clear by his creating and controlling all elements of nature.

It is also possible that the reference may be to Israel's crossing the sea at their exodus from Egypt. The description of the mighty sea is reflected in Exodus 15:10. And the language of creation is used by Malachi for the establishing of the covenant people (Mal. 2:10). The polemical element would then be focused more specifically on the gods of Egypt (see Num. 33:4). In any

---

31. N. C. Habel, *Yahweh versus Baal: A Conflict of Religious Cultures* (New York: Bookman, 1964), pp. 52–71, especially p. 66.

case, the point of the psalm is that it is Yahweh, not some pagan god, who is sovereign over the chaotic forces of nature.

Verse 4 is the answer to verse 3 (and perhaps it was sung antiphonally). It begins with the comparative construction "More than the sounds of many waters" but then adds "majestic, breakers of the sea." The word "majestic" (or "mighty") is here in the plural (אַדִּירִים; s.v. Ps. 8:1); if the form stands as it appears in the MT, then it may be taken as a modifier of the "breakers," reading "the mighty breakers of the sea" in apposition to "many waters" (see the note on the text).[32] But however this part is translated the main point of the comparison is in the last colon: "the LORD on high is majestic (more than . . .)." "On high" (בַּמָּרוֹם; s.v. Ps. 46:10) exalts the LORD above all the chaos of the many waters on earth; in that exalted position he is majestic (אַדִּיר)—more than all the impressive forces and sounds of mighty waters.[33] He is above all things.

III. The holy LORD rules faithfully forever (5).

The transition between verses 4 and 5 at first seems abrupt, a change from the LORD's majesty displayed in his control of creation, to revelation through his word (see the same type of change in Psalm 19). The point makes sense in the context: this sovereign king of creation has given his people his testimonies (עֵדֹתֶיךָ; s.v. Ps. 119:2). The term "testimonies" is probably a reference to the covenant as a whole, including the revelation of God's wonderful acts along with his laws. Some commentaries suggest interpreting this word as referring to an aspect of God's enthronement ("appoint" meaning to establish kingship); for example, Dahood links it to a word for "throne" (עַד) and suggests

---

32. Eaton suggests that verse 4b might even be interpreted to include titles and not just descriptions, in the same way that Ugaritic refers to (prince) Sea (Yam) and (judge) River (Nahar). This he argues would account for the plural form of majesty: the LORD is more exalted than "the Majesties," or "the Breakers of the Sea" (see J. H. Eaton, "Some Questions of Philology and Exegesis in the Psalms," *JTS* 19 [1968]:688, 9).
33. This imagery is also used in the book of Revelation where the voices of great companies of people are compared to the sounds of many waters, a roaring sound.

that the line states that God's throne has been firmly established.³⁴ But the normal meaning of "testimonies" or "decrees" makes good sense. Broyles suggests it refers to the royal decrees of the king and not simply a codified legislation.³⁵ Whatever the specific content of "testimonies" might be, it clearly refers to God's revelation. And these testimonies the psalmist states are "faithful" (נֶאֶמְנוּ; s.v. Ps. 15:2). God's words, his revelation, are true and reliable—a point made repeatedly in the book of Psalms (see Pss. 12, 19, and 119). Not only is the LORD majestic and powerful, he is also trustworthy in all that he says.

The second half of the verse then considers the holiness of the LORD's house: "holiness is befitting for your house" (לְבֵיתְךָ נַאֲוָה־קֹדֶשׁ). This indicates that "holiness" is the beauty of the house of the LORD (see Isa. 52:7 and Song 1:10). The emphasis in the line is the word "holiness" (s.v. Ps. 22:3): it refers to the uniqueness or distinctiveness of the LORD's dwelling place. There is no place comparable to his sanctuary because there is no one comparable to the LORD—he is holy. This expression too may be polemical against Canaanite myths in which Baal ascended the mountain in the north to his house, which was filled with debauchery and profane celebration—it was base and low, all too human. But the LORD's house is holy! And this is not a seasonal quality re-enacted each fall with an enthronement ceremony, but an eternal quality of his house—"for ever" (literally, "for the length of days"; see Ps. 23:6).³⁶ The wording of the text may not clearly state that it is eternal, only that it continues for all time. But the New Testament will clearly confirm that it is eternal (Rev. 21:22–22:5).

MESSAGE AND APPLICATION

The message of this short psalm is clear enough. It may be

---

34. *Psalms*, II:342.
35. *Psalms*, p. 369,
36. See also J. D. Schenkel, "An Interpretation of Psalm 93:5," *Bib* 46 (1965):401–16. He translates the verse to say, "Your throne has been firmly established; in your temple the holy ones (taking the word collectively) glorify you, Yahweh, for length of days."

worded this way for an exposition: *The LORD reigns from his eternal, holy throne with majesty, power, and faithfulness over the world he established.* The exposition will no doubt dwell on the aspects of the LORD's reign, how he established his authority at creation, how he is the king over all creation, how his reign is majestic and powerful, how he is enthroned in holiness, and how he rules by decrees. In doing so the exposition will also have to show the stark contrast between all this and pagan contaminations. Believers will gladly acclaim that the LORD God reigns, both in the celebration of worship and in daily witness; but as they do so, they will be reminded of their allegiance to their sovereign and their responsibilities in his kingdom.

And this commitment to the divine king will increase daily in the lives of the people of God, for they realize that while he now reigns on high, he has not yet put down all his enemies and solidified his majestic power throughout all the earth. That will take place when the Lord comes in power and glory. Til then the acclamation "the LORD reigns" is both a present reality to the believer and a future hope for the world.

Furthermore, the expositor should add the clarification that just as the LORD established Israel as his people through the sovereign display of his power over the world system, he also built his church and ensured that it would never be destroyed by the gates of hell (Matt. 16:18). And so until the saints enter into the LORD's holy presence in glory, they must demonstrate the power of their divine king as they serve him on earth (1 Cor 3:17).

PSALM 94

Vindication through Divine Retribution

INTRODUCTION

Text and Textual Variants[1]

1 O God who avenges,[2] O LORD,
   O God who avenges, shine forth.[3]

---

1. The Greek manuscripts include: Ψαλμὸς τῷ Δαυιδ, τετράδι σαββάτων, "A Psalm of David, for the fourth day of the week."
2. The text has this order: "O God who avenges, Yahweh, // O God who avenges, shine forth." It could also be translated, "O LORD, the God who avenges." The Greek version translates the line as "The Lord is God of vengeance."
3. The form in the text is הוֹפִיעַ, the *hiphil perfect* of יָפַע, "shine forth" (if it is an imperative it does not follow the expected short form). Most interpretations would read the form as an imperative, suggesting the form was הוֹפִיעָה, as in Psalm 80:2, explaining the loss of the ה by haplography. There is substantial support for the imperative in the later versions—Aquila, Symmachus, Theodotion, Quinta, Jerome and the Syriac. However, the Greek version reflects a perfect tense: ἐπαρρησιάσατο, "spoke openly." Dahood retains the perfect tense of the MT as well, rendering it as "has shone forth" (comparing Psalm 50; see *Psalms*, II:346).

2 Rise up, O judge of the earth;
   put back on the proud what they deserve.

3 How long *will* the wicked, O LORD,
   how long will the wicked celebrate?
4 They pour out, they speak[4] arrogant[5] *words*;
   all the evildoers speak boastfully.[6]

5 They crush[7] your people, O LORD;
   they oppress your inheritance.
6 They slay the widow and the alien[8];
   and they kill the fatherless.[9]
7 And they say, "The LORD[10] does not see;
   the God of Jacob does not consider."

8 Consider *this,* you senseless ones among the people;
   and you fools, when will you act wisely?[11]
9 He who implanted the ear, does he not hear,
   or he who formed the eye, does he not see?

---

4. Several versions include "and" here.
5. The Greek translation uses "injustice," $\dot{\alpha}\delta\iota\kappa\iota\alpha\nu$.
6. The MT has a stronger form of the verb "speak," the *hithpael* יִתְאַמְּרוּ; which occurs only here; it would seem to have a meaning of "say to themselves." The Greek translation uses $\lambda\alpha\lambda\eta\sigma\sigma\upsilon\sigma\iota\nu$, which would be a translation of the simple *qal,* יֹאמְרוּ, "they speak." It may be that the verb is not the verb "to say." There are nouns that reflect the idea of loftiness or height: אָמִיר is a high branch, and אָמֹרִי a mountaineer. And there is an Arabic cognate that means "carry oneself as a ruler." Perhaps this line should read "carry themselves proudly," even though that does not parallel the motif of speaking in the first colon. The translation "speak boastfully" fits the verse well.
7. The Greek translation interpreted this idea with the more general "they humbled," $\dot{\epsilon}\tau\alpha\pi\epsilon\iota\nu\omega\sigma\alpha\nu$.
8. The Greek version translated this with "convert" or "proselyte," $\pi\rho\sigma\sigma\eta\lambda\upsilon\tau\sigma\nu$.
9. The Greek translation reverses "alien" and "fatherless" in the word order.
10. The form in the MT is the abbreviated word יָהּ.
11. For MT's מָתַי תַּשְׂכִּילוּ Greek version has $\pi\sigma\tau\dot{\epsilon}\ \varphi\rho\sigma\nu\eta\sigma\alpha\tau\epsilon$, which may be rendered, "think for once."

Vindication through Divine Retribution

10 He who disciplines[12] nations, does he not punish,
    even he who teaches humans[13] knowledge?[14]
11 The LORD knows the intentions of humans,[15]
    that they are futile.

12 Blessed is the one[16] whom[17] you discipline, O LORD,[18]
    and *whom* you teach[19] from your law,
13 giving such a one calmness[20] from days of trouble,
    till a pit is dug for the wicked.
14 For the LORD will not reject his people;[21]
    neither will he forsake his inheritance.

---

12. MT has the interrogative particle with the participle, הֲיֹסֵר, "does he who disciplines." The Greek version has ὁ παιδεύων, "he who disciplines," reading the participle with an article (הַיֹסֵר). This resolved the more difficult construction of the MT that has the interrogative particle twice in the line: "does he who disciplines nations, does he not punish."
13. The Hebrew text uses the general word אָדָם, "man" or "humankind." Some manuscripts add the preposition to it.
14. To make a better parallel construction in the verse some propose reading the word "knowledge" (דָּעַת) with the preposition: "Is the one who teaches human beings without knowledge?" The same idea may be obtained by simply supplying a word like "lack" based on the parallel constructions: "does he who teaches human beings *lack knowledge*?" (see NIV). But the clause is best left as it is in the MT and taken to be explanatory: *"even* he who teaches human beings knowledge."
15. MT has אָדָם.
16. MT is הַגֶּבֶר, "the man."
17. The MT has the relative pronoun, even though it is not necessary to translate it. But two manuscripts do not have it.
18. Hebrew יָהּ.
19. The form in the MT is תְּלַמְּדֶנּוּ, "you teach him" (referring to "the man/the one"). A relative pronoun may be understood here, making the suffix a resumptive pronoun: who + him, becoming "whom."
20. The verb שָׁקַט here is the *hiphil* infinitive construct form, לְהַשְׁקִיט; the word would mean "to give [him, i.e., the person] relief" or "inner calmness." Tate suggests translating it as a circumstantial clause, "giving them assurance" (*Psalms 51–100*, p. 484).
21. The Qumran scroll (*4QPs^b*) adds the sign of the accusative before "his people."

15 For unto righteousness justice will return,[22]
    and all the upright in heart *shall follow* after it.[23] [24]

16 Who will rise up for me against the wicked?
    Who[25] will take a stand for me against evildoers?
17 Unless the LORD *had been* my help,[26]
    I[27] would soon have dwelt in *the* silence *of death*.[28]
18 When[29] I said, "My foot is slipping,"
    your loyal love, O LORD, supported me.
19 In the abundance of anxious thoughts[30] *that were* within me,
    your comforts brought joy to my spirit.[31]

---

22. This line is rather abstract. The editors of BHS propose reading with two manuscripts, Symmachus, and the Syriac the form צַדִּיק, "righteous," in place of MT's צֶדֶק, "righteousness." The idea then would be that justice will turn back on or to the righteous. However, the same meaning could be derived from the text without making a change: "righteousness" could be a metonymy for the righteous. But the idea of justice returning to righteousness also makes sense.
23. This colon is cryptic: "and all the upright in heart after it." The translation of אַחֲרָיו could have the meaning "with him" or "after him"—in like manner (see Dahood, *Psalms,* I:275, 302; II:195). Tate follows this and translates it "likewise"—Justice will return to the righteous, and to the upright of heart likewise (*Psalms 51–100,* p. 482).
24. The Greek version reflects a *"selah"* here.
25. Two manuscripts and the Greek and Syriac versions have a conjunction here.
26. The Greek version (and some modern versions) translates this as a verb, ἐβοήθησέν μοι, "had helped me."
27. MT has נַפְשִׁי, "my life," meaning "I."
28. The MT simply has the word "silence" (דוּמָה), which in this verse means death. I have added the word "death" to ensure the meaning of the word "silence." The Greek verse added "in Hades," τῷ ᾅδῃ.
29. The particle אִם could also be translated "if" ("If I said . . . .") and then the imperfect in the second colon "would support me."
30. For the word שַׂרְעַפַּי many manuscripts have ס instead of שׂ.
31. The Greek version is clearly reading the words in the Hebrew text, but translating the line differently: "The pains of my heart were as many as your consolations that loved my soul."

Vindication through Divine Retribution

20 Can a corrupt throne be allied with you—
    one that forms trouble by decree?[32]
21 They band together[33] against the life of the righteous
    and condemn *to death*[34] innocent blood.
22 But the LORD has become[35] my fortress,
    and my God, the rock of my refuge.[36]
23 He will repay them[37] for their sins
    and destroy them[38] for their wickedness;
    the LORD our God will destroy them.

---

32. The word is simply חֹק, "decree" or "statute." The Syriac adds the second person suffix, "your statute," probably giving the meaning that they form trouble against the LORD's law—"against your statute." But it could also be referring to the ordinances of the iniquitous rulers that create trouble.
33. MT has יָגוֹדּוּ, but many manuscripts have the spelling as יָגֻדוּ—"they gather in troops." The Greek translation uses θηρεύσουσιν, "they will hunt down."
34. The verb יַרְשִׁיעוּ means "they declare guilty," i.e., condemn. Their condemnation may not always be to death, but this psalm has spoken of how they destroy the righteous and here condemn innocent blood.
35. The form וַיְהִי continues the sequence within the context.
36. MT has לְצוּר מַחְסִי, "(and has become) for a rock of my refuge," a rock in whom I take refuge. But the Greek version again interprets "rock" with "helper," reading "helper of my hope" or "my hoped-for helper," εἰς βοηθὸν ἐλπίδος μου.
37. The form in the text is וַיָּשֶׁב which would at first glance be translated "and he has returned/brought back (their iniquity against them)". The Greek translation has καὶ ἀποδώσει, "and he will recompense" (reading a simple *waw* on the imperfect). Some commentators suggest emending the text to וְ to read a future tense here with a normal conjunction, as the verbs in verse 23 should be taken to refer to the future. There are other possibilities for the form. It could continue the present tense, affirming that God repeatedly turns their iniquity back on them. This does not work very well because the next verbs are simple imperfect tenses speaking of the certain future destruction. Another proposal is to take the *waw consecutive* form as referring to the future: "he has become my rock of refuge, and he will turn their iniquity back on them." This interpretation (like a prophetic perfect) would have the same effect as the emendation. The use is not very common; and some of the passages cited for its use have other plausible explanations (see e.g., Pss. 16:9; 22:30; 41:13). Either by emending the text slightly, or taking an unusual classification for the form, the text is probably best translated in the future.
38. The Greek text does not have the verb written twice; it reads "in their wickedness the LORD our God will destroy them."

Composition and Context

Psalm 94 is a prayer for the LORD, the judge of the whole world, to vindicate the oppressed by destroying the oppressors. The theme is divine retribution, which is a more precise term than vengeance. The psalmist, speaking for countless believers then and now, lives in the midst of danger and destruction, but anticipates the fulfillment of the promises. Accordingly, on the one hand he exhorts the righteous to live faithfully until the judgment comes, and on the other, the wicked to realize the folly of their way.

The structure of the psalm itself is easily followed: the first part is a corporate prayer for judgment on the oppressors (vv. 1–7), the second is an admonition for these senseless oppressors to come to their senses and act wisely (vv. 8–15), and the third part is an individual lament with extensive words of confidence (vv. 16–23). Some commentators see the psalm in just two parts, the national lament (vv. 1–15) and the individual lament (vv. 16–23). But the central section has a distinct wisdom emphasis that calls for separate attention.

The location of Psalm 94 in the collection is well-placed. It has close ties to Psalm 93, as 93 has to 92; in short, Psalms 90–94 form a unit within the collection of Psalms 90–99. And verses 12–15 in Psalm 94 come at the center of the section 90–99.[39]

It is difficult to identify the precise occasion for the psalm. The oppression described here could fit almost any time in Israel's history. The psalm's inclusion in Book IV of the collection indicates that it retained great value for the nation suffering oppression from other nations.[40] The psalm, in fact, Psalms 90–99, served to revive the faith of the people living under the effects of God's wrath. Accordingly, most commentators would take a late date for the psalm; A. A. Anderson briefly surveys some possible times, such as that of Isaiah or Micah, before concluding that

---

39. In a more technical study, Howard also notes that the structure and syllable count is comparable to acrostic psalms (as Psalm 119), making it a non-alphabetic acrostic (see Howard, *The Structure of Psalms 93–100*, pp. 50–51; see also D. N. Freedman, "Acrostic Psalms in the Hebrew Bible: Alphabetic and Otherwise." *CBQ* 47 [1985]:624–42).
40. The Midrash says that the Levites were singing the conclusion of this psalm when the temple was destroyed (*Psalms* 2:135).

the late Persian date is "a reasonable guess."[41] But the original composition may have been much earlier than its use in this section, for there is no clue in the passage that the oppressors are a foreign power. Dahood claims it is early because of the use of prefixed verb forms for the past tense. And Howard says that while a pre-exilic date is plausible, although not as certain as Psalm 93, the psalm still could have come from the 9th century, even though it is later than Psalm 93.[42]

Whenever the exact date of the composition, the psalm would have found constant use in the worship of the faithful. Weiser suggests that it was used in the festival cult of the community in the sanctuary, where the psalmist hoped for judgment on evil doers and where he gained confidence from previous vindications.[43] The psalm was later designated for use on the fourth day of the week, according to the superscription in the Greek version.

Exegetical Analysis

Summary

The psalmist calls on the LORD to render vengeance on the proud who have wickedly oppressed the righteous, expressing his confidence that the LORD will not forsake his people but will deliver them when he destroys those who have no part with the LORD's righteousness.

Outline

I. Speaking on behalf of the people, the psalmist calls on the LORD to take vengeance on the proud who have wickedly oppressed and afflicted the righteous (1–7).
  A. He calls on the LORD (to whom vengeance belongs) to render to the proud the punishment they deserve (1–2).

---

41. *Psalms 73–150*, p. 670.
42. *Structure*, p. 189.
43. *Psalms*, p. 623.

B. He laments the oppression the proud have insolently inflicted on them (3–7).
   1. He wonders if the triumph of the wicked will never end (3).
   2. He describes how in their arrogance and blindness they demolish God's people, especially the needy and the oppressed (4–7).
II. The psalmist warns the proud to consider their foolish ways, because the LORD, who fully knows their deeds, will not forsake his people (8–15).
   A. He calls on the wicked to consider their folly (8–11).
      1. The foolish and senseless enemies should become wise (8).
      2. God sees their oppression and is fully aware of their vanity (9–11).
   B. He expresses his confidence that God will deliver his people from the wicked (12–15).
      1. Those whom God chastens are blessed (12).
      2. God intends to give them rest when the wicked are destroyed (13).
      3. The LORD will not forsake his people but will vindicate them (14–15).
III. The psalmist confidently announces that the righteous LORD will deliver his people and bring retribution to the wicked (16–23).
   A. He praises the LORD for deliverance, preservation, and comfort (16–19):
      1. Only the LORD can deliver as he has done before (16–17).
      2. The LORD has protected and preserved his people along the way (18).
      3. The LORD comforts them in their thoughts (19).
   B. He confidently anticipates the vindication of the believers and the divine retribution against the wicked (20–23).
      1. Those who deal out wickedness have no part with God (20).
      2. Those who trust in the LORD for refuge will be vindicated when the wicked are destroyed (21–23).

COMMENTARY IN EXPOSITORY FORM

I. The faithful trust the LORD to bring judgment on the arrogant who wickedly oppress people (1–7).

A. *They appeal to the LORD to judge the wicked for their deeds (1–2).*

The first part of the psalm is the prayer for God to bring retribution on the wicked—it is God alone who can do this, and not people. If anything at all is understood from the beginning of this psalm it is that it is the LORD who avenges. Not only is the idea repeated, but it is also put first in each colon: "O God who avenges, O LORD; // O God who avenges, shine forth." The precise construction is "God of avengings" (אֵל־נְקָמוֹת). The word is difficult to translate; "vengeance" sounds vindictive and arbitrary, when the context here speaks of rendering to the wicked what they deserve. The word includes the senses of "retribution" and "vindication" (s.v. Ps. 18:47). And here it is put in the plural form for intensification (GKC 124a; although Howard suggests a plural of totality).[44] The point in this psalm is that Yahweh, as the covenant God, will vindicate his people by bringing judgment on the enemies.

The prayer is for God to "shine forth." This is the language of epiphany (see Pss. 50:1 and 80:1). The psalmist desires the LORD to appear in divine splendor to judge the wicked; he wants a glorious intervention to bring an end to all this trouble. The petition is continued in verse 2 with the verb "rise up"; but the term used is the verb "lift up" or "be lifted up" (הִנָּשֵׂא, s.v. Ps. 24:7) which is not the normal word in such a prayer (the verb expected would be from רוּם; s.v. Ps. 46:10). Nevertheless, the meaning of God's rising up is that he get started in his work of judgment. The desired activity of this petition is clear because it is addressed to the judge of the earth (שֹׁפֵט הָאָרֶץ; s.v. Ps. 9:4), the earth being a figure for the people in the earth (a metonymy of subject), the object of this judgment. God's being the judge of all the earth means that he

---

44. *Structure*, p. 46.

makes the decision regarding all people, vindicating the righteous and condemning the wicked.

Here the immediate focus is on the wicked, described as the "proud" (גֵּאִים).[45] These are people who have no recognition of God's authority, as the psalm will reveal; and by setting God's laws aside, they decide to do as they please. The prayer is that God will "pay back" (literally, "put back"; הָשֵׁב < שׁוּב; s.v. Ps. 126:1) the wicked what they deserve. And what they "deserve" (גְּמוּל) is judgment for their sins (see also Ps. 28:4).[46]

B. The wicked deeds of the arrogant oppress and destroy God's people (3–7).

The writer next describes what these wicked people do. The section begins with the rhetorical question, "How long?" in each colon of verse 3. "How long?" expresses the lament of the psalmist that the oppression of the wicked seems never to let up—God seems not only to be letting them continue their evil acts but also to be jubilant in their power. How long will God let the wicked "celebrate" (יַעֲלֹזוּ; ironically, a word also used in Psalm 28:7 for the joy of the righteous)? This form, and the subsequent imperfect tenses, yield the sense that from the writer's point of view the wicked activities were presently going on and would continue until God stopped it.

The psalmist now focuses on the delight that the wicked have in their uncontested activities. The description starts with their arrogant words (v. 4). Two verbs are used in the first colon: "they gush forth" and "they speak" arrogantly (עָתָק). The two verbs may be translated separately for intensification; but they also may be taken together, the second verb may be subordinated to the first as a temporal clause, so that the verse would say that they gush forth arrogant words when they speak. The verb "gush forth" (יַבִּיעוּ) can be used for any words, words of the

---

45. This word "proud" can be used in a good sense in referring to the LORD's majesty (s.v. Ps. 93:1). Here, of course, it refers to the wicked, who are proud. The pride here is hubris; according to Psalm 123:4 these people act without regard for God.
46. The word is neutral; it can also be used to refer to the rewards for the righteous (Ps. 13:6). The context will decide what they actually deserve.

wise (Ps. 78:2) as well as of the fool (Ps. 59:7)—here clearly of the wicked. The arrogance of their speech comes from their (naive) belief that God does not pay attention to them. So they speak boastfully. The verb used is unusual (יִתְאַמְּרוּ), but probably has the sense that they speak their words repeatedly about themselves and to each other.[47] What makes this talking boastful is that they are full of themselves, and in their arrogant words promote themselves and deny God's attention to what they are doing—and what they are doing is considerable since they are called "doers of evil"(for אָוֶן; s.v. Ps. 28:3).

Now the focus is on what they were doing—specifically, they crush (יְדַכְּאוּ), they oppress (יְעַנּוּ), they slay (יַהֲרֹגוּ), and they kill (יְרַצֵּחוּ). These four verbs in the section rapidly describe evil (vv. 5–6). And the arrangement of the words underscores the intensity. The first word "crush" is intensive (a *piel*); and the last word "kills" (also a *piel*) probably signifies plural activity—they kill like assassins. The second word "oppress" joins with the first verb to complete the idea that the crushing is part of their oppression; and the word "slay" joins with the intensive "kill" to stress that they destroy people.

These words could be taken figuratively (hyperbole), although the literal cannot be ruled out (there were both individual and state-sanctioned oppressions and murders). If the verbs were taken to be figurative, the verse would mean that the wicked were destroying the rights of other people, or depriving them of the things necessary to their livelihood—they effectively crushed them and destroyed their lives.[48] And what is so disturbing to the psalmist is who they destroy: in verse 5 the focus is on the people of God; in verse 6 the focus is on people of God who are vulnerable, the widow, the alien, and the fatherless. In short, they were attacking people that God promised he would protect, that he required the people to protect, but since they refused, then only he now would protect.

According to verse 7, these wicked people thought that they were safe in their wicked acts—which is why the psalmist will proceed to call them senseless fools. The verse begins with

---

47. Goldingay, *Psalms 90–150*, p. 77.
48. Anderson, *Psalms 73–150*, p. 672.

"they say" (literally "and they said," וַיֹּאמְרוּ); this form of the verb (the preterite with *waw* consecutive) carries the same nuance as the other verbs in this section, but is used here stylistically to close of the section: "They say, 'The LORD does not see; the God of Jacob does not consider'." By using the verbs "see" (יִרְאֶה) and "consider" (or "understand," יָבִין; s.v. Ps. 49:3), they were claiming that God was unaware of what they were doing, or not interested in judging them, or unable to do so.

II. The faithful warn the wicked to abandon their foolish ways because the LORD is fully aware of their deeds and will destroy them (8–15).

A. *They appeal to the wicked to abandon their ways because God is preparing to judge them (8–11).*

The second section of the psalm uses wisdom terms to warn the wicked to abandon their foolish ways. The section begins with an imperative from the same verb used at the end of verse 7; here it is "consider *this*" (בִּינוּ). They claimed that God did not understand or discern what they were doing; now the psalmist tells them to consider the truth—God does know all about them! He first addresses them as "senseless ones" (בֹּעֲרִים), a word that describes them as the dullest and densest of people. Parallel to this he calls them "fools" (כְּסִילִים), a word that describes them as stubborn and rebellious.[49] The words are appropriate; as VanGemeren puts it, they foolishly establish their little kingdom on earth as if there is no God who calls them to account.[50] So the psalmist tells them to act wisely (he uses the rhetorical question, "when will you act wisely?"). This verb (תַּשְׂכִּילוּ; s.v. Ps. 36:4) is a common word for acting wisely or prudently (and therefore becoming successful in God's plan). For them to act prudently would mean to take into account that God does see and evaluate everything they are doing and therefore to change their ways before it is too late (compare Ps. 2:10–12). In short, the psalmist wonders when they will come to their senses.

---

49. The word כְּסִיל is a common designation of the fool in Proverbs.
50. *Psalms*, p. 713.

There follows a series of rhetorical questions designed to make affirmative statements: God hears, God sees, and God punishes. The reasoning is so simple that even a foolish simpleton should be able to understand it. If God can make people able to do something, he surely can do that something himself.[51] He made the human ear, he surely can hear; he formed the eye, he can see; and he disciplines (for the verb יָסַר s.v. Ps. 6:1) nations and teaches people knowledge (s.v. Ps. 139:6), he surely can punish (for the verb יָכַח s.v. Ps. 38:1). These kinds of statements bring many passages to mind; one that stands out is the report in Exodus 2:24–25 that says God heard the groaning of his people, he looked at them, and he knew them. And the result was that he took retribution on those who had been oppressing his people.

The sum of these points is that God knows the intentions of humans, that they are futile (v. 11). The "intentions" are the thoughts and plans that people make (מַחְשְׁבוֹת, from חָשַׁב; s.v. Ps. 32:2); and the word "futile" means "empty, meaningless" (הֶבֶל, as in Eccl. 1:1). The word "futile" could refer to the word "man" (אָדָם), here translated "humans," or to their intentions. The plural pronoun "they" would suggest that it goes with "intentions," even though that is a feminine plural word, and "man" here is collective for people. Weiser takes it to say "their thoughts are nothing",[52] which would mean all their plans, their self-promotion, and their activities are futile. In a sense, then, they are meaningless.

B. The faithful take comfort in God's chastening because he will not abandon them to the wicked (12–15).

The psalmist contrasts the warning to the fools with words of blessing and encouragement to the righteous. This little section begins with the assertion that the one whom the LORD disciplines and teaches is blessed (for אַשְׁרֵי, "blessed," s.v. Ps. 1:1). The verbs "disciplines" and "teaches" repeat the themes from

---

51. Broyles, *Psalms*, p. 371.
52. *Psalms*, p. 624

verse 10; but the contrast is also clear: those who respond to divine discipline wisely and receive additional revelation faithfully will be blessed. The people of God may have to endure oppression and danger for some time, but in it all they will come to know more about God through his revelation. And that knowledge they gain will bring them an inner calmness (לְהַשְׁקִיט from שָׁקַט) to enable them to endure until the judgment is set for the wicked. That calmness is essentially relief, a relief that is characterized by confidence because it is based on divine revelation that reminds them of the coming vindication, a vindication that must include the destruction of the wicked, expressed here in the imagery of a pit being dug (an implied comparison), signifying that God is preparing a way to destroy the wicked who are presently causing so much trouble.

The assurance that brings such relief is based on the covenant truth that God will not reject his people, nor forsake his inheritance (v. 14). The righteous are God's people by covenant; and in the covenant God's people are his inheritance. The two verbs are in negative statements ("he will not reject" [לֹא־יִטֹּשׁ], and "he will not forsake" [לֹא יַעֲזֹב]); to make the point positively one would simply say that God will remain loyal to his people because they belong to him—he will take care of them through all the trouble of this life and guide them to glory. It may seem at times that God has abandoned his people to the ruthless oppressors of this world, but Scripture affirms that he has not. This constantly repeated truth keeps hope alive for the believers until the judgment of God brings them vindication.

The last verse (15) in this section is difficult. The first colon says justice will turn or return (יָשׁוּב) to righteousness. That probably means that judicial decisions would once again be made with righteousness (צֶדֶק; s.v. Ps. 1:5). But if this word "righteousness" is taken to mean "the righteous," it would mean that righteous people will once again be treated with justice. There is very little difference between the two meanings. If God judges the wicked and restores righteousness to the land, those who are righteous will be the chief beneficiaries of it anyway.

The second colon of the verse only says "and all the upright in heart after it." These words have received a number of suggested interpretations. Most commentators supply a verb before "after it" to say that the upright will pursue after this righteousness that will return. Kraus and others emend the text ("after it," וְאַחֲרָיו) to read "and a reward" (וְאַחֲרִית): "a reward shall come to all who are upright in heart."[53] There is no support for this change; and the reading in the text makes good sense.

III. The faithful are confident that the LORD will deliver them and bring retribution to the wicked (16–23).

A. They put all their trust in the LORD because he delivers, defends, and comforts them (16–19).

The next few verses record the individual lament and prayer for vindication. The questions asked earlier now lead to additional rhetorical questions: "Who will rise up (יָקוּם; s.v. Ps. 3:1) for me against the evil doers (מְרֵעִים; s.v. Ps. 10:15)?" Earlier he called on the LORD to rise up on his behalf, and so this question is meant to appeal to the LORD to be the one to rise up because there is no one else who can do it. The parallel colon adds another rhetorical question designed to state that it is the LORD who will take a stand against workers of iniquity (פֹּעֲלֵי אָוֶן). And to confirm that the LORD is the one to do this, the psalmist provides his personal experience in verse 17: "Unless the LORD *had been* my help (עֶזְרָתָה; s.v. Ps. 46:1), I would soon have dwelt in *the* silence *of death*." The verse simply means that the LORD intervened and kept him alive. He apparently had been in serious trouble and could have entered that land of silence, the grave (see Ps. 115:17). The beginning particle translated "unless" (לוּלֵי) introduces the exceptive clause; without divine help he would have dwelt (שָׁכְנָה, the perfect tense completing the hypothetical idea) in the silence which is death ("silence" being a metonymy of adjunct for the grave).

This event is specified in the next two verses. He describes the danger of his dilemma, his foot was slipping, and the despair it caused; his anxieties were abundant. The foot slipping is a frequent figure for the lack of stability and confidence in a time of trouble (if it refers to something that happened on the pilgrim

---

53. *Psalms 60–150*, p. 242.

way it could be a metonymy, otherwise, it is an implied comparison). The idea is intensified in verse 19: his anxious thoughts (שַׂרְעַפַּי)[54] were so numerous that he was nearly overwhelmed with doubts and despair. But what sustained him through the trouble was the LORD's loyal love (חֶסֶד; s.v. Ps. 23:6), meaning the way that God intervened in his life to protect him and provide for him (so "loyal love" is a metonymy of cause). Then, in verse 19b the psalmist provides the effect of the loyal love—the LORD's comforts soothed his spirit. The word "your comforts" (תַּנְחוּמֶיךָ; s.v. Ps. 119:76) is then a metonymy of effect, the cause being the loyal love. It is put into the plural to intensify the idea. Because in his faithful love God intervened in his distress, his spirit was lifted from a crippling anxiety to a delightful comfort (יְשַׁעַשְׁעוּ).[55]

B. They are confident that God will repay the wicked, destructive people for their sins (20–23).

The last few verses express the confidence that God will not tolerate the wicked and their evil domination. These words of confidence are meant to inspire other troubled believers to put all their trust in the LORD, their rock, because he will judge the world in righteousness. In verses 20 and 21 the psalmist states the foundational principle that the kingdom of evil cannot co-exist with the kingdom of God—it must come to an end. And in making this firm assertion, the psalmist also explains the

---

54. The plural noun שַׂרְעַפִּים may be related to a verb שָׂעַף, "to divide," which in the Arabic cognate has a meaning "be disquieted" by something. The regular noun is שְׂעִפִּים means "disquieting thoughts" in Job 4:13 and 20:2. The form in the text here and in Psalm 139:23 has essentially the same meaning, but it has been written as a quadriliteral with the insertion of the letter ר, which is common in Aramaic (GKC, #85w). Goldingay interprets the word to mean a consuming anxiety, or anxious doubts (III:83).
55. The assumed verbal root behind this duplicated (*pilpel*) form is שָׁעַע, which has the meaning "take delight in, sport." The verb is used in Isaiah 11:8 for the infant playing at the cobra's hole; it is also used in Psalm 119:70 for taking delight in the law (also verses 16 and 47). The noun form, a plural of intensification, is used a little more frequently. It is found in the allegory in Isaiah 5:7 to describe Israel as the planting of God's delight. In Proverbs 8 wisdom speaks, saying, "My delight was with the sons of man" (v. 31).

Vindication through Divine Retribution

occasion for his many anxious thoughts. The focus is on a "corrupt throne," literally, a "throne of destructions" (כִּסֵּא הַוּוֹת), the word "throne" being figurative (a metonymy of subject) for the one ruling. The genitive "destructions" could be classified as attributive, "a destructive throne," or objective, a "throne that brings destructions." The latter would fit this psalm better (and still include the former): these enemies have been oppressing and destroying righteous and vulnerable people. Moreover, their destructive reign carries out trouble by decree (עֲלֵי־חֹק), probably indicating that the regime makes decrees that oppress the people and deprive them of their livelihood. Using another rhetorical question the psalmist asks if such a reign of corruption can be allied to God, because the wicked human kingdom destroys what God establishes. The answer of course is "no" (not for long at any rate, only long enough to test or develop faith), for God will destroy such wickedness. And so the question serves to prompt the LORD to end the trouble and establish the longed-for righteousness.

But until God does so, the wicked band together against the righteous and condemn the innocent (נָקִי; s.v. Ps. 19:13). The verb "condemn" is literally, "declare guilty" (יַרְשִׁיעוּ; s.v. Ps. 1:1); the line is a vivid description of the miscarriage of justice, for innocent people are condemned. The word "innocent" is qualified with "blood," to portray more graphically their condemnation; it is metonymical for the innocent people who suffer under wicked rulers—their lives are subject to oppressive and destructive people. Until the judgment comes, the faithful must put their confidence in the LORD and leave retribution to him.

That confident faith is stated powerfully in verses 22 and 23. He uses two images to describe God: "a fortress" and "a rock of my refuge." These metaphors emphasize the safety and security that God provides for those who take refuge in him. This noun "refuge" is appropriate; the word, along with its verb, has the sense of finding shelter (מַחְסִי < חָסָה, s.v. Ps. 7:1), either from a storm, or from wicked enemies. The LORD is the secure refuge in times of wicked oppression and corrupt government, because the faithful can pray with confidence, knowing that the LORD will never abandon them, but will care for them until the time comes to make everything right. And that hope is the point of verse 23: God will turn their evil back on them (the verb is שׁוּב again, but now in the preterite form with the force of future certainty, perhaps as a prophetic perfect). This certainty is confirmed with the repeated statement that the LORD will destroy them (יַצְמִיתֵם). The repetition of this verb "destroy" recalls the repetition in verse 1 of "avenges." This affirmation also is a call for faith to be renewed, for it is a faith in the God of vindication.

MESSAGE AND APPLICATION

The issue that this psalm brings up is the perversion of justice and apparent triumph of legalized oppression and destruction; and the challenge is how the righteous will endure it. The psalm moves from the initial cry to God in the distress to a comforting confidence that God will destroy the wicked and restore righteousness. The source of this confidence is the nature of the LORD, the covenant God. Accordingly, the psalm is filled with clear statements about God: he is the God who avenges, he is the judge of the earth, he does not reject his people, he is their help, his loyal love comforts his people, he is their rock and refuge, he knows what the wicked are doing and planning, he will destroy them for their wickedness, and he will bring in universal righteousness. In view of this the righteous must endure the evils of this world for a little while, and look ahead to the day of vindication. They must simply turn their fears and their frustrations over to the Lord, for he will bring retribution on the wicked. The expository idea may be worded this way: *Believers must pray for the LORD to avenge the oppression of the wicked, knowing that he will surely vindicate his people when he destroys those who oppose his righteousness.*

To say that God avenges wickedness is to say that he brings retribution in judgment—he will give to the wicked what they deserve, and in the process vindicate those who trust in him for deliverance. Human vengeance is different; it is often vindictive and unforgiving, a desire to get even. But vengeance, or retribution, belongs to the LORD; he will repay.

The Bible clearly teaches that God will destroy all wickedness in the judgment—he may intervene with judgments before then, but ultimately he will establish his righteous reign by destroying the reign of wickedness. But the Bible also teaches that God is patient, desiring that people come to repentance. And so believers must endure the destructive and oppressive works of wickedness until it is time for God to judge. They may seek to champion righteousness in the world, but they will find that their final recourse is prayer, for their comfort and hope is in the LORD. The psalm is a prayer by believers who are oppressed by wicked people in power; it is not about one social system or one country versus another.

Psalm 94:11 is cited in 1 Corinthians 3:20; and 94:14 is used in Romans 11:1–2. This prayer is not just an Old Testament prayer; even in the New Testament prayer continues for the LORD to avenge the death of the saints (Rev. 6:9–11). The fact that the righteous turn this over to God shows that they trust his righteousness in ending violence and oppression. And they can then find calmness in his comforting loyal love.

PSALM 95
Unbelief or Rest

INTRODUCTION

Text and Textual Variants[1]

1 Come, let us sing joyfully to the LORD,
    let us shout aloud to the rock of our salvation;[2]
2 Let us come before his presence[3] with thanksgiving,
    with psalms[4] let us shout aloud[5] to him.

---

1. The Greek version has a superscription: Αἶνος ᾠδῆς τῷ Δαυιδ, "A Praise. Of an Ode. Of David."
2. Many manuscripts have יְשָׁעֵינוּ for the MT's יִשְׁעֵנוּ. The Greek version interprets "to the rock of our salvation" as "to God our Savior," τῷ θεῷ τῷ σωτῆρι ἡμῶν.
3. The MT has נְקַדְּמָה פָנָיו, "let us come before his face/presence" or "let us approach his presence." The verb could even be interpreted as "to meet" with God.
4. Greek and Syriac have "and with psalms."
5. The form in the text is נָרִיעַ, but a few manuscripts have the cohortative form נָרִיעָה.

3 For the LORD is a great God,[6]
    and[7] a great king over all gods,[8]
4 in[9] whose hands are the deep places[10] of the earth,
    and the heights of the mountains are his.
5 To whom the sea belongs, for[11] he made it;
    and his hands formed the dry land.

6 Come, let us worship and bow down;[12]
    let us kneel[13] before the LORD our maker.
7 For he is our God,
    and we are the people of his pasture,
    and the sheep of his hand.[14]

Today, if only you will hear his voice:

---

6. The usage of this expression in Psalms 47 and 48 indicates that the idea is meant to be definite: it does not mean he is a great God, but that he is the great God (Anderson, *Psalms 73–150*, p. 677).
7. A few manuscripts and the Syriac do not have the conjunction.
8. The Greek version (not in A) has an additional line: "for the Lord will not cast off his people."
9. In the Hebrew text both verses 4 and 5 begin with אֲשֶׁר, which could be taken as causal—the Greek translation used ὅτι, "for, because," in both places. But here it is taken as a relative pronoun, and with the resumptive pronoun it is translated as "in whose hands."
10. The rare form in the MT is מֶחְקְרֵי; it refers to places unexplored, the lowest and most inaccessible places. The Greek version (and one Hebrew manuscript) has "distant parts/ends (of the earth)," τὰ πέρατα, probably reading the form as מֶרְחַקֵּי.
11. The conjunction "and" is here explanatory.
12. The Greek has "to/before him."
13. The MT has the form נִבְרְכָה, "let us kneel"; this verb is not to be confused with the verb בָּרַךְ, "to bless," even though some dictionaries have put them together. It is a homonym. The Greek translation has an entirely different idea, "let us weep," καὶ κλαύσωμεν, probably reading the form as וְנִבְכֶּה.
14. One manuscript and the Syriac version read these lines as "we are his people and the sheep of his pasture."

8 "Harden not your heart as at Meribah,[15]
    as in the day of Massah[16] in the wilderness,
9 when your fathers tried me,
    proved me, although they saw my work.[17]
10 For forty years I was disgusted with *that*[18] generation.
    And I said, "It is a people[19] that wander away *in their* heart,
    and they do not know my ways;
11 so that[20] I swore in my anger,
    they shall not enter into my rest."[21]

Composition and Context

Psalm 95 has been included in the collection of enthronement psalms, although it does not have some of the distinguishing features of that group. Mowinckel took the first part to be an enthronement psalm, and the second part to be a renewal of the covenant through a cultic prophet;[22] but there is no support for this to be a covenant renewal liturgy, even though it could have been used in that kind of a service. Sabourin calls it a psalm of prophetic exhortation;[23] Anderson says it is a prophetic liturgy, a double hymn with a prophetic warning (similar to the structure

---

15. The name "Meribah" means "strife, controversy" (related to the verb רִיב); the Greek version simply translated the word with ἐν τῷ παραπικρασμῷ, "in the provocation" or "embittering."
16. The name "Massah" means "trial" (related to the verb נָסָה); the Greek version also translated this word with τοῦ πειρασμοῦ, "trial"– according to the day of trial.
17. The form is plural in the versions.
18. The Greek translation has "that" (τῇ γενεᾷ ἐκείνῃ), clarifying the line (followed by the Syriac and Jerome), whereas the Hebrew only has בְּדוֹר, "with a generation."
19. MT has עַם תֹּעֵי לֵבָב, "a people that wander away *in their* heart"; but one manuscript has עַד and the Greek version has ἀεὶ, making the translation "always are they straying in *their* heart."
20. This is a rare use of the pronoun אֲשֶׁר to express result.
21. The Greek makes a literal translation here: "if they shall enter my rest." One would assume that they were familiar with the forms of oaths when they retained the precise wording of the MT.
22. *The Psalms in Israel's Worship*, I:156.
23. *The Psalms*, p. 404.

of Psalm 81).[24] The psalm certainly has enough praise to warrant a hymnic classification, that is, a descriptive praise psalm (vv. 1–7a). And the structure of the psalm fits the descriptive praise pattern fairly well: a call to praise (1–2); the cause for the praise (3–7a) emphasizing God's greatness (vv. 5–6) and his grace (v. 7a); then, instead of a concluding praise there is the didactic element, the prophetic oracle of warning (vv. 7b-11).[25]

The language of the psalm clearly fits a worship setting, for the people are called to enter the LORD's presence in the temple courts with praises, hear his voice, and resolve to obey.[26] The work could have been used for a fall festival of some kind, perhaps a covenant renewal ceremony; but it could have been written for worship at any time when the nation was in need of a reaffirmation of the greatness of the LORD God over all gods and all creation. There were many such occasions in Israel's experience, and so it could have been composed at any time before the exile. No matter when the psalm was composed, it apparently held a special meaning for the exilic or post-exilic community, and so was included in this part of the collection of psalms. Kaiser focuses on the psalm as eschatological, which would harmonize with the ultimate fulfillment of enthronement psalms in general.[27] But the psalm is primarily praise with an oracle, even though it would serve well in the setting of Israel's worship.

The commentators propose a wide range of dates for the composition, at least in its final form; most date it in the exilic

---

24. *Psalms 73–150*, p. 676.
25. Biblical scholars since the time of Wellhausen have debated the structure because of its apparent fragmentation (see Anderson, *Psalms 73–150*, p. 676). But a close analysis of the design of the psalm confirms its fundamental unity—or at least explains why the parts have been put together if indeed they were originally separate. See Marc Girard, "The Literary Structure of Psalm 95," *Theology Digest* 30 (1982):55–58; Samir Massouh, "Psalm 95," *Trinity Journal* 4 (1983):84–88; C. B. Riding, "Psalm 95:1–7c as a Large Chiasm," *ZAW* 88 (1976):418; and Howard, *The Structure of Psalms 93–100*, pp. 74–84.
26. A number of commentators focus on the worship aspect in some detail, isolating in the psalm several calls for the worshipers to draw nearer to God in stages. See, for example, G. H. Davies, "Psalm 95," *ZAW* 85 (1973):183–98.
27. Walter C. Kaiser, Jr., "The Promise Theme and the Theology of Rest," *BibSac* 130 (1973):135–150.

period because of parallels with Deuteronomy and Isaiah 40–66 (assuming late dates for these works). Tate places it in the early post-exilic period,[28] but other writers put it to the later post-exilic period because of similarities with Malachi 2 and Isaiah 57–59. However, Mowinckel argued that the desert tradition used here in the psalm is older than Amos or Isaiah (II:72). The evidence from the psalm leans a little more toward a pre-exilic date for the composition—the sense that the temple was still standing (with no hint that it might have been the rebuilt temple in the later period), the subtle allusions to Canaanite ideas, and the use of the desert tradition to warn people not to rebel against the LORD and, therefore, not to enjoy his rest. The exilic community had failed to obey, and so could only hope to be restored to the promised land; the post-exilic community was already back, and no longer hoping to enter the land. But whenever the psalm was composed, its message is timeless: it is always "today" for those who hear the warning not to harden their hearts. Limiting its meaning to a particular period of time is not only difficult to do, it is something the psalmist chose not to do.

Exegetical Analysis

Summary

Having acknowledged the greatness of the LORD as king above all gods, and having exhorted the congregation to worship their maker, the psalmist instructs the people to hear and obey God's warning not to rebel, lest they fail to receive the promised blessing as their ancestors did.

Outline

I. Descriptive Praise: The psalmist acknowledges the greatness of the LORD as King above all gods, and exhorts the congregation to worship him (1–7a).
   A. The congregation should sing praises to their saving God (1–2).

---

28. *Psalms 51–100*, p. 500.

B. The faithful should acknowledge the greatness of the LORD as King over all his creation (3–5).
C. The congregation should worship the LORD because he is their God and they are his people (6–7a).
II. Prophetic Oracle: The psalmist reports God's warning to his people not to rebel against his word as their ancestors did and were prevented from obtaining their full inheritance (7b–11).
A. Wish: He desires that "today" they should hear his warning (7b).
B. Warning: God's oracle warns them not to harden their hearts as did their forefathers in the wilderness who were hindered from entering the rest (8–11).

COMMENTARY IN EXPOSITORY FORM

I. God's people must praise him as the great king above all gods because he made them, saved them, and takes care of them (1–7a).

The first part of the psalm is a call for the people of God to offer praise to the LORD because of his majestic sovereignty over all creation and his gracious provision of a covenant for them (vv. 1–7a). The emphasis throughout this part is on the close relationship the faithful have with almighty God. Accordingly, their response must be endless praise.

A. Believers must sing praises to the LORD because he is their sure salvation (1–2).

The first two verses form the call proper. The exhortation begins with "Come" (לְכוּ), followed by the hortatory "let us sing joyfully" (נְרַנְּנָה, from רָנַן, "sing, give a ringing cry"[29]; s.v. Ps. 33:1). The parallel verb is "let us shout aloud" (נָרִיעַ; s.v. Ps.

---

[29]. It is possible that the word carries the connotation of "pay homage" through the acclaim when the word is used in a coronation context (see 1 Sam. 10:24; Anderson, *Psalms 73–150*, p. 677).

100:1). The English translations are for the most part too calm: both verbs call for loud, enthusiastic, joyful praise to be given to the LORD.

And the description of the LORD in the verse provides an initial reason for the praise: he is "the rock of our salvation." The metaphor "rock" is frequent in the book of Psalms,[30] emphasizing that the LORD is the solid foundation of the faith, providing safety and security and stability for those who trust in him. The qualifying word, "our salvation" (יִשְׁעֵנוּ, s.v. Ps. 3:2), could be an attributive (genitive), "our saving rock" or "the rock that is our salvation"; but it is more likely objective, referring to the LORD as "the rock saved us" (an idea that is implied in the other classifications). This means that the people who are being called to praise are recipients of his grace—they are the redeemed, not just in the sense of being delivered from enemies or exile, although that may be a part of it, but in being brought into a covenant relation with the LORD. This spiritual dimension to the redemption will be confirmed in verse 7a.

B. Believers must acknowledge God's sovereignty because he rules over all creation (3–5).

The second section of the psalm provides the reason for praise, God's greatness (vv. 3–5) and grace (vv. 6–7a). Verse 3 is the summary statement: "For the LORD is a great God, and a great king above all gods." Since he is the king over all gods, he is the great God—there are none over him. The adjective "great" (גָּדוֹל; s.v. Ps. 34:3) is used twice in the verse, emphasizing the LORD's superiority as God and as king over all gods;[31] the word itself would signify his majesty, but when used to affirm

---

30. For example, see Psalms 18:2; 31:46; 10:14; 28:1; 78:35 and others. There may be a didactic intent in this psalm's use of the metaphor "rock" since the later references to Exodus 17:1–7 and Numbers 20:2–13 in verse 8 remind the reader that in the desert tradition Moses struck a rock.
31. The verse is not an acknowledgment of polytheism. It is a declaration of the supremacy of Yahweh over everything and anything people might claim as deities. But they are not true gods, as the Psalter will make clear (see Ps. 115).

his sovereignty over all gods it stresses his incomparability. All the gods that the pagans worshiped were, after all, part of the LORD's creation—they worshiped the sun, the moon, the stars, rivers, animals, and forces of nature. But the LORD is the great king over all that they worshiped, because any gods they worshiped were part of his created dominion. And to worship the creature and not the creator is not only an insult to the living God but also futile.

Verses 4 and 5 are formed as relative clauses to illustrate the greatness of this king of gods. The first colon says "in whose hands are the deep places of the earth." "Deep places" would be the remote and dangerous abysses of the earth, the unexplored depths. But the figurative use of "his hands" (an anthropomorphic expression) signifies that these places—and what happens in them—are still in his power (compare Psalm 139:7–12). The mention of the "heights of the hills," that is, the mountain peaks, in the second colon forms a merism with the "depths" in the first—from the unexplored depths to the highest points on earth—everything is under his control. There is also a subtle polemical note here as well: the "depths" could also refer to the underworld, the realm of many pagan gods, and the "heights" to the abode of the higher gods. So the simple, general way the verse is stated would undermine the belief in any such "powers" in the depths or in the heights.

Then, the first colon of verse 5 adds that the sea also belongs to him, because he made it; and this is paralleled with the statement that his hands formed the dry land. Now we have a horizontal merism, the sea and dry land—everything is his because he made it. If the line is alluding to the supposed conflict with the sea or primeval chaos, it does so by simply sweeping such an idea away with the declaration that God made the sea. So the depths and the heights, the sea and the dry land, and everything contained in these, are all his and under his control because he created them. Because these places are under the LORD's dominion, no one or nothing in them, especially spirit forces, can act independently of the true and living God. His great sovereignty, demonstrated by his creation of the world and dominion over it, would be reason enough to praise him. But there is more —his grace.

C. Believers must bow down before their maker because he is their God and they are his people (6–7a).

The next two verses focus on the LORD's relationship with his people, a gracious provision of this sovereign Lord. Verse 6 begins with a call as well: "Come, let us worship and bow down, let us kneel before the LORD our maker." The first verb is the imperative (בֹּאוּ), parallel to the imperative in verse 1 (לְכוּ, "come"); but that first invitation was a general exhortation, this is a specific invitation to enter. True believers willingly do this, so this is more of a call to worship than a command to submit. The imperative is followed by three cohortatives all having to do with bowing down before the LORD. The first, translated "let us worship" (נִשְׁתַּחֲוֶה), basically has the idea of bowing oneself low to the ground, the proper and natural posture of the devout in the presence of the living God.[32] The second verb, "and let us bow down" (וְנִכְרָעָה), intensifies the aspect of reverential obeisance in worship. The second colon of the verse uses a third verb in the same semantic field, "let us kneel" (נִבְרְכָה),[33] adding to the growing intensity of the line, but finally including the object of the obeisance: "before Yahweh our maker" (עֹשֵׂנוּ).

The designation of the LORD as "our maker" could be referring to creation in general; but in this psalm with its focus on the covenant relationship the people have with the LORD, it probably refers to the making of the nation.[34] If it is taken as a reference to the formation of the nation, then it would have the idea of

---

32. The word הִשְׁתַּחֲוָה was taken to be from the root שָׁחָה in the older dictionaries; it would be a *hithpael* with metathesis. More recent scholarship relates it to a verbal root חָוָה, and analyzes it as a *hishtaphel* form, a causative (שׁ) and reflexive (ת) stem that is rare in Hebrew. But this explanation would account for all the letters in the word. The meaning would be to cause oneself to be low (to the ground), or bow down, or worship. For the arguments, see John Emerton, "The Etymology of *Hištaḥawāh*," *OTS* 20 (1977):41–55.
33. Older dictionaries list one root בָּרַךְ with the meanings of "bless" and "kneel down." But it is more likely that there were two different roots with the same letters. Here the meaning is clearly "kneel down" and not "bless" (for the discussion of "bless," s.v. Ps. 45:12).
34. See also Malachi 2:10. There, too, it is possible that the reference is to creation in general, but seems to refer more specifically to the formation of Israel by covenant.

God's forming the people into a covenant community, a kingdom of priests and a holy nation (Exod. 19:5–6). Thus the psalmist affirms: "For he is our God, and we are the people of his pasture, and the sheep of his hand."[35] Just as everything else that God made is in his control, the people he formed into a nation also are in his powerful control. Simply put, he is their God —this is the covenant relationship. And the figures used (metaphors) emphasize this covenant relationship: the people are God's "sheep," and his domain, i.e., the land of promise, is the "pasture" of the LORD. Elsewhere Scripture makes the connection clear that the LORD is the shepherd of his people Israel (see Ps. 23:1). Verse 7 seems to echo the covenant promise of God: "I will be their God, and they shall be my people" (see Exod. 19:5–6; 2 Sam. 7:24; and Jer. 31:33). The point of this section, then, is that the faithful are called to bow in his presence because he is their God, the one who graciously elected them to be his people and who takes care of them like a shepherd.

II. God's people must hear and obey God's word rather than stubbornly refuse and fail to receive his promises in full (7b–11).

A. Believers must always be ready to obey the voice of the LORD (7b).

With this part of verse 7 we begin the oracle section of the psalm. Anderson expresses the transition well by saying that while it is right that God's people should rejoice in their king and his care, they must not forget that they have covenant responsibilities as well.[36] One can imagine the scene here of worshipers kneeling before the LORD in his temple and being advised to respond properly to his voice.

The prophetic oracle begins suddenly: "Today, if (only) you would hear his voice." There are two difficulties here; first, how should the clause with "if" (אִם) be interpreted; and second, is

---

35. The wording of the verse is a little unusual, but the meaning is clear; and the Hebrew text has the support of the Greek translation and the Latin Vulgate.
36. *Psalms 73–150*, p. 679.

the clause to be connected to the first part of verse 7 or verse 8? The particle "if" can introduce a conditional clause: "Today, if you hear his voice." But it can also introduce a wish (or desiderative) clause: "Today, if only you will/would hear his voice." Either is possible and both fit the context of the psalm, but the choice depends on the relationship of the clauses.

In the Hebrew text this clause is part of verse 7. If verse 7b is interpreted as belonging to 7a, then the sense might be that the people were God's people if they heard his voice. But since the psalm does not indicate that their position as the people of God was contingent upon hearing his voice (indeed, the reference to God as the rock of their salvation indicates that they were his covenant people), it is preferable to join 7b with verse 8. This has the support of the translation in the Greek text and therefore the citation in Hebrews 3:7 as well. So if the clause is linked to what follows, then it would mean that as the people of God they should obey him.

Now if the clause is taken as a conditional clause it would be connected to verse 8 in this way: "Today, if you will hear his voice, do not harden your heart." In other words, if the assembled people heard from God, they should not make the mistake of their ancestors but obey. It may be that "his voice" refers to a message or a song preceding Psalm 95.

But, if "his voice" refers to the oracle of verses 8–11, then the desiderative interpretation of the clause beginning with "if" would work well. It would mean this: "Today, if only you would hear his voice *(that is)*: 'Do not harden' . . . ." The psalmist would be desiring that they would obey God's warning to avoid the sin of their ancestors.

In either case the use of "today" expresses the urgency of his desire for their immediate obedience—the current audience is being called to participate (see also Deut. 4:40; 5:2–3; 6:6; 7:11). Kirkpatrick says that "today" is "*now*, while the door of opportunity lies open before you."[37] He adds that the reference is not to a particular incident in history, but any time the psalm is read.

---

37. *Psalms*, p. 574.

B. Believers must take heed not to resist his word and thereby fail to receive his full promise (8–11).

Verses 8–11 form the prophetic oracle from the LORD. It begins with the negated jussive, "Do not harden (אַל־תַּקְשׁוּ) your heart." Since the heart represents the will (a metonymy of subject), the image of hardening it would mean a stubborn refusal to obey the word of the LORD. This is not a matter of ignorance, nor uncertainty over the meaning; rather, it is a deliberate choice to refuse to obey God's instructions. And the illustration for this warning is "as at Meribah" (כִּמְרִיבָה, related to רִיב,[38] "to strive") and "as in the day of Massa" (מַסָּה, related to נָסָה, "to test"; s.v.

---

38. רִיב basically means "to quarrel" or "dispute." The verb occurs 65 times in the Old Testament, the main noun רִיב occurs 60 times, and some other forms and related names (such as מְרִיבָה) just a few times. The word is found in non-legal settings as well as legal; a study of the first setting helps understand the use in the second.

In its non-legal usages, the word refers to a dispute between people (Exod. 21:18; Deut. 25:1). Some of the better-known examples are Genesis 13:8 (between the herdsmen of Abram and of Lot), Genesis 31:36 (between Jacob and Laban), and Judges 8:1 (Gideon and the Ephraimites). A common use concerns disputes that occurred over wells of water (e.g., Gen. 26:20ff.). These disputes border on being conflicts or wars and easily lead into such. In fact, the word is used for warfare (Judg. 11:25).

In legal settings, or settings leading up to legal decisions, the word is used for formal complaints and charges. Gideon's defense for destroying the altar of Baal gives rise to a nickname using the verb, Jerubbaal, for his statement was, "Let Baal contend." It was a call for the defendant to appear and respond. The term is also used for a legal hearing before a court where the matters of dispute are resolved (see the arrangement of matters in Deut. 17:8). In the normal legal sense, those in the dispute are basically equals under the law.

When the word is used in theological contexts, the balance changes dramatically. In a number of psalms it forms part of the prayer of lament (see Ps. 74:22), or a prayer for judgment on the enemies (Jer. 25:31). When people pour out their complaint, their dispute before the LORD, the LORD becomes both the accused and the judge in the matter (see Num. 20:13). When God has a dispute with his people, then of course they are the accused and he is the accuser and the judge. In line with this we have the prophetic judgment speeches in which the LORD in fact brings an indictment against the people (Isa. 3:13; Hos. 4:1; and Mic. 6:2). See further J. Limberg, "The Root *ryb* and the Prophetic Lawsuit Speeches," *JBL* 88 (1969):291–304; and B. Gemser, "The *rîb*- or Controversy-Pattern in Hebrew Mentality," *VT Supp* 3 (1955):122–25; and G. Liedke, "רִיב *rîb*.

Ps. 26:2).[39] These names formed a perpetual reminder of the disobedience of Israel in the wilderness when the people strove with God over the lack of food and water. Their complaint in the wilderness started with murmuring,[40] but escalated to formal accusations and charges at Meribah. At Massah they put God to the test, the word "test" always being concerned with doubts and questions, in this case betraying a very weak and doubting faith.[41] The point is that they had God's word of promise, and they had the experience of his miraculous provisions, but they still refused to trust him and challenged him instead—his words of promise, his ability to meet their needs, even his desire to keep them alive. So verse 9 explains that in the wilderness the ancestors put God to the test in unbelief—"although they saw his work."

Verses 10 and 11 record the divine discipline of that generation, a discipline that was well known in the nation. For forty years God was disgusted (אָקוּט) with them. This word has been given various translations; it describes the outraged sense for what is shameful as opposed to what is fitting,[42] and so "disgusted" fits, although "loathed" would also be appropriate given the situation. The LORD said, "They are a people erring in heart,

---

to quarrel," *Theological Lexicon of the Old Testament*, ed. by Jenni and Westermann, III:1232–37.

39. There is a critical problem connected with these two names in Exodus 17:1–7. Meribah may be connected with Kadesh Barnea, but it is joined with Massa in the wilderness tradition and so in the psalm. There is either a double name for the same place, or two locations with similar events that are brought together to make the point (Exodus 16 does this with the manna and the quail).
40. A careful study of this verb in the wilderness passages will show it does not refer to ordinary complaining or grumbling—so it is a difficult word to translate. What the people included in their "murmurings" were accusations against the LORD's integrity, expressions of unbelief in his ability to meet their needs, and statements of disloyalty to the covenant. The controversy (רִיב) started with such rebellious attitudes and accusations.
41. If God tests people, there is some question about their faith. How they respond to the divine test will demonstrate whether they have a strong faith or not. When people put God to the test, it is usually out of unbelief or a weak faith, they demand a sign or proof that he can be trusted rather than take his word on faith and wait for his provision.
42. Kidner, *Psalms 73–150*, p. 346.

and they do not know (יָדְעוּ; s.v. Ps.139:1) my ways." "Erring" is literally "wandering" (תֹּעֵי, the participle going with heart, a genitive of specification: straying in their decisions and affections). Because of their waywardness and rebellion, the LORD swore an oath in his anger (בְאַפִּי; s.v. Ps. 30:5).

The oath begins with "if" (אִם again), but in this formula the sentence is elliptical ("[may such or so happen] if they enter...," meaning, "they shall by no means enter"). In the oath God staked his life on the fulfillment of the oath, so to speak. If the rebellious people entered the rest, then the LORD was not the great God.

This "rest" (מְנוּחָה)[43] referred to in the last verse is in the present context the promised land of Canaan. And since the promised land was the LORD's, his oath prevented them from entering "my rest"; only those who observed the covenant had the right to dwell in the LORD's inheritance and enjoy his rest.[44] So although it refers to the land of inheritance, there is more to it than that. As the fulfillment of God's promise to Israel, entering the land also meant receiving the blessing of God and enjoying the experience of his presence. To enter the land as the people of God would have meant full participation in his theocratic program on earth. The term "rest" in the psalm does not immediately refer to spiritual salvation, even in an eschatological

---

43. The noun מְנוּחָה, "rest," is related to the verb נוּחַ. The verb can be used for setting things at rest, as in settling down or remaining in a place (the ark after the flood, Gen. 8:40; or insects, Exod. 10:14; or the rod of wickedness on the righteous, Ps. 125:3). It is also used for reposing, being quiet, or having rest, such as on the Sabbath day (Exod. 20:11), or from enemies (Est. 9:16). The *hiphil* verbal system simply makes these meaning causative. For examples: Israel set down stones when crossing the Jordan (Josh. 4:3); or the LORD placed the man in the garden (Gen. 2:15).

There are numerous derivatives with the emphasis on quietness or rest. The word used in this psalm means "rest" or a "resting place." It can refer to the sanctuary, the LORD's resting place (Ps. 132:8, 14; and Isa. 66:1), or to a resting place on a journey (Jer. 51:59). The emphasis on tranquility and restfulness comes through in the use in Psalm 23:2 with the waters of restfulness(es). It is also used for rest from all the enemies (1 Kings 8:56). And in Ruth 1:9 it refers to marriage as a place of rest. These and other uses show the many and varied connotations. But as a description of the blessed life in the land that God promised to Israel, the word is most effective.

44. Anderson, *Psalms 73–150*, p. 680.

sense, for the majority of the people who came out of Egypt were already believers (e.g., Moses and Aaron for sure). Rather, "rest" is the full blessing of the promised inheritance in the land that they were denied because of their unbelief; it is both a physical and spiritual rest in the covenant blessings.

And that warning was applicable to the audience of the psalmist: "today," if they rebelled against the LORD, they too would forfeit their full inheritance rights as the people of God in the promised land.[45] But since the "rest" included both temporal and spiritual enjoyment of the LORD's presence and provisions,[46] people could be physically dwelling in the land but not in his rest (just as people could be in a church but not in his kingdom). Kidner notes that this warning would sound a note of realism to the participants in the worship (especially if they were gathered together for the feast of tabernacles that recalls the experiences of the wilderness): they were not to romanticize those events and miss the warning.[47]

MESSAGE AND APPLICATION

Psalm 95 is therefore a call for praise from God's redeemed people for his greatness over all his creation and his grace in making them into a covenant people. But in addition to offering their Lord the praise that is due him, the worshipers are reminded of their responsibility to obey his word. These themes are still relevant for the church. So we could word the expository idea this way: *Believers must acknowledge the sovereignty (greatness) and salvation (grace) of the LORD their maker while taking heed to obey his word so as not to jeopardize their full participation in the promised inheritance.* The New Testament time and time again confirms the divine imperatives to praise the LORD and to obey his word.

The psalm is treated at length in the book of Hebrews. The

---

45. Tate observes that this type of prophetic preaching is Levitical, and more common in the later periods, especially after the exile (*Psalms 51–100*, p. 503).
46. See further Kaiser, "The Promise Theme and the Theology of Rest," pp. 135–150.
47. *Psalms 73–150*, p. 345.

message of the oracle in the psalm is carried over by the writer to teach that *perseverance in the faith brings certainty of the promised "rest."* It is an analogical application of the Old Testament passage; accordingly, "rest" is applied on a higher, spiritual level in Hebrews—it is salvation "rest," even though the principles are the same between the passages. This New Testament application does not exclude other aspects of the promises; it simply makes it clear that if people do not find "rest" (salvation) with God, they will receive no other "rest" (the fulfillment of all the promises) in his kingdom.

The book of Hebrews was written for Jewish people who came to faith in Christ, but under the pressures and persecutions of the time began to waver in their commitment to the new faith. On the one hand, those who were wavering needed the exhortation to hold fast to the faith revealed in Christ Jesus, for faithfulness to God's word would ensure participation in Christ's kingdom through salvation, the ultimate promised rest. And on the other hand believers needed to be reminded to persevere because their promised rest had not yet fully come. So the writer used the theme of "rest" for his analogical application (what is called a *midrash*): the term had a primary interest in the promised blessing of the land of Canaan in the psalm, but in the application in Hebrews it has its greatest and fullest meaning of salvation and communion with God in the world to come. The main idea in either context is clear: *those who hear and obey God's word demonstrate that they are the people of God and will have a share in the promised inheritance to come; but those who do not respond properly to his word may not enter into that rest.* To make the point more vivid, the illustration of the ancestors failure to enter the land as God's people because of unbelief serves the purpose.[48] So the use of the word "rest" focuses on its eschatological, salvific connotations, connotations that find fulfillment in part when people believe in Christ (Matt. 11:28 and Heb. 4:3), but in full ultimately in the age to come. The message

---

48. Hebrews' use of the Psalm is illustrative, an application made by analogy. It is not saying those who failed to enter the land were all unbelievers, for that would eliminate people like Moses and Aaron. It is making the principle that obedience to God's word is necessary to receive the promises.

remains the same in both the psalm and the epistle, namely, that people who profess to be believers must remain steadfast in their obedience to the faith.

Obedience to God and his word is evidence of a living faith—and this is what enables people to know that they have a share in the promised rest. Disobedience to God brings the stern warning of judgment—and this is how someone might miss the promised rest. At the end of the fourth chapter the writer to the Hebrews states the means of entering the rest: the word of the LORD. If it is not believed, if people harden their hearts and refuse the message from God, the blessing will not be given to them. All professing believers must persevere in their faith, or they will not receive the promised blessings, now and in the age to come. The application is serious; every worshiper should be reminded of this warning from God based on the Israelites' lack of faith at Meribah and Massa. Tate says, "The old trek through the wilderness toward the promised land always passes Meribah, where hearts may be hardened and the pilgrimage be lost."[49]

---

49. *Psalms 51–100*, p. 504.

PSALM 96
The Exalted King

INTRODUCTION

Text and Textual Variants[1]

1 Sing to the LORD a new song;
   sing to the LORD all the earth![2]
2 Sing to the LORD! Bless[3] his name![4]
   Proclaim his salvation from day to[5] day!
3 Declare his glory[6] among the nations,

---

1. The Greek version has a superscription: Ὅτε ὁ οἶκος ᾠκοδομεῖτο μετὰ τὴν αἰχμαλωσίαν· ᾠδὴ τῷ Δαυιδ, "When the house was being built after the captivity. An Ode. Of David."
2. This psalm appears in 1 Chronicles and has parallel expressions in Isaiah. In 1 Chronicles 16:23 "a new song" in the first colon and "sing to the LORD" in the second are not there.
3. The Syriac and Vulgate have a conjunction, "and bless."
4. This colon is not in 1 Chronicles 16:23.
5. Many manuscripts and 1 Chronicles 16:23 use אֶל־יוֹם instead of לְיוֹם which is in the MT.
6. The sign of the accusative is present in many manuscripts and 1 Chronicles 16:24.

his wonders among all the peoples!
4 For great is the LORD and greatly praiseworthy;[7]
   he *is to be* feared[8] above all gods.
5 For all the gods of the peoples are idols;[9]
   but the LORD made the heavens.
6 Honor[10] and majesty are before him;
   strength[11] and beauty are in his sanctuary.[12]

7 Give to the LORD, O families of peoples;
   give to the LORD glory and strength;[13]
8 Give to the LORD the glory of his name;
   bring a gift[14] and come into his courts.[15]
9 Bow down to the LORD in holy attire;[16]

---

7. The form in the MT is a plural *pual* participle, literally reading "ones greatly (to be) praised." The plural may be interpreted as a superlative and rendered, "most worthy of praise" or "greatly praiseworthy."
8. The second colon begins with a conjunction ("and feared . . .") in several manuscripts, the Syriac, Targum and 1 Chronicles 16:25.
9. The Greek version translates אֱלִילִים with δαιμόνια, "demons," but the word basically means "nothings" or "worthless things." It can, however, mean false gods—and so the gods of the nations are "nobodies" in comparison with the LORD.
10. The Greek version has here ἐξομολόγησις, "acknowledgment," perhaps assuming הוֹד was from יָדָה.
11. The Greek version here uses ἁγιωσύνη, "holiness," instead of "strength" (עֹז).
12. In place of MT's וְתִפְאֶרֶת בְּמִקְדָּשׁוֹ, a few manuscripts and 1 Chronicles 16:27 have וְחֶדְוָה בִּמְקֹמוֹ; unless this was simply a confusion of words, it may have been a way of generalizing the word in a psalm attributed to David.
13. The Greek translation has τιμήν, "honor" (for עֹז in the MT).
14. The verb means "take up," which was translated literally in the Greek. The form of the noun is singular; in the Greek it is plural: "(raise) offerings."
15. Many manuscripts and 1 Chronicles 16:29 have לְפָנָיו, "before him," instead of "into his courts."
16. For MT's בְּהַדְרַת־קֹדֶשׁ. the editors of BHS propose reading "his holiness," קָדְשׁוֹ, instead of "holiness," based on some versions and Psalm 29:2. The Greek version (and Syriac) has ἐν αὐλῇ ἁγίᾳ αὐτοῦ, "in his holy court," the word "court" reflecting a Hebrew form בְּחַצְרַת. An attractive proposal has been made for a different rendering than "attire." The word חדרה may be linked to a Ugaritic term with the sense of "dream," which would mean here a "revelation" or a "theophany," some oracle or revelation in the sanctuary (see P. R. Ackroyd, "Some Notes on Psalms," *JTS* 17 [1966]:396). It

The Exalted King

tremble before him,[17] all the earth.
10 Say[18] among the nations, the LORD reigns![19]
    Yes, the world is established[20] that it cannot be moved.
    He shall judge the peoples in uprightness.[21]

11 Let the heavens rejoice and the earth exult;
    let the sea thunder and all that is in it.
12 Let the field[22] exult[23] and all that is in it.
    Then[24] all[25] the trees of the forest[26] will sing for joy
13 before the LORD,[27] for he comes,[28]

---

would be translated, "Bow down to the LORD at his holy appearing," or perhaps, "at the appearance of the Holy One." This would fit the parallelism well. However, Craigie points out that there is a major problem: in the Ugaritic texts the word occurs only once, and may even be an error for $d\,(h)\,r\,t$, "dream," and so this is not a very compelling suggestion (Psalms 1–50, p. 242, n. 2; see also Howard, *The Structure of Psalms 93–100*, pp. 88–89).

17. MT has מִפָּנָיו; many manuscripts and 1 Chronicles 16:3 have the expression, מִלְּפָנָי.
18. For MT's imperative אִמְרוּ 1 Chronicles 16:31 has an imperfect or a jussive, וְיֹאמְרוּ, "and they will say" or "and let them say."
19. A few manuscripts and 1 Chronicles 16:31 have the entire colon placed after verse 11a.
20. MT has the *niphal* form תִּכּוֹן, "is established" (see Psalm 93:1). The Greek, Symmachus, the Syriac, Targum and Jerome have an active verb, reading the form as *qal*, תָּכֵן. The Greek version also has the active, κατώρθωσεν. "he has established," or "he set (the world) right."
21. This colon is not in 1 Chronicles 16:31.
22. MT has שָׂדַי; a few manuscripts and 1 Chronicles 16:32 have הַשָּׂדֶה.
23. MT has the word spelled יַעֲלֹז, but 1 Chronicles 16:32 has it יַעֲלֹץ.
24. A number of commentators change "then" (אָז) to "also, the more so" (אַף). But "then" is in the Greek version.
25. A few manuscripts and 1 Chronicles 16:33 do not have "all."
26. MT has כָּל־עֲצֵי־יָעַר; several manuscripts and 1 Chronicles 16:33 have the article: הַיָּעַר. One manuscript and the Vulgate also have the word plural: הַיְעָרִים.
27. MT has לִפְנֵי and 1 Chronicles 16:33 has מִלִּפְנֵי, "from before."
28. The form בָא could be taken as a perfect tense, "he has entered," perhaps reflecting a cultic setting; but it is more likely the participle, "he comes" or "he is coming."

for he comes[29] to judge the earth;[30]
he shall judge the world in righteousness
   and peoples in his faithfulness.[31]

Composition and Context

Psalm 96 is another song of praise for the LORD's kingship, the so-called enthronement psalms (see Introduction). But any discussion of its origin and composition is complicated by the fact that it borrows motifs and lines from other similar psalms, shows several parallels with passages in the book of Isaiah, and is used in Chronicles.

Even though it draws in material from other psalms, Psalm 96 was put together as a separate composition for sanctuary worship. Briggs argued that Psalms 93 and 96–100 were originally a song of praise for the advent of the LORD, the universal king, for judgment.[32] There is no proof for such a composite work; but the suggestion does underscore the fact that the psalms in this group all have common themes and motifs. Mowinckel and those who followed him described these psalms as cultic and connected them to the annual enthronement festival. As an enthronement psalm, the composition would then be eschatological as well. Commentators who do not accept such a reconstruction, are satisfied that these psalms were used at the festivals, particularly in the fall at the Feast of Tabernacles in celebration of the LORD's reign, perhaps as part of a covenant renewal ceremony.

But Psalm 96 is clearly composite; the analysis of the text will show it uses passages from such psalms as Psalms 29 and 93. The superscription found in the Greek version ascribes the psalm to David, which may mean that it belonged to the Davidic psalms, or that much of its material was originally Davidic. The fact that the superscription also says the psalm was a celebration for the building of the house after the captivity indicates

---

29. The clause "for he comes" is not repeated in many manuscripts, the Syriac, and 1 Chronicles 16:33.
30. Several manuscripts and 1 Chronicles 16:33 add the sign of the accusative.
31. These last two cola of the verse are not in 1 Chronicles 16:33.
32. *Psalms,* II: 296.

that the translators thought it was put together later, at least in its final composition, or that it was simply adapted to that use later.

The psalm also shows some similarities with passages in the book of Isaiah. Verse 11 is close to Isaiah 44:23 and 49:13; verse 12, to Isaiah 43:23 and 55:12; and verse 13 to Isaiah 40:10, 50:19, 20, 60:1 and 62:11. There are three possible explanations for these similarities. First, one could argue that these are just common cultic expressions that occurred frequently in various worship contexts in Israel's experience. But here the material seems to be more specific, focused on certain aspects of worship. Second, the most common view is that the psalm was dependent on Isaiah 40–66 for its conceptions and images, supporting the conclusion that the final composition of the psalm was later than that portion of Isaiah. This interpretation usually assumes a post-exilic date for the material in the book of Isaiah. Third, it may also be possible that the author of Isaiah 40–66 was influenced by the cultic language that was in existence at the time, notably that which was preserved in the psalms.

So any suggestion concerning the date of the final form of Psalm 96 has to be tentative. The psalm was used by the Chronicler in a composite hymn in conjunction with the report of the removal of the ark. Briggs says the fact the psalm was inserted there indicates that it was older than Chronicles and had been used for a considerable time in liturgy as Davidic (II:299). Anderson, while concluding that it is not impossible that the present psalm was post-exilic, allows that some of it is far more ancient in origin.[33] Tate also concludes the psalm was post-exilic, or at least read as such; but he acknowledges that the parallels with Isaiah are not that determinative, and so there is still some uncertainty.[34] Howard concludes from his

---

33. *Psalms 73–150*, p. 681.
34. Tate concludes that (1) there was a long tradition of kingship-of-Yahweh poetry in Israel, reaching back to early pre-exilic periods, probably represented in Psalm 93; (2) the dates of origin for Psalms 95 and 96–99 as individual psalms are uncertain—possibly pre-exilic, but more probably post-exilic in their present final forms; and (3) the cultic situations of Psalms 93–99 in the Psalter are mostly post-exilic, and these should be considered the primary contexts for their interpretation (*Psalms 51–100*,

study of Psalms 93–100 that Psalm 96 is pre-exilic, most likely a post-ninth-century work (see Ps. 98:9).[35] The point is that the ideas expressed in the psalm are ancient, and not limited in their meaning to a later period after the exile. While it is possible the final form of the composition was late, there is no compelling reason it had to be. Its placement here in the collection does show at least that the final editor(s) saw its message as particularly relevant to the post-exilic experience and emphases. But this is the value of the psalms even for believers: the psalms, and particularly Psalm 96, are meaningful in every age, including the modern age when there is so much uncertainty about the doctrines of the faith. The psalm proclaims the ancient truths that the LORD is the creator, the king, and the coming judge, and at his coming there will be righteousness on the earth.[36] Therefore, his greatness, displayed in his saving power, should be praised in all the earth. And the call for the nations to praise the LORD is essentially a call for them to come to faith.

Exegetical Analysis

Summary

The prophet calls upon all the people of the earth and all the elements of nature to praise the LORD who is infinitely greater than all the gods of the nations because he created all things, rules over all things, and is coming to judge the world in righteousness.

---

p. 507). This is a plausible approach; however, if we cannot say for certain that the psalm in its present form was post-exilic, it would be unwarranted to make that period the primary context for the interpretation. It would be safer to interpret the message of the psalm first and then consider its connections to the different settings.

35. *Structure*, p. 191. Howard argues that Psalms 93–100 form a logically coherent unit in Book IV.
36. See also H. Ringgren, "Behold Your King Comes," *VT* 24 (1974):207–11.

The Exalted King

Outline

I. The psalmist calls all people to sing praises to the LORD and proclaim his marvelous work of salvation because he is infinitely greater and more majestic than the gods of the nations (1–6).
   A. The call to praise: He calls upon all the earth to sing a new song to the LORD and proclaim his marvelous salvation day by day (1–3).
   B. The cause for praise: The LORD is greater than all the gods because he created everything and his temple is characterized by majesty, strength and beauty (4–6).
II. The psalmist calls the tribes of the nations to give glory to him and worship him because he is the sovereign ruler and by his reign the world will finally be righteous (7–10).
   A. The call to praise: He calls the tribes of the nations to give God the glory, worship him in holiness and fear, and submit to his sovereign authority (7–9).
   B. The cause for praise: With the LORD's reign the earth will finally be established in righteousness (10)
III. The psalmist calls upon all creation to rejoice because the LORD is coming to judge the earth in righteousness and truth (11–13).
   A. The call to praise: He calls nature to rejoice (11–12).
   B. The cause for praise: The LORD is coming to judge the world in righteousness and faithfulness (13).

COMMENTARY IN EXPOSITORY FORM

I. The whole world should acknowledge the LORD's great work of salvation because he is greater than the gods the world proposes (1–6).

A. Everyone should praise the LORD for his marvelous provision of salvation (1–3).

The first three verses form an emphatic call for people in all the world to praise the LORD, a call that assumes the response will be an act of faith. There are six imperatives here: sing, sing,

sing, bless, publish, and declare. The first colon calls for all the earth to sing (שִׁירוּ; s.v. Ps. 33:3) a new song to the LORD. The song should be new in that it would reflect a new event, a new experience of divine intervention. This emphasis may lie behind the composition of this psalm itself, for even though it included many lines from other passages, it too was a new song for a new reason. The reason the psalms frequently call for a new song to be sung is that God's faithfulness is new every day, making praise for him inexhaustible.[37] Here the call goes out to all the earth, meaning people in all the earth (a metonymy of subject). The intended audience for this call would be believers; but if others now acknowledged the greatness of the LORD and sang praises to him, they would also be numbered among the believers.

The call to sing a song is clarified in verses 2 and 3. First, people are to "bless his name." "Bless" (בָּרְכוּ; s.v. Ps. 5:12) here is a synonym for praising; the word adds the emphasis of enhancing or enriching God's reputation in the world through the praise. The idea of reputation comes from the meaning of "name": it means his nature, who he is and what he does (s.v. Ps. 20:1).

But two additional expressions further clarify what exactly the focus of this praise will be. First, people are to "proclaim" or "publish" (בַּשְּׂרוּ) his salvation, meaning, they are to tell the good news about it. A noun related to this verb means "messenger" in 1 Samuel 4:17; people who tell of the LORD's wonderful works are like messengers who bring the good report. What they will publish will be about "his salvation" (יְשׁוּעָתוֹ; s.v. Ps. 3:2), that is, the salvation he has wrought ("his" being a subjective genitive). In this context the term could describe some recent victory the nation had experienced, or some great victory in the past, or even the LORD's great triumph at creation.[38] It probably refers to some victory Israel experienced that demonstrated to the world that the LORD was a saving God; but since the psalmist does not identify what that was, it is futile to try to identify one.[39]

---

37. See further Anderson, *Psalms 73–150*, p. 682.
38. Ibid.
39. Briggs had concluded that it referred to some great event that would give joy to the world, and so he suggested the overthrow of Persia by Alexander (II:303). That is most unlikely.

The other clarification of the praise is stated in verse 3: they were to declare (סַפְּרוּ) his glory (כְּבוֹדוֹ; s.v. Ps. 19:1) among the nations, his wonders (נִפְלְאוֹתָיו; s.v. Ps. 139:5) among the peoples. "Glory" is that attribute that signifies one's importance; it is an attribute that is demonstrated through actions and therefore can be seen and appreciated by others. The word "glory" here refers to God's unparalleled importance that is revealed through his works. The glory of the LORD was displayed in the work of creation, in his kingship, and also in acts of salvation and judgment. Yahweh is simply the most important person in existence, ever. And the songs and praises of people should acknowledge this. The parallel term "wonders" focuses on the amazing things the LORD does that demonstrates his glory (so "glory" is the metonymy of cause, and "wonders" the metonymy of effect). His works are incomparable, surpassing, extraordinary—they are truly wonders (s.v. Ps. 139:5). To speak of the glory of the LORD, therefore, is to speak of his wonders, and to tell of his wonders is to declare his glorious nature.

B. Because the LORD created all things, he is infinitely greater than any other gods people worship (4–6).

The next four verses record the reason for this praise; they affirm that the LORD is infinitely greater and more majestic than any other "gods." Verse 4 introduces the theme: "Great (גָּדוֹל; s.v. Ps. 34:3) is the LORD." Because he is great, he is greatly (to be) praised (וּמְהֻלָּל מְאֹד; s.v. Ps. 33:1). Down through the ages the faithful have praised the LORD continually and enthusiastically because they know that he is the great God. But not only is he greatly praised, but he is to be feared (נוֹרָא; s.v. Ps. 2:11) above all gods. Because of his greatness seen in his wonderful works, the LORD is both awe-inspiring—and terrifying. The term "feared" would carry different connotations for believers than for unbelievers who rebelled against him. The point of this verse, though, is that the LORD is to be feared more than other gods, because he is greater than those gods. The word "gods" (אֱלֹהִים) can refer to human leaders, or angels; but here it most likely means the so-called gods of the nations since the next verse will explain that they are worthless objects of trust.

They are "worthless" (literally "nothings," אֱלִילִים, v. 5). Some choose to translate this word as idols, which is in part what the word is describing; the Greek version chose "demons." The word is a descriptive term of contempt and should be retained if possible to capture the psalmist's tone. The false gods are "nothings," "non-entities." Briggs says this is appropriate because these gods have done nothing for their people, can do nothing, and are in reality nothings; they have no real existence and are not gods at all (II:303–4). There was no reason to fear or worship those gods, for they failed the nations that worshiped them.

Then, in the strongest contrast, the psalmist states that the LORD made the heavens—the very place where these pagan gods were said to reside. The pagan gods were man-made and therefore weaker than humans—they were impotent. But the LORD created everything and therefore he is greater than all things.

And further strengthening the contrast the psalmist heaps up descriptions of the magnificence of the LORD. He uses four important terms:

"honor" (הוֹד),[40]

---

[40]. The word הוֹד means "highness, majesty." The difficulty of translating the word can be seen in the fact that for the 24 occurrences the Greek version used a dozen different words. The meaning is connected to its use for royalty (e.g., Ps. 21:5; Dan. 11:21). This quality of majesty or highness for kings is a gift from God (such as in Psalm 45:3 and 21:5, where the splendor was from God; and in the sample of the LORD's conferring it on Solomon according to 1 Chronicles 29:25). The idea of "splendor" also is applied to people in a few other places, such as for the splendor of Israel blessed by God (Hos. 14:7), or of famous people like Moses (Num. 27:20). It has the sense of honor in the warning of Proverbs 5:9, perhaps referring to the product of a lifetime that could be wasted. In Daniel 10:8 it describes the radiance of the face.

Most importantly it describes the majesty of God as seen in his mighty works in creation and history. Because of these marvelous works, people praise God for his highness or grandeur. The word speaks of the dignity and majesty of God here in Psalm 96:6. It may also include the connotations of glory and brilliance. God wears his splendor as a king (Ps. 104:1); his actions are with glory and splendor (Ps. 111:3); his voice is majestic (Isa. 30:30); and his majesty or highness is in the heavens (Ps. 8:1). See further "הוֹד *hôd* **highness**, **majesty**" by D. Vetter, in *Theological Lexicon of the Old Testament*, ed. by Jenni and Westermann, I:355, 6.

"majesty" (הָדָר),[41]
"strength" (עֹז; s.v. Ps. 29:1),
and "beauty" (תִּפְאֶרֶת).[42]
These are presented in terms of attendants (and so

---

41. This second word הָדָר means "splendor." Here too there are several connotations, which led the Greek version to use some 20 words in the 42 occurrences of the Hebrew word. The related verb may have the sense of "adorn" (Isa. 63:1), "honor" (Lev. 19:32) and perhaps "swell" (as of the land, Isa. 45:2)." The verb is probably a denominative formation from the substantive.

    The noun הָדָר means "splendor, grandeur" and even "adornment." In Proverbs 20:29 it refers to gray hair as the beauty of an old man; in Leviticus 23:40 it describes nature's beauty in the fruit on the trees. In the sense of majesty the word is an attribute of earthly kings (Ps. 21:5). In Psalm 110:3 the plural may refer to royal finery, perhaps ornaments or sacred garments. Human splendor was conferred on mankind at creation (Ps. 8:5); it also is present in the wise, such as the dignity and majesty of the noble woman (Prov. 31:25). The sense of "honor/glory" is found in Psalm 149:9 for the saints, and in Micah 2:9 for the LORD's glory as the possession of his people. Human beauty and dignity and honor exists because God gives it.

    Here of course it refers to the LORD's majesty. He is said to be clothed with it in Psalm 104:1. So splendor and grandeur describe his nature in terms of clothing—and in the Bible clothing often signifies the character or the condition of the person (clothed with righteousness, or clothed with filthy garments). The noun הֲדָרָה only occurs in the construct state. When followed by "holy" it qualifies the worship of the LORD (Ps. 29:2; Ps. 96:6; 1 Chron. 16:29; and 2 Chron.20:21); it may mean to worship the LORD "in the splendor of (which is) holiness," or "in the adornment of holiness" (in holy ornaments). Worship of the holy God must be covered with holiness.

    When the term is part of the praise for the LORD, it refers to his majesty and splendor as king. The description is naturally prompted by the marvelous works God does, even his acts of judgment. See "הָדָר *hādār* **splendor**," by G. Wehmeier, in *Theological Lexicon of the Old Testament*, ed. By Jenni and Westermann, I:353–355.

42. The word "beauty, glory" is תִּפְאָרָה. It is related to a verb פָּאַר which means "to beautify, glorify." It occurs in the *hithpael* stem, meaning "glorify oneself," i.e., "boast" in Isaiah 10:15, or "assume the honor over me" (to make the decision) in Exodus 8:5, or "be glorified" as of the LORD in Isaiah 44:23.

    More helpful is the way that the noun is used. First, it can describe beauty or finery, as of jewels (Ezek. 16:17), garments (Isa. 3:18), the form of a man as a pattern for an idol (Isa. 44:13), or a city (Isa. 28:1). There is a related noun that means "turban," an ornament of people of position or luxury.

personifications); wherever the LORD is, these qualities are there. They signify the majesty and power of his court (certainly in contrast to the imagined pantheons of the pagan religions). Honor, majesty, strength and beauty set the LORD apart as infinitely greater than all gods—and if all gods, then certainly all who worship such gods. Not only is he worthy to be praised, but he is to be feared and obeyed.

II. All people should give glory to God and worship him because by his reign the world will finally be established in righteousness (7–10).

A. *Everyone should give God the glory, worship him, and submit to his authority (7–9).*

The next section of the psalm also includes a call to praise and a cause for the praise. The call is expressed in three verses, two of which are very similar to Psalm 29:1–2. But this call to give glory to the LORD differs in two ways from Psalm 29. First, it is not addressed to the "sons of the mighty," i.e., angels (see Ps. 29), but to the families of peoples. And second, it includes the instruction to bring a gift, a dedication offering to the LORD. These changes make the expressions found in Psalm 29 more suited to this context which is calling the people of the world to praise and fear the LORD. Now the psalmist calls them to worship him. He first tells them to bring a gift to the LORD (מִנְחָה; see Lev. 2), enter his courts, and then bow down (הִשְׁתַּחֲווּ; s.v. Ps. 95:6), or worship him "in holy attire" (or, as some texts have it, "in the beauty of holiness"; see Ps. 29:2). This holy attire usually refers to garments that are ritually clean and acceptable in the sanctuary (see Lev. 11:24–8); the imagery means that those who would praise the LORD and bring him a gift of gratitude and dedication must be properly prepared to come into his

---

Second, it can mean glory pertaining to a rank. Here it describes the robes of the high priest (Exod. 28:2), or the greatness of a king (Est. 1:4). It can also mean glory of renown, such as the nature of the LORD (Ps. 71:8). The house of the LORD is so designated (Isa. 60:7), as well as the ark of the covenant (Ps. 78:61). These are beautiful because they are attached to the presence of the LORD, who is all glorious—beautiful.

presence. These instructions mean that the nations are being called to submit to the LORD in worship by faith. And this obeisance includes fear, not simply reverence, but trembling (חִילוּ, v. 9). Because the idea of trembling does not seem to many to be well-suited to the context of thanksgiving in worship, some commentators suggest that this is a word that refers to whirling in dance, meaning, the people are called on to take part in a sacred dance (see Ps. 87:7; 1 Sam. 18:6). But this change is not necessary; a call for people to submit to the LORD is not out of harmony with a call for them to tremble in the LORD's presence (see Ps. 2:10–12). After all, the psalmist has taken some time to describe the nature of this God that they must approach, and all of his descriptions should cause people to tremble in the presence of such a God, and if not for that, for the prospect of the judgment to come.

B. Because the LORD reigns, the earth will finally be established in righteousness (10).

The cause for this call to give God the glory and to worship him is stated in verse 10: "the LORD reigns." This fact is placed within the instruction: "Say among the nations, 'the LORD reigns'" (for מָלָךְ in these psalms, see Ps. 93:1; 97:1).[43] Like the messenger in Isaiah 52:7, here a company of messengers will take the news to the world. The LORD is the sovereign king; there is no one with more authority than he. And because the LORD is the creator and king, the world is established in uprightness. His reign has not yet been fully realized, for he must yet come to judge the wicked; but his sovereignty has firmly established the world with uprightness (or equity, מֵישָׁרִים; s.v. Ps. 67:4). All creation is based on divine equity. As Kidner observes, this verse is

---

43. Briggs (II: 304–5) includes a note of passing interest that later versions, especially the old Latin, had "the Lord reigned from the tree," which was cited by Latin fathers as a prophecy of Christ, and was used by Justin Martyr in his charge that the Jews were erasing things from the text (*Apol.* I:41). The reading was clearly a later, Christian gloss; nevertheless, it gained currency through its use in the hymn of Fortunatus at the beginning of the 7th century, Vexilla regis prodeunt, "The royal banners forward go." It was translated by Neale.

a "prophecy of perfect government, not a pronouncement on—of all things!—the earth's rotation."[44] The wonderful saving works of the LORD have revealed that he is the sovereign ruler; but at the great Day of the LORD that is coming the people of the world will finally realize his absolute, eternal reign; and then people will have no choice but to acclaim his kingship.[45]

III. All creation should rejoice because the LORD is coming to judge the world in righteousness and faithfulness (11–13).

A. *The whole creation should be joyful (11–12).*

Now the psalmist issues a call for all of nature to share in the acclamation of the sovereignty of the LORD. The call is recorded in verses 11 and 12: the heavens, the earth, the sea, and the fields should rejoice, and then the trees of the forest (wood) will sing for joy. These images (personifications) signify that everything will thrive and flourish in the coming the reign of the LORD—all singing and rejoicing is an acclamation of God's blessing in one way or another. These motifs are found in eschatological passages in the psalms as well as the prophets; they predict the time when the effects of the curse will be replaced by divine blessing, or to put it another way, they declare the expected corrective for the apostle's description of the whole world's groaning, waiting for the day of redemption (Rom. 8).

B. *The LORD is coming to judge the world in righteousness and faithfulness (13).*

The cause for this third call is presented emphatically in the last verse: the LORD is coming to judge the earth. The expression "he is coming" is repeated to underscore the certainty of it.

---

44. *Psalms 73–150*, p. 349.
45. The expression "the great Day of the LORD" refers to the coming of the LORD in glory to judge the world and establish his universal reign of peace and righteousness. In the prophetic literature (e.g., Joel and Amos) it is usually described in epiphany language (see Ps. 97).

And the purpose of his coming is to judge (לִשְׁפֹּט; s.v. Ps. 9:4) the earth, also repeated. This prospect of judgment could refer to some expected divine intervention at the time, an expected reality in the experience of the psalmist. But ultimately it refers to the great Day of the LORD, the eschatological expectation of the final judgment (see Isa. 40:10). This judgment will destroy wickedness and those who are wicked, but will vindicate the righteous—in other words, the LORD is coming, and his reign over all the earth will be absolute. And because his decisions will be characterized by righteousness and faithfulness, his reign will finally make everything right.

MESSAGE AND APPLICATION

The composite nature of this psalm makes the expository presentation easier. Moreover, its themes are easily united for a central message: *Because the majestic LORD of creation comes to judge and rule the world, all people should worship him in fear and praise him in holy array for his great salvation.* It is a song of praise for the reign of the LORD, which has been demonstrated again and again throughout history in his mighty saving acts, but will be fully revealed when he comes to judge the wicked and to establish his righteous reign over all the earth. The series of calls in the psalm makes the application clear and direct; but the reasons for the calls to praise and worship form the theological substance of the praise. Here we have his great salvation, creation, his majesty and beauty, and his coming to judge with righteousness and faithfulness. These explanations provide evidence for the greatness of the LORD, for indeed, there is no god like him; and they should prompt in us fear and trembling as well as praise and worship. Those who refuse to acknowledge his sovereign kingship in this life, who refuse to do obeisance to him in holiness now, will find themselves the objects of his judgment when he comes. For the Christian, the witness of Scripture is clear: Jesus Christ, the Son of God, created all things (John 1), and will judge all things (John 5); he came and brought salvation to us, and he will come again to judge the world and establish his righteous reign over it. When he comes to fulfill all things, he will be identified as Faithful and True (Rev. 19).

PSALM 97

Preparing for the Coming of the LORD

INTRODUCTION

Text and Textual Variants[1]

1 The LORD reigns![2] Let the earth rejoice;
 Let the many isles be glad!
2 Clouds and darkness surround him;
 righteousness and justice are the foundation of his throne.
3 A fire goes before him
 and burns up his enemies round about.[3]

---

1. The Greek version has a superscription for this psalm: Τῷ Δαυιδ, ὅτε ἡ γῆ αὐτοῦ καθίσταται, "of David, when his land is being brought to order." Briggs thinks that the superscription refers to the return of the exiles, obviously meaning that the first part would have to be "for David," even though this is the form traditionally translated "of David" (*Psalms*, II:300).
2. The form in the MT is the simple perfect tense, מָלָךְ. The Greek version uses ἐβασίλευσεν, "became king" or "reigns."
3. A few manuscripts and versions read "around him" (סְבִיבָיו); this is not necessary since the pronoun is implicit (Howard, *Structure*, p. 97).

PSALM 97

4 His lightnings light the world;
    the earth sees and trembles.
5 The mountains melt like wax at the presence of the LORD,
    at the presence of the Lord of the whole earth.
6 The heavens declare his righteousness,
    and all the peoples see his glory.
7 Let all who serve[4] carved images be put to shame,[5]
    who boast in idols.
    Worship him all you gods![6]
8 Zion hears and is glad,
    and the daughters of Judah rejoice
    because of your judgments, O LORD.

9 For you, LORD, are most high above the earth;
    you are exalted far[7] above all gods.
10 You who love the LORD, hate evil![8]

---

4. The Greek version properly understood this as spiritual service and interpreted it with, "(Let all) those who worship" or "do obeisance" (προσκυνοῦντες).
5. Some commentators take the verb (יֵבֹשׁוּ) to be indicative and not jussive, "they are (will be) put to shame," and harmonize the word "worship" (in 7c) with this by taking it as an indicative and not imperative (the form is the same), so that the verse has a run of indicatives without being interrupted by an imperative (see further Tate, *Psalms 51–100*, p. 517). But if this verb "shame" is a jussive ("let them be put to shame") then the imperative "worship" is not the lone volitive in a run of indicatives.
6. Instead of "(you) gods" (אֱלֹהִים) the Greek version interpreted the word as οἱ ἄγγελοι αὐτοῦ, "(all you) his angels."
7. The form is the adverb, מְאֹד. Some commentators wish to read it as an epithet for God—the Mighty One (see Howard, *Structure*, pp. 99, 100).
8. The MT is clear; it uses the participle in construct אֹהֲבֵי, "lovers of (the LORD)," and then the plural imperative שִׂנְאוּ, "hate (evil)." Many scholars think that Yahweh must be the subject. And so the editors of BHS propose changing the latter to a plural participle in construct, שֹׂנְאֵי, to read "haters of (evil)." This would yield the translation "lovers of the LORD *are* haters of evil." But they also propose changing the first form to a singular participle אֹהֵב (suggesting there was a dittography), and this would make the line read, "the LORD loves those who hate evil." But the changes are gratuitous; and the Greek translation agrees with the MT.

He[9]preserves the lives of the saints;
He delivers them out of the hand of the wicked.
11 Light is sown[10] for the righteous,
and gladness for the upright in heart.
12 Rejoice in the LORD, you righteous,
and acknowledge his holy memorial.[11]

Composition and Context

This psalm also is classified as an enthronement psalm in many commentaries. The designation is useful if by it one means that the psalm is a celebration of the evidence of the reign of the LORD as well as the expectation of his future reign over all the earth. The work may have been a liturgical piece, but owing to the lack of evidence, we cannot easily say what kind of celebration used it. There certainly were great festivals; the festival in the fall was a time of thanksgiving for the summer harvests as well as prayer for future blessings. In it the people probably acknowledged the kingship of the LORD and renewed their commitment to him (see Introduction, vol. 1).

Whatever the setting for the composition was, this psalm uses "epiphany" language in its acclamation of the LORD's sovereignty. Such language is striking; it describes spectacular changes in nature that accompany the LORD's intervention. The psalm may have been written to celebrate some experience of the nation, perhaps a victory over an enemy that could only be attributed to God's intervention. But in reflecting on the victory, in which

---

9. The form in the text is simply the masculine singular participle; so the Greek version adds "the Lord" as the subject.
10. The image of light being sown is difficult; these words are never elsewhere used together. One Hebrew manuscript and the versions read a form זָרַח, "to arise," instead of MT's figurative זָרֻעַ, "(is) sown": "light has dawned sprung up/arisen" (Greek has ἀνέτειλεν). Dahood thought to solve the difficulty by rendering the first word (אוֹר) "field" instead of "light": "a sown field awaits the just" (*Psalms*, I:222, and II:362). This conjecture is unnecessary.
11. The line could be read "acknowledge the remembrance of his holiness," but "remembrance" or "memorial" is often used for his name, especially when uttered in cultic worship (see B. S. Childs, *Memory and Tradition*, p. 71). The Greek has a fairly literal rendering of the line with "the remembrance of his holiness" (τῆς ἁγιωσύνης αὐτοῦ).

perhaps some of the elements of nature were employed by God, the psalmist used the language of epiphany first witnessed at Sinai (Exod. 19) to describe the recent intervention. And the use of that language is understandable; after all, that event at Sinai was the culmination of the greatest deliverance Israel ever had—victory over Egypt with signs and wonders in heaven and on earth.

There are samples in the Bible where the LORD used elements of nature in his defeat of Israel's enemies. In Judges 4 we have the report of the battle against Sisera and the Canaanites. Judges 4:15 tells us that the LORD routed Sisera's army by the edge of the sword; but Judges 5:20 and 21 restate the record in poetic form, saying the stars from heaven and the brook Kishon fought against Sisera. What happened is that there was a tremendous storm that along with the overflow of the Kishon flooded the valley, miring the iron chariots of Sisera in the mud and leaving the armies vulnerable to Israeli foot soldiers. So in the poetic account of the event, nature fought for Israel because God sovereignly controlled it. The writer of Psalm 97 could easily have used dramatic descriptions of nature to say that God fought from heaven.

But the use of such elaborate language here also anticipates an even greater victory to come at the end of history. To the psalmist, the present victory may have revealed the LORD's power through nature in some way, but it was not the final victory, only a preview of the final victory. And the psalmist knew what the prophets foresaw, that in the eschatological fulfillment the victory and the manifestation of his appearance will be glorious beyond anything imaginable. Some prophets used epiphany language in detail to describe the great day of the LORD that is to come at the end of the age (Joel 2:28–32; Amos 5:18–20). It is to be a time of judgment when mountains will melt like wax, when the moon will turn to blood (perhaps appearing so through the flames on earth), and lightning and thick clouds will accompany his appearance. They do not simply have in mind natural phenomena that would be interpreted as divine intervention; rather, they foresee dramatic changes in nature, reminiscence of the extraordinary phenomena at Sinai, that will accompany his coming. They draw on epiphany language from that foundational event at Sinai to show what the intervention at the end of the age is going to be like.

So in this psalm some significant divine intervention probably inspired the writing of the psalm, but the elaborate language used to describe it transcends the historical event and will become historically and literally fulfilled at the coming of the LORD to establish his reign.

Therefore, the exposition of a passage like Psalm 97 has two things to consider. First is the vivid description of an experience that occurred in the time of the psalmist that gave rise to this psalm; and the second is language used in the psalm harmonizes with prophecies of the final great day of the LORD, i.e., the eschatological meaning of the psalm. Such a twofold emphasis is fairly common in the exposition of the psalms; after all, every act of God's deliverance and judgment in the past is a harbinger of the future deliverance that will finally put down all sin and rebellion. When people witnessed a great deliverance from the LORD, they would have naturally turned their thoughts to the long-awaited final deliverance.

Exegetical Analysis

Summary

The saints should rejoice and renew their commitment to righteousness in view of the revelation of the awe-inspiring epiphany of the LORD who comes to judge his adversaries and to rule with righteousness.

Outline

I. The psalmist calls upon all the people in the world to rejoice at the establishment of the LORD's reign (1).

II. The psalmist describes the LORD's intervention and its effects on all moral creatures (2–9).
   A. He describes the event as an awe-inspiring epiphany (2–5).
      1. The LORD's administrative judgments are ominous and righteous (2).
      2. The LORD's judgment destroys his adversaries when he begins to rule (3).

3. The evidence of the LORD's power is displayed throughout the earth (4).
   4. All barriers and opposition disappear before the LORD as he establishes his rulership (5).
  B. He describes the righteous effects of the coming on all moral creatures (6–9).
   1. All phenomena of nature bear witness to the glory and righteousness of the LORD's kingdom (6).
   2. All idol-worshipers will be destroyed and their idols proven inferior (7).
   3. Believing Israel will rejoice before the LORD (8–9).
III. The psalmist calls on the saints to live righteously and to acknowledge gladly their holy savior (10–12).
  A. He calls upon those who love the LORD to reject evil because the LORD delivers his people from the wicked (10).
  B. He calls upon the righteous to acknowledge the LORD with gladness because of the widespread joy of their blessed estate (11–12).

COMMENTARY IN EXPOSITORY FORM

I. People throughout the world must acclaim the sovereign rule of the LORD (1).

As with the other psalms in this group, Psalm 97 begins with the declaration "the LORD reigns." And as explained in Psalm 93, this verb (מָלָךְ, the perfect tense) could be interpreted as an instantaneous perfect or a gnomic perfect to gain an English present tense, "the LORD reigns" (here and now, or, he always reigns); but it could also be taken as a present prefect, "the LORD has become king." In the immediate experience of the psalmist the verb could refer to the LORD's establishing of his sovereignty through some amazing victory, and so these translations fit easily. But they also fit with the eschatological direction of the psalm, for the psalm anticipates the acclamation that will be given when the LORD reigns in fact.[12]

---

12. In the historical context the verb would declare that the LORD has demonstrated his sovereignty through a victory, and that expression would be

Preparing for the Coming of the LORD

The wording of my first point uses "must" because of the force of the verbs in the sentences—praise is the natural and necessary response to the LORD's reign. When the psalmist uses these (jussive) forms to call the world to praise the LORD, he is expressing more than a wish or desire—he is calling for people to make acclamation of his glorious kingdom. To refuse to acclaim the LORD as king is to refuse to live in his kingdom, that is, under his blessings now and in his salvation in the world to come. Frequently, when the psalmists use calls for praise, they are in fact extending calls for faith.

The psalm makes it clear that the scope of the LORD's reign is universal; this is a common emphasis in the psalms of Book IV. So here the writer calls for the earth to rejoice (תָּגֵל; s.v. Ps. 13:6) and the isles to be glad (יִשְׂמְחוּ; s.v. Ps. 48:11). The two expressions "earth" and "islands" are figurative, referring to the people who live in them (thus, metonymies of subject). Islands may not rejoice, but people living in them can and must.[13] The two words also balance each other (as a merism): those who are far off, and those who live near. All people everywhere are called to rejoice at his reign.

II. The LORD appears in majestic power and glory to establish his righteous kingdom (3–9).

A. *The LORD reveals himself in an awe-inspiring epiphany (2–5).*

The description of the LORD's sovereign intervention uses epiphany language. First are "clouds and darkness," or (as a hendiadys), "dark clouds." Here is an ominous note about the LORD's presence, for the intervention is not with clear blue skies, nor the brilliance of the luminous cloud that guided the

---

typological of the eschatology. But the verb could also be taken as a prophetic perfect without any historical reference in mind, and the glorious future intervention of the LORD to judge the world would then be the only interest of the writer.

13. In some psalms the elements of nature are said to rejoice, meaning to flourish or prosper. In the context of this psalm the focus seems rather to be on what the people of the world will say.

Israelites in their journey, but rather with thick, dark clouds that represent judgment.[14] Broyles remarks: "Yahweh's kingship is here exhibited, not by a static deity sitting on a throne, but by the dynamic appearance (i.e., a theophany) of the God of the storm (cf. Pss. 18:7–15; 29:3–10; 68:1–4, 32–34; 104:32; Exod. 19:16–19; Deut. 4:11; Judg. 5:4–5; Hab. 3:3–15)."[15]

The question for the expositor is whether there were actual thick dark clouds in the event that formed the basis of this psalm. If there were, then the clouds would have accompanied the divine presence (and these words would be metonymies of adjunct). This interpretation would harmonize with the eschatological passages that describe the coming of the LORD with clouds to judge the world. But on the other hand, if the event behind the psalm did not actually have these manifestations of nature, then the psalmist would be using them poetically to speak of judgment (and so they would simply be implied comparisons). Whichever view is taken will influence the interpretation of the other images in the psalm as well—the fire, the lightning, and the melting of the mountains. The first view makes the most sense of the descriptions, and can be supported from accounts in the Bible where the LORD's coming was accompanied by, or accomplished through, some natural phenomena. It seems more likely that if there was an actual event there was some reality to these images.

The second half of the verse clarifies the point of the manifestation: his judgment is right. The text uses two common theological words, righteousness and justice. The word "justice" (מִשְׁפָּט; s.v. Ps. 9:4) may be translated "judgment," representing the decisions of God, even though the word is also used for the Law itself (throughout Ps. 119) or a portion of the Law (Exod. 21–23). The word often has a positive connotation of vindication, but also (and especially in this psalm) it retains the idea of condemnation or punishment. Here it is joined with "righteousness" (צֶדֶק; s.v. Ps. 1:5); and the two words together (as a hendiadys) form one idea, "righteous judgment." The word "judgment" is repeated in

---

14. The impression is that because of the thick, dense clouds, the LORD is not seen directly; rather, he dwells in the clouds (see also 1 Kings 8:12–13).
15. *Psalms*, p. 379.

verse 8 where the righteous are said to rejoice over it. So the point is that the LORD's reign will be established when judgment is meted out on the inhabitants of the world. Accordingly, the imagery of "the foundation of his throne" is used to convey this point. Righteous judgment is equated with the foundation of a throne, meaning that the basis of his rule is righteous judgment. His administration will be just in all its decisions, but especially in putting down wickedness and rebellion (see Pss. 101 and 45:6–7).

Verse 3 continues the picture of judgment, now using the imagery of "fire," which is used often in Scripture in conjunction with God's wrath (e.g., Ps. 2:10–12). Here the fire goes before him and burns up his adversaries. A devastating fire may have been part of the victory behind the writing of the psalm. God had made his presence known in judgment with fire in previous events, such as the judgment of Nadab and Abihu (Lev. 10), or the judgment on the camp at Taberah (Num. 11). It could refer to fire from heaven such as lightning, or from the earth such as an eruption, or a breakout of fire from some other cause. But it signifies judgment and purification, because this fire burns up the LORD's enemies. Whatever the reality was here, in the fulfillment at the coming of the Lord fire will play an important part in the judgment at the end of the age, even if it applies to devastating wars (see Zech. 14:12–15).

In verse 4 the focus is on lightning that lights up the world, which may be an elaboration on the fire in the preceding verse. The "world" in this line could refer to the physical land as well as the people living in it, for his lightning will light up everything. The second colon of the verse, then, states the effect of this: the earth (meaning the people in the earth, a metonymy of subject) sees and trembles. In the ancient world lightning was interpreted as divine fire, a weapon of the gods. For that and for practical reasons it would strike fear in the hearts of people, especially when related in their minds to the power and wrath of God.

All three verbs in the verse may be interpreted with the same nuance as the verb "reigns" in verse 1, an English present tense reflecting the event at the moment, but which would have a future fulfillment when the LORD's victory will be so acclaimed.

For an original setting the language would have been hyperbolic, but in the fulfillment the whole world will be terrified at his glorious appearance.

Then, in verse 5, we have the last element of the epiphany—the hills melt like wax at the presence of the LORD. In a description of some natural event like a landslide or volcano the simile of "like wax" is easy to understand. If the language is merely poetic and no mountains were actually involved, then the whole verse would form an implied comparison with the devastating effect of the presence of the LORD—all opposition in the world will disappear. But if some such phenomena occurred (suggested also in Psalm 46, at least as a possibility), then the image of melting like wax would form a very real picture in the minds of the people. Under the intense pressure of the presence of the divine judge, nothing can hold up. And so in a similar way the prophets anticipate major geological changes will take place when the Lord comes at the end of the age (see Ezek. 47: Zech 14). Accordingly, the ultimate application of these verses is to the coming of the Lord in glory with all the manifestations of his powerful presence in nature. The psalmist may have been describing a miraculous deliverance poetically, but his descriptions will go way beyond his present experience and will be fully realized at the end of the age.

B. The psalmist records the effects of this epiphany (6–9).

Verse 6 could be put with the preceding section as a summary statement, or here as a transition to the general effects of the epiphany. It announces that the heavens declare God's righteousness and glory (compare Ps. 19:1). "Heavens" refers to all the phenomena of nature in the heavens just described (so a metonymy of subject). And the verb "declare" is therefore figurative (a personification), for such phenomena can only reveal his power and glory in non-verbal communication. But this "declaration" is powerful, for what is revealed to the people in the earth is the majestic power of the sovereign Lord of the universe.

"Glory" (כָּבוֹד; s.v. Ps. 19:1) and "righteousness" refer to the Lord's nature and therefore to his reign as well. "Glory" may speak of the brilliant aspects of nature that surround God's presence, attesting to his importance; but more specifically it refers to his intrinsic nature as the most important person ever. "Righteousness" summarizes the justice, equity and fairness of God by which he judges sinners, redeems his people, and rules over all his creation. So these two attributes are the ones to which the phenomena of nature point.

After this general statement the psalm turns to the establishment of the LORD's sovereign reign over the earth. First is the destruction of idolaters (v. 7). The first verb in the verse may be taken as a jussive, "let them be put to shame" (יֵבֹשׁוּ; s.v. Ps. 31:1), to harmonize with the imperative, "worship" or "bow down" (הִשְׁתַּחֲווּ; s.v. Ps. 95:6). But because this latter verb overlaps with the perfect tense in form, some commentators take it that way and correspondingly take the first verb as a regular imperfect, "they are/will be put to shame." The line then would assert that all who served images were put to shame, even all the gods bowed down to him. The Greek translation understood the verbs as volitional moods, however, and that still makes better sense in the passage—because the psalmist understands the implications of the appearance of the divine judge he desires that the wicked be destroyed, but calls for submission to the LORD.[16] The verb "put to shame" is a figure of their defeat (a metonymy of effect); it means shamefully destroyed (s.v. Ps. 31:1). The verb has idolaters in mind, here described as those who "serve carved images." The second colon adds "who boast in idols."

With an abrupt change the psalmist boldly calls the "gods" of these idolaters to submit to the LORD. The pagans worshiped inferior and therefore worthless things because the very gods they worshiped must now and in the end will bow before the LORD. The imperative "worship" (or "do obeisance") is probably rhetorical, expressing the inferiority of false religions by calling them to bow before the LORD. The word "gods" (אֱלֹהִים) can, of course, also mean "God," "angels," and even human "judges." It is unlikely that angels are meant here because the verse is about

---

16. The psalmist is praying for something that he knows is going to happen, and so the prayer is more of a statement of faith and hope in God's word, much like a Christian's prayer for the Lord to come quickly.

idolatry. And the first meaning, "God," would be nonsensical. So the word may refer either to human judges or false gods—or both as in Psalm 82. Because there are no clues that human judges are meant, and because the verse is talking about idols, and because "gods" is clearly meant in verse 9, false "gods" is the better interpretation here. Thus, even the gods that idolaters worship are inferior to God—so they are called on to submit to the LORD. The focus certainly refers to the spirit forces behind the false gods. Perowne says, "As all the worshipers [of idols] are confounded, so must all the objects of their worship be overthrown, as Dagon was before the Ark of the Lord; all must yield before him who is the Lord of the whole earth."[17] This call for all to bow before him is most emphatically a proclamation of the sovereignty of the LORD (see, for example, Phil. 2:10–11).

The contrasting verse 8 focuses on the joy of the righteous when the LORD judges wickedness and idolatry. "Zion" is a mountain, of course; here it is used figuratively (a metonymy of subject) to refer to the people living and worshiping on Mount Zion. And the "daughters of Judah" is also figurative, probably referring to the villages in Judah that grew up in the land around the main city of Jerusalem; these settlements of people appear to be what Judah produced (so an implied comparison between daughters and villages, the feminine "daughters" being used because words for cities and villages are feminine). The point is that all the people in the land, in the city and the surrounding villages, rejoice when they hear the news of God's judgments. The verbs "hears" (a perfect tense) and "is glad" (a preterite with the *waw*) are to be treated in the same way that "reigns" (the perfect tense) was in verse 1. They rejoice now; but the rejoicing will be greater in the final deliverance.

The reason that the unbelievers (and their gods) are put to shame and that believers rejoice is that the LORD is high above everyone and everything (v. 9). Some oppose the high God to their everlasting shame; some trust him to their eternal salvation. The repetition of the verb (עָלָה) "to go up, be high," in the forms "Most High" (עֶלְיוֹן) and "you are exalted" (נַעֲלֵיתָ), the repetition of the word "all," and the use of the adverb "very," all

---

17. *Psalms*, II:201.

add a greater intensity to the description of the sovereign majesty of the LORD. Not only is he high above all the earth, but he is exalted over all that are called "gods." There is no god like the LORD. His appearance to judge the world and redeem his people proves that he is the only true God. And when this begins to happen, the righteous will be filled with joy. Perowne adds, "In the same spirit our Lord, when speaking of the signs of fear which shall be the precursors of His second coming, says, 'When ye shall see these things begin to come to pass, then lift up your heads: for your redemption draweth nigh.' "[18]

III. Those who love the LORD and expect his glorious reign must remain loyal to him (10–12).

The last three verses of the psalm present a didactic force: the psalmist instructs the righteous to live in a way that anticipates their ultimate redemption and participation in the kingdom of righteousness. The first part of the instruction is addressed to those "who love (אֹהֲבֵי; s.v. Ps. 11:7) the LORD," literally, "lovers of Yahweh." This word "love," includes the idea of affection, to be sure, but has at the heart of it the connotation of choosing or preferring. To love the LORD means to be devoted to him in service and worship; it is the key term used in the covenant to express a willing compliance with the LORD's commandments (Deut. 6:4–5; see also Jesus' call: "If you love me, keep my commandments" [John 14:15]).

The natural instruction for those who love the LORD is to "hate evil." "Hate" (שִׂנְאוּ; s.v. Ps. 139:21) is the antonym of love, and so includes the idea of rejecting something, usually along with feelings of disgust or even loathing. Here we have the exclusivity of the covenant: one cannot love the LORD and evil as well. Loving one means rejecting the other; here it is evil that is to be rejected. And the word "evil" (רָע; s.v. Ps. 10:15) refers to any activity that is destructive and harmful to life—sin and corruption that causes pain and destruction.

The second half of the verse declares that the LORD preserves and delivers his people. It parallels the verbal use of the

---

18. *Psalms*, II:202.

active participle "preserves" (or "keeps," שֹׁמֵר; s.v. Ps. 12:7) with the imperfect tense "delivers them" (יַצִּילֵם; s.v. Ps. 22:20), giving the latter tense the nuance of a progressive or habitual imperfect. The half-verse expresses the continual activity of the LORD: he protects and delivers his saints—those who have entered into covenant by faith. The call to hate evil is therefore a critical call for believers to demonstrate their loyalty to God, especially if they are looking for his preservation and deliverance.

Verse 11 is complicated by the textual problem over unusual figurative language. The overall meaning seems clear enough: great rejoicing is the provision for the righteous. The primary image used here is "light." In the Bible it can mean holiness, truth, understanding, joy, life, as well as a few other ideas. Here the parallelism with "gladness" suggests that the idea is bliss or joy—the happy estate of the kingdom of light. But the difficulty comes in that the second word is the passive participle "[is] sown" or "scattered" (זָרֻעַ). Nowhere else is the word for "light" joined with the word "sown." So the variant reading has "dawns" (צָרַח) instead of "sown"—light dawns on the righteous. This draws on the prophetic image of "the sun of righteousness" rising with healing in its wings (Mal. 4:2). Although this variant reading presents a clear idea, it seems to be a deliberate harmonization and therefore secondary. It is too easy and too obvious; if it was the original reading it would be hard to explain the insertion of such an unusual figure as "sown." The Hebrew reading of "sown, scattered" should therefore be retained; but it will have to be explained as a figure of speech, an implied comparison. So light, meaning joy and bliss of the kingdom of light (a metonymy of adjunct), is scattered all around (an implied comparison with sowing seed).

The psalm then closes with a second instruction for the faithful: "rejoice (שִׂמְחוּ; s.v. Ps. 48:11) in the LORD, you righteous, and acknowledge (or give thanks to; הוֹדוּ; s.v. Ps. 6:5) his holy memorial (name)," or "at the remembrance (זֵכֶר; s.v. Ps. 6:5) of his holy name" (שֵׁם; s.v. Ps. 20:1). The name of the LORD means his nature, the divine attributes revealed in word and deed. In this psalm the focus has been on his righteousness, his glory, and his majestic sovereignty as judge of the whole world. Whenever these are remembered, that is, called upon by faith or

158

displayed by divine intervention, believers truly have reason to praise and rejoice in the greatness of their God and Savior.

MESSAGE AND APPLICATION

The psalm, then, is instructive for saints of all times. The central idea of the exposition may be worded this way: *In response to the dramatic intervention of the Lord to deliver and preserve them and to establish his sovereign rule, the saints joyfully renew their commitment to serve and worship him.* They do this after every divine intervention, whether as spectacular as this or not; and each time they do they will anticipate the great and final deliverance at his coming. So their acclamation of his reign, and their portrayal of his glorious intervention, is all in anticipation of their greater celebration at the end of the age. But only the righteous who are eagerly awaiting his coming to judge the world do this.

Thus, in the eschatological fulfillment when the heavens open and the Lord descends with the clouds, then, according to the psalmist and the prophets, fire will consume around his presence, the mountains will split apart and melt away, the heavens will be lit up for all to see, and he will come to judge those who rejected him to worship vain images and false ideas—as well as the things they worship. This great coming of the Lord will cause endless praise and celebration by the righteous who will then realize the answer to the prayers of the saints down through the ages that his kingdom come and his will be done on earth as in heaven. But now we have the words of the apostle John to those who claim to have a share in this kingdom of righteousness and glory: "Whoever has this hope in him purifies himself" (1 John 3:5). Or, as the psalm puts it: "You who love the Lord, hate evil."

PSALM 98
Celebration of the LORD's Reign

INTRODUCTION

Text and Textual Variants

A Psalm[1]

1 Sing to the LORD a new song,
    for he[2] has done marvelous things;
    his right hand and his holy arm
    have worked salvation for him.
2 The LORD has made his salvation known
    and revealed his righteousness in the sight of the nations.
3 He has remembered his loyal love[3]
    and his faithfulness to the house of Israel.

---

1. The Greek version has "of David" also.
2. The Greek version adds "the Lord" as the subject.
3. The Greek version adds "to Jacob," forming a parallelism with "to the house of Israel" in the second half of the verse. However, if that full parallelism had been in the original, it is hard to explain why it was deleted.

> All the ends of the earth have seen[4]
> the salvation of our God.
>
> 4 Shout for joy to the LORD, all the earth;
> break forth and sing joyfully, and sing praises;
> 5 sing praises to the LORD with the harp,
> with the harp[5] and the sound of singing praises,
> 6 with trumpets and the sound of the ram's horn–
> shout for joy before the king, Yahweh.[6]
>
> 7 Let the sea resound, and everything in it,
> the world, and those[7] who live in it.
> 8 Let the rivers clap their hands,
> let the mountains sing joyfully together,[8]
> 9 before the LORD,[9]
> for he is coming to judge the earth.
> He will judge the world with righteousness
> and *the* peoples with equity.[10]

Composition and Context

Psalm 98 is entirely praise. Perowne summarizes the subject matter as "the last great revelation, the final victory of God, when His salvation and His righteousness, the revelation of which He has promised to the house of Israel, shall be manifested both to

---

4. The verb comes at the beginning of the line in the MT. Many manuscripts and a couple of versions have the conjunction: "and have seen" (see Isa. 52:10).
5. A few manuscripts and versions do not have "with the harp" a second time.
6. The MT has לִפְנֵי הַמֶּלֶךְ יְהוָה, which may be translated as "before the LORD, the King," or "before the King, the LORD."
7. MT has "and those who live in it," וְיֹשְׁבֵי בָהּ. Some Greek texts have "all"– all who live in it.
8. The Greek translation interprets the verbs in this verse as indicatives and not jussives. It also joins "together" with the clapping of hands in the first colon: "The rivers will clap their hands together."
9. The phrase "before the LORD" is not in the Greek version (only in A).
10. This last verse is almost identical to Psalm 96:13; the major changes being that Psalm 96 has "he comes" twice, and has "faithfulness" instead of "equity." One Greek manuscript (A) has "he comes" twice.

His own people and to all the nations of the earth."[11] Psalms 96 and 98 capture the sheer delight of the prospect of the coming LORD, who will make all things right; in between them Psalm 97 brings out the darker side, the doom that awaits those who rebel against the LORD.[12]

Psalm 98 is very similar to Psalm 96; in fact, it has been described as a mere echo of Psalm 96, almost a variant of it. But the similarity of expressions in the two psalms is probably due to the use of common language in the liturgy of the LORD's kingship.[13] It is a celebration of God's deliverance of his people; and this great deliverance was made manifest to the people of the world, so that they too would be expected to acclaim the sovereignty of the LORD.[14] What God did for his people Israel is therefore relevant to the whole world, for it attests to the fact that the LORD keeps his covenant promises, and at the same time confirms that he will ultimately redeem his people and judge the world in the process.

The celebration in this psalm could fit the time of the deliverance of Israel from the exile when the nations acknowledged that the LORD had done great things for them (Ps. 126).[15] But there is no historic reference in the psalm, and therefore the expositor should not force it into a setting such as the exile or even the exodus. It could have been written for any marvelous deliverance the LORD brought to his people, for every one of them was a cause for great celebration and a harbinger of the great deliverance to come at the end of the age. Weiser suggests that

---

11. *Psalms*, II:203.
12. Kidner, *Psalms 73–150*, p. 349.
13. Anderson, *Psalms 73–150*, p. 690.
14. See additionally T. Longman, III, "Psalm 98: A Divine Victory Song," *JETS* 27 (1984):267–74. Longman takes the view that this is a victory song or hymn of triumph of the returning divine warrior; he also stresses that there is no special reference to any event.
15. Goldingay notes that the ideas of the psalm match the themes in Isaiah 40–55 very well; but he correctly adds that there is no clear reference to that event, and so the psalm should be a given a broader meaning (*Psalms 90–150*, p. 120).

the psalm is a cultic representation of God's saving acts, both in the past and in the future.[16]

The eschatological emphasis is present in all the so-called enthronement psalms; but here (and in Psalm 96) with the grand announcement that the LORD is coming to judge the world it is strikingly clear. When he does come to make everything right, all of the people of the earth and all of nature will respond in ways that will reflect his majesty.

Exegetical Analysis

Summary

The psalmist calls upon all the people of the earth to sing a new song and all of nature to respond because the LORD has revealed his salvation and righteousness to the world by delivering his people Israel and will therefore come to judge the whole world with righteousness and equity.

Outline

   I. The psalmist calls for a new song to be sung to the LORD because he has demonstrated his loyal love and faithfulness by saving Israel in the sight of all the nations (1–3).
      A. He calls for a new song (1a).
      B. He explains that the LORD should be praised because he has demonstrated his powerful salvation to the world and his loyal love and faithfulness to Israel (1b-3).
  II. The psalmist calls upon all the people of the earth to rejoice enthusiastically before the LORD who is the king (4–6).
      A. He calls for everyone to praise the LORD with all kinds of music (4–6a).
      B. He explains that this praise is for Yahweh, the king (6b).
 III. The psalmist calls for all of nature to respond joyfully because the LORD is coming to make everything right (7–9).

---

16. *Psalms*, p. 637.

A. He calls for everything in nature to respond appropriately to the sovereign power of the LORD, the creator (7–8).
B. He explains that the LORD should be acclaimed with shouts of joy because he will come to judge the world in righteousness and equity (9).

COMMENTARY IN EXPOSITORY FORM

I. God's people must sing a new song to the LORD who has revealed his righteous salvation to the world (1–3).

A. A new song will praise the LORD for new and marvelous works (1a).

The psalmist calls the congregation to sing (שִׁיר) a new song (שִׁיר; s.v. Ps. 33:3) to the LORD. Praise must never be routine and common, but always new and fresh. But this call is not simply to sing something different; it is a call to have new reasons for the singing (a metonymy of effect). "Sing a new song" means to experience the Lord's presence and blessing in a new way so that there will be new substance for the praise. If the people prayed and God answered their prayer, then they too could say that the LORD had put a new song in their mouths (Ps. 40:3). Apparently the congregation had experienced a marvelous new victory from the LORD, and that experience should therefore fill them with new songs of praise. This is the point of the explanatory clause in the first line: "because he has done marvelous things" (a *niphal* participle נִפְלָאוֹת; s.v. Ps. 139:5). These things[17] that the LORD had done were extraordinary, surpassing, wonderful in the truest sense—that which would fill people with wonder. The rest of the verse will clarify what these marvelous things were.

---

17. The form may be a numerical plural, of course, referring to many things the LORD has done. But it could also be a plural of intensification, referring to one great act of deliverance.

B. This new song will proclaim how the LORD revealed himself to the nations by saving his people (1b–3).

Now we have the central content of these marvelous things: powerful works of salvation. But the way the report is worded puts the emphasis in the content of the praise on the nature of the LORD, not the details of the salvation. This is instructive: the LORD is to have the pre-eminence in all praise.

In this regard the psalm makes three clear points. First, the salvation itself was a mighty act of God. The noun "salvation," and its verb "save," do in fact describe God's saving acts, but in the Psalter this salvation is more often some deliverance from danger, affliction, or death, such as on the battlefield, than spiritual salvation (although it is still also a spiritual victory). Whatever translation is used the saving act must be explained as a victorious deliverance. Here the text says: "his right hand has worked salvation for him, and his holy arm." The figurative use of "hand" and "arm" (anthropomorphic terms) signifies that the salvation was by God's power. That his arm is called holy (s.v. Ps. 22:3) emphasizes that there is no comparable power or ability on earth. God "worked salvation/deliverance" (הוֹשִׁיעָה, the perfect tense from יָשַׁע; s.v. Ps. 3:2) for himself, meaning essentially, he got himself the victory over the enemies. His people benefitted, of course, but he won the victory. Whatever event was behind this psalm, it was clearly a powerful deliverance of the people by God alone.

The second point is that by this "the LORD has made his salvation known" (v. 2). This is the second reference to "salvation" in the psalm; now it is the noun (יְשׁוּעָה): when he accomplished this salvation, he made it known (הוֹדִיעַ; s.v. Ps. 67:2). This great act of salvation on behalf of his people, as well as all his acts, was designed to reveal to the world his power as the saving God. The third colon parallels and completes this point: "and has revealed his righteousness in the sight of the nations." The verb translated "revealed" is specifically "uncovered" (גִּלָּה). And what he unveiled for the world to see (to their eyes, לְעֵינֵי) was his righteousness (צִדְקָתוֹ; s.v. Ps. 1:5). Here the word designates what his righteousness does (so it is a metonymy of cause): it refers to the act of salvation in the positive sense of putting right what is wrong.[18] The nations would not only come to know that the LORD is the powerful God, but that his righteousness provides for his people's benefit.

The third point in this section focuses on the reasons for his mighty act: "he has remembered his loyal love and his faithfulness to the house of Israel." The verb "remembered" (זָכַר; s.v. Ps. 6:5) means that he acted on what he remembered, i.e., he implemented his covenant promises to his people. The two attributes mentioned here are common descriptions of the LORD's keeping covenant promises: "his loyal love" (חַסְדּוֹ; s.v. Ps. 23:6) "and his faithfulness" (וֶאֱמוּנָתוֹ; s.v. Ps. 15:2), the two together often forming a single idea (as a hendiadys): "his faithful covenant love." These attributes also stand for what they produce, the resultant actions (so they are metonymies of cause): "loyal love" means the acts of love God bestows on his covenant people, and "faithfulness" means his deliverance was in keeping with his promises. So then God had remembered his covenant, that is, he had fulfilled his promises to his people, thereby showing himself to be trustworthy.

And this he did in clear view of the nations, thus revealing his victory, his great act of salvation, to everyone. Verse 3b reads "all the ends of the earth have seen the salvation of our God." In the immediate context the language used here is elaborate; it is a generalization to say that everyone saw or witnessed this great deliverance. The "ends of the earth" refers to people living in distant lands (metonymy of subject); they witnessed what the LORD did for his people, how he showed himself faithful to his covenant people by saving them from the oppressors of the world.[19] The revelation of this salvation (the third use of "salvation") to the people of the world provided the opportunity for them to come to faith in the LORD—or gave them the warning that salvation comes through the LORD alone. But as will be noted later, the psalm has an eschatological meaning as well, and so the verb could also be taken as a prophetic perfect, the full realization of these lines being in the future.

---

18. Kidner, *Psalms 73–150*, p. 352.
19. After the return from the exile the nations said, "The LORD has done great things for them" (Ps. 126:2).

II. (Therefore) all the people of the earth should also rejoice enthusiastically before the LORD, the king (4–6).

A. Everyone should praise him (4–6a).

There now follows an extended call for the people of the world to praise the LORD with enthusiasm. Their compliance with this call would demonstrate that they received the revelation and responded to the LORD by faith.

The section begins with the forceful "Shout for joy (הָרִיעוּ; s.v. Ps. 100:1) to the LORD," addressed to all the earth, meaning all the people in the earth (a metonymy of subject). The verb should be interpreted as a call for people to declare their homage to the divine king (see 1 Sam. 10:24).[20] The second colon in the verse has three imperatives: "break forth" (פִּצְחוּ) "and sing joyfully" (וְרַנְּנוּ; s.v. Ps. 33:1) and "sing praises" (וְזַמֵּרוּ; s.v. Ps. 33:2). The first imperative is always found with the second verb, and so the two together might be rendered "break out in joyful song" (as a hendiadys). These expressions recall the enthusiastic praise that occurred at the great festivals. But now the call is for people everywhere to join in praise. After all, they have seen the salvation of the LORD, and so they must acknowledge it with praise—and not a half-hearted praise either. If they do not show such faith, they will have no share in his coming kingdom.

Verses 5 and 6 continue the call for praise, now adding some of the means by which it should be given. They are to sing praises (repeated from the end of verse 4) with the[21] harp, with the harp and the sound of singing praises, with trumpets and the ram's horn. The trumpets (חֲצֹצְרוֹת) were metal tubes made of bronze or silver (Num. 10:2), as opposed to the horn (שׁוֹפָר) which was made from animal horns. The latter instrument especially was used to signal the divine presence (see Exod. 19:16, 19; Ps. 47:6;

---

20. Here we have a metonymy of effect: the shouting for joy is the effect of their faith (the cause), for there would be no such homage from those who do not believe.
21. The text does not use the article, but the class of instruments is what is meant.

Joel 2:1). So with words, harps, trumpets and horns, the people are called to offer praise to the LORD.

B. They should praise the LORD as king (6b).

The last colon of verse 6 completes this point of the call but provides the main reason for it. Here again we have the imperative "shout for joy," which is a call to offer homage joyfully and enthusiastically, and they are told to do this "before [in the presence of] the king, Yahweh." He has demonstrated his power and his righteousness to the world by saving his covenant people. He is certainly Israel's king; but he is also the king over all creation by his dominion over all the people and all the forces of the world.[22]

III. All of creation should respond joyfully because the LORD is coming to make everything right (7–9).

A. All creation must (and will) flourish in response to the glad news of his coming (7–8).

Verses 7 and 8 turn the attention to the forces of nature. The section makes the point that although this world now groans, as it were, waiting for its redemption, the coming reign of the Lord will set everything right, so that all creation will sing, as it were, in the flourishing abundance of a new world order (see Rom. 8:19ff.).

The first call is for the sea and everything in it ("its fulness") to resound (or roar; see Ps. 96:11); and this is joined with a call for the world and all who dwell in it. Since this section focuses on nature, Briggs suggests that the word "inhabitants" of the world does not refer to people but to animals and plants.[23] More plausible is the idea that the mention of the sea may recall the

---

22. To explain the psalms' focus on Israel with a design for the world, Goldingay says that God never relates to the world independently of relating to Israel. Ultimately, his relation to Israel is the model of his relation to the Church (*Psalms 90–150*, p. 124).
23. *Psalms*, II:308.

primeval chaos alluded to in other enthronement psalms; at that time the forces of nature were seen as enemies of God, but in the future they will roar in homage.[24] But the verse may simply be calling everything in the sea and on the land to respond to the glad news.

The figurative language continues in verse 8. The first is that the rivers clap their hands. The poetic language (personification) may refer to high waves cast up by full rivers flowing into and hitting one another like hands clapping. It is the language of abundance, as with the trees clapping their hands[25] (Isa. 55:12); everything in creation will flourish, and that flourishing will be in response to the coming of the LORD, who by his power will rejuvenate all of creation. In addition to being an expression of joy, clapping is also an appropriate sign of acclamation for a king (2 Kings 11:12). The second half of the verse includes the mountains: "let the mountains sing joyfully together." The personification of the mountains singing joyfully similarly reflects the abundant growth and flourishing life on the mountains that comes from the influence of the sovereign and powerful reign of the LORD over all creation (see Ps. 65:9–13).

B. All creation must (and will) respond because the LORD is coming to make everything right (9).

This is the second main reason for praise, hinted at in the first: there is to be a new song because there will be a new victory, and verse 9 prophesies that divine intervention: "for he is coming to judge the earth." Kidner offers two points to contemplate in this psalm, God's day of power at his coming, and the anticipation of that culmination in every act of worship.[26] The expectation of the coming of the Lord (with the participle, "for he is coming" [כִּי בָא]) was introduced in Psalm 96:13; and the ending of this psalm is almost identical to that. Perowne explains

---

24. Anderson, *Psalms 73–150*, p. 693.
25. The idea of the trees clapping their hands may picture a time of abundant growth so that when the wind blows the leafy limbs hit against each other—nature is celebrating the blessing of God.
26. *Psalms 73–150*, p. 353.

that the participle is used to express more vividly the coming of the LORD;[27] it sounds as if the coming is actually occurring at the time of speaking, but the point is that it is imminent—he is coming!

The purpose of his coming is "to judge" the earth, meaning everyone in the earth. The expression (לִשְׁפֹּט; s.v. Ps. 9:4) includes both aspects of divine judgment, punishing the wicked and vindicating the righteous, that is, those who belong to God by faith. All of God's decisions or judgments are fair and just, for he will judge with righteousness (בְּצֶדֶק; s.v. Ps. 1:5) and with equity (מֵישָׁרִים; s.v. Ps. 67:4). No one will say his decisions are unjust or unfair; everything the Judge of the whole earth does is right (see the emphasis on the righteous judgments of the Messiah, Isa. 11:1–9).

MESSAGE AND APPLICATION

The message of this psalm is very clear and needs little additional concluding discussion: the LORD has displayed his salvation and therefore his righteousness to the world in his deliverance of his people, and he will some day come to save his people, judge the whole world, and renew all creation, just as he promised. All of creation should, and will eventually, respond to his majestic power enthusiastically. Specifically, though, the faithful are called to sing a new song to the LORD, a song proclaiming new works of God, for when he comes to judge the world they will sing a new song in celebration of the fulfillment of the promises. Until then their praise is offered for what he has done, but with the expectation of what he will do at his coming.

An expository summary idea could be worded this way: *God's people should be singing new songs that attest to his continuing wonderful works on their behalf and that anticipate the greatest saving act that will take place when he comes to make all things right.* The call to praise the LORD is a call for people to trust in him for his wonderful acts of deliverance so that they might offer new songs of praise; it is also a call that is inspired by the hope of his coming when all of his creation, all people and all of nature,

---

27. *Psalms*, II:198.

will respond spontaneously and enthusiastically to the sovereign Lord of all creation. For creation to flourish as God intended it to do will be a tribute to his power; and so it can be said that nature will sing and rejoice when God makes everything right.

PSALM 99

Exalt the Holy One of Israel

INTRODUCTION

Text and Textual Variants

1 The LORD reigns![1]
 Let the nations tremble.
 He sits[2] enthroned above[3] the cherubim!
 Let the earth shake.[4]
2 Great is the LORD in Zion;

---

1. The Greek has a superscription attributing this psalm to David.
2. The two halves of the verse appear simply to be parallel constructions, "the LORD reigns" paralleled with "he sits enthroned above the cherubim," and then the two jussive clauses are also parallel. This is the clearest and probably correct way to understand the verse. It may be, however, that a full title of the LORD was intended ("Yahweh who sits enthroned"), but was split between verses 1a and 1b, but still reflected in the Greek version's "he who sits upon the cherubim" (Greek has "cherubin"). Verse 1b would then be a further qualification of 1a.
3. There is no preposition in the text. One could supply "upon" or "above" or "between." The Greek version has ἐπὶ "upon" probably.
4. The verb in the MT is תָּנוּט. It and the verb in the first colon, יִרְגְּזוּ, could be taken as imperfect tenses, but in this section of the psalm and especially

173

and he is exalted over all the nations.[5]
3 Let them praise[6] your great and awe-inspiring name![7]
   It[8] is holy.

4 And the strength of the king loves justice—[9]
   you have established equity;
   you have executed judgment and righteousness in Jacob.
5 Exalt the LORD our God
   and bow down at[10] his footstool.
      He is holy.[11]

---

   in light of verses 5 and 9, it is likely that they are jussives. The versions have optatives; the Greek is σαλευθήτω, "let (the earth) shake."
5. A few Hebrew and Greek manuscripts have "gods" instead of "nations" (עַמִּים). This was no doubt influenced by the expressions in Psalms 95:3, 96:4, and 97:9. But in this psalm the nations are called to tremble, and the peoples to praise.
6. The verb יוֹדוּ could be taken as an imperfect; but the jussive harmonizes with verses 5 and 9.
7. It may be possible to translate this colon as, "Let them praise your name, O Great and Awesome One!" But the attributive use of these words retains the focus on the nature of the LORD just as readily.
8. The last clause, קָדוֹשׁ הוּא, could be translated "it is holy" or "he is holy." "He is holy" harmonizes with later verses, but "it is holy" fits the verse more readily. The Greek version has ". . . your great name, for it is awesome and holy."
9. This first colon in the verse is difficult because it seems unlikely that "strength," עֹז, should be the subject of "loves." However, this is what the versions have: the Greek version has "and the king's honor (τιμή) loves judgment." Some commentators try to ease the difficulty by dividing the line into two clauses: "The king is mighty; he loves justice," or, "The victorious one (for "strength") is king; he loves justice (see Howard, *Structure*, p. 121). The RSV interprets "king" as a genitive of specification, translating the two words as "mighty king" (king, specifically strong). Another suggestion is to subordinate the clause to the previous call for praise for his name, "and for the strength of the king [who] loves justice." If the traditional rendering is retained, then it will have to be explained poetically.
10. There may be a slight problem here with the preposition, whether translated "to" or "at" his footstool. If the psalm was written after the captivity began with the destruction of the temple, there would be no ark. In that case Zion would simply represent the throne of God (see Tate, *Psalms 50–100*, p. 527).
11. A few manuscripts, the Greek version, and Jerome, also have "for (he is holy)."

> 6 Moses and Aaron *were* among[12] his priests,
>> Samuel *was* among those calling on his name;
> calling to the LORD
>> and he would answer them.[13]
> 7 He would speak to them from the pillar of the cloud;
>> they kept[14] his testimonies and the statute he gave them.[15]
> 8 O LORD our God,
>> you answered them;
>> you became to them a forgiving God,[16]
>> though you took vengeance on their misdeeds.
> 9 Exalt the LORD our God
>> and bow down at his holy mountain,
>>> for the LORD our God is holy.

Composition and Context

This is the last of the so-called enthronement psalms. It declares that the LORD reigns, and then calls on everyone to fear and tremble because of his sovereign majesty, but also to acknowledge and exalt him. The repeated refrain is that the LORD is holy. Because he is holy, he alone should be worshiped and served. And so to demonstrate his holiness, the psalmist delineates how the LORD rules over his people.

All of these psalms tell of the establishment of a righteous kingdom on the earth—on this earth. It can only be a righteous kingdom because the king is holy—he is the LORD. Whatever occasion may have prompted the writing of this psalm, ultimately

---

12. The preposition can be translated "among"; it may, however, be a *bêt* of essence, "as his priests" (Anderson, *Psalms 73–150*, p. 696). Johnson suggests separating the name Moses from the line, and reading, "Moses, and Aaron his priest, and Samuel as one who. . . ." (*Sacral Kingship*, pp. 62–3). This would require making "priests" a plural of excellence. The proposal is plausible, but the MT and the Greek translation put the words together.
13. The imperfect tense יַעֲנֵם is taken here as a customary imperfect because the context is referring to what people regular did in past history. The Greek version has ἐπήκουσεν, "he hearkened (to them)."
14. A few manuscripts have the conjunction: "and they kept."
15. Or, "they kept his testimonies; and he gave them a statute."
16. The Greek version interprets אֵל נֹשֵׂא הָיִיתָ לָהֶם as ὁ θεός, σὺ εὐίλατος ἐγίνου αὐτοῖς, "O God, you were / became propitious / merciful to them."

it too is eschatological: a righteous and holy king will rule over all the earth. And so in these historic events people were given a foretaste of that glorious time.

There is no indication of the authorship of this work. There is nothing in the psalm that argues for a late or early date. As Anderson notes, there is very little here that is dependent on Deuteronomy or Isaiah, so nothing to militate against a pre-exilic date.[17] It may have been used at the Feast of Tabernacles, for there seem to be some similarities to covenant renewal ritual. But here too there is nothing in the psalm that strongly expresses that.

The composition appears to have two parts with a refrain in verses 5 and 9, calling for people to exalt the LORD and bow before him (before his holy footstool, the ark, or before his holy mountain). So the connection to sanctuary worship is clear. But there is another refrain that occurs three times in the psalm: he (or his name) is holy (vv. 3, 5, and 9). Delitzsch suggests that this threefold motif is reminiscent of the seraphic trisagion of Isaiah 6: "holy, holy, holy."[18] There may be even more to connect the passages, because in Isaiah 6 the LORD is exalted, high and lifted up, and he is the king over all; and yet he condescends to remove the sin of the young prophet who cries out to him. The connections may be deliberate, but they might also be due to the fact that Isaiah 6 includes the central aspects of sanctuary worship to which this psalm refers.

The structure of Psalm 99 may be arranged differently for the exposition: verses 1–3 may be taken as a separate unit because they announce the LORD's reign and describe his greatness in Zion; then verses 4 and 5 explain that his reign is characterized by his love for justice and righteousness which he has established; and finally, verses 6–9 provide samples of his covenant faithfulness in answering prayer, revealing his will, and forgiving sin. Each of these sections ends with a reminder of his holiness.

---

17. *Psalms 73–150*, p. 694.
18. *Psalms*, III:100.

Exegetical Analysis

Summary

Stressing that the LORD, the God of Israel, is holy, the psalmist calls for all people to praise and worship him for his righteous reign in the world and his merciful dealings in answering prayers.

Outline

I. The psalmist calls for all the people of the earth to tremble and praise the LORD for his righteous reign throughout the earth (1–3).
   A. He calls people to tremble before the LORD who reigns from Zion over all people (1–2).
   B. He calls people to praise his great and terrible name because it is holy (3).
II. The psalmist exhorts the faithful to exalt and worship their righteous God because he is holy (4–5).
   A. He declares that the LORD establishes justice and equity in the land (4).
   B. He exhorts believers to exalt and worship God because he is holy (5).
III. The psalmist praises the LORD for his faithful and merciful dealings with the ancestors, and then exhorts the faithful to exalt and worship God because he is holy (6–9).
   A. Praise: He praises the LORD for his faithfulness and mercy to the ancestors (6–8).
      1. The LORD answered the prayers of those who called on him—Moses, Aaron and Samuel among them (6).
      2. The LORD spoke to his people and they obeyed (7).
      3. The LORD answered his people with forgiveness, even though he punished them at times (8).
   B. Exhortation: He exhorts believers to exalt and worship God because he is holy (9).

COMMENTARY IN EXPOSITORY FORM

I. All people must fear the sovereign majesty of the whole earth and praise his great and holy nature (1–3).

A. *He is to be feared because he reigns over all the world (1–2).*

The psalm begins with the now familiar exclamation, "the LORD reigns" (for the interpretation of the verb מָלָךְ see the discussion with Ps. 93:1). Here, however, the second half of the verse provides a parallel description of his sovereign majesty: "he sits enthroned *above* the cherubim." The participle "he sits" (יֹשֵׁב) is figurative (anthropomorphic) for sitting enthroned as king. This further description of the manner of his rule focuses on the throne room, which for the psalmist is on Mount Zion (expressed in v. 2). On this holy mount stood the sanctuary with the holy of holies, the throne room; and in this room was the footstool, the ark of the covenant with the cherubim carved on its lid. The LORD sat enthroned above the cherubim. So the throne of God is associated with the ark of the covenant; and all of this was the earthly representation of the heavenly scene.

The logical and necessary response to this sovereign majesty is fear and trembling. The two verbs are best taken as jussives in the light of other exhortations in the psalm:[19] "Let the peoples tremble" (יִרְגְּזוּ) and "let the earth be moved" (תָּנוּט). The first verb means to be in tumult, and even to rage (see Ps. 2:1); the psalmist desires that the people of the whole world tremble because he is the divine king of the universe. Of course they will do this in the culmination of the promises—and then this desire will be realized. The other verb is unusual, being used only here. But it also calls for the earth to be moved in the light of the LORD's sovereignty.

Verse 2 summarizes the LORD's exalted majesty: he is great (גָּדוֹל; s.v. Ps. 34:3), and he is exalted (וְרָם; s.v. Ps. 46:10) above

---

19. Some commentators take the verbs to be indicatives, describing the immediate and necessary effects that follow the acclamation of the LORD's sovereignty (e.g., Perowne, *Psalms*, II:207).

all the peoples. The kingdom of the LORD covers the whole universe, even though its center is in Zion—the earthly Zion to the psalmist.

B. He is to be praised because he is holy (3).

The psalmist then expresses his desire that all the people of the world praise the LORD, but here his words are addressed to the LORD directly ("Let them praise your name"). Once again some commentators take this verb to be an imperfect; but the jussive harmonizes better with verses 5 and 9. This word for praise (יוֹדוּ; s.v. Ps. 6:5) has the sense of a public acknowledgment: since the LORD is exalted above all the peoples, then all of them should acknowledge his sovereign nature. The object of their praise is the LORD himself, his nature and his works, expressed here in the familiar use of the word "name" (s.v. Ps. 20:1). This "name," i.e., this majestic God, is then further described: people should praise his "great (גָּדוֹל) and terrible (וְנוֹרָא; s.v. Ps. 2:11) name." The realization of who this God is and what he is like is terrifying. Those who trust in the LORD find him awe-inspiring; but those who refuse will discover how terrifying he will be.

The last colon of the verse is brief: "it is holy" (קָדוֹשׁ; s.v. Ps. 22:3). While some commentators would make this a reference to the LORD himself, "he is holy," it is more likely that the subject is the name—it is holy. Obviously there is no difference in meaning; the suggested change is simply the desire of some to harmonize the line with the repeated refrain.[20] The choice of the word "holy" for the refrain is perfect, for it means that there is no one like the LORD, anywhere, ever. In this psalm the focus so far has been on his great and exalted majesty—he alone is the exalted, majestic sovereign over all creation. So verses 1–3 powerfully introduce the reader to the universal sovereign of the world who established the center of his reign in Zion.

---

20. The Greek translation took the syntax a little differently, and this has influenced some interpreters today: "Let them praise your great name, for it is terrible and holy." Others have suggested making "great" and "terrible" substantives: "O Great and Awesome One."

II. The holy LORD must be exalted and worshiped because he loves justice and establishes uprightness in the land (4–5).

A. *He loves justice and establishes righteousness in the land (4).*

Now the psalmist will focus on the righteous character of the LORD's reign in Israel. We are first told in the poetically unexpected expression that "the strength of the king loves judgment." His power is exerted in establishing what he loves, justice (מִשְׁפָּט, s.v. Ps. 9:4). Because he loves (אָהֵב; s.v. Ps. 11:7) justice, he established (כּוֹנַנְתָּ; s.v. Ps. 93:1) uprightness (מֵישָׁרִים; s.v. Ps. 67:4) and executed judgment and righteousness (צְדָקָה; s.v. Ps. 1:5) in Jacob. These are the frequent descriptions of the works of the LORD; everything he does, and especially all his decisions, are just, right and fitting. God established and sustained a just and righteous order for his people; therefore, his people should not only live by it but champion it as the only solution to a fallen world.

B. *He is to be exalted and worshiped because he is holy (5).*

If people have not done so before, now they should exalt the LORD our God. Here we have the imperative form of the verb "exalt" (רוֹמְמוּ; s.v. Ps. 46:10): in their praise and adoration people should lift up the LORD, meaning he should be the focus of their praise. Anything short of this is not praise at all. The idea of lifting him up is contrasted here with the idea of making oneself base and low: "bow down at his holy footstool." The verb "bow down" (i.e., causing oneself to be low; for וְהִשְׁתַּחֲווּ s.v. Ps. 95:6) is the word used frequently for worship in the Old Testament. The act of bowing down to the ground represents worship and obeisance, so the term was used for all aspects of worship. Here people are called to bow at his footstool. The footstool is the ark; it signifies that the throne is above it, so that the focus of the veneration is the one who sits on the throne—people bow down before the LORD, at his feet, so to speak.[21] To bow before his

---

21. The footstool is the ark in Psalm 132; but it may be the lower step of the

footstool, that is, before the throne, is to acknowledge that he is the sovereign Lord and divine King.

The section then ends with the refrain: "He is holy."

III. The holy LORD must be exalted and worshiped because he has proven himself to be faithful, merciful and righteous (6–9).

A. *He answered the cries of the ancestors with instruction, forgiveness and justice (6–8).*

Because the holy God calls for people to bow before his holy footstool on his holy mount, all acts of worship must likewise signify that submission and dependence on the LORD. And so the psalmist now singles out a few of the better known servants of the LORD as samples. In verse 6 he mentions Moses and Aaron among his priests, or better, "as his priests" (taking the preposition as the *bêt* of essence). Aaron was certainly a priest; but since people do not normally think of Moses as one of the priests there have been attempts to re-word the colon to isolate Moses from Aaron. But if Moses did not continue to function as a priest when Aaron was ordained, he certainly did before that as he established all Levitical worship and offered the consecrating sacrifices. Next, the psalmist names Samuel with them, "as those who would call on his name." These servants of the LORD would cry out to the LORD,[22] and he would answer them. The verb "call" used here is in the participle form in both places: they were "among / as the callers of his name (בְּקֹרְאֵי), calling (קֹרְאִים) unto the LORD." The activity of calling to the LORD was a continuing aspect of their service. And because of the use of the participle to express this aspect, the final verb should be taken as a customary imperfect: "he would answer them" or "he used to answer them" (יַעֲנֵם). Here we have the primary example of the manner of the sovereign reign of the LORD in the affairs of people—he

---

throne according to Isaiah 66:1. The LORD's "footstool" represents much more—it represents his sovereign presence.

22. See among other passages Exodus 17:11–12; 32:30–32; Num. 12:13; 1 Sam. 7:8–9; 9:12–13.

responded to their cries to him. They submitted themselves to him and cried out to him, and he revealed his majesty in answering them.

The psalmist next provides an example of his sovereignty and his love for justice: he spoke to them and gave them his laws (v. 7). The revelation came at first to the Israelites in a pillar of a cloud; from this manifestation of his glory he would speak to them (another customary imperfect). And in submission they kept his testimonies (עֵדֹתָיו; s.v. Ps. 119:2) and the statute (חֹק; s.v. Ps. 119:5) he gave them.[23] The full explanation then is that when God responded to their cries he revealed his will to them; and when he did they trusted him and kept his laws. All of this is presented by the psalmist as the cycle of faith for the devout.

The focus then turns to the LORD's forgiveness in verse 8. The psalmist repeats the fact that God answered them, but he adds the clarification: "you were / became a forgiving God (אֵל נֹשֵׂא) to them." The implication, then, is that there were cries for forgiveness, and those cries were answered with forgiveness (not specifically to these three men mentioned, but to ancient Israel in general). Because God was their sovereign Lord they had to receive forgiveness from him, and they did. But since God was also their righteous Lord, no unconfessed sin would go unpunished. So he adds the expression, "and yet taking vengeance (נֹקֵם; s.v. Ps. 18:48) on all their doings (עֲלִילוֹתָם)." The addition of this clause is troubling in view of the preceding statement that God proved to be a forgiving God. The line may be taken to mean that God punished the sinful acts of the people but then forgave those who called on his name. Their understanding of forgiveness would be inadequate if they never knew of his anger against sin.[24] Or, it may mean that those who did not find forgiveness were punished.

---

23. Or: "they kept his testimonies; and he gave them a statute."
24. The addition of the idea of vengeance seems to some commentators out of place in the verse. See further C. F. Whitley, "Psalm 99:8," *ZAW* 85 (1973):227–30. Whitley suggests: "he cleanses (from נקה) from their evil deeds." Whybray takes the suffix as an objective genitive, and reads "as an avenger, on account of the evil deeds done to them." R. N. Whybray, "'Their Wrongdoings' in Psalm 99:8," *ZAW* 81 (1969):237–39.

B. He is to be exalted and worshiped because he is holy (9).

The last verse of the psalm repeats verse 5, except now the command is to bow down to his holy mountain—Zion (Ps. 2:6). The mountain was holy only because the LORD was there, and so approaching the holy mountain always meant approaching the LORD. He alone is holy; his sanctuary is therefore holy, as well as the mountain on which it was located. So whether the psalmist refers to the footstool or the mountain, the call is actually to bow down to the holy LORD God. And this is the concluding statement of the psalm: "for the LORD our God is holy."

MESSAGE AND APPLICATION

Psalm 99 continues the series of enthronement psalms, calling for people to praise and exalt the sovereign king. But the psalmist wants everyone to understand what kind of a king this is, and so he tells of his sovereign majesty over all people, his establishment of justice and righteousness through his people, and his response to their cries for help and his provision of guidance in the law, revealing him to be a forgiving God but also a God who judges wickedness. These essential aspects of the LORD set him apart from all others–in a word, he is "holy."

So these things may be gathered together in a summary expository statement: *The holy LORD must be praised and exalted in worship because he reigns over the whole world, loves and establishes justice, and meets the physical and spiritual needs of his people.* Here we see the greatness and the grace of God, the two common causes in the psalms for praising him.

By singling out Moses, Aaron and Samuel as examples to follow, the psalmist is reminding us of the priestly character of true worship. All who call upon the LORD in time of need are functioning as priests; all who receive his commandments and obey them are participating in their spiritual service. And the perpetual reminder in the psalm that the LORD is holy, a covenant theme seen frequently in the Law (e.g., Lev. 19), is a reminder that to praise and exalt him properly requires that we bow before him in submission and reverence. Because he is the sovereign king, he has established a covenant of righteousness and justice; and because he has fixed this order for his people, he meets the needs of his people, guiding them according to his will and responding to their cries, especially their cries for forgiveness, so that the order of righteousness may be retained.

All of this will ultimately find its fulfillment in the coming of Jesus the Messiah. When he puts down all his enemies and establishes his righteous reign, then the acclamation and praise of his greatness and his grace will be fully realized and fully appreciated.

PSALM 100
Jubilant Praise to the LORD Our Maker

INTRODUCTION

Text and Textual Variants

A Psalm.[1] For Thanksgiving.[2]

1 Shout for joy to the LORD, all the earth!
2 Serve the LORD with gladness;
   enter his presence[3] with jubilation.
3 Know that the LORD is[4] God.
   He made us, and we are his;[5]
   we are his people, and the sheep of his pasture.

---

1. The psalm is entitled "Jubilate" in the Anglican *Book of Common Prayer*.
2. The Hebrew word תּוֹדָה can be translated "thanksgiving" (meaning a public acknowledgment); the word could also be used for the "sacrifice of praise" (s.v. Ps. 6:5).
3. Or, "before him" (לְפָנָיו).
4. Literally, "he is God."
5. The *Kᵉthiv* is וְלֹא (*wᵉlō'*), making the line read: "He made us, and not we [ourselves]." This has the support of the Greek version, the Syriac, and Symmachus. The *Qᵉre'* is וְלֹו (*wᵉlô*) with the reading: "He made us, and to him are we," or "we are his." This has the support of Aquila, Jerome, and

4 Enter his gates with thanksgiving
   and his courts with praise;[6]
  Give thanks to him, bless his name.
5 For the LORD is good; his loyal love *endures* forever,
   and his faithfulness through all generations.[7]

Composition and Context

Psalm 100 is to be classified as a hymn, perhaps a short entry hymn sung by the worshipers preparing to enter the sanctuary and offer their praise. The composition may have been part of the formal worship of Israel, but since it is not restricted to any particular season or service it may have been used more widely. It was possibly a pre-exilic composition because the temple was still standing, although some would argue that the rebuilt temple was meant. At any rate, its placement in the collection reflects its valuable application in the post-exilic community.

This placement serves as a hymnic summation or sequel to Psalms 96–99, or perhaps even Psalms 90–99, in which the collapse of the Davidic monarchy serves as the background for the call for the whole world to acknowledge the kingship of the LORD and the anticipation of his glorious appearance to judge the world. The theme of the faithfulness of God in Psalm 100 recalls the sevenfold use of this theme in Psalm 89 which closed the last collection. But Psalm 100 is more tightly connected to

---

the Targum. Moreover, 15 times in the Bible the text has לֹא where לוֹ is meant (see BDB, p. 520).

The first reading has the difficulty of being a unique idea–nowhere do we find such a reference to self-creation. The second reading fits the context better, but it has the difficulty of being slightly tautological. Most translations, however, accept this as the better reading of the line. But the questionable word has also been taken as an asseverative, with the meaning "and indeed" and the rest of the line connecting with the next, "we are his people" (see J. O. Lewis, "An Asseverative לֹא in Psalm 100:3?" *JBL* 86 [1967]:216). Another interpretation is similar, but takes it as the particle לֻא, usually "if only" but here "indeed" (C. F. Whitley, "Some Remarks on *lu* and *lo*," *ZAW* 87 [1975]:212–14).

6. The Greek translation uses ὕμνοις, "hymns," for תְּהִלָּה.
7. The reading is, "to generation and generation," translated literally in the Greek version.

Psalm 95 in its setting with the motifs of the shout, the thanksgiving, the call to enter, and the relationship of the LORD and his people. Psalms 95 and 100 frame Psalms 96–99, which stress the reign of the LORD.[8] By its placement in Book IV, Psalm 100 most likely was used in the same festival celebrations as the preceding psalms.

This short hymn has two parallel sections: a call to acclaim the kingship of the LORD with a celebration of the covenant relationship he has with his people (1–3), and a call to give thanks to the LORD with a celebration of the benefits of the covenant relationship (4–5).[9]

Exegetical Analysis

Summary

The psalmist calls the people to serve the LORD with gladness because he made them and provides for them, and to enter his courts with thanksgiving because he is good and faithful to his covenant people.

Outline

I. The psalmist exhorts the people to serve the LORD with gladness because he made them and provides for them (1–3).
   A. Call to praise: People everywhere should serve the LORD with gladness (1–2).
   B. Cause for praise: They should praise him because he is God, because he made them, and because he cares for them (3).
II. The psalmist exhorts the congregation to enter his courts with thanksgiving because he is good and faithful (4–5).

---

8. Tate, *Psalms 51–100*, p. 535.
9. See also J. L. Mays, "Worship, World, and Power: An Interpretation of Psalm 100," *Int* 23 (1969):315–30; and W. Bruegemann, "Psalm 100," *Int* 39 (1985):65–9.

A. Call to praise: Worshipers should enter his courts with thanksgiving and praise (4).
B. Cause for praise: They should praise him because he is good and because he is faithful to his covenant people (5).

COMMENTARY IN EXPOSITORY FORM

I. Those who acknowledge the LORD as their maker and master should worship and serve him with jubilation (1–3).

Praise is the evidence of a living faith because it reveals how well people know the LORD and how loyal they are to him. And so in this brief hymn we have the clear link between the repeated call for people to praise him and their knowledge of who he is and what he has done. Accordingly, the first half of the psalm has the call to praise (vv. 1–2) and the cause (v. 3).

A. *People everywhere should praise the LORD and enter his presence with jubilation (1–2).*

The first two verses form an emphatic call with the threefold "shout," "serve," and "enter."

The main point of the psalm is thus captured from the beginning, namely, that entering into the presence of the LORD in the sanctuary to worship and serve him is to be accompanied by shouts of praise and acclamation. The first imperative is "shout for joy" (הָרִיעוּ; it is from רוּעַ, "raise a shout, give a blast" with clarion or horn).[10] This call is addressed to "all the earth," meaning everyone in the earth (a metonymy of subject); it

---

10. The word stresses the loudness of the shout, as it can be used for sounding the alarm for battle or giving a war-cry (Josh. 6:10), or shouting in triumph over enemies (Zeph. 3:14). It is used to describe the angelic shout for joy at the creation of the world (Job 38:7). In public worship it refers to shouts of joy (Ps. 100:1), or blasts of sound on musical instruments. The related noun (תְּרוּעָה) is similar in usage; it is a shout or blast given in jubilation but also to sound an alarm, especially in time of war.

therefore signifies that he is to be recognized as sovereign over all the earth by an acclamation of praise, a homage shout or fanfare as Kidner puts it.[11]

Verse 2 makes the call more specific. The imperative now is "serve (עִבְדוּ; s.v. Ps. 134:1) the LORD with gladness." This verb can be used for any kind of work, but in a religious context it is another word for worship. In this case it refers to worship as spiritual service, such as participation in the formal worship in the sanctuary. Kidner notes that it is a word that leaves no gap between worship and work (p. 356). The word may have a political connotation as well, especially since the LORD is acclaimed sovereign over the earth (see Ps. 2:11). Here the service is to be performed with gladness (שִׂמְחָה; s.v. Ps. 48:11). There must be a heartfelt response to the LORD's greatness and goodness, and that response will be manifested in joyful service. VanGemeren further explains that this gladness signifies a joy in living in harmony with the creator, redeemer, and king.[12]

The second half of the verse has traditionally been rendered "Come before him with joyful songs." The verb "come" (בֹּאוּ) is the same word that is used in verse 4 with the sense of "enter." Here the entering would be into the LORD's presence—before him. No doubt the sanctuary is meant, for there the faithful would gather before him in worship. This entering is to be with "jubilation" (בִּרְנָנָה, from רָנַן; s.v. Ps. 33:1), a word that also signifies a shout or ringing cry of celebration. So the emphasis of these first lines is clear: entrance into the presence of the LORD for worship should be characterized by genuine jubilation.

B. They should praise him because he is God who made them and takes care of them (3).

Verse 3 introduces the reasons for the exuberant praise with the imperative "know" (דְּעוּ; s.v. Ps. 67:2). The word "to know" has a wide range of meanings; here it could mean "learn," that is, come to know, or it could mean "be assured." It probably is

---

11. *Psalms 73–150*, p. 356.
12. *Psalms*, p. 742.

closer to the latter—a recognition formula;[13] but it also has a confessional tone to it in that the expressions are statements made about God. So in general, the knowledge of the LORD is a prerequisite for praise. And here there are three things that the people must acknowledge about the LORD: 1) that he is God, 2) that since he made them they are accountable to him; and 3) that they have a privileged position in the covenant.

First, people should come before him with praise because he is God. That in itself is sufficient reason. The LORD is God—there is no one else. People may think that they are independent of the LORD, but they are not. Because he is God, everything they are and everything they have came from him. This is particularly relevant to worshipers because the psalm has several references to the covenant; thus, Yahweh is the covenant God, their covenant God.

The second reason for the call to praise builds on this simple fact: if the LORD is God, then he is the creator—"he made us" (הוּא־עָשָׂנוּ). The expression is broad enough to include the creation of people in general, and more specifically, the creation of the nation. If people focus their attention on this truth, then they will be filled with wonder and praise. But more importantly, they will also realize that they belong to him and are therefore accountable to him, their Maker.

The third reason believers should praise the LORD is that they have a special, covenant relationship with him: "we *are* his people, and the sheep of his pasture." People who have entered into covenant with the LORD by faith are "his people," i.e., the people of God. They are also called here the "sheep of his pasture," a common figure (an implied comparison) that signifies the care and protection and provision he gives to his people. The image of a shepherd can also be a monarchical figure (see Jer. 23:1; Ezek. 34:41; Ps. 77:20–21). It stresses the fact that the LORD cares and provides for his people.

When faithful people fully know and acknowledge that

---

13. The formula may be reduced from the more formal "and you shall know that . . . ." For a detailed study, see W. Zimmerli, "Knowledge of God according to the Book of Ezekiel," in *I Am Yahweh*, tr. by D. W. Stott (Atlanta: John Knox, 1954 and 1982), p. 30.

Yahweh is God, that he made them, and that he is their shepherd, their response will be jubilant praise.

II. Those who enjoy God's goodness and faithfulness should enter his courts with praise and thanksgiving (4–5).

A. *The people of God should enter his courts with praise and thanksgiving (4).*

The second half of the psalm also begins with a call to praise, now specifically calling believers to acknowledge the person and works of the LORD. In the first part we had "shout," "serve," and "enter"; now we have "enter," "thanksgiving" and "praise."

The verb "enter" is repeated from verse 2; here the people are called to enter his gates and courts. This is the area inside the entrance to the sanctuary and around the holy shrine; it is the place of worship activity. So the call is for communal worship in the sanctuary. Here is a hint that the psalm may have been pre-exilic in its origin.

The people are to enter with thanksgiving and praise. The first word "thanksgiving" (תּוֹדָה, also used in the superscription; s.v. Ps. 6:5) means "acknowledgment"; it refers to a public acknowledgment or proclamation about the LORD. It might also here include the giving of the peace offering for praise—but at least the colon calls for public praise in the sanctuary. The traditional translation "thanksgiving," while accurate enough, does not capture the full emphasis of the word—the expositor will have to explain the full meaning. The second qualifier is "praise" (תְּהִלָּה; s.v. Ps. 33:1), that is, an enthusiastic, glowing report. These words describe what the faithful will be expressing when they enter the sanctuary.

And once there, they are called on to "give thanks" and "praise." The first imperative (הוֹדוּ) is related to the noun "acknowledgment / thanksgiving" mentioned above. Thus, the faithful who enter with expressions of their thankfulness are now called on to acknowledge them in public worship. The second imperative (בָּרְכוּ; s.v. Ps. 5:12) may be translated "praise" in general, but it means "bless." It is a public praise that elevates and enhances the LORD in the minds of the people. The object of this blessing is "his name," that is, his character and his acts (s.v. Ps. 20:1). The clear understanding of his "name" reminds worshipers of the proper focus and emphasis of praise. The public acknowledgment and blessing of the LORD God is based on his nature that is revealed through his wonderful works. These great works the faithful are to acknowledge publicly, in a way that he receives all the glory.

B. They should praise him because he is good and faithful to his covenant people (5).

Now we turn to the reasons for this call to praise. The first is that the LORD is good (v. 5a). In verse 3 the psalmist affirmed that the LORD is God; now he states that the LORD is good. In the Bible the word "good" (טוֹב; s.v. Ps. 34:8) usually describes people or things that promote, enhance, protect, and preserve life. In creation everything God made was called "good." His work of forming Israel was also good (Isa. 30:15); in fact, everything he did for his covenant people was life-giving and beneficial. To say God is good is the fundamental way of explaining the blessings and benefits of life; as Tate says, God is the source of all that makes life enjoyable and worthwhile.[14]

This affirmation is followed by the second attribute of God: "his loyal love [endures] for ever." The line seems to be an excerpt from the common formula: "Give thanks to the LORD, for his loyal love endures forever" (Pss. 106:1, 107:1, 118:1; 136:1). The word "loyal love" (חֶסֶד; s.v. Ps. 23:6), refers to that faithful love God manifests on behalf of his covenant people; it is the attribute of God that most clearly states the basis for his faithful acts on their behalf. The word is often joined with "truth" or "faithfulness," forming a hendiadys to express "faithful love"; here the second half of the verse adds "and his faithfulness" (אֱמוּנָתוֹ; s.v. Ps. 15:2). And this faithfulness and loyal love endure from age to age. Thus, God is completely dependable. He keeps his promises; he fulfills his plans; he never fails. People can say this of no one else—only God. But the problem is, they do not say it enough.

---

14. *Psalms 51–100*, p. 538.

MESSAGE AND APPLICATION

The message of this psalm is very clear: God is worthy to be praised because of who he is and what he has done. And the applications are direct: there is the call for praise expressed in the imperatives "shout for joy," "give public acknowledgment," and "bless," and in the qualifications "with gladness," "with jubilation," "with thanksgiving," and "with praise." And they must do this in community as they enter the sanctuary to worship (i.e., serve) him with gladness. The faithful must praise the LORD with enthusiasm and understanding.

This understanding is basic to worship and service, and so the imperative to know that the LORD is God, that he made us, and that he cares for us, is central to the psalm. But it is the nature of God that lies behind these acts, as the conclusion of the psalm reminds us: he is good, loving, and faithful.

If a summary idea is necessary for this short, clear psalm, it could be worded this way: *Believers should praise God enthusiastically and serve him with delight because in his goodness and faithful love he made them and he takes care of them.*

There are many doxologies and acclamations in the New Testament; but the hymns and anthems in Revelation 4 and 5 capture some of these ideas and relate them to the Lord Jesus Christ. In Revelation 4:8 the Lord is praised because he is holy, powerful, and eternal, or in the words of the psalm, he is God. The next hymn (Rev. 4:11) declares that the Lord is worthy to receive praise because he made everything by his own will, an expansion on the psalm's point that he made us. In Revelation 5 the Lord is praised because he redeemed people to be a kingdom of priests (5:9–10); the covenant language of the psalm anticipates the covenant love demonstrated in our redemption. And the last two hymns (5:12 and 5:13) affirm the worthiness of the Lord to receive praise.

PSALM 101

The King's Righteous Reign

INTRODUCTION

Text and Textual Variants

A Psalm of David.

1 I will sing *of your* loyal love and justice;
   unto you, O LORD, I will sing praises.
2 I will behave wisely[1] in a blameless way.
   When[2] will you come to me?
  I shall walk about[3] in the midst of my house
   with a perfect heart.
3 I will not set a vile thing[4] before my eyes;

---

1. A few manuscripts have "to you."
2. MT has מָתַי; the Greek version renders it "when," πότε (ἥξεις πρός με).
3. The form in the MT is the imperfect tense, אֶתְהַלֵּךְ. It and the subsequent imperfect tenses may be translated as either future tenses, stating what he will do, or present tenses, stating what he is now in the habit of doing. The Greek version translated most of these as past tenses.
4. The text uses דְּבַר־בְּלִיָּעַל. The qualifying word describes that which is worthless and wicked. The Greek version used a much milder word for it: "unlawful," παράνομον.

195

I hate the practice of unfaithfulness;[5]
It shall not cling to me.[6]
4 A perverse heart shall depart from me;[7]
   a *wicked* person I will not know.
5 Whoever slanders[8] his neighbor in secret,
   him will I destroy;[9]
   a high look and a proud[10] heart
   him I will not endure.[11]
6 My eyes are on the faithful of the land,
   that they may dwell with me;
   whoso walks in a perfect way
   shall minister for me.[12]
7 *Whoever* works deceit[13] will not dwell within my house;
   whoever speaks lies[14] will not be established[15] before my eyes.

---

5. The MT has עֹשֵׂה סֵטִים, "doing evil (faithlessnesses, apostasies)." The Greek version has the plural form for the participle, "doers of evil" ($\pi\alpha\rho\alpha\beta\acute{\alpha}\sigma\epsilon\iota\varsigma$). An alternate reading is with the participle, עֹשֵׂי, "doers of faithlessness(es)."
6. The Greek version has the next phrase, "a perverse heart," as the subject of this clause.
7. This clause is made a subordinate clause in the Greek for the following statement: "when the wicked kept turning from me (I would no longer know him)."
8. The Q°re' form is מְלָשְׁנִי, possibly a *piel* participle (for מְלַשְּׁנִי), although it could be a shortened form of the *poel*. It is followed by most manuscripts and the Targum. The K°thiv form is the *poel* participle, מְלוֹשְׁנִי. There would be no difference in the meaning. For the *hîreq yôd* ending see Gesenius (*GKC*, par. 90m).
9. The form is an imperfect; the Greek version again makes it refer to the past: $\dot{\epsilon}\xi\epsilon\delta\acute{\iota}\omega\varkappa o\nu$, "I have driven (from me)," or, "I would drive away."
10. This is translated in the Greek as $\dot{\alpha}\pi\lambda\acute{\eta}\sigma\tau\omega\ \varkappa\alpha\rho\delta\acute{\iota}\alpha$, "an insatiable heart."
11. The Hebrew is לֹא אוּכָל. This line was translated in the Greek version (and Syriac) as $\tau o\acute{\upsilon}\tau\omega\ o\dot{\upsilon}\ \sigma\upsilon\nu\acute{\eta}\sigma\vartheta\iota o\nu$, "with him I have not eaten" ("would not eat"), as if the Hebrew had אִתּוֹ לֹא אוֹכַל.
12. The Greek translation has "he that walked" and "ministered" or "would minister" ($\dot{\epsilon}\lambda\epsilon\iota\tau o\acute{\upsilon}\rho\gamma\epsilon\iota$).
13. The Hebrew is עֹשֵׂה רְמִיָּה, "worker of deceit"; but the Greek version has $\pi o\iota\tilde{\omega}\nu\ \dot{\upsilon}\pi\epsilon\rho\eta\varphi\alpha\nu\acute{\iota}\alpha\nu$, "proud doer (did not dwell)."
14. The Hebrew is דֹּבֵר שְׁקָרִים, "speaker of lies"; the Greek has it $\lambda\alpha\lambda\tilde{\omega}\nu\ \ddot{\alpha}\delta\iota\varkappa\alpha$, "unjust speaker."
15. For the MT's לֹא־יִכּוֹן the Greek version has a free interpretation, $o\dot{\upsilon}\ \varkappa\alpha\tau\epsilon\acute{\upsilon}\vartheta\upsilon\nu\epsilon\nu$, "prospered not."

8 Every morning[16] I will destroy all the wicked of the land,
   that I may cut off all evil-doers from the city of the
   LORD.

Composition and Context

There is widespread agreement that the psalm is about the king and his righteous rule; but there is some disagreement about the occasion for its writing. The most likely setting would be the coronation of the king, at which time he would acknowledge his loyalty to the covenant and vow to maintain righteousness in his reign. But we cannot rule out the possibility that the psalm might have been used at an annual festival during which loyalty to the covenant would be renewed.[17] The passage presents God's justice and mercy as kingly virtues; as such it is a mirror for kings and all who are in authority under God.[18] If the king was to rule over God's holy nation, then only those who were faithful to the way of the LORD could be admitted to places of honor and trust.[19]

The work must come from the time of the monarchy. Many commentators suggest a date later in the monarchy, such as 620 B.C.[20] The superscription of the psalm preserves the tradition that it was written by David. It would make sense for David to have written a piece like this because the new state had to be organized and officers of state had to be chosen.[21] Those who do not think David wrote it note that David did not do this in his court as far as we can tell, and that the psalm has been placed in Book IV of the collection and not the earlier book with so many Davidic psalms. Accordingly, the psalm was instructive for future rulers on how to have a righteous reign. But of course the

---

16. לַבְּקָרִים may be translated "at the mornings," "by mornings," or more freely as "morning by morning." The Syriac has the word in the singular.
17. See, for example, S. Mowinckel, *The Psalms in Israel's Worship*, I:67–68.
18. Perowne, *Psalms*, II:212.
19. See J. E. Weir, "The Perfect Way," *EvQ* 53 (1981):54–59; and Michael L. Barré, "The Shifting Focus of Psalm 101," in *The Book of Psalms*, ed. by Flint and Miller, pp. 206–223.
20. See, for example, A. A. Anderson, *Psalms 73–150*, p. 700.
21. Perowne, *Psalms*, II:212.

need to remove the slanderer, the proud, the deceitful, and the liar would be as important in the early monarchy as in the late. Many of the evil characteristics that the king was trying to avoid are also found in various passages in the book of Proverbs.[22]

The poem begins with the king's affirmation of loyalty—he will sing of the LORD's loyal love and justice (v. 1). The king then resolves to be faithful to God (v. 2). This verse could be taken with verse 1 or joined to the rest of the psalm as a summary statement. I have chosen to make it a separate point about the king's own integrity. Then, in the rest of the psalm we have a clarification point-by-point of the way of purity he will maintain in his administration (vv. 3–8).[23] What it adds up to is a description of the ideal king, for none of the kings of Israel were able to live up to this. But as a royal psalm the description also looks ahead to the ideal king who will reign with righteousness, the promised Messiah (see Pss. 45 and 72).

Exegetical Analysis

Summary

The king resolves to maintain purity in his realm by purging evil from his personal life, from his court and from his capital, in order that loyal-love and justice might prevail and that the LORD might be pleased to dwell in their midst.

Outline

I. The king extols the virtues of loyal-love and justice (1).
II. The king resolves to follow the perfect way with a perfect heart (2).
III. The king clarifies how he will apply God's standards to his reign (3–8).
   A. He will keep himself pure by tolerating no evil act or thought (3–4).

---

22. See Helen Ann Kenik, "Code of Conduct for a King," *JBL* 95 (1976):391–403.
23. The pattern seems clearly consistent throughout; but for the suggestion that the latter part may be an oracle, see John S. Kselman, "Psalm 101," *JSOT* 33 (1985):45–62.

1. He will not tolerate a vile or faithless person.
   2. He will not tolerate a perverse thought.
   B. He will keep his court pure by exterminating the evil ministers and surrounding himself with pure ones (5–6).
      1. He will annihilate ministers who are slanderers, arrogant and proud.
      2. He will surround himself with men like himself.
   C. He will keep his capital pure by purging it of all evildoers (7–8).
      1. He will not consciously tolerate the presence of an evil person.
      2. He will rigorously purge evil men from Jerusalem.

COMMENTARY IN EXPOSITORY FORM

I. Truly spiritual leaders praise the LORD for his faithful love and justice (1).

The king begins the psalm with an affirmation of his loyalty to the LORD. He resolves to sing (אָשִׁירָה; s.v. Ps. 33:3) and praise (אֲזַמֵּרָה; s.v. Ps. 33:2) the LORD for his faithful covenant love (חֶסֶד; s.v. Ps. 23:6) and his justice (מִשְׁפָּט; s.v. Ps. 9:4). The loyal love would refer to acts of love that God did for him, proofs of his loyal love (so metonymy of cause). And because the word is primarily a covenant word, then the immediate focus would be on God's faithfulness to the covenant he made with the king. Both covenant love and divine justice would have been given to the king to enable him to judge rightly during his reign.[24] This little hymnic introduction then lays a solid foundation for the vows that follow.

II. Truly spiritual leaders maintain a spiritual relationship with the LORD (2).

Praise for God's faithful love must be accompanied by a commitment to live faithfully, and that is what the royal psalmist

---
24. Anderson, *Psalms 73–150*, p. 701.

does in verse 2. His first vow could be translated "I will be wise," with the intended effect of "I will expound," that is, teach (אַשְׂכִּילָה; s.v. Ps. 36:4).[25] He will think and act in a way that is prudent, that is pleasing to God and successful in life, so that others will know what a righteous reign is like. This will take thoughtful consideration and personal discipline—it will not happen instantly. And the primary evidence of Godly wisdom is expressed in the prepositional phrase, "in a perfect way." The word translated "perfect" (תָּמִים; s.v. Ps. 7:8) here describes a life of integrity, that is, being forgiven for sin and living free from sin. This requires constant vigilance and frequent maintenance. The colon is paralleled by the last part of the verse: "I shall walk about (אֶתְהַלֵּךְ)[26] with a perfect heart," the heart signifying his choices and affections (a metonymy of subject; s.v. Ps. 111:1). His regular activities, where he goes and what he does, will be with pure and proper motives.

In between these two cola is the expression, "When will you come to me?" Here in his affirmation of obedience he includes a brief prayer for God's presence with him. It may simply be a prayer for God to make his presence known to his people at the altar during worship,[27] or perhaps to the psalmist privately in a vision.[28] But in David's case it is not impossible that he has in mind the bringing of the ark to the holy city.[29] At any rate, in the midst of all his vows the psalmist voices his desire for LORD to draw near to him, that is, to make his presence known in the reign.[30]

---

25. See Goldingay, *Psalms 90–150*, p. 141.
26. The form is not now a cohortative. It may express a simple future, but Briggs takes it as a habitual imperfect, expressing his claim for the way he lives (*Psalms*, II:314).
27. Broyles, *Psalms*, p. 389.
28. T. J. Booij, "Psalm ci.2," *VT* 38 (1988):458–62.
29. In 2 Samuel 6:9 we have a similar desire expressed: "How shall the ark of the LORD come to me?" But several commentators who take the setting as a festival event suggest this brief prayer might be part of the ritual humiliation of the king for the people (see Anderson, *Psalms 73–150*, p. 701). There is little or no evidence for such a view.
30. Goldingay suggests that the purpose of this coming was to exercise authority in the world (p. 142).

III. Truly spiritual leaders ensure the spiritual nature of their leadership (3–8).

A. *They maintain personal purity by not tolerating evil (3–4).*

For spiritual leaders to maintain such integrity necessarily involves how they conduct their lives before other people and deal with them. First, they must not tolerate or condone evil.

1. *Vile and evil people must be removed.*

The "vile thing" (דְּבַר־בְּלִיָּעַל; s.v. Ps. 18:5) is something that is both wicked and worthless. The Greek version rendered it with "unlawful," which by its usage is certainly true; but the word stresses more the worthlessness of the person and what he does. Here the word may obtain some specific clarification by virtue of the parallel expression, "doing evil" (עֲשֹׂה־סֵטִים). This word translated "evil" only occurs here; the probable etymology would suggest a connection with a verb (סוּט) that has the idea of falling away; this would yield the meaning of "doing apostasies" or "acts of unfaithfulness." Such a person would be worthless and wicked in the king's administration. And so the psalmist declares that he will not have such a person in his presence ("before my eyes")—he hates (s.v. Ps. 139:21) such a sin and will not permit it to cling to him. There will be no tolerance for a person who might appear faithful but is an apostate.

2. *Perverse things must not be tolerated.*

In verse 4 the focus is on a perverse heart (עִקֵּשׁ), that is, a person whose choices and affections are twisted. The king needs people in his court who are upright and forthright. The wicked person will have to go—he will depart from the king. In the parallel line the king determines not to "know" such a wicked person (אֵדָע; s.v. Ps. 67:2). This kind of knowledge is personal and experiential; it especially belongs to people who share a covenant relationship. But he will maintain no personal relationship, no familiarity, with such an untrustworthy person, especially since that one will depart.

PSALM 101

B. They maintain purity in their leadership by surrounding themselves with spiritual people (5–6)

1. Slanderers and arrogant people must be removed (5).

Just as dangerous in court is the slanderer (מְלָשְׁנִי, Q.). But this is even more insidious because the slanderer in mind does his evil deed in secret, a whisperer of malicious words about people. The king will not merely expel or avoid this one—he will destroy him (אַצְמִית).

This description is paralleled with arrogance, probably because someone with a superior attitude would be prone to destroy others with slander. The first description is "a high look," literally, "lofty of eyes" (גְּבַהּ־עֵינַיִם). The expression is used only here in the Old Testament, but is similar to Proverbs 21:4 and Psalm 18:27. The expression describes someone who is ambitious, and who looks down on other people. Here it is linked with "a proud heart, literally, "broad of heart." This signifies someone who is insatiable or greedy; his desires are never satisfied (Prov. 28:25). Of such an arrogant person the psalmist says, "I cannot" (אֹתוֹ לֹא אוּכָל). The Greek version assumed the word was "eat," and translated it accordingly: "I have not eaten with him." But the Hebrew expression finds a parallel construction in Isaiah 1:13, "I cannot (bear)."

2. Faithful and blameless people must be chosen (6).

Verse 6 provides the contrast: he cannot tolerate these wicked and vile people, but he chooses people who are faithful. The expression, "my eyes are on" means that he looks after and cares for the right kind of people (see Gen. 44:21). Here the right kind are the "faithful of the earth" (בְּנֶאֶמְנֵי־אֶרֶץ; s.v. Ps. 15:2), people on whom he may depend, not the apostates, slanderers, or self-serving ambitious people.

His eyes are on the faithful so that they may dwell with him (לָשֶׁבֶת, from יָשַׁב), meaning, be his associates and servants. The parallel line describes them also as people whose life (walk) is "perfect" (or "blameless," תָּמִים)—the same term he used for his own way of life. A king who lives a blameless life must necessarily surround himself with people who live with the same integrity. And these people will minister for him (יְשָׁרְתֵנִי). This verb describes different kinds of service, either of people or of angels. It can be used of serving God in the sanctuary; but here it is serving the king in his righteous administration.

C. They maintain purity in the work by purging evil from the place of service (7–8).

1. The presence of evil people must not be tolerated (7).

According to verse 7 the king will not abide liars. Two expressions are used for them: they are "workers of deceit" (עֹשֵׂה רְמִיָּה; for "deceit" s.v. Ps. 5:7) and "speakers of lies" (דֹּבֵר שְׁקָרִים; for "lies" s.v. Ps. 144:8). These people will not dwell in his house, meaning, either the royal court, or the whole land itself. No liar should ever be put in a position of authority or honor. The king will not allow such people to become established (לֹא־יִכּוֹן; s.v. Ps. 93:1).

2. Evil people must be removed from the place of service (8).

Finally, the royal psalmist determines to destroy (אַצְמִית)[31] the wicked from the land "morning by morning" (לַבְּקָרִים, "by the mornings"). Judgment was usually made in the morning (2 Sam. 15:2), with the king taking the difficult cases and setting the standard (1 Kings 3:16–28). This expression may simply mean that it will be his primary concern—first thing. The point is that the king will mete out justice every day so that he may cut off (לְהַכְרִית) all evil-doers ("all doers of evil," כָּל־פֹּעֲלֵי אָוֶן; s.v. Ps. 28:3) from the city of the LORD. These are people who characteristically do evil things. They have to be cut off from Jerusalem, because what is done in Jerusalem would affect the way people live in the land.[32]

---

31. The verb (צָמַת) is a strong word, meaning "exterminate, annihilate, bring an end to" someone or something. An Arabic cognate means "to silence, make speechless."
32. Anderson, *Psalms 73–150*, p. 703.

MESSAGE AND APPLICATION

Here we have an inspired pattern for a king and his court. In order to maintain a righteous administration, the king will have to be ruthless in rooting out all evil, for it would not take much to bring down the monarchy. What is true of an Israelite king is also true of anyone who desires to maintain purity and integrity in leading people in the service of God. If God does not tolerate evil, if wicked activities like those mentioned here prevent people from entering God's presence to worship (Ps. 15), then those who are chosen by God to lead his people must be sure to maintain that level of righteousness. The central expository idea could be worded this way: *Truly spiritual leaders will purge evil from their own lives and remove evil and perverse people from their "court" so that the LORD will make his presence known to the righteous.*

The difficulty is, and always has been, that many people seek offices or places of leadership who do not have the spiritual qualifications. And unfortunately, those entrusted with the task of ensuring that the work is led by righteous people often look only at skills and training. Today as much as ever before ministries need to be purged of people who try to serve without integrity.[33] And since the standard is seldom met, we have to look beyond our approximation to the Messiah to see the perfect fulfillment.[34] This does not mean leaders today should do nothing; they must purge evil from their own lives and evil people from their place of service so that their ministries will have integrity and be effective in a world that has lost the way. Accordingly, the Apostle Paul made sure that he and his fellow workers renounced all the hidden things of shame so that the light of the Gospel would illumine those who were yet in darkness (2 Cor. 4:1–6).

---

33. Jaki advises that we should use this principle with caution; rather than being hell-bent on rooting out evil we should follow justice and wisdom (Stanley L. Jaki, *Praying the Psalms* [Grand Rapids: Eerdmans, 2001], pp. 177–179).
34. Kidner, *Psalms 73–150*, p. 358.

PSALM 102

An Urgent Plea to the Eternal God of Heaven

INTRODUCTION

Text and Textual Variants

A prayer of an afflicted man
when he is faint and pours out his lament before the LORD.

1 O LORD, hear my prayer,
   and let my cry come to you.
2 Do not hide[1] your face from me when I am in distress;
   incline your ear to me when I call;
   answer[2] me quickly!
3 For my days vanish in smoke,[3]
   and my bones burn like a firebrand

---

1. For the MT's אַל־תַּסְתֵּר, "do not hide," the Greek version interprets with ἀποστρέψῃς, "(do not) turn away (your face)."
2. For "answer" the Greek version uses "hear (εἰσάκουσόν)."
3. For clarification the preposition בְ was changed to כְ, "like (smoke)," by the majority of manuscripts—as well as the Greek, Targum and Jerome.

PSALM 102

4 My heart is struck[4] and withered like grass
    for I forget to eat my bread.
5 Because of the sound of my groaning
    my bone(s) stick to my skin.[5]
6 I am like an owl of the desert;
    I have become like a screech owl among the ruins.
7 I lie awake, and I am[6]
    like a lone bird[7] on the roof top.
8 All day long my enemies reproach me;
    those who rail[8] against me use my *name* as a curse.[9]
9 For I eat ashes like[10] bread;
    I mingle my drink with weeping,
10 because of your great indignation and your wrath,
    for you have taken me up and cast me away.
11 My days are like a shadow *that has* declined,[11]
    and I wither like grass.

12 But you, LORD, sit enthroned[12] forever;

---

4. The form in the MT, הוּכָּה, is an unusual writing for הֻכָּה, the *hophal* perfect of נָכָה, "(it) was smitten."
5. Literally, "my flesh"; the image is that of emaciation where bones can be seen against the skin.
6. The Hebrew form וָאֶהְיֶה has the disjunctive accent here, which makes a break in the clause.
7. MT has כְּצִפּוֹר בּוֹדֵד, but a few manuscripts, the Syriac, and Targum, read "a wandering (נוֹדֵד) bird."
8. Hebrew מְהוֹלָלַי, "those who rail against me," is a passive form (*poal*) with a suffix (see *GKC* 121). It was translated by the Greek (and Syriac) as "they that [used to] praise me" *(καὶ οἱ ἐπαινοῦντές με)*, reading it as מְהַלְלָי. Leslie Allen suggests the word be repointed as an active verb, a *poel* form מְהֹלְלָי, "those who made a fool of me" (*Psalms 101–150* [Waco: Word, 1983], p. 15).
9. The idea may be that when they swear they use him as an example: "God do to me as he did to him if I (do such and so)."
10. Instead of "like" ("like bread," כַלֶּחֶם), a few manuscripts have "without," בַּל; the form may have been taken at first as בַּלֶּחֶם, "in bread."
11. MT has נָטוּי, "declined," a passive form modifying the shadow as having declined, perhaps of an evening shadow. The Greek (Syriac and Jerome) make it the active verb: "my days have faded" *(ἐκλίθησαν,* perhaps for נָטְיוּ).
12. The Greek version interprets the line with "remain" *(μένεις).*

An Urgent Plea to the Eternal God of Heaven

and your renown[13] *endures* to all generations.
13 You will arise, you will have compassion on Zion,
for it is time to be gracious to her,
because the appointed time has come.[14]
14 For your servants desire her stones
and have pity for her dust.
15 And nations will revere[15] the[16] name of the LORD,
and all the kings of the earth will revere your[17] glory.
16 Because[18] the LORD has built[19] Zion
he[20] has appeared in his glory.[21]
17 He had regard for the prayer[22] of the destitute,
and has not despised their prayer.
18 This shall be written for a generation to come,
that a people *to be* created may praise the LORD:
19 For the LORD[23] has looked down from his holy height,[24]
from heaven he looked intently at the earth,
20 to hear the groans of the prisoner,[25]

---

13. For MT's וְזִכְרְךָ, "and your memorial / renown," Allen follows Childs in suggesting that this may have been a cultic invocation of the name. One manuscript has וְכִסְאֲךָ, "and your throne," and a few other manuscripts have כִּסְאֲךָ, "your throne" (Lam. 5:19).
14. The Syriac shortens the last part to say, "the time to be gracious to her is come."
15. For וְיִירְאוּ in the MT 4Qps*b* omits the copula; and most manuscripts read "and they will see" instead of "and they will fear."
16. The Syriac has "your name."
17. 4QPs*b* has "his glory."
18. If this is taken as a temporal particle, "when the LORD . . . ," then the following perfect should be translated as a future perfect (Allen, p. 15).
19. The NIV translates the verbs in verses 16 and 17 as future tenses, taking them as prophetic perfects.
20. The Greek and Syriac have "and."
21. 4QPs*b* simply has "in glory."
22. Qumran has a strange corruption here—"worm"; it may have come from a marginal note.
23. This translation reflects a move in the disjunctive accent. MT has "For he was looked down from his holy height, from heaven the LORD looked intently at the earth."
24. For מִמְּרוֹם in the MT 4QPs*b* has ממעון (see מְמְעוֹן, Deut. 26:15).
25. The Greek has a plural form for "prisoners."

PSALM 102

to set at liberty those about to die,[26]
21 *that* in Zion the name of the LORD will be declared,
and his praise in Jerusalem.
22 When the nations are gathered together
and the kingdoms, to serve the LORD.
23 He has brought down[27] my strength[28] in the way,
he has shortened my days.[29]
24 I said, O my God,[30] do not cast me away in the midst of my days,
while your years continue to all generations.
25 In the beginning[31] you laid the foundation of the world;
and *the* heavens are the work[32] of your hands.
26 They will perish, but you will stand;
and all of them will wear out as a garment,
like[33] clothing you will change them
and they will be discarded.
27 But you are the same,[34]

---

26. The Hebrew has the expression "the sons of death."
27. MT has עִנָּה, the *piel* perfect, which would have the sense "he afflicted" or "he humbled." The Greek has ἀπεκρίθη, "he answered (him in the way of his strength)," reading the unpointed text as a simple *qal* form. The editors of BHS propose עֻנָּה, "(my strength) was brought down."
28. The *Qᵉre'* is כֹּחִי, "my strength"; this is the reading in the majority of the manuscripts, *4QPsᵇ*, the Syriac, Targum and Jerome. The *Kᵉthiv* is כֹּחוֹ, "his strength," which is the reading in the Greek: "he answered. Him in the way of his strength."
29. Targum has "my days were shortened." The Greek takes the verbal form "he has shortened" as a noun, "shortness, paucity"—τὴν ὀλιγότητα τῶν ἡμερῶν μου, "the paucity of my days."
30. For MT's אָמַר אֵלִי, the Greek version has ἀνάγγειλόν μοι (אֱמָר אֵלִי), "tell me," and joins it with the last clause from the preceding verse: "tell me the shortness of my days." Allen also puts the expression with the last verse but repoints the two words to read: "He has decreed for me a short life" (pp. 15–16).
31. The Greek version adds σύ, κύριε, "(In the beginning) you, O LORD (laid the foundation of the earth)."
32. The form is singular, "work (of)"; but one manuscript, the Greek, the Targum and *4QPsᵇ* have a plural construct, "works (of)."
33. Several versions have a conjunction.
34. The MT says, "But you are he." The translation here is interpretive to be sure, but it conveys the meaning of the construction—"you are he" means

and your years shall have no end.
28 The children of your servants shall live *in your presence*,[35]
and their descendants will be established before you.[36]

Composition and Context

Psalm 102 is a little unusual and so has received varying proposed interpretations. A large part of it (verses 2–12 and 24 and 25a) appears to be an individual lament psalm in form and function; however, the personal griefs and troubles recorded in verses 3–11 lead to a concern for Zion, whose destiny is nonetheless glorious. And so these other parts are more communal.

The relationship between these two concerns: the personal suffering and the national future, has been given a good deal of attention. It is possible that an individual lament was adapted for communal use with the additional national concerns. Childs suggests that a pre-exilic lament was joined with an exilic word of promise to the community.[37] Weiser simply classifies the whole psalm as a pre-exilic individual lament. Eaton proposes that the psalm was the lament of a leader, perhaps the king, who represented the community in his lament; it was then used in the fall festival.[38]

Many commentators who try to fit the psalm into a specific historical setting place the writing late in Israel's history. Anderson dates it in the exile or post-exilic period; he argues that the psalmist laments his own troubles against the background of the destiny of Jerusalem and the hope for restoration.[39] Perowne

---

"you are the same" (the ever-present "I AM"). This is the same expression found frequently in the prophets: Isaiah 41:4, 43:10, 46:4, and 48:12 for example.

35. This phrase has been supplied from the parallelism for a smoother reading.
36. The MT has לְפָנֶיךָ, "before you," but the Greek version has εἰς τὸν αἰῶνα, "for ever."
37. B. S. Childs, "Analysis of Canonical Formula: 'It Shall Be Recorded for a Future Generation,'" in *Die Hebräische Bibel und ihre zweifache Nachgeschichte*, FS R. Rendtorff, ed. E. Blum et al (Neukirchen-Vluyn: Neukirchener Verlag, 1990), pp. 357–64.
38. J.H. Eaton, *Kingship and the Psalms* (London: SCM Press), pp. 80–81.
39. *Psalms 73–150*, p. 704.

also had concluded that the psalm was written in the exile, at a later time in the exile when the hope of returning to Zion was no longer doubtful. Accordingly, the suffering psalmist looked past the sorrow to the glorious prospect ahead at the appointed time of Zion's deliverance. Then the kingship of the LORD would be manifested; and a new nation would be born in Jerusalem and nations gathered to praise the LORD. He adds that until that happens, suffering prevails.[40] The description of the glorious future of Zion uses expressions that appear frequently in the prophets, especially portions of Isaiah. The conclusion is then that the communal section seems to fit that period the best. Briggs had gone further and suggested a Maccabean setting for the prayer of restoration from the devastations of Antiochus.[41]

There are a few difficulties in placing the psalm in the later periods. First, there is no mention in the psalm of the exile, or the fall of Jerusalem. This is why some put the individual lament portion earlier. Second, the individual suffering in the lament section (vv. 3–11) does not seem to describe life in the exile, unless the language is highly figurative. There no doubt was suffering in the war and the deportation; but by the end of the exile many Jews did not want to leave when they could have done so. Third, the use of expressions similar to the prophets again raises the question of which text was borrowing from the other. The emphasis on the restoration to Zion, the rebuilding of the city, and the drawing of nations to worship the LORD in Zion, certainly were words of promise and hope expressed during the exile; but these ideas were expressed in the pre-exilic period as well.

It is difficult to say with certainty exactly when the psalm was written, or when it was put in its present, final form. The liturgical approach stresses the movement here from the lament of an individual to the petitions and concerns of the community. This would make the entire psalm useful for times when individual concerns merged with the national hope (when was this not the case, especially in Davidic psalms?). It makes good sense here to see how the community may have adopted an earlier,

---

40. *Psalms,* II:217–219.
41. *Psalms*, II:320.

individual lament and developed it for liturgical purposes. If the latter part of the psalm employed an exilic message of promise, then with the joining of the parts the individual making the lament might have been seen to be speaking on behalf of the suffering community. This would then open the possibility that the first part of the lament was intended to be a figurative description of Israel in Exile,[42] an idea that surfaces in other passages that refer to national crises (Isa. 1; Isa. 52–53). However, without a copy of the lament section as an individual psalm, we can only observe how the parts differ and suggest how they may have been connected in this final form, showing how the lament leads into the communal material.[43] We may only speculate. Be that as it may, the message of the psalm is timeless—it would provide anyone enduring a traumatic experience the hope of a glorious future with the LORD, and thereby encourage the suffering saints to pray confidently.

The early church listed this passage as the fifth of the seven penitential psalms. There is no mention of penitence in it, but the description of suffering due to the wrath of God suggests that the psalmist was acknowledging such.

Whatever the circumstances of the original writing were, and however it was put to liturgical use, the psalm also fits as a messianic psalm with its emphases on personal suffering and the future glory of Zion (see Ps. 22, and Isaiah 52:15–53:12). The use of the psalm for Jesus in the book of Hebrews confirms the messianic themes that are here.

Exegetical Analysis

Summary

Crying out to the LORD for urgent help, the psalmist explains that he is in grave physical danger and reproached by unbelievers, but finds comfort and encouragement in the fact that

---

42. Leopold Sabourin, *The Psalms, Their Origin and Meaning* (New York: Alba House, 1974), p. 256.
43. See further R.C. Culley, "Psalm 102, A Complaint with a Difference," *Semeia* 62 (1993):19–35.

the ever-living and unchanging God desires to be with his people and will not forsake them, a truth that will lead future generations to praise.

Outline

I. Call to God: The psalmist prays that God will answer him speedily (1–2).
II. Complaint: The psalmist laments that he is overwhelmed by the reproach of the enemies (3–11).
   A. He describes his lamentable condition (3–7):
      1. His days consume away like smoke, his heart like grass withers (3–4).
      2. He groans in great physical agony (5).
      3. He is forced to desolate places as a bird in search of food and water (6–7).
   B. He describes how the reproach of the enemy has bound him to ashes and tears in mourning (8–9).
   C. He is convinced that God's wrath has consumed him so that he withers like grass (10–11).
III. Consolation: The psalmist finds consolation in the fact that the LORD, who abides forever in Zion, will not forsake those who love him but deliver them so that others will praise (12–22).
   A. The LORD abides forever and will have mercy on Zion (12–13).
   B. The LORD, who built up glorious Zion, will not forsake those who love him (14–17).
      1. The LORD's servants love Zion (14).
      2. The nations will fear the LORD who has built Zion (15–16).
      3. He has not despised their prayer (17).
   C. The LORD will be praised by future generations because he will look on their sighing and deliver them from death (18–22).
      1. Future generations will praise the LORD (18).
      2. The LORD will look down from heaven to their plight to loose them from death (19–20).
      3. People will therefore praise and serve him (21–22).

IV. Conclusion: The LORD had weakened him, but since the LORD dwells forever, the psalmist prayed not to die prematurely (23–28).
   A. He announces that the LORD had weakened him and shortened his days (23).
   B. He prayed that he would not be taken prematurely (24a).
   C. He confesses that although man perishes like a garment, the LORD abides forever (24b-28).
      1. God is eternal, having laid the earth's foundation.
      2. People, like old garments, shall perish; God shall remain the same.
      3. The LORD's servants shall continue.

COMMENTARY IN EXPOSITORY FORM

I. Devout believers cry out to the LORD in their crises (1–2).

In a short invocation the psalmist employs a variety of expressions and images that are common to prayer, drawn from several lament psalms. In doing so he emphasizes the urgent need for the LORD to deliver him from his day of distress. He begins with "hear (שִׁמְעָה; s.v. Ps. 45:10) my prayer" and parallels it with "let my cry come to you." Then in verse 2 he prays to God, "Do not hide your face from me when I am in distress (in the day of my distress)," and parallels that with "incline your ear to me when I call (in the day I call)." The image of God's hiding his face would signify his withholding favor; and the image of inclining the ear would stress that God should listen very closely to him, as if leaning over to hear better. His use of the word "day" in this verse ("in the day I call") introduces a leitmotif for the psalm: as the psalm unfolds we will read how his days are full of trouble and will be cut short, whereas the days of the LORD are eternal and glorious.[44]

The urgency of the prayer is then underscored with the brief

---

44. Broyles, *Psalms*, p. 390.

but forceful "answer me quickly"; the clause using two imperatives, "hasten, answer me" (מַהֵר עֲנֵנִי; the construction forms a hendiadys, "answer me quickly"). The need is urgent, as the superscription reflects: "A prayer of the afflicted (לְעָנִי; s.v. Ps. 9:12), when he is faint (overwhelmed[45]) and pours out his lament (שִׂיחוֹ; s.v. Ps. 119:15) before the LORD."

II. The devout believers' greatest urgency comes from grave physical suffering intensified by the opposition of unbelievers as well as their own awareness of God's wrath (3–11).

A. *Their physical suffering may bring them to desperation and possible death (3–7).*

The supplicant now laments his desperate condition using a variety of images. He begins by affirming that his "days" are consumed in / as smoke, and his bones are burnt up as a firebrand. In short, his life is ebbing away in suffering, day by day as it were; it quickly is vanishing like smoke. The verb "consumed" (כָּלוּ; s.v. Ps. 90:7) simply means it is finished, coming to an end. The prepositional phrase "in smoke" could be taken as an implied comparison (which is why some manuscripts and versions read "like smoke" instead); but it is also possible that it could be referring to a burning fever, especially with the parallel image of a firebrand (מוֹקֵד, a burning mass of fire, or a furnace). His statement that his bones are burnt up would then be figurative of either a burning fever or an aching in his bones. And "bones" may refer to his bony framework, his whole body (see Pss. 22:16; 31:11; 32:3), or to his spirit within the bony frame (so a metonymy of subject). In either case, he means that he is fading quickly, probably with a burning fever.

The fourth verse focuses on the loss of his will to fight. His

---

45. The third root עָטַף means "to be feeble, faint." It is used for weakness in animals (Gen. 30:42) or in people due to war (Lam. 2:12; Pss. 77:4, 107:5). The word is used in the description of the drowning Jonah (Jon. 2:8) when his life was about to fail. The choice of this verb is an appropriate summary for the description that follows in the lament.

heart, the center of his will and his affections (s.v. Ps. 111:1), has been struck down like grass and withered. The simile of grass withering in the field under the heat of the sun (see Ps. 121:6; Isa. 49:10) provides a vivid description of his will withering under the intense suffering he has to endure (see Jonah 4:8 where under the glistening sun the prophet becomes faint and ready to die). As evidence that he has almost given up the will to survive, he says that he has forgotten to eat his food. His sorrow and suffering has been so overwhelming that food is the last thing he thinks about (compare Job 33:20).

Consequently, he has become emaciated as well as weak (v. 5). Because of (from) his groaning, meaning the suffering that causes the groaning (a metonymy of effect), his bones[46] stick to his flesh, or specifically, his skin (see Ps. 22:17, "I can count all my bones"). This image is not only of an emaciated person who is wasting away, but also of one who has the corresponding loss of power that such a pathetic weakness brings.

In verse 6 the psalmist compares himself to various birds to underscore his desolate condition. He forms the similes using first the verb "I am like" (דָּמִיתִי) and then in the second colon the prepositional phrase. The identity of the type of birds referred to here is not clear. The first word (קָאַת) may refer to a desert owl. The Greek text used "pelican" (πελεκᾶνι); if that is the meaning the image would also include his being out of his natural place, a place that would sustain its life—a pelikan in the desert would not find water sufficient for it. But if it is an owl the term would be paralleled with a second word (כּוֹס) that may mean "a screeching owl," described here as dwelling among the ruins. Whatever the exact translations, the idea seems to be that of isolation or loneliness. The locations of the desert and the ruins add to the similes that portray him as solitary and trying to survive in spite of adverse surroundings.

The imagery of birds continues in verse 7. Here he begins by saying, "I lie awake" (literally, "I have watched" [שָׁקַדְתִּי], meaning that he watched early and intensely, lying awake and looking for relief. He has become like a solitary bird (צִפּוֹר) that perches on high places, perhaps a bird of prey that constantly watches.

---

46. The word is singular, but taken as a collective to refer to his bones.

The word "lonely, solitary" (בּוֹדֵד) captures his isolated, weakened, and watching condition better than the variant reading of "wandering" (נוֹדֵד) found in a few manuscripts and assumed in a couple of versions. All he can do is wait and watch from his desperate circumstances.

B. Their mourning may be intensified by the opposition of unbelievers (8–9).

Personal suffering would be had enough, but with people taunting him it becomes almost unbearable. In these two verses the lament focuses on enemies (the "they" portion of a lament). He begins by stating that all his enemies have reproached or derided him (חֵרְפוּנִי; s.v. Ps. 22:6). Their cutting taunts even take on the form of a curse: "those who rail against me use my *name* as a curse." The verb translated "rail" here (a *poal* participle מְהוֹלָלַי) is related to the verb "praise" (s.v. Ps. 33:1). The Greek version reflects the connection more clearly as it translated the form with—"they that praised me" (assuming the active מְהַלְלַי). The form in the text has been questioned by commentators. If it is changed to the active verbal stem (*poel*), it would have the meaning "make a fool of"; if the passive form that is in the MT (*poal*) is kept, it would probably mean something like "those mad against me," that is, those consumed with the desire to exploit his folly. Then, when he says they swear he probably means that they use his name in a curse formula: "May God do to me as he did to . . . ." The sufferer had become their prime example of a curse.

Further figures amplify the description of his condition which his enemies exploit. He says, "For I eat ashes like bread." He does not mean that he literally eats ashes as food; the symbolism of ashes refers to grief and humiliation; so just as ashes would be useless and destructive as a normal diet, so the grief was destroying him. The image is probably taken from the lamentable plight of sitting on the ash heap and pouring ashes on the head (Lam. 3:16)—his life has become worthless. Ashes had become a regular and intimate part of his life, as food had been before.[47] Then, if ashes symbolized his nourishment, tears filled

---

47. Allen, Psalms 101–150, p. 20.

out his drink (see Ps. 80:6). His weeping mingles with his grief. So the desperate circumstances of his plight fill up his life more than normal food and drink.

C. They fear that it is God's wrath that consumes them (10–11).

The psalm now records the common concern in such suffering: God's great wrath has led to his being abandoned by him. This is the "you" section of laments, which is the more serious part. When he attributes his suffering to God's wrath, he is indicating that sin is the cause of his pain (even though he does not actually say that) and that God is in collusion with the enemies. The language in the text gives the picture that in his wrath God had picked him up only to cast him away, perhaps dash him to the ground forcefully. The idea may be illustrated with a whirlwind that seizes an object and casts it away as worthless; this may indicate the imagery if not the use of a storm in the description of God's wrath. In any case, it is ultimately God who has brought this on.

The effect of God's powerful wrath is that his days are like a shadow that has declined (נָטוּי, the disappearance of the evening shadow from the setting of the sun; see Jud. 19:9). His life is all but gone—only the shadow that has receded is witness to his existence. And the parallel colon picks up the earlier image of withering like grass; it too captures his sense of the near approach of death.

The lament reads like a personal lament. But the psalmist does not explain if his suffering is personal and physical, resulting from illness or a battle, or if it signifies in some way what the nation was going through in figurative language.[48] A straightforward reading of the lament leads to the conclusion that it is the lament of an individual over the painful and life-threatening effects of God's wrath for sin; it describes a serious judgment to be sure.

---

48. Compare this with the vivid personification of the nation as a beaten and bruised man in Isaiah 1.

III. Devout believers remain confident in all their suffering that the everlasting God will deliver those who love him and bring glory to his name (12–22).

A. *The sovereign LORD will demonstrate his compassion at the appropriate time (12–13).*

The tone of the psalm changes abruptly here from complaint (vv. 3–11) to consolation (vv. 12–22). The first part was written as an individual lament, but this part looks to the LORD's meeting the needs of the nation and the world. It is in effect a hymn to the permanence of the LORD and his redeeming compassion.[49]

The contrast with the first part of the psalm begins in a striking fashion: whereas the psalmist's life was fading away like a shadow that has just declined, the LORD sits enthroned forever. Verse 12 introduces this idea with the strong contrastive "But you, O LORD" and then makes the affirmation that the LORD sits enthroned forever. The meaning is not simply that the LORD is eternal, but rather that the LORD is sovereignly reigning over the affairs of mankind. Whatever was happening to the psalmist, or later to the nation, was under the dominion of the king of glory. This great thought enables devout believers to find comfort in suffering, for their hope rests on the eternal King and not the present circumstances. No matter what they experience in this life, they will dwell with him in glory.

Parallel to this affirmation is the equally strong statement that the LORD's renown is to all generations. The word "renown" (וְזִכְרְךָ; s.v. Ps. 6:5), often translated "memorial," refers to the person and the works of the LORD; it is in this way similar to the actual word "name" (שֵׁם)—his name is timeless. Saying that his memorial name is to all generations indicates that every generation will remember his wonderful deeds and place their trust in him.

The psalmist then expresses his confidence that God will intervene for his people. "You will arise" (תָּקוּם; s.v. Ps. 3:1) expresses in human terms the idea that God will begin to act (rise up against). And the next verb expresses what that action will be: "you will have compassion" (תְּרַחֵם; s.v. Ps. 25:6) on Zion, meaning

---

49. Broyles, *Psalms*, p. 392.

the city on the hill of Zion and all the people in it (so a metonymy of subject). This confident anticipation indicates that the city was in some trouble, and may have been in ruins, although the text does not say that. The reason for this confidence is that the time is right. The psalmist says "for it is time to be gracious to her." The word "to be gracious" (לְחֶנְנָהּ; s.v., Ps. 4:1) confirms his lament that the suffering was due to the wrath and indignation of God—all the guilty sinner can hope for is grace. The psalmist takes it one step further, though, explaining "because the set time has come." Several views have been put forward for this expression. Some have suggested that the set times refers to the 70 years prophesied by the prophet (Jer. 25:11,12); others say it refers to the time when warfare is accomplished (see Isa. 40:1). So the line could mean that God appointed a set time to show compassion for Zion, perhaps meaning to restore and rebuild the city, or simply that since the suffering had almost destroyed the psalmist, it is time for the LORD to act.

B. The LORD, who has established his presence with his people, will not abandon them (14–17).

To add to the appeal, the psalmist now reports the peoples' love for Zion. The servants of the LORD "find pleasure" (רָצוּ; s.v. Ps. 30:5) in the old city. The use of the images "stone" and "dust" may indicate the city was in ruins, but it may not. There is no mention of the destruction of Jerusalem in the entire psalm, and so in keeping with that, figures of speech were used here. Stones and dust could be reminders of past glorious victories and present defeats. The faithful love these stones because of the memories they provide—how the LORD redeemed his people in Jerusalem time and time again.

If the LORD now has compassion on Zion, he will strengthen the nation and rebuild the city. But it will not simply be a rebuilt city! It will be the center of the LORD's administration and the location of the central sanctuary. Nations shall revere the name of the LORD, and all the kings of the earth will fear the name of the LORD and his glory (כְּבוֹדֶךָ; s.v. Ps. 19:1).

Verse 16 could be taken in one of two ways: it could be declaring that because the LORD has built Zion, he has appeared in his glory—the psalmist would be looking back to the history of the faith; but in this context it is more likely that the psalmist is looking to the future when the LORD will build (or will have built) Zion. The line is written in the past tense (a prophetic perfect) to express the certainty of what will be. The Greek version made the tenses future. But while the idea looks to the future primarily, the message could apply to the past as well. When God establishes the center of his theocratic kingdom in Zion, that is where his glory appears. The allusion is likely to the luminous cloud of glory that was in the sanctuary; but that token of his presence only looked forward to a far greater appearance of the glory of the LORD. Until then devout worshipers expected to see only the evidence of his glory (Ps. 63:1). And the greatest glory was manifested in his bestowal of grace upon his people, particularly in answering their prayers. And so verse 17 states that the LORD "had regard for the prayer of the destitute; and has not despised their prayer." To "have regard," literally "to turn," means to respond favorably to prayers, to regard them pay attention to them; and the parallel line adds that "he has not despised" them (forming an understatement, tapeinosis), meaning he has honored their prayers and gloriously delivered them. If he had despised their prayers (בָּזָה; s.v. Ps. 22:6), he would not have turned in favor to them.

C. When the LORD delivers his people from suffering and death he will be glorified (18–22).

The great answer to prayer will be recorded for future generations to read (this is the only place in the Psalter where events are said to be written down to preserve them). People not even born yet, a new creation, shall read of it and praise the LORD. If the psalmist has reference to the Babylonian exile as the place of his suffering, then the return from the captivity will be like a new beginning (although such a reversal would fit other divine acts of deliverance as well). The new creation would stand in a dramatic contrast to the present devastation.

The answer to their prayer is now delineated in terms that draw upon the beginning of the exodus experience. The LORD looked down from his holy height, from heaven, and observed the earth, meaning the people in the earth (v. 19). The purpose of this intense observation was to "hear the groans of the prisoner, and to set at liberty those about the die" (v. 20). The first colon may allude to Exodus 2 where the LORD said that he had heard the sighing of his people in bondage and had come to deliver them. Then the second colon states what Isaiah 61 announced, that the messiah would open (set at liberty) those doomed to die.

But the purpose of their being delivered was to declare in Zion the name of the LORD, and his praise (s.v. Ps. 33:1) in Jerusalem (v. 21). Spontaneous praise is the natural response to any answer to prayer, especially for the great deliverance of the people and their restoration to the holy city. They will offer this praise when people and kingdoms gather to worship the LORD (v. 22). Such a gathering of the redeemed from the nations to serve the LORD in the holy city is prophesied elsewhere in Scripture (Gen. 49:10; Isa. 45:14; and Ps. 22:21–31).

IV. Believers know that even though the everlasting LORD God may bring life-threatening affliction on them, they still may be confident in praying to him for deliverance from death (23–28).

A. *The LORD may weaken them and shorten their lives (23).*

The psalmist turns now to contrast his sufferings and the brevity of his life with the eternality and power of the LORD. He acknowledges that the LORD brought down (or afflicted, עִנָּה) his strength on the journey of life ("in the way"), with the result that he has shortened his days—he will die soon. Believers do not always know the reasons for this, but they all have to deal with this truth sooner or later, either in their own experience, or in the experiences of people they know. Our lives are in his hands; even our suffering is part of his plan—but we have a glorious future.

B. *They still pray that they would not die prematurely (24a).*

The faithful still may pray confidently that this weakening

not result in a premature death. It may be one of God's purposes that they pray for life when confronted with what seems like certain death: "I said, O my God, do not cast me away in the midst of my days." The urgent plea is reminiscent of the prayer of Hezekiah who was told he was going to die in the middle of his days (Isa. 38). The psalmist wants to live; but perhaps more than anything else he wants to see the LORD manifest his glory in Israel's restoration (much like old Simeon who was waiting for the consolation of Israel in Luke 2).

C. They put their confidence in the One who is eternal and unchanging (24b-28).

The psalmist's appeal and its motivation is based on and in contrast to the cardinal truth that God's "years continue to all generations." God's presence is eternal; but he manifests it in glorious ways—in the past in creation, and in the future in the new creation. And so the psalmist recalls that in antiquity God laid the foundation of the world, and that the heavens are the work of his hands. That was in the beginning; but there will also be an end, a consummation, because all of creation has the impress of death and decay. The heavens, he explains, shall perish (v. 26); they will not remain as they now are. But God will—they will perish, but the LORD shall stand (תַעֲמֹד), an expression signifying immovability and sovereignty. All of creation, he adds, shall grow old like a garment; and God will change them—all of it is passing away. Everything in creation will decay and deteriorate, even the psalmist in his fast approaching death. But God remains the same. In fact, he is the one who will change things. And the New Testament will expand on this hope with details of the promise of a new creation (2 Pet. 3:13).

So the psalmist's faith is in the God of eternity: "But you are the same (lit., you are he); and your years shall have no end." The LORD is the same; he does not grow old or weak. And the New Testament will clarify that we know this one to be the Lord Jesus Christ. He is the creator; he is the redeemer; and he is the eternal Lord.

And because he is the eternal God and savior, the future descendants of the servants of the LORD will continue in his presence, and their seed shall be established before him (v. 28). There will be a glorious new creation some day; but in the meantime, faithful believers from age to age will maintain their fellowship with the living God.[50] So every time the faithful came to the sanctuary "to see" the LORD, their thoughts would leap forward to the time when they will be in his glorious heavenly presence eternally.

MESSAGE AND APPLICATION

Most people will in their lifetime experience something of what the psalmist had to endure: great distress from physical and emotional suffering. It may be serious enough to weaken and discourage them so that they can hardly function apart from moaning as they appeal to the LORD to restore them to health and vitality. Their confidence, indeed, their only hope, is that the LORD who reigns from heaven will rise to the occasion and have compassion on them, as he has done countless times before. So they pray continually that he will answer their prayer and set them free from suffering and possible death. The expository idea that ties this psalm together may be worded as follows: *Those who love and serve the eternal LORD know that he will not forsake them in times of grave physical danger because he desires to be with them and in his compassion will deliver them from death.*

What was true for the psalmist remains true today, but with more clarity. We too pray for healing, knowing that the fervent prayer of the righteous is effectual, as demonstrated by Elijah in the Old Testament (James 5:13–18). And so we cast all our cares upon the Lord (1 Peter 5:7). The fact that Psalm 102:25–27 is applied to Jesus Christ in Hebrews 1:11 also gives us more confidence. Not only is Christ's reign eternal and cannot be hindered by any human crisis, it is also the reign of someone who was dead and is alive forever more. Christians then know that the Lord is powerful enough to restore them to health now, and

---

50. There may be an allusion here to the festivals of the year when people came to the holy city to see the power and the glory of the living God, because the verb "shall continue" is the verb "to dwell in a tent (יִשְׁכּוֹנוּ).

certainly will in the age to come. Just as the psalmist was convinced of a glorious future for himself and generations to come when God delivered his people, so too do we know that when the Lord delivers us all from the suffering and death of this world will we join the rest of God's people in singing praises to him in glory.

PSALM 103

God's Gracious Benefits for Frail and Sinful Believers

INTRODUCTION

Text and Textual Variants

Of David

1 Bless[1] the LORD, O my soul,[2]
    and all that is within me[3] *bless* his holy name.
2 Bless the LORD, O my soul,
    and by no means forget all his benefits,

---

1. The NIV chose to translate this word as "praise," to communicate the meaning more clearly; but while that may prove helpful on one level, it does not include the distinct idea of the word "bless."
2. I retain the word "soul" here because of its parallelism with "within me"; the praise is not just with his voice, but it is coming from deep within his being, where the emotions and the will were located. See Allen, *Psalm 101–150,* p. 26.
3. The Hebrew text has a plural form here, קְרָבַי, "my inner parts"; the editors of BHS propose the more common form, קִרְבִּי, "my inner being." Perhaps the Hebrew was simply harmonizing the form with "all."

3 who[4] forgives all your[5] iniquities,
   who[6] heals all your diseases;
4 who redeems your life from the pit;[7]
   who crowns you with love and tender mercies;
5 who satisfies your mouth[8] with good *things*,
   so that your youth renews itself[9] as the eagle.

---

4. The NIV again clarifies the psalm by using "he" instead of a relative pronoun that reflects the article.
5. The form in the text is עֲוֺנֵכִי, the noun plus the 2nd feminine singular suffix, "your iniquity"; many manuscripts and the Greek version have a plural form reading עֲוֺנַיְכִי, "your iniquities." The spelling follows an archaic spelling for the pronominal suffixes (which came to be ךְ for the 2fsg). The form in Qumran (*4QPs^b*) is simply עונך.

   The psalmist is speaking to his own soul, and so uses the feminine suffix. To clarify the line the NIV has changed "your" in these verses to "my" (adding a footnote recording what the Hebrew actually has). The change may make the meaning clearer for many, but it seems unnecessary if the reader understands he is encouraging himself to bless the LORD.
6. The Qumran scroll does not have the article ("who heals"), only a conjunction ("and heals").
7. The term for "pit" was used in Psalm 16:10 in parallelism to *she'ol*. The Greek version rendered the word here as "corruption" (ἐκ φθορᾶς).
8. The form in the text, עֶדְיֵךְ, is difficult to translate. There are several major suggestions for the word. The first relates the word to a verb meaning "to put on," עָדָה. This would then have the sense of "what is put on, ornaments." A similar idea occurs in Psalm 32:9 where the meaning "harness" or "trappings" describes what is put on the horse to control it. But the verb "satisfy" does not go well with this meaning. A second suggestion comes from the Greek translation: "desire" (τὴν ἐπιθυμίαν). This does fit the line fairly well. It is the reading chosen by the NIV. A third idea relates it to time: the Targum renders it "old age." But the most likely understanding is that it refers to the mouth. This reflects the use in Ezekiel 16:7 for "cheeks," here inside the cheeks. This was the view followed by the commentators Ibn Ezra and Qimchi. The Syriac uses the general word "body." Anderson says that "mouth" is unlikely, preferring "ornament" as a picturesque way to describe the life (*Psalms 73–150*, p. 714). Allen suggests making a slight change to the text to obtain the meaning "existence" (p. 26).
9. The verb "renews itself," תִּתְחַדֵּשׁ, is a third feminine singular form, whereas the subject is a plural noun. This is not uncommon in the Bible (see GKC 146.3), so there is no need to change the form or make its translation passive, "is renewed." Greek has, "will be renewed" (ἀνακαινισθήσεται).

6 The LORD does righteousness[10]
    and justice for all *who are* oppressed.
7 He made known[11] his ways to Moses,
    his deeds[12] to the people of Israel.
8 The LORD *is full of* compassion and gracious,
    slow to anger and abounding in loyal love.

9 He will not always accuse,
    neither will he retain *his anger* for ever.
10 He has not dealt with us according to our sins,
    neither according to our iniquities has he repaid us;
11 for as high as the heavens are above the earth,
    so great[13] is his loyal love toward those who fear him;
12 as far as the east is from the west,
    so far has he removed our transgressions from us.
13 As a father shows compassion for *his* children,
    so the LORD shows compassion for those who fear him;
14 for he knows our frame,[14]
    he remembers[15] that we are *but* dust.
15 As for man,[16] his days are like grass;
    like a flower of the field, so he flourishes;
16 for the wind passes over it and it is gone,

---

10. The form in the text is plural, "righteousnesses." It could be interpreted as a plural of intensity to stress the righteousness; or it may refer to acts of righteousness. The word may be a metonymy, the cause for the effect, with the intended meaning of "vindication" in this context, meaning the LORD brings vindication and justice to the afflicted.
11. The form in the text, יוֹדִיעַ, is a *hiphil* imperfect; it could be interpreted as a customary imperfect, indicating what the LORD used to do, or it could be treated as a preterite without the *waw* and given a simple past tense translation.
12. Greek has "his will" (τὰ θελήματα αὐτοῦ).
13. For MT גָּבַר the Greek version has "(the LORD) strengthened" (גִּבַּר).
14. The text has יִצְרֵנוּ, "our frame." There is a variant reading that takes the word as a plural, "our frames," יְצָרֵינוּ, but it is not well-supported. The NIV clarifies the word with "how we are formed."
15. The form in the text is a passive, זָכוּר; the Greek text has μνήσθητι, "remember," which would reflect זְכֹר. But the form in the text can be given the active sense (see GKC #50).
16. אֱנוֹשׁ may indicate "ordinary man" or "frail man."

and its place remembers it no more.
17 But the loyal love of the LORD is from everlasting[17]
    to everlasting with those who fear him,
    and his righteousness with children's children—
18 to those who keep his commands,[18]
    and to those who remember his precepts to do them.[19]

19 The LORD has established his throne in the heavens,
    and his kingdom rules over all.
20 O bless the LORD, *you*[20] his angels,
    who are mighty in strength, *who* carry out his word,[21]
      obeying his word.[22]
21 Bless the LORD, all you his *heavenly* hosts,
    you ministers of his, who do his pleasure.
22 Bless the LORD, all you his works, in all places[23] of his dominion.
    Bless the LORD, O my soul.

Composition and Context

Allen describes Psalm 103 as an individual thanksgiving with a number of hymnic features, adding that since it was probably to be sung in a liturgical setting it was meant to inspire others (p. 27)—which it has done and continues to do. Eaton proposed that it was a hymn for the fall festival.[24] We may not be able to be that specific, but we can say that it was an individual hymn sung

---

17. The editors of BHS suggest deleting "from everlasting" and simply reading "the loyal love of the LORD is everlasting."
18. The Greek version has "his covenant."
19. This last word, an infinitive construct with the preposition, could be taken epexegetically and translated "by doing them," indicating how they remember the precepts and forming a closer parallel with the first colon.
20. The Greek version and a few Hebrew manuscripts add "all" (all his angels).
21. Qumran has a plural, "his words."
22. The Hebrew literally says, "by listening to the voice of his word," which is idiomatic for "obeying his word." The noun is plural in the Qumran scroll, and in the Greek version (τῶν λόγων αὐτοῦ).
23. The Greek, Syriac and Targum have a singular noun, "in every place."
24. *Kingship*, pp. 246–7.

for the community. Concerning the impact of this composition, Perowne writes:

> This beautiful psalm is the outpouring of a full heart in thanksgiving to Jehovah for His grace and compassion, both as experienced by the Psalmist in his own life, and also manifested to his nation in their history. It celebrates especially God's mercy in the forgiveness of sin, and that tender pity, as of a human father, wherewith He remembers the frailty, and stoops to the weakness, of His children. It is a hymn of which the text and motto are to be found in that revelation of Himself which God gave to Moses when He proclaimed Himself as "Jehovah, tenderly compassionate and gracious, long-suffering, and abundant in goodness and truth' (Exod. xxxiv. 6).[25]

Concerning the authorship of and occasion for the psalm, very little can be said with certainty. The superscription applies it to David, perhaps written in his old age (Syriac). The setting is also uncertain. Attempts to fit it into a precise setting, such as after the death of Uriah, or the much later time at the end of the exile, have failed for lack of compelling evidence. The later date is supported by noting that some forms in it are considered later (i.e., they do not appear in David's time but do appear in 2 Kings 4:1–7), and by observing allusions to other passages. But dating passages based on the occurrence of words that are considered late, or early for that matter, is in many cases an assessment based only on existing texts and their assumed dates. The argument of allusions to other passages seems to be more compelling, but even it is debatable. The decision of which passage was borrowing from the other can work both ways; for example, Kidner maintains that some of the expressions are early, and that several echoes of the psalm are found in Isaiah and Jeremiah rather than prophetic expressions being found in the psalm.[26] The better approach is to deal with the theological message of the psalm and then determine if it has reference to a specific time or event or must be treated as a timeless piece.

---

25. See Perowne, *Psalms*, II:224–5.
26. *Psalms* 73–150, p. 364.

After all, the exposition will focus on the message of the psalm in the canon.

The psalm unfolds in three parts: in verses 1–5 the psalmist stirs up praise within himself for God's benefits; in verses 6–18 the psalmist is more reflective concerning the covenant and sin; in verses 19–22 there is a triumphant conclusion: joy issues into praise.

Exegetical Analysis

Summary

After reviewing the mercies of God towards him, the psalmist finds hope in the covenant relationship with the LORD even though people are sinful and frail, and then calls on all creation to bless their LORD.

Outline

I. With gratitude from deep within him, the psalmist rehearses the mercies of God granted to him (1–5).
   A. He exhorts his own soul to bless the LORD (1–2).
      1. He exhorts himself with his whole being to bless (1).
      2. He exhorts himself not to forget the benefits (2).
   B. He blesses the LORD for the mercies he has received (3–5).
      1. God forgives his iniquities (3a).
      2. God heals his diseases (3b).
      3. God redeems him from destruction (4a).
      4. God crowns him with loyal love and mercy (4b).
      5. God satisfies his desire with good things and renews his strength (5).

II. While reviewing the facts of history, the psalmist realizes that the covenant relationship the LORD made with frail sinners gives hope (6–18).
   A. He reviews the covenant of the LORD with Moses (6–8).
      1. God executes righteous judgments (6).
      2. God revealed himself to Moses as a gracious and merciful God (7–8).

B. He recalls that the LORD mercifully forgives sins (9–12).
     1. God is slow to anger, and so does not deal with us according to our sins (9–10).
     2. God's love is great, and so he separates our sins from us completely (11–12).
  C. He realizes that although people are transitory, they are established by the covenant (13–18).
     1. People are frail and transitory and in need of divine care (13–16).
        a. God, like a father, pities his children (13).
        b. God remembers how frail they are (14).
        c. They wither away and are gone like the wind (15–16).
     2. People are established by God's covenant of love (17–18).
        a. The everlasting covenant is with those who love him (17).
        b. The everlasting covenant is with those who obey him (18).
III. In view of the LORD's dominion, the psalmist calls all of creation to bless him (19–22).
  A. The LORD has established his eternal dominion over all (19).
  B. All angelic and heavenly hosts should bless the LORD (20).
  C. All ministers should bless the LORD (21).
  D. All his works, everywhere, should bless the LORD (22).
Epilogue: "Bless the LORD O my soul!"

COMMENTARY IN EXPOSITORY FORM

I. With joyful gratitude the righteous must rehearse the many gracious benefits granted to them (1–5).

A. We must exhort ourselves to bless the LORD with everything we have (1–2).

Praise should be but is not very often natural; the psalms

are filled with calls and exhortations for the people to praise, but here it is a self-exhortation to praise (Psalms 42:5, 11; 43:5; and 104:1). This brings a forceful emphasis to the line that strengthens his resolve to praise. In this case the word for praising is the word "to bless"—"Bless the LORD, O my soul" (בָּרְכִי נַפְשִׁי אֶת־יְהוָה). "Bless" has a distinct meaning of expressing joyful gratitude as an enrichment of God (s.v. Ps. 5:12). The praise given will make more people aware of the person and works of the LORD, and so God's reputation will be enriched. The fact that he exhorts his own "soul" to bless indicates that he will bless with his whole being, his whole spiritual being, his will, his reason, and his affections. "Soul" is paralleled here with "everything inside me"; and "the LORD" is matched with "his holy name" (s.v. Ps. 20:1 for "name"; and Ps. 22:3 for "holy"). The name signifies his nature and actions, and the attribute "holy" summarizes the uniqueness of everything about him.

Verse 2 at first repeats the first colon of verse 1 and then adds, "and do not forget all his benefits." As in many other passages, the verbs "to remember," and "to forget"[27] mean more than

---

27. The verb is שָׁכַח is fairly common, occurring 122 times, 104 in Hebrew and 22 in Aramaic. It is the antonym of זָכַר, "to remember" (s.v. Ps. 6:5), and the understanding of that verb will therefore help clarify this one. The verb "forget" can have the obvious meaning of not retaining something in memory, something that slipped from memory because no one cared any longer to be involved with them (for the cup-bearer forgetting Joseph, Gen. 40:23; see also Ps. 31:13; Isa. 23:15 for example).

In the lament psalms the verb "forget" is used with reference to God's failure to respond: "How long, O LORD, will you forget me forever?" (44:25). The lack of divine attention is lamentable because of the promise of the covenant that God will not forget the cry for help of the suffering (Ps. 9:13; see also Isa. 49:15). When the LORD is said to forget it does not mean the human trait of not remembering, but practical behavior. For the LORD to forget signifies an active turning away and even opposition to the one praying.

Likewise the human resolve not to forget involves more then a mental activity of remembering, although that is part of it. In Psalm 137 the exiled psalmist vows never to forget Jerusalem; he will hope and pray for the restoration to Zion. In the Law the people are exhorted not to forget the LORD (Deut. 6:12; 8:11, 14, 19) and his salvation (Deut. 4:9), his provisions (Deut. 8:10–14), or their own rebellions and covenant duties. To forget these things would mean that they were not living by faith, or worse,

mental activities; they have to do with actions. So here "forgetting" is not a slip of the memory, but a deliberate act of ignoring God's goodness and disobeying his will.[28] The word "benefits" (גְּמוּלִים) refers to gracious and charitable deeds. The psalmist's message here is: Do not forget them (almost, stop forgetting them)—that is, start acting on them.

B. We must never, ever, forget the LORD's gracious and generous benefits for us (3–5).

1. He forgives all our sins (3a).

As the psalmist records his list of divine benefits, he begins with forgiveness: "who forgives all your[29] iniquities (עֲוֹנֵכִי; s.v. Ps. 32:5)."[30] The text uses the participle to stress the nature of forgiveness and its repeated action—he is a forgiving God because he constantly forgives. The article serves as the relative to link the description to the LORD (הַסֹּלֵחַ; a clear, explicit word for forgiveness; s.v. Ps. 130:4). The forgiveness of sins is the first and greatest of God's benefits, for without this none of the other benefits matter.

2. He heals our diseases (3b).

Parallel to forgiveness is healing. Theologically we might ask, "Is there always forgiveness of sin?" Yes. But then, "Is there always healing of diseases?" Not always—at least not

---

that they were turning to other beliefs. Not to forget God's benefits would mean to act on them by faith; this is the equivalent of remaining loyal to the covenant in word and deed. And so when the unexpected tragedy of military defeat struck the nation, the people appealed to the LORD for help by affirming that they had not forgotten the LORD, meaning they had not gone after other gods (Ps. 44:18, 21). It was their protestation of innocence. But because Israel occasionally did turn to other deities and corrupt practices, the abiding warning is not to forget the LORD and his benefits (Pss. 78:7; 103:2).

28. Anderson, *Psalms 73–150*, pp. 712–13.
29. Throughout the psalmist is addressing his own soul, so the pronoun is "your"; we may word it differently for the clarity of the exposition.
30. See further H. McKeating, "Divine Forgiveness in the Psalms," *SJT* 18 (1965):69–83.

automatically, and perhaps not in this life. The difference can be seen in God's covenant relationship with his people. Sin can ruin it and must be dealt with immediately. But suffering with disease can actually deepen the relationship, which is why God may not heal immediately.[31] The verb "to heal" (רָפָא) can be used for physical or spiritual healing. In fact, the physical healing of diseases or adverse situations is often the outward sign of inward healing (see Exod. 15:22–27; Matt. 9:1–7).

3. He preserves our lives (4a).

The participle is actually "who redeems" (הַגּוֹאֵל; s.v. Ps. 19:14); it has the basic sense of "protect" and is often used for practical care and defense of the family rights (as in the book of Ruth). But with God as the subject the ideas of rescue or redeem are more pronounced. Here he redeems our life from the pit, another term for *she'ol,* meaning death or the grave or hell. The Greek version translated the word "pit" with "corruption"; the Targum used "Gehenna." The sequence in this psalm leads to the idea that illness brings us close to death, so healing is being rescued from death or something worse.[32] Believers know that God preserves their lives so that they may live a full and meaningful life; but they also know that he has redeemed them from the pit (Ps. 16:10).

4. He crowns us with love and compassion (4b).

The psalmist now declares that God crowns believers ("you" in the text) with loyal love and tender compassion. By using "who crowns you" (הַמְעַטְּרֵכִי), the psalmist is signifying how God honors his people—he makes them feel like kings, as Anderson paraphrases it (p. 713). By so crowning them he fits them to reign; and to do that, as Perowne says, he weaves the crown out of his own attributes.[33] The two words in the text (adverbial accusatives) are well-known divine attributes: "loyal love" (חֶסֶד; s.v. Ps. 23:6) and "tender mercies" (רַחֲמִים; s.v. Ps. 25:6). In creation God imparted these attributes to people, so that like him humans could show love and compassion. In redemption, God

---

31. Kidner, *Psalms 73–150*, p. 364.
32. *Psalms 73–150*, p. 713.
33. *Psalms*, II:227.

restored what was lost and enabled the redeemed to share in his righteousness.

5. *He provides good things for us so that we may be strengthened (5).*

This entire verse now lists the next benefit. God satisfies (הַמַּשְׂבִּיעַ; s.v. Ps. 90:14) with good things "our mouth." For the word translated "mouth," the text has an unusual word. Many take it as the word "desire," which is a fairly good interpretation. Anderson prefers "your ornament" as a figure for the soul or life;[34] but that does not seem to work as well. "Mouth" makes good sense in the context. A general reference to one's life is a possible interpretation. In any case the point is understandable: God satisfies us with good things, i.e., things that enhance and benefit our lives, so that we may be renewed (spiritually and/or physically).

II. By rehearsing God's dealings with his people, the righteous find renewed hope in spite of their own frailty and sinfulness (6–18).

A. *Even though the LORD executes justice he is gracious and merciful (6–8).*

The next three verses focus on the nature of the LORD by recalling his revelation and mighty works with Moses. The first verse declares that the LORD does righteousness and justice for the oppressed. The verb is still a participle, but without an article; it serves as the predicate with "Yahweh" as the subject. He does "righteousness" (righteous acts, perhaps, since it is plural; s.v. Ps. 1:5) and justice (just acts, perhaps, since it is also plural; s.v. Ps. 9:4). It means that God's righteousness and justice are in his gracious acts. It is possible that "righteousness" here might be figurative for "salvation" or "vindication" (a metonymy of cause), so that the verse would mean that he works vindication and justice for the afflicted. While this may be helpful, vindication is only a part of what he does for the afflicted. It may be that

---

34. Psalms 73–150, p. 714.

the two words together form one idea: he makes "right decisions" for the afflicted.

The psalmist next relates the divine attributes to history. God made known his ways to Moses, and his deeds to the Israelites. By his miraculous intervention, Moses and the people learned the ways of God, that is, his modes of action, his grace and power, both in redeeming and caring for his people and in judging the rebellious (see Exod. 33:13).[35]

Verse 8 is taken from Exodus 34:6; the material became a creedal formula for the people of God (see Joel 2:13; Neh. 9:17, 31; and Ps. 86:15 for a few references). Four descriptions of God are listed here: he is "compassionate" (see above), "gracious" (s.v. Ps. 4:1), "slow to anger" and "abounding in loyal love" (see above). In Exodus this revelation was given to the nation after the sin of the golden calf—when they needed it the most. The attributes listed refer to the ways that God deals with his sinful people. Such descriptions have been a comfort and relief to all subsequent sinners in their guilt and fears.

B. Rather than give people what they deserve the LORD lovingly seeks to remove their sins (9–12).

Here we have an elaboration of these comfortable words. Verse 9 reminds us of the good news that while God may be angry over sin, his anger does not last forever (see Isa. 57:16). He will not always strive (or chide; the verb רִיב means "dispute, strive, contend, go to law"; s.v. Ps. 95:8). Neither will he keep (נָטַר, "guard, keep") his anger forever, meaning, he will not always maintain his anger, leaving no hope of relief. Moreover, in verse 10, the psalmist declares that God has not actually dealt with us according to our sins. If he did, if he dealt with us only in justice, none of us could stand (see Ps. 130:4)

Rather, God's anger and discipline is tempered by his grace and mercy. In verse 11 the psalmist praises the greatness of God's loyal love to those who fear him—it is unlimited, higher than the heavens above. No matter what we do, we know that

---

35. P. E. Dion, "Psalm 103: A Meditation on the Ways of the LORD," *Eglise et théologie* 21 (1990):13–31.

the faithful love of God will forgive and restore us.[36] His word guarantees this because of his nature to forgive. And according to verse 12, in forgiving us God completely removes our sin—as far as the east is from the west. People need to be assured that when they repent and confess to the LORD, the forgiveness they are given is complete. God will never bring up those sins again.

C. Even though people are frail and transitory the LORD cares for his own with an everlasting love (13–18).

1. Because people are frail and transitory the LORD cares for them (13–16).

God's compassion and forgiveness are now focused on human frailty. The text first draws the analogy between a human father's compassion for his children and the LORD's compassion for his people, people who are in covenant with him. The word "compassion" (רָחַם again) is appropriate in this context; it describes the tender care and nourishing that a parent gives to a child (although often in the analogy of a mother and her child). This compassion is explained by the fact that God knows our frame (s.v. יֵצֶר, Ps. 33:15), how we are made (according to the Greek version), and remembers that we are but dust. The use of the words "frame" and "dust" recalls the account of creation in Genesis 2:7 and 3:19. God "formed" the man from the "dust" of the ground; and God declared, "Dust you are and to dust you shall return." God deals with us according to what he knows we are—mortal and frail. And this point is repeated in verses 15 and 16, but with the imagery of grass and flowers. The grass and flowers flourish in all their glory, but they fade and the wind blows it all away and it is gone and forgotten. So too are humans. The contrast in these verses is striking: God's love is everlasting (v. 17), but we are quickly dying and disappearing; God is

---

36. See further T. M. Willis, "So Great Is His Steadfast Love: A Rhetorical Analysis of Psalm 103," *Bib* 72 (1991):525–37; and N. H. Parker, "Psalm 103: God Is Love. He Will Have mercy and Abundantly Pardon," *CJT* 1 (1955):191–196.

healing us, but we are still fading away. God knows all of this; in fact, he knows us better than we know ourselves. And so his understanding of our frailty informs his compassion and his love.

2. The LORD cares for his own with an everlasting love (17–18).

The psalmist declares that God's love and righteousness endure forever and ever—good news to the weak, frail, and dying human beings. Suffering and death cannot separate us from the love of God, as the prophets and apostles remind us frequently. But it is important to note that in these verses the recipients of God's benefits are true believers. For the third time they are described as people who fear the LORD, a common expression for obedient faith. And in clarification of that we read that they keep the commands and remember (act on) the precepts. The love of God that is described in these verses is only known by those who have received the grace of God.

III. Those who truly appreciate all the wonderful works of the LORD will naturally desire that he be praised in heaven and on earth (19–22).

A. The righteous acknowledge that the LORD rules over everything from heaven (19).

The emphasis of the psalm changes here; now the psalmist extols the greatness and the majesty of the one who has taken pity on sinful, mortal creatures. Placing the divine name first in the sentence signals the change: "Yahweh in the heavens has established (הֵכִין; s.v. Ps. 93:1) his throne." Throne is a symbol of his reign; and its location in the heavens places his reign far above and over all the earth and all mortal beings. The LORD himself established his rightful authority by creation and by redemption. Everything belongs to him; and he rules over it all.

B. They desire that the LORD be blessed in heaven and on earth (20–22).

The psalm closes with an exhortation to bless the LORD, as it did in the beginning. The psalmist started by exhorting himself to bless the LORD; now he calls the angels who are mighty in strength, who carry out God's word, to bless the LORD. The description of them as "mighty ones of strength" is unusual; it is here taken as a genitive of specification, mighty in their strength.

Then he summons all the heavenly hosts who are his ministers to bless the LORD (see Ps. 104:4; Dan. 7:10; and Heb. 1:14). To this he adds the exhortation for "all his works," all of creation, everywhere, to bless the LORD.

The last line of the psalm parallels the first line: "Bless the LORD O my soul!" But now, as Kidner says, "His song is no solo, for all creation is singing—or will sing—with him; but his voice, like every other voice, has its own part to add, its own 'benefits' (2ff.) to celebrate, and its own access (*cf.* Ps. 5:3) to the attentive ear of God."[37]

MESSAGE AND APPLICATIONS

Psalm 103 is filled with solid doctrinal statements of faith, so much so that it would be difficult for the expositor to exhaust this material in one exposition. Although the doctrines that are listed here are not fully developed in the psalm, they are nonetheless clear; and later Scripture confirms and expands them. Of the many passages that might be correlated with this psalm, several from the book of Romans may be cited. Paul details the sinfulness and weakness of human beings in Romans 1–3, and especially in 8:14–20. The provision for forgiveness and salvation he explains in Romans 3:21–26. The covenant relationship that we have in the Lord gives us hope, according to Romans 8:1 and 8:31–39. And the response to all this marvelous provision from the Lord should be endless praise (Rom. 11:33–36). For a summary expository idea of the psalm, we could say something like this: *Even though people are sinful and frail, when they remember the mercies of the LORD toward them they renew their hope in his covenant love and their commitment to praise and serve him faithfully.*

---

37. *Psalms 73–150*, p. 367.

PSALM 104

The Wisdom of the LORD's Manifold Creation

INTRODUCTION

Text and Textual Variants[1]

1 Bless the LORD, O my soul!
  O LORD[2] my[3] God, you are very great;
    you are clothed with splendor and majesty.
2 You cover[4] yourself with light as with a robe,
    you spread out[5] the heavens like a tent,
3 *You are the one who* lays the beams of his chambers in the waters,
    who makes the clouds his chariot,
      who rides on the wings of the wind;

---

1. The Greek version and Qumran have "Of David."
2. A few manuscripts do not have the holy name.
3. Qumran reads "our God."
4. The Hebrew text has the participle עֹטֶה; the pronoun is understood following the perfect tense; the editors of BHS propose the imperfect תַּעֲטֶה, basing it on a possible haplography with final ה of the preceding word.
5. The MT has נוֹטֶה; the editors of BHS propose הַנּוֹטֶה, also suggesting haplography with final ה of the preceding word.

PSALM 104

4 who makes *the* winds his messengers,
   flames[6] of fire[7] his ministers.
5 *You are the one who* established[8] *the* earth on its foundations,
   that it should not be moved *for*[9] ever and ever.
6 You covered it[10] with the deep as with a garment;
   above the mountains the waters stood.
7 At your rebuke they fled,
   at the voice of your thunder they were scattered;
8 They flowed *over the* mountains, they went down *into* the valleys,
   to the place which you had established for them.
9 You have set them a boundary that they cannot pass;
   never again will they cover the earth;

10 *You are the one who* sends forth springs along the river-beds,
   they flow between *the* mountains;
11 they give drink to all the animals of the field;
   the wild donkeys quench their thirst.
12 Above them the birds of the sky have their nest,
   and sing among the branches.[11]
13 *You are the one who* waters *the* mountains from his upper chambers,
   so that the earth is satisfied with the fruit of your work;[12]

---

6. The Greek and Syriac version begin the line with "and."
7. The Hebrew is אֵשׁ לֹהֵט; the Greek version has πῦρ φλέγον, "flaming fire," and Qumran has לוהטת to match the gender of "fire".
8. The Hebrew is simply יָסַד; the Greek[AL] has ὁ θεμελιῶν, indicating a participle יֹסֵד was assumed. Others have ἐθεμελίωσεν, "he established."
9. With עוֹלָם a few manuscripts add the preposition לְ, "for ever."
10. The Hebrew is כִּסִּיתוֹ; the Greek version has τὸ περιβόλαιον αὐτοῦ, "(the deep . . .) is his clothing," perhaps for כְּסוּתוֹ. Other versions indicate a feminine suffix.
11. The Q^ere' reading is עֳפָאיִם and the K^ethiv is עֳפָאִים. The Greek version has τῶν πετρῶν, "rocks."
12. In place of MT's מִפְּרִי מַעֲשֶׂיךָ the editors of BHS propose something like מִפְרֹשׁ עָבֶיךָ. Briggs says an ancient copyist mistook the form for "fruit," and then was obliged to explain it by the addition of "your works" (*Psalms*, II:334).

The Wisdom of the LORD's Manifold Creation

14 *who* makes grass grow for the cattle,
    and plants for the service of mankind,
        that he may bring forth food from the earth,
15 and wine that makes glad the heart of man;
    oil to make *his* face shine.
    and bread that may strengthen man's heart.
16 The trees of the LORD[13] are well-watered,[14]
    the cedars of Lebanon that he planted;
17 there[15] the birds make their nests;
    as for the stork, cypresses[16] are her dwelling.
18 *The*[17] high mountains are for the wild goats;
    The steep precipices are a refuge for the rock badgers.

19 *You are the one who* made the moon for seasons;
    the sun knows when to set;
20 when you make darkness—then it is[18] night,
    wherein all the beasts of the forest prowl.
21 The young lions roar after their prey,
    and seek their food from God.
22 The sun rises—they[19] go away;
    they return and lie down in their dens.
23 People[20] go out to their work,

---

13. Instead of the holy name, the Greek translation has τοῦ πεδίου, "(the trees) of the plain," equal to Hebrew שָׂדַי (see Ps. 8:8). Was this a corruption of שַׁדַּי, "the Almighty"?
14. The text simply says that they "are satisfied," meaning they have enough water.
15. Hebrew has אֲשֶׁר־שָׁם, but several versions have simply "there" שָׁם (alone).
16. The text has בְּרוֹשִׁים, but the Greek version reads ἡγεῖται αὐτῶν, "(the home of the heron) leads them," perhaps interpreting the word as if it were בְּרֹאשָׁם, "on top of them."
17. The editors of BHS propose restoring the article, which they think was lost by haplography.
18. The Hebrew text has וִיהִי, the short form (volitive form). The Greek (and Jerome) has the preterite translation, καὶ ἐγένετο, "and it became," which would reflect וַיְהִי. Both the main verb (תָּשֶׁת) and this form are shortened (apocopated) forms to mark the prodosis and apodosis: "when you make darkness, then it is light." (See Perowne, *Psalms*, II:248).
19. The Greek version and Qumran have the conjunction.
20. The text literally has "a man," but it is intended to be generic. The following pronouns had to be changed to the plural to harmonize with "people."

and to their labor until the evening.

24 How many are your works, O LORD!
   In wisdom have you made them all—
      the earth is full of your creatures.
25 There[21] is the sea, great and broad,
      teeming with creatures, beyond number,
         living creatures both small and great.
26 There go the ships,
      and there leviathan
         which you formed to play in it.
27 All of them wait for you
      to provide[22] their food in its season.
28 *When* you give *it* to them, they[23] gather;
      when you open your hand, they are satisfied with good
         things;[24]
29 *when* you hide your face, they are terrified;
      when you take away their breath,[25]
         they die, and return to their dust.
30 When you send forth your Spirit, they[26] are created,
      and you renew the surface of the ground.

31 May the glory of the LORD be for ever!
      May the LORD rejoice in his works!
32 He looks to the earth, and it trembles;
      he touches the mountains, and they smoke.

33 I will sing to the LORD, all my life,
      I will sing praises to my God, while I remain.
34 May my meditation be pleasing to him
      as I rejoice in the LORD.

---

21. The Hebrew starts the verse with זֶ֤ה, literally "this." It is not in the Qumran text.
22. The verb is "to give"; Qumran adds "to them."
23. Qumran has "and."
24. The text simply says "good."
25. Instead of "their breath," רוּחָ֣ם, Qumran has "your Spirit" or "breath," רוחכה.
26. Qumran and some versions have the conjunction "and."

The Wisdom of the LORD's Manifold Creation

35 *But* may sinners[27] be destroyed from the earth,
    and the wicked be no more.

Bless the LORD, O my soul!
Praise the LORD![28]

Composition and Context

Psalm 104 is a descriptive praise psalm, a hymn to the LORD, the sovereign creator and sustainer of all things. It is similar to Psalm 103; but whereas Psalm 103 focused on the redeemer king, Psalm 104 is about the creator king.[29]

The psalm shows some features in verses 20–30 that are similar to the Egyptian hymn to Aten.[30] But the differences between the two texts are also significant.[31] Accordingly, there is insufficient evidence to show direct borrowing. Israel's theology of creation was unique in the ancient world; for example, the sun was merely a creation of Yahweh God, and not a god, and all the glory belongs to the LORD who is over all creation, not part of it.

The psalmist was immersed in Hebrew cosmology; Gunkel said the psalmist used Genesis as the model.[32] The passage does follow the Genesis record in general: light and the heavens, the earth from chaos to creation, the heavenly bodies, and the birds and living things. Essentially, this psalm is not merely about the

---

27. For "sinners" the MT has חַטָּאִים; Qumran took it as a participle, חוטאים.
28. The Hebrew here is spelled differently: it may be הַלְלוּ־יָהּ or הַלְלוּיָהּ.
29. VanGemeren, *Psalms*, p. 762. Craigie suggests that the psalm is to be linked to Solomon's temple; the poem is in fuller form in the Greek of 1 Kings 8:12–13 (*Psalms 51–100*, pp. 19–21).
30. See Allen, *Psalms 101–150*, p. 40. See also P. E. Dion, "YHWH as Storm-god and Sun-god: The Double Legacy of Egypt and Canaan as Reflected in Psalm 104," ZAW 103 (1991):43–71; and P. C. Craigie, "The Comparison of Hebrew Poetry: Psalm 104 in the Light of Egyptian and Ugaritic Poetry," *Semitics* 4 (1974):10–21.
31. The Egyptian hymn diverges into the mystery of birth and the diversity of lands and people. The psalm presents the contrast by calling for worship of the creator and not the creation.
32. Gunkel, *The Psalms*, p. 453. See D. J. McCarthy, "'Creation' Motifs in Ancient Hebrew Poetry," *CBQ* 29 (1967):393–406.

LORD's creation, but about his provision for it to sustain life.[33] The tone here is not as matter-of-fact as the account in Genesis. Perowne says it is a "bright and living picture of God's creative power, pouring life and gladness throughout the universe."[34]

Exegetical Analysis

Summary

Portraying the LORD's creation in poetry, the psalmist traces the stretching out of the heavens in light, the sovereign control of the chaotic deep, the adornment of the earth as a dwelling place, the arrangement of night and day for life, and the preparation of the sea for its life, and then praises God who gloriously rules the creation and renews by his Spirit, calling for that final purging of sinners who are out of harmony with the wisdom of his creation.

Outline

I. The psalmist exhorts himself to praise the LORD's majesty in creation (1–23):
   A. He exhorts himself to praise the LORD who is great and majestic (1).
   B. The LORD stretched out the heavens and all of their hosts after light is formed (2–4).
      1. He is clothed with majesty (1b)
      2. He covers himself with light and stretches out the heavens as a curtain (2).
      3. He builds his heavenly palace and makes the elements his servants (3–4).
   B. The LORD created the foundations of the earth and covered it with the deep under his control (5–9).
      1. He laid the firm foundations of the earth (5).
      2. He covered it with the deep and controlled it (6–9).
   C. The LORD adorned the earth as a place to live (10–18).

---

33. B. Janecko, "Ecology, Nature, Psalms," in *The Psalms and Other Studies in the Old Testament*, FS J. I. Hunt, ed. by J. C. Knight and I. A. Sinclair (Nashotah, WI: Nashotah House Seminary, 1990):96–108.
34. *Psalms*, II:232.

The Wisdom of the LORD's Manifold Creation

      1. He put the springs in the valley for life (10–12).
         a. He sends springs in the valleys (10).
         b. They give drink to animals (11).
         c. The birds sing among them (12).
      2. He gives food for all of life (13–15).
         a. He waters the mountains so that fruit grows (13).
         b. He causes grass and herbs to grow (14).
         c. He brings wine, oil and bread to man (15).
      3. He makes dwelling places for life (16–18).
         a. The trees are flourishing.
         b. Birds nest in the tall fir trees.
         c. Animals live in the rocky slopes.
    D. The LORD made the heavenly bodies (19–23).
      1. He appointed the sun and the moon for their times (19).
      2. In the darkness of night, animals prowl for food (20–21).
      3. In the light of day, people labor for food (22–23).
II. In admiration of the wisdom of God's creation, the psalmist turns back to see all of creation under the total dominion of the LORD (24–32).
    A. He admires the marvelous wisdom of the LORD's creation (24).
    B. He looks to the creatures of the sea that wait for the LORD for life and food (25–30).
      1. Innumerable and various creatures are in the sea (25–26).
      2. The LORD feeds and sustains all of them and controls their life (27–30).
    C. He calls for the glory to continue since the LORD has such powerful control over creation (31–32).
III. Vowing to sing praises to the God of creation in sweet meditation, the psalmist calls for sinners to be consumed by his powerful God who can thereby restore harmony to creation (33–35).
    A. He praises God with song and meditation (33–34).
    B. He prays to God for the consummation of wickedness in the earth (35).
Epilogue: The psalmist exhorts his soul to bless the LORD. "Praise the LORD!"

COMMENTARY IN EXPOSITORY FORM

I. The faithful must resolve to bless the LORD because the wonders of creation reveal the LORD's splendor and majesty (1b–23).

A. *They praise the LORD for his majesty (1).*

The first part of verse 1 could be taken as a prologue because it begins the psalm the same way Psalm 103 did: "Bless (בָּרֲכִי; s.v. Ps. 5:12) the LORD, O my soul!" But it also functions here as a call to praise, a self-exhortation to bless the LORD. The rest of the verses gives a summary statement of the cause for praise: Yahweh is very great and clothed with majesty and honor (for הוֹד and הָדָר s.v. Ps. 96:6). He uses the imagery of clothing to portray the honor and majesty of the LORD. Clothing in the Bible often is used to describe the nature of the person; clothed with filthy garments signifies a sinner, clothed with white raiment indicates a saint. Here the meaning is that God is majestic.

B. *The LORD, who is light, formed the heavens (2–4).*

1. *He covered himself with light (2a).*

The greatness of the LORD is most frequently revealed in his great works, and here the work is creation. The line corresponds to the first day in the Genesis account of creation (1:3–5). Clothing is again used to reveal the true nature of LORD: he is light. Light in the Bible is symbolic of many things, including holiness, understanding, joy, and life itself. The LORD is everything that light is (see also 1 John 1:5 and John 1:4–9); and according to this verse it is he who covered himself with light. Because light is vital to life, the one who is the true light created light first.

2. *He spread out the heavens (2b).*

The second half of the verse corresponds to the making of the "firmament" or expanse in Genesis on the second day (1:6–8). There the separation is portrayed as something of a beaten out metal cover; here it is pictured as a tent curtain. But the point to be made from this passage is the ease with which the LORD did this, simply spreading it out. This too reveals his sovereign majesty.

3. He makes his palace above the heavens (3–4).

These verses reflect on the glory above the firmament. The imagery begins with building a palace—its foundations, here compared to beams, are in the waters above the skies. In the culture upper chambers were above the main house, and they were known for their seclusion and privacy. The palace of the heavenly king is high and inaccessible to mankind.

Not only is his "palace" in the heavens, but the clouds are his chariots, and wind and lightning are his messengers. Like a king who rides a chariot throughout his kingdom, so the LORD oversees everything in his kingdom—but he rides the clouds above. The kingship of Yahweh is therefore completely distinct from our earthy existence. And his sovereignty is unfathomable: he is surrounded by servants, for everything he has made in the heavens and on the earth stands ready to do his will, to be his messengers and the agents of carrying out his will. All of creation displays the glory of the LORD (Ps. 19).

C. The LORD created the foundations of the earth and the great deep (5–9).

Now the focus of the hymn is on the earthly domain (corresponding to the third day, Gen. 1:9–10). The LORD established (יָסַד; s.v. Ps. 87:1) the earth on its foundations (see Ps. 24:1–2), so it was not moveable (מוֹט; s.v. Ps. 66:2); at first he covered it with water, even over the mountains. The "oceans' deeps" (תְּהֹמוֹת) were the surface of the earth. The solid land was there but needed to emerge, which it did in an upheaval so that the waters receded. This is a poetical description of the early separation of land and sea; it portrays Genesis 1:9. The imagery harmonizes with the note in Genesis that there was an early chaos in which the earth was covered by water (Gen. 1:2; 2 Pet. 2:5) and in darkness and disorder. Then the LORD began to bring about the creation we enjoy.

This separation of land and sea was brought about by the LORD's command. The verb used here is stronger than the verbs of decrees in Genesis: he "rebuked" the water (גָּעַר; s.v. Ps. 76:6),[35] and it fled to its place. In the ancient Near East the pagan stories of creation often envision a cosmic battle between the creator-god and the goddess of the deep water; but there is no hint of a fight here, just a simple rebuke and the chaotic waters withdrew. It has been likened to a military scene: by his powerful command the sovereign scatters the water into reservoirs. The thundering sound of God's rebuke caused the waters to flow from mountains through valleys to the seas. Once in place the LORD set a boundary for the water so that it could not again cover the earth (Job 38: 10–11).

D. The LORD made all the earth to support life (10–18).

It should be pointed out that in surveying the different arenas of creation the psalmist dwells on the activity within each sphere. So here when the LORD causes springs to flow through the frequently dry torrent beds (*wadis*), it is so that the animals ("living creatures") of the field and especially the wild donkeys can drink (10–11). Above them the birds make their homes in the branches and sing ("give sound"). He also sends water from above to the mountains to make things grow for food, so he feeds his creatures[36] (v. 13)—grass for domesticated animals, green herbs for the service of people so that bread can be made, wine to cheer the heart, oil for appearance and comfort for the skin, and food for health (vv. 14–15). There is a great interest here in all the activity of life on the earth.

The bounty of the earth continues: the greatest trees (literally, "the trees of the LORD," a superlative construction) are well-watered, even the famous cedars of Lebanon. And in these trees the birds make their nests, in particular the majestic stork whose home is in the cypresses. Also, the high mountains are

---

35. See P. J. Van Zijl, "Discussion of the Root *Ga'ar* ('Rebuke')," in *Biblical Essays*, edited by A. H. Van Zyl (Potchefstroom: Pro Rege-Pers, 1969), pp. 56–63.
36. Thijs Booij, "Psalm 104:13b: The Earth is Satisfied with the Fruit of Your Works," *Bib* 70 (1989):409–12.

home to the wild goat (the ibex), and the rocky precipices are a refuge to the rock badger (the coney). The depiction of active life in the mountains and the trees shows a creation that is alive and not static (see also Job 38:39–39:30). So God provides water and therefore food for all his creation.

E. The LORD created all the heavenly bodies (19–23).

The psalmist now focuses on the heavens (corresponding in order to the fourth day of creation). He begins with the moon, perhaps because Israel followed the lunar calender as the structure of the annual cycle. The sun also he made to be visible in its time (figuratively, "the sun knows its going down"; for another figurative description, see Ps. 19)—it all runs harmoniously by days and years and seasons. The cycle of sun and moon prompts the psalmist to think of the darkness that is night. In that world the darkness was considered to be dangerous and oppressive; but to the psalmist it is a time filled with animal activity—the cycle provides for life in its times. In the night animals move about the forests, and young lions roar as they find their prey, given to them in the order of creation. But during the daytime, the night hunters scurry away to their dens; when the sun rises, people go to their work (lit. "man to his work") and their labor until the evening. As with Genesis, the climax of the survey ends with mankind, the crown of creation.

So in every time and setting in God's creation there is constant activity; plants and animals and people all depend on God's ordering of life to meet their needs. The plan of God has worked out the life-cycle for the different living things in their habitats.[37]

II. The LORD's dominion over all creation reveals his wisdom (24–32).

A. The wisdom of God is revealed in creation (24).

A burst of praise comes from the psalmist at this point as

---

37. W. Harrelson, "On God's Care for the Earth: Psalm 104," *CTM* 2 (1975):19–22.

he contemplates the many works of God: how marvelous they are, how intricately interwoven and so dependent on the cycle of life. Creation is clearly the work of God's wisdom (חָכְמָה; s.v. Ps. 19:7; compare Prov. 8:22–31). So the verse records a pause for the psalmist to review in wonder what he has just surveyed.

B. The creatures of the sea are fed and controlled by God (25–30).

In verses 25 and 26 the psalmist considers the sea, that vast area ("great and broad"), teeming with life of every size and without number. Here too the attention is given to the activity: "There go the ships, *and there is* leviathan which you formed to play in it." Leviathan in the pagan world was deified as a god of the underworld; but in the text it is simply a very large sea creature.[38] The last clause of verse 26 has often been taken to mean that God put leviathan in the sea "to play with it" (לְשַׂחֶק־בּוֹ). But it probably means that the creature was put in the sea to sport in it, alongside other fish and the ships. Weiss fits this explanation into the flow of the psalm by asking what the poet sees: when he looks at the springs of water, he sees animals drinking; when he looks at the plants, he sees their use for living creatures; and when he looks at the luminaries in the heavens, he thinks of their function in relation to everything on earth. In other words, the poet sees how the various parts of creation function together with other aspects of creation. So when he looks to the sea, he sees a path for ships and a place for fish. He mentions the ships and the great sea creatures together because he sees them next to each other, the great fish swimming alongside the ships. So just as the trees are where the birds nest and sing, the sea is the playground for these great creatures. The verb "to play" prompts the reader to envision them spouting water high into the air like a fountain in a garden, or leaping from the water in rows as they accompany the ships.[39] This analysis by Weiss not only clarifies

---

38. So there may be a polemic here against pagan mythology: what they feared and venerated the Israelites saw to be part of God's animal creation.
39. See M. Weiss, "*liwyātān* (Psalm 104:26)," in *The Bible From Within* (Jerusalem: Magnes Press, 1984), pp. 78–92.

a difficult clause but also helps us see the way the hymn focuses on life in God's creation.

The psalmist summarizes the message so far by saying that all creation is dependent on God for life (vv. 27–30). He presents the animals in human terms as if they wait for the LORD to give them food, and when[40] he does they gather to receive it and are satisfied. But when he does not show them this favor ("hides his face"), they are terrified (see Ps. 30:7; for בָּהַל, s.v. Ps. 83:15); and when he takes away their breath, they die and return to their dust. Everything depends on God's care and provision. In fact, their very existence is by his power: when he sends his Spirit (lit. "you send your Spirit," although the word could also be rendered "breath"), they are created (יִבָּרֵאוּן; s.v. Ps. 51:10). This verb could be translated "created" or "revived / renewed." Both would be true. Parallel to this colon is the statement that God "renews" the face of the earth (the surface of the ground). Thus, the order of creation is restored and continues. God is the source of all life; he created it, and he sustains it.

C. The glory of the LORD should last forever because he has absolute control of all creation (31–32).

These thoughts prompt another burst of praise: "May the glory (s.v. Ps. 19:1) of the LORD be forever! May the LORD rejoice (s.v. Ps. 48:11) in his works." The psalmist seems to be drawing on the statements in Genesis 1 that report that God saw what he had created and declared that it was all good; and when it was done he rested, i.e., celebrated and enjoyed his creation (see Gen. 1:31–2:3; and Prov. 8:31). God takes delight in his creation; and because of this he cares for it, from the highest mountain to the smallest bird. All creation reveals the power and glory of God; but most majestically earthquakes and volcanoes result from his "touch." Here the psalmist turns these thoughts into a prayer or a wish that this glory would continue forever. It is characteristic of the faith that believers anticipate the plan of God and express

---

40. All the clauses in this section are written in the text as independent clauses; but they may be subordinated as temporal clauses in view of the sequence of ideas in each verse.

their confidence in it by prayer, such as in praying for the Lord to come.

III. Believers respond to God's marvelous works with praise and pray that he will renew harmony to creation by removing wickedness (33–35).

The conclusion of the psalm answers the beginning: the psalmist is determined to sing praises to the LORD as long as he lives (see Ps. 146:2). The closing prayer is that his meditations (שִׂיחַ; s.v. Ps. 119:15) will be pleasing to the LORD as he rejoices. At the very least his praise for the God of all creation should now be elevated and elaborate; it should be filled with rich descriptions of the work of the creator, insofar as he has the language to do so. But by simply describing the wonders of heaven and earth and everything in them, he is in fact giving praise to the maker.

The prayer also expresses the desire that sinners (for חָטָא, s.v. Ps. 51:2) be removed[41] from the earth—that they will come to an end and disappear. The wicked (s.v. Ps. 1:1) and sinners are unbelievers who live independently of God—they offer no acknowledgment that the LORD is the source of all life. They are not only outside the covenant, but are also harmful to the faith. The psalmist is not merely interested in their punishment but in their removal from the earth. His primary intent is to protect God's program within the word; he longs for a perfect world free from outside interference.[42]

Epilogue: "Praise the LORD!"

MESSAGE AND APPLICATION

Kraus provides an excellent summary of the message of this psalm:

---

41. The verb יִתַּמּוּ is the *qal* of the verb תָּמַם, "to be complete, finished, destroyed, come to an end." Some geminate verbs follow a pattern similar to I *nun* verbs.
42. VanGemeren, *Psalms*, p. 771.

The entire world is supported and controlled by deeds of God, toward which all elements and creatures are oriented. Close and emphatic are the metaphors. Yahweh creates the world like a master builder: he "lays the beams" of his heavenly dwelling. Like a family father, he stretches the tent roof. Like a field general, he thunders at the primeval waters—they flee. Like a farm manager, he leads the quickening waters to the living beings and the fields. Like the father of a household, he distributes his goods and gifts. And all of this is done with sovereign, world-transcending power, profound wisdom, and gracious goodness. The conception of the heavenly king stands behind the whole psalm. But the entire creation is open to Yahweh; it is absolutely dependent on him, it dies without him. It lives on a creative act which is constantly effective in renewal. With Yahweh's כבוד [glory] there lies on the world as Psalm 104 sees it the brightness of the royal glory of God, the light of a new, other world, in which evildoers no longer have a place. In this world the human being can react to the deeds and gifts of Yahweh only with daily praise that is conscious of its dependence.[43]

The primary application of the psalm is to praise the LORD; the content of the psalm is the LORD's creation; and the way to do this is by contemplation and meditation on all the marvelous aspects of his care and provision for creation. We can state most of this as a summary expository idea: *When believers consider the amazing and wonderful works of God in all the aspects of creation, they will praise him as the giver and sustainer of life and anticipate the promised new order of creation without sin.*

---

43. *Psalms 60–150*, p. 304.

PSALM 105

Praise for the Fulfillment of the Promises of the Covenant

INTRODUCTION

Text and Textual Variants

1 Give thanks to the LORD, proclaim his name;
    make known among the nations what he has done.
2 Sing to him, sing praise to him,
    tell of all his wonderful acts.
3 Glory[1] in his holy name;
    let the heart of those who seek the LORD rejoice.
4 Seek the LORD and his strength;
    seek his face always.[2]

5 Remember his wonders that he has done,
    his miracles and the judgments of his mouth,

---

1. The MT has הִתְהַלְלוּ, the passive-reflexive of the verb "to praise" which is difficult to translate. The Greek version reads "be commended," ἐπαινεῖσθε. Allen suggested a translation of "praise with pride" (*Psalms 101–150*, p. 50).
2. The parallel words for "seek" are דִּרְשׁוּ and בַּקְּשׁוּ.

PSALM 105

6 O descendants of Abraham, his servant,[3]
   sons of Jacob, his chosen ones.[4]

7 He is Yahweh[5] our God;
   his judgments are in all the earth.
8 He remembers his covenant forever,
   the word he commanded for a thousand generations,
9 which he made with Abraham,
   even his oath to Isaac.
10 He established it to Jacob as a decree,
   to Israel as an everlasting covenant,
11 saying:[6] "To you I shall give the land of Canaan,
   the portion for your inheritance."

12 When they were few in number,
   a small group,[7] and temporary residents in it,
13 wandering[8] from nation to nation,
   from one kingdom to another people,
14 he allowed no one to oppresshem,
   but warned kings for their sake:
15 "Do not touch my anointed ones;
   do my prophets no harm."

16 Then he called down famine on the land
   and destroyed all their supplies of food.
17 He sent a man before them—
   Joseph, *who was* sold as a slave.

---

3. The Greek version has a plural here, "his servants," understanding it to refer to the descendants and parallel to "his chosen ones."
4. Two manuscripts and Qumran (*11QPs^a*) have a singular form to match "his servant."
5. I have retained the proper name here instead of "the LORD" to represent more precisely the statement of faith within the covenant.
6. The Greek translation clarifies the reading by beginning this verse with "saying," λέγων.
7. The MT has כִּמְעָט, "just a little"; the Greek version has "of little account," ὀλιγοστοὺς
8. The text literally reads, "and they wandered"; it is here taken as a temporal clause with the following verse as the independent clause.

Praise for the Fulfillment of the Promises of the Covenant

18 His feet were bruised[9] with shackles,
   his neck was put in irons,
19 until his word came to pass,
   until the oracle of the LORD proved him true.[10]
20 The king sent[11] and released him,
   the ruler of nations, and he set him free.
21 He made him master of his household,
   and ruler over all he possessed,
22 to instruct[12] his princes as he pleased[13]
   and teach his elders wisdom.
23 Then Israel entered Egypt;
   and Jacob lived as an alien in the land of Ham.

24 The LORD made his people very fruitful;
   and he made them too numerous for their foes.
25 He turned their hearts to hate his people,
   to conspire against his servants.

26 He sent Moses his servant
   and Aaron, whom he had chosen.
27 They announced[14] among them the words of his signs
   and wonders in the land of Ham.
28 He sent darkness and made it dark—

---

9. The verb is עִנּוּ; in this stem the verb means "oppress, afflict." With no expressed subject the form is taken as a passive. Some interpret the verb to mean "forced into" with "his feet" as the subject.
10. For MT's צְרָפָתְהוּ the Greek reads closely "purified (ἐπύρωσεν) him."
11. The construction שָׁלַח מֶלֶךְ would normally be "a king sent," but it could just as easily be "he sent a king," maintaining the LORD as the subject here. But the king as the subject fits verse 21 the best, and also the passage in Genesis 41.
12. The form in the MT is לֶאְסֹר, "to bind," which does not fit the parallelism. It is usually emended to לְיַסֵּר, "to instruct," based on the Greek version's τοῦ παιδεῦσαι.
13. Hebrew is בְּנַפְשׁוֹ, "in himself," meaning essentially "as he pleased." The Greek version has "as himself" (ὡς ἑαυτὸν).
14. The verb שָׂמוּ means "they set, put"; but the object in the MT is "words." The expression of setting words before them must signify that they announced or proclaimed them. The Greek has "to them he committed the words of his signs."

PSALM 105

and they did not rebel[15] against his word.
29 He turned their waters into blood
   and killed their fish.
30 Their land swarmed with frogs,
   even in the chambers of their rulers.
31 He spoke, and there came swarms of flies,
   gnats throughout their country.
32 He turned their rain into hail,
   with lightning throughout their land.
33 He struck down their vines and fig trees
   and broke in pieces the trees of their country.
34 He spoke, and locusts came,
   grasshoppers without number;
35 and they devoured all the vegetation in their land,
   and ate the produce of their soil.
36 Then he struck down all the firstborn in their land,
   the firstfruits of all their virility.[16]

37 He brought them out with silver and gold,
   and there was none from among their tribes that faltered.
38 Egypt was glad when they went out,[17]
   because the dread of them had fallen on them.
39 He spread out a cloud for a covering,
   and a fire to give light at night.
40 They[18] asked, and he brought them quail
   and satisfied them with bread from heaven.
41 He opened a rock, and water gushed out;
   as a river it flowed in arid places.
42 For he remembered his holy word
   to Abraham, his servant.
43 So he brought his people out with rejoicing,
   with shouts of joy his chosen ones.
44 And he gave them the lands of the nations;

---

15. The sense of these two clauses together is not readily clear. The negative is not in all the Greek manuscripts (or Syriac): "they embittered (παρεπίκραναν) his words," or, "they did not embitter his words."
16. For MT's אוֹנָם the Greek has "their toil" (πόνου αὐτῶν).
17. The Greek translation has "at their exodus" (ἐν τῇ ἐξόδῳ αὐτῶν).
18. The form in the text is "he asked."

>   and they fell heir to the labor of *other* peoples,
> 45 so that they would keep his decrees
>   and observe his laws.
>
> "Praise the LORD!"[19]

Composition and Context

Psalm 105 is a hymnic celebration of the mighty works of the LORD on Israel's behalf. Both Psalms 105 and 106 address this aspect of the history of redemption but they do it differently: Psalm 105 tells of God's faithful love in Israel's early history, but Psalm 106 delineates Israel's failures in that period of time. The last three psalms of Book V form a fitting closure: Psalm 104 focused on the LORD the creator, then Psalm 105 emphasizes his redemption of Israel from bondage, and Psalm 106 provides a penitential memory of the events. All three emphases would have been instructive to the Jews in exile.

While the passage may be classified as a hymn, Anderson suggests a more precise description would be a history psalm in the style of a hymn.[20] The psalm does not cover all the events, such as those at Sinai, perhaps because other passages provided that historical remembrance for Israel's worship. But Psalm 105 does cover the sending of Joseph into Egypt to be raised to power and deliver his people, a theme that would also provide hope for the exiles. In this and in several other ways Psalm 105 would have been instructive for the people of Israel, no matter how difficult their situation was.[21]

Much of the psalm proved useful on other occasions as well. Psalm 105:1–15 was recorded by the Chronicler (1 Chron. 16:8–22) as part of the report of David's moving of the ark to Jerusalem. The LORD's choice of Zion as his resting place would

---

19. This is not in the Greek or Syriac.
20. *Psalms 73–150*, p. 725.
21. See further R. J. Clifford, "Style and Purpose in Psalm 105," *Bib* 60 (1979):420–7; and A. R. Ceresco, "A Poetic Analysis of Psalm 105, with Attention to Its Use of Irony," *Bib* 64 (1983):20–46.

have been seen as a culmination of some of the promises of the covenant.

The expositor will not find the analysis of this passage complicated; it is the retelling of the ancient history with an emphasis on God's mighty works. But it will be a challenge nonetheless due to its length. The expositor will have to focus on the theological principles and not spend a lot of time retelling the details of the history.

Exegetical Analysis

Summary

By tracing the history of Israel as the LORD moved his people miraculously in fulfillment of the covenant promises, the psalmist praises the greatness of the LORD's love to his people in history as he remembered his covenant.

Outline

I. The psalmist praises the LORD for his greatness and love to Israel as he remembered the promise of the land (1– 11).
   A. Call to Praise: People must acknowledge the mighty works (1–6).
      1. Israel should sing and praise the glorious works of his name (1–3).
      2. Israel should remember his works for the nation (4–6).
   B. Reason for Praise: They should praise him for his remembrance of the covenant promises (7–11).
      1. The LORD's judgments are in all the earth (7).
      2. The LORD fulfilled the oath he swore to the fathers concerning the land (8–11).

II. The psalmist traces the history of the ancestors from the sojourn in Canaan to the bondage in Egypt (12–23).
   A. The LORD protected the patriarchs when they were sojourning in other lands (12–15).
   B. The LORD sovereignly brought Joseph to Egypt so that at the time of the famine the family could move to Egypt (16–23).

1. The LORD called a famine onto the land (16).
2. The LORD sent Joseph into bondage in Egypt (17–18).
3. The LORD fulfilled his promise and raised Joseph to power (19–22).
4. Then the family of Israel entered Egypt (23).

III. The psalmist recalls how the LORD prepared for the deliverance by judging Egypt and the Egyptians (24–36).
   A. The LORD blessed his people abundantly (24–25).
   B. The LORD gave them leaders and brought great plagues on Egypt by his powerful word (26–36).

IV. The psalmist rehearses how the LORD delivered his people from bondage, provided for them in the wilderness, and gave them the promised land (37–45).
   A. The LORD brought them out of Egypt with spoil (37–38).
   B. The LORD led them through the wilderness with marvelous works (39–41).
      1. He spread a cloud and fire before them (39).
      2. He gave them quail and manna (40).
      3. He brought water out of the rock (41).
   C. The LORD kept his promise of the land for Israel (42–45).
      1. He remembered his promise to the fathers (42).
      2. He brought them out with rejoicing (43).
      3. He gave them the land so that they would keep his word (44–45).

Epilogue: "Praise the LORD!"

COMMENTARY IN EXPOSITORY FORM

I. The LORD must be praised for his mighty works and his faithfulness to his word (1–11).

A. Praise him for his mighty works (1–6).

The first six verses provide the call to praise with a variety of words for praise; each one has a distinct emphasis and together they reveal the richness of the celebration of worship.[22]

---

22. They are הוֹדוּ, "give a public acknowledgment"; הוֹדִיעוּ, "cause (them) to know"; זַמְּרוּ, "sing praises (with musical accompaniment"; שִׁירוּ, "sing"; שִׂיחוּ,

Almost all the verbs in verses 1–5 are imperatives, three in verse 1, three in verse 2, 1 in verse 3, 2 in verse 4, and 1 in verse 5. The piling up of these directives would have been very effective in calling the attention of the worshipers to the necessity of praise. In addition, in the first verse there is the command, "call (קִרְאוּ) upon his name"; in the context it probably is to be given its meaning of making proclamation (cf. Exod. 34:5–7, Gen. 12:8). Making proclamation along with making known what he has done and telling of his wonderful acts all make clear the contents of the praise—the wonderful works (נִפְלְאוֹתָיו; s.v. Ps. 139:5) of the LORD. Many of these works will be delineated in the psalm.

The call for praise is addressed to the descendants of Abraham through Jacob, that is, the people Israel (v. 6). But the address is not simply to the physical descendants of the patriarchs, for in verse 3 the call is to those who seek the LORD (מְבַקְשֵׁי יְהוָה; s.v. Ps. 83:16). The verbs "to seek" (דָּרַשׁ and בָּקֵשׁ) give the sense of seeking help or guidance from the LORD in prayer, in worship, or in making enquiry through priests or prophets. So describing the faithful as those who seek the LORD prompts the psalmist to instruct the people to seek the LORD and his strength, to seek his face always. By doing so they will receive his favor, their faith will be strengthened and they will have more occasions to praise the LORD. This focus on the faithful in Israel is also indicated in that they are called descendants of Abraham, the LORD's servant (for עֶבֶד, s.v. Ps. 134:1). They are therefore the physical and spiritual descendants of Abraham—they also serve the LORD. And this is what they were called to do because they are "his chosen ones" (בְּחִירָיו). They are those whom God chose to be his holy, priestly people. As so they are expected to praise and proclaim, sing and tell, and rejoice and remember (or bring to everyone's memory) all God's mighty works in their history. They are also to "glory" in his holy name (v. 3). This verb is the reflexive form of the verb "to praise" (for הָלַל, s.v. Ps. 33:1). This form of the word has often been translated "boast," but that may have the wrong connotation. Allen's

---

"tell (your musings)"; הִתְהַלְלוּ, "glory, make it all your praise"; and יִשְׂמַח, "let them rejoice, be glad."

translation, "praise with pride," may catch something of the meaning (see fn 1.). The word indicates that the worshiper is to be caught up in the praise, making the praise a personal celebration or glorying. And while all this praise will be for all the wonderful miracles on Israel's behalf, those works also brought God's judgments on the antagonistic nations, notably Egypt and the Canaanites (v. 5).

B. Praise him for his faithfulness to his word (7–11).

The main section of the hymn begins with an affirmation of faith based on the word of the LORD. The psalmist declares, "He is Yahweh our God." The holy name is the covenant name that God demonstrated and enlivened by delivering Israel from bondage. He made a covenant with them in his name, and that name ever after signified his special relationship with his people. But he was not merely a national God like the pagans had; his judgments are worldwide. In carrying out his promises to his people he had to deal with the pagan nations that sought to destroy his people and the covenant.

Verse 8 states that the LORD remembers (זָכַר; s.v. Ps. 6:5) his covenant forever. To remember something means to act on it, to be loyal to it—here to be faithful to his covenant promises. And the covenant is unlimited—its promises are for a thousand generations. They are valid forever because their fulfillment depends on the LORD and his plan for the ages. The covenant was initiated with the patriarchs by God's grace—he chose them and gave his promises to them; but those promises were not fulfilled in the time of the patriarchs. At the core of the covenant is the promise recorded here in verse 11: "To you I shall give the land of Canaan, the portion for your inheritance" (see e.g., Gen. 15:18; 17:2–8; 22:16; 26:3–5; 28:13–15). So the psalm will trace the history of redemption from the promises made to the patriarchs to the conquest of their divinely appointed share, the land of Canaan. For the LORD to give the inheritance to his people necessitated bringing judgment on the world that opposed God and his covenant.

II. The LORD must be acknowledged for his guidance of his people through suffering to glory (12–23).

A. Acknowledge his protection of his people (12–15).

The report begins with the tiny family of Abraham before the bondage in Egypt. They were a very small group of people and they had no land of their own. The text says they were "men of number," very few—easily numbered (as opposed to a people without number). And they were temporary residents (גָּרִים, "sojourners") in the land. They had to deal with the jealousy of kings (Gen. 21 and 26), invasions (Gen. 14), and the corruption of pagans (Gen. 34 and 38), to name a few crises. But as a weak and seemingly insignificant band they were under God's protection. The LORD did not allow anyone to oppress them; in fact, he warned kings off (Gen. 20:2). This divine protection of the people is expressed in the decree, "Do not touch my anointed ones; do my prophets no harm."[23] Calling them "my anointed ones" (מְשִׁיחָי, the plural of "messiah," from מָשַׁח) indicates that they were chosen by God for a purpose. And God would ensure that this purpose was fulfilled, which is why he often delivered them even when they failed (e.g., Gen. 12:10–20). The designation "my prophets" is a little more difficult. It is true that Abraham was called a prophet in Genesis 20:7; but the designation here is probably for the Israelites in general. As the chosen people they would speak for God. So the reference should not be restricted to the classical prophets.[24] The point of the section is that God protected his people because he chose them and made a covenant with them so that they would be his representatives in the earth.

B. Acknowledge his provision of a deliverer (16–23).

The praise of God must include serious reflection on his mysterious ways. He protects his people, but he also brings adversity

---

23. We are left to wonder if this warning was actually declared to anyone in this way, or if it is a poetic way of saying what the LORD was thinking, an expression of the LORD's plan to protect his people.
24. Anderson, *Psalms 73–150*, pp. 730.

in order to carry out his plan and in the process deliver his people. In verse 16 the new section begins with the acknowledgment that the LORD brought a famine on the land (Gen. 41:54). As the Lord of all creation, he simply called down or summoned it (וַיִּקְרָא). As the whole account in Genesis made clear, and this psalm recalls, there was a purpose for the adversity. God would send his people to Egypt so that he might demonstrate his power over nature and over the earthly kingdoms.

The psalm only briefly recalls the story of Joseph. The LORD sent Joseph into Egypt as a slave before the rest of the family. Joseph at the time did not understand what was happening to him, but after his exaltation he could see that God meant it for good (Gen. 45:5, 7; 50:20; see also Rom. 8:28). But before he rose to power he suffered as God was preparing him to fulfill his calling (Gen. 37:5–11). The psalmist says that his feet were bruised (a general word for affliction, עִנּוּ) with shackles and his neck (נַפְשׁוֹ) put in iron. We have no mention of this in Genesis, other than that he was taken as a slave to Egypt and did spend time in prison. It is not likely that this is simply narrative embellishment of his suffering; he very likely experienced some of this, but it was not all physical suffering because his wisdom and faithfulness enabled him to be entrusted with duties even in his time of imprisonment. He had to endure being a slave until the oracle (אִמְרָה; s.v. Ps. 119:11) to him was fulfilled. This is a reference to the dreams that God gave him (Gen. 37:5–11). Verse 19 says his suffering lasted until the time the LORD "proved him true." If this is the best translation of the verb (צְרָף), it would mean that his calling and his faithfulness were confirmed by his rise to power. But the verb has the sense of refining and proving, so it could be taken to mean that his bondage "purified him." This would indicate that his suffering was a time of testing to prepare him to rule Egypt.

Once this period was over, Pharaoh sent for Joseph, set him free, and made him lord and master (מֹשֵׁל; s.v. Ps. 66:7) over all that he possessed (vv. 20–21; see Gen. 41:14, 40). The king was therefore an instrument of God's plan for Joseph and for Israel's entrance into Egypt as well—even though he was not aware of it. The ruler of Egypt made Joseph ruler under him, in order to instruct his princes as he pleased and teach them wisdom. The king was pleased to find a wise man in whom the Spirit of God dwelt. It is not likely that formal instruction was given to the princes; rather, by his decisions and his integrity Joseph would help them to see what it meant to be wise. He would rule wisely and in the process save the land of Egypt; in so doing he became the prime example of how wisdom rules, not just to the princes of Egypt, but for all who would rule in ages to come (Prov. 8:15).

III. The LORD must be remembered for his blessings on his people and his judgments on the wicked (24–36).

A. Remember his blessings for his people (24–25).

The survey turns now to the great deliverance from bondage.[25] The first three verses give an overview of the early chapters of Exodus. God made Israel so fruitful that they became more numerous than their enemies (Exod. 1:7–12). Their growth was the work of the creator (compare the language here with Gen. 1:20–26), creating a great nation. But their blessing brought jealousy and fear to their captors. It was God, then, who turned Egyptian hearts to hate (שָׂנֵא; s.v. Ps. 139:21) Israel and conspire against them, meaning that in making Israel fruitful he gave occasion for the Egyptians to hate them—and their hatred led them to try to control the Israelite populations by the conspiracy to kill the males. The way the psalm is written, then, continues to stress the sovereignty of God in all these events.

B. Remember his judgment on oppressors (26–36).

The turning point came when the LORD sent Moses and Aaron to the people. The verb "send" signifies a calling to service with divine authority (God had already sent Joseph to Egypt). Moses would become great, but he would be great because he was the servant of the LORD (Exod. 14:31), an expression that emphasizes his loyalty to the LORD above all else. God also sent Aaron, whom he had chosen. There is no mention here of Moses'

---

25. See S. Holm-Nielsen, "The Exodus Tradition in Psalm 105," *ASTI* 11 (1978):22–30.

hesitancy that was partly the reason for the calling of Aaron, only that he was chosen by God. He was to be the spokesman for Moses (see Exod. 4:14–16).

The psalm now rehearses the miracles God did in Egypt when he delivered his people from bondage in accordance with the promises. The psalmist lists eight of the ten plagues, leaving out the 5th and 6th, the severe plague and the plague of boils.[26] He also changes the order, beginning with the darkness (the 9th plague) and ending with the death of the first born (the 10th); these two frame all of the other plagues with their significance for judgment, first on the sun god and then on Pharaoh.[27]

Verse 27 uses the verb "they set, put" (שָׂמוּ). It has been interpreted to mean "they wrought"; but it has also been changed in some versions to read the singular, "he wrought (his signs by his words, דִּבְרֵי אֹתוֹתָיו)." The verb as it stands would indicate that Moses and Aaron set the judgments before the king and his people, meaning they announced or predicted the signs. The plagues were designed to be "signs" and "wonders" (מֹפְתִים) in the land of Ham.

After the plague of darkness is mentioned, the text says, "and they did not rebel (מָרוּ) against his word" (v. 28). As it stands the line means that Moses and Aaron were faithful in fulfilling their task. But the expression still seems out of place here. And so many follow the Greek and Syriac versions and omit the negative; this would then mean that the Egyptians rebelled against his word, by hardening their hearts. It has also been suggested that the negative is actually in an interrogative sentence, and the meaning would be "Did they not rebel?" Still others suggest the verb should be "they did not keep" (שָׁמְרוּ instead of מָרוּ). It would certainly be a smoother reading to say that the Egyptians rebelled; but such a change suggests a secondary reading. The clause in the Hebrew Bible does makes sense, even though unexpected.

According to verse 29, the LORD turned the water to blood and killed the fish; then in verse 30 the swarms of frogs came,

---

26. See S. E. Loewenstamm, "The Number of the Plagues in Psalm 105," *Bib* 52 (1971):34–38.
27. See Th. Booij, "The Role of Darkness in Psalm cv 28," *VT* 39 (1989):209–14.

even in the royal chambers; flies and gnats are mentioned in verse 31; hail and lightning and the devastation to vines and trees are recalled in verses 32–33; locusts that devoured everything that was left are the subject of verses 34–35; and finally, the death of the first born, the first fruits of their strength, is reported in verse 36. The psalmist did not need to go into great detail on these plagues, or to show how each one destroyed the economy and the religious beliefs of the land. The people were well-versed in all that through their retelling of the wonders in their festival liturgies. The simple mentioning of the plagues was sufficient to remind people of the greatness of God in the world and his grace toward Israel. To redeem his people from bondage, God would judge the nations that held and oppressed them. This he could do again when the people who were in exile, waiting to renew their covenant relationship with the LORD and enjoy the blessing of everlasting promises.

IV. The LORD must be acknowledged for redeeming his people, providing for them in the way, and bringing them to their inheritance (37–45).

A. *He delivers his people from bondage (37–38).*

In the last section the psalmist touches on events concerning Israel's wandering in the wilderness and conquest of the land. Verses 37–38 report the exodus, but emphasize the blessing of the people and the response of the Egyptians. The LORD brought them out with silver and gold. In the historical account the people demanded these things from the Egyptians, as if they were to be spoils of war. And when they left Egypt, none of them faltered; they were all convinced of the word of the LORD that called them to leave, and of the power of the LORD that would enable them to leave.

But the Egyptians were glad when they left. They had endured months of plagues because of the refusal of their king to release the Israelites. They were afraid to harm or hinder Israel in any way because they were terrified that some dread thing would happen (the "dread of Israel" had fallen on them).

Praise for the Fulfillment of the Promises of the Covenant

B. He provides for them in the way (39–41).

Once the LORD brought them out of Egypt, he spread out a cloud for a covering for them. If this is a reference to the cloud of fire that went before them to light their way at night and to protect them from danger, it may also have served to shelter then from the burning sun of the desert.[28]

Then, when they asked for food, he brought them quail and gave them manna from heaven. There is no mention here of the murmuring that informed their request, or the judgment on their craving, only the wonderful provision of the LORD. The focus remains on his sovereign power and goodness. When they were thirsty he provided water from the rock—again no mention of the failure of the people that led to this provision. The point of the psalm is that God was protecting them and providing for them as they journeyed through the wilderness (see Exod. 13:21–22; 15:22–27; 16:13–16; 17:1–6; etc.).

C. He brings them to their promised inheritance so that they would keep his word (42–45).

The simple explanation of God's intervention is stated clearly: he remembered his holy word (of promise) given to his servant Abraham. Two observations may be helpful here. First, the verb "remembered" does not mean he had forgotten and then called it to mind; it means that he acted on what he remembered—it refers to his active involvement to fulfill the covenant (זָכַר; s.v. Ps. 6:5). Second, he remembered his "holy" word. To describe the promise of his word as holy means that it is not a common promise, but set apart from the ordinary because it is God's word. If God had not kept his promises, his promises could not be called holy—they would be common, like our promises that may or man not be kept.

Because he "remembered" his promises he brought his people out triumphantly, with rejoicing and shouts of joy (e.g., Exod. 15:1–21). It was a great deliverance. Then he gave them their inheritance, the land that was promised to them was their possession. They even fell heir to all that the inhabitants had built

---

28. Kirkpatrick, *Psalms*, p. 623.

and labored over—they simply took it over. For God to fulfill his promise to Israel of the land, he also had to fulfill his warning to the people in the land that he would remove them because of their wickedness.

Finally, we have a statement of God's purpose for redeeming and caring for Israel in the way, and giving them the land for their inheritance. He did this so that they would observe his decrees and keep his laws. God's purpose in redemption is to have a people on earth who will do his will. He had done all these wonderful things for Israel because he was faithful to his word; now he required that his people be faithful to his word in response.

MESSAGE AND APPLICATION

The message of this psalm is clear: *Recalling the miraculous works of the LORD throughout the history of the faith will inspire greater confidence in the LORD's covenant promises and greater praise for his faithful love.* Through the teaching of their family and congregational leaders and in their historical festivals the Israelites were able to keep the traditions of the faith alive and meaningful. But hymnic compositions such as this one made their memory of and meditation on the wonderful works of God much easier. The many details in each of the events mentioned here would come to mind as the devout believer relived in his meditation at least the history of the faith. And in thinking through the great saving acts and provisions of the LORD, they understood full well that they benefitted all the people of God because they were partial fulfillments of the great promises that the LORD made by covenant with the ancestors.

The Christian can also be inspired by recalling God's great works on behalf of his people Israel. Their historical faith is also our historical faith, and their anticipation of the fulfillment of the covenant promises guaranteed in their new covenant is our anticipation because we have been grafted into that new covenant. But what Christians can do now is follow up on this psalm with additional meditations on the history of the Christian faith, beginning with the great redemption from bondage in the crucifixion of Christ Jesus, his resurrection and his exaltation, but continuing with the miraculous ways he has cared for his saints down through the ages. Some parts of Christendom have done so with their meditations on the lives of the saints. But there is more, much more, that needs to be called to mind that will inspire greater adoration for our great God and Savior.

PSALM 106

God's Great and Gracious Acts for His Rebellious People

INTRODUCTION

Text and Textual Variants[1]

1 "Praise the LORD!"[2]

   Give thanks to the LORD, for he is good;
      his loyal love endures forever.
2 Who can proclaim the mighty acts of the LORD
      or declare all his praise?[3]
3 Blessed are they who maintain justice,[4]
      who constantly do[5] what is right.

---

1. In conjunction with this study of the text, see G. J. Brooke, "Psalms 105 and 106 at Qumran," *RevQ* 14 (1989–90):267–92.
2. This is not in a few manuscripts or the Syriac.
3. The form is plural in the versions.
4. The Syriac has a plural form with a suffix "his."
5. The participle is singular in the text, a collective; a number of manuscripts and the versions have it plural.

4 Remember me,⁶ O LORD, when you favor your people,
    attend to me⁷ in your salvation,
5 that I may see the prosperity of your chosen ones,
    that I may rejoice in the joy of your nation
        and glory⁸ with your inheritance.

6 We have sinned, along with⁹ our ancestors;
    we¹⁰ have done wrong, we are guilty.
7 Our ancestors in Egypt
    gave no thought to your wonders;
    they did not remember the abundance of your acts of love,¹¹
    and they rebelled¹² by the sea,¹³ the Red Sea.¹⁴
8 Yet he saved them for his name's sake,
    to make his mighty power known.
9 He rebuked the Red Sea, and it dried up;
    he led them through the depths as¹⁵ *through* the desert.
10 He saved them from the hand of *those* who hated *them*;
    he redeemed them from the hand of the enemy.
11 The waters covered their adversaries;
    not one of them survived.

---

6. The Greek version and others make the pronouns plural to match the plural confession: "We have sinned" (v. 6).
7. The MT has פָּקְדֵנִי, "visit me," "attend to me"; the Greek version interprets with "regard (ἐπίσκεψαι) us."
8. The word is in the *hithpael* stem of הָלַל; the Greek renders it "be commended," τοῦ ἐπαινεῖσθαι.
9. The Greek translation follows the Hebrew literally: "with (μετὰ) our fathers."
10. Many manuscripts and the Syriac have a conjunction here.
11. The word for "loyal love" is in the plural; a few manuscripts have the singular form.
12. For the Hebrew word, the Greek version has "embittered (παρεπίκραναν)."
13. The phrase in the MT, עַל־יָם, "by the sea," seems unnecessary to the line. The Greek translation read it as if it were עֹלִים, "ascending," for it uses ἀναβαίνοντες. Two Hebrew manuscripts, Aquila and Symmachus do not have it, reading only "by the Red Sea." Some suggest that the words in the text displaced an original עֶלְיוֹן, "the Most High" (see Allen, *Psalms 101–150*, p. 65). But there is no evidence.
14. Hebrew has יַם סוּף, "sea of reeds," perhaps a tributary of the Red Sea or an inland body of water from it.
15. A number of manuscripts have the preposition בְּ instead of כְּ.

God's Great and Gracious Acts for His Rebellious People

12 Then they believed in his words;
      they[16] sang his praise.
13 But[17] they soon forgot his works;
      they did not wait for his plan.
14 In the desert they were consumed with craving;[18]
      and they put God to the test in the wasteland.
15 So he gave them what they asked for,
      and sent a wasting disease[19] upon them.

16 They grew jealous[20] of Moses in the camp,
      of Aaron, the holy one of the LORD.
17 The earth opened[21] and swallowed Dathan;
      it covered over Abiram's group.
18 Fire burned among their group;
      flames consumed *the* wicked.

19 They[22] made a calf at Horeb
      and worshiped an idol of cast metal.
20 They exchanged their glorious one[23]
      for an image of a grass-eating bull.
21 They forgot the God who saved them,
      who had done great things in Egypt,
22 wonders in the land of Ham
      and awesome deeds by the Red Sea.

---

16. There is no conjunction in the MT, but there is in a few other Hebrew manuscripts and the major versions.
17. There is no conjunction in the verse; there is in a few Hebrew manuscripts and the Syriac and Vulgate.
18. The Hebrew has the cognate accusative construction: וַיִּתְאַוּוּ תַאֲוָה, "and they craved (with) a craving."
19. MT has רָזוֹן; the Greek version has "surfeit," πλησμονὴν, as if the form was thought to be either מָזוֹן or רָוֹן. The context needs a judgment word, however.
20. The MT has וַיְקַנְאוּ; the Greek version has "they angered" (Moses), παρώργισαν, which would represent a form וַיַּקְנִיאוּ.
21. The Greek translation makes the verb passive, "was opened," ἠνοίχθη, equal to תִּפָּתַח.
22. One manuscript and the Greek version have the conjunction.
23. The expression is "their Glory," כְּבוֹדָם, a reference to the LORD.

23 So he decided[24] to destroy them—
　　had not Moses, his chosen one,
　stood in the breach before him
　　to turn away his wrath from destroying *them*.
24 Then they refused the pleasant land;
　　they[25] did not believe his word.
25 And they grumbled in their tents;
　　and would[26] not obey the LORD.
26 So he lifted up his hand against them,[27]
　　swearing to make them fall in the desert,
27 to scatter[28] their descendants among the nations
　　and disperse them throughout the lands.

28 They yoked themselves[29] to the Baal of Peor
　　and ate sacrifices to dead things;[30]
29 they provoked anger[31] by their wicked deeds,
　　and a plague[32] broke out among them.
30 But Phinehas stood up and intervened,
　　and the plague was stopped.
31 This was credited to him as righteousness
　　for generations ever after.

---

24. The text literally has, "And he said."
25. The conjunction is found in a few Hebrew manuscripts and the versions.
26. A few Hebrew manuscripts and the versions have a conjunction "and."
27. The Hebrew only says, "he raised his hand against them to cast them down . . . ." The idea is that he swore an oath by raising his hand. See also other passages concerning this oath (Ps. 95: 10–11).
28. To avoid the repetition in the verses, many commentators follow the Syriac and emend the text here from וּלְהַפִּיל, "and to make fall," to וּלְהָפִיץ, "and to scatter," which forms a better parallelism. Allen says that the MT suffered assimilation to the preceding verb (p. 65).
29. The Greek translation has "they were initiated," ἐτελέσθησαν.
30. The Hebrew has מֵתִים, and the Greek translation follows with "(sacrifices of) the dead," νεκρῶν.
31. The line simply says "they provoked." A few manuscripts and the versions add a pronoun הוּ.
32. The Greek translation has "a falling," ἡ πτῶσις.

God's Great and Gracious Acts for His Rebellious People

32 By the waters of Meribah[33] they provoked wrath,[34]
    and trouble came to Moses because of them;
33 for they rebelled[35] against his spirit,
    and harsh words came from his lips.[36]

34 They did not destroy the peoples
    as the LORD had commanded them,
35 but they mingled with the nations
    and learned to do their works.
36 They served their idols,
    which became[37] a snare to them.
37 They sacrificed their sons
    and their daughters to demons.
38 They shed innocent blood,
    the blood of their sons and daughters,
  whom they sacrificed to the idols of Canaan,
    and the land was defiled by their blood;
39 and they became unclean[38] by their works;
    they became unfaithful[39] by their deeds.

40 Therefore the LORD was furious with his people
    and abhorred his inheritance.
41 He gave them into the hand of the nations,

---

33. The Greek version does not have the name but a translation of it, "Contention," ἀντιλογίας.
34. The Greek and Syriac versions have "him": "they provoked him to wrath."
35. The MT has הִמְרוּ, "they rebelled, defied." Many suggest repointing the word to הֵמֵרוּ, "they made bitter (his spirit)." This follows the Greek version—"made his spirit bitter" (also the Syriac, Jerome, and two Hebrew manuscripts). This issue is related to the interpretation of "his spirit." If it is the Spirit of the LORD, "rebelled" would be the likely choice; if it is the spirit of Moses, then "embittered" might be preferable, although they could still rebel against his spirit as well.
36. The Hebrew simply says "and he parted with his lips," an idiom referring to his rash and emotional response.
37. The form in the text is plural, וַיִּהְיוּ, "and they (idols) became." Many manuscripts, the Greek and the Targum, have the singular form, וַיְהִי, "and it became."
38. The Hebrew form is the simple *qal* stem, "and they were defiled."
39. The expression is literally "they prostituted themselves."

and those who hated them ruled over them.
42 Their enemies oppressed them
   and they were subjected[40] to their power.
43 Many times he would deliver them,
   though they rebelled in their counsel,[41]
      and sank deeper[42] in their sin.

44 But he took note of their distress
   when he listened to their cry;
45 and he remembered his covenant with them,
   and relented according to his loyal love.
46 He caused them to be pitied
   before all their captors.

47 Save us, O LORD our God,
   and gather us from the nations,
   that we may give thanks to your holy name
   and glory in your praise.[43]

48 Blessed be the LORD, the God of Israel,
   from everlasting to everlasting.
   And all the people shall say, "Amen!"[44]

"Praise the LORD!"

Composition and Context

This psalm that closes Book IV of the Psalter makes people reflect on human rebellion in spite of the glorious works of the LORD. In conjunction with Psalm 105, it fills out two sides of the reflection on the historical traditions of Israel: Psalm 105 surveys the marvelous acts of God with no emphasis on the sins

---

40. The Greek translation has "and they were brought low," ἐταπεινώθησαν.
41. Allen translates this line as "they persisted in a policy of rebellion" (p. 64).
42. The Hebrew has וַיָּמֹכּוּ, "they sank"; the editors propose וַיָּמַקּוּ, "and they pined." The change is unnecessary.
43. Several versions have "with your inheritance" instead of "in your praise."
44. The Greek version interprets "Amen" with "may it be" repeated: γένοιτο γένοιτο.

of the people, but Psalm 106 continually reminds the reader of their sins in spite of God's works, which, in fact, necessitated many of those wonderful works. Perowne says it well when he explains that all the glory of Israel's history is confessed to be due, not to her heroes, her priests, her prophets, but to God; all the failures which are written upon that history, all discomfitures, losses, reverses, the sword, famine, exile, are recognized as the righteous chastisement which the sin of the nation has provoked.[45]

To keep the proper perspective he also points out that there is not a single ode that sings the praises of Moses, or Aaron, or Joshua, or David, or of the nation itself; the historical accounts of Israel are almost always retold to warn or to rebuke the people.[46] Psalm 106 has just such a didactic purpose: it mingles hymnic material with lament in such a way as to move people to repentance and a renewed obedience while inspiring their praise.[47] Allen identifies the passage as a communal complaint marked by hymnic features; it follows in general the structure of a hymn, but in this case Israel's rebellious acts are inserted into the context of praise for the LORD, who is therefore their redeemer and judge.[48] The tension throughout is between Israel's disobedience and God's merciful acts, or as Anderson terms it, Israel's disgrace and God's grace.[49] He adds that it is somewhat of a liturgical sermon, perhaps preparing people for confession of sin.

The aspects of a hymn occur in verses 1–2, 8–12, and 43–46; and the lament material is found in verses 6–7, 13–21, and 24–39. The structure in general is not difficult to outline: there is the call to praise with an introductory statement of the reason (vv. 1–5); then the cause for praise is laid out in a rehearsal of God's dealings with Israel, first in the wilderness (vv. 7–33) and then in the land (vv. 34–46). Finally, a prayer for deliverance concludes the psalm (v. 47). Such a prayer after this material

---

45. *Psalms*, II:257.
46. See further F. C. Fensham, "Neh. 9 and Pss. 105, 106, 135, and 136: Postexilic Historical Traditions in Poetic Form," *JNSL* 9 (1981):35–51.
47. VanGemeren, *Psalms*, p. 780.
48. *Psalms 101–150*, p. 50.
49. *Psalms 73–150*, p. 735.

indicates that the people who were now praying had in some way failed like their ancestors and needed divine help. Verse 48 is a concluding blessing for Book IV; but such a final blessing would also be appropriate for this psalm as it would any psalm.

The setting and occasion of the psalm is generally taken to be in the exile, or immediately after. The bulk of the psalm traces historical events from the exodus to the conquest, and then quickly jumps at the end to the experience of the psalmist which is much later. It is clear that the psalmist is applying all the earlier material to a current dilemma from which he prays for deliverance for the nation. The setting is probably the exile, even though portions of the material were likely used much earlier. It would not be difficult to see ancient hymnic forms and expressions carried forward to different crises. Anderson concludes that the psalm was put together after the completion of the Pentateuch but before Chronicles[50]—but when the Pentateuch was completed raises another question as well.

Exegetical Analysis

Summary

Before praying that the LORD would deliver his people from captivity, the psalmist voices a national confession of sin that traces the rebellious activities of the Israelites throughout their history along with the LORD's corresponding judgments.

Outline

I. Praising God for his goodness, the psalmist prays for help from the captivity (1–5).
  A. He praises God for his incomparable power and loyal love (1–2).
  B. He pronounces a blessing on all those who do righteous works (3).
  C. He prays for saving favor so that they might prosper, rejoice and glory (4–5).

---

50. *Psalms 73–150*, p. 736.

God's Great and Gracious Acts for His Rebellious People

II. The psalmist confesses the nation's sin by tracing their rebellious acts from Egypt to Canaan (7–33).
   A. He confesses on behalf of the nation that they have sinned (6).
   B. He acknowledges the nation's sin at the crossing of the sea (7–12).
      1. The ancestors rebelled at the sea.
      2. The LORD saved them to show his power.
      3. They believed and sang his praise.
   C. He acknowledges their sin as they passed through the wilderness to the land (13–33).
      1. They craved different food and God judged them (13–15).
      2. Many rebelled against Moses and were destroyed (16–18).
      3. They worshiped their golden calf but Moses interceded for them (19–23).
      4. They despised the land and God judged them (24–27).
      5. They sinned at Baal-Peor and Phinehas stayed the plague (28–31).
      6. They sinned at Meribah and prompted Moses to sin (32–33).
   D. He acknowledges their sin as they settled in the land (34–46).
      1. They mingled with the pagans and worshiped their idols with gross practices (34–39).
      2. The LORD judged them many times and dispersed them among the nations (40–42).
      3. Yet the LORD often delivered them when he heard their cry (43–46).
III. The psalmist prays for deliverance from the present captivity so that they may praise the LORD (47–48).
   A. He prays that they will be delivered so that they might praise (47).
   B. He announces the closing benediction by blessing the everlasting God of Israel (48).
Epilogue: "Praise the LORD!"

COMMENTARY IN EXPOSITORY FORM

I. Appealing to the power and the love of God the righteous may pray with confidence for deliverance and blessing (1–5)

A. The righteous must praise God for his loyal love and incomparable works (1–2).

Following the introductory "Praise the LORD," the psalmist calls the assembly to "give thanks (הוֹדוּ; s.v. Ps. 6:5) to the LORD, for he good (s.v. Ps. 34:); his loyal love (s.v. Ps. 23:6) endures forever." This is the formula used in a number of praise psalms; and it is especially fitting here to remember that the covenant love is eternal in spite of the sins of the people. It was most appropriate to sing it after a great deliverance or restoration that confirmed that the covenant was intact.

The initial call is followed by a rhetorical question, "Who can proclaim the mighty acts (גְּבוּרוֹת; s.v. Ps. 45:3) of the LORD?" This and its parallel expression are designed to say that the praiseworthiness of the LORD is too great for mere mortals to understand let alone adequately express. No one can fully declare his mighty works; and yet his mighty works demand praise.

B. The righteous may pray with confidence for deliverance and blessing (3–5).

The call to praise gives way to a prayer for deliverance, which implies that the psalmist (and the nation for whom he speaks) may have gotten themselves into difficulty by their own rebellions. The appeal is prefaced by a word of blessing on the righteous: the significance of this is that people who are the recipients of God's goodness and covenant faithfulness respond with obedience—they maintain justice (מִשְׁפָּט; s.v. Ps. 9:4) and constantly do righteous deeds (צְדָקָה; s.v. Ps. 1:5). God expects his people to persevere in doing right (see Ps. 15:1–5). These are said to be blessed (אַשְׁרֵי; s.v. Ps. 1:1); they are filled with joy because they are right with God. But placing this blessing here before the prayer serves a didactic purpose: maintaining righteousness must be seen as a prerequisite to answered prayer.[51]

And so in verses 4 and 5 the righteous psalmist prays to be included in the deliverance (יְשׁוּעָה; s.v. Ps. 3:2). Seen in the whole context of the psalm a confession of sin (vv. 13–39) will inform this petition. Just as the ancestors rebelled and suffered, and then in contrition prayed for deliverance, the psalmist is praying for deliverance. He identifies with the ancestors in both the need of and cause for deliverance. He may be speaking on behalf of the nation, but his prayer is now for himself: "remember me, O LORD, when you favor your people." The prayer to be remembered (for זָכַר s.v. Ps. 6:5) is a prayer for God to act on what he remembers, namely, the covenant relationship he has with his people who believe in him. He wants God to take care of him (for פָּקַד, s.v. Ps.8:4) in his salvation, or, when he delivers the people. The appeal is clearly to the covenant God of Israel, for the writer refers to them as "your people," "your chosen ones," "your nation" and "your inheritance." The psalmist wants to share in the great deliverance and restoration, so that he might witness their prosperity and rejoice in their celebration when God shows them favor (רָצוֹן; s.v. Ps. 30:5). The divine favor is the cause of the salvation (which is here a metonymy of effect). While the psalm might fit a number of occasions in Israel's history, one can certainly see how well this would fit the situation of someone in the exile.

II. In order to appreciate the LORD's gracious provisions for his people, believers must acknowledge their sinfulness (6–33).

A. Summary: They confess their sins to the LORD (6).

This lengthy section begins with a communal confession of sin: "We have sinned" (for חָטָא; s.v. Ps. 51:2). And the reason for the subsequent listing of the rebellious acts of the ancestor is here expressed in the line with "even as our ancestors did," or more literally, "with" or "along with our ancestors." The people

---

51. Allen, *Psalms 101-150*, p. 70.

recognized their own ungrateful and rebellious acts in the sins of their ancestors; the implication is that they shared in them. They were not entirely separate from their ancestors; they regarded the people of God as a whole. For example, when they celebrated the festivals they were to do it as if they had been there in the beginning ("he delivered us from Egypt"). And so now they acknowledge that they are one in guilt and one in punishment with their ancestors.[52] Their confession had a familiar ring; they acknowledged that from the beginning they went astray. They admit that they have done wrong (for עָוֺן s.v. Ps. 32:5) and so are guilty (for רָשַׁע s. v. Ps. 1:1)."[53]

B. They identify with the sins of the nation when the LORD set them free (7–12).

The psalm begins the historical recollection of the ancestors in Egypt—and the way it is told suggests their part with them. Verse 7a refers to their experience prior to the exodus, and 7b to the exodus. They witnessed all the plagues and miracles that God did in Egypt, but gave them no thought (הִשְׂכִּילוּ; s.v. Ps. 36:4); they did not remember his many acts of love, and so rebelled by the sea. In spite of all the wonders they had seen, when faced with the crisis at the sea they were afraid and demonstrated a lack of faith. This verse then sets the tone for the entire psalm; the contrast will be between the LORD's wonderful works and abundant love and their indifference and rebellion, as incredible as that might seem.

In spite of their failure, he saved them (v. 8). Why? He did it for his name's sake and to make his power known. The reasons for God's mighty works are greater than we often imagine. He delivers his people in order to sanctify his name, that is, to preserve his reputation throughout the world (see also Ezek. 36:22–36). The Egyptians would see, and others hear, that his

---

52. Perowne, *Psalms,* II:260.
53. The verb is frequently translated as "we have acted wickedly." In that case the two verbs in the colon could be taken as a verbal hendiadys, "we have done wrong, we have acted wickedly," becoming something like "we have done exceedingly wickedly." But the verb has more of the sense of being guilty and so probably expresses the results of their sin.

power is greater than anything they claimed for their gods (Exod. 14:12). And Israel would see it as well, and hopefully strengthen their faith. And so in verses 9–11 the psalmist recalls the main features of the exodus, salvation to Israel and judgment to the Egyptians. It occurred by the LORD's rebuke (for גָּעַר s.v. Ps. 76:6) of the sea, a command of the LORD that brought immediate results. The pathway through the sea became as dry as the desert. The LORD led them through the depths "like a horse in an open field"—they did not stumble (Isa. 63:13). Thus he saved his people from the power of those who hated them (for שָׂנֵא s.v. Ps. 139:21), redeemed them (for גָּאַל s.v. Ps. 19:14) from their enemies. And that salvation brought death to their adversaries—no one survived who tried to follow the Israelites into the center of the sea.

Then they believed in his words and sang praises to him (v. 12; see Exodus 15:1–18). How could they not have believed after walking through that miracle (for "believed," וַיַּאֲמִינוּ s.v. Ps. 15:2)? The report that they believed now underscores their weak faith—they could not believe the LORD for his word, but believed only when they saw the results. Such a faith would not do well in the tests that lay ahead for them.

C. They identify with the failures of the ancestors when the LORD led them through on their journey (13–33).

Here we have the long record of Israel's sin in spite of God's marvelous works, and also necessitating further acts of God on their behalf. The main purpose for rehearsing these accounts is theological reflection. At every step of the journey, so to speak, the people forgot God and his wonders; but God had pity on them. In the process they also came to realize that the savior is liable to turn to be their judge.[54]

The first instance in their memory is the sin of craving (vv. 13–15). The people forgot (for שָׁכַח s.v. Ps. 103:2) God and did not wait for his plan, that is, his intention to meet their needs; instead, they craved food and water (see Exod. 15:22–25; 16:1–17:1;

---

54. Allen, *Psalms 101-150*, p. 71.

Num. 11; and Psalm 78:28–29). Desiring (אָוָה) food and water is not sinful by itself; but here they were consumed by their desire ("they craved a craving") and so rather than trust the LORD they put him to the test (נָסָה; s.v. Ps. 26:2). They did not believe his word; as Anderson explains, they wanted to dictate to God rather than trust him.[55]

So God gave them what they asked for, but he did it in a way that what they craved became a wasting disease upon them. Some commentators do not think "wasting disease" (רָזוֹן; see Isa. 10:16) fits the line; they suggest a slight change to "abundance" (מָזוֹן). But in the historical account when God sent the quail they gorged themselves so greedily that in the process many of them became ill and died. God could have provided for them so easily; but because of their attitude he used what they demanded to judge them.

The second episode concerns the sin of jealousy (vv. 16–18). The section refers to Numbers 16 and 17 and the rebellion of Korah, Dathan and Abiram and 250 of their group. They became envious (for קָנֵא s.v. Ps. 37:1) of Moses and Aaron, of their position as leaders and their closeness to the LORD. They not only wanted to be the leaders, but they also wanted to go back to Egypt. So God judged them: first, the earth opened up and swallowed the ring leaders and their group; then a fire burned among the rebels and the wicked were destroyed. God demanded trust from the people, not only for his provisions but also for his choice of leaders.

Third, there was the grave sin of idolatry with the golden calf (vv. 19–23). They made the calf in Horeb, or Sinai, and worshiped (וַיִּשְׁתַּחֲווּ; s.v. Ps. 96:6) a cast metal idol (Deut. 9:7–29). A man-made god! How foolish and how spiritually blind! They exchanged "their Glory," meaning the LORD ("their glorious one"; s.v. Ps. 19:1), for an image of a grass-eating bull—an animal dependent on the LORD's provision of food to survive (see Jer. 2:11). These actions are explained by verse 21: they forgot (s.v. Ps. 103:2) the God who saved them. They ceased to act faithfully in response to the great wonders he had done on their behalf; instead they became idolatrous and were almost destroyed.

---

55. *Psalms 73–150*, pp. 740.

Idolatry is that serious, because it denies the true nature of the God of revelation and salvation.[56] They chose to worship the creature rather than the creator (Rom. 1:18–22).

So God said he was going to destroy them (v. 23); but Moses stood in the breach to turn away his wrath from destroying them. Standing in the breach seems to be a military figure, describing someone who would stand in a gap or hole in a wall to fend off the foe, that is, he was someone who was willing to die so that others could escape. Through the intercessory prayer of Moses the destruction of the nation was prevented, so that only the ringleaders were destroyed.

Fourth, we have the costly unbelief of the nation at Kadesh Barnea (vv. 24–27). The psalm says they refused the pleasant land. This is a reference to the unbelief over the report of the spies (Num. 13:25–29). They refused it because they did not trust the word of the LORD to go and get it. They believed the negative report of the majority of the spies that taking the land was impossible; and they were not convinced by Joshua and Caleb that God was able to give them the land. So because they would not go when the LORD told them to go but only complained over his provision, they would never see the land. Verses 26 and 27 record the LORD's oath that he swore in his wrath (Ps. 95:8–11; Num. 14:3). The oath was directed to that generation, dooming them to live out their lives in the wilderness. But verse 27 expands the scope of the judgment of the divine oath against unbelief to the age of the exile—the descendants in the future would lose the land and be scattered throughout the lands. The point is because Israel forgot the LORD and did not act on his promises they forfeited the right to live in the land of promise.

In the fifth episode (vv. 28–31) the psalmist gives his attention to the rebellion of the nation on the steppes of Moab (Num. 25:3). On the verge of entering the promised land, the people defected, devoting themselves to Baal of Peor. There they ate sacrifices offered to dead things (וְזִבְחֵי מֵתִים) either meaning to false gods or for some funerary cult. It was this text, based on this event, that led to the later prohibition in Jewish literature not to eat things offered to idols (see in the Talmud, *Avodah*

---

56. VanGemeren, *Psalms*, p. 785.

Zarah 29b; see also 1 Cor. 10:28–29). In Numbers their corruption went beyond yoking themselves to Baal by ritual sacrifice to engaging in open fornication. So a plague broke out in the camp (Num. 25:8–9), and many died. The plague was stopped when Phinehas killed the Israelite and the Midianite woman engaged in a sexual act (Num. 25:7–8). The text says he intervened (וַיְפַלֵּל); the verb (פָּלַל) has the idea of mediate, arbitrate; and in this (*hithpael*) stem, intervene or intercede.[57] Phinehas was the one who arbitrated between the sinful people and the LORD and stopped the catastrophe. The act was ever after this credited to him as a righteous act—he stopped the plague and the immorality, preventing the destruction of the people of God at the entrance to the land.

In verses 32–33 we have the last report from the time of the wandering. It is the rebellion at Meribah when Moses had to bring water from the rock for the rebellious people. The sin of the people provoked the LORD to anger and ensured their death in the desert (Ps. 95:10–11). But the psalmist focuses on the effect it had on Moses: trouble came to Moses because of them. When Moses was instructed to bring water from the rock, he became angry and used harsh words against the people, calling them rebels and claiming to be the one who could bring water from the rock. All of his actions to produce water failed to bring about true faith in the people and did not sanctify the LORD in their eyes (Num. 20:8–13). So Moses was not permitted to enter the promised land. Verse 33 explains that the people "rebelled against his spirit." Some commentators take this as a reference to the Spirit of God. Perowne, e.g., argues for this;[58] see also Isa. 63:10 and Ps. 78:40. This is certainly a plausible interpretation with good support. Others suggest that it is Moses' spirit, and this makes the best sense in the verse.[59] Arguing that the verb "defy" does not fit very well here, some choose to follow the reading in the Greek text and slightly change the vowels in the Hebrew verb: "they had made his spirit bitter." In either case the result was that harsh words came from his mouth.

---

57. E. A. Speiser, "The Stem *PLL* in Hebrew," *JBL* 82 (1963):301–6.
58. *Psalms*, II:265.
59. Allen, *Psalms 101-150*, p. 73.

God's Great and Gracious Acts for His Rebellious People

D. They identify with their ancestors unfaithfulness when they settled in the midst of pagans (34–46).

1. The defilement of pagan idolatry (34–39).

Now the survey gives attention to the sins of the ancestors in the land of Canaan. First, they failed to destroy the Canaanites as the LORD had commanded (Judg. 1:18–36 and 2:1–3); and failing to do this meant the danger remained. So they quickly mingled with the pagans (Judg. 3:5–6) and learned their practices (Judg. 2:16–19). The false belief quickly led to corrupt practices: they served the pagan idols and sacrificed their children to demons (שֵׁדִים may be related to Akkadian *šēdu,* subordinate spirits with powers for good or evil). It is hard to imagine how quickly the Israelites embraced these horrible sins of idolatry and murder of the innocent in the name of religion. But they did, and as a result they defiled the land with the shedding of innocent blood (v. 38) and became unclean themselves (v. 39). By following the pagan ways in their religious observances they were unfaithful to the LORD—or as the psalm puts it, they prostituted themselves (זָנָה; see Hos. 2:2–13). This expression could be metaphorical for their unfaithfulness to the LORD; but it is likely saying more than that, for pagan religion did involve fornication in Canaanite places of worship. This was not just a primitive stage in history for what the ancestors did, their descendants did the same and more so, and as a result forfeited their right to the promised land.

2. The judgment on the corrupt people (40–43).

Because of these serious rebellious acts of the nation, the LORD was angry and abhorred (for תָּעַב, s.v. Ps. 14:1) them; they were just as displeasing to him as the Canaanites were. So he gave them into the power of other nations who ruled over them and oppressed them. These verses could refer to any number of experience in the history from the period of the judges down to the exile. The psalm seems to focus on the period of the Judges as a prophetic warning for the nation, because verse 43 summarizes this material by saying that the LORD would deliver them many times, but they persisted in their rebellions and sank deeper into sin (see for example, Judg. 2:18–19).

3. *The compassion of the LORD (44–46).*

But God took note of their distress when he listened to their cry (v. 44—as he had done in Exodus 2:24). As a result he remembered (s.v. Ps. 6:5) his covenant for their sake and relented of his judgment (inspired by passages like Judg. 3:9). God's covenant love for his own restrains his judgment on sin. There was judgment—invasion of the land, foreign control, and oppression of the people—both in the time of the judges and in the last, dark days of the nation on the eve of the exile. But there was deliverance as well: he heard their cries and remembered his covenant and relented (וַיִּנָּחֵם ; s.v. Ps. 119:76) of the evil he had sworn to bring on them. He even caused them to be pitied before the nations.

III. Confessing believers continue to pray for deliverance from their troubles so that they might glory in and praise his holy name (47).

The prayer at the end of the psalm provides us with a window into the occasion for this psalm: the psalmist, on behalf of the nation, prays for the LORD to gather them from the nations so that they may give thanks to God and glory in his praise.

Benediction: The LORD is to be blessed enthusiastically (48).

MESSAGE AND APPLICATION

The psalm gives praise to the LORD for his wonderful works for his people, but the praise is surrounded by the darkness—guilt and judgment seem to overshadow the praise. In the end, praise for God's wonders turns into a review of human failure. The testimony of God's faithfulness and mercy in Psalm 106 is reflected in Luke 1:68f., but it must be read with Romans 11:22 and 1 Corinthians 10:11.[60] It is important for believers to remember that when praising God for his glorious acts they also

---

60. Kraus, *Psalms 60–150*, p. 322.

account for the needs of those acts, the sins of the people. The expository idea could be worded in a number of ways, but this one may serve the purpose: *When believers acknowledge the way that God redeems his people, provides for them and takes them to the promised land in fulfillment of the covenant promises, they must also confess that the need for his great acts was the sinfulness of the people—as well as their own sinfulness.* They must correlate divine intervention with the human need for salvation. Then the grace and love of God will be better understood. He forgives and restores his people for his name's sake and for his glory. As the apostle Paul said to the young Timothy, even if we are unfaithful, he remains faithful because he cannot deny himself (2 Tim. 2:13). The praise of God must be a regular part of the believer's life; but praise must include an acknowledgment of sin. We may look to the cross and glory in Christ's victory over sin and death; but we know it was for our sins that he did it.

PSALM 107

Praise from the Redeemed of the LORD for His Loving Care

INTRODUCTION

Text and Textual Variants[1]

1 Give thanks to the LORD, for he is good;
  his loyal love endures forever.
2 Let the redeemed of the LORD say *this* –
  those he redeemed from the hand of the adversary,
3 and those he gathered from *the* lands,
  from east and from west, from[2] north and overseas.[3]
4 They wandered in the desert wastelands
  and found no way to a city where they could settle.[4]

---

1. The expression "Praise the LORD" that ends Psalm 106 is put here at the beginning of Psalm 107 in the Greek version.
2. The Greek and Syriac versions have "and" here.
3. "Overseas" is the translation given by Allen (*Psalms 101–150*, p. 81); the Hebrew text simply says "from sea." Others translate it "from south" to fill out the directions.
4. This translation is a little interpretive; the Hebrew says "a city of habitation" (מוֹשָׁב, a settlement).

PSALM 107

  5 They were hungry, also thirsty,
     and their life[5] fainted away.
  6 Then they cried to the LORD in their trouble;
     and[6] from their distress he delivered them.
  7 He led them by a straight way
     to go to a city where they could settle.
  8 Let them give thanks to the LORD for his loyal love
     and his wonderful works before humankind,
  9 for he satisfies the thirsty[7]
     and fills the hungry with good things,
10 people who sat in darkness and death's shadow,
     prisoners in affliction and in iron,
11 for they had rebelled[8] against the words of God
     and despised the counsel of the Most High.
12 So he wore them down[9] with hard labor;
     they stumbled,[10] and there was no helper.
13 So they cried to the LORD in their anguish,
     and[11] he saved them from their distress.
14 He brought them out of darkness and death's shadow
     and broke away their chains.
15 Let them give thanks to the LORD for his loyal love
     and his wonderful works for humankind,
16 for he breaks down gates of bronze
     and cuts through bars or iron.

17 *Some became* fools[12] because of their rebellious ways

---

5. The Hebrew is נַפְשָׁם בָּהֶם, "their life within them," meaning their inner vitality and spirit.
6. The conjunction is not in the MT; it is in a few manuscripts and the Greek.
7. The Hebrew expression uses the word נֶפֶשׁ, "life, soul" (נֶפֶשׁ שֹׁקֵקָה, "the thirsty), and the same kind of construction for "the hungry." The Greek version rendered it, "he fed an empty soul," ψυχὴν κενὴν.
8. For MT's הִמְרוּ the Greek version uses παρεπίκραναν, "they embittered."
9. The verb in the text is in the active voice, וַיַּכְנַע, "he subjected them, forced them down"; but in the Greek version it is passive, "and they were brought low," ἐταπεινώθη (= וַיִּכָּנַע, the *niphal*).
10. The Greek has "they became weak," ἠσθένησαν.
11. The conjunction is in a few manuscripts and the Greek; see verse 6.
12. For MT's "fools," אֱוִלִים, the Greek translation has "he aided them (ἀντελάβετο αὐτῶν = עֲזָרָם) from their rebellions." Many commentators

Praise from the Redeemed of the LORD for His Loving Care

and because of their iniquities they suffered affliction.[13]
18 They loathed all food
    and drew near the gates of death.
19 Then they cried to the LORD in their trouble,
    and he saved them from their anguish.
20 He sent forth his word and healed them;
    and so he rescued them from the pit.[14]
21 [15]Let them give thanks to the LORD for his loyal love
    and his wonderful works before humankind.
22 Let them sacrifice sacrifices of praise
    and recount his works with songs of joy.

23 Others went out[16] on the sea in ships;
    they were doing business on the mighty waters.
24 They saw the deeds[17] of the LORD
    and his wonderful works in the deep.
25 For he spoke and stirred up[18] a tempest
    that lifted high[19] its waves.
26 They mounted up to the sky, they[20] went down to the depths;

---

    follow the suggested emendation to חוֹלִים, "sick." But the change is not necessary.
13. The Hebrew has "suffered affliction," יִתְעַנּוּ; the Greek has "they were brought low," ἐταπεινώθησαν.
14. The Hebrew word is מִשְּׁחִיתוֹתָם, "from their pit(s)," but means "the grave." The Greek version took it to mean "their destruction," διαφθορῶν αὐτῶν. Allen suggests that it is an intensive plural of "pit" (*Psalms 101–150,* p. 83).
15. Verses 21–26 and verse 40 are bracketed in the text by the scribes with an inverted letter *nûn* (נ) to indicate the lines were transposed.
16. The verb is "went down" (see Jonah 1:3); it probably means to go and embark on sea journey.
17. A number of manuscripts have the singular.
18. The MT has וַיַּעֲמֵד, "and he caused to stand," meaning he brought into his use" the tempest. The Greek text has the tempest as the subject, and it happened, equivalent to the *qal* "and (it) stood."
19. Here too the Greek translation has a different subject: "its waves were raised on high," ὑψώθη, the equivalent of וַיָּרֹמוּ perhaps, instead if MT's וַתְּרוֹמֵם
20. The Greek and the Syriac have a conjunction here.

PSALM 107

      their courage[21] melted away in their peril.
27 They reeled and staggered like a drunken man;
      they were at their wits' end.[22]
28 Then they cried to the LORD in their trouble,
      and he brought them out of their anguish.
29 He silenced[23] the storm to a whisper;
      their waves[24] became quiet.
30 And they were glad when they grew calm
      when he guided them to their desired haven.
31 Let them give thanks to the LORD for his loyal love
      and his wonderful works before humankind;
32 and let them exalt him in *the* assembly of *the* people
      and praise him in the assembly[25] of the elders.

33 He made[26] rivers into a desert,
      flowing water into thirsty ground,
34 a fruitful land into a salt marsh,
      because of the wickedness of those who lived in it.
35 He made a desert into pools of water
      and a parched ground into flowing water;
36 and there he settled the hungry,
      and they founded a city where they could settle.
37 They sowed fields and planted vineyards
      and produced a fruitful harvest;
38 So he blessed them, and their numbers greatly increased,
      and he did not let their herds diminish.
39 Then they became few in number and were humbled

---

21. The form is נַפְשָׁם, "their soul, life, life force."
22. Literally: "their wisdom (i.e., skill as mariners) was swallowed up."
23. The text has יָקֵם, usually "to raise," but here "cause to stand," meaning cease from raging. The Greek version has "he commanded," ἐπέταξεν.
24. The text has "their waves/rollers" (גַּלֵּיהֶם). Because the suffix is plural leaving the referent in question, the Syriac has "the waves of the sea" instead of the suffix. Qumran has "the waves of their sea." Many modern translations follow this.
25. The word is מוֹשָׁב again, a "settlement, habitation, a sitting or dwelling place."
26. It is possible to interpret the verbs in verses 33–41 as timeless, expressing things that the LORD does frequently.

>   by oppression, calamity and sorrow;
> 40 he who pours contempt on nobles
>   made them wander in a trackless waste.[27]
> 41 But he lifted up the needy out of their affliction
>   and increased their families like flocks.
> 42 The upright see and rejoice,
>   but all wickedness shuts their mouths.
>
> 43 Whoever is wise, let him heed these things
>   and consider the loyal love of the LORD

Composition and Context

As the initial psalm of Book V, Psalm 107 calls for praise for the God who redeems people from their various conditions and crises. It has been classified differently because of its two main parts: verses 1–32 form a declarative praise or thanksgiving psalm, and verses 33–42 a wisdom psalm. This description may be sufficient for our concerns, but to unify the psalm we could call it a thanksgiving wisdom psalm. The psalm has a number of similarities with Psalms 105 and 106; they all include the suffering of the people, their turning to God, their deliverance, and their praise.[28]

Psalm 107 begins with the formulaic call to praise (v. 1) directed to the redeemed of the LORD (vv. 2–3). There follows then a lengthy report of the LORD's deliverance in various circumstances: travelers (vv. 4–9), released prisoners (vv. 10–16), recently healed people (vv. 17–22), and seafarers (vv. 23–33). The pattern followed is a report of the dilemma, prayer, details of deliverance, and finally communal thanksgiving with each group speaking out.[29] There is a double refrain in verses 6 and 8, 13

---

27. Some suggest that verses 39 and 40 should be reversed; that would mean verse 39 would be describing the nobles the LORD punished. It would give two verses concerning the wicked (39–40), and then two concerning the upright (41–42). It is not very compelling to change the order of the verses to form a preferred pattern.
28. The question has been raised whether the three were written by one author or not.
29. Anderson, *Psalms 73–150*, p. 749.

and 15, 19 and 21, and 28 and 31. The last part of the psalm, verses 33–42, is a concluding hymn on the theme of the providence of God.[30]

The origin and use of the psalm has been given a good deal of attention. Many commentators conclude that the psalm was post-exilic, identifying the redeemed of the LORD in verses 2 and 3 as the returned exiles from Babylon who were now taking part in the liturgical thanksgiving service in the sanctuary. The psalm follows the prayer in Psalm 106:47 for the LORD to gather the exiles from the nations; Psalm 107 would then be the thanksgiving for answering that prayer. This interpretation has been pressed even further with the idea that the situations covered in verses 4–32 describe the Israelites' journeys back to the land. Snaith says the psalm traces the Israelite experience from the wilderness to Canaan to the exile in Babylon where the nation was almost dead; but God regathered the "bones" (Ezek. 37) and brought the nation back from the four corners of the world. Within this section the storm at sea is interpreted as an allegory of Israel's return experience.[31] Others give the seafaring section a more literal meaning, taking it to refer to the return of Jews to the land from the diaspora by sea.[32] Allen's structure of the entire psalm shows how the psalm is geared for the returning exiles: the call for the redeemed (1–3), braving the return overland (4–9), freed from exile (10–16), healed from punishment for sin (17–22), braving the return by sea (23–32), enjoying God's control of life in the land (33–41), and call for reflection (42–43).

On the other hand, Kraus thinks that the psalm could be very old; the reference to the "diaspora" (if that is the best term for the Babylonian exile) in verse 3 would be a later amplification (similar to Isaiah 62:12) with the saved from the exile entering the celebration of praise in groups.[33] Anderson also allows that the psalm may be a pre-exilic composition adapted to the

---

30. See additionally J. Mejia, "Some Observations on Psalm 107," *BTB* 5 (1975):56–66.
31. N. H. Snaith, *Five Psalms* (London: Epworth Press, 1964), pp. 17–21.
32. Allen, *Psalms 101–150*, p. 90.
33. *Psalms 60–150*, p. 327.

needs of the restored people.[34] Allen too concludes that it is a repackaged psalm for a later generation.[35]

The detailed working out of the aspects of the return from captivity has not been received by everyone. Perowne concluded that the interpretation that the central part of the psalm illustrates the different ways the Jews journeyed home "can scarcely be maintained." He agrees that the Babylonian exile was uppermost in the mind of the writer in verses 2 and 3, but argues that it is unnatural to take all the experiences in this psalm as figurative or illustrative of the journey home. In particular, the allegorical explanation of the seafarers as the suffering of the people in exile is forced. Perowne concludes that the psalm is not a historical tracing of experiences, but a description of the many ways that God delivers his people from trouble.[36] This would not mean that the psalm had no relevance for the returning exiles; they would recall the ways the LORD had answered prayers and therefore strengthen their faith.

The Targum sought to link the episodes in the psalm with appropriate events; so as a preface to each section they state the connection: with verse 4 it says "concerning the house of Israel"; with verse 10, "concerning Zedekiah and the princes" who went into captivity and darkness; with verse 17, "concerning Hezekiah"; with verse 23, "concerning the sailors in Jonah," and with verse 33, "concerning the generation of Joel, son of Pethuel."

The interpretation of the cases that demonstrate the LORD's deliverance of people in need cannot be made that specific; the verses provide general descriptions of how great and varied the redemption of God is.

Exegetical Analysis

Summary

By portraying how the LORD delivers out of the barren wilderness, breaks the bonds of prisoners, restores the sick, and shows

---

34. *Psalms 73–150*, p. 749.
35. *Psalms 101–150*, p. 91.
36. *Psalms,* II:272.

his power to mariners in the sea, and by demonstrating God's providential government of the world, the psalmist motivates the redeemed to praise the LORD forever.

Outline

I. Call to praise: The psalmist calls the redeemed of the LORD to praise the LORD (1–3).
   A. The people should give thanks to the LORD for his loyal love which endures (1).
   B. Those who have been redeemed from all over the earth should praise him (2–3).
II. Cause for praise: The psalmist portrays the loyal love of the LORD by wonderful interventions (4–32):
   A. The LORD delivered out of the weary wilderness (4–9).
      1. They wandered wearily in the wilderness (4–5).
      2. They cried to God and he led them out (6–7).
      3. People should praise the LORD because he satisfies the hungry soul (8–9).
   B. The LORD delivered the rebellious prisoners out of their bonds (10–16).
      1. They were bound in prison darkness because they rebelled (10–12).
      2. They cried to God and he brought them out (13–14).
      3. People should praise the LORD because he broke the bonds (15–16).
   C. The LORD delivered the sick from the grave (17–22).
      1. Sinners were afflicted and near death (17–18).
      2. They cried to God and he brought them up from the pit (19–20).
      3. People should praise the LORD because of his work, and sacrifice to him (21–22).
   D. The LORD showed his marvelous works to those who work on the seas (23–32).
      1. The mariners who go down to the sea saw his works as he called up a storm (23–27).
      2. They cried to God and he stilled the storm (24–30).
      3. People should praise the LORD in the assembly of the righteous (31–32).

Praise from the Redeemed of the LORD for His Loving Care

III. Second cause for praise: The psalmist demonstrates the LORD's providential government of the world (33–43).
   A. The LORD can turn the fruitful land into a smitten land and the wilderness into a prosperous land (33–39).
      1. He turns the fruitful land into a smitten land and a salt marsh (33–34).
      2. He blesses the wilderness with increase and produce (35–38).
      3. He also turns the circumstances of people into oppression and sorrow (39).
   B. The LORD can reverse the fortunes of people (40–42).
      1. He brings down the princes and makes them wander aimlessly (40).
      2. He exalts the needy and blesses them so that the upright will rejoice (41–42).
   C. Conclusion: The wise will consider these things (43).

COMMENTARY IN EXPOSITORY FORM

I. The redeemed of the LORD must praise him for his everlasting loyal love (1–3).

Following the traditional call to give thanks (הוֹדוּ; s.v. Ps. 6:5) to the LORD for his goodness (טוֹב; s.v. Ps. 34:8) and his everlasting loyal love (חֶסֶד; s.v. Ps. 23:6), the psalmist focuses his call on the redeemed (גְּאוּלֵי; s.v. Ps. 19:14) of the LORD. The expression by itself could refer to anyone redeemed from any situation, for the word applies to both physical and spiritual deliverance in different circumstance. All the redeemed can share in giving thanks to the LORD for their particular redemption. But with the clarification of verse 3 that this redemption is of those gathered from distant lands, the writer likely has in mind the returning exiles (see Isa. 62:12). They had experienced great adversity in exile; but they were delivered by their redeemer. And according to the verse, they came from every direction: east, west, north, and–"sea." The word "sea" (יָם) is frequently emended to "right hand" (יָמִין), also meaning "south" (as one faces east in orientation). While that change may make the four directions complete, the reading of "sea" in the Hebrew Bible is supported by Isaiah 49:12.[37] The prophets did predict that in the great regathering people will come from "overseas" in fulfillment of the covenant promises. Whether that was partially fulfilled after the Babylonian captivity or awaits the final regathering at the end of the age is another but related issue.

II. The LORD's loyal love is displayed in the wonderful ways that he delivers people from their distressing and sinful conditions (4–32).

A. *He delivers his people from their displacement and deprivation (4–9).*

The first episode concerns journeying over land. The section begins with "they wandered" (תָּעוּ > תָּעָה); without an expressed subject it may be rendered "some wandered." The verb fits the wilderness wandering after the exodus better than the return of the exiles; the psalm may be using that experience as a prime example of God's protection for the traveler, albeit traveling in extreme conditions. The "desert wastelands" could literally mean the wilderness after Sinai; but if taken figuratively, it could describe the time of the exile, especially since the verb "wander" can be used in the Bible for a prolonged stay (see Ps. 95:10). But the normal sense would refer to traveling aimlessly, especially since the text says that they found no way to a place suitable for living (מוֹשָׁב), no city that was habitable. Along the way they were hungry and thirsty and completely exhausted.

But they cried to the LORD and he came to their assistance (vv. 6–7). When he heard their cry from their trouble (צַר; s.v. Ps. 120:1), he delivered them (יַצִּילֵם; s.v. Ps. 22:20). He did this by rescuing them in the way and leading them straight to a place where they could dwell. For this they should give thanks. Verses 6–7 ("they cried . . . and he delivered them") and verses 8–9 ("Let them give thanks . . . for he satisfies") form a refrain that will be used several times in the psalm, but with variations in the explanation of the reasons for the praise. The point of verses 6–9 is that God hears prayer, delivers people from their trouble,

---

37. See also J. Jarick, "The Four Corners of Psalm 107," *CBQ* 59 (1997):270–87.

and blesses them—here specifically he makes the way straight to the inhabitable city and cares for them along the way (see Jer. 31:25; Luke 1:53). The praise for this should therefore emphasize his faithful covenant love (חֶסֶד; s.v. Ps. 23:6) and his wonderful works (נִפְלָאוֹת; s.v. Ps. 139:5). These wonderful works of the LORD were not done for Israel alone, for they were revealed before all mankind (אָדָם; v. 8).

B. He delivers his people from their bondage due to sin (10–16).

Now the psalmist focuses on the suffering of his people in bondage or captivity. They sat in darkness as prisoners in affliction and in iron (v. 10). The "darkness" (חֹשֶׁךְ) is forcefully worded with the familiar "shadow of death" (צַלְמָוֶת), meaning as dark as death or the deepest darkness. The Targum associated this description with King Zedekiah who was afflicted in exile; but the Israelites on the whole did not experience this. Some dwelt in darkness (Isa. 42:7) in the exile; whether that means in some dark prison with chains or in spiritual ignorance is hard to say, although the latter would fit the exile better (see Isa. 61:1–3, where the LORD's anointed sets the prisoners free among other things). But it is safe to say that their time in Babylon was not pleasant; as VanGemeren says, they found out what life was like without the love of the LORD.[38] After all, they were in that situation because they rebelled (הִמְרוּ) against the words of God and despised his counsel. He is the Most High God; all the authority is his. So when they rebelled against his authority, it proved to be costly. The LORD broke down their spirit or will ("their heart") with bitter labor; and when they grew weak and faltered they had no helper (עֹזֵר; s.v. Ps. 46:1)—no one who could do for them what they could not do themselves—i.e., set themselves free.

The refrain appears again in verse 13: they cried to the LORD in their distress and he saved them from their trouble (now "saved," יוֹשִׁיעֵם; s.v. Ps. 3:2). This salvation, or deliverance, is explained in verse 14: he brought them out of darkness and broke their chains. If this is referring to the nation as a whole,

---

38. *Psalms*, p. 798.

then the language is figurative, hyperbolic even, suggesting that they were existing in captivity as if the darkness of death was hovering over them while they were chained.[39] They were not free; and they were waiting to die. The other part of the refrain is a call to praise God for his loyal love and wonderful works (v. 15), which is explained in verse 16–he breaks through bronze gates and iron bars, symbolic of delivering people (see Isa. 45:2).

C. He delivers his people from folly and self destruction (17–22).

Some became fools (אֱוִלִים) because of rebellious ways. The idea is unexpected here, and so one suggestion is to emend the text to read "sick" (חוֹלִים) to parallel the second colon. But "fools" fits the passage well enough and offers a clear indictment of people who chose to rebel against God and ended up suffering affliction—they were fools to rebel and go their own way (see Prov. 1:7). All they accomplished was to draw closer to the grave. Verse 18 says that in their affliction they lost their appetite and so loathed food, and that is what brought them to the brink of death. The "gates of death" refers poetically to entrance into death itself as if it was a prison.

Verse 19 repeats the refrain. Again they cried to the LORD in their trouble and he saved them. He did this by sending his word and healing (רָפָא; s.v. Ps. 30:5) them and rescuing (מָלַט; s.v. Ps. 41:1) them from the pit (meaning the grave). The "word" of the LORD is personified as a messenger; God sent forth his word, probably an "oracle of salvation," and it was fully able to succeed (see Isa. 55:11; and John 1:1). It was this same word of God that they had refused to believe and had rebelled against; but it now became salvation and comfort to them. So the refrain ends with the call to praise—and here with additional call to sacrifice sacrifices of praise (זִבְחֵי תוֹדָה). To do this they would stand

---

39. In Psalm 2 we have a similar use of the figurative description: the kings of the earth resolve to break free from the chains and fetters with which they were bound by the king of Israel. If they were literally chained, they could not rebel, not even conspire. They were held in check by the power of the king and not free to act.

at the altar and while the animal was roasting on the fire for the communal meal tell everyone what God had done for them.

D. He delivers his people from the dangers of nature (23–32).

In verses 23–32 the psalmist focuses on sea-faring merchants. Such travel was not a major part of Israelite life; and it does not seem to describe the returning exiles. Perhaps in the great regathering at the end of the age there will be such a flow of people from all places. Here the attention is given to the sea-faring trade to show the majesty of the creator. With the ease of a command the LORD raises a fierce storm. The mariners on board very quickly lose their courage and control. Like drunken men they stagger along the deck; and they are at their wits' end (literally, their "wisdom" or "skill" [חָכְמָה; s.v. Ps. 19:7] was nullified by the LORD's storm at sea).

This is followed by the refrain (v. 28): they cried to the LORD again and he delivered them from their trouble. He silenced the storm so that the waves stood still. The mariners were delighted in the calm and made way for the harbor. For this they should praise the LORD in the assembly (vv. 31–32) for his faithful love and amazing wonders.

III. The LORD's loyal love is displayed in his providential governing of the world (33–43).

A. He changes the fruitful land into desert and the desert into a prosperous land (33–39).

The second part of the psalm is a wisdom psalm that lays out different ways that the providence of God is displayed. The first two verses (33–34) declare that as a punishment for sin the LORD has the power to change things: rivers into a desert, flowing water into a dry and thirsty land, and a fruitful land into a salt marsh. The wicked may think they are safe in their rebellion, but they soon discover that their good land has become a waste land. On the other hand, as a blessing for the righteous, the LORD can turn the desert into pools of water and flowing streams (v. 25). The righteous may be faced with obstacles, but that never hindered the LORD. So in verses 36–38 the psalmist explains how the LORD settled the hungry in this good land he was providing with water. There they founded a city that they could inhabit; there they sowed the fields and produced a harvest. Thus he blessed them with the good life, and their numbers increased while the number of their animals did not decrease. These verses may be compared to Isaiah 55:1–2, which calls for the exiles to return to the land where, rather than buying their supplies for money (as in Babylon), they could live off their own land that the LORD blessed. So we see the providential dealings of the LORD, who is the creator, after all: he can change nature in line with his blessing for righteousness or punishment for sin.

B. He reverses the fortunes of people (39–42).

After telling how the LORD can change nature for the detriment or benefit of people, he now tells how the LORD changes people. Verse 39 describes the divine discipline given to the people for their failures (unless the verse is transposed with verse 40 and then describes corrupt leaders). Rather than flourish under God's blessing, they became few in number and were humbled by God's judgment so that they had to endure oppression, calamity and sorrow. And as for the nobles, the LORD pours contempt (בּוּז; s.v. Ps. 22:6) on them, making them wander aimlessly (תָּעָה again). The nobles, or princes, are "men of rank" in Israel; this could include the last two kings of Judah, among other nobles, who were taken in disgrace to Babylon. They had contempt for God's word, and so God poured contempt on them—they wandered without their authority or their respect.

On the other hand, the LORD lifts the needy out of their affliction and raises them on high (vv. 41–42). The "needy" are contrasted with the wicked, and are the objects of God's favor, so the psalmist has the believers in mind. The verb "lifted" (שָׂגַב) means to be "inaccessibly high"; it is often used figuratively for security and protection in the LORD—out of reach of the enemy. But it is not limited here to protection; it describes their rescue and the blessing of their families and flocks. The upright will see this transition and rejoice, while the wicked (wickedness) will shut their mouths.

C. The wise will consider the ways of God (43).

The natural conclusion to draw from all this is that if people are wise (חָכָם), they should heed (שָׁמַר; s.v. Ps. 12:7) these things and consider the loyal love of the LORD. The fools rage against the LORD, but the wise take all these things to heart. Those who are wise, according to Proverbs, are people who believe in the LORD, fear (worship and obey) the LORD, and lives a life that is characterized by righteousness, justice, and equity (Prov. 1:1–7).

MESSAGE AND APPLICATION

A psalm like this is rather easy to develop into an exposition. It is a call for the redeemed to praise the LORD. And the reason for their praise is inspired by recalling all the marvelous works of the LORD in answer to their prayers. In whatever situation the people of God might have found themselves, they could always cry out to the LORD, knowing that he would answer them because of his faithful love for them. The episodes that are traced here may have been written to describe the difficulties of the returning exiles; but they are written in a more general way to describe the many different ways that the LORD has redeemed his covenant people. The episodes could be used as categories to allow people to identify with the people who cried out to the LORD, and to praise the LORD for what he has done for people in biblical history as well as for them today. Prayer and praise will be strengthened the more people reflect on the wonderful works of redemption by the LORD. One way to express a summary expository idea is this: *The redeemed of the LORD—those who have been delivered from futile wandering, set free from bondage, restored to health, brought through many dangers, and enjoyed the blessing of God who can change life's circumstances—would be wise to consider all of God's ways and then praise him forever.*

The primary application will be to offer praise in the assembly for all the wonderful works the LORD has done through the ages to redeem and take care of his people. But that instruction assumes another, based on the fact that those wonderful works were in answer to the cries of needy people. And so a second application will be to pray to the LORD from any need; and that prayer will be made with confidence if people know what God is able to do—what he has done for countless others. The exposition can easily include references to biblical stories that illustrate each of the categories covered by the psalm.

PSALM 108

Victory through God's Faithful Love

INTRODUCTION

Text and Textual Variants

A Song. A Psalm of David.

1 O God, my heart is steadfast;[1]
  I will sing and give praise, even[2] *with* my glory.
2 Awake, lute and harp!
  I will awaken the dawn.
3 I will praise you, O LORD,[3] among the nations,
  and[4] I will sing praises to you among the peoples.
4 For your loyal love *is* great above[5] the heavens,
  and your truth *reaches* to the clouds.
5 Be exalted, O God, above the heavens,
  and[6] your glory above all the earth;

---

1. In Psalm 57:7[8] the expression is repeated.
2. MT has אַף; Greek has "in my glory." Psalm 57:8[9], "awake."
3. Psalm 57:9[10] has "Lord" instead of the holy name.
4. There is no conjunction in Psalm 57:9[10] and in a few manuscripts here.
5. Here the MT has עַל, but Psalm 57:10[11] has עַד.
6. There is no conjunction in Psalm 57:11[12].

6 that your beloved may be delivered,
>   save *with* your right hand and answer me.

7 God has spoken in his holiness:
>   "I will rejoice;[7]
>   I will divide Shechem
>   and measure out the Valley of Succoth.
8 Gilead is mine; Manasseh[8] is mine;
>   Ephraim also is the helmet for my head;
>   Judah is my lawgiver.
9 Moab is my washpot;
>   over Edom I will cast my shoe;
>   over Philistia I will triumph."[9]

10 Who will bring me *into* the fortified[10] city?
>   Who has guided me to Edom?
11 Is it not *you*,[11] O God, *who* spurned us?
>   And *you*, O God, who do not go out with our armies?
12 Give us help from *the* adversary,
>   for the deliverance of man is vain.
13 Through God we will do valiantly,
>   And he will trample our enemies.

Composition and Context

Psalm 108 joins two sections from previous psalms, Psalm 57 and Psalm 60. Both of those psalms had the superscription attributing the work to David. But that does not mean that David put these parts together here. A later poet may have

---

7. The Greek text has "I will be exalted," ὑψωθήσομαι; this may reflect a division of the Hebrew word אֶעְלֹזָה into אַעַל־זֶה. Or, it might simply be an interpretation.
8. Psalm 60:7[9] has a conjunction with this second clause.
9. Psalm 60:8[10] has "because of me, Philistia, rejoice." The editors of BHS suggested changing Psalm 60 to match Psalm 108; but the Greek version changes 108 to read with 60.
10. For MT's מִבְצָר most manuscripts read with Psalm 60:9[11], מָצוֹר.
11. Psalm 60:10[12] has the pronoun "you," and so here a few manuscripts and versions include it.

adapted the material to fit his circumstances in facing regional conflicts; he prays for God's deliverance. The need to praise the LORD, and the assurance of the oracles of God, are timeless in their meaning, whether for the compiler of Psalm 108 or for subsequent believers who face opposition. The commentary below is a simplified treatment of the basic ideas; for the more detailed discussion of the texts, see Psalm 57 and Psalm 60 themselves.

Exegetical Analysis

Summary

Singing a song of triumph to the LORD's loyal love in the expectation that his enemies will be destroyed, the psalmist is convinced that God will exult in the subjugation of nations and so calls on the LORD for leadership since man is weak and vain.

Outline

I. The psalmist sings his song of triumph to God's loyal love and truth in the expectation his enemies will be destroyed and God exalted (1–6).
  A. He vows to sing his triumphant song of victory to God's loyal love and truth (1–4).
    1. David is determined to sing praises (1).
    2. David vows to awake and sing to the LORD (2–3).
    3. David will praise his loyal love and truth (4).
  B. He expresses his desire for God to be exalted over the earth so that the beloved may be delivered (5–6).
    1. God should be exalted above the earth (5).
    2. The beloved should be saved (6).
II. The psalmist reiterates the promise of God that he would exult in the subjugation of the tribes of the earth (7–9).
  A. God exults because both the land and the tribes of Israel are his (7–8).
  B. God promises to subjugate Moab, Edom and Philistia (9).
III. After discovering the necessity of the LORD's leadership, the psalmist prays for help against the adversaries in the absolute confidence that he will tread them down (10–13).

A. By rhetorical questions he demonstrates the necessity of the leadership of the LORD (10–11).
B. He petitions the LORD for help since human deliverance is vain (12).
C. He concludes in absolute confidence that God will tread down their adversaries (13).

COMMENTARY IN EXPOSITORY FORM

I. The righteous who remain steadfast in their faith sing praises to God's faithful love in the expectation of the removal of evil and with the desire for God to be exalted over all the earth (1–6).

A. *They are resolved to praise God for his faithful love (1–4).*

In verses 1–4 we have the resolution of the psalmist to sing praises to God for his faithful covenant love. He begins with an affirmation of his loyalty to God: "O God, my heart is steadfast," which means that he is firmly established in his faith so that his affections and actions are loyal to God. Such unwavering faith means that no circumstances could disturb his trust in God.

Accordingly, he vows to sing praises. The first verb indicates that he will sing his praise to God, which is clearly a celebration of victory, and the second indicates he will sing praises or make melody in his praises. His praise will be no simple word of thanks, but a celebration in the sanctuary.

Verse 2 varies the vow with the exhortation, "Awake lute and harp" and then resumes his vow, "I will awaken the dawn." He calls for the musical instruments to awaken, as if they had been sleeping and needed to become active (a personification). And in the parallel colon he says that he will awaken the dawn. The dawn, the time just before the sunrise, was normally what would awaken people to a new day, but here the psalmist will awaken the dawn. He will arise before the dawn and it will appear that his singing praises will stir the dawn to a new day. The entire verse energizes the vow of praise with its eagerness and enthusiasm for bringing to life those things that have too long been silent and by offering praise early.

And this praise will be not only to the glory of God but for the benefit of the nations. And so verse 3 says, "I will acknowledge you among the nations, O Lord, I will sing praises to you among the peoples." The psalmist would normally plan to go to the sanctuary and praise God in the midst of the congregation. But here he has a much wider audience in mind, all peoples and nations. Verse 4 gives the central theme of the praise and the basis for his salvation: the faithful love of God. The psalmist fully anticipates that God will save him, and so here he praises the LORD by saying that there is no limit to his faithful love.

B. They express their desire for God to be exalted over all the earth (5–6).

The section ends with an appeal for God to be exalted above the heavens, and his glory above the earth. It is a call for God to act in such a way that all the earth will attest to his majesty. His exaltation will reflect his mighty works displayed for all to see, especially when he delivers his people from adversaries. So he prays for God to answer the prayer so that God's beloved may be delivered.

II. In praying for deliverance from adversaries, the righteous may find encouragement from the guarantees of God's word (7–12).

A. The oracle of God guarantees the security and success of God's people in adversity (7–8).

These next verses record an oracle of God in which by a bold figure God speaks as an earthly warrior and as a leader—he is the king. The oracle is introduced with the formula: "God has spoken in his holiness." The sure promise is from the holy God; it is not a human wish or word of encouragement. If in the psalm the speaker is the psalmist, then he is simply declaring the oracle God gave to him. And the oracle confirms the promises of God established from the time of the conquest. The oracle was most likely an old oracle from God that was applied to a present crisis. It may have had reference to material found in passages like Genesis 49, Numbers 24, and Deuteronomy 33 because it refers to the conquest and distribution of the land. The use of the oracle at later times (both in Psalm 60 and here in Psalm 108) simply applies the declaration God made for the settlement of the land. The meaning would have been timeless—every time the nation's stability and possession of the land was threatened the people would be reminded of God's oracle for victory.

It is an oracle of triumph, as the first word indicates: "I will exult" fits the portrayal of God as a victor who has won the land. Now he will distribute it to his people. He says, "I will divide Shechem, and I will measure out the Valley of Succoth." The two verbs are appropriate for the division of the land into inheritances for the people. Shechem and Succoth represent Israelite territory on both sides of the Jordan, Shechem in the land (40 miles north of Jerusalem) and Succoth in transJordan. The names are best known from the patriarchal history, for Jacob first came to Succoth, and then settled in Shechem. They were meant to represent the allotment of the entire land as an inheritance for Israel. Because the settlement in the land was a fulfillment of the promises to the fathers, anytime the land was invaded—or lost—the people would be reminded of God's word.

In verse 8 the LORD announces that Gilead and Manasseh belong to him, as well as Ephraim and Judah. The point is that he owns the land—and this means he has the right to allocate it to whomever he wants. Gilead was the region in transJordan, roughly between the rivers Arnon on the south and Yarmuk on the north. It was allocated to the Israelite tribes of Reuben, Gad and half of Manasseh. The rest of the tribe of Manasseh settled on the west of the Jordan River in the north part of the hill country. Judah, of course, is in the south, and always identified with the Davidic dynasty and judicial authority. Ephraim is the name of the central part of the country north of Jerusalem. It became one of the names used for the kingdom of Israel that was later centered in Samaria. Here it is called "the helmet (defense) of my head." The image indicates that since Judah was the center of the kingdom it was the head, and the northern part of the country was its defense against invasion. Ephraim was to the state what a helmet was to a warrior.

By selecting these representative sections, the psalmist was recalling the ancient allotments of the land by the LORD in order to reiterate the fact that the land belonged to the triumphant Lord; and in his rejoicing he delighted in allocating the land to his people.

B. The oracle of God guarantees the subjugation of nations to him (9).

In the last part of the oracle the psalmist describes the expansion of the kingdom over surrounding states, Moab, Edom, and Philistia. These were states that gave Israel so much trouble during the times of the judges and throughout the early part of the monarchy, but they belonged to the LORD. These countries were never fully incorporated into Israel; they were merely subjugated and controlled. David reduced their power and kept them under control. But the prophets foresaw a time when the monarchy would be restored and the nations part of the kingdom (see Amos 9:12; Isa. 11:13–14; Zeph. 2:4ff., and Zech. 9:7).

Moab is described as a vessel for washing; it may refer to washing the feet, but in any case it is a metaphor signifying a servant coming with a pot for washing. Moab is a servant, living in bondage to the LORD and his kingdom. Then "upon Edom I cast my shoe." This points to the servitude of Edom as well, in the sense of a warrior casting his shoes to the slave to have them cleaned. Then triumph over Philistia is announced. In Psalm 60 Philistia is called on to shout. That passage may be irony in which the LORD was saying, "shout all you want, but the triumph is mine"; or it could refer to forced homage. Ultimately the line in Psalm 60 harmonizes with Psalm 108:10 in which the LORD says "over Philistia I shout in triumph" because that land is subjugated.

III. In praying for God to deliver them from their distress, the righteous may anticipate the fulfillment of the promises when the LORD leads them to victory (10–13).

A. *The promises of God will be fulfilled when he leads his people to their promised victory (10–11).*

The psalmist now will pray with confidence for victory over the oppressors, a prayer that is based on the oracle of God. It seems that the nation was planning an attack into Edom, and so applied the ancient oracle to the present situation. But the first two verses of the section raise the question of how it can be done. Verse 10 begins with the question, "Who will conduct me into the fortified city? Who has guided me unto Edom?" The parallelism locates the city in Edom; it is unclear which city is intended, but it may be meant as a general reference to the fortified cities. The major difficulty of the verse is the relationship between the two halves. They both begin with "who," and while it is possible that these could be expressing his wish ("O that someone would lead me"), the change in tenses from the imperfect to the perfect in the two parts indicates otherwise. It makes more sense to see the first half as the question, "Who will conduct me into the fortified city?"; and the second half as the answer, "who (i.e., the one who) has guided me to Edom?"—the LORD of course.

The conquest of Edom would have been possible only if the LORD enabled them to do it. But the problem is that the LORD seems to have spurned them: "Is it not you, O God, who spurned us? And you, O God, do not go out with our armies." The question is rhetorical—it is the LORD who spurned them who can guide them into the fortified city. So here is the psalmist's dilemma.

B. *The people of God must acknowledge that their need for divine intervention is total (12).*

The prayer, then, is straightforward: "Give us help from the adversary." It asks for the LORD to intervene fully, for the word "help" indicates that they cannot possibly gain the victory without him. The word is figurative for the intended result of the help, victory (a metonymy of cause) over the adversary. And the reason they need God's intervention is explained in the parallel clause, "the deliverance of man [the deliverance man can provide] is vain"—it is worthless. So it is vain to trust in man for deliverance (see Ps. 33:16–17. In spite of the fact that God seems to have spurned them, they pray to him out of desperation for victory as they mounted the attack—and they were confident of the answer because they were relying on the oracle of God.

C. The power of God will give the people of God the victory over their adversaries (13).

Because they had the oracle of God, they knew that their prayer was right and that the LORD would answer them. So the last verse of the psalm expresses that certainty: "In God we will do valiantly." Without God they would fail; but with God's help they will win—valiantly. And the second colon illustrates just how successful they would be: the LORD "will trample our oppressors." The emphatic beginning of the clause, "and he" (וְהוּא) keeps the readers attention on the LORD—he is pictured as a warrior trampling the enemy under foot (the figure is a bold anthropomorphism to signify the complete defeat of the enemies), probably meaning that he will enable them to do it.

MESSAGE AND APPLICATION

For the expository idea and suggested applications for each section, see the two psalms themselves. In the way that the parts have been joined here, we could simply unite the major ideas in this way: *Because God's word guarantees it, those who are steadfast in the faith may be confident that God's faithful love will deliver them from the adversary so that the LORD will be exalted over all the world.*

PSALM 109

Divine Vengeance and Vindication

INTRODUCTION

Text and Textual Variations

For the chief musician. A psalm of David.

1 O God of[1] my praise, do not be silent![2]
2 For a wicked and a deceitful mouth have they opened[3]
    against me;
   they have spoken against me with a lying tongue.

3 With words of hatred they surround me,
    and fight against me without a cause.

---

1. A few manuscripts, the Syriac and Targum have "God" (אֱלֹהִים) and not the construct form.
2. The line in the Greek version reads, "do not pass over (μὴ παρασιωπήσῃς) my praise in silence."
3. The Greek version makes this passive, but that is not necessarily a textual variant since there is no definite subject in the verse.

4 In return for my friendship they are adversaries[4] to me,
    but as for me—prayer.[5]
5 They have repaid me evil for good,
    and hatred for my love.

6 Appoint a wicked man over him,
    and let an adversary stand at his right hand.
7 When he is tried let him go out condemned,
    and let his appeal fail.
8 May his days be few;
    and may another take his position of leadership.
9 May his children be orphans
    and his wife a widow.
10 May his children wander about and beg[6]
    and ask,[7] from their ruined houses.
11 May a creditor seize[8] all that he has;
    and may strangers plunder his earnings.
12 May there be no one to extend kindness to him;
    neither let his fatherless children have any to show *them* favor.
13 Let his descendants be cut off;
    may their name be blotted out in the next[9] generation.
14 May the iniquity of his fathers be remembered before the LORD;
    and the sin of his mother never be blotted out.

---

4. The verb שָׂטַן means "to be an adversary"; it is often translated as "accuser" (as it is connected to the name Satan). The Greek version has "slander" (ἐνδιέβαλλόν); and the NIV uses "accuse" (me).
5. The verse in the Hebrew Bible simply says, "and I prayer" (see the constructions of Ps. 110:3 and 120:7). NIV smooths it to read "I am *a man of prayer.*"
6. The line is literally, "may his children also be continually wandering and beg"; the Greek version has "as they totter, let his sons wander about (σαλευόμενοι μεταναστήτωσαν) and beg."
7. The second half begins with "and seek," וְדָרְשׁוּ. This is usually emended to a passive form of גָּרַשׁ, "driven out." The second colon of the verse includes the understanding of "may his children wander" (now from their ruins) and supplies a parallel word for "ask."
8. The Greek translation interpreted this verb with "seek out," ἐξερευνησάτω.
9. The Greek took אַחֵר to be אֶחָד and read it as "in one generation."

> 15 May they always be before the LORD,
>   that he may cut off[10] the memory of them from the earth.
> 16 Because he did not remember to show kindness
>   but pursued the afflicted and the needy
>   and the brokenhearted, to put *them* to death.[11]
> 17 Since he loved cursing, then may it come[12] to him;
>   since he had no delight in blessing, may it be far from him.
> 18 Since he clothed himself with cursing as his raiment,
>   may it come[13] like water into his body
>   and into his bones like oil.
> 19 May it be to him like the garment he wears,
>   and like the belt always tied around him.
> 20 This is the reward[14] from the LORD for my adversaries,
>   and for those who speak evil against my life.
>
> 21 But you, O Lord Yahweh,[15] deal[16] with me for your name's sake;
>   because your loyal love is good, deliver me.[17]
> 22 For I am afflicted and needy,
>   and my heart is wounded[18] within me.
> 23 Like a shadow when it lengthens I fade away;

---

10. For the active verb יַכְרֵת, "may he cut of," the Greek (and Jerome and 2 manuscripts) has "and may their memory be destroyed," ἐξολεθρευθείη (= וְכָרַת).
11. The NIV translates the expression with "hounded them to death," but the text may be stronger than that—they pursued them to kill them. The Greek version has "to their death."
12. To translate this verb form as a jussive, as well as the verb "may it be" in the second half, requires a slight repointing of the conjunction to replace the *waw consecutive* (which would read "and it came").
13. See note 12.
14. Allen translates פְּעֻלַּת as "punishment" (p. 99).
15. The Greek translation of course has to use κύριε κύριε, "Lord, Lord."
16. It makes a smoother reading to have some adverb or object with the verb "do / deal." Some versions say "deal *well with me.*" The Greek used "steadfast love": "show your steadfast love to me."
17. This is put with the next verse in the Greek translation.
18. The verb חָלַל is a little difficult. It may have been written to say "one has pierced my heart within me." A passive form would be more natural here, such as the *polal*, חֹלַל, "my heart was pierced within me." Allen suggests

I am shaken off like a locust.
24 My knees have become weak through fasting,
and my body has grown thin with weight loss.[19]
25 Moreover,[20] I have become an object of scorn to them;
they see me, they shake their head.

26 Help me O LORD my God;
save me according to your loyal love,
27 so that they may know that this is your hand,
that you, O LORD, have done it.
28 They may curse, but you bless;
w*hen* they rise up, they are put to shame,[21]
and so your servant rejoices.
29 My adversaries will be clothed with disgrace
and covered in their own shame *as in* a cloak.[22]
30 I will fully acknowledge the LORD with my mouth,
and in the midst of a multitude I will praise him.
31 For he stands at the right hand of the needy
to save *him* from those who condemn his life.[23]

Composition and Context

The striking feature of Psalm 109 is the extended imprecatory

---

the root חול, "to writhe, throb," is expected here: "my heart within me beats wildly with distress" (pp. 98 and 100).

19. This translation may be a little too free, but "failed of fatness" is hard to understand. For the body to lack fatness means it has become thin and gaunt (NIV translation). The Greek version has "changed because of oil."
20. Hebrew: "But I" or "But as for me."
21. This colon reads: "they arose and they were put to shame, but your servant will rejoice." Some commentators subordinate "they arose" to form a contrast with "put to shame," matching the first part. Others suggest changing קָמוּ, "they arose," to קָמַי, "my adversary," "the one rising against me." Allen translates the words as "may my assailant be confounded," (changing the conjunction again on the second verb to allow the jussive translation. But the verb "confounded" is plural.
22. Some commentators take the verbs in verse 29 as petitions (jussives) as well.
23. The Greek translation has the pronoun "me" in this colon; it also translates it as "to save me from those who keep pursuing / persecuting (ἐκ τῶν καταδιωκόντων) my life," perhaps a necessary paraphrase.

section, verses 6–19. Because of this it seems unlikely that the psalm was not used in Israel's worship; it is more suited to be a prayer or some ritual for a person being slandered and falsely accused.[24]

The psalm may be classified as an individual lament with this extended section of curses included. The structure of the passage can be laid out in a number of ways. VanGemeren suggests: an invocation (v. 1), an introductory lament of the words and works of the wicked (vv. 2–5), the imprecation (vv. 6–15), a further lament over the acts and words of the wicked (vv. 16–20), a petition for God's love and vindication (vv. 21–29), and a closing benediction (vv. 30–31).[25]

The date of the composition is uncertain. Kraus concludes that there is nothing here that prevents a pre-exilic date. But Anderson says that a post-exilic date is better because the maledictions are close to Jeremiah 18:19–23.[26] Older commentators found some compelling evidence for placing the occasion in David's experience with the adversary Shimei. At least the psalm may be illustrated by this narrative in 2 Samuel 16. Verses 1–5 describe accurately the words and works of Shimei. In addition it is further argued by some that the curses in verses 6–19 of the psalm may well be the words of Shimei that David is reporting (because, in part, there is a change to the singular at the beginning and a change back to the plural after the imprecations).[27] The idea that the imprecations are quotations from the adversary has found support in a number of commentaries over the years, perhaps in part because it removes such curses from the mouth of the pious believer.[28] One major difficulty with this view is the

---

24. See further D. P. Wright, "Ritual Analogy in Psalm 109," *JBL* 113 (1994):385–404.
25. *Psalms*, p. 804.
26. *Psalms 73–150*, p. 759.
27. One presentation of this historical connection is summarized by Perowne, *Psalms*, II:288.
28. Booij, "Psalm 109:6–19 as a Quotation: A Review of the Evidence," in *Give Ear To My Words: Psalms and Other Poetry in and around the Hebrew Bible," FS* for N. A. van Uchelin, ed. by J. Dyk, et al (Amsterdam: Societas Hebraica Amstelodamensis, 1996), pp. 91–106. Allen concludes that verses 6–19 are a quotation and summarizes the reasoning (pp. 72–3).

reading of verse 20 in the Hebrew text (without being changed to fit the view): "This is the punishment from the LORD for my adversaries, and for those who speak evil against my life." This certainly sounds like what has just been imprecated is an announcement of judgment on the wicked. Verse 16b seems also to refer to the psalmist as the victim—he is not pursuing people to kill them. To say this of the psalmist would be a wild accusation. It may also be noted that since with curses there was an understanding that power was attached to the words, it would be less likely for the psalmist to repeat them if they were from the wicked.

While the suggestion that the curses came from the wicked is somewhat appealing, it does not completely satisfy the way this psalm is presented, nor answer the question of imprecations elsewhere in the Psalter (see the introductory section in volume 1). This is an imprecatory psalm in which the psalmist, i.e., David, prophetically prays for the end of evil.[29] The psalmist is bold in his appeal because he looks at right and wrong very seriously, and knows that eventually God will destroy the wicked. He is therefore praying for God to fulfill his plan to enable righteousness to triumph. His prayer is written with the force of one who knows by experience what it means to be hounded to death, suffer malicious slander, and be repaid with evil for all the good he has done. But it ceases to be personal vengeance as he turns all his wishes over to the LORD in a prayer, thereby leaving it to the LORD to deal in justice with his adversary.[30]

Exegetical Analysis

Summary

After calling to the LORD for help against those who fought him with evil devices, and after laying curses on the enemy so that

---

[29]. See Martin J. Ward, "Psalm 109: David's Poem of Vengeance," *AUSS* 18 (1980):163–168.
[30]. See also R. Althann, "The Psalms of Vengeance against Their Ancient Near Eastern Background," *JNSL* 18 (1992):1–11.

Divine Vengeance and Vindication

he would be desolate and dispossessed because he (the enemy) loved cursing, the psalmist prays that the LORD will help him by avenging his shame and dishonor.

Outline

I. David calls for help from the LORD against his malicious enemies who surround him with evil (1–5).
   A. Call: He calls for help against the deceitful enemies who opened against him (1–2).
   B. Complaint: He complains about the evil enemies (3–5):
      1. They have surrounded him with words of hatred (3).
      2. They are his adversaries who repayed friendship with malice (4).
      3. They have rewarded his kindness with evil hatred (5).
II. David pours out his imprecations upon the enemy, appealing to God to make the wicked desolate and dispossessed because of their love for destruction and cursing (6–20).
   A. Curse: He details his desire for the enemy to be cursed (6–15):
      1. Let an adversary be against him and let him be judged as guilty (6–7).
      2. Let his days be few so that his wife is a widow and his children fatherless beggars (8–10).
      3. Let him be ruined by the creditor (11).
      4. Let no one pity him (12).
      5. Let his posterity be cut off by the next generation (13).
      6. Let the ancestral sins be remembered on him (14–15).
   B. Cause: He explains the reason for the curses (16–19):
      1. He hounded to death the broken-hearted and the needy (16).
      2. He loved heaping curses on other people (17–19).
   C. Conclusion: This is the punishment from the LORD on the wicked (20).
III. David prays to the LORD for help in defending against his enemies because he is in great need (21–31).
   A. He prays for help since he is in great need (21–25).
      1. The LORD should deal with him according to love (21).
      2. He is in need since he is weak and perishing (22–25).

B. He prays for help so that they will know the truth (26–27).
C. He anticipates the outcome (28–31).
   1. They will be cursed and shamed (28–29).
   2. He will rejoice because the LORD will save the needy (30–31).

COMMENTARY IN EXPOSITORY FORM

I. The people of God must cry out to God when they are persecuted by malicious adversaries (1–5).

A. Prayer is necessary when deceitful enemies attack (1–2).

The psalmist appeals directly to "the God of my praise," meaning the God whom he praises because he so often has delivered him. The petition is bold: "do not be silent." God appears to be "silent" when he does not answer; he "speaks" when he intervenes to save and to judge. The reason for this urgent prayer is that David is the victim of malicious talk: "a wicked (רָשָׁע; s.v. Ps. 1:1) mouth and a deceitful (מִרְמָה; s.v. Ps. 5:7) mouth have opened against me." The mouth is the instrument of speech (a metonymy of cause); he means that someone or some people were making wicked and deceitful accusations against him. David is under an all out, malicious attack on his character, which, as the psalm will show, has taken a great toll on him.[31]

B. Prayer includes the lament to reveal the wickedness of the adversaries (3–5).

The details of the malicious acts of the adversary justify the psalmist's plea for the LORD to act on his behalf. The simple fact is that they have come after him to destroy him: not only are their words wicked (רָשָׁע; s.v. Ps. 1:1) and deceitful (מִרְמָה; s.v. Ps. 5:7), they are also hateful (שִׂנְאָה; s.v. Ps. 139:21)—their deception came from the hate in their hearts. But their attack is

---

31. Kidner, *Psalms 73–150*, p. 388.

completely unwarranted, "without a cause" (חִנָּם; s.v. Ps. 4:1). He had done all that he could to show "kindness" to them (the term אַהֲבָה, "love," is a deep friendship or kindness here; s.v. Ps. 11:7); but they had not responded in kind. On the contrary, they are his adversaries (יִשְׂטְנוּנִי can also be translated "they accuse me"). Verse 5 elaborates further on this: they have repaid him with evil for his good, hatred for his friendship. The line contrasts the depth of his kindness to them with their unlimited hatred of him. And the evil they bring to him is intended to cause pain and destruction (for רָעָה, s.v. Ps. 10:15). He has done the right thing, but it has only met with increased animosity. Nonetheless he has done what is right.

The only recourse he has is to appeal to the LORD for intervention. In verse 4b he says "I—prayer," or, "but as for me—prayer." The cryptic nature of the expression fits the intensity of the crisis. But commentators and translators prefer to supply what is missing to make a clear sentence: "but I *give myself to* prayer," or "but I *am a man of* prayer," or just "I *have* prayer" (as the only recourse). Be that as it may, the emphasis is clearly on "prayer" (תְּפִלָּה; s.v. Ps. 5:2); what is his only course of action? Prayer.

II. The prayers of the righteous rightly appeal to God to take vengeance on those who are bent on destroying the afflicted and needy (6–20).

A. They should appeal to God to repay the wicked for their deeds (6–15).

The psalmist's commitment to prayer in the light of his unreasonable enemies flows naturally into the next section of the psalm, the imprecations. It is a prayer for God to turn their evil and malice back on them. The first petition (v. 6) is that the wicked will find no help when put in the position of the accused—as is the psalmist now. It is a call for evil to punish or destroy evil (as the plan of God so frequently carries out). The scene is a legal setting; a wicked man should be appointed over him, an accuser should be at his right hand. And when a decision is reached he should be found guilty ("when he is judged, he goes out wicked"), meaning guilty. The point is that wicked people will decide his case and he will have no chance of being acquitted. In addition to that, the psalmist asks that his appeal (literally "prayer" or "petition") fail. The text simply says "let his prayer become sin." However, the word "sin" (חֲטָא; s.v. Ps. 51:2) literally means "to miss" (the mark or the way). In the legal setting, if that extends this far, the line could be taken to mean "let his appeal fail."

The curse in verse 8 is for his early death: "may his days be few." The longer wicked people live the longer they will be venting their hatred for the LORD and the righteous. It would be better for them to perish soon so that someone else could take their position of leadership (פְּקֻדָּה; s.v. Ps. 8:4). This verse is well known to those who read the New Testament carefully. Judas Iscariot had betrayed the Lord and in the end hanged himself, thus becoming a curse. The apostles decided to find a replacement for him, and this passage which laid out imprecations on the adversaries confirmed that his office should be given to another (see Acts 1:20).

Verses 9 and 10 direct the imprecation to the family. It would be a great disgrace if the children became fatherless and the wife a widow; but if they were also reduced to living in ruins and wandering about begging,[32] as often happened for such people, it would be a fate worse than death. The second colon carries the idea of begging a little further by providing the background: "and seek (by begging) from their ruined places."[33]

He also wishes that a creditor seize all his possessions, and that strangers plunder his earnings, the result of his labor (v. 11). The meaning is that the wicked should also be subjected to ruthless and unlawful treatment. In the process, he should find no one to show him kindness (חֶסֶד; s.v. Ps. 23:6), nor to show his children any favor (חוֹנֵן; s.v. Ps. 4:1). Should this happen, then

---

[32]. The infinitive absolute intensifies the verb: "wandering about, may his children wander about." And the verb "to ask" is here in the intensive stem, "beg."

[33]. See additionally A. Guillaume, "A Note on Psalm 109:10," *JTS* ns 14 (1963):92–93.

the wicked will feel what they have inflicted on poor and helpless people.

Their descendants should also be cut off and their names soon forgotten (v. 13). Death was the lawful punishment for those who so wickedly violated the covenant; for their name to be forgotten means that they will cease to exist. It is a prayer that the line of the wicked should come to an end. The thinking may be that the evil the wicked do will continue generation to generation unless God intervenes (see Exod. 20:5).

But the curse includes the idea that the sins of the wicked would be remembered (זָכַר; s.v. Ps. 6:5) before the LORD, so that they would remain guilty (vv. 14–15). Their names might be blotted out, meaning they will cease to exist, but the memory of their sins will remain and continue to condemn them. Anderson notes that unatoned sins will not be forgotten by God.[34]

B. They must explain the reasons for their appeal (16–19).

In the next section the psalmist focuses more on the evil that these people have done to show that his appeal for God to judge them is not only just but urgent. The wicked pursued their sins because they did not remember (זָכַר; s.v. Ps. 6:5) to show kindness (חֶסֶד, faithful covenant love). Ignoring their covenant responsibilities, they pursued a policy of destruction, persecuting the afflicted and the needy and the broken-hearted, "to kill them." The NIV interprets this to mean they hounded them to death, which communicates one aspect of their pursuit but may soften their intent "to kill them." Seeking to gratify their own desires for power and possessions they destroyed people. So not remembering, or deliberately forgetting the covenant, means that they acted in violation of it (see Lev. 19:10; Mic. 6:8): they continued to hate, curse, oppress, and harass people, especially the needy. These wicked people deserved to be punished. They will be punished. The psalmist wants it soon.

The prayer in verse 17 takes on a clear talionic tone. Since

---

34. *Psalms 73–150*, p. 763.

he loved cursing[35]—may it come to him; since he had no delight in blessing—may it be far from him. The psalmist expands on this, wishing that the curse affect his body and soul, that it fill his body like water and his bones like oil. Anderson suggests there may be a reference here to some ordeal of magic.[36] At least

---

35. The noun comes from קָלַל, "to be light, slight, trifling" in the basic *qal* stem, and in the causative *hiphil* it means "to make something light" or "to curse," and in the *piel* stem "to curse, make something contemptible" or "treat as unimportant." The word "curse" with its meaning of treat as light and unimportant may be understood in contrast to the word "honor," which is from the verb "to be heavy," and thus to treat someone as important or give him the proper respect.

    The basic meaning can apply to a number of things, such as warriors that are swift (1 Sam. 1:23) or matters that are trifling (1 Sam. 2:30), or in the passive of being lightly esteemed (2 Sam. 6:22).

    The word in the *piel* can be either declarative or factitive. The translation of "curse" then would have the sense of treating someone or something as trifling or of no importance, or making something contemptible. In Genesis 12:2 the LORD declares that he will curse (אָרַר, to remove from the place of blessing) anyone who curses Abram (קָלַל, treats with contempt). In Psalm 109 this cursing is linked to malicious words of hate and destructive accusations, showing utter contempt for those cursed. The effects of a scornful word like this could be damaging if not life-threatening.

    The verb in the *hiphil* can have the simple meaning of making something light, such as the mariners throwing the cargo overboard to lighten the load in the storm (Jon. 1:5). But in a few places it can also have the meaning of treating someone with contempt or bringing dishonor on them (Isa. 8:23).

    The noun קְלָלָה, "curse," occurs 33 times in the Bible. It became the proper word for the curse execrating another person. It may describe an expressed curse on someone, a denunciation or expression of contempt (Prov. 26:2). In Genesis 27:12 Jacob was concerned that if his father discovered who he was he would be given a curse, and not a blessing. Blessing is occasionally placed opposite the word for curse, such as in Ps. 37:22 where those blessed by God will inherit the land but those cursed by him will be removed. A curse could be made as an oath or a prophetic warning that would come to fulfillment (Judg. 9:57). The LORD can pronounce a curse on wickedness that will be fulfilled if they persist in disobedience (Deut. 27–30). So the word can have the sense of making something contemptible or treating someone as contemptible, that is, worthless and deserving of no recognition at the least and ruin at most. The curse brings with it the aspect of having so little regard for something that it is despised and abused accordingly.

36. *Psalms 73–150*, 764.

we can say that the appeal is that whatever he does will continue to fill him with every kind of effect of the curse and become so closely associated with him as to cover him like clothing bound tightly to him (v. 18). He should not simply be cursed, but become a curse.

C. They must be correct that this is the punishment due the wicked (20).

Verse 20 signifies a change from the imprecations to a summary explanation: "This is the punishment (פְּעֻלַּת, often translated "reward") from the LORD for my adversaries." All of the curses for which he has prayed in the preceding section record what the LORD has in store for the wicked who speak evil against the righteous.

III. The people of God must continue to pray that the LORD will help them find vindication in their struggle with the wicked (21–31).

A. Because they are in great need the faithful pray for help (21–25).

After the lengthy section of imprecations, other aspects of the lament psalm emerge: the petition to the LORD for deliverance and the lament proper. The prayer is simply "But you, Yahweh Lord, deal with me," although some versions and commentaries add something like "do *loyal love* with me." It is a petition for God to act on his behalf. The prayer is a righteous prayer offered in faith as he begins with an emphatic addition to the LORD's name (Hebrew is יְהוָה אֲדֹנָי), makes his appeal for the sake of the LORD's name, and then bases it on the LORD's goodness and loyal love.

The petition is urgent because of his failing condition—he is afflicted and needy (and so he identifies himself again as the object of the malice of the adversaries). His weakness is described with the use of two similes: he is fading away like the disappearing shadow in the evening, and he is shaken off as a locust is brushed off. The wicked would rather be rid of him as easily as that than to show him any kindness. But their persecution has been drawn out so that he has been weakened and grown unstable on his feet because of his lack of food and made frail with weight loss. In addition to his physical weakness, his spirit is grieved by their cutting taunts (חֶרְפָּה; s.v. Ps. 22:6) and gestures of contempt.

B. Their desire is that God's response will reveal the truth (26–27).

In his weakness and desperation the psalmist cries for help (עָזְרֵנִי; s.v. Ps. 46:1) and salvation (הוֹשִׁיעֵנִי; s.v. Ps. 3:2), meaning deliverance. His prayer is confident because of his trust in the LORD's loyal love; but his prayer for deliverance has an additional purpose, namely, that they will know that it is the LORD who has taken vengeance on them and vindicated his servant. Their punishment must come with understanding: it is God Almighty who is taking vengeance on them for their wickedness against the afflicted and the needy. They have not simply attacked such people, but in doing so they have attacked the creator (Prov. 14:31; 17:5).

C. They make their petition in the hope that they will rejoice in their salvation (28–31).

The psalmist is filled with confidence that the LORD will reverse the evil that they do (although some translations make verses 28 and 29 prayers). On the one hand the wicked may curse (קָלַל), but they cannot carry out the curse if it is baseless and not of God (Prov. 26:2); and on the other hand God will bless the righteous (בָּרַךְ, "enrich, enable, empower"; s.v. Ps. 5:12). When the wicked rise up against him, God puts them to shame (for בּוֹשׁ; s.v. Ps. 31:1). In the end the servant of the LORD, the righteous believer, will rejoice (for שָׂמַח s.v. Ps. 48:11) as the adversaries are clothed with (identified completely as) disgrace (כְּלִמָּה) and shame (בָּשְׁתָּם).

Then, and finally then, the psalmist will publicly acknowledge (אוֹדֶה; s.v. Ps. 6:5) the LORD and praise him (אֲהַלְלֶנּוּ; s.v. Ps. 33:1) in the midst of many people. And the substance of the praise is that the LORD stands at the right hand of the needy to save him from those who are condemning (for שָׁפַט s.v. Ps. 9:4) his life. Here is a significant contrast: the curse was for a wicked man to stand at the right hand of the wicked (so there was no hope of deliverance), but the blessing is that the righteous LORD stands at the right hand of his people to deliver them. The presence of the LORD as his defender will vindicate him by bringing vengeance on the wicked.

MESSAGE AND APPLICATION

The basic structure of this psalm follows the familiar pattern of a lament, with the suffering saint crying out for help, pouring out the lament, appealing to God to deliver, and anticipating praise. But here we have the additional aspect of the extended curse. Many believers today are troubled by this because it seems so unrighteous. But even in the Old Testament such imprecations presented a tension with the love and kindness the Law prescribed (Lev. 19:17–18; Prov. 24:17; 25:31). But divine judgment for serious violations of the Law of God were not dealt with kindly (see Deut. 19:16–21). The Israelites lived as a nation under divine law, and that law called for punishment for sin. A prayer such as this, albeit somewhat shocking by its detailed imprecations, is not out of harmony with that situation. And while the modern believer may pray for the enemies in a different light, and may find the idea of vengeance difficult to accept, the truth of the matter is that the Lord has declared that vengeance belongs to him and he will repay. We may word it very differently because of the emphasis of the New Testament, but to pray for the Lord to bring about justice and righteousness necessarily includes the removal of all wickedness from the world. That is the desire of this psalm. An expository idea that fits the psalm and is, with clarification, useful in prayers today, is as follows: *In situations of extreme danger and malicious attacks by people who hate them, it is natural and not inappropriate for the righteous to pray that the LORD avenge their suffering and shame by delivering and vindicating them.* But because of the teachings of the New Testament, the prayers of suffering saints should also pray for the salvation of evil people, as Christ did from the suffering and shame of the cross.

PSALM 110

The Exaltation and Glorious Victory of the Coming King

INTRODUCTION

Text and Textual Variants

A Psalm of David

1 An oracle of Yahweh to my lord:
   "Sit at my right hand
      until I make your enemies a footstool for your feet."[1]
2 Yahweh shall extend your mighty scepter[2] from Zion:
   "Rule[3] in the midst of your enemies!"
3 Your people shall offer themselves willingly[4]

---

1. A few manuscripts have "your feet" without the preposition; others, "your foot."
2. MT has מַטֵּה־עֻזְּךָ, "scepter of your might," meaning "your mighty scepter."
3. MT has the imperative, רְדֵה; one manuscript, the Greek and Targum have the conjunction, "and rule." The Syriac reads "and he will rule."
4. The Hebrew עַמְּךָ נְדָבֹת is "your people (are) willing," the plural emphasizing that they are willingness itself. This is the word for a freewill offering in the Law, and so some translations suggest "offer themselves

PSALM 110

> on the day of your power;
> > *arrayed* in the beauty of holiness,[5]
> > from the womb of the dawn,[6]
> > your youth shall be to you like the dew.[7]
> 4 Yahweh has sworn and will not relent:
> > "You are a priest forever
> > > according to the order of[8] Melchizedek."

---

freely" or "willingly." The words are translated differently in the Greek version: μετὰ σοῦ ἡ ἀρχή, "with you is dominion," or "with you is nobility [pl]." This would reflect עִמְּךָ, "with you," and נְדִבֹת, the feminine plural of the noun "nobility."

5. The MT has בְּהַדְרֵי־קֹדֶשׁ, "in the beauty of holiness." But Symmachus, Jerome and a good number of manuscripts read it as "mountain of holiness," probably confusing the "d" (ד) of "beauty" for the "r" (ר) of mountain (הַר may be written in the plural with two letters "r"); "beauty, splendor, honor" is הָדָר. The Greek version agrees with the MT, but interprets with plurals: "in the splendors of [your] holy things / your saints (τῶν ἁγίων [σου])."

6. The Masoretic text has a difficulty with the spelling of the second word: "dawn" has a letter *mem* prefixed to it. MT has מֵרֶחֶם מִשְׁחָר. If the second word had the מ repointed it would be another preposition: "from the womb, from the dawn"; if the letter were deleted, the words would read "from the womb of the dawn" (most English Bibles do this). Support comes from the spelling of "womb," which indicates a construct ("womb of"). Either a letter was accidently added to the second word (dittography), or we have a variant spelling of the noun. The Greek has "out of the womb before the dawn" or "morning star," ἐκ γαστρὸς πρὸ ἑωσφόρου, suggesting it read the preposition on the second word. The editors of BHS suggest the מ on the second word came by dittography and should be deleted.

7. This line also has some difficulties. The MT has לְךָ טַל יַלְדֻתֶיךָ. The Greek version does not have "to you [is] the dew" (i.e., "you have the dew"), but reads the line as "From the womb, before the morning star, I have begotten you." The word "your youth" was taken as a verb יְלִדְתִּיךָ and translated as such: ἐξεγέννησά σε. This translation may have been influenced by the mention of "womb" in the first part of the line, and perhaps by recalling the royal coronation Psalm 2 with its "I have begotten you." But Psalm 110 is not parallel to Psalm 2. Moreover, everything here is addressed to the king with an emphasis on "you"; it would be difficult to change to a verb with the subject "I" at this place.

8. The MT has עַל־דִּבְרָתִי. A few manuscripts have the ending וֹ, "his," and two have the construct ־ת.

338

The Exaltation and Glorious Victory of the Coming King

  5 The Lord[9] at your right hand
      shall shatter kings in the day of his anger.
  6 He shall judge among the nations;
      he shall fill *the land* with corpses;[10]
      he shall shatter the head(s) over a broad[11] land.
  7 He shall drink from a brook by the way;
      therefore shall he lift up[12] his[13] head.[14]

Composition and Context

Psalm 110 is one of the most fascinating psalms in the entire collection. It is a royal psalm that is rich in language and profound in theological content. It is no surprise that this passage is the most frequently cited psalm in the New Testament.

And yet, its interpretation has some major difficulties. We classify it as a royal psalm because it focuses on a high point in the life of the king, his being enthroned and then sent forth by God to conquer the land, putting down his enemies and establishing his dominion. But how this psalm was understood and used in Israel's experience is difficult to determine. First, how could the Davidic king be said to sit at the right hand of Yahweh before receiving the mandate to rule over his enemies? And

---

  9. The form in the text is not the *tetragrammaton* יהוה, but "Lord." However, it is vocalized as the substitute word for the holy name, אֲדֹנָי. The majority of the manuscripts therefore have the letters of the holy name. So it is the LORD at his right hand.
10. "Corpses" is גְוִיּוֹת; this is the reading in the Greek version. But in Aquila, Symmachus and Jerome it is "valleys," φάραγγες, which in Hebrew would be גֵּאָיוֹת. The editors of BHS proposes both, "the valleys he fills with corpses," avoiding the need to supply "the land" as the object. But it may have the sense "he shall fill up (the number of) corpses."
11. The Greek version took רַבָּה in the sense of "many," "he shall shatter heads of many in the land," or "he shall shatter heads in the land of many." One would have expected רַבִּים in that case.
12. This is the meaning of the *hiphil* form in the text, יָרִים; a few manuscripts and the Syriac have *qal*, יָרוּם.
13. MT simply has "head," ראש, probably meaning his head; the Greek version has "head" ("his" being supplied); and two Hebrew manuscripts and the Syriac have supplied the pronoun "his."
14. Three Hebrew manuscripts add הַלְלוּ־יָהּ to the end of the psalm; and two manuscripts omit it from the beginning of Psalm 111.

second, how could he be called a priest? And why after the order of Melchizedek? No king in Israel was also an established priest; in fact, if a king tried to usurp the role of the priest he was dealt with severely (see 2 Chron. 26:18). And as long as the Levitical priests from the line of Aaron were in power, no one from another priestly line or tribe could have served. To complicate the understanding of these lines the Hebrew text uses unusual forms and constructions that have proved hard for translators and commentators to explain.[15]

Commentators are divided on whether there was an event behind this psalm or not. If there was an actual event that gave rise to this psalm, it most likely would have taken place in the time of David. The New Testament witness supports the early date for psalm when it refers to it as David's.[16] Most commentators would not follow that view; a number at least allow that it came from the early monarchy. Anderson says that the psalm may be one of the oldest in the collection because of its ideas.[17] He and others see this as an ancient royal psalm, perhaps written for the enthronement of the king, or as a cultic piece for the fall festival of enthronement, that later was taken to be messianic. Eaton argues for its being a coronation psalm, perhaps sung at the end of the ceremony, with verses 5 and 6 reflecting a dramatic reenactment of the defeat of the king's enemies.[18]

The psalm could have been written after some battle that

---

15. The difficulties in the text harmonize with an early date; see E. R. Hardy, "The Date of Psalm 110," *JBL* 64 (1945):385–390.
16. Not many would be willing to say David wrote it. Briggs, for example, says that when Jesus raised the question of what David meant in this psalm (e.g., Matt. 22:43–45), he says that the argument rests upon David's having said these words in the Psalm, and it is justified if the author of the psalm lets David appear as spokesman. But he adds that it does not require Davidic authorship; Jesus was simply following common opinion about the authorship of the psalm, and if he knew otherwise he did not care to correct the idea (*Psalms*, II:376). This kind of reasoning is unconvincing since there is no good reason why David could not have written the psalm, even if some of the words had been given to him by an oracle.
17. *Psalms 73–150*, p. 767. The setting of Solomon's coronation is one suggestion; see T. N. D. Mettinger, *King and Messiah, The Civil and Sacral Legitimation of the Israelite Kings* (Lund: C. W. K. Gleerup, 1976).
18. *Kingship and the Psalms*, p. 124.

Israel had to fight and for which a divine oracle declared victory. But it may fit more precisely the time of David's conquest of the city of Jerusalem; it would then be a celebration of his enthronement on the ancient seat, so to speak, of Melchizedek. Verse 4 seems to point to this occasion with the reference to Melchizedek who was both king and priest of Salem (old Jerusalem); and verses 5 and 6 may lend support as the description of the victory and taking of the city through the watercourse. The psalm then could have been used by subsequent kings for royal celebrations, perhaps coronations or preparations for battle, the psalm reminding them of the LORD's promise of victory (as in Ps. 2). Allen notes that for this to work the priesthood of verse 4 has to be harmonized with David's reign.[19] If this can be demonstrated, then the psalm may have been written to legitimize the priestly prerogative of the Davidic dynasty—David as the new Melchizedek.[20] It may be that David himself could have claimed some link to Melchizedek in this way because he was the first Israelite to occupy the throne of Melchizedek, and because he appears to have been involved in the sanctuary ritual, wearing an ephod and making a sacrifice.[21] The idea would be that his throne was set up next to the holy site where the tabernacle would be, so he could be pictured at the right hand of the LORD (facing east as the temple did). But this seems forced; it would be better to say only that sitting at the LORD's right hand is figurative for a position of honor rather than to try to locate a physical arrangement. It would also be complicated if David did write the psalm about his descendant—what he did with ephod and sacrifice may not have applied to the dynasty. But the fact that Psalm 110 as well as Psalm 109 are Davidic psalms in Book IV shows an interest in the future fulfillment of the Davidic monarchy.

Rowley proposed a solution to the Davidic priesthood

---

19. *Psalms 101–150*, p. 85.
20. Ibid., p. 81.
21. It is possible that Davidic kings had some role in priestly activities (see C. E. Armerding, "Were David's Sons Really Priests?" in *Current Issues in Biblical and Patristic Interpretation*, ed. by G. F. Hawthorne [Grand Rapids: Eerdmans, 1975], pp. 75–86).

connection.[22] He suggested that in the first three verses of the psalm Zadok addressed David, his lord, and delivered the oracle of enthronement and conquest to him. Then, David addressed Zadok in verse 4 declaring his new status as the priest in Melchizedek's place. Verses 5–7 again were the words of Zadok, blessing David. Commentators may not all agree with Rowley's construction; however, most would allow that the psalm might be an oracle delivered by a court prophet to the king whom he called "my master," perhaps as part of a coronation ritual in which he declared the promise of victory in coming battles.

There are other suggestions for the date of this psalm. One view is to place it in the time of Simon Maccabeus, who reigned as king and priest from 142–134 B.C.—but his right to reign was challenged by the devout. Another would be to place it in the post-exilic period because of the prophecy of the unity of the offices of priest and king in Zechariah 3 and 6. But most would place the event in a time when there was a monarchy; suggestions range from David, to Solomon to Azariah (Uzziah) to Josiah.

On the other hand, there is the view that the psalm does not reflect any specific event, a coronation or a victory. In this understanding the psalm has no actual connection to an earthly king but is purely prophetic of the Messiah.[23] The emphasis on the union of the priesthood with the monarchy would then be entirely prophetic, being carried forward by Zechariah (chapters 3 and 6) under the figure of the Branch. Delitzsch classifies it as purely prophetic, and suggests that it may have been one of the last things David wrote because of the similarities with the last words of David in 2 Samuel 23.[24] Allen rejects the idea that it is only Messianic, noting that while this interpretation is a

---

22. H. H. Rowley, "Melchizedek and Zadok," *FS für Alfred Bertholet,* ed. by. W. Baumgartner, et al (Tübingen: J. C. B. Mohr, 1950), pp. 461–72.
23. For example, see E. J. Kissane, "The Interpretation of Psalm 110," *Irish Theological Quarterly* 21 (1954):103–14; Kidner, *Psalms 72–150,* pp. 391, 2; and see further on the Messianic value, David M. Hay, *Glory at the Right Hand: Psalm 110 in Early Christianity* (Nashville: Abingdon, 1973).
24. *Psalms,* III: 185–186.

worthy effort, it is not the way the Old Testament works[25]; this would be the only royal psalm that would do this because all the others have a primary reference to an event in the life of a king that becomes typological of the greatest of the Davidic kings, the Messiah. This qualification must be taken seriously; but then, Psalm 110 is unique in several ways, and a purely prophetic interpretation is not out of the question.

It is certainly possible that a court prophet addressed this message to the king, his master, and promised great success over his enemies. It may have been at the time David took Melchizedek's seat and appropriated priestly functions with his kingship. But the psalm itself would have been written by David, perhaps incorporating the oracle, with a view to a far greater fulfillment in the future. However this worked in the origination of the psalm, ultimately the psalm's prophetic message is the chief concern. On this almost all Christian commentators agree, especially since with the ascension of Jesus the Messiah and the promise of his second coming to put down all rebellion the apostles saw how the exact meaning of the psalm applied to him alone. From the perspective of Jesus and the apostles, David received a revelation from God in which his descendant, his Lord, would be exalted to the right hand of God and given the power and the authority to put down all his enemies. This descendant would go forth in the day of battle with all his armies who willingly offer themselves for his service. David expected the promises God made to him and his dynasty to be fulfilled in subsequent kings, because his reign had not exhausted the promises (see further Ps. 72). Moreover, the psalm goes beyond all this to announce that this future king will be a high priest as well, not after Aaron, who was a Levitical priest, but after Melchizedek's order, which was a royal priesthood. The king being from Judah could never be a priest under the old dispensation; there would have to be major changes. But it was certain, because God swore that it would happen.

Regardless of whether there was an actual historical event behind the writing of this psalm or not, we know from the clear

---

25. *Psalms 101–150*, p. 84.

exposition of the New Testament writers that it fits perfectly into the flow of the Messianic passages in the Old Testament that all come to fulfillment in the person and work of the Messiah. Psalm 110, however, finds its fulfillment in his exaltation in glory and in his certain coming to judge the world (Zech. 14 and Acts 1).

Exegetical Analysis

Summary

The psalmist receives a revelation that his descendant, who is his lord, will be enabled by Yahweh and assisted by his willing subjects to establish dominion over the nations and reign in honor and glory as a royal priest.

Outline

I. The psalmist receives a revelation that his lord sits enthroned at the LORD's right hand until the day of battle when he will be empowered to establish his dominion over his enemies (1–3).
   A. The revelation tells of the lord's exaltation to the right hand of Yahweh (1a).
   B. The revelation promises that God will establish his dominion in the earth (1b–2).
   C. The revelation predicts that the people will willingly and enthusiastically offer their service to the king in that holy and awesome day (3).
II. The psalmist records the oath of Yahweh that makes this king a priest after the order of Melchizedek (4).
III. The psalmist anticipates that the king will defeat his enemies with a crushing blow, refreshing himself from a brook and being exalted to a position of honor and dominion (5–7).
   A. God himself will destroy the opposing rulers in the world (5).
   B. His judgment on his enemies will be final and complete (6).
   C. The king will be refreshed and established in his dominion (7).

The Exaltation and Glorious Victory of the Coming King

COMMENTARY IN EXPOSITORY FORM

I. The king will be exalted at God's right hand where he will await the establishment of his dominion over his enemies (1).

The first verse establishes the meaning of the psalm and sets the tone for it. It is a majestic psalm that affirms the future victory of the king over his enemies; but the certainty of that victory does not come from the king himself, but from Yahweh who will exalt him and enable him to succeed. The verse literally reads:

"An oracle of Yahweh[26] to my lord:
'Sit at my right hand
   until I make your enemies a footstool for your feet'."

A. *God speaks to the future king (1a).*

The human speaker of verse 1 may have been a prophet speaking to the king, or David speaking about his descendant; but the focus is on Yahweh as the speaker. The word rendered "oracle" (נְאֻם) is a prophetic term that means "utterance, declaration, revelation" (it was used in Ps. 36:1; it is an actual oracle from God in this psalm). The word is usually translated with the English verb "says" or "said" because the noun is followed by a qualifying genitive that gives the source of the oracle. Thus, "an oracle of Yahweh" is simply another way to say "the prophetic word of Yahweh" or "Yahweh declares." This term is much stronger than the verb "said" or even the noun "word," although anything God says is true and reliable. The term emphasizes that this is a divine oracle, an announcement of the will and plan of God; and it ensures the certainty of its being fulfilled (see Joel 2:12; Isa. 49:18; 56:8). We are not told how the psalmist heard or received this oracle; but prophets did receive divine words in a number of ways. Matthew 22:43 simply indicates it came by the Holy Spirit.

---

26. In some psalms, and especially this one, it would be clearer to use the actual name than the conventional translation. "The LORD said to my Lord" is not very clear to most readers.

The certainty of the oracle is based on the speaker—God. The personal name "Yahweh" is used, but it was translated "LORD" in English bibles, which is not a name but a title, making the point of the line confusing since "Lord" is also used. "Yahweh" is the personal name of God; when used it emphasizes that he is a person who makes his will known to his people, that he is the sovereign God,[27] and that he has a covenant with Israel.[28] Yahweh speaks.

But the unusual part of this verse concerns the term for the direct recipient of the oracle that David was allowed to hear: Yahweh says "to my lord." Here the word "my lord" (אֲדֹנִי) simply means "my lord" or "my master."[29] The title emphasizes the authority and superiority of the king. A prophet addressing David as his master would not be difficult; but David was referring to his descendant as his master, which would be more unusual in dynastic pronouncements. David clearly sees this future coming king, who is the one to whom God is speaking, as his sovereign master. His use of the word "my lord" does not indicate that the king was divine, only that he is lord and master. If it is referring to David's descendant, it means he will be greater than David.

B. God exalts the king (1b).

In this revelation God said to David's lord, "Sit at my right hand." Sitting (שֵׁב, from יָשַׁב) is a sign of honor and majesty (1 Kings 2:19). Kings (Deut. 17:18; Isa. 10:13) or judges (Exod. 18:14; Mal. 3:3) sit, and their attendants and servants stand to wait upon them or do their will; but sitting at the right hand of a higher authority is also the position of power and prestige. Here,

---

27. This is based on his own explanation of the meaning of the name as "I Am that I Am"—he is sovereignly independent of all creation.
28. Throughout the Law the divine revelation is constantly begun with "I am Yahweh your God" (see for example the repetition in Leviticus 19).
29. The word in the singular most often refers to human superiors; when the word refers to God it is usually put in the plural (אֲדֹנָי, literally "my Lords); this is the word that is pronounced instead of the holy name in Jewish custom, and so when put into English as "LORD" it represents the holy name of God, "Yahweh." But here in the first verse of the psalm the text says "Yahweh said to my lord."

sitting at the right hand of Yahweh means that this king was to be exalted to the power and dominion and honor of heaven itself—before he establishes dominion in all the earth.[30] No one would have more authority and power than he, apart from the Majesty on High himself. It is hard to know what David thought about this expression, even if he first heard it applied to him, but especially as he thought of the future king. His descendant would have all the authority of heaven for his reign. Later Scripture would make it clear that he would actually come from heaven to reign (Dan. 7), but this probably was not in David's mind at the time. Jesus tried to get his critics to explain this idea as well, but they had no answer.

C. God will defeat the enemies of the king (1c).

The first verse continues the words of Yahweh, saying that the king was to sit enthroned at God's right hand until his enemies would be put down. The word "until" is used to mark a future turning point (see Gen. 49:10; Ps. 71:18; Ps. 112:8; see also GKC 164f.). That turning point will come when Yahweh makes the king's enemies his footstool. The verb "I make" (אָשִׁית) has the idea of "set, appoint, constitute" as well as "make"; here it is with the double object (see also 1 Kings 11:34; Ps. 88:9). The first object is "your enemies" and the second is "footstool." The word for "enemies" is a participle (אֹיְבִים), the verb meaning "to be hostile"; for example, it is etymologically connected to "enmity" referred to in Genesis 3:15. Those who oppose God's work on earth through his Messiah are the enemies; but because Yahweh has promised to put down all opposition their hostility will come to an end (compare Psalm 2).

The second object is the image used for the end of that hostility, "a footstool," "a stool for your feet." The word "stool" occurs only six times in the Old Testament, always with the

---

30. Those looking for a specific reference suggest that the ark may have been brought to the throne near the Gihon spring (H. W. Wolff, "Psalm 110:4," in *Herr, tue meine Lippen auf*, ed. by C. Eicholz, 2nd Edition, 5 Volumes (Wuppertal-Barmen: Müller, 1961):5:310–23; see p. 314), or the throne may have been placed by the ark in the temple (Kraus, p. 931). Allen says the reference is metaphorical (p. 80).

word for feet. The picture is that the enemies will be trampled under foot—completely forced into submission. Conquerors would put their foot on the neck of a defeated enemy (e.g., Josh. 10:24) to signify complete victory. But the language here is figurative (an implied comparison); it describes the complete subjection of the king's enemies in vivid terms (see also Ps. 47:4; 18:39). So the oracle in this first verse speaks of the divinely-given authority of the king: the first line speaks of honor next to God, and the second line speaks of his assuming his complete rule.

II. The king will be given authority and power to establish his rule on earth (2–3).

A. *Yahweh will give him the kingdom (2).*

The beginning of that rule on earth is the focus of verse 2. The verse has two halves, the first declaring what Yahweh will do, and the second recording the divine commission to rule. The psalm first declares: "Yahweh will extend your mighty scepter from Zion." The sentence actually begins with "your mighty scepter," focusing on the absolute and powerful rule of the king. The word "rod" is parallel in the verse to the verb "rule," so "scepter" is the meaning; and the scepter was the symbol (a metonymy of adjunct) of the authority to rule. This authority given to the king will be powerful, as the modifying word (genitive of attribute) indicates: "the rod of your strength" means "your mighty rod" (in Psalm 2:9 it is a rod of iron). Great power will be given to the king to rule, and that power includes the ability to crush the wicked and establish kingship.

The reason that he will be successful, of course, is that Yahweh will extend his rule. The verb means "he will stretch out, extend, reach" (יִשְׁלַח). A good number of commentators have been troubled by the presence of the imperfect tense here ("he will extend") when the parallel verb is an imperative ("rule"). Some of the ancient versions rendered the second verb with a conjunction (*waw* consecutive), making it read the same tense as the first verb. But such changes are not necessary; the construction is similar to what was found in the first verse:

The Exaltation and Glorious Victory of the Coming King

    1. A declaration of Yahweh / "sit"
    2. Yahweh will extend / "rule"

The verb "extend" simply means "send" when it takes an object that is complete in itself (see 2 Sam. 22:15 [arrows]; Num. 20:16 [a person]); Isa. 55:11 [the word]). But it means "to extend" when it refers to something attached to something else (such as a hand [1 Chron. 13:10], or a finger [Isa. 58:9]). Here the object is the scepter, which the king holds in his hand; and so the translation is "extend." The idea of extending the scepter may indicate a demonstration of authority, or the declaration of a sovereign decree, or the transference of power to destroy opposition (such as Moses stretching out the staff over the Red Sea [Exod. 14:16]), or raising his staff to defeat Amalek [Exod. 17:9, 11]). Yahweh is going to establish the king's powerful reign on earth. This idea is captured nicely by the prophecy of Daniel 7:13–14 (NIV):

> In my vision at night I looked, and there before me was one like a son of man, coming with the clouds of heaven. He approached the Ancient of Days and was led into his presence. He was given authority, glory and sovereign power; all nations and peoples of every language worshiped him. His dominion is an everlasting dominion that will not pass away, and his kingdom is one that will never be destroyed.

The administrative center of this kingdom is called "Zion." The name originally designated the southeast hill of Jerusalem, the place of the city of David and the temple of Yahweh (2 Sam. 5:7). Later "Zion" came to designate the whole city of Jerusalem (Isa. 40:9; Mic. 3:12), and even the whole land (Zech. 2:7). But in prophetic passages "Zion" refers to Jerusalem, the capital of the kingdom. For example, the Bible says that the king will reign in Mount Zion (Ps. 2:6), the people of Zion will be comforted (Isa. 30:19), those who are left in Zion will be holy (Isa. 4:3), the nations will go to Zion to learn (Isa. 2:2–3), and Zion will never again be troubled (Isa. 33:20).

Following this declaration that God will extend the rule of the king, the verse dramatically instructs the king, "Rule (וּרְדֵה)

in the midst of your enemies."[31] The imperative in this passage may not have the force of a direct command, but more of the idea of promise or permission for there is a certain consequence in the imperative in this sentence.[32] If God says to the king, "Rule," then the king will rule; but this word also implies that the king will have absolute authority and that he will be honored and obeyed by his subjects.[33]

The interesting thing in this prophecy is that he will not only subjugate his enemies but will rule among them. Messiah will establish his rule by destroying his enemies at the start of his reign (Matt. 25:31–46), and will punish whatever enemies rise up against him (Ps. 2:9; Zech 14:17–18), until he delivers the kingdom up to the Father (1 Cor. 15:24–26) with only the righteous having a share in it.

B. The people will offer themselves willingly in holy service to the king (3).[34]

The expressions in verse three have proved to be the most challenging to scribes and scholars down through the ages. There are textual problems in the ancient manuscripts and versions

---

31. The verb רְדֵה means "have dominion, rule, dominate." It may be cognate to Arabic "trample, tread," and Syriac "chastise." But usage in the Hebrew Bible simply conveys the meaning of having dominion. It was first used in the Bible in Genesis 1:28 for humans to rule in the earth. It was then more specifically attached to the reign of kings (Ps. 72:8, Num, 24:19, as well as Ps. 110:2), the reign of Messiah being a restoration of what was lost to the human race because of sin. The reign is often portrayed as forceful (Isa. 14:2; see also the noun in v. 6, "dominion," מִרְדָּה), but Israel was not permitted to rule over servants ruthlessly (Lev. 25:46). Ruling over enemies was seen as the ultimate triumph, as the righteous will rule over the wicked in the future (Ps. 49:14).
32. The same imperative is used in Genesis 1:28, "Rule and have dominion over every living thing." Humans were given the authority over all creation, but they lost it by sinning; so we do not see all things under their feet—but we see Christ. Christ will receive that dominion at his second coming (Heb. 2).
33. See Thijs Booij, "Rule in the Midst of Your Foes!" VT 41 (1991):396–407.
34. See W. P. Brown, "A Royal Peformance: Critical Notes on Psalm 110:3a-b," JBL 117 (1998):93–96.

The Exaltation and Glorious Victory of the Coming King

that need to be considered, and there are unusual expressions in the clauses themselves that must be explained.

The first clause has been translated, "Your people offer themselves willingly in the day of your power." The focus is on the loyal subjects of the king who willingly join their king in the day of battle. The immediate reference in Israel would be the people of Israel, as opposed to the nations that oppose the Messiah. In the wider scope, taking all of Scripture into view on the ultimate event, "your people" would refer to all who are followers of the king, Jews and Gentiles, who have entered his kingdom by faith. Here it is said that they will offer themselves willingly. The actual word in the text is "freewill offerings" (נְדָבֹת), the plural amplifying the idea to mean willingness in all its aspects.[35] This is figurative then, meaning that those who belong to the king willingly offer themselves to him in service, and as other Scripture specifies, service in his kingdom to come (Rev. 5:10).

This will take place in the day of the king's "strength." This word (חַיִל; s.v. Ps. 49:6) can refer to economic, political, physical, or military strength. In the context of this song it is military-political power (in Judges, "a mighty man of valor / strength,"

---

35. The word נְדָבָה is from נָדַב, which has a fairly wide range of meanings in the cognate languages, from incite, be noble, be willing, and generous; the noun is a freewill offering in other languages as well as Hebrew. The verb is used for volunteering for war (Judg. 5:2) and making freewill offerings for the temple (1 Chron. 29:5).

The noun can mean in general "voluntariness," such as in Hos. 14:5, "I will love them freely," and perhaps here in Ps. 110 meaning the people will be all voluntariness. It can also be used for the freewill offering made in the sanctuary (Lev. 7:16), an offering not made under compulsion or duty, or for expiation or thanksgiving, but freely. For example, the expression "freewill offering" was used in the Old Testament for monetary gifts given for the building of the sanctuary (Exod. 35:29) or sacrificial offerings (Deut. 16:10). It refers to things offered to God based purely on love and devotion.

The adjective נָדִיב means "inclined, willing," as well as "noble" in rank, princely, perhaps someone who acts freely (Ps. 118:9). The emphasis on willingness is in the use in Exodus 35:5 and 22 for the offerings for the building. It is also used in Psalm 51:14 in the prayer for God to enable the sinner to develop a "willing spirit," someone whose self-will is broken and who willingly obeys the LORD.

גִּבּוֹר חָיִל). But the psalm uses the word "strength" (a metonymy of cause) in place of the intended effect of that strength—the victory that establishes his sovereignty. When the king unveils his strength and establishes his dominion, his people will eagerly serve him.

The next clause declares that the king has the "dew of his youth"; to qualify this it uses two prepositional phrases: "in the beauty of holiness" and "from the womb of the dawn." The Hebrew is very cryptic: "to you, the dew of your youth," or "you have," the preposition expressing possession. The noun "your youth" (יַלְדֻתֶיךָ, "your young men") is parallel to "your people" in the first half of the verse. Then with the figure of "dew" David is comparing (an implied comparison) the king's young servants to the dew. At dawn dew is discovered all over the ground, instantly appearing, fresh and innumerable. The willing servants of the king will be with the king suddenly, and in abundance. In 2 Samuel 17:12 there is the additional connotation of dew as an irresistible force.

This figure draws on the preceding prepositional phrase: "from the womb of the dawn." The figure of "womb" is an implied comparison with beginning of the day—the break of dawn is like the birth of the day from a womb. He also uses "dawn" in the same figurative way to mean the beginning of the time of the display of the king's power. Whether that begins literally at dawn is impossible to say (although Malachi says that he, the "sun of righteousness," will rise with healing in his wings); but it is possible to say that the coming of the king to establish his reign on earth is the "dawning" of a new day. And just as the dawn gives birth to the dew in splendor and great number, the future king will appear with all the company of his host.

The other prepositional phrase has been translated "in the beauty of holiness." The word "beauty" (הַדְרֵי), that is, "splendor, adornment," or "beauty" (s.v. Ps. 96:6), describes something that inspires admiration and appreciation.[36] The fact that it is in the plural may mean that it refers to beautiful garments such as

---

36. The variant reading of "mountain" draws a parallel to Mount Zion in Psalm 2:6; moreover, the image of "dew" fits the idea of "mountains" better than "splendor." So the variant reading is attractive.

those that the priests would wear (see 1 Chron. 16:29; 2 Chron. 20:21; Ps. 29:2; 96:9). The qualifying word "holiness" (an attributive genitive) explains that these beautiful adornments are holy. This may be drawing on the beautiful, holy garments used by the priests in the holy place, indicating they are properly prepared for serving the holy one.

Thus, when the king appears to put down his enemies and establish his earthly reign, he will be accompanied by a myriad of willing servants who will be adorned in holy array, meaning that they have been set apart to his service and are characterized by holiness.

III. The king will also be a high priest forever (4).

The psalm takes an unexpected turn in the fourth verse to announce that Yahweh has ordained that this future king be a high priest as well. The text says,

> "Yahweh has sworn, and will not relent:
> you are a priest forever, after the order of Melchizedek."

"Melchizedek" (מַלְכִּי־צֶדֶק) means "king of righteousness." In the Bible Melchizedek was the Jebusite priest of "the Most High God" who ruled over the ancient city of Salem, generally believed to be Jerusalem in the days of Abram (Gen. 14).[37] This person appears on the scene rather mysteriously[38] to bless Abram after the battle; and Abram, recognizing him as a spiritual authority, pays tithes to him. Because he was both a king and a priest, and because he was reigning in old Jerusalem, he made the perfect prophetic type of the Messiah, whom the prophets declared would be a king and a priest (see Zech. 3 and 6).

In Israel there could be only one order of High Priest (or priests), and in biblical times that was the order of Aaron, in

---

37. See also P. J. Nel, "Psalm 110 and the Melchizedek Tradition," *JNSL* 22 (1996):1–14.
38. When the book of Hebrews says that he was without father or mother, it may be speaking of his single appearance—in a book (Genesis) given to genealogies and historical connections, this man appears without any reference to tribe and lineage, and remains in our minds without such.

the line of Levi. The Davidic kings came from the line of Judah, and any function they had in the sacrificial ritual would have been under the authority of the priesthood. The only way that a descendant of David could become the official priest was for the order of Aaron to come to an end, which happened at the death of Christ according to New Testament teaching. The saints now have a new High Priest and King. And God declared with a solemn oath that this king would be a priest forever, a royal priest—making his loyal subjects a kingdom of priests. The verb "swore" draws on a very human enterprise, that is, confirming the words of a promise or an agreement by invoking the higher power. But since there is none higher than God, he swore by himself. The reason for the use of a divine oath was to communicate to people that God was obligating himself to fulfill his word—his life and reputation were hereby put on the line (not that he ever lied or went back on his word—the oath was for their benefit). For our greater confidence in his promises, he bound himself by solemn oath.

To reiterate this point the text uses another very human expression: "he will not relent" (or "repent"). The volitional aspect of the verb (נחם; s.v. Ps. 119:76) means "to change one's mind"; and the emotional aspect means "to grieve, regret" (see Exod. 13:17 for the former, and 1 Sam. 15:11 for the latter). Here the expression confirms the oath with the volitional meaning: God will not alter his plan or his purpose. The use of this verb is figurative where God is concerned (an anthropomorphism); it is designed to emphasize the absolute certainty of the promise.

The declaration "You are a priest forever" is significant for a number of reasons. God chose the priests in Israel, and when God chose them, no one could challenge that choice. God has chosen the king, our Lord, to be the eternal high priest. But as this appointed priest of God, the king will not be limited to Salem as Melchizedek was, but will rule over and be priest for the whole world.

This fourth verse then indicates why the king's youthful servants will be clothed in holiness—their king is their priest. As a priest, he will sanctify the people and make them spiritual servants, or, as the original intention for Israel put it, a kingdom or priests and a holy nation (Exod. 19:5–6).

The Exaltation and Glorious Victory of the Coming King

IV. The king will crush all opposition to his reign (5–6).

A. *The victory will be convincing (5–6).*

The psalmist now turns to describe the victory of the coming king. It will be a crushing and convincing victory over the king's enemies. The first statement made is that "The Lord is at your right hand." The Hebrew text now uses the word "lord" (אֲדֹנָי, *'ădōnāy*, not the letters *YHWH* with the vowels for "Lord" under them as usual for God). To whom does this refer? The similarity to *'ădōnî*, "my lord," and the reference to the right hand in verse 1, would seem to indicate it is the king who is at God's right hand who will be the victor. But it appears here that the image is reversed, that God will be at the king's right hand in the battle. Many of the ancient manuscripts simply changed it to "Yahweh" to say that it was God at the king's right hand who would give the victory.

The passage is probably referring to Yahweh and not the king because of this spelling. But more compelling is the fact that the theme of the psalm is that Yahweh was going to make the enemies of the king his footstool. The king will go to battle, but Yahweh will crush the heads of the enemies, judge the nations through this victory, and inflict a great defeat (indicated by the corpses). Yahweh will do the work, and the king will receive the kingdom and the glory. Morever, verses 1–4 refer to Yahweh's exaltation of the king, and verses 5–6 the means by which he will enable it to take place. The use of *'ădōnāy* in this verse may serve as a structural marker, beginning a new section, and making a contrast between "the LORD" and "my Lord."

The fact that God is at the right hand of the king now carries a slightly different nuance than the place of honor: it now signifies a place of powerful activity (metonymy of adjunct). God is ready to enable the king to be victorious (see Ps. 16:8, 45:10, 109:31, and 121:5). The king will be victorious in the day of his strength, the day of battle, because it will be the day of judgment. The expression "in the day of his anger" harmonizes with the prophecies of the "Day of the LORD" (in Joel and Amos). And the effect will be that God will shatter (מָחַץ is a prophetic perfect) kings in that day. To shatter or crush is to deliver a fatal blow which will completely disarm and incapacitate the enemies. A graphic illustration is the use of this verb in Judges 5:26, which tells how Jael crushed the skull of Sisera with the nail.

Not only will the LORD destroy kings in this day of wrath, the psalm tells us that he will judge among the nations, filling the valleys with the bodies and destroying the heads of many countries. The picture is of a total victory in battle. It sounds unpleasant and bloody, but then war is unpleasant and bloody. The Bible prophesies a great final battle which the coming of the Messiah will bring to an end (see Zech. 14). In this victorious battle the LORD will judge (יָדִין; s.v. Ps. 140:2) among the nations, probably meaning he will execute judgment (1 Sam. 2:10; Jer. 21:12). This will be among the nations, or Gentiles; many from all the nations will have believed and become part of his kingdom, but the wicked will not, and so will be judged (see Matt. 25:31–46). This is a scene that has been played out in many conflicts in human history; but the ultimate judgment will come at the end of the age with a final victory for the Messiah (compare Ps. 2:10–12).

The graphic description of filling the land with corpses is a natural battle-field description.[39] If there were specific settings in the history of Israel to which this psalm applied, there would have been battlefields strewn with the dead. Some may, however, interpret these lines to be Old Testament imagery of the future triumph of the king—so mostly figurative language. But the words still have to be explained as to what they mean, even if they were figures; and it is hard to get around the fact that judgment will bring death. Besides, the Bible says that at the end of the age when the great and final battle is fought it will be severe—the description being that it will take months to bury the dead (Ezek. 39:12).

Finally, we are told that he will "crush the head over a broad country." The same word "crush" is used here that was used above; now the object is "head," a singular form. The expression

---

39. The text has an ellipsis: it does not say what will be filled. Some of the early versions and recensions change the word "corpses" to "valleys" since the text does not say what is filled with the corpses. Later scholars wanted to include both, that he will fill the valleys with bodies. The text just says that he will fill . . . with corpses. The understanding must be the battle-field, or the land.

"to crush the head" may simply signify a devastating destruction in all the earth, i.e., crushing every head. However, it could be taken to refer collectively to the leaders of the enemies (Ps. 68:22), or with the singular the main leader of the opposition, one antagonistic ruler. The book of Revelation seems to favor this latter idea (Rev. 19:20; 20:2). The promise was first made in Genesis 3:15 which said that the head of the serpent would be bruised.

The expression "a broad country" probably refers to the land of Israel: there he will destroy the armies of the wicked one and judge the unbelieving and rebellious Gentiles (Rev. 19:19--20:15). The language of the psalm is somewhat cryptic, but when joined with other passages about the war at the end of the age and the coming of the Messiah to judge the world and begin to transform it into his kingdom of righteousness and peace, then the lines make very good sense as they stand. Whatever immediate application there may have been in the conquests of the king, the ultimate meaning of the oracle concerned the end of the age.

B. The victorious king will be refreshed (7).

The psalm concludes by stating that "he shall drink from the brook by the way; therefore he shall lift up his head." The subject here is ambiguous. The king enjoys victory because God fights for him and in him; but he will tire in the battle, and the LORD will not. So the focus shifts here to the king who will be exalted in the victory. The "brook" is the often-dry river bed that flowed with water in the rainy season; they were therefore taken as a sign of God's blessing on the land. VanGemeren suggests that the drink the king takes here may be more ceremonial, an expression of his confidence in the LORD's provision.[40] The picture of the conquering king drinking from such a brook is a sign that in his kingdom the streams will flow in great abundance (see Isa. 35:6). It is a significant touch of Scripture also to remind us that this glorious future king is human enough to drink from the brook.

And the "way" that he follows in the verse refers to the "way"

---

40. *Psalms*, p. 817.

of the activity that he is following (and so the idiom). His way is doing the work of God, bringing righteousness to the earth through judgment of wickedness. Isaiah uses the imagery of a highway to refer to the righteous service of God (see Isa. 40:1–11; 35:8).

Consequently ("therefore") this king will find honor and glory. The imagery of "lifting up the head" is used in the Bible to refer to exaltation to, or restoration to, the position of honor and dignity in the kingdom (see the cup-bearer in Genesis 40:13; and David's description of God as the lifter-up of his head in Psalm 3). The meaning of the verse seems to capture the theme of the psalm, the exaltation of the king over his domain. Not only will Yahweh enjoy honor and glory when all enemies are defeated, but his king will receive honor and glory—quite a contrast to the shame and abuse he suffered in the history of the world.

MESSAGE AND APPLICATION

This marvelous psalm is a prophecy of the coming victory of the Messiah over the world. It declares that he has been exalted to God's right hand, that he will come to establish his dominion over the world, and that he will put down all his enemies with a sudden and final blow. But he will be much more than a king—he will be a high priest, so that his followers will be sanctified and prepared to worship and serve the LORD. The expository idea may be worded this way: *God will enable his chosen king, whom he has also declared to be a royal priest, to carry out his judgment throughout the world when he sends him forth with all his faithful servants to destroy the enemies of God.*

Unless there is some immediate event that inspired David to use such elaborate expressions, the passage is pure prophecy.[41] According to the New Testament when Jesus rose from the dead he ascended to heaven and, in the language of the Bible, was seated at the right hand of the Father (Acts 2:33; Eph. 1:20; Heb. 1:3; and Heb. 10:12–13). The language is intended to say that at his ascension Jesus, the Son of God, was exalted to the place

---

41. If there was an event, then the psalm would be typological like the other Royal Psalms.

of authority and power in heaven (not that he has been literally sitting down for this time). The six New Testament passages that cite Psalm 110 (Matt. 22:44, Mark 12:36, Luke 20:42, Acts 2:34, Heb. 1:13, and 10:13) refer to Jesus's exaltation between the ascension and the second advent. He now awaits the second coming to receive his kingdom (Matt. 26:64). 1 Corinthians 15:25 describes Christ's reign upon his own throne; and at the end of that age his kingdom will be delivered up to the Father, so that in the eternal state God will be all in all.

The book of Hebrews explains how Melchizedek was a type of Christ because he did not owe his priesthood to his physical lineage, because he was both a king and a priest in Jerusalem, and because he remains a priest forever in human memory. The Aaronic priesthood did come to an end when Jesus the Messiah completely satisfied the demands of the Law and made the perfect sacrifice, fulfilling all the temple ritual once and for all. No longer was there a need for sacrifices, or the temple, or the Levitical sacrificing priests. Jesus became the high priest, consecrated by his own blood, and confirmed[42] forever when he went into the heavenly sanctuary. Because his sacrifice was made once and for all, and because it remains the basis for salvation and sanctification forever, his priesthood will never end.

The sequence of the prophecies about Messiah in the psalms is captured nicely by the writer to the Hebrews. At Jesus's resurrection and ascension, he was coronated, and so Psalm 2 declares to him, "You are my Son, this day I have begotten you." The "today" is the day of his exaltation to glory after the resurrection. Psalm 110 says that the Father said to him, "Sit at my right hand until I make your enemies your footstool." Psalm 2 says that the Father will say to the Son, "Ask of me and I will make the nations your inheritance." Only the Father knows that time, Jesus said. The writer to the Hebrews says that then the Father again brings his firstborn into the world, and declares, "You shall smash your enemies with a rod of iron" (Ps. 2), and "Rule in the midst of them (Ps. 110). Psalm 45 clarifies that his

---

42. When Hebrews says that Jesus was made perfect, it probably is drawing on the Greek text of Leviticus in the description of the ordination of priests (Lev. 8); in other words, Jesus was installed, as it were, as the high priest.

rule will be one of righteousness and equity, because he is the righteous king.

Passages like this offer hope and comfort to believers, because no matter how evil or troubling the world might appear, the final outcome is certain. Those who believe in Jesus the Messiah, and who have been sanctified by his sacrificial blood, have nothing to fear. They will be with him as he comes to rule on earth, for they will be like the dew that suddenly appears in the morning when the shadows flee away and the "sun of righteousness" rises with healing in his wings (Mal. 3). Because of that hope, believers should (1) comfort and encourage one another, (2) purify themselves to be clothed in white linen, which are the righteous acts of the saints (Rev. 19), and (3) be about the work of the kingdom, obeying the king, serving the king, and extending his kingship to people in the world.

In addition to this, because he is the great High Priest, believers also ought to be drawing near to God with their prayers because the Mediator has made that possible. He has made the perfect sacrifice, so it is possible for us to be in holy array; and he prays for us, so that we need never fear. We have a glorious high priest, but that fact is lost on the way most Christians live day in and day out. His priestly ministry was to involve representing the people to God (Heb. 2:17), making the perfect and eternal sacrifice (Heb. 7:27), and making intercession for the people (Heb. 7:24–25).

In the New Testament we have the full revelation, however; it clarifies that this king is the divine Son of God; and there can be no work of God in which all persons of the Godhead are not present and actively involved. For the Son to defeat his enemies is for God the Father to defeat the enemies.[43] The power and authority comes from the Son, who submits to the Father; the working out of the plan is through the agency of the Son, by the power of the Spirit.

---

43. The same tension occurs in Psalm 2. The psalmist advises the people to submit to the Son "lest he be angry and you perish in the way." Who will be angry—Yahweh who crowned the Messiah, or the king? Probably Yahweh because of the earlier use of "anger" in the passage. But the two are inseparable: if Yahweh is angry and destroys the rebels, he will do it through the anger and the victory of the Son.

PSALM 111

Adoration and Praise for the LORD's Great and Gracious Works

INTRODUCTION

Text and Textual Variants

    1 Praise the LORD![1]

א   I will praise the LORD[2] with all *my*[3] heart
ב   in the assembly of the upright and in the congregation.

ג   2 Great are the works[4] of the LORD;

---

1. הַלְלוּ יָהּ is probably not part of the original composition since it stands outside the acrostic arrangement (see Introduction, I:107). It was likely a liturgical addition.
2. The Greek version correctly renders אוֹדֶה as "I will acknowledge," but adds the pronominal object and makes "the LORD" vocative: ἐξομολογήσομαι σοι κύριε, "I will acknowledge you, O Lord."
3. The pronoun is not in the Hebrew; it was supplied in the Greek translation to complete the idea.
4. A few manuscripts have the singular.

PSALM 111

ד		*they are* sought out[5] by all who delight in them.[6]
ה	3	Glorious[7] and majestic are his deeds,
ו		and his righteousness endures[8] forever.
ז	4	He has made his wonders a memorial;
ח		gracious and compassionate is the LORD.
ט	5	He provides food for those who fear him;
י		he will remember his covenant forever.
כ	6	He has declared the power of his works to his people,
ל		giving[9] them the heritage of other nations.
מ	7	The works[10] of his hands are faithfulness and justice;
נ		all his precepts are sure.
ס	8	*They are* fixed for ever and ever,
ע		made in faithfulness and uprightness.[11]
פ	9	He sent redemption to his people;
צ		he commanded his covenant forever–
ק		holy and awesome is his name.
ר	10	The fear of the LORD is the beginning of wisdom;
ש		all who do them[12] have good understanding.[13]
ת		His praise endures forever.

---

5. The word in the MT is דְּרוּשִׁים; Allen, following Jouon (§ 121 e, i), translates it with a gerundive force: "worth studying" (*Psalms 101–150*, p. 121).
6. The Greek version understood the word "(all who) delight (in them)" as "his will" (τὰ θελήματα αὐτοῦ) and has the line read: "his will is sought out regarding all things."
7. For Hebrew הוֹד, "glorious," the Greek version has "acknowledgment," ἐξομολόγησις, perhaps confusing the word with תּוֹדָה.
8. The form here and in verse 10 is the participle עֹמֶדֶת, which could be translated "stands firm, fast."
9. The infinitive could also be translated to reflect what he declared, "that he would give."
10. A few manuscripts and a couple of versions have the singular.
11. The Hebrew text has the adjective, וְיָשָׁר; a few manuscripts and the versions have the noun form וְיֹשֶׁר.
12. The MT has לְכָל־עֹשֵׂיהֶם, "(to) all doers of them." The plural suffix would suggest a reference to the works of the covenant. But the Greek, Syriac and Jerome have a 3fsg suffix, translated "it," probably referring to wisdom, or the covenant itself. Translations that retain the MT usually provide an interpretive clarification, such as "all who do *his works*."
13. The word שֵׂכֶל could be translated "prudence, understanding" or even "success." See the discussion of the word in Psalm 36:4.

Adoration and Praise for the LORD's Great and Gracious Works

Composition and Context

This psalm is a hymn, a descriptive praise song of the marvelous, gracious and righteous works of the LORD. The psalmist summons all believers to praise God for these things. And so down through the ages as believers have been uplifted by this and similar hymns they have been prompted to think of God's goodness in their own lives. And the joy they experienced in rehearsing psalms like this is then enhanced by their own personal enjoyment of God's benefits. Ultimately such praise must acknowledge that what enables believers to experience such great and good acts in their lives is the grace of God.

This psalm is arranged as an acrostic, an alphabetically arranged piece, as the translation indicates. Each half-verse begins with a word that begins with a letter of the alphabet in succession. It is a way of remembering the themes of God's person and works to be sure, but it also is an attempt to show the completeness of the message.

Besides this alphabetical arrangement, the psalm can be divided into three parts according to its literary classification as a descriptive praise psalm, a hymn: there is an introductory resolve to praise (1), then a detailed summary of the cause for praise (2–9), and finally a conclusion to the praise (10). In my exposition I have chosen to join verses 2 and 3 with the introductory resolve: they form a general summary of the praise—the enumeration of the reasons to praise follows.

The psalm is closely linked to Psalm 112; both are acrostics and have 22 lines. Psalm 111 describes God through his mighty works, and Psalm 112 picks up the theme of fearing God from the end of Psalm 111. The psalm is generally understood to be post-exilic, largely because of its acrostic structure and its emphasis on the works of God in hymnic form. But there is nothing in the psalm that could not have been composed earlier.

Exegetical Analysis

Summary

The psalmist vows to praise the LORD in the assembly for his great and marvelous works, which are his established and redemptive ways that lead people to worship.

PSALM 111

Outline

I. The psalmist praises the LORD in the council for his great and marvelous works (1–3).
   A. He will give thanks to the LORD in the council of the upright (1).
   B. He will praise the marvelous works of the LORD that were sought by people (2–3).
      1. The LORD's works are great and sought by people (2).
      2. The LORD's work is majestic for his righteousness endures forever (3).
II. The psalmist enumerates the marvels of the LORD's wondrous works to people which are gracious, redemptive and established by covenant (4–9).
   A. The LORD has made his wonderful works to be remembered (4).
   B. The LORD has done marvelous things for those who trust in him (5–6).
      1. He gives food to them that fear him in accordance with his covenant (5).
      2. He gives the people the heritage of the nations (6).
   C. The LORD has done works that are established by covenant and are redemptive (7–9).
      1. His works are truth and his precepts sure (7).
      2. His works are established forever (8).
      3. He gives redemption to his people because his name is holy and awesome (9).
III. The psalmist concludes that the fear of the LORD is the beginning of wisdom, and that his praise endures forever (10).

COMMENTARY IN EXPOSITORY FORM

I. The devout praise the LORD in the congregation for his marvelous works (1–3).

A. *This praise should be given in the assembly of the righteous (1).*

Adoration and Praise for the LORD's Great and Gracious Works

The writer begins by expressing his resolution[14] to acknowledge the LORD in public praise (אוֹדֶה; for יָדָה s.v. Ps. 6:5). Because the word is used in the Bible for both confession of sin and public praise, "acknowledgment" is probably its basic meaning. The exposition should stress this idea of public acknowledgment more than the common translation of "give thanks," for the activity of giving thanks may be done in private without edifying the assembled people, and it may not elaborate as much on the reason for the praise. In this passage we can see clearly that the setting for the praise is in the midst of the congregation of the righteous—it is a public activity. The worshipers here are described both as the "company of the upright" and an "assembly." By describing the assembled people as "upright" (יָשָׁר; s.v. Ps. 67:4) the psalmist means that they are the faithful believers, those who are living according to God's word. So the praise will be given in the presence of God's faithful worshipers.

And the psalmist says that this praise will be offered "with all *my* heart." The heart is a common figure for the will and affections (a metonymy of subject), and so this praise will be offered willingly and enthusiastically.

B. The praise should acknowledge his great works and enduring righteousness (2–3).

Following this introductory verse, there is a summary of the praise that will be offered. The rest of the psalm will enumerate the LORD's actions and attributes; but in these verses we have a general description of God's great works. The psalm begins with an affirmation that the works of the LORD are great! "Works" is a very general word, referring to everything God has done, including creation (see Pss. 8:3, 19:1, 102:25, for example), or his dealings with Israel (Deut. 11:3, 7). But the description of God's works in this psalm will show that the interest is mainly in God's wonderful works in history on behalf of his covenant

---

14. The form is therefore interpreted as a cohortative of resolve, even though with this type of verb there is no clear spelling for a cohortative. The cohortative makes the speaker's plan to praise more resolved than a simple future.

people. The works are so great that those who delight in them, that is, true believers,[15] seek them out (v. 2b; literally, the works are "sought out," דְּרוּשִׁים). This is the response of every devout believer; and it is appropriate, because the great works of God are worthy of careful, diligent study.[16] Moreover, a careful, diligent study of God's great works will lead to greater praise.

Additionally, in verse 3 the psalmist affirms that such a study of God's glorious and majestic deeds will reveal the righteous nature of God. He first affirms that the deeds are glorious and majestic (הוֹד־וְהָדָר; s.v. Ps. 96:6). While the writer has not yet stated specifically what the deeds (פָּעֳלוֹ) are, he has prepared his audience for something amazing by describing them as gloriously majestic (taking the two words as a hendiadys). Moreover, these majestic works confirm that "his righteousness endures forever." The word "righteousness" (צְדָקָה, s.v. Ps. 1:5) speaks in part of the integrity of the LORD—as Judge of the world he will do what is right, and so then all of his marvelous works are linked to his righteousness in the world—he brings salvation to his people and judgment on the world.

II. The devout should praise the LORD for his gracious, redemptive works that were established by his covenant with his people (4–9).

A. *The LORD has established his works as a memorial (4)*

In these next verses the hymnist enumerates specific works to be praised—and they focus on the heart of the faith, redemption. This redemption is alluded to in a few verses and then explicitly stated at the end of the section. Verse 4 begins by stating that God made his wonderful works a memorial (s.v. Ps. 6:5). Not only would the people retain the knowledge of the great acts of deliverance, they would have opportunity to celebrate them in

---

15. Psalm 1:2 notes that it is the righteous who delight themselves in the Law of the LORD.
16. The verb used (דָּרַשׁ) means "seek, enquire"; it used for the interpretation of Scripture, the word *midrash*, exposition and application generally, is related to the verb.

the feasts that memorialized them, for at the great feasts the Israelites relived the experience of the ancestors while telling of their own salvation. The most appropriate of the festivals for this remembrance of redemption was the Passover (Exod. 12:14; 13:8ff.), for in that celebration the story of the Exodus was retold year after year. Such memorial occasions were designed to retain the heritage of the faith from generation to generation, a heritage centered on redemption (cf. Ps. 78:11). This retention was ensured by the people's participation in the telling of the account, and not just in hearing about it. In each generation the participants were to think of themselves as having been there, being redeemed from Egypt with the others (Exod. 12:14; 13:8–16). The mighty works would have been unforgettable in and of themselves (unless wilfully forgotten), but this dramatic means to retain the memory of them was most effective.

In that great deliverance, and in so many other occasions of Israel's deliverance, the LORD's attributes of grace and compassion were evident (4b; see also Exod. 33:9; 34:5–7). God's grace (חַנּוּן; s.v. Ps. 4:1) confirms that the works of God, especially in salvation, are unmerited. His beneficial works are bestowed freely. Moreover, his redemption is a demonstration of his compassion (רַחוּם; s.v. Ps. 25:6), that tender, loving care that God has for those who are helpless and dependent. These two attributes are present in all God's saving acts, but they were very clearly revealed in the Exodus.

B. The LORD has fulfilled his covenant promises by providing his people with food and a land (5–6).

Verse 5 declares that the LORD provides food for those who fear him. In this context, and in light of the parallel colon mentioning his faithfulness to the covenant, it is likely that the primary reference would be to the LORD's provision of manna and quail in the wilderness (Exod. 16; Num. 11). But the meaning of the line cannot be limited to that provision, for the LORD continually met the physical needs of his people.[17]

---

17. The perfect tense could be classified as a gnomic perfect, if not a definite past referring to a wide period of time.

The LORD's provision is directed to those who fear him, another description of those who delight in his works (v. 2). The description of the faithful as God-fearers is frequent in the Bible. The word "fear" (s.v. Ps. 2:11) may be rendered "reverence" or "reverential fear" in passages like this. The term includes the idea of being drawn to something powerful (and dangerous) in awe and wonder, but shrinking back in fear and respect. It describes the true believer as one who is drawn to the LORD in adoration, but who in reverence seeks to live obediently before the sovereign LORD.

The verse continues the praise of God's attributes and works by stating that he will remember his covenant forever (5b). He delivered Israel from bondage in Egypt in partial fulfillment of his covenant promises, and at Sinai he established the covenant with them, making them his covenant people. Because this covenant was the foundation and expression of the faith, the people could count on the LORD to act in faithfulness to his promises. This is because to "remember" a covenant means to act on the basis of what was remembered, i.e., the covenant promises and stipulations.

Then in verse 6 the hymn praises the power of God for dispossessing the Canaanites and settling Israel in the land promised to the fathers. The Bible makes it clear that the inhabitants of the land had become so evil that God was ready to judge them; and he used Israel as his instrument to do this in the conquest. God then gave the land to his people, with the warning that if they became disobedient and corrupt he would also expel them.

So in these verses we have moved from the exodus to the wilderness provisions and the conquest. Only the power of God could have done these things. And so the praise attributes all of it clearly to his power. But the powerful acts of God were also evidence that he acted in accordance with the promises he made, and so the hymn now turns to praising his faithfulness.

C. In faithfulness to his covenant promises the LORD brought redemption to his people (7–9).

The psalmist now links the word of God to the works of God in his praise. The works are both faithful and just, and so his

Adoration and Praise for the LORD's Great and Gracious Works

word is trustworthy. In this immediate context, settling Israel in Canaan's land was a demonstration of his faithfulness to the covenant promises, his word, but by driving out the Canaanites he also revealed his justice. The LORD judged the Canaanites because of their wickedness (Deut. 32:4). In fact, the reason for Israel's being in Egypt for so long was in part due to the fact that the Amorites were not evil enough yet to be judged (Gen. 15:16).

When God made the covenant with Israel, he included more than wonderful promises. He gave them the Law, their obligations to the covenant. If all God's works are faithful and just, then what he demanded in the Law was also trustworthy and upright, established forever. These laws and precepts were both forceful and pleasing to believers (Ps. 19:7–9); and since they revealed the faithfulness and righteousness of God, they were not temporary or changeable—they were fixed forever. God's word is right—it is reliable and appropriate if the people wanted to live under God's continued gracious and mighty works. When God revealed his mighty works he also demonstrated the reliability of his word which he guaranteed with covenants.

But the one major event in which the faithfulness of the word of God and the power of the work of God could be seen most vividly was redemption. So in verse 9 the psalmist makes his climactic point: "He provided redemption for his people; he ordained his covenant forever." Israel's redemption from bondage was a provision from heaven. And when it came to pass in accordance with his revealed word, he ordained (literally "commanded") his covenant forever. The mighty redemptive work of God on earth was the working out of the eternal plan of God; and the work of redemption was ordained in covenant form forever.

And that plan was a manifestation of God's nature: "Holy and awesome is his name." The word "name" represents his nature (as a metonymy of subject; s.v. Ps. 20:1). First and foremost he is holy (s.v. Ps. 22:3); he is unique, set apart, distinct from anything in creation. There is no one like him—in power, in justice, or in faithfulness. No power in Egypt, physical or spiritual, could prevent or forestall the exodus; when he delivered his people from the bondage of the world, he destroyed all the gods of Egypt (Exod. 33:6). And no power on earth could prevent his giving the land of Canaan to them as their inheritance. There simply was no one like him, in heaven or on earth. Moreover, the many ways that God revealed his holiness were so amazing that they also showed him to be awesome (s.v. Ps. 2:11). Israel naturally responded with fear and adoration—they worshiped him and him alone. Such is the natural and fitting response of the redeemed to their God.

III. The life of wisdom begins with the fear of the LORD and will lead to everlasting praise (10).

Having celebrated the LORD's wonderful works and holy character, the psalmist concludes with a principle from wisdom literature, one that flows from the immediate description of God as awesome, that is, to be feared! He reminds everyone that "the fear of the LORD is the beginning of wisdom." The word "fear" includes the ideas of adoration and awe of something powerful and majestic, as well as the fear of getting too close to the dangerous power (s.v. Ps. 2:11). The fear of the LORD describes those who are obedient worshipers. In reverence and respect they shrink back from God almighty, the consuming fire and judge of all the world; but they cannot help but be drawn closer in adoration and wonder to their redeemer.

The effect of fearing the LORD includes many things, but here as in Proverbs it is the beginning of wisdom. "Wisdom" is the ability and discipline to live a productive and honorable life in compliance with the Word of God (s.v. Ps. 19:7). All such ability or skill is God-given, and so by faith the believer will seek to live a moral and righteous life. And submitting one's will to the sovereign will, that is, living in the fear of the LORD, is the way one begins to cultivate Godly wisdom. Then, that wisdom will increase the more the believer understands the will of God and commits to doing it. And so, all who follow God's precepts have good understanding (for שֵׂכֶל, s.v. Ps 36:4). The word can mean understanding, but it often is wisdom or prudence that proves to be successful. The success, however, is ultimately from God, and not from people themselves (see the use of the word in Isaiah 52:12 for the Messiah, who ultimately is successful).

MESSAGE AND APPLICATION

The message of this psalm is that *Devout worshipers must praise the LORD in the sanctuary for his marvelous and gracious works that bring redemption and blessing to his people.* In fact, the purpose of his wonderful works is to inspire greater praise and obedience.

Believers have every good reason to praise the works and the words of the LORD; they are powerful and awesome, because he is mighty and majestic. There are many, many examples of the amazing works of the LORD, but those attached to his work of redemption come to the fore. And if that was true of Israel's experience in Egypt, how much more for the believer today who has been set free from the bondage of sin and the world, entered into an eternal covenant through Christ Jesus, and has found that the Lord of the covenant is faithful to his people. The Church accordingly has used this psalm at Easter and Eucharistic services, because the redemption provided by Jesus Christ includes his resurrection from the dead, guaranteeing that the promises of the covenant are sure, and that our redemption is eternal.

PSALM 112

The Blessings for the Righteous

INTRODUCTION

Text and Textual Variants

	1	Praise the LORD![1]
א		Blessed is the one[2] who fears the LORD,
ב		who delights greatly in his commands.
ג	2	His descendants will be mighty in the land;
ד		*each* generation of the upright will be blessed.
ה	3	Wealth and riches are in his house,
		and his righteousness endures forever.
ו	4	Light dawns for the upright in darkness;
ח		h*e is* gracious and compassionate and righteous.[3]

---

1. הַלְלוּ יָהּ
2. The Hebrew text has אִישׁ after אַשְׁרֵי instead of הָאִישׁ as in Psalm 1:1.
3. Only a few times in the Bible are these attributes of the LORD ascribed to a human. Consequently, some Hebrew and Greek manuscripts include God as the subject.

ט	5	Good *is the* man[4] *who* deals graciously and lends freely,
׳		*who* sustains his affairs with justice.
כ	6	Surely he will never be shaken;
ל		a righteous person will be in everlasting memory.
מ	7	He will not fear a bad report;
נ		his heart is steadfast, trusting in the LORD.
ס	8	His heart is firm, he will not fear;
ע		in the end he will look *in triumph* on his foes.
פ	9	He has given generously[5] to the poor,
צ		his righteousness endures forever;[6]
ק		his horn will be exalted in honor.
ר	10	The wicked man will see *it* and be troubled,
ש		he will gnash his teeth and melt away;
ת		the desire of wicked *people*[7] shall perish.

Composition and Context

Psalm 112 expands the last verse of Psalm 111; but whereas Psalm 111 recorded the mighty works of the LORD, Psalm 112 will focus on the blessings of the LORD on those who fear him. There are a number of connections between the two psalms, notably the acrostic style and eleven terms or expressions from Psalm 111 used in 112. The poems are close enough in style and contents that they could have been the work of the same poet.[8] Allen does not go that far though; he thinks it is more likely that the writer of Psalm 112 used 111.[9] We cannot know for certain.

---

4. The Hebrew verse begins simply with טֽוֹב־אִ֭ישׁ, and there are a number of ways this could be translated. The Greek has, "He who deals . . . is a kind man." The simplest would be: "A good man deals graciously . . . ." But it may also be translated, "Good will come to the man who deals graciously . . . ," or, "It is good for a man to deal graciously . . . ."
5. The text reads: "he has scattered, he has given to the poor." The two verbs may be taken together, the first modifying the second to describe his giving as widespread or generous.
6. The Greek version has "forever and ever."
7. The word "wicked" in the MT is here in the plural. The Greek translation has "sinners."
8. Kraus, *Psalms 60–150*, p. 362.
9. *Psalms 101–150*, p. 128.

The Blessings for the Righteous

The psalm is a wisdom psalm, having most of the characteristic features of wisdom and showing parallels with the book of Proverbs.[10] And the psalm frequently employs well-known lines in its survey of the blessings of the LORD. But the scope of wisdom included in this brief psalm presents a realistic portrayal of wisdom. It embraces the proverbial idea that there are wonderful blessings for those who fear the LORD and follow wisdom, but in its allusions and images it also reminds us that the wise are not immune from adversity.[11] As with other wisdom literature that deals with adversity and suffering Psalm 112 promises a successful and blessed outcome for the righteous in the end, and divine retribution for the wicked.[12]

The acrostic pattern the psalm follows is like Psalm 111, beginning each colon or half verse with the successive letters of the alphabet rather than each verse. The acrostic pattern creates some difficulties for the analysis of parallelism as well as specific emphases in the lines.

There have been several attempts to find the setting for this psalm. A few argue that the psalm is also a royal psalm, and this would put it early, at least pre-exilic. But there is no consensus of the setting—was it for a royal wedding, righteous administration, a priestly blessing, or a liturgy at the gate for worshipers. And in general most commentators see no clear evidence for its setting; but they assume the work originated in the late exilic period—although there is not much evidence for this either.[13] Allen says the psalm is a fine example of post-exilic piety and caring for others in the community.[14] One wonders, though, where such piety and caring is recorded—not much in the writing of Ezra,

---

10. See further M. E. Thomas, "Psalms 1 and 112 as a Paradigm for the Comparison of Wisdom Motifs in the Psalms," *JETS* 29 (1986):15–24.
11. VanGemeren, *Psalms*, p. 824. Broyles, in addressing Brueggemann's idea of orderliness, says, "Order needs to be affirmed most strongly in times of disorder, and there are indications of current disorder in this psalm and of a tension between what the world should and will be and what the world is now" (*Psalms*, p. 421).
12. See J. K. Kuntz, "The Retribution Motif in Psalmic Wisdom," *ZAW* 89 (1977):223–33.
13. Kraus, *Psalms 60–150*, p. 363.
14. *Psalms 101–150*, p. 132.

Nehemiah and Malachi—quite the reverse. There is simply no compelling reason to place the psalm in the later period.

Attempts to find a detailed structure for the verses have not been convincing. We do have introductory and concluding verses and in between a listing of divine blessings for the righteous.

Exegetical Analysis

Summary

The psalmist enumerates the blessings of the one who fears the LORD because his righteousness endures forever, and then anticipates the exaltation of the righteous and the grievous destruction of the wicked.

Outline

I. The psalmist announces the heavenly bliss of the one who fears the LORD (1).

II. The psalmist enumerates the blessings for those whose righteousness endures (2–9).
   A. He is blessed with physical and material blessings for he is righteous (2–3).
   B. Light is given to him because he is gracious and righteous (4).
   C. He maintains his affairs because he is gracious and generous (5).
   D. He shall be held in everlasting remembrance because he is solidly established without fear (6–8).
      1. He shall never be moved but always remembered.
      2. He shall not fear a bad report but always be fixed in trust.
      3. He is established and in the end shall see his foes destroyed.
   E. The righteousness of the believer will endure because he has given to the needy and his position will be exalted with honor (9).

III. The psalmist anticipates that the wicked who are about to perish will witness the exaltation of the righteous with grief and anger as their own desires perish (10).

COMMENTARY IN EXPOSITORY FORM

I. Those who worship and obey the LORD are blessed (1)

The psalm begins with "Praise the LORD" (הַלְלוּ־יָהּ); but it is a prologue and not part of the acrostic pattern. That begins with the first line: "Blessed (א–אַשְׁרֵי) is the one ("a man") who fears the LORD." The word "blessed" (אַשְׁרֵי) should not be simply taken to mean "happy"; more fully it describes the inner joy of knowing one is right with the LORD (s.v. Ps. 1:1). Literally it could be read as "O the blessednesses of the one . . . ," the plural emphasizing the bliss. And the one blessed is the one who fears the LORD. "Fear" refers to reverential obedience (יָרֵא; s.v. Ps. 2:11). A God-fearer is a faithful believer, a devout worshiper. This line would be an encouragement to the faithful worshipers of the LORD, and a motivation to persevere.

And the verse indicates they will do just that. The second half says that they are people who greatly delight (חָפֵץ) in his commandments (see also Ps. 1:2). The word "delights" indicates either the motivation for obedience (a metonymy of cause), or the pleasure the faithful derive from obeying the commands (a metonymy of adjunct). To the devout the commandments of the LORD are not a burden but a joy because they know them to be the way of a full and fulfilling life (for מִצְוָה s.v. Ps. 119:6).

II. Those who maintain their righteousness will enjoy abundant blessings in every aspect of their lives (2–9).

A. Those who are righteous will enjoy physical and material blessings (2–3).

The psalm now records a series of blessings that come to the righteous. The first is that the descendants will be mighty. His descendants are referred to here as "his seed" and "*each generation of the upright.*" "Generation" (דּוֹר) could refer to any group of people characterized by uprightness, but in the parallelism of this verse it probably means the family of the upright, each successive generation descended from those who fear the LORD, that is, the upright. The description "upright" (יְשָׁרִים; s.v.

Ps. 67:4) is another way of saying they are obedient people, following the way of the LORD. To them God is a living reality, and his word a lamp for their way to lead them through and out of darkness. The fact that they are the upright means that their successive descendants will more than likely embrace the faith.

The promise to these descendants is that they will be "mighty" (גִּבּוֹר; s.v. Ps. 45:3). The term is at home in military contexts where it describes people as valiant ("the mighty man of valor"). But it also describes people as powerful by virtue of wealth, position, and ability (wisdom). Others will look up to them as successful and influential leaders. This specific promise is balanced in the second colon by the general verb "will be blessed" (יְבֹרָךְ; s.v. Ps. 5:12).[15] They will see their lives enriched materially and spiritually by God's intervention.

The listing of blessings continues in verse 3. "Wealth and riches" (הוֹן־וָעֹשֶׁר) are in his house, i.e., in his family and its living conditions. The word "wealth" (הוֹן), often translated "honor," actually refers to wealth and sufficiency, a synonym of "riches" in this line. This psalm like wisdom in general will use a number of paired words. The two together are emphatic, and may be interpreted as a hendiadys to get the full force. In that construction one of the words becomes a modifier of the other—"sufficient riches." The righteous will live lives that are comfortable and pleasing. See also Proverbs 3:16, 8:18, 22:4, and Matthew 10:29–30.

The second half establishes that obedience is the reason for God's blessings: "and his righteousness endures (stands) forever." This expression usually refers to the LORD, but here it is applied to people; so "righteousness" (s.v. Ps. 1:5) refers to the character and the works of the faithful. By adapting a description of God (see Ps. 111:3) the psalmist is showing the connection between God's righteousness and the believers' righteousness. As Perowne notes, this is not simply about an individual striving to copy God; it is stronger than that (II:320). He explains that righteousness is a gift, an empowerment for the believer, and in

---

15. Note the chiastic structure of the line: "Mighty / in the land / will be/ his seed // a generation / of the upright / will be blessed." See A. R. Ceresko, "The Chiastic Word Pattern in Hebrew," *CBQ* 38 (1976):303–311.

this we see the link between divine and human righteousness. The believer is living out the righteousness of God and therefore enjoys a blessed life.

B. Those who are gracious and compassionate will receive light in darkness (4).

Verse 4 introduces a hint that life even for the righteous is troubling and confusing—there is darkness. But the good news is that "Light dawns for the upright in the darkness"; it says "light glistens" (אוֹר . . . צָרַח). The image of "light" is difficult to interpret because it is used for so many things in Scripture. For example, in Psalm 97:11 the figure was used for the joy and prosperity of God's kingdom. Here it is possible that "light" refers to the LORD; this would be reflected by translating the line as "He arises as a light in the darkness to the upright, *being* gracious . . . ." But in Psalm 112 some descriptions of the LORD are applied to humans (from Ps. 111:4). So we read that "light" is given to the righteous. They are not the light, but what the light signifies is given to them. The idea would be that the upright go through many times of darkness, opposed by wicked people and beset by troubled bad reports (vv. 7 and 8); but God's provision of light enables them to live righteously and successfully in dark times.

The connection of the second colon to this line is difficult in that it simply lists three adjectives. They probably describe the upright in this psalm, even though elsewhere they are descriptions of the LORD. If they are taken to refer to the LORD's attributes here as well, then these words would be in apposition to the light, defining God's provision of ways through the darkness. But even then they would be describing the character and conduct of believers who are so empowered. The point of the line is that the faithful are gracious, compassionate and righteous. They maintain their integrity and virtue in times of trouble. The adjectives used are "gracious" (חַנּוּן; s.v. Ps. 4:1), "compassionate" (רַחוּם; s.v. Ps. 25:6), and "righteous" (צַדִּיק; s.v. Ps. 1:5). The psalmist is then describing how the upright live in harmony with the nature of God; and accordingly he would be giving us the reason why God would bless the upright.

C. Those who are generous and just will enjoy good things from God (5).

The focus in verse 5 is on the grace and generosity of the righteous. The verse begins with "good" ("Good is *the* man," טוֹב־אִישׁ, s.v. Ps. 34:8). The expression is similar to the psalm's beginning, "blessed is *the* man." The term indicates the well-being of the person—circumstances that are beneficial for a full and prosperous life. The one whose life can be characterized as good is one who is gracious and generous (compare Prov. 16:10). "He deals graciously (חוֹנֵן) and lends freely (מַלְוֶה)." Here the word-pair means the generosity is gracious; in other words the upright do not look for returns in their giving.

And the counterbalance to this gracious giving is that he sustains his affairs (his words, his acts, דְּבָרָיו) with justice (מִשְׁפָּט; s.v. Ps. 9:4). All his activities are secured because he acts with justice, or simply put, he makes the right decisions.[16]

Kidner also notes that the psalm mentions generosity here, and in verse 9, and slightly in 4b. He relates three temptations that go with the possession of money: 1) to abuse the power that money brings, hence the commending of grace and justice; 2) to fear (vv. 7–8) for much can go wrong with the wealthy; and 3) to be a miser (vv. 5, 6 and 9). Righteousness based on the fear of the LORD will bring about the proper use of money.

D. Those who are firm in their faith will not fear for in the end they will triumph over their foes (6–8).

These three verses stress the security and steadfastness of the righteous. First we read that the righteous will never be shaken (לֹא־יִמּוֹט; s.v. Ps. 62:2). There will be no wavering, no slipping; no matter what comes his way he will not be dislodged from his faith or his integrity. Not only will his security endure forever, so will the memory of him ("memorial, remembrance," זֵכֶר, s.v. 6:5; and for the word "ever," עוֹלָם, s.v. Ps. 61:4). His memory will continue as people talk about his faith and his deeds. See Psalm 111:3 and Proverbs 10:7.

According to verse 7, the righteous will not fear an evil

---

16. Kidner, *Psalms 73–150*, p. 400.

report (מִשְׁמוּעָה רָעָה). "Evil" news is disastrous news, reports of calamities, losses, or antagonism. The righteous person is not exempt from such things (see Prov. 10:24). He will not fear because his heart is steadfast (נָכוֹן; s.v. כּוּן in Ps. 93:1), trusting in the LORD (בָּטֻחַ; s.v. Ps. 4:5). The passive participle (usually rendered "trusting") might be better translated "made secure" or "secure" in the LORD. Here we have another word-pair: steadfast and secure: his heart (mind, will; s.v. Ps. 111:1) is securely steadfast in his faith in the LORD.

Verse 8 completes the trilogy. His heart is "steady," or better, "sustained" (due to the passive participle of סָמוּךְ, "to lean, rest, support"; s.v. Ps. 51:12), and so he will not fear. The emphasis on not fearing in this section therefore is the result of fearing the LORD—if the righteous fear the LORD, they will be secure in their faith and have nothing to fear in this life. They trust in the LORD, not themselves; they fear the LORD, not their enemies or the circumstances of life. They lean on and are supported by the LORD.

In the end the righteous will "look on their [his] foes." The emphasis of this expression is not the pride and gloating of the victor, but rather the simple fact that the righteous will see their enemies destroyed. Here is the hope that balances the present dark days, the evil reports, and the presence of antagonists. Ultimately the righteous will enjoy the victory of the LORD.

E. The righteous who give generously to the poor will see their position exalted with honor (9).

Generosity is the evidence of gratitude for God's gifts. And so the psalmist returns to the theme again. The text says that the righteous gives generously to the poor. The literal construction has a pair of verbs, "he scatters (פִּזַּר) he gives (נָתַן)" to the poor; this would yield the sense of "he gives generously" (see Prov. 11:24, which uses the verb in the same way). This giving is broadly dispersed and freely given without holding back. Here we have the spirit of giving that the LORD loves. Appropriately, Paul cites the verse in his appeal for people to contribute to the collection for the poor (2 Cor. 9:9).

Two blessings are promised for such a generous person. First, his righteousness endures forever. The meaning of righteousness is the same as above, i.e., the works of righteousness that he does and that will remain forever; but in this verse the focus may be narrowed to his acts of generosity. Not only will people remember his generosity, but his acts could also set different things in motion that will continue from age to age. No one can foresee the long-range effect of generous acts of righteousness.

The other blessing uses the figure of the horn: "his horn will be exalted forever." In the animal world, the horn, rising high, is a symbol of superior strength. It was used frequently for a powerful king (see 1 Sam. 2:1, and frequently in Daniel 7). Here it refers to the power and preeminence of the faithful, which also will be everlasting (see Ps. 75:5; Ps. 92:10).[17]

III. Wicked people will be consumed with grief when they see the righteous exalted and their desires perish (10).

The final verse forms the contrast to all of the above; it foresees the grief and anguish of the wicked on the day of judgment when they will see the triumph of righteousness and the destruction of wickedness. "The wicked (רָשָׁע; s.v. Ps. 1:1) will see and be troubled," or "indignant" (וְכָעָס; the verb means "to be troubled, angry, indignant). "He will gnash his teeth and melt away." Anderson describes the gnashing of teeth as a response of powerless rage.[18] The result is that he will "melt away," a figure (implied comparison) that signifies his making himself weak or ill from his anger, so that he ceases to be a threat to anyone. In fact, the psalm ends by announcing that the desire of the wicked will perish. The choice of this word for "desire" is significant; it (תַּאֲוָה) is a strong desire that usually leads to taking things. It is used of the desire of Adam and Eve in the garden; and it is used in the Decalogue with the meaning "covet." It was the desire of the wicked that prompted them to overstep their bounds and

---

17. See further Margrit L. Suring, *The Horn-Motif in the Hebrew Bible and Related Ancient Near Eastern Literature and Iconography*. AUSDDS 4 (Berrien Springs, MI: Andrews University Press 1980).
18. *Psalms 73–150*, p. 779.

exploit others, reliving the primal sin. It is the exact opposite of giving generously and graciously to the poor and needy.

MESSAGE AND APPLICATION

Psalm 112 is a wisdom psalm that parallels the teachings in Proverbs closely. It enumerates the blessings that God gives to people who fear him (which is the beginning of wisdom) and who do works of righteousness (which are the characteristics of wisdom). They will flourish, become wealthy, be kept safe and secure, find honor and fame, and ultimately see victory over the wicked. In describing the blessings, however, the psalmist gives some hints that they are not necessarily immediate or untroubled. The psalmist lives in darkness and needs light; he has enemies and needs victory, he hears reports of disaster and must remain steadfast. The blessings may come in and through the difficulties of this life, but they will come for sure in the end. So the main thrust of this psalm may be captured for exposition in this way: *Whoever fears the LORD will be blessed abundantly in this life and in the end witness the destruction of the wicked because the LORD's righteousness endures forever.*

The blessings and promises of God portrayed here may seem to focus on earthly and physical things, but that is not entirely true since much of what is given will last forever; conversely the New Testament seems to focus more on the spiritual and eternal blessings, but that is not entirely true either since much of it begins here and now (see Matt. 6:33; 2 Cor. 9:11, and Phil. 4:19). And, just as the psalm signifies, so the New Testament affirms that when blessings are given, whether material prosperity or spiritual enrichment, they bring obligations for the righteous. So the psalm is a great encouragement for the righteous, but also a reminder of their obligations (1 Tim. 6:17–19). The applications then should be drawn from the character and conduct of the person God blesses.

PSALM 113

God's Greatness Displayed in His Grace

INTRODUCTION

Text and Textual Variants

1 Praise the LORD![1]
   Praise, O servants of the LORD;[2]
      praise the name of the LORD.
2 Let the name of the LORD be blessed
      from now and forever more.
3 From the rising of the sun to[3] the place where it sets,
      the name of the LORD is to be praised.[4]

---

1. Throughout the psalm I have retained the use of "the LORD" as a substitute for the holy name "Yahweh," although a translation with the exact name would make some of the expressions clearer, and the main call to praise, "praise Yah[weh]" or *hallelû-Yāh* (הַלְלוּ־יָהּ), is well-known to most students of the Bible.
2. The Greek Old Testament, Aquila, Symmachus, Theodotion, and Jerome make "the LORD" the object of the imperative and "servants" (not in construct now) is the vocative: "Praise the LORD, O servants."
3. Many manuscripts, some of the Greek manuscripts, and Aquila and Symmachus have a conjunction: "and unto."
4. Instead of the passive מְהֻלָּל in the MT, the Greek version makes it an imperative: "praise the name of the LORD" (αἰνεῖτε τό ὄνομα κυρίου)."

4 The LORD is high above all the nations;
    above the heavens is his glory.
5 Who is like the LORD our God,
    who sits enthroned on high,
6 who comes down to look[5]
    on the heavens and the earth?
7 He raises the poor from the dust[6]
    and[7] from the ash-heap he lifts up the needy,
8 to seat *them* with princes,
    with the princes of his people.[8]
9 He settles the barren woman in *her* home
    as a joyful mother of children.
    Praise the LORD![9]

Composition and Context

Psalm 113 is part of a group of psalms later designated as the *Hallel*, Hymns of Praise to be sung at the great festivals, especially at Passover which celebrated the deliverance of Israel from Egypt. This collection includes Psalms 113–118. In the first century, for example, at a typical Passover Psalms 113 and 114 would be sung before the meal, and Psalms 115–118 after it, when the final cup had been filled.[10]

It is difficult to know when this custom of singing Psalms 113–118 at the festivals began. It is certainly pre-Christian in origin, but how much earlier is unclear. It looks like it was operative before the closing of the canon because these passages have

---

5. The Greek translated this line as, "and looks down upon that which is lowly" (καὶ τὰ ταπεινὰ ἐφορῶν).
6. For "dust" in the Hebrew text the Greek version used γῆς, "earth" of ground."
7. The conjunction "and" is found in a few manuscripts, the Greek version, and Jerome.
8. The Syriac and one manuscript do not have "with the princes"; and the Syriac does not have "his" with "his people."
9. The final "הַלְלוּ־יָהּ" is not found in the Greek version; instead it comes at the beginning of Psalm 114.
10. The designation Great *Hallel* is also used, but there is disagreement over what it includes: some say it refers to Psalm 136, others to Psalms 120–136, and others to Psalms 135 and 136.

been placed together. Later the Church incorporated Psalms 113, 114 and 118 to sing at Easter not only because Jesus inaugurated the New Covenant at a Passover meal but also because they saw the fulfillment of the festivals of Passover and First Fruits in the death and resurrection of Jesus.

Psalm 113 is clearly a descriptive praise psalm, a communal hymn; it begins with the call to praise (1–3), the cause for the praise (2–9b), and a concluding call to praise in the form of one expression (9c). Its intended setting may have been cultic with the plural call to worship addressed to the "servants of the LORD." A common interpretation is that the psalm was written to celebrate God's gracious intervention to restore Israel after the exile, putting the date of the composition late, of course.[11] This interpretation is based in part on the Targumic explanation of the section drawn from the song of Hannah (1 Sam. 2) that the barren woman represents Israel after the restoration (also from Isa. 54).

Other views place the writing of the psalm much earlier. J. T. Willis says it is a song of victory that originated in the north and was later taken over by the Temple musicians; he argues that parallels with the song of Hannah indicate that both pieces came from the sanctuary at Shiloh.[12] D. N. Freedman dated the composition even earlier, to the 12th century with the song of Hannah, coming in the monarchical period.[13] On the other hand, Allen notes that there are forms in the psalm (vv. 5 and 6) that are most likely late; he follows the view that the psalm is the end of a long process of critical development, and verses 7–9b make use of the song of Hannah in an archaized form.[14] If this is correct it would make the dating of the psalm impossible because it would include both early and late elements.

The basic message of the psalm is certainly ancient, namely that the God of heaven comes down in some way to intervene in

---

11. See, for example, Kirkpatrick, *Psalms*, p. 677; Anderson says the date is uncertain, but possibly post-exilic (*Psalms 73–150*, p. 780).
12. "The Song of Hannah and Psalm 113," *CBQ* 35 (1975):139–54.
13. "Psalm 113 and the Song of Hannah," in *Pottery, Poetry, and Prophecy, Studies in Early Hebrew Poetry* (Winona Lake, IN: Eisenbrauns, 1980):243–61.
14. *Psalms 101–150*, p. 134.

the affairs of humans to lift them out of their dire circumstances and restore to them freedom, prosperity and dignity. It would be appropriate for this theme to be revived for the post-exilic community. But we have no solid evidence to determine the origin of the composition or how it might have been revised to fit the later period.

The structure of the psalm is fairly easy to identify. Verses 1–3 record the call to praise the name of the LORD ("name" is mentioned three times). Verses 4–9a provide the cause for the praise, and typically focuses on the greatness of the LORD (vv. 4–5) and his grace (vv. 6–9b). There is no didactic conclusion, only a renewed call to praise with "Praise the LORD" (v. 9c). This expression, however, may belong at the beginning of the next psalm instead. I will follow this structure, making two sub-points for the second section on the cause for praise. But others wish to divide the psalm into three strophes of three verses each. Verses 1–3, of course, form the first. The second, verses 4–6, describes the greatness of God. And the third, verses 7–9, record examples of his grace. In support of this structure is the use of the verb "to be high" (רום) at the beginning of verses 4 and 7, as well as the framing of the second section (vv. 4–6) with an emphasis on the nations in the earth. Verse 6 is a difficulty in this analysis because it describes God's gracious condescending and belongs better with the latter section. Allen arranges it with 1–3 the call, 4–6 the glory and grace, and 7–9 two cases of grace.[15] That is certainly workable, although the division between greatness and grace can be maintained within a second major section on the cause for the praise (vv. 4–9b).[16] How the psalm is divided is less important than a clear explanation of the development of the message. The expositor may find it more effective to discuss the greatness as a unit (vv. 4–5) and then the grace (vv. 6–9).

---

15. *Psalms 101–150*, p. 135.
16. For further discussion see J. A. Loader, "A Structural Analysis of Psalm 113," *OTWSA* 19 (1977):64–8; and P. L. Graber, "The Structural Meaning of Psalm 113," *OPTAT* 4 (1990):340–52.

Exegetical Analysis

Summary

The psalmist calls upon all the servants of the LORD to praise him because although he sits enthroned on high he comes down to lift the lowly to high places and fill up the life of the barren.

Outline

Introduction: "Praise the LORD!"
I. Call to praise: The psalmist calls upon the servants of the LORD to praise the one who is worthy of all praise for all time in all the earth (1–3).
   A. He summons the servants of the LORD to praise his name (1).
   B. He announces that the LORD is worthy of praise for all time (2).
   C. He announces that the name of LORD is worthy of praise in all the world (3).
II. Cause for Praise: The psalmist reports the fact that the LORD, who set himself above all things, comes down to deliver people from their degradation and distress (4–9b).
   A. His greatness: He sits enthroned in glory above all nations and heavens (4–5).
   B. His grace: He condescends to meet the needs of people (6–9b).
      1. He comes down to care for his creation (6).
      2. He exalts the miserable poor and needy to places of honor and dignity (7–8).
      3. He makes the barren woman to dwell in a home as a joyful mother (9).
III. Conclusion: "Praise the LORD!"

COMMENTARY IN EXPOSITORY FORM

I. The servants of the LORD must praise him at all times and in all places (1–3).

The prologue *hallᵉlû-Yāh*, "praise the LORD [Yah]," leads naturally into the call for praise as the same form of the verb is repeated twice without the abbreviated form of the name: "praise." This word for "praise" (הָלַל; s.v. Ps. 33:1) signifies enthusiastic and spontaneous praise, a glowing report. The object of the praise in the different contexts will indicate just how enthusiastic the praise might be. Here, in the first verse the object is the LORD—the direct object appears at the end of the line, after the identification of those being called to praise: "praise, O servants of the LORD, praise the name of the LORD."

The call is addressed to the "servants of the LORD" (עַבְדֵי יְהוָה). It is possible that the reference is to the priests and Levites, perhaps the Levitical singers and musicians (see Pss. 134:1 and 135:18); but it more likely refers to worshipers in general, true believers who belong to the covenant community called to be the servants of the LORD. The designation of "servant of the LORD" for a worshiper is a high title, the highest that people can have. But it reminds them of their covenant obligations as well as their privileges as the people of God.

One obligation is to praise the name of the LORD throughout the world. The "name" refers to the person and works of the LORD and not simply the personal name "Yahweh"—the expression refers to the "name" of the name Yahweh (so a metonymy of subject; s.v. Ps. 20:1). Yahweh has a name—and "name" refers to all that God has revealed himself to be. Kraus elaborates even further by saying that "everything that has taken place and is taking place is comprehended in the divine שֵׁם [name] alone: in the secret and the wonder of the personal, actual presence of the God of Israel. His name distinguishes itself from all phenomena of wonder and wishful thinking. His name is the free and sovereign self-determination of his salutary activity."[17]

Kidner observes that the motif of "name" is complemented by that of "servants." He explains that for worship to be acceptable to God it must be more than flattery and more than guesswork. Worship expressed in praise is the homage of the those who are committed to that which has been revealed.[18]

In the second verse the psalmist calls for praise to be offered at all times. The "name of Yahweh" is repeated in the verse, but

---

17. *Psalms 60–150*, p. 369.
18. *Psalms 73–150,* p. 400.

the verbal construction has changed. The verse uses the jussive "let it be" (יְהִי) with the passive participle (מְבֹרָךְ), "blessed" (s.v. 5:12). The verb, "to bless," essentially means "to enrich"; and while it is in the same semantic range as other verbs for praise, it brings a distinct emphasis. By their witness and their praise they make God known in the world, they enrich his reputation. The words used in offering such a blessing would naturally tell all of the things the LORD has done. And this report will continue to be enlarged as successive people of God witness his mighty works "from now and forever more."

But it is not enough that praise be offered only in one small place by one small community; God is sovereign over the whole world, and so people throughout the world should praise him. The verbal form is another passive participle (מְהֻלָּל), but no verb is expressed here. Based on the previous construction, the verb to be supplied would be "may it be." Then the psalm uses a figurative expression (a merism) to refer to the totality of people: "from the rising of the sun unto its setting [going in] *may* the name of the LORD be praised." The figure lists two opposites to indicate the totality. The place of the rising of the sun is in the East, and the time is the morning; the place of the setting of the sun is in the West, and the time is the evening. It means, everyone, everywhere, from east to west, and all the time, from morning til evening, should be praising him.

It was always the plan of God that his servant Israel should be the channel of blessing to the world (Gen. 12:3); he made them into a kingdom of priests (Exod. 19:6). God's plan from the outset included the nations in his kingdom. This came to be expressed more and more as Israel had to deal with the nations (from about 750 B.C. through the captivities and the return). Malachi finally reiterated the prophecy that the nations will eventually be offering pure worship to the LORD and proclaiming his name (1:11). This psalm harmonizes with that prophecy.

II. They should praise the LORD for his greatness and his gracious acts (4–9).

A. The LORD reigns over all from heaven (4–5).

Beginning with verse 4 we have the lengthy report of

the cause for the praise, God's greatness and his grace. The psalmist first describes the exalted greatness of the LORD: "The LORD is high above all the nations." The verb "high" (רָם) designates his unparalleled greatness over all the nations (see Isa. 40:12–18; and 52:13). The nations are nothing before him; he transcends all created beings and all nations, for he is Lord over them all due to his exalted position (see Pss. 46:10; 99:2 and Isa. 40:17).

What is more, "his glory is above the heavens." The word "glory" (s.v. Ps. 19:1) in this passage means all the supernatural manifestations of his presence. He who sits enthroned in the highest heavens is surrounded by brilliant and radiant light; and all of it means that there is no one more important than he, no one more honorable, no one more powerful.

The natural response to this comes in the form of a rhetorical question in verse 5: "Who is like Yahweh our God?" The personal name Yahweh and the epithet "our God" are central to the covenant God made with Israel. The point of the expression is to affirm that there is no one like him; he is totally incomparable. No powerful nation on earth, no acclaimed god in the pagan skies, can even come close to the glory of the God Yahweh.

What makes him incomparable is his sovereign majesty. He reigns above all gods, and all nations, for the (anthropomorphic) expression "he sits" in reference to God means that "he sits enthroned above."[19] And it is he himself who has exalted his throne above all else because of his innate power and authority.

---

19. The Hebrew construction is a little difficult, but a common grammatical one. הַמַּגְבִּיהִי לָשָׁבֶת is the *hiphil* participle, "he makes high," followed by the *qal* infinitive construct, "to dwell." In such a construction (called hendiadys) the infinitive serves as the main verb, and the participle modifies it. Hence: "he sits on high."

The final *hîreq-yôd* on the participle is not a pronominal suffix. Older works labeled it *hîreq campaginis*, a long connecting vowel. It occurs several times in this psalm. It appears to add nothing to the meaning or force of the word. Some folks have suggested it is an old form, perhaps originally used to mark the genitive. But there is little information. A conclusion that we have here an attempt by the psalmist to bring back an old form is based on too many assumptions.

B. The LORD comes down to meet the needs of people (6–9ab).

In verse 6 we have a transition to the grace of God. It connects with the last verse by using the same construction, but now in contrast to the previous one: "he comes down to see" is literally "he makes low (הַמַּשְׁפִּילִי) to see (לִרְאוֹת) in the heavens and on/in the earth." The expression could be rendered "he looks far down" on what is happening in the heavens and the earth, but the emphasis on his care and intervention in human affairs may be more clearly expressed by reference to his condescension—he comes down to care for his creatures.[20] This condescension in no way diminishes his greatness; in fact, it is the evidence of his greatness.[21] Kirkpatrick records some lines from John Keble to summarize this point (p. 678):

> Exalting still His holy place,
> Low bending still His eye of grace,
> In heaven above, in earth below.[22]

Now the psalm will provide two examples of the grace of God. The first is that he raises the poor from the dust and lifts up the needy from the ash-heap." The verb "he raises" (מְקִימִי; s.v. Ps. 3:1) is paralleled with "he lifts up" (יָרִים), the latter forming a word play with the previous use of the verb in verse 4. The LORD is "high"; and what does he do with his high and lofty position? He descends to raise up the poor and needy, described as being in the dust and ash-heap. It is a picture of utter degradation and misery. Poor people would sort through the rubbish heaps for anything useful, and warm themselves by the constantly smoldering fire. But God delights in raising them up from such a low and degrading estate, to seat them with the nobility of his people, the rich and the powerful of the land (see Ps. 146:3 and Prov. 19:6). The picture is that of reversing the fortunes of people, either individuals (like Job) or the nation out

---

20. Anderson, *Psalms 73–150*, p. 781.
21. See I. W. Slotki, "Omnipresence, Condescension and Omniscience in Psalm 113:5–6," *JTS* 32 (1931):367–370.
22. The source of the lines is difficult to find; Kirkpatrick does not provide it.

of war and exile, and raising them to a higher estate of honor and dignity—it is a transition from a living grave to glory. The verse is not intended to say that God always does this—there are many situations and circumstances involved; neither does it say he chooses to do it quickly (as we learn from the case of Job). In fact, it may be an exaltation after death, as in the case of Lazarus in Jesus' parable (Luke 16:19–31). The picture of the exaltation of the poor to the place of nobility is given here as an example of the grace of God, what he can do, what he delights in doing, and what he will do for the saints in the end.

The second illustration tells how he can change the estate of the barren woman so that she will become a joyful mother of children in a home: "He causes the barren woman to dwell in her home *as* a joyful mother of children." The verse is from the song of Hannah (1 Sam. 2); there is therefore no reason to doubt that it was intended to speak to the basic stigma of a barren woman, telling how God can resolve that dilemma and give her children.

The Targum, however, again relates the passage to a major historical event for the whole nation, not just a lowly barren woman. It reads, "He gives a home to the Assembly of Israel, which may be compared to a barren woman who sits looking anxiously at the men of her house, *to be* full of crowds, like a mother who rejoices over her children." Support for this interpretation (or application) was no doubt derived from the language of Isaiah 54 which compares exiled Israel to a barren woman and promises in the restoration an expanding population. That restoration and reversal was, of course, a great work of grace by the sovereign God. But it was no more supernatural than opening a barren womb and providing a woman like Hannah with children. So the psalmist is using the lines from the Song of Hannah to apply to all such case where God meets the needs of the oppressed and lonely.

III. Praise the LORD (9c).

The third part of this type of psalm usually has a conclusion, either a lesson, or a renewed call to praise. Having said all that he has said, the psalmist needed no further elaboration and so simply called the congregation to praise the LORD.

MESSAGE AND APPLICATION

This little psalm reveals so clearly the greatness and the grace of the LORD: The gracious acts of the LORD reveal his greatness, for as sovereign Lord he cares for his creation. That care is portrayed in two arenas, the miserable poor people who have no hope of a better life, and the lonely barren woman who is filled with sadness. By his power and through his grace he can change these things. *The LORD who reigns above all the world comes down to earth to exalt the lowly and care for the needy.* He can lift up the poor from the ash heap and enable them to enjoy a royal life; and he can change the fortunes of a barren woman so that she will be a joyful mother of children. The two samples focus on the circumstances in society and the joy in the home.

The psalm provides a glimpse of things to come. In the fulness of time God sent forth his Son to redeem people; and so to fulfill the eternal plan, the Son laid his glory by and became incarnate in order to meet the needs of people (Phil. 2). He demonstrated in his earthly ministry that he is able to meet all the physical needs that people have, but in so doing he revealed he could meet the greater need of redemption, delivering us from the bondage and emptiness of this world to dwell with him in glory and enjoy his eternal blessings. Such grace and power certainly require that people everywhere and at all times praise the name of the Lord.

PSALM 114

The Supernatural Formation of the Nation

INTRODUCTION

Text and Textual Variants[1]

1 When Israel went forth[2] of Egypt,
   The house of Jacob from a people of a strange language,[3]
2 Judah became his sanctuary
   Israel his dominion.[4]

---

1. The Greek version provides an initial "Hallelujah," Αλληλουια, taken from the end of Psalm 113. That creates a sequence of four psalms with the same heading, but the pattern is secondary.
2. The MT uses the infinitive construct in a temporal clause: "When Israel went forth (בְּצֵאת)." The Greek version renders this as ἐν ἐξόδῳ, "At the Exodus (of Israel from Egypt)."
3. MT's לֹעֵז is translated in the Greek version as ἐκ λαοῦ βαρβάρου, "from a barbarian people"—people speaking a different language.
4. For the MT's מַמְשְׁלוֹתָיו the Greek (Syriac and Jerome) has ἐξουσία αυτοῦ (= לְמֶמְשַׁלְתוֹ), "his seat of authority." The versions indicate a singular word, but that may be their translation and not indicative of a singular form they were translating.

3 The sea saw and fled,
    Jordan turned backwards;
4 the mountains skipped like rams,
    the[5] hills like young sheep.
5 What ails you,[6] O sea, that you flee;
    You, Jordan,[7] that you turn backwards?
6 You mountains, *that*[8] you skip like rams;
    You hills, like young sheep?

7 Before the Lord tremble,[9] O earth,
    Before God,[10] *the God of* Jacob,
8 Who changed the rock into a pool[11] of water,
    The flint stone into a fountain of waters.

Composition and Context

The psalm is essentially a descriptive praise psalm, a historical hymn, but it does not follow that type very closely. Kidner addresses its unique imagery and style of the hymn by saying, "Here is the Exodus not as a familiar item in Israel's creed but as

---

5. The Greek version adds the conjunction, "and the hills."
6. This charming traditional rendering is a little free; the MT has מַה־לְּךָ, literally "What to you?" but perhaps meaning "What does it mean to you?" or, "What is wrong with you?" The Greek has τί σοί ἐστιν, "Why was it (O sea, that you fled)?"
7. The Hebrew text simply has the article on "sea" and "Jordan." The Greek clarifies the vocative sense: καὶ σοί Ιορδάνη. . . , "and you, O Jordan, that . . . ."
8. The Greek version has "that."
9. The MT has the imperative חוּלִי, "tremble"; the Greek (and Syriac) has ἐσαλεύθη, "(the earth) was shaken." Kraus suggested changing the text to what he thought was the original form כֹּל, reading "all the earth," to make it harmonize better with Joshua 3:11, 13, to which Psalm 114 alludes (see also Ps 97:4). The conclusion would then be that the form was later changed to חוּל (*Psalms 60–150*, p. 371). But why would a common expression like "Lord of all the earth" be changed to a very different word calling the world to tremble?
10. The Hebrew has אֱלוֹהַּ; it reads roughly: "before God Jacob." A few manuscripts have אֱלֹהֵי, which would read "before the God of Jacob," which is what the Greek has.
11. The Greek version interprets as plurals, "pools" and "fountains."

The Supernatural Formation of the Nation

an astounding event: as startling as a clap of thunder, as shattering as an earth quake."[12] Indeed, the theme of the psalm is the supernatural presence of the LORD in delivering his people from bondage and establishing them in the land. Whereas the historical records relate the events and circumstances, here the well-known events have been converted to lyrical poetry to celebrate more widely God's dominion in history and nature.[13] The psalm was therefore appropriate for use at the great festivals, but especially Passover.

Concerning the age or occasion of the psalm, Perowne concludes there is no clue; the only hints of a later date would be in parallels with Deuteronomy or unusual forms in verse 8 of the psalm.[14] So based on the contents of the psalm commentators have speculated about the occasion, such as its being part of the enthronement festival, or the covenant renewal festival, or Passover liturgy. One view links the psalm to Joshua 3–5 as part of the Gilgal tradition.[15] Another suggests that the origin was in the north at Bethel and that verse 2 indicates a Judean expansion, probably in the time of Josiah.[16] Anderson says the date of the composition is uncertain and that it may be pre-exilic, as early as before 721 as Weiser thought—but then he adds that it is more likely to be later.[17]

There are also varying opinions over the structure of the passage. On the surface it appears to be four strophes with each having two bicola; and this arrangement may be the easiest for

---

12. *Psalms 73–150*, p. 403. See also S. A. Geller, "The Language of Imagery in Psalm 114." FS W. L. Moran, ed. by T. Abusch, et al. *HSS* 37 (Atlanta: Scholars Press, 1990), pp 179–94.
13. Weiss, *The Bible from Within*, p. 353.
14. *Psalms*, II:325. But psalms may have been classified as late in part because of these forms, making the argument circular. The forms in question have the article and the final "I" vowel; they are also described as being archaized forms.
15. Kraus, *Psalms 60–150*, p. 373. He adds that the Judean perspective and the emphasis on one central sanctuary does not demand a post-Deuteronomic date.
16. L. Ruppert, "Zur Frage der Einheitlichkeit von Psalm 114," in *Altes Testament: Forschung und Wirkung*. FS H. Graf Reventlow, ed. P. Mommer and W. Thiel (Frankfurt am Main: Long, 1994):81–94.
17. *Psalms 73–150*, p. 783.

the expositor to follow. Allen summarizes the sections: vv. 1–2 record Israel's exodus and origin, vv 3–4 tell of nature's reaction to the adversary, vv. 5–6 seek an explanation from nature, and vv. 7–8 provide the answer—it is due to God's theophany and power.[18] Among other suggestions, VanGemeren says verses 1–2 describe the covenant people, verses 3–6 tell of the witness of nature, and verses 7–8 describe the covenant God.[19] He lays this structure out as a chiasm.

Exegetical Analysis

Summary

Recalling how the sea fled and the mountains trembled when Israel was delivered from Egypt, the psalmist interrogates the mountains and the sea concerning their reaction, and calls the earth to tremble at the presence of the LORD who brought water from the rock.

Outline

I. The people of Israel became God's sanctuary when they came out of bondage in Egypt (1–2).
   A. Israel came out of bondage to a foreign people (1).
   B. Israel became God's sanctuary (2).
II. The waters fled in fear and the mountains trembled when Israel became a new creation (3–4).
   A. The sea fled in fear at the Exodus, and the Jordan ran back (3).
   B. The mountains and hills shook and quaked at the beginning of the nation (4).
III. The psalmist challenges the waters and the hills to explain their reaction (5–6).
   A. He asks the sea and the river why they fled (5).
   B. He asks the hills and mountains why they quaked (6).
IV. The earth should also tremble at the presence of the LORD who brought water from the rock (7–8).

---

18. *Psalms 101–150*, p. 140.
19. *Psalms,* p. 835.

A. The psalmist instructs the earth to tremble at the presence of the LORD (7).
B. It is the LORD who brought water from the flinty rock (8).

COMMENTARY IN EXPOSITORY FORM

I. When God delivered his people from bondage they became his sanctuary and dominion (1–2).

The psalm begins in an unusual way—it focuses on Israel rather than on God. Other psalms might say, "When God brought Israel out of Egypt," but here it says, "When Israel went out of Egypt." The LORD is not referred to until the pronoun "his" is used in verse 2. Delaying mention of the LORD in this way builds anticipation—the people knew from learning the ten commandments that it was the LORD: "I am the LORD your God who brought you out of the land of Egypt."

The deliverance from the bondage of Egypt was from "a people talking unintelligibly" (i.e., speaking a strange language"; מֵעַם לֹעֵז). Dwelling in bondage in another land is bad enough, but the language barrier would have been a constant reminder to the people of Israel that they were aliens in a strange land, and this would have deepened their feeling of isolation and hopelessness.

Verse 2 tells us that at the exodus "Judah became his sanctuary (holy place / holy one), Israel his dominion." The line seems clear enough at first glance, but the details need clarification. Here we have Judah and Israel paralleled. Were they meant to be synonymous in some way, or did they refer to different things? One interpretation is that they refer to the two kingdoms, Judah in the south and Israel in the north. But the passage is looking at the exodus and settlement in the land. Another possibility is that the two names refer to all the people, yet giving honor to Judah specifically. This is similar to another view that says the verse refers to all Israel, but the mention of Judah denotes the greater Israel, the people of God. So Judah represents the whole of Israel.[20]

---

20. Allen suggests that the two words mean all the land; he suggests that the fall of the northern kingdom is presupposed and Judah is left as the sole

Weiss sees a little more going on here with the parallel expressions: Judah // Israel, sanctuary // dominion.[21] The two words, "his sanctuary" (קָדְשׁוֹ; s.v. Ps. 22:3) and "his dominion" (מַמְשְׁלוֹתָיו;[22] s.v. מָשַׁל, Ps. 66:7), recall the revelation of God that Israel was to be a holy nation and a kingdom of priests (Exod. 19:6). The Israelites were to be both a religious people (holy nation) and a political union (kingdom). The names may have been used to reflect the idea that Judah became the theocratic center of the nation, and Israel was the designation for the nation as a whole. Weiss notes that the word plays in the line endorse this interpretation. "Judah" would have an auditory association with the *tetragrammaton* "Yahweh," and "Israel" would yield a word play with the verb "to rule, have dominion." The word plays may not be that clear without close analysis; but the link between the names of "Judah" and "Israel" with "sanctuary" and "dominion" is more helpful in tracing the message of the psalm. By the deliverance from bondage, from a place where they were not at home, the Israelites entered a special relationship with the LORD and became a new order of creation. Their new status would mean that they would be the sanctuary and the dominion for God almighty.

These ideas are reflected in the writings of the New Testament typologically. In what the apostles view as the greater exodus the Lord delivered people from bondage and made them a new creation. And that new order meant that the redeemed were now the temple of the LORD.

II. When God made the people his sanctuary the waters fled and the mountains quaked to prepare for the new creation (3–4).

The psalm now tells what happened in nature when Israel

---

heir of the religious designation "Israel" (*Psalms 101–150*, p. 141). This idea forces the text to say more than it appears to say. The two names seem to be a standard formula for the covenant people of God (Exod. 13:3; 19:1; Deut. 16:3). See also Jer. 2:3. See VanGemeren, *Psalms*, pp. 835–36 and Anderson, *Psalms 73–150*, p. 784.

21. *The Bible from Within*, p. 359.
22. The form is a plural, which must be interpreted to be something like a plural of extension or composition or intensification to stress the idea of dominion.

was delivered from Egypt. Verse 3 focuses on the water: "the sea saw and fled, Jordan turned backwards" (Exod. 14:21; Josh. 3:15–16). The sea is a reference to the sea that parted to enable the Israelites to escape on dry ground, and the Jordan is the Jordan river that backed up and allowed the people to cross over into the land. Weiss makes two important observations here (pp. 360 ff.). First, in contrast to the historical accounts, the change in the sea and the river are described in the active voice, not the passive (see also Ps. 77:17). They saw, and they fled away. Second, what the sea saw (realized) was most probably the whole of verses 1 and 2, the creation of a new order by the deliverance of Israel from bondage in the world.

In the psalm's focus on the sea and the river, many commentators see an allusion to creation (see Ps. 104:1–7; Ps. 66:5–7). They suggest that the idea of the LORD's victory over chaos is implicit because of similarities to Canaanite myth where Baal defeats the god "Sea" (*Yamm-*) and another god "River" (*Nahar-*). Imagery from poetic accounts of creation may be reflected here, but it is applied to Israel's history to express supernatural manifestations. But the point is that there was no need for God to fight the sea and the river—the presence of the sovereign creator of the universe was enough for the elements of nature to flee. And they are presented as active—they saw, and they fled. It was fear that caused them to run away, even though they had nowhere to go. Allen says, "How formidable must have been the foe that they acted in such demoralized terror."[23] So these elements of nature "saw" in the exodus the creation of a new order, and against that the old order could not stand firm.

The fourth verse adds the report of the mountains and the hills skipping like young animals. This is a poetic description of earthquakes, most likely referring to Mount Sinai and the region around. When the LORD made his redeemed people into a holy nation, the new beginning was signified by changes in the old created order (Exod. 19:18; Judg. 5:5; Ps. 68:9). God was shaking the earth when he established a new order for his redeemed people (Exod. 19). What is to be noted is that each element, the sea, the river, the mountains and the hills, each did

---

23. *Psalms 101–150*, p. 141.

what was contrary to its nature, what was contrary to the old order of creation. The supernatural changes were due to the Creator's terrifying presence on the earth to establish a new order.[24] Weiss reiterates that these phenomena in nature were the result of the choice of Israel (p. 366). The mountains and hills were considered to be the foundations of the natural world, the most solid elements in the world. But through the events that made Israel God's sanctuary and dominion, transformations in the existing world of nature were the result of the transformation of history. Weiss offers further support for this idea in the thematic parallel connections between verses 1–2 and 3–4 (pp. 367–8). Verses 1 and 3 describe a change of place; verses 2 and 4 a change of state. So verse 1 is carried forward in verse 3, and verse 2 is reflected in verse 4.

The vivid and dramatic descriptions of the events around the establishment of the nation were designed to make it live in the minds of the people. The psalmist was reenacting for his audience the well-known story of the exodus, reminding the people of supernatural events by giving nature personal reactions. Both the vivid imagery and the personifications were meant to bring past history forward to be present for the experience of the people.[25] All of this is true of other great acts of redemption that are told and retold with vivid descriptions: the greatest acts were accompanied by supernatural changes, and in telling of these events the psalmists and the apostles look forward to the greatest change in nature and history at the end of the age.

III. When God delivered and established his people the great changes in creation were necessary but unexpected (5–6).

Flowing naturally from the imagery in the preceding section is rhetorical questioning. The questions reflect the sense of excitement in the psalmist as if he was there observing the changes and finding it difficult to believe his eyes.[26] The ques-

---

24. Broyles, *Psalms*, p. 427.
25. Kirkpatrick, *Psalms*, p. 681.
26. Weiss, p. 368.

tions are addressed to the sea / river and the mountains / hills, as if they could answer; the questions were designed to help the reader come to an understanding of the way nature responds to the presence of the LORD. "What is the matter?" "Why did you flee?" In this dramatic analysis of the history, it seems as if the psalmist pretends not to know why nature responded as it did. By putting himself in the past he makes the listeners feel it as if it had just happened[27] so that they too will have to answer the questions. The questions are the kind that would be found in a taunt song; they demand the elements of nature to explain their response. They cannot, of course, but he can—it was the shock over the intervention of the Creator to prepare a new order.

IV. When the Lord God supernaturally changes nature in making his people his sanctuary all the world should tremble (7–8).

The psalmist now calls the earth (or land) to tremble before the God of Jacob. The questions paved the way for this imperative; and the revelation of God's works not only gives reason to tremble but also provides the answer to the questions in the last section: the sovereign Lord God of creation was present and supernaturally taking care of his people. Something new was unfolding from the exodus to the occupation of the land: the kingdom of God was breaking in on the old order, and supernatural events had to accompany and demonstrate the divine plan. The new order was not simply a good plan that Israel developed; the LORD was actively present, and that should cause the whole world to tremble. The imperative "tremble" addressed to the earth is also figurative (personification); it calls for the earth to quake and shift before the LORD.

Twice in verse 7 we have the expression translated "from before," followed first by the "Lord" and then by "God." The usual way that this is interpreted is that in the presence of the Lord the whole world should tremble. Weiss suggests taking a less common use of the expression, translating it "on account of" as

---

27. Allen, *Psalms 101–150*, p. 142.

in 1 Samuel 8:18 (p. 372).[28] This gives a different emphasis, not necessarily a better one.

The earth, meaning the land and everything in it (a metonymy of subject) is to tremble before "the Lord" // the "God of Jacob." The emphasis here is on the power of God, he is "Lord" and he is "the God of Jacob" (see Ps. 20:2). And that power is illustrated with the miraculous event of bringing water from the rock at Kadesh (Exod. 17:1–7; Numb. 20:1–11). Here too we have a pattern in the choice of words: "rock" and "flint," and "pool" and "fountain." Matching these with the earlier description, Weiss links the "sea" and the "Jordan" with the "pool" and the "fountain" respectively. Then, "rock" and "flint" are located on the wilderness side, the "mountain" and the "hills" on the other. These connections join the beginning and the ending of the psalm to stress the idea of the transformation of nature at the creation of this new order (p. 370). Here the water produced from the rock underscores the Lord's power to change the nature and function of creation. So prior to the conquest the Lord demonstrated to his people that he was fully able to meet all their needs because he was sovereign over all nature and people.[29] These wonders in the wilderness were proofs of God's absolute creative power that changes the prospect of death into the prospect of life, and of his grace, that chooses a people to be his sanctuary and dominion.[30]

So the earth should tremble because there was the sovereign Lord God of creation using all of nature in bringing about a new order. God brought his people out of Egypt, sustained them in the wilderness, and gave them the promised land. The message for later generations of Israelites, and for us as well, is that one day the Lord will redeem his people from the bondage of the world, accompanied by staggering supernatural events in nature that will

---

28. He also suggests emending the imperative חוּלִי to read מְחוֹלֵל meaning "creator." This he argues makes a better parallelism: "On account of the Lord, the creator of the world // on account of God, the God of Jacob." This is too much of a rewriting; and there is no reason why the two lines have to be synonymously parallel.
29. These supernatural works indicate essential changes in his work at the time of creation. His new creation will require a different use of nature and a different direction in history.
30. Perowne, *Psalms*, II:327.

shape the world, and in that new creation the people will enjoy the promises of God Almighty (1 Chron. 28:8; Neh. 9:36–37).

MESSAGE AND APPLICATION

The exposition of this psalm will have to tie together its two major motifs, the LORD's shaking creation and his making Israel to be his sanctuary and dominion. The sanctuary and dominion will connect easily to the call of Israel to be a holy nation and kingdom of priests so that the LORD can dwell with them; and the shaking of creation can be connected to the LORD's creation of the world as he controlled the seas and formed the dry land. It is clear in the Bible that at the exodus the LORD created the nation of Israel. And as creator, he demonstrated his power and authority over nature in the way he redeemed his people. So the exposition could be summarized in this way: *The Sovereign LORD God moves heaven and earth when he forms his people into a new kingdom of priests.*

These motifs also appear in Genesis at the Flood; there God created a new order with those he saved from the deluge, but the supernatural nature of the Flood clearly revealed the sovereignty of the LORD over all creation. We find the same two emphases in the LORD's establishment of the Church in the death and resurrection of Jesus. Darkness, earthquakes, and the dead rising demonstrated this was a new creation of a kingdom of priests, a people in whom the LORD could dwell. And we know that the promises of the coming of the LORD in glory will also be accompanied by massive changes in this creation as he comes to establish the new order of his kingdom.

All of this should remind believers that the formation of the redeemed into a kingdom of priests is a supernatural work from beginning to end. It should also inspire believers to greater faith as they learn that God is able to change all of creation to make room for his program. Surely nothing is impossible for our Creator and Redeemer. Therefore we should trust him fully, and praise him eternally.

PSALM 115

The Trustworthiness of the LORD Versus the Futility of Idols

INTRODUCTION

Text and Textual Variants[1]

1 Not unto us, O LORD, not unto us,
    but unto your name give glory,
  because of your loyal love,
    because[2] of your truth.
2 Why[3] should the nations say,
    "Where now is their God?"

---

1. Psalm 115 is a continuation of Psalm 114 in many Hebrew manuscripts, the Greek version, Theodotion, the Syriac version, Jerome and Qumran. In the MT they are separate psalms, and rightly so since the tone and contents are different.
2. Many manuscripts and versions have a conjunction here: "and because."
3. The Greek version did not read this as an interrogative sentence, but rendered it "so that the nations do not say."

PSALM 115

3 But our God is in the heavens;[4]
  he does[5] whatever he pleases.
4 Their idols[6] are silver and gold,
  the work[7] of the hands of man.
5 They have mouths, but they do not speak;
  eyes they have, but they do not see;
6 they have ears, but they do not hear;
  noses they have, but they do not smell;
7 they have hands,[8] but they do not handle;
  feet they have, but they do not walk;
    nor do they mutter through their throat.
8 Those who make them are[9] like them;
  so is everyone who trusts in them.

9 O Israel,[10] trust[11] in the LORD;
  he is their help and their shield.
10 O house of Aaron, trust in the LORD;
  he is their help and their shield.
11 You who fear the LORD, trust in the LORD;
  he is their help and their shield.

12 The LORD has remembered us;

---

4. The Greek translation adds "above" to this line, and then inserts after it an additional colon: "in the heavens and in the earth."
5. Some commentators translate the verb as a past tense, following the Greek version. But an English present tense fits the ongoing activity of God indicated here in contrast to the impotence of the gods.
6. The Greek version (followed by the Syriac and Jerome) has "The idols of the nations" (see Ps. 135:15).
7. A few manuscripts and the Greek have "works."
8. The Hebrew Bible has "their hands"; the Greek and Jerome follow the pattern of verses 5 and 6 with "hands to them," meaning "they have hands."
9. The verb in the text is the imperfect or jussive form, יִהְיוּ. It could be translated "they are" or "they will be" or as some prefer, "may they be" (as the Greek version has it).
10. Many manuscripts, the Greek and the Syriac add "house (of Israel)" to harmonize with the following verses.
11. The Greek (Syriac and Jerome) translated the imperative בְּטַח as if it were the perfect tense: ἤλπισεν, "hoped." This was also done in verses 10 and 11; and in verse 12 ("and he blessed" for Hebrew יְבָרֵךְ).

> he will bless us;
> he will bless the house of Israel;
> he will bless the house of Aaron.
> 13 He will bless those who fear the LORD,
> the small with the great.
>
> 14 May the LORD give increase,
> for you and your children.
> 15 May you be blessed by the LORD,
> *the* maker of made heaven and earth.
>
> 16 The heavens, *even* heavens,[12] are the LORD's;
> but the earth he has given to mankind.[13]
> 17 The dead will not praise the LORD,[14]
> nor will any who go down into silence.[15]
> 18 But we[16] will bless the LORD
> from this time forth and forevermore.
>
> Praise the LORD![17]

Composition and Context

Psalm 115 is not easy to classify; it seems to be a liturgical prayer with a strong note of assurance; but in the collection it was probably used more for its praise.[18] Allen calls it a communal or liturgical lament;[19] but VanGemeren calls it a psalm of communal confidence, while noting its varied parts of lament, liturgy and confidence.[20] The exposition will explain the different motifs of

---

12. The word is repeated in apposition to the first, expressing the highest heavens; the Greek version assumed a construct form, "the heavens of heavens," to get to the same meaning.
13. Literally, "to the sons of man."
14. Hebrew has יָהּ; the Greek has "will not praise you, O Lord."
15. For MT's דוּמָה, "silence," the Greek version used "Hades."
16. The Greek translation adds "who are alive," οἱ ζῶντες.
17. The Greek version joins this exclamation to the beginning of Psalm 116.
18. Anderson, *Psalms 73–150*, p. 785.
19. *Psalms 101–150*, p. 146.
20. *Psalms*, p. 838.

the psalm that have prompted these classifications, and as a result the label will be of less value. Verses 1–2 fit a national lament motif; verses 3–8 are more hymn-like. Then in verses 9–1 there is also a changing of pronouns that indicate different voices, making the psalm liturgical. There seems to be a prophetic voice in verses 12–13; and it is followed by praise (vv. 14–18).

The general understanding is that the psalm came from the exile or post-exilic experience because it reflects a period of national difficulty when nations oppressed them, but also when they found assurance in this world. The exchange between the pagan taunts of the faith and Israel's mocking of their idols certainly would capture the experience of the exile and deliverance (see Ps. 137). Even though the contents of the psalm reflect such an opposition from the nations, the full psalm is part of the liturgy and praise in the temple,[21] in which the people hear God's blessing and express their confidence.

While the psalm may fit that experience, some of its emphases are not new to the exilic period; as Weiser points out, the denunciation of pagan gods had been in the cult since ancient times (see Josh. 24:14 et al).[22] Accordingly, Kraus cautions that the detailed circumstance of the setting cannot be ascertained.[23] And so all we can say for certain it that it is a liturgical prayer sung antiphonally with an emphasis on assurance.[24]

Exegetical Analysis

Summary

After calling on the LORD to vindicate his honor among the nations, and after demonstrating the sovereignty of the LORD and pouring contempt on pagan idols, the psalmist exhorts all to

---

21. Perowne says the psalm was composed when the taunts were still ringing in their ears (*Psalms*, II:327).
22. *Psalms*, p. 714.
23. See further K. Luke, "The Setting of Psalm 115," *ITQ* 34 (1967):347–57.
24. Kraus, *Psalms 60–150*, p. 378.

The Trustworthiness of the LORD Versus the Futility of Idols

trust in the LORD who will bless them abundantly so that they may praise.

Outline

 I. Address to God: The psalmist calls for God to vindicate his honor among the nations (1–2).
    A. He confesses the unworthiness of the congregation (1a).
    B. He calls for God to vindicate the worthiness of his great name (1b–2).
 II. Satirical Song: The psalmist demonstrates God's sovereignty over idols by pouring out contempt on them and on those that made them (3–8).
    A. He declares the sovereignty of God in the heavens who does as he pleases (3).
    B. He pours out contempt on idols and those that make them (4–8).
       1. Idols are silver and gold, but they are the work of man's hands (4).
       2. Idols have mouths, ears, hands and throats, but they are impotent (5–7).
       3. Those who make them and those who trust them will be like them (8).
 III. Exhortation: The psalmist exhorts the congregation to trust in the LORD for he is their help and shield (9–11).
    A. Israel should trust in the one who is their help and shield (9).
    B. Priests should trust in the one who is their help and shield (10).
    C. Those that fear should trust in the one who is their help and shield (11).
 IV. Blessing: The psalmist promises that the LORD will bless them and increase their children's heritage since he has been mindful of them and they shall praise in response (12–18).
    A. The LORD has been mindful of them and will bless them (12–13).
    B. The LORD should bless them and their children because the earth is given to the children of men (14–16).

C. The people that die cannot praise, but the psalmist and his fellow believers will praise forever (17–18).

Epilogue: "Praise the LORD!"

COMMENTARY IN EXPOSITORY FORM

I. The afflicted saints long for the LORD to vindicate his honor in an antagonistic world (1–2).

The psalm begins with a protestation: "Not unto us, O LORD, not unto us, but unto your name give glory."[25] The verse indicates the people are still in some difficulty and so pray for the LORD's deliverance, a deliverance that will bring glory to him—not them. This is an acknowledgment of their own unworthiness, and of the fact that because they have suffered as God's people the glory of God is at stake. They do not pray primarily for their own sake, and certainly not for any credit to them. They are more concerned with his glory (for כָּבוֹד, s.v. Ps. 19:1). And so the imperative "give" means more than it says (it is a metonymy of effect); they are praying: "Act on our behalf to magnify your reputation."[26]

What is at stake is the loyal love (חֶסֶד; s.v. Ps. 23:6) and truth / faithfulness (אֱמֶת; s.v. Ps. 15:2) of the LORD. These two words often work together, the latter modifying the former: the faithful loyal love of the LORD. If God does not act, his reputation for faithful love for his people will be called into question, to say the least. To make this point more strongly, the psalmist asks God why the nations should say, "Where is their God?"[27] Both of these are rhetorical questions: his asking why they should say this means they should not be allowed to say it; and their question was meant to say that Israel's God was unable or unwilling to help. Obviously,

---

25. Kidner reminds us of how these words have been used in significant times. For example, at the battle of Agincourt the army was told to kneel and say, "Non nobis, Domine . . . ." And, it was used by Wilberforce at the passing of the bill in parliament to abolish the slave trade (*Psalms 73–150*, p. 404).
26. Anderson, *Psalms 73–150*, p. 786.
27. Moses used this appeal in his intercession for the nation; see Exodus 32:12 (as well as Numb. 14:13–15).

the situation was serious enough for these questions to be raised.[28] Serious adversity casts doubt on God's power.[29]

II. The saints know that the LORD is sovereign over all creation, especially over the foolish beliefs of the pagans (3–8).

A. *The LORD is omnipotent and free (3).*

In this section is the response of the faithful. They first affirm the sovereignty of God, and then denounce the folly of idolatry (in a way responding with their own question, "What are their gods?")

The psalmist declares, "But our God is in heaven," stressing the fact that "it is our God who is in heaven"—their gods are limited to earth. Such a statement emphasizes the infinite distance and therefore sovereignty of the LORD.[30] As the true God, he does as he pleases! Not only is he omnipotent, but he is also free—his ability to act and fulfill his plans distinguishes him from pagan gods.[31]

B. *The gods of the pagans are impotent and confined (4–8).*

This section is similar to Psalm 135:15–18, which may have been borrowed from this piece. And this indicates that because of the frequent clash with people antagonistic to the faith the denunciation of their gods may have been common.

The idols of the pagans are man-made; but the LORD is the sovereign creator who made humans as his image. Idolatry reverses creation as its devotees try to make gods in their own image (see Isa. 44:9–20). Their idols were covered with gold and silver, making them look more magnificent than the actual material underneath; but both materials are from God's creation!

---

28. Anderson, *Psalms 73–150*, p. 786.
29. VanGemeren, p, 838.
30. Weiser, *The Psalms*, p. 716.
31. Anderson, *Psalms 73–150*, p. 787.

This text does not mention that pagan idols were often understood to be representations of spirits; it simply is a condemnation of the crude form of idolatry.[32] Perowne, however, notes that the pagans themselves did not distinguish between the idol and the god they worshiped.[33] This is no doubt due to the spiritual blindness that fed the folly of idolatry (see Isa. 44:9–20); turning to idols "their foolish heart became darkened" like their idols (Rom. 1:21–23).

In verses 5–7 the psalmist underscores the impotence of the gods of the nations. They had a similarity to human appearance, but they did not, could not function, not even as humans do. This forceful polemic against idols is essentially a praise of God by contrast. All these things that the idols could not do, he can do because he is the living God—he sees, he hears, he speaks, and he acts on behalf of his people.

The psalmist adds that those who make idols and worship them are like them (v. 8). Thus idolatry is not harmless; it diverts people from serving the living God and demoralizes them to live on the same base level as their corrupt gods. Those gods were lifeless and ineffective; and their use made the devotees empty and degraded (Isa. 44:19).

So the confession of confidence in the LORD is set against the foolishness of idols; in contrasting "our God" and "their idols," the faithful can see the point clearly: "Idols are limited in power because they are human artifacts, share in human limitations, and are made of materials that come out of the earth."[34] In the end, God will bring all idolaters to judgment because if their gods could not hear, speak, walk, or handle, they certainly could not deliver their blind and foolish worshipers from the wrath to come.

III. The saints call for everyone to put their faith in the LORD because he alone can help and protect them (9–11).

These observations of worthless, pagan practices prompt the psalmist to call for the righteous to put their trust in the

---

32. *Ibid.*, p. 787.
33. *Psalms*, II:329.
34. VanGemeren, p. 840.

LORD completely. This is not a blind faith; it is the antithesis of the foolish faith in lifeless idols because it is a faith in the living God who acts. The righteous do not come to the LORD carrying idols and images; they are the image of God, who comes to them with redeeming love and provides them with reasons to praise.

In this section the change of persons is unexpected: the psalmist addresses Israel, but then someone refers to them in the third person. The likely reason for this is that it is antiphonal: the psalmist calls Israel to trust in the LORD, and another voice, perhaps of a priest or even the Levitical choir, responds with the assurance that the LORD is their help and shield. Such antiphonal singing fits liturgical worship. So in this psalm we have a threefold call to trust, and a threefold word of assurance given to encourage people to trust.

The command is "trust (בְּטַח; s.v. Ps. 4:5) in the LORD"—rely completely on him for security and safety. And this word goes out to different groups in the assembly (see Ps. 118:1–3): the Israelites, the priests, and all who fear the LORD. The antiphon is: "he is their help and their shield." As "helper" (עֹזֵר; s.v. Ps. 46:1) the LORD does for his people what they cannot do for themselves—whereas the pagans have to do everything for their gods who can do nothing for themselves. And as a "shield" (a metaphor), the LORD protects his people from attacks.

IV. The saints are confident that the LORD is mindful of them and so they praise him for his many blessings (12–18).

A. The LORD has been mindful of them and will bless them (12–15).

The confident tone expressed in the antiphon of verses 9–11 now inspires believers to anticipate the blessing of God. In verses 12–13 we have a threefold blessing that repeats the groups mentioned in verses 9–11. First, he will bless the house of Israel, that is, all Israelites who trust in him. Then, he will bless the house of Aaron, that is, all the priestly families who lead the worship. Finally, he will bless all who fear the LORD, devout worshipers, no matter what their position in society might be.

The blessing will come because "the LORD has remembered us." The holy name is placed first in verse 12 to emphasize that it is Yahweh alone who can do this. The meaning of "remembering" is that God has acted on their behalf—he has been mindful of them (for זָכַר s.v. Ps. 6:5). Because they as a nation have experienced his faithful, saving presence, he will bless them (יְבָרֵךְ; s.v. Ps. 5:12).

In verse 14 the psalmist prays specifically that the LORD "add (יֹסֵף) upon you, upon you and upon your children." In this text the verb means "increase"; and it may very well refer to the increase of the population at the return (see Isa. 54:1–3; Ps. 127), but it could also include increase in their material substance (Isa. 55:1–2). The fulfillment of this appeal for blessing is not at all impossible or unlikely, because the LORD is the maker of heaven and earth.[35] The primary evidence of the omnipotence and love of God is creation; if he could produce the world in which we live, he can bring salvation, increase children, crops and cattle, and provide health and security for those who trust in him.

B. The believers will praise him forever (16–18).

The rest of the psalm is the praise of the community; verse 16 provides the substance of the praise.[36] Emphatically, "the heavens, heavens, are the LORD's"; his dominion is above everything on earth and without limit. The statement is also polemical, because even though the pagans attempted to lift the sphere of their gods above the clouds and to the heavens, they are worthless idols, earthy and limited. The sovereign creator is in heaven. But if heaven is his dominion, he has sovereignly given the earth to people so that they would serve him; the earth only belongs to them because of the grace and goodness of God.

Those who trust and serve the LORD will enjoy his blessing, and that blessing promises a glorious, unending future in his presence. In contrast to the righteous, the dead will not praise the

---

35. See N. C. Habel, "'Yahweh, Maker of Heaven and Earth': A Study in Tradition Criticism," *JBL* 91 (1972):321–37.
36. Some arrangements put verse 16 with 15 to speak of his sovereignty, but that would not take away from the praise which is evident throughout the psalm.

LORD—they are going down to silence (דוּמָה). The reference here is to the shadowy existence in the life to come for unbelievers (e.g. Ps. 49:13–15). They had no relation with the living God; they will go down to the land of silence, still excluded from the covenant people of God and from God himself. But the righteous will not be silent; they will bless the LORD from now throughout eternity. The psalmist is here showing the perspective from which it is possible to overcome the power of evil and death: believers have a life and a future through faith in the LORD, but the idol worshiper has no meaningful life and no future.[37]

MESSAGE AND APPLICATION

Psalm 115 renews the faith and confidence of believers by contrasting the living God with the worthless idols of the pagans. The people of God must live in a world that has rejected the creator to worship and serve created things, and that defection has made them boldly antagonistic to the historic faith. So the psalmist reminds us all that: *Although believers are opposed and afflicted by the world that mocks God, God is sovereign, omnipotent and loving, and he will rescue his honor when he pours contempt on those opposed to the faith and redeems his people.*

We worship the true and living God, the sovereign over all his creation, and the redeemer of his people. But rather than worship and obey an invisible God the people of the world desired to have a god like them, with hands, ears, eyes, a mouth, and feet. They wanted their god to be like them. But it was more than that, for the Son of God had hands, ears, eyes, a mouth, and feet, but they nailed his body to a cross to silence him forever. They did not want a God who made demands of them; they wanted a god to serve them. It is the same spiritual blindness of ancient idolatry: those who make gods, or religions, can only make something weaker than they. True believers acknowledge that only a higher power, the God of heaven who made them, can save them, care form them, and take them to glory.

---

37. Weiser, p. 717.

PSALM 116

Precious in the Sight of the LORD is the Death of His Saints

INTRODUCTION

Text and Textual Variants

1 I love the LORD, because he heard
   my voice, my supplications.[1]
2 Because he turned his ear to me
   I will call *on him* as long as I live.[2]

3 The cords[3] of death entangled me,

---

1. The line in the MT is difficult: אֲהַבְתִּי כִּי־יִשְׁמַע יְהוָה אֶת־קוֹלִי תַּחֲנוּנָי, "I love, because the LORD heard // my voice, my supplications." "LORD" is not in the MT or the Greek as the object of the verb; so normally the words are transposed so that it is: "I love the LORD, because he heard." The second colon has the direct object of the verb, "my voice." But in the Greek and Syriac and Jerome's versions it is put as in construct (= קוֹל), to read "the voice of my supplications. But "my supplications" could be in apposition to "my voice" to get the same result. Furthermore, the editors of BHS suggest the verb should be שָׁמַע, clearly "he heard"; the prefix *yôd* being explained as dittography with the preceding כִּי. But this change is not necessary as the verb could be interpreted as a preterite.
2. The MT literally reads "and in my days." The verb "I will call," אֶקְרָא, could be interpreted as prayer, calling on him, or praise, making proclamation of him. See the discussion in the commentary.
3. The Greek translation has "pangs," ὠδῖνες.

PSALM 116

    and the anguish of the grave[4] found me;
    I found trouble and sorrow.
4 Then I called on the name of the LORD:
    "O LORD, rescue me!"

5 The LORD is gracious and righteous;
    and our God acts with compassion.
6 The LORD protects the simple;[5]
    when I was in great need he saved me.
7 Return to your rest, O my soul,
    for the LORD has been good[6] to you.
8 For you have delivered[7] my life from death,
    my eyes[8] from tears,
        my feet from stumbling,
9 that I may walk before the LORD
    in the land[9] of the living.
10 I believed; therefore, I spoke,[10]
    "I am greatly afflicted."[11]
11 I said in my dismay,[12]
    "Every man is a liar."

12 How can I repay the LORD
    for all his goodness to me?
13 I will lift up the cup of salvation
    and call on the name of the LORD.
14 I will pay my vows to the LORD

---

4. Hebrew שְׁאוֹל.
5. For "simple" the MT has פְּתָאיִם but many manuscripts have פְּתָיִם; the Greek translation interprets with "infants," τὰ νήπια.
6. MT has גָּמַל עָלָיְכִי; the Greek version has "acted on your behalf."
7. The Greek, some Syriac and Jerome have the form 3rd msg, "he delivered."
8. In the text "eye" is singular; and "foot" also is singular, but plural in the Greek, Syriac, and Jerome's versions.
9. The MT has the plural, "lands"; the Greek, Syriac and Jerome have the singular.
10. This verse starts a new psalm in the Greek version and Jerome.
11. MT has עָנִיתִי; the Greek version (Symmachus and the Syriac) has ἐταπεινώθην (= עֲנֵיתִי), "I was brought low."
12. For the MT's form חָפְזִי the Greek version has "alarm," ἐκστάσει.

422

Precious in the Sight of the LORD is the Death of His Saints

    in the presence[13] of all his people.
15 Precious[14] in the eyes of the LORD
    is the death of his saints.
16 O LORD, truly[15] I am your servant;
    I am your servant, the son of your handmaid;
        you have freed me from my chains.
17 To you I will offer the sacrifice of praise
    and call on the name of the LORD.[16]
18 I will pay my vows to the LORD
    in the presence[17] of all his people,
19 in the courts of the house of the LORD,
    in your midst, O Jerusalem.

Praise the LORD![18]

Composition and Context

There is general agreement that this is an individual thanksgiving psalm in which the psalmist praises the LORD for delivering him from some life-threatening situation. But there is less agreement on the structural arrangement because there are so many diverse elements that represent other types of psalms. The verses at times alternate between deliverance and praise, and there is a frequent use of couplets, making a straightforward analysis complicated. Various commentators chart the sections a little differently, but the overall meaning is not changed. I have chosen to divide the psalm into three parts: verses 1–4 have the

---

13. The Hebrew text has the unusual construction נֶגְדָה־נָּא for "before" or "in the presence of." The editors of BHS propose: . . . לְנֶגֶד עֵינֵי כָל, which makes clear sense, but is only a suggestion. The particle נָא is an intensifying particle.
14. For Hebrew יָקָר, "precious," Allen suggests an Aramaic meaning, "grievous" (p. 152).
15. Hebrew כִּי can be rendered "truly," or "that." The Greek and Syriac do not have it.
16. This second half of verse 17 is not in the Greek version.
17. See footnote 13.
18. In the Greek version this is joined to the next psalm as a superscription. It is not in the Syriac.

introductory declaration of love and devotion based on the fact that the LORD answered his prayer, followed by the report of his trouble, and his prayer for help. Verses 5–11 form much of the thanksgiving: verses 5–6 rehearse the nature of the LORD revealed in his salvation of the simple, verses 7–9 tell how the psalmist found rest in God's deliverance from death, and verses 10–11 clarify that God alone and not man is trustworthy. The third section (vv. 12–19) records the psalmist's vow of praise: he can only offer praise in gratitude for God's goodness (12–14), he has come to know that God carefully guards the lives of his saints (15), and he vows to praise the LORD publicly because he is a true servant of the LORD (16–19). It will become clear in the exposition that much of the report and of the praise is didactic in nature, which is what praise should be.

Exegetical Analysis

Summary

Recalling how the LORD delivered him from the peril of death by his love and grace, the psalmist vows to acknowledge the LORD with the sacrifice of praise in the temple because the death of a saint is not a matter of indifference to the LORD.

Outline

I. The psalmist announces that he loves the LORD for answering his prayer to be rescued from the suffering and peril of death (1–4).
   A. He affirms his love for the LORD who hears him when he cries out to him (1).
   B. He resolves to call on him as long as he lives because he is dependable (2).
   C. He reports his life-threatening dilemma and his cry to the LORD for deliverance (3–4).
II. The psalmist describes the LORD as gracious, righteous, compassionate and completely trustworthy because he delivered him from death (5–11).
   A. The LORD's marvelous attributes were displayed in the answer to his prayer (5–6).

B. The LORD's deliverance of his life from death brings comfort and commitment (7–9).
   C. The LORD is the only one who is trustworthy (10–11).
III. The psalmist can only offer grateful praise to the LORD in the presence of all the assembly (12–19).
   A. The grateful believer vows to praise the name of the LORD for his goodness (12–14).
   B. The believer knows that the death of a saint is something the LORD holds dear (15).
   C. The believer, the true servant of the LORD, will offer the sacrifice of praise publicly in the sanctuary (16–19).

COMMENTARY IN EXPOSITORY FORM

I. The faithful praise the LORD for delivering them from the peril of death in answer to their prayer (1–4).

A. They love the LORD for hearing their cry and so commit to a life of trusting him (1–2).

Filled with gratitude and joy over being delivered from the danger of death, the psalmist proclaims his love for and commitment to the LORD. "I love the LORD" (אָהַבְתִּי; s.v. Ps. 11:7) is not only an expression of grateful joy, but also of loyalty to the LORD, for the verb "love" is used as the essential description of faith and obedience in Israel (see Deut. 6:5; Exod. 20:6). The believers' love for the LORD is based on the LORD's goodness and faithfulness to them—and so, we also love him because he first loved us (1 John 4:19). The reason for the psalmist's renewed devotion and loyalty is that God heard (יִשְׁמַע; s.v. 45:10) the prayer, i.e., God answered "his cry for mercy" (literally, "his voice, supplications"; "voice" is metonymical for the prayer, and "supplications" modifies the voice by apposition). His prayer made supplications, which are appeals for mercy (for the noun, s.v. חָנַן in Ps. 4:1). And because the LORD paid close attention to his plea ("inclined his ear" is the anthropomorphic expression), he promises to call on him throughout his life. The verb "call" (קָרָא) has a wide range of meanings in the Bible; it can refer to prayer, but it can also refer to proclamation (Gen. 4:26; 12:9; Exod. 34:5–7). The basic meaning here is that the psalmist is promising to be a faithful worshiper the rest of his life; and at the heart of worship is the proclamation of the name of the LORD (which always as here is the result of answered prayer).

B. They recall how they cried out to him from their anguish and suffering (3–4).

In the next two verses the psalmist details the dilemma. We do not know the occasion for the psalm, but whatever the experience, he was sensing the loss of his hold on life. It was as if "the cords of death" entangled him. The image may be taken from hunters who lie in wait with ropes and nets to capture the prey.[19] At least we can say that death is treated as a person in some way to say that he was in its clutches—it seized him and entangled him and began a process of taking his life away. He may not have been on his deathbed, but he felt he was in great peril for his life and in need of immediate deliverance. The psalmist adds in the second colon that "the anguish of the grave (מְצָרֵי שְׁאוֹל; for *she'ol*, s.v. Ps. 6:5) found him." He was overtaken with anguish and distress, the fearful prospects of passing from life to the grave. All he found in life was trouble and sorrow (צָרָה; s.v. Ps. 120:1; and יָגוֹן).

Then he called on the name of the LORD (v. 4). Here the meaning is clearly prayer, prayer based on the person and works of the LORD, as the "name" indicates (s.v. Ps. 20:1). His only hope in the face of life-threatening peril was this "name" of the LORD (s.v. Ps. 20:1). So he continually called to the LORD: "O LORD, rescue me" (מַלְּטָה; s.v. Ps. 41:1). The great need for deliverance is emphasized by the variety of words used in the prayer: save (יָשַׁע), rescue (מָלַט), deliver (חָלַץ).

II. The faithful acknowledge that the LORD is gracious and righteous and completely trustworthy because he alone can deliver from death (5–11).

---

19. Allen, *Psalms 101–150*, p. 155.

A. The LORD displayed his nature in answering prayer (5–6).

There is a dramatic shift in the tone of the psalm in verse 5, changing from the terrifying descriptions of his peril to the glorious nature of the LORD. The list of attributes indicate what the LORD revealed about himself when he delivered the suffering saint. These descriptions were revealed to Israel through Moses when the people were in need of words of grace (Exod. 34:5–7). The LORD is "gracious" (חַנּוּן; s.v. Ps. 4:1), because he forgives and cares for his needy people in spite of their failures; he is "righteous" (צַדִּיק; s.v. Ps. 1:5), because he is faithful to his word to keep his covenant promises to his people; and he "acts" with "compassion" (now a participle, מְרַחֵם; s.v. Ps. 25:6) toward his people, because he is tender and understanding of their difficulties in this world. And because of all of this, the psalmist can declare that the LORD protects (שֹׁמֵר; s.v. Ps. 12:7) the "simple" (פְּתָאִים). In Proverbs this word describes people who are naive, gullible, and foolish; but here the meaning is more likely just simple, helpless, or inexperienced.[20] This simplicity may leave people open to attacks, but if they know this, then they can always cry out to the LORD immediately—even with a simple faith. The psalmist is painting himself in this way: when he was growing weak and was in great need (דָּלַל means "languish, be low, weak") the LORD saved him (for יָשַׁע s.v. Ps. 3:2). So the psalmist's contemplation on the nature of God immediately brings to mind his own experience.

B. The LORD's deliverance from death brings comfort and commitment (7–9).

Now that he has been rescued the psalmist can speak to himself with comfortable words (for another self-exhortation, see Ps.42:5). He says to himself: "return to your rest" (שׁוּבִי נַפְשִׁי לִמְנוּחָיְכִי; for "return," s.v. Ps. 126:1; and for "rest," s.v. Ps. 95:11). In the midst of the dangers and troubles in life, the faithful can be at rest in the confidence that the LORD who has been good to them, cares for them, and will help them. They will be free from anguish and

---

20. Anderson, *Psalms 73–150*, p. 792.

fear because the dangers and difficulties of life may be turned over to the LORD in prayer.

Then the focus returns to deliverance (vv. 8–9). In verse 8 he elaborates on the deliverance with a threefold description: "for he has delivered my life from death, my eyes from tears, and my feet from stumbling." By this report he is actually instructing the congregation that the LORD can deliver people from everything that causes sorrow—death, anguish, and falling in the way. Thinking of delivering his feet from stumbling the psalmist is moved to reflect on the purpose of God's deliverance: "that I may walk before the LORD in the land of the living" (v. 9). To walk before the LORD is an expression that signifies a life of close harmony and careful obedience (see Gen. 17:1, "and be perfect"; and Isa. 38:15–19, "I will walk humbly"). Only the LORD can turn the troubled life into a life filled with joy in fellowship with him.

C. The LORD alone is trustworthy (10–11).

In times of tension and trouble the suffering saint knows that humans will fail them, but the LORD is completely trustworthy. The psalmist says, "I believed, therefore I said, 'I am greatly afflicted'." This statement is in contrast to verse 11 in which he says, "in my dismay I said, 'Every man is a liar'." "Liar" (כֹּזֵב) may carry the sense of being deceitful, or false, and so in a word, unreliable.[21] In the time he was panic-stricken, he became very aware of the failures of people in their willingness and ability to help him. He learned that he could not rely on people; but he could trust the LORD with confidence. That is why he states, "I believed" (הֶאֱמַנְתִּי; s.v. Ps. 15:2). This confession has to be interpreted within the whole line. It may have the sense of "I kept my faith when I said, 'I am greatly afflicted.'"[22] He held fast to his faith in the LORD and so he prayed. Other commentators take it in a slightly different sense: "I believed *even when* I said, 'I am greatly afflicted'."[23] The point is that he demonstrated

---

21. Allen, *Psalms 101–150*, p. 112.
22. Anderson, *Psalms 73–150*, p. 793.
23. Perowne takes it a little differently by saying that a living faith in the heart will utter with the mouth the strong convictions. He had looked to

genuine faith: because he believed, he poured out his complaint to the LORD—he learned the lesson of true faith that only the LORD is able and willing to save him. In times of great danger and distress the believer knows to cry out to the only one who is completely reliable.

III. The redeemed cannot repay the LORD for delivering them from death but they can acknowledge him in the midst of the congregation (12–19).

A. The grateful believer can only offer praise to God in the assembly (12–14).

Now that the LORD saved him the psalmist wonders how he can repay him for all his goodness. He cannot, of course. His question is most likely rhetorical, acknowledging this fact. There is no way anyone can repay the LORD; but one can acknowledge in the congregation what the LORD has done. He says, "I will lift up the cup of salvation." The cup in the Bible is often a symbol of one's lot in life; but in this case the cup may be more specifically related to sanctuary ritual, i.e., pouring out libations at the altar in conjunction with his sacrifice of praise (see Exod. 29:40–41; Numb. 28:7). The qualifying word "salvation" may indicate that "the cup is for (his) salvation," or the taking up of "the cup (in praise was the effect of his) salvation." The parallel colon harmonizes with the link to the ritual, stating, "and call on the name of the LORD." It would not be prayer here, because this is the celebration of the answer to prayer made in the sanctuary. It is a proclamation of "the name of the LORD," a public declaration of the person and works of the LORD on his behalf. Such public praise was accompanied by the sacrifice of praise and a libation of wine. At that occasion he will "pay" or "fulfill" (אֲשַׁלֵּם; s.v. Ps. 38:3) his vows to the LORD in the presence of all the people. When people prayed to the LORD from their distress, they included in their prayers vows to praise the LORD when he answered them; the "vow of praise" built their own confidence and also served

---

others for help, but they were all false and deceitful. So because he believed in the LORD, he said, "I must speak, I am greatly afflicted" (II:334).

to motivate the LORD to answer, to provide a reason he should answer—"LORD, this is what I will say when you deliver me." Once delivered, the person is by oath bound to deliver his praise in the sanctuary—to pay his vows (see Ps. 50:14; 66:13–20). No one can repay God for his grace (it would not then be grace if it was even possible); but they can tell others all about it.

B. The rescued believer knows that the LORD holds dear the deaths of his saints (15).

All praise has a didactic element to it; it is based on what the individual learned in the experience and concerns what the congregation should learn from it. In his case it was, "Precious[24] in the sight of the LORD is the death of his saints." The word "precious" (יָקָר) means prized, highly valued, or rare; in this verse it indicates that God does not treat the deaths of saints with indifference—they are highly valued by him. He cares so deeply for the lives of the saints that he allows no one to die apart from his plan or without his approval. Allen says the psalmist learned "how reluctant Yahweh is to suffer by premature death the loss of human partners in the covenant relationship, and how quickly God rushes to avert such a tragedy."[25]

C. The believer, the true servant of the LORD, will offer praise publicly in the sanctuary (16–19).

In the final four verses the psalmist vows to offer the praise. But first he affirms his loyalty to the LORD: "I am your servant, and the son of your handmaid" (for "servant," עֶבֶד, s.v. Ps. 134:1). In faith and humility the psalmist is confirming his status as a vassal; he is avowing obedient service and loyalty to the LORD. But many people have a little difficulty understanding the additional

---

24. Some accept the Aramaic meaning for the word and translate it "grievous" instead of "precious." For the discussion, see John A. Emerton, "How Does the LORD Regard the Deaths of His Saints in Psalm cxvi 15?" *JTS* 34 (1983):146–156. Another attempt to make better sense of the line is to emend "death" to "faith," which would be precious (see M. Barré, "Psalm 116: Its Structure and Its Enigmas," *JBL* 109 (1990):61–78.
25. *Psalms 73–150*, p. 155.

expression, "(I am) the son of your handmaid." Some follow the suggested emendation: "your faithful son" in place of "son of your handmaid" ("your handmaid" is אֲמָתֶךָ, and "your faithful [son]" is אֲמִתְךָ).[26] There is, however, a more satisfactory understanding to be found in Scripture and in the culture of ancient Israel. Weiss says that the second clause is meant to emphasize the first—"I am your servant, but also the servant of your handmaid." The expression, "son of your handmaid" describes someone who does not go free with his father (Exod 21:4), and so it describes someone who remains loyal—it emphasizes the absolute servitude of the psalmist.[27] Weiss also connects this verse to the next as cause and effect, citing the analogy with the words of R. Nehunya ben Haqqana: "Whoever takes upon himself the yoke of the Torah, from him the yoke of the kingdom and the yoke of worldly care will be removed" (Mishnah, *'Avot* III:6). And so the the true servant is loyal to the LORD who has freed him from his chains.

We may at least say that the psalmist acknowledges that the LORD has set him free from the tensions and anxieties of the world by delivering him from death, and so now he belongs to the LORD as a servant, a loyal servant—the redeemed belong to the LORD.

As a result, the psalmist will praise the LORD (vv. 17–19). He will offer the sacrifice of praise and make proclamation of the name of the LORD (see again Ps. 50:14; 66:13–20; and also Lev. 7:12–15 and Heb. 13:15–16). In so doing he will pay his vow to praise the LORD in the assembly and in offering the sacrifice of praise provide for the communal feast of the worshipers.

MESSAGE AND APPLICATION

Here we have a celebration of praise, an enthusiastic thanksgiving to God for deliverance from almost certain death. The application from this psalm as with other praise psalms must be for the people of God to give praise and glory to him. But what informs this praise is the arena of faith presented in this passage: the suffering saint was in great anguish and sorrow to the point

---

26. Dahood, *Psalms*, 3:150.
27. *The Bible from Within,* pp. 106–108.

that death seemed to be claiming him—but when in faith he prayed, the LORD answered his prayer and restored him to full life. The primary application of this psalm would be for people who are restored to health, whose lives are spared, to give praise to God in the congregation. This is all they can do, because they cannot repay God for his grace. Their praise, then, will necessarily focus on the LORD's grace, righteousness and compassion that were all displayed in his answer to prayer to preserve the life of his saint. For an expository idea to express the message of the psalm we may say something like this: *Because the death of his saints is precious in his sight, the LORD is faithful to deliver them from suffering and premature death by his grace and compassion so that they might acknowledge his goodness in the presence of all the saints*. The principles displayed in this psalm are timeless: the LORD's grace and compassion for his people, his power to heal and restore through prayer, the effectual prayers of the righteous, and the necessity to offer the sacrifice of praise for all his goodness.

PSALM 117

Universal Praise for God's Faithful Love

INTRODUCTION

Text and Textual Variants[1]

1 Praise the LORD, all you nations;
    laud him, all you peoples.[2]
2 For his loyal love toward us is great,[3]
    and the faithfulness of the LORD endures forever.

   Praise the LORD.[4]

---

1. In the Greek version $Αλληλουια$, "Praise the LORD," is a prologue to the psalm, whereas in the MT it comes at the end of Psalm 116.
2. The MT has הָאֻמִּים, which seems to be an Aramaic form for אֻמּוֹת. The editors of BHS propose לְאֻמִּים, for "peoples." One manuscript has הָעַמִּים, "the nations" or "peoples."
3. The Greek version interprets the line with $ὅτι ἐκραταιώθη τὸ ἔλεος αὐτοῦ ἐφ' ἡμᾶς$, "for his mercy has been abundant toward us."
4. In the Greek version $Αλληλουια$, "Praise the LORD," is put at the head of Psalm 118, whereas in the MT it comes at the end of Psalm 117.

Composition and Context

This short psalm follows the form of a descriptive praise psalm with its call for praise and then the cause for the praise, here the LORD's faithful covenant love. The passage is joined to Psalm 116 in many manuscripts, but serves well as an individual praise, especially with its inclusion of the nations in the call. It is best to take it as it is, a short doxology for Psalms 111–116, even though it might have had a separate use in the festivals of Israel.

Most commentators date the psalm to the period of the exile because it has certain linguistic features that are late and there are similarities to the latter part of Isaiah. Dahood, still, argued that the psalm was pre-exilic, seventh or sixth century B.C.[5]

Exegetical Analysis

Summary

The psalmist calls all nations and peoples to praise the LORD for his faithful loyal love.

Outline

I. Call to praise: All nations and peoples must praise the LORD (1).
II. Cause for praise: They must praise the LORD for his faithful loyal love (2).
III. Conclusion: The LORD is to be praised.

COMMENTARY IN EXPOSITORY FORM

I. All nations and people must praise the LORD (1).

The call to praise begins with the familiar expression, "praise the LORD" (הַלְלוּ אֶת־יְהוָה; s.v. Ps. 33:1), usually addressed to the covenant community, but here to the nations as well. The imperative is generally understood as a call or invitation, as are many

---

5. *Psalms*, III:152.

imperatives that call for people to respond correctly to the grace and goodness of God; but in view of the consequences of refusing to acknowledge the LORD, it is closer to a command. This first imperative is addressed to all the people (גּוֹיִם), a word that has come to refer to Gentiles but was originally used in the promise to Abram of a great nation (Gen. 12:2).

The parallel half of verse one uses another imperative for "praise him," or if we wish to show that the text uses a different Hebrew or Aramaic word, "laud him" (שַׁבְּחוּהוּ). This verb appears to be an Aramaic word for "praise, laud"; and unless it was also Hebrew but not used much in the psalms, it may indicate that the psalmist chose it to address the nations since Aramaic was spoken in the non-Israelite world and became the dominant language at the time of the captivity. A "Gentile" word would complement the first imperative, a Hebrew word, that would have spoken to the Israelites. And with this second verb we have the object "all peoples" (הָאֻמִּים), perhaps also an Aramaic spelling. The two words, "nations" and "peoples," clearly show that the call is addressed to the people of the whole world; and if the call is expressed in both Hebrew and Aramaic forms, the universal appeal would be made stronger.

II. They must praise the LORD for his faithful covenant love (2a).

Verse 2 provides the reason for the praise: the faithful, covenant love of the LORD. It divides the cause into two parts, the first focusing on the covenant love and the second on his faithfulness. The first half declares that God's loyal love (חֶסֶד; s.v. Ps. 23:6) is great. The verb used here (גָּבַר; s.v. Ps. 45:3) has the basic meaning of being strong or mighty; it is easily illustrated by its connections to related forms.[6] In the other verbal stems the verb can mean to confirm a covenant (Dan. 9:27, the *hiphil* stem), or

---

6. These words are discussed with the use of גִּבּוֹר, "mighty," in Psalm 45:3. The noun גֶּבֶר refers to man as strong (see 2 Sam. 23:1, with the sense of a combatant who defends the people). The cognate Arabic means "compel, force, play the man." The verb has the basic meaning of being strong or mighty (Ps. 65:4), but can have the sense of prevailing (as in the war in Exod. 17:11, or the waters of the flood in Gen. 7:18).

show oneself mighty (Isa. 42:13, the *hithpael* stem). But in this context it may have the connotation of prevailing (although עַל would be expected as in Ps. 103:11). Often when the Israelites praised God's faithfulness and loyal love, it was because he acted on their behalf to demonstrate his love. Accordingly, the "loyal love" would be understood as a figure (a metonymy of cause), signifying what that loyal love did for the covenant people. The word is essentially a covenant word, emphasizing that God is loyal to his covenant people whom he loves.

The second colon adds the idea of "truth" (וֶאֱמֶת; s.v. Ps. 15:2). The verse could be translated with this meaning as in the Greek version. In that sense it would be saying that whatever God said, especially in his covenant promises, is completely reliable—eternally true (the idea of faithfulness or reliability being at the heart of its meanings). But the two words "loyal love" and "truth" are frequently found together in the psalms, and may form a single idea with "truth" modifying "loyal love": "true / faithful loyal love" (a nominal hendiadys). If God's loyal love is demonstrated in the fulfillment of the covenant promises, then his faithfulness is also displayed, faithfulness to his word. So the second colon makes the idea of the first colon much stronger: God's faithful loyal love is eternal—he fulfills all his covenant promises.

III. The LORD must be praised (2b).

The psalm closes with the familiar call to praise: "Praise the LORD" (הַלְלוּ־יָהּ). Although this has become an exclamation in worship, it remains an imperative. Everyone must praise the LORD.

MESSAGE AND APPLICATION

The psalm is a call for all nations to praise the LORD for his faithful covenant love. Here is another confirmation that from the very beginning God's plan included Gentiles (see Gen. 12:3). The apostle Paul quoted this psalm to reiterate the point in Romans 15:11: in Christ the love of God is now fully revealed to both Jews and Gentiles.

The wording of the expository idea for this psalm is uncomplicated: *Everyone everywhere must praise the LORD for his faithful covenant love*. This is not only a call for believers to acknowledge his faithful love; it is also a call for people to come to faith, to acknowledge the greatness of God's love—and, how could they praise him for his faithful love without believing in him? But even if in this life people refuse to praise the LORD, they will in the end have to acknowledge his lordship even though they may have no share in his eternal kingdom (Phil. 2).

For believers today living in the light of the new covenant, the faithful love of God has been made manifest in a far more glorious way—in the redemption through Christ Jesus at the cross. This display of the love of God was the fulfillment of many of the promises given to the world through Israel in the Old Testament; and what the love of God in Christ accomplished is our eternal salvation. Such love did indeed prevail as the victory over sin and death. This fact alone should inspire believers to praise God throughout this life, and the life to come.

PSALM 118

Jubilant Praise for Deliverance and a New Beginning

INTRODUCTION

Text and Textual Variants

1 Give thanks to the LORD, for he is good,
    for his loyal love endures forever.
2 Let Israel now say:[1]
    "His loyal love endures forever."
3 Let the house of Aaron say:
    "His loyal love endures forever."
4 Let those[2] who fear the LORD say:
    "His loyal love endures forever."

---

1. In verse 2, 3, and 4, the Greek version adds "he is good" before "his loyal love endures forever."
2. The Greek text adds "all," "all those who."

PSALM 118

5 Out of my anguish I cried to the LORD;[3]
   the LORD answered me[4] by liberating *me*.[5]
6 The LORD is for me; I[6] will not be afraid.
   What can man do to me?[7]
7 The LORD is for me; *he is* my helper.[8]
   And I will look in triumph on those who hate me.

8 It is better to take refuge[9] in the LORD
   than to trust in mortals.
9 It is better to take refuge in the LORD,
   than to trust[10] in princes.

10 All the nations surrounded me;
   in[11] the name of the LORD I cut them off.[12]
11 They surrounded me on every side;[13]

---

3. The form here is יָהּ in both places in the verse, and also in verses 14, 17, 18, and 19.
4. The Greek, Syriac and Symmachus have "and" at the beginning of the colon.
5. The Hebrew text literally says, "he answered me in a broad place."
6. Some versions add "and."
7. The Greek version reads these clauses as: "I will not fear what man can do to me."
8. The Hebrew has a plural form, but most interpret it as a singular following the Greek and Syriac versions..
9. *4QPs*ᵇ has "trust," בְּטַח, to fit the following lines; see also the Greek and Syriac.
10. The Greek translation has "hope."
11. The Greek and Syriac have "and / but."
12. The Hebrew text has the verb אֲמִילַם, from מוּל, "to circumcise," rendered here "I cut them off." A few manuscripts do not have the *yôd*, perhaps suggesting a form אֲמֹלֵל, unless the spelling is simply defective. The Greek translation used ἠμυνάμην, which has a meaning something like "I fended them off." Since the form in the text is unusual, Allen suggests it comes from a verb that is a *hapax legomenon*, and that it should be given a translation like the Greek version. There is not much support for this; it is a proposal based on the Greek interpretation. But the Greek translation may have been struggling with the difficult form and interpreted it that way. At any rate, the form is to be taken as a preterite, meaning that the crisis was over. How exactly the psalmist (Israel) achieved that victory is unclear from this difficult word.
13. The Hebrew text says "they surrounded me, also they surrounded me."

Jubilant Praise for Deliverance and a New Beginning

      in the name of the LORD I cut them off.
12 They surrounded me like bees;[14]
      they died out as quickly as burning thorns;
      in the name of the LORD I cut them off.

13 I was pushed back[15] and about to fall,
      but the LORD helped me.
14 The LORD is my strength and my song;
      and he has become my salvation.
15 The sound of rejoicing and salvation
      is in the tents of the righteous:
    "The right hand of the LORD does valiantly;
16 The right hand of the LORD is exalted high;[16]
    The right hand of the LORD does valiantly."

17 I shall not die, but I shall live
      and will proclaim the works[17] of the LORD.
18 The LORD chastened me severely,
      but he has not given me over to death.
19 Open for me the gates of righteousness;
      I will enter through them,[18] I will give thanks to the LORD.

20 This is the gate of the LORD,
      through which the righteous may enter.
21 I will give you thanks for you answered me;
      And you have become my salvation

22 The stone *which* the builders rejected

---

14. The Greek translation adds "a honeycomb."
15. The Hebrew text has a 2nd msg verb: "You pushed me back." Allen says that this is hardly possible; God is not addressed directly until verse 21 (p. 162), and the parallel line switches to God as the subject. For דְּחִיתַנִי the Greek translation (and the Syriac and Jerome) has a passive (= נִדְחֵיתִי).
16. The MT has רוֹמֵמָה; the Greek translation (and Syriac) have an object, representing a suffixed pronoun: "exalted me."
17. Many manuscripts have the singular form.
18. The Greek version reads: "When I enter through them," probably interpreting the relationship between the two clauses.

has become the head of the corner;[19]
23 This is from the LORD,
it[20] is marvelous in our eyes.
24 This is the day *that* the LORD made;[21]
let us rejoice and be glad in it.

25 O LORD, save *us*;
O LORD, grant *us* success.
26 Blessed is the one who comes in the name of the LORD–
we bless you[22] from the house of the LORD.
27 The LORD is God
and he has made *his* light shine upon us.
Bind the sacrifice[23] with cords[24]
to the horns of the altar.

---

19. The Hebrew word is פִּנָּה, probably referring to the capstone; the Greek version has "chief cornerstone," κεφαλὴν γωνίας. See M. Cahill, "Not a Cornerstone! Translating Ps 118, 22 in the Jewish and Christian Scriptures," *RB* 106 (1999):345–57.
20. The Greek and Syriac have "and."
21. Or, "This today is what the LORD has done."
22. The suffix "you" in the Hebrew is plural.
23. The word is חַג (from חָגַג); it refers to the pilgrimage to the festival to make a sacrifice.
24. The expression in the Hebrew is: אִסְרוּ־חַג בַּעֲבֹתִים, "bind the festal sacrifice with cords." The Greek version has "arrange the feast with branches," συστήσασθε ἑορτὴν ἐν τοῖς πυκάζουσιν. The reading in the Hebrew has some difficulties that have led many to find different interpretations or follow variant readings. The word חַג is normally the pilgrimage to the festival to make sacrifices. Some suggest that the word עֲבֹת is "rope," but עֲבוֹת is "branches." This is not entirely compelling, for both words can mean "leafy, interwoven foliage," whereas the first can also mean "cord, rope." BDB translates it "cords" in this passage. These considerations, as well as the absence of any evidence that they tied sacrifices to the horns of the altar, have led people to conclude that this was referring to the Feast of Tabernacles; but this would require a change in meaning of the initial verb because it clearly is "bind." Several commentators following Gunkel and Kraus and others have suggested that dancers at the festival were roped together: "Link the pilgrims with ropes . . . ." But there is certainly no evidence for that at all. At least the existence of horns on the altar makes a translation "bind" plausible.

Jubilant Praise for Deliverance and a New Beginning

28 You are my God, and I will give you thanks;
    my God, and I will exalt you.
29 Give thanks to the LORD, for he is good,
    for his loyal love endures forever.

Composition and Context

This psalm may be classified as a communal thanksgiving for a great deliverance from the oppressing enemies that surrounded and almost destroyed the people of Israel in what appears to have been divine chastening, but it includes a liturgical section. The first part introduces the praise and reports the deliverance (1–4). The next part turns to praise (the verses could be variously divided for the structure): the psalmist first announces the intention to praise, and then does it (5–18). The last part of the psalm describes a cultic procession to the altar, the blessing by the priests, the praise of the psalmist, and the acclamation of the people (19–27). The psalm closes by repeating the initial praise (28–29).

The passage appears to be a little confusing at first glance. For example, the verbs of the psalm change from singular to plural on occasion; but this probably indicates that the psalmist was speaking on behalf of the nation—hence a communal thanksgiving. Also, parts of the work are antiphonal. A number of commentators suggest that the individual was the king, or if there was no king, a Davidic prince or some other leader. A study of the whole psalm will lead to the conclusion that the "I" of the first part of the psalm is the leader of the worship procession in the final part who speaks on behalf of the people. From the report of the deliverance in the first part one can learn that the people suffered greatly under the oppression of the nations but were then delivered by God in an amazing victory. And from the liturgical section to follow, one can also learn that they had returned to their own place to start anew as the people of God and so made their way to the sanctuary to praise the LORD.

There is some disagreement on the occasion or setting of the psalm. A number of commentators do agree that the psalm was written to celebrate the victory of the king and his people in battle with a liturgical procession to the sanctuary to offer praise to the LORD (along the lines of the account in 2 Chron. 20:27–28).[25] Exactly what victory that was is left open for speculation. Anderson does not think any particular victory is in view here; rather, he suggests that the psalm was written for the annual fall festival's cultic ritual.[26] A more common and more plausible view is that the psalm represents a post-exilic liturgical thanksgiving. Perowne proposes four possible times for this: 1) the first Feast of Tabernacles after the return (Ezra 3:1–4); 2) the laying of the cornerstone (Ezra 3:8–13); 3) the consecration of the completed temple (Ezra 6:15–18); or 4) the great Feast of Tabernacles after the completion (Neh, 8:13–18). He prefers the last option, noting that the Jewish tradition says the psalm itself was used at the Feast of Tabernacles (*b. Sukkah,* 45a–b) and that the psalm indicates that the temple was complete.[27] However, in Jewish tradition the psalm was part of the Hallel and used at all the festivals, Passover especially. Furthermore, the fact that later Judaism used the psalm at the Feast of Tabernacles does not prove it was written for that occasion. The use of the psalm in the Gospels witnesses to its use for Passover as well.

The general understanding is that the psalm was post-exilic, although Anderson concludes it is most likely from pre-exilic times.[28] during the monarchy. Oosterhoff concludes that the psalm was old but given a new interpretation after the exile.[29] And we may add here that the psalm would also receive new but related meanings in the fulfillment in the Gospels.

The ideas of the psalm fit the return from the exile better than any other occasion in Israel's history. It is not just about the king's (people's) victory over oppressing enemies. The oppression was divine chastening for the nation. And when the nation was able to gain victory over her enemies, the faithful praised the LORD for establishing a new beginning for his kingdom program

---

25. Kidner, *Psalms 73–150*, p. 412.
26. *Psalms 73–150*, p. 797. He follows Mowinckel in this; he suggests it was part of a liturgical drama performed at the temple gates.
27. *Psalms,* II:339.
28. *Psalms 101–150*, p. 797.
29. B. J. Oosterhoff, "Het Loven van God in Psalm 118," in *Leven en Geloven*, ed. by M. H. van Es, et al (Amsterdam: Ton Bolland, 1975):175–90.

Jubilant Praise for Deliverance and a New Beginning

in which they would all share. Other details will fall into line in the survey of the passage.

Exegetical Analysis

Summary

In praising the LORD for his marvelous loyal love, the psalmist rehearses how the LORD dealt valiantly in overcoming the powerful nations that threatened their lives, and how he restored them to the center of his program so that they could once again enter the sanctuary in great jubilation and anticipation.

Outline

I. The leader of the people (speaking to the congregation) calls the people to praise the LORD's loyal love that endures forever (1–4).
   A. General: He calls for praise to be given to the LORD for his loyal love (1).
   B. Specific:
      1. All Israel must praise him for his loyal love (2).
      2. All priests must praise him for his loyal love (3).
      3. All worshipers who fear him must praise him for his loyal love (4).
II. The leader of the people (now speaking for the nation) reports how the LORD answered their prayer in the time of distress and gave them victory over the enemies, enabling them to live and not die (5–18).
   A. The LORD answered them out of their distress (5).
   B. The people learned to trust the LORD in the process (6–9):
      1. When the LORD is on their side, they have nothing to fear because they are assured of victory (6–7).
      2. It is better to take refuge in the LORD than in human resources (8–9).
   C. The LORD gave them victory over the nations that had surrounded them (10–13).
      1. In the name of the LORD they were able to cut off the nations that surrounded them (10–12).
      2. The LORD is their strength, song and salvation (13).

- D. Because the LORD has done mighty things, they will live to proclaim his mighty works (14–18).
  1. The LORD has become their strength, doing mighty things (14–16).
  2. The LORD let them live to proclaim his works (17).
  3. The LORD chastened them, but they survived (18).
III. The leader of the people (now leading the communal praise) expresses their desire to enter the sanctuary to praise the LORD for giving them such a great victory over the nations and a share in his renewed program (19–27).
- A. Desire to Praise: They desire to enter the holy sanctuary to offer praise to the LORD who has become their salvation (19–21).
  1. They want to enter the sanctuary to praise God (19).
  2. The priests remind them that the righteous may enter (20).
  3. They will praise God who has given them salvation (21).
- B. The Praise: The LORD has made this their time of salvation by exalting them over their oppressors to have a share in God's renewed program (22–24).
  1. The insignificant nation (and its prince) which the foreign powers rejected has become the center of the LORD's kingdom program (22).
  2. This is what the LORD has done (23).
  3. It inspires praise and celebration (24).
- C. The Procession: The redeemed enter the sanctuary to worship the LORD with the sacrifice of praise (25–27).
  1. They pray for complete salvation and restored prosperity (25).
  2. The priests bless everyone who comes in the name of the LORD (26).
  3. The thankful people present their festal sacrifice at the altar in praise of the LORD's victory (27).
IV. The psalmist reiterates the vow to praise the LORD God because his loyal love endures forever (28–29).

Jubilant Praise for Deliverance and a New Beginning

COMMENTARY IN EXPOSITORY FORM

I. The faithful love of the LORD endures forever in spite of the circumstances of life (1–4).

The first few verses of this psalm follow a form for calling the whole assembly to praise the LORD; but that does not in any way weaken the theology that is expressed again and again in it, that the loyal love (חֶסֶד; s.v. Ps. 23:6) of the LORD is everlasting (עוֹלָם; s.v. Ps. 61:4). Everything expressed in the verses to follow will demonstrate the working out of God's faithful covenant love to his people. So after the initial call "give thanks" (or "acknowledge," הוֹדוּ; s.v. Ps. 6:5) and the reason, "for he is good (טוֹב; s.v. Ps. 34:8), for his loyal love endures forever," the call is for different groups in the assembly, Israelites, priests, and then all who fear the LORD, to repeat the anthem, "his loyal love endures forever."

II. The amazing power of the LORD brings deliverance from the oppression of the world (5–18).

This section records the cause for praise, namely, that the LORD demonstrated his loyal love by delivering his people from a life-threatening oppression from the great nations in order that they might live to proclaim his powerful and amazing works.

A. Cause for Praise: The LORD answers their prayers from distress (5).

The main reason for the praise is stated succinctly: the psalmist (i.e., the people) cried to the LORD from his anguish and the LORD answered him and set him free. On the surface this appears to be the thanksgiving of an individual, but as the report of the dilemma and then of the deliverance unfolds it will be clear that the individual is the spokesman for the people, perhaps the king if this was written in the time of the monarchy, but more likely if written after the return then a Davidic prince or some other leader of the people. Thus, it was not a personal dilemma and deliverance, but a national disaster. Here he simply says "from my anguish" (הַמֵּצַר; s.v. Ps. 120:1), which he will explain later, "the LORD answered by setting *me* free" (literally, "he answered me in a broad place"), which the psalm will also explain.

B. Lesson: They have nothing to fear if the LORD is on their side (6–9).

The psalmist immediately acknowledges that the deliverance was due to divine intervention. Twice he declares "the LORD is for me," meaning that in the conflict the LORD was on his side. If the LORD was for him, who could then be against him and succeed (see Rom. 8:31)? So he states that he will not fear (for יָרֵא; s.v. Ps. 2:11) because there is nothing that man can do to him (an affirmation expressed by the rhetorical question). The second occurrence of this declaration (v. 7) explains how the LORD was for him, "as my helper."[30] The word "helper" (עֹזֵר; s.v. Ps. 46:1) does not minimize God's part in the victory at all; it means that God did for his people what they could not do for themselves—get free from captivity. And the result of this "help" from the LORD is a triumphant celebration: "I will look *in triumph* on those who hate me" (שָׂנֵא; s.v. Ps. 139:21). The psalmist is anticipating the celebration of the victory; to look on one's enemies is to look from the perspective of the victor.

Out of this theological explanation the psalmist advises the people: "It is better to take refuge (חָסָה; s.v. Ps. 7:1) in the LORD than to trust (בָּטַח; s.v. Ps. 4:5) in man." There is no comparison between the LORD's ability and that of mortal man; and yet the nation did "put confidence" in other nations on the eve of the deportation to Babylon rather than trust in the sovereign LORD. The lesson is repeated in verse 9 with the change now to "princes." It is a reminder to believers that no matter how serious the crisis may be they must trust in the LORD who is "for them" rather than human allies who may not be for them and may not be able to withstand a common enemy either.

---

30. The form in the text uses a *bet* of essence, not "in" but "as my helper" (בְּעֹזְרִי).

C. Report of Deliverance: The LORD gave them victory over the nations (10–12).

With this report we learn more of the dilemma: "all nations surrounded me." Clearly he is speaking on behalf of the people for nations do not surround one man. By "all nations" he means the surrounding tribes and especially the great empires that were their enemies. He will repeat this report of the dilemma two more times in these verses: they surrounded him on every side (v. 11), and they surrounded him like bees (v. 12). In verse 12 he adds that they died out as quickly as burning thorns.

Corresponding to these three reports of the dilemma he says three times, "in the name of the LORD I cut them off." The ability to gain victory over and freedom from the nations came from the "name of the LORD," that is, his powerful intervention (s.v. Ps. 20:1).

Whatever "victory" the psalmist has in mind is explained by the verb "I cut them off." The verb is an unusual choice; it literally says "I circumcise them" (אֲמִילַם from מוּל, which here could be taken as a future tense, but preferably in the report of the deliverance a preterite). A number of commentators and translations retain this meaning: Dahood, Hengstenberg, Briggs, Delitzsch, and Rosenbloom[31] do so with varying explanations, such as forced conversion (by forced circumcision) or figuratively for changing the mind. Others who find this verb too difficult follow the reading in the Greek version, something like "fend off" or "ward off, disperse." On the basis of that they posit a Hebrew verb (מוּל II), a homonym with the meaning "ward off," a word that they say occurs only here.[32] It would be more compelling if there was support from Hebrew usage. As it stands it is possible that the translator of the Greek version found the word as troubling as we do and offered a paraphrase that fit the context. If we retain the meaning "I cut them off," the psalmist would then be saying something like this: he (i.e., the nation under his leadership) was surrounded by enemies (more powerful nations) and almost perished, but that LORD ended that crisis with a great

---

31. Joseph R. Rosenbloom, *Conversion to Judaism, From the Biblical Period to the Present* (New York: KTAV Pub. Inc., 1979), p. 25.
32. See for example Allen, *Psalms* 101–150, p. 162.

victory which he describes with the word "circumcised" and not one of the many verbs for military victory; he did not have the literal sense in mind, but rather the significance of circumcision, circumcision of the heart (Deut. 30:6[33]), meaning that by supernatural intervention that changed their minds with regard to Israel the nation was able to gain freedom. Now if the occasion for this psalm is the release of the people from the Babylonian captivity the choice of this word would make better sense, for there was no military battle at all. There was a change of heart by their captors, the Persians under Cyrus the Great, so that they restored the Jews to their land.

Whatever the precise meaning of the verb is, it clearly describes an amazing deliverance from an impossible situation, a deliverance that could only have been by the power of the LORD and not by Israel's abilities. Furthermore, since the one (leader of the people) who "cut them off in the name of the LORD" is also the one who leads the assembly to praise the name of the LORD, then additional information about the deliverance will be found there.

D. Praise: The LORD let them live to proclaim his mighty works (13–18).

Now we learn that the nation was almost destroyed but that the LORD let them live; and more importantly, the danger they were in was part of the LORD's chastening of them. The Hebrew text in verse 13 says "you pushed me down" (the 2nd person of the verb). Because this does not read smoothly with the second half, "the LORD helped me," many follow the versions and make it a passive, "I was pushed down." That does give a better flow to the verse; but yet it will be clear according to verse 18 that the dilemma, this pushing down, was the severe chastening by the LORD. Verse 13a simply explains that the LORD pushed them down to the point of falling, the imagery suggesting an

---

33. It is interesting to note that this meaning of circumcision in Deuteronomy 30:1–10 is in a passage telling about how the LORD would deliver his people from exile, only in the passage the people's heart would be circumcised.

Jubilant Praise for Deliverance and a New Beginning

overpowering defeat. But the LORD helped them, and so they were not destroyed—he became their strength (עֹז; s.v. 29:1), their song (זִמְרָה; s.v. Ps. 33:2), and their salvation (יְשׁוּעָה; s.v. Ps. 3:2). This line seems to be drawn from Exodus 15:2a, the song of Moses when the LORD defeated Egypt at the Sea. The LORD became their strength, because they were weak; he became their song (a metonymy of effect) because he gave them reason to sing (he has become the subject of their praise), and he became their salvation because he set them free. These descriptions are explanations of the statement in verse 13b that the LORD "helped" them (עָזַר; s.v. Ps. 46:1). As a result there was the sound of rejoicing and victory (literally, salvation). The reference to tents has been taken to refer to the temporary dwellings of the people at the Feast of Tabernacles, but there is no support for that in the text. It seems more likely it is referring to the dwellings of the people, who, if they are returning exiles, had temporary dwellings but still occasion for great rejoicing.[34]

In verses 15b–16 this rejoicing is expressed in a threefold praise for the power of the LORD, using the idiom of "the hand of the LORD." He has done valiantly (חַיִל; s.v. Ps. 49:6), an expression used in the first and third cola. What the LORD's power has done is amazing to all who know it. And it is so far above anything humans could do that he can only exclaim, "the hand of the LORD is exalted" (רוֹמֵמָה; s.v. Ps. 46:10).

The effect of this great power was life over death: "I shall not die, but I shall live, and proclaim the works of the LORD" (v. 17). It is not sufficient to say his troubles were like death; he means that actual death was inevitable, for the nation and certainly for the individual, until the LORD delivered them. It is still the nation for whom he speaks—the nation did not die out, as all the other little states that were attacked and carried off. No, Israel survived, amazingly, to live and to proclaim his works. Of course the singular verb also makes sense here, because the praise would begin with the leader's proclamation, and the people would follow him in this, everyone testifying to

---

34. See further S. E. Loewenstamm, "The LORD Is My Strength and Glory," *VT* 19 (1969):464–70.

his or her renewed life. The last clause could be subordinated to mean, "I shall live in order that I might proclaim."

The LORD had power over their circumstances, because their suffering was divine chastening: "the LORD chastened me severely (יִסַּר; s.v. Ps. 6:1) but he has not given me over to death." If the suffering came from the LORD's chastening, and not simply from overpowering nations, then the LORD would also easily be able to limit the chastening and bring about the deliverance. The LORD is therefore sovereign over the nations, and over the life of his people; to him they pray, and of him they speak in their great thanksgiving.

III. The great salvation of the LORD guarantees a glorious future in God's renewed program, for which the redeemed assemble to offer their praise (19–27).

A. Desire to Praise: The redeemed are eager to offer praise to God (19–21).

In the rest of the psalm we have recorded the liturgical procession of the faithful to the altar to celebrate the great salvation they have received from the LORD and to pray for the fulfillment of God's program which has now begun anew. The section begins with a short entrance or gate liturgy. The leader of the congregation speaks on behalf of the people when the congregation approaches the gate of the temple: "Open to me the gates of righteousness" (צֶדֶק; s.v. Ps. 1:5). Some commentators take these gates to be symbolic of the completion of the salvation, that is, drawing near to the LORD. That symbolism is certainly possible, but the gates may still be the actual gates of the temple. The qualification of the gates as "gates of righteousness" means that righteous people will enter into the presence of the LORD for a righteous purpose. Here it is to praise the LORD. Verse 20 provides the clarification of this expression (and may be the response of the Levitical gate keepers): "This is the gate of the LORD through which the righteous may enter"—and only the righteous. People who were believing members of the covenant community and serious about following the Law of the LORD were admitted into the holy place after meeting with the

Jubilant Praise for Deliverance and a New Beginning

gatekeepers (see Pss. 15 and 24). Here the psalmist's response to the standard appears to be a claim to his qualification; it is a testimony of salvation from the LORD and therefore his right to enter. He desires to praise the LORD for answering his prayer. So, if the LORD heard the cries of his people, ended their chastening, delivered them from their enemies, and restored them to their land to renew the covenant, then surely they were acceptable to the LORD and had the right—and the necessity—to enter his courts to offer their praise.

B. Praise: The redeemed declare that the LORD delivered his people to be part of his renewed program (22–24).

These three verses form the praise that the people would offer to the LORD. It begins with the declaration that "the stone *which* the builders rejected has become the head of the corner." The language is figurative, probably inspired by the rebuilding of the temple where some of the existing stones were discarded and others used. But such a stone probably reminded the psalmist of other prophetic passages in which the image of the stone was prominent. Isaiah 28:16 prophesied that the LORD would lay in Zion a stone for the foundation when he restored the people. And other passages identified the Messiah and his kingdom as a stone (see Isa.8:14; Dan. 2:34 and 45; and Zech. 3:9).

Perowne summarizes the symbolic and typological aspects of this passage clearly: The stone was a type of what was happening to the nation and its leader; the stone symbolizes Israel, represented by the Judean prince; and the builders symbolize the empire builders, the great powers of the world. As these nations swept through the land to establish their empires, they considered the little country of Judah to be of no value to them—they rejected it and would have destroyed it. But now that which was rejected by them as worthless has been chosen by God. It not only was restored to the land, but was also made the center of God's theocratic program—and Babylon no longer existed! (II:343).

According to the usage of the passage in the New Testament, Israel represented by its prince, was a type of Christ. Jesus is presented in the Gospels as the true Israel, the promised seed. What was true of the nation was therefore true of him on the highest level.[35] And so in Matthew Jesus claims to be the "stone" of the psalm, the true king and representative head of the nation (Matt. 21:42–44). And the "builders" then are the political and religious leaders, the chief priests and Pharisees (see Matt. 21:45), the kings, and the Romans, most of whom who rejected him and tried to destroy him. In spite of their efforts, this stone became the center of God's new program, a new kingdom that would produce fruit (unlike the Jewish people from whom the kingdom was taken). This came about through the resurrection. And so the day of deliverance and renewal of the covenant program in the Psalm point to the resurrection and the beginning of the new covenant. According to the New Testament, this is the day the LORD has made.[36] Renewed Israel may have been the head of the corner at the return from the exile; but Jesus is the stone of the eternal covenant (Eph. 2:20).

What was marvelous (נִפְלֵאת; s.v. Ps. 139:5) in their eyes, as great as that was, is not as marvelous as the fulfillment on Christ; and so also the rejoicing and celebration over the day of salvation should be far greater as well (for גִּיל s.v. Ps. 13:6; and for שָׂמַח s.v. Ps. 48:11).

C. Worship: The redeemed assemble to give thanks to the LORD and to pray for complete salvation (25–27).

After recording the praise that would be given, the psalm then traces the procession of the people into the sanctuary. They enter, calling on God to save completely and to grant success. The deliverance marked a new beginning; but the deliverance was only the beginning. Their prayer is "save *us*" (הוֹשִׁיעָה נָּא; s.v. Ps. 3:2); it is a prayer familiar to Christian worshipers as

---

35. This emphasis occurs frequently in the narratives. When Joseph and Mary returned from Egypt with the child Jesus, Matthew says the passage in Hosea that says "Out of Egypt have I called my son" (Matt. 2:15) received its fullest meaning, for Hosea was primarily referring to the Exodus.
36. See also A. Berlin, "Psalm 118:24," *JBL* 96 (1977):567–68.

"Hosanna," based on the Greek translation of the acclamation of Jesus's followers who proceeded into the temple with him (see Matt. 21:9 and Mark 11:9–10). To this is added "grant *us* success" (הַצְלִיחָה נָּא; s.v. Ps. 45:4). For the returning exiles the need was still great, and so these petitions were made in their approach to the temple. Likewise Christians also pray this prayer, believing that the one who has begun a good work in them will perfect it.

Verse 26 records a blessing, probably delivered by the priests to the whole assembly of worshipers collectively: "Blessed is the one who comes in the name of the LORD." To bless (s.v. Ps. 5:12) in the name of the LORD means that the blessing comes with divine authority—only God can bless. All who entered received a priestly blessing: "we bless you," "we" indicating the priests spoke, and the pronoun "you" is plural (בֵּרַכְנוּכֶם). Now, in the New Testament account of the triumphal entry of Jesus, the people begin to acclaim the Lord with these words. Jesus was by now believed to be the "coming one" (see Matt. 11:3 and John 11:27), understood by his followers as a Messianic title and not merely a true worshiper. So they praise him and call on him to save them in the highest (Matt. 21:9).

In verse 27 the worshipers respond to the blessing with confidence. They say, "The LORD is God, and he has made his light shine upon us" (וַיָּאֶר). The image of "light" is often used with the blessing of salvation and the joy of being in the kingdom of God (see for example, Psalm 97:11). The instruction in the verse is "bind the (festal) sacrifice with cords to the horns of the altar." Although there is no mention of such a practice in the Old Testament, the existence of the horns and the need for securing the sacrifices in place makes perfectly good sense. Other suggestions made are also without scriptural support, such as binding the sacrifice and taking it to the altar (NIV). This interpretation would fit well the New Testament correlation with the arrest of Jesus to be taken to his sacrificial death. Very unconvincing is the idea of the peoples' binding or joining themselves together in a festal dance to the altar.[37] The word for sacrifice (חַג) usually refers to the festival as a whole but can also refer

---

37. Among others, see Anderson, *Psalms 73–150*, p. 803.

to the festal sacrifice; here the sacrifice is the object of the verb "bind" with ropes.

IV. The LORD is worthy of praise for his everlasting love (28–29).

The faithful finally make their approach to the altar where they will repeat their praise for the everlasting faithfulness of the love of God. The psalm concludes with the acclamation that the LORD is their God and the resolution to praise and exalt him forever. He has shown himself to be their God by answering their prayer, delivering them from bondage, and renewing their covenant relationship in his developing program. Verse 29 repeats the refrain that summarizes all of this: the faithful covenant love of the LORD is eternal.

MESSAGE AND APPLICATION

The argument of the psalm need not be restated here in detail; it is a thanksgiving for the LORD's amazing deliverance of his people from the nations in order to establish them anew as the covenant people. The psalm is filled with important details that need to be explained in the development of the exposition; but the central section of praise brings the main motifs of the psalm together and explains the other parts. And it is here that we have the primary link to the Gospels. There are many ways that the expository statement for the psalm could be expressed; I would suggest something like this: *The LORD has redeemed his people by his amazing power and in accordance with his everlasting love so that they might have a share in his glorious theocratic kingdom.* For this they offer praise and thanksgiving; for this they assemble regularly to enter his sanctuary in adoration of his faithful love, amazing power, and redeeming grace.[38]

---

38. There is so much in this psalm that one idea cannot do justice to the whole; but it does at least help the expositor organize the development of the exposition. See further S. B. Frost, "Psalm 118: An Exposition," *CJT* 7 (1961):155–66.

Jubilant Praise for Deliverance and a New Beginning

Most importantly for Christian expositors is the fact that the psalm is quoted or referred to three times in the Gospels, all within Holy Week. That the words of this psalm were used at the triumphal entry of Jesus (Matt. 21:9) can easily be explained by the fact that it was the time of Passover and people would be familiar with the Hallel Psalms. Many who had heard his teachings and believed he was the Messiah readily saw his entry into Jerusalem as a triumph. He was not now just a prince leading a congregation to worship "in the name of the LORD"; rather, he was "the coming One." Their hope for salvation lay in this one coming in the name of the LORD, this one rejected by his own people, especially the leaders.[39] Accordingly, the cultic language of the psalm took on new meaning as the followers of Jesus cried out to him as their Lord.

The second place the psalm is used is during the middle of the week when Jesus was teaching. He gave an explanation that the meaning of the psalm was that the kingdom would be taken from Israel and given to a nation bearing fruit. The Pharisees—who rejected Israel's stone—knew he was talking about them (Matt. 21:42–45).

Finally, because this psalm was a Hallel Psalm, it would have been sung at the celebrations, certainly including the Passover. Tradition tells us that for a Passover meal Psalms 113–116 were sung before the meal, and Psalms 117 and 118 closed the evening. This psalm, then, was the hymn that Jesus and the disciples sang in the upper room after the last supper (Matt. 26:30). After the evening concluded with the line "Bind the sacrifice with cords to the horns of the altar," Jesus and his disciples went out into the Garden of Gethsemane to watch and pray—and await the fulfillment of their hymn.

The exposition of the psalm must therefore work on two levels, the Old Testament meaning and the New Testament fulfillment. But in both cases it is a song of praise. And because the Lord Jesus Christ clearly appropriated it to himself, the early

---

39. Jubilantly they acclaimed him to be the Messiah, laying branches in his path. This does not mean it was the time of Tabernacles; we have from the Maccabean period this custom to hail the mighty king as he traveled to Jerusalem.

Church made much of it in the formation of the Eucharistic Liturgy. "Hosanna," "Blessed is he who comes in the name of the LORD," the "Stone the builders rejected," all have figured prominently in the prayers and praises of the Church.

PSALM 119
The Word of the LORD and the Life of Faith

INTRODUCTION

Psalm 119 has not received the kind of attention that it deserves. For many students of the Bible its massive size and apparent repetition is off-putting. This is reflected in a number of commentaries and studies as well. Leopold Sabourin, for example, says, "Tedious repetitions, poor thought-sequence, apparent lack of inspiration reflect the artificiality of the sition."[1] Anderson calls it monotonous, but impressive in many ways.[2] Weiser considers it a purely literary composition that is wearisome in its repetition of motifs—and one that opens the way for later legalism; he offers no commentary on the text.[3] But most would agree with Breuggemann that it is a massive achievement.[4]

---

1. Sabourin, *The Psalms, Their Origin and Meaning*, p. 381. He does, however, survey other works that present a more positive appreciation of the psalm.
2. *Psalms 73–150*, p. 806.
3. *Psalms*, pp. 739–41.
4. *The Message of the Psalms*, p. 39.

PSALM 119

Composition and Context

The first thing even a casual reader would notice is that it is an alphabetic acrostic psalm similar to Psalms 111 and 112, or Lamentations 3 (which has 22 strophes of 3 lines, each three beginning with letters in the order of the alphabet). Psalm 119, however, is the greatest acrostic passage, for each stanza has eight verses beginning with the same letter of the alphabet.[5] For example, with the first, the "'*Aleph* stanza," each verse begins with a word that begins with the letter *'āleph* (א); with the second, the "*Bet* stanza," each verse begins with the letter *bêt* (ב), and so on through the alphabet in 22 stanzas. That Lamentations uses an acrostic pattern throughout has been taken as one argument in favor of dating Psalm 119 to that time or later; but the acrostic pattern is not necessarily limited to that period.

That each stanza has eight verses is no doubt linked to another stylistic feature of the psalm, namely that it uses eight different words for the law throughout the psalm. The word "law" (תּוֹרָה) is used 25 times, "word" (דָּבָר) 24 times, "decision" (or "judgment," מִשְׁפָּט) and "testimony" (עֵדוֹת) 23 times, "command" (מִצְוָה) 22 times, "statute" (חֹק) and "precept" (פִּקּוּד) 21 times, and "saying" (or "oracle" or "promise," אִמְרָה) 19 times. All eight synonyms occur in four stanzas: verses 57–64 (*Het*, ח), verses 73–80 (*Yod*, י), verses 81–88 (*Kaph*, כ), and verses 129–136 (*Pe'*, פ). The other stanzas use seven or six of the words, sometimes repeating one or two of them. So there is no apparent attempt at a perfect symmetry.[6] But the word "law" (תּוֹרָה) receives prominence because it is used more than the others and is found in the first verse, which sets the focus for the entire psalm.[7] And far from being needlessly repetitious, the psalmist uses repetition as part

---

5. This arrangement is a way of saying this is the full revelation on the nature of the law (a rhetorical device used elsewhere in Scripture, even in abbreviated form such as "the alpha and the omega."
6. For a detailed analysis of the use of these words see David Noel Freedman, *Psalm 119, The Exaltation of Torah* (Winona Lake, IN: Eisenbrauns, 1999).
7. Allen notes that the word has a wide meaning in the psalm, embracing in its references the Pentateuch, Isaiah, Jeremiah, and Proverbs as canonical texts (*Psalms 101–150*, p. 141).

of the grand plan; and the main theme of the structure of the psalm is the inexhaustibility of the *tôrāh*.[8]

Since the psalm uses so much of the language of Deuteronomy, it has been classified as a *tôrāh* psalm. In its wording and arrangement of themes, however, it recalls much of Proverbs as well. So it may be best to call it a wisdom psalm, but clarify that this is the branch of wisdom literature that extols the law. There are so many different features in the psalm, such as lament, prayer, protestation of innocence, and vow of praise, that Allen calls it a medley of praise, prayer and wisdom features; he adds that it is both a hymn in praise of *tôrāh* and a prayer expressing the need for the master's care.[9]

There is also a frequently appearing note of lament—references to oppression and harassment by powerful people—that drives the psalmist's need for God's word and prompts him to pray for the fulfillment of the promises in it. The language of his affliction recalls Jeremiah's language of suffering. Although there is not enough here to suggest a date for the composition, it seems to come from a time of serious trouble. And yet the affliction as well as the meditation in the law is personal, not national or corporate. Ordinary individuals may not have had access to copies of the Law for such meditation, before or after the exile; but the psalmist is not an ordinary person. These, his written meditations, were accordingly delivered to the sanctuary for use by other worshipers in their spiritual journeys.

Most commentators would date this work in the post-exilic period, at least after the writing of Deuteronomy (which date is debated). Some would put it after Ezra or even later. There is no reason, however, why the psalm could not have been written just prior to the exile, because there is an absence of post-exilic literary references in the work.[10]

Whenever it was actually written is less important than its value in the collection. It may have been composed to close an earlier arrangement of the psalms, serving as a counterpart

---

8. Freedman, p. 89.
9. *Psalms 101–150*, pp. 140, 142.
10. See further Leo Perdue, *Wisdom and Cult* (Missoula, MT: Scholars Press, 1977), pp. 305, 328.

to Psalm 1. It currently stands as the dominant psalm in the final book (Pss. 107–150). There is some debate about its being written to serve some cultic purpose, perhaps for the priests in Jerusalem whose concern was for teaching the law. But there does not seem to be sufficient evidence for identifying this as the purpose, even though it most likely was used in such ways since it was added to the collection.

Meditation and Exposition

If people simply read through Psalm 119 quickly they most likely will conclude it is a repetitious and random collection of meditations on the Word of God. But if they take time to study each stanza in sequence, they will discover how each of the stanzas forms a complete meditation with certain themes and emphases. They will also see how the collection builds on the themes from stanza to stanza to develop a general flow to the message. To gain a full appreciation for this amazing work one must study it carefully from beginning to end, stanza by stanza.

As a major resource for meditation this psalm is superb. It reveals how divine revelation is the basis for everything that the believer does; but it also shows how the Word of the LORD is applied in all the circumstances of life. VanGemeren aptly says, "This is a psalm not only of law but also of love, not only of statute but also of spiritual strength, not only of devotion to precept but also of loyalty to the way of the Lord. The beauty in this psalm resounds from the relationship of the psalmist and his God."[11] The acrostic arrangement no doubt served as a mnemonic device; but it was also a way of organizing the thoughts on various themes in the meditation, themes often introduced in the first verses of each stanza.

It is most unlikely that an expositor would ever preach a sermon on the entire psalm, unless as a general, introductory message. What I have done, therefore, is to treat each stanza separately, providing for each a discussion of the text, an exegetical analysis, and an expository treatment (outline, central idea, and New Testament correlations). In this way an expositor

---

11. *Psalms*, p. 858.

could use one stanza for a lesson or a sermon in its own rights, or an individual could meditate on one stanza at a time and understand how to draw the timeless truths and applications from it. In time the expositor could work stanza by stanza through a section of the psalm in a thematic series.

In the translation I have inserted each of the eight words for the law where they occur, using the lexical form as a simple notation. I have also tried to give each a consistent translation so that the reader would be reminded of which word is used; in the commentary, though, I will on occasion clarify the translation with more contextual precision. My interpretive comments on Psalm 119 are not exhaustive because of the length of the passage; they will not, for example, repeat discussions of the words and their meanings every time they occur. In studying through the psalm, the reader will be able to recall the meanings of words and the repetition of motifs. My comments will focus on the most important words and expressions in each stanza in order to clarify their distinct emphases.

Exegetical Summary

A general summary message of the entire psalm might at least help the expositor keep the major themes in mind. It may be expressed in this way:

> Finding himself in persecution from powerful people who ridicule his faith in an effort to shame him into abandoning it, the psalmist strengthens himself by his detailed meditations on the Word of the LORD, which is his comfort, his prized possession, his rule of life, his resource for strength, and his message of hope, all of which inspire him to desire it even more, to live by it, and to pray for its fulfillment.

While there is no clear and simple development of one particular theme throughout the psalm, there are nevertheless general developments that can be identified to some satisfaction.[12]

---

12. Here I have used the general framework presented by Richard J. Clifford, *Psalms 73–150*, pp. 211–216, who in turn was influenced by other

The first two stanzas (*'Āleph*, א, and *Bêt*, ב) form a prologue to the entire psalm; the first announces a blessing for obedience to God's law and the psalmist's commitment to obey it, with the expectation of praising him for his protective care—a theme reiterated in the last stanza; but the second stanza raises the issue of cleansing one's ways. The psalmist knows this to be an issue in God's word, so he desires to know more through meditation.

In the next four stanzas (*Gîmel*, ג, *Dālet*, ד, *Hē'*, ה, and *Wāw*, ו) there is a movement from complaint to petition and piety. In the first (*Gîmel*) the psalmist complains that powerful people conspire against him and condemn him; he therefore needs to see wonderful things in the law that will give him direction. This is followed (in *Dālet*) by an appeal for restoration from his lamentable condition to vitality so that he can learn to be more faithful. In the third stanza (*Hē'*) of this section, the psalmist has a growing awareness of and disdain for this world, and so prays for understanding and guidance to live without being caught up in selfish gain and worthless ways. He desires confirmation from the word by the removal of his reproach and renewal of his life. Finally, living in hope the psalmist prays for deliverance so that he can answer his enemies with fulfillments from God's promises, promises he loves and promises to proclaim (stanza *Wāw*).

Following this the psalmist looks at God's plans and provisions in the past as the basis for hope and petition for the future. In the first section (stanza *Zayin*, ז) he speaks of comfort and hope against the world and prays for the fulfillment of God's word, because it alone brings comfort and hope in affliction. When the faithful are scorned, God inspires obedience and his word brings joy. This is followed by an affirmation that everything belongs to God and the believer is under his care (stanza *Hêt*, ח). Because of the certainty of divine care, the psalmist commits himself to obey and prays for intervention in the current life-threatening situation. Then, recalling the goodness of God and the well-being of his people, the psalmist expresses his desire for more knowledge and understanding because of the affliction of the arrogant who lie about him—their opposition simply drives him back to God's

---

commentators. I have modified it a bit, and added my summary themes for each stanza.

word (stanza *Têt*, ט). This section closes with a reminder that God made us all, and that affliction is part of the Creator's plan (stanza *Yôd*, י). The psalmist prays accordingly for more understanding, for deliverance from the arrogant, and for a blameless heart so that his prayer will be valid.

In the next few stanzas we find the psalmist reaching his lowest point, but it turns out to be the turning point, leading to more positive reflections. The first part (stanza *Kaph*, כ) explains how the psalmist was almost overwhelmed while waiting for vindication from those who were destroying him. Even in his great trouble, however, he remained faithful to God's law. His confidence is strengthened in the next stanza (*Lāmed*, ל) when he acknowledges that God's word was firmly established forever in heaven. Although the wicked tried to destroy him, the promise of deliverance provides security. Hope in God's word enables believers to overcome the world. This leads him to consider further the superiority of God's word (*Mēm*, מ). God's word is superior to earthly knowledge and wisdom; and so meditation on his word brings more understanding than the learned or aged of the world. Here he finds renewed confidence. Then in the last stanza of this part (*Nûn*, נ) the psalmist announces that God's law is a light to his path—he will follow divine instruction through the dangers of this world because it brings understanding and leads to joy.

The next four stanzas all express his confidence and loyalty in one way or another. In the first part (stanza *Sāmek*, ס) the psalmist declares his hatred for ungodly and untrustworthy people; he will remain separate from them, knowing that God will judge them. There is safety in God's word, not in the world that God will judge. This prompts him to pray, for it is time for the LORD to act to vindicate him (stanza *'Ayin*, ע). But even though he is still in danger, he is confident to appeal to God's faithful love because he has been faithful to God in his life. In the next stanza (*Pē'*, פ) the prayer continues for God to turn to him and establish him through his word. He desires to be vindicated in the eyes of those who hate God's word, because he himself delights in the wonderful words of life. Still, he is saddened to see so many hate divine revelation; but ultimately the righteousness of the LORD will triumph (stanza *Tsādē'*, צ). The

LORD is righteous: the law of the LORD is everlastingly right. This truth brings comfort in affliction, and inspires zeal for the LORD and his word.

The conclusion of the psalm in the last four sections records a cycle of petitions with affirmation of loyalty and promise to praise. In the first part (stanza *Qôph*, ק) he prays for deliverance because he trusts in the word of the LORD. The key is that the LORD, and his word, is near; but the wicked are far from God. God's presence in time of trouble ensures God's word will be fulfilled. His prayer for vindication continues (in stanza *Rêš*, ר) and is based on the fact that he loves and keeps the law. He may be weakened by affliction, but is confident that God will deliver him from his enemies who are far from salvation. The nature of the affliction is described in more detail in the next stanza (*Śîn/Šîn*, שׂ/שׁ): powerful princes are attacking him without a cause—whether Israelite or foreign is unstated. But in spite of wickedness in high places the psalmist rejoices in God's word that brings him peace. Finally, in a fitting conclusion (stanza *Tāw*, ת) the psalmist confesses that he has gone astray, meaning that he has not always followed the LORD's guidance; he desires therefore restoration and deliverance through God's word, for which he will offer praise.

א *'Aleph*

The Blessing of Protective Care

Text and Textual Variants

א 1 Blessed are those whose way is blameless,
    who walk in the law (תּוֹרָה) of the LORD!
א 2 Blessed are those who keep[13] his testimonies (עֵדוּת),
    they seek him with a whole heart;
א 3 they also do not do[14] wrong,

---

13. For MT's נֹצְרֵי the Greek version has οἱ ἐξερευνῶντες, "who search out."
14. The form in the MT is the negated perfect tense לֹא פָעֲלוּ, but the Greek version has a participle οἱ ἐργαζόμενοι, reading the form as פֹּעֲלֵי, following the pattern from verse 2. But the sense of the verse is taken differently

אֲ 4 You have commanded your precepts (פִּקּוּד)
         for us to keep[15] diligently.
אֲ 5 O that my ways may be steadfast
         in keeping your statutes (חֹק)!
אֲ 6 Indeed, I shall not be put to shame,
         when I fix my eyes on all your commandments
         (מִצְוָה).
אֲ 7 I shall praise you with an upright heart
         when I learn your righteous decisions (מִשְׁפָּט).
אֲ 8 I shall keep your statutes (חֹק);
         do not utterly forsake me!

Exegetical Analysis

Summary

Having declared the truth that God's blessing is with those who live in obedience to the law, the psalmist commits himself to keeping the commandments, anticipating that he will praise the LORD for his protective care (119:1–8).

Outline

I. He announces that those who live in accordance with God's law are blessed (1–3).
II. He declares his desire to live more faithfully in the light of God's commands so that he will be successful in life (4–6).
III. He anticipates praising the LORD with an upright heart as he learns more of God's word and trusts in God's care (7–8).

---

 in the Greek version: "they that practice lawlessness did not walk in his ways."
15. The ESV translates this line "to be kept." The form in the MT is לִשְׁמֹר, the active "to keep," which is a difficulty in the line. The intent of the line is: "you have established / commanded your precepts *for us to keep*."

Commentary in Expository Form

I. Those who are obedient to God's word are blessed (1–3).

The first stanza begins with a twofold declaration of the blessing of God on people whose lives are characterized by integrity. The word "blessed" (אַשְׁרֵי; s.v. Ps. 1:1) begins both verses 1 and 2. The expression (literally "O the blessednesses of") signifies the spiritual and heavenly bliss of those who are right with God. But it is not limited to an inner, spiritual joy; there is often external, physical evidence of God's blessing on such a proper relationship, blessing that may take the form of provisions and protective care.

Their conduct is first described as blameless ("those blameless of way," תְמִימֵי־דָרֶךְ), that is, those who in their lives are forgiven for sin and free from sin (s.v. Ps. 7:8). The idiom of "way" is then expanded in the second colon with the participle "who walk" (הַהֹלְכִים) in the law of the LORD, that is, who live out their lives in obedience to God's instructions (for תּוֹרָה, s.v. Ps. 1:2).

The second declaration of blessing offers further explanation of their obedience (v. 2). First, they are "keepers of his testimonies." The participle "keepers [of]" (נֹצְרֵי) describes them as people who carefully observe God's word.[16] Here the term used for the law is "testimonies" (plural, עֵדוֹת), a word that emphasizes

---

16. Related forms of the verb נָצַר (I), "to watch, guard, keep," occur frequently in Psalm 119. The word is very close in meaning to שָׁמַר, "to watch, keep" (s.v. Ps. 12:7). For the usage of נָצַר the lexicon by Brown, Driver and Briggs (pp. 665, 6) lists five categories. First, it has the basic meaning of guarding something, such as a vineyard (Job 27:18). The participle actually means "watchmen" (2 Kings 17:9; Jer. 31:6). It can be used with this meaning in an ethical sense, as in guarding the mouth (Prov. 13:3) or tongue from evil (Ps. 34:14).

Second, the word can have the meaning of guarding from danger or preserving something. In wisdom literature it has a meaning to guard wisdom (Prov. 4:6) or understanding (Prov. 2:11). In Isaiah 49:6 the passive participle means "the preserved of Israel."

Third, it has the sense of guarding something with fidelity, that is, keeping or observing. Here we have the uses for keeping the covenant (Deut. 33:9) or the commandments (Psalm 78:7); here would be all the uses of the word in Psalm 119.

The Word of the LORD and the Life of Faith

the legal stipulations of the covenant.[17] Second, they seek the LORD with their whole heart. The imperfect tense (יִדְרְשׁוּהוּ) is parallel to the participle and so stresses that this is an ongoing pursuit. To seek the LORD with a whole heart means that they are completely occupied with the discernment of the LORD's will revealed in his word. It is the people who keep God's laws and diligently seek him who are blessed by him.

The effect of their determined obedience is expressed clearly in verse 3: "they do not do wrong." The perfect tenses in this verse (פָּעֲלוּ and הָלָכוּ) continue to describe their consistent activities (and may be classified as characteristic perfects). They do

---

The last two categories do not have a lot of uses. The fourth is "to keep secret." The passive participle can mean "secret things, or secret places (see Isa. 48:6; 65:4). And the fifth has the sense of blockading (a city in Isa. 1:8). People who blockade a city are enemies who guard its entrances.

17. The plural word עֵדוֹת is related to the (denominative) verb עוּד, "to bear witness." Another related form עֵד is a "witness," and the noun עֵדָה is "testimony." The nouns עֵדוּת and תְּעוּדָה both mean "testimony." There is some difficulty over the identification of the word in the text. עֵדוֹת is the plural of עֵדָה, and עֵדְוֹת is the plural of עֵדוּת. BDB (p. 730) suggest that either the plural of the first was artificially borrowed from the latter, or that the first plural is a contraction of the latter. The conclusion would be that the word in the text is עֵדוּת in the plural (except 119:138). This technicality does not make much difference in the meaning since both words mean "testimony."

The noun עֵדוּת, "testimony" (or "law"), describes the legal contents of the ark. Moses placed the "testimony," the two tablets of the Decalogue, into the ark (Exod. 25:16; 31:7). It would thus be known as the ark of the testimony, and would be inside the tent of testimony. Because the word refers to the tablets, it clearly describes the essence of the law in written form. The law therefore functioned as a witness or testimony of God's covenant with his people, reminding the people of his saving acts and their obligations. The term came to be a general designation of moral and religious ordinances that formed the divine standard of conduct for the covenant people (see Driver, *Deuteronomy*, p. 81).

The plural עֵדוֹת almost always has a suffix and always refers to the LORD's testimonies or covenant stipulations. It may primarily focus on the terms of the treaty or law that the sovereign LORD placed on his people. The word "covenant" may include the reciprocal agreements, but this word focuses on the legal conditions placed by God on his people, laws they must keep to remain loyal to the covenant. See further C. Van Leeuwen, "עֵד *'ed* **witness**," in *Theological Lexicon of the Old Testament*, edited by Jenni and Westermann, II:838–846.

not practice wrong-doing (עַוְלָה; s.v. Ps. 43:1), a word that focuses on wronging someone else, in general, crimes or injustices. The second half forms a contrast: *"but* they walk in his ways," repeating the idea of verse 1.

II. Those who determine to live more faithfully will be safe and secure in the LORD (4–6).

The emphasis shifts slightly in the next three verses to the psalmist's determination to keep the commandments God has made. Verses 1–3 described the integrity of those people blessed by God; but verse 4 begins with a new subject: "You have commanded your precepts *for us* to keep diligently." The verb "commanded" (צִוִּיתָה) is related to the word for the commandments (מִצְוֹת) used in verse 6 (see the word study there). The point being stressed here is that all of God's laws are divine orders. The word for the law in this verse is "precepts" (פִּקֻּדִים; s.v. Ps. 8:4); this noun only occurs in the Psalms and refers to the appointed laws of God in general. It is connected to the idea of an overseer who is responsible to appoint and carry out the destiny of the people; it points therefore to God's instructions that give attention to details in the care and development of his covenant people.[18] These precepts were commanded for the people of God to keep or observe diligently (לִשְׁמֹר מְאֹד; s.v. Ps. 12:7).

And so in verse 5 the psalmist expresses his desire to be faithful in keeping God's commandments. His wish is that his ways (continuing the idiom) would be steadfast (יִכֹּנוּ; s.v. Ps. 93:1). The infinitive of the last verse is now repeated, but is used to explain the first colon: "in keeping your statutes." The word for "statutes" here and in verse 8 (חֻקִּים, from חֹק) emphasizes the binding nature of God's laws.[19] By keeping these statutes one's conduct will be steadfast.

---

18. Kidner, *Psalms 73–150*, p. 418.
19. The verb חָקַק means "to inscribe, prescribe"; it occurs 12 times in the Old Testament. More common are the derivatives: the noun חֹק occurs 128 times; חֻקָּה occurs 104 times, and מְחֹקֵק 7 times. The verb has the sense of carving out, digging, inscribing, and from thence "to write, prescribe, determine." The clearest sample is found in Isaiah 22:16 where it is used for the excavation of a grave in the rock; Ezekiel 4:1 also uses it for engraving

The expected result of this steadfast obedience is deliverance. The psalmist words it as an understatement: "I shall not be put to shame" (אֵבוֹשׁ; s.v. Ps. 31:1). The expression anticipates verse 8 that suggests the psalmist is in some kind of difficulty, but does not expect to be left there if he is faithful to God's word. Eventually the blessing will be realized in that he will not be put to shame. The rest of verse 6 is a temporal clause, "when I look on all your commandments." The verb "look" or "gaze intently" (נָבַט); in this passage (with the following preposition אֶל) probably has the nuance of regarding or paying attention to something.[20] And the focus of this attention is expressed by the prepositional phrase: "to all your commandments (אֶל־כָּל־מִצְוֹתֶיךָ)."[21] When be-

---

on a brick, and Job 19:23 for engraving on a rock. In Isaiah 49:16 it refers to tattooing on the hand.

In the legal realm the verb has the sense "to establish justice" or "to govern" (see Prov. 8:15; Judg. 5:9). In connection to this, מְחֹקֵק means "staff" or "scepter" in Genesis 49:10 and Numbers 21:18.

The word חֹק may be illustrated from its meaning of something "inscribed" such as marked out boundaries that must not be crossed (see Jer. 5:22). So the word describes the boundary lines that a sovereign prescribes for his subordinates. In Job 38:10 it is the boundary of the sea that cannot be crossed, and in Proverbs 8:27 and 29 the circle of the earth. In Psalm 148:6 the noun is the boundary of the heavenly ocean. And in Micah 7:11 it refers to the boundaries of the territory of Zion. In relation to this the word can refer to the quota of work required (Exod. 5:14).

The word comes to mean then an "established order" (Judg. 11:39). In its usage, especially when it is the LORD's statute, the word refers to the laws that the sovereign makes which no one dare cross over. The word signifies the nature of the law as it establishes binding regulations. But חֹק can be used for God's promises as well (Ps. 2:7).

In legal contexts this word overlaps with מִשְׁפָּט, "decision" or a casuistic statement of law, and מִצְוָה, "commandment," most frequently. The different words usually refer to the whole of the law of God in its various aspects and characteristics. חֹק emphasizes the legally binding statutes, the boundaries God places on his people.

For a full discussion, see G. Liedke, "חקק hqq **to inscribe, prescribe**" in *Theological Lexicon of the Old Testament*, edited by Jenni and Westermann, II:468–472.

20. Brown, Driver, and Briggs, *A Hebrew and English Lexicon of the Old Testament*, p. 613.
21. The word "commandments," מִצְוֹת (singular מִצְוָה), is connected to the verb "command," צִוָּה. The verb occurs almost 500 times, and the noun

lievers stay focused on the commands of the LORD, they will be confident that they will find deliverance.

III. Believers who experience God's righteous decisions and obey his statutes can expect to praise the LORD for his protective care (7–8).

In the last two verses we find an emphasis on the psalmist's anticipation of praising the LORD. The reason for the praise has been hinted at in verse 6 with "I shall not be put to shame," and now more specifically expressed in the closing prayer, "do not utterly forsake me." It appears that the psalmist was in some

---

approximately 181 times. The verb "command" is a verb of speech, a specific kind of speech—a superior's discourse ordering and commanding a subordinate (see G. Liedke, "צוה *ṣwh pi.* **to command**," in *Theological Dictionary of the Old Testament*, edited by Jenni and Westermann, II:1062–1065).It has a fairly wide range of nuances, but all with the emphasis of orders given by a superior. For example, it can have the sense of "lay a charge upon" people, meaning to set commandments for them (Gen. 2:16; Exod. 1:22). This is closely related to the idea of appointing people (2 Sam. 7:11) or putting people in charge of some service (Gen. 12:20). This may be a lifelong commission (Exod. 6:13).

The meaning appropriate for this context is its normal meaning of "command." It is used in general for the commandments that God gives in the law (Deut. 4:40; 6:2, 6). God's commands are not limited to the law code in the Old Testament: he also commanded creation (Ps. 33:9), redemption (Ps. 68:29), and blessing (Ps. 133:3).

The noun מִצְוָה may be used for the orders given by humans who are in places of authority, such as a father to his children (Prov. 6:20), or a king to his people (1 King 2:43). But again the noun most often refers to the LORD's commandments. When the word is used in the singular it refers to the whole law (Deut. 30:11); when used in the plural it refers to individual commands (Lev. 26:14).

These words then stress God's sovereign authority over all creation; everything that happens is based on God's commands. The law especially is the result of his command (as stated in verse 4): The LORD commands *tôrāh* (Num. 19:2), *bᵉrît* (covenant; Josh. 7:11), *ḥuqqîm* (Deut. 6:20), and *mišpāṭ* (Ps. 7:7). God's prophetic word (Jer. 1:7 and Ezek. 37:7) is also by commandment (Liedke, p. 1065).

These words then emphasize that the law is the decree of the divine sovereign; they are commands to be obeyed. The word is one of the main descriptions of the law in the Pentateuch.

danger or difficulty (which will unfold gradually throughout the psalm); but knowing that the LORD blesses the righteous, he was determined to live obediently to the law and thereby anticipate praising the LORD for his protective care, i.e., the blessed life.

"I shall praise / acknowledge you (אוֹדְךָ; s.v. Ps. 6:5) with an upright heart" expresses his anticipation of enjoying God's blessing (v. 7). The phrase "with an upright heart," or literally, "in *the* uprightness of *the* heart" (בְּיֹשֶׁר לֵבָב; for יָשָׁר see Ps. 67:4), indicates that he will have lived obediently to the law—in other words, the praise will come from an obedient believer. But the anticipation of praise is qualified by the temporal clause, "when I learn of your righteous decisions" (or, "the decisions of your righteousness"). God's decisions (often translated "judgments"; for מִשְׁפָּט, s.v. Ps. 9:4) refers to decisions that concern right and wrong and that put into execution the righteousness of God.[22] Such divine decisions would ultimately bring deliverance to the righteous who are in danger or difficulty. In this sense the word "righteous" might be figurative of deliverance (a metonymy of cause). Therefore, when the believer learns of these decisions, meaning experiencing the acts that come from God's decisions (so also a metonymy of cause), he will praise him.

In verse 8 the psalmist reiterates his commitment to keep the law: "I shall keep (אֶשְׁמֹר) your statutes." But then he prays "do not utterly forsake me" (אַל־תַּעַזְבֵנִי עַד־מְאֹד). This urgent petition (expressed by the jussive with אַל) indicates that the psalmist was in some kind of difficulty and wanted God to set him free. The petition is an understatement (tapeinosis); he says "do not forsake me" but means the opposite, that God intervene to take care of him.

Message and Application

This first stanza of the series of meditations that make up Psalm 119 sets the pattern and tone for the entire collection: in the midst of some serious difficulty or dilemma, the psalmist knows that the blessing of God is with the faithful, and so he determines to

---

22. Delitzsch, *Psalms*, III:245.

keep the commandments of God, anticipating that he will have reason to praise the LORD for his protective care. We may word this in the form of an expository idea: *Because of the revelation that God's blessing is with those who are devout, the faithful will commit themselves to obey his word, anticipating that they will praise him when he blesses them with his protective care.*

The themes in this first stanza will appear frequently throughout the entire psalm; but they are timeless truths. James instructs us with these words: "Do not merely listen to the word, and so deceive yourselves. Do what it says . . . . the man who looks intently into the perfect law that gives freedom, and continues to do this, not forgetting what he has heard, but doing it—he will be blessed in what he does" (1:22, 25).

ב *Bet*

Preservation from Sin

Text and Textual Variants

ב 9 How can a young man keep his way pure?[23]
By guarding *it* according[24] to your word[25] (דָּבָר).

ב 10 With all my heart[26] I seek you;
do not let me wander[27] from your commandments (מִצְוָה).

ב 11 I have stored up your word[28] (אִמְרָה) in my heart,
that I might not sin against you.

ב 12 Blessed are you, O LORD;
teach me your statutes (חֹק)!

---

23. MT has יְזַכֶּה, "keep / make pure"; but the Greek version has κατορθώσει, "keep straight / direct."
24. The Greek version does not have the preposition: "by guarding your words."
25. Many manuscripts and some versions have this word plural.
26. Instead of לִבִּי, "my heart," a few Hebrew manuscripts have simply לֵב, "heart."
27. The Greek version renders אַל־תַּשְׁגֵּנִי with μὴ ἀπώσῃ με, "do not cast me aside."
28. Several manuscripts, the Greek and the Syriac have this word plural.

ב 13 With my lips I declare
          all the decisions (מִשְׁפָּט) of your mouth.²⁹
ב 14 In the way of your testimonies (עֵדוֹת) I delight
          as much as in all riches.
ב 15 I will meditate on your precepts (פִּקּוּד)
          and fix my eyes³⁰ on your ways.
ב 16 I will delight³¹ in your statutes (חֹק);
          I will not forget your word (דָּבָר)!³²

Exegetical Analysis

Summary

The psalmist affirms that devotion to the word of God cleanses one's way in life, prompting him to desire to learn more from God and to determine to meditate with delight in his word (119:9–16).

Outline

I. The psalmist affirms that devotion to the word of God cleanses the life (9–11).
   A. Using a question and answer he affirms that the disciple keeps his way pure by guarding it with God's word (9).
   B. He expresses his intention to avoid sin by asking God to keep him from wandering and by making the word a part of his whole life (10–11).
II. The psalmist prays for the LORD to teach him his statutes and confirms that he declares God's decisions and delights in his testimonies more than in riches (12–14).
III. The psalmist vows to meditate on and delight in the law of the LORD (15–16).

---

29. A few manuscripts and some versions have "your righteous" here.
30. The Greek version reflects this idea with κατανοήσω, "put my mind (on your ways)."
31. The form in the MT is אֶשְׁתַּעֲשָׁע (see below in the commentary); the Greek version interprets this (regularly) with "meditate" (μελετήσω).
32. The majority of Hebrew manuscripts, the Greek, Syriac, and Jerome, all have "words."

Commentary in Expository Form

I. The faithful learn to live by God's word because it keeps them pure (9–11).

A. *They guard their lives by God's word in order to remain pure (9).*

The focus of this second stanza of the psalm is on keeping pure throughout life. According to this passage as well as others in the Bible, it is only possible to do this with a wholehearted commitment to God's word.

The stanza begins with a question and answer, reminiscent of proverbial constructions (Prov. 1:4; 25:12–13). The question is addressed to God, and so is rhetorical, introducing the issue of remaining pure. In using "young man" as the subject, the question also recalls wisdom literature with its emphasis on the disciple as a "son." The matter does not only concern a young man, but any concerned disciple.

The issue raised in the question is how anyone can keep his way pure. "His way" (אָרְחוֹ) is idiomatic for all the activities of life, and so the need for purity would be felt in many ways. The verb rendered "keep pure" (יְזַכֶּה; s.v. Ps. 51:4) has the idea of being free from sin or from the tarnish of sin.[33] The word does not mean he is sinless; it means he is acquitted or free from it, i.e., righteous.

The way to keep one's way pure in all of life's activities is by guarding (לִשְׁמֹר; s.v. Ps. 12:7) it according to God's word ("your word" in this address to God). Guarding one's way would mean to protect or safeguard it from all sinfulness and impurity; it calls for a consistent diligence in applying the word of God to the activities of the day. And so the guarding is clarified with "according to your word" (דְּבָר).[34]

---

33. Delitzsch, *Psalms*, III:246.
34. The word דָּבָר has a fairly wide range of uses in the Bible. It can be used for an utterance, saying, speech or word, either by a human, or by God. Almost 400 times is it used for the divine word, whether it refers to a command, or a prophecy, or a message of help and encouragement. But it can also signify an event, an affair, or a matter of some importance—or even some way or manner. But in this psalm the word refers to the law

B. Prayer and devotion to the word are the means of guarding their lives (10–11).

The psalmist details in the next two verses what this guarding requires. The first is "with all my heart I seek you" (דְּרַשְׁתִּיךָ). To seek the LORD means to look for his place and his will in every aspect of life; it describes a life lived for the sake of God. The use of the perfect tense here stresses that this is the characteristic activity of the devout; and the expression "with all my heart" means that this pursuit is carried out with the utmost sincerity and diligence. Because this diligent search will primarily be in the word of God, the prayer is that God not let the faithful wander (אַל־תַּשְׁגֵּנִי) from his commandments. Proverbs informs us that when people stop listening to instruction they wander from the words of knowledge (19:27). The prayer is that in their study of Scripture God will sustain his people in their will to obey.

Verse 11 expresses beautifully how the word of God has become an important part of the psalmist's life: "I have stored up (צָפַנְתִּי) your word in my heart." The verb has traditionally been translated "hidden," but it has more the sense of "laid up, stored up," or "treasured," indicating that it is so valuable it will be preserved in the heart (that is, the mind) for any appropriate use. The psalmist has done this so that the word will be continually at his disposal to determine his actions. Perowne adds that the word was no mere outward rule of conduct; it was in the heart as a power and a life within.[35] The term used for "word" (אִמְרָה) is a poetic variant of the term used in verse 9.[36] And the purpose for treasuring up the word in the heart is "so that I might not sin (אֶחֱטָא; s.v. Ps. 51:2) against you." By learning and living the word of God the faithful will keep pure.

---

of God; and its emphasis is on the nature of God's law as a divine word or utterance.
35. *Psalms*, II:351.
36. The word means "utterance, speech, word," and so is a close synonym of דָּבָר. This term is used in poetry as a variant for the other word. It appears mostly in the singular as a collective for God's word (see Ps. 119:103 with the plural verb). It is used throughout the psalm for the saying(s) and word(s) of the LORD, i.e., his commands and promises, and at times his oracle, usually given through a prophet.

II. The faithful desire to learn more of God's word because it is more delightful than riches (12–14).

There is a sudden change in tone with verse 12—praise: "Blessed (בָּרוּךְ; s.v. Ps. 5:12) are you, O LORD." This is the language of praise and thanksgiving; it is usually followed by a reason for praising the LORD, but here it is followed by an imperative of request, a prayer: "teach me your statutes." The point of the verse is the desire to learn more of God's law, but a teachable spirit begins with a proper regard for God—hence, the praise for the teacher.[37]

The point of this verse is enhanced by the next two. In verse 13 the psalmist says that he declares (סִפַּרְתִּי) all God's decisions with his lips. The perfect tense again is characteristic of his life. The meaning of the verb, "declare, recount," is related to the idea of counting; thus the NEB renders it "say them one by one."[38] This telling of God's word is a natural result of having them treasured within and used for every aspect of life. It is a vocal declaration ("with my lips"), which finds correspondence with the source of God's decisions—"your mouth" (an anthropomorphism, but one that recalls that the word given was audible; see Deut. 4:12).

To this the psalmist adds a statement of the value of God's testimonies to him: "I delight" (שַׂשְׂתִּי, שׂוּשׂ or שִׂישׂ) in them "as much as in all riches"– this explains why he is constantly proclaiming them. The idea of delighting in spiritual things more than physical things anticipates the teaching of Jesus that people should seek first the kingdom of God and not all the riches of life (Matt. 6:33).

III. The faithful will meditate on and delight in God's word (15–16).

This stanza closes with two resolutions. The first is to pay attention constantly to God's precepts. Verse 15 uses two cohortatives, "I will meditate" (אָשִׂיחָה) and "and I will pay attention to" (literally, "fix my gaze." וְאַבִּיטָה). The meditation will be on God's

---

37. VanGemeren, *Psalms*, p. 862.
38. The verb סָפַר in the basic *qal* system means "to count"; in the *piel* it means "to proclaim, tell, narrate," among other meanings.

precepts, the attention will be paid to God's ways (recalling verse 9) that Scripture reveals. If believers make God's ways their ways, then their ways will be pure.

The verb translated "meditate" (שִׂיחַ) is a little more involved.[39] It can refer to a loud and enthusiastic form of speaking, either lamenting or declaring something significant. Here it seems to mean a thoughtful concentration on God's word[40]; but Briggs suggests that in this context it is the musing, talking, or even singing to oneself about a joyous theme.[41] The emphasis in this section certainly is on the psalmist's delight, so whatever form the meditation may have taken, it would be joyous.

The last verse completes this idea with the psalmist's anticipation: "I will delight in your statutes." The unusual verb is an intensive formation (אֶשְׁתַּעֲשָׁע, the *hithpalpel* of שָׁעַע), "I take

---

39. The verb שִׂיחַ is used three ways in the Old Testament: to declare, to meditate or ponder, and to complain or lament. The dictionaries define the word accordingly, with an array of sub-categories—to be concerned with, to muse, to consider.

    The sense of "speak, declare" or "tell" can be seen in Judges 5:10 which says, "speak, you who ride on white donkeys," and in Psalm 105:2, "tell of all his wondrous works" (see also Isa. 53:8).

    The category of "meditate, ponder" is found here in Psalm 119:15 for meditating on the ways of the LORD, and Psalm 143:5 with the same meaning (parallel to "remember").

    The meaning "lament, complain," is found in Proverbs 23:29, referring to the one who has sorrow, woes, and complaints. Job also will give free expression to his complaints (10:1).

    Along with the idea of "lament, complain" is the subcategory of "plead, entreat," as in Psalm 55:17, "I will pray and cry aloud and he will hear my voice."

    One single English translation will not capture the range of this word, but all the uses have the idea of rehearsing or recalling, whether a complaint, a praise, or a meditation. Perhaps it is better to define the word by its various uses. The Greek Old Testament used various words to translate it in the distinct contexts: for "declare" it used "to talk, to meditate, to babble, to practice, to rehearse" and "to study'; the idea of "complaint" is rendered with words like "unpleasant, disagreeable;" and the meaning of "plead" is translated with "supplicate, entreat".

40. VanGemeren, p. 862.
41. *Psalms*, II:420.

delight in."[42] The verse recalls the first psalm's statement that the blessed are those whose delight is in the law of the LORD, in which they meditate day and night. But in this passage, because the psalmist delights in God's statutes, he is determined to live out the word of God (repeated from verse 9) that he has treasured in his heart: "I will not forget (לֹא אֶשְׁכַּח; s.v. Ps. 103:2) your word."

Message and Application

This "*Bet* Stanza" has to do with keeping our lives pure by avoiding sin, which is done by knowing the word of God so well that it is always on our minds to correct and to guide us through life. But this is no fixed duty; for the believer the word is like a treasure, more delightful and useful than riches. The LORD is the teacher, his word and his way the lesson, and righteousness the result. The summary statement would be: *Because the word of God is the means by which the faithful maintain purity in life, they desire to learn more from God and enjoy meditating in his word.* The point of this stanza is reflected in the prayer of Jesus for us: "Sanctify them by your truth; your word is truth" (John 17:17). The apostle Paul also reminds us that the righteous are those who hear and do the word of God (Rom. 2:13), for the law of God made us aware of sin (Rom. 3:20). As we learn more and more from the word of God and put it into practice, we will become aware of sins that need to be overcome, and righteous practices that need to be incorporated. Through this process we will be able to maintain a righteous way of life.

---

42. שָׁעַע (II) occurs in the *pilpel* stem; some commentators have tried to link it with שָׁעַע (I) that means "smear" or "smooth over," but that verb is used with the idea of blindness. This word, at least in this stem, has the sense of "sport, take delight in." It is used in Isaiah 11:2 for the infant playing (וְשִׁעֲשַׁע) at the cobra's hole. In other places it is the law of the LORD or the LORD's consolations that bring delight. The related intensive, plural noun, "delight" (שַׁעֲשֻׁעִים) is used frequently in Psalm 119 to describe God's law as the object of delight.

The Word of the LORD and the Life of Faith

ג *Gimel*

Comfort and Counsel in Distress

Text and Textual Variants

ג 17 Deal bountifully[43] with your servant that[44] I may live,
and I will keep your word (דְּבָר).[45]

ג 18 Open my eyes that I may perceive
wondrous things out of your law (תּוֹרָה).

ג 19 I am a sojourner on the earth;[46]
do not hide your commandments (מִצְוָה) from me!

ג 20 I am[47] consumed with longing
for your decisions (מִשְׁפָּט) at all times.

ג 21 You rebuke the insolent,[48] accursed ones,
who wander from your commandments (מִצְוָה).

ג 22 Take[49] from me reproach and contempt,[50]
for I have guarded[51] your testimonies (עֵדוּת).

ג 23 Even though princes sit and[52] conspire against me,
your servant will meditate on your statutes (חֹק).

---

43. For Hebrew גְּמֹל the Greek version has ἀνταπόδος, "requite."
44. A few manuscripts have the conjunction with the verb; the MT does not.
45. Many manuscripts and the versions have the plural "words."
46. Instead of this prepositional phrase the Syriac has "with you" (עִמְּךָ, as in Ps. 39:13).
47. MT has נַפְשִׁי with the feminine form of the verb.
48. For the MT's זֵדִים, a few manuscripts have זָרִים, "strangers." The Greek and Syriac redivide the line: "You rebuke the insolent; cursed are they who turn away from your commandments."
49. MT has גַּל from גָּלָה, "to uncover" (as in verse 18). The editors of BHS propose reading גֹּל, the imperative of גָּלַל, "to roll away." But the verb "uncover" can mean to uncover the eyes (the accusative being the thing uncovered), or "take off" (with the accusative of the covering taken off), e.g., the reproach that lies on a person (Perowne, *Psalms*, II:367). The Greek version has περίελε, "remove."
50. "Contempt" is not in the Syriac version.
51. The verb נָצַרְתִּי has the sense of "I have guarded, treasured." The Greek version translated it ἐξεζήτησα, "I sought."
52. The Greek and Syriac have the conjunction.

481

נ 24 Also, your testimonies (עֵדֹוּת) are my delight;[53]
   they are my counselors.[54]

Exegetical Analysis

Summary

The psalmist prays for God to show him wonderful things from his word, things that bring him delight and give him direction, because powerful, wicked people conspire against him and pour contempt upon him (119:17–24).

Outline

I. The psalmist calls for God to enable him to discover even more wonderful things in his word so that he might be delivered and live as God intended (17–18).
II. The psalmist attests that in his earthly sojourn he desperately needs God to reveal his will and way to him (19–20).
III. Knowing that God destroys the arrogant, the psalmist prays for God to remove the reproach of the wicked from him, affirming in the meantime his delight in and direction from God's word (21–24).
   A. He knows that God brings to an end those who arrogantly refuse his word (21).
   B. He prays for God to remove their reproach of him now (22).
   C. He affirms that even though he must endure their evil conspiracy against him, he finds delight and counsel in God's word (23–24).

---

53. The Greek has μελέτη μου, "my meditation."
54. The Hebrew construction is אַנְשֵׁי עֲצָתִי, literally "men of my counsel," meaning "my counseling men." The Greek version adds τά δικαιώματά σου to form a subject: "your statutes are my counsels / counselors." The Greek version used this word to translate "statutes" (חֹק) in the previous verse.

Commentary in Expository Form

I. God's faithful servants pray for the provision of life and the ability to understand the riches of divine revelation (17–18).

In these eight verses we see a new motif, the difficulty of living in a world that is not only opposed to the faith but conspires against it. The passage shows us that in response to this the faithful will affirm that the word of God, properly understood and consistently obeyed, brings comfort and guidance in the difficulties and distresses of life.

The first two verses (17–18) are prayers; they each have an imperative followed by a purpose clause. The first is "deal bountifully (גְּמֹל) with your servant that I may live" (אֶחְיֶה). In this line, and in verse 23, the psalmist refers to himself as God's servant; such a designation signifies a close, spiritual relationship with the LORD (not all believers are called "the servant of the LORD" in the Bible). The appeal for divine bounty at first seems rather general; but the word is used in the Psalter with the connotation of deliverance (see 13:6; 116:7; 142:7). The word would then be a figure (a metonymy of cause or adjunct), implying the kind of bounty intended. Given the tension that this stanza addresses, the psalmist would be desiring God to deal bountifully with him by ending the reproach he suffers at the hand of the arrogant. If God does this, then he will live, meaning live a full life in the land as God intended. Briggs notes that the writer thinks the only true life is knowing and obeying God's laws.[55] In addition to this prospect, the psalmist adds, "and then I will keep (וְאֶשְׁמְרָה; s.v. Ps. 12:7) your word." He will diligently obey God's word as he lives out his life.

The second verse in the section is a prayer for divine illumination—he needs to understand more fully what God's will and ways are, especially in the present tensions. The prayer is for God to "open" his eyes (the verb גַּל means to "uncover") so that he might "perceive" (וְאַבִּיטָה; the verb means "gaze intently, regard, pay attention to"). The intent of the prayer is for divine help in understanding and regarding the intended meaning of

---
55. *Psalms*, II:421.

the text—not everyone who reads God's word has the spiritual understanding to appropriate it correctly (see Matt. 6:22–23; 7:3–5; John 9:39–41). What the psalmist wants to "perceive" is wondrous things from the law. "Wondrous things" (נִפְלָאוֹת; for פֶּלֶא s. v. Ps. 139:5) are the profound and amazing things of God revealed in the word. Delitzsch says the description refers to "everything supernatural and mysterious which is incomprehensible to the ordinary understanding and is left to the perception of faith."[56]

In this context it would probably include revelation concerning the arrogant who are accursed and awaiting the judgment as well as God's marvelous plans for the righteous. While there are scores of wondrous things in God's word, some of them are more relevant to the tension of living in a fallen world; but the psalmist needs divine illumination to see it all and be reassured in his faith.

II. God's faithful servants know this world is a temporary home and therefore need to know more of God's will (19–20).

In the next two verses of the stanza the psalmist focuses on himself. He first expresses his need for guidance because this world is not his true home—it is an alien land. His initial statement, "I am a sojourner (גֵּר) on the earth" (or: "in the land"), asserts that his time on earth is temporary—it is a strange land to him. The word "sojourn," although somewhat archaic, means to dwell in a land without many of the rights of citizenship; the sojourner is an alien. This fact, joined with his description of himself as a servant of the LORD, shows that his allegiance is above the earth. What this means for the psalmist, and to the countless numbers of believers throughout history, is that this alien land is often hostile to God's will and ways. This statement of fact lays the foundation for his prayer, a prayer that reveals a desperate need: "Do not hide (אַל־תַּסְתֵּר) your commandments from me." The prayer is for the continued revelation and

---

56. *Psalms*, III:246.

illumination of God's word—instructions to guide him in his dangerous journey in the world.

What he feels is stated more clearly in verse 20: "I (my soul) am broken with longing for your decisions at all times." The verb (גָּרְסָה) means "to crush in pieces" (compare Lam. 3:16). Anderson translates it this way: "I am (practically) shattered by (the intensity of my) longing."[57] His longing is for God's word, but here specifically the "decisions" or "judgments" in it. The emphasis is on the need for guidance and hope in this world—what does God want him to do, and what is God going to do?

III. God's faithful servants pray for relief from the persecution of the arrogant while they find comfort and counsel in God's word (21–24).

A. They know that God will judge those who reject his word (21).

What the psalmist is looking for is God's intervention in his current distress. And so in the final verses he will lay out the problem, beginning with the principle of God's dealings with the disobedient. "You rebuke" (גָּעַרְתָּ; s.v. Ps. 76:6) refers to a verbal activity that causes an effective end to the activities (it is a metonymy of cause). By his rebuke, his powerful word, God easily stops the activities of the arrogant. By using the word "arrogant" (זֵדִים)[58] the psalmist is referring to those who despise God and

---

57. *Psalms 73–150*, p. 814.
58. זֵדִים is the participle of the verb זִיד, "to boil up, seethe, act proudly, presumptuously." The Arabic cognate means "to increase, exaggerate." The verb in the basic (*qal*) stem means to act presumptuously. It is in Exodus 18:1 of Egypt's treatment of the people of God, and in Jeremiah 50:29 of Babylon's presumptuous actions against the LORD.

But it is in the *hiphil* form that we have a helpful, non-theological usage to serve as an illustration. It is used in Genesis 25:29 for Jacob's boiling the lentil soup. It means "boil." But the word may have been chosen in the passage for a couple of other reasons: 1) to form a word play with the word for "hunter" (צַיִד)—Jacob too was hunting; and 2) to describe Jacob's activity as presumptuous. As water in a pot will overflow when boiled too much, so Jacob has overstepped his bounds to get what he wants.

treat his cause with contempt. They are described in the Bible as oppressors, liars, and destroyers, people who have no regard for God's laws. Hence, they are "accursed" (אֲרוּרִים).[59] If God's blessing is on the obedient, his curse is on those who are disobedient ("curse" meaning removed from the place of blessing), who wander away from God's commandments.

B. They pray for God to remove the reproach of their persecution (22).

The people of God, like the psalmist, pray for the painful persecution to stop. Verse 20 says, "Take (גַּל as in verse 18) from me reproach and contempt" (s.v. Ps. 22:6). The use of this verb indicates that the taunts and contempt of the arrogant are like a covering to be removed. The use of this word draws verses 18 and 22 together: the psalmist needs understanding to deal with this, and so when he affirms what God's plan is for the wicked (v. 21), he prays for the difficulty to be removed. The reason for the appeal is that he has guarded (נָצַרְתִּי, s.v. 119:2) God's testimonies. In other words, he has been obedient, and the reproach is therefore because of the faith (cf. Matt. 5:11–12). Briggs concludes from this passage that the writer was living at a time when there were a number of proud, arrogant men accursed of God (II:422). It would be hard to find a time where there were none; but the point here is that they were creating serious problems for the psalmist.

The word has the sense of acting presumptuously in this (*hiphil*) system as well. The Israelites acted presumptuously by trying to conquer the land without the LORD's help (Deut. 1:43). Likewise, the false prophet acts presumptuously when he attempts to speak for God (Deut. 18:20).

The adjective זֵד, "insolent, presumptuous," refers to activities in opposition to the LORD, such as the scorner in Proverbs 21:24. The noun זָדוֹן, "insolence, presumptuousness," was used of the lad David by his brothers when he was confident he could fight Goliath (1 Sam. 17:28).

These words, then, describe an arrogant attitude of self-sufficiency, a pride that runs contrary not only to God but to reality. The "arrogant" are unbelievers who think they are capable of doing what they want.

59. The word is in apposition to "arrogant" in the MT. But some versions and commentators prefer to join it with verse 21b, "cursed *are they who wander*."

C. They affirm their delight in and dependence on God's word in the face of persecution (23-24).

The last two verses bring the two themes together: powerful people were conspiring against the psalmist, but he finds comfort and counsel in the word. This is what the righteous of all ages do. These last two verses were intended to be looked at together because they both begin with the same particle (גַּם), translated "even" in verse 23 and "also" in verse 24. The description of the arrogant is further explained here—they are magistrates (שָׂרִים, "princes," a word that can be used for civil authorities, officers, or leaders of tribes). They naturally have power, but they are a problem because they are arrogant; the psalmist, on the other hand, is a servant of the LORD (here and in v. 17).

The power of the arrogant is turned against the psalmist, for they conspire against him. The verb translated "conspire" (נִדְבְּרוּ) simply means they deliberate or talk with each other (it has a reciprocal nuance); but it forms a powerful contrast to the "word" (דְּבָר) of the LORD. The psalmist trusts the LORD's word, for it reveals the truth, sustains believers, and counsels in the way of life; but the words of unbelieving leaders are troublesome and destructive. Even if they conspire against him he will meditate on God's statutes—this is what the faithful always do. Therefore he finds delight (s.v. 119:14) and counsel in God's statutes, which he calls his counselors (אַנְשֵׁי עֲצָתִי; "men of my counsel," meaning "men who counsel me").

Message and Application

This stanza (vv. 17–24) stresses the importance of God's word in the difficulty and distress of this world. It describes the experience of the psalmist, but what is described is universal; so the psalmist speaks on behalf of us all. The tension he unveils here is that arrogant powerful leaders are conspiring against him, bringing reproach and distress on him. His recourse is the word of the LORD, in which he delights and to which he looks for counsel. He desires that God will enable him to understand it more as he awaits God's will in resolving the difficulty of this world.

The tension was real; it still is. And the only way to find

PSALM 119

comfort and guidance in dealing with it is to discover more profound and amazing things in God's word concerning his provisions and his promises. *When faced with reproach and contempt from unbelievers, the faithful find comfort and counsel as they learn to live by his word.* Believers then should be instructed by this to meditate in God's word, seeking greater understanding of it and looking deeper in it for God's provisions. In the New Testament Paul reminds us that in our spiritual conflicts with the world we need to learn how to use the sword of the Spirit, which is the word of God (Eph. 6:17).

ד *Dalet*

The Restoration of Vitality for the Faithful

Text and Textual Variants

ד 25 I[60] cling to the dust;
 renew my life according to your word (דָּבָר)![61]

ד 26 I declared my ways, and you answered me;
 teach me your statutes (חֹק)!

ד 27 Make me understand the way of your precepts (פִּקּוּד),
 and I will meditate on your wondrous works.

ד 28 My life[62] melts away[63] because of grief;
 strengthen me according to your word (דָּבָר)![64]

ד 29 The way of deceit[65] remove from me,
 and be gracious to me *through* your law (תּוֹרָה)!

---

60. MT has נַפְשִׁי with the feminine verb.
61. Many manuscripts and the Targum have the plural "words"; and a few manuscripts and the Greek version have "in" or "by" instead of "according to."
62. A few manuscripts have עֵינַי, "my eyes," instead of נַפְשִׁי.
63. The form in the MT is דָּלְפָה, perhaps meaning "melt away, crumble"; it is rendered by the NIV as "is weary." The Greek version has ἔσταξεν, "was drowsy / slumbered."
64. Many manuscripts have the plural again; and a few manuscripts and the Greek have the preposition "in."
65. The MT has דֶּרֶךְ־שֶׁקֶר, "a way of falsehood" or deceit; the Greek interprets it more widely as ὁδὸν ἀδικίας, "the way of injustice."

ד 30 The way of faithfulness I have chosen;
I set[66] your decisions (מִשְׁפָּט)[67] before me.
ד 31 I cling to your testimonies (עֵדוּת), O LORD;
do not let me be put to shame!
ד 32 I run[68] in the way of your commandments (מִצְוָה)
for you have enlarged my heart.

Exegetical Analysis

Summary

Revealing his lamentable condition, the psalmist asks for God to restore his vitality and to teach him more of his truth because he has chosen to be faithful (119:25–32).

Outline

I. In near death circumstances the faithful psalmist prays for renewed vitality and understanding (25–27).
   A. Because his life is in danger he prays for renewed vitality (25).
   B. Because God answered him, he prays for greater understanding so that he might meditate on God's wondrous works (26–27).
II. In a weakening condition because of grief the faithful psalmist prays for strength and purification from deceitful ways (28–29).
   A. He prays for strength because his life is fading (28).
   B. He prays for purification from deceitful ways (29).
III. Because he has chosen to be faithful and is devoted to obeying God's word the psalmist prays that God will not let him be put to shame (30–32).

---

66. The verb in the MT is שִׁוִּיתִי; the Greek translation has οὐκ ἐπελαθόμην, "and I did not forget your judgments." It seems to be an attempt to translate a difficult line; or it may reflect אִוִּיתִי.
67. Several manuscripts and the Syriac have a conjunction: "And your decisions I set . . . ."
68. MT has אָרוּץ, which the Greek rendered ἔδραμον, "I ran" (but perhaps "I run"). The ESV translates the verse: "I will run in the way of your commandments when you enlarge my heart."

A. Because he has chosen to be faithful he keeps God's word before him (30).
B. Because he holds fast to God's word he asks that he not be put to shame (31).
C. He eagerly complies with God's word because God has enabled him to do so (32).

Commentary in Expository Form

I. In life-threatening circumstances the faithful pray for renewed vitality and spiritual understanding (25–27).

A. They pray for renewed vitality (25).

The first two sections of this psalm begin with a description of the psalmist's lamentable condition. He is apparently in deep trouble, a life-threatening situation, and so he prays for renewal of his strength, then understanding, then the removal of deceitful ways from himself by God's grace. But since he has chosen to live faithfully, he also prays that God will not let him be put to shame.

Verse 25 begins with his first lament: "I cling (דָּבְקָה, feminine with the subject נַפְשִׁי) to the dust." This statement seems to continue the description of his plight in verses 21–23. Clinging to the dust is a graphic depiction of being in a life-threatening condition (see Ps. 44:25 where it indicates that the people were defeated, dying, and unable to raise themselves from their situation). The prayer therefore is naturally fitting: "renew my life." The verbal expression (the *piel* imperative חַיֵּנִי from the verb "to live," hence "renew life" or "cause life") is a prayer for God to renew his vitality, to restore him to the fullness of life.

Critical to the meaning of the line is "according to your word." This could mean that God would simply restore him to health by divine intervention. But in a psalm that is so focused on the law, it is probably a reference to the principle in the law that the fulness of life comes from obedience to the law (Lev. 18:5, which asserts that if people obey the laws they will live). The psalmist would then be praying for God to fulfill his word by restoring his life.

B. *They pray for spiritual understanding (26–27).*

But the psalmist wants more than a restoration of his life; he wants to increase his understanding of God's word and ways. In verse 26 he says, "I have declared (סִפַּרְתִּי) my ways, and you answered me (וַתַּעֲנֵנִי)." He has reviewed the troubles ("my ways") of his life, noting that when he spoke to God of his distress God answered his prayers. Because he is now praying for renewed life, this statement that God has been faithful to him before would build his confidence now.[69]

In addition his desire is that God teach him his statutes and give him understanding (הֲבִינֵנִי; s.v. Ps. 49:3). If he gains more knowledge and understanding of God's word, he will be able to make more sense of this life and renew his commitment to live faithfully in spite of the dangers. When he gains more understanding, then he will meditate (וְאָשִׂיחָה; s.v. Ps. 119:15) on all God's wondrous works. With the increase in knowledge and understanding there will be increase in devotion and praise.

II. In increasing weakness from grief the faithful pray for strength and purification (28–29).

A. *They pray for strength (28).*

The motifs of the first section are repeated in verses 28 and 29: first the lament of his condition, and then the prayer for strength and spiritual change. In verse 28 he states that he (his life) melts away. The verb (דָּלְפָה) means "to drop, drip"; when the eyes "drop" it refers to tears, and so in this passage it may have the sense of "my life weeps itself away." Allen translates it, "I have collapsed," following the suggestion that the verb means "crumble" based on use in Ugaritic.[70] In any case, the reason for this lamentable state is "grief" (תּוּגָה).[71] We cannot tell ex-

---

69. VanGemeren interprets this to mean that he opened his life to the Lord in the belief that God answers prayers (*Psalms*, p. 865); but this does not fully reflect the sequence of the verbs.
70. *Psalms 101–150*, pp. 127, 135; see also Dahood, *Psalms*, III:177.
71. The noun is תּוּגָה, "grief." It is related to the verb יָגָה, "to suffer." The verb is used in conjunction with the suffering over the destruction of Zion (Lam. 1:4) and the exile (Zeph. 3:18). It is also used in Job 19:2. There

actly what his condition was, but he was physically weakened (clinging to the dust) and sensing his life was falling apart with grief. He was either dying or in serious danger of dying; he therefore prays for strength. The verb used is a little unusual here; it literally means "set me up *again*" (קַיְּמֵנִי; s.v. Ps. 3:1), meaning to raise him up and establish him. It is parallel to the prayer for God to renew his life (v. 25); and here too it is "according to your word."

B. *They pray for purification (29).*

The second petition in the section is for purification: "remove (הָסֵר, from סוּר) the way of deceit from me and be gracious to me through your law." The word "deceit" (שֶׁקֶר; s.v. Ps. 144:8) may be "falsehood" or "deception." It also describes something as having no real basis and therefore will collapse sooner or later; thus, it not only means "deceit" but "worthless" or "pointless" as well.[72] The psalmist wants all that is false and pointless removed from his life—because he has chosen the "way of faithfulness" (v. 30). His appeal, then, is for God to be gracious to him (s.v. Ps. 4:1); and this too would be through the law. VanGemeren says, "The word of God is also a means of grace, as it keeps one away from the ways of the world . . . and as it renews an inner, burning desire to live a life of devotion to God (vv. 30–32)."[73]

III. Those who are committed to living faithfully pray for deliverance (30–32).

A. *They have chosen to love faithfully (30).*

The final section records the psalmist's claims of devotion to the word of God. All of the verbs emphasize his active involvement in obeying the LORD: "I have chosen, I set, I cling, I run." First, he has chosen "the way of faithfulness" (דֶּרֶךְ־אֱמוּנָה; s.v.

---

is a masculine noun יָגוֹן, "grief, sorrow" (for example, it is used of Jacob's sorrow over the possible loss of his son in Genesis 42:38).

72. Anderson, *Psalms 73–150*, pp. 817–8.
73. *Psalms*, p. 865.

Ps. 15:2). This expression is placed in the text in a way to underscore its contrast with "the way of falsehood." The "way of faithfulness" summarizes a life that is characterized by obedience to the will of God—he is consistently dependable. His choice is clarified by the second colon: "I set your decisions before me." His spiritual focus is on the way that the word of God determines the right course of action on the issues of life so that he might live by them.

B. They pray to be vindicated (31).

The psalmist also testifies that he clings to God's testimonies. The verb (דָּבַק) is chosen to contrast its use in verse 25: there his life was clinging to the dust, but even in such a distressing situation he clings to God's covenant stipulations. His prayer, therefore, is for deliverance from his plight, expressed in the negative as "do not let me be put to shame" (אַל־תְּבִישֵׁנִי; s.v. Ps. 31:1), which is a figure expressing the effect of being left in his condition (a metonymy).

C. They obey God's word eagerly (32).

His eagerness to please God is expressed in another figure, "I run in the way of your commandments" (an implied comparison). It intensifies the normal idiom of walking in the way of the commandments—he eagerly and swiftly obeys God's word. And his reason for this enthusiastic response is that God has enlarged (תַחְרִיב) his heart. This expression probably means that God has given him greater understanding (1 Kings 4:29); but it might also include greater happiness, a sense of freedom from his troubles (Isa. 60:5).

Message and Application

There are enough references in this psalm to indicate that the psalmist was living at a very dangerous time; it could have been a time when the nation lost its independence and was ruled by the ungodly, or it could have been simply a time when powerful people were trying to destroy his faith. We do not know. But we do know he was being taunted and oppressed, so much so that his life was in danger. He is not the only believer to have suffered this way—the history of the faith to this very moment is filled with such circumstances. For people in many parts of the world the opposition is open and life-threatening. For many in the West, the opposition is in a milder and more subtle form; but it still seeks to destroy the faith. In this the psalmist serves as a guide for us all. He prays not only for deliverance from his plight, which is natural, but also for spiritual understanding to know what to do, and for purification so that he will not be like the world. The expository idea would then say: *In life threatening circumstances those who are committed to being faithful to God's word pray for restoration, discernment, and purification.*

The themes of this stanza also are echoed by the New Testament. We are reminded that we have been born again through the living and enduring word of God (1 Pet. 1:23); and not only did God's word bring us life, it brings us spiritual discernment and direction because it is living and active (Heb. 4:12). In any time, but certainly in troubled times, we must follow the psalmist into meditation in the word of God, for there we find our assurance of salvation. And in the process of using the word of God daily, we must also be careful not to use it deceitfully, especially as we proclaim it to the world as truth (2 Cor 4:2).

ה *He'*

Spiritual Growth and the Desire for Confirmation

Text and Textual Variants

ה   33   Teach me, O LORD, the way of your statutes (חֹק),
and I will keep[74] it as a reward.[75]

---

74. The MT's use of נָצַר, "keep, treasure" (וְאֶצְּרֶנָּה) is here and elsewhere rendered in the Greek version with "seek" (εκζητήσω).
75. The word עֵקֶב should be translated "reward," but some take it to mean "continually" after the Greek version that has, (καὶ ἐκζητήσω αὐτὴν διὰ παντός, "and I will seek it out) continually."

ה 34 Give me understanding,[76] and I will keep your law
(תּוֹרָה)
and observe it with a[77] whole heart.
ה 35 Lead me in the path of your commandments (מִצְוָה),
for I delight in it.
ה 36 Incline my heart to your testimonies (עֵדוֹת)
and not to unjust gain![78]
ה 37 Turn my eyes from looking at worthless things;
and renew my life in your ways.[79]
ה 38 Confirm your oracle (אִמְרָה) to your servant,
that you may be feared.[80]
ה 39 Turn away my reproach that I dread,[81]
for your decisions (מִשְׁפָּט) are good.
ה 40 Behold, I long for your precepts (פִּקּוּד);
in your righteousness renew my life.

Exegetical Analysis

Summary

After praying for knowledge, understanding, and guidance so that he might live more obediently and not be drawn to selfish gain and worthless ways, the psalmist asks for confirmation of the word so that his reproach would be removed and his life renewed (119:33–40).

---

76. The Greek version has a general translation: συνέτισόν με, "instruct me."
77. The Greek translation reads more smoothly with "my (whole heart)."
78. The interpret εἰς πλεονεξίαν, "(not) to greediness / covetousness."
79. Many manuscripts take the word as a plural. In this verse not one of the eight key words for the law is included; and so two manuscripts and the Targum (and the NIV) have "by your word" instead of "ways," following the structure in v. 25. Allen translates it, "give me life in your ways" (*Psalms 101–150*, p. 127).
80. The translation provides a smooth reading; the Hebrew simply has אֲשֶׁר לְיִרְאָתֶךָ, "that for your fear." The Greek version is literal: εἰς τὸν φόβον σου, "for fear of you."
81. "That I dread" is not in the Syriac version.

PSALM 119

Outline

I. Instruction: The psalmist asks God for knowledge, understanding, and guidance in the way that the word reveals, so that he might observe it wholeheartedly (33–35).
  A. He asks to be taught the revealed way so that he might keep it (33).
  B. He prays for understanding so that he might obey wholeheartedly (34).
  C. He requests guidance in the way of the commandments (35).
II. Commitment: The psalmist asks God to cause him to desire the word over selfish gain, and to turn his attention from worthless things and be renewed (36–37).
  A. He wants the LORD to cause him to desire the word and not selfish gain (36).
  B. He wants the LORD to turn him from worthless things and renew his life (37).
III. Confirmation: The psalmist asks for confirmation of God's word by the removal of his grievous reproach and the renewing of his life because he longs for God's precepts (38–40).
  A. He prays for the word to be confirmed to him so that God might be feared (38).
  B. He prays for his dread reproach to be turned away and prays for renewal (39–40).

Commentary in Expository Form

I. Believers need to know and understand the word so that they may keep it wholeheartedly (33–35).

A. Believers need to know the word in order to obey it (33).

This stanza is characterized primarily by (*hiphil*) imperatives: there are seven petitions and one affirmation (v. 40). The nature of these petitions reveal the psalmist's humility and dependence on the LORD. The first request is "teach me (הוֹרֵנִי; s.v. Ps. 1:2), O LORD, the way of your statutes." The verb is connected to the noun "law, instruction" (תּוֹרָה), and has the sense of instructing or directing. Briggs renders the imperative more specifically, "Show me the way."[82] The psalmist wants to know how to live according to the statutes; and he knows that the LORD himself must interpret and apply his own revelation. God is the teacher (see Pss. 25:4, 9; 27:11), but he delegates the task to others who must faithfully speak for God (Deut. 24:8; 33:9–10; Mal. 2:7).

The result of God's teaching the psalmist the way is that he will keep or treasure it (וְאֶצְּרֶנָּה; s.v. Ps. 119:2). Divine instruction has the goal of inspiring obedience; here the psalmist is ready to observe what the LORD teaches him. This obedience is qualified by a word (עֵקֶב) that has been translated "continually" (the Greek version; followed by the NIV and RSV), or "to the end" (ESV, but with a note for the previous other view). Usage indicates that a better translation would be *as a reward* (see Ps. 19:11; 40:15; this is the view of Briggs, Weiser, Anderson, and others). Briggs explains that "the law itself is the reward for the servant of God; the very keeping of it is its own reward, as 19:12 [11], and gives delight to the heart whose whole affections are set upon it."[83]

B. Believers need to understand the word in order to keep it wholeheartedly (34).

The next verse continues to focus on learning more about the word; here the request is "give me understanding" (הֲבִינֵנִי; for בִּין, s.v. Ps. 49:3). In addition to being taught the word, the psalmist knew he needed discernment to know how to understand and apply it. When he has understanding he will keep the law (< נָצַר again) and observe it (< שָׁמַר again) "with a whole heart," meaning, to the utmost of his ability and commitment. The addition of "whole heart" qualifies the idea—the more he knows and understands of God's word and way the more enthusiastically will he obey it.

---

82. *Psalms*, II:423.
83. *Psalms*, II:423.

C. Believers desire guidance in its ways because they delight in it (35).

The third petition is "lead me (הַדְרִיכֵנִי, the verb connected to דֶּרֶךְ, the "way") in the path of your righteousness, for I delight in it." The request is followed not by a result clause, but a causal clause. He desires to follow the way of righteousness because it is delightful to him; but he will need to be taught and made to understand it before he can follow God's leading fully.

II. Believers need divine help in order to prefer God's word over covetousness and vanity (36–37).

A. Their devotion must avoid personal gain (36).

In the next two verses the petitions are different; here the psalmist wants the LORD to turn his attention away from the things of the world and toward the things of God. The first request is "incline (הַט) my heart to your testimonies and not to unjust gain." The word for "unjust gain" (בֶּצַע) has been given the interpretation of "covetousness" or "greediness" (after the Greek translation). No doubt wrong desires are involved, but this word says more (unless the word covetousness is understood in its contextual meanings where it includes the taking of what was coveted). It refers to the plunder or gain one gets by means of violence and damage done to someone else. The psalmist knows it will take a supernatural influence on his affections and will to make him prefer the good and reject the bad. He cannot have both, mammon and the stipulations of the covenant (see also Matt. 6:24; Luke 16:13); and if he wants to follow the LORD's way, there is no place for unjust gain. In this prayer the psalmist reveals that he is completely dependent on God to change his heart; and this will be accomplished through God's word.

B. Their devotion must avoid worthless things (37).

The other verse in this section of the stanza has a similar focus. Here the psalmist wants God to turn his eyes from looking at worthless things. The final word (שָׁוְא; s.v. Ps. 127:1) can mean "a worthless thing, vanity," something without divine contents or intrinsic value. It can also mean something vain or profitless in the sense of morally unsound, or, as Perowne puts it, all that is against God or without God.[84] He does not want even to look at such things for they weaken his faith. Instead, he wants the LORD to renew his whole life, even the way he lives (חַיֵּנִי). This prayer for renewed life in God's ways suggests at least that he had been inclined more to unjust gain and worthless things (two categories that cover almost everything in the pagan world) than to the way of God. These two verses may record the resultant prayers when God gives people understanding of the word.

III. Believers need divine confirmation that God removes their reproach and renews their lives (38–40).

A. Confirmation inspires reverence (38).

In the last three verses the prayer requests change to calls for God to act on his behalf. The first is for God to confirm his oracle or promise to his servant (again stressing the humility of the psalmist). The verb "confirm" or "establish" (הָקֵם; s.v. Ps. 3:1) has the sense of acting so that the divine promise would be realized. And when the word is fulfilled, the result will be that God will be feared (the expression in the text is cryptic, but the sense is clear). The devout especially will be filled with reverential awe and be drawn to greater faith in his word.

B. Confirmation removes reproach and restores life (39–40).

What the psalmist specifically desired is that God would confirm his word by removing the reproach he dreaded. This is most likely a reference to the troubles he introduced in verse 22. There are two ways to explain this reproach, and both are probably true: first, those who deny God scorn loyalty to the law,[85] and second, these worthless men heap reproaches on him for

---

84. *Psalms*, II:363.
85. Kirkpatrick, *Psalms*, p. 711.

not sharing in their worthless conduct.[86] As long as they continue with their reproach, God's promises of blessing for obedience seem not to be fulfilled. But the psalmist is persuaded of better things, because he knows God's decisions are good.

He closes the stanza therefore with an affirmation of his desire for God's precepts. In this context the "precepts" must refer to those aspects of the law that result in divine acts—this is what he longs for in his prayer ("precepts" then may be interpreted as a metonymy, signifying what the effect of these precepts would be). That he desires divine acts of judgment that bring help for the afflicted[87] is confirmed by the second colon of verse 40 in which he prays for God to renew his life in righteousness. This word "righteousness" signifies the righteous acts of God (and so it is another metonymy of cause, the attribute being put for the effect).

Message and Application

The psalmist prays for God to teach him, give him understanding, and guide him so that he might faithfully keep God's ways. But he is faced with two difficulties that make these petitions urgent: the allurement of the world in which gain at any cost and worthless activities compete for his attention, and the reproach he suffers from those who reject God and the way of righteousness. As he learns and understands more of God's revelation, he desires to remain focused on the way of God; but as he stays focused on this way, he desires that God would confirm the promises by removing the dreaded reproach he receives. This pattern is played out again and again in the lives of believers: the more we grow in the word, the more we avoid the wicked and worthless ways of the world; but the more we focus on the ways of God, the more we suffer the reproach of the world. It is the desire of the devout to grow in grace and knowledge, but it is also the desire of the devout that God confirm his word by removing the reproach of the wicked and renewing the lives of believers. The expository idea of the psalm could be laid out in the same sequence of ideas:

---

86. Briggs, *Psalms*, II:423.
87. A. A. Anderson, *Psalms 73–150*, p. 820.

Increased knowledge and understanding of God's revelation leads to obedience; greater obedience leads to disdain for the wicked and worthless ways of the world; and greater awareness of the world leads to the desire for God to confirm his promises.

The themes of this stanza are also expressed in the New Testament. We are reminded that the law is good (Rom. 7:16), and that all Scripture is profitable for instruction in righteousness (2 Tim. 3:16). We are commanded to study the word so that we might be approved (2 Tim. 2:15). Our task is to keep the word of God, even though there is much yet to be fulfilled (1 John 2:5; Rev. 3:8). But Jesus said that not one part of a letter would pass away until it was all fulfilled (Matt. 5:17–18). The application is therefore straightforward: we should pray the prayers of this stanza, noting the intended result of the petitions. The only difference is that today we have more revelation than the psalmist had received, and so our focus is on understanding and obeying the whole word of God.

ו *Waw*

Living in Hope

Text and Textual Variants

ו 41 And[88] let your loyal love come[89] to me, O LORD,
      your salvation according to your oracle (אִמְרָה);
ו 42 then shall I have an answer for the one who taunts me,
      for I trust in your word (דָּבָר).[90]

---

88. Each verse in this section begins with the conjunction *waw*, for there is nothing else that could be used for this letter in the acrostic. A translation "and" for each line would be wooden, and so some variation has been attempted.
89. The form in the MT is the plural verb וִיבֹאֻנִי to go with the plural noun חֲסָדֶךָ (written without the *yôd*). The Greek version uses a singular verb since "mercy" is a singular noun, probably based on the consonantal text that looks like a singular noun. The editors of BHS suggest reading it as singular.
90. Many manuscripts, the Greek, Syriac, and the Targum have the plural. The form is regularly singular in the Hebrew text.

PSALM 119

ו 43 And do not take the word of truth utterly from my mouth,
>for I hope in your decisions (מִשְׁפָּט).[91]

ו 44 So I will keep your law (תּוֹרָה) continually, forever and ever,[92]

ו 45 and I will[93] walk about at liberty,[94]
>for I have sought your precepts (פִּקּוּד).

ו 46 I will also speak of your testimonies (עֵדוּת)[95] before kings
>and shall not be put to shame.

ו 47 I also delight[96] in your commandments (מִצְוָה), which I love.[97]

ו 48 And I lift up my hands toward your commandments (מִצְוָה),
>which I love;[98]
>and I will meditate on your statutes (חֹק).

Exegetical Analysis

Summary

The psalmist prays for deliverance from those who reproach him so that he can answer them with the fulfillment of God's sure

---

91. The vowels in the MT suggest a plural noun, without the *yôd* (מִשְׁפָּטֶךָ), the normal form in the psalm. This is supported by many manuscripts, the Greek, Syriac and the Targum, that clearly have the plural.
92. The Greek translation has "forever and forever and ever."
93. The Greek version translates the main verbs in verses 45–48 ("walk," "speak," "meditate," and "lift") as past tenses. But they are cohortatives for the most part, and require a future translation at least.
94. MT has "in a wide place."
95. The Syriac version has "righteousness."
96. The Greek version has ἐμελέτων, "meditate."
97. The Greek version adds σφόδρα, "completely" (= מְאֹד).
98. Because of the unusual repetition of "which I love," and the use of "commandment" along with "statute" in the verse, the editors of BHS propose deleting "your commandments which I love." They also propose a suffix for the preposition, to have the first colon read "I lift up my hands to you." But there is no support for these changes.

word, which he promises to obey and proclaim because it is his delight and the object of his meditation (119:41–48).

Outline

I. The psalmist prays for deliverance in accordance with the promises of God, so that he will have an answer for the one who taunts him—the declaration of God's faithfulness (41–43).
   A. He asks God to deliver him by his loyal love according to his promises (41).
   B. He knows that when God does this he will have an answer for his taunter; he looks forward therefore to declaring God's faithfulness (42–43).
II. When the LORD delivers him, the psalmist will continue to obey God's law, live at liberty, and proclaim God's testimony because of this deliverance (44–46).
   A. He will keep God's law and live at liberty because of his obedience (44–45).
   B. He will testify even before kings and not be ashamed (46).
III. Because the psalmist delights in and longs for the commandments of God which he loves, he will meditate in them (47–48).

Commentary in Expository Form

I. Believers should pray for God's promises to be fulfilled so that their proclamation of God's faithfulness will silence skeptics (41–43).

A. They should pray for the promises of God to be fulfilled (41).

What the psalmist does in this stanza is what all believers should do, pray for the promises of God to be fulfilled. The focus of the request here is on the promised deliverance from the opposition and reproach of the world. The psalmist first asks that God's "loyal love" (s.v. Ps. 23:6) come to him. As noted already, the noun is plural; it may be so to emphasize the nature of divine love, or it may refer to the many acts of love that God has displayed and promised. This word "love" signifies what divine love will do for him—fulfill the covenant promises (and so it is a metonymy of cause). The parallel colon adds "your salvation" (or "deliverance"; s.v. Ps. 1:5); this clarifies that the prayer for loyal love is a prayer for a deliverance that would vindicate the psalmist as the next verse will make clear. The psalmists knew only the salvation of the LORD could do this, for no human power was sufficient (see Pss. 37:39; 33:16–17; 60:12). Besides, this deliverance based on God's faithful love would be a fulfillment of divine promises (אִמְרָה referring to God's oracle or promise). In the covenant God had promised to deliver his people from their enemies and thereby vindicate his word of promise. It is for this the psalmist prays; it is for this believers today pray as they say the Lord's prayer.

B. They should pray for deliverance so that their praises will silence the skeptics (42–43).

In verse 42 the verb (an imperfect with the *waw*) in sequence with the preceding imperative expresses the result of this deliverance: "then I shall answer" or "have an answer" (וְאֶעֱנֶה). By "answer" he means that a deliverance would be a refutation of the scorner, who may have been challenging his faith as those in Psalm 3:2.[99] While in his difficulty he had to endure their reproach; but he knew that when God delivered him the disgrace would be removed and he would rebuke his taunters. The description of the scoffer adds the term "word" for a full expression: "the one reproaching me *by* word" (חֹרְפִי דָבָר; s.v. Ps. 22:6). The words of that cutting taunt will be silenced by the fulfillment of the divine word. The psalmist knows that the words of the enemy are false, but God's word is trustworthy: "I trust (בָּטַחְתִּי; s.v. Ps. 4:5) in your word." The action of the verb is characteristic of the psalmist; he is here affirming his confidence that God's word is true, that God is able and willing to fulfill what he has promised.

In the meantime, he prays that God not take the word of

---

99. Anderson, *Psalms 73–150*, p. 821.

truth from his mouth (v. 43). The verb "take away" has more of the sense of "snatch away" (וְאַל־תַּצֵּל; s.v. Ps. 22:20); but here it probably means "do not withhold" your word. He does not want to be deprived of the fulfillment of God's word; so this is a restatement of the prayer in verse 41. But he uses "the word of truth" in the verse. "Truth" (אֱמֶת; s.v. Ps. 15:2) signifies that which is reliable and firm; in this construction God's word is being described as faithful and reliable; but the petition is that the word of truth not be taken from his mouth. He does not want to be deprived of the privilege of praising God's faithfulness[100]; Perowne puts it in a positive way: "Give me the power faithfully to witness for Thy truth, and so to answer him that reproacheth me."[101] And the reason for this is that he hopes in God's decisions ("I hope," יִחָלְתִּי; s.v. Ps. 31:24).

II. Believers who pray for God's word to be fulfilled must also commit themselves to obey and proclaim his word (44–46).

A. They must live obediently by his word (44–45).

There is a sequence between the last section's petitions and this verse, expressed by the cohortative verb with the conjunction (וְאֶשְׁמְרָה; s.v. Ps. 12:7), "so I will keep your law continually." Since he is praying for God to keep his word and deliver him from the one taunting him, he will promise to keep God's word as well, continually. Verse 45 adds to this the expectation of living at liberty when the LORD fulfills his word and because the psalmist is faithful. The expression used is "and I will walk about" (וְאֶתְהַלְּכָה), using the idiom of walking with a different emphasis, living life fully, expressed here as to be "in a wide place." He anticipates living a good life without the hindrances of opposition or misfortune (see Pss. 4:1; 118:5). And the reason for this anticipation is that he has sought (דָרַשְׁתִּי) God's precepts. Such seeking could be to obtain an oracle (Gen. 25:22; and possibly Ps. 24:6), or to study and apply God's word more fully (as later the

---

100. Anderson, p. 821.
101. *Psalms*, II:354.

word was used for this with the label *midrash*). In this context both make sense, but ultimately in the psalm it would refer to his focus on studying and applying God's word (specifically, his precepts). His prayer for deliverance intensifies his resolve to obey; and his anticipation of deliverance is based on his determined investigation of God's word.

B. They must boldly proclaim his word (46).

The psalmist also vows to declare God's testimonies, even before kings. The faithful do not keep silent when God makes promises, and certainly not when he fulfills them (see Ps. 40:9–10). Here the verb is a form of "word" (דָּבָר), keeping the theme in the forefront: "I will speak" (וַאֲדַבְּרָה) is the public declaration of what God has said and done; and he will do this before kings, which impresses us with the boldness of it (even if the king was over a city or province). It is not possible to determine what kings he might have had in mind, if any; but the line would be appropriate if he was under foreign rule (one thinks of Daniel speaking before the kings of the east; see also Acts 4:29). The psalm has already indicated that some of those threatening him were powerful leaders. Nevertheless, speaking God's word was and is a part of the believers' duty (Exod. 19:6; Deut. 6:7; Deut. 20:10). And here, the psalmist is confident that he will not be put to shame in doing so (וְלֹא אֵבוֹשׁ; s.v. Ps. 31:1). It will be a time of victory in which the true God will be credited for the deliverance. Kidner rightly notes that the word spoken is first the word appropriated (v. 41), trusted (vv. 42–43), obeyed (v. 44), sought (v. 45), and loved (vv. 47–48).[102]

III. Believers who love God's word and long for its fulfillment must meditate in it (47–48).

The stanza closes with the psalmist's expression of delight in and love for God's word. In verse 47 he declares his delight in the commandments; the verb (וְאֶשְׁתַּעֲשַׁע; s.v. Ps. 119:14) is the imperfect tense, expressing his present and continuing enjoyment

---

102. *Psalms 73–150*, p. 425.

of God's commandments. The relative clause takes it a step further: "which I love" (אָהָבְתִּי, the characteristic perfect tense agreeing with the progressive nuance of the imperfect). His love for God's commandments will be evident in his doing God's will (Deut 5:10; 6:4–5).

To this he adds an expression of his longing for God's word. The image, "and I lift my hands" (וְאֶשָּׂא־כַפַּי, the verb also expressing his present activity), intensifies the point that he has a longing for God's revelation. Lifting the hands could refer to prayer, and in this passage perhaps praying for grace to keep the commands; it probably is being used here for the fervent longing or desire (as in a prayer) for God's word.[103] It is in the words from God that he will meditate (אָשִׂיחָה; s.v. Ps. 119:15)

Message and Application

The continuing flow of references to the psalmist's distress appear in this stanza as well with the reference to the one reproaching him. The stanza develops with this issue in mind: he prays for deliverance so that he can answer the taunts; and as he contemplates God's fulfillment of his word this way, he himself resolves to obey God's word and proclaim it without shame. For devout believers this is not a difficult commitment to make, for they believe the word, love the word, and long for the word to triumph. Meditation on passages like this reminds believers of their duty. The theme of the stanza could be expressed in this way: *Those who long for God's promises to be fulfilled (so that skeptics may be answered) must commit themselves to obeying and proclaiming God's word to the world.* It stands to reason that people who put all their hope in God's word would also study it and proclaim it to others.

The fulfillment of God's promises continues to be the desire and expectation of all believers. Jesus declared that every detail would be fulfilled (Matt. 5:18); but Paul explained that this was so because Christ himself is the "yes" to all the promises of God (2 Cor. 1:20). As believers today long for the complete fulfillment of all the promises, they are called on to obey the word of God (John

---

103. Delitzsch, *Psalms*, III:250; Kidner, p. 425; see also Psalms 63:4 and 141:2).

14:15; 1 John 2:5) and proclaim it to the world (Matt. 10:18; Acts 26:1, 2). It is surely hypocritical to pray for God to fulfill his promises in the word and not be committed to obeying that same word.

ז Zayin

Comfort and Hope Against the World

Text and Textual Variants

ז 49 Remember *your*[104] word (דָּבָר) to your servant,[105]
      in which you have made me hope.

ז 50 This is my comfort[106] in my affliction,
      that your promise (אִמְרָה) renews my life.

ז 51 The arrogant utterly[107] scorn me,[108]
      but[109] I do not turn away from your law (תּוֹרָה).

ז 52 I remember your decisions (מִשְׁפָּט) from of old,
      and I take comfort, O LORD.

ז 53 Burning indignation[110] seizes me because of the wicked
      who forsake your law (תּוֹרָה).

ז 54 Your statutes (חֹק) have been *my* songs
      in the house[111] of my sojourning.

ז 55 I remember your name in the night, O LORD,
      and will keep your law (תּוֹרָה).

ז 56 This has fallen to me,[112]
      that I keep[113] your precepts (פִּקּוּד).

---

104. דָּבָר has no suffix in the MT. But in the versions there are a number of variations: G* and Syriac have the 2msg suffix; G^L and Theodotion have a plural noun with the 2msg suffix, "your words"; Symmachus has the word with a 1sg suffix, "my word."
105. One manuscript, the Greek^s and Aquila have "servants."
106. MT has נֶחָמָתִי, but the Greek translation has a verb με παρεκάλεσεν, "(this) has comforted me," which would be equivalent to נִחֲמַתְנִי.
107. This expression is not reflected in the Syriac translation (see Ps. 119:43).
108. The verb in the MT is הֱלִיצֻנִי; the Greek version has παρηνόμουν, "transgress the law." The editors of BHS propose אָלְצֻנִי.
109. The conjunction is present in one manuscript, the Greek and the Syriac.
110. The Greek version interprets this word as "despair," ἀθυμία.
111. The Greek version gives a general translation of "house" as "place," τόπῳ.
112. The ESV translation has, "This *blessing has befallen* me."
113. Again the Greek translation has "sought" for this verb.

Exegetical Summary

Summary

The psalmist prays for the fulfillment of God's word because it is his comfort and hope in affliction, affirming his faithfulness even when scorned, explaining that God's word fills him with joy and God's name inspires his obedience (119:49–56).

Outline
  I. The psalmist prays for God to fulfill his word because it has given him comfort and hope in the midst of his affliction (49–50).
  II. The psalmist affirms his faithfulness to God's word, which comforts him, even when he is scorned by the wicked who rebel against God's word (51–53).
    A. He is faithful to God's word even though he is scorned (51).
    B. He finds comfort when he remembers God's ancient word (52).
    C. He burns with indignation at the disobedience of the wicked (53).
  III. The psalmist explains that the word of the LORD has filled him with singing and the name of the LORD has inspired his obedience (54–56).

Commentary in Expository Form

I. Believers pray for God to fulfill his word because it is their hope and comfort in affliction (49–50).

The "*Zayin* Stanza" begins with a prayer for God's word to be fulfilled. The key word is "remember" (זָכַר; s.v. Ps. 6:5), which does not mean that God, like a human, needs to remember. The verb signifies acting on the basis of what was called to mind.[114] It is a prayer for God to fulfill the promises he made to his people, here, specifically the psalmist, who refers to himself as God's

---

114. It is helpful to review Brevard Childs' *Memory and Tradition in Israel*, p. 34.

servant. The psalmist may be praying for a specific application of the divine promises to protect and bless the covenant people, or perhaps for the fulfillment of some special word of promise.[115] Whatever the specific reference, it is a word of promise in which the psalmist has put his hope (the verb יִחַלְתָּנִי is causative, yielding the literal meaning of "you have caused me to hope"). Delitzsch suggests a comparison with the opposite idea of God's causing someone to forget the immediate afflictions, as in Genesis 41:51.[116]

The second verse of the stanza declares that God's promises keep him going, as it were. The line begins with the affirmation, "This is my comfort in my affliction." This noun "comfort" (נֶחָמָה; s.v. Ps. 119:76) is rare, occurring only here and in Job 6:10; but the meaning of consolation and relief is clear from the use of the verb and other related words. In the midst of his affliction (עָנְיִי; s.v. Ps. 9:12) the psalmist's comfort comes from the promises that God renews life (חִיָּתְנִי). This does not simply mean preserving his life; the promises revive his spirit with fresh courage to remain faithful. The point is that the promises God made to his people in his word bring comfort and courage—it is the nature of the word to revive the spiritual life (Ps. 19:7).

II. Believers remain faithful to God's comforting word even when they are scorned by those who rebel against God's word (51–53).

A. *They remain faithful when scorned (51).*

In the heart of this stanza the psalmist lays out the tension that he faced, a tension that all the faithful will experience in their earthly journey. He states that the arrogant (זֵדִים; s.v. Ps. 119:21) scorn him relentlessly (עַד־מְאֹד). The verb "scorn" (הֱלִיצֻנִי) is related to the word "scorners" in Psalm 1:1.[117] Proverbs 21:24

---

115. Perowne, *Psalms*, II:355.
116. *Psalms*, II:250.
117. The word "scorn," לִיץ, has both positive and negative connotations. On the positive side the word is used for an interpreter. Genesis 42:23 is the best illustration as Joseph spoke to his brothers through an interpreter.

says, "The proud and arrogant man—'Mocker' is his name; he behaves with overweening pride." The psalmist and his faith were treated with derision by arrogant unbelievers. If the setting is the time of the captivity, there are passages like Psalm 137 that reveal some of this. Such scorn however is not limited to any one period or circumstance. The psalmist then demonstrates how true believers respond: he affirms that even though this happens he does not turn away from God's laws.[118]

B. They remain faithful because they find comfort in his ancient word (52).

The psalmist's faithfulness is expressed with the verb "remember" (זָכַרְתִּי); the action implied by this word is his meditation on and obedience to the word of God. The use of the verb here is instructive: if people want God to "remember" (i.e., fulfill) his word, they must "remember" (i.e., obey) his word. What he remembers are the laws and decisions of God in all matters, which are here described as "ancient" (מֵעוֹלָם, "from antiquity"; s.v. Ps. 93:2). They have stood the test of time with all its conflicts and

---

In a similar way it can describe intermediaries between God and man (Isa. 43:27), and ambassadors (2 Chron. 32:31).

But on the negative side it describes mocking, deriding and scorning. This refers to a malicious and sarcastic verbal attack or ridicule. Proverbs has many descriptions of the scorner: proud, arrogant, incapable of discipline, does not respond to rebuke, and is an abomination to be avoided. Judgment awaits him. An interesting use of the word is in Proverbs 20:1 which says that wine is a scorner or mocker, indicating that the effect of wine makes the drinker look foolish.

The word is used in the cognate Arabic with the sense of speaking obliquely or indirectly. Perhaps this is behind the noun מְלִיצָה, a satire, mocking poem, or an enigma in Proverbs 1:6. The scorning or sarcastic mocking may be indirect at times, direct at other times.

118. There is no formal indication of the contrast between the two halves of the verse, but the implication is that in spite of their scorn he remains faithful. Psalm 125 may be compared: there the pilgrim attests that wicked government will not be sufficiently wicked to cause the righteous to turn aside to crookedness.

pains; God's word is eternal—ever reliable and ever binding. In this the psalmist takes comfort (וָאֶתְנֶחָם).[119]

C. Their faithfulness causes them to burn with indignation against wickedness (53).

But with the comfort there is also a burning indignation (זַלְעָפָה). This is a rare word (Ps. 11:6; Lam. 5:10); it can mean a burning, or the effects of the burning (faintness). The Greek version interprets it with "despondency" and the Targum has "trembling." So Briggs says he means that their scorn is like a burning wind (sirocco) that has seized him—the word would refer to his affliction and not his anger.[120] But it seems more likely in this context that the psalmist is expressing his reaction to the prevailing wickedness of the world; the verb "seized" fits better with the building indignation than the idea of scorn ridiculing him. Anderson suggests the meaning "horrified."[121] When the psalmist considers his affliction at the hands of the arrogant, he seems to be more angered that they have no regard for the word of God than for his own plight. The truly devout naturally have a moral outrage over the ungodly who forsake God's laws.

III. Believers find their inspiration for joy in the word of the LORD and their motivation for obedience in the person of the LORD (54–56).

A. They rejoice in the word of the LORD (54).

The last part of this stanza provides the psalmist's explanation. He first states that God's word brings him joy: "your statutes have been *my* songs" (זְמִרוֹת; s.v. Ps. 33:2).[122] Either he sings

---

119. Anderson notes that the verb in this stem could be reflexive, "I comforted myself," or passive, "I was comforted" (*Psalms 73–150*, p. 824).
120. *Psalms*, II:425.
121. *Psalms 73–150*, p. 824.
122. The suggestion that this word is cognate to an Arabic word for "strength" may be appealing but is not very convincing (M. Pope, *Job*, Anchor Bible, 1965, pp. 228–29).

God's word, or God's word inspires him to sing.[123] Singing has always been an effective way to comfort the troubled soul and renew hope and confidence. The psalmist's singing is said to be in the house of his sojournings (בְּבֵית מְגוּרָי), probably an expression meaning wherever he lodges. The choice of the word "sojourn" reiterates his earlier emphasis that he is a stranger in the earth, a passing guest (v. 19). The words that he sings are filled with hope that transcends the sins and sorrows of this world.

B. They meditate on the name of the LORD (55).

The word of the LORD may fill him with comfort, hope and joy, but it is the name of the LORD that inspires his faithfulness. After all, the word reveals the LORD to him. Here we have the third use of the verb "remember" in the stanza—he remembers the name of the LORD. The statement includes at least his meditation on the name of the LORD (see Ps. 20:7 where the verb "remember" in the *hiphil* is used with the "name of the LORD" to indicate meditation on and confident trust in the person and works of the LORD. When he does this, he is inspired to live in obedience to the law. It should be so for all believers that the focus of their meditation should be on the Lord himself.

C. They acknowledge this as God's gift (56).

The last verse seems to be the sum of the matter. It is expressed somewhat ambiguously: "This *has fallen* to me" (literally, "this was to / for me," זֹאת הָיְתָה־לִּי) raises the question of the reference for "this." It could refer to God's blessings as a reward for obedience (translating the last part as "because I have kept your precepts"). The Targum adds the word "blessing, reward" (see the RV). Or it could refer to the remembrance of God's name in the last verse. However, "this" most likely refers to verse 56b, requiring the translation "that (כִּי) I have kept your precepts." In other words, he would be saying that this keeping of God's precepts was by divine enablement—it was a gift allotted to him

---

123. This does not fit well with the pain of the exiles who could not find it in themselves to sing the songs of Zion (Ps. 137).

to obey (Perowne, II:356). This view harmonizes with the overall emphasis of the Psalm that God has renewed and inspired him in spite of his circumstances.

Message and Application

The ongoing affliction that the psalmist was experiencing is at the center of this stanza too. But in spite of the scorn and affliction, he finds comfort in God's word, hope in his promises, and inspiration in the revelation of the name of the LORD. So there is comfort, hope and joy from the LORD through his word, in spite of the wickedness around him. This all can be expressed in an expository idea: *The faithful who endure the scorn of the world pray for the fulfillment of God's word because God is the inspiration of their obedience and his word the source of their comfort and joy.*

All believers sooner or later have to deal with the scorn and opposition from the world, as well as the awareness of how the world continues to transgress God's laws openly and shamelessly. They will pray therefore for God to end the trouble by fulfilling his promises; but in the meantime, they must focus their attention on his word and live out their faith with joy in the midst of evil. The New Testament confirms that the word of God is eternal (Matt. 24:35) and that it will be fulfilled. In the meantime we who believe find comfort in the "God (who) comforts us in all our troubles, so that we can comfort those in any trouble with the comfort we ourselves have received from God" (2 Cor. 1:4). One passage that captures the spirit and details of this stanza comes from one of Paul's prison epistles; from that unpleasant circumstance, he wrote, "Let the word of Christ dwell in you richly as you teach and admonish one another with all wisdom, and as you sing psalms, hymns and spiritual songs with gratitude in your hearts to God. And whatever you do, whether in word or deed, do it all in the name of the Lord Jesus, giving thanks to God the Father through him" (Col. 3:16, 17).

ח *Het*

Divine Provision and Human Commitment

Text and Textual Variants

ח 57 The LORD is my portion;[124]
I say I will keep[125] your words (דְּבָר).[126]

ח 58 I entreat your face with all my heart;
be gracious[127] to me according to your promise (אִמְרָה).

ח 59 I think on my[128] ways
and I turn my feet to your testimonies (עֵדוּת);

ח 60 I hasten[129] and do not delay[130]
to keep your commandments (מִצְוָה).

ח 61 *Though* the cords of the wicked surround[131] me,
I will not forget your law (תּוֹרָה).

ח 62 At midnight I rise to praise you,
because of your righteous decisions (מִשְׁפָּט).

ח 63 I am a companion to all who fear you,
to those who keep your precepts (פִּקּוּד).

ח 64 The earth, O LORD, is full of your loyal love;
teach me your statutes (חֹק).

---

124. The Greek version reads the line slightly differently: Μερίς μου (εἶ) κύριε, "You are my portion, O Lord." This is followed by some commentators as well as the NIV. The translation requires the addition of the pronoun.
125. The MT has אָמַרְתִּי לִשְׁמֹר, "I say to keep." ESV has, "I promise to keep"; NIV, "I have promised."
126. Many manuscripts and Jerome have a singular form; the Greek version reads τὸν νόμον σου, "your law."
127. MT has חָנֵּנִי; the Syriac has "preserve me alive" (= חַיֵּנִי).
128. In the Greek translation the suffix is 2sg, "your ways."
129. MT has חַשְׁתִּי, but the Greek version has ἡτοιμάσθην, "I was prepared" or "I prepared myself."
130. For the MT's הִתְמַהְמָהְתִּי the Greek has και ουκ ἐταράχθην, "and was not troubled / terrified."
131. The MT form is עִוְּדֻנִי; a few manuscripts manuscripts have עִוְּתֻנִי, two have עָרְךָ רוּנִי and two others have עִוְּרֻנִי. The verb עוד in the *piel* means "surround"; עות in the *piel* means "bend, make crooked"; עָוַר I, "make blind" (and two hollow roots עוּר, which would not occur in the *piel*, "rouse oneself" and "be exposed").

Exegetical Analysis

Summary

The psalmist commits himself to keeping the LORD's commandments faithfully and enthusiastically as he prays for gracious intervention in his life-threatening situation, acknowledging that everything he has is in the LORD and everything in the world is under his care (119:57–64).

Outline

I. Because everything he has is in the LORD, the psalmist promises to keep his word (57).
II. The psalmist seeks God's grace in fulfilling his word because he wholeheartedly keeps God's commandments (58–60).
   A. He seeks divine favor in accordance with the promises (58).
   B. He commits himself to live his life in obedience to God's word without hesitation (59–60).
III. The psalmist affirms his faithfulness to and praise for God's rulings even while the wicked come close to destroying him (61–62).
IV. In fellowship with faithful believers who fear the LORD, the psalmist desires to know more of the word of the LORD because the earth is under the LORD's loving care (63–64).

Commentary in Expository Form

I. Believers must make a commitment to obey God's word because everything they have comes from God (57).

In this stanza the psalmist's appreciation of the LORD provides the frame: in verse 57 he speaks of the LORD as his portion (חֶלְקִי) and in verse 64 he mentions the LORD's loyal love (חֶסֶד).

The declaration that the LORD is his portion is familiar (see Pss. 16:5, 73:26, 142:6). The metaphor signifies that everything he possesses is bound up in his relationship with the LORD. It may be that this expression reflects the circumstances of the

Levites; they were not allocated any land for their possession but had to depend on the LORD (see Num. 18:20). The expression would have been true of every Israelite; even if they had a plot of land, everything they possessed was to be found in God. It was something every devout believer would acknowledge. If the LORD is one's portion, then that certainly calls for a commitment to obey the LORD's word. So the second colon has, "I say (or "I have said," אָמַרְתִּי) to keep (לִשְׁמֹר; s.v. Ps. 12:7) your words." This could be translated as "I said that I would keep," or, "I have promised to keep," or "I say, I will keep." In any case, commitment is the appropriate response to the provision of God.

II. Believers must demonstrate their eagerness to be faithful when they pray for God to be faithful to his promises (58–60).

A. They should pray for God to fulfill his promises (58).

The next verse records a prayer for gracious intervention. The first colon describes the prayer, the second records the appeal. "I entreat your face" (חִלִּיתִי פָנֶיךָ) is a poetic description of prayer; it basically means to stroke or caress the face, that is, appealing to God's good pleasure with a flattering entreaty.[132] There is no false flattery here, however. The devout have a close, personal relationship with the LORD, so that they may make their appeal on the basis of God's love and compassion for them. Here the appeal is with the whole heart—it is urgent and sincere; it is a prayer for God to be gracious (חָנֵּנִי; s.v. Ps. 4:1) according to

---

132. The verb חָלָה (II) means "to mollify, appease, entreat the favor of." It seems to have the basic sense of making the face sweet or pleasant, perhaps illustrated with a child's stroking of a parent's face; the intent, though, is to appeal favorably to the LORD in prayer. This meaning is found in Proverbs 19:6 where the verb is used for entreating the favor of a prince. In Exodus 32:11 it is used for the urgent appeal to God to show favor in place of the wrath for the idolatry. And in Malachi 1:9 the hypocritical worshipers are urged to entreat the LORD so that he might be gracious to them. The purpose of entreating the LORD's favor is to appeal for safety, success, and prosperity through his favor.

his promise. The verb expresses the cause (a metonymy), but implies the effect, i.e., that God by his grace would act to fulfill his promises. The reason for the urgent appeal will be spelled out in verse 61. In view of that we may say it is a prayer for God to rescue him from the wicked who are about to destroy him.

B. Believers must commit themselves to obey God's word enthusiastically (59–60).

The next two verses describe the commitment to obey the word of the LORD. The psalmist begins with a time of self-examination ("I consider" חִשַּׁבְתִּי; s.v. Ps. 32:2). As a result of his careful consideration of his ways, he turns (וָאָשִׁיבָה; s.v. Ps. 126:1) his feet to the word of the LORD. Briggs says this turning is the positive side of repentance, even though there is no indication in the stanza of the negative side because he does not say he uncovered sin.[133] The mention of feet draws in the idiom of the believer's walk, i.e., the way of life—here is a commitment to live in obedience to God's word. And according to verse 60, he hurries to do this and does not delay. His eagerness to keep God's commands corresponds to his urgent prayer for God to fulfill his promises. There is something hollow about people pleading for God to fulfill the promises in his word when they pay little attention to keeping his word.

III. Believers need to renew their loyalty to God when their lives are in danger by the opposition of the wicked (61–62).

We now learn something of the crisis of the psalmist. He reports that "the cords of the wicked surround" him (חֶבְלֵי רְשָׁעִים עִוְּדֻנִי). These "wicked" (s.v. Ps. 1:1) are no doubt the arrogant scorners he has referred to before. Here he uses an implied comparison: they are like hunters who have snared him with ropes (see Ps. 116:3); but even though his life is in imminent danger, they cannot destroy his commitment to the LORD. His "I will not forget" means that he will continue to act on the word he

---

[133]. *Psalm*, II:426.

knows, i.e., he will remain faithful to God's law. In fact, he rises at midnight to praise (לְהוֹדוֹת; s.v. Ps. 6:5) the LORD for his righteous rulings. Here we see the spiritual discipline of the devout, keeping hours of prayer and praise, intentionally rising at midnight to acknowledge the decisions of the LORD in his word.

IV. All believers who fear the LORD desire to know his word because the whole earth is in his loving care (63–64).

The psalmist's loyalty to the LORD also finds expression in his association with other believers—he is a companion (חָבֵר) to all who fear (s.v. Ps. 2:11) the LORD, meaning those who keep his commandments. The tie that binds the devout together is the commitment to keep God's commands.

In the last verse of the stanza he declares that the earth is full of God's loyal love (חַסְדְּךָ; s.v. Ps. 23:6). The earth belongs to the LORD and is under his loving care (see also Ps. 24:1; 33:5; 104:24; and Isa. 6:3). If the whole world benefits from the LORD's loving care, then how much more his faithful people! This care is the chief benefit of having God as one's portion. The psalmist therefore desires to know even more about God's revelation. He prays, "Teach me your statutes." Goldingay notes that the prayer would at first glance seem to be superficial, since anyone can know the word that is available to them. But, he further explains, not everyone does so; and besides, the divine teacher has ways of impressing the word on the heart that goes beyond a simple study of the text.[134] The Spirit of the LORD might so instruct him as he meditates on the word or may use faithful teachers. In any case, his desire for the LORD to fulfill his word, and his commitment to live in obedience to it, prompted his prayer to be taught more.

Message and Application

This stanza emphasizes the LORD's "portion" and "loyal love," which frame the passage. Within the stanza we have the

---

134. *Psalms 90–150*, p. 406.

psalmist's urgent prayer for grace in the light of his crisis, and his commitment to live in obedience to God's word. Delitzsch suggests that understanding and keeping God's word is the heart of the psalmist's portion and the object of his prayer and praise.[135] We may word the expository idea this way: *When praying for God to deliver them from danger by his grace, believers must demonstrate their faithfulness by acknowledging his loving care and by renewing their commitment to obey his word.*

This is true for the New Testament believer as well. Scripture warns us again and again that the world will hate those who believe in the Lord and will try to destroy their faith with false teaching and persecution. But believers know that the Lord has made every provision for them by the love of Christ (Eph. 1:3–14) and promised them the hope of glory (2 Cor. 4:16–18). It is because of this hope that they persevere in their commitment to do the will of God, to keep his commandments (John 14:15; 15:10; and 1 John 2:5). As they persevere they pray for his protection, and for the fulfillment of his promises, knowing that every word will be fulfilled (Matt. 5:18). When they find their lives threatened or the faith attacked, they know that nothing can separate them from the love of God in Christ Jesus; and so they demonstrate their faith by their praise. It is the faith that was demonstrated by the apostles in prison, praying and singing praises to God (Acts 16:25)–and they were marvelously delivered for the glory of God.

ט *Ṭet*

God's Goodness and Our Well-Being

Text and Textual Variants

ט 65 You have dealt well[136] with your servant,
O LORD, according to your word (דְּבָר).[137]

---

135. *Psalms*, III:251.
136. The NIV takes the perfect tense in an imperative nuance: "Do good to your servant."
137. A number of manuscripts have this form in the plural.

The Word of the LORD and the Life of Faith

ט 66 Teach me good judgment[138] and knowledge,
   for I believe in your commandments (מִצְוָה).

ט 67 Before I was afflicted[139] I was going astray,
   but now I keep your word (אִמְרָה).

ט 68 You are good[140] and you do good *things*;[141]
   teach me your statutes (חֹק).

ט 69 The arrogant have put together[142] a lie against me,[143]
   but I with my whole heart will keep[144] your precepts (פִּקּוּד);

ט 70 their heart is unfeeling like fat,[145]
   but I delight in your law (תּוֹרָה).

ט 71 It was good for me that I was afflicted,[146]
   that I might learn your statutes (חֹק).

---

138. MT has טוּב טָעַם, literally, "goodness of perception (taste)," but reading it as a genitive of specification yields "good perception." The psalmist is praying for a fine sense of apprehension of God's word (Perowne, *Psalms*, II:357). Some propose deleting טוּב as a repetition of verse 65. The Greek version has: χρηστότητα καί παιδείαν καί γνῶσιν, "(teach me) kindness, and instruction, and knowledge."

139. The form is the active אֲעֶנֶה; the editors of BHS propose the *niphal* אֵעָנֶה, which is required here, and which is supported by the Greek version's πρό τοῦ με ταπεινωθῆναι, "I was afflicted." The imperfect is treated as a preterite after טֶרֶם.

140. The Greek version adds Κύριε, "O Lord."

141. The form is the *hiphil* participle מֵטִיב, "doing good." In the Greek version it is treated as a noun and connected to the next section: ἐν τῇ χρηστότητί σου, "in your goodness (teach me . . .)."

142. The word literally means "patch together"; Perowne suggests "forged" (*Psalms*, II:357).

143. The MT has the noun שֶׁקֶר, "a lie," next to the subject of the sentence, זֵדִים, "the arrogant." The line in this order would be "they have forged against me a lie, the insolent." The Greek version has the line read: "*The injustice of the proud* (taking the two nouns together for ἀδικία ὑπερηφάνων) has filled out (ἐπληθύνθη) against me."

144. The Greek version again translates the verb נָצַר, "keep, treasure," as "examine" or "search out."

145. The MT has טָפַשׁ כַּחֵלֶב, "(their heart) is unfeeling like fat." The Greek version reads: ἐτυρώθη ὡς γάλα, "(their heart) has been curdled like milk." Along with the Greek (and Syriac), one manuscript has כֶּחָלָב. The NIV has "(their hearts) are callous and unfeeling."

146. The MT has the passive כִּי־עֻנֵּיתִי, "that I was afflicted." But the Greek translation has ἐταπείνωσάς με, "you humbled (or afflicted) me" (= עִנִּיתָנִי).

ט 72 The law (תּוֹרָה) of your mouth is better to me
            than thousands of gold and silver *pieces*.

Exegetical Analysis

Summary

Acknowledging that the LORD has treated him well by his word, the psalmist prays for knowledge and understanding of the word that he believes in and obeys even though arrogant people lie about him, concluding that the affliction he endured forced him to learn more of God's ways (119:65–72).

Outline

I. The psalmist declares that the LORD has treated him well in accordance with his word (65).
II. The psalmist asks the LORD, who is the source of all good things, to teach him knowledge and understanding because he believes in the word (66–68).
  A. He prays for knowledge and insight because he believes in the word (66).
  B. He recalls how he used to wander but affirms he now keeps the word (67).
  C. He asks the LORD, who is the source of all good, to teach him his statutes (68).
III. The psalmist affirms his delight and obedience in God's word even though insensitive and arrogant people lie about him (69–70).
IV. The psalmist acknowledges that his affliction forced him to learn God's law, which is his most prized possession (71–72).

Commentary in Expository Form

I. God is good to his servants, just as his word says (65).

The point of this first verse is that the believer's loyal service brings divine blessing. It begins with the affirmation "you have dealt well" (טוֹב עָשִׂיתָ), an acknowledgment of the faithfulness of the LORD (for the meaning of "well," literally "good," s.v. Ps. 34:8). This favor was directed to God's servants (s.v. Ps. 134:1), just as the LORD's word had promised (Deut. 30:15–16).

II. God's people desire to understand more of his word because he is the source of all good things (66–68).

A. They pray for knowledge and understanding of the word that they believe (66).

The psalmist's prayer is for God to teach (לַמְּדֵנִי) him "good judgment and knowledge." The good judgment is "good taste" (טוּב טַעַם), meaning that then his preferences and decisions will be appropriate to a Godly life.[147] Joined with "knowledge" (דַּעַת; s.v. Ps. 67:2), this is a practical prayer for spiritual growth and not just the best information. The petition is explained by his affirmation of faith: "for I believe in your commandments." This kind of faith (הֶאֱמָנְתִּי; s.v. Ps. 15:2) includes a commitment to live according to the revealed word of the LORD that is believed.

B. They testify that even though they once wandered they now keep God's word (67).

The psalmist's personal experience is related in verse 67—an experience shared by so many believers. The verse provides more background to his statement "I believe." "Before I was afflicted" clarifies his present situation: one may suppose that references to the hostility of enemies in this psalm may be at the heart of his affliction; before this affliction, he had wandered. The verb (שָׁגַג) is used in Leviticus for unintentional sins; but here it probably includes rationalized, deliberate sins because he was wandering from the way of God. He was not walking by faith in obedience to the word, and so he suffered some affliction at the hands of the wicked; but now he was keeping God's oracle, the word "keep" (שָׁמַר; s.v. Ps. 12:7) referring to a meticulous observance of all that God required in his covenant.

---

147. See the use of "taste" for the decision and ruling of the king in Jonah 3:7.

C. Because the LORD is the source of all good things, they ask for direction (68).

The psalmist's desire to learn the statutes of God is based on the realized truth that God is good and that he does good things (וּמֵטִיב). This little section of hymnic praise must surely reflect the personal experience of the psalmist: to live according to the word of God is to experience the goodness of God; but wandering from God there is no such display of goodness. He therefore repeats, "teach me." This teaching could come through the ministry of priests who were to teach the laws of God (Deut. 33:10); but it could also include the LORD's impressing the reality and significance of his word on the heart of the psalmist in times of meditation (see Ps. 16:6–7).

III. God's people delight in doing God's word even though arrogant unbelievers lie about them (69–70).

The next two verses provide information about both his affliction and the goodness of God. The focus turns to the arrogant, godless people around him (זֵדִים; s.v. Ps. 119:21) who have patched together (טָפְלוּ) a lie (שֶׁקֶר; s.v. Ps. 144:8) against him. Their attempt to smear him with fabricated lies is set in stark contrast to God's goodness. To escape this danger and enjoy God's goodness, the psalmist will keep or treasure (אֶצֹּר; s.v. Ps. 119:2) God's precepts wholeheartedly—no doubting, no wavering, no divided loyalties. He adds another description of the arrogant: their heart (contrast with his heart's loyalty to God) is as unfeeling as fat. They have no sensitivity to the things of God, no inclination to keep his precepts, and no concern for those who do. This verb (טָפַשׁ) occurs only here in the Hebrew; but its cognate in the Aramaic Targum of Isaiah 6:10, "make fat," clearly signifies unbelief and indifference to God's message. They are the arrogant unbelievers. But the psalmist's delight, his belief and enjoyment, is in God's instructions.

IV. God's people acknowledge that affliction forces them to learn more of God's revealed ways (71–72).

The psalmist is able to acknowledge that his affliction

worked for his good because it forced him to learn more of God's plan revealed in his word. In learning through adversity he discovered the word God personally revealed in human language was far more valuable than silver or gold.

Message and Application

This meditation focuses on the goodness of God—he is good, he does good things for his people, and even the afflictions they endure are for their good. When the faithful study God's word and pray to understand his ways, they realize that his word is good—better than riches. The message for these verses may be worded this way: *Because the LORD does good things for his people in accordance with his word, even through affliction, the faithful pray for more knowledge and understanding of his revealed ways.*

The apostles warn us that there will be false teachers who are arrogant unbelievers, slanderers of the people of God and blasphemers of God himself (1 Pet. 2:1, 10–12). Even in times when the arrogant oppose us and our faith, we know that God is good and good to his people. He loves to give good gifts to his people; as James reminds us, every good gift comes from him (1:17). When there is opposition to the faith, God uses such times of affliction as a means of developing our faith (James 1:2), even if it is an affliction we brought on ourselves. It is our task to study the word to know and understand the ways of God, and therefore know him better in the process. When we study his word, it should be our prayer that he teach us, either directly by his Holy Spirit as we meditate on the word, or through properly appointed and spiritually directed teachers. The substance of our prayer is that we learn "good taste," i.e., what is the pleasing and right way to live, so that we will not wander away in our beliefs or activities.

י *Yod*

Affliction in the Creator's Plan

Text and Textual Variants

י 73 Your hands have made me and established me;
     give me understanding[148] that I may learn your commandments (מִצְוָה).
י 74 Those who fear you shall see me and shall rejoice,[149]
     because I have hoped in your word (דָּבָר).[150]
י 75 I know, O LORD, that your decisions (מִשְׁפָּט)[151] are righteousness,
     and in faithfulness you have afflicted me.
י 76 Let your loyal love be to comfort me,
     according to your oracle (אִמְרָה) to your servant.
י 77 Let your tender mercies come to me, that I may live;
     for your law (תּוֹרָה) is my delight.[152]
י 78 Let the arrogant be put to shame,
     because they have wronged me *with* falsehood;[153]
     as for me, I will meditate on your precepts (פִּקּוּד).
י 79 Let those who fear you turn to me,
     those who know[154] your testimonies (עֵדוּת).
י 80 May my heart be blameless in your statutes (חֹק),
     that I may not be put to shame!

---

148. For MT's חֲבִינֵנִי the Greek provides a more general idea: συνέτισμόν μου, "instruct me."
149. Some translations take the verbs as jussives: "may they see" (cf. NIV).
150. Several manuscripts and the Greek version have a plural here.
151. Jerome has a singular noun; the other versions have plural.
152. The Greek again uses μελέτη, "meditation," in place of "delight."
153. The NIV translates this as "without a cause."
154. The text has a K^ethiv–Q^ere' reading. The K is וידעו, וְיֵדְעוּ, "and (that) they may know," providing a purpose clause for their returning. The other form, the Q, the correction of the text, is וְיֹדְעֵי, "and/even those who know (your testimonies)." This latter reading is supported by many manuscripts, the Greek (καὶ οἱ γινώσκοντες), Syriac and Jerome. It would then be a parallel expression. Even though most follow this reading, a few modern commentators and translations prefer the purpose clause, "that they may know."

Exegetical Analysis

Summary

Knowing that the LORD created him for a purpose, and acknowledging that his affliction was part of God's faithful dealings with him, the psalmist confidently prays for understanding to learn God's commandments, deliverance from the arrogant who have wronged him, and a blameless heart so that he might not be put to shame (119:73–80).

Outline

I. The psalmist prays that the God who created him give him understanding (73).
II. The psalmist prays that God will deliver him from the arrogant who have wronged him and thereby give believers the occasion to rejoice in the faith (74–79).
  A. He is confident that believers will rejoice when his faith is vindicated (74).
  B. He acknowledges that God who makes right decisions has afflicted him for a purpose (75).
  C. He prays that God will comfort and restore him by his loyal love and compassion (76–77).
  D. He prays that God will destroy the arrogant who have wronged him (78).
  E. He is confident that believers will turn to him when he is vindicated (79).
III. The psalmist prays that his heart would be blameless so that he is not put to shame (80).

Commentary in Expository Form

I. The plan of the creator is that we gain understanding to know his will (73).

The "*Yod* stanza" begins with a strong statement of faith: "Your hands have made me (עָשׂוּנִי) and established me" (וַיְכוֹנְנוּנִי; s.v. Ps. 93:1). This meditation therefore begins with the foundational truth that God made us. The verb is the common word "to do, make," but it becomes powerful when used for creation, particularly of human life (Pss. 95:6, 100:3, and 138:8). The idea is underscored with the second verb, "to establish" (see Deut. 32:6). This first half provides the foundation for the prayer in the parallel part: "give me understanding" (הֲבִינֵנִי; s.v. Ps. 49:3). It is a prayer for God to finish his work of creation: God made us for a purpose, and to fulfill that purpose we need spiritual understanding to learn God's commandments. Delitzsch says, "It is impossible that God should forsake man, who is His creature, and deny to him that which makes him truly happy, viz. the understanding and knowledge of His word."[155] In the psalmist's mind, since God made him, God must instruct him. And because of the crises that he faced in life, he realized his need for understanding was urgent if he was to live blamelessly (v. 80).

II. The plan of the creator includes testing us with affliction so that we seek comfort and deliverance in his faithful love (74–79).

A. Other believers will rejoice when our faith is vindicated (74).

The heart of this stanza is concerned with the psalmist's present affliction. He begins the section with a confident expectation of the outcome, that those who fear the LORD will see and rejoice. The verb "see me" (יִרְאוּנִי, forming a word play with the preceding "those who fear you," יְרֵאֶיךָ) means see him delivered, for then they will rejoice (וְיִשְׂמָחוּ; s.v. Ps. 48:11). The reason for this anticipated celebration is his faith: "because I have hoped (יִחָלְתִּי; s.v. Ps. 31:24) in your word." Here is the basic truth that the salvation of the afflicted is the outcome of faith in God's word.

B. In our faith we recognize God's purpose in our afflictions (75).

The expected deliverance is from the affliction God has brought upon him. He knows that God's decisions or rulings are "righteousness" (צֶדֶק; s.v. Ps. 1:5), meaning that all of God's acts

---

155. *Psalms*, III:253.

The Word of the LORD and the Life of Faith

of judgment, all his decisions, are sure to be right. He is never wrong, never incomplete, never arbitrary. With this in mind the psalmist acknowledges, "*in* faithfulness (אֱמוּנָה; s.v. Ps. 15:2) you have afflicted me (עִנִּיתָנִי)." The affliction he has been experiencing came from God, even though it was through arrogant oppressors. The principle was laid down in the experience of Israel in the wilderness: God tested them to see if they would obey or not (Deut. 8:16).[156] Those who understand the ways of God know that ultimately it is his plan to exalt the righteous and destroy the wicked, but that in his wisdom he often humbles the righteous before exalting them. This affliction is therefore qualified by "in your faithfulness." The text does not clarify what this means; it may mean that God was being faithful to his covenant, or to his word in general (see Ps. 89:28–37), or it may mean that he was faithful in his intentions for the psalmist (as well as us). God has made it clear in Scripture that he develops faith and spiritual understanding with such means. Delitzsch says it well: "it is just in the school of affliction that one first learns rightly to estimate the worth of His word and comes to feel his power."[157]

C. In our faith we pray for God's love and mercy to bring comfort and deliverance (76–77).

And yet, even though the faithful know this, they still may pray for comfort in the affliction and deliverance from it. The prayer for comfort is in verse 76: "Let your loyal love (חַסְדְּךָ; s.v. Ps. 23:6) be to comfort me (לְנַחֲמֵנִי)."[158] He desires that God's

---

156. Nothing is said in this stanza about the affliction being a punishment for sin. While that may be a possibility, it is more likely the affliction was God's way of testing him for obedience.
157. *Psalms*, p. 253.
158. The word נָחַם means "to comfort, console." In the *niphal* stem it means "be sorry, console oneself, repent"; and in the *piel* system, "comfort, console." There are a couple of related nouns, and a number of proper nouns, but they do not provide any additional information to the verb. See H. J. Stoebe, "נהם *nhm pi.* **to comfort**," in *Theological Lexicon of the Old Testament*, edited by Jenni and Westermann, II:734–739.

In the *piel, pual* and *hithpael* stems the meaning is "comfort, console." It has a wide array of applications; in the various contexts, the type of comfort given depending on the means of the comforter. For example, in

faithful, covenant love serve to bring him comfort in his affliction. The word "loyal love" is figurative, signifying what God's love does (a metonymy of cause); what God does out of his love will be to comfort him; and the demonstration of this love will be according to the promises of God. The word of God promises what God in his love will do for his people, both during affliction and in ending it.

Ending the affliction is the intent of the prayer for deliverance

---

Psalm 23:4 the LORD's rod and staff comfort the psalmist in the face of danger; in Genesis 37:35 the sons tried to comfort the grieving patriarch Jacob, but he refused to be comforted; in Ruth 2:13 Boaz comforts the Moabitess, but in this passage the comfort is closer to the idea of showing mercy to the foreigner; and in Isaiah 40:1 the remnant is commanded to comfort the rest of the nation in the exile, assuring them that the punishment for sin is complete. It can also refer to one's comforting oneself with the prospect of retribution, as in the case of Esau planning to kill his brother (Gen. 27:42). In this passage the comfort would not be seen in the presence of a comforting companion, but in the removal of a vexing one.

When God comforts, the connection with the idea of showing mercy is implied. For example, in Isaiah 12:1 when the LORD comforts he renews his grace relationship with those he had punished. Here in Psalm 119 the psalmist prays for God's loyal love to bring him comfort in his affliction, meaning sustaining him in the affliction and bringing it to its desired end.

In the *niphal* the word means "be sorry, feel pain, regret." It has the sense of being comforted as well, such as in the marriage of Isaac (Gen. 24:67). In most uses however it expresses the idea of repenting over evil or some calamity that has been planned or done, a sorrow or regret that leads to changing the actions (see Jon. 3:9, 10; 4:2). In Jonah and elsewhere the LORD is most often the subject in this category. It is a figurative use (an anthropomorphism); it appears that the LORD repented making man, or promising judgment, but the meaning of the expression is designed to communicate God's grief and sorrow in human terms. When God repents (or relents as some have it), there are always concrete consequences. This means that if the text says that God repented over the evil he said he would do, it signifies that he is gracious and merciful. Because he is gracious and merciful, voiced plans for disaster need not be his immediate plan, but serve to communicate his pain over the cause for the disaster. In Jonah when the people repented over their evil and changed, God is said to have repented over the evil (judgment) he had said he would do—but Jonah knew all along that God was not going to destroy them.

The word can also simply indicate changing; in Psalm 110:4 it refers to God's resolute determination: he has sworn and will not repent (Ps. 110:4).

(v. 77). Now the motivation in the prayer is God's compassion: "Let your tender mercies (רַחֲמֶיךָ; s.v. Ps. 25:6) come to me that I may live (וְאֶחְיֶה)." Here too the divine attribute is put for what God in his mercy does (another metonymy of cause). The psalmist wants God's compassion to be demonstrated in the way he will enable him to overcome the affliction and live. These attributes, then, refer to the basis for God's acting on his behalf. The basis for his prayer is that the law is his delight (שַׁעֲשֻׁעָי; s.v. Ps. 119:16); even in affliction the psalmist delights in God's law—the divine test has proven his faith, and so now it is time for relief.

D. In our faith we pray for righteousness to prevail over evil (78).

The other side of the prayer for relief is for God to deal with the agents of his affliction, the arrogant who were all too happy to inflict suffering on him. He prays that they be put to shame (יֵבֹשׁוּ; s.v. Ps. 31:1), meaning soundly destroyed. The immediate reason for their judgment is how they treated him: "they have wronged me with falsehood." The verb (עִוְּתוּנִי) means they have perverted his cause, or subverted him (see Lam. 3:36). This they did with falsehood; the word (שֶׁקֶר; s.v. Ps. 144:8) could mean they wronged him using falsehood, or they wronged him for no purpose.[159] In spite of their ongoing attempts to ruin him, however, he will continue to meditate (אָשִׂיחַ; s.v. Ps. 119:15) on God's precepts. He prays for comfort and deliverance, but in the meantime he remains faithful to the word of God.

E. In our faith we pray for other believers to unite with us in the faith (79).

In the last line of this section the psalmist prays for other believers to turn, or return, to him (יָשׁוּבוּ; s.v. Ps. 126:1). This prayer (although some translate it as a simple future, expressing his confidence) assumes that the righteous people have at least

---

159. The line simply reads: "for falsehood they have wronged me." The word "falsehood" is functioning adverbially. Either classification of the adverbial use is workable.

stood away from him in his affliction. It may be that they were deceived by the arrogant into thinking the psalmist was at fault. But when they see the deliverance of the LORD they will turn back. The colon then is expressing the result of the deliverance (it functions as a metonymy of effect): the prayer is that God will deliver him from the arrogant, but the effect of that prayer is stated here.

The parallel half in verse 79 is difficult due to the textual variant. Most of the support is for the reading "those who know," which would make the second half of the verse parallel to "those who fear you" in the first. A number of commentators and translations prefer the other reading, "that they may know," providing a purpose clause to the verse—they will turn to him for the purpose of learning God's testimonies. This would mean that the community would benefit from his deliverance—they all would learn more of God's will and ways.

III. The purpose of the plan of the creator is that we live blamelessly according to his word (80).

The stanza closes with a final prayer and a reason. The prayer is that his heart would be blameless (תָמִים; s.v. Ps. 7:8), that is, in all his decisions and affections he would be unwavering in his adherence to God's word. To be blameless would mean to be free from sin, forgiven and faultless. The reason for this petition is that he not be put to shame. He knows that if he is not loyal to God's word God might not deliver him. He may put his faith in the LORD's promises, but that faith must be demonstrated by a blameless walk.

Message and Application

In this stanza we are reminded that God has created us with a purpose, and that purpose is that we might understand and obey his commandments. And, as part of the process God afflicts us, perhaps allowing arrogant unbelievers to cause us great difficulty, so that we may demonstrate our loyalty to him and his word. In such times God's faithful love and tender mercy brings us comfort and restores our lives. In the end other believers will rejoice and renew their commitments. At the center of this stanza is the emphasis on the sovereignty of God, how he afflicts us in his faithfulness, and how we look to him to meet our needs. The expository idea could be worded this way: *Believing that their creator has tested them according to his word, the faithful may pray for God's love and compassion to bring them comfort in and deliverance from their affliction.*

The psalmist also prays for God to teach him wisdom and understanding concerning his ways. This too is a prayer of the Christian, to ask wisdom from God in the time of suffering (Jas. 1:5). In many ways the apostolic teaching provides much of the sought after understanding of the ways of God. We know that even though God created us with a plan (Col. 1:16), he tests our faithfulness with affliction (Jas. 1:12). In all our difficulties, however, we know that he has a greater purpose, so that when we endure the suffering by his love and compassion our faith is strengthened (Jas. 5:10–11). This brings us comfort in the midst of trials (2 Cor. 1:4); and if the suffering is engineered by adversaries of the faith, we know that in God's plan they will be put to shame. And so when we pray for deliverance from affliction, Scripture reminds us to pray for wisdom, for it is more important for us to learn what God desires of us through the affliction than merely to find relief.

כ *Kaph*

Overwhelmed but Faithful

Text and Textual Variants

כ 81 My soul faints[160] *with longing* for your salvation;
      I hope in your word (דְּבָר).[161]

כ 82 My eyes fail[162] *looking* for your oracle (אִמְרָה);

---

160. The MT simply has the verb כָּלְתָה, "fails" or "faints"; the Greek text used ἐκλείπει, "faints."
161. A few manuscripts and the Greek version have the plural, "words."
162. The MT has the same verb, now כָּלוּ.

asking,¹⁶³ "When will you comfort me?"
כ 83 For I have become like a wineskin in the smoke,¹⁶⁴
        yet I have not forgotten your statutes (חֹק).
כ 84 How long must your servant endure?¹⁶⁵
        When¹⁶⁶ will you do justice (מִשְׁפָּט) on those who persecute me?
כ 85 The insolent have dug pitfalls for me;¹⁶⁷
        they do not live according¹⁶⁸ to your law (תּוֹרָה).¹⁶⁹
כ 86 All your commandments (מִצְוָה) are sure;
        they persecute me with falsehood;¹⁷⁰ help me!
כ 87 They have almost made an end¹⁷¹ of me on earth,
        but I have not forsaken your precepts (פִּקּוּד).
כ 88 By your loyal love renew my life,
        that I may keep the testimony (עֵדוּת) of your mouth.

Exegetical Analysis

Summary

The psalmist admits that his soul fainted away in waiting for the great vindication from those who almost consumed him, but he did not forsake the law (119:81–88).

---

163. The MT has the frequent לֵאמֹר; Greek has λέγοντες, "saying."
164. The phrase in the Hebrew is כְּנֹאד בְּקִיטוֹר; the image is that of a wineskin that is blackened and shriveled and so useless by the smoke of the fire by which it is hung (Perowne, *Psalms* II:358). The Greek translation uses ἀσκὸς ἐν πάχνῃ "(as a) bottle / wineskin in the frost").
165. The line actually says, "How many are the days of your servant?" (כַּמָּה יְמֵי־עַבְדֶּךָ). The Greek renders it faithfully: πόσαι εἰσὶν αἱ ἡμέραι, "How many are the days (of your servant)?"
166. MT has מָתַי, "how long?"
167. The MT has כָּרוּ־לִי זֵדִים שִׁיחוֹת; the word order probably influenced the translation of the Greek: διηγήσαντό μοι παράνομοι ἀδολεσχίας, "transgressors told me lies / tales."
168. A few mss plus the Targum have "in" your law.
169. The Greek translation adds Κύριε, "O Lord."
170. The MT has שֶׁקֶר; the Greek uses ἀδίκως, "unjustly."
171. The verb is כִּלּוּנִי, repeating the word used in verses 81 and 82.

Outline

I. He admits that his soul almost fainted away waiting for God's word (81–83)

II. He asks God how long it will be before he is finally vindicated (84–86).

III. He testifies that while they almost consumed him he did not forsake God's law (87–88).

Commentary in Expository Form

I. True believers do not abandon hope even though they might feel overwhelmed waiting for the fulfillment of the promises (81–83).

In this stanza the suffering of the psalmist is the predominant theme, a suffering made worse because God seems to have abandoned his servant. He begins with the report that he wastes away (כָּלְתָה; s.v. Ps. 90:7), that is, his strength is failing, while he waits for deliverance (תְּשׁוּעָה; s.v. Ps. 3:2). His faith is expressed in terms of hoping for God's word (for "hope," יִחָלְתִּי, s.v. Ps. 31:24). He believes in God's word and all that it promises, but with the use of this term he reveals that there is a good deal of tension and uneasiness as he waits for the LORD.

The emphasis on his failing strength is repeated in verse 82, now with reference to his eyes: "my eyes fail" (כָּלוּ). The eyes reflect his weariness in watching for a sign of God's answer; so under a prolonged strain of waiting, the psalmist acknowledges that he is worn out. The word he is looking for now is the oracle, God's promise to protect and bless his people—he is waiting for God's promises to be fulfilled. To put it another way, he asks the LORD, "When will you comfort me?" (תְּנַחֲמֵנִי; s.v. Ps. 119:76). Here begins a series of interrogatives that express the psalmist's suffering and frustration. This first one asks when God will comfort him. It is when God delivers him from his oppressors and revives his life that he will feel comforted. Similarly, the faithful remnant was called on to comfort the exiled nation, announcing that their sins were forgiven and the war was over (Isa. 40:1–2). As long as this psalmist suffers at the hands of the wicked, he will not sense all of God's comfort; when God ends the persecution and sets his servant free, then he will be truly comforted.

He further describes his lamentable condition with a comparison (a simile): he is like a wineskin in the smoke.[172] We are not absolutely sure of the meaning of this comparison. The image may be that of a wineskin hung up by the fire that becomes shriveled, blackened and therefore unpleasant and practically useless. The point of the figure would be that he himself has become emaciated, disfigured, and useless by his suffering and sorrow; but he has not forgotten the statutes of the LORD. He has remembered them, meaning, he has complied with them. Here is faith persevering in the midst of persecution that God is permitting.

II. True believers remain loyal as they pray for vindication from the oppression of the arrogant and godless enemies (84–87).

The suffering psalmist asks another question; but his questions are essentially laments (so rhetorical questions). "How long must your servant endure?" means "Your servant (I) has been enduring long enough." The first half of the verse laments his prolonged endurance. The second is concerned with the cause of his condition "When will you execute justice on those who persecute me?" People were openly persecuting him, which was the cause of his horrible condition; but if God were to execute justice on them, meaning destroy them for their evil activities, the psalmist would no longer feel that he was fading away. Instead, his life would be renewed.

But in the meantime, the persecution of the arrogant enemies (s.v. Ps. 119:21) was taking a vicious turn: they were hunting him down like an animal. The idea of their digging pits signifies laying some sort of trap for him. Their arrogance is evidenced in the fact that they do nothing in compliance with God's word. They completely ignore it and have no tolerance for those who seek to live by it.

---

172. The fact that some versions used "frost" and some "smoke" shows that there was a good deal of uncertainty over the description.

All the psalmist can do is rely fully on God's commandments which he knows to be reliable (אֱמוּנָה; s.v Ps. 15:2). This means that all the commandments are trustworthy when they promise life will be better for those who live according to God's laws. In contrast to the *truthfulness* of all God has said, the psalmist notes that his enemies persecute him *falsely* (שֶׁקֶר; s.v. Psalm 144:8). Because they persecute him for no purpose, or with lies, he can but cry for God to do for him what he cannot do for himself: "help me" (עָזְרֵנִי; s.v. Ps. 46:1).

To conclude his description of his plight he returns to the key word of verses 81 and 82, only now he uses the *piel* form of the verb: "they have almost made an end of me" (כִּלּוּנִי). The plain meaning is that he is almost dead—finished, on this earth. However, to the very end if need be, he affirms his faith: "I have not forsaken your precepts" (note the contrast in Jer. 16:10 where the LORD accused the people of this very thing).

III. True believers pray to be preserved alive in order that they may keep the covenant (88).

Finally, the afflicted psalmist prays for God to renew his life. The verb (חַיֵּנִי) could mean "restore me (my life)" or "preserve me (my life)" or "revive me." In this passage it is more than a prayer for preservation or survival; he wants to come out of this persecution victoriously so he can enjoy all aspects of living. The translation should then be: "renew my life"; and the basis for this petition is God's loyal love (חֶסֶד; s.v. Ps. 23:6). It is an appeal to God to act in his faithful covenant love on behalf of his people. The purpose of the petition is likewise connected to the covenant: "that I may keep the testimony of your mouth." The testimony refers to all of God's instructions, the whole covenant law, which came by direct revelation from God. The psalmist wants to be revived, so that he would be able to keep the covenant fully, without weakness, suffering and distractions due to constant persecution.

Message and Application

This stanza provides us with a meditation on the problem of serious suffering due to the persecution of wicked people. The suffering is serious because the psalmist is almost dead—his strength and vitality are almost gone. The difficulty is worsened in God's delay to save him. In the midst of it all, the suffering psalmist continues to cry out to God to deliver him and renew his life so that he might live out the law of God more readily. The meditation is applicable to believers at all time; we may word the principle this way: *Even though believers feel overwhelmed by the oppression of the world, they must remain faithful to the covenant but they may also pray for vindication.*

Jesus told his followers, including us, that he was sending them out as sheep among wolves (Matt. 10:16); and then by his own suffering at the hands of his enemies, he left us an example of how to suffer in this life for the glory of God (1 Pet. 3:13–18). And yet the suffering is still real, and painful. The apostle Paul explained it in words that are similar to many laments, that we groan inwardly, waiting for the day of redemption to come (Rom. 8:23). Since we do not know exactly how to pray, the Spirit of God intercedes with groaning on our behalf (Rom. 8:26); and like the psalmist we may appeal to the love of God (Rom. 8:38–39) when we pray for deliverance from our afflictions.

ל *Lamed*

Secure in the Sure Word of God

Text and Textual Variants

    ל 89 Forever,[173] O LORD,
                  is your word (דְּבָר) firmly fixed[174] in the heavens.
    ל 90 Your faithfulness[175] *endures* to all generations;[176]

---

[173]. The Greek version forms two sentences: "Forever are you, O Lord; your word endures in the sky." The Syriac adds the 2msg pronoun "you" here.

[174]. The MT has נִצָּב, "fixed, settled, firmly standing"; the Greek simply has διαμένει, "endures / abides."

[175]. For אֱמוּנָה the Greek translation uses ἀλήθεια, "truth."

[176]. Literally, "to generation and generation."

The Word of the LORD and the Life of Faith

ל   you have established the earth, and it stands fast.[177]

ל 91 According to your decisions[178] (מִשְׁפָּט) they stand fast[179] *unto*[180] this day,
for all things[181] are your servants.[182]

ל 92 Unless your law (תּוֹרָה) had been my delight,[183]
I would have perished in my affliction.

ל 93 I will never forget your precepts (פִּקּוּד),
for by them you have preserved my life.[184]

ל 94 Yours I am; save me,
for I have sought your precepts (פִּקּוּד).

ל 95 The wicked wait for me to destroy me,
but your statutes (עֵדוּת) I consider.

ל 96 I see an end to all perfection,
but your commands[185] (מִצְוָה) are completely boundless.

Exegetical Analysis

Summary

The psalmist declares that although the wicked tried to afflict

---

177. The form is וַתַּעֲמֹד, but the Syriac version reads it as a *hiphil* with a suffix, "and you caused it to stand."
178. לְמִשְׁפָּטֶיךָ has the sense of "with reference to your ordinances." The Greek and Jerome have the singular form of the noun; the word is not in the Syriac.
179. The subject of עָמְדוּ is probably the heaven and the earth, i.e., what God created (v. 90). The Greek version has "the day" as the subject, and the verb singular to go with it. Others suggest "decisions" is the subject.
180. The MT simply has הַיּוֹם; Jerome has the preposition "unto (the / this day)." The Greek translation makes this the subject: τῇ διατάξει σου διαμένει ἡ ἡμέρα, "by your arrangement the day continues."
181. MT הַכֹּל means "the whole," everything—the universe and everything in it (Perowne, *Psalms*, II:359).
182. Instead of a noun Jerome has the verb, "they serve you."
183. The Greek version again has "meditation" instead of "delight."
184. The form in the MT is חִיִּיתָנִי, but the Syriac reads "my life." The Greek version adds κύριε, "Lord."
185. The form in the text is singular, as it is in the Greek version; but the plural may be intended if this is to harmonize with other uses in the psalm.

him, God brought him out of it because the word is settled in heaven (119:89–96).

Outline

I. He declares triumphantly that the word is settled in heaven and is attested by God's faithfulness (89–91).
II. He states that his delight in the law enabled him to have the victory because the wicked attempted to destroy him (92–95).
III. He concludes that the law is exceedingly broad (96).

Commentary in Expository Form

I. God's word is eternally established and faithfully displayed in his sovereignty over creation (89–91).

In this stanza the focus is on the word of the LORD, its nature and its trustworthiness. The first assertion of the meditation is that it is eternal: God's word is firmly fixed forever. We do not know what the psalmist had in mind with this declaration, but taking it at face value it means that God's word is eternal (לְעוֹלָם; s.v. Ps. 61:4); it was preexistent before given to humans. The term (דָּבָר) would here refer to the full expression of God's nature, purpose and will, and subsequently apply to the revealed and written word.[186] The New Testament similarly presents this in the light of the incarnation: "In *the* beginning was the word, and the word was with God, and the word was God" (John 1:1–2).

Here God's word is said to be firmly established (נִצָּב) in the heavens. God created everything by his word, and once creation was fixed, God's word was also established. The whole creation is evidence of God's powerful, eternal word.

The second verse in the stanza affirms that God is eternally faithful (s.v. Ps. 15:2). If God is constant in his works through his creative word, then he is faithful in his revealed word. God's faithfulness, that is, his dependability to do what he says he will do, lasts forever. This constancy is reiterated in the last colon of verse 90: "You have established (כּוֹנַנְתָּ; s.v. Ps. 93:1) the earth,

---

186. Anderson, *Psalms 73–150*, p. 831; see also Deut. 4:2.

and it stands fast." God's work is dependable, because God is dependable; and the permanence of the earth, which he created, is an emblem and guarantee of his faithfulness.[187]

The emphasis on creation's standing is repeated in verse 91. "They stand" probably is to be interpreted with the heavens and the earth as the subject because the emphasis is on the established creation. The verb "stand" (< עָמַד) emphasizes that what God created is fixed and permanent; it may also have the connotation of standing by to do the will of the sovereign, as attendants might present themselves before their king (Gen. 43:15) with the sense of becoming servants to a lord (1 Sam 16:22). This is confirmed in the second colon: "for all things are your servants." All of creation exists because of obedience to God's word; all of creation, therefore, exists to do his will. As Ruskin put it so elegantly, "From the ministering of the Archangel to the labour of the insect, from the poising of the planets to the gravitation of a grain of dust, the power and glory of all creatures, and all matter, consists in their *obedience*, not their freedom."[188]

II. Delight in obeying God's word brings preservation from the wicked who would destroy the faithful (92–95).

In the next section the psalmist brings this meditation to bear on his affliction. He affirms that his relationship to the LORD and delight in his word sustained him when people sought to destroy him. The point is that if God's word created and controls everything, then living in harmony with that word enables the believer to not only survive but overcome opposition.

In verse 92 he states clearly that he would have perished in his affliction had it not been for his delight in the law of the LORD. The word "delight" signifies also that he meditated in the word ("delight" being a metonymy, either of cause or adjunct; see also Ps. 1:2). This inspired further loyalty to God: "I will never forget your precepts." The verb "forget" would mean that he did not study

---
187. Kirkpatrick, *Psalms*, p. 719.
188. From *The Two Paths*, Lecture V, cited from another source by Kirkpatrick, *Psalms*, p. 719.

and apply the word of God to his life—but he will not forget. It is like the verb "remember," which usually means to act on what is remembered. The psalmist determines that he will not forget—he will remember and do what God's laws say. The reason for this is that they are the words of life: "by them you preserved my life" (חִיִּיתָנִי, the *piel* form meaning either "preserve life," or "renew life" or "revive"—it is not always easy to know which nuance to use). But in this meditation he is still in difficulty and praying for God to save him. We may say that he has been sustained in the midst of the persecution, but his life has not been fully restored.

The word that he received from God and sustained him in life is in itself a confirmation of the covenant relationship he has with God. Therefore, he states, "I am yours!" God redeemed Israel from bondage and gave them his law; subsequent believers are also recipients of his word because they too belong to the covenant. Because of his consciousness that he belongs to God, the psalmist has confidence to pray for deliverance.[189] The prayer, "Save me" (הוֹשִׁיעֵנִי; s.v. Ps. 3:2), is a prayer to be delivered from the people who were trying to destroy him. The psalmist then adds, "for I have sought your precepts," strengthening the statement of faith that he belongs to God with the statement of his loyalty to his covenant God.

In verse 95 he reiterates his affliction: proud, scornful, slanderous enemies wait[190] for the opportunity to destroy him.[191] They were almost succeeding, according to verse 92. But during this time of trouble the psalmist was considering (אֶתְבּוֹנָן; s.v. Ps. 49:3) God's statutes. This verb would have the connotation of trying to understand them and their relevance to his life. On the outside the wicked were lying in wait to destroy him, but he was discerning and faithfully following God's revealed plan for him.

III. In contrast to the limitations of earthly things God's word is boundless (96).

The last verse is the summary statement of this stanza. On

---

189. Briggs, *Psalms*, II:430.
190. Here the word "wait" (קִוּוּ) has a negative connotation, lying in wait to destroy the faithful (s.v. Ps. 25:3).
191. Briggs, *Psalms*, II:430.

the surface it seems unclear, but on further reflection the point is clear. He says, "I see an end to all perfection." The word "end" (קֵץ) means that there is a limit; and the word "perfection" (a word occurring only here, תִכְלָה; s.v. Ps. 90:7), possibly meaning "completeness," refers to the completion of all things. What he is saying is that all things, however complete they are, however perfected, have their limit—they all come to an eventual end.[192] On the other hand, the commands of God are not limited but boundless (spacious, רְחָבָה). All earthly perfection is limited—God's word is not. His commands have no limits, because his word is eternal and established.

Message and Application

The meditation reminds us of the eternality, immutability, and comprehensiveness of God's law. Moreover, for believers enduring persecution and suffering, this word of God has provided them with comfort and security. The expository idea might be stated: *There is security for those who love and live according to God's eternally established, faithful and boundless decrees.*

Two passages in the New Testament speak to these points more fully. In John 1:1–3 we have the revelation of the divine Word who created everything, a Word that was preexistent, powerful, and in time revelatory. This Word confirmed that he gave his disciples the word that the Father had given him (John 17:8), a word that would provide their safety and sanctity (vv. 11–17). Because the world that was created by the word has been established, the word that has been revealed to us from the creator is trustworthy. And so time and time again believers in danger or affliction return to the word of God to renew their hope and their commitment.

---

192. Briggs, *Psalms*, II:430.

מ *Mem*

The Superiority of God's Word over Earthly Wisdom

Text and Textual Variants

מ 97 Oh, how I love your law! (תּוֹרָה)[193]
       It is my meditation all day long.
מ 98 Your commands (מִצְוָה)[194] make me wiser[195] than my enemies,
       they[196] are mine forever.
מ 99 I have more insight than all my teachers,
       for your testimonies (עֵדוּת)[197] are my meditation.
מ 100 I understand more than the elders,
       for I have securely guarded[198] your precepts (פִּקּוּד).
מ 101 I have refrained my feet from every evil path

---

193. The Greek version adds κύριε, "O Lord."
194. The word in the MT is a plural but written defectively, מִצְוֹתֶךָ; and so the Greek version has it as a singular. Allen suggests that it be repointed in the text to a singular as well, in view of the verb's being singular, and the singular pronoun "it" that follows—considerations that no doubt led the translators of the Greek version to assume the consonants represented the singular form (*Psalms 101–150*, p. 137).
195. The MT has a singular verb תְּחַכְּמֵנִי, taken here as the 3fsg verb with "command(s)" as the subject. For the use of a singular verb with the plural noun, see GKC Par. 143, 3. The versions take the noun as a singular (as does one Hebrew manuscript), and the verb as the 2msg form (the Greek has ἐσόφισάς με, "you made me wiser [than my enemies] regarding your command)." Then, the following pronoun "it" (הִיא) would refer to the command. Perowne explains that the singular pronoun "it" could mean that the law as whole is meant—but he allows that the noun may be pointed incorrectly as a plural (*Psalms*, II:368). The use of the singular pronoun may in fact be a way of showing the unity of God's word (Kirkpatrick, Psalms, p. 720). The meaning of the line may not be significantly different with each reading: the commands or command of God make him wiser, or, God makes him wiser by the commands.
196. The pronoun is the singular "it," but probably refers to all God's commands, or, Scripture in general.
197. The Syriac has the singular, "your testimony."
198. For Hebrew נָצַר, "keep, treasure," the Greek translation again uses "sought out."

The Word of the LORD and the Life of Faith

              that I might keep your word (דָּבָר).[199]
מ 102 I have not turned aside from your decisions (מִשְׁפָּט), for you have taught me.
מ 103 How sweet is your oracle[200] (אִמְרָה) to my taste,[201] more than honey to my mouth.[202]
מ 104 I get understanding from your precepts (פִּקּוּד); therefore I hate every false[203] path.

Exegetical Analysis

Summary

The psalmist meditates on the sweet word of God that brings him more understanding than the learned of the world and the aged (119:97–104).

Outline

I. He declares his love and everlasting devotion to the law which brings him understanding and wisdom more than the aged teachers (97–100).
II. He testifies that he has kept himself pure (101–102).
III. He extols the precepts of God as having a pleasant taste (103–104).

Commentary in Expository Form

With this stanza we have a change: there are no petitions, only the psalmist's statements concerning his wisdom and

---

199. Many manuscripts and the versions have "your words."
200. Here the form in the text is singular, but a few manuscripts, the Greek, Syriac, and Targum, all have the plural to harmonize with the plural verb. Allen suggests it be changed accordingly to the plural (p. 137). If the singular is retained, it can be explained as representing all the oracles—the sense would be plural.
201. The MT has חִכִּי, literally "my palate"; the Greek has λάρυγγί, "throat."
202. The Greek version adds καὶ κηρίον, "and the honeycomb," probably influenced by Psalm 19:10.
203. The word is שֶׁקֶר; the Greek version has a general translation, ἀδικίας, "injustice."

discernment gained from divine revelation. These statements are partly wisdom and partly confessions. At first glance they might sound presumptuous but taken in context, affirm what everyone who is spiritual ought to be able to affirm.

I. Those who are spiritual love the word because it has brought them more wisdom and understanding than the world could ever offer (97–100).

The main theme of this stanza unfolds in the first few verses. The psalmist exclaims how he loves divine instruction, a love that speaks of devotion and commitment (אָהַבְתִּי; s.v. Ps. 11:7; see also Ps. 119:113 and 163). This love for God's law prompts him to meditate in it all day long (see Ps. 1:2), meaning that he reads it, interprets it, and prayerfully applies it to his life.

The primary benefit of such deep study in God's word is that it brings him a wisdom that is superior to any earthly knowledge. In verse 98 he begins by stating that God's commands make him wiser (תְּחַכְּמֵנִי; s.v. Ps. 19:7) than his enemies. This wisdom is from above; it is characterized by righteousness, justice, and equity; and begins with the fear of the LORD. It opens up a way of living skillfully in a fallen world, helping people to avoid the dangers and pitfalls of life. Living by God's command, i.e., the law, has made the psalmist wiser than his enemies, for by rejecting the law of God they have proven to be fools. The psalmist is never without the instructions of God—they are his everlasting possession.

The study of God's word not only makes him wiser than his enemies but also gives him more insight (הִשְׂכַּלְתִּי; s.v. Ps. 36:4) than all his teachers! The psalmist's words in this verse and the next seem at first to be presumptuous. Goldingay wonders if the meaning is that these teachers are people who did not base their instruction on the law of God.[204] Even though the text does not say this, he is probably correct because the psalm is extolling the value of the law. And besides, there no doubt were teachers who did base their teachings on God's word. The psalmist is not claiming to have more insight than every teacher but that the

---

204. *Psalms 90–150*, p. 418.

true source of wisdom and spiritual insight is divine revelation; and any instruction in spiritual and ethical matters, as well as in basic issues of life not based on God's law, is inferior. He is rightly acknowledging that God is the great teacher, and that his law is superior to all other sources of wisdom and knowledge.[205] Therefore, knowledge alone is not enough; faith in God's word and the commitment to obey it is what brings spiritual insight and wisdom.

The psalmist adds that he has more understanding (אֶתְבּוֹנָן; s.v. Ps. 49:3) than the elders. Again, it is the word of God that gives such prudence (Deut. 4:6) and not traditional wisdom. The reference here is probably not to the qualified, godly elders of the community, but simply to "old men" (as Briggs translates it). These folks base their decisions on lifelong experiences, but true prudence comes from using the word of the LORD in all decisions. Here too the point is that obedience to the law of the LORD is better than the knowledge of the world. Proverbs tells us that the beginning of proper knowledge is the fear of the LORD (1:7).

The psalmist claims to be wiser than his enemies, have more insight than his teachers, and understand more than the old men. The repeated reason for this is his meditation on and obedience to the law of the LORD. He is never without it. It is an integral part of his thinking.

II. Those who are spiritual avoid the evil ways of the world because God has taught them by his word (101–102).

The result of this meditation in God's word, and the evidence of his wisdom and understanding, is an obedient life. Very simply stated, by God's word he has learned to avoid evil. He first states that he has refrained his feet from every evil path (i.e., he has kept himself from entering into ways that are evil). The purpose of this avoidance of evil ways is obedience to God's word. He then adds that he has not turned aside from God's decisions (i.e., the

---

205. Briggs, *Psalms*, II:430. This passage also provides a helpful complement to Jeremiah 9:23–24, which tells people not to glory in their wisdom or strength, but to glory in the fact that they know and understand God.

decisions he makes in life conform to the decisions of God in the word). The reason that he stays on the right path and chooses to do the right things is that God has taught him to do so. "You have taught me" (הוֹרֵתָנִי; s.v. Ps. 1:2) is etymologically related to the noun "law" (תּוֹרָה). His instruction in life comes from God through his word.

III. Those who are spiritual find God's word pleasing because it brings them understanding to avoid false ways (103–104).

For the psalmist this devotion to the word of the LORD is no fixed duty. It is his delight. He states in verse 103, "How sweet (מַה־נִּמְלְצוּ) are your oracles to my taste, more than honey to my mouth." This image was first introduced in Psalm 19:10; it describes the word of the LORD as desirable and enjoyable—what honey was to his palate, God's oracles were to his spirit. And the pleasure derived from meditation in God's word translated into spiritual understanding (אֶתְבּוֹנָן again) that caused him to spurn ("I hate," שָׂנֵאתִי; s.v. Ps. 139:21) every false path. By "false" (שֶׁקֶר; s.v. Ps. 144:8) he means any course of action that is wrong or unprofitable—every path that leads away from the will of God is false. Similarly, Proverbs reminds us that one of the results of fearing the LORD is to hate evil (8:13).

Message and Application

This meditation reminds us that true wisdom and understanding comes from the knowledge and study of the word of God and will be displayed in a life of obedience to God. Those who cultivate wisdom and understanding from God's instruction will be wiser than those who gain their knowledge and insights from what may be called conventional wisdom. It is often the sad case that even those entrusted to teach the word of God fail to gain spiritual wisdom and understanding from it (see Mal. 2:1–9). In the secular world, teachers of subjects like ethics and qualities like integrity, often approach the subject from pragmatic or culturally-oriented theories, frequently nullifying holy Scripture. Faithful believers in the LORD, however, live according to a higher standard, and the wisdom they gain from the word of God is superior and eternal. They may learn much from secular sources, but it is the divine instruction that will teach them how to please God. Paul says that the wisdom of the world does not know God; and even the foolishness of God is wiser than human wisdom, and the weakness of God is stronger than human strength. But God takes the foolish things of the world and makes them wise, so that they may confound those who think they are wise. Therefore, all our boasting should be in the Lord (1 Cor. 1:20–31). Paul adds that none of the rulers of the world had Godly wisdom, for if they had they would not have crucified the Lord (2:8). Similarly, the psalmist knows that godly wisdom was superior to the worldly wisdom of the wicked who were trying to destroy him.

The apostles also emphasize that true Christians have an anointing by the Spirit so that they do not need a teacher (1 John 2:27). God is the teacher; his word is what is taught. It brings life, understanding, and discernment (Heb. 4:12–13; and 5:11–15). The message is clear from both testaments: *Meditation in the word of God and commitment to obey it lead to wisdom and understanding that is superior to what the world has to offer.* A simple knowledge of the Bible is not sufficient however; the believer must be devoted to the word, meditate on it daily, and obey it faithfully.

נ *Nun*

Light for the Journey through a Darkened World

Text and Textual Variants

נ 105 Your word (דְּבָר)[206] is a lamp to my foot[207]
and a light for my path.[208]

---

206. Many manuscripts have the plural "your words." Some Greek manuscripts have νόμος, "law."
207. The MT has "foot"; one manuscript, the Greek, and Syriac have "feet."
208. The Greek and Syriac versions have "paths."

| | 106 | I have taken an oath and am resolved in it,[209]
| | | to keep your righteous decisions (מִשְׁפָּט).
| | 107 | I have been very greatly afflicted;
| | | O LORD, revive me according to your word (דָּבָר).
| | 108 | Be pleased, O LORD, with the freewill offerings of my mouth,
| | | and teach me your decisions (מִשְׁפָּט).
| | 109 | My life is constantly in my hand,[210]
| | | yet I have not forgotten your law (תּוֹרָה).
| | 110 | The wicked have set a snare for me,
| | | but I have not wandered from your precepts (פִּקּוּד).
| | 111 | I have inherited your statutes (עֵדוּת).
| | | for they are the joy of my heart.
| | 112 | I have inclined my heart to keep your statutes (חֹק);
| | | the reward is everlasting.[211]

Exegetical Analysis

Summary

The psalmist recognizes that the law is the light for his path and therefore he will joyfully follow it through the present affliction (119:105–112).

---

209. MT has וָאֲקַיֵּמָה, "and I am resolved." The Greek version translates this with ἔστησα, "determined."
210. The line in the MT is: נַפְשִׁי בְכַפִּי תָמִיד, "my life is in my hand continually." This is probably also the reading in the Greek version, but some Greek manuscripts have ἡ ψυχή ἐν ταῖς χερσί σου δια παντός, "my soul / life is constantly in your hands."
211. The word עֵקֶב can mean "end" or "reward (outcome)." Some translations prefer the former and read the colon "for ever (even unto) the end." But the meaning of "reward" may be the intended meaning. The Greek version has δι' ἀντάμειψιν, "(I inclined my heart to perform your statutes forever) on account of an exchange in return," i.e., for the sake of a return or recompense. But in the MT "forever" goes with the word, and so "reward is forever."

Outline
 I. He recognizes that the law is his light and vows to obey it (105–106).
 II. He laments his present affliction that ensnares him and calls for divine help (107–110).
 III. He joyfully will follow God's testimonies (111–112).

Commentary in Expository Form

This section is filled with praise for the law of the LORD. But the psalmist's complaints are interwoven with the praise. Allen says that these complaints were introduced in this way to enhance the psalmist's devotion to the word of God.[212]

I. Believers resolve to keep God's word because it provides guidance and understanding (105–106).

The distinctive motif of this psalm is stated in the first verse: "Your word is a lamp to my foot, and a light for my path." As Kirkpatrick puts it, the psalmist knows the value of God's law as the guide of his life and resolves to keep it.[213] The comparison of the word of God to a "light" and a "lamp" (metaphors) indicates that divine revelation brings spiritual guidance for the faithful who live according to it. The figures of "foot" and "step" (implied comparisons) refer to what Scripture elsewhere calls the believer's walk, the course of actions in life. The image of light in the Bible also has the connotation of joy and happiness in life. On the other side, the world is enveloped in darkness because of the presence of evil and what it produces. Kidner stresses that the concern here is for truth for moral choices and not secular guidance as in the choice of a career—although that on occasion may be involved. He suggests that the temptation of Christ Jesus (Matt. 4) is a fitting illustration of light from the word in a place of snares.[214]

Because God's word is a light, the psalmist has taken an oath

---

212. *Psalms 101–150*, p. 143.
213. *Psalms*, p. 721.
214. *Psalms*, II:427.

to obey it. The first part of verse 106 is stated strongly: "I have taken an oath (נִשְׁבַּעְתִּי) and am resolved (וָאֲקַיֵּמָה; s.v. Ps. 3:1)." It essentially says "I have sworn and ratified it"; the two verbs could be taken together to express one idea emphatically: "I have undertaken a solemn oath." The reference may be to an oath of loyalty to the covenant taken at the entrance to the sanctuary, or as part of a renewal ceremony. Since there is no clear statement concerning this, it is equally possible that the psalmist made such a commitment on a different occasion. The important part of the oath is what he swore to do: "to keep your righteous decisions." These "decisions," another word for the laws of God, were rulings that would guide him in right choices. He took an oath to live according to the laws of God. It is a foundational part of a believer's life to make a binding commitment to obey the Lord.

II. Believers maintain their loyalty to God's word as they pray for deliverance from constant dangers (107–110).

In the next four verses the psalmist speaks of his difficulty while reiterating his dependence on God's laws. He first makes the general statement that he has been greatly afflicted (v. 107). Perhaps his zeal to live according to God's laws has exposed him to this persecution. He does say in verse 109, "My life is constantly in my hand." The expression refers to the great risk and peril he has brought on himself by his life of faith. Kirkpatrick explains that a treasure carried in hand is not concealed but is easily snatched.[215] This individual has not concealed his faith, but lived openly in accordance with God's laws. In verse 110 he clarifies that wicked people have set a trap for him, which explains the hazards he faced by living faithfully. The trap is a bird trap (פַּח), the kind that would spring up and capture the prey (see Amos 3:5). These people had been trying to find ways to ruin the psalmist, or at least his integrity.

However, they have not been successful. He attests that he has not forgotten God's law, meaning that he has remained consciously obedient to it (v. 109). The wicked with all their devices

---

215. Kirkpatrick, p. 722.

have not succeeded in making him wander from God's precepts (v. 110). The imagery of wandering away from the path signifies falling into sinful disobedience, and in this psalm, not following the light for the pathway.

And yet, his spiritual success is a constant struggle. Because he has been seriously afflicted, meaning he has suffered greatly, he prays for God to revive his life (v. 107). Every affliction brings him nearer to death, as verses 81–88 made clear; and so he prays for his life to be revived and renewed.

With his prayers the psalmist brought freewill offerings to the LORD, which here are called freewill offerings of his mouth (v. 108). This is clearly a reference to praises, but such praises if offered in the sanctuary were to be accompanied with an offering, hence, "the sacrifice of praise" (Ps. 50:14; Heb. 13:15). His prayer is that God would be pleased with them (רְצֵה־נָא; s.v. Ps. 30:5), that is, accept them (v. 108). If God accepts his praise, God will be favorably disposed toward answering his prayer for renewal (see Ps. 20:3). The psalmist does not simply want a deliverance from his affliction; he wants to know the LORD better; and so he also prays, "teach me (לַמְּדֵנִי) your decisions" (v. 108). This is part of what it means to walk in the light, for following the LORD's guidance obediently will open up other areas that need to be addressed as well.

III. Believers keep their commitment to obey God's word that they have received because it brings joy (111–112).

The last two verses of this meditation record some of the blessings that come from living a life committed to obeying the LORD. The psalmist says that he has inherited God's testimony or covenant forever. The inheritance is God's holy word, and the everlasting life of holiness that it brings (Briggs, II:431). This inheritance is more sure than the inheritance of the land of Canaan; for the word of the LORD is eternal and always dependable. The covenant is a delightful inheritance—it brings salvation and joy to the believer. Obedience to God's word was never seen as a drudgery or fixed duty by the devout; to them it was a life of joy and blessing. The psalmist restates his commitment by saying "I have inclined my heart" to keep God's statutes (v. 112). He has determined to do it; and the reward is never ending. Keeping the law is reward in itself, because it brings blessings to the faithful, both now and in the world to come.

Message and Application

All this is true for the New Testament believer as well, but with the clarification that we have more light because we have the full revelation from God. John says that if we walk in the light, as God is in the light, then we have fellowship with one another, and the blood of Jesus, his Son, purifies us from every sin (1 John 1:7). The symbol of light has several meanings in Scripture, including holiness and truth. The instruction to walk in the light surely includes the idea of living in obedience to the truth, to the word of God. It is the word of God, at least the law as far as the psalmist was concerned, that is a light to our way. Such divine illumination is certainly needed in a world where the wicked attempt to ruin the righteous. This kind of spiritual conflict can leave the saints drained and discouraged; but God can revive them again and teach them what they should do. Walking in the light is more than obedience; it is a life of faith in God's word empowered by prayer and devotion. This calls for a total commitment to the way of the LORD, a way that is filled with joy and blessing. The theme of the meditation may be worded in this expository statement: *Because God's word brings understanding and joy in a world fraught with dangers, the people of God must keep their commitment to live by it.*

ס *Samek*

Hope in God's Word and not the Words of Untrustworthy Unbelievers

Text and Textual Variants

    ס 113   The double-minded[216] I hate,
                  but your law (תּוֹרָה) I love.

---

216. The MT has סֵעֲפִים; the Greek version uses the general word Παρανόμους, "transgressors of the law."

ס 114 You are my hiding place and my shield;[217]
     I hope in your word (דְּבָר),[218]
ס 115 Depart from me, you evil-doers,
     that I may keep[219] the commandments (מִצְוָה) of my God.
ס 116 Uphold me according to[220] your oracle (אִמְרָה), that I may live,[221]
     and let me not be ashamed of my hope.
ס 117 Hold me up, and I shall be saved
     and shall have regard[222] for your statutes (חֹק) continually.
ס 118 You spurn all who wander from your statutes (חֹק),
     for their deceit[223] is falsehood.
ס 119 *Like* dross[224] you remove[225] all the wicked of the earth,

---

217. The Greek version translates סִתְרִי, "my hiding place," as βοηθός μου, "my helper," and מָגִנִּי, "my shield," as ἀντιλήμπτωρ μου, "my supporter."
218. Some Greek manuscripts have plural, "words."
219. The verb means "keep, treasure, preserve"; the Greek version again renders it "examine."
220. Instead of the preposition כְּ (supported by the Greek version), many manuscripts have בְּ (see also Aquila, the Syriac, and Targum).
221. The MT has וְאֶחְיֶה, "that (and) I may live"; Greek manuscripts have either ζῆσόν με, "quicken me," or ζήσομαι, "I shall live."
222. The MT form is וְאֶשְׁעָה. The Greek (followed by the Syriac, Targum, and Jerome) has καὶ μελετήσω, "and shall meditate." The editors of BHS suggest this reflects וְאֶשְׁתַּעֲשַׁע.
223. The form תַּרְמִיתָם is "cunning, deceit"; the Greek version has τὸ ἐνθύμημα αὐτῶν, "their notion" or "inward thought." Some suggest that the Greek version may have read תַּרְעִיתָם, "thought" or "purpose"; but it is also possible that the word in the MT was interpreted more loosely, given the range of usage for this Greek word in the translation. Allen concludes that a different *Vorlage* for the Greek version is unlikely *(Psalms 101–150,* p. 138). See also Theodotion and Quinta (the Syriac and Jerome).
224. The MT begins the verse with סִגִים, "dross." The Greek version has παραβαίνοντας, "sinners" (= סָגִים).
225. The word הִשְׁבַּתָּ in the text means "you cause to cease" (< שָׁבַת). A few manuscripts, Aquila, Symmachus and Jerome have "you reckon," reflecting חָשַׁבְתָּ, "you reckon." The Greek version and 11Q Psa has "I reckoned"—ἐλογισάμην, "I have reckoned (all the wicked of the earth as sinners)," which would represent חָשַׁבְתִּי. Allen concludes that while a reading "you

therefore I love your testimonies (עֵדוֹת).²²⁶

ס 120 My flesh trembles²²⁷ for terror of you,
and I am afraid because of your decisions (מִשְׁפָּט).

Exegetical Analysis

Summary

The psalmist announces his hatred for double-minded evildoers and acknowledges that God, in whom he trusts for salvation, removes the wicked of the earth by his judgments (119:113–120).

Outline

I. He states his hatred of double-mindedness and that his refuge is in the word (113–114).
II. He demands the wicked to leave him (115).
III. He prays that God would uphold him with salvation and remove the wicked of the earth (116–119).
IV. He trembles at the judgments of God (120).

Commentary in Expository Form

I. Believers find security and hope in God's word and not in the inconsistency of the words of people (113–114).

The first verse of this meditation unveils its theme, a contrast between those who are dedicated to God's word and those who are double-minded. In the first colon the psalmist declares that he hates (שָׂנֵאתִי; s.v. Ps. 139:21) the double-minded. This word "double-minded" (סֵעֲפִים) occurs only here; but it describes people who are fickle, who cannot decide what they believe. It can be illustrated with 1 Kings 18:21 where the prophet Elijah

---

reckon" (not "I reckon") makes good sense, the reading in the MT reinforces verse 118 and prepares nicely for verse 120 (p. 138).
226. Some Greek witnesses add "continually" (διὰ παντός).
227. The MT has סָמַר. The Greek version renders this with καθήλωσον, "penetrate / nail (my flesh from fear of you)."

accuses the nation of halting between two opinions—they could not decide between Yahweh or Baal!

In verse 113b the psalmist states what he loves (אָהַבְתִּי; s.v. Ps. 11:7): the law of the LORD. These two verbs, love and hate, are antithetical, but they are also words that include acts. To "hate" includes the idea of rejecting, and "love" the idea of choosing. Goldingay suggests interpreting them as "being against" and "being dedicated to."[228] The psalmist has little patience with those who are double-minded.

The next verse explains why the psalmist loves the law of the LORD—it is because of what the LORD means to him. He uses two figures (metaphors) to describe the LORD, "hiding place" and "shield." Both of these are common in the psalms: "hiding place" occurs in Psalms 27:5, 31:20, 32:7 and other places, and signifies safety in the LORD; "shield" occurs in Psalms 28:7, 33:20, 84:11 to name a few, and signifies protection. The use of these figures indicates the psalmist learned these things about the LORD by being in the midst of assault and oppression. Because of what he has learned, he puts his hope (יִחָלְתִּי; s.v. Ps. 31:24) in God's word. By "word" he probably means primarily the covenant promises of God to protect and preserve him. His love for the law of the LORD is therefore based in part on his experiencing protection according to God's word.

II. Believers desire separation from evildoers so that they can follow God's commands (115).

Typical of laments in general, the psalmist turns to address the evildoers (e.g., see Ps. 6: 8). He says, "Depart from me . . . that I may keep the commandments of my God." It is a demand for the wicked to leave him alone so that he can hold to God's word in his life. He could maintain such a commitment to the word even if they did not depart; but if they left him alone, however, he would be free to do more in his service of God.

---

228. *Psalms 90–150*, p. 423.

III. Believers pray for God to sustain them by his word because he opposes the wicked (116–119).

The psalmist now turns to prayer: there are two verses in which he makes petitions, followed by two verses that express his confidence in God's justice concerning wicked enemies. The first petition is for God to uphold him so that he might live. This verb (סָמְכֵנִי, from סָמַךְ; s.v. Ps. 51:12) can be used for divine help in general (see Pss. 3:5, 37:17, 71:6). Since he is praying this that he might live, the more specific meaning of "uphold" is appropriate. The petition appeals to God's oracles, a reference to the promises God made to his people in the covenant. Parallel to this petition is his request not to be ashamed because of his hope. The verb "ashamed" (וְאַל־תְּבִישֵׁנִי; s.v. Ps. 31:1) means much more than being embarrassed or made to look silly; it is commonly used for humiliating defeats at the hands of the enemies. He does not want to be so humiliated and have his belief in God's word seriously discredited. The word "hope" (שֵׂבֶר) occurs only here in verse 116 and in Psalm 146:5; it refers to his expectation that the promises God made will be fulfilled. If he has put his trust in God's word for help, and no help came, he would be put to shame—and God would be discredited because his word would appear to be unreliable.

In verse 117 he prays again in a similar way: "Hold me up (סְעָדֵנִי) and I shall be saved" (וְאִוָּשֵׁעָה; s.v. Ps. 3:2). The verb is an appeal for divine help (as in Pss. 20:3; 41:3). If the LORD sustains him in his faith, he will eventually be delivered from his enemies. With this appeal he affirms his esteem for God's statutes. The verb "have regard" (וְאֶשְׁעָה) has the idea of acceptance; it was used in this way in Genesis 4:4–5 to say that God had regard for the sacrifice of Abel but not for Cain's. The psalmist pays close attention to God's statutes because they are his life.

Following these two petitions, the psalmist makes two observations that express his confident expectation of deliverance. The first (v. 118) is that God rejects those who reject him, those who wander away from his statutes (meaning disregard and disobey). The verb used (סָלָה) is a rare word, but probably has the sense of "spurn" or "throw out." Those who abandon the law of God have no future with God. The reason for this is that "their deceit is falsehood" (כִּי־שֶׁקֶר תַּרְמִיתָם). Because the clause seems tautologous, Goldingay suggests a paraphrase: "because of their deceitfulness, their falsehood."[229] The expression could be taken to mean that their deceit (s.v. Ps. 5:7) proves to be false (s.v. Ps. 144:8)—that it serves a false purpose because in the end they will be discovered for what they are.

The second statement is that God causes the wicked to cease (v. 119), that is, removes them like dross (for שָׁבַת, s.v. Ps. 46:9, where God makes wars to "cease"). Dross is the worthless material removed in the refining process (NEB renders the word "scum"). Because God removes the wicked, the psalmist declares his loyalty to him: "therefore I love your testimonies." The word "love" (אָהַבְתִּי) is used here with its sense of showing loyalty to the covenant God has made. This statement comes immediately after his report that God removes the wicked, the ungodly who are not part of the covenant (s.v. Ps. 1:1). It is followed by a statement of his personal response to the thought of divine judgment (v. 120).

IV. Believers stand in fear of the judge of the whole world (120).

Verse 120 does not emphasize that the psalmist responds with reverential fear, i.e., worship, but rather with genuine fear. Believers of all people know best how fearful the divine judge is. The verb (סָמַר) means "to tremble, shiver"—"my flesh trembles" (see Job 4:15); Kraus translates it "shudder."[230] The reason for this is "because of your fear" (מִפַּחְדְּךָ [231]), meaning, "because of

---

229. *Psalms 90–150*, p. 425.
230. *Psalms 60–150*, p. 419.
231. The word פַּחַד means "dread." The related verb simply means "to be in dread, in awe of." The basic idea seems to be "to shake" (Akkadian, *pahadu*, "to be frightened, shake"), and the noun then would mean a "shaking terror." The word can be used in a good sense of shaking with joy (Isa. 60:5); but the dominant meaning is shaking with terror (Deut. 28:66, "filled with dread day and night"; Jer. 36:24, the king and his attendants "showed no fear"; and Prov. 3:24, "when you lie down you will not be afraid").

H. -P. Stähli lists four important considerations for the theological use of these words ("פחד *phd* **to shake**," in *Theological Lexicon of the Old Testament*, ed. by Jenni and Westermann, III:979–981). First, they are

dread of you." It could mean his feeling of dread of the LORD ("you" being objective), but in view of the parallelism the word may refer to the dread thing from the LORD, i.e., the judgment. The second colon says, "I am afraid because of your judgments" (decisions, but in this context judgment on those who refuse God's decisions). The psalmist is not afraid that he might be swept away in the judgment; he is overwhelmed and terrified at the thought of divine justice on all the ungodly.

Message and Application

The faith and the fear of the psalmist is true of believers in all ages. Those who are openly devoted to the LORD and love his word become more aware of the presence of people who are double-minded and deceitful about their beliefs and their actions. They pray earnestly for God, who is their hiding place and their shield, to sustain them in their faith. They pray for this knowing that God will judge the ungodly who disobey his word—just the thought of this brings terror even to the believer. The righteous try to warn evildoers of God's dealing with the ungodly in the hopes that they would depart, that is, cease trying to ruin the faith.

To put this meditation in an expository principle that is applicable to today, we may say: *Separating themselves from ungodly and untrustworthy people whom God will judge, believers pray for God to sustain them in their faith by his word.* Christians

---

used as terms for the numinous terror of God, especially in the presence of his mighty works (Exod. 15:16, "terror and dread will fall on them"). Second, they characterize God's frightfulness in relation to his majesty and kingship (Isa. 2:10, "hide . . . from dread of the LORD and the splendor of his majesty"; also vv. 19, 21). Third, the reference is to terror produced by God, and so the usual expression is that dread fell upon people (2 Chron. 20:29, "the fear of God came upon all the kingdoms of the countries when they heard how the LORD . . . "; see also Exod. 15:6). This seems to be the idea behind the wicked person who ignores God because there is no dread thing from God that has shaken him (see Ps. 36:1). Fourth, the words may have a weakened sense of ethical fear of God (2 Chron. 19:7, "Now let the fear of the LORD be upon you). Here too we may place the description of the LORD as "the fear of Isaac" (Gen. 31:42), although it may have a stronger significance.

The Word of the LORD and the Life of Faith

who love the LORD and his word cannot be comfortable in a world of double-minded and deceitful people who have no intention of following God's ways. Many of these ungodly people are false teachers and deceivers, or have been influenced by them, over whom the judgment of God hangs (1 Pet. 2:3). The chief concern of Christians is to remain faithful in their lives and honest in their words; they must renounce all secrets and shameful things and deception because their witness is to people who are perishing (2 Cor. 4:2). They know that God will judge the unbelievers with a terrible judgment, and so they try to warn them (2 Tim. 4:2).

ע *Ayin*

The Appeal to God's Faithful Love for Vindication

Text and Textual Variants

ע 121 I have done[232] what is just (מִשְׁפָּט) and right;
    do not leave me to my oppressors.

ע 122 Give a pledge[233] of good[234] to your servant;
    let[235] not the arrogant oppress me.[236]

ע 123 My eyes fail for your salvation
    and for your righteous oracle (אִמְרָה).

ע 124 Deal with your servant according to your loyal love,
    and teach me your statutes (חֹק).

ע 125 I am your servant; give me understanding,

---

232. For the MT's עָשִׂיתִי, "I have done," a few manuscripts and the Syriac have the 2msg form, "you."
233. The MT form is עֲרֹב. The Greek version has ἔκδεξει, "accept/receive (your slave for good)."
234. This verse and verse 132 are unusual in Psalm 119 because they do not include one of the words for the Law. However, "good" has been understood as referring to the Law (see b. *Berachoth*, 5a).
235. A few manuscripts and the Syriac have a conjunction in the second colon: "and let not . . . ."
236. "Let them (not) oppress me" is יַעַשְׁקֻנִי; the Greek version renders this with μή συκοφαντησάτωσάν με, "let not (the proud) accuse me falsely" or "extort from me."

that I may know your testimonies (עֵדוּת)!
ע 126 *It is* time for the LORD to act,
for they have broken your law (תּוֹרָה).
ע 127 Therefore I love your commandments (מִצְוָה)
above gold, above fine gold.[237]
ע 128 Therefore I consider all your precepts (פִּקּוּד)[238] to be right;[239]
every false way I hate.

Exegetical Analysis

Summary

Asserting that it is time for the LORD to act to defend him and destroy the oppressors, the psalmist appeals to God to deal with his servants in love and enable them to know and love the commandments (119:121–128).

Outline

I. He calls for God to deal with him, his servant, in justice and on the basis of loyal love because he is righteous (121–124).
II. He motivates the LORD to work by explaining his loyalty as a servant (125–126).
III. He loves the LORD's laws and hates false ways (127–128).

---

237. For פָּז the Greek version has τοπάζιον, "topaz."
238. The MT has כָּל־פִּקּוּדֵי כֹל, "(Therefore I consider) all the precepts of all (to be right)." The second part, "all (things)" is awkward and therefore questionable. As the text stands, it would be translated: "all the precepts of everything." It is often compared to Ezekiel 44:30, but the usages are not the same. Briggs says that the last כֹל is erroneous, and should be ךָ, leaving only "all your precepts" (*Psalms*, II, p. 442). Allen further suggests that the remaining letter (l) from the word "all" (*kol*) could be an emphatic lamed on the following verb: "I indeed find agreeable (all your precepts)" (*Psalms 101–150*, p. 138). There is little difference in the meanings. It will either read, "I consider all the precepts of all (things) to be right," or "I consider all your precepts to be right."
239. The verb is יִשָּׁרְתִּי means "make straight, right," in the sense that he is setting himself straight by the precepts. The Greek version has interpreted the verb as κατωρθούμην, "I directed myself" or "I set myself straight."

Commentary in Expository Form

I. Those who trust in the LORD and obey his word may pray with confidence for deliverance from oppressors (121–124).

Devout believers who trust the LORD for deliverance know that they are servants to their master, the LORD God; and so the word "servant" (עֶבֶד; s.v. Ps. 134:1) occurs several times in the psalm—"I am your servant" is at the center of this meditation. The point of this meditation is that it is time for the LORD to intervene on behalf of his servant and end the oppression of the arrogant people, whose faithlessness prompts the psalmist to confirm his love and devotion to the law of the LORD. He begins the meditation by stating that he has done what is just and right (or, "I have done justice [מִשְׁפָּט; s.v. Ps. 9:4] and righteousness [צֶדֶק, s.v. Ps. 1:5]."). These are qualities that God loves and honors (see Ps. 33:5). Because he has been loyal to the law of the LORD, he is confident to pray for God to deliver him from the oppression of the lawless; his petitions begin with, "Do not leave me (בַּל־תַּנִּיחֵנִי; s.v. Ps. 95:11) to my oppressors (לְעֹשְׁקָי, to those crushing me," often in the sense of extortion).

In an unusual request, he asks God for a pledge of good to his servant. The word "give a pledge" (עָרֹב) is normally used with the legal sense of surety, when one person takes the responsibility for another to guarantee the deal. Here it is used figuratively because the psalmist is asking God to provide surety for him (a comparison with the legal activity). He is asking God to guarantee his welfare. Kraus suggests "Vouch for me" as a more helpful rendering;[240] he is essentially asking God to do something that will ensure his protection and deliverance. The parallel colon simply asks God not to let the arrogant (זֵדִים, s.v. Ps. 119:21) oppress him (< עָשַׁק). It is only right that God champion the righteous and not allow the arrogant unbelievers to gain the upper hand.

In verse 123 the psalmist inserts a lamentation over his condition, repeating expressions he has used before. He says, "my eyes fail (כָּלוּ; s.v. Ps. 90:7) for your salvation." The idea is that

---

240. *Psalms 60–150*, p. 407.

of longing for something to the point of weakness (see v. 82). He weakens, waiting for God's deliverance, that is, for "the oracle of your righteousness," which could be understood as "your righteous oracle." By oracle he probably means the fulfillment of the promise of salvation that God made to his people (so a metonymy of cause for the effect). He has obeyed God's word, and the enemies have not; therefore he prays for God to keep his word to him. He appeals to God to deal with his servant by his faithful covenant love (כְּחַסְדֶּךָ; s.v. Ps. 23:6) and teach him his statutes.

II. Those who pray for God to act must confirm their loyalty to him and submission to his word (125–126).

The use of the term "loyal love" and the repetition of the word "servant" stress the covenant relationship the psalmist enjoys with the LORD, a relationship he correctly understands; in verse 125 he states, "I am your servant." This is not only the language of the personal covenant relationship he has with the LORD (see Mal. 1:6), but also the expression of his dependence on God. The believer in covenant with God is always the servant, always to be dependent, always to be obedient; and as a servant the believer waits for God's word that gives him instructions. Here the psalmist prays for God to give him understanding (הֲבִינֵנִי; s.v. Ps. 49:3) that he might know (וְאֵדְעָה; s.v. Ps. 67:2) God's covenant laws. This emphasis on knowing is also covenant terminology, or at least, fitting for a covenant relationship; his prayer expresses his willingness to accept the claims of God made in the law.[241]

Because as a servant of the LORD the psalmist knows the promises of the covenant, he states that it is time for[242] the LORD to act, which goes beyond confidence to boldness. Briggs says it is like saying it is high time for God to do something (II:433). He explains that this is not simply because he is in peril, but because God needs to vindicate his own laws which the arrogant have broken (or nullified by their actions: הֵפֵרוּ, from פָּרַר). The

---

241. See also H. B. Huffmon, "The Treaty Background of Hebrew YADAʿ," BASOR 181 (1966):37. See also Anderson, Psalms 73–150, p. 838.
242. Anderson notes that it is also possible to take the preposition (לְ) here as a vocative: "It is time, O LORD, to act" (p. 839).

infinitive "to act" (simply עֲשׂוֹת, "to do" something) in this and similar contexts means to judge the wicked and deliver the righteous (see Jer. 18:23; Ezek. 31:11).

III. Those who affirm their loyalty to God will demonstrate it by loving God's word and hating every false way (127–128).

Having made his appeal to God to act, now, the psalmist closes his meditation with attestations of his love for and loyalty to the commands of God. He begins (v. 127) with "therefore" (עַל־כֵּן), which gives the idea that the more the arrogant break God's laws the more he loves the them.[243] Several commentators follow the old suggestion to change "therefore" to "above all" (עַל־כֹּל) in verse 127, but there is no support for this, and the Hebrew reading makes sense. These verses may be the conclusion to the whole meditation, including the repeated emphasis on being a servant. At any rate, the verse is clear: he loves God's commands—more than fine gold (an expression that is reminiscent of Proverbs).

In the last verse he repeats "therefore," but now followed by a statement that he regards God's precepts as right, and so he hates every false way.

Message and Application

Effectual prayer requires an affirmation of faith, an obedient life, and a demonstration of loyalty to God. The New Testament will confirm this idea by stating that the fervent prayer of the righteous is efficacious. The expository idea may then be expressed this way: *People who pray for God to act on their behalf must demonstrate their loyalty to him by their obedience to his word and rejection of false ways.*

The standard for effective prayer is therefore righteousness, that is, faith, commitment and obedience (James 5:16). In praying for divine intervention, the faithful look for some sign, some indication that like a pledge would be a guarantee that God was hearing their prayers and would answer them. This

---

243. Kirkpatrick, *Psalms*, p. 725.

might be a partial fulfillment of the prayer, or a word of encouragement from someone else; but since the Holy Spirit has been given to us as a pledge or seal of our salvation, then perhaps the sign that the faithful desire may come through the inner conviction that God had heard the prayer.

פ *Pe'*

Delight in the Wonderful Words of Life

Text and Textual Variants

פ 129 Wonderful are your testimonies (עֵדוּת);
        therefore my soul treasures[244] them.

פ 130 The unfolding[245] of your words (דָּבָר)[246] gives light;
        imparting understanding[247] to the simple.

פ 131 I open my mouth and pant,
        because I long for your commandments (מִצְוָה).

פ 132 Turn[248] to me and be gracious to me,
        as is your custom (מִשְׁפָּט)[249] with those who love your name.

פ 133 Establish my steps in[250] your oracle (אִמְרָה),

---

244. For נָצַר, "treasure, keep," the Greek version again uses "searched out."
245. The MT has פֵּתַח, a noun meaning "opening, unfolding"; accordingly, the Greek version has ἡ δήλωσις, "the manifestation" or "exposition." It means revelation or illumination here. The Syriac read it as פִּתַח; Symmachus (and Jerome) has ἡ πύλη, "doorway." The editors of BHS suggest reading פֶּתַח, "opening, door."
246. Many manuscripts and the Syriac have singular, "your word."
247. The MT has the participle, מֵבִין; the Greek and Syriac have a conjunction with it.
248. The Greek version interprets this with ἐπίβλεψον, "look on (me)."
249. The word, often translated "judgment" or "decision," has the sense of "custom." Here it refers to the way that the LORD treats those who love his name. The Syriac interprets the word as "your ways."
250. The preposition בְּ is in the MT. Some manuscripts and the Greek and Vulgate have "according to," כְּ, which is followed by several modern translations.

and let no iniquity gain dominion[251] over me.
פ 134 Redeem me from man's oppression,[252]
that I may keep your precepts (פִּקּוּד).
פ 135 Make your face shine upon your servant,
and teach me your statutes (חֹק).
פ 136 In streams of water my eyes run down,
because they[253] do not keep your law (תּוֹרָה).

Exegetical Analysis

Summary

The psalmist calls for God to turn to him and establish him through the word because it is the light for which he longs (119:129–136).

Outline

I. He declares his delight for the law of light which is wonderful (129–131).
II. He prays for the LORD to turn to him and establish him (132–135).
III. He expresses concern over those who hate the law (136).

Commentary in Expository Form

1. Those who are spiritual love and long for God's wonderful words because they give understanding (129–131).

---

251. MT reads וְאַל־תַּשְׁלֶט־בִּי. "Let no (iniquity) gain dominion over me" (a *hiphil* form). The Greek version has κατακυριευσάτω, "it will not master." The editors of BHS notes this represents a *qal* form, יִשְׁלַט, perhaps a jussive.
252. For Hebrew עֹשֶׁק the Greek interprets with συκοφαντίας, "extortion" or "accusation."
253. The verb is simply שָׁמְרוּ, "they (do not) keep." The subject in the line appears to be the same as the first colon, "my eyes"—they run down with tears because they do not observe God's law. The Greek version understands the line to mean this, and clarifies the translation with οὐκ ἐφύλαξαν, "I kept not." Others suggest the reference is to people in general, and supply the subject: "because people do not keep your law" (ESV), or make it passive.

The psalmist begins this meditation with the declaration that the testimonies of the LORD are "wonderful" (פְּלָאוֹת; s.v. Ps. 139:5), that is, extraordinary or surpassing. Because of their amazing value, he treasures them, meaning that he stores them up for future use. The value of God's testimonies is identified in the statement that the opening of God's words gives light (יָאִיר), a figure for illumination (an implied comparison), which is clarified in the second colon of the verse with "giving understanding" (מֵבִין; s.v. Ps. 49:3) to the simple.[254] The book of Proverbs describes the troubles that the simpleton will encounter if there is no spiritual understanding from the word; but for the psalmist that understanding has been a life-changing experience. Because the word of the LORD is so beneficial, the psalmist desires more (he pants for, or strongly desires [וָאֶשְׁאָפָה] and longs for [יָאָבְתִּי] the commandments of the LORD).

II. Those who are spiritual desire God to establish them in a life of increasing obedience to his word (by grace) (132–135).

The psalmist has already experienced the blessings of divine illumination through the word; but he wants more influence on his life from the word. He begins this section of petition with the request that God turn to him (פְּנֵה־אֵלַי) and be gracious to him (וְחָנֵּנִי; s.v. Ps. 4:1). The petition for God to turn to him (an anthropomorphism) simply is an appeal for God to pay attention to him and deal favorably with him. This is not a unique petition; it was the LORD's custom (מִשְׁפָּט; s.v. Ps. 9:4) to favor those who love (לְאֹהֲבֵי; s.v. Ps. 11:7) his name, that is, who he is and what he does (s.v. Ps. 20:1). The petition proper is essentially twofold, that God establish his ways and redeem him from the oppression of men. The request for God to establish (הָכֵן, from כּוּן; s.v. Ps. 93:1) his steps by the word means that God should make his life safe and secure, for when God establishes such things

---

254. Luke 24:32 provides an interesting correlation; there the Lord Jesus opened the Scriptures to the two disciples and they began to understand the plan of God. For the idea of "unfolding" Goldingay suggests the image of a scroll being unrolled (*Psalms 90–150*, p. 429).

he makes them fixed and firm. The parallel colon offers further detail here: "and let no iniquity (אָוֶן; s.v. Ps. 28:3) gain dominion over me." He will have to deal with iniquity as it comes against him, but if the LORD establishes his ways then iniquity will not gain dominion over him.

His prayer is that the LORD redeem him (פְּדֵנִי; s.v. Ps. 25:22) from the oppression of man (מֵעֹשֶׁק אָדָם) so that he might keep God's precepts, no doubt meaning give full attention to keeping them without being opposed and oppressed. Oppressors might easily gain dominion over him and change his focus on spiritual understanding from the word—although the experience of facing opposition is in itself an occasion for growth, for here he must pray for God's grace to redeem him.

The prayer was for God to be gracious to him (v. 132); and that is now reiterated figuratively with "Make your face shine (הָאֵר) on your servant." Here the word for "shine" is the same verb used earlier for giving him light through the word, thereby linking the two lines: if God is gracious to him (causing his face to shine on him), meaning that he will teach the psalmist his statutes, then he will find in them spiritual illumination for his life in spite of the presence of oppression.

III. Those who are spiritual are truly saddened to see God's word hated (and rejected) by people (136).

That there are people who oppress the righteous is indeed troubling for the devout, not simply because they must endure it, but because it means that God's word is being disobeyed. This meditation closes with the psalmist's confession that he weeps (poetically expressed in hyperbolic language that his eyes, meaning tears from his eyes [a metonymy of subject] run down in streams of water) because these oppressors do not keep the law. For someone who loves the word of God, lives obediently by it, and finds hope in its promises, to see the world mistreat it and reject it is very painful. Their attitude to the word is completely the opposite of the devout, who have found so much delight and benefit in it that they desire more from the LORD.

Message and Application

The theme of this stanza is the appreciation of the Law, which necessarily includes sadness over the fact that so many do not appreciate God's word. His appreciation of God's word prompts him to desire more understanding. Accordingly, the message of this meditation may be worded this way: *Because those who are spiritual long for God's word and are saddened to see it hated by the world, they desire God to sustain them in an increasing obedience to his word.* Like the Old Testament, the New Testament tells believers to grow in the grace and knowledge of the word, for through it they will learn how to discern all things, especially how to live in a wicked world (1 Tim. 4:5; Heb. 4:12). These are they whom the LORD establishes in the faith, of whom it will be said in the final analysis that they kept his word (Rev. 3:8).

צ Tsadhe

The Righteous LORD and His Righteous Word

Text and Textual Variants

    צ 137 Righteous are you, O LORD,
                and upright are your decisions (מִשְׁפָּט).[255]

    צ 138 You have appointed your testimonies (עֵדוּת) in righteousness
                and in all faithfulness.

    צ 139 My zeal[256] consumes me,
                because my[257] foes have forgotten your words (דְּבָר).[258]

    צ 140 Your oracle (אִמְרָה) is well tried,
                and your servant loves it.

    צ 141 I am small[259] and despised,

---

255. A few manuscripts, the Greek and Jerome have a singular noun.
256. The MT has קִנְאָתִי, but the Greek has ὁ ξῆλος τοῦ οἴκου σου, "the zeal of your house," as in Ps. 69:10.
257. Syriac has "your" foes.
258. The majority of manuscripts and the Syriac have the singular, "your word."
259. Hebrew צָעִיר is translated νεώτερος, "young," in the Greek version.

צ 142 *yet* I do not forget your precepts (פִּקּוּד).
צ 142 Your righteousness is an everlasting righteousness,
and your law (תּוֹרָה) is true.
צ 143 Trouble and anguish[260] have gotten hold of me,[261]
but your commandments (מִצְוָה) are my delight.[262]
צ 144 Your testimonies (עֵדוּת)[263] are righteous forever;
give me understanding that I may live.

Exegetical Analysis

Summary

The psalmist announces that because the LORD is righteous the law is everlastingly righteous and this is a comfort in time of affliction (119:137–144).

Outline

I. He declares that because the LORD is righteous his law is righteous (137–138).
II. He testifies to his own zeal for the word which is pure (139–142).
III. He finds comfort in the righteous law when he is in affliction (143–144).

Commentary in Expository Form

I. God's word is dependably righteous because God is righteous (137–138).

Here we focus on the everlasting righteousness of God: the righteousness and reliability of God's word inspire love and reverence in the faithful. The section begins with the declaration:

---

260. These first two words have been translated as plural nouns in the Greek.
261. מְצָאוּנִי is often translated "have found me (out)."
262. Hebrew שַׁעֲשֻׁעָי, "my delight," is again translated μελέτη μου, "my meditation," in the Greek.
263. Syriac has a singular noun.

"Righteous are you, O LORD; and upright are your decisions." "Righteous" (צַדִּיק; s.v. Ps. 1:5) essentially has the meaning of corresponding to the standard, i.e., the Law of God, to indicate what is right; and here the standard is affirmed: "Righteous are you, O LORD." Kirkpatrick states that this is the fundamental attribute of the Author of the law as it necessarily determines the character of the law in all its aspects.[264] Parallel to this affirmation is the statement: "and upright (יָשָׁר; s.v. Ps. 67:4) *are* your decisions." This is the natural result in the revelation of the one who is righteous. Moreover, the psalmist affirms that the LORD appointed (צִוִּיתָ; s.v. Ps. 119:6) his testimonies in righteousness and faithfulness (וֶאֱמוּנָה; s.v. Ps. 15:2) to the uttermost. The words "righteousness" and "faithfulness" are here taken adverbially, "in righteousness" and "in faithfulness," indicating the manner and purpose of the law that God established. God's commandments, then, are the expression of his absolute righteousness and his faithfulness to his covenant that is an inseparable element of his righteousness.[265] The word of the LORD is always right and completely dependable.

II. God's word has been proven true by those who are zealous for his truth in a world that has forgotten it (139–142).

The writer now explains that these truths have been validated by his own personal experiences. He first asserts that he is consumed by zeal because his foes have forgotten God's word. "Zeal" (קִנְאָה; s.v. Ps. 37:1) is that passionate intensity over things that matter, such as God's holy institutions, or the holy place itself. Here it is zeal to defend God's word because the enemies have forgotten it, meaning they have not paid attention to its revelation or regulations. The psalmist is consumed with this passion: it has almost destroyed him; he could not however stand by while the word of the LORD was being nullified, for it is truth. The reliability of the word of the LORD is not something he had heard, or had been taught—it has been proved by him. He had

---

264. *Psalms*, p. 726.
265. Kirkpatrick, *Psalms*, p. 727.

been in situations where he was forced to rely on the promises of the LORD, to discover that the LORD keeps his word.[266] He could state therefore that God's oracle is "very pure" (or, well-tried; צְרוּפָה); by his application of the LORD's word he has proven it to be pure, like gold that has been refined (see Ps. 12:6). Because it is perfect, he loves it (for אָהֵב; s.v. Ps. 11:7). He acknowledges that even though he is insignificant, yet he remains faithful to God's word. By saying he is "small" (צָעִיר) and "despised" (וְנִבְזֶה; s.v. Ps. 22:6) he means that in the opinion of the world he is considered insignificant and treated as worthless. In this context the implication is that he is viewed in this way because of his zeal and love for the word of the LORD, which the wicked treat as worthless; but he remains faithful. As Kirkpatrick writes, "neither the glamor of worldly power nor the sting of worldly contempt can move him from his allegiance."[267] He will never forget God's precepts because he knows that God's righteousness is an everlasting righteousness, and that God's law is true. God does not change; and his word does not change—it is truth.

III. God's word brings delight in the midst of trouble and anguish (143–144).

Most significantly, the word of the LORD has brought him comfort in his time of need. He has been seized with trouble and anguish (צַר־וּמָצוֹק). He does not state what the difficulty is, but the cause of his problem is "trouble" and the effect is "anguish." From the context of this stanza as well as the previous stanzas the difficulty most likely has been caused by his enemies in high places who are oppressing and demeaning him. Briggs says that his zeal for the law and its observance has brought persecution from his adversaries who violate it.[268] This opposition would have been overwhelming, if it had not been for the word of the LORD that brought him delight ("my delight," שַׁעֲשֻׁעָי; s.v. Ps. 119:14). When he meditated on God's word he knew not only that he was living in harmony with God's righteousness

---

266. See Goldingay, *Psalms 90–150*, p. 432.
267. *Psalms*, p. 727.
268. *Psalms*, II:434.

and truth; but also that the promises of God revealed in it would be fulfilled eternally because God's righteousness is eternal. The testimonies of the LORD were not simply right for his time; they are righteous forever. The psalmist concludes with the prayer that God give him understanding in order that he might live. He desires a fuller understanding of the divine revelation, because through it he will truly live—fulfill the purpose for his existence.

Message and Application

This stanza stresses the integrity and reliability of the word of the LORD: it is eternally righteous because the LORD is righteous; it is true and faithful because the LORD is. The point may be stated this way: *Because God is (dependably) righteous, his word is everlastingly righteous and a comfort in times of anguish.* For the psalmist anguish here comes from people who ignore and violate the word of the LORD; when he is zealous for the word of the LORD, his adversaries oppose him and cause him grief. Nevertheless, it is the word that brings him comfort and joy, and so he will not abandon it. The New Testament confirms that the law was holy and just and good (Rom. 7:12–16); Jesus declared that the word of the LORD is truth and the means of salvation and sanctification (John 17:17; see also 2 Cor. 6:7 and 1 Pet. 1:23). Believers today build their lives on the word; but the more they do, the more they find that people around them are uncomfortable with it. If believers are zealous to defend and proclaim the word, they will find strong opposition. And so they should do as this psalmist did, prove it to be true by relying on it, so that in times of opposition the word will increase their joy and comfort.

ק *Qoph*

God Is Near His People but Far from the Wicked

Text and Textual Variants

ק 145 I called with *my* whole heart,
   "Answer me, O LORD,

The Word of the LORD and the Life of Faith

ק 146 *so* I will keep[269] your statutes (חֹק)."
I called to you, "Save me,
that I observe your testimonies (עֵדֹות).[270]

ק 147 Early in the morning dawn did I cry for help;
I waited for your words (דְּבָר).[271]

ק 148 My eyes are awake before[272] the watches[273] of *the night*,
that I may meditate on your oracle (אִמְרָה).[274]

ק 149 Hear my voice according to[275] your loyal love;
O LORD, according to your justice (מִשְׁפָּט)[276]
renew my life.

ק 150 They who follow after evil intent[277] draw near;
they are far from your law (תֹּורָה).

ק 151 You are near, O LORD,
and all your commandments (מִצְוָה) are truth.

ק 152 Long have I known from your testimonies (עֵדֹות)[278]
that you have founded them forever.

Exegetical Analysis

Summary

When the enemies follow after him, the psalmist calls for

---

269. Again the Greek version translates this word with "search out."
270. The Syriac has the singular.
271. The form in the text is לִדְבָרֶיךָ; the K*e*thiv is לִדְבָרֶיךָ, "for your words," but the Q*e*re' is לִדְבָרְךָ, the singular form. The Greek reads with K, but the majority of Hebrew manuscripts and some version with the Q.
272. Or, "my eyes prevented" (קִדְּמוּ, "to act before, prevent"). The same verb was used in verse 147, literally, "I arose before the dawn," or, "early in the morning dawn" (קִדַּמְתִּי) and cried for help," but there it was used as part of the hendiadys, modifying "I cried for help."
273. The MT has אַשְׁמֻרֹות, "watches"; but the Greek has simply ("prevented) the dawn" πρὸς ὄρθρον).
274. A few manuscripts, the Greek and Jerome, have the plural form.
275. A few manuscripts have בְּ, "in," instead of כְּ.
276. Some manuscripts have the plural.
277. The MT has רֹדְפֵי זִמָּה, "followers of evil (purpose)." Some manuscripts, the Greek, Symmachus and Jerome have "they who persecute me" (רֹדְפַי). And the Greek version translates זִמָּה with the general ἀνομία, "unlawfully."
278. The Syriac reflects the singular (עֵדוּתְךָ).

575

deliverance because he trusts in the word of the LORD who is near (119:145–152).

Outline

I. He calls for deliverance because he meditates in and hopes on the word (145–149).
II. The enemies who are far from the law follow him and are near him (150).
III. He confesses that he has kept the commandments of the LORD who is always near (151- 152).

Commentary in Expository Form

In this stanza we read of the psalmist's diligent prayer to remain faithful in the midst of faithlessness. This section reflects a lament; but the psalmist's means of overcoming it is his fervent prayer and his awareness of the closeness of God.[279]

The passage not only uses the letter *qoph* ("q," ק) for each line as is the pattern of this psalm, but repeats words in pairs: verses 145 and 146 begin with "I called" and "I called to you" (קְרָאתִי and קְרָאתִיךָ); verses 147 and 148 begin with the verb "to act beforehand" or "early" (קִדַּמְתִּי and קִדְּמוּ); and verses 150 and 151 begin with the words "be near" and "near" (קָרְבוּ and קָרוֹב respectively), and then verse 152 begins with "before, long before," related to the verb used in verses 147 and 148 (קֶדֶם). All of these strengthen the meaning of the meditation: he prays to the LORD who is near, and he prays early and often, because his enemies are drawing near.

I. God's people pray earnestly and expectantly for God's word to be fulfilled so that they may reflect on it and be renewed in their spiritual lives (145–149).

The first part of the stanza focuses on his fervent praying. He begins by declaring that he called on the LORD with a whole heart (בְּכָל־לֵב), earnestly and fervently. His prayer was that the LORD would answer him (עֲנֵנִי, "answer me") and save him

---

279. Allen, *Psalms 101–150*, p. 144.

(הוֹשִׁיעֵנִי, "save me," s.v. Ps. 3:2), no doubt from the unbelievers who were following after him with an evil intent (v. 150). The answer to this prayer will mean that he will be able to continue keeping the statutes and testimonies. It may be that the oppression he was facing hindered him from fully and freely keeping the law, having to spend more time concerned with dealing with the wicked. At any rate, the two purpose clauses offer a valid reason for God to deliver him.

According to verses 147 and 148 the psalmist awakens early to pray. He first says (v. 147) that he acted beforehand in the dawn to cry out of his distress to God; and then second (v. 148) he says his eyes were awake before the watches of the night so that he could meditate on God's oracle. There were therefore early meditations in the word and early prayers to the LORD. That the text mentions the night watches may indicate he prayed frequently through the night. It may be that he was a Levite who awakened early in order to start his turn as a watchman. Whatever the circumstances of his prayers in the night, his early meditation in God's word not only led to early prayers but also prompted him to hope (יִחָלְתִּי; s.v. Ps. 31:24) for God's word to be fulfilled. The line is similar to the statement in Psalm 130 that the psalmist waited for the LORD, more than the watchmen for the morning, and hoped in his word, perhaps an oracle of deliverance. Here the psalmist hopes for God's word as he meditates in the law and prays for deliverance from his enemies; surely the word he waits for is something that will give him confidence in his prayer.

He then reiterates his prayer in verse 149: "hear (שִׁמְעָה ; s.v. Ps. 45:10) my voice," meaning, answer my prayer. He now however bases his appeal on the loyal love of the LORD (חֶסֶד; s.v. Ps. 23:6), that faithful covenant love that God has for believers. The prayer then is for God to be faithful to his covenant people and to his covenant promises. The prayer specifies that God should renew his life (חַיֵּנִי), or possibly "preserve him," because of his justice (מִשְׁפָּט; s.v. Ps. 9:4). God's decisions are always right and true; therefore he should intervene to vindicate his people who are being persecuted by wicked people. If the people of God are living faithfully, then they may be confident that God's faithful love and justice will deliver them from trouble and vindicate them.

II. God's people confirm that their dangerous enemies are far from God (150).

The complaint is now introduced briefly. He is being hounded by wicked people who are getting closer and closer to him. He describes them as "followers of evil (purpose)." The construction (רֹדְפֵי זִמָּה) may be interpreted in different ways.[280] The word "evil (purpose)" (s.v. Ps. 10:2) may be best classified as an objective genitive, meaning that they seek out evil. Some versions have it with a pronominal suffix and not a construct ending, translating it as "who persecute me *with* lawlessness."

There is a contrast here with the words "near" and "far"— these enemies draw near (קָרְבוּ), that is, they are in a position to inflict evil on him. The second colon of the line makes it clear that there is little that they would not do, because they are far (רָחָקוּ) from God's law. They have no intension of obeying the law of the LORD, and so as they draw near to him he feels the danger.

III. God's people know that the LORD is near them because his word is reliable (151–152).

Kidner observes that the threat is not glossed over, but is put in proper perspective by a greater fact: the psalmist affirms, "You are near (קָרוֹב) O LORD."[281] This expression, like the affirmation "the LORD is with us," speaks of divine intervention and not location. The language is similarly used in Psalm 22 where the psalmist prays for God not to be far off because trouble is near. When God does not intervene, it seems that he is far away. The psalmist is convinced the LORD is near, because his meditations in the word have constantly reminded him of God's presence and of other interventions, and because in his own life he has experienced divine protection and deliverance. In this situation his confidence in the LORD's presence more than nullifies the anxiety of the approaching wicked.

A parallel statement of confidence forms the second colon: "and all your commandments are truth" (אֱמֶת; s.v. Ps. 15:2). The

---

280. The Targum reads it as "those who pursue prostitution," reading *znh* for *zmh*.
281. *Psalms 73–150*, p. 428. Briggs chooses to supply an imperative and have the verse read, "Be near, O LORD" (*Psalms*, II:435).

line helps explain his confidence that the LORD is near—he knows that all the decrees from God are reliable, including all the promises of provision and protection that are part of the covenant. The testimonies of God may be ancient, founded long ago, but they are not obsolete; and most germane to this stanza, the assurance of God's presence with the believer and all that implies is an eternally valid promise.

Message and Application

The stanza focuses on the believers' response to a present danger from people who have evil pursuits: they do not minimize the danger, but focus instead on the presence of the LORD and the reliability of his word. The message of this section may be worded as follows: *When threatened by those who are far from God, the faithful may pray with confidence for deliverance because the LORD is near them and his promises are sure.* I used the word "faithful" to describe the believers here, because in the stanza the psalmist's confidence is related to his obedience to God's word. In order for the people of God to claim God's promises in times of need, they must demonstrate their faith with faithfulness. In the New Testament the LORD Jesus declared that even though he ascended to heaven he would be with us always (Matt. 28:20). That promise and countless others in the word of God have given believers the confidence to live by faith in the midst of wickedness. The word of Christ dwells in the saints, so that they are constantly made aware of his presence (Col. 3:16). Moreover, they are reminded that the one who is in them is greater than the one who is in the world. Prayer for spiritual victory over the world requires a close communion with the ever-present Lord through his word.

ר *Resh*

A Plea for Vindication and Renewal of Life

Text and Textual Variants

ר 153 Look on my affliction and deliver me,
       for I do not forget your law (תּוֹרָה).

ר 154 Plead my cause, and ransom me;
      revive me according to your oracle (אִמְרָה)!
ר 155 Salvation is far from the wicked,
      for they have not sought your statutes (חֹק).
ר 156 Many are your tender mercies, O LORD;
      revive me according to[282] your decisions[283] (מִשְׁפָּט)
ר 157 Many are my persecutors and my adversaries,
      but I do not turn from your testimonies[284] (עֵדוּת).
ר 158 I look at the faithless and I am grieved,[285]
      because they do not keep your oracle[286] (אִמְרָה).
ר 159 See how I love your precepts (פִּקּוּד)!
      O LORD, according to[287] your loyal love revive me.
ר 160 The sum[288] of your word[289] (דָּבָר) is truth,
      and every one of your righteous decisions[290] (מִשְׁפָּט) endures forever.

Exegetical Analysis

Summary

The psalmist calls for God to vindicate and deliver him from

---

282. The Syriac has "(and) in," reading בְּ rather than כְּ, "according to."
283. The MT has the plural noun; a few manuscripts and the Greek version have the singular.
284. A few manuscripts and the Syriac have the singular noun.
285. The MT has וָאֶתְקוֹטָטָה; the Greek translation used ἐξετηκόμην, "I pined away."
286. The MT has the singular noun, "oracle, spoken word"; but the Greek version has a plural, "oracles."
287. The Greek version has ἐν τῷ ἐλέει σου, "in your mercy" (reading a בְּ instead of a כְּ preposition).
288. The MT has רֹאשׁ, "head, sum"; the Greek version translated this as ἀρχή "beginning."
289. One manuscript, the Greek version, and Jerome have a plural noun.
290. The MT has the singular noun, which makes a difficult translation: "every righteous decision of yours." The majority of the manuscripts, the Greek version, the Syriac and the Vulgate, have the word as a plural, as if the form in the text were מִשְׁפְּטֵי, "all (of) decisions of your righteousness," or, all your righteous decisions." This is the intent of the line because of the use of "all."

oppression because he loves and keeps the law but his treacherous adversaries are far from salvation (119:153–160).

Outline

I. He calls for God to plead his cause and deliver him (153–154).
II. He announces that salvation is far from the wicked (155).
III. He recognizes that God's mercies are great (156).
IV. He laments that he has many adversaries who do not keep the law (157–158).
V. He calls for God to consider how he loves the law of truth (159–160).

Commentary in Expository Form

I. The righteous who are afflicted pray for God to plead their cause and set them free (153–154).

In this stanza the lament element of the psalm is intensified with more urgent prayers for deliverance from the debilitating oppression of the wicked. Three times the psalmist will make his appeal to God for life, indicating that the oppression is not a small concern. In the first two verses he uses five imperatives. The first is "look on / see" (רְאֵה) my affliction; and the effect of that attention is expressed in the second, "and deliver me" (וְחַלְּצֵנִי). Parallel to these requests verse 154 uses "plead my cause" (רִיבָה רִיבִי; s.v. Ps. 95:8), followed by the desired effects, "and redeem me" (וּגְאָלֵנִי; s.v. Ps. 19:14) and "revive me" (חַיֵּנִי). The appeal for God to look is a request for God to respond to his affliction, no doubt all his troubles caused by malicious enemies ("look" is the cause, and "deliver" the effect). The basis for his appeal is his continued obedience to the law (for "forget," שָׁכַח, s.v. Ps. 103:2). In the second verse the appeal to God to plead his cause is a call for vindication; the language used is that of a lawsuit, for God will champion his cause. The effect of God's pleading his case is that he will be redeemed from bondage. This word for "redeem" is well-known for its use in kinsman-redeemer passages; but it essentially refers to setting someone free from bondage and adversity, here caused by the wicked. This request to be redeemed is joined with the request for God to revive him. The verb is the causative stem (*piel*) of "to live" (חָיָה); it could be translated "preserve my life" or "restore my life," both of which would fit the passage. In either case he wants deliverance from the oppression of the wicked so that he can live his life fully in the service of the LORD. This appeal is not based on his faithfulness to the Law, but on the LORD's fulfilling the promises in his oracles. The law declared that the LORD would protect and defend his covenant people if they lived faithfully—and since he is a faithful covenant member, his prayer appeals to the promises of God to be carried out.

II. The righteous know that God will not save those who refuse his word (155).

The motivation for God to act is made more explicitly in verse 155. His confidence that God will deliver him from the wicked indicates that the wicked are far from God's deliverance. Since the wicked do not seek God's statutes, that is, they are far from the law (see v. 150), then salvation (יְשׁוּעָה; s.v. Ps. 3:2) is far from them. This victory comes from God; it will not come to those who reject God's authority, but to those who trust in him and seek to live in harmony with his will.

III. The righteous may pray for reviving because of God's tender mercies (156).

Having discarded the hope of the wicked for victory, the psalmist reiterates his appeal to God to revive his life (the second use of חַיֵּנִי), which he bases on God's compassion. This word (רַחֲמֶיךָ), translated "your tender mercies," refers to that tender care and protection God has for those who are helpless and dependent—like a mother for her child (s.v. Ps. 25:6). The psalmist knows God has compassion on the weak and oppressed, especially those who are believers; and so he appeals to God to act on this tender mercy and revive him according to his decisions (v. 149). Using "decisions" to refer to the law, he is carrying forward his appeal for God to plead his cause—in his case the decisions of God will bring deliverance.

IV. The righteous who are faithful to God's word will be opposed by faithless adversaries (157–158).

To bolster his appeal the psalmist next affirms his loyalty to God in the midst of adversity. He is assailed by many persecutors and adversaries, people responsible for his affliction, but he remains loyal to God—he does not turn from his testimonies. Nothing these people can say or do will make him abandon the path of righteousness laid down in God's word.

The psalmist not only follows this way, but also he is grieved to see those who do not. He sees the "faithless," people who are treacherous—who cannot be trusted to keep their word (בֹּגְדִים; s.v. Ps. 78:57), and he is grieved. The verb translated "grieved" (וָאֶתְקוֹטָטָה) probably has more of the sense of loathing and disgust (see Pss. 139:21 and 95:10); people who do not obey God's oracles disturb him tremendously. No doubt he was grieved over it, but it also angered him and he felt a disgust and loathing for it—the word of God is being ignored and violated every day!

V. The righteous who affirm their love for the truth of God's eternal word may appeal to God's faithful love to revive them in their faith (159–160).

In the last two verses of the stanza, he returns to his appeal for God to "see / look on" (רְאֵה). Whereas in verse 153 he wanted God to see (become involved with) his affliction, here he wants God to see (recognize and approve) his faithfulness, which is not due to a forced obedience, but to his love for God's precepts: "See how I love" (אָהָבְתִּי; s.v. Ps. 11:7). Using this terminology is an expression of faithfulness to the covenant, for "love" is the foundation and motivation of obedience to the word of the LORD (see Deut. 6:5 and Jesus's "if you love me" in John 14:15). For the believer obeying the law of God was not an unpleasant, burdensome task; it was the natural life style of those who loved the LORD and his word. The psalmist's appeal for God to revive him (the third use of the imperative) is based on God's faithful, covenant love (חֶסֶד; s.v. Ps. 23:6). At the heart of the covenant is love, the love of the believer for the LORD, and the LORD's faithful love to the beloved. Every believer in any difficulty may appeal to God to act on his faithful, covenant love for his people to vindicate them by delivering them from affliction and restoring their lives.

He concludes the stanza with a summary statement: "The sum of your word is truth, and all your righteous decisions are eternal." The word translated "sum" is literally "head"; here it means the chief characteristic of God's word is truth. Everything God has said is reliable, because he himself is the truth (see John 14:6). This is not simply a reality for the writer's current predicament—the word of God is eternal, and therefore eternally true.

Message and Application

This stanza captures the main features of many lament psalms: a cry to God for vindication and restoration, a lament over the affliction of the oppressors, confidence in God's mercy and love, and a petition based on God's covenant love. The issue is clarified here by the fact that the wicked reject the word of God and are therefore without any hope of victory from God, but the righteous love the word of God and remain loyal to it. The stanza is essentially an appeal for God to redeem his own faithful people. We may say: *When the faithful find themselves weakened by the affliction of adversaries who reject God's word, they may confidently pray for God to vindicate and revive them.*

This division between the righteous and the wicked is continued throughout the New Testament. The righteous, that is devout believers, keep the word of God (1 John 2:5; Rev. 3:8). They do this in part because of their love for Christ, who said, "If you love me, keep my commandments" (John 14:15; 15:12; 1 John 3:23). Believers know the law of love leads them to fulfill the commands (Rom. 13:10). "Love" remains the operative word for the New Covenant: to be loved by the Lord means to be redeemed; and to love the LORD is to believe in him, adore him, and be faithful to him.

God's word is powerful, because it brings life and understanding (Heb. 4:12). Because we are redeemed by the word, live by the word, and trust in the promises of the word, we may expect the Lord to vindicate us when the world opposes and oppresses. We therefore pray that it will happen immediately, but know it will happen ultimately since not even death can sever us from the love of God (Rom. 8:37–39).

The Word of the LORD and the Life of Faith

שׂ שׂ *Śîn Šîn*

Rejoicing in God's Word that Brings Peace

Text and Textual Variants

שׂ 161 Princes have persecuted me without cause,
   but my heart stands in awe because of your word (דָּבָר).[291]

שׂ 162 I rejoice because of your word (אִמְרָה)[292]
   like one who finds great spoil.

שׂ 163 Falsehood[293] I hate and abhor,[294]
   but[295] your law (תּוֹרָה) I love.

שׂ 164 Seven times a day[296] I praise you
   for your righteous decisions (מִשְׁפָּט).

שׂ 165 Great peace have those who love your law (תּוֹרָה);
   and there is no stumbling-block before them.

שׂ 166 I hope for your salvation, O LORD,
   and I do[297] your commandments (מִצְוָה).

שׂ 167 I[298] keep your testimonies (עֵדוּת)[299]
   and I love them exceedingly.

---

291. The MT form is וּמִדְּבָרֶיךָ; the *Qᵉrê* is וּמִדְּבָרְךָ, "and because of your word," but the *Kᵉthiv* is וּמִדְּבָרֶיךָ, "and because of your words." The majority of the manuscripts, the Syriac and the Targum read with Q. But the Greek version and Jerome have the plural.
292. A few manuscripts and the Greek version have the plural.
293. The Greek translation uses ἀδικίαν, "unrighteousness," for שֶׁקֶר.
294. Instead of MT's וָאֲתַעֵבָה, the imperfect / cohortative form with the simple conjunction, the majority of the manuscripts and collected editions have וְ, the *waw* consecutive, making the nuance equivalent to the verb before it. The translation of an English present tense may be derived in either case.
295. There is no conjunction in the MT. The Greek version has δέ, indicating a conjunction (likewise a few manuscripts and the Syriac have "and / but").
296. The text literally says "seven in the day."
297. The MT has עָשִׂיתִי, but the Greek version has ἠγάπησα, "I loved." One manuscript has חָפַצְתִּי.
298. The MT has נַפְשִׁי, usually translated "my soul" with the feminine verb. The parallel colon captures the meaning with "I love."
299. One manuscript and the Syriac have the singular.

שׂ 168 I keep your precepts (פִּקּוּד) and your testimonies (עֵדוּת),
for all my ways are before you.³⁰⁰

Exegetical Analysis

Summary

In spite of being persecuted by princes without a cause, the psalmist rejoices in the word of God, declaring that it brings peace to those like himself who trust and obey (119:161–168).

Outline

I. He attests that princes have hated him without a cause (161).
II. He rejoices in the word with great praise (162–164).
III. He affirms that there is great peace and hope in the word for salvation (165–166).
IV. He testifies that he has observed the law (167–168).

Commentary in Expository Form

I. The faithful remain in awe of God's word even when powerful leaders persecute them unjustly (161).

The stanza begins with a lament about powerful persecutors. These "princes" (שָׂרִים) appear to be civil authorities, Israelite nobility (cf. 119:23; Jer. 26:10ff.; and Ez. 9:1–2). Their continuing persecution of him (the present perfect רְדָפוּנִי was gratuitous hostility (חִנָּם, "without a cause," "for no reason"; s.v. Ps. 4:1). However, this note of lament quickly changes as the second colon records the psalmist's deeply felt awe ("my heart stands in awe") over God's words. The word rendered "stands in awe" (פָּחַד) essentially means "fear, dread, stand in terror or awe" (see Ps. 119:120) and here must have its positive connotation of reverential fear or awe, a combination of fear and faith.

---

300. The Greek translation ends the verse with Κύριε, "O Lord."

II. The faithful rejoice in the truth of God's word and regularly praise him for it (162–164).

The psalmist's attitude toward the word of God prompts him to express his faithfulness to and zeal for the word of the LORD. He first complements his awe with rejoicing (שָׂשׂ)[301] over God's oracles, comparing his joy to finding (מוֹצֵא) great spoil (שָׁלָל). The word "spoil" may have been chosen with a view to the expected victory over his persecutors the psalmist anticipates. However, his joy is a present reality; it is both the motivation for and effect of his obedience to the law (cf. Ps. 1:2).

In verse 163 the psalmist states his hatred of falsehood (שֶׁקֶר; s.v. Ps. 144:8) with the strongest of terms (שָׂנֵא, "hate"; s.v. Ps. 139:21; and תָּעַב, "abhor"; s.v. Ps. 14:1)—totally rejecting falsehood with loathing and disgust. These are terms that are used elsewhere for rejecting paganism and its corrupt tendencies—they are an abomination (תּוֹעֵבָה), so that the psalmist's reference to falsehood was more serious than ordinary dishonesty. In fact, he contrasts this hatred of falsehood with his love (< אָהַב; s.v. Ps. 11:7) for the law. Because the contrast is between what is false and the teaching of the LORD, whatever the falsehood was, it was contrary to God's word. By affirming his desire and enjoyment is in God's teaching, the psalmist confirms his loyalty to God.

His love is demonstrated by his constant praise for God for giving him his righteous decisions (v. 164). He expresses this with "seven times a day I praise you" (הִלַּלְתִּיךָ; s.v. Ps. 33:1), literally, "seven in the day" (שֶׁבַע בַּיּוֹם). The number "seven" may convey the sense of completeness or fulness, so that the psalmist probably means he praises God constantly and repeatedly, all day long, and not necessarily a specific number of times;[302] his praise for God is for God's righteous decisions (מִשְׁפְּטֵי צִדְקֶךָ, "the decisions of your righteousness"). The teachings in God's word that provide proper guidance in making decisions are righteous, because they come from his righteousness and therefore have

---

301. This verb is the *qal* perfect from the root שׂושׂ or שִׂישׂ, "to exult, rejoice" (see Ps. 119:111). In Psalm 51:14 the noun is used in reference to the rejoicing in the sanctuary that the penitent desires to hear once again.
302. Kirkpatrick, *Psalms*, p. 731.

the character of righteousness (for צֶדֶק, s.v. Ps. 1:5). To reject God's righteous decisions would be to follow the wrong choices and the wrong way, wrong because unrighteous and therefore false.

III. The faithful find great peace and the promise of salvation in God's word (165–166).

According to these two verses believers possess peace and the hope of salvation. They have peace because of their faith in and devotion to the word of the LORD; and they have hope for salvation because they trust in the promises of the word of the LORD. First, he announces that those who love God's law have great peace (שָׁלוֹם; s.v. Ps. 38:3). The indication they have peace is that there is no stumbling block (מִכְשׁוֹל) before them, the figure referring to things that would interrupt or hinder spiritual progress.[303] The faithful have great peace because, as Kirkpatrick puts it, "'they walk firmly and safely on the clear path of duty without stumbling and falling into sin."[304] Perowne adds: "When God's law is loved, instead of being struggled against, the conscience is at peace, and the inward eye is clear; a man sees his duty and does it, free from those stumblingblocks which are ever occasion of failing to others."[305]

There may not be any stumbling block to this psalmist's faith, but there is the challenge of persecution; therefore he hopes (שִׂבַּרְתִּי) for God's deliverance (לִישׁוּעָתְךָ; s.v. Ps. 3:2; see also Gen. 49:18). Because hoping for deliverance from the LORD is based on the promises of the word of the LORD, those who hope must also be obedient to his word—how could they expect what the word promises and refuse to do what the word requires?

---

303. The verb כָּשַׁל means "stumble, stagger, totter." It often has the figurative sense of failure, defeat, or wavering in pursuing the right way. The related noun may be literally a stone that causes someone to stumble (see Lev. 19:14); but it too has a figurative sense (an implied comparison) that means an occasion for stumbling in a spiritual quest (as in Isaiah 8:14). The figure signifies some misfortune, calamity or hindrance; it could refer to idols as the stumbling stone.
304. *Psalms*, p. 731.
305. *Psalms*, II:366.

Thus the psalmist affirms his loyalty with his trust: "I hope for your salvation" is followed by "I do your commandments."

IV. The faithful affirm that they love and keep God's word (167–168).

The last two verses of the psalm continue the affirmation of loyalty; Kraus calls this the psalmist's (self) description of the righteous.[306] Both verses 167 and 168 begin with the verb "keep," the first using the feminine form (שָׁמְרָה) with the stated subject ("my soul keeps," i.e., "I keep"), and the second simply "I keep" (שָׁמַרְתִּי; for the word s.v. Ps. 12:7). The first has "your testimonies" as the object, and the second has "your precepts and your testimonies." In the first (v. 167) the explanation for his obedience is that he loves the testimonies of God exceedingly; and in the second (v. 168) it is that his ways are before the LORD. In a sense, he is coming to the LORD in his appeal for deliverance with a clear conscience—he is at peace with God and is obedient to God's word; and he is appealing to God's conscience about him—God knows that his persecution is unwarranted because he is obedient to the word. The expression "all my ways are before you" means that everything he does and everywhere he goes is fully known to God. This would be true even if he were sinful because he could not hide from God; but here his "ways" refers to his obedience in the midst of trouble. He lives obediently because God knows everything about him. Goldingay concludes that "our living obedient lives means God keeps an eye on us."[307] That may be true, but in this passage the psalmist says he kept God's word *because* his ways were before God. It was another motivation for faith and righteousness.

Message and Application

Once again the motif of persecution appears in this mostly positive meditation. The writer of Psalm 119 finds great comfort in

---

306. *Psalms 60–150*, p. 419.
307. *Psalms 90–150*, p. 440.

the word of the LORD and is able to commit his difficulty to the LORD in a prayer for deliverance and rest in the peace of God and the promise of salvation. The expository idea can capture this easily: *When powerful leaders persecute them unjustly, committed believers remain faithful to God's word for in it they find peace and the promise of salvation.* These same ideas are confirmed in the New Testament, but with greater detail and certainty. Christ's beatitudes included those who suffer persecution for his sake (Matt. 5:10–12); their persecution comes from the world that does not believe in Christ (John 16:1–4), but if it is endured it will bear fruit and increase joy, especially when he comes again (John 16:20–22). In the meantime, he has given us a peace that is beyond what the world can understand (John 14:27).

ת Taw

An Urgent Plea for Deliverance and Restoration

Text and Textual Variants

ת	169	Let my cry come near before you, O LORD; give me understanding according to[308] your word (דְּבָר)!
ת	170	Let my supplication come in before you; deliver me according to[309] your oracle (אִמְרָה).
ת	171	Let my lips pour forth praise, for you teach me your statutes (חֹק).
ת	172	Let my tongue sing of your oracle (אִמְרָה),[310] for all your commandments (מִצְוָה) are right.
ת	173	Let your hand *be ready* to help me, for I have chosen your precepts (פִּקּוּד).
ת	174	I long for your salvation, O LORD,

---

308. A few manuscripts and the Syriac have "in," בְּ, instead of כְּ, "according to."
309. A few manuscripts and the Syriac have "in" here as well.
310. A few Hebrew manuscripts and some Greek manuscripts have this word plural.

and your law (תּוֹרָה) is my delight.³¹¹

ת 175 Let me³¹² live, and praise you,
and let your decisions (מִשְׁפָּט)³¹³ help me.

ת 176 I have gone astray like a lost sheep; seek your servant,
for I do not forget your commandments (מִצְוָה).

Exegetical Analysis

Summary

Confessing that he has gone astray like a lost sheep, the psalmist calls for God to deliver him according to his word so that he may praise and sing to God (119:169–176).

Outline

I. He calls for God to hear his supplication and deliver him (169–170).
II. He desires to praise and sing of God's word (171–172).
III. He calls for God's hand to be near and to enable him to live since he loves his law (173–175).
IV. He confesses that he has gone astray like a lost sheep and asks God to rescue him by his word (176).

Commentary in Expository Form

I. Penitent believers pray for deliverance and understanding (169–170).

With this final stanza the lengthy meditation of Psalm 119 comes to its proper conclusion; but the desire for understanding

---

311. As before, the Greek version translates this word as "meditation."
312. The Hebrew is נַפְשִׁי, usually translated "my soul."
313. The form in the MT is singular, "your decision," but the verb following it is plural: "let them help me," meaning "your decision." The noun would have to be taken collectively. However, the Syriac version makes the verb singular to match the subject; but the majority of Hebrew manuscripts and the versions have the noun as the plural. The English translation requires this.

God's word and deliverance from adversaries have not yet been realized, as the petitions of the stanza make clear. In all but two of the lines of this section the third feminine form of the volitional mood (the jussive) is used (hence the letter *taw*, ת), expressing his desire for understanding, deliverance, and spiritual renewal.

In the first two verses of the stanza he prays for understanding and deliverance. In verse 169 he asks that his cry (רִנָּתִי; s.v. Ps. 33:1) draw near (תִּקְרַב) before the LORD; and then he specifies the intended result with "and give me understanding" (הֲבִינֵנִי; s.v. Ps. 49:1) that will be based on and in harmony with the word. In verse 170 his desire is that his supplication (תְּחִנָּתִי; s.v. Ps. 4:5) come before the LORD, so that the LORD would deliver him (הַצִּילֵנִי; s.v. Ps. 22:20). The combination of "supplication," an appeal for grace, and "before you," literally "before your face," signifying grace, stresses the need for God's favor for deliverance. This appeal, to be delivered, along with the former need, to gain understanding, are two frequent petitions made in Psalm 119. Here the provision of deliverance from outward circumstances would give him freedom to learn and apply God's word; and accordingly, provision of understanding would enable him to discover God's promise and provision of deliverance in the word.

II. They desire to praise God for his word he has taught them (171–172).

The desire of the psalmist in the next two verses is to praise God; but making this a petition indicates that God must give him the reason to praise (the prayer is a metonymy of effect). The appeal uses "my lips" in verse 171 and "my tongue" in verse 172, both figurative of his capacity to speak (metonymies of cause). With the first he uses a verb of exuberance: "pour forth" (תַּבַּעְנָה), like a gushing spring of water; and with the second he uses "sing" (תַּעַן, from עָנָה), which is more controlled than the former.[314] He wants to sing praises to the LORD upon his

---

314. The verb commonly means "to answer," but in some contexts and in some cognate languages it has the sense of singing, perhaps antiphonally.

deliverance—spontaneously and enthusiastically, and certainly in the sanctuary before the assembly. The focus of his praise will be twofold: God enables him to know the word, and the word is righteous.

The enablement to know is expressed in the causal clause: "for you teach me (כִּי תְלַמְּדֵנִי) your statutes." How would this happen? Certainly a good deal of the teaching would come from the priests, who were expected to teach the law to Israel (Mal. 2:7). But in the Psalter another way was through the meditations of the heart (=mind), especially in the night seasons on his bed (Ps. 63:6–7). Just the thought of the sovereign LORD teaching him the eternal word inspires in him the desire to praise.

III. They pray for saving help and spiritual renewal because they love and seek to obey God's word (173–175).

Now the psalmist urges God to deliver him. The precise words are: "Let your hand *be ready* to my help" (to help me"; לְעָזְרֵנִי, s.v. Ps. 46:1); the verb "be ready" is added for clarification. The "hand" of God (an anthropomorphism) signifies God's power; and that power will be needed to "help" the psalmist, i.e., do for him what he cannot do for himself. The basis for this appeal is that the psalmist has chosen God's precepts—he wanted to know and observe them. Then, in the next verse (174) he states that he longs for God's deliverance, adding, "and your law is my delight" (שַׁעֲשֻׁעָי; s.v. Ps. 119:14; compare Ps. 1:3).

The reason the law is his delight is that it in part promises salvation to the saints. His prayer to be delivered will be answered, one way or another. Accordingly, in verse 175 the psalmist longs for spiritual renewal: "Let me live and praise you; and let your decisions help me." The verb "let me ('my life') live" (תְּחִי־נַפְשִׁי) is problematic in that we would expect "revive me (my life)." To translate it that way, or as "preserve my life" or "restore my life," is too developed for the basic (*qal*) verbal form used here. He simply wants to live.

Miriam and the women apparently responded line-by-line in singing the song of Moses at the sea (Exod. 15:21).

With the three petitions—for help, for deliverance, and for life, there are four reasons stated for the prayers to be answered: 1) he has chosen God's law and is resolved to obey it; 2) he has longed for deliverance from all hindrances so that he might obey freely; 3) the law is his devotion and delight; and 4) he desires to praise God for the answers to his prayer. In short, he is a believer who trusts the LORD for salvation, is committed to obeying his word, and will praise him throughout his life. Scripture teaches that God will bless such saints because this is what he desires from them.

IV. They pray for God to seek and find them because they have gone astray (176).

In verse 176, we have a personal confession: "I have gone astray (תָּעִיתִי); seek your servant as a lost sheep." We cannot interpret these words as we would the parable of the lost sheep in the New Testament, for here the psalmist has repeatedly said that he is faithful to the LORD. This is likely describing some outward situations that have forced him to wander and not merely his spiritual condition.[315] As he travels through life he is exposed to dangers, and those dangers often force him off course. Perowne explains it this way:

> In what sense can one who has so repeatedly declared his love of God's word, who has asserted that he has kept God's precepts, make this confession? The figure cannot be employed here in the same sense, for instance, in which it is employed in our Lord's parable. He who is the lost sheep here is one who does not forget God's commandments. The figure, therefore, seems in this place to denote the helpless condition of the Psalmist, without protectors, exposed to enemies, in the midst of whom he wanders, not knowing where to find rest and shelter. But in the 'I have gone astray,' there is doubtless the sense of sin as well as of weakness, though there is also the consciousness of

---

315. Kirkpatrick, *Psalms*, p. 733.

love to God's law, 'I do not forget Thy commandments.' Comp. with this xix. 12–14 [13–15].³¹⁶

He has wandered, he acknowledges, "like a lost sheep." The word translated "lost" has the sense of "perishing" or "ready to perish" (אָבַד). This clarifies his appeal to God to let him live. Even though he has wandered and has come close to perishing, he remains God's faithful servant (עַבְדֶּךָ; s.v. Ps. 134:1) and so petitions God to seek and find him. And God should do this because he is an obedient believer, one who does not forget the commandments.

Message and Application

The people of God are a praying people; they pray continually for the LORD to hear and answer their prayers. But as they meditate in his word they also come to see more areas of their lives that are not right, for the Word of the LORD convicts them of their sin. Their prayers therefore necessarily include an appeal for forgiveness. The exposition of this stanza could then be summarized in this way: *When those who love God's word and seek to obey it do wander away from him, they must acknowledge their sin as they pray for him to rescue and restore them.* The believers today know that if they confess their sins he will be faithful and just to forgive them because forgiveness is based on the shed blood of Christ (see for example 1 John 1:5–10).

---

316. *Psalms*, II:367.

PSALM 120

Longing to Dwell in Peace

INTRODUCTION

Text and Textual Variants

A Song of the Ascents[1]

1 In my distress[2] I called to the LORD
   and he answered me.[3]
2 Deliver me, O LORD, from lying lips,[4]
   from[5] a deceitful tongue.

---

1. The word is from the verb "to go up" (עָלָה), and so means "goings up" or "ascents." The Hebrew word is הַמַּעֲלוֹת and the Greek rendering is τῶν ἀναβαθμῶν, perhaps "(An Ode) of the Steps."
2. The construction in the MT, בַּצָּרָתָה לִּי, is rendered in the Greek version with ἐν τῷ θλίβεσθαί με, "when I was being afflicted."
3. The word order in the text is: "To the LORD in my distress // I called and he answered me."
4. MT has שָׁקֶר. The Greek text used a general word in place of "lying," ἀδίκων, "unjust." Both Aquila and Symmachus use "false" in harmony with the MT.
5. Greek adds the conjunction: "and from."

3 What more shall be done to you,[6]
   O[7] deceitful tongue?[8]–
4 sharp arrows of the warrior
   with hot coals from broom trees![9]
5 Woe is me, that I stay in Meshech,[10]
   that I dwell among the tents of Kedar!
6 I[11] have dwelt too long
   with those[12] who hate peace.
7 I am for peace,[13]
   but when I speak, they are for war.[14]

Composition and Context

With Psalm 120 we begin the study of the pilgrim psalms (Pss.

---

6. The Hebrew text uses a wish formula: מַה־יִּתֵּן לְךָ וּמַה־יֹּסִיף לָךְ, "what shall he give to you, and what shall he add to you," which the Greek version translated fairly literally, albeit as passives ("What might be given to you, and what might be added to you"). Here the two verbs have been taken as a hendiadys construction and translated as one clause.
7. The Greek version adds a preposition πρὸς to form the reading "against (a deceitful tongue)."
8. The word "tongue" is לָשׁוֹן and not written as a construct; "deceitful" is either in apposition to it or functions as an adjective.
9. For רְתָמִים, "broom trees," the Greek version has ἐρημικοῖς, "desert," which may be taken as "desolating coals" instead of "desert coals." BDB lists a proper name רִתְמָה as a station in the desert (Num. 33), which the translator may have known about, especially in view of the other place names in the psalm, and generalized the word to refer to the desert or a desolate area.
10. The Greek text has a verb, ἐμακρύνθη, "prolonged, put at a distance" a translation of the verb מָשַׁךְ that means "to prolong." It also takes the first verb to be a verbal noun with a subject suffix, reading, "Woe is me, that my place of sojourning was put at a distance." The verb in the MT, גַּרְתִּי, is translated ἡ παροικία μου, "my place of sojourning."
11. MT has נַפְשִׁי, "my life" = "I."
12. MT has a singular form; a few manuscripts, the Greek and other versions all have the plural.
13. The Greek translation redivides the line, taking this colon with the last part of the preceding line: "With those who hate peace (7) I was for peace."
14. The Greek version reads: "(when I would speak to them,) they would fight me without a cause," ἐπολέμουν με δωρεάν, a verb was read instead of the noun "war," and the independent pronoun "they" (הֵמָּה) was read as "without a cause" (for the form חִנָּם), confusing the two words.

Longing to Dwell in Peace

120–134), which are also part of the *hallel* psalms (Pss. 120–136). All fifteen of these psalms have the heading "ascents," which has been given several different interpretations. One is the old view that these psalms in the collection were for or by Jews in the Diaspora, making their way back to the sanctuary to worship.[15] But there is no compelling support for this; in fact, the collection includes pre-exilic as well as post-exilic psalms. In Psalm 120 the mention of Meshek and Kedar do not necessarily indicate that the psalmist was dwelling in a different country; the names may be taken figuratively.

These psalms most likely were collected for use in festal processions on the way to the sanctuary and perhaps in the sanctuary as well.[16] It is not clear why Psalm 120 was used to begin the collection; perhaps it was because it set the tone for the difficulty of worshiping the LORD with militant opposition.[17] It expresses the tension of trying to live in peace when surrounded by enemies who only want conflict until they get what they want. Unfortunately, this tension has characterized life in the land of Israel for ages. And since this psalmist found no resolution, all he could do was pray that the LORD would deliver him from deceitful enemies. The situation was (and always has been) so frustrating that prayer was the only truly workable resource.

The psalm may be classified as a lament, although some take it as a thanksgiving. The decision is related to the interpretation of the first verse: if the verse refers to something that happened previously (and the verbs translated as past tenses), then this will be a lament that draws confidence from that experience; but if the verse refers to the present crisis (whether the verbs are translated as past tenses or present), then it would be

---

15. See Perowne, *Psalms,* II:369.
16. Mowinckel, *The Psalms in Israel's Worship,* II:208. Eaton, however, notes that there is little evidence that the reference to "ascents" means pilgrims' journeys *(Psalms,* p. 279). See further Cuthbert Cubitt Keet, *A Study of the Psalms of Ascents* (London: The Mitre Press, 1969), pp. 1–17; he surveys the views and concludes it is a pilgrim psalm.
17. After raising this question, Weiser concludes that concerning the occasion for the psalm we are as much in the dark as in many other psalms *(Psalms,* p. 742).

a thanksgiving song, verse 1 stating the thanksgiving and the rest of the psalm reporting what happened.[18]

Verse 1 may at first sound like a thanksgiving ("I called . . . he answered"), but there is nothing else in the psalm that follows a praise pattern. The verse is probably a reference to an earlier answer to prayer from which the psalmist draws confidence.[19] The people of God often rehearse how the LORD has answered them in the past when they are looking for deliverance in the present.

Exegetical Analysis

Summary

Hoping for peace among treacherous neighbors who are constantly for war, the psalmist can only pray to the LORD for deliverance, but he may do so in confidence because of past answers to prayers.

Outline

I. The psalmist finds confidence from answered prayer (1).
II. The psalmist prays for deliverance from deceitful neighbors and longs for their destruction (2–4).
   A. The LORD should deliver him from people who are deceitful (2).
   B. The LORD should defeat his recalcitrant enemies.
III. The psalmist laments his predicament and longs for peace (5–7).
   A. He must dwell among people who hate peace (5–6).
   B. He longs for peace but they are for war (7).

---

18. Anderson, *Psalms 73–150*, p. 848.
19. See Keet, *A Study of the Psalms of Ascent*, p. 18; see also Allen, *Psalms 101–150*, pp. 147–8; and Weiss, *The Bible from Within*, pp. 275–7, who argues for a lament on the basis of the form of the psalm.

COMMENTARY IN EXPOSITORY FORM

I. God's people build confidence through answered prayer (1).

The first line is a declaration that God has answered the prayers of the psalmist in the past, an encouraging way to begin an individual petition like this; the two verbs are accordingly translated with the past tense, "I called" and "he answered." The psalmist is beginning this prayer with an acknowledgment that the LORD answered other prayers when he called to him from his distress.[20]

The word order gives prominence to the LORD, the verse beginning with "to the LORD in my distress." Then, by placing the two verbs together at the end of the line the psalmist stresses the simple fact: "I cried and he answered." What that distress was we do not know, especially if this refers to an earlier prayer. The word "distress" (צָרָה) means a "strait, narrow place"; it simply indicates that he was in a bind when he prayed.[21] Because the

---

20. The first verb is a perfect tense (קָרָאתִי) and the second a preterite with *waw* consecutive (וַיַּעֲנֵנִי). Some translations make them both English present tenses, meaning they would refer to this prayer. The NIV makes the second verb a regular imperfect and therefore a purpose clause, "so that he may answer." For a survey of various translations see Broyles, *Psalms*, p. 447.
21. The noun is related to the verb צָרַר, "to bind, tie up, be restricted, narrow, cramped." The verb can have the basic meaning of referring to things tied up or wrapped up, like the kneading troughs in Egypt (Exod. 12:34), or of people being cramped in the land too small for them (Isa. 49:19). But it can also have the sense of something distressing, something pressing in on one, such as the distress of Jacob at the prospect of the advancing Esau in Genesis 32:8: it was narrow for him—he was in straits, i.e., distress. The adjective צַר means "narrow, tight"; it too can have the sense of a place that is too narrow, too small for people (2 Kings 6:1). A noun צַר means "distress, straits," and the feminine noun צָרָה has these same basic meanings (it occurs some 24 times in the Psalms). In general, it refers to the distress that comes from some pressure or difficulty that presses in on the person—the sufferer would be in a bind. It is impossible in most cases to determine exactly what the distressing situation was, because it is often used for "the day of trouble" (Ps. 50:15) or the like. It is used for the distress that the brothers caused Joseph when they threw him into the pit and then they themselves were plagued with that distress (Gen.

LORD answered his prayer, the difficulty must have been a previous one. And this recollection provides the psalmist with confidence in the current crisis. This is a reminder that believers need to pray so that they may receive answers to their prayers that will build their confidence.

II. God's people hope and pray for deliverance from treacherous enemies (2–4).

A. *They pray for deliverance from deceitful enemies (2).*

The psalm reminds us that the presence of deceitful enemies is a perennial problem, and so the people of God must regularly and earnestly pray for protection and deliverance for them.[22] Verse 2 is just such a prayer; it begins with the vocative, "O LORD." And the urgency of the request is expressed by the imperative "deliver" me[23] (הַצִּילָה, perhaps with the sense of "snatch away"; s.v. Ps. 22:20); in this case the appeal is for deliverance from treacherous people and their false words. The prepositional phrases that complete the verse clarify the difficulty: "from the lip of falsehood, from the deceitful tongue." Both "lip" and "tongue" are the instruments of speech and therefore signify what the enemies say (metonymies of cause). The first phrase uses an attributive genitive (מִשְּׂפַת־שֶׁקֶר, "from lip of falsehood"; for "falsehood," s.v. Ps. 144:8), "false lip," meaning false speech; and the second phrase uses a simple attributive adjective (מִלָּשׁוֹן רְמִיָּה, "from a deceitful tongue"), meaning deceitful speech (for "deceitful," s.v Ps. 5:7). The repetition of the description

---

42:21). The trouble could be physical, such as in travail (Jer. 49:24); but it often affects the spirit with an overwhelming sense of anguish. In general, it depicts any kind of trouble from which the psalmist cries for help to be set free—he is in a bind, we might say. There is another related noun, מֵצַר, "distress, straits," such as the anguish of being drawn towards *She'ol* (Ps. 116:3).

22. Some commentators suggest the enemies are those after the exile who prevented the people from returning to the sanctuary; Keet rightly finds this unconvincing (p. 19).
23. The MT has נַפְשִׁי, which could also be translated "my life."

underscores the problem: what the enemies say is purposefully false and intended to deceive. And in this context that refers to the psalmist's desire for peace. He may have in mind the false treaties and deceitful promises that these enemies make regarding peace. But the descriptions certainly would apply to any deceitful people, not just those dishonestly negotiating treaties.

B. They long for the defeat of treacherous enemies (3–4).

In conjunction with his prayer, the psalmist expresses his longing in the next two verses. The line is put in the general form of an oath using a question and an answer.[24] The verse reads literally "what will he give to you," but since the subject is not expressed, the form can be translated with the passive voice (as the Greek version does with, "what will be given to you [τί δοθείη σοι]," as if the form were יֻתַּן). Likewise, the second clause, "what will he add to you," would come to mean "what will be added" (as if from יוּסַף instead of יֹסִיף). Then, "what will be given" and "what will be added" together form one idea (a verbal hendiadys): "What will be done to you, and more?" or "What more will be done to you?" Since the psalmist is longing that something more will be done to the deceitful enemies to bring about peace, it could be translated, "O that something more will be done to you."

Verse 4 completes the desired punishment. The first part is relatively easy to understand; he wants them to be destroyed with sharpened arrows of a warrior. If literal, "arrows" would be a reference to war (metonymy of adjunct): if they want war, then they should die in war. But the psalmist is for peace and not war. If "arrows" can also be used figuratively for speech (an implied comparison; see Ps. 57:4; 64:3; Prov. 25:18), then the psalmist would be desiring that they be destroyed by retributive words, or their own deceptive words coming back on them.

The second half adds "with hot coals of broom trees." The

---

24. Weiser, p, 742. See 1 Sam. 3:17 and 2 Sam. 3:35. Keet says that if this is so then it would indicate the enemies were sworn to destroy him, but his prayer is that what was resolved would be turned on them (p. 20).

wood from the broom tree burns easily and retains heat; and then when the fire appears to go out it can quickly flame up with a bit of wind. Perhaps the psalmist envisions them in the desert under attack where the use of broom trees would be useful in making campfires. But his allusion to broom trees is fitting for it matches their deception: the deceiver would be deceived, thinking the fire was out, only to have it flare up and burn him.

III. God's people must promote peace while living among people who hate peace (5–7).

A. They often must endure people who reject peace with them (5–6).

The Israelites certainly had to live in the midst of antagonistic enemies all through their history; likewise, many faithful believers in the world today also find that they live among people who oppose them and hate their faith. The psalmist therefore speaks for many when he laments that he must dwell in the midst of people who are violent. He says, "Woe to me that I stay *in* Meshek,[25] *and* dwell among the tents of Kedar." The two verbs used indicate that he recognized he was not a permanent resident among them; the first verb (גַּרְתִּי, from גּוּר, "to sojourn, stay, dwell") usually means a temporary stay, and the second verb (שָׁכַנְתִּי, "to settle down, dwell") indicates the dwelling is only a little more settled. Both verbs (perfect tenses) are put in the English present to reflect the psalmist's current lamentable situation. VanGemeren says the psalmist felt as though he were an alien.[26]

There is some difficulty with the locations mentioned here. Unless some other place is meant by the word Meshek, the reference is to the steppes of Russia (see Gen. 10:2; Ezek. 38:2); and Kedar is in the remote south wilderness of Arabia (see Isa. 21:16–17; Ezek. 27:21). Because these are too far apart to be close by the psalmist's probable location in the land, the Greek

---

25. Briggs concludes that this word is improbable and must have been a later conjecture (*Psalms*, II:444).
26. *Psalms*, p. 892.

version took the letters in the manuscript (מֹשֶׁךְ, for Meshek [מֶשֶׁךְ]) to be a verb ("prolonged," מָשַׁךְ) and not a place. But if the proper names are retained, the verse need not be saying that the psalmist lived near both places; it is possible they were meant to have an expanded significance. He may have meant that he lived among people just like them, that is, hostile barbarians.[27] Or, by choosing these two names, the psalmist may have meant that the nation was situated between these northern hordes and southern tribes, both of whom were known for their hatred of Israel. It could also be that by choosing places so far apart the psalmist was accounting for remote places Israelites lived, and therefore difficulties that the pilgrims had to overcome (a theme in the collection). The point is that the people had to deal with hostile opposition all around them.

The psalmist then appeals to the LORD that he has dwelt[28] among people who hate him far too long (v. 6). The participle "hater of" (שׂוֹנֵא) should be taken as a collective noun, representing people who hate peace. It is like saying, "I have to dwell with the terrorists." The verb "hate" (שָׂנֵא; s.v. Ps. 139:21) includes the idea of rejecting something; to the wicked, peace with Israel was loathsome and unacceptable unless it was under their terms completely. But for Israel that meant no peace at all. Weiser says, "Even the most devout man will not be left in peace if it does not please his wicked neighbour."[29]

B. They long for peace but are met with hostility (7).

Verse seven provides the sum of the matter for God's people.

---

27. This is the view of Anderson (p. 850), Briggs (p. 445), Allen (p. 146) and many others. The psalmist was comparing his foes to these vicious enemies. Dahood suggests taking the sentence as a conditional clause, saying that even if he were to reside among this or that group, he would still be among those who hate peace (*Psalms,* 3:194, 197). Others have suggested that the psalm reflects the feelings of the people during the Diaspora, when they were scattered among the nations. But there is no hint of that here.
28. The verb "dwelt" (שָׁכְנָה) is the 3rdfsg perfect tense, agreeing with the subject "my life" (נַפְשִׁי), here rendered simply as "I." The verb has a prepositional phrase attached to it (לְהּ־) which serves as an ethical dative to emphasize the subject.
29. *The Psalms,* 744.

The first two words simply say "I peace," perhaps "I *am* peace" (compare Ps. 109:4, "I am prayer"), meaning "I am all about peace." But in view of the parallelism it can be read "I [am for] peace." This cryptic expression is then a longing for peace, and in the context essentially a prayer for the LORD to restore peace. The word "peace" (שָׁלוֹם; s.v. Ps. 38:3) can also mean well-being, welfare, or wholeness. Here in contrast to war it would signify at the least an end to hostilities, but more than that, a condition in the land where they could live out their lives undisturbed. Apart from brief periods of respite, the land has never enjoyed such peace—the world has never seen it.

The godly long for this peace and pray for it; whereas the wicked sow discord. So the rest of the verse reads "but when I speak, they are for war."[30] There is some question about where to divide the verse into its parallel units. The temporal clause would go nicely with the first clause ("I am for peace when I speak") were it not for the conjunction (וְכִי, "but when") that breaks it up. The idea is essentially the same, though, for it would be peace that he promotes. But his words are met with threats of war.

MESSAGE AND APPLICATION

The writer, most likely a Davidic king, was faced with the tension of living among warrior tribes who were not interested in peace. But what made it so frustrating was that they lied and deceived, making any dealings or agreements with them meaningless. So for the psalmist the only solution was for God to deliver him from them and deal with them in the way that they dealt with other people. Not much has changed since the days of the psalmist.

New Testament believers are not as bold in their expressed desires for deliverance from enemies by divine judgment, even though they long for the same peace. This may be in part because Christians are not a nation living in one area that has to deal with deceitful, militant enemies all around them as Israel

---

30. Some commentators say that "war" here is symbolic. That is no doubt true, but if it is symbolic of all hostilities, then it would still include war.

did—at least not Christians in the West. But in some areas of the world, and certainly down through history, many groups of Christians have been hated and persecuted by people around them. Jesus said that in this life we will have enemies who hate us. We certainly should pray for deliverance from such people, and for peace; but we are also now called to pray for them, that they might come to repentance (Matt. 5:45). Like the psalmist we may see no lasting resolution to terror and conflict on the personal or international level, not yet anyway. But we know that when the Lord comes he will judge the world and bring in everlasting peace. For that day of deliverance we pray (as in the Lord's prayer). But in the meantime, we must try to live peaceably with all people (Rom. 12:18–20).

The message of the psalm, therefore, may be worded to express the desire of the righteous who must endure this difficulty: *When the LORD intervenes to deliver the faithful, he will destroy the deceivers who are hostile to believers and refuse peace with them*. This hope for vindication is a comfort to the righteous who often find themselves in the midst of hostile and deceptive people; and it is for this longed for deliverance they pray.

PSALM 121
Protection on the Pilgrim Way

INTRODUCTION

Text and Textual Variants

A Song for the Ascents.[1]

1 I lift up my eyes to the hills—
   from whence[2] comes my help?

---

1. The Hebrew now uses the preposition: שִׁיר לַמַּעֲלוֹת. A number of manuscripts do not have it.
2. Instead of using an interrogative pronoun, the Greek version used the relative pronoun ὅθεν for the Hebrew מֵאַיִן, giving the meaning that the help would come from the hills. Later Greek revisions changed it to πόθεν, the interrogative. This relative pronoun was used in the KJV, leading to studies and sermons on help from the hills, such as Sinai and Calvary.

   If the interrogative is correct, then the "hills" are to be interpreted in a negative sense, a source of anxiety for the journey, or perhaps a reference to the high place of false gods along the way, who can provide no help at all This interpretation that travel through the hills posed a problem makes the best sense.

2 My help *comes* from the LORD,
    the maker of heaven and earth.
3 May he not give[3] your foot[4] to slipping;[5]
    may he who protects you not slumber.
4 Indeed, he who protects Israel
    will neither slumber nor sleep.
5 The LORD is your protector;[6]
    the LORD[7] is your shade over your right hand.
6 The sun will not strike you by day,
    nor the moon by night.
7 May the LORD protect[8] you from all calamity;

    Taking the word as a relative pronoun puts the idea of the "hill" in a positive light. Briggs took it to refer to the mountains of Jerusalem, the location of the sanctuary (*Psalms* II:446). A case has also been made for the word to refer to the cosmic mountains of the LORD (see Ps. 48:1–3 and 87:1–3; see Allen, *Psalm*, 151). T. H. Weir suggested that the question of the verse be taken as an indirect question, which would give a positive emphasis to the hills ("Psalm 121:1," *ExpT* 27 [1915/16]:90, 91). It would read something like "I lift up my eyes to the hills (to see) where my help is to come from." The sanctuary in Zion would then be intended as the source of help. The Syriac reads the word "help" as a participle, "my helper," and not the noun "help."

3. This translation of verse 3 takes the verb forms with אַל as negated jussives, in contrast to the forms in verse 4 that use לֹא (see also Goldingay, *Psalms 90–150*, p. 457; Jerome F. D. Creach, "Psalm 121," *Int 50* [1996]:47–51). Verse 4 provides the confidence for the prayer of verse 3. The Greek version agrees with "let not (your foot) be moved": "do not give (your feet) to stumbling," μὴ δῷς εἰς σάλον. Others leave it as an imperfect and explain that the form with אַל has additional emphasis, or that it is a negative statement with subjective conviction (see GKC 107p, 109e).

4. Many manuscripts have "your feet"; the singular fits the idiom well enough.

5. The form in the MT is a noun, לַמּוֹט, pointed with an article to ensure the form. The editors of BHS suggest changing it to an infinitive, לְמוֹט, "to slip," as in Psalm 66:9 (but see 118:18).

6. The MT has a participle with a suffix, שֹׁמְרֶךָ; but the Greek reads φυλάξει, "shall keep (you)," and the Targum and Jerome agree with a future tense translation, suggesting the imperfect tense. The Qumran scroll has the participle, clearly agreeing with the Hebrew text. But Qumran also adds "in the night" (בלילה).

7. This is not in the Qumran scroll.

8. The verbs in verse 7 could just as easily be translated as imperfect tenses and not jussives, as most translations do. The Greek translation also uses the future. The meaning of the psalm as a whole is not affected by this

may he protect your life.
8 The LORD will protect
your going out and your coming in,
from this time forth, and even forevermore.

Composition and Context

This is a psalm of encouragement or blessing prompted by the concern of the pilgrim for safety on the journey up to Jerusalem.[9] The comforting promise is that the LORD who required the people to come and worship him in the sanctuary would watch over the faithful on the journey, as well as in all the activities of their lives. Thus, the theology of the passage concerns divine protection for God's faithful people.[10] The tension and the truth expressed in the psalm would fit any period of Israel's history, but it is impossible to identify the particular occasion for it.[11]

The passage has a change in the personal pronouns, indicating that it may record a dialogue between two people on a pilgrimage. It is possible that it is a literary dialogue, meaning that the psalmist is the speaker throughout. Support for this

---

choice, only the way the meaning is laid out. I suggest reading verse 7 as a prayer, with verse 8 as the confidence. This would reflect the pattern in the psalm: verse 1 is the concern, verse 2 the answer; verse 3 the prayer, verses 4–6 the comforting answer; verse 7 a prayer, and verse 8 the comforting assurance.

9. The psalm could also be applied to the journey home; in that case it would form something of a farewell liturgy spoken by the priest (see Anderson, *Psalms 73–150*, p. 851). But in the sequence with Psalm 122 that celebrates the arrival in the city, it seems more likely that the primary intent was the journey to the sanctuary. David G. Barker takes the "going out" as departure and the "coming in" as the returning to the next festival ("The LORD Watches over You," *BibSac* 152 [1995]:163–81).

10. For a different emphasis, see John T. Willis, "Psalm 121 as a Wisdom Poem," *HAR* 11 (1987):435–51.

11. The suggestion that the psalm was of a post-Deuteronomic origin (see Anderson, p. 851) is intended to say the psalm was late, assuming the Deuteronomic material is late. Anthony Ceresko suggests it is about the king going out on a campaign and returning safely, which would mean the psalm would be pre-exilic ("Psalm 121: Prayer of a Warrior?" *Bib* 70 [1989]:496–510).

view is based on the lack of decisive information about the participants and the comparison with Psalms 42 and 43.[12] But the dialogue with the inner self of Psalms 42 and 43 is made clear by the clarification of the "addressee": "why are you cast down, O my soul." If this is the correct interpretation for Psalm 121, then the psalmist would have to be encouraging himself with the pronoun "my,"[13] and then speak to himself with "your" in the rest of the psalm. But in Psalm 121 there is no clarification of the pronoun as in Psalm 42:5. It seems more likely, then, that there is an actual dialogue between two speakers recorded in the passage, the psalm reflecting some occasion of concern or perhaps frequent concerns. Kraus suggests, for example, that verse 1 is spoken by the individual, verse 2 by the priest, verse 3 by the individual again, and verse 4 the priest again.[14] I would interpret the interchange a little differently: at the outset the pilgrim expresses both the concern and confidence for the trip (vv. 1, 2); but the rest of the psalm (vv. 3–8) appears to be from someone else, an accompanying pilgrim or priest, who both prays for the traveler and assures him of the LORD's continual protection. Such a distinction, or one similar to it, allowed for the psalm to be sung or said antiphonally on all journeys to the holy city. So the individual pilgrim speaking in the psalm represents all concerned pilgrims, and the accompanying pilgrim or priest all those who give the words of comfort.

There is another pattern that is helpful for the interpretation of the psalm. It was written in simple verse pairs, and the second verse of each pair (vv. 2, 4, 6, 8) answers the first with what the LORD's action would be.[15] This pattern is clear enough in the first two pairs; a specific translation of the verbs in verse 7 in the last pair would carry the established pattern to the end; the third pair is less clear, but the addition of verse 6 to verse 5 provides an expansion of the concern that the principle provides.

---

12. VanGemeren, *Psalms*, p. 894.
13. Many commentators delete the suffix "my" as a copyist's error (see Briggs, II:446). There is no support for this deletion.
14. *Psalms 60–150*, p. 427.
15. Broyles, *Psalms*, p. 449.

Protection on the Pilgrim Way

Exegetical Analysis

Summary

Faithful pilgrims who journey to Jerusalem to worship the LORD take comfort in the fact that the LORD, the creator of heaven and earth and the protector of Israel, will protect them on their journey and at all times.

Outline

I. The Pilgrim's Concern: The pilgrim expresses his need for help as he contemplates the journey to Jerusalem, but consoles himself that the LORD, the creator of heaven and earth, will help him (1–2).
   A. He asks for the source of help for the journey through the hills (1).
   C. He affirms that the LORD, the creator, is his source of help (2).
II. The Blesser's Assurance: The blesser prays for and gives assurance of the LORD's protection for the pilgrim on his mission and in his activities throughout life (3–8).
   A. He gives assurance that the protector of Israel is never indifferent to his people (3–4).
      1. The concern is that the LORD not be indifferent to their needs (3).
      2. The assurance is that the LORD is never indifferent to their needs (4).
   B. He affirms that the LORD protects his faithful people at all times (5–6).
      1. The LORD is the protector of the pilgrim's activities (5).
      2. The LORD protects him from harm day or night (6).
   C. He anticipates that the LORD will always protect the pilgrim (7–8).
      1. He prays that the LORD protect the pilgrim from all harm (7)
      2. He is confident that the LORD will protect him in his activities at all times (8).

COMMENTARY IN EXPOSITORY FORM

I. The faithful worshipers of the LORD, the creator, need not be anxious about dangers as they do the LORD's bidding (1–2).

A. Dangers in life raise concerns for God's people (1).

The first verse presents the concern and raises a question. The concern in this situation is over the perceived danger of the journey through the hills to Jerusalem. The first verb (נָשָׂא > אֶשָּׂא, s.v., Ps. 24:7) should then have the nuance of the present tense, "I lift up" (a progressive imperfect), with the whole expression, "I lift up my eyes," expressing the pilgrim's present and intense contemplation of the journey. After all, the way to the holy city would be through hills fraught with danger—slippery paths and loose rocks and deep valleys, as well as robbers and wild animals. This would have been a concern for anyone who had to travel, but certainly for the pilgrims who were required to go to the festivals (which, no doubt, led to their traveling in caravans).[16]

The second half of the verse raises the obvious question, "From whence comes my help come?" The verb could be given the same translation value as the first verb, but it could have more of a future nuance—"from whence will my help come?" The pronoun suffix on the subject, "my help" (עֶזְרִי; s.v. Ps. 46:1), serves as an objective genitive since God would help him. And this word "help" is a term that is used frequently for divine intervention in which the LORD

---

[16]. The hills could be the hills right around Jerusalem, but that would probably not raise concern—it would be a positive prospect. It is more likely that the hills refer to all the hills along the journey to the holy city, all of them possible places of danger. Other commentators suggest a more spiritual application to the idea. Ibn Ezra said it is the custom of anyone in straits to lift up his eyes to see if help will come to repel the enemy. Some take the hills to be a reference to the provision of help, that is from shrines to pagan gods in the hills, or for a sense of security from the everlasting hills (e.g., see Jer. 3:23; 1 Kings 20:23). In such cases the psalmist might be contemplating how false worship in those places would offer no help, only the LORD who made it all can protect (Keet, *Psalms of Ascents*, p. 26; see also Broyles, pp. 448, 449; and E. H. Blakeney, "Psalm 121:1–2," *ExT* 56 [1944/5]:111). See additionally John T. Willis, "An Attempt to Decipher Psalm 121:1b," *CBQ* 52 (1990):241–51.

provides what the people were lacking, or does for them what they cannot do for themselves. So it is more than simple assistance that is meant—without this help the psalmist would not be safe at all.

B. Protection comes from the LORD, the creator (2).

But the concerned pilgrim knows the answer: "my help *comes* from the LORD." The noun "help" is repeated to begin the line, and the verb "comes" is understood, based on the first verse. The confidence is that this needed help comes only from the LORD. But it is the parallel expression that clarifies why this is so: the LORD is "the maker of heaven and earth" (see Pss. 124:8; 134:3 115:5; 146:6). The participle "maker" (עֹשֵׂה) stresses the characteristic of the LORD as the creator; and the expression "heaven and earth" (a merism) signifies the whole universe and everything in it as his creation (the words are objective genitives after the construct participle).[17] The point is that if the LORD created everything, then he created the hills through which the pilgrim must walk; and whatever the LORD has created he can control. The doctrine of creation, therefore, is relevant for the life of faith in every detail. If pilgrims were faithfully obeying the sovereign LORD of creation by going up to Jerusalem to worship him, then they could be confident that he was able to overcome any difficulty on the way.

II. Those who trust the sovereign LORD God for protection find reassurance that he protects them from harm in every way (3–8).

A. They are assured that the LORD is never indifferent or unavailable (3–4).

The next two verses record the reassurance that the LORD never fails to watch over his people; the form this affirmation

---

17. Kraus says this is the language of Deutero-Isaiah (*Psalms 60–150*, p. 428). But the idea of the LORD being creator of heaven and earth is not only found in later texts (see Gen. 14:19; Ps. 65:6). Goldingay says the worship of the Maker of heaven and earth had long been central to the Jerusalem sanctuary (p. 457). See also Norman C. Habel, "', Maker of Heaven and Earth': A Study in Tradition Criticism," *JBL* 91 (1972):321–37.

takes is a prayer followed by an assuring answer. And because the pronouns now change, it is likely that these words were spoken to the pilgrim either by an accompanying priest or another pilgrim who was strong in the faith (especially if verse 3 is a prayer). At least in the arrangement of the psalm the lines lend themselves to antiphonal singing. Even today words of assurance from spiritually mature leaders are comforting, even if those words are written for all to read in the Scriptures.

Although most translations use a future tense in verse 3, the change between verses 3 and 4 suggests that it is more likely verse 3 is a prayer or a wish using the form of the negative that goes frequently with the jussive (אַל with יִתֵּן): "May he not give" (i.e., permit), paralleled with "may he not slumber" (again אַל with the verb יָנוּם).[18] The prayer is that the LORD would not permit the pilgrim's foot to slip, i.e., that he not fall or be harmed in any way (foot being a synecdoche for the whole person). The noun "slipping" (מוֹט, s.v. Ps. 62:2) would represent any accident along the journey. This concern is easy to understand given the treacherous walking in those hills and valleys even today. It is a prayer that any pilgrim would appreciate.

Such protection from slipping would require attention be given to every step of the way; and so if God is to prevent it then he must be attentive always. The parallel request, then, is that God not slumber.[19] The image may have suggested itself as the pilgrims made camp, knowing that God would not sleep. But the idea of slumbering is a figure (an implied comparison) for lack of attention or indifference and not merely a reference to being asleep. The subject of the verb is "your protector" or "your

---

18. Briggs says the negative of the jussive certainly implies a petition (II:447). Driver suggests it is an interrogative particle like Akkadian *ali*, meaning here "Will he not . . . ?" (*JSS* 13 [1968]:37). Others take it as an emphatic particle, "surely" (Perowne, *Psalms*, II:376); but see Psalm 25:1–3 where the אַל form is answered. The form of the second verb, יָנוּם, is the normal spelling of the imperfect, the jussive being a different spelling in hollow verbs, although not always.
19. There were times when the psalmists found themselves in grave danger and prayed as if the LORD had slumbered: "Rouse yourself . . . awaken . . ." (see Ps. 44:24). The figure is anthropomorphism, comparing God's apparent inactivity to being asleep. See also Pss. 7:6 and 35:23.

keeper" as it is often rendered (שֹׁמְרֶךָ; s.v. Ps. 12:7), referring to the LORD. Here the participle as a substantive stresses the idea of "protecting" and all that it involves. The prayer, then, is that the divine protector be vigilant in his care.

Because this word "protect / keep" (שָׁמַר) is used six times in these eight verses it is clearly the focus of the passage. God's protection of his people at times came through direct, divine intervention, such as through angels who were given charge over people lest they dash their foot on the way (Ps. 91:11), or through unexpected supernatural events (Judg. 5:4), or through the circumstances of life in which the LORD was clearly at work but remained hidden (Gen. 12:10–20), or through the agency of other believers (leaders such as kings and priests who were to shepherd the people) who were the LORD's instruments for guiding and protecting the people. This promise of divine protection was so basic to the well-being of Israel that it was part of the priestly blessing given in the sanctuary: "The LORD bless you and keep you . . ." (Num. 6:22–27). This psalm about protection for the pilgrimages to the sanctuary may have been a meditation on that oracle; and if the psalm was also used at the dismissal for the journey home, the words of the blessing would be fresh in their minds.

Verse 4 presents the response to verse three; it is a strong affirmation that the LORD is never unattentive. The wording in the text shows a clear contrast to verse 3. Beginning with the emphatic particle "indeed" (הִנֵּה), the construction expresses the truth (now it is the other negative לֹא with the imperfect tense): "Indeed, he will not slumber" (לֹא יָנוּם). A second verb is added, parallel to the first, to strengthen the point: "and neither will he sleep" (וְלֹא יִישָׁן). And the subject of these two verbs is placed in the second half of the verse–"the protector of Israel." Here it is the participle again, but now with a clarifying object that broadens the application from "your protector" to the "protector of Israel." God is not like the pagan gods—he does not need to rest, eat, or sleep; he is always there and always protecting.[20]

---

20. VanGemeren, *Psalms*, p. 896.

B. The LORD is vigilant at all times (5–6).

The next two verses elaborate the consistency and the extent of the divine protection the faithful can expect. The content of these two verses indicates the concerns of the pilgrims, but the attention is given fully to the assurances that will set them at ease. The section now begins with the subject clearly stated, the LORD; the name is then repeated in the second part to emphasize it further. The LORD, i.e., Yahweh, the maker of heaven and earth and the covenant God of Israel, is now expressly identified as the protector of Israel: "the LORD is your protector."

After this brief first exclamation, the verse develops the idea of protection. First, the blesser states that "the LORD is your shade over your right hand." The figure "shade" (a metaphor) compares divine protection to shade to signify constant and complete coverage. Shade for the pilgrim would be a real and delightful image. By stating that the shade is "over your right hand," the speaker means that the protection would be on all the pilgrim does—whatever he puts his hand to (a metonymy of cause).

This constant coverage would ensure that nothing would harm the pilgrim (v. 6). Here the words "sun" and "moon" form the expressed subjects of the verb. But they are to be explained as figurative (metonymies of subject), intending to convey what goes on under the sun and the moon; they also complement the merism expressed in "day" and "night," meaning all the time.[21] God will protect the faithful from any harm that strikes (נָכָה, a common word in military contexts, meaning "to strike, smite, attack") in the daytime or in the night time. This too would comfort the pilgrims since the journeys to the holy city often meant traveling for a day or two.

---

21. Some commentators still suggest that the psalmist believed that God would protect the pilgrim from sunstroke or from becoming moonstruck, or a lunatic; but it is much more likely that the line is referring to anything that happens night or day. E.g., the prophets say that the "day" of the LORD will burn with fire as an oven; it means the judgment that will occur on that day (see Mal. 4:1). Interestingly, the Targum has, "When the sun has dominion by day the morning demons shall not strike you; nor the night demons when the moon has dominion by night."

C. The LORD is able to protect from all harm (7–8).

The theme of the psalm is brought to a powerful conclusion in the last two verses—the verb "protect" (יִשְׁמֹר) is used twice in verse seven and once in verse eight. The precise translation of the last two verses is not certain, even though their meaning is clear. Most English versions translate it in all three places as the simple imperfect tense expressing the future.[22] That is certainly a legitimate translation, and in a psalm filled with expressions of confidence it is plausible. There is no indication in the form of the verb or the syntax to indicate it should not be the simple imperfect (and there is no indication that it must be the simple imperfect). But if simple futures, the interpretation would be that God will protect them from all evil at all times.

Such a promise would need to be explained in the light of the constant difficulties of life. The word "evil" (רַע; s.v. Ps. 10:15) can refer to any kind of calamity or misfortune in life, anything that brings pain and distress to a person, including sin, of course. For the psalm to assure the pilgrim that God will protect him from "all evil" will have to be harmonized with other passages that focus on the "evil" that the psalmists had to endure—hence we have the lament psalms.

But the other way to interpret the verse is to translate the verbs in verse 7 as jussives, expressing the concern in prayer, and leave verse 8 as imperfects, providing the response. It is a translator's choice because the verb form would be the same for an imperfect and a jussive. This means that verse 7 is the prayer or wish, and verse 8 its reply—which would follow the pattern of the verses with verses 2, 4, 6, and 8 as replies. In either case, whether two statements of confidence, or a prayer and the confidence, the point is that the LORD protects his people.

In both verses the holy name has been placed first for prominence in thought. In verse seven the prayer (or if preferred, the promise) is for protection from "all evil," any harm—sin, disaster, or trouble. The parallel expression in the verse assures that the LORD will protect the pilgrim's very life (נַפְשֶׁךָ; s.v. Ps. 11:5), now

---

22. The shift from the use of participles to the use of the imperfect / jussive marks the change from the present expression of the character of God as protector to the future manifestation of it.

and always. The two halves express the whole idea that the life be protected from all harm.

Then, in verse eight the priest, perhaps, responds with assurance of the LORD's protection, He uses two merisms. The first is "your going out and your coming in";[23] the two together refer to all activities in the daily course, especially going out on the pilgrimage and returning home, and including all movements in between (see Deut. 28:16; 31:2). The second merism is "from now and forever" (literally "from now and unto perpetuity"; for עוֹלָם, s.v. Ps. 61:5), which means "from now on"—always.

MESSAGE AND APPLICATION

So the theme of the psalm is divine protection, even though the passage does not clarify how God will do this. The message is that the pilgrim, the true worshiper who is obeying the LORD's word and making his way to the sanctuary to appear before the LORD and to praise him for his many benefits, may have confidence that the LORD will see him safely there and back—and in all activities of life. The expository idea is: *Believers may confidently trust in the LORD to protect them in their spiritual journey*. I have broadened the idea of a pilgrim journey to Jerusalem to apply the psalm to the spiritual journey of the believer today, which could of course include a sacred pilgrimage to a holy place to worship, but would refer to any spiritual activity such as ordinary services or special trips with a mission. Believers in their spiritual activities will build their confidence through prayer over their concerns and with the help of words of assurance from the LORD, both in his written word and through other believers. This assurance of the LORD's protective presence does not mean that life will be free of danger or difficulty; rather, believers will

---

23. The use of the verb "come" in verse one and now in verse eight forms an inclusio, a bracket effect for the entire psalm, bracketing the message of the psalm with the idea that if help comes from the LORD the pilgrim will safely come home. It could, of course, apply to a king going out to battle, but there is no support for that as the primary meaning (see A. C. Ceresko, "Psalm 121: A Prayer of a Warrior?" *Bib* 70 [1989]:496–510.)

be protected throughout the struggles of life.[24] In fact, the use of this psalm in Israel's pilgrimages to the holy city as well as my corresponding wording for its use in our spiritual journeys limits the application. It is when believers are obeying God in their activities that they can be confident in praying for his protection. But assurance of divine protection cannot be expected when people live in disobedience.

The New Testament reiterates the truth of the divine presence protecting faithful believers wherever they go (Matt. 28:20; Rom. 8:37–39). We read that the LORD is with us, from now to eternity; he will never leave us nor forsake us as we make our journey through life to the presence of the Lord.

---

24. If some harm should come to us, then that must be analyzed by faith to discern the divine purpose in it, with the conviction that ultimately the LORD will deliver us from all evil. The lament psalms often ask why calamity and suffering come upon the righteous who have been faithful (see Ps. 44 for example).

PSALM 122

The Joyful Journey to the City of God

INTRODUCTION

Text and Textual Variants

A Song of Ascents. Of David.[1]

1 I rejoiced with those who were saying[2] to me,
   "We will go to the house of the LORD!"
2 Our feet[3] are standing
   within your gates,[4] O Jerusalem–

---

1. The old Greek and the Targum and two Masoretic manuscripts omit "of David" from the superscription; but the Qumran scroll has it.
2. The form in the text is a participle: בְּאֹמְרִים; to obtain the meaning "when they said," the form would have to be repointed as an infinitive construct: בְּאָמְרָם, "in the saying of them," or, "when they said."
3. The Syriac and Qumran have רגלי, "my feet," to harmonize with the preceding verse. But the change to the plural "our" preserved in the better manuscripts to agree with "we will go" is to be retained.
4. The Greek has ἐν ταῖς αὐλαῖς σου, "in your courts," for בִּשְׁעָרַיִךְ, "in your gates." This seems to be a translation choice rather than a variant reading, since the Greek Old Testament uses this word for translating Hebrew

PSALM 122

3 Jerusalem, which is built
    as a city that is compacted[5] together;
4 where[6] the tribes go up,
    the tribes of the LORD
    (in accordance with the statute[7] for Israel),
    to praise the name of the LORD.
5 For there the thrones[8] for judgment stand,
    the thrones[9] of the house of David.

6 Ask for the peace of Jerusalem:
    "May those who love you[10] prosper.[11]
7 May there be peace within your walls,[12]

    "gates" elsewhere (e.g. Esther). But Aquila and Symmachus did change it to "gates" (πυλαις). Some Greek manuscripts do not have the pronoun "your," and read "courtyards of Jerusalem." Qumran has "gates."
5. The MT has שֶׁחֻבְּרָה־לָּהּ יַחְדָּו. The Greek version, as well as Symmachus and Jerome, took the word as a noun (the *pual perfect* verb being rare) meaning "fellowship, partnership" (= שֶׁחֶבְרָה); the Greek has ἧς ἡ μετοχη. αὐτῆς, meaning "whose fellowship is complete," or "that is shared in common." The translator may have had trouble with the rare passive and so used the common noun. The Qumran scroll simply has לו instead of לה יחדו, "(which is bound) to itself," or bound firmly.
6. MT has שָׁם, "where" (which + there); Qumran and the Syriac version have "there" (שָׁמָּה; there + the directive ending).
7. The Greek version agrees with the MT with μαρτύριον, "testimony." But Symmachus has ἐκκλησία, thinking of "assembly" rather than "testimony." Qumran also has "assembly" (עדת), without the following preposition: "assembly of Israel." For this meaning see Rick R. Marrs, "Psalm 122, 3. 4," *Bib* 68 (1987):106–9; and Th. Booij, "Psalm cxxii 4," *VT* 51 (2001):262–6.
8. The word "throne" in both places in this verse is plural in the MT. I have taken it as a plural of intensification and not a numerical plural as if there was a complex judicial center.
9. Qumran has the singular, "throne."
10. Instead of "those who love you," אֹהֲבָיִךְ, one manuscript has "your tents," אֹהָלָיִךְ, which the editors of BHS propose reading because it conforms to the pattern of the lines to follow, with walls and citadels.
11. MT has the verb יִשְׁלָיוּ, "may they prosper." The Greek text uses a noun εὐθηνία and not a verb; it reads: καὶ εὐθηνία τοῖς ἀγαπῶσίν σε, "prosperity to those who love you." This may have been influenced from verse seven which uses the noun שַׁלְוָה, unless it is a translation of a form וְשַׁלְיוּ.
12. The Greek version has ἐν τῇ δυνάμει σου, "within your host," apparently

624

The Joyful Journey to the City of God

      prosperity[13] within your citadels."
8 For the sake of my brothers and my companions,
    I will now say,[14] "Peace *be* within you."
9 For the sake of the house of the LORD our God
    I will seek[15] your good.

Composition and Context

This psalm begins where the last one left off—the pilgrims are now standing in the city of Jerusalem, recalling the delight at the prospect of going to the sanctuary, and observing in amazement all the wonders of the holy city. Because the psalm celebrates Jerusalem and its value for the people of God, it may be classified as a song of Zion as well as a pilgrim psalm. Jerusalem was the civic and religious center of the nation because the LORD had chosen it for his dwelling place, that is, to be the place where he would meet with his people. And it is no surprise, therefore, that the well-being of the nation was tied to the peace and safety of this city. Thus, the psalm is not simply a description of an amazing city, but rather it is a reminder for the people of God to pray for its well-being.

The superscription preserves a tradition that the psalm is David's. Most commentators note the difficulties with this connection: the psalm seems to have been written by a visitor to the city, the temple appears to be in operation, and Jerusalem has become the religious and political center of the country where "the thrones of the house of David" are in place. These all suggest a later time when the dynasty was established. These difficulties may explain why the superscription is not found in some versions and manuscripts (but it is in the Masoretic Text and Qumran). If it was written by David it would have to come from the latter part of his reign when the holy city had become the

---

      thinking חֵילֵךְ, "your walls," was the homonym חַיִל, "host, army." The parallelism favors the MT reading.
13. A number of manuscripts and the Greek and Syriac versions add "and."
14. The Greek version uses a past tense, "I have indeed spoken." But Symmachus brought it into conformity with the cohortative of the MT, changing it to the future, "I shall speak."
15. The Greek version has a past tense translation, "I have sought"; Symmachus changed it to the future to conform with the cohortative.

religious and political center of the nation.[16] But some of the details in the psalm still seem to require a later date, such as the thrones of David being in place.

Exegetical Analysis

Summary

After recalling his joy at the prospect of going to the sanctuary and his amazement at the complexity and significance of the holy city, the psalmist calls others to pray for the peace and prosperity of Jerusalem, both for the sake of the godly and God.

Outline

I. The pilgrim recalls his joyful anticipation of going to the house of the LORD and his wonder at being there (1–2).
   A. The prospect of going to the sanctuary was delightful (1).
   B. Actually being there was amazing (2).
II. The pilgrim describes the holy city as the spiritual and civic center of the nation (3–5).
   A. Its compactness is amazing (3).
   B. It is the center of worship for the tribes (4).
   C. It is the center of justice (5).
III. The pilgrim calls for prayer for the peace and prosperity of Jerusalem (6–9).
   A. He calls for prayer for the peace of the city and offers a blessing for those who love it (6).
   B. He prays for its peace and prosperity (7).
   C. He prays for its peace and well-being, for the sake of the godly and for the sake of God whose presence is there (8–9).

---

16. To support this connection one could argue that David drew upon his own experience to write the psalm to be used by pilgrims in the future. But the psalm does not actually say the pilgrim-psalmist came from a long distance, only that he was delighted when it was time to go to the house of the LORD. There, within the sacred courts, he marvels at the beauty and value of the city and prays for peace. Later the psalm was added to the collection of pilgrim psalms.

The Joyful Journey to the City of God

COMMENTARY IN EXPOSITORY FORM

I. The devout are delighted to go to the LORD's sanctuary to worship him (1–2).

A. *The prospect of worship brought them joy (1).*

The psalm begins with the recollection of the anticipation of going to the house of the LORD, most likely to one of the great festivals. To understand this excitement, one should imagine farmers in places like Galilee or the nearby hill country who have been laboring night and day to get their harvests in, and finally when the work is done they and their families are able to make their way to the holy city for a week or two of celebration—praising God for the harvest, feasting, singing and celebrating in the busy city with its crowds, its attractions, and the chance to see friends and relatives once again. Anyone who has worked on a farm can appreciate the kind of joy and relief at the harvest that lay behind these pilgrimages (see Isa. 9:4); but adding the festive time in Jerusalem greatly increases the joy. An application of this verse to our going to church would be more appropriate if the service was a glorious celebration on par with the festivals of Israel, perhaps a special seasonal festival on the holy calendar, rather than a routine service. The words of the psalm do not fit most of the modern experiences of attending a worship service.

The initial verb (שָׂמַחְתִּי; s.v. Ps. 48:11) can be translated as it has for centuries, "I was glad"; but given the meaning of the context and the modern connotation of "glad" it would be better rendered "I rejoiced" or "I was filled with joy." That joy began when people were getting ready to go to the holy city. The temporal clause "when they said to me" is the traditional way the verse reads; but it is difficult to get this translation from the unusual construction in the text that has a preposition and an active participle followed by the prepositional phrase (בְּאֹמְרִים לִי). It would more precisely be translated as "with / among those saying to me" or "with those who said to me," the participle functioning as a substantive, the object of the preposition.[17] There were people saying it was time to go to

---

17. Keet, *Psalms of Ascents,* p. 31.

the city, and no doubt making preparations; the psalmist was filled with joy and excitement with them in that prospect.

The second half of the verse tells what they were saying. The word order places the verb at the end of this clause, perhaps to give prominence to the place they were going—the house of the LORD,[18] meaning the sanctuary in Jerusalem.[19] The verb has been traditionally translated "let us go." While one might make a case for that translation, the word is formally an imperfect tense (נֵלֵךְ) and not the clear cohortative spelling (נֵלְכָה). A simple translation would be "we will go (future) or "we are going" (a progressive imperfect). The pilgrims were preparing to go on the journey.

B. The holy city, the setting of the sanctuary, was inspiring (2).

The psalmist next recalls the amazement that he and his fellow pilgrims felt when they were actually standing in the place.[20] The construction (עֹמְדוֹת הָיוּ, the feminine [with the subject "feet"] participle with the verb "to be") emphasizes the durative activity. The subject of this sentence, "our feet," is figurative for the whole person (a synecdoche), but chosen to give emphasis to the feet of the pilgrims: "Our feet are actually standing" in the holy city.[21]

---

18. The word "house" has no preposition before it; it is an accusative in an adverbial use, indicating the place to which they were going (a terminative accusative). A preposition must be supplied in the translation: "[to] the house . . . ."
19. The expression "the house of the LORD" came to be the description of the Solomonic temple, but it was used before that for the sanctuary (see the discussion under Ps. 5:7). Wherever the ark of the covenant was located was the place of worship. One would have to say that because the psalm is about Jerusalem, it would have been written after the ark was moved up to the threshing floor which later became the temple. And because of the details about Jerusalem, most would conclude the psalm was written sometime later.
20. Keet suggests that it was sung as the pilgrims entered the gate-complex at the end of their journey (p. 31).
21. The clause could also be translated with a past tense if the verse is a recollection: "our feet were actually standing" (in the midst of the city).

The idea is completed in the second half of the verse which uses a prepositional phrase and then a vocative to address Jerusalem: "within your gates, O Jerusalem." In ancient cities the word "gates" often refers to larger areas between and behind a series of gates that provided places for animal stalls, open markets, gathering places, and seats for the elders ("gates" would be a metonymy of either adjunct or subject); such plazas immediately inside the entrance were hubs of activities. Because of all that was going on in the gates, the city would have made an immediate impression on a pilgrim from the countryside.

II. There is wonder over the complexity and significance of the place where God chose to be with his people (3–5).

A. *Its physical complexity was amazing (3).*

This section begins with the response of the pilgrim to the city—it was busy and compacted together as a capitol city might be. The verse continues the contemplation of Jerusalem, the city that God chose for his dwelling[22] and therefore the central place of worship. In view of the importance of the place, the compact buildings were necessary and appropriate for all the people who needed to be there.

"Jerusalem" is repeated from verse 2 in order to qualify the city now with further descriptions: "Our feet are standing in your gates, O Jerusalem—Jerusalem, which is built together . . . ." The name is first modified by "which is built" (הַבְּנוּיָה), the feminine participle, to describe its physical circumstances.[23] And this is followed by a prepositional phrase with a relative clause to describe it further: "like a city that is compacted together." The construction in the relative clause is rare, using the shortened pronoun (שֶׁ)

---

22. References to the LORD's "dwelling" among his people in Zion are anthropomorphic; even Solomon acknowledged that the heavens could not contain him (1 Kings 8). The "dwelling place" is a way of describing the place where the LORD chose to manifest his presence with his people in a special way and where they were to assemble to worship him.
23. With the article on the form it would not be translated simply as "Jerusalem is built."

and the passive verb (חֻבְּרָה, a *pual* perfect tense). The picture is that of a city with its buildings all stacked up on top of each other, compacted and jammed together in a complex way—because so many people needed to stay in the city, permanently as well as temporarily.

B. It was the spiritual center of the people of God (4).

The psalmist then acclaims the spiritual significance of the city: It was where the tribes go up to worship the LORD. The verb "go up" (עָלוּ) here has the value of a present tense because the psalmist means that the tribes go up regularly every year (a characteristic or gnomic classification of the perfect tense). The subject of the clause is then reiterated by the appositional expression, "the tribes of the LORD" (שִׁבְטֵי־יָהּ), the word "tribes" referring to the families and people of the twelve tribes. But the construct relationship in the text clarifies that they were more than united tribes—they were the tribes of the LORD. They belonged to the LORD and therefore owed him their allegiance. This is why the Law required them to go up to Jerusalem and appear before the LORD three times a year. And so this explanation was inserted in the psalm as a parenthesis. The construction simply has the noun "statute" (עֵדוּת; s.v. Ps. 119:2) at the beginning of the clause; it serves as an adverbial accusative to specify the reason, and so may be translated "[in accordance with] the statute for Israel." The Law required the people of Israel to go up to the holy place at the three harvest festivals to pay tribute to him for his blessings.

The next clause expresses this purpose of their going up to Jerusalem: "to give praise to the name of the LORD." The infinitive (לְהֹדוֹת; s.v. Ps. 6:5) is often translated "to give thanks"; but it is stronger than that. It means "to make a public acknowledgment" or "to give praise." It is related to the noun in the expression "the sacrifice of praise" (תּוֹדָה). The main purpose for the Israelites' going up to Jerusalem at each harvest festival was to pay tribute to God for their harvests and other blessings they had received from him; and that praise would be expressed tangibly in paying their tithes. In this way praise and all it included was an expression of allegiance to the LORD.

And here, as well as elsewhere in the psalms, the praise is

focused on "the name of the Yahweh." Since the name "Yahweh" is mentioned in this expression, the word "name" (שֵׁם; s.v. Ps. 20:1) refers to something else—his nature, his attributes, and his acts ("name" being a metonymy of subject). The faithful would worship God by acknowledging who he is, what he is like, and what he has done. And they would do this as a united congregation in the LORD's presence.

C. It was the administrative center of the kingdom (5).

Jerusalem was also the central government of the nation. But here the specific focus is on "the thrones for judgment (or justice; מִשְׁפָּט; s.v. Ps. 9:4), the thrones of the house of David." There is little information in Scripture concerning such a place of justice, but it appears that the king set up a court to make decisions and settle hard cases. "Thrones" is a figure of speech (metonymy of subject or adjunct) referring to the judges in the court system who would sit on the thrones; to speak of thrones, or halls and courts of justice, is to speak of the people who will be in power there to make the decisions. And the mention of "David" indicates that David set them up, unless they were simply named after David since he established the dynasty ("the house of David"). But there is another way to interpret the expression. The plural "thrones" might not be a numerical plural; the plural might be used for emphasis and the expression then used for the "throne of David," or Davidic king, who would sit and make decisions (as Solomon did in I Kings 3:16–28).

III. The people of God should pray for the well-being of the sanctuary city (7–9).

A. They should pray for its peace and prosperity (6–7).

The psalmist now asks people to pray for Jerusalem, meaning the people in the city, their activities, security and prosperity. The exhortation uses the imperative "ask" (שַׁאֲלוּ) to formulate an urgent request. Of all the words used for prayer in the Old Testament, this word "ask" expresses the basic idea of prayer, for prayer is asking. And what the people were to ask for was "peace" (שָׁלוֹם; s.v. Ps. 38:3).[24] The word refers to more than the absence of war; it indicates a condition in which everyone and everything can live undisturbed and flourish. So it has the ideas of well-being, health, peace, and prosperity in its usage. If the city of Jerusalem were to have such peace, the whole nation would too. Down through history the prayer has been offered again and again, even though Jerusalem is not presently the religious and political center of God's program. But the tensions in the region still exist, and to pray for the peace of Jerusalem today is a way of praying for peace in the Middle East. Of course for the Christian to pray for the peace of Jerusalem is to pray for spiritual peace as well, both the turning of people to the prince of peace so that they might find salvation and the culmination of all the promises.

A blessing is then pronounced on those who love (אֹהֲבָיִךְ; s.v. Ps. 11:7) Jerusalem. Those who love Jerusalem are those who value its spiritual significance for the kingdom of God; they are the people of God who will pray for the peace of the city of God. The verb used, "let them prosper" (the jussive, יִשְׁלָיוּ), may be described as a blessing in that it indirectly invokes God to prosper them.

The desired blessing continues in verse 7: "May there be peace within your walls, and prosperity in your citadels." The line parallels "peace" and "prosperity" with "walls" and "citadels." Again, it is God who will enable them to prosper in an environment of peace.

B. They should pray for the sake of the godly and God (8–9).

Both of the last two verses begin with the same particle meaning "for the sake of"(לְמַעַן). In verse eight the psalmist resolves to pray "peace be in you" (שָׁלוֹם בָּךְ) for the sake of his brothers and his friends. His prayer is focused on his family and friends; but peace will be a benefit for all who come to Jerusalem to worship and conduct business. The prayer is introduced with the verb, "I will now say" (the cohortative, אֲדַבְּרָה־נָּא), which

---

24. There are several words similar in sound and meaning in this line that form a paronomasia: "Ask for the peace of Jerusalem, let those who love you prosper," שַׁאֲלוּ שְׁלוֹם יְרוּשָׁלָםִ יִשְׁלָיוּ (sha'ălû shᵉlôm yerûshālāyim yishlāyû).

expresses his resolve to pray. This corresponds to his appeal for others to pray.

And in the last verse, the text uses the same construction: "For the sake of the house of the LORD our God, I will seek (the cohortative אֲבַקְשָׁה) good for you." The verb "seek" would include any effort to promote the well-being of the city, especially through prayer. Whereas in verse 8 the psalmist resolved to pray for "peace" within the city; now he is determined to seek "good" for it. "Good" (טוֹב; s.v. Ps. 34:8) is a broad term; its meaning includes anything that promotes, preserves or enhances life. Here the psalmist is resolving to seek the best for the city. And his efforts are for the sake of the "house of the LORD." If the city enjoys peace and prosperity, the worship of the LORD in the sanctuary will thrive.

MESSAGE AND APPLICATION

The psalm was clearly written in the spirit of enthusiasm for Jerusalem which was the center of Israel's religious and civic activities. As the pilgrim surveyed the city and considered its significance for the people of God, he felt compelled to pray for its peace and prosperity, and to exhort others to pray as well—and Jerusalem needed a good deal of prayer down through its troubled history.

The application of a song of Zion like this will have to make an analogy between what was the center of worship for Israel and what our places of worship are today, although there are major differences in that Israel was a theocracy. But this is the procedure that has to be followed when expounding any Old Testament passage that deals with Israel's worship in Jerusalem, whether the sanctuary itself or the ritual procedures. And so for the expository idea I would make the statement more general to be applicable: *The people of God should pray for the peace and well-being of the place where they eagerly gather to offer their praise to God.*

But there are two significant ways to apply this principle. The first way, and no doubt the primary purpose of the psalm, concerns prayer for the holy city of Jerusalem. This application could certainly be made literally so that people would pray for the peace of Jerusalem, for such a prayer would be a part of God's program for Jerusalem as revealed in prophecy.[25] Moreover, that war-torn part of the world certainly needs peace, and the issue of Jerusalem is at the center of the conflicts. But since the city is not the center of true worship today, nor the center of the theocratic program presently, to pray for the peace of Jerusalem would necessarily include praying that its inhabitants would come to know the Prince of Peace, without whom there can be no lasting peace in that region, or anywhere else for that matter. And in the fullest meaning of the words, a prayer for the peace and prosperity of the holy city is a prayer for the coming of Christ to end all trouble and strife.

But the psalm lends itself to a secondary application as well, that is, to pray for the peace and prosperity of centers of true worship under the new covenant as well. Wherever the people of God gather to worship the LORD, it would benefit the ministry greatly to have peace and prosperity, especially in lands today where the church is persecuted and the most in need of peace. If God blesses those cities and countries with peace and prosperity, the people will be able to praise God more freely and worship him more securely. Prayers for such peace and prosperity should be motivated primarily by concern for other believers and for the work of the Lord, so that praise to God may abound.

The psalm also addresses the eager anticipation of going to worship. An additional application would be appropriate here: spiritual leaders today must make worship so joyous, meaningful, uplifting, and life-changing that people will eagerly anticipate being there.

---

25. Goldingay rightly emphasizes the need for peace in that troubled place, and peace would benefit everyone. But his identifying the brothers and friends as Jews, Christians and Muslims goes beyond this particular text, for it is highly unlikely that the psalmist meant warring people when he said "for the sake of my brothers and my friends" (*Psalms 90–150*, p. 468).

PSALM 123

Earnestly Expecting Divine Favor

INTRODUCTION

Text and Textual Variants

A Song of the Ascents.

1 Unto you I lift my eyes,
   you who sits[1] *enthroned* in the heavens.
2 Indeed, as the eyes of servants
     look to the hand[2] of their masters,
   as the eyes of a maid
     look to the hand[3] of her mistress,
   so our eyes *look* to the LORD our God,
     until he has mercy[4] on us.

---

1. For the exceptional spelling with the *hireq-yôd* ending, הַיֹּשְׁבִי instead of הַיֹּשֵׁב, see GKC 90m. The vowel is classified as a *hireq campaginis*, but there is no satisfactory explanation for it.
2. The Greek version has "hands."
3. The Greek version has "hands."
4. The MT has the verb חָנַן here as well as twice in the next verse. The Greek translation used ἕως οὗ οἰκτιρήσαι ἡμᾶς here and ἐλέησον in the next verse: "until he has compassion on us. Have mercy (upon us, O Lord), have mercy (upon us)."

3 Have mercy on us, O LORD, have mercy on us,
   for we are exceedingly filled with contempt.
4 We are exceedingly filled[5]
    with scorn from[6] those who are at ease,
       contempt from the proud.[7]

Composition and Context

At the heart of the psalm is a short prayer for divine mercy; it comes after an elaborate affirmation of dependence on the LORD, and before a lament that the faithful have had enough scorn and contempt from the world. Because they had about all of this opposition that they could handle, they cried to the LORD to be merciful to them.

Exegetical Analysis

Summary

Eagerly expecting the sovereign LORD's response, the psalmist prays for his merciful intervention because the people of God have endured more than enough scorn and contempt from the proud.

Outline

I. The faithful eagerly await for the sovereign LORD's merciful intervention (1–2).

---

5. The Greek version ends the colon here, using "our soul is exceedingly filled" to parallel the last colon. Then, the rest of the psalm is made a prayer: "Let the reproach be to them that are at ease, and contempt to the proud." The Syriac has "we heard," thinking of שָׁמַעְנוּ, instead of "we were filled," שָׂבַעְנוּ.
6. Instead of the construct relationship here, the Greek version and one manuscript have the preposition "for (those who are at ease)."
7. The form in the MT is written לִגְאֵיוֹנִים. The *Qᵉre'* is לִגְאֵי יוֹנִים but the *Kᵉthiv* is לִגְאֲיוֹנִים. The *K* reading means "proud"; this is reflected in the versions and is the preferred reading. The *Q* reading has the word "proud" (גֵּאֶה) in the plural, construct, followed by the noun יוֹנִים, "violent, cruel." Briggs favors the latter reading and translates it "proud oppressors" (*Psalms,* II: 451–2).

A. Under the similes of servants and maidservants, the psalmist attests to his eager anticipation of the answer to his prayer (1–2a).
   B. On behalf of the congregation, he continues to pray until the LORD has mercy on them (2b).
II. The faithful pray for divine mercy because they have had enough scorn and contempt from the proud (3–4).
   A. They pray for deliverance because they have endured much contempt (3).
   B. They lament that they have had more than enough scorn and contempt from the proud (4).

COMMENTARY IN EXPOSITORY FORM

I. Faithful believers eagerly watch and pray for their sovereign LORD's merciful deliverance from trouble (1–2).

A. Their prayer is to the sovereign LORD (1).

The first part of the psalm asserts the psalmist's constant attentiveness to prayer. It begins with the direction of that prayer to the LORD, who sovereignly reigns in heaven. By this expression of his focus on God the congregation would be reminded that prayer addressed to the king of heaven is in itself an expression of confidence in his sovereignty. He alone reigns on high above all the difficulties of this life. The confidence comes in understanding and depending on this.

The psalmist emphasizes the intensity of his praying with a figure (a metonymy of adjunct): "I lift my eyes to you." Looking up to heaven is a physical act that focuses on the spiritual direction of the prayer (e.g., Jon. 2:4). Since the answer to the prayer had not come yet, the psalmist must have been continuing praying. That is why the verb (נָשָׂאתִי; s.v. Ps. 24:7) is best translated as a present tense, "I lift" (a characteristic perfect).

In the sentence the prepositional phrase "unto you" is placed first to draw attention to the LORD. In the second half of the verse we have an additional description of the LORD as "the one who sits [enthroned] in the heavens." To describe the LORD as sitting (anthropomorphism) is a common expression for his sovereignty (e.g., Ps. 2:4); it indicates that he reigns, i.e., sits enthroned. And the phrase "in the heavens" emphasizes his exalted dominion: he reigns over all the earth from heaven above and no one can challenge his dominion. The psalmist, therefore, rightly places his hopes in the highest power, the sovereign Lord of heaven and earth.

B. Their prayer is vigilant and attentive (2).

To describe the anticipation of the answer to their prayers, the psalmist uses two figures (similes): "as the eyes of servants *look* to the hand of their masters" and "as the eyes of a maid *look* to the hand of her mistress." There is no verb in these clauses, but because of the idea of lifting up the eyes used in verse one, we may supply the verb "look" in these expressions. The point is that in each case the servants cannot do anything on their own initiative or authority, but are constantly looking to their superiors for directives and provisions. They eagerly wait for them. The psalmist is saying that the faithful have the same kind of attentiveness to God with their prayers.

The play in each comparison is between the "eyes" and the "hand"; the "eyes" represent the attention given to the masters or mistresses; and the "hand" represents the activity and direction of the masters or mistresses. The "eyes" are part of the attentiveness of the whole person (metonymy of adjunct); and the "hand," a word that indicates power and authority, represents what the person does (metonymy of cause). The final line of the verse completes the comparison: ("as . . .) so our eyes *look* to the LORD our God." Thus, the idea of the "eyes" looking to the LORD as illustrated with these figures represents giving full attention in prayer to the LORD. Their prayers are complemented by their eager expectation of the LORD's answer.

And this attentiveness will continue until God in his mercy acts on their behalf. The temporal clause uses the preposition "until" with the abbreviated form of the relative pronoun prefixed to the verb (עַד שֶׁיְּחָנֵּנוּ). The verb simply expresses the future confidence: "until he will have mercy on us." The verb (חָנַן; s.v. Ps. 4:1) may be translated "be gracious, show favor, be merciful."

Earnestly Expecting Divine Favor

It usually refers to favor that is undeserved, which is why it is the focus of prayer. And by praying for God to be merciful, the psalmist was asking for what that mercy would provide, namely, deliverance from the oppressors (so "mercy" is a metonymy of cause).

II. They pray eagerly for merciful deliverance from the contempt of the world (3–4).

Now the need of the psalmist is made clear. Unbelievers were scorning the faithful and treating them with contempt. The prayer for divine intervention has the same tone as prayers that cry out, "How long, O LORD!" (Ps. 13:1; see also Rev. 6:10). And it uses repetition to underscore the urgency of the request. The imperative in the request, "have mercy on us" (חָנֵּנוּ), is also from the same verb used in the preceding clause.

The reason for the urgent prayer is "because we have had more than enough contempt." The verb used (שָׂבַעְנוּ) means "to be sated, satisfied, full, have enough." The clause literally says, "for we are exceedingly full of contempt." So here the verb does not have a good sense of being satisfied, but a bad sense of having their fill of contempt from the world.

"Contempt" (בּוּז; s.v. Ps. 22:6) is an arrogant, condescending attitude that considers something worthless; it is manifested by contemptuous acts—they did things to show their contempt (and so "contempt" is a metonymy of cause). In the psalms contempt is often verbal ridicule, but occasionally persecution and mistreatment.

The next line adds scorn to what they must endure. The parallel expression strengthens the subject by calling attention to it: we (traditionally translated literally as "our soul") have had more than enough."[8] The nouns "scorn" (לַעַג) and "contempt" (בּוּז) follow the verb "filled" and specify its contents, so we must translate it as "we are exceedingly filled [with] scorn" and "[with]

---

8. Moreover, the pleonastic form *lah* further draws attention to the inner anxiety—"we [our soul] is filled within it." Gesenius calls this a *dativus commodi* or *dativus ethicus*, meaning that it gives emphasis for the significance in question for a particular subject (GKC 119s).

contempt." The word "scorn" has the meaning of "scoffing, mocking, scorning, deriding, laughing at" (see Psalm 2:4). So this brief lament (and motivation for God to be merciful) is that the people had all the ridicule they could take.

Who were these scorners? Two descriptions are given in the last line. The first means "those who are at ease" (הַשַּׁאֲנַנִּים);[9] and the second word means "the proud" (לִגְאֵיוֹנִים). This word for pride is related to the description of the majesty or exaltation of God (s.v. Ps. 93:1); but in this description of the wicked it has to do with self-sufficiency and independence of God. The use of these descriptions may refer to the mistreatment of the lower classes by the arrogant upper class people (Amos 6:1). So the faithful have had to put up with the wealthy, self-sufficient, unbelievers and the proud oppressors who have treated them with contempt and scorned their faith.

MESSAGE AND APPLICATION

The message of this psalm is: *The faithful give full attention to watching and praying for God's merciful deliverance from the contempt of this world.* The attention to prayer has the same diligence and focus as that of servants' paying attention to their masters and mistresses. The emphasis is similar to the instruction of Jesus, "Watch and pray." But because the actual petition does not come until near the end of the psalm, the focus is more on the attentiveness to prayer to the sovereign God.

God calls his people to be diligent in their praying. This intense praying is not for the casual or the careless, and neither is it for the arrogant or self-sufficient. It is for the faithful servants of the LORD who are attentive to their sovereign LORD and his provisions. Prayer is the means by which a servant seeks favor from the master. And even though in Christ, the true Servant of the LORD, we may come boldly before the throne of grace, we still humble ourselves as servants and pray for his will to be done.

---

9. Because it is a duplicated noun form, a *pe'alal form*, it means "totally at ease."

PSALM 124

The LORD Is On Our Side

INTRODUCTION

Text and Textual Variants

A Song for the Ascents. Of David.[1]

1 If it had not been the LORD who was for us[2]–
   let Israel now say–
2 if it had not been the LORD who was for us,
   when men[3] rose up against us,
3 then[4] they would have swallowed us up alive,
   when their anger was kindled against us;
4 then the waters would have swept us away,

---

1. A few Hebrew manuscripts and the oldest text of the Greek version do not have "of David."
2. The MT has לָ֫נוּ, "for us," or as some render it, "on our side." The Greek translation has ἐν ἡμῖν, "among us," which may simply be an interpretation of the text to clarify the point of divine intervention.
3. MT has the collective singular אָדָם.
4. The form אֲזַי is used for אָז only here in verses 3 and 4; it does appear in extra-biblical literature.

PSALM 124

    the torrent[5] would have gone[6] over us;[7]
5 then the raging waters[8]
    would have gone over us.[9]

6 Blessed be the LORD
    who has not given us as prey to their teeth!
7 We[10] have escaped as a bird[11] from the snare of the fowlers;[12]
    the snare was broken and we have escaped!
8 Our help is in the name of the LORD,
    maker of heaven and earth.[13]

Composition and Context

The LORD's deliverance of his people and his care for them is the substance of this psalm. The writer acknowledges that the people are completely dependant on the LORD for their safety and security, for it was only because the LORD was on their side

---

5. For MT's נַחְלָה, "torrent," the Targum has "sickness," apparently taking the word as a *niphal* participle of the verb "to be sick," חָלָה.
6. MT has עָבַר, "to go over"; the Greek version has here and in the next verse διῆλθεν, "(our soul) would have passed through (a wadi)," perhaps interpreting the meaning of the image.
7. MT has נַפְשֵׁנוּ. Some commentators take the noun in its primary literal sense and translate it as "our neck" (see Wolff, *Anthropology and the Old Testament*, p. 13).
8. This translation reverses the Hebrew order of the cola, which reads: "then would have gone over us, the raging waters." The verb is singular for the subject, literally "the raging waters." The Greek version has this verse translated as "then our soul would have passed through the irresistible waters." This follows the interpretation in verse 4c. But in both places the translation that makes "our soul" (or, "us") has the preposition "over"; to make the word the subject requires ignoring this preposition.
9. MT has נַפְשֵׁנוּ, "our soul / life."
10. MT has נַפְשֵׁנוּ, "our soul / life (has escaped)."
11. MT simply has צִפּוֹר, "bird"; but the Greek translation specifies στρουθίον, "sparrow."
12. The form יוֹקְשִׁים means "fowlers," those who bait traps. But the Targum translated this as "snares," i.e., reading the traps of snares, apparently thinking of it as מוֹקְשִׁים. But see also G. R. Driver, "Reflections on Recent Articles. 2. Hebr. *môqēš* 'Striker.'" *JBL* 73 (1954):131–6.
13. The Greek translation has definite articles: "the heaven and the earth."

that they were able to break the oppression of their enemies and escape the "trap" laid for them.

The psalm may be classified as a thanksgiving psalm, even though it reads more like a praise psalm in its content. It seems to have been written for, or adapted for, community worship, the first two verses forming the bidding of the leader, and the next three verses expressing the testimony of the community. Verses 6–8 fit the praise patterns loosely: they begin with the praise for the LORD (v. 6), explain what the LORD has done (v. 7), and conclude with a didactic summation (v. 8). In its very brief form this little psalm shows the faithful how to praise the LORD in the light of his great deliverance.

The exact deliverance the psalmist has in mind is not clear. The emphasis on the "name of the LORD" and the LORD as the "maker of heaven and earth," as well as the similarity of the first two verses to Psalm 118, might indicate a date after the exile. The psalm would certainly have been appropriate for the returning exiles, but whether it was composed at that time, or simply adapted to that time,[14] is impossible to say. The psalm could also fit the time of the deliverance of Hezekiah from the Assyrians; the language of a flood used for the invasion is found in both Isaiah 8 and 43:2. If it was originally Davidic, then the crisis would have come because of enemies like the Philistines. There is nothing in the psalm that would demand any particular time or setting.

Exegetical Analysis

Summary

Acknowledging that if the LORD had not been on their side the enemies would have destroyed them completely, the pilgrim psalmist blesses the sovereign LORD, who enabled them to break free from the trap that was set for them.

---

14. Kirkpatrick, *Psalms*, p. 744.

Outline

I. The psalmist reminds the people that if the LORD had not been for them their enemies would have completely destroyed them (1–5).
  A He acknowledges on behalf of the people that their victory was due to the LORD's being for them (1–2).
  B. He acknowledges that the enemies would have completely destroyed them if the LORD had not been for them (3–5).
II. The psalmist praises the LORD who enabled them to go free when he destroyed the plans of their enemies (6–8).
  A. He praises the LORD who did not abandon them to their enemies (6).
  B. He acknowledges that the LORD, the maker of heaven and earth, helped them escape the traps their enemies had set for them (7–8).

COMMENTARY IN EXPOSITORY FORM

I. The faithful people of God acknowledge that they are totally dependent upon the LORD for their survival (1–5).

A. Believers acknowledge their dependence on the LORD who is for his people (1–2).

Speaking on behalf of the faithful believers, the psalmist begins by acknowledging that if the LORD had not been for them (often translated "on our side"), they would never have survived. The first line of his acknowledgment reads, "If [it had not been] the LORD who was for us (שֶׁהָיָה לָנוּ)." It forms the protasis of a conditional clause (לוּלֵי, "unless . . .") with the apodosis coming in verses 3–5 (אֲזַי, "then . . . ," an emphatic form of אָז). The conditional clause requires the past perfect: "If not [was] the LORD who had been for us," or, "If it had not been the LORD who was for us." Moreover, in this case the particle used to introduce the conditional clause ("if not, unless") introduces a conditional clause where the condition has not been fulfilled in the past, or is not capable of fulfillment in the present or future, and so the

The LORD Is On Our Side

consequences can never occur (GKC, #159 l, m). In other words, it was not possible that the LORD was not for them, and so it could never be that the enemies would destroy them.

The psalmist calls the people to join him in acknowledging the LORD's saving presence: "Let Israel now say" (using the jussive יֹאמַר־נָא for instruction). What they are to say is what he said at the start, but with a temporal clause added: "when men[15] rose up against us" (בְּקוּם עָלֵינוּ אָדָם; for קוּם s.v. Ps. 3:1). Rising up against them is a figurative expression (a metonymy of adjunct) that refers to the beginning of the attack (e.g., see Gen. 4:8 where Cain "rose up" against his brother and slew him). There is no specific reference in this line to the situation; "men rising against them" could refer to any kind of attack against the nation or a substantial part of the nation.

B. Believers acknowledge that they are totally dependent on the LORD to protect them (3–5).

The next three verses complete the conditional clause in verses 1 and 2 (forming the apodosis section). The verb carries out the hypothetical condition (hypothetical perfect): if such and such had not happened, they would have done such and so. Here he explains how they might have been destroyed. Using the figure of ravenous beasts (an implied comparison), he says, "they would have swallowed us alive (living)" (חַיִּים בְּלָעוּנוּ). The word "alive" is the noun "life, lifetime"; here it functions as an adverbial accusative explaining their state when being "swallowed"– swallowed alive. Without God's being for them the enemies would have completely destroyed them, as thoroughly as if something swallowed them whole.

The second half of the verse qualifies this with a temporal clause: "when their anger burned against us." The infinitive in the clause (חֲרוֹת) is from a verb meaning "burn, kindle, be angry" (חָרָה; s.v. Ps. 37:1). It strengthens the idea of the subject (subjective genitive, אַף), which also conveys the sense of heat: "when their hot anger was kindled / burned." The noun "anger" is a

---

15. The form is the masculine singular "man," but it here is a general reference to people, so "men."

figure (a metonymy of cause), signifying what the anger caused, the attack.

The text changes figures in verses 4 and 5: the enemies are now compared to a surging and raging river (another implied comparison). The language is reminiscent of Isaiah 8:5–12 in which the massive invasion by the Assyrians is described in terms of the Euphrates River overflowing its banks and flooding the whole land of Israel. Since verse 4 is still part of the conditional sentence, the nuance of the verb would match that of the last verb: "then the waters (הַמַּיִם) would have swept us away" (hypothetical perfect). And parallel to this is the expression that "the torrent (נַחְלָה) would have gone over us." Verse 5 then pulls these motifs together: "Then over us would have gone the raging waters" (הַמַּיִם הַזֵּידוֹנִים).[16] The two verses are connected by the use of "passed over us" (i.e., our life, עָבַר עַל־נַפְשֵׁנוּ). Under the two images then, being swept away and being drowned (the water passing over them), the psalmist is reiterating that if the LORD had not delivered them they would have been destroyed suddenly and swiftly without leaving a trace.

II. The faithful people of God praise the LORD for enabling them to escape the plans of the wicked (6–8).

A. Believers praise God for their deliverance (6–7).

The beginning of verse 6 clearly signals this as a section of praise: "Blessed [be] the LORD" (בָּרוּךְ יְהוָה; s.v. Ps. 5:12). The verb is a passive participle, serving as a predicate adjective; and the verb to be supplied would be a jussive: "Blessed [be] the LORD," which in reality is saying "may the LORD be blessed." This word for praise carries the aspect of enrichment; praising as enriching the LORD would mean that the reputation of the LORD would be enriched, that through the praise the person and works of the LORD would be better known in the world. In

---

16. The word זֵידוֹנִים is not found elsewhere (normally זֵד is used). The verb זוּד means "to be proud." Here it would have the idea of surging or swelling up (Keet, *The Psalms of Ascent*, p. 43).

time this particular construction became a fixed exclamation of praise (as did "*hallᵉlû-Yāh*").

The reason that the LORD is to be blessed is expressed in the relative clause modifying "the LORD": "who has not given us as prey to their teeth!" The nuance of the verb, a present perfect, indicates that the deliverance was completed in the past and the results continue—he has not given them over to them, and so they were not in their power. The figures used in the line are drawn from the animal world. The first is the implied comparison of the people with the "prey" (טֶרֶף) of wild beasts (following the comparison of the enemies with beasts in verse 3). The word "prey" is an adverbial accusative, indicating the product, or the indirect object: he has not given us *to be* prey, or *as* prey. The second figure compares the threat of destruction by the enemies with the "teeth" of the wild animals. The enemies were not actually going to devour them with their teeth, but they were about to destroy them just as ruthlessly and completely.

But God did not let them do that; rather, he enabled his people to escape. The psalmist now uses a qualified comparison (a simile): "We have escaped like a bird from the snare of the fowler." They are compared to a bird; and the qualification is that the bird escaped the fowler's net. So the enemies' attempt to destroy them is implicitly compared to a fowler spreading a net to catch a bird. Then the second half of the verse extends this figure to emphasize how complete the escape was: "the snare was broken, and we have escaped" (for מָלַט, s.v. Ps. 41:1). The writer does not say specifically what the enemy tried to do, but we may conclude it was some kind of a planned trap to destroy the people of God. But God somehow intervened so that the plan was foiled and the people escaped.

B. They acknowledge that their help is from the sovereign Lord of creation (8).

The final verse focuses attention on the nature of the one who delivered them. The theme of help from the maker of heaven and earth is expressed here as well as in Psalm 121:1–2. We first read: "Our help (עֶזְרֵנוּ; s.v. Ps. 46:1) is in the name of the LORD."

"Help" is a figure (a metonymy of adjunct or effect) which has the intended meaning of what the help was, namely, deliverance from the enemies. And the common expression "in the name of the LORD" refers to the nature of the LORD (e.g., see Ps. 118:10–12, 26; see also Exod. 34:5–7), "name" being a figure (a metonymy of subject) that means all the attributes of the LORD (s.v. Ps. 20:1). The psalmist is declaring that they were delivered because of the power, love, faithfulness, and righteousness of God, to name a few of the relevant attributes. The text uses a preposition, "our help is in the name of the LORD," which if translated "in" has a significant meaning. But the line may also be translated to read, "our help is the name of the LORD" (the preposition [בְּ] would be a *beth* of essence, meaning that the object of the preposition is essentially the help—the help is the LORD himself).

The last half of the verse is in apposition to the first and completes the description of the "LORD" as the "the maker of heaven and earth." "Heaven and earth" are the objects of the participle (objective genitives after the construct form); they also should be taken together (as a merism), meaning God made the whole universe and everything in it. The point of this ending to the psalm is to underscore the sovereignty of the LORD as the basis for the security and the deliverance that the faithful experienced. Breaking the "traps" of the wicked is no problem for the one who made everything.

MESSAGE AND APPLICATION

The unique emphasis of this psalm of praise concerns the complete dependency of the people of God on the LORD. The main idea could then be put this way: *When the faithful are delivered from the destructive plans of the wicked by the LORD, their praise must include the acknowledgment that they are completely dependent on him for their survival.* What makes our praise genuine and powerful is the confession that unless the LORD was for us, we would not survive. But the LORD is for us, and so we can trust him for deliverance from danger. The apostle Paul makes the same point with the rhetorical question, "If God is for us, who can be against us?" (Rom. 8:31).

PSALM 125

The Security of the Believer

INTRODUCTION

Text and Textual Variants

A Song for the Ascents.

1 Those who trust in the LORD *are* like[1] Mount Zion
which cannot be moved, *but* remains[2] forever.

---

1. Instead of MT's כְּהַר, some Hebrew manuscripts and the Syriac read בְּהַר. This would change the meaning of the line considerably, restricting the focus on those who trust the LORD to Jerusalemites.
2. The MT has the imperfect יֵשֵׁב, "it [Mount Zion] abides/remains." The Greek version has ὁ κατοικῶν Ιερουσαλημ, "the inhabitant of Jerusalem," reading the form as if it were the participle in construct, יֹשֵׁב. The MT has "Mount Zion" as the subject of the verb "cannot be moved," qualifying the simile. The Greek version has the participle as the subject of the verb, "the inhabitant (of Jerusalem) cannot be moved."

The reading in the Qumran scroll indicates the scribes there probably knew of the textual difficulty and wished to clarify the proper understanding. The entire line is not preserved intact, but the existing part of the scroll does have the relevant part. The scribe or scribes prefixed a relative pronoun to the negative, giving the form שׁלוא. The verse would

649

2 Jerusalem[3]– as the mountains are around her,
   so the LORD is around his people
   from this time forth and forever.
3 For the scepter of wickedness[4] shall not rest[5]

---

then be translated: "Those who trust in the LORD [are] like Mount Zion, which cannot [be moved, but forever d]wells." The reading in the Dead Sea Scroll, then, supports the MT by clarifying the proper subject of the verb. It is Mount Zion that cannot be moved.

3. The textual problem of verse 1 continues with the beginning of verse 2. In the MT verse 2 begins with "Jerusalem," which is an independent nominative absolute. This main word is isolated at the beginning of the sentence (the earlier grammars called it a dangling case, *casus pendens*), and the following clause refers to it with a resumptive pronoun: "Jerusalem—as the mountains are around her . . . ." This construction is not that common, but occurs frequently enough and its distinctive emphasis should be reflected in the translation. The psalmist wanted the reader/listener to focus on "Jerusalem" briefly before proceeding. To translate it "as the mountains are around Jerusalem" misses the emphasis entirely.

But the Greek version, apparently not recognizing the construction, and having read the verb at the end of verse 1 as a participle, thought "Jerusalem" was the genitive after the construct participle. This gave the common reading "the inhabitant of Jerusalem," which was then made the subject of "cannot be moved" (the participle being the subject of the verb). This would limit security to those who lived in Jerusalem.

4. The noun is the less common word רֶשַׁע, "wickedness"; the Greek and Syriac versions, the Targum, and a few Hebrew manuscripts assumed it to be the common word רָשָׁע, "[the] wicked," i.e., "sinners." In the MT the noun "wickedness" would be a metonymy of adjunct describing the rule (i.e., scepter) as wicked; in the variant reading it would refer to the wicked (i.e., people) who were ruling. Because the MT has the less common word and the versions, working without vocalization, assumed it was the common word, the MT most likely preserves the original reading.

5. The verb in MT is יָנוּחַ, the imperfect tense of the *qal* stem: "will (not) rest." It has "the rod (of wickedness)" as the subject. The DSS as well as Jerome's PIH agree with this.

The Greek version has οὐκ ἀφήσει, "he will not allow," and some Greek mss express the subject by adding Κύριος, to read "the Lord will not allow." This is not a translation of the *qal* imperfect of the verb, but of a *hiphil* imperfect, יָנִיחַ, "(not) cause to rest" or "allow to rest." This Greek translation then makes "rod" the object: "For the LORD will not allow the rod of sinners to rest upon . . . ."

Since the MT and Qumran agree, the external evidence is initially in favor of the first reading. Then the internal evidence convincingly supports the *qal* form. First, since "the LORD" is the subject throughout the

650

The Security of the Believer

    on the lot[6] of the righteous,
to the extent that the righteous
    stretch out their hands to evil.

4 Treat well, O LORD, those who are good,[7]
    and to those who are upright in their hearts.
5 But as for those who turn aside to their crooked ways,
    the LORD shall lead them away
        with the workers of iniquity.

Peace *be* upon Israel!

Composition and Context

This psalm of trust seems to have been written when the nation was under a wicked government, either corrupt Israelite leaders or Gentile dominion. The text does not indicate that it is a foreign power as in the time of post-exilic Judaism, even though that seems to be a common assumption.[8] Perowne suggests that verses 3, 4, and 5 refer to the threats that came to the people in that time.[9] But all that there is to go on in the psalm is the expression "the scepter of wickedness," which refers to the government. The "rod of wickedness" certainly could mean Gentile rule over the

---

    psalm, the Greek translation apparently sought to bring this verse into conformity with the rest of the psalm, perhaps already assuming the verb was a *hiphil* (the letters *yod* and *waw* often being similar). Second, it is more likely that a scribe would add the holy name to clarify the subject than to delete the name if it had been there. And third, the reading with "rod" as the direct object accordingly made more sense than the more difficult MT reading with it as the subject. So the MT most likely preserves the original reading: "for the rod of wickedness will not rest . . . ."

6. This word can be used figuratively for one's portion, but it can also refer to allotted land, which is the preferred understanding in a number of commentaries (see Allen, *Psalms 101–150*, p. 167).
7. The literal translation of the line has repetition to form a word play: "Do good, O LORD, to those who are good (to the good)." But such a translation does not employ the best English usage.
8. See Allen, pp. 167–8; and Anderson, *Psalms 73–150*, p. 862.
9. *Psalms,* II:388. For an example of the demands of an occupying regime, see Nehemiah 5.

post-exilic community, but that identification is far from certain because the people of Israel had enough wicked kings of their own down through history.[10] If it does refer to the later Gentile domination of the land, then the prayer for those who turn aside to sin is that they will be expelled from the land with these wicked foreign governors. Support for this view comes from a couple of comparisons with expressions in other texts, such as an enemy occupation as "evil-doers" (Isa. 14:5, 29), or the verb "lead away" referring to exile (Deut. 28:36; 2 Kings 24:15; Hos. 2:16 [14]). But these may be too general to be compelling. In fact, a pre-exilic date could be supported in the same way, taking the wicked rulers as Israelite, and the warning of judgment to be exile. And the designation "evil-doers" can refer to Israelites as well as foreigners. There is no clear indication of the setting of the psalm.

Whatever the occasion, the psalmist was convinced that those who lived faithfully would not be caught up in the wickedness of the state under such leaders. But those who might get caught up with the wickedness would suffer the same fate that God had in store for the wicked. The main emphasis of the theology of the psalm, then, concerns the security of the believers, especially in trying times—and the insecurity of the make-believers who will be exposed at those difficult times. The focus of Psalm 124 was on deliverance; but the focus of Psalm 125 is perseverance, first stated positively, then negatively.

The psalm may be classified as a national song of confidence for it is not the faith of an individual that is at stake, but of the whole people.[11] Broyles takes it to be more of a corporate prayer with confidence, the first part expressing the confident trust of the people and then verse 4 forming the prayer and verse 5 a warning.[12] The predominant emphasis is on the security of the believers, but the prayer and warning remind the believers of the need for perseverance. The psalm has a lengthy confession

---

10. But see further Carol Bechtel Reynolds, "Psalm 125," *Int* 48 (1994):272–5. See also Loren S. Crow, *The Songs of Ascents*, SBL Dissertation Series 148 (Atlanta: Scholars Press, 1996).
11. VanGemeren, *Psalms*, p. 905; Weiser, *Psalms*, p. 757.
12. *Psalms*, p. 455.

of trust or confidence, lengthy for such a short psalm, followed by intercession (v. 4) and warning (v. 5).

Exegetical Analysis

Summary

Believers are as secure as the mountains around them because the LORD who surrounds them will not allow them to be tested beyond their endurance; but those who turn aside to wicked ways will endure the same fate as the wicked.

Outline

I. The psalmist asserts the unshakable security of the believers even under the dominion of wicked governments (1–3).
  A. Comparing believers to Mount Zion he affirms their security (1).
  B. Comparing the LORD to the mountains around Jerusalem, he shows the protection the believers have (2).
  C. Describing the government that the righteous must endure as wicked, he assures that God limits such oppression to their endurance (3).
    1. Wicked dominion may rule over the righteous.
    2. But it will be limited to their endurance so that they should not abandon their trust in the LORD.
II. The psalmist prays for the prosperity of the righteous (4).
III. The psalmist predicts that those who turn aside to wickedness under such dominion will suffer the same fate as the wicked (5a).
Epilogue: There should be peace on Israel (5b).

COMMENTARY IN EXPOSITORY FORM

I. Those who trust in the LORD are secure because the LORD's presence protects them (1–3).

A. Believers are as secure as the mountains (1).

The first part of the psalm concerns the security of those

who put their trust in the LORD (1–4); the psalm will end with the contrasting insecurity of the unfaithful (5). Both parts are introduced by participles, the parallel structure strengthening the contrast: verse one has "Those who trust in the LORD," and verse five begins with "But those who turn aside."

First, the faithful are introduced with the participle "those who trust" (הַבֹּטְחִים; s.v. Ps. 4:5). This word "trust" is a strong word, meaning to find security, feel secure or confident, or to rely on something. But because this word can be used for confidence in false gods or other things as well, the text specifies the object of their trust as "the LORD."

The rest of the verse describes their security in the LORD with a figure (a simile): they are like Mount Zion. The image of Mount Zion conveys the strength, security, and durability of their life of faith in the LORD. "Mount Zion" made a good comparison, for this was the location of the temple in Jerusalem. The rocky hill that was the foundation has stood securely for ages.

The rest of the verse qualifies the figure; the sentence is cryptic, but understandable. It simply says ". . . like Mount Zion [it] cannot be moved [it] dwells forever." The two verbs (יִמּוֹט[13] and יֵשֵׁב) are both singular forms and so cannot have "those who trust" as their subject. "Mount Zion" is the subject, and so this last part of the verse must be a relative clause without the relative pronoun (although it was supplied in the Qumran scroll): "[which] cannot be moved [but] remains forever." The true believer is as secure and immoveable in the faith as the rocky Mount Zion.

B. The believers' security comes from the LORD (2).

The second verse is also cryptic and a little difficult grammatically. "Jerusalem, mountains around it, and the LORD around his people, from now and forever." This may be rendered more smoothly: "Jerusalem—*as the* mountains *are* around it, even *so* the LORD *is* around his people, from now and forever."

---

13. The verb means "totter, slip, shake" (s.v. Ps. 62:2). In Arabic it means "to deviate from the right course." In the Bible it may be used as a figure of insecurity (an implied comparison)–the believer will not slip or be shaken. The word can be illustrated with the related noun מוֹט which is the "bar" or "pole" used for carrying things (a cluster of grapes); it gives and bends to make the carrying easier.

The word "Jerusalem" is an independent nominative absolute; it is placed first as an independent word to call particular emphasis to it, and then it will be referred to with a resumptive pronoun: "Jerusalem—as the mountains are around it." But it should not be smoothed out to read: "As the mountains are around Jerusalem," for that destroys the force of the construction that focuses on Jerusalem first. The parallelism then clarifies that the comparison of believers with Mount Zion is here extended: "mountains *are* around it //and the LORD *is* around his people." Believers are as secure as Mount Zion; and as the mountains around Zion provide the security, the LORD around his people makes them secure. The old city of Jerusalem was built on Mount Zion; on three sides there were valleys, but on the other side of the valleys a ring of mountains or hills that provided a natural defense for the city.[14] Zion was not the highest point; the Mount of Olives on the eastern side was about 216 feet higher in elevation, and Mount Scopus on the other side was 250 feet higher than the holy city. Mount Zion was nestled in between these protective ridges.

C. Their faith will survive wicked domination (3).

It is in this verse that one finds the major issue of the psalm, and the reason that the people needed to know how secure they were in the LORD. The nation was apparently suffering under wicked leaders, either unbelieving Israelites or Gentile powers (it is hard to know which was the case simply from the word "wickedness"). Such rulers would make life difficult for the righteous to hold to their integrity. But the psalmist was convinced that God would not let such wickedness become so severe that even the elect would turn aside from the faith. The verse is paralleled by the apostle Paul's dictum that the Lord will not permit us to be tested above that which we are able, but with the testing will make a way of escape (1 Cor. 10:13). Here, basic to that way of escape is the wholehearted trust in the LORD that brings security in the faith.

---

14. The simile is a general description because on the north side there was no mountainous area that made a complete ring around the city.

The first half of verse 3 reads, "For the rod of wickedness will not rest on the lot of the righteous." The "rod" signifies governmental rule or dominion; leaders had the scepter of the administration to show their authority (so "rod" is a metonymy, either of subject or adjunct). But here "rod" is followed by an attributive genitive: "the rod of wickedness" (רֶשַׁע; s.v. Ps. 1:1). The government is wicked. To have this wicked rule lie (יָנוּחַ, "rest"; s.v. Ps. 95:11) on the "lot" of the righteous means that the righteous had to live under the burden of a government characterized by wickedness until the LORD broke the rod. Here "lot" (גּוֹרָל) could simply refer to the land that was allotted to them. But it likely means more than that in this psalm; it is a figure (an implied comparison) for their life, what they received and have in life. Their whole life in their land would have to endure a wicked government.

But the verb is negated, and so the sense is that this wicked rule will not continue to rest on the lot of the righteous. And this promise is qualified by the following result clause (with לְמַעַן, "that"): this wickedness will not burden the righteous to the extent that, or "so that," they would turn away from their integrity. The "rod of wickedness" will be over them, but it will not be so powerful that the righteous will abandon their integrity. The idiom that is used here for abandoning their integrity is "they stretch out their hands in evil" (יִשְׁלְחוּ . . . בְּעַוְלָתָה יְדֵיהֶם). The expression could mean that they might participate in evil using their hands (a metonymy of cause), or that their sinning would be like someone stretching out the hand to something (an implied comparison). The point is that the true believer would not begin to get involved in evil activities just because there is a wicked government making it difficult for them to hold to their integrity or appealing to change. The word for "evil" (עַוְלָתָה; s.v. Ps. 43:1) means "wickedness" or "lawlessness." The assurance of the psalmist is that the wicked government would not be able to pressure the faithful to comply with evil practices, or influence them to live on a lower standard of righteousness. This assurance does not mean that believers would not be persecuted or reproached for their faith; it means that they will not waver in their faithfulness. The world system, ancient or modern, allows and promotes practices that are contrary to the will of God, and to live by the higher law often brings persecution.

II. God's people need divine favor (4).

The people of God need divine favor in any age, but especially when wickedness rules the land. So verse 4 is a prayer, literally saying: "Do good, O LORD, to the good [people], and to those who are upright in their hearts." The imperative is a prayer, and the use of an imperative stresses the urgency of the prayer. The verb (הֵיטִיבָה; s.v. Ps. 34:8) means "do good." The translation may be put into smoother English, such as "show favor" or "treat well," but the literal translation captures the emphasis from the repetition. The verb means to cause good things to happen; and the recipients are "those who are good." This use of the cognate adjective "good" (טוֹבִים) as a noun ("to the good [people]") underscores that this favorable treatment would be a reward for faithfulness—God will do good to the good. There are good people being tested severely and suffering under wicked governments, trying to hold to their integrity; so the prayer is that the LORD do good things for them. And the verb "do good" is also figurative (a metonymy of cause or adjunct), signifying what that goodness is that God should do for them—give the faithful what is needed for their lives, freedom from oppression and prosperity.

These good people are also described as the "upright in their hearts." In the Old Testament the word "heart" is commonly used (as a metonymy of subject) to represent the will or the innermost capacity of making choices (for "heart," s.v. Ps. 111:1). It is the aspect of the spiritual capacities that combines the mind and the affections. These people live their lives, make their choices, and desire things in harmony with what is upright and righteous (for יָשָׁר s.v. Ps. 67:4). They do not pervert what is right nor conform to the life of their wicked world.

III. Unbelievers who turn aside from the faith to wickedness have no security in the coming judgment (5).

In contrast to those who believe in the LORD and are not shaken from their faith or their faithfulness, the psalm now focuses on those people who do turn aside to wickedness. In view of the message of the psalm so far, these must be people who in the final analysis are not the upright in heart. It is as the apostle

John says, "They went out from us, but they were not of us; for if they had been of us, they would no doubt have continued with us" (1 John 2:19).

The first word of the verse uses the participle to form the contrast: "But those who turn aside" (וְהַמַּטִּים, *hiphil* participle from נָטָה). This participle also functions as an independent nominative absolute, for the suffix on the main verb (יוֹלִיכֵם) resumes the idea as the direct object—"But (as for) those who turn aside . . . the LORD will lead them out." The idea of "turning aside" is figurative (an implied comparison) for abandoning the faith and following the way of the world and for ancient Israel also the gods of the world.

The word "their crookednesses" (עַקַלְקַלּוֹתָם) following the participle functions as an adverbial accusative ("turn side *to* their crookednesses"). It is put into the plural to intensify the idea of their activities as crooked or perverse; and the form is a reduplicated form to add to the intensity. So this verse is not referring to a small infraction of God's law or a sin of ignorance; it describes giving oneself over to corrupt activities.

For these people the future is bleak if they do not repent of their sin. The LORD will lead them away with[15] the "practitioners of iniquity" (פֹּעֲלֵי הָאָוֶן). The participle is used to show that these are not simply people who sin, but they are doers of evil (and "evil" is an objective genitive; for "evil," s.v. Ps. 28:3)—it is their continual activity to do sinful things that cause pain. The verb "lead away" could be taken literally to refer to causing them to go into some captivity; or, it may be figurative (a comparison) for destroying them in judgment.

The psalm closes with the simple prayer: "Peace upon Israel" (for "peace," s.v. Ps. 38:3). In the context this is likely to be a prayer, and so a (jussive) verb must be added: "Peace *be* upon Israel." The benediction is on those who trust, not on all those who turn aside from the LORD to live in wickedness. This peace

---

15. Goldingay takes the view that אֵת is not here the preposition "with," but the sign of the accusative: "the LORD will lead them away, (i.e.,) the practitioners of iniquity" (*Psalms 90–150*, p. 487). The change is not necessary for the implication is clear enough: if they do wickedness they will be judged like the wicked.

will finally come when the LORD removes the wicked rulers from the land—and with them the wicked people in general. For them there is no prospect of peace. In the exposition of the psalm this verse could be made a separate point or simply a summing up of the desire expressed in the prayer.

MESSAGE AND APPLICATION

The psalm ends with the desire for better times; but in the meantime it reminds the faithful of their security in the LORD in contrast to the unfaithful who will be judged. The main idea can be worded in a number of ways, but the psalm is essentially saying: *Those who are secure in their faith will hold to their integrity in spite of pressure from wicked government; but those who turn to evil will be judged with the wicked*. The instruction to be drawn from this would be on making sure that one's faith is in the LORD, and that it is a faith that is growing so that it can withstand such tests. A strong faith will be secure in the LORD and will be characterized by a righteous life and an upright heart.

On the other hand, there are many people who profess to be in the covenant community (today, even church members), but there is no evidence of genuine faith. And in evil times when there is either subtle pressure or outright oppression they will conform to the lifestyle of the world, even if the standards of righteousness have to be set aside as outdated or irrelevant.

The test of living under wicked systems is limited, for God will not allow us to be tested beyond what we are able, but will make a way of escape.

PSALM 126

The Great Joy and Chief Concern of the Redeemed

INTRODUCTION

Text and Textual Variants

A Song of Ascents

1 When the LORD brought back the captivity[1] of Zion,
 we were like those who are restored to health.[2]

---

1. The form here in the text is שִׁיבַת. The word is taken by most to be a scribal error for שְׁבוּת or שְׁבִית, and its derivation traced either to שָׁבָה, "to take captive," or שׁוּב, "to return." If the connection is to "return," the line would then say "when the LORD turned the turning," It then would refer to the LORD's reversing their fortunes after some adversity, but not necessarily the captivity.

 But it could also be understood to mean "the returned," i.e., those who returned to Zion from the captivity (שָׁבָה, "to take captive"). The Greek has "captivity." The difference is not great: the idea would either be that of the LORD's restoring the people from the captivity, or restoring the fortunes of the people after some disaster (like the exile). See further J. M. Bracke, "Šûb šebût," ZAW 97 (1985):233–44.

2. The traditional translation is "we were like dreamers." The Masoretic Text reads הָיִינוּ כְּחֹלְמִים, "we were like dreamers." The form is the *qal*

active participle, plural, from the root חָלַם, "to dream." The idea that this would have is that the restoration was too good to be true—it was like a dream. But the significance of dreaming in the Old Testament is different; dreams were more ominous and important. They were often prophetic, and so if "dreamers" is the original, one would expect some anticipation of a future restoration (see also anticipatory dreams in Isa. 29:7–8). Goldingay agrees that the idea of dreaming does not fit this context since dreams were usually revelation (*Psalms 90–150*, p. 492; he allows that it could refer to a visionary dream the LORD gave them that came true).

The Greek ὡς παρακεκλημένοι is a passive participle; it cannot therefore have any connection to the active voice, or the meaning "dreamers," but may be rendered as "(we became) as those comforted." The Qumran scroll appears to agree with the Greek translation's idea, for it writes the form חלומים, a passive participle (the waw indicating a šûreq), or possibly a stative adjective. In biblical Hebrew there is another root חָלַם which means something like "recover health, restore to life." It is used in Isaiah 38:16 where Hezekiah was restored to life and health after a threatening illness. This verb probably is what is reflected in the Qumran scroll as well as the Greek translation, and not the verb "to dream." The Targum on the Psalm also reflects this other verb; it reads "like the sick who are cured." There is, however, one manuscript of the Targum that includes both choices: "we shall be like those who sleep (and) are awakened from their dreams." Another translation: "Like the sick who have been cured of their sickness" (David M. Stec, *The Targums of Psalms* [Collegeville, MN: Liturgical Press, 2004], p. 223). If this reading is correct, it would mean that in their circumstances it looked like they would die, but now they were full of life again, "as men who had been healed" (John Strugnell, "A Note on Ps. cxxvi.i," *JTS* 7 [1956]:239–43).

The external evidence seems to be strongly in favor of the Greek, Qumran, and Targum understanding based on a different root than what is in the MT. And the internal evidence favors this reading as well. If the commonly known word "dream" was the original reading, why would someone change it to the passive of a verb that is very rare? But if the passive of a rare verb was the original, one can more easily explain how a scribe might have assumed it was the common word for "dream." Scribal variants often exhibit a movement toward the common, better-known word or form rather than to the rare and difficult. And if this form was written defectively (that is, without the *waw*), a form חלמים could have been understood to be the active *hôlᵉmîm* or passive *ḥălûmîm* participle.

Most modern versions stay with the MT's reading "dreamers." But it seems to me that the evidence and the textual critical procedures would support the variant reading; the translation should be something like "we were like those restored to health." VanGemeren says the evidence for this word is relatively weak (*Psalms*, p. 909); but the Greek version, Qumran, Targum and Vulgate follow it. On the whole, the better reading seems to

2 Then our mouth was filled with laughter,
   and our tongue with joyful singing.
  Then it was said among the nations,
   "The LORD has done great things for them."
3 The LORD has done great things for us;
   we are rejoicing.

4 Bring back our captivity,[3] O LORD,
   as streams in the desert.
5 Those who sow with tears
   shall reap with shouts of joy.
6 *Whoever* goes forth continually, weeping,
   carrying seed for sowing,
  shall doubtless come back with shouts of joy,
   carrying his sheaves with him.

Composition and Context

Psalm 126 appears to be a post-exilic pilgrim psalm because of the reference to the restoration of the captivity. The translation with restoring the "fortunes" is more general and could be pre-exilic in origin; but it would also fit as a reference to the return from the exile—Isaiah 52:8 uses the idea in conjunction with the return to Zion after the exile with shouts of joy.[4] To capture the intensity of this passage one must imagine what it would have been like to have lived in the Babylonian captivity and not have been free or able to worship in the way the nation had been accustomed to before, and then imagine what it would have been like to be free to go once again to Jerusalem for the festivals. Psalm 137 captures the sadness of the exiles who could not sing

---

  be "we were like those who are healed" or "restored to health." See also D. Winton Thomas, *Text of the Revised Psalter* (London: SPCK, 1963).
3. The form in the text is a *Kethiv-Qere'* reading. The *K.* reading is שְׁבוּתֵנוּ. The *Q. is* שְׁבִיתֵנוּ. It has the support of the Targum and the majority of the manuscripts.
4. Dahood takes the psalm as pre-exilic because of the use of some of the terms (*Psalms*, III:217–18). But if verses 1–3 are interpreted in the past tense, then the psalm most likely refers to the restoration to the land.

the songs of Zion; Psalm 126 captures the joy of the people who returned and were able to celebrate once again.

But those who returned were faced with some major obstacles to the rebuilding of the nation. The historical records tell how they had to deal with lands that had not been farmed for a good fifty years or more, were opposed by different groups in the land, and were dismayed by the fact that only a small portion of the people came back. So this psalm both celebrates the initial restoration and prays for more people to come back and join in the rebuilding of God's program.[5]

Many commentators classify Psalm 126 as a communal lament. It begins with a report of celebration to be sure, but turns on the prayer for God to restore the captives to Zion (similar to the gratitude and prayer pattern of Psalm 85). The use of parallel words shows the pattern of the psalm with two parts, verses 1–3 and then 4–6.[6] The prayer with its principle from the world of agriculture in the second half overshadows the celebration of the first half. The first exiles returning to the land were filled with joy; but they were deeply concerned that more did not return with them. The prayer focuses on God's part in the complete restoration, and the principle drawn from agriculture focuses on their efforts. So the prayer and the principle represent the community's expectation of a greater restoration to help in adverse conditions.[7] Weiser and others suggest it was associated with the autumnal festival in view of the reaping imagery, but there were other harvests.

Exegetical Analysis

Summary

Joyful because the LORD restored them to their land, the first exiles pray and labor for the full restoration of the captives and

---

5. Broyles notes that the psalm could also apply to any instance where God restored believers who, in turn, sought to ensure that the restoration was all that God wanted it to be (*Psalms*, p. 457). See also Allen M. Harman, "The Setting and Interpretation of Psalm 126," *RTR* 44 (1985):74–80.
6. J. Magne, "Répétitions de mots et exégèse dans quelques Psaumes et la Pater," *Bib* 39 (1958):177–97.
7. Weiser, *Psalms*, p. 760.

the prosperity of the land, finding encouragement in the principle that perseverance in sowing will yield a good harvest.

Outline

I. Praise: The restored exiles recall their great joy for the LORD's restoration of them to their land (1–3).
   A. They tell of their joy when they returned to Zion (1).
   B. They report how the nations acknowledged that the LORD had done great things for them (2).
   C. They express their joy because the LORD had done great things for them (3).
II. Prayer: The restored exiles pray for the full restoration of the captivity to Zion and find encouragement from the principle of sowing and reaping (4–6).
   A. They pray for the full restoration of the captives (4).
   B. They find encouragement in the principle of sowing and reaping (5–6).
      1. Principle: Those who persevere will succeed (5).
      2. Reiteration: Those who continually labor in spite of difficulties will most certainly succeed (6).

COMMENTARY IN EXPOSITORY FORM

I. Redemption fills the saints with joy and the world with amazement (1–3).

A. *The LORD restores the life of his people when he sets them free from bondage (1).*

If the setting of the psalm is the deliverance of the people of Israel from their exile in Babylon, then that deliverance according to the prophets was a redemption, not in the New Testament spiritual sense of salvation, but redemption as in the deliverance of the people of God from bondage. The exiles who returned to Zion were for the most part believing members of the covenant already, and so it was for them a restoration to their life in the land. The New Testament uses the redemption of Israel from Egypt and later from Babylon to illustrate our spiritual redemption: after all, it was a deliverance from the bondage of the world by the grace of God through the forgiveness of sins. I have worded the points of the outline to bridge the two testaments because the principle is the same: Israel's deliverance from bondage (forgiveness and restoration) filled them with joy and a new life, and our redemption from the bondage of sin (forgiveness and salvation) should fill us with joy and life as well.

The psalm begins with a temporal clause referring to Israel's great deliverance: "When the LORD brought back (בְּשׁוּב יְהוָה) the captives of Zion."[8] The following object is: "captivity of Zion." Zion is the mountain on which Jerusalem was situated; here it signifies the nation by referring to its capital of Jerusalem (a metonymy of subject). In the phrase the "captives of Zion" it could be either a genitive of termination, "the captives to Zion," or a

---

8. The word שׁוּב is a very common word in the Bible, occurring over a thousand times. It has the basic idea of "turn back, return." Derived nouns include תְּשׁוּבָה which means "return, answer," including the returning of the year or springtime; מְשׁוּבָה, "turning back" in the sense of apostasy; as well as the adjectives שׁוֹבָב and שׁוֹבֵב, both meaning "back-turning, apostate."

The verb has both literal and figurative meanings. Literally, it is used for any simple act of turning back (Ruth 1:16), returning (Gen. 14:17), or returning to something (Exod. 4:20, 21).

In the figurative uses it can be used of human relations and conditions, such as returning to a physical condition (Job 33:25; 1 Kings 13:6), being refreshed (Ps. 23:3), returning to a divorced wife (Jer. 3:1), or restoring allegiance to a leader (Judg. 11:8). But it has more uses here for the spiritual relationship with God. The verb, as well as nouns and adjectives, can be used for turning away from God in apostasy (Judg. 2:19), and returning to God, meaning seek penitently (Hos. 6:1; Ps. 51:15). In this light the word can mean to repent, that is, change the mind and direction (Jer. 3:7). The object of repentance is to return to the original covenant relationship with the LORD. It is not completely a restoration of the old, but more a starting point of a new or renewed relationship. Closely related is the emphasis on turning back from evil (I Kings 8:35; Jon. 3:9), especially in the prophets where there is an urgent need to turn away from idolatry and corruption.

The verb is also used of the LORD's returning to his people, meaning to show them favor and bless them once again (Gen. 18:10; Isa. 63:17). There are also a number of uses concerning inanimate subjects, such as a prayer turning back (Ps. 35:13), or the word returning (Isa. 45:23), or judgment (Ps. 94:15). See further W. L. Holladay, *The Root ŠUBH in the Old Testament* (1958); and "שׁוּב *šub* **to return**," by J. A. Soggin, in *Theological Lexicon of the Old Testament*, ed. by Jenni and Westermann, III:1312–17.

partitive genitive, "the captives (who are part of the people) of Zion," or simply possession, "Zion's captives."

The response to this restoration was joy, first in a subdued sense of joyful relief, and then a more exuberant joy. The relief is expressed in this verse with "we were like those restored to health." The participle in the text (חֹלְמִים) is "dreamers"; it functions in a nominal use as the object of the preposition; and the preposition "like" makes the participle also a figure of comparison (a simile). It would say, "We were like dreamers." If the variant reading is accepted, then in this construction the participle would be passive (חֲלוּמִים), and the line would read, "We were like those restored to health." In the general exposition of the psalm this distinction would not alter the point the verse is making; but in the precise exegesis, the latter seems more likely the original reading.

B. The great deliverance brings joy to the redeemed and recognition from the world (2).

In the second verse the psalmist tells of the joy that the returning exiles had. The first verb in verse two is "filled" (יִמָּלֵא); this would normally be taken as an imperfect, but after the adverb (אָז), "then," it has a preterite nuance (or definite past tense), "then was filled." Verbs of filling usually are idiomatic, followed by the description of what filled them. The accusative is "laughter" (שְׂחוֹק), but the translation must supply the preposition "with" to capture the sense of the expression: "(then our mouth) was filled *with* laughter." The mouth is the organ of expression, and so it is used figuratively (metonymy of cause) for the sounds and words of celebration. The word "laughter" (שְׂחוֹק) represents the general sense of rejoicing and celebrating.

The parallel expression is "and our tongue [was filled] with joy." "Our tongue" and "our mouth" are used the same way (as metonymies of cause), the instruments of speech being put for what they said—so their words, their speech or the things they said, were filled with joy and laughter. The word that is parallel to "laughter" here is "joy"; this word (רִנָּה; s.v. Ps. 33:1) refers to great joy, a ringing cry or shouting for joy. This was no subdued celebration; it was a great celebration of freedom from captivity (contrasting with the sadness and grief described in Psalm 137). This word for "joy" is used both for joyful shouts as in a victory in war, and for cries of lamentation. It often is identified with the sound made by flicking the tongue from side to side in the mouth and shrieking or crying out as loud as possible.

In the second half of the verse we have the report that people in other nations acknowledged the great things the LORD did for his people. This does not mean (necessarily) that they came to faith, only that they recognized something supernatural had been at work to do what must have seemed to be the impossible. It would be comparable to people's responses to a healing today against all medical odds—they might not trust the Lord, but they must recognize something supernatural happened.

Both halves of the verse begin with "then" (אָז) followed by the verb expressing the past time, here, "then it was said" (יֹאמְרוּ, literally "they said," but rendered as a passive because there is no expressed subject). The following prepositional phrase identifies who the speakers were, but only generally: "among the nations" means that non-Israelite people in the nations observed this amazing deliverance and concluded that Israel's God had done something for his people. The rest of the verse provides a summation of the kind of thing that was being said: "Yahweh has done great things with these [people]." The construction uses two verbs to express the one idea (a verbal hendiadys): the first verb is "he did great" or "he made great" (הִגְדִּיל; s.v. Ps. 34:3) and the second is the infinitive "to do" (לַעֲשׂוֹת, from עָשָׂה), so together they say "he made great to do." But the first verb becomes adverbial in this construction and the infinitive becomes the main verb: "he did greatly" or "he did great things."

C. The redeemed acknowledge the LORD's deliverance (3).

The first part of verse three is a restatement of what the nations were saying—the people of God could not say it any better. The only difference is in the prepositional phrase: the nations had said "with these" but the redeemed say "with us." The line closes with a construction similar to the end of verse one (the verb "to be" and the participle): "we are glad" (הָיִינוּ שְׂמֵחִים). The translation "glad" is far too weak for the form (שְׂמֵחִים; s.v. Ps. 48:11) given the circumstances; it would convey more of the sense of joy, rejoicing, or taking delight in what the LORD had done.

II. The saints pray for God to restore many others from bondage (4).

The fourth verse could certainly be taken together with the last two verses, but since it seems to form the major contrast with verse one it may be more effective to deal with it as a separate point, and then deal with the principle from agriculture as the responsibility of the people to promote participation in the program of God.

Verse 4 forms a transition between the first and last parts of the psalm. As a prayer it introduces the theme of the second part, the concern over influencing others yet in bondage to be restored to the land. It also forms a link to the first half of the psalm by repeating the word "restore" (שׁוּב), now as an imperative. So the psalmist prays that the LORD restore to the land others who were still in captivity. The concern is like the evangelistic concern of the church, except that the psalmist is praying for people who are in the covenant to be prompted to return to the land to do the work of God. The desire is that they too will catch the vision that the future of God's program is in Israel, not in captivity in a foreign land.

The form "restore" (שׁוּבָה) is the alternative masculine singular imperative from the verb (שׁוּב): "Restore, O LORD, our captivity."[9] If in the first part they were relieved and filled with joy because the LORD had restored them, they now pray that he will restore the rest of the people who had not yet heeded the call. The illustration the psalmist uses is in the comparison (simile), "as streams in the desert." This word "streams" (אֲפִיקִים) refers to the dry river beds in the wilderness. They are dry in the dry season; but in the rainy season they become rushing torrents of water. Most of them are then filled with water running down from the mountains and high plateaus of the land; they can be

---

9. Dahood argues for a past tense translation of this verb based on a comparison with cognates, but it is not convincing (*Psalms*, III:220).

strong enough to wash buses off the roads when they overflow their banks. The psalmist compares the road from Babylon to such a river bed. It is now dry, meaning, there are no people coming down the road. He prays for God to bring the rest of the people back so that those roads would be "overflowing their banks" like streams in the desert.

III. The saints who labor for the kingdom find encouragement in the principle of sowing and reaping (5–6).

The principle recorded in these last two verses encouraged the people who were praying for the full restoration of the captivity to persevere in their efforts. No doubt the people who first returned found agriculture difficult in a land that had not been worked for decades; but they knew that perseverance would eventually bring a harvest. But because these verses are joined with the prayer of verse 4, we know that the psalmist's concern was not with a harvest of wheat, but people. Therefore, the entire two verse section is figurative (an implied comparison), referring to the labor for God's restored program. Delitzsch says it well:

> The tearful sowing is only an emblem of the new foundation-laying, which really took place not without many tears (Ezra iii. 12), amidst sorrowful and depressed circumstances; but in its general sense the language of the psalm coincides with the language of the Preacher on the Mount, Matt. v. 4: Blessed are those who mourn, for they shall be comforted. . . . As by the sowing we are to understand everything that each individual contributes towards the building up of the kingdom of God, so by the sheaves, the wholesome fruit which, by God bestowing His blessing upon it beyond our prayer and comprehension, springs up from it.[10]

The principle is expressed in both verses: verse 5 states it, and verse 6 elaborates on it in more detail. In other words, there

---

10. *Psalms*, III:290–291.

is a designed intensification between the two verses, as if to say that as the difficulties increase, the perseverance must increase, and the resulting joy will be all the greater.

Verse 5 begins the principle with "the sowers" or "those who sow," a participle (הַזֹּרְעִים) that serves as the subject of the verb in the second colon, "shall reap" (יִקְצֹרוּ). The imperfect tense states the future expectation: those who sow shall reap. But the other words in the line highlight both the labor and the reaping. The first is "tear" (דִּמְעָה), taken collectively for "tears." It is figurative (a metonymy of adjunct), used to explain the sowing as "with tears." It stresses that the work would be difficult, frustrating, and at times disappointing. The idea is drawn from the struggle of the people to get crops to grow in a land that had been largely left uncultivated for many years: the labor was hard and the results meager at first. The psalmist, therefore, is making a comparison: in the spiritual task of promoting God's renewed program back in the land, whether by prayer or by direct appeals, the effort will be disappointing and frustrating at times but must be tireless—the "sowing" must continue.

The outcome of the labor is expressed in the prepositional phrase "with a ringing cry" (רִנָּה; see v. 2; s.v. Ps. 33:1); it forms a dramatic contrast with the "tears." In fact, the arrangement of the line (as a chiasm) highlights the contrast: "Those who sow / with tears // with a ringing cry / will reap." This ringing cry is also figurative (a metonymy of effect or adjunct), signifying that they shall not only reap a great harvest, but that harvest will cause them to shout with joy and excitement.

As an implied comparison, the sowing represents any effort expended for the kingdom of God, and the tears indicate it will be hard and frustrating, sometimes discouraging; the reaping refers to any success in convincing others to return and join God's program of renewal and restoration in the covenant, and the joy will then not be joy of a harvest, but greater joy like that mentioned in verse 2.[11]

The point of verse 5 is expanded in verse 6 to draw out all

---

11. Attempts to link the laughing and the weeping with Canaanite ritual acts for the New Year are not convincing; see F. F. Hvidberg, *Weeping and Laughing in the Old Testament* (Leiden: E. J. Brill, 1962).

these themes. The first half of the verse expands the idea of sowing in 5a, and the second half develops the idea of reaping in 5b. The verbal construction for the participle ("those sowing") is now expressed with a singular verb that refers to any and all: literally "he goes forth continually" (הָלוֹךְ יֵלֵךְ). This imperfect tense may be given a progressive or habitual nuance ("he goes") in view of its parallelism with the participle "sowing." But the nuance of an imperfect expressing possibility also works very well in the context: "he may indeed go forth while weeping." The first may be preferable since this infinitive absolute (from הָלַךְ) often adds the adverbial sense of "continually." So the two words would say, "He [who] goes forth continually" or "Whoever continually goes forth" to sow. The nuance of the verb and the infinitive emphasize the important point of the perseverance of the sower.

A second infinitive (וּבָכֹה) is then added to express simultaneous activity: "while weeping." A literal translation of the line is: "he goes out, going and weeping"; but it means he continually goes out while weeping. This expression captures the "sowing with tears" in the preceding line so that the tears and the weeping are meant to express the difficulty and frustration of the work. There would be actual weeping from time to time, but the words more likely signify the difficulty (metonymy of adjunct).

The second colon of the verse uses an active participle "carrying" (נֹשֵׂא; s.v. Ps. 24:7). This participle further modifies the action of the subject (as an adverbial accusative): he goes out but as he goes he is carrying his bag of seed. The picture is of the individual continually going out while weeping, carrying his bag of seed.

The contrast is in the second half of this verse. Parallel to the first colon (v. 6a) the third colon has an infinitive absolute and an imperfect tense (בֹּא יָבוֹא [from בּוֹא]); but now in view of the context this imperfect tense will have the nuance of specific future, and the modifying infinitive will stress the certainty: "(whoever continually goes forth . . .) shall surely come in." The verbs "go out" and "come in" represent the activities of sowing and reaping. He may go out with sorrow and frustration, but he will return with great joy. For the third time in this psalm the word for "ringing cry" (רִנָּה) is used. If the sower perseveres in the sowing, no matter how difficult or frustrating, there will be a harvest—there will be a coming in with rejoicing. This reason for the rejoicing is expressed in the final colon: "carrying his sheaves." This last part of the second half of the verse parallels the last part of the first half, repeating the participle (נֹשֵׂא) and forming another contrast: he goes out carrying a seed pouch; he comes in carrying sheaves. Obviously, time passes between the going out with seed and the coming in with sheaves. But the point is clear: perseverance will pay off, the seed will produce a harvest, and the struggle will be replaced by celebration. This principle is true of agriculture; but it is also true of labor in God's kingdom.

MESSAGE AND APPLICATION

The psalmist is concerned with spiritual matters. But living in a time when agricultural work had been made difficult by the exile, he could draw on that setting to bring encouragement to the people. The people had been set free from bondage by the LORD, a deliverance that brought great joy to them and even acknowledgment from people in the nations around them. The LORD truly had done great things. But there were so many more people who needed to respond to the word of the LORD and return to build God's program in the land once again. To that end the faithful prayed; to that end they labored in what was obviously every bit as difficult as the physical labor in the fields. But they knew if they kept at it, more and more people would return to the land.

In the New Testament Jesus used the figure of the sower in his parable (Matt. 13) to represent those who proclaim the message of the kingdom of God. All that any sower had to do was remain faithful to his task to sow the seed. God prepared the kind of ground that would receive it. Since the success of doing the work of God depends on God's preparing people to receive the word, the faithful pray that the LORD will bring the people into his program; and since the means of their coming is the word of the LORD, the faithful will keep proclaiming the message (sowing the seed). Because the psalmist uses the agricultural image for spiritual matters, and because our Lord Jesus Christ expanded the point to preaching the message of the kingdom so people would come to faith, the modern exposition can apply this psalm to redemption as well as to spiritual renewal, first recognizing that the psalm was primarily intended to draw people, who may have already been believers, back to the land to get involved in the service of the LORD.

So a Christian exposition of this passage could word the main expository idea in this way: *Those who have experienced the great salvation of the LORD will not only be filled with joy but will desire that others come to share in his kingdom.* As a corollary we might add, *To that end they will pray; to that end they will do whatever they can to ensure that there will be a "harvest" of people coming to serve the LORD.* The applications would include both praying for others to turn to the LORD, and using whatever gifts one has to work for the kingdom. To put it in the words of the psalmist, the task of the redeemed is to sow the seed. That includes sharing the word of God with people and imploring people to respond to it. The motivation for this kind of spiritual service is the joy of redemption. The more that redemption is appreciated, the greater the service will be.

This psalm may also be used to focus on the need of spiritual restoration. Within the believing community there are people for whom the world has too much of a hold. They need to show their commitment to the LORD by getting involved in his program rather than remain comfortably in the world (as many Israelites did at the time of the return from the exile). This focus was uppermost in the mind of the psalmist, but his prayer for people to return was broad enough to refer to people who may not have been believers as well as those who were.

PSALM 127

Living under Divine Providence

INTRODUCTION

Text and Textual Variants

A Song of Ascent. Of Solomon.

1 Unless the LORD builds the house,
   they who build it labor in vain;
   Unless the LORD protects the city,[1]
   the watchmen awake in vain.
2 It is vain for you to rise up early,
   to stay up late,[2]
   to eat the bread of toil;

---

1. The Targum clarifies with "city of Jerusalem," likely following the view that the house is the temple and the city is Jerusalem.
2. The MT has מְאַחֲרֵי־שֶׁבֶת, "making late to sit" or "sit up late." Paralleled with the first idea of rising early, the two lines seem to refer to lengthening the day artificially. The Greek version has ἐγείρεσθαι μετὰ τὸ καθῆσθαι, perhaps meaning "to get up after sitting down." And the Targum gives an entirely negative interpretation, stating that it was vain to get up early to do robbery, or stay up late to commit fornication, or to eat the bread of hard-working poor people.

for he gives rest[3] to his beloved.[4]
3 Behold, children are a heritage from the LORD,
and the fruit of the womb is his reward.
4 As arrows in the hand of a mighty man,
so are the children of youth.[5]
5 Blessed is the man who has his quiver[6] full of them;

---

3. The MT's שֵׁנָא, translated "rest," has been questioned by many commentators; it seems to run contrary to wisdom literature where hard labor is rewarded with success rather than rest. Trying to harmonize the line with the whole psalm no doubt, D. Winton Thomas and others have interpreted the word "rest" to mean sexual intercourse and so fertility ("A Note on זַרְמָתָם שֵׁנָה יִהְיוּ in Psalm 90:5," *VT* 18 [1968]:267–8). Emerton makes a plausible suggestion that it be translated "honor." He draws this from the identification of שֵׁנָא with שָׁנָה in cognate Syriac and Arabic; this sense can be noted for passages in Proverbs as well (such as 5:9 and 24:21). See John A. Emerton, "The Meaning of *šēnā'* in Psalm cxxvii 2," *VT* 24 (1974):15–31.
4. MT has לִידִידוֹ, "to his beloved." The Greek version, the Syriac and Jerome have a plural, "those he loves." They may have thought the form in the text was written defectively: דָ- instead of דָיו-. The singular form would harmonize better with the association with Solomon (see below in the commentary section).
5. The Hebrew is הַנְּעוּרִים, but the Greek text introduces a curious idea with its reading "children of those who were outcasts." There is another Hebrew root נער that means "to shake off, shake free," and it is possible that because of the plural form in the text and the *šûreq* vowel, the translator assumed it was that word and identified it as a passive participle instead of the abstract plural noun "youth time." The Greek word used, ἐκτετιναγμένων, "outcasts," usually refers to a solid or even violent shaking out, like winnowing, or knocking fruit off the branches, or running people out. The translator may have thought it referred to the nation of Israel as those who were run out of other lands. The reading is certainly unusual.
6. For MT's אַשְׁפָּתוֹ, "his quiver," a form that occurs only here in the Psalter, the Greek version has τὴν ἐπιθυμίαν αὐτοῦ, "his desire." The Greek text reads, "Blessed is the man who shall satisfy his desire with them." The translator may not have known this particular word for "quiver" since it is not very common. And, there is a word meaning "long for, pant for, desire," that uses the same letters, but in different order: שָׁאַף. It may simply be a case of confused letters. One could argue that "desire" was the original, and the Masoretic (or earlier) scribe wished to continue the simile with arrows and introduced (accidentally or deliberately) the idea of "quiver." But it is more likely that the rare word that was in the MT was overlooked and the common word "desire" put in its place.

they shall not be put to shame
when they speak with their enemies in the gate.

Composition and Context

Psalm 127 is a pilgrim song about divine providence in domestic activities. The passage focuses on the hidden activity of the LORD in building a house, protecting a city, prospering one's labor, and providing children for the family. These daily cares of the ancient Israelite were eased by the belief that the LORD was sovereignly working through all the circumstances to bless his people.

Most commentators note the wisdom motifs that are found here; Allen describes the psalm as popular, didactic religious wisdom literature.[7] If it is wisdom literature, then like Proverbs the ideas would be timeless and not easily identified with a historical occasion. The superscription associates the psalm with Solomon. There is no reason to dismiss out of hand this traditional notation; in fact, the internal features of the psalm support the connection. Perowne says that there is not a word in the psalm to guide us to the time of the composition.[8] He enumerates the features of the psalm that led people to think it was Solomon's: (1) the psalm talks about the LORD's building a house, and certainly the thought of building the house of the LORD cannot be forgotten in applying this text to the activities of life;[9] (2) the psalm places a heavy emphasis on the motif of vanity, a motif best known from the book of Ecclesiastes, which was also traditionally attributed to Solomon;[10] (3) the psalm refers to the LORD's giving (in) sleep to his beloved, and this may have some reference to the fact that Solomon was granted wisdom in such a way; and (4) the mention of "his beloved" may reflect the name the LORD gave to Solomon, Jedidiah, which

---

7. *Psalms 101–150*, p. 178.
8. *Psalms*, II:393.
9. Eaton says linking the house with Solomon's temple may be a correct insight (*Psalms*, p. 286). See further P. D. Miller, "Psalm 127–The House that Yahweh Builds," *JSOT* 22 (1982):119–32.
10. Modern critical scholarship would not credit Ecclesiastes to Solomon, but place it much later in time.

means "truly beloved of the LORD."[11] Of course, these features by themselves are not that compelling, but together they tend to support the note; so the idea that Solomon wrote Psalm 127 is not that far-fetched. If he did not, at least a connection with him provides a useful link between the psalm and other teachings on the life of wisdom.

Most modern commentators, however, reject the idea that the work is Solomon's. Anderson simply says it is unlikely Solomon was the author and that the psalm was probably post-exilic.[12] Some commentators conclude that Psalm 127 is composed of two different psalms that were joined together because the subject matter is so different in each half. The argument, however, is not convincing; the psalm should be taken as a unit—which it certainly is in its canonical form (see Anderson, Miller and others who argue for the unity).

Commentators offer various suggestions for the setting of the psalm. One common view is that it was associated with the Feast of Tabernacles in the fall when the people would look for God's blessings. But the concerns of the psalm would be applicable to many occasions in life. It seems best to avoid trying to fit it into a specific setting. As a wisdom psalm its principles would be timeless. It contrasts the blessings of God with the futility of life without God: without God's blessing all human effort and precautions are in vain (Perowne, II:394).

Exegetical Analysis

Summary

The psalmist affirms that total dependence on divine intervention alone ensures worthwhile and successful domestic enterprises and safeguards, and then he epitomizes the divine blessing in the gift of children who can defend the interests of the family.

---

11. The name Jedidiah was given to David's child after the first one died. It was a sign that the LORD had completely forgiven David and Bathsheba and would bless their marriage (2 Sam. 12:25).
12. *Psalms 73–150*, p. 867.

Living under Divine Providence

Outline

I. The sage affirms that domestic enterprises are meaningless without the divine intervention of the LORD (1–2).
   A. The domestic life independent of the LORD is futile (1–2a).
      1. It is meaningless to build any house independently of God (1a).
      2. It is pointless to guard a city without divine protection (1b).
      3. It is futile to prolong the days with anxious toil to earn a living (2a).
   B. The domestic life dependent on the LORD is satisfying (2b).
II. The sage epitomizes the blessing of the LORD in the provision of children who are capable of defending the family (3–5).
   A. The divine provision of children is both a blessing and a trust (3).
   B. The divine provision of children is beneficial for the security of the family (4–5).

COMMENTARY IN EXPOSITORY FORM

I. Only when domestic enterprises are pursued by faith are they worthwhile and satisfying (1–2).

A. Domestic activities are pointless and powerless apart from divine intervention (1–2a).

The first two verses stress the necessity of divine providence. The point is first made negatively (1–2a) and then positively (2b). The negative aspect focuses on building (1a), guarding (1b), and laboring (2a). Verse 1 is a long verse of two lines of text. It contains two separate but related ideas, one on building a house and the other on guarding a city. The parallel "Unless the LORD" (אִם־יְהוָה) at the beginning of each half stresses the point that the LORD must be involved for these activities to be worthwhile. Likewise, the repetition of "vain" (שָׁוְא) at the beginning of the third and the fourth cola stresses the futility or worthlessness of actions without the LORD's involvement.

679

1. Building without faith in and dedication to the LORD is pointless (1a).

The verse states that if the LORD does not build the house, the builders labor in vain. It is presented as an observation in general terms. The clause's beginning with the particle "unless, except" (אִם),[13] helps in the classification of the tenses. The imperfect tense "builds" (יִבְנֶה) works best as a progressive imperfect, receiving the English present tense translation (although a modal nuance might also work: "Unless the LORD should build a house"). The present tense is preferable because the second unit uses the perfect tense and then a participle, suggesting that the work is going on: "its builders (those who are building it) labor in vain."[14] The perfect tense "labor" (עָמְלוּ) would then be classified as a characteristic perfect (or possibly a gnomic, in which case it would be saying that they always labor in vain if the LORD is not in it).

The word translated "vain" (שָׁוְא) is difficult to translate precisely.[15] "Vain" conveys the idea of empty or futile; the Hebrew word does indeed mean "futile, worthless, meaningless," but it

---

13. The particle usually introduces a conditional clause; but here with the negative adverb preceding the imperfect tense ("if not") it is restrictive, or exceptive–"Unless the LORD builds a house."
14. This particular verb stresses the agony and the anxiety of the work—it is a true labor.
15. The word שָׁוְא occurs 53 times in the Bible; it has as its basic meaning "deceit" or "wickedness" or "falsehood." In the Law it can refer to a false report (Exod. 23:1), a false witness (Deut. 5:20), or idol worship (Isa. 1:13). The commandment not to take the name of the LORD "in vain" (לַשָּׁוְא) would then mean speaking the name for a false or deceitful purpose.

    The verb seems to have the sense of "be evil, foul," although it occurs more in the cognate languages. There are a couple of rare uses where the verb (in the *hiphil)* means "to treat badly" (Pss. 55:16 and 89:23).

    The idea of "vain" may have come into English from the Latin rendering. BDB suggested that the basic meaning of the word was "emptiness" rather than deceit, meaning that false witness or idolatry was empy and therefore vain. Sawyer says that the meaning of "deceit" has been narrowed to the idea of "nothingness" or "for naught, in vain." He says that in contrast to other words meaning "vain" or "worthless," this word would retain the connotation of "evil" or "deceit." The usage in Psalm 127 does not go this far; rather, it seems to mean that building without the LORD's participation is futile or worthless, closer to the idea of emptiness

also means "false." Any secular or pagan building, no matter how grand or glorious, is meaningless because it is of no use to God and neither does it bring him any glory. So for a building to be meaningful the LORD must build it. The expositor must here explain how the LORD builds a house. The text is clear that there are builders who are doing the actual building. So to say the LORD builds it must be a theological interpretation of the work. It is the language of faith that attributes causality to the LORD (a metonymy of cause). We may say that the LORD builds the house if (1) the people build it by faith in the LORD's provisions for it, (2) in accordance with his will, (3) in a way that is pleasing to him, honest and fair, (4) dedicate it to his use and purpose, and (5) give glory to him for the accomplishment. When these things happen, then the faithful may say that the LORD built the house.

2. *Seeking security for something God does not protect is powerless (1b).*

The same constructions and tenses are now used in the second example which focuses on guarding and keeping. The first half begins with the particle "unless" (אִם), and the second half begins with "vain" (שָׁוְא). The "watchman" (שׁוֹמֵר), a participle, parallels "builders" in the first part. And the perfect tense "stays awake" (שָׁקַד) matches the nuance of the verb "labor" in the first part. Unless the LORD protects the city, the watchman wakes in vain.

Here too we must ask how the LORD guards the city? It may be through watchmen of course. But in this verse we still have the language of faith. One can hire watchmen, and probably should particularly in evil times, for that would be wise—but that is of little value if the LORD does not protect it. In Israel when God did not protect his people from invading armies, all their fortifications and defenses were of no avail. The believer recognizes that true security comes from God. One can live wisely and cautiously in this world, but must acknowledge that it is ultimately God alone who protects. Therefore, people must place their trust

---

(see J. F. A. Sawyer, "שָׁוְא *šāw'* **deceit**," in *The Theological Lexicon of the Old Testament*, ed. by Jenni and Westermann, III:1310–12.

in him: they must pray to him for protection, trust in him for safety, and give him the glory for daily preservation. So while the psalmist uses these exceptive clauses to make the point of the futility of godless enterprises, he is also instructing people to submit to the LORD's providence in the daily activities.

3. Anxious toiling to earn a living is pointless and powerless (2a).

Verse 2 is a very difficult verse from several aspects. First, like verse 1, it is a quatrain; but in the Hebrew text the first three cola make up the half-verse or one idea, and the fourth the other half with a contrasting idea. The division, or dichotomy, does not come in the middle of the verse, but three-quarters of the way through.

Second, the syntax is also more complex. Modified adverbial constructions (verbal hendiadys) are used in the first two cola. The first is "to rise up early," literally "making early of rising" or "[to] rise" (מַשְׁכִּימֵי קוּם). The infinitive becomes the primary verb, and the preceding participle becomes adverbial: "rising early." And this infinitive construction functions in the sentence as the subject with "vain" as the predicate. It may be translated either "It is vain for you to rise up early" or "Rising up early is vain for you." Likewise the second construction expresses a parallel topic: "(it is vain for you) to stay up late." Here too the text is literally "making late of sitting" or "[to] sit" (מְאַחֲרֵי שֶׁבֶת). The infinitive is "to sit" (from יָשַׁב); it also becomes the verbal idea and the preceding participle becomes adverbial: sitting up late. Here too the construction functions as the subject: sitting up late is vain.[16]

The two cola together also form a merism as rising up early and sitting up late together refer to the artificial lengthening of the day on both ends. This is futile. The implication from verse 1, however, would qualify this to mean that it is futile if the LORD is not in it. There are sufficient cases where in Godly pursuits people lengthen the day, either by getting up a great while

---

16. In both cases the *hiphil* participle is a plural construct, which is impossible to translate literally. The first one means "doing something early (to rise)" so would be literally "early doers of—rise"; and the second would then mean "late doers of—sit."

before dawn to pray (as our Lord did), or by having God prolong the day (as for Joshua).

The next clause, however, explains the circumstances that make this artificial lengthening of the day vain. The colon is also difficult grammatically and conceptually: "eating the bread of sorrows," literally, "eaters of the bread of sorrows" (אֹכְלֵי is the participle in construct). The word "bread" is an objective genitive: (it is vain) to eat the bread of sorrows." And "sorrows" is also a genitive after the construct "bread," referring to the struggle that produced the bread. "Sorrows" would be a figure (a metonymy of adjunct) describing the labor as filled with anxious fears and painful toil.[17] So the picture is one of someone laboring with anxieties and painful toil to be able to eat bread. This artificial lengthening of the day in anxiety is vain.

Grammatically the expression appears parallel to the two construct participles before it; but syntactically this expression is different. Those two participles were part of the hendiadys constructions and became adverbial to their following infinitives (the subjects of the sentence). This participle could serve as a subject: "eaters of the bread of sorrows [are] vain" also. But it seems more likely that this colon is stating the purpose[18] of the lengthening of the day and thus explaining why it is vain to lengthen the day artificially. A long, industrious day is not wrong. In fact, this is held up as profitable in wisdom literature. But if the food is produced through tiring labor, anxiety, and stress, and the family eats of food so produced, it is a life of fear and worry without trusting the LORD and it is futile. More than that, it is lethal, physically and emotionally, for such anxiety kills the body just as easily as it kills the spirit.

B. A life dependent on the LORD is secure and satisfying (2b).

The third difficulty in the verse is the interpretation of the

---

17. This is the same word used in Genesis in the "curse" oracles; the pain for the woman would be in childbirth, but the pain for the man under the curse would be toiling by the sweat of the brow. The psalm, then, is referring to the drudgery of life under the curse.
18. The participle would be a substantival use, functioning adverbially to indicate the purpose of the activity.

last of the four cola in verse 2. It expresses a contrast with everything that has been said before (and so the dichotomy in the text marked out by the Masoretes after the third colon makes sense). The last part of the verse then forms a contrasting conclusion, explaining the difference, and clarifying why the other way of life is vain.

The particle "thus" signals this logical conclusion in view of the vanity of the vain activities. Those who live independently of the LORD and who labor under their own strength have futile lives as far as God is concerned, and they may be frustrating and unhealthy too. On the other hand, the LORD blesses his beloved (לִידִידוֹ> יָדִיד > ידד). The "beloved" are the devout believers who live by faith and enjoy the blessings of their relationship with the LORD by covenant. In this case the LORD gives them "sleep."

The difficulty in this clause is the understanding of the word "sleep" (שֵׁנָא). Some commentators think that the word "sleep" is unsatisfactory in the verse and so offer different explanations. The most plausible is the suggestion of a meaning "honor," based on Syriac and Aramaic cognates; this would certainly provide a sensible meaning to the line.[19] But "sleep" can be interpreted in a way that it fits the verse fairly well too, and so it need not be abandoned too readily. The word is an accusative in the sentence after the verb "he gives" (which here may be classified as a habitual imperfect). One way to explain it would be to take the accusative adverbially—"He gives to his beloved *in* sleep." This would not say what the LORD gives his beloved, only that it is during sleep. It would mean that material goods prosper even during the time of sleep (so that people do not have to work so hard for their food). While there is truth to this idea to be sure, I would prefer taking the noun as the accusative of direct object, and translating it "He gives to his beloved sleep." This is the way the Greek text interpreted it. The word "sleep" would be symbolic (perhaps a metonymy of adjunct or effect), referring both to literal sleep and to what sleep represents, resting in the security,

---

19. See J. A. Emerton, "The Meaning of *šēnā'* in Ps cxxvii 2," *VT* 24 (1974):15–31. For the interpretation "in sleep," see Booij, "Psalm 127,2b," *Bib* 81 (2000):262–8.

confidence, and satisfaction of knowing that one's life is in God's hands.[20] In other words, those who place their complete trust in the LORD may rest assured that he knows their needs and will provide for them, and that agonizing and laboring in fear and anxiety will not get any more done than what he chooses to give. The life of faith is a life that rests in him; it may be diligent and industrious but will be free of the restless anxieties.

II. The LORD's provision of children ensures the happy security of the family (3–5).

A. *The divine provision of children is a blessing and a trust (3).*

The second half of the psalm shifts to focus on children as a prime example of the LORD's provision of a meaningful life. The picture is drawn from the world of the ancient Israelites, where family was treasured, and many children were seen as a true blessing, and where the family would have to be protected from generation to generation in legal disputes and claims. The values and perceived needs of modern families do not always share the outlook of Israel presented in this psalm, much to their detriment.

Verse 3 introduces the theme of children as a trust from God. Literally it could be read, "Behold, children are an inheritance from the LORD, the fruit of the womb is a reward." "Children"[21] in the line is paralleled with "fruit of the womb," and "inheritance" is paralleled with "reward." The beginning particle (הִנֵּה) need not be translated "behold," but the gloss is still useful in getting attention. If it has that force (the deictic use[22]), it serves to focus greater attention on the statement to follow. But the

---

20. Allen suggests that "rest" has the connotation of arriving home after a days work (cf. 2 Sam. 7:1 for a military context; *Psalms 101–150*, p. 176).
21. The text has בָּנִים, literally "sons," but in wisdom literature and in the wider use of the Old Testament can refer to males and females. The well-known "children of Israel" (בְּנֵי יִשְׂרָאֵל) means the whole nation.
22. The term "deictic" comes from the Greek word δεικνύμι, "to show, point out." So this use of the Hebrew particle is the pointing out use—"look, behold," although "behold" is archaic (it is an imperative meaning "see").

particle could also function emphatically in the sentence and be translated "indeed."

Two metaphors are used in this verse. The first says that children are a "heritage" (נַחֲלַת) from the LORD. Usage of this word "inheritance" gives the picture of something left to an heir, or something that was an allotment given to another person as a possession and trust (sometimes left in trust). An inheritance brings with it a great opportunity, but it also requires responsible use. On the one hand it is the heir's possession, a gift; but on the other hand it is a trust to be developed, improved, and enjoyed by all. So children are such a gift from God, but a gift that requires care and development if the child is to grow up to be righteous and wise. The metaphor suggests something of the responsibilities of parents as well as the value of the child.

The second metaphor focuses more on the aspect of a gift: children are a "reward" (שָׂכָר), the word meaning "recompense" or "pay" as well as "reward."[23] This figure stresses the joyful benefit from God for the marriage. The Israelites saw children as the greatest enrichment God could give their married lives. And in the ancient world where life was fragile and infant mortality high, a child who lived and flourished was something for which the parents would praise God. No devout believer would dare neglect or abuse such a gift from God.

Children are described in the second part of the verse as "the fruit of the womb." The word "fruit" (פְּרִי) is a figure that compares children to fruit from trees or plants (an implied comparison). The figure fits with the general appreciation of fruitfulness in Israel, starting with the instruction for Adam and Eve to be fruitful and multiply. "Fruit" describes the marriage as alive and productive; and by frequent use over time the expression "fruit of the womb" became an idiom for children.

B. The divine provision of children is beneficial for the security of the family (4–5).

The last two verses extend the focus on children,

---

23. When God told Abram that his reward would be very great (Gen. 15:1), Abram responded by saying, "What will you give me, since I remain childless?"

demonstrating their value to the family. The way the verses use the figurative language (a simile) with the construction "as . . . so," followed in the next verse with "blessed is the man," is all reminiscent of Proverbs. The simile establishes the comparison of children with arrows. "Arrows" in the Psalms may refer to words as well as weapons.[24] In view of the last verse of this psalm which mentions defending the family in the gate, the place of legal and business disputes and transactions, the psalmist may have "words" in mind as the point of the comparison with arrows. This would involve a double image: children compared to arrows is the simile, but arrows meaning words in legal or business debate would be an implied comparison. Just as a warrior would feel safe with arrows in his hand (at his disposal, ready to be used if not already in use), so would the parent who had children who could defend the family honor and possessions in court or business.

The psalmist refers to the children as "(the children of) youth" (הַנְּעוּרִים) to signify that these are the offspring of the youthful vigor of the parents and not children of their old age. They would represent the strength of the family because they grew up during and participated in the early activities and development of the family. The parents are at full strength to share with their children and train them in the process. The word "youth" is a plural noun as it embraces all that goes on in and makes up what is known as the time of youth, here the early years of married life.

The blessing is pronounced in verse 5: "How blessed is the one[25] whose quiver is full of them." The word "blessed" (אַשְׁרֵי) is frequently translated "happy," but that does not convey its full meaning. The noun celebrates the benefits of a right relationship with the LORD; it refers to the feeling one has who knows that all is well with God. And since it is a plural in the construct form, it might more accurately be rendered, "O the heavenly bliss (O the blessednesses) of the one whose quiver is full of them." The line is linked to the preceding verse by the use of

---

24. See Daniel J. Estes, "Like Arrows in the Hand of a Warrior," *VT* 41 (1991):304–311.
25. The word is הַגֶּבֶר, "the man," but may be taken in the general sense of the parent(s).

"quiver." The simile there introduced the themes of arrows and a warrior; now they are extended by introducing the idea of the "quiver." This figure could be classified as a continuation of the simile, qualifying that the home full of children is like a quiver full of arrows. But taken as an independent verse, it would be an implied comparison.

The blessing is that whoever has such a family will not be put to shame (לֹא־יֵבֹשׁוּ; s.v. Ps. 31:1) when they speak with enemies in the gate. This verb "not be ashamed" is figurative (a metonymy of effect), the cause being that they will not lose the argument or challenge. The reference is probably to legal or financial disputes, because the action takes place in the gate—and the action is "speaking."[26] The gate, meaning the entrance plaza area with the rooms off to the sides, was the location for business and legal transactions (see Ruth 4 for an illustration of where the elders sat to decide who would buy Naomi's field and marry Ruth). The well-being and honor of the family would be defended there if there were sufficient family representatives who could do it.

MESSAGE AND APPLICATION

I would word the expository idea of this psalm in general terms to cover the domestic life, rather than detailing building, guarding, working, sleeping, and building a family. These individual aspects of the idea will be fully explained in the exposition. But the homiletic idea could be worded this way: *The providence of God ensures the full success and safety of domestic activities for those whom the LORD loves.* I am including the samples from both halves of the psalm under the heading "domestic activities." And I included the idea of the beloved as those whom the LORD loves, because the psalm implies that success with God in domestic activities is a life of dependence on God's providential intervention. Leaving the statement somewhat general allows the

---

26. There is a rare verb with the same letters which means "drive away, destroy"; if that is the verb the setting would be combat. But the more likely understanding within the domestic life of Israel would be the verb "speak."

expositor to speak of the principle involved here, and then use the samples as cases in which the principle can be seen working.

In this way one need not be so tight with the correlations to the New Testament, for finding verses about building a house or guarding a city or having children may not be that easy. But one could certainly go first to the teachings of Jesus in which he instructed people to trust in God's providence, for anxieties about the daily cares cannot help—God cares for the flowers and the animals better than Solomon could adorn his throne room. Jesus also instructed that building one's life should be on the rock rather than the sand, meaning by faith in him, so that the works of life would be safe and serviceable when trouble should come, and that the believer need not be anxious about life. Likewise one could correlate James who stresses that in daily planning one should be careful to affirm that things will be done if the LORD wills. Or, if something more specific is desired for the correlation, one could connect Paul's teachings on the place and value of children in the home, salvation for the mother and sanctification for the children, as well as the orderly home. But some of these passages correlated may raise more questions than the expositor has time to answer in a message on Psalm 127.

I would think that the overall emphasis would be on the life of faith under God's providence. Most of the believer's life is lived without visions, revelations, or words from heaven; it is lived wisely and righteously, trusting in the LORD's provision and guidance. So whatever one does in life must be by faith in the LORD and bring glory to his name. Verses in the New Testament that emphasize this would indeed capture the theology of the psalm. The message would call for believers to understand the balance between human responsibility and divine providence, and in understanding that begin to live out their faith in a practical and satisfying way.

PSALM 128
The Blessed Life

INTRODUCTION

Text and Textual Variants

A Song of Ascents.

1 Blessed is everyone who fears the LORD,
    who walks in his ways.
2 When[1] you eat the labor of your hands,
    you *shall be* blessed, and *it shall be* good for you.[2]
3 Your wife *shall be* like a fruitful vine
    in the innermost parts[3] of your house;
your children like olive plants
    around your table.

---

1. This is the temporal translation of כִּי; others take it to indicate an emphatic force and translate the line as "you will surely eat" (as in the Greek translation).
2. The Targum's translation reflects the interpretive approach of taking each of two parallel ideas to refer to different things: "blessed" is therefore in this world, and "good" is in the world to come.
3. More specifically, "on the sides of" your house.

4 Indeed, thus[4] shall the man be blessed
   who fears the LORD.

5 May the LORD bless you out of Zion
    that[5] you may look on the good of Jerusalem
      all the days of your life;
6 and see your children's children.
   Peace be upon Israel!

Composition and Context

Psalm 128 continues the theme of the providence of God with a focus on family life; it includes praise for the blessings of God in life, but it also includes a prayer for the blessing of peace and prosperity to continue for the good of the domestic life. Because the psalm introduces the subject matter with "blessed," and describes the good life of the *faithful*, it may be classified as a wisdom psalm. Kraus says it is a didactic poem shot through with wisdom elements.[6] But being part of the collection of pilgrim psalms, it certainly had a liturgical use as well. Weiser says that the beatitude at the beginning and the benediction at the end show it was used in communal worship.[7]

We do not know the occasion or date for the psalm. Some commentators simply state it is a post-exilic psalm because it seems to have a mixed genre and because of its use of the "peace" formula, but this is not very compelling.

Exegetical Analysis

Summary

Having declared those who fear the LORD blessed, the pilgrim

---

4. The MT has הִנֵּה כִי־כֵן, but a few manuscripts do not have the particle כִּי; the Greek has ἰδοὺ οὕτως, "look, thus."
5. In this verse "and look" as well as "and see" are imperatives with the conjunction—taken here to express the consequence of the LORD's blessing. The Greek translation made them equal to the jussive "may he bless" with "may you look" and "may you see."
6. *Psalms 60–150*, p. 458.
7. *Psalms*, p. 767.

psalmist enumerates some of the basic blessings of the good life and prays for even greater blessings.

Outline

I. The pilgrim declares the blessedness of those who fear and obey the LORD (1).
II. The pilgrim enumerates some of the basic blessings of those who fear the LORD (2–4).
   A. They shall find prosperity from their labor (2).
   B. They shall find prosperity in their families (3–4).
III. The pilgrim prays for further blessings on those who fear the LORD, and for the peace of Jerusalem (5–6).
   A. He prays that the LORD bless them from Zion and that they see the prosperity of Jerusalem (5–6a).
   B. He prays for the peace of Jerusalem (6b).

COMMENTARY IN EXPOSITORY FORM

I. God's blessing rests on faithful and devout believers (1).

The first half of the first verse signals the main theme of this psalm, namely, that God's blessing is on those who are faithful and devout. But the expressions used must be clearly defined to understand the point being made. The word for the blessing (אַשְׁרֵי; s.v. Ps. 1:1) can include the idea of happiness, but it has the basic meaning of the joy or bliss that comes from knowing that one is right with God, and that the blessings are from heaven. The plural form stresses the abstract quality and could be rendered: "O the blessednesses of all who fear the LORD."

The expression "everyone who fears the LORD" (כָּל־יְרֵא יְהוָה) refers to devout worshipers. This fear is a reverential fear for the LORD; it is exhibited by worship and obedience. The term (s.v. Ps. 1:2) indicates both an attraction to and a shrinking back from the object. The attraction to the LORD is adoration for the majesty and power and glory of the LORD; the shrinking back is the acknowledgment that he is the sovereign judge of all the earth and must be obeyed. Parallel to this is a relative clause "who walks in his ways." The participle (הַהֹלֵךְ) modifies "everyone" (כָּל)," clarifying that those who fear the LORD are also obedient. The participle is the masculine singular form, serving collectively. The Greek translation made it plural to clarify the collective idea. The expression "walking" is figurative (an implied comparison), but it is so frequent it has become idiomatic; it signifies all the activities of life. The word "ways" has also become idiomatic; but it forms a comparison between roads or ways and the course of life revealed in the Law. Walking in God's ways means living in harmony with the standard of God.

So the first half of the verse gives the basis for living out the faith: fearing the LORD; and the second half of the verse gives the result of the fear: living obediently before God. The two halves can be fully explained in relation to the other: the first colon stresses the cause (a metonymy of cause) and the second the effect (a metonymy of effect). The two halves make up the whole picture of the devout and obedient worshiper.

II. God's blessings are evident in the good life (2–4).

A. God prospers the labors of the devout (2).

The psalm now turns to list a few evidences of the blessing of God on those who trust and obey. The first theme concerns labor: "when you eat the labor of your hands, you shall be blessed and you will *receive* good [things]." The verb "when you eat" (תֹאכַל) is in a temporal clause with the particle "when"; it lays down the premise for the next clause: "you shall be blessed." The verb "eat" is figurative (a metonymy of effect), for eating is the satisfying result of the labors that produced something to eat. A greater sense of divine blessing will rest on people when they enjoy the beneficial results of their labor.

The object, "the labor of your hands," is placed first in the sentence for emphasis. It too is figurative (now a metonymy of cause); to eat the "labor" of the hands means to eat what the labor produced. The psalmist asserts that those who were faithful to God and diligent in their work would enjoy the blessing of divine provision. This is expressed with two words: "you *shall be* blessed" (אַשְׁרֶיךָ) and you will receive "(what is) good" (טוֹב; s.v. Ps. 34:8). The first reiterates the heavenly bliss that comes from knowing that the good things of life came from God; the second concerns the well-being of life in general that is evidence of the blessing.

B. God causes the family to flourish (3–4).

The psalmist now turns his attention to the family and how God blesses it. In verse 3 we read, "Your wife *shall be* like a fruitful vine in the innermost chambers of your house." The point of the comparison (a simile) is to say that the spouse will flourish and be productive, just like a fruitful vine. The image also suggests grace and beauty. The simile is further qualified by the location as "in the innermost chambers of your house." The word (יַרְכְּתֵי), literally "sides of," refers to the most private place of the lodging, probably the private room of the wife. Here the "fruitful vine" can flourish and be productive.

The second half of the verse specifies the blessing of children, using another simile: "Your children *shall be* like olive plants round about your table." The picture is of young olive trees springing up from the parent stem, fresh, vibrant, and full of promise. The olive tree was an emblem of vigor and vitality in the Old Testament, and naturally a symbol of long endurance since they last for such a long time. They also were very productive, the oil being used for many important things.

These ideas are then summarized by verse four. The text has an emphatic construction: "Indeed, for thus" or "indeed, thus." Then the verb "shall be blessed" (יְבֹרַךְ; s.v. Ps. 5:12), a future in this context, anticipating divine blessing: "Indeed, for thus shall a man (גֶּבֶר) be blessed." But the important part of the verse is the last part, which is in apposition to the "man": "[who] fears the LORD" (יְרֵא יְהוָה; literally, "fearer of the LORD"). In line with what was said in verse 1, to be a fearer of the LORD is to be a faithful, obedient worshiper. So the wonderful blessings of produce and posterity are bestowed on those who are devout and obedient. This is in harmony with the promises of wisdom literature; there may be exceptions, but the normal expectation is blessing for faithfulness.

III. The faithful trust the LORD for divine blessing (5–6).

The major question in verse 5 is whether the verb (יְבָרֶכְךָ) is an imperfect tense ("he will bless you") or a jussive ("may he bless you"). If it is taken as an imperfect tense, then it would be a promise or expectation of blessing; if it is a jussive, it would be a prayer for blessing. The choice may be decided by the following imperatives (רְאֵה twice). These may indicate a sequence of the volitional mood, the jussive followed by the imperative to show purpose or result: "May the LORD bless you . . . that you may see . . . ."[8] And this blessing is to come from Zion, the mountain on which the temple stood (a metonymy of subject). The temple was the place of prayer and praise for the people of God; and so the blessing would come from the LORD in his sanctuary.

The divine blessing would enable the people to "look on" (וּרְאֵה) the goodness of Jerusalem all the days of their lives. The blessing is the goodness or well-being of Jerusalem (including the people who live and work there); but to look on it all their lives means that they will enjoy a lifetime of peace and prosperity in the land because all would be well with the city of God. But the verb "look" followed by the preposition "on" is an expression of triumph. This would be their enjoyment throughout life.[9]

Verse 6 gives a second, parallel purpose of the blessing: "and that you may see your children's children." This whole line is figurative, expressing the result in place of the cause (a metonymy of effect): the blessing is to live long enough to see the grandchildren—the epitome of a full and rich life.

The psalm then closes with an additional and standard prayer for the pilgrims: "Peace [be] upon Israel." If God's peace is granted to the nation, then the people would be able to work, their families would flourish, and they would enjoy the good things of life.

MESSAGE AND APPLICATION

As with Psalm 127, Psalm 128 is an acknowledgment of the blessings of the domestic life on the righteous; its central point may be summarized as follows: *Those who are devout and faithful*

---

8. However, the purpose idea could also work if the first verb was an imperfect: "The LORD will bless you . . . in order that you may see . . . ."
9. The last clause begins with the noun "all" (כָּל) is an adverbial accusative specifying the time of the looking. The substantive is in construct, and so the following string of genitives ("of the days of the life of you") answer the question "all what?"–all of the days of your life.

may confidently anticipate the LORD's blessing on their labors and on their families. And that blessing will take the form of the enjoyment of the good life, the flourishing of the marriage, the vigor and vitality of the children, and long life under God's peace and prosperity.

While the psalm is a contemplative one, there are nonetheless "wisdom" ideas here that need to be applied if the passage is expounded. The main emphasis must be on the theme of fearing the LORD, for that is found twice in the psalm. And obedience is the evidence of fearing the LORD. People therefore must be exhorted to fear the LORD if they desire the blessings of God in their life. The exposition will have to be very clear as to what the fear of the LORD is: devout worship and reverential obedience.

PSALM 129

Faith that Overcomes Affliction

INTRODUCTION

Text and Textual Variants

A Song of Ascents.

1 "Many a time have they afflicted[1] me from my youth *up*,"
   let Israel now say.
2 "Many a time have they afflicted me from my youth up;
   yet they have not prevailed over me.
3 The plowers[2] plowed upon my back;
   they made their furrows long."[3]

---

1. The Greek version interprets this with "made war," ἐπολέμησάν.
2. The Hebrew has the active participle "the plowers," חֹרְשִׁים. The Greek text has "the sinners," οἱ ἁμαρτωλοί. They apparently thought the word was הָרְשָׁעִים. Later Greek translations knew it was a participle and adjusted the reading accordingly.
3. The Masoretic Text has a K*ethiv-Q*re' reading in this place (לְמַעֲנוֹתָם). Many Hebrew manuscripts and the Targum read with Q, לְמַעֲנוֹתָם, "their furrows." The Greek and Latin follow K with "their iniquity" (the Greek has

4 The LORD is righteous;
    he has cut asunder the cords[4] of the wicked.
5 Let them be put to shame and turned backward,
    all they that hate Zion.
6 Let them be as grass upon the housetops,
    which withers before it grows up;[5]
7 Wherefore the reaper fills not his hand,
    nor he that binds sheaves his bosom.
8 Neither do they that go by say,
    "The blessing of the LORD be upon you;[6]
    We bless you in the name of the LORD."

Composition and Context

Israel looks back on what it has survived by the grace of God, and those incidents provide hope: time and time again they were persecuted and plundered by their enemies, but the LORD never allowed them to be destroyed. Now, as before, the psalmist is confident that the LORD will utterly destroy those who hate Zion and have plotted against her.

In the first four verses the piece has the form of a communal thanksgiving; but then it turns to imprecation in the rest of the psalm. Weiser suggests it was intended as a liturgical formulary

---

τὴν ἀνομίαν αὐτῶν), reading לַעֲוֹנוֹתָם. This variant uses a common word in place of a rare word with an unusual poetic usage.

4. The MT is עֲבוֹת, "cords"; the Greek text has "neck" (עֲרוֹף) instead of "cords." Either there was confusion of letters, or the Greek translation attempted to interpret the figure.
5. The Hebrew שָׁלַף means "to shoot up." G. R. Driver suggest a meaning similar to the cognate languages, "produce a stock" ("Studies in the Vocabulary of the Old Testament. 1." *JTS* 31 [1930]:275–84). The Greek has "(which withers before) it is plucked up" (ἐκσπασθῆναι), maybe representing the verb (שָׁדַף). Perhaps the translator of the Greek version was simply trying to smooth out a difficult text. The editors similarly propose reading the clause as שֶׁקִּדְמֹ תִשְׁדֹף. Aquila, the Targum, and Jerome render it "before it has shot up."
6. The MT has אֲלֵיכֶם, but many manuscripts have the expected form עֲלֵיכֶם. Following this the Targum has inserted the expression "and they do not answer them" before the final statement, to capture a dialogue between reapers and passers-by.

700

of Israel's covenant community; it formed a piece of liturgy that was used in worship, and ends with a curse for those who hate Zion and a blessing for the righteous.[7] It may have been put to this kind of use in time, but it seems instead to have been written originally to anticipate another deliverance from God in a present crisis.[8] Kraus simply classifies it as a communal prayer song where confidence dominates.[9] The faith of the people of God has experienced the renewal of stability and peace time and time again; and because of that the people may pray again with confidence for God to deliver them from those who hate them. But here, as occasionally before, the prayer for deliverance is emboldened with the desire for the wicked to be suddenly and finally removed. The severity of this imprecation is due to the nature and acts of the enemies; Kraus says, "It needs to be emphasized that the enmities directed against Israel in the last analysis apply to Yahweh himself (v. 5b). . . . It is hatred against the place of God's revelation and presence that Israel has to bear and suffer" (p. 463).

Exegetical Analysis

Summary

After describing the various ways that the LORD had delivered them from the ravages of the wicked, the people of God pray confidently that the LORD put to shame those who hate Zion.

Outline

I. Praise: The people of God attest that God often delivered them from the wicked (1–4).
   A. Using the imagery of warfare, they testify that their adversaries did not prevail over them (1–2).
   B. Using the imagery of plowing, they describe their period of extreme suffering (3).

---

7. *Psalms*, p. 770.
8. See further A. J. O. Van der Wal, "The Structure of Psalm cxxix," *VT* 28 (1988):364–7.
9. *Psalms 60–150*, p. 461.

C. Using the imagery of harnessing, they report how the LORD delivered them from bondage (4).
II. Petition: The people of God petition the LORD to put to shame those who hate Zion (5–8).
   A. Using the imagery of warfare, they pray that those who hate Zion will be repulsed (5).
   B. Using the imagery of harvesting, they pray that those who hate Zion will wither up (6–7).
   C. Using the occasion of greeting, they pray that no blessing be pronounced upon those who hate Zion (8).

COMMENTARY IN EXPOSITORY FORM

I. The faithful acknowledge that God has a history of delivering them from enemies (1–4).

A. The wicked have not prevailed over them (1–2).

The first two verses of this psalm start with the parallel expression: "Many a time." The use of "many" (רַבַּת) stresses both the magnitude of the persecution as well as the number of the times it occurred. Some translations use "greatly" while others stay with "many a time." The point is that the persecution has been repeated—relentlessly! And this persecution has plagued the righteous from the early days: "from my youth." The verb (צְרָרוּנִי) would then be best translated as a present perfect: "they have afflicted me from my youth."

The experiences of the nation of Israel are often expressed in terms of an individual (see Ps. 118; Isa. 54). Here "youth" refers to the time when the nation was young and developing (so an implied comparison). Israel can look back to the time of its bondage in Egypt and trace its history of persecution. The evidence that this is the correct interpretation of the verse now comes with the liturgical directive, "let Israel now say" (יֹאמַר־נָא יִשְׂרָאֵל). It is the nation of Israel that reflects on how they have been afflicted from the nation's youth.

After the initial colon is repeated, then the outcome of the affliction is reported: but the enemies did not win. The verb (יָכְלוּ, a simple perfect, classified also as a present perfect), followed by the preposition (*lamed*), has the meaning "prevail over"—"they have not prevailed over me (i.e., the nation)." And the asseverative particle (גַּם) provides the emphatic assurance "yet, in fact, surely."

B. The persecution has often been extreme (3).

This line provides a figurative description (an implied comparison) of their intense suffering during such persecution. The writer uses a participle (for the subject) and a perfect tense (expressing perhaps an indefinite past) from the same verb (חָרַשׁ): "The plowers plowed upon my back." And the obvious result of their "plowing" was that "they made their furrows long." The back is compared to a field that was plowed; the enemy has left wounds and lacerations like deep furrows (see Isa. 51:23). The use of this imagery may have been suggested to the psalmist by the people's close identification with the land, or perhaps by prisoners' backs being torn open by the lash—or both. But the point is clear: the wicked have persecuted the people of God ruthlessly and cruelly, physically and emotionally (see Mic. 3:12). The verb "made long" or "lengthened" (הֶאֱרִיכוּ) is a past tense, but perhaps with the nuance of an indefinite past again because there were many different events that could have been included. The "furrow" is the strip of land that is plowed at one time. The enemies did their cruel work thoroughly and spared nothing.

C. The LORD has delivered his people (4).

The psalmist now focuses his attention on the LORD's deliverance. The first two words go together, but there is some uncertainty as to how they do. The words (יְהוָה צַדִּיק) could be translated "The LORD is righteous" or "The LORD, the righteous, . . ." Whether "righteous" is taken as a predicate or as an appositive, the meaning is clear. But some commentators think a verb has dropped out from the line, noting that the adjective "righteous" is antithetical to "wicked" at the end of the verse; one idea is that it may have read, "The LORD *vindicated* the righteous, he cut off the backs of the wicked." But while that might sound smoother, it requires unwarranted changes. The simplest rendering would be: "The LORD is righteous." This brief, clear declaration is the basis for the vindication: because he is righteous, he did not permit their persecutions to run their course.

So the psalmist says, "he has cut asunder the cords of the wicked." The word for "cords" may refer to the straps or bands by which the yoke was fastened on to the neck of the oxen. If this verse is continuing the implied comparison of the last verse, then it is saying that the LORD broke the plower's harness so that the work of plowing could not continue. Or, it is possible to see a new illustration, namely that Israel is like an ox, and the cords refer to that which fastens the yoke of servitude upon her neck. At any rate, God has delivered his people from bondage.

II. God's people may pray with confidence for deliverance (5–8).

A. They pray for the defeat of their enemies (5).

The psalmist uses military terminology in his prayer for the destruction of their enemies. The prayer is that "they may be put to shame and turned backward." The verb "put to shame" (יֵבֹשׁוּ; s.v. Ps. 31:1) is figurative (a metonymy of effect), referring to the shame from their defeat. The second petition is for the enemies to be turned back in battle. The verb (the *niphal* jussive from סוג) may also be a figure, referring to the result of being defeated—turned back. So the prayer is that the enemies will be repulsed in their attack.

The second half of the verse identifies the subjects of these verbs: all those who hate Zion. The subject of the verbs is specifically "all" (כֹּל), but "all" is then explained by the genitives "haters of" and "Zion." The participle "haters (of)" (שֹׂנְאֵי; s.v. Ps. 139:22) describes the enemies as people who despise and reject Zion. And since "Zion" is a figure of speech (metonymy of subject) referring to all that is on the mountain, the people, the city, the temple, their hatred is for all these things.

B. They pray for the wicked to vanish (6–7).

The psalmist compares the wicked to grass that will die and disappear on the roof tops. People used to make their flat roofs with branches and dirt packed together in layers. In the rainy season in the spring grass would begin to grow from the dirt that was used. But when the rains stopped and the dry season began the grass that had sprung up quickly would wither and die even more quickly—without a trace. The second colon explains that it "withers" (יָבֵשׁ, forming a word play with the first verb of verse five) "before it has unsheathed." This may be a figurative way of saying before it shows signs of growth, or it may refer to their unsheathing the cutting instrument to cut long grass. The point of the figure, at any rate, is the wish that the enemies, who may be flourishing for the moment, would just disappear suddenly.

The picture is further explained in the seventh verse by another relative clause following the relative clause in verse six. Both clauses modify the first colon, "Let them be like grass on the housetop." The reaper (active participle) would grab a handful of stalks of grass or wheat, and with the other hand cut them off at the ground. The psalmist is saying that this grass will not get high enough for a reaper to fill his hand with the grass, meaning that the enemies should be destroyed before they can come to full strength. The verb "fill" (מִלֵּא) is understood in the last colon: "nor the binder [fill] his loose fold" (in the garment where he would carry the cut stalks). The prayer is that the enemies will disappear before anyone has to deal with them.

C. They pray for the rejection of the wicked (8).

The psalmist concludes this prayer for the judgment on the enemies by praying that no blessing be given to them. The verse is referring to people who pass by the reapers in the field and offer their blessing (see the greetings in the book of Ruth); they would say, "The blessing of the LORD *be* upon you" or "We bless[10] you in the name[11] of the LORD." This kind of greeting or exchange of greeting would be said particularly with the prospect of a great harvest in mind. But here the psalmist is praying that

---

10. The form is the *piel perfect*. Since it is given a present tense translation, the classification would be instantaneous perfect. For the meaning of the verb and its main noun "blessing," s.v. Ps. 5:12.
11. For the meaning of "name," s.v. Ps. 20:1.

the enemies would be destroyed and that they would wither like the grass on the rooftops, so that no one would give them the greeting as if the LORD were to prosper their way. No, they are all enemies of the LORD, haters of Zion, and there should be no blessing or note of congratulation extended to them. Far from any such praise or false flattery there should be only words that warn of judgment and condemnation.

MESSAGE AND APPLICATION

The psalmist is confident that the LORD will deliver his people. This confidence is based on the past dealings of the LORD with them: time and time again they have been persecuted, but he has always delivered them. Because of those experiences the psalmist is confident in his prayer for deliverance from present enemies. Believers today also should pray for deliverance from the wicked and from evil; but they will do so with confidence if they have often experienced his intervention. If they rehearse how God has delivered them in the past, and if they remember that he will ultimately destroy the wicked in the future, their prayer in the present threatening time will be with confidence. Accordingly, the message of the psalm may be summarized in this expository idea: *Knowing that God has delivered his people time and time again will build confidence in praying for deliverance from evil.* Jesus taught us to pray for deliverance from evil; and the history of the faith is filled with accounts of divine interventions in such times. Jesus taught that in this life there would be hatred and persecution for those who follow him (so in Acts we read how James was beheaded, and Peter and Paul were imprisoned at times); but that the suffering saint must not despair because he has overcome the world (John 15:18–24; 16:33 and others). But even though we have the words of comfort from the Lord, we still may pray to be delivered from evil, knowing that the prayer may not be answered in the crisis but will certainly be answered at the coming of the LORD.

PSALM 130

There is Forgiveness with God

INTRODUCTION

Text and Textual Variants

A Song of Ascents.

1 Out of the depths I cry to you, O LORD.[1]
2   Lord,[2] hear my voice;
    let your ears[3] be attentive

---

1. The Qumran scroll may have read this line differently. At the beginning of verse 1 the scroll has אדוני, "Lord"; in the Masoretic Text that begins verse 2. Then, the space in the broken part of the scroll does not seem to be wide enough to allow the rest of the letters of verse 1; there is only room for 16 slots (not enough for קראתיך יהוה אדוני שמ). It may be that "Yahweh" was not included; but without the material in the *lacuna* the matter cannot be resolved.
2. For MT's אֲדֹנָי many manuscripts have יהוה.
3. In verse 2 of the Qumran scroll there is another variant. Because of the singular verb ("hear") the scribe has written the singular "ear" and not the plural "ears" of the Masoretic Text (Qumran writes words with the vowel letters, but here there is no *yôd* before the suffix which should be there for a plural). This required that the jussive also be in the singular form, תהי

to the voice[4] of my supplications.
3 If you, LORD,[5] should mark iniquities,
O Lord, who could stand?
4 But with you there is forgiveness
in order that you may be feared.[6]

נא, in contrast to the plural verb in the Masoretic Text, תִּהְיֶינָה. This change may have been an unintentional confusion of *tehi na'* for *tihyenah.* It looks like Qumran has tried to harmonize the verse with a consistent singular number, as well as with common usage since the plural "ears" is used nowhere else for the LORD. Because common usage calls for a singular "ear," and because the imperative was singular, this line was written with the singular. That meant the predicate adjective ("attentive") was made singular as well, for Qumran would otherwise have written it plene, קשובות.

4. The Qumran scroll has לי, "to me," where the MT has "my voice." It is likely that "supplications" completed the verse. And that would be what was needed to fill the 18 slots in the *lacuna* on the next line.
5. The MT uses the abbreviation, יְ in this place.
6. The Hebrew text has the *niphal imperfect* תִּוָּרֵא, "(that) you may be feared"; apart from the participle this is the only use of the verb in the *niphal*. The Greek translation has τοῦ νόμου σου, "your law," which would be תּוֹרָתֶךָ; the translator apparently assumed תורא in the text to be the well-known תּוֹרָה. It joins the word with the next verse. There is also an inner Greek variant that reads "name" (τοῦ ὀνόματός) instead, perhaps adjusting the word for "law" by adding the omicron. Both Symmachus and Theodotion revise the Greek to "law" (νομου); and this is corroborated by Theodoret, Jerome, and Chrysostom. All these indicate, therefore, that the original Greek translation was "law." For this section, then, it reads: "for with you is forgiveness, [5] for your law I have waited for you O Lord, my soul has waited for your word. [6] my soul has hoped in the Lord, from the morning watch till the night." This has realigned subjects and verbs in a chain reaction after the problem with verse four. The verb "I hope" had to be changed to the feminine singular to match "my soul."

The translator(s) of the old Greek thought of the common word "law" (תּוֹרָה; final א and ה interchanging) more readily than a rare, irregular verb (*niphal* imperfect from a I *Yod* verb). In addition, "your law" formed a better parallelism with "your word" in the next clause. The Targum and Vulgate took the word to be the *niphal* imperfect but of the verb "to see": "that you may appear."

The MT most certainly preserves the original reading of the psalm. It is the reading that best explains the other reading, for it is more difficult, and the more obtuse theology. If the common word "law" was the original reading, it would be harder to explain why it was changed to the irregular verb "that you may be feared." Moreover, Aquila corrected the Greek to φοβου, to bring it into line with the official temple text.

5 I wait for the LORD, my soul waits,
    and in his word do I hope.[7]
6 My soul *waits for* the Lord
    more than watchmen *wait* for the morning,
    y*ea, more than* watchmen for the morning.[8]
7 O Israel, hope[9] in the LORD,
    for with the LORD there is loyal love,
    and with him is abundant redemption;[10]
8 And he will redeem Israel
    from all its iniquities.

Composition and Context

Psalm 130 is one of the six penitential psalms in view of its emphasis on the forgiveness of sin.[11] The doctrine is so clearly stated in this passage that Martin Luther described it as a

---

7. This word was made feminine singular in the old Greek because it was connected to "my soul"; but the MT has the masculine singular "I wait," which is supported by the DSS—except that the DSS duplicates the verb (compare Pss. 42:6, 42:12, and 43:5).
8. The MT has מִשֹּׁמְרִים, "more than the watchmen." The Greek has ἀπὸ φυλακῆς πρωίας μέχρι νυκτός, "from the [morning] watch (till the night)," apparently reading the noun "watch," מֵאַשְׁמֹרֶת, instead (and not thinking of a comparative *min* prefixed to the form, but the normal use of the preposition). And so to finish out the thought they had to add "night [watch]," covering the duplication of "watch" ("watchmen" in the MT). The Targum adds the interpretation that the watchmen were waiting to make the morning sacrifice. See further S. Porúbčan, "Psalm cxxx 5–6," *VT* 9 (1959):322–23; and N. Tromp, "The Text of Psalm cxxx 5–6," *VT* 39 (1989):100–103.
9. The Greek has "Let Israel hope in the Lord." The verb ἐλπισάτω indicates that they interpreted the verb form יַחֵל as if it were a jussive יְיַחֵל, perhaps thinking the *yôd* was a prefix. That would have made more sense to them in view of the word order of the verse.
10. The MT has וְהַרְבֵּה עִמּוֹ פְדוּת. The Greek version made the infinitive form an adjective for redemption—with him is abundant redemption"; but this is not possible; it is used adverbially, "plenteously." The Qumran scroll appears to have a singular adjective הרב to go with the simple פדה. But the editors of the published edition of the scroll separate the two words, and suggest that the scroll is not reading "with him" (*'immô* [עִמּוֹ]), but "his people" (*'ammô* [עַמּוֹ]).
11. See N. H. Snaith, *The Seven Psalms* (London: Epworth Press, 1964).

Pauline psalm.[12] The simplicity of the theological point and the beauty of the composition make this passage all the more memorable.

Anderson classifies the psalm as an individual lament because of the petition of the first two verses;[13] but Denton calls it a psalm of trust because most of it focuses on the expectation of forgiveness and redemption.[14] This latter designation makes sense since the psalm has more to do with assurance of forgiveness than the difficulty in which the psalmist found himself. He is sure of forgiveness, but longs for the word from the LORD. The closing verses form an exhortation for the people to wait in faith on the LORD because the future deliverance from all their sins is sure.[15] Kraus says that "Ps 130 is a model that shows an individual pious person takes his place with his prayer in the reality of the community that surrounds him."[16] The psalm may have been used as an adaptation of the entrance liturgy at the gate.[17]

The psalm falls into four sections of two verses each. The first two verses record the psalmist's cry to the LORD out of trouble. The next two verses express his confidence that there is forgiveness for sins, indicating that the dilemma was probably due to sin. The third section tells of the psalmist's eager waiting for an oracle telling him he is forgiven. And the final two verses is a call for the people to hope in the LORD because some day he will redeem them from all their sins. The psalm is saying that the present (and repeated) cycle, for the remedy

---

12. See also John Owen, "A Practical Exposition upon Psalm cxxx," in *The Works of John Owen* (Edinburgh: T. & T. Clark, 1862). 6:325–648.
13. *Psalms 73–150*, p. 875.
14. See Robert C. Denton, "An Exposition of an Old Testament Passage," *Journal of the Bible and Religion* 15 (1947):158–161.
15. See Rick R. Marrs, "A Cry from the Depths," *ZAW* 100 (1988):81–90.
16. *Psalms 90–150*, p. 465.
17. W. H. Schmidt, "Gott und Mensch in Ps. 130. Formsgeschichtliche Erwägungen," *ThZ* 22 (1966):241–53. For the church's use of the psalm in the holy calendar, see Richard J. Pettey, "Psalm 130," in *The Psalter and Other Studies in the Old Testament*, edited by Jack C. Knight and Lawrence A Sinclair (Nashotah, WI: Nashotah House, 1990):45–53.

of sin—forgiveness and deliverance—is a harbinger of the final and complete deliverance from all sin.

In other words, every deliverance is a preview and a pledge of that great day of redemption, and every experience of forgiveness is a foreshadowing of the final redemption from sin and everything connected to it.

Exegetical Analysis

Summary

Assured that God forgives iniquity and delivers his people from their dilemmas, the psalmist waits for the word from the LORD and exhorts the nation to join him in waiting for the time when the LORD will redeem them from all their iniquities.

Outline

I. Addressing the LORD: The psalmist confidently petitions the LORD to deliver him from his dilemma because he knows the LORD forgives sin (1–4).
  A. Petition: He cries to the LORD for deliverance (1–2).
    1. He asserts his great need of help (1).
    2. He petitions the LORD to answer his prayer (2).
  B. Confidence: He finds confidence that his prayer will be answered because he knows that God forgives sin in order that people might be devoted to him (3–4).
    1. If God did not forgive sin, no one would survive God's judgment (3).
    2. But God does forgive sin, that people might be devoted to him (4).

II. Addressing the Congregation: The psalmist affirms that he is waiting patiently for the LORD's oracle of forgiveness, and exhorts Israel also to hope for their redemption from all iniquity (5–8).
  A. Affirmation: He testifies that he is earnestly waiting for the oracle from the LORD (5–6).
  B. Exhortation: He exhorts the people to hope in the LORD because he has loyal love for them and will redeem them from all their iniquities (7–8).

COMMENTARY IN EXPOSITORY FORM

I. Petition: Penitent believers cry out to God in times of trouble (1–2).

It will probably be easier and more effective in an exposition of this psalm to break it down to four units of two verses each, even though it is clear that the first two units address God and the last two address the congregation. The four parts are petition, confidence, testimony, and exhortation.

In the first two verses the psalmist petitions the LORD to answer his prayer. He does not say what the need is, only that he cries out from the depths. The word "depth" or "valley" (s.v., עֹמֶק) is a figure (an implied comparison) for the trouble he was in, not unlike the "valley of the shadow of death" in Psalm 23, although there some actual dangerous valley is probably in mind. Images like a pit, a valley, miry clay, and the like, were popular for any kind of trouble. Whatever the trouble was in this case, the psalm simply refers to it as the depths; it was a difficulty or circumstance that could only be resolved by crying out to God. The argument of the psalm will lead to the conclusion that his plight was the result of his sin, perhaps divine discipline for his sin.

The verbs in his petition stress the urgency. Verse 2 uses the imperative "hear" (שִׁמְעָה; s.v. Ps. 45:10) and then the jussive, "let your ears be (תִּהְיֶינָה) attentive." The first form, the imperative of "hear," means "respond"; with the expression "in my voice" (בְּקוֹלִי) it means "respond to what I say." He wants an answer, not an audience. Likewise, the prayer (jussive), "let (your ears) be" with the predicate "attentive" or "answering" (קַשֻּׁבוֹת) is a strong appeal to God to pay close attention to his supplication. The use of "your ears" is a bold figure (anthropomorphism) to make the appeal more vivid: it is as if he wants the LORD to lean over to hear better.

In view of these forms we may now interpret the first verb in the psalm, the perfect tense (קְרָאתִיךָ), as a present tense, "I cry."[18] The point is that he is still in the need of an answer to his prayer—he wants the LORD to be attentive to his prayers,

---

18. It could also be classified as a present perfect, "I have cried to the LORD,"

literally, the voice of "my supplications" (תַּחֲנוּנָי, from the verb "to show favor, mercy" (חָנַן; s.v. Ps. 4:1). This noun depicts petitions or supplications for grace. In other words, what he is requesting is undeserved, a gracious provision from the LORD in the midst of a great difficulty. And since the form of the noun is plural, his prayers are frequent and intense.

II. Confidence: Believers know that there is forgiveness of sin (3–4).

The confidence section begins with a conditional clause followed by a rhetorical question forming the independent clause: "If you, O LORD (יָהּ), should mark iniquities, Lord (אֲדֹנָי), who could stand?" The two verbs are imperfect tenses; the first "mark" (תִּשְׁמָר; s.v. Ps. 12:7), being in the conditional clause, may be given a modal nuance: "if you should mark." It is a condition that is contrary to fact, but raised as a possibility for the sake of the clear affirmation that there is forgiveness. The other verb, "stand" (יַעֲמֹד), should be classified as a potential imperfect in the interrogative clause: "who could stand?" This rhetorical question is intended to affirm that no one could stand if the LORD kept sins on the record, that is, held them against them. In addition to this, the verb "stand" is idiomatic (an implied comparison) for surviving divine judgment for sin (cf. Ps. 1:5). The idea is that if the LORD kept a meticulous record of iniquities, or marked the sins themselves and did not remove them, no one could hope to escape judgment.

The LORD is addressed first as "Yah" (יָהּ), the abbreviation for the holy name, and then with "Lord" (אֲדֹנָי), the title.[19] "Yah" is the short spelling of the covenant name; and it is set in an immediate contrast to the word "iniquities" (s.v. Ps. 32:5) that is placed prominently first: "If iniquities, O Yah, you should mark." The title for lord or master completes the emphasis on

---

meaning he still was crying, or a very recent past, "I have [just now] cried to the LORD"—therefore, LORD, answer my prayer.

19. The title is simply "lord, master"; but it is written in the text with the vowels that fit the holy name, indicating that this Lord is the LORD, i.e., Yahweh.

the sovereignty of God and underscores the idea that no one could survive the judgment where the charges against them, their sins, would be enumerated.

Against this disheartening prospect verse 4 stands as the antithesis; it is introduced with the adversative "but" (כִּי).[20] By this the psalmist immediately asserts that the condition he raised in the previous line need not be a concern—God does not preserve the sins against the penitent; rather, he forgives. This line has neither subject nor verb, only the predicate adjective: "But with you *there is* forgiveness." The key word of the psalm is this "forgiveness" (הַסְּלִיחָה); the article is commonly written with abstracts to emphasize the subject matter.[21] It is a word that means excusing, removing, forgiving sin; it is used in Leviticus for the forgiveness that accompanies the sin offering.[22] This glorious declaration is followed by a purpose clause—the purpose of the forgiveness (לְמַעַן): "in order that you may be feared." The verb "feared" (s.v. Ps. 2:11) in this line is a rare form of the irregular verb (a *niphal* imperfect of the *I Yod* root: תִּוָּרֵא), occurring only here. In the purpose clause it would function as a final imperfect. The point is that God forgives people in order that they might fear, meaning, that they might become his faithful, obedient worshipers. Weiser says that since God is more powerful than sin and only he can overcome it, he is to be feared.[23]

---

20. Anderson suggests this is an indirect prayer for forgiveness (*Psalms 73–150*, p. 876).
21. Goldingay says the article identifies the subject: "pardon is with you" (*Psalms 90–150*, p. 521).
22. The word "forgiveness," סְלִיחָה, occurs only here and in Nehemiah 9:17 (in the abstract plural form). The verb סָלַח occurs fairly frequently; it means "pardon, forgive." It is used most frequently in the passive voice (*niphal* stem) in Leviticus 4 and 5, as well as Numbers 15, in connection with the ritual for the sin and reparation offerings. The word is used in Exodus 34:9 in the intercession for forgiveness for the people. It is used in Numbers 14:19 where forgiveness is granted even though the people will not see the land. And when Solomon dedicated the temple, he prayed that when people came to pray the LORD would forgive them (1 Kings 8:20). So the word is pretty straightforward in its meaning. Interestingly, the word *s^elikhah* is appropriately used in modern Hebrew for "excuse me" (as we might use "pardon me" in English).
23. *Psalms*, p. 774.

The one who has power over the soul is to be feared beyond any who only have power over the body. But the good news is that there is forgiveness; and forgiveness frees the penitent from the fear of the judgment.

III. Testimony: Believers wait patiently for the LORD's word (5–6).

These verses in the Hebrew text read:

"I wait for the LORD, my soul waits,
   and for his word I hope.
My soul [waits] for the Lord,
   more than the watchmen [waits] for the morning,
   watchmen for the morning."

The first word of verse 5 is "I wait" (קִוִּיתִי; s.v. Ps. 25:3); it has the idea of eager expectation for something.[24] The idea of waiting is strong in the line, for the verb is repeated immediately with "I" (literally "my soul," נַפְשִׁי) as the subject. The repetition and the enhancement of the subject point to the complete focus and eager anticipation of the psalmist—he waits with his whole being.

Parallel to this word is the synonym "I hope" (הוֹחָלְתִּי, the *hiphil* perfect of יָחַל; s.v. Ps. 31:24). This word also has a connotation of restlessness—not anxiety, but an unsettled expectation of the realization of what is hoped for. It stresses that the waiting is in hope; Job 13:15 says, "Though he slay me, yet will I hope in him"—never giving up the expectation or hope of divine intervention. So the word "wait" (קָוָה) looks at the endurance aspect of the waiting, and hope provides the strength or inspiration of the waiting. Waiting on the LORD, or hoping in the LORD, calls for constant vigilance, eager preparation, and no relaxation of efforts until the hope is realized.

The object of the hope is God's "word." Probably what is

---

24. This waiting in hope may have a certain amount of tension if the cognate noun signifies anything for it. The noun is the word for a cord or rope, perhaps with the idea of twisting and tightening.

meant by "his word" in this psalm is the oracle of forgiveness from the LORD through a prophet or priest, declaring that the sin had been removed and the punishment for the sin was ended. It would be the word of forgiveness, as for example the prophet's word to David, "The LORD has put away your sin" (2 Sam. 12:13), or as in the message of comfort to the exiles, "Speak comfortably to Jerusalem: cry unto her . . . that her iniquity is pardoned" (Isa. 40:2). Thus, the "word" would be a figure (a metonymy of cause, or subject), for the psalmist is eager for what the word of forgiveness will bring—relief from the crisis. Kraus sums it up by saying that such a proclamation of salvation from a priest or prophet would bring forgiveness to the one who has hope.[25]

Waiting for the LORD is the same as hoping for his word. It is the eager anticipation of the LORD's intervention in his affairs. He waits for this more than the watchmen wait for the morning. The figure of comparison with watchmen (a simile) is a good one. For much of the time watchmen do little besides wait for the morning, checking for it regularly, looking for that first bit of dawn, and then the light. In the line the repetition enhances the diligence of the watchmen looking again and again for the light. And the use of "morning" (metonymy of subject) represents the time of the sunrise they eagerly expect. It is not impossible that the watchmen in mind here are priests, waiting for that first glimmer of light on the eastern horizon so that they might make the early morning sacrifice. The waiting in such a case would be most focused.

IV. Encouragement: God's people may expect complete redemption (7–8).

The last section addresses the nation, encouraging them to keep hoping in the LORD, because there will be abundant redemption for them when the LORD removes their iniquities. Individual experiences of forgiveness reveal the nature of the LORD God and provide a preview of the great deliverance to come.

---

25. *Psalms 60–150*, p. 467.

There is Forgiveness with God

Verse 7 begins with the imperative "hope" (יַחֵל; s.v. Ps. 31:24): "Hope in the LORD, O Israel." This imperative expresses encouragement along with exhortation—the psalmist desires that they hope in the LORD, and he is indicating that if they do they will find complete redemption in the end. The nation apparently was in the same difficulty from time to time as the psalmist, and therefore was not to lose hope. The rest of the verse is a causal clause, giving two reasons for the hope. The first is that with the LORD there is "loyal love" (חֶסֶד; s.v. Ps. 23:6). This figure (a metonymy of cause) signifies the acts that the LORD's loyal love produces, and the loving act in this line is "redemption" (perhaps to be taken as the corresponding metonymy of effect). The verse modifies this redemption as "abundant" (using the *hiphil* infinitive absolute form הַרְבֵּה). Its use is adverbial: "with him is redemption plenteously (abundantly)." The two prepositional phrases are parallel: "with the LORD is loyal love, with him is redemption plenteously." The penitent believer need never lose hope because God's loyal love that brings redemption is always present and active.

Verse 8 reiterates the point: "And he will redeem Israel from all its iniquities." Here the imperfect tense expresses specific future: there is coming a time when the LORD will deliver his people from their sins, once and for all; accordingly, until then every act of forgiveness, every deliverance, is but a preview or a harbinger of that time. So Israel is called to keep on hoping for this, expecting it, looking for it, preparing for it. In that regard this expectation falls in line with the New Testament emphasis on the hope of the believer for the second coming of the Messiah.

The final word of the psalm, "its [Israel's] iniquities" (עֲוֹנֹתָיו; s.v. Ps. 32:5) is a figure as well (a metonymy of cause). The iniquities caused the crisis out of which the psalmist cries; moreover, this expression of redemption is not used for sin alone, but for deliverance from some crisis or catastrophe, often caused by sin. Thus, in the future, the LORD will redeem his people from all their crises. How so? By removing any iniquities that caused them and setting them free. So once again the emphasis is that there is forgiveness with God, a forgiveness that will be realized through redemption from all sin and its effects.

MESSAGE AND APPLICATION

In this psalm the psalmist cries to the LORD from his trouble, takes comfort in the fact that there is forgiveness of sins, eagerly waits for the oracle of forgiveness, and knows that ultimately the LORD will remove all iniquities and their effects—that is, from those who believe in him and seek his forgiveness.

Every act of deliverance and every occurrence of forgiveness of sin are but harbingers of the final deliverance from sin and its effects. The glory of the love of God that brings such redemption must not be minimized. With the LORD there is forgiveness of sin! Full forgiveness! Believers, therefore, can have this same hope and confidence in the LORD, that someday there will be no more confession of sin necessary, and no more need to pray for deliverance (John 16:23). But in the meantime, every prayer and every confession should hasten the hope. And that hope, that waiting for final redemption with the return of Christ, should likewise lead us to be seeking forgiveness for our sin. The apostle said, "Whoever has this hope purifies himself" (1 John 3:3).

The lessons and applications for a passage like this are straightforward. If we make the homiletic idea *Because the LORD forgives sin he will one day remove all sin and its effects,* then the immediate application would be to find forgiveness for sin (cry to the LORD as the psalmist was doing), and live in the hope of future, abundant redemption. Living in that hope involves fearing the LORD (the purpose of forgiveness) and glorying in his assurance of forgiveness, now written in Holy Scripture once for all. Every experience of forgiveness is a sign not only that all is well with the LORD, but also that a final ultimate forgiveness lies ahead.

PSALM 131
Humility and Trust

INTRODUCTION

Text and Textual Variants

A Song of Ascent. Of David.[1]

1 O LORD, my heart is not proud,
    nor my eyes raised high;[2]
  neither do I involve myself in great matters,
    or, in things too wonderful for me.

---

1. The name "David" is in the MT, the Greek, Symmachus, Aquila and the Syriac; it is not in some Greek manuscripts or the Targum.
2. The MT has רָמוּ, "they are high, raised"; the eyes being high means ambitious and arrogant. The Greek version translated this fairly literally with ἐμετεωρίσθησαν, "(neither have my eyes) been raised."

2 Surely[3] I have stilled[4] and quieted[5] my soul,
　　like a weaned child with its mother–
　　like[6] the weaned child *is* my soul within me.[7]
3 O Israel, hope in the LORD
　　from this time forth and forever more.[8]

---

3. An oath or asseverative may be introduced with אִם or אִם לֹא and the complete sentence may be expressed: "[may the LORD do so to me] if I have not stilled . . . ," and means, "Surely, I have stilled . . . ." The Greek (and Vulgate) appear to have a protasis and apodasis of a conditional sentence, translating it as: "If I have not been humble (εἰ μὴ ἐταπεινοφρόνουν) but exalted my soul" (you will recompense my soul).
4. The verb שִׁוִּיתִי, if taken from one root שָׁוָה, would mean "to level off" (as in Isa. 28:25); if it is taken from a second root, which seems to have been the preferred connection, it would have the sense of "cause to lie down," hence, the translation "I have stilled (myself)."
5. The MT has the *poel perfect* וְדוֹמַמְתִּי from דָּמַם, "to make level, calm." The Greek (and some Hebrew manuscripts) apparently took the verb to be רוֹמֵם, a simple confusion of letters, because it renders the verse with ὕψωσα, "have exalted (my soul)." Perhaps the previous use of this verb influenced the choice.
6. The two prepositions could be interpreted in the sense of "as (a weaned child with its mother) so . . . " (P. A. H. DeBoer, "Psalm cxxxi 2," *VT* 16 [1966]:287–92).
7. The word גָּמֻל, "weaned," occurs twice in this verse, and many commentators think that may be an error, that a different form should be present. The Greek version does not have "like a weaned child" repeated. It reads: "like a weaned child to his mother, so you will recompense (ὡς ἀνταπόδοσις) my soul." The translation of the second verb may represent a verb תִּגְמֹל, meaning "be kind, benevolent, or act justly." This does not fit the verse very well, but the editors propose following it. They also propose reading עֻלִי in place of עָלָי. But as Perowne observes, the resumption of the previous expression is in accordance with the rhythmical structure of many of the pilgrim psalms. As the text stands it makes the poetry climactic and has a designed parallelism with the use of the preposition in the two lines: "as a weaned child (lies) upon (the breast of) its mother, as (so) the weaned child (I say) is my soul within me" (*Psalms*, II:408; see also Keet, *Psalms of Ascent*, p. 84; and see additionally Willem A. VanGemeren, "Psalm 131:2–*kᵉgāmul*," *Hebrew Studies* 23 [1982]:51–57).
8. Some commentators suggest that verse 3 may have been added to the short psalm to give it a fitting conclusion for liturgical use. But Kraus says that the verse fits the passage well as an example of the righteous man who sets his own sample before the community and exhorts them to hope (*Psalms 60–150*, p. 470).

Composition and Context

Psalm 131 is one of those short little psalms that seldom receives attention; it is just not profound enough for some expositors—so it seems. But it is a significant passage that contrasts faith with pride. The psalmist sets his own case before the community to give the people hope. And that example is of a confident psalmist who has put aside worldly ambition and rests in comfort in divine security.[9] It should be classified as a psalm of confidence or trust of an individual because of the personal language,[10] although Kraus suggests it is a prayer song.[11]

Exegetical Analysis

Summary

Expressing his avoidance of proud and overly ambitious endeavors, the pilgrim expresses his humble faith and calm confidence in the LORD and encourages others also to hope in the LORD.

Outline

I. The pilgrim expresses his humility in that he has avoided proud and ambitious endeavors (1).
   A. He asserts that he is not proud and does not have lofty ambitions.
   B. He asserts that he does not attempt anything too high for him.
II. The pilgrim describes his simple but secure faith in the LORD (2).
   A. He attests that he has calmed his spirit in his faith.
   B. He attests that he is secure in his life of faith.
III. The pilgrim encourages the people to hope in the LORD forever (3).

---

9. Keet, p. 84.
10. Anderson, *Psalms 73–150*, p. 878.
11. *Psalms 60–150*, p. 469. See B. P. Robinson, "Form and Meaning in Psalm 131," *Bib* 79 (1998):180–197; and H. Stephen Shoemaker, "Psalm 131," *Rev Exp* 85 (1988):89–94.

COMMENTARY IN EXPOSITORY FORM

I. Those who trust in the LORD remain humble (1).

A. *They are not proud or presumptuous.*

This psalm is a meditation addressed to the LORD in which the writer asserts his sincere faith. The first verse is a quatrain, the first two cola dealing with attitudes and desires (the heart and the eyes), and the second two with actions. The sentence is expressed negatively as the psalmist distinguishes himself from the proud and arrogant who have ambitious schemes: "O LORD, my heart is not proud, / nor my eyes haughty; // neither do I involve myself in great matters, / or in things too extraordinary for me." In the first colon David says his "heart," meaning his will (a metonymy of subject), is not "proud," the word "proud" (גָּבַהּ) means "be exalted" (in one's own eyes); it stresses an arrogant attitude and presumptuous activity. The parallel verb is "raised" or "high" (רָמוּ; s.v. Ps. 46:10). The idiom "haughty" or "high eyes" expresses ambition, an overreaching ambition; it is the "proud look" of Proverbs 6 that the LORD hates. The term "eyes" means more than an arrogant look; it includes the ambitious thoughts (so it is a metonymy of adjunct). The context indicates that the "high eyes," or "ambition," is not ordinary, harmless ambition. Joined with the proud heart the line is talking about presumptuous ambition.

B. *They do not attempt things too extraordinary for them.*

The next two cola are about action. The first part says, "neither do I involve myself (literally, go about) in great things." The verb is idiomatic; it is based on a comparison of the activity of walking about with being involved in great things. The stem used here (a *piel,* הִלַּכְתִּי) makes the action plural, i.e., he (does not) go about, or busy himself with grand things. And the perfect tense expresses activity that is continual (a characteristic perfect). Others characteristically are involved in such things, but the psalmist is not.

What is meant by "in great things" (בִּגְדֹלוֹת) is not made clear. There is nothing wrong with wanting to do great things; but in this psalm with its emphasis on "proud" and "haughty" in the first line, the word here refers to acts of hubris—great activities that are beyond one's abilities. And the implication is that being busy trying to accomplish things beyond one's abilities is foolish.

This point is reiterated with the parallel idea: "things too extraordinary for me." The word used here (וּבְנִפְלָאוֹת) is a substantival form of the feminine participle; the verb (פָּלֵא; s.v. Ps. 139:5) means "to be wonderful, extraordinary, surpassing, incomprehensible." It is used regularly in the Bible to describe some work of God that is amazing or surpassing. It is occasionally translated as "difficult" or "arduous," but it describes something that is extraordinary, beyond human abilities, and not just too hard to do. Along with the use of the word the psalmist adds the superlative idea (with the comparative *min*)–they are too wonderful for him.

II. Those who trust in the LORD are secure in their faith (2).

A. They have calmed their hearts in faith.

David now expresses the corollary of the first point: not only does he not exhibit arrogance and ambition beyond his abilities, but has a simple but secure trust in the LORD. The verse begins with the oath formula (אִם־לֹא שִׁוִּיתִי), which would literally say "if I have not stilled . . . ." The formula has an understood ellipsis: "[May God do so to me] if I have not . . . ," which means "I surely have. . . ." If the verb in the clause is taken from the first root (שָׁוָה), it would mean "to level" (used of leveling the ground for sowing); but if it is from the second root which means "to cause to lie down," it would more naturally have the idea of calming oneself within: "Surely I have stilled (and quieted my soul)." The parallel verb enhances the point; the form (וְדוֹמַמְתִּי, the *poel* perfect of the geminate verb) means "and quieted."

B. They are secure in the faith.

The second half of the verse uses an explicit comparison (a simile), and so the entire verse may be classified as emblematic parallelism. The emblem, "like a weaned child upon his mother," is meant to illustrate the kind of quiet, secure and safe trust the psalmist has in the LORD. There are two main ways to interpret the parallel expressions as one line: "as a weaned child upon his mother, so my soul is like the weaned child within me"; or, as two parallel expressions: "like a weaned child upon his mother, like the weaned child is my soul within me." In the last part the prepositional phrase "within me" (עָלָי) appears to be redundant; but it forms a designed parallelism with the form in the preceding colon (עָלָי). And the repetition (of "weaned") fits the style of the pilgrim's psalms.

III. Those who trust in the LORD encourage others in their faith (3).

In the final verse of the song David encourages the people of Israel to "hope" in the LORD. This word "hope" (יָחַל; s.v. Ps. 31:24) is the same word used in the exhortation in Psalm 130; there the people were encouraged to hope for full forgiveness of sin. Here it is more general, encouraging people to put their full trust in the LORD rather than delude themselves into thinking they have the ability to solve all the problems of life. A call to trust is therefore a call to humility; a refusal to trust is pride. It seems that behind the encouragement is the expectation that the LORD would intervene on their behalf—they were waiting in hope for the LORD, and he wanted the whole congregation to exhibit the kind of humble yet secure faith that he had.

The last colon extends the encouragement beyond any present need to "from this time and for ever" (a merism). It is a call for faith to wait for the LORD at all times.

MESSAGE AND APPLICATION

The psalmist is in general exhorting the nation to exhibit such a basic, childlike faith in the LORD that enjoys complete rest and security, rather than follow an arrogant and ambitious approach to the needs and desires of this life. After all, God resists the proud, but gives grace to the humble. *Genuine faith is demonstrated by a calm confidence in the Lord and not in self-sufficient ambition.* The ambition of a true believer should be to please the Lord; and it is impossible to please him without faith.

PSALM 132

The Glorious Future of God's Program

INTRODUCTION

Text and Textual Variants

A Song of Ascents.

1 O LORD, remember for David's sake[1]
   all his affliction:[2]
2 how he swore to the LORD,
   and vowed to the Mighty One[3] of Jacob:

---

1. The Greek translation has a clarifying reading, making the name the direct object: "remember David."
2. The MT has עֻנּוֹתוֹ, but the Greek version has τῆς πραύτητος αὐτοῦ, "his meekness," apparently reading the form as עֲנָוֹתוֹ. The Hebrew word "affliction" might refer to David's self-affliction (1 Chron. 22:14).
3. The form in the MT is לַאֲבִיר, "to the Mighty One (of Jacob)"; the Greek version interprets this with θεῷ, "to the God (of Jacob)." The title refers to the LORD and may recall the narratives about Jacob, or it may be an epithet that refers to the ark (see T. E. Fretheim, "Psalm 132: A Form Critical Study," *JBL* 86 [1967]:289–300). Theories that suggest connecting the Hebrew term to אָבִיר, "bull," in comparison with Canaanite terminology, are not compelling.

PSALM 132

3 "I will by no means enter the tent of my house,
   nor go up to the couch of my bed;
4 I will not give sleep to my eyes,
   or slumber to my eyelids;[4]
5 Until I find a place for the LORD,
   a tabernacle for the Mighty One[5] of Jacob."

6 "Behold, we heard of it[6] in Ephrathah;
   we found it in the Field[7] of Yaar![8]
7 Let us go into his tabernacle,
   let us worship at his footstool.[9]
8 Arise, O LORD, to your resting place,
   you, and the ark of your strength."[10]
9 Let your priests be clothed with righteousness,
   and let your saints shout for joy![11]
10 For the sake of your servant David,
    do not turn away the face of your anointed.

11 The LORD has sworn to David in truth
    (he will not turn from it):[12]
    "Of the fruit of your body

---

4. The Greek text adds the colon: καὶ ἀνάπαυσιν τοῖς κροτάφοις μου, "nor slumber to my temples."
5. The Greek translation again has θεῷ, "for the God (of Jacob)."
6. The suffix in the MT is feminine, referring to the ark (in verse 8); Jerome has masculine.
7. The MT has בִּשְׂדֵי, "in the fields of (the wood)," as does the Greek version. But most manuscripts and the other versions read a singular (שְׂדֵה).
8. The Targum has "of the forests of Lebanon, the place where the fathers of old prayed." But the reference is probably to Kiriath-jearim (1 Sam. 6:21–7:2).
9. The Greek version has οὗ ἔστησαν οἱ πόδες αὐτοῦ, "the place where his foot stood."
10. MT has עֻזֶּךָ, "your strength"; but the Greek version reads τοῦ ἁγιάσματός σου, "your holiness."
11. A few manuscripts add רַנֵּן to the verb יְרַנֵּנוּ in accordance with the fuller construction found in verse 16.
12. The Greek version offers a strong interpretation: καὶ οὐ μὴ ἀθετήσει αὐτήν, "and he will by no means annul it."

will I set¹³ upon your throne.
12 If your sons will keep my covenant
    and my testimony¹⁴ that I shall teach them,
  their children also shall sit upon your throne
    for evermore."
13 For the LORD has chosen Zion;
    he has desired it for his habitation:
14 "This is my resting place forever;
    here will I dwell, for I have desired it.
15 I will abundantly bless her provision;
    I will satisfy her poor¹⁵ with bread.
16 Her priests also will I clothe with salvation;
    and her saints shall shout aloud for joy.
17 There I will make the horn of David to bud;¹⁶
    I have ordained a lamp for my anointed.
18 His enemies I will clothe with shame;
    but upon him shall his crown¹⁷ flourish."

Composition and Context

This long pilgrim psalm is a prayer for the LORD to honor the commitment of David by fulfilling the promises to David. David had vowed to find a resting place for the ark of the covenant, and the LORD vowed to make an everlasting covenant with his house. It is the fulfillment of this latter vow, based on the completion of the former vow, for which the psalmist prays.

The faithfulness of David is not only remembered in this psalm, but relived by the faithful in the use of the psalm. A ritual procession seems to lie in the background of the psalm

---

13. The editors of BHS propose a noun here for clarification, either "a king" or "kings" or "sons."
14. MT has עֵדֹתִי זוֹ, "this my testimony," with one manuscript reading זֶה. The Greek translation has plural: καὶ τὰ μαρτύριά μου ταῦτα, "and these my testimonies."
15. Some manuscripts and versions have a conjunction with this noun (which comes at the beginning of the Hebrew clause): "and her poor."
16. The Greek renders this with ἐξανατελῶ, "spring up, sprout up."
17. The MT has נִזְרוֹ, "his crown"; but the Greek version has τὸ ἁγίασμά μου, "my holiness."

as the composition celebrates finding the ark and proceeding to Jerusalem (2 Sam. 6:12–19).[18] The work may very well be from the tenth century; Chronicles incorporates verses 8–10 in its record of Solomon's prayer (2 Chron. 6:41, 2); but it was not included in 1 Kings 8, opening the possibility that it was a liturgical composition used in later festivals, leaving open the question of when the psalm was written and then adapted for such use.[19] The Scripture does affirm that Solomon included these ideas, and so he was comfortable praying that the LORD would not reject his anointed one, probably in reference to himself in the first place.

But as one might expect in such a complex composition, there are numerous views that have been put forward concerning its writing. The traditional view is that it was written by David after receiving the covenant (2 Sam. 7). The psalm then may have been composed for the actual transference of the ark to Jerusalem (or to commemorate it with a psalm to be used in the future); and it would have included an early prayer for God to fulfill the promise he had made to David. A second view is that the psalm was written a little later, perhaps by Solomon or a poet of his time, in commemoration of David's faithful act—which Solomon completed by building the temple. Anderson represents a third view, that the psalm was pre-exilic, but not Solomonic.[20] Still another proposal is that it was written by someone at the time of Zerubbabel's rebuilding and rededication of the temple. But this one is more difficult to support because Zerubbabel was never anointed as king, and the ark apparently did not return from the exile. Moreover, the psalm does not mention or lament any lack of kingship. This latter point also applies to

---

18. Allen suggests the psalm may be a prayer of a Judean king on the anniversary of moving the ark to Jerusalem (*Psalms 101–150*, p. 209). For further discussion, see J. R. Porter, "The Interpretation of 2 Samuel vi and Psalm cxxxii," *JTS* ns 5 (1954):161–73.
19. See also Antti Laato, "Psalm 132 and the Development of the Jerusalemite/Israelite Royal Ideology," *CBQ* 54 (1992):49–66; and "Psalm 132," *CBQ* 61 (1999):24–33.
20. *Psalms 73–150*, p. 880.

the suggestions that the psalm was written in the exile, or later during the Maccabean period.[21]

There is no information in the psalm about its setting or occasion.[22] One would gather from the passage that the Israelites were living in the land, that the central sanctuary was operating, and that they prayed for the Davidic covenant to be fulfilled. This may or may not indicate that kingship was in difficulty at the time. Likewise the prayer for the priests to be clothed with righteousness may or may not indicate the priesthood was corrupt. These points have been argued in different ways. If there were problems with the monarchy and the priesthood at the time, the faithful could still commemorate the finding of the ark and carrying it up to the sanctuary. Whether people actually carried the ark or not in a historical reenactment is not clear from the passage.[23] But the psalm does in some dramatic way rehearse the finding and transference of the ark as part of the appeal that God will make the crown of David flourish. The psalm may reflect a time of spiritual and political trouble when the promises to David seemed to be waning rather than being fulfilled, but how serious that trouble may have been is not detailed. Whatever the circumstances, the prayer called for the fulfillment of the promises, and so ultimately looked to that glorious future known as the Messianic age.

The classification of the psalm is not at all easy.[24] Its length is unusual for a pilgrim song, and yet it is part of that collection. It focuses on three main themes: the ark, Zion, and the House of David; but it uses liturgy and narration in its poetic

---

21. For a more detailed analysis of the possible redactional issues of the psalm, see Cornelius B. Houk, "Psalm 132," *JSOT* 6 (1978):41–48; and R. E. Bee, "The Textual Analysis of Psalm 132," *JSOT* 6 (1978):68–70.
22. Goldingay thinks we should give up the "pointless effort" to discover when psalms were written (*Psalms 90–150*, p. 544). But the effort serves to engage the expositor in the precise understanding of what the psalm is saying, and what it is not saying.
23. Mowinckel and those who followed his approach used this passage for part of the reconstruction of the annual enthronement festival wherein people carried the ark to the sanctuary.
24. See T. E. Fretheim, "Psalm 132: A Form Critical Study," *JBL* 86 (1967):289–300.

presentation. The emphasis on the temple and kingship harmonize with royal psalms; and the emphasis on the holy city reflect the songs of Zion. In fact, Gunkel classified it as a song of Zion and suggested that the setting was a dedication festival to the memory of the establishment of the temple and the palace. Kraus agrees that there are motifs in it from Zion songs but also acknowledges the elements from royal psalms.[25] Some have suggested that the psalm might have been used as a coronation psalm,[26] or perhaps as a festival to the kingship of the LORD.[27] How the same work may have been used over the centuries is very difficult to determine. It would have been very important to the post-exilic community who looked for the restoration of God's program; this accounts for its inclusion in Book V of the collection.

We can say for certain that the psalm commemorates the founding of the sanctuary with the ark and assures the future of the Davidic dynasty. If we review the whole context of the movement of the ark, we gain a framework for the motifs of this psalm. 2 Samuel 6 records the moving the ark to Jerusalem; 2 Samuel 7 then reports the making of the covenant with David. These are the two prominent motifs in this psalm. So the composition serves as a royal festival of Zion.

As mentioned above, the structure is arranged with two vows. For exposition the psalm could be divided into three parts to give more focus to the final part: the prayer to remember David's vow (vv. 1–5), the liturgical procession and prayer for blessing (vv. 6–10), and the anticipation of God's response to the prayers (vv. 11–18). But it may be easier to leave it in two sections to fit the two vows: the prayer and procession of the faithful (vv. 1–10) and the response of God, which ends with the anticipation of God's answer to the prayer (vv. 11–18).[28] The anticipation motif still

---

25. Kraus suggests that the psalm is late, pre-exilic, but that it combines older traditions (*Psalms 60–150*, p. 479). He also takes the view that 2 Samuel 7 is a composite of prophetic traditions (pp. 476–7).
26. See D. R. Hillers, "Ritual Procession of the Ark and Psalm 132," *CBQ* 30 (1968):48–55.
27. See Porter, pp. 161–73.
28. C. B. Houk, "Psalm 132, Literary Integrity and Syllable-Word Structures,"

will receive more focus because it will be the final section of the second part, and of the whole psalm.

Exegetical Analysis

Summary

In answer to the prayer of Israel that he remember the vow of David concerning the permanent dwelling place for the ark, and in response to their resolution to worship him there by seeking a visitation of glory, righteousness, and power, the LORD solemnly reiterates his promise of an eternal throne to David's line, his eternal dwelling in Zion, and the appearance of Messiah.

Outline

I. The faithful petition the LORD to remember the vow of David concerning a permanent dwelling place for the ark, resolving to worship him there in the expectation that he will visit them with glory, righteousness and power (1–9).
   A. They petition the LORD to honor David's vow to find a dwelling place for the LORD among his people (1–5).
   B. They resolve to worship the LORD with a ritual re-enactment of the transference of the ark, praying that the LORD will visit them with power and righteousness (6–10).
      1. Resolve: Actualizing the past event, the people resolve to go to the sanctuary to worship (6–7).
      2. Request: The people call upon the LORD to visit them with glory, and clothe their priests with righteousness, and endow their king with power (8–10).
II. The LORD responds to the prayer of the faithful by reiterating his oath to David, affirming his choice of Zion, and promising that kingship will flourish with the Messiah (11–18).
   A. He reiterates his oath to David for an eternal throne (11–12).

JSOT 6 (1978):41–48 ; see also C. Brekelmans, "Psalm 132: Unity and Structure," *Bijdr* 44 (1983):262–65.

B. He affirms his choice of Mount Zion (13–16).
   C. He promises the appearance of Messiah (17–18).

COMMENTARY IN EXPOSITORY FORM

I. The faithful pray for the fulfillment of the promises as they commemorate the historical events of the faith in their worship (1–9).

A. They pray for the covenant promises to be fulfilled (1–5).

The psalm begins with a call for the LORD to "remember." An explanation of "remember" (זָכַר; s.v. Ps. 6:5) is necessary because it forms a key motif in the psalm.[29] The word includes the meaning of acting on what is remembered, and so this is a prayer for the LORD to fulfill his promises to David who was faithful to the LORD. Here we see the direction of the psalm: it begins with a prayer to remember David's oath, and then re-enacts David's fulfillment of his oath by moving the ark; it will then record the LORD's oath to David, guaranteeing its fulfillment.

This call for the LORD to remember is "for David's sake." The direct object is in the next colon: "all his affliction"–everything that David suffered for the LORD. The form translated "his affliction" is literally "his being afflicted" (עֻנּוֹתוֹ, a *pual* infinitive construct specifying the substantive "all"). The Greek translation took the word (the consonants ענותו) to be the more common and simpler word "his humility"; but while there is some overlap in these meanings, the idea of "being afflicted" is the more difficult form in the text and is most likely correct (see 1 Chron. 22:14).

Verse 2 begins with the pronoun (אֲשֶׁר) which may be taken as explanatory and translated "how," making what follows essentially the affliction. It could also be the simple relative use of the pronoun and translated "who (swore)." The reference is to a past act (the perfect tenses indicating definite past); and

---

29. See the study of this word in Brevard Childs' *Memory and Tradition*, pp. 1–8.

although the psalm will include a vow that David swore, there is no record in the historical books of this particular vow. While it is certainly probable that he would make such a vow, the wording here uses hyperbolic language and is probably a poetic representation of David's determination to find a resting place for the ark.[30] The oath is made to the LORD, the mighty one of Jacob (לַאֲבִיר יַעֲקֹב). The use of "Mighty One" is probably a reference to Jacob's words in Genesis 49:24; he was the first to vow (at least the first one recorded as vowing), and the first to establish a holy place known as the house of God (Bethel). The epithet "mighty one" became a poetic substitution for the holy name, stressing God's power. While some commentators have attempted to interpret the epithet as "Bull" to reflect an old reference to God as in the Canaanite literature, the word in the text (אֲבִיר) is "mighty" (not אַבִּיר).[31]

In the oath David swore not to rest until he found a dwelling place for the LORD.[32] The oath formula uses the particle "if" (אִם): "if I go into the tent of my house." The statement is elliptical; it means something like "[God do to me] if I go," which is a strong way of saying, "I surely will not go." The verse then uses pleonastic constructions for the oath, and in the process indicates that he had a dwelling place but God did not. The full wording repeats the point with "tent of my house" and "couch of my bed." The use of the word "tent" might refer to his private, inner chamber, since he lived in a palace.[33] The point is that he could not rest when the LORD did not have a resting place, so that in verse 4 the image in the vow is changed to sleeping with

---

30. The record of the vow may have been derived independently of other passages, or it may be part of a cultic celebration to commemorate his determination (Anderson, *Psalms 73–150*, p. 880).
31. See further on this VanGemeren, *Psalms*, p. 927.
32. For literary links between the psalm and the Davidic covenant in 2 Samuel 7, see Elizabeth F. Huweiler, "Patterns and Problems of Psalm 132," in *The Listening Heart*, FS for R. E. Murphy, ed. by K. G. Hoglund et al, *JSOT* Supplement 8 (Sheffield: Sheffield Academic Press, 1987), pp. 199–215.
33. Because the words seem to refer to a bedroom, some commentators have seen in this a vow to abstain from sexual relations and not sleep (see further Anderson, *Psalms 73–150*, p. 881). But the text seems clearly to be referring to sleep.

"I will not give sleep to my eyes, or slumber to my eyelids." This clarifies the meaning of going into his bedchamber. The images (metonymies of adjunct) underscore his determination in the vow not to rest until he finds a resting place for the LORD. The language is hyperbolic: since it took some time to negotiate the land acquisition, it is unlikely he did not sleep; but the point is made forcefully that he would not rest until he had found the place.

The fifth verse provides the point of the oath: "until I find a place for the LORD, a tabernacle for the mighty one of Jacob." The object of this search is expressed by the parallel terms "place" (מָקוֹם) and "tabernacle" or "dwelling place"(מִשְׁכָּנוֹת). The first is the general word, but the second is the technical term for the old sanctuary (the plural form may be taken to amplify the dignity of the LORD, or it may be a plural of composition for all the things in the tabernacle). In such a dwelling place the glorious presence of the LORD would remain in the midst of the people, and not move about in a portable shrine.

B. They worship in expectation through the re-enactment of historical events in the history of the faith (6–9).

In verse six there is a liturgical section that forms a dramatic break from the prayer:

"Behold, we heard of it in Ephrathah;
　we found it in the Field of Yaar."

The psalmist appears to be introducing the people of David's time as the speakers, expressing their eagerness and joy at locating the ark to move it to Jerusalem.[34] With David's transference of the ark to Zion the period of its wanderings came to an

---

34. The word "it" refers to the ark, or the report of its whereabouts. The ark had been kept in Kiriath-Jearim for about twenty years after the Philistine episode (see 1 Sam. 7:2). The verse says they heard of it in Ephratah and found it in the Field of Yaar; but these may be references to the same place.

end.³⁵ But the way this is written, the current readers could reenact the event, much as they did with all their festivals.

The names pose a problem. The ark was never in Ephrathah, that is, the region of Bethlehem. And the word (אֶפְרָתָה) is not the same as Ephraim (אֶפְרַיִם), which would encompass Shiloh where the ark had been at one time.³⁶ It is probably best to follow Delitzsch and take the name to refer to the district of Kiriath-Yearim as well as Bethlehem (*Psalms* III:311–13). The expression in this passage, "the Field/Fields of Yaar" (שְׂדֵי־יָעַר, "the fields of the wood") is probably a reference to (Kiriath-Yearim), "the city of forests/woods," where the ark had been kept prior to the move.

The next verse records the words of the Israelites as they exhorted one another to come and worship at the newly chosen place for the ark. The two verbs in verse seven are plural cohortatives expressing the exhortation. The first is the simple "let us go" (נָבוֹאָה), and the second, "let us worship" (נִשְׁתַּחֲוֶה, from חָוָה, "to bow down"; s.v. Ps. 95:6).³⁷

Their desire was to go to the dwelling place and worship at his footstool (an anthropomorphic reference to the ark).³⁸ The LORD was enthroned above the ark, with the cherubim on either side and the ark below as his footstool, as it were. But the reference here is general for the sanctuary (a metonymy of adjunct), because pilgrims could get nowhere near the ark of the covenant, only to the outer courts.

Then in verses 8 through 10 we have their request to God as they come to bow before him: they call on God to act, so that the priests might be righteous and the king empowered. The language of verse eight is also figurative (anthropomorphic): "arise (קוּמָה; s.v. Ps. 3:1), O LORD, to your resting place." This

---

35. VanGemeren, *Psalms*, p. 927.
36. Weiser suggests it is a reference to Shiloh where the ark was located for a while (*Psalms*, p. 780).
37. The older lexica list this latter word under a root שָׁחָה and explain it as a *hithpael* with metathesis.
38. Allen raises the question concerning the ark's being both a burden to carry and the goal of the journey; he suggests when the ark was put down at the end of the journey (in reality or reenactment), then the obeisance began (*Psalms 101–150*, p. 202).

request for God to "arise" is in effect a call for God to act powerfully and demonstrably, usually on behalf of the nation (see the use of these words in the old battle cry, Numbers 10:33–36 and Psalm 67:1). God's willingness to do this would be evidenced by his movement to the sanctuary of Zion. The description "your resting-place" (מְנוּחָתֶךָ; s.v. Ps. 95:11) is a reference to the sanctuary in the holy city. The designation should not be taken to mean that God needed rest, only that he settled in that place in fulfillment of his plan. And if God blessed the people with his presence, then they and the city would be protected and prosper.

The LORD is always present everywhere; but the psalmist is focusing on the movement of the ark to the holy place, as if there was to be a grand procession as in the days of David. The ark had become the symbol of the presence of the LORD among his people, and so the prayer for God to come to his resting place is made with the ark included: "you and the ark of your might" (עֻזֶּךָ; s.v. Ps. 29:1). The ark now takes on the attribute of God's might (as if to say, "your mighty ark"), signifying the LORD as the divine warrior.

A central focus of the prayer is that the priests be clothed with righteousness (צֶדֶק; s.v. Ps. 1:3). The figure of being clothed (an implied comparison) signifies the nature or condition of the person. For example, to be clothed with white raiments would mean doing righteous acts; clothed with filthy rags means the person is sinful. So here, to be clothed with righteousness would mean that the priests should be righteous. And this word "righteousness" could have the connotation of "salvation" (by metonymy of cause) as the phrase probably harmonizes with the repeated refrain in verse 16. It would mean that promised salvation would be the effect of this righteousness. Note how the two words are juxtapositioned in Psalm 98:2. But even if taken this way, their "righteousness" would still be necessary to the blessing. So it means "Let them be clothed with righteousness and its result."

This petition may indicate that things had not gone well for the priests or the nation. If this prayer had been written at the time of the transference of the ark, then the account of the corrupt priests under Eli and the loss of the ark to the Philistines would still be in the memory of the people. A new beginning would require a prayer for those who care for the ark to be in harmony with the will of God. If the psalm was used at the time of the exile, then this prayer would be obviously necessary. We may think of the dark days that led up to the exile wherein the prophets and the priests were living in disobedience and unrighteousness. Perhaps this is one reason why the psalm was put in Book V. And yet it is also true that at any time when there was a need for God to restore his program, the righteousness of the "spiritual leaders" was the major concern.

Parallel to this request is the clause "let your saints shout for joy." The "saints" are the devout or pious ones (חֲסִידֶיךָ; s.v. חֶסֶד, Ps. 23:6), technically, the beloved, those who are in covenant with God. Thus they are called "your saints" in the prayer.[39] The verb, literally "give a ringing cry" at the change of fortunes (for רָנַן, s.v. Ps. 33:1) can be translated as a second petition, or as the intended result of the petition in the first half ("and / so that your saints may shout for joy"). The difference would only be slight in the interpretation, for in both cases God would be bringing about the changes in the spiritual condition of the priests and the joy of the saints. But if the second clause is subordinated, then the first clause would be the means of God's causing the saints to shout. And verse 10 is the request for the king: "For the sake of David your servant, do not reject your anointed one." The use of "anointed one" (מָשִׁיחַ)[40] here is probably not a reference to David,

---

39. The use of this possessive pronoun throughout underscores the fact that it is all God's program: your resting place, your mighty ark, your priests, your saints, your servant David.
40. The verb "anoint," מָשַׁח, is used extensively throughout the Old Testament, mostly in cultic or religious contexts. But it is used in secular contexts also, such as with the sense of smearing paint on a house (Jer. 22:14) or rubbing a shield with oil (Isa. 21:5; 2 Sam. 1:21).

But its main use is for the solemn setting apart of something or someone by consecration, i.e., anointing with oil. The prophet Elijah anointed Elisha to succeed him (1 Kings 19:16). David was anointed king with holy oil (Ps. 89:20). The priests were anointed to holy office (Lev. 8:12). And even the standing stone was anointed with oil (Gen. 31:13). The custom in the land was to give guests water with which to wash and oil for anointing their skin –this was the gracious host. It may be that the custom of anointing religious leaders was intended to show that the LORD was welcoming them into his house. The anointing oil came to symbolize

since the prayer is "for David's sake";[41] it could refer to Solomon or any subsequent king. The mention of David, though, is a reference is to his faithfulness to God referred to in the first part of the psalm, how loyal he was in finding a resting place for the ark—a sanctuary for God among his people. The request is: "Do not turn away (אַל־תָּשֵׁב) the face of your anointed," meaning that God not reject his appeals for favor. The psalm is essentially a prayer for God to honor the covenant that he made with David, based on how David was faithful to the covenant. We may conclude that the anointed king might have been in some kind of trouble, or at least concerned that something would threaten his kingship; and so the prayer is that God would respond favorably to him. This is connected in some way to the (perceived) need of righteousness (that would result in deliverance) in the priesthood.

Thus the people renewed their devotion to God, possibly retracing the movement of the ark to the holy spot. They prayed for God to accept the king and favor him. If the psalm was used at a commemoration for the founding of the temple, then these requests would be general ones for God's deliverance and preservation of the institutions of the kingdom.

II. The LORD assures his people of his faithfulness to his word (11–18).

A. *The Lord's covenant promises are repeated (11–12).*

Parallel to the first half of the psalm which recorded David's vow to the LORD, the second half of the psalm records the LORD's vow to David—a vow that will yet be fulfilled. Verses

---

the Holy Spirit (Zech. 4:6), so that a believing king might be empowered by the Spirit when anointed (for an unbelieving king the ritual was just so much oil on the head).

מָשִׁיחַ, "anointed," would describe anyone anointed to office, or even more loosely anyone chosen by God for a duty, such as Cyrus the king of Persia (Isa. 45:1). But most importantly it described the Messiah, the prince (Dan. 9:25). As most serious students of the Bible know, "Christ" is simply the Greek translation of Hebrew "Messiah."

41. See Perowne, *Psalms*, II:415.

11 and 12 simply restate the Davidic covenant in its form as an oracle. It is introduced, though, with an emphasis on its reliability: "The LORD has sworn to David *in* truth (he will not turn from it)." The word "truth" (אֱמֶת) is cognate to the verb, "to be sure, reliable, dependable" (אָמַן; s.v. Ps. 15:2), and so indicates that what is described as "truth" is dependable. Here the noun is adverbial in use.

This is a description that applies to all God's covenant promises, not just the covenant to David. New Testament believers are reminded that in establishing the new covenant God swore by himself and will not change. Usually it is humans who are not trustworthy who need to take a solemn oath so that what they say will be considered reliable. The idea of God's taking an oath or swearing by himself is figurative (anthropomorphism), meant to communicate to us the complete trustworthiness of God's words.

The promise to David was that his descendants would continue on the throne after him. The language of the text uses "fruit" (an implied comparison between fruit and physical descendants) to describe the subsequent heirs to the throne. The choice of the word also stresses their prosperity under God's blessing.

The conditions of the covenant are laid out in verse twelve: the promises were sure, but individual participation in the covenant and its promises required faithfulness. The line of Davidic kings sitting on the throne would continue as long as those kings kept the covenant. The psalmist seems to sense the danger that they might not remain faithful, and so prays for God to honor his covenant promises for David's sake. The implication in the psalm is that they must have had a king who was faithful and so were calling on God to preserve his reign or his right to reign in view of this covenant.

But we know that apart from a few exceptions Israel's kings did not keep the covenant of God, but disobeyed his word, and so their rule came to an end with the captivity. But according to the New Testament, when Jesus was born the word from heaven was that he would inherit the throne of David his father. The covenant promise was still intact, for it guaranteed an eternal kingship. Thus Jesus would inherit the throne and reign for ever, for he is both righteous and eternal.

B. The presence of the LORD is affirmed (13–16).

The psalmist returns to his theme that the LORD chose Zion as his desired dwelling. "Zion" is the area, and so the temple on mount Zion would become the dwelling place ("Zion" is a metonymy of subject where the word is substituted for what is on Mount Zion). "Dwelling place" (מוֹשָׁב > יָשַׁב) is figurative as well (an implied comparison)–when Solomon dedicated the temple, he stated very clearly that this was not to be a place where God was located, because the heavens of heavens could not contain him. The "dwelling-place" was to be the place that God would make his presence known among his people; it was where they could come to appear before him, to meet with him, to hear from him, and to find strength for their lives in the knowledge of his presence.

This is a truth that comes to its fullest meaning in the New Testament when the Son of God comes into the world to dwell with people, fulfilling the meaning of the promise of "Immanuel," "God with us." And at his ascension to glory he promised, "I am with you always, even to the end of the world."

The next few verses of the psalm explain the meaning of this desired dwelling place. In verse 14 we read that it was to be his "resting place" (מְנוּחָה), the place he chose for his dwelling, where he would sit enthroned (אֵשֵׁב). Both ideas presented here are important for the promise of the Messianic kingdom—the eternal rest and eternal reign. The LORD's resting place in Zion anticipates the restoration of the rest that had been interrupted by sin. It is the same place of rest that the people of God sought to enter but were denied because of their disobedience and hardness of heart (Ps. 95:11). But when the LORD dwells among his people it will be a place of rest. And that rest will be due to his sovereign reign—he will sit enthroned in the glorious Zion. The fulfillment of the Davidic covenant therefore calls for a divine kingship centered in the holy dwelling place.

Part of the sovereign's reign will be to guarantee the abundance of food (v. 15). Because the LORD will reign, he will bless the people with abundant provisions and satisfy the poor with bread. The force of the promise "I will bless" needs to be made clear to reflect the construction: "I will surely bless" (בָּרֵךְ אֲבָרֵךְ, an imperfect tense with an infinitive absolute). This is the divine resolution, sworn to with an oath.

And then in verse 16 we have the promise that the LORD will clothe the priests with salvation, and her saints will ever sing for joy. Earlier the prayer was that the priests be clothed with righteousness; here the assurance is that they will be clothed with salvation (יֵשַׁע; s.v. Ps. 3:2). As mentioned before, it is possible to take the meaning of "righteousness" in verse 9 to mean the result, "salvation" or "victory." In fact, both words should be explained figuratively (as metonymies) to refer to the LORD's intervention to provide the healthy restoration of the Davidic kingship. "Righteousness" in verse 9 would be the stated cause, and the salvation the intended effect. Then in verse 16 the use of "salvation" would be figurative (a metonymy of effect), stating that the effect of God's clothing them with righteousness was victory or salvation from all their troubles. So the LORD should clothe the priests with righteousness, and the effect would be salvation or victory.

C. The future of the Davidic Covenant is assured (17–18).

The psalm concludes with a promise from God that the Davidic covenant will continue in the person of the promised Messiah. The psalm does not say this is "the" Messiah, only that there will be a glorious future king who will flourish and put down all their enemies. All Davidic kings were "anointed" because of the covenant; but the ultimate king was to be known as "the anointed," i.e., the Messiah. And the language used here to describe that future king is language that appears in other passages about the promised Messiah as well.

The section begins with "there" (שָׁם), a word that looks to the future place of fulfillment. Then, the first thing that is said is "I will cause to sprout a horn for David." The figure "horn" (an implied comparison, or a symbol because of its frequent use) comes from the animal kingdom and represents power—the bigger the horn the more powerful and important the animal. In Daniel the imagery of the horn is used for powerful kings. This "horn" in Psalm 132 will grow for David, that is, in line with the promises to David there will be a descendant, a future king. And the imagery emphasizes the power and the vigor of the dynasty under his reign (see Luke 1:69–75). The choice of verbs is also significant: "I will cause to sprout" (אַצְמִיחַ). The verb is related to the same word for "branch" (צֶמַח), which is a Messianic symbol in the Bible (see Zech. 3:8 and 6:12 as well as Jer. 23:5).

The second figure is that of a lamp (implied comparison): "I will set up a lamp for my anointed one." The verb can also be translated "I will set in order (עָרַךְ) the lamp of my anointed one." Is the lamp (נֵר) the king himself or someone or something that will be provided for the king? Since the line is parallel to the first half of the verse ("I will make flourish a horn for David, I will set up a lamp for my anointed one"), the horn and the lamp both refer to the descendant of David, the anointed one himself (see 2 Sam. 21:17). To refer to the king as a lamp focuses on one of his major tasks—to be a guide to the nation.

Once again the image of clothing is used in the prediction of the victory over the enemies. Now the LORD will clothe the enemies with shame. The figure of clothing (an implied comparison) is now given a negative sense, for the enemies will be clothed with shame (בֹּשֶׁת; s.v. Ps. 31:1), meaning that they will be completely destroyed to their everlasting shame.

On the other hand, the king will be glorious. The final reference is to his crown which will be resplendent: "but on him shall his crown (נִזְרוֹ) flourish (be resplendent [יָצִיץ])." The crown is the symbol of kingship in all its glory and joy; and here the joy of kingship will flourish because of the victory over the enemies.

MESSAGE AND APPLICATION

The psalm, then, is a wonderful liturgical piece that is constructed around two oaths, one by David and the other the LORD's covenant with David. The psalm is an appeal for God to prosper the nation in the person of the anointed king, based on the faithfulness of David in moving the ark to the resting place in Zion—which the participants now seem to be re-enacting. Such a ritual is a way of carrying the obedience and faithfulness forward to their generation, as if they would do the same thing David did; and since they have ritually entered into that historic act, they too can pray for its fulfillment with great confidence.

The original occasion for the psalm was typological of the

Messianic fulfillment, as all the royal and enthronement psalms are. And yet because this psalm includes the sure word of God's promise in his covenant with David, it is more directly prophetic than other psalms. The expository idea will therefore reflect the theology of the oracle of God specifically: *God used the faithfulness of people to reveal his covenant promises, and those promises guarantee a future kingdom of righteousness that will flourish under the reign of the Messiah.*

The faithful congregation of believers still pray for God to fulfill his covenant promises to bring in the kingdom of righteousness in the establishment of the reign of the Messiah. Christians may not identify with the movement of the ark in their ritual worship, but they do demonstrate through ritual acts their identification with those who first received the covenant promises from the Lord Jesus Christ in the upper room. And the significance of this reenactment is that it confirms the inauguration of the new covenant and looks forward to the coming kingdom. On the basis of this and included with it we continue to pray that God will fulfill the promises that he made to us in the new covenant. The promises of the new covenant bring together all the promises that were made in the past, so that the Davidic covenant will ultimately be fulfilled as Jesus the Messiah comes to reign in power and glory to the everlasting joy of the saints and the everlasting shame of his enemies. It is right for us to pray for that, as indeed Christ taught us to do in the Lord's Prayer. To this we may add, "Even so, come quickly, Lord Jesus."

PSALM 133

The Blessing of Unity

INTRODUCTION

Text and Textual Variants

A Song of Ascents. Of David.[1]

1 Indeed, how good and how pleasant it is
   for brothers to live together in unity![2]
2 *It is* like[3] the precious oil *poured* upon the head,
   that runs down[4] on the beard, the beard of Aaron,

---

1. Two manuscripts and some manuscripts of the versions do not have the ascription "of David," but the Qumran scroll does.
2. The Targum has "for Zion and Jerusalem to dwell like two brothers together."
3. The central message of the psalm is developed with the use of similes. For the idea that the latter part of verse 2 is another simile, see Wilfred G. E. Watson, "The Hidden Simile in Psalm 133," *Bib* 60 (1979):108, 9.
4. The MT has יֹרֵד, but one manuscript has the form with the article. The editors of BHS propose reading the participle with the relative pronoun as it appears in verse 3: שֶׁיֹּרֵד, suggesting that in this case the omission was by haplography, the word before יֹרֵד ending with שׁ: הָרֹאשׁ

that runs down upon the edge of his robes.[5]
3 *It is* like the dew of Hermon,
that comes down upon the mountains of Zion;
for there the LORD commands the blessing,
life[6] forevermore.

Composition and Context

Here is a celebration of the blessings of covenant fellowship seen in the unity of brothers. The idea of brothers dwelling together is expressed in rather general terms; nevertheless it has occasioned a good deal of speculation on the original setting of the psalm. It probably was written simply in praise of the ancient custom of brothers dwelling together. But it may reflect a time when tensions between Israel and Judah were still high and Hezekiah was trying to bring them together with his reforms. It could also fit the time when the nation was repopulated after the exile—it certainly would have been appropriately used at such a time. So it would have found great use in the pilgrimage festivals. Anderson says that it is probably post-exilic, but offers no compelling reasons.[7]

The psalm is a pilgrim psalm, but it also has the kinds of expressions, figures of speech, and interest in divine blessing that fit wisdom psalms. It may not be a wisdom psalm precisely, but

---

5. The MT's reading of the "edge of his robes" (מִדּוֹתָיו) is most probably the correct reading, even though this form would normally mean "his measurements" or "his size" and so here might suggest "according to his measurements." Accordingly, some commentators take it to refer to "his body" and not his robes, noting also the difficulty of oil running on the collar under the beard (see O. Keel, "Kultische Brüderlichkeit—Psalm 133," *FZTP* 23 (1976):68–80. But the word can be used for clothing (see Dahood, *Psalms* III, p. 252).
6. The word "life" in the text may be in apposition to "blessing," some translations supplying "even" before it. One manuscript as well as the Greek and Syriac have a conjunction.
7. *Psalms 73–150*, p. 885. See also S. Norin, "Zusammenhang und Datierung," *ASTI* 11 (1978):90–95; Thijs Booij, "Psalm 133," *Bib* 83 (2002):258–67; and Adele Berlin, "On the Interpretation of Psalm 133," in *Directions in Biblical Hebrew Poetry*, JSOT Supplement 40, ed. by Elaine R. Follis (Sheffield: Sheffield Academic Press, 1987):141–47.

it has some of the features of that genre and blends them with worship.[8]

The structure of the psalm may provide a key to its main point. There may be a chiastic structure with a central emphasis on the priesthood of Aaron:

  A. Blessing (1)
     B. Comparison with oil (2a)
        C. Aaron's Ministry (2b)
     B' Comparison with dew (3a)
  A' Blessing (3b)

The text does not readily lend itself to a full chiastic structure, but there certainly is a symmetrical balance to the brief poem with a central focus on Zion and the ritual that took place there.

Exegetical Analysis

Summary

The psalmist extols the blessing of unity that has come down from heaven by comparing it to the anointing oil flowing down on the priest's head and beard and to the dew of Hermon that comes down on Zion where the LORD bestows his blessing.

Outline

  I. The psalmist expresses the appropriateness and the delight of brothers' dwelling together (1).
  II. The psalmist compares their dwelling together to the anointing oil of the priests and the dew of Mount Hermon (2–3a).
     A. It is like the anointing oil that flows down from the priest's head to his beard to his collar (2).
     B. It is like the dew of Mount Hermon falling on Zion (3a).
  III. The psalmist emphasizes that Zion is where the LORD bestows the blessing of life (3b).

---

8. VanGemeren, *Psalms*, p. 935.

COMMENTARY IN EXPOSITORY FORM

I. It is fitting and pleasing for brothers to dwell together (1).

The first verse of the psalm expresses a blessing of sorts, not a formal blessing but certainly an announcement of approval for the inherent goodness and pleasantness of brothers' dwelling together. The verse appears to be a wisdom saying about the life of the extended family in antiquity, but it is used here to make a more important point for the people.

The issue for the verse is the meaning of "dwelling together" (שֶׁבֶת אַחִים גַּם־יָחַד). Many translations use the English "in unity" to capture the meaning, but that may need to be qualified. The expression of dwelling together occurs in Genesis 13:6 and 36:7 where it refers to relatives and related tribes residing as an extended family in an area (not in the same tent). They would do this to defend the family interests and ensure its future. In other words, the expression reflects the responsibilities of those dwelling together and does not simply refer to a peaceful settlement. The expression can be used to refer to sitting down and having a meal together (Judg. 19:6), which is a more specific idea. Another use of this expression is found in Jeremiah 31:24 where it refers to the restoration of Judahites to their land to live together once again. This third sample is essentially the same as the first, but has a specific reference to the time of the restoration.

The psalmist seems to be drawing on this idea of relatives living in a shared area under the paternal roof, so to speak, to share common interests and meet common needs. This kind of unity reflects a greater unity, a spiritual one that will be demonstrated in the pilgrimages to Zion where the blessing of God will be bestowed. Since this is a pilgrim psalm that eventually focuses on the blessing in Zion, it will take the idea to that spiritual level. What is pleasant is the spiritual harmony that brings people together, not just a common relationship or pact.

The pilgrims enjoyed a sense of unity as they traveled from their homes together for the main purpose of worshiping one God, the LORD, in the holy city. When the Israelites went to Jerusalem they celebrated their common heritage and spiritual unity in the covenant. And in the sanctuary they would receive God's blessings on their lives back where they dwelt together. In a sense the unity of the people was both a prerequisite for the blessing and part of the blessing itself.

This "dwelling together" is declared "good" (טוֹב; s.v. Ps. 34:8) and "pleasant" (נָעִים).[9] The unity and harmony that this dwelling together exhibited was conducive to a productive life ("good") and was an enhancement of it ("pleasant" or "delightful"). When this was true, it was one of the most cherished blessings from God. It still is.

II. Unity is a blessing that flows from God (2–3a).

A. *It is like the anointing oil for the priests (2).*

The psalmist first compares the people's dwelling together to the oil that was used to anoint the priest, Aaron. The reference to Aaron, who here represents all priests, immediately brings in the idea of the sanctuary and the blessing that comes from God in anointing the priests. Unity among brothers, then, according to the simile, is from God and sets their relationship apart as spiritual and useful to God.

The anointing oil was a special oil prepared for sanctuary use (Exod. 30:22–33). The ceremony of anointing recalls the wilderness experience described in Leviticus 8. The scene that this brings to mind is of the central tabernacle where the anointing took place and all the tents of the tribes of Israel set up around it.

---

9. The word נָעִים is connected to the verb "be pleasant, delightful, lovely." The verb is used in the Song of Solomon to describe the woman as lovely (7:7); but it also has other uses: the land can be pleasant (Gen. 49:15), a friend can be delightful (2 Sam. 1:26), and words can be pleasant (Ps. 141:6). In the cognate languages the meanings for the verb include lovely, agreeable, pleasant, and plentiful.

The noun נֹעַם, "delightfulness, pleasantness," is used in Psalm 27:4 to describe the LORD as contemplated in the sanctuary. The adjective נָעִים means "delightful, pleasant"; it describes the friendship of David and Jonathan (1 Sam. 1:23), words (Prov. 23:8), wealth (Prov. 24:4), singing praises to the LORD (Ps. 135:3), and of spiritual delights in general (Ps. 16:6, 11). So brothers dwelling in unity is a delightful and pleasant circumstance.

So the unity of the tribes in that place was based on the centrality of the sanctuary; and the importance of the sanctuary was made clear from the divine appointment of the priesthood. Here the comparison emphasizes the "running down" of the oil from the head to the beard to the collar (lit., the edge of the robe, probably the top edge and not the bottom hem). So the two main points of the comparison are that the anointing oil flowed down, and that it covered the head, beard and collar. Thus, the unity of the people was a blessing that came down from heaven and was all-encompassing.

B. It is like the dew from Hermon (3a).

The second simile is the dew of Mount Hermon. This 9,000 foot mountain is in the far north of the land in an area that is known for its moist air, rain, and in the colder season, snow. And the benefit of this much moisture in the air is lush greenery. The problem with this simile if read in a straightforward manner is that the dew of that mountain does not actually descend on Mount Zion, which is Jerusalem, well over a hundred miles to the south. Some scholars try to alleviate the difficulty by changing the text from "Zion" (צִיּוֹן) to "Iyon" (עִיּוֹן), a place in the foothills of Mount Hermon. There is a similarity between the initial letters (a צ for Zion, and ע for Iyon); but there is no real support for this suggestion. A better proposal is to take the line as hypothetical; so the NIV translates it as: "It is as if the dew of Hermon were falling on Mount Zion." The idea would then be that the unity of brothers, perhaps from the northern regions, who were gathered together at the festivals in Zion, was as refreshing to the dry region of Jerusalem as the dew would be in Hermon.

But the text says that it is like the dew that comes down. So perhaps the best explanation is to take the "dew of Hermon" as a fixed expression with "Hermon" qualifying the "dew" (an attributive genitive)–"Hermon-type dew" (טַל־חֶרְמוֹן). Anderson concludes it would be proverbial for heavy dew.[10] However the

---

10. *Psalms 73–150*, p. 886. J. P. M. Van der Ploeg argues against this view, against the idea that it was known for its heavy dew ("Psalm cxxxiii and Its Main Problems," in *Loven en geloven*, *FS* for N. H. Ridderbos [Amsterdam:

The Blessing of Unity

difficulty is explained, the points again are the same as the anointing oil: as the dew comes down from heaven and covers everything, so the unity of brothers is a blessing from God and draws them all together.

Some scholars see here a theme emerging of the binding together of the north (Hermon) and the south (Zion). The point is that Zion, or Jerusalem, is the place where the LORD bestows his blessing, and so the LORD's gifts of unity and life are expected there. But by bringing in Mount Hermon the psalmist was also identifying the bounty of the north with a blessing from the LORD.

If this is taken to be from Hezekiah's time or later, the idea makes sense. But a simple simile in a statement about the blessing of unity is not a lot of evidence for such a view. The psalm is far too brief to build a definitive case. It could have been written at any time to express such a blessing from God, even in the Davidic time; but its message is timeless and so would have been applicable at many times.

III. The LORD bestows the blessings of life in the sanctuary (3b).

The final verse is linked to the contemplation of this unity with the word "there." The immediate reference would be to Mount Zion, the place of the sanctuary and the Aaronic priesthood, and by implication the place where the unity of the people would be the most noticeable. So where there was unity, God would bestow his blessings, even life and all its common joys. The psalm has made a transition from the simple idea of people dwelling together to the sanctuary where the blessings are bestowed. The transition was facilitated by the use of the simile of the anointing oil that made the reader think of the priesthood, and then the application of the dew to Zion as if that were the place all material blessings would begin to be realized.

The verb used in this line is forceful: "he commands" a blessing (צִוָּה; s.v. Ps. 119:6). This construction is rare, being used

---

Ton Bolland, 1975], pp. 191–200). Goldingay suggests the idea of dew with the mention of oil refers to the rains (*Psalms 90–150,* p. 568).

in Leviticus 25:21 and Deuteronomy 28:8 (see also Psalm 42:9). In both Pentateuchal passages it refers to the fertility that God gives for faithfulness to the covenant. So the expression of commanding a blessing may be a priestly idea for the bestowal of covenant blessings for the fertility of the land. At any rate, the whole idea of this blessing harmonizes with the emphasis on their dwelling together in their lands.

Part of this blessing is "life for evermore" (חַיִּים עַד־הָעוֹלָם). It probably does not have as its main idea what we call "eternal life" or "immortality." The emphasis of the blessing in the psalm is on life that continues, the duration of life which includes the perpetuation of the family. And the essence of that blessing of life is the unity of brothers that is good and pleasant.

MESSAGE AND APPLICATION

What at first seems to describe the benefits of an extended family dwelling together in harmony is actually the manifestation of the greater spiritual unity of the people gathered in Zion to receive God's blessing. The psalm is not so much about fraternal harmony (or assembled pilgrims, or reunited tribes) or the unity of brothers as it is about the descent of the blessing from God that truly binds people together in the covenant. As Kidner says, community is praiseworthy, but dependent on the LORD.[11] That blessing is bestowed in the sanctuary, the place where people come together to worship and to pray for it; it is a blessing that brings all the common joys of life to the people who dwell together. The exposition of this psalm could be summarized this way: *The blessing of God brings a delightful and enriching unity to his people.*

Both testaments emphasize the importance of living in peace and harmony with others, most certainly others in the covenant. And that unity should be most evident as people gather in fellowship in the presence of the Lord to worship in common and to realize his renewed blessings. If the blessing of God is not the cause of the unity, then there is very little basis for it. But if that unity is from God, then it brings with it the responsibilities of a community.

---

11. Psalms *73–150*, p. 486.

PSALM 134

Blessing the LORD and Blessing His People

INTRODUCTION

Text and Textual Variants

A Song of Ascents.

1 Come,[1] bless the LORD, all you servants[2] of the LORD
 who stand in the house of the LORD[3] by night.[4]

---

1. The particle הִנֵּה before an imperative is unique; some commentators think it a scribal error, but Allen suggests it was inserted for redactional adaptation, forming a continuity with Psalm 133 (*Psalms 101–150*, p. 216).
2. If the first verse is directed to the priests, this would be the only place the participle of the verb "serve" is used for them—the noun "servant" and the verb "serve" are used frequently for the priests.
3. The Greek version adds a parallel colon ἐν αὐλαῖς οἴκου θεοῦ ἡμῶν, "in the courts of the house of our God," probably from Psalm 135:2.
4. The Greek translation then joins "in the night" to verse 2.

2 Lift up your hands[5] to the sanctuary[6]
 and bless the LORD.
3 May the LORD, the maker of heaven and earth,
 bless you[7] from Zion.

Composition and Context

We come now to the final pilgrim psalm, a "liturgy in miniature" as Anderson calls it,[8] that forms a conclusion to the collection.[9] The psalm falls into two parts: verses 1 and 2 form a hymnic exhortation to praise, and verse 3 records the priestly blessing. In the first two verses the psalm appears to be addressed to the priests in what may be some kind of night vigil, perhaps a concluding blessing at one of the festivals or some other service. It is also possible to interpret these verses as an address to the congregation, although the people would not be standing in the sanctuary through the night. Even if the first part of the psalm is directed to the priests, it would indirectly apply to the congregation because it would call the priests to lead in praising God.

Then, after the call to bless the LORD, a blessing is pronounced either to an individual (the form is singular) or to the assembly addressed collectively. This blessing may be the words of the priests, the servants of the LORD: after they bless the LORD they bless the worshipers. Their blessing may form a benediction for the departing pilgrims.[10]

---

5. Lifting the hands was either a gesture accompanying prayer or praise, here praise, as in Psalm 63:4. The Targum adds here: "O you priests on the platform of (the sanctuary)."
6. The MT is קֹדֶשׁ, "sanctuary," probably meaning the main temple building; but the Greek version uses a plural, τὰ ἅγια, "to the holy places" or precincts.
7. The form in the MT is singular. Either an individual is now being blessed, or the congregation or perhaps the cultic personnel is being addressed collectively (see Num. 6:24).
8. *Psalms 73–150*, p. 887.
9. Psalm 133 does not seem to come to a proper conclusion; and Psalm 134 does not seem to have a proper beginning. The psalms seem to flow together (see Ziony Zevit, "Psalms at the Poetic Precipice," *HAR* 10 [1986]:351–66).
10. See Pierre Auffret, "Note on the Literary Structure of Psalm 134," *JSOT* 45 (1989):87–89.

There is no way to know for sure when the psalm was written, for there is nothing in it that demands an early or a late date.

Exegetical Analysis

Summary

The psalmist calls for the priests who minister in the house of the LORD to praise and bless the LORD with lifted hands, and then records the priestly blessing from Zion.

Outline

I. The psalmist calls for the servants of the LORD who attend to the services in the night seasons to bless the LORD in the sanctuary (1–2).

II. The psalmist records the blessing of the people from Zion (3).

COMMENTARY IN EXPOSITORY FORM

I. The servants of the LORD who attend to the worship regularly must bless the LORD in the sanctuary (1–2).

In the first verse the psalmist addresses the priests directly and calls on them to bless the LORD; the significance of this is that those who are in the sanctuary are there to praise God. The call is expressed in an unusual construction: it begins with the particle (הִנֵּה) that was traditionally translated "behold." Here it is followed by the imperative "bless" (בָּרְכוּ; s.v. Ps. 5:12); it has an added force of calling attention to the command, either "Come, bless the LORD," or "O, bless the LORD."[11] The word "bless" expresses the idea of "praise" here; but it might refer to a specific form of praise to be offered (such as recorded in Deut. 26:1–15). It is praise designed to enhance or enrich God's reputation in the minds of the people.

Those who are called on to bless him are the "servants of the

---
11. Briggs, *Psalms*, II:477.

LORD" (עַבְדֵי יהוה). The expression is rather general; the word "servants" can be used for worshipers in general (see Ps. 135:1; and Isa. 54:17) as well as for priests.[12] In this psalm the details of the text may fit the priests, or temple servants such as Levitical singers better than the general congregation (although it would certainly apply to all who serve the LORD). Psalm 135:19–20 includes the priests as well in its call for praising.

The servants are people "who stand by night in the house of the LORD." The participle "who stand" (עֹמְדִים) means "wait upon, serve" or "minister" (NIV). The expression of "standing" in the sanctuary or at the altar is used elsewhere for the priests (see Deut. 10:8 which says they are to stand before the LORD to minister and to pronounce blessings; see Ezek. 44:15 where they stand to make sacrifices; see also Zech. 3:7; Judg. 20:28 and 2 Chron. 29:11). The priests were chosen to minister in the sanctuary, the house of the LORD, and their serving is described as

---

12. The verb עָבַד "to work, serve," is a common word but has a wide range of application. It can mean labor in the secular sense, as referred to in the Sabbath law (Exod. 20:9). A specific example is the mention of "workers in flax" (Isa. 19:9). This kind of service can also refer to serving another person, such as Jacob's serving Laban (Gen. 31:6), or Israel in bondage (Exod. 1:14). It can have a political application as well, such as serving as subjects of the king (1 Sam. 11:1), or even of kings serving other kings as vassals (Jer. 27:7).

But the religious sense is of more interest here. This word is used in the call of Moses in the sign that the Israelites would serve, i.e., worship, the LORD in the holy mountain (Exod. 3:10). In general it is a word for worship (Ps. 22:31) as people could serve God with sacrifices (Isa. 19:21). It is used for the Levitical service of the LORD in the sanctuary and all that entailed (Num. 3:7, 8; see also 2 Chron. 16:11, 13). The word can also refer to serving other gods (Judg. 2:10 and 10:13).

The noun עֶבֶד has essentially the same range of meanings. It can be used for a household slave (Gen. 38:17, 19), or of a nation as abject slaves (Gen. 9:25), or servants of a king (Gen. 40:20).

In the religious sense the word can describe worshipers in general (Ps. 135:14), which would allow Psalm 134 to refer to people in general. But it more often refers to spiritual leaders such as priests or other temple personnel (Pss. 113:1; 135:1, and possibly 134:1) or prophets (2 Kings 9:7). The title "servant of the LORD" appears to be used for people of particular spiritual magnitude, usually leaders like Moses or David. The title is used in Isaiah for Israel as God's servant, which in places is typological of the Messiah (see e.g., Isa. 42:10; 43:10; 45:4; 49:3; and 52:13).

"standing before the LORD" as an attendant, ready to act on the LORD's instructions.

This passage says that they minister in the house of the LORD, the temple, "in the nights"; the plural may signify "during the nights" or "night after night" (NEB). It is possible that this is a reference to evening services during the great festivals (and so could apply to all worshipers); but according to Psalm 92:3 the priests were to be in the sanctuary (when it was their turn) to proclaim God's faithful love in the morning and in the evening. Their service was to be day and night; they were to give thanks morning and evening, and the musicians were to play morning and evening (1 Chron. 9:33; 23:30). And some of the priests served as watchmen in the sanctuary through the night.

Psalm 134 seems to have been addressed to a group of cultic personnel who were responsible for the evening blessings in the sanctuary. At least we can say that the language suits the ministry of the priests as worshipers in general might not be in the temple precincts at all these times.

In verse 2 the psalmist calls on the priests to bless the LORD in the sanctuary. The line uses a physical description in its call: "Lift up your hands" (a metonymy of adjunct), a gesture that accompanies their praising. People would raise their hands for a number of reasons, such as taking oaths (Numb. 14:30; Deut. 32:40; Gen. 14:22) or making an entreaty (see Lam. 2:19; Isa. 1:15; Ps. 28:2; and 1 Tim. 2:8) as in 1 King 8:30 when Solomon dedicated the temple with his lengthy prayer, or in giving the priestly benediction (Lev. 9:22). But in this psalm it goes with the praising of the LORD (Ps. 63:4).

This was to take place in the holy place (קֹדֶשׁ; s.v. Ps. 22:3), the sanctuary. This word could also be taken in an abstract sense, "in holiness." But in the context it is more likely an accusative of location, "in the sanctuary," the temple.

II. Ministers of the LORD are to declare the blessing of the people (3).

After this call for the LORD to be blessed, the psalm includes the blessing for the people. Here too it could be argued that the worshipers may have given this blessing to one another, but it was the place of the priests to do this and so they are likely the speakers. According to the sequence of this psalm, then, there is a close connection between praising God and bestowing the blessing: the praise would have been offered for how the LORD had already blessed the people and the blessing would express the expectation of continued blessings.

When the priests lifted their hands in the sanctuary it often accompanied the giving of the priestly blessing (see Lev. 9:22 when Aaron blessed the people). Here it seems that the priests were being called on to bless God with their praise, and then bless the people (see Psalm 128:5; 118:26). The great priestly blessing recorded in Numbers 6:24–25 is an oracle announcing the blessing of the LORD on the participants in worship: "The LORD bless you and keep you, the LORD make his face shine upon you and be gracious unto you, the LORD lift up his face towards you and give you peace." Here the blessing is much simpler: "May the LORD, the maker of heaven and earth, bless you from Zion." This wording is similar to that used in the blessing of Abram by Melchizedek in Genesis 14. Whoever voiced the blessing, it was worded in such a way as to remind people that it is God who blesses, not the speakers. He is described here as "the maker of heaven and earth," a description that recalls Psalm 121:2, an earlier pilgrim psalm. "Heaven and earth" is a common figure (a merism), meaning the whole of creation and everything in it. As a description of the one who is the source of all blessing this epithet is significant: God had already blessed the world in and through creation—that is why they were there giving thanks; now God's anticipated action of blessing them and their flocks and fields would recall the substance of their praise and thanksgiving to him at the festival.[13]

As noted previously, the word "bless" (בָּרַךְ; s.v. Ps. 5:12) has the basic idea of enrichment; and that enrichment God provides could be material or spiritual. Here the verb (a jussive for the blessing) has a singular suffix "you" (יְבָרֶכְךָ; see Ps. 128:5), probably functioning as a collective to refer to the congregation. This blessing would come from the LORD from Mount Zion, the

---
13. See N. C. Habel, "Yahweh, Maker of Heaven and Earth: A Study in Textual Criticism," *JBL* 91 (1972):321–37.

chosen place for the sanctuary of the LORD. The proclamation fits the understanding that the temple in Jerusalem was the religious center from which God's blessings flowed, and so the very place to which the pilgrims ascended regularly for the great festivals (see Isa. 2:3 and Mic. 4:2). This is the kind of blessing that would form a benediction as the pilgrims began to depart from the holy city, and so the verse appropriately ends the collection of the pilgrim psalms.

MESSAGE AND APPLICATION

This little psalm, then, addresses the priests, and at least indirectly the worshipers; it calls for them to praise the LORD and then records the blessing of the people. Such words of blessing, to God and to the people, were at the heart of all worship in the sanctuary. The point is that out of the praise for the LORD would come blessing for the people: when priests led the people in giving thanks and praise to God they would be focusing on God's bounty to them; and as the people had come to the sanctuary to offer their thanksgiving to God for the bounty of life, they would expect to receive an oracle of further blessing. The psalm may have been an extended summons to worship, perhaps a summons to the final benediction or the closing of an evening vigil (see Isa. 30:29), or perhaps as part of an ordinary service (1 Chron. 9:33). But it reflects the wider liturgy in use in the services.

The expository point of the psalm is straightforward: *When the servants of the LORD bless the LORD in the sanctuary they will in turn proclaim the LORD's blessing on his people.* This has not changed over the years, even though the external forms of worship have. Ministers, leading the worshipers, must bless the LORD in the sanctuary; and as they bless him for his bounty they will anticipate his continued blessing on the people. Or to put it another way, those who proclaim God's word of blessing on others do so as a part of their offering blessing to God for all his bounty. So as faithful messengers they only bless what God promises to bless, and what God promises requires faith.

PSALM 135

Praise for the Lord of Creation and History

INTRODUCTION

Text and Textual Variants

Praise the LORD![1]

1 Praise the name of the LORD!
   Praise, O servants of the LORD,[2]
2 who stand in the house of the LORD,
   in the courts of the house of our God!
3 Praise the LORD, for the LORD is good;
   sing praises to his name, for it is pleasant![3]
4 For the LORD[4] has chosen Jacob for himself,
   Israel for his own possession.[5]

---
1. הַלְלוּ־יָהּ
2. The Greek does not take this as a construct, "servants of the LORD," but translates it as "Praise, O servants, the LORD" (δοῦλοι Κύριον).
3. The MT has נָעִים, "pleasant, fitting"; the Greek has καλόν, "good, beautiful."
4. The text has יָהּ here.
5. The Greek has "for his peculiar treasure."

761

PSALM 135

5 For I know that greater is the LORD,
    even our Lord, than all gods.
6 All that the LORD pleases, he does;
    in heaven and on earth
    in the seas and all[6] the deeps.
7 *It is he who* brings up the clouds from the end of the earth,
    who makes lightning for the rain
        and brings the wind out of his storehouses;
8 who struck down the firstborn of Egypt,
    from people to animals;
9 he sent into your[7] midst, O Egypt, signs and portents
    against Pharaoh and all his servants;[8]
10 who struck down many nations
    and killed mighty kings,
11 Sihon, king of the Amorites,
    and Og, king of Bashan,
    and all the kingdoms of Canaan,[9]
12 and gave their land *as* an inheritance,
    an inheritance for his people Israel.

13 O LORD, your name *endures* forever,
    O LORD, your renown throughout all ages.
14 For the LORD will vindicate his people
    and have compassion[10] on his servants.

---

6. The majority of the manuscripts, Greek and Syriac have "and in all."
7. Because the direct address to Egypt with the pronoun "your" seems out of place in the contextual sequence, many commentators have tried to find ways to explain the pronominal suffix כִי differently. Allen suggests it is an emphatic particle, and so the line should just read "the midst of Egypt" (*Psalms 101–150*, p. 286). There is no strong support for such a change; the MT finds confirmation in the Greek text. The more difficult reading should be retained; it is perfectly clear; its only problem is it does not make for a consistent pattern in the lines.
8. If the text was following the historical chronology, verse 9 (the plagues) should precede verse 8 (the death of the firstborn). But these are simply poetic recollections of major events at the time of the exodus.
9. Each of the three cola in this verse is prefixed with a *lamed*. It is probably to be taken as an emphatic particle and not the preposition.
10. The MT has יִתְנֶחָם; the Greek translation has "comfort himself" or "be consoled (concerning)" ($\pi\alpha\rho\alpha\kappa\lambda\eta\vartheta\dot{\eta}\sigma\varepsilon\tau\alpha\iota$).

15 The idols of the nations are silver and gold,
   the work[11] of human hands.
16 They have mouths, but cannot speak;
   they have eyes, but cannot see;
17 they have ears, but cannot hear,
   nor is there[12] any breath in their mouths.
18 Those who make them will be like them,[13]
   so *will*[14] all who trust in them!

19 O house of Israel, bless the LORD!
   O house of Aaron, bless the LORD!
20 O house of Levi, bless the LORD!
   You who fear the LORD, bless the LORD!
21 Blessed be the LORD from[15] Zion,
   he who dwells in Jerusalem!

Praise the LORD![16]

Composition and Context

This psalm is a hymn, praising God as the sovereign creator and the Lord of history. Its message is an expansion of Psalm 134; and its contents are composed of many citations from and allusions to other scriptures. Kirkpatrick describes it well when he writes, "Though the psalm is little more than a mosaic of fragments and reminiscences from the the Law, Prophets, and other Psalms, it possesses real vigor of rhythm and spirit."[17] Anderson

---

11. The Greek and a few manuscripts have "works."
12. The line makes use of a pleonastic form, אַף אֵין־יֶשׁ־רוּחַ, "there is not - there is - breath (in their mouth)." Some commentators propose deleting יֶשׁ, but there is no reason to do so because while the form is difficult it is not impossible. And besides, the pleonastic form makes no difference in the translation.
13. The Greek text interprets יִהְיוּ as "let them become." The jussive would be expected in a lament, but not in a hymn like this.
14. Several manuscripts and versions have "and."
15. The Greek translation has "in."
16. The Greek version joins this word to the next psalm as a prologue.
17. *Psalms,* p. 773.

suggests that the apparent dependence on passages like Psalms 115 and 136 may be largely due to familiarity with liturgical expressions.[18] The psalmist may have drawn on many passages, but in the final analysis his composition makes a distinct contribution to the collection.

The psalm formed part of a collection that was called the Great Hallel, although there was some disagreement among Jewish scholars concerning what psalms were to be included. This psalm's classification as a Hallel psalm indicates that it would have been used regularly at the great festivals, Passover in particular.

Psalm 135 follows the pattern of a descriptive praise psalm, or hymn. There is the call to praise in verses 1–4, the cause for the praise in verse 5–18, and the conclusion in verses 19–21. The cause for praise first declares that the LORD is sovereign over creation and history (vv. 5–14) and then greater than all gods (vv. 15–18). This latter section focuses on the uselessness of idols in contrast to the LORD.

Exegetical Analysis

Summary

The psalmist calls upon the priests of Israel to praise the LORD because he is the true and living God, the lord of creation and history.

Outline

    Praise the LORD!
I. The Call to Praise: The psalmist calls ministers in the sanctuary to praise the LORD because he is good and because he chose the people of Israel for himself (1–4).
    A. All servants of the LORD should praise him (1).
    B. Priests who minister in his presence should praise the LORD (2).
    C. Praise is appropriate for the LORD because he is good (3).

---

18. *Psalms 73–150*, p. 889

D. The LORD should be praised because he chose the people of Israel for himself (4).
II. Cause for Praise: The psalmist explains that they should praise the LORD because he is the only true and living God, the lord of creation and history (5–18).
   A. The LORD, who is greater than all gods, controls his creation as he pleases (5–7).
      1. He is greater than the pagan gods (5).
      2. He is sovereign over heaven and earth, the sea and the deeps (6).
   B. This sovereign LORD delivered his people from bondage and gave them the land of Canaan for an inheritance (8–12).
      1. He delivered Israel from Egypt with signs and portents (8–10).
      2. He destroyed the Canaanites to give Israel its inheritance (11–12).
   C. The LORD is praised because he has compassion on his people and vindicates them (13–14).
   D. The LORD, who is mightier than the pagan gods, is the only true God (15–18).
      1. Pagan idols were created by men (15).
      2. The LORD is the only true and living God (16–18).
III. The Conclusion: The psalmist calls all ministers to bless the LORD who dwells in their midst in Jerusalem (19–21). Praise the LORD!

COMMENTARY IN EXPOSITORY FORM

I. Those who minister in the sanctuary should praise the LORD because of his goodness in choosing a people for himself (1–4).

The beginning of the call to praise is a continuation of Psalm 134:1–2, and similar to that of Psalm 113:1. Those called to praise are the "servants of the LORD who stand in the house of the LORD." In light of Psalm 134, the descriptions given here would apply to ministering priests, although it is not impossible that others who worship and serve the LORD in the temple are included. The foundational reason that they should praise is that the LORD is good (טוֹב; s.v. Ps. 34:8), which is paralleled with "it [his name] *is* pleasant" (נָעִים; s.v. Ps. 133:1). The last statement of the verse could be interpreted to mean that singing praises is pleasant or appropriate, or that the name is pleasant, in which case "pleasant" is a synonym for "good." Both make very good sense, and so commentators and translators are divided over the way to read it. A tight parallelism would favor taking it as a description of the LORD, making the goodness and pleasantness of the LORD the foundational reason for praise (see Prov. 23:8).

The evidence of God's goodness lies in what he does, namely his gracious works. Verse 4 provides a specific example of this: The LORD chose the people of Israel for his own possession (see Exod. 19:5; Deut. 7:6; 14:2; Mal. 3:17; and Ps. 114:2)—the redeemed belong to the LORD! Anderson observes that this is the true value of Israel—it was a nation chosen by God.[19] To be chosen to be the LORD's "special possession" has a number of ramifications.[20] Allen gathers from the study of the term (סְגֻלָּה) that its uses in extra-biblical texts shows overtones of alliance and worship.[21] Such a special relationship with God naturally requires that the redeemed be a holy nation in order to serve as a kingdom of priests.

II. The LORD should be praised because he is the true and living God, the Lord of creation and history (5–18).

A. *Praise the LORD because he is sovereign over all creation (5–7).*

Public praise now begins with a personal expression, "For I know." The use of the pronoun with the verb makes the psalmist's confession of faith emphatic. What he knows is that the LORD is greater than all gods. These are words that Jethro

---

19. *Psalms 73–150*, p. 890.
20. See further B. E. Shafer, "The Root *bhr* and Pre-exilic Concepts of Chosenness in the Hebrew Bible," ZAW 89 (1977):20–42.
21. *Psalms 101–150*, p. 290.

used in Exodus 18:11 when he met Moses and Israel after the great deliverance from Egypt. It is the kind of confession of faith that any believer could make, especially the Israelites as they remembered the events at Passover. The faithful Israelites—for whom the psalmist speaks—certainly knew this truth. But the nations who worship false gods do not know the greatness of the LORD, for they are blinded by their belief in worthless gods. The psalmist at this point is not allowing that their gods are actually gods; he is simply stressing the point that the so-called gods the nations worship were nothing compared to the greatness of the LORD.

To portray the greatness of the LORD, the psalmist turns directly to creation, the most important and the greatest work of God, especially in response to pagan beliefs (vv. 6–7). Here we read that in all of creation—in heaven and on earth, in the seas and in the deeps—the LORD has unlimited authority because he made everything. He does just as he pleases (see Ps. 115:3). He brings up the clouds, makes the lightening for the rain, and brings out the wind, as if from storehouses. All of these things are caused by the sovereign LORD God, not by some pagan gods, and not by chance. These descriptions of the sovereignty of the LORD were used elsewhere in the Bible, especially in the prophets, to show the impotence of idols (compare Jer. 10:13; 51:16; Ps. 33:7 and Job 38:22).

The people of God in any age must never lose sight of the fact that the LORD is the creator, and as the creator he has absolute power over all of nature. Without the doctrine of creation, there is no fall, no sin, no need for redemption or resurrection, and no reason to praise the LORD. But because the LORD is the creator and the redeemer, he is to be praised forever.

B. Praise the LORD because he is lord of history (8–12).

He is also sovereign over history, a truth constantly demonstrated in the Bible with regard to Israel. Verses 8 and 9 focus on the deliverance of Israel from Egypt—an amazing demonstration of the power of God over nature and of his desire to create a new people for himself. The verses are in the reverse order for the historical chronology, but then this whole section is a poetic reflection on a few selected events from Israel's history—the plagues in Egypt (vv. 8–9), the defeat of the Canaanite kings (vv. 10–12), and the gift of the land as Israel's inheritance (v. 11). Very few details of the exodus are given here, but believers would naturally recall all the details related to the great plagues and the death of the firstborn of Egypt, because they rehearsed them at Passover when this psalm was also being recited.

Verses 10–11 recall victories over the kings of Transjordan, Sihon and Og and the other kingdoms of Canaan. These were Israel's strategic victories in the conquest; but the names Sihon and Og stand out and serve to focus the memory on the great events of this period (see Num. 21:21–4; 21:33f.; Deut. 2:30–33; and 3:1–6).

Finally, the last verse of this section (11) mentions Israel's inheritance. The people were the possession of the LORD, but he gave the land to them as their inheritance. And these are both clear manifestations of the goodness and grace of God for which he is to be praised.

C. Praise the LORD because in compassion he vindicates his people (13–14).

The psalmist breaks into praise at this point, addressing the LORD directly. He proclaims, "O LORD, your name endures forever, O LORD, your renown throughout all ages." His "name" (s.v. Ps. 20:1) and his "renown" (s.v. Ps. 6:5) recall the revelation of the LORD to Moses in Exodus 3:15, 6:3, 6–8. The renown, the fame, of the LORD increases with every intervention. And the psalmist knows that there are many of these: he says with confidence, "The LORD will vindicate (יָדִין; s.v. Ps. 140:2) his people and have compassion (יִתְנֶחָם; s.v. Ps. 119:76) on his servants" (see Deut. 32:36). God's compassion for his people motivates him to vindicate them by delivering them from their enemies, now and finally at the end of the age.

D. Praise the LORD because he is the only living and powerful God (15–18).

The LORD is the only true God, a fact that his been proven

again and again by his mighty works on Israel's behalf. The psalmist makes this point by describing the worthlessness of the false gods. The verses form a polemic against pagan beliefs; they come from Psalm 115:4–8. First, we are reminded that false gods are made by human beings out of silver and gold—they are created matter, and to worship them is to worship what was created and not the creator. Moreover, they are made by men and have all the limitations of humans (see also Isa. 44:9–20). Secondly, they are impotent—worthless (vv. 16–17). The idols have mouths, but they cannot speak (the potential imperfect fits the idea the best); eyes, but cannot see; and ears, but cannot hear. In fact, there is no breath at all in them. They are lifeless, manmade statues.[22] The faithful could see the contrast immediately: the LORD is the only true God; he speaks and reveals his will, he watches over his people, he hears their cries and prayers and does mighty works on their behalf. He is the living God.

The devotion of the pagans to their gods is futile (v. 18). Those who make these gods, and those who trust in them, will become like them. In other words, what is true of their gods is true of them (see Isa. 44:19). Perowne adds that the pagans turned from worshiping the creator to worshiping created things, and consequently they became spiritually blind, deaf and dumb, like the gods that they worshiped, even though they did not realize this even when their impotent gods could not help them.[23] They were destined for destruction by the living judge of the whole world.

III. The LORD should be blessed by all who serve him in the sanctuary because even though he is the sovereign Lord of creation and history he dwells in the midst of his people (19–21).

In the last three verses of the psalm we have a renewed call for praise. This final appeal for adoration corresponds to the

---

22. The Israelites knew that there were many evil spirits in the world that posed a serious threat to life, but they were not in fact real gods. In passages like this the writers affirm that pagan beliefs in such "gods" was futile, for there is only one true God—Yahweh.
23. *Psalms,* II:330.

prayer at the end of Psalm 134 (and is similar to Pss. 115:9ff. and 118:2ff). Five times the section uses the imperative "bless" (בָּרְכוּ; s.v. Ps. 5:12), the natural response to the way that the LORD blesses his people (see Pss. 133:3, 134:3). The call is addressed to all who fear the LORD, the congregation of Israel (literally, "house of Israel") and the priests (literally, "house of Aaron"). Another group is specified: the Levites ("the house of Levi"). By using the figure of "house" to represent people, the psalmist is emphasizing their unity and common origin, much as one might refer to the royal family descended from David as the house of David.

The last line of the psalm offers the praise, "Blessed be the LORD (בָּרוּךְ יְהוָה) from Zion" and provides a fitting reason in the epithet, "who dwells in Jerusalem". The living God chose Israel as his people, settled them in their land as his possession, and chose to dwell among them as their God. Kirkpatrick explains that the blessings of God came "from Zion," where the people assembled to worship; and so from that holy place must ring out the people's answer of adoring praises.[24]

When the nation rebelled against the LORD the praises were not ringing out (see Ps. 137), and the LORD was not present with the people; but the righteous were steadfast in their faith that God's desire to dwell among his people in the holy city would yet be fully realized (see Ps. 132:13–16). And when the LORD delivered his people they rejoiced that the LORD had done great things for them (see Ps. 126). So this hymn could be sung in times of trouble to inspire hope; but it could also be sung with great enthusiasm when God delivered his people, thus revealing his sovereignty over creation, history and the gods of the pagans.

The psalm ends with an epilogue to match the prologue: "Praise the LORD."

MESSAGE AND APPLICATION

The psalm focuses on the greatness and the goodness of the LORD displayed in his sovereignty over creation, history and pagan beliefs. The exposition, therefore, will encourage believers

---

24. *Psalms*, pp. 775–76.

to praise the LORD for these and related mighty acts of God: *All servants of the LORD, his ministers especially, must praise the LORD as the one true and living God who is lord of creation and history.* The ministers of the congregation must lead in the praise and inspire and instruct the people to praise as well. When the people of God remember his mighty works, the redemption of Israel from Egypt, the protection of them on the way to the promised land, and the granting to them an inheritance, they will find much to say about God in praise. And with each additional divine intervention should come further praise. Kidner notes that the creeds of the church follow the same pattern as Israel's ancient hymns and use the same language: creation, redemption, and then the consummation of the promises at the second coming (see Tit. 2:14; 1 Pet. 2:9–10).[25]

Now, though, in the new covenant the household of faith must praise God for the great redemption in Christ, for the provisions and protection God gives his people along the way, and for the inheritance that he has given to his people—all due to the goodness and grace of the Lord (see Eph. 1–2).

---

25. *Psalms 73–150*, p. 456.,

PSALM 136
Praise for the LORD's Enduring Love

INTRODUCTION

Text and Textual Variants

1 Give thanks to[1] the LORD, for he is good,
   for his loyal love endures forever.
2 Give thanks to the God of gods,
   for his loyal love endures forever.
3 Give thanks to the Lord of lords,
   for his loyal love endures forever;

---

1. I have retained this familiar translation here even though the modern understanding of giving thanks is not what the verb fully means. The word used (והדו; s.v. Ps. 6:5) would more accurately be rendered "acknowledge (the LORD)," for it refers to a public acknowledgment of who the LORD is and what he has done.

PSALM 136

4 who[2] alone does great[3] wonders,
   for his loyal love endures forever;
5 who by understanding made the heavens,
   for his loyal love endures forever;
6 who spread out the earth above the waters,
    for his loyal love endures forever;
7 who made the great lights,
   for his loyal love endures forever;[4]
8 the sun to have authority over the day,
   for his loyal love endures forever;
9 the moon and stars to have authority over the night,
   for his loyal love endures forever;

10 who struck down Egypt with their firstborn,
   for his loyal love endures forever;
11 and brought Israel out from among them,
   for his loyal love endures forever;
12 with a strong hand and an outstretched arm,
   for his loyal love endures forever;

13 who divided the Red Sea in two,
   for his loyal love endures forever;
14 and brought Israel out through the midst of it,
   for his loyal love endures forever;
15 and swept Pharaoh and his army into the Red Sea,
   for his loyal love endures forever;
16 who led his people through the wilderness,

---

2. The translation requires something to be supplied or changed; the text literally has "to the doer," or "to the one doing," that is, "give thanks . . . to the one doing . . . ." Some translations simply paraphrase what the preposition and participle say and translate the construction throughout as a verb: "he does . . . ." I have chosen to use "to *the one who* does . . . ," and then follow it up in the other occurrences with "*who* made," etc., leaving the preposition out of the translation because it is clear that the praise is to be given to the one who did this or that
3. Many commentators delete the word "great" to achieve a better meter for the line. Qumran (*11QPs^a*) omits it, but there is not very much strong support for its removal..
4. The Qumran scroll adds a verse between verses 7 and 8: "the sun and the moon, for his loyal love endures forever."

> for his loyal love endures forever;
> 17 who struck down great kings,
>   for his loyal love endures forever;
> 18 and killed mighty kings,
>   for his loyal love endures forever;
> 19 Sihon, king of the Amorites,
>   for his loyal love endures forever;
> 20 and Og, king of Bashan,
>   for his loyal love endures forever;
> 21 and gave their land as a heritage,
>   for his loyal love endures forever;
> 22 a heritage to Israel his servant,
>   for his loyal love endures forever;
>
> 23 It is he who remembered us in our low estate,
>   for his loyal love endures forever;
> 24 and rescued us from our foes,
>   for his loyal love endures forever;
> 25 who gives food to all flesh,
>   for his loyal love endures forever;
> 26 Give thanks to the God of heaven,
>   for his loyal love endures forever.

Composition and Context

In later Jewish tradition, Psalm 136 is listed as the last psalm in the collection known as the Great Hallel, if not the Great Hallel psalm itself. Hallel psalms were designated to be sung at the festivals of Israel, especially the Passover. Some scholars who identify many of the psalms with the fall festival, naturally think that it was originally to be used at New Years or Tabernacles.

We do not know when this hymn was actually written, but its meaning and intended use are clear nonetheless. It is a hymn that was written for antiphonal use in a communal setting. The unique feature about it is that the second colon in each line has the refrain, "for his loyal love endures forever." This repeated liturgical response may have been said or sung by a Levitical choir or the congregation. In a simple reading of the psalm it may seem to be a monotonous repetition, but it is actually a forceful refrain.[5] It focuses the attention of the congregation on the LORD's intervention by his loyal love.[6]

The structure follows the pattern of a hymn: there is a call to praise (vv. 1–3), a lengthy cause for the praise (vv. 4–25), and a concluding call for praise (v. 26). So the beginning (vv. 1–3) and the ending (v. 26) call for praise, leaving no doubt what the primary application must be. The cause for this praise embraces some of the greatest acts of God: creation (vv. 4–9), redemption (vv. 10–16), provision for his people (17–22), and finally an actualization of the love of God seen in his care for his creation (23–25).[7]

There have been other proposals for the structure. VanGemeren sees a chiasm here: creation (vv. 4–9), redemption (vv. 10–22), redemption (vv. 23–24), and creation (v. 25).[8] These labels must be used in a wide sense for this to work. Others simply divide the section into cosmic features (vv. 4–9) and historical references (vv. 10–22). And as far as the metrical pattern goes, Kirkpatrick noted that the first six sections have three lines each (through verse 18), and then the last two have four lines each through verse 25.[9]

Exegetical Analysis

Summary

The psalmist calls for praise to be given to the LORD who performed the great wonders of creation and redemption through his loyal love.

---

5. Anderson, *Psalms 73–150*, p. 893. For many in the congregation (then and now) it would be monotonous if simply read routinely. But with devoted concentration it is life-giving—as with all Scripture.
6. Kidner names the psalm "His love has no end," after the translation by Gelineau (*Psalms 73–150*, p. 457).
7. This basically follows the arrangement Allen has for the psalm (*Psalms 101–150*, p. 297).
8. *Psalms*, p. 944.
9. *Psalms*, p. 776; see further J. Bazak, "The Geometric-Figurative Structure of Psalm cxxxvi," *VT* 35 (1985):129–38.

Praise for the LORD's Enduring Love

Outline

I. Call to praise: The psalmist calls for praise to be given to the LORD for his everlasting love (1–3).
  A. He calls for praise to the LORD because he is good (1).
  B. He calls for praise to the LORD who is the supreme God of all (2).
  C. He calls for praise to the LORD who is the absolute sovereign (3).
II. Cause for praise: The psalmist delineates the marvelous acts of God in creation, redemption, and conquest as the cause for praising him for his loyal love (4–25).
  A. The LORD did great wonders when he created everything (4–9).
    1. He does great wonders because of his loyal love (4).
    2. He did wonderful works of creation through his loyal love (5–9).
      a. He made the heavens (5).
      b. He stretched out the earth over the seas (6).
      c. He made the great lights in the heavens (7–9).
  B. The LORD did wonderful works in redeeming Israel by his loyal love (10–16).
    1. He triumphed over Egypt because of loyal love (10–15).
      a. He smote the first born and led Israel out (10–12).
      b. He severed the Red Sea (13–15).
    2. He triumphed over the wilderness because of his loyal love (16).
  C. The LORD did wonderful works in conquering the land through his loyal love (17–22).
    1. He struck down many great kings (17–20).
    2. He gave Israel the land and preserved them in it (21–22).
  D. The LORD does wonderful works in protecting and caring for his people (23–25)
    1. He is faithful in protecting his people (23–24).
    2 He provides food for his creation (25).
III. Conclusion: The psalmist calls everyone to praise the LORD because of his loyal love (26).

COMMENTARY IN EXPOSITORY FORM

I. The LORD should be praised for his everlasting love because he alone is the sovereign Lord God (1–3)

The call for praise uses a familiar expression repeatedly: "Give thanks to the LORD . . . for his loyal love endures forever" (e.g., Ps. 107:1; 2 Chron. 7:3, 6). The verb "Give thanks" calls for a public acknowledgment of what the LORD has done (for the verb הוֹדוּ, s.v. Ps. 6:5). The initial reason for this call is that the LORD is "good" (טוֹב; s.v. Ps. 34:8). Everything about the LORD and everything that he does is gracious and life-giving. The second colon, the refrain, links his goodness to his covenant faithfulness. "Loyal love" (חֶסֶד; s.v. Ps. 23:6) refers to God's faithful covenant love, even though it has been given more general translations. The point of the refrain is that God is faithful to his covenant and to his covenant people—"his Covenant loyalty is endless."[10]

Verses 2 and 3 focus on the supreme majesty of the LORD. He is described as the "God of gods" and the "Lord of lords" (from Deut.10:17). The constructions are superlative genitives, meaning that he is God over all, and he is the supreme Lord. Referring to other gods does not mean that the psalmist was acknowledging them as real gods; it is simply his way of saying that Yahweh is the one true God and Lord over all.

What did the LORD do for his people that prompted them to sing praises for his faithful covenant love? Since we have no clear indication of the occasion for the psalm, we can only speculate. But because of the emphasis on the LORD's absolute sovereignty as well as his faithfulness to the covenant, it must have been written in celebration of a great deliverance. It may fit the best with the community of believers who survived the exile and were restored to the land (as Psalm 118). However, that was by no means the only event in Israel's history that was a marvelous display of God's faithful love.

---

10. Anderson, *Psalms 73–150*, p. 894.

II. The LORD deserves praise for his loyal love because of the mighty works he has done for his creation (4–25).

A. Because of his loyal love he created the heavens and the earth (4–9).

The heart of a hymn is the reason for the praise; it not only motivates the worshipers to praise but gives them the content of their praise.[11] Verse 4 reads like a general summary for the section: "(to the one who) alone does great wonders, for his loyal love . . . ." The following verses will recall many of these wonders, works that were surpassingly extraordinary—supernatural (נִפְלָאוֹת; s.v. Ps. 139:5).

The next few verses describe the wonders of creation.[12] The statement that he made the heavens by understanding recalls Proverbs 3:19. Creation is the result and evidence of the wisdom and understanding of God (see Prov. 8). The LORD also spread out the earth above the waters. The verb "spread out" (רָקַע, "to beat out") suggests the image of a thin sheet of metal spread over the subterranean waters (compare Psalm 24:2).[13]

Verses 7–9 mention the heavenly hosts. The "great lights" in the heavens reminds the congregation of the creation account of Genesis. These lights are the sun to rule the day and the moon and stars to rule the night. Several commentators prefer to delete "and the stars" to improve the meter and to harmonize the idea with Genesis 1:16—the stars were not said to rule the night.

At any rate, the basic point in this section is that God alone created everything in all its wondrous glory as a display of his everlasting covenant love. Believers needed to be reminded that they entered into covenant with the sovereign creator of the universe—and this is true today as well. All God's works are wonderful and purposeful; the lights in the heavens are not only glorious, but have their dominion as well.

---

11. See P. D. Miller, "Psalm 136:1–9, 23–26," *Int* 49 (1995):390–93.
12. See further N. C. Habel, "'Yahweh, Maker of Heaven and Earth': A Study in Tradition Criticism," *JBL* 91 (1972):321–37.
13. See Anderson, *Psalms 73–150*, p. 895. The cognate word in Genesis 1 is translated "firmament."

B. Because of his loyal love he redeemed his people from bondage (10–16).

The subject now changes to the LORD's redemption of Israel out of bondage,[14] singling out the tenth plague, the exodus, and the conquest. The text here repeats motifs found in Psalm 135:8–12. The hymn is not designed to be complete; it is a poetic reflection on significant examples of God's wonders. This section begins by recalling how the LORD struck down Egypt and its firstborn and brought Israel out from among them (vv. 10–11). This was done, verse 12 explains, "with a strong hand and an outstretched arm," a frequent poetic description of the powerful intervention of the LORD (see for example Exod. 6:1, 6; and Deut. 4:34, 5:15, and 26:8); the figures (anthropomorphisms) are idiomatic of God's powerful acts; it is as if he stretched out his hand to strike Egypt.

Then we are to recall that he divided the sea and brought Israel through it (vv. 13–14). The word "divided" (גֹּזֵר) literally means "to cut," and so the expression could be interpreted to say he cut the sea in pieces, perhaps hinting at a polemic against pagan beliefs concerning the sea god. Then, when the text says that he "swept" Pharaoh and his army into the sea (v. 15), the choice of words emphasizes how effortless this act was, for the verb (נִעֵר) means to "shake off." The LORD was simply shaking off Pharaoh and his army—they were powerless before him. In his hymn on "The Hundred-Thirty-Sixth Psalm," Milton writes: "The floods stood still like walls of glass, / While the Hebrew bands did pass. . . . / But full soon they did devour / The tawny king with all his power."[15] There was no real challenge from Pharaoh and his gods to the God of gods.

Verse 16 continues the account of the deliverance from bondage with an emphasis on the LORD's leading his people through the wilderness (see Deut. 8:15). It is a plain statement of fact, but the people would remember the many events that

---

14. See B. S. Childs, "Deuteronomic Formulae of the Exodus Traditions," *VT* Supplement 16 (Leiden: Brill, 1967), pp. 30–39.
15. *The Poets' Book of Psalms,* edited by Laurance Wieder (Oxford: Oxford University Press, 1995), p. 201.

made up that wilderness trek, notably how the LORD again and again provided for and protected his people.

C. Because of his loyal love he provided an inheritance for his people (17–22).

Reasons for praise now come from the mighty works that the LORD did in the period of the conquest. Verses 17 and 18 simply report that the LORD destroyed many mighty kings. The historical texts describe how Israel fought the battles, but it was God who was enabling them to do this (for example, see Exod. 17:1–7). The psalmist singles out Sihon, the king of the Amorites, and Og, the king of Bashan, the two powerful kings in Transjordan that represent the Canaanite kingdoms (vv. 19–20). Israel had to fight these kings in order to gain access to the land. Here the names are grammatically in apposition to the great kings that the LORD defeated, identifying significant kings. Israel had to fight these kings in order to gain access to the land.

The result of these victories was that God gave the land of Canaan to Israel as its inheritance (see Ps. 135:12). Once he dispossessed the Canaanite kings, the LORD enabled Israel to possess their land. This inheritance was the intended culmination of the redemption from Egypt and the conquest of the Canaanite kings. But it was an inheritance that came with responsibilities, for the nation is referred to here as "his servant Israel," an expression used frequently for the nation in Isaiah 41. The people would learn that obedience to the Lord of the covenant would allow them to remain in the land and enjoy their inheritance.

At every point along the way the antiphon would affirm that the LORD's loyal love is everlasting. Every wonderful and amazing work that he did was a demonstration of his faithful love. The psalm did not dwell on Israel's failure to trust the LORD that led to the wilderness wandering, the open rebellions, the constant murmuring against the LORD, and the sin with the golden calf—the people knew all about those events. Rather, it focused on the LORD's wonderful acts of covenant love—which were even more praiseworthy considering how many times Israel failed.

D. Because of his loyal love he protects and provides for his people (23–24).

The last two verses of the central section of the psalm convey how the LORD has demonstrated his faithful love to the nation in general. No longer does the psalmist provide historical examples; rather, he actualizes the love of God for the immediate congregation. It is the LORD "who remembered us in our low estate . . . and rescued us from our foes." God acted on behalf of this, his people. The description "our low estate" could fit any number of occasions, for Israel was in many life-threatening difficulties, many of them of their own making. The reference could be to one of them, possibly to the time of the Judges (since the historical sequence ends with the settlement in the land), or, as most would say, it could simply be a general reference covering from the time of the settlement in the land until the restoration from the exile. No matter what low estate the Israelites experienced, even exile, the covenant program of God continued for his loyal love endures forever.

Furthermore, the LORD provides for his creation: he "gives food to all flesh." The reference to "all flesh" extends the provision of the LORD far beyond Israel, and may include the animal world as well as the human. The bounty of the earth is the food that God in his love provided.

III. The LORD should be praised for his everlasting love (25).

The conclusion of the psalm reiterates the call from verse 1: "Give thanks to the God of heaven, for his loyal love endures forever." This is the only place in the Psalter that this designation is used, even though it occurs in other books (such as Jon. 1:9; Ezra 1:2; and Neh. 1:4). It reiterates the earlier description of the LORD as the sovereign God over all, creator, redeemer, and provider, especially for his servant Israel.

MESSAGE AND APPLICATION

The point of Psalm 136 is obvious: acknowledge the LORD in the assembly for his faithful love displayed in his mighty works,

Praise for the LORD's Enduring Love

especially in creation and redemption. These two themes for praise stand out frequently in Scripture, even in the great heavenly anthems recorded in Revelation 4 and 5. But a listing of God's works can never be complete, and so a psalm like this should prompt believers to add more or form their own song of praise for antiphonal use. But the message still must remain clear: *The LORD alone is to be praised for his marvelous works of creation, redemption and provision for his people.*

PSALM 137

By the Rivers of Babylon

INTRODUCTION

Text and Textual Variants[1]

1 By the rivers of Babylon,
    there we sat down and[2] wept
        when we remembered Zion.
2 On the poplar trees there[3]
    we hung up our harps.
3 For there our captors
    demanded of us words of a song,
    and our tormentors[4] *required* gladness, *saying*,

---

1. The Greek text has a superscription, τῷ Δαυὶδ Ἰερείου, "of David" with the (Lucianic) addition of "(through) Jeremiah," probably comparing the attacks on Edom and Babylon in Jeremiah 49–50 (Allen, *Psalms 101–150*, p. 234).
2. MT has גַּם, "also," instead of the simple conjunction "and."
3. MT has בְּתוֹכָהּ, "in the midst of it."
4. MT has the form וְתוֹלָלֵינוּ. It seems to be from the verb יָלַל, "to howl, lament" (the form developing like תּוֹשָׁב from יָשַׁב); the idea of "those howling," with the sense of "cruel exultations," would be a metonymy for the idea of

"Sing to us one of the songs[5] of Zion."
4 How can we sing the LORD's song
    in a foreign land?
5 If I forget you, O Jerusalem,
    let my right hand forget[6] *its skill*!
6 Let my tongue stick to the roof of my mouth,
    if I do not remember you,
    if I do not set Jerusalem
        as the chief of my joy!

7 Remember, O LORD, against the Edomites[7]
    the day of Jerusalem,
  who were saying, "Lay it bare, lay it bare,
    down to its foundations!"
8 O daughter of Babylon, *doomed to be* devastated,[8]
    blessed *shall he be* who repays you
        with the treatment with which you treated us!

"tormentors." However, the Greek version (and Syriac) has "and our plunderers," καὶ οἱ ἀπαγαγόντες ἡμᾶς, which Allen suggests may be a guess (p. 236); the editors of BHS suggest it reflects something like וּמוֹלִיכֵינוּ. A similar idea is found in the explanation of the form as Aramaic in Targum (the ת representing שׁ), וְשׁוֹלְלֵינוּ. Other proposals are less convincing: "those who mock us" from הלל (Dahood, *Psalms*, III:271), and "those who took us prisoners" from Arabic *talla* (A. Guillaume, "The Meaning of *tôlēl* in Psalm 137:3," *JBL* 75 [1956]:143–4).

5. MT is singular; the versions have the plural form.
6. MT has תִּשְׁכַּח without an object. The Greek has ἐπιλησθείη, which may reflect a *niphal* form, תִּשָּׁכַח, "(let my right hand) be forgotten" (see also Jerome). There have been proposals for the word to get around the difficulty. One is to read the form as תִּכְחַשׁ, or תְּכַחֵשׁ, "grow lean," "wither" (Kraus, *Psalms 60–150*, p. 501). Another is to emend to תִּכָּשֵׁשׁ, "wither," "be crippled" (I. Eitan, "An Identification of *tiškaḥ yemînî*," Ps. 137:5," *JBL* 47 [1928]:193–5).
7. MT reads "(to) the sons of Edom." The preposition could be taken as introducing the direct object, and "the day" as an adverbial accusative: "Remember, O LORD, the Edomites *in* the day of Jerusalem."
8. MT has the form הַשְּׁדוּדָה, a passive with the meaning "destroyed," or "devastated," here with the meaning "*that shall be* destroyed" (Perowne, *Psalms*, II:433). The Greek text has a modifier for "daughter of Babylon" as "wretched," ἡ ταλαίπωρος. Most commentators follow Symmachus, the Syriac and the Targum in taking the word as active, written something like הַשּׁוֹדְדָה, "you devastator."

9 Blessed *shall he be* who takes your little ones
    and dashes them against the rock!

Composition and Context

Psalm 137 does not fit any category very well, but it comes the closest to a communal lament. The first four verses are certainly such a lament; the next two verses may be taken as a commitment to Zion by a spokesman; and the rest of the psalm is an imprecation (such imprecations are not uncommon in laments). Allen calls it a modified version of a song of Zion (p. 241). Ogden retains the classification of a communal lament psalm, but one that includes a prophetic oracle of judgment on the nations.[9] The psalm records the prayer of the community both looking back to their captivity and looking forward through the oracle to their vindication.

We can be more sure of this occasion for the composition. In fact, Kraus says that it is the only psalm that can be dated reliably.[10] The psalm was clearly written during the exile to express the pain and grief of the people. And although the Babylonian empire still existed, the community looked back to the painful beginning of their captivity. So as the community gathered they rehearsed their plight, vowed their allegiance, and invoked the LORD to fulfill the ancient oracles of judgment on the nations.

Exegetical Analysis

Summary

In the language of pathetic beauty, the psalmist rehearses the lamentation of those who wept in the strange land and could not sing their songs of Zion, voices his oath to remain loyal to Jerusalem, and then calls on the LORD to repay the deeds of the wicked, against whom he utters an imprecation.

---

9. Graham S. Ogden, "Prophetic Oracles Against Foreign Nations and Psalms of Communal Lament: The Relationship of Psalm 137 to Jeremiah 49:7–22 and Obadiah," *JSOT* 24 (1982):58–97.
10. *Psalms 60–150*, p. 501.

PSALM 137

Outline

I. The exiled people mourn the plight of the nation in captivity (1–4).
   A. The people sat down by the rivers of Babylon and wept (1).
   B. They could not sing their songs of Zion in a foreign land (2–4).
      1. They hung their harps on the trees (2).
      2. They could not sing their songs when taunted by their captors to sing (3–4).
II. Speaking for the community, the psalmist vows never to forget Jerusalem (5–6).
   A. He would rather that this right hand forget its skill than he forget Jerusalem (5).
   B. He would rather be struck dumb than forget Jerusalem, his great joy (6).
III. The psalmist calls for the LORD to remember the evil done to his people and to repay it (7–9).
   A. He calls for the LORD to repay the evil part that Edom had in the invasion and devastation of Jerusalem (7).
   B. He adds imprecations on Babylon as part of his desire for justice to be exacted on them for what they had done (8–9).
      1. Babylon should note that because of their destruction of Jerusalem they would be repaid in measure (8).
      2. Babylon should expect that their little ones also would be destroyed (9).

COMMENTARY IN EXPOSITORY FORM

I. When the world seeks to destroy the faith by mocking the forms of worship of believers, the faithful will strengthen their resolve to remain loyal to God (1–4).

A. The faithful can only weep when they recall the ruin of their holy place and their worship (1).

It is difficult to say much, if anything, that would enhance the beauty and power of the words and images of this psalm.

Kirkpatrick observes that at the beginning of the psalm the tender pathos of the mourning exiles enlists our sympathy; but at the end the bitter denunciation shocks and repels us—and yet it stretches pain to the limit.[11] The language is intense because the experience was overwhelming. "By the rivers of Babylon, there we sat down and wept." Babylon was a land of rivers and canals and trees, so the present images provided a natural setting for the lamentation. Normally rivers and trees are sources of delight, but not for exiles. For many of them life in Babylon was comfortable enough, but it amounted to nothing because they were aliens in a strange land. The statement that they sat down could refer to the simple act of a company of them sitting by a river; or it could mean that they dwelt there by the rivers. Briggs suggests that there is a stronger implication in the verb "we sat down," namely, that in this context it serves as a description of their despair and sorrow—they were simply overwhelmed and sat down in grief.[12] Likewise, another simple act was used in verse 2 with a greater significance—they hung their harps on the tree.

The weeping and the discouragement was brought on when they remembered Zion (meaning the city of Jerusalem on Mount Zion, so a metonymy of subject). No doubt they relived again and again the catastrophe of the destruction of their land and the holy city throughout the exile. No one familiar with the Bible would have to be told what must have been running through their minds in Babylon; their memory would be consumed with grief, much like we read in the book of Lamentations.

B. The faithful cannot sing the LORD's song when the wicked taunt them to sing the songs of Zion (2–4).

Israel had always enjoyed singing, especially the songs of Zion during the great festivals. Accordingly, the psalms had gradually become the largest collection of lyrical poetry in antiquity, easily set to music and well-known to the people. But now singing was inappropriate, out of the question. They hung their

---

11. *Psalms*, p. 779.
12. *Psalms*, II:485.

harps (lyres) on the trees, signifying that their days of singing had come to an end. The Authorized Version used the translation "willows," but the word probably means poplar trees. The imagery of the weeping willow tree harmonized so well with the sorrow these people were feeling; but the location was Babylon, not England. They hung up their harps on the trees where they lived because they thought there was no further use for them.

According to verse 3 they were taunted with a demand to sing one of the songs of Zion. These songs focused on Zion, not for Zion's sake, but because the LORD was there in the midst of that place. They were joyful songs because they proclaimed the security and triumph of Jerusalem. But now the people were in exile, far from Zion; they were not secure or triumphant, and so everything looked hopeless. And when they were asked to sing, they knew that the enemies, described here as "our captors" (שׁוֹבֵינוּ) and "our tormentors" (תוֹלָלֵינוּ), were not interested in hearing their songs. They were simply mocking the Jews by demanding that they sing one of their victory songs. It is as if they were saying, "Where is your God now?"

The Jews refused to sing, thinking in their hearts, "How can we sing the LORD's song in a foreign land (v. 4). Not only did the content of those songs seem inappropriate now that the people were in exile, but it also seemed to them to be a profane thing to sing the LORD's song for the amusement of the wicked. Moreover, they were dwelling in a foreign land because of God's judgment on them. How can people who are "unclean" sing a holy song in a land that is unclean?[13] So they could not sing, would not sing, for their captors.

II. When the world seems to be destroying the faith, the afflicted believers resolve never to forget their highest joy, the city of God (5–6).

In the next two verses we have a shift from lament to confidence and hope. The psalmist, speaking now in the first person as no doubt everyone did in the community, focuses on Jerusalem; and in remembering the holy city he was renewing

---

13. Anderson, *Psalms 73–150*, p. 899.

his commitment to the faith. He says, speaking to the city, "If I forget you, O Jerusalem, let my right hand forget—." He cuts his sentence off before finishing it (which is an aposiopesis) because of the intensity of the thought—forget Jerusalem?—that would be tantamount to abandoning the faith. The verbs "forget" (s.v. Ps. 103:2) and "remember" (s.v. Ps. 6:5) express more than mental activity or inactivity. If remembering means acting on what is remembered, then forgetting would refer to a decision not to act.[14] For the psalmist to say that he might forget Jerusalem, even in a hypothetical clause, would be disloyal. Loyalty to the faith comes in remembering Jerusalem, even if (or perhaps especially if) it leads to grief and sorrow (and guilt).

But here the psalmist uses two serious self-maledictions to affirm his loyalty. "Let my right hand forget" (probably its skills). The curse means that he would be paralyzed and unable to act. The second malediction is in verse 6, "Let my tongue stick to the roof of my mouth." He would be better off dumb and unable to speak.[15] With such self-maledictions on his ability to act and speak, the psalmist is avowing his loyalty to Jerusalem, the chief of all his joys. But he is not merely expressing his pleasure in a city. It is the city of God, the city that God chose for his dwelling place forever. He may not sing the songs of Zion now, but he will not abandon his loyalty to the faith or his hope for deliverance. If he abandoned his faith, it would be better to be dumb and unable to sing, or paralyzed and unable to play the harp. So he will maintain his loyalty and "set" Jerusalem as his chief joy.[16]

---

14. For example, when we confess sins the Bible says the LORD will forget them and remember them no more. He cannot forget because he knows everything; it means he will not act on them in judgment.
15. VanGemeren lays this material out in a chiasm (*Psalms,* p. 951):
    A. If I forget;
    B. My right hand;
    B'. My tongue; and
    A'. If I do not remember.
16. The verb used is a simple one, "I will bring up" (the *hiphil* אַעֲלֶה), meaning "consider" Jerusalem as the chief joy. Freedman suggested emending the verb to read it as a *qal,* "I will ascend Jerusalem with joy upon my head." D. N. Freedman, "The Structure of Psalm 137," in *Near Eastern Studies, FS* for W. F. Albright, ed. By H. Goedicke (Baltimore: Johns Hopkins, 1971), pp. 187–205.

III. Because the wicked ruthlessly tried to destroy God's program the faithful may rightly appeal to the LORD to repay their barbaric deeds (7–9).

A. *The righteous pray for the LORD to take vengeance on all who complied with the persecution (7).*

The psalmist now employs the verb "remember" in an appeal for the LORD to act on what the Edomites did, to take vengeance on the them: "Remember, O LORD, (against) the Edomites, *in* the day of Jerusalem." According to the biblical records, the Edomites had sided with the Babylonians against Judah and had taken great pleasure in the destruction of Zion (see Obadiah, Lam. 4:21; and Ezek. 25:12f., 35:5f.). They had shouted for the Babylonians to tear the city down to its foundations. The foundations were literal, of course; but the implication is that in doing this they would also destroy the social and spiritual foundations, the order of life and justice. They wanted the complete destruction of Jerusalem and all it stood for—which would be the historic faith. So the psalmist prays to the LORD to "remember," to secure judgment on Edom for what they did.

Here we see the influence of the judgment oracle in the psalm. God's faithful love for his people, for his chosen dwelling place, and for the future of the faith, will necessarily mean judgment on the nations. He starts with Edom because the Edomites were closely related to the Jews and their treachery therefore was inexcusable.

B. *The righteous express their desire for justice by means of imprecations on the guilty (8–9).*

Finally the imprecation focuses on the Babylonians themselves, referred to poetically as the daughter of Babylon. Subsequent generations of the original culprits shared the same animosity to the Jews and therefore the same guilt.[17] They are

---

17. A study of "Babylon" in Scripture will discover how it became the symbol of godless society. God would destroy the Babylonians by the Persians in the immediate reference; but Babylon reemerges as the city to be destroyed at the end of the age (Rev. 18–19).

destined for destruction, as many prophecies make abundantly clear (Isa. 13:16; Hab. 1). And so the psalmist prays that when they are destroyed they will be given the same treatment they gave to Judah; that would be about the only thing that such a ruthless people like the Babylonians would understand.

But then he adds a blessing for anyone who participates in the destruction of Babylon and of their little ones, the most painful part of warfare. Warfare is always cruel and barbaric, even when waged by civilized nations. In ancient warfare the killing of the young was considered a necessary step to prevent future retaliation (Briggs, II:486); that, of course, does not make it right but only explains why they did it. Here in Psalm 137 even though the desire is for God to exact justice, the offering of a blessing for those who kill the children is rather chilling for us to read. It is not that it does not happen today, for it does and probably more than in antiquity. But for the psalmist to say this is jarring for believers.

There are several things that need to be considered here. First, this imprecation is not an isolated occurrence. Scattered throughout the Psalter there are communal prayers in the form of curses that express the desire for God to avenge the suffering of his people. These are all part of inspired Scripture, so we have to try to understand why they used them and how they harmonize with the rest of Scripture. But the wording itself of Psalm 137 has been most troubling to modern day readers.

Second, it is important to keep in mind that the nation had almost been completely destroyed by the ruthless Babylonian army with a portion of the population carried off into a strange land where they would remain for seventy years, living without their sanctuary, sacrifices, festivals, or Zion itself. This was a major catastrophe. No wonder the people could not sing the songs of Zion because of their lamentable existence. In light of all this, Psalm 137 ends with the expressed desire that all the Babylonians, even their little ones, be destroyed in the same way that the Babylonians had slaughtered their families.[18]

While the imprecation has troubled most people because it

---

18. One additional resource for this aspect of the communal lament is Graham S. Ogden, "Prophetic Oracles Against the Nations and the Psalms of

seems so primitive and barbaric, in the context of the shared pain of the nation, these expressions form an emotional longing for divine justice. The Israelites had experienced such atrocities by the pitiless Babylonians and treacherous Edomites, so that they now cried out for vengeance.[19]

Third, the destruction of Babylon had been prophesied before this prayer—it was part of the way that God judged nations. Israel itself had experienced and even practiced these violent things in warfare (see 2 Kings 8:9–12; Amos 1:30; and 2 Kings 15:14–16). But God's people had been warned that they would suffer from this ruthless practice if they rebelled against these nations and also against the LORD (Hos. 13:16; Nah. 3:10; Hab. 1); but they rebelled anyway. And so the powerful invaders utterly destroyed the people and the land because they did not keep the covenants—not only with the LORD, but also with Nebuchadnezzar (Ezek. 17:11–15). But in his divine justice, God promised the same judgment would fall on Babylon—what they did to others would be done to them (Isa. 13:16). All of this is to say that the communal prayer of Psalm 137 was a prayer in harmony with the prophetic oracle concerning the coming judgment on Babylon. They were actually praying for God to do what he said he was going to do, bring punishment on the Babylonians that was a just recompense for their barbaric activities.

Fourth, why did they use such language to pray for divine justice? Kidner suggests there was at least a rhetorical element to the imprecation. It was designed more to express the outrage and pain than to spell out the penalties the psalmist desired.[20] And since it was written to be sung the impact of the ideas would be even greater. Breuggeman says, "On reflection it may be the voice of a seasoned religion which knows profoundly what it costs to beat off despair. . . . It is an act of profound faith to

---

Communal Lament: The Relationship of Psalm 137 to Jeremiah 49:7–20 and Obadiah," *JSOT* 24 (1982):88–97.

19. It is important to note that these "atrocities" are found routinely in vassal treaties of Assyria; they were to be administered to people who rebelled against the overlord. See James B. Pritchard, *Ancient Near Eastern Texts Relating to the Old Testament*, 3rd edition with supplement (Princeton: University Press, 1969), pp. 228, 539–40
20. *Psalms 1–72,* p. 27.

entrust one's most precious hatreds to God, knowing they will be taken seriously."[21]

Finally, then, we are to remember that this is a communal prayer. It is a cry by the nation for justice, from a context of anguish, pain and humiliation.[22] Very few modern believers have experienced the kind of treatment the Israelites received, other than people who were sent to concentration camps or endured ethnic cleansing or brutality at the hands of terrorists. Certainly people who have suffered so severely deserve more understanding. In fact, what believer has not desired that God destroy the merciless and murderous enemies of the people of God? But the point is that Psalm 137 is a prayer; it turns the painful desires and expressions over to God, the supreme judge of the whole earth. Their desire is clear; but as it is left in God's hands, it ceases to be personal revenge and becomes a prayer for God to punish the ruthless in kind.[23]

MESSAGE AND APPLICATION

It is easy to discard such prayers as primitive or "un-Christian," which in some way is true. The new covenant teaches us to love our enemies and pray for them. But saints of all ages have had similar prayers for divine vengeance when powerful nations and governments commit such atrocities in their attempted persecution and annihilation of believers. When the people of God pray for the persecuted church, or for nations and tribes that are being annihilated whether Christian or not, they certainly should pray for a change of heart in the oppressors who need the grace and love of God; but they also should pray urgently

---

21. *Message of the Psalms*, p. 77.
22. Here we have a contrast with the ruthlessness of the Babylonians. We read in Daniel how the king would rip people limb from limb and make their house a dunghill if they did not interpret a dream, bow down to a statue, or violate some other minor law. But the punishment desired here in the Psalm is for justice—the severe punishment should fit the seriousness of the crime.
23. See further John N. Day, *Crying for Justice, What the Psalms Teach Us about Mercy and Vengeance in an Age of Terrorism* (Grand Rapids: Kregel, 2005), pp. 62–72.

for relief for those who are suffering, knowing that that relief is likely to be the outworking of divine justice in the removal of the wicked. As long as the inner desire for God to judge the world is cast in the form of prayer, then we have surrendered our will to his will to be done. And so when we pray, "thy kingdom come, thy will be done," we are actually praying for the Lord to come and destroy the wicked. And this will also be in answer to the prayers of the martyred saints in glory, who cry out, "How long, O Lord, until you avenge our deaths?"

A summary expository idea that would capture the point of this psalm would be: *When wicked people in power begin destroying the faith and persecuting believers maliciously, the righteous must strengthen their resolve to keep their hope alive and must submit their desires for vengeance to the LORD in prayer.* It is frequently the case that grave periods of suffering and persecution have inspired greater loyalty to the faith. When they come, whether as a divine punishment for disobedience as in the case of Israel, or as a divine test for the faithful, it is natural and appropriate for the faithful to express their pain and confusion in laments such as this. But it essential that they surrender their desires to the LORD in prayer, knowing that he will judge wickedness righteously. And for believers today who live under the new covenant, the Holy Spirit will influence their prayers so that they are in harmony with the will of God. There is no room for indiscriminate hatred and personal vengeance, even though it is hard to jettison these things in the midst of suffering. But the overall desire of the prayer should be for righteousness to triumph and the hope of the redeemed be fulfilled. There is no easy and smooth answer for the cruelty of humans; and there is no virtue in ignoring the problem. The Lord listened to the cries of his people which often bordered on blasphemy (as in the case of Job), remembering that they were but flesh. And the Lord is the only one who can make things right, for he himself endured the brutal cruelty of the cross. And through that painful suffering sinners of every degree can find forgiveness and the hope of glory.

We do not know exactly when this psalm was written in the exile, but it is not impossible that the writer was still living at the time of the return to the land. Certainly the generation of people who were alive knew and sang this psalm. It is interesting to note that the deliverance from exile and the restoration to the land changed everything for them. Then they could sing, "When the LORD brought back the captives of Zion . . . , then was our mouth filled with laughter, and our tongue with songs of joy. Then they said among the nations, 'The LORD has done great things for them.' The LORD has done great things for us, therefore we are glad."

PSALM 138

The Demonstration of the LORD's Glory in His Care for the Lowly

INTRODUCTION

Text and Textual Variants

Of David.[1]

1 I give you thanks[2] with my whole heart;[3]
     before[4] the gods[5] I sing your praise;

---

1. This is not in a few manuscripts, Aquila, or Sexta. Some Greek manuscripts add "Haggai and Zechariah," or just "Zechariah." This may indicate that they thought the psalm was from that time, or that the psalm expressed the feelings of that time (see Kirkpatrick, *Psalms,* p. 783).
2. A number of Hebrew manuscripts, Qumran, and the versions have here "O LORD." The reading in the MT is shorter and harder, and so to be preferred.
3. The Greek version has an extra line here: "because you heard the words of my mouth." Allen suggests that this was a marginal correction for 4b that was attached to this verse (*Psalms 101–150,* p. 311).
4. The Greek and Syriac have "and before . . . ."
5. The Greek version interpreted אֱלֹהִים as "angels" (ἀγγέλων). The Syriac has "kings," perhaps a corruption; the Targum has "judges."

PSALM 138

2 I bow down toward your holy temple
   and give thanks to your name
      for your loyal love and your faithfulness,
  for you have magnified above all
   your name *and* your word.[6]
3 In the day that I called, you answered me;[7]
  You made me courageous[8] with strength in my soul.

4 All the kings of the earth shall[9] give you thanks, O LORD,
   for they will hear the words of your mouth,
5 and they shall sing of the ways of the LORD,
   for great is the glory of the LORD.
6 For *though* the LORD is high, he sees the lowly,
   but the proud he knows[10] from afar.

7 If I walk in the midst of trouble,
   you will preserve my life;
   you will stretch out your hand[11] against the wrath of my enemies,
   and your right hand shall save me.[12]

---

6. The Hebrew is difficult: "for you have magnified over all your name your word." The Greek version has "for you magnified your oracle above every name." The editors of BHS suggest a change to "you have exalted above all names your name." See the discussion in the commentary below.
7. The Greek version makes this a petition: "On the day I call, hearken to me (ἐπάκουσόν μου) quickly." The Hebrew text has a preterite with a *waw* consecutive.
8. The MT's תַּרְהִבֵנִי is related to the word "pride," רֹהַב. The Greek version has "you will care for me" (πολυωρήσεις). The Hebrew verb has many shades of meaning; but Perowne suggests a root meaning "to act with spirit." So here "You have infused spirit into me" meaning "you put strength in me" (*Psalms*, II:437).
9. The Greek version took the verbs in verses 4 and 5 to be jussives: "Let all the kings . . . give you thanks."
10. The form in the MT, יֵדָע, is a *qal* but is formed after the analogy of the *hiphil* forms, retaining the first letter of the root whereas in the normal paradigm it is lost altogether. There have been attempts to find a better meaning for the verb; see the discussion in the commentary.
11. Many Hebrew manuscripts have "your hands."
12. Or: "you save me with your right hand" (Allen, *Psalms 101–150*, p. 311).

8 The LORD will perfect[13] that which concerns me;
   your loyal love, O LORD, endures forever.
   Do not forsake the works of your hands.

Composition and Context

Psalm 138 appears to be an individual thanksgiving, but its classification is by no means assured. It follows the form of an individual praise in the first three verses, but in verses 4–6 it becomes more communal. This has led a number of commentators to conclude that the psalm was the thanksgiving of the community, with an individual speaking on behalf of the people.[14] Accordingly, many suggest that the setting for the praise was in the forecourt of the temple because of a few hints in the passage, such as the psalmist's praising "before / in the presence of" the LORD or bowing toward the temple. But it can be demonstrated that such phrases were used for prayers offered in other places but directed to the LORD (e.g., Jonah 2).

There is not much agreement on the date of this composition; Perowne says that neither language nor allusions will warrant any conclusion as to the date or authorship.[15] And Allen chose to leave the question of the date open.[16] One common view is that the community was praising God in the sanctuary for deliverance from the exile. Support for this interpretation comes from similarities with Isaiah 40–66, including the ideas of Israel's role as a witness to the pagans, and of kings responding to the glory of the LORD. This interpretation assumes a later date for the Isaianic material; but that aside, the ideas expressed in the psalm are not limited to the later periods.

Some commentators like Eaton and Dahood classify the psalm as a royal psalm because of its similarities to passages like Psalm 18; this would fit the superscription of the psalm and make the date pre-exilic at least.[17] The use of "temple" in the

---

13. The Greek version has "will repay" (ἀνταποδώσει).
14. Anderson, *Psalms 73–150,* p. 901; Kirkpatrick, p. 783. Kirkpatrick does allow for the possibility that the individual psalmist could have borrowed from communal songs (p. 783).
15. *Psalms,* II:434.
16. *Psalms 101–150,* p. 314.
17. Eaton, *Kingship and the Psalms,* p. 68; and Dahood, *Psalms,* III:276.

psalm would not nullify the idea of Davidic authorship, because the word was used for the tabernacle as well (s.v. Ps. 5:7). Then, concerning the setting of the praise, Eaton placed it in the forecourt of the temple, but Dahood said the psalmist was away but looking toward the sanctuary.

What we have is a final collection of psalms attributed to David placed here at the end of the Psalter, Psalms 138–145. VanGemeren explains how these fit the flow of the book. The Psalter is moving to the grand finale, the praise of the LORD in psalms 146–150, but not without a last burst of lament. These eight psalms bring forward the major motifs of the earlier collection of Davidic laments, namely, the awareness of enemies, the need for divine help, and prayer for deliverance. Psalms 138 and 145 provide a framework of praise for these eight; Psalm 139 is a meditation in the midst of enemies, and the remaining five are laments. Even Psalm 138, a praise psalm, ends with an appeal for the LORD not to abandon his people. Moreover, Psalm 138 clearly develops the major theme of this section, namely that the LORD watches over all who love him, but will destroy all the wicked.[18]

The psalm can be divided into three sections: verses 1–3 record the praise of an individual; verses 4–6 expand to a communal praise; and verses 7 and 8 express the confidence. The psalmist may be speaking for the community, but the words of verses 4–6 could be part of an individual praise just as well. But as far as the message of the psalm goes, it matters little if the psalm is individual praise, or communal expressed by an individual.

Exegetical Analysis

Summary

After encouraging himself to praise the LORD's loyal love and goodness for the answer to prayer, and after announcing the hope that all kings acknowledge God's favor to the lowly, the psalmist voices his confidence that the LORD will deliver him.

---

18. *Psalms,* p. 955.

The Demonstration of the LORD's Glory in His Care for the Lowly

Outline

I. The psalmist praises the LORD's loyal love and goodness because he has answered his prayer (1–3).
   A. He worships and praises the LORD's loyal love and truth (1–2).
   B. He acknowledges that the LORD answered his prayer and strengthened him (3).
II. The psalmist prophesies that all the kings will also praise the LORD for his greatness and glory displayed in his delivering the lowly and not judging by human standards (4–6).
   A. Kings will acknowledge his greatness when they hear of his glory (4–5).
   B. They will sing of his greatness and glory in delivering the lowly and not making decisions by human standards (6).
III. The Psalmist expresses his confidence that the LORD will deliver him from his enemies according to his loyal love, and perfect his plan for his life (7–8).
   A. He trusts that the LORD will deliver him from trouble (7).
   B. He trusts that the LORD will perfect his plan for him, but prays that he will not forsake it (8).

COMMENTARY IN EXPOSITORY FORM

I. Those who have experienced the love and faithfulness of the Lord will naturally declare their praise before the world (1–3).

A. They will witness to the LORD's love and faithfulness before the world and its false beliefs (1–2).

The psalm opens with the psalmist's acknowledgment of the loyal love and faithfulness of the LORD. He simply states, "I give you thanks" (or, "I acknowledge you," אוֹדְךָ, s.v. Ps. 6:5); the thanksgiving is a public acknowledgment of the LORD. And it will be set forth in song (אֲזַמְּרֶךָּ, s.v. Ps. 33:2). The object of the praise is not named until verse 4; here only a pronominal suffix is used. Perowne suggests that the absence of the vocative (O LORD) brings a certain emphasis, as if the psalmist was saying there could only be one object of praise (II:435).

This praise, we are told, is given "before *the* gods" (נֶגֶד אֱלֹהִים). Understandably, the word "gods" has been given different interpretations. First, it has been interpreted to mean "angels." This was the view of the Greek Old Testament, accepted by Calvin and Luther. One difficulty is that in the Old Testament angels are not said to be witnesses to praise. Second, it has been interpreted to mean "judges" or "kings." This is the understanding in the Targum, the Syriac, Rabbinic literature and a number of modern translations and commentaries. This would mean that the leaders of the country, or perhaps of the worship in the sanctuary, witness the praise. It is unclear what the significance of the expression would be in this case. Third, it has been rendered "before God," meaning before the ark, or in the sanctuary. But this would be awkward as the verse would then say, "before God and I give you thanks." The fourth and most likely interpretation, especially in view of verses 4–6 is that it refers to pagan gods. Other passages in this part of the Psalter refer to the pagan gods as well (Pss. 95:3; 96:4–5; and 115:3–8). The psalmist praises the greatness and glory of Yahweh "in the face"—so to speak, of false gods. This would render the false gods as witnesses to the glory of the true God, and therefore bring confusion to their devotees. David himself had been among such pagans and no doubt felt the tension between the religions as well as the demonic power—but the LORD proved superior (1 Sam. 26:19). The point would be that Yahweh's power was greater than the nations and their gods. If this is the correct understanding, the verse does not restrict the setting to Israel's sanctuary.

Verse 2 also seems to locate the praise in the forecourt with the mention of the temple, but bowing down to the LORD's holy temple can mean looking toward the sanctuary in prayer just as easily (Jonah 2). The word "bow down" (אֶשְׁתַּחֲוֶה, s.v. Ps. 95:6) depicts the obeisance of the worship—making oneself low to the ground in worshiping the LORD. Here we see the other side of the psalmist: in addition to his boldness in acknowledging the greatness of God before the gods, we see his humility in bowing

The Demonstration of the LORD's Glory in His Care for the Lowly

down toward the temple.[19] In bowing down towards the temple, the psalmist meant that he was bowing to the LORD in his holy temple (a metonymy of subject).

This praise is given to the name of the LORD. "Name" is a common designation for the nature of the LORD ("name" is a metonymy of subject; s.v. Ps. 20:1). What he specifically focuses on here are the attributes of his loyal love and his faithfulness. These two words, "loyal love" (חֶסֶד; s.v. Ps. 23:6) and "faithfulness" (אֱמֶת; s.v. Ps. 15:2), are often together and can be taken as a hendiadys, one idea through two words wherein one of the words is a modifier—"faithful covenant love." But there is also a relationship between these words that must be clarified. God has been faithful to his covenant promises because of his steadfast love.

The last colon of verse 2 is difficult. The sentence reads in English: "for you have magnified over all your name, your word" (כִּי־הִגְדַּלְתָּ עַל־כָּל־שִׁמְךָ אִמְרָתֶךָ). The line appears to mean that the LORD's fulfillment of his promise to the psalmist surpasses all other manifestations of God's works.[20] This idea would work well with praise for the return from the exile, if that were the sure occasion. But the line has been given different readings. The Greek version read, "for you magnified your oracle above every name." And there have been many suggestions to reconstruct the line. Some have reworked the text a little too much. One view is to read it as "you have made great your name above the heavens." The editors of the Hebrew Bible proposed "You have exalted above all names your name." More cautiously, Allen suggests reading, "you have magnified "your name and your promise above all [else]."[21]

C. Their praise will be for answered prayer (3).

In verse 3 we have the reason for the praise: "In the day that I called, you answered me." That is clear enough, but the second

---

19. Kidner, *Psalms 73–150*, p. 461.
20. Ibid., p. 462 and others.
21. *Psalms 60–150*, p. 311. The Hebrew term for "word" here may specifically be defined as an oracle or a promise. See the discussion of the word under Psalm 119:11.

colon requires more attention. One translation of it is, "You made me courageous with strength in my life" (תַּרְהִבֵנִי בְנַפְשִׁי עֹז). The verb is related to a noun "pride"; it has a variety of meanings but essentially means in this stem: "give boldness, ability." The line probably means that God gave the psalmist the boldness or courage as the means for answering the prayer. On the other hand, some have followed the Greek translation and read a different verb, such as רָבָה, "to be many," and in this *hiphil* stem, "to increase," reading תַּרְבֵנִי, "you increased strength in my life." The Hebrew Bible has a more difficult form and therefore most likely retains the original.

II. Powerful rulers will acknowledge the greatness of the LORD because he does not judge by human standards but delivers the lowly (4–6).

A. *Rulers will acknowledge the glory of the LORD (4–5).*

The focus of the psalm turns now to a prophecy concerning the nations.[22] The psalmist reiterates the prophecy that all the kings of the earth will also give thanks to the LORD and sing of his ways (see also Pss. 68:29–32; 72:10–11; and 102:15–16). In a sense he is indicating that it is not enough for praise to come from him, or even the community in Israel. Such a great God must be acknowledged by kings and their kingdoms the world over.

The reason that they will praise the LORD is that they will hear the words of his mouth and realize how great he is. The verb "hear" is a perfect tense in the passage, but should be taken as a prophetic perfect looking to the future reality. It means they will respond with understanding and faith to what God is doing. What they will hear is the revelation of the works and the will of God. This would include God's fulfillment of the promises he has made to his people, individually and collectively. The "ways" of

---

22. It is possible that the verbs used in verses 4 and 5 could be taken as jussives, as in the Greek version. This would make the section a prayer or wish.

the LORD that will fill their songs refers to his glorious acts. No more will they sing of love and war but of the glory of the LORD (Ibn Ezra).

B. His glory is displayed in his gracious dealings with the lowly (6).

The "glory" of the LORD is a broad expression; it embraces all the wonderful works and amazing revelations that attest to his greatness and importance above all others (for the word, s.v. Ps. 19:1). But in this section verse 6 explains (כִּי) what form the revelation of God's glory took in their experience: his heavenly majesty and greatness were displayed by his grace. And so we read that although the LORD is high (רָם; s.v. Ps. 46:10), he sees the lowly (compare Ps. 113). The term used simply refers to what is low (שָׁפָל), but it must have reference to their humble and lowly status, which would indicate that they do not have the ability to deliver themselves from oppressors. But God sees them. The verb "see" used with God as the subject can mean evaluate, superintend, oversee, and provide (see also 1 Pet. 5:6). Here it means he is aware of their plight and takes care of them—he provides for them by his grace (see the use of the verb in Gen. 22:8, 14, the LORD will provide / see). Almighty God is exalted high above all things; he has all the greatness and the glory; and yet he cares for the lowly (see Isa. 57:15).

On the other hand, he knows (s.v. Ps. 67:2)[23] the proud from afar. The idea that God knows the proud is not in itself difficult, for he knows everything and everyone (see Ps. 139). But how he knows them in this context must be explained. To know them

---

23. There have been some attempts to find a better meaning for this context than "know." D.W. Thomas found the meaning of being humbled or humiliated in the cognate Arabic language that seemed to fit very well ("The Root ידע in Hebrew. 2." *JTS* 36 [1935]409–412; and "Some Rabbinic Evidence for a Hebrew Root ידע = [Arabic] *wd'*," *JQR* ns 37 [1946–47]:177–178; see also J. A. Emerton, "A Consideration of Some Alleged Meanings of ידע in Hebrew," *JSS* 15 [1970]:145–180). For the argument against the connection, see W. Johnston, "YD' II, 'Be Humbled, Humiliated'?" *VT* 41 (1991):49–62; and J. A. Emerton, "A Further Consideration of D. W. Thomas's Theories about *yada'*," *VT* 41 (1991):145–63.

from a distance means that they are not near him, either by their refusal to draw near or his rejection of them because of their pride. Unlike the lowly in spirit who must rely on the LORD, these are the people who think they are self-sufficient and need no divine help. The expression that he knows them from afar according to Allen describes the "ill-boding omniscience of the behavior of the self-willed."

III. The faithful may be confident that the LORD will deliver them from their enemies and perfect his plan for them (7–8).

A. The faithful trust the LORD to protect and deliver them from their enemies (7).

In the last two verses the psalmist expresses his confidence, the confidence of every believer who "walks in the midst of trouble." In a psalm that praises the LORD for answer to prayer and anticipates that praise will be given by the kings of the earth, the psalmist must return to the present reality. His course of life may very well take him into situations where he is again in trouble, in a bind as it were (צָרָה). But even there he is confident that the LORD will preserve his life (תְּחַיֵּנִי from חָיָה, "to live"). No doubt his present experience of being delivered has built his confidence to face the future. He is confident that the power of God will oppose his enemies. He expresses this by the (anthropomorphic) statements that God will stretch out his hand (see Prov. 31:20), i.e., the power of God will be against them, and that God's right hand will save him (יָשַׁע > וְתוֹשִׁיעֵנִי; s.v. Ps. 3:2). This salvation could be by direct intervention; but it could also be by God's strengthening of the psalmist as attested in this psalm.

B. The faithful are confident that the LORD will perfect his plan for them (8).

So here we see the balance of the spiritual life: even while praising the LORD for delivering him and reiterating the confidence that the kings of the world will submit to the LORD, the faithful know that times are still difficult. But they are also confident that God is not finished yet with his plan of redemption. They know he will finish it. Verse 8 says, "The LORD will perfect that which concerns me" (יִגְמֹר בַּעֲדִי)—i.e., he will fulfill his purpose on my account. The LORD made a covenant with his people and in it promised them his faithful and everlasting love which would mean their complete and eternal salvation from everything evil. And so the psalmist rehearses this cardinal creed of the faith, "Your loyal love, O LORD, endures forever" (a common doxology in the psalms; see Ps. 118:1–3; and Ps. 136).

But faith in the love of God is to be expressed in prayer. And so in the last line the psalmist prays, "Do not forsake the works of your hands." Prayer is the expression of faith by those appropriating the promises of God—it is praying according to the will of the LORD. On the human level the psalmist knows that if God "forsook" his works, then his purpose for the redeemed would not be fulfilled. But it will be; this is what the righteous believe, and this is what they pray for in the midst of trouble.

MESSAGE AND APPLICATION

Here we have the confident faith of a believer who is trusting the LORD to deliver him from his enemies and perfect his plan for his life. And this is what every believer desires. But the psalmist bases his confidence on the LORD's loyal love and goodness, displayed so clearly in his answering the prayers of the saints and in his championing the needs of the lowly. Here is the point of the psalm, namely, that the grace of God is his greatness—not something that the kings of the world embrace, but that they will acknowledge in the end when they see his glory. The expository idea may be worded this way: *Because the LORD by his grace answers prayer and rescues the lowly, those who trust in him know that he will perfect his plan for them and inspire universal acknowledgment of his greatness.* The point is expressed powerfully in Isaiah 52:13–53:12, which prophesies that the kings of the earth will be astounded and shut their mouths when they see the glory of the Lord, for his greatness and his glory is due to the fact that he suffered and died for the sins of the world so that he could justify many and bring them everlasting peace. No king in the world could have even dreamed of doing all of this.

The Gospel of John emphasizes the idea that the glory of Christ Jesus is his gracious work of redemption at the cross where he conquered sin and death (see John 1:14; John 17:1–5) and made provision to lift up the lowly to bring them to glory. But the believers now remain in this world and must endure opposition and trouble. And so they pray for deliverance, but they pray with confidence, for like the psalmist they trust the Lord and so "are confident of this one thing, that he who has begun a good work in them (you) will complete it until the day of Jesus Christ" (Phil. 1:6).

PSALM 139

The Perceiving, Pursuing, Planning God

INTRODUCTION

Text and Textual Variants

For the Chief Musician. A Psalm of David.

1 O LORD, you have searched me and you know *me*.
2 You know my sitting down and my rising up;
    you discern my intentions[1] from afar.
3 You winnow[2] my journeying forth and my lying down,[3]

---

1. A number of manuscripts and the Greek and Syriac seem to have taken this word to be "my thoughts" (דֵּעִי) from the verb "to know." The word in the Masoretic Text is רֵעִי, which probably means "striving after things, intentions." The Hebrew word occurs only here; it may be equivalent to the Aramaic word. The Hebrew word רְעוּת occurs frequently in Ecclesiastes with the sense of striving after something, perhaps the will or the intention of the thought.
2. The MT has זֵרִיתָ, "to scatter, spread, winnow, sift," figurative here for discernment. The Greek translation has ἐξιχνίασας, "traced."
3. The Greek version has σχοῖνόν, "miles" (traveled).

PSALM 139

    and you have become acquainted[4] with all my ways.
4 For *before* there is a word on my tongue,[5]
    indeed,[6] O LORD, you know it altogether.[7]
5 You have besieged me behind and before,
    and you have placed your palm over me.
6 *Such* knowledge[8] is too wonderful[9] for me;
    it is high, I cannot prevail over it.

7 Where can I go from your Spirit?
    Or where can I flee from your presence?
8 If I ascend into heaven, you are there;
    if I spread out my bed in hell, indeed, you *are there*.
9 *If* I take the wings[10] of the dawn,[11]
    a*nd*[12] settle down in the uttermost parts of the sea,
10 even there your hand shall lead me,
    and your right hand shall hold me.

---

4. The Greek has προεῖδες, "you foresaw."
5. The MT literally reads: "For *there is* not a word on my tongue, *but* indeed, O LORD, you know it altogether."
6. Hebrew has הֵן. The verse can be read as "There is no word on my tongue (which) you do not know altogether," or, "A word is not (yet) upon my tongue, (but) lo, you know it altogether." This second reading is preferable because of the Hebrew particle (Perowne, *Psalms,* II:444). The sentence can be worded for easier understanding, however.
7. The Greek version arranges the clauses differently. Verse 4a stands alone. Then verse 5 reads: "O LORD, you know all things, the last and the first // you shaped me and laid your hand on me."
8. The MT simply has דֵּעָה. The word without the article or pronoun draws attention to the meaning, hence, "*such* knowledge." The Greek translation has a second masculine singular suffix.
9. "Wonderful" is in the text a K°*thiv-Q°re'* reading. The *K* is פְּלִאיָה, the feminine of the adjective פִּלְאִי. The *Q* is פְּלִיאָה, which has the support of most of the manuscripts.
10. Instead of the construct form כַּנְפֵי, "the wings of," the Greek has "my wings (at the dawn)"
11. Here the Syriac has "like an eagle" (= כְּנֶשֶׁר).
12. The conjunction is found in a few Hebrew manuscripts, the Greek and the Syriac.

The Perceiving, Pursuing, Planning God

11 I said,[13] "Surely the darkness shall bruise me,[14]
    and the light shall be night about me."[15]
12 Indeed, the darkness shall not be too dark for you,
    but the night shall shine as the day;
    the darkness and the light are both alike to you.

13 For you created my inner being;
    you knit me together[16] in my mother's womb–
14 I acknowledge you, for I am uniquely[17] and fearfully made;[18]
    wonderful are all your works,
    and that I[19] know very well!–
15 My frame was not hidden from you
    when I was made[20] in the secret place,

---

13. The MT is pointed with a *qāmes* under the *waw*, וָאֹמַר, clearly making the form a *waw* consecutive with a preterite: "and [so] I said." This is also the wording in the Greek version. But the editors of BHS propose without manuscript support changing it to a *shewa* and reading it as an imperfect in a conditional clause, "if I say." NIV adopted this reading.
14. The MT has יְשׁוּפֵנִי, "will bruise me," but the NIV and many other versions have a translation based on Symmachus, "conceal me" (ἐπισκεπάσει με). This proposal does not take the verb to be שׁוּף, but from שָׂכַךְ (said to be equivalent to סָכַךְ). This proposal involves changing a שׁ to a שׂ, a פ to a כ, doubling the כ, and retaining the *šûreq* before the doubled letter (an anomaly). The form would be יְשֻׂכֵּנִי. There are too many changes here to be convincing. Besides, there is no manuscript evidence to support it (the Greek has καταπατήσει, "trample"). And I am not convinced that the new reading is even necessary. Another suggestion is to take it from a word נֶשֶׁף, "gloomy" (Targum [= חָשַׁךְ], and perhaps behind Symmachus).
15. The Greek translation is "the night became light to my delight."
16. The Greek has "you supported me."
17. The form in the MT is נִפְלֵיתִי, "I am unique, distinct." Some Greek mss, the Syriac, and Jerome have a 2nd person singular, reading "you are wonderful," as if from פֶּלֶא.
18. The Dead Sea scroll has rearranged נוֹרָאוֹת to obtain the pronoun "you" with the verb. The scroll as נורא אתה, "you are awesome."
19. MT has נַפְשִׁי.
20. The Hebrew text uses an old *qal* passive form (pointed like a *pual*), "I was made." The Greek version made it active, "you made," ἐποίησας, reading עָשִׂיתָ.

813

PSALM 139

when I was skillfully woven[21] in the lowest parts of the earth.
16 Your eyes saw my unformed substance;
and in your book they were all written,
the days ordained for me,[22]
when *as yet there were* none of them.
17 How precious also are your intentions[23] for me, O God!
How great are the sums of them![24]
18 *If* I could count them, they would be more in number than the sand–
When I awake, I am still with you.

19 O that you would slay the wicked, O God!
Depart from me, therefore, you bloodthirsty men!
20 For they speak of you[25] for evil intent;
your enemies[26] take[27] *your name* in vain.
21 Do not I hate them, O LORD, who despise you?

---

21. The Hebrew has רֻקַּמְתִּי. But the Greek does not have a verb, but reads this as καὶ ἡ ὑπόστασίς μου, "and (nor) my substance," perhaps וְקׂמָתִי.
22. This line was translated in the Greek version with "in a day they will be formed."
23. The Greek text has "your friends," apparently thinking of רֵעַ.
24. The Greek version has a different understanding of the letters: "the beginnings of them were strengthened." The translator may have been looking at the letters, but without vowels.
25. The form in the text, יֹאמְרֻךָ, is difficult. It appears to read "they speak [of] you." There is no other place where the verb with the accusative means to speak of a person. Perowne suggests the correct reading should be יַמְרוּךָ (in line with the Quinta rendering, παρεπίκραναν) with the meaning "they provoke you" or "they rebel against you." Then the next word, he suggests, is used adverbially, to mean something like "foolishly" (*Psalms*, II:445). But the context seems to emphasize the speech of the bloodthirsty people.
26. The form in the MT is עָרֶיךָ, which would be "your cities," and not make any sense in the passage. Some would simply change the form to a pronoun such as עָלֶיךָ, "against you." But the word may be an Aramaic word, which would be equivalent to Hebrew צָרֶיךָ, "your enemies". This is the reading found in several of the versions. The normal phonological correspondences include the Aramaic ע corresponding to the Hebrew צ (unless in this case the word is from a different root altogether, perhaps עוּר).
27. The MT has נָשֻׂא, apparently abbreviated from נָשְׂאוּ, for "they take."

>   And do not I loathe[28] those who rise up against you?
> 22 I hate them with complete hatred;
>   they have become my enemies.
> 23 Search me, O God, and know my heart;
>   try me, and know my anxious thoughts;[29]
> 24 and see if there is any wicked[30] way in me,
>   and lead me in the everlasting way.

Composition and Context

Psalm 139 is surely one of the most beautifully written psalms in the collection, and one of the most profound as well. Moreover, we have here perhaps the most intimate psalm in the collection.[31] And according to many commentators (following Gunkel) it is this inner attitude that breaks the form and content free from standard patterns. There are so many views on the genre and setting of this psalm that it would be a study in itself to work through them. Many are satisfied with saying that it is a compilation using mixed types and motifs (see Allen, p. 323). There is some agreement over the contents of the major sections: verses 1–18 are more hymnic, and verses 19–24 more like a lament psalm. Allen suggests it is a individual lament in a developed form, the entire first part providing the psalmist with relevant support for his prayer.[32] Anderson suggests it is an individual thanksgiving psalm written after the psalmist was accused and then acquitted of the charge of idolatry, making verses 19–24

---

28. The Greek translation reads "was I not wasting away," ἐξετηκόμην.
29. Greek reads "paths."
30. The word in the text has the meaning of "pain" or "hard." Because this does not seem to fit very well, the word has been given different interpretations, such as "iniquity" in the Greek (and so "wicked" in modern versions), "deceit" in Jerome, or "lying" in the Syriac. Allen suggests reading a homonym, "idolatry." He adds that this would mean understanding the next line as "ancient way" and not "everlasting way," the ancient way being the historic faith (pp. 318, 320).
31. Broyles, *Psalms,* p. 483.
32. L. C. Allen, "Faith on Trial: An Analysis of Psalm 139," *Vox evangelica* 10 (1977):5–23.

an affirmation of innocence.[33] Eaton was more specific: it was written for the king who was beset by enemies.[34] And most commentators note the wisdom motifs in the psalm; Kraus suggests that the psalm came from the intellectual sphere of wisdom poetry,[35] but notes that it is not quite a wisdom psalm, and not technically a hymn, but didactic poetry instead.

As a result, one cannot be dogmatic about the genre of this passage. Neither is there enough evidence to establish the occasion or date. It may be that the psalmist had been accused of idolatry, or it may simply be that he is avowing his loyalty to the LORD to avail himself of divine protection. The theology of the psalm is often considered too advanced for David (the superscription), and that along with Aramaic words leads most scholars to take it as a post-exilic composition. But Allen raises the question of whether an older psalm from a Davidic collection might have been brought forward and adapted to a later set of circumstances.[36] There is no strong evidence that the ideas of the psalm had to be late.

Whatever the setting was, students of the Bible are drawn to this passage when studying the omniscience and omnipresence of the sovereign God, the creator and redeemer. The psalm however is far more than a theological study; it uses the theological ideas to form a powerful message for those who trust in the sovereign LORD God—it is applied theology, and so always relevant.

As the analysis of this psalm will show, there are four strophes of six verses each. In each of the first three strophes a clear pattern emerges: a summary statement, then a development of this theme with examples, and then a conclusion. The concluding idea of each section forms the transition to the next strophe. And the final strophe records the psalmist's conclusion based on the meditation, an affirmation of his loyalty to the LORD.[37]

---

33. *Psalms 73–150*, p. 904. This is an old view of Bentzen, followed by Würthwein, Weiser, Kraus and others.
34. *Kingship*, pp. 83–84.
35. *Psalms 60–150*, p. 511–13.
36. *Psalms 101–150*, p. 327.
37. See J. C. M. Holman, "Analysis of the Text of Psalm 139," *BZ* 14 (1970):37–71; and "The Structure of Psalm cxxxix," *VT* 21 (1971):298–310.

The Perceiving, Pursuing, Planning God

Exegetical Analysis

Summary

Knowing that the LORD superintended his development in the womb and foreordained the events of his life with loving intentions, David acknowledges that the LORD knows every detail of his life in advance and that it is impossible to hide from that penetrating presence, all of which leads him to affirm passionately his loyalty to the LORD and to seek divine guidance.

Outline

I. David realizes that every aspect of his life is known and controlled by the LORD's penetrating knowledge (1–6).
   A. He avows that he is the object of the LORD's penetrating knowledge (1).
   B. He explains that the LORD knows every detail of his life (2–4)
      1. The LORD knows his every move and discerns the motivation for each of them (2)
      2. The LORD has become familiar with and concerned over his life (3).
      3. The LORD knows his words before he can say them (4).
   C. He concludes that the LORD's penetrating knowledge is insuperably controlling him (5–6).
      1. The LORD restricts his actions and imposes his will on him (5).
      2. The LORD's knowledge is so extraordinary that it is beyond his control (6).
II. David realizes that it is impossible to escape from the LORD's controlling presence, no matter how far or fast he may go, in the dark or in the light (7–12).
   A. He avows that there is no place he can go to escape the LORD's presence (7).
   B. He explains that there is no place in the universe where he can escape the control of this omnipresent God (8–10).
      1. The LORD is present everywhere from the heavens above to *she'ol* below (8).

2. The LORD is present everywhere from the east to the west, continually guiding him (9–10).
   C. He concludes that even the darkness cannot separate him from the LORD (11–12).
      1. David proposes the possibility that he might be in danger in oppressive darkness (11).
      2. David concludes that since darkness and light are the same to him, darkness will not separate him from the LORD's presence (12).
III. David joyfully acknowledges that the LORD superintended his physical and spiritual formation in the womb and foreordained his life with loving intentions (13–18).
   A. He avows that the LORD created his inner being and carefully planned his physical constitution (13).
   B. He praises the LORD because he is one of God's many marvelous works, explaining that the LORD superintended his formation in the womb and ordained his life (14–16).
      1. The LORD is continually praised for this and all his unique and awesome works (14).
      2. The LORD superintended his intricate formation within the secrecy of the womb (15).
      3. The LORD foreordained all his life's details before he was even born (16).
   C. He joyfully concludes that the LORD's innumerable intentions for him are comforting, even in the reality of life (17–18).
IV. David exhibits his loyalty to the LORD by passionately rejecting the wicked enemies of God and by submitting his life to the penetrating examination of the LORD to determine his loyalty to God, whom he asks to lead him in the right way (19–24).
   A. He longs for God to slay the wicked rebels who use religion for their own evil purposes (19–20).
   B. He affirms his loyalty to God by passionately dissociating himself from God's enemies (21–22).
      1. The psalmist rejects those who oppose God.
      2. The psalmist affirms that his rejection of them is complete.

C. He petitions God to examine his life and prove his loyalties, asking to be guided in the everlasting way of God (23–24).
   1. The psalmist calls on God to examine him for loyalty (23).
   2. The psalmist desires that God expose anything grievous (24a).
   3. The psalmist asks God to guide him in the everlasting way (24b).

COMMENTARY IN EXPOSITORY FORM

I. The LORD knows and evaluates every aspect of our lives (1–6).

A. Summary: The LORD knows us thoroughly (1).

The first line of the psalm is the summary statement of the first strophe: "O LORD, you have searched me and you know [me]." The use of the personal, covenant name "Yahweh" ("LORD") is appropriate, for it harmonizes with the emphasis on God's intimate knowledge and superintendence of the life of the psalmist as well as his protecting presence.

To describe this personal knowledge the psalmist has to rely on figurative language: "you have searched me" (חֲקַרְתַּנִי) compares the process and findings of a diligent human search to the immediate and complete knowledge God has of the psalmist. The verb "to search" is used for such human activities as spies searching out the land, miners searching for precious ore, or scribes searching the laws. Divine knowledge, of course, does not require that God engage in such a search, and so the expression is figurative (an implied comparison)–it is as if God has made such a search of him and discovered all there was to know. The figure gives the reader a clearer understanding of the thorough, diligent, and determined knowledge that the LORD has of people. The verb should be classified as a present perfect, stressing the lasting result of the "search."

The last verb in the line clarifies the result: "and [as a result] you know [me]." The direct object of this verb has to be supplied from the previous, parallel verb. David is saying that if God has searched "me," then he knows "me." And this is personal, intimate, and experiential knowledge (יָדַע; s.v. Ps. 67:2). The rest of the strophe will now develop the completeness of the LORD's knowledge of David and likewise of us.

B. Development: The LORD's knowledge is penetrating (2–4).

In these three verses the psalmist will give some specifics about the knowledge of the LORD. He begins with the repetition of the verb "to know," here introduced with the emphatic pronoun: "[As for] you, you know when I sit down and when I arise." The object of the verb is formed with two infinitives with pronoun suffixes, "my sitting down and my rising up" (שִׁבְתִּי וְקוּמִי). The two forms together form a unified idea (a merism), expressing the totality of his movement: God knows every move he makes (including sitting down and rising up, but much more than those two movements).

God's knowledge extends beyond awareness of the movements to the reasons for them. "You discern my intentions from afar." The translation "intentions" or "motivations"(רֵעִי) is based on an Aramaic equivalent and a similar noun in Hebrew meaning "striving" (רְעוּת). Other translations read the word as "thoughts" (from דֵּעִי). The point is that God not only knows every move people make, but knows their motivations as well, what they are striving for in them. All of these things God evaluates, for the verb is "to discern, to perceive" (בִּין; s.v. Ps. 49:1). He not only knows everything we do but also evaluates all of it. And he does this "from afar" (רָחוֹק), a word that can mean "afar" in either space or time. Because in this context the emphasis is on God's intimate knowledge of the activities of the psalmist, it is unlikely that far off in space could be meant; and because he will say that God knows what he is trying to say before he says it, it is likely "afar" in time is meant. In other words, God knows all this from a distance in time, meaning—beforehand.

Verse three develops the idea of discerning with a figure: "You winnow my journeying forth and my lying down." The verb "winnow, sift" (זֵרִיתָ) compares God's evaluating, penetrating knowledge to the process of winnowing grain– separating what is worthless from what is valuable. And the focus of this activity is expressed in another merism, the opposite ideas of "journeying forth" and "lying down on a bed" meaning one's entire daily routine. The parallel colon states how thorough God's knowledge is: "You have become familiar with all my ways." "Ways" is the idiom for activities and characteristics. And the verb selected here has the sense "become familiar" or "habitual." The psalmist is therefore saying that the LORD is completely familiar with all his daily activities, as familiar as one might be for whom they are habitual.

The psalmist now provides one specific example of God's knowledge—what we say (v. 4). The construction employs a causal clause followed by a clause introduced with the particle "indeed" (הֵן): "for there is not a word on my tongue, indeed O LORD, you know all of it." The first part lays out the condition, and the second the consequence. A smoother rendering is "Before there is a word on my tongue, you, O LORD, know it completely." The idea is that the psalmist has not yet been able to frame the words that he wants to say (tongue being a metonymy of cause, for speaking), but God knows everything that will be said. The point of the illustration is that if God knows this much about this detail of life, he certainly knows all the activities and intentions we have.

C. Conclusion: Such knowledge seems overwhelming and restrictive (5–6).

Because of the way these two verses have been translated, one can easily take them in a positive sense. But in fact they do not have that emphasis. The psalmist feels trapped and overwhelmed by God's knowledge, so much so that his next thoughts will be to escape from it. The first half of verse 5 says "you have besieged me behind and before." The verb used here (צוּר) means "to confine, besiege" (NIV, "hem in"). It definitely has the sense of being surrounded and restricted. Its object is another merism, "behind and before," meaning "on all sides."

The parallel unit in the verse confirms this troubled sense: "you have placed your palm over me." The word for "hand" here is not the ordinary word (יָד) that would express the power of God; rather, it is the "palm" (כַּף) of the hand. The bold figure (an anthropomorphism) of "you place your hand over me" gives the picture of "cupping" something with the hand, like a bug on the table. This image fits the parallelism and expresses the uneasiness the psalmist has about the controlling and evaluating knowledge of the LORD.

The psalmist can only conclude that this kind of knowledge is completely beyond his ability to understand, let alone control: "[This type of][38] knowledge is too wonderful for me." The word translated "wonderful" (פְּלִא) does not express a pleasing and happy response. The word means something is full of wonder, surpassing, extra-ordinary, or incomprehensible.[39] The kind of knowledge he has been describing is not human; it is supernatural and surpassing, wonderful in the sense of extraordinary and incomprehensible.

This meaning is complemented by the parallel military expression: "it is high, I cannot prevail over it." The verb "it is high"

---

38. The word without the article stresses the essential meaning of the word.
39. The word פֶּלֶא means "a wonder," something extraordinary or hard to be understood, such as God's dealings with his people (Isa. 29:14) or the testimonies of the Law (Ps. 119:129). The acts of God's judgment and redemption are called wonderful (Ps. 88:11, 13; 89:6). The word is used for one of the throne names of the Messiah in Isaiah 9:5. If the LORD has the kind of knowledge this psalm says he has, then he will need no counselors or advisors, but will be a wonder of a counselor himself.

The denominative verb פָּלָא means "to be extraordinary, surpassing." For example, in Genesis 18:14, where the LORD promises a child for the dead womb of Sarah, we read: "Is anything too hard [extra-ordinary] for the LORD?" The sense is that of something beyond one's power—and nothing is beyond God's power. The verb can also be used for things too difficult to understand, such as aspects of nature listed in Proverbs 30:18. It certainly can describe the marvelous acts of God, but also the presumptuous words of the pagan king (Dan. 11:36). As it describes the wonderful works of the LORD, the emphasis is on their being so extraordinary as to be almost incomprehensible (Exod. 34:10; Josh. 3:13; Ps. 78:11). When the LORD is the subject the meaning is always on his doing something truly amazing; what is impossible for people is possible for God.

The psalmist here is not actually delighted in the knowledge of the LORD—it is so amazing, so extraordinary that it is beyond his control or capacity to understand. So he wanted to flee.

(נִשְׂגְּבָה) describes something that is unattainably high, like a wall of a fortress. And "prevail over" (the verb "to be able" followed by a *lamed* preposition with the pronoun object) has the sense of conquering or controlling. God's knowledge is like a high fortress before which he stands powerless. God has all the controlling knowledge; and so the psalmist feels trapped and powerless.

II. The LORD is present everywhere we go, no matter how remote or dangerous that might be (7–12).

A. *Summary: There is no place we can go to flee from the LORD (7).*

In view of this confining knowledge the LORD has, the psalmist's first inclination was to flee, to get out from under the besieging hand of God. But that impulse raises the question of where he should go, which leads to a second meditation on the omnipresence of God. Not only does God know everything about us, he is everywhere we go or even think of going.[40]

Verse 7 uses rhetorical questions to affirm that there is no place one could go to flee from his presence. The two verbs, "go" (אֵלֵךְ) and "flee" (אֶבְרָח) have the nuance of potential imperfects, for the question asks "where can I go / where can I flee," i.e., where is it possible to go to get away from God's controlling knowledge? The escape would be from God's Spirit and presence (literally, "from your face"). These two rhetorical questions are designed to express the negative idea that there is no place to go where he would not be in the presence of God.

B. *Development: The LORD is present everywhere in the universe (8–10).*

David poses hypothetical situations to illustrate and elaborate on this point. Verse 8 uses a pair of conditional clauses followed by their affirmations: "If I ascend to the heavens, you

---

40. See E. J. Young, *A Study of the Omnipresence of God* (London: Banner of Truth Trust, 1965); and W. I. Wolverton, "The Psalmists' Belief in God's Presence," *CJT* 9 (1963):82–94.

are there; if I spread out my bed in *she'ol*, you are even there." "Heavens" above and *"she'ol"* below form a merism, meaning everything from one place to the other; and the verbs "ascend" and "spread out my bed" recall the earlier merism of getting up and going out in the morning and coming back to lie down at night. God was thoroughly familiar with all of that, according to verse 3; now the point is that God is there in every place the psalmist could go or even conceive of going, from heaven above to *she'ol* below.

In verse 9 he introduces another conditional clause using further merisms. Now the merism signifies east to west, but still retaining the idea of the heavens above and *she'ol* below in the words of "the wings of the dawn" (above) and "the uttermost part of the sea" (below) respectively. The conditional particle "if" is understood from the context to begin verse 9: "[If] I take the wings of the dawn," which employs other figures. "Wings" is used because of the similarity in appearance of the early morning rays of the sun and the great outstretched wings of a bird (zoomorphism). The image would point to the swiftness of flight as well as the appearance of the rays at dawn. The "dawn" is a figure for the time of the sunrise (a substitution, for the word for the time of the sun rise has been put in place of the word sun). The psalmist is here raising the hypothetical idea that he might mount up in flight at dawn and streak across the sky with the speed of light from east to west. Even if he could do that, he could not escape the presence of God.

The second part of this condition is the arrival in the distant west: "[and] settle on the far side of the sea . . . ." Still using the image of a bird in flight, the psalmist envisions the destination in the uttermost west, the far side of the Mediterranean Sea, the place of the sunset. But the sea also was for the biblical writers a place of chaos and death, very much like *she'ol* or the abyss. So both verses 8 and 9 have movement from the place of light and life to the place of darkness and death. From heaven to hell, from east in the morning to the west at dusk, there is no place that he could go to escape, no matter how fast or how far he might travel.

Now, in verse 10, we have the final statement, the apodasis (גַּם־שָׁם): "even there your hand will guide me, and your right hand will hold me fast." The tone of the psalm now changes completely, perhaps because of his thinking about the places he might go without God—*she'ol*, or the dark, uttermost parts of the sea. These are places he would not want to be without God. Two things show the change. First, he now uses the other word for "hand" (יָד) which refers to the hand and forearm and signifies the power of God. Second, the verbs are not now verbs of besieging but of leading and guiding. The verb "lead, guide" (נָחָה) is the word used in Psalm 23 (s.v. Ps. 23:3); it is definitely favorable and comforting. The other verb is "hold fast, seize" (אָחַז); in any place of danger, in any remote or dark land, it would be a comfort to know that God was holding him firmly in his power. God is not only present with him everywhere, but holding him and guiding him with loving intentions.

C. Conclusion: Nothing hinders the protective presence of the LORD (11–12).

David now proposes the possibility that darkness might create barriers for him from the knowledge and presence of God. He sets forth his thinking with "[So] I said," 'Surely the darkness will bruise me'." While the idea of darkness bruising someone is difficult, in a poetic composition it is not that difficult. The "darkness" may be a figure referring to what happens in the darkness (so a metonymy of subject); and perhaps bruising has the added connotation of darkening him as well. But the connection is to *she'ol* (opposite of heaven) and the dark uttermost part of the sea (opposite the sun rise), places of danger (and places therefore deified by the pagans). The line could be translated in a number of ways. It could be a simple future: "Surely the darkness will bruise me"; or it could be with the nuance of possibility: "Surely the darkness would bruise me"; or even the jussive: "Only[41] let the darkness bruise me." Any of these could fit the context well, but the first would be preferable if he is contemplating the dangerous places in which he could find himself.

---

41. The particle *'ak* (אַךְ) may be an asseverative "surely" or a restrictive "only"; the latter works better if a jussive is taken for the nuance of the verb.

Whatever nuance is selected for the verb must be used for the nominal sentence to follow: "Only the darkness will bruise me // and the light [will become] night around me." The text literally has "and [the] night / light / around me." In such a nominal clause, the predicate nominative is often put first; this fact, plus the parallelism with the first part, indicates that "light" is the subject of the sentence. The construction is difficult, but the psalmist is laying out the possibility that everywhere he went could become oppressive darkness. And the idea of the oppression expressed in the bruising would darken him with wounds. Clearly, there are very dangerous places where one might be.

But he affirms that even if that were the case, it would be no problem for the LORD. Verse 12 provides the *apodasis* for the preceding verse: "even the darkness will not be too dark for you; the night shall shine like the day, for darkness is as the light to you." The last clause simply has "like the darkness, like the light," meaning, "as is the darkness, so is the light." Nothing in the darkness can harm him, for neither darkness nor distance can separate him from God's powerful presence and penetrating knowledge.

III. (All of this is so because) the LORD lovingly superintended our development and planned out our lives from the womb itself (13–18).

A. Summary: The LORD has made us (13).

The third strophe of the psalm explains the first two: God knows everything about us and is always present with us because he made us. Thus, verse 13 begins with "for": "For you created my inmost being, you knit me together in my mother's womb." The two halves credit the LORD with the formation of the soul and the body. The first uses the verb "create" (קָנִיתָ)[42] with the object "my kidneys" (כִּלְיֹתָי). "Kidneys" is used commonly (a metonymy of subject) for the internal emotional being, the soul or spirit. It was understood that a person was formed in the womb

---

42. The verb *qānāh* (קָנָה) is a homonym; the other verb means "to acquire, possess," which would not be the idea here.

by natural reproductive processes; but the believer emphasizes that God is the cause of it all (a metonymy of cause). Ultimately, God is the one who created him.

The parallel colon focuses on the physical body. The verb "to weave together, knit" is figurative (an implied comparison), picturing the formation of the body as the weaving of a beautiful tapestry. The body truly is a work of art.

B. Development: The LORD superintended our development in accordance with his plan for us (14–16).

Before David goes any further he breaks forth into praise (v. 14). The initial verb is "I acknowledge you" (אוֹדְךָ, from יָדָה; s.v. Ps. 6:5). This is the common word in the Psalter for "acknowledge, give thanks, confess." Here the imperfect tense must be translated as an English present tense since it is parallel to the active participle (יֹדַעַת), "I know"—the psalmist is breaking forth into praise. And the reason for the praise is because he realizes that he is "uniquely made" (נִפְלֵיתִי) in a "fearful manner" (נוֹרָאוֹת; s.v. Ps. 2:11). The participle "fearful" is used adverbially here. He is saying, "I am extraordinary in a way that produces fear" (following the reading in the MT). This statement is followed by an expansion: all God's works are wonderful. So one half of the verse acknowledges that the psalmist is marvelously made; the other half declares that all God's works are wonderful—and that he (lit. "my soul") knows full well.

The psalm turns to expand on the way that God has made us. The focus is on the LORD's superintendence over the birth process: "My frame was not hidden from you, when I was made in the secret place, when I was woven together in the depths of the earth" (v. 15). The subject of the first part is "my frame" or more literally, "my boney structure" (עָצְמִי), a figure for his structure and all that is contained within in (a metonymy of subject). His whole body was not hidden from God when he was developing in the womb—because the darkness and remoteness is no barrier to God. The verb "was not hidden" is of course an understatement, meaning the opposite, that God saw his body in the womb. The positive statement will be made in verse 16.

PSALM 139

The second half of the verse clarifies when he was not hidden. The two verbs are "I was made" (a *qal* passive perfect tense) and "I was woven together" (רֻקַּמְתִּי, a *pual* perfect). This latter verb is another figure, comparing the idea of "weave together, embroider (in variegated colors)" with the development of the body in the womb under God's superintendence. The womb in this verse is described as "the secret place" (a metonymy of adjunct) and "the lowest part of the earth." This last figure (an implied comparison) is unusual; but it was probably chosen to make a link with the preceding strophe in which he spoke of descending to *she'ol* or going to the uttermost part of the sea. In the psalmist's day inside the womb would have been as remote to the human eye and knowledge as any region in the netherworld.

In verse 16 the psalmist details the divine superintendence over his formation. He writes: "Your eyes saw my unformed body; all of them were written in your book, the days ordained for me, before one of them came to be." The verb "saw" in this context has the nuance of "to oversee, superintend."[43] And what was being superintended was the fetus, the unformed body (גָּלְמִי is a shapeless form, rolled up ball, fetus).

The next part of the verse is a little difficult because the suffix on "all of them" is proleptic, referring ahead to "days" in the second half of the verse—the days were written in the book.[44] The "book" is a figurative reference to the omniscience of God (an implied comparison) because God does not need to write in a book the record of our lives. The word "days" is also figurative (a metonymy of subject), meaning the things that were done on the days (which would include the number of days as well). And modifying "days" is the verb "ordained" (a *pual* perfect, יֻצָּרוּ); a relative pronoun must be supplied to form the smooth English rendering "which were ordained."[45] In this intensive stem, the

---

43. With God as the subject, the verb "to see" can have the meaning of "to evaluate," "to pity," or "to superintend."
44. The word order in the Hebrew is: "and in your book / all of them / were written, / the days / they were ordained / and there was not one of them.
45. The verb means "to form, fashion" with a plan or design. It is used in the creation account for the forming of Adam from the dust, forming by design. The idea of intent is included in this word, as the use of its related noun "plan, intent" (יֵצֶר) would clarify. The participle from this word is the

828

psalmist is saying that the LORD planned all the activities of his life before he was even born.

C. Conclusion: The LORD's loving intention for us are precious and innumerable (17–18).

The third strophe concludes on a much more positive note than the first—this divine omniscience of his entire life is precious. "How precious" is expressed with the adjective (יָקָר) which means "rare," and is used often to describe precious gems. If it is rare, it is precious and valuable. But what is precious are God's intentions (רֵעֶיךָ is the same word that was used in verse 2, which was translated "intentions, motivations"). The intentions God has for us would be a figure of speech (a metonymy of cause for the effect), because the text mentions God's intentions but means the effect of them, what God does in our lives.[46] And the emphasis in the text is on "to me," which comes first in the line.

The second half of the verse exclaims that the "sums" (plural, as if many sums) of them are vast. The word for "vast" (עָצְמוּ) may form a word play on the word for "boney framework" in verse 15–as the LORD superintended the development in the womb, he did so with innumerable intentions for the life that was to be lived. The idea of their vastness is then developed in the last verse of the section: "Were I to count them, they would be more numerous than the grains of sand." This expression is hyperbolic for emphasizing any large number. At the very least this section would call for a healthier consideration of how God has plans for the child being formed in the womb; and in addition to that, the section calls for people to evaluate every aspect of their lives to ensure that they are fulfilling God's intentions.

The last colon of verse 18 forms the transition to the next section. David says, "When I awake, I am still with you." The verb "awake" (קִיץ) can refer to awakening from sleep, from drunkenness, from death, or in this case from meditation. He

---

Hebrew term for "potter." The verb's idea, then, is to form with a design, a plan.

46. For the meaning "your designs," see Liudger Sabottka, "Rē'eykā in Psalm 139:17," *Bib* 63 (1982):558–9.

829

has been meditating, and in those meditations he came to be filled with comfort. Now, when he comes back to reality, as it were, he knows that all his thoughts are still true. And the final section will apply them to his predicament.

IV. We will find great comfort and security in the LORD if we remain loyal to him (19–24).

This section forms the conclusion of the entire psalm: The psalmist can find comfort in the knowledge and presence of the LORD, and even in the midst of enemies find security—if he is loyal to the LORD. If people are unfaithful to God, then God's knowledge and presence will be sources of conviction; but if people are loyal, they bring comfort. So the psalm will end with the psalmist making sure of his loyalties. We have in this psalm, then, the antinomy that is found in all of Scripture. On the one hand the Bible teaches clearly that God is absolutely sovereign in all things; and on the other hand it teaches that he has given to us the responsibility of our choices. This keeps the doctrine from becoming fatalism. We do not know the details of God's sovereign will for our lives; but we do know that we must live by faith in accordance with his will. But our faith must be strengthened by the knowledge of the perceiving, pursuing and planning God.

A. Those who are loyal to the LORD distance themselves from the LORD's enemies (19–22).

Verse 19 breaks into the meditation with the force of a rude interruption: "O that you would slay the wicked, O God. Turn away from me you men of blood." Apparently David was being harassed by men intent on killing him (their intentions conflicted with God's intentions). And so he called for intervention. The imprecation is the standard wish formula, literally, "if you will kill," meaning, "O that you would kill." The address is to God (now in the form of the poetic variant אֱלוֹהַּ); this use of "God" stresses the authority and strength of the sovereign LORD God (earlier the use of the personal name had stressed the intimate knowledge).

The description of these people begins with the word "wicked" (רָשָׁע; s.v. Ps. 1:1), the word for the ungodly, someone who is a guilty person, not a member of the covenant community, not a believer, and one who is capable of all manner of evil against God and people. This word does not mean that their wickedness is easily detected, for such people can be hypocritical as well and appear to be very nice. But not in this case, as the next lines make clear.

First, David turns to address them directly as "men of blood[s]." The genitive "blood" is attributive, meaning that they are bloody men, or bloodthirsty men—killers. His imperative in the direct address to them to "depart" is more of a warning than anything else: God is with him, and therefore opposed to them. Second, they justify their schemes with religion. Verse 20 is fraught with difficulties. The line in the Hebrew text says, "who speak of you for evil intent; your adversaries take your name." The first half has the difficulty of the verb "they speak [of] you," which is a smooth rendering of "they say you" (יֹאמְרֻךָ). This line can be interpreted to mean that these folks mention the LORD for a false or deceptive purpose, as the parallelism will show.[47] The translation "for evil intent" is an accurate representation of the text (לִמְזִמָּה; s.v. Ps. 10:2). The words connected to this root often have the connotation of false or deceptive practices.

The second half of the verse also has some textual difficulties. The verb ("they take") itself is written in an unusual form (נָשֻׂא).[48] With the following expression "to falsehood, vanity," one would expect the meaning here to be "they take [your name] in vain" (for שָׁוְא s.v. Ps. 127:1). That would form a good parallelism with the first half. If the reference is to the third commandment, then we have an ellipsis of the word "name" and the meaning would be understood from the suffix on the preceding verb. To take the name of the LORD in vain would be to give false testimony or to swear falsely. Their religious expressions are hollow

---

47. The variant reading is with the verb "to rebel" (מָרָה). But the evidence as well as the parallelism support the MT reading.
48. The form expected would be $nāś^{e}\hat{u}$ (נָשְׂאוּ), but with the weaker letter 'aleph the suffix has been written immediately after the preceding consonant.

and vain—they use them to cover their malicious attacks on the psalmist.

The final word is also difficult. In Hebrew this word (עָרֶיךָ) would be translated "your cities"–but that would make no sense in the line. Some commentaries have suggested changing the second letter to a "d" or an "l" to get a preposition "against you." But a better solution allows for us to leave the text alone. If the word in the text is viewed as an Aramaic word, then it means "your enemies." The line then says, "your enemies take [your name] in vain."[49]

The psalmist now affirms his loyalty to the LORD by expressing passionately his total rejection of those who oppose his Lord (v. 21). He does this with a rhetorical question to affirm his hatred of them: "Do not I hate those who hate you." For many today this sounds very harsh. But there are several things to consider here. First, at the heart of the word translated "hate" (שָׂנֵא) is the idea "to reject" (as opposed to the word for "love" which has an emphasis on choosing).[50] Second, the form that the

---

49. Gene Rice translates the line: "they have carried away the cities to destruction" ("The Integrity of the Text of Psalm 139:20b," *CBQ* 46 [1984]:28–30).
50. The verb שָׂנֵא means "to hate"; it occurs some 164 times in the Bible. There are very few words that have the same emphasis or range of meanings. The verb "hate" can have varying levels of intensity from hate with great hatred to feeling aversion to something or someone. Sometimes "hate" means "to love no longer" (see Judg. 14:16; 15:2). Leah, for example, was hated (Gen. 29:31, 33), meaning less loved or neglected. Many times its distinct force can be measured by the presence of its antonym, אָהַב, "to love."

The word is used frequently with God as the subject. Things he hates are many: abominations (Jer. 44:4), hypocritical worship (Isa. 1:14), a serious of troubling sins (Prov. 6:16), divorce (Mal. 2:16), and heathen practices (Deut. 16:22). But in addition to these it can be used for God's sovereign rejection: Jacob have I loved, but Esau I hated (Mal. 1:3). God chose Jacob before he was born and so personal feelings were not the issue; he did not choose Esau. Accordingly, most things hated are rejected; whereas things loved are chosen. God commands those who love the LORD to hate evil (Ps. 97:10), meaning reject it, but no doubt with feelings of revulsion.

People who reject the LORD and his Law are said to hate him (Exod. 20:5). Similarly the psalmist's enemies are often called his "haters," and their hatred may be a mixture of loathing and rejection. Conversely, the

psalmist uses for their hatred of the LORD is a more intensive form *(a piel* participle), underscoring their intense hatred of God; whereas the form used to describe his hatred of them is not intensive (only the *qal* imperfect), with the progressive or habitual nuance to get the English present tense. Third, the word order places the wicked first to emphasize the fact that they are first the LORD's enemies, and then became his also. A clear way to translate this would be: "Those who utterly despise (totally reject) you, O LORD, do not I hate (reject)?" The Psalmist knew what the apostles affirmed later, namely, that to be loyal to the Lord one cannot have fellowship or even close friendship with the avowed enemies of the Lord (2 Cor. 6).

The second half of the verse restates the point but in stronger terms. Parallel to "I hate" is the verb "I abhor" (קוּט), meaning a loathing or abhorrence. The object of this verb is the participle "those who rise up against you" (וּבִתְקוֹמְמֶיךָ).[51] This word clarifies their hatred of the LORD as open opposition.

These rhetorical questions are followed with an affirmation in versed 22: "I hate them with a complete hatred." He uses the adverbial accusative "complete" (תַּכְלִית, from כָּלָה; s.v. Ps. 90:7), followed by the genitive after the word of entirety and totality, to strengthen the verbal idea– "[with] completeness of hatred I hate them." His is a total rejection of God's enemies. The point is clarified by the parallel expression stating that they have become his enemies. Again, the point is important: they were first God's enemies, and since he is loyal to God, they have become his enemies.

B. The faithful desire to maintain their integrity throughout life (23–24).

Now the psalmist turns the meditation into a prayer. He prays for the LORD to continue his search of him in order to

---

people of Israel were warned not to hate their brothers in their hearts (Lev. 19:17). See E. Jenni, "שָׂנֵא *śn'* **to hate**," in *The Theological Lexicon of the Old Testament,* ed. by Jenni and Westermann, III:1277–79.

51. The form is a *hithpolel* participle; the *mem* of the prefix for the participle was dropped (aphaeresis) to avoid the labials (*mem* and *bet* of the preposition) coming together at the beginning.

uncover any disquieting thoughts. In addition to his request "search me" and "know my heart," he adds the prayer "test me" (בָּחַן).⁵² The word means "to examine" in order to discover any spiritual weaknesses in him. Just as one would refine a metal to remove impurities, so God should test his life for impurities. The impurities are called "my disquieting thoughts" (שַׂרְעַפָּי, from the root שָׂעַף); the idea is that of anxious, excited thoughts, disquietings, and therefore weaknesses in his faith that might lead to sin (s.v. Ps. 94:19). David wants his loyalty to match his understanding of the God he has been describing.

The psalm closes with the completion of this short prayer for examination. "See" goes with the [omniscient] search requested in the last verse; it too is a human expression (an anthropomorphism), as if God has to look closely to see any false ways. The object of this examination is to determine if there is any "way of pain" in him. The way refers to any activities or mannerisms in his life; and the qualifying word "pain" modifies this word to mean any activity that causes pain (a metonymy of effect, "pain" being put for the activity that causes the pain).

His final request is to be guided (which he earlier described as God's work wherever he might be)⁵³ in "the everlasting way." This expression refers to the right way of living that will endure. It is comparable to seeking first the kingdom of God and its righteousness. It is the course of life that results in rest and blessing, but which if abandoned results in destruction (cf. Ps. 1:6; Jer. 6:16; 18:18).

---

52. The verb בָּחַן means "examine, try." One of its categories of meaning is simply "examine, try," such as the eyelids of the LORD examining the sons of man (Ps. 11:4). This is probably the emphasis here in Psalm 139.

    The verb can also mean "test, prove" someone or something. God is said to test people, as one tries gold (Zech. 13:9). It is also found in passages where the analogy with gold or silver is not present but implied; in Malachi 3:10 and 15 God will test his people to make them fit for service. In this line the noun בֹּחַן, "testing," is used: Isaiah 28:16 refers to a tested stone, one that was approved to be used in the foundation.

    The word can also be used for man testing or tempting God (Ps. 95:9, for the wilderness experience). They tested God even though they had seen his works. So in that case their testing God came from their unbelief or weak faith; when God tested people it was to discover faith in them.

53. Prayer, then, is the expression of faith and submission to the will of God.

The Perceiving, Pursuing, Planning God

MESSAGE AND APPLICATION

The expository idea of this complex psalm may be expressed in this way: *The omniscience and the omnipresence of the sovereign creator is a great comfort to those who are loyal to him (and a stern warning to those who oppose him).* The psalm is certainly a holy meditation on doctrine, but as a meditation it is more than theological reflection—it is an application of doctrine to life. The psalm not only probes the nature of God but also shows the significance of it all to the way we live.

The message of the psalm is reiterated throughout Scripture. The emphasis on God's knowledge is repeated in many passages. In the book of Revelation the letters to the churches have a constant theme: "I know your works." God truly does know everything about us. For the second stanza we again have many passages in the Bible to stress the presence of the Lord, one of the strong points from the exodus on. The Bible echoes the promise "I will be with you" again and again. We also have the words of Jesus at his ascension, promising that he is with us always, even to the end of the world. He will never forsake us. The focus on the Lord as the sovereign creator and sustainer of all life is also repeated in the Bible. Here the emphasis is on human birth as part of the divine plan. Acts 17:24–28 comes pretty close to Psalm 139:13–18, showing not only divine creation but control of our lives. The final stanza is the psalmist's application. It stresses the psalmist's loyalty to the LORD and opposition to those who hate God; any of the passages on separation could be mentioned here, but 2 Corinthians 6:11–18 is perhaps the most forceful.

The application would then be that believers in the Lord must demonstrate their loyalty to God and his cause, praying for continued evaluation and guidance, and submitting to his leadership into eternal paths of righteousness.

PSALM 140

An Imprecation against the Ungodly

INTRODUCTION

Text and Textual Variants

For the Chief Musician. A Psalm of David.

1 Deliver me, O LORD, from *the* evil man,
   from[1] the violent man preserve me,
2 who have devised evil things in *their* heart;
   all[2] day they stir up[3] wars.
3 They have sharpened their tongue[4] like a serpent,
   adder's poison is under their lips. S*elah*

---

1. A few manuscripts and the Syriac version have a conjunction here.
2. In a few manuscripts and the Greek version there is an article: "all the day."
3. MT has יְגוּרוּ, "they attack"; the dictionaries list this as a distinct root, but it is not very compelling. The Greek has παρετάσσοντο πολέμους, "they kept waging wars." BHS suggests reading יְגָרוּ, from גָּרָה, "they incite wars."
4. It will be noticed that this psalm alternates between the singular and the plural; the use of the singular is probably meant to be collective.

PSALM 140

4 Keep me, O LORD, from the hands[5] of the wicked,
    from the violent preserve me,
        who have purposed to thrust aside my steps.
5 The proud have hidden a snare for me, and cords,[6]
    they have spread a net by the side of the road,
    they have set traps for me. S*elah*
6 I said to the LORD, You are my God,
    give ear, O LORD,[7] to the voice of my supplications.[8]
7 O Yahweh, Lord,[9] *the* strength of my salvation,
    you have covered my head in *the* day of battle.
8 Do not grant, O LORD, the desires[10] of the wicked;
    do not further his wicked device,

---

5. The Greek translation has the singular, probably an interpretation as a collective.
6. The line is difficult due to the placement of the accents. The MT reads:

טָמְנוּ־גֵאִים פַּח לִי וַחֲבָלִים / פָּרְשׂוּ רֶשֶׁת לְיַד־מַעְגָּל / מֹקְשִׁים שָׁתוּ־לִי.

    There appear to be three clauses here: "The proud have hidden a snare for me, and cords"; "they have spread a net by the side of the road"; and "traps they have set for me." The difficulty is the inclusion of "and cords." As it stands in the MT it would be in apposition to "snare." But if the disjunctive accent is placed after "net" instead of after "road," then the second and third clauses could be read: "and they have spread cords *as* traps for me, by the side of a path they have set a trap for me." But for the word "cords" some have suggested a slight variation in the form to חֹבְלִים, "those who stretch out a cord," i.e, parallel to the "arrogant." The verse then reads: "The arrogant have hidden traps for me, and the corrupt spread nets; along the path they have set snares for me" (Allen, p. 332–3). None of this changes the clear meaning of the verse; it only sets out the phrasing differently and reworks the difficult word.
7. This is not in the Syriac.
8. The Greek has the singular.
9. The MT uses both the tetragrmmaton and the word "Lord" pointed with the vowels for the holy name: it reads יְהוִה אֲדֹנָי, and so may be rendered "LORD, Lord," or "Yahweh Lord." The vowels with the holy name are the vowels for "God," אֱלֹהִים, indicating that it was officially to be read, "O God, Yahweh."
10. The MT text has the plural construct form מַאֲוַיֵּי, "desires of." But the Greek translation has "from my desires," ἀπὸ τῆς ἐπιθυμίας μου, perhaps representing a form מַאֲוָתִי. The version translates: "Do not hand me over, O LORD, to a sinner as a result of my desire."

An Imprecation against the Ungodly

    that they be lifted up.[11] *Selah*
9 The head of those who surround me—[12]
    Let the trouble of their own lips cover them.[13]
10 Let burning coals fall on them,[14]
    Let them be cast into the fire,[15]
        into a miry pit[16] that they rise not again.
11 Do not let[17] an evil[18] speaker be established in the earth,

---

11. This part of the verse has זְמָמוֹ אַל־תָּפֵק יָרוּמוּ סֶלָה, "his [wicked] device do not further, they rise up. *Selah*. "His device" in the text is זְמָמוֹ. The Greek has "they schemed against me," διελογίσαντο κατ' ἐμοῦ, which would represent a verbal construction זְמָמוּ עָלַי. But the sequence of "do not further they rise" is the greater problem. Allen suggests reading the line "as for his plots, O God, wrench them away. *Selah*." He suggests as the verb תְּפֵ־רְקֵמוֹ, and the negative he takes as the word for "God." Others suggest more of a change: "may those who despise me not raise (their head)," constructing ". . . סֹלְיִ לֹא יָרִימוּ. But the word "heads" belongs with the next line: "the heads of those who surround me."
12. This cryptic expression does not seem connected very well to the rest of the verse. As it stands, it the expression could be a nominative absolute, resumed by the pronouns to follow: "the heads of those who surround me—let the trouble of their own lips cover them." The Greek version simply translated what was there: "the head of their encirclement—(the mischief of their lips will cover them).
13. The form in the text is a *K-Q* reading: יְכַסּוּמוֹ. The majority of manuscripts and the versions follow the *Qʳrē'* writing יְכַסִּימוֹ., "let it [the harm *done* by their own lips] overwhelm them."
14. The Greek version reads: "Coals will fall on them."
15. The text says, "Let him cast them," יַפִּלֵם, which may be interpreted as a passive. Greek reads, "With fire you will throw them down (καταβαλεῖς αὐτούς). Instead of reading "into the fire let them be cast," some have suggested that בָּאֵשׁ may not be "in / with fire," but an Aramaic word for evil (BDB). It would then say "may evil plunge them into . . . ."
16. The MT has בְּמַהֲמֹרוֹת, a word that seemed to be connected to an Arabic cognate that gave the sense of watery place. The word may mean a miry pit. Greek has "misery," ταλαιπωρίαις, "in misery they will not bear up."
17. The verbs in this verse could be translated as future indicatives or as jussives. The jussive translation fits this section of the psalm a little better.
18. The text simply says "a man of tongue." In the context the implication is that it is the enemy who is laying a trap—but speaking smoothly to cover it over. The Greek has a fairly literal rendering, ἀνὴρ γλωσσώδης, that may be interpreted to mean "a garrulous man."

the violent man—let evil hunt him to crush *him*.[19]

12 I know that the LORD will maintain the cause of the afflicted,
    the right[20] of the poor.
13 Surely the righteous shall give thanks unto your name;
    the upright shall dwell in[21] your presence.

Composition and Context

The psalmist in this case is apparently being wrongly accused of something serious by malicious slanderers bent on ruining him. So his prayer to the LORD describes his dilemma in great detail and then his desired justice in equally vivid terms. The psalm is an individual lament, but there is no complaint here that the LORD was not answering his prayer (no "you" section in the lament, only "I" and "they"). It is essentially a prayer with the repetition of descriptions of the dilemma and expressions of confidence.

The superscription ascribes the psalm to David; it is one of a series of psalms in this part of the collection that is Davidic. The contents of the prayer could fit any time in the life of David, or any period of Israel's history. Anderson, and most commentators, prefer a late date for the composition, suggesting that the language favors a late date.[22] Eaton argues that the psalm is a royal psalm, but there is not a lot of evidence for that other than the fact that such malicious slander would be more common in a context of a power struggle, especially if it included trumped up charges. Dahood places the psalm early because of the rare forms;[23] and Oesterley places it in later Judaism).[24]

The psalm can be outlined in a number of ways, but it seems

---

19. MT has לְמַדְחֵפֹת. The Hebrew verb has the sense "to push down" and so here the derivative word might have the meaning "[with a view] to pushing down." The Greek version reads "to destruction," διαφθοράν.
20. A few manuscripts, the Greek and the Syriac have a conjunction
21. The Greek translation rendered this "with your presence."
22. *Psalms 73–150,* p. 913.
23. *Psalms*, III:301.
24. *Psalms*, p. 558.

to fall into a pattern of prayer and confidence. In verses 1–5 we have the cry to God and the lament, in verses 6–8 the confidence, in verses 9–11 the prayer again but with imprecations, and verses 12–13 the confident expectation of praise. I chose for the exposition the pattern of prayer—confidence—prayer—confidence;[25] but it could easily be developed in the basic structure of the lament: introductory cry, lament, confidence, petition with imprecation, and anticipation of praise.

Exegetical Analysis

Summary

Certain that the afflicted will be maintained in their cause by the LORD, the psalmist prays for deliverance from evil people and includes in his prayer harsh imprecations on the wicked who gather together against him with poisonous accusations and destructive snares.

Outline

I. Crying out to God: The psalmist prays for deliverance from evil people who seek to destroy him with poisonous accusations and who set traps for him (1–5).
   A. Call for Help: He calls on the LORD to deliver him from the wicked (1–2).
   B. Lament: He describes the wicked who would destroy him (3–5):
      1. They have prepared their verbal attacks like a poisonous serpent (3).
      2. They have planned evil things to thrust him aside so he needs the LORD's help (4).
      3. They have laid traps for him in his daily activities (5).
II. Confidence in Praying: He reiterates his prayer for help from the LORD, voicing his confidence in the LORD, the strength of his salvation (6–8).
   A. The LORD is the strength of his salvation and therefore he prays to him (6–7).

---

25. This is similar to the arrangement by VanGemeren, *Psalms,* p. 965.

B. He prays that the LORD will not let the wicked have their way (8).
III. Petition with Imprecation: The psalmist announces his harsh imprecations on the wicked (9–11):
  A. He hopes the mischief of their lips will cover them (9).
  B. He hopes that burning coals will be cast on their heads as they are thrust into the fire (10).
  C. He is convinced that evil shall hunt the violent man to overthrow him (11).
IV. Confidence for Praising: The psalmist expresses his confidence in the LORD, certain that the righteous will rejoice in the deliverance (12–13).
  A. He knows that the LORD will maintain the cause of the afflicted (12).
  B. He is certain the upright shall give thanks to God's name in His presence (13).

COMMENTARY IN EXPOSITORY FORM

I. Crying out to God: When evil assailants try to destroy the righteous by slanderous accusations and dangerous traps the primary recourse for believers is to pray for deliverance (1–5).

A. *They must pray for God's deliverance from the destructive attacks of evil people (1–2).*

The psalm begins with the expected cry to the LORD for deliverance. In the first verse the verbs of the appeal, "deliver me" (חַלְּצֵנִי) and "preserve me" (תִּנְצְרֵנִי; s.v. Ps. 119:2), begin and end the line, forming a bracketing (inclusio) of the line by the chiasm. Within the verbs we have the two parallel prepositional phrases: "from *the* evil man" (רָע; s.v. Ps. 10:15) and "from *the* violent man (man of violences," חֲמָסִים; s.v. Ps. 58:2). The plural of "violence" could indicate "violent acts,"[26] or "exceptional violence."[27] And as the psalm will indicate, the word "man" in these phrases is to be

---

26. Van Generen, *Psalms*, p. 916.
27. Anderson, *Psalms 73–150*, p. 914.

taken collectively—evil and violent people. The variant in the poetic balance of the line is the addition in the first colon of the holy name, "Yahweh," which does double duty in the verse.

Verse 2 provides a relative clause to clarify what makes these people evil and violent. First, they plan evil things in their heart. Here the verb is plural, showing that it is a group of enemies that are in view (for חָשְׁבוּ, s.v. Ps. 32:2). Evil men devise evil things (רָעוֹת). And these schemes come from their heart, meaning it is their full intent to destroy the psalmist (for לֵב, s.v. Ps. 111:1). And how they put their plans into action is explained in the second colon: "all day (continually) they stir up wars." As noted before, the verb has been translated as "they attack" (a second root גּוּר), but the evidence for that verb and its meaning is not strong. Many therefore follow the variant with "provoke, stir up wars" as the meaning. The point would not be changed greatly in either case; however, if it means to stir up wars it might indicate that the psalmist is not a mere individual citizen but perhaps the king who would be susceptible to military attacks.[28] Whatever it is that they are doing, and the psalm will continue to specify that, they are doing it relentlessly—all the day, or, continually.

B. They need God's help because the wicked make slanderous accusations to destroy them (3–5).

The nature of the activities of the assailants further explains why the psalmist so desperately needs divine intervention. Believers of all ages have found themselves in similar situations where prayer becomes indispensable (as it always should be) because all human efforts have either failed or cannot adequately deal with the nature of evil.

The focus of the lament is on their malicious slander. "They have sharpened their tongue" may apply a military idea, sharpening a sword or arrows, to speech, for the object is their tongue, meaning what they say (a metonymy of cause). The point is that

---

28. Anderson said that this and the mention of a battle later could be hints that the psalmist was a king; but he rather suggests that the words were borrowed from the royal setting and applied to individuals (p. 914).

they carefully prepare and hone what they want to say so that it will destroy and inflict pain. We know this was their intent from the simile, "like a serpent," which is taken further by saying "adder's poison is under their lips." The image of the serpent conveys stealth and danger—they are preparing to attack; but the additional colon speaks of poison. Their intention was clearly evil, i.e., to say things that would be carefully intended to bring painful ruin and death. So the psalmist has to face their malicious and slanderous accusation, and because they are so clever, so well-prepared, he is not able to deal with it alone.

In verse 4 the psalmist turns immediately to prayer, repeating the first verse of the psalm essentially, but changing the first request to "keep me" (שָׁמְרֵנִי; s.v. Ps. 12:7) and the first prepositional phrase to "from the hand (power) of the wicked." After these two requests he clarifies their wickedness with a relative clause: "who have planned to thrust aside my steps." Their wickedness was a carefully thought-through plan (for חָשַׁב s.v. Ps. 32:2), designed to disrupt and destroy his course of activity, his life. The word means "to thrust, push" (לִדְחוֹת from דָּחָה); it has the sense here of pushing aside or down, tripping up, or overthrowing.

How they will bring this about is revealed in verse 5: like trappers they have prepared traps to catch him unaware (see Pss. 31:4; 119:110, 142:3 and 141:9). Three times over he says that they have laid traps: they have hidden a snare, they have spread a net, and they have set traps. While it is possible that there might have been physical ambushes planned to destroy him, it is more likely that slanderous accusations have been carefully prepared to catch him and destroy his daily activities, i.e, his life. Who are these people? They are "the proud" (גֵּאִים; s.v. Ps. 93:1). The word used means "rise up"; it can have a good sense, such as in describing the majesty of the LORD, but it can have a negative sense, such as people who think too highly of themselves and leave no room for God. They are evil and violent because they are self-sufficient and seek to obtain their goals by any means.

II. Confidence in Praying: The righteous may pray with confidence that the LORD prevent such wicked attacks because he is their God and their savior (6–8).

In the next three verses the psalmist still presses his appeal

An Imprecation against the Ungodly

to the LORD to listen to his supplications and not permit the wicked to achieve what they planned and be exalted over the righteous. But the confidence of the psalmist comes to the fore in these verses. His first announcement is, "You are my God." Here is a simple but profound contrast to the clever wording of the arrogant. He is acknowledging his faith and loyalty to the LORD (to Yahweh), the God of the covenant. And on the basis of this covenant relationship he appeals to the LORD to listen carefully (the common anthropomorphic expression is "give ear," as if he would have the LORD lean over to hear better) to the voice of his supplications. The construction may be interpreted as an objective genitive, a voice producing supplications, or appeals for mercy (תַּחֲנוּנָי; s.v. Ps. 4:1). As with laments in general, those praying are always aware that they need God's gracious intervention; they know they do not deserve it, but because the LORD is their God they know that he delights in showing compassion and grace to his people—especially in face of malicious attacks from the proud.

The psalmist also describes the Lord ("O Yahweh, Lord") as the "strength of my salvation" (v. 7). This expression (עֹז יְשׁוּעָתִי) explains "Lord" by apposition. The second word, "salvation," is the genitive; it could be taken as an attributive genitive, "my saving strength," or as a genitive of specification, "my strong deliverer."[29] The suffix on "salvation" would then be objective—the saving of me. For "strength" s.v. Ps. 29:1; and for "salvation" s.v. Ps. 3:2.

In the parallel line the psalmist affirms that God has covered his head in the day of battle. The idea of covering the head may suggest with a shield or a helmet for defense. The reference to a battle and to salvation may raise the possibility that the slanderous accusations were linked to a possible insurrection. In any case, the LORD here appears as a divine warrior, avenging and delivering his people with might on the day of battle. But the expressions may simply be used figuratively for the conflict with the wicked.

The appeal in this section is for God to prevent evil from succeeding and wickedness being exalted because of it. The

---

29. Anderson, *Psalms 73–150*, p. 915.

prayer is for God to prevent the proud from achieving their "desires," namely, to thrust the psalmist down and destroy him. The second half of the verse, difficult as it may be, still makes sense in the text: "Do not further his (their) plan *that* they rise (or, are lifted up)." God should disrupt what the wicked are doing without delay, for if they continue they might succeed in their desires and exalt themselves more than they already do (being swelled with pride). The verb used (יָרוּמוּ; s.v. Ps. 46:10) simply means "they lift up," but would have the connotation here of exalting themselves or becoming proud.

III. Petition with Imprecation: The people of God may pray that the LORD will deliver them by turning the malicious devices back on the wicked (9–11).

The psalmist's petition becomes more intentional now due to the specific nature of what his malicious enemies are doing. The prayer includes imprecations, prayers that the evil they do will come back on them and they will be afflicted with the kind of pain they have inflicted on others. It is a prayer in harmony with the idea of talionic justice—may they reap what they sow. But it is not an expression for personal revenge, but an expression of concern for God's just rule. The answer to his prayer should clearly display divine justice on evil people.

Verse 9 begins with a description of the wicked that seems disconnected. But taken as an independent nominative absolute it actually focuses attention on the subject matter of the imprecation—"(as for) the head of those who surround me—let the trouble of their own lips cover them." The use of the word "head" might be collective for the proud who attack him, or it may refer to the leadership of the group. In any case, his prayer is that the troubling accusations they are bringing cover them instead. "Trouble" could in general refer to the harm that they have done, but since the text mentions lips specifically, it is probably the slanderous accusations. The prayer is that they will be overwhelmed as their own words will be turned against them.

In verse 10 the text uses the image of "burning coals" for divine judgment, perhaps alluding to Sodom. And if the Hebrew text of the next line stands as it is, the petition would continue with a

An Imprecation against the Ungodly

similar image of divine wrath, "let them be cast into the fire." The third clause has been translated as "watery place," which does not fit comfortably with this verse. It may mean "miry pit" instead of "watery place." The lines would then say that the wrath (coals) of God would fall on them, that they would be thrown into the great suffering (fire) of divine judgement, and that they would be completely destroyed (cast into the pit and never rise again).

Following this the psalmist appeals for divine justice on the earth: "Do not let an evil speaker be established in the earth, the violent man—let evil hunt him to destruction (or the place of the dead)."[30] For "an evil speaker" the text simply says "a man of tongue"; but given the previous references to the tongue and lip, it is likely that this description refers to the wicked who are skilled at saying things that are destructive and painful. The "man of tongue" could be a slanderer, a false witness, or a malicious liar. The petition is that such a person is not to be established (יִכּוֹן; s.v. Ps. 93:1) but rooted out before he consolidates his own position. People may be gifted in logic and rhetoric and communicative skills, but if it is put to evil purpose and employed slanderously and maliciously, it is dangerous to all and becomes a matter for urgent prayer, especially in this modern age where people can post comments and opinions so easily. Some people will be persuaded by liars and flatterers and follow them; but God will not allow them to succeed—there will be divine retribution. Here the righteous pray that "evil (רָע)" will hunt them down to destruction. It is a prayer that the violent man who is so involved with evil be ruined in his own devices. The psalmist is only praying for what he knows God does, and will do, in restoring justice to the land.

IV. Confidence for Praising: The people of God may rightly anticipate giving praise for their deliverance because the LORD champions the cause of the afflicted (12–13).

The last two verses also express confidence, but now it is

---

30. מַדְחֵפֹת may be a term for a hunter's corral, which would be figurative then of the place of the dead. See Moshe Greenberg, "Two New Hunting Terms in Psalm 140:12," *HAR* 1 (1977):149–53.

confidence in the future of the righteous—God will champion their cause so that they will offer praise to him and enjoy living in the blessings of his presence. This is what the righteous of all ages look forward to, even in the midst of serious crises and opposition. The psalmist's "I know" expresses the certainty of his faith (see Ps. 20:6), a certainty based on his personal knowledge of how the LORD defends the afflicted. Here the text says that "the LORD will maintain (literally "do," יַעֲשֶׂה) the cause of the afflicted (דִּין עָנִי), the right of the poor (מִשְׁפַּט אֶבְיֹנִים)." The two terms, "cause"[31] and "right" (s.v. Ps. 9:4) are legal terms. For the LORD to maintain righteous causes means that he will champion the cases in a society that are unjust, cases in which the poor and the needy have no one to defend them or take up their cause. Israel's leaders had not only failed to do this, but on the contrary were seeking to destroy the righteous. Accordingly, they had forfeited their own rights and would have to receive divine justice. And when this happens, the righteous will be able to enjoy life as God intended. Verse 13 is directed to the LORD himself, and forms both an expression of praise and of confidence. He says the righteous "will give thanks (יוֹדוּ; s.v. Ps. 6:5, or "acknowledge") your name,"—the name of the LORD, who the LORD is and what he has done for them (s.v. Ps. 20:1). As that praise is offered up, he adds, "the upright shall dwell in (with) your presence." They will live in safety and security in the presence of the LORD, their God, their savior, and their defender.

---

31. The verb דִּין means "to judge," and its substantive means "a legal case." The verb occurs some 22 times in the Old Testament (8 in the Psalms), and the noun another 20. The word basically described authoritative, binding judgment in a legal procedure. The subjects of the verbs are always people in authority, namely the king, the high priest, or tribal leaders. The objects of such judgment (or vindication as the case may be) are frequently the poor, needy, widow and orphan (Ps. 72:2 for example).

Where the LORD is the subject of the verb, the meaning might be "to pronounce judgment" or "to judge," meaning "create justice." The LORD will judge the nations (Ps. 96:10; Gen. 15:14) and the nation of Israel (Ps. 50:4). The LORD also creates justice for the suffering (Ps. 140:13). So the word may mean to meet for legal procedures and settle cases, it extends to the carrying out of legal decisions.

An Imprecation against the Ungodly

MESSAGE AND APPLICATION

Confidence in the LORD is essential for the believer in this world system. Because those who are opposed to the faith, to righteousness, and to integrity will attempt to destroy believers by malicious accusations and plots to bring them down, the righteous will have to spend much time in prayer. To do that they will have to build their confidence in the LORD and in his promises; then they will hold to their integrity and continue to pray with faith. In this psalm we also have a section of imprecations, curses to be carried out on the wicked by the LORD. As we have seen with other imprecatory psalms, Christians are cautious about praying down such wrath on their enemies. They have been taught to forgive and to pray for their enemies. And yet when the persecution becomes unbearable, as it is in parts of the world today, praying for God to do now what we know he is going to do eventually seems appropriate. In fact, an imprecatory prayer might sound a warning for those who oppose the faith.

An exposition of this psalm today will emphasize the confident prayer for deliverance from the wicked and the confident praise for God's care and deliverance of his people, the confidence being based on the LORD's being our strength and salvation. That deliverance ultimately will be at the expense of the wicked; praying for that simply means that we are turning vengeance and judgment over to the LORD. The message could be summarized in this way: *Because the LORD provides strength and salvation to his afflicted people, they may pray with confidence for protection and deliverance from the wicked (a prayer which will ultimately be answered in the destruction of the wicked).* The applications should include two important messages: believers must build their confidence in the LORD, and they must pray and praise regularly with that confidence. The focus on the LORD will enable them to overcome a world that hated the Lord before it hated them.

PSALM 141

A Righteous Prayer for Protection from a Sanctified Believer

INTRODUCTION

Text and Textual Variants

A Psalm of David

1 O LORD, I call to you; hasten to me;[1]
   listen[2] to my voice when I call to you.
2 May my prayer be set[3] before you *like* incense,
   the lifting of my hands *like* an evening offering.

3 Set a guard before my mouth, O LORD;

---

1. For the MT's "hasten" (חוּשָׁה), the Greek version has "listen to me" (εἰσάκουσόν μου) which is clearly interpretive but duplicates the next colon.
2. The form in the Hebrew text is הַאֲזִינָה, traditionally rendered "give ear," a denominative verb based on the noun "ear."
3. MT uses תִּכּוֹן (from כּוּן; s.v. Ps. 93:1), "set in order" or just "set." The Greek text interprets this as "succeed" (κατευθυνθήτω).

PSALM 141

keep watch [4] at the door of my lips.
4 Do not let my heart incline to an evil thing,
   so that I participate in wicked activities
      with those *who are* evildoers;[5]
   and do not let me eat of their delicacies.[6]
5 Let a righteous man strike me—*it shall be* a kindness,
   and let him reprove me—*it shall be as* oil on my head;[7]
   Let not my head refuse *it*,
      for my prayer will still be against the deeds of
         wickedness.

6 *When* their rulers[8] are hurled down the sides of the rock,
   then they shall realize that my words are pleasing.
7 *They will say*,[9] "As one ploughs and breaks up the earth,
   our bones have been scattered at the mouth of the grave."

---

4. The form in the text is the imperative נִצְּרָה (see Prov. 4:13); the editors of BHS propose reading a noun וּנְצָרָה. to parallel "a guard" in the first colon. The Greek version slightly rearranges this colon and reads it as, "and a door of constraint about (καὶ θύραν περιοχῆς περί) my lips."
5. The colon in the text literally has "with men (אֶת־אִישִׁים), workers of iniquity."
6. The MT has for "do not let me eat" וּבַל־אֶלְחַם; but the Greek version has "and I shall not team up with" (καὶ οὐ μὴ συνδυάσω). And for "delicacies" the Greek version reads "(their) chosen ones" (ἐκλεκτῶν).
7. The first half of this verse is cryptic and requires something to be supplied to make it understandable. Taking the first parts of each of the lines as conditional clauses makes the best sense. The Greek version, however, reads the first three cola as, "A righteous man will discipline me with mercy and shall correct me. But let not the oil of a sinner anoint my head." The translation appears to have read the second "head" (רֹאשׁ) as "sinner" (רָשָׁע).
8. The text has "judges," but it means the leaders of the enemies.
9. This has been inserted for clarification. The MT has "our bones," suggesting that the verse describes the devastation on the psalmist and his supporters. Others read "their bones," clearly referring the devastation to the rulers of the wicked. It seems more likely that it will be the rulers/judges who will be hurled down the rocky slopes (if it is not indicating they already have been so destroyed). Other than changing the text, an additional clause to lead into the words makes this view clear.
   For a different interpretation Briggs suggests reading the line as "O that . . . their bones . . ." (*Psalms*, II:509), although the MT has "our bones." Kraus as well as others simply conclude that the verse makes no

A Righteous Prayer for Protection from a Sanctified Believer

8 But my eyes are *fixed* on you, Yahweh, Lord;[10]
    in you have I taken refuge—do not end[11] my life.
9 Protect me from the traps they lay for me,
    from the snares of the evildoers.
10 Let the wicked fall into their own nets,
    while I pass by safely.[12]

Composition and Context

This is a psalm of petition, a prayer for sanctification and protection.[13] Its structure follows the normal pattern of the individual lament fairly well: an address to God, a lament, a confession of trust, and the petition itself; but this psalm has no final vow of praise which would normally be in a lament. Moreover, this psalm's main emphasis is on the petition, so that the other sections are abbreviated. In verses 1 and 2 we have the introductory cry with the lament; in verses 3–5 the petition to be preserved from sinning, in verses 6–7 the confident anticipation that the wicked be punished; and finally, in verses 8–10, the concluding petition for deliverance from the pernicious plans of the wicked and for the wicked to fall by their own devices.

It is difficult to construct the setting for such a psalm. Kirkpatrick says that the writer seems to be on guard against lapses in his confidence and enjoyment of the pleasures with the wicked.[14] He may have been praying at a set time for worship, perhaps the evening prayers, unless his prayer simply alludes

---

  sense (*Psalms 60–150*, p. 526). And Perowne says these two verses are obscure, and that all we can do is guess at their meaning (II:453).
10. The MT uses the holy name "Yahweh" with the designation "Lord"– "Yahweh (my) Lord." The holy name is pointed with the vowels for "God" so that in public reading 'Adonay would not be said twice. The Greek version had little choice but to render them the same: κύριε κύριε, "Lord, Lord."
11. The verb in the text means "pour out (my life)," meaning to bring it to an end. The Greek version reads "(do not) erase (me)" (ἀντανέλῃς).
12. The Hebrew has יַחַד אָנֹכִי עַד־אֶעֱבוֹר, "while I pass by in safety"; the Greek version reads "I am alone (κατὰ μόνας) until I pass by."
13. Booij, "Psalm 141: A Prayer for Discipline and Protection," *Bib* 86 (2005):97–106.
14. *Psalms,* p. 527.

to such times. It is hard to say. He does express his piety and his confident faith; but from the first verse he indicates how sharply his piety is under trial.[15] His brief references to aspects of ritual procedures in the law has led some to conclude that the final form of the composition is late. But this is surely insufficient evidence for such a conclusion, especially since the laws of the sanctuary are early. In fact, the danger the psalmist faces, his confidence in the LORD, and the form of his appeal for deliverance matches various Davidic psalms.

Exegetical Analysis

Summary

Offering his evening prayer, the psalmist prays that he be prevented from speaking against the LORD or falling into the alluring temptations the wicked offer, but that he will be kept from the traps of the wicked so that their rulers will finally listen to his message.

Outline

I. The psalmist asks the LORD to answer his evening prayer speedily (1–2).
   A. God should answer his prayer quickly (1).
   B. God should pay attention to his prayer at the time of the evening oblation (2).
II. The psalmist asks that the LORD guard him from saying the wrong things, and from the alluring temptations of the wicked (3–5).
   A. He prays that God guard his words (3).
   B. He prays that God preserve him from the alluring temptations of the wicked (4).
   C. He asks that if the righteous rebuke and correct him he would accept it as a loving act—for his prayer remains against the deeds of wickedness (5).

---

15. Kidner, *Psalms 73–150*, p. 470.

A Righteous Prayer for Protection from a Sanctified Believer

III. The psalmist expresses his confidence that the wicked will realize his words were appropriate when their leaders are cast down and they are left to die (6–7).
   A. He is sure that when the rulers of the wicked are thrown down their followers will finally realize that his words are correct and pleasing (6).
   B. Their bones will be scattered disgracefully at the entrance of the graves (7).
IV. The psalmist confidently petitions the LORD to deliver him from the traps of the wicked by destroying them with their own devices (8–10).
   A. Because he has taken refuge in the LORD and remains constant in his faith, he confidently prays that God will extend his life (8).
   B. He asks specifically to be kept from the traps of the wicked (9).
   C. He desires that the wicked will be caught in their own traps while he escapes (10).

COMMENTARY IN EXPOSITORY FORM

I. The righteous pray for God to answer them quickly as they faithfully keep their prayer vigil (1–2).

In his introductory cry for help, the psalmist appeals to the LORD to respond quickly. This emphasis on the quick response indicates the urgency of his situation: the imperative itself would call for an immediate response, but the word chosen, "hasten" (חוּשָׁה), intensifies the appeal. Apparently he (perhaps he and his companions) is in a life-threatening crisis and needs God to act immediately.

The cry for help is extended through the other cola in the first two verses. Twice in the first verse he calls out to the LORD (the first verb, a perfect tense nuance, indicates he began to call out in the past and continues now, as the adverbial clause that follows indicates). In the second colon of verse 1 he calls for God to listen closely, the Hebrew verb asking God to "give ear" to his voice when he calls on him, a fairly common figure of speech in the psalms that appeals to God to pay the closest attention (an anthropomorphism, picturing God's leaning over to listen more closely). Then in verse 2 he uses more detail to motivate God to answer: he asks that his prayer be set before the LORD *"like* incense" and the lifting of his hands (a metonymy of adjunct for the prayer) *"like* an evening sacrifice." In other words, this is not just a call for help from anyone—it is a call from a devout believer who is not only praying continually but is following the prescribed sanctuary ceremonies for evening prayer. The main verb in verse 2 is "may (my prayer) be set (before you)," or, arranged properly (תִּכּוֹן; s.v. Ps. 93:1). The verb is used for having things in proper array or readiness, especially in the sanctuary ritual (2 Chron. 29:35; 35:10, 16); its use here expresses the desire that everything connected with his prayer be in proper order for God to see and honor.

The figures used in verse 2 (comparing his prayer to incense and the evening offering) may indicate the setting of the prayer was in the sanctuary, or at the least, indicate the prayer comes from someone who regularly worships in the way God prescribed. The incense (the adverbial accusative קְטֹרֶת) could be the ordinary incense put to either the morning or evening oblation,[16] or it could refer to what was added to any memorial dedication offering (the מִנְחָה of Lev. 2).[17] But here the offering is identified as the evening oblation (עֶרֶב). The gesture of lifting up of the hands is connected to praying in general, especially in sanctuary ritual. Here, then, the prayer with the gesture seems to be linked to the time of the evening offering (מִנְחָה) with the prayers (Lev. 2:1; Ps. 40:6) when incense was added to the oblation (the *tamid;* see Exod. 29:38–42; Num. 28:3–8). All that can be said for sure, however, is that the lifting of the hands and the mention of incense alludes to the sanctuary oblations, reflecting the psalmist's devout participation in the cycle of prayer.[18] The use of incense with the sacrifice signified that the prayer was

---

16. Perowne, *Psalms,* II:452.
17. Delitzsch, *Psalms,* III:362. See also M. Haran, "The Uses of Incense in the Ancient Ritual," *VT* x (1960):113–129.
18. But it is still possible that the prayer was not being made in the sanctuary as part of the ritual for prayer, but that the psalmist is merely alluding to the incense and gestures in his appeal to the LORD to accept his prayer.

pleasing to God. So the psalmist desires that his prayers would be as acceptable to God as the daily sacrifices were.

II. The righteous pray that God will guard their words and keep them from participating with the wicked in their activities (3–5).

A. They want God to guard their words (3).

The prayer is specifically for God to preserve his faithful servant from falling into sins of speech (see Prov. 13:3, for example).[19] Two imperatives express this first petition: "set (שִׁיתָה)" a guard, and "keep watch (נִצְּרָה)." The editors of BHS and some commentators suggest changing this second word to a noun to parallel "a guard" (שָׁמְרָה; s.v. Ps. 12:7) in the first colon: "Set a guard at my mouth, O LORD, a watch at the door of my lips." But there is no warrant for such a change. At any rate, what the psalmist wants is for God to guard what he says ("mouth" and "lips" are metonymies of cause for what he says). This could mean that he is afraid that he might murmur against God, or that he might lash out against his persecutors and thereby indulge in rash and possibly malicious words as the wicked do.[20] It would be easy to succumb to cynical and vindictive attitudes that are not really what God wants. As Delitzsch says, he prays for the grace of silence.[21] Just how the LORD will do this is not stated. It may be that God would work through his word in the mind of the psalmist to prevent him from saying anything foolish or wicked. In Proverbs this control of speech takes discipline and wisdom.

B. They want God to prevent their turning to wicked works (4).

The petition now is expanded to include separation from the wicked, that is, avoiding any temptation to get involved with them. He first asks God not to let his heart incline to any evil

---

19. Anderson, *Psalms 73–150,* p. 919.
20. See Perowne, *Psalms,* II:452.
21. *Psalms,* III:363.

thing.[22] The verb "incline" (the jussive אַל־תַּט, from נָטָה) specifically has the meaning of "turning" towards something, "let my heart not turn to an evil thing." The prayer is that God will not allow his heart (i.e., his mind, his will and affections) to go after any evil thing. The result of such turning is expressed in the second colon clearly: "so that I participate in wicked activities." The infinitive "participate" (לְהִתְעוֹלֵל) has the sense of "busy oneself," and here that would be with "wicked activities" (עֲלִלוֹת). The connection of these two words underscores the fact that he does not want to be readily active in wicked things. If his heart was inclined to turn toward this evil, then he would easily become active in doing the kinds of things that the wicked do. It all begins with the will and the affections. The way that the LORD would prevent this would be to enable him to keep his heart focused on obedience to the will of God.

The second request of the verse is that God not let him eat of their pleasurable things, or as some older versions had it, "dainties." These things are representative of the prosperity the wicked gain from their misdeeds; in general, the word refers to any things that the wicked take pleasure in, any luxuries and pleasures. Such things may surface in hospitality that the wicked provide. The psalmist is afraid that if he tastes of their pleasing but ill-gotten food or other provisions, he would enjoy it all and not be able to free himself from that allurement.[23]

C. They desire to receive correction from the righteous as they pray for judgment on the wicked (5).

This and the next two verses are challenging to the expositor because the situations presented in them do not seem to fit easily into the flow of the psalm. In verse 4 the psalmist prayed not to be swayed by evil; now he prays to accept appropriate rebuke. The

---

22. As Anderson correctly observes, the psalmist is not attributing sin to God when he asks that God not let his heart incline to evil; rather, he is expressing his dependence on the LORD to retain separation from it all (p. 920).
23. Anderson suggests that it is not impossible that "delicacies" be intended metaphorically to refer to the seductive and deceptive words they speak, as in Proverbs 5:3 (*Psalms 73–150*, p. 920).

858

idea exemplifies the attitude of the wise who receive correction well (Prov. 9:8). The main verbs may be taken as jussives setting forth the situation to which he must respond appropriately, although they could be explained as imperfect tenses in understood conditional clauses. There is no real difference between these two ways of reading the verse. The situation imagined is that if a righteous person smites him, (it will be) loyal love (in action), and if he reproves him, (it will be as) oil on the head. The supplied verbs could also be jussives as he would be praying that such rebuke would be received by him ("let it be"); or, they could be imperfects expressing his willingness to receive it ("it shall be"). The striking parallels the reproving, and the loyal love the oil. The idea seems to be that if or when a righteous person corrects him and prevents waywardness in him or in what he says, it will be seen by him as an act of faithful love and not simply criticism. And the image of oil on the head reflects the custom of joyfully welcoming a guest into one's house—the rebuke will be welcomed gladly as a genuine blessing that will keep him set apart to God. To accept such rebuke in this way would signal genuine faith and wisdom—to receive this will contribute to the way that he prays for protection from the wicked. And prayer is the best defense against wickedness—the prayers of a righteous person.

He then adds the request that his head not refuse the correction. The verb (יָנִי, a *hiphil* from נוא) means "to refuse"; here it expresses the subjective feeling and sympathy of the speaker. The reason he does not want to refuse it is that it will enable him to continue to pray about the deeds of wickedness that he faces. This latter word (בְּרָעוֹתֵיהֶם) means "in their evils," but could include "in their distresses" in light of the following context that reveals the terrible destruction that is coming upon their leaders as a result of their wickedness. If he accepts rebuke from the righteous it will be spiritually beneficial for him in that it will keep him in the right attitude and focus of prayer. This is one way in which his request in verses 3 and 4 will be answered. The rebuke of the righteous will check his words and keep him praying about the deeds of the wicked—that he will be delivered from the snare of the wicked, and that those who follow the wicked leaders will see his faith at work in what he says.

III. The righteous anticipate the fate of the wicked and its impact on the people (6–7).

The psalm then anticipates the destruction of the wicked rulers, and the realization of the survivors of the truth and appropriateness of his words. The verbs in this verse are perfect tenses, but since they probably refer to the future they should be taken as prophetic perfects. The first line tells of the destruction of the rulers. The verb "are hurled down (נִשְׁמְטוּ)" means that the leaders of the wicked will be harshly slain, here against the sides of the rocky cliffs. Once the leaders are gone, their followers will listen to David's words—they will realize that his words are correctly pleasing. This could refer to words of kindness and amnesty that he would extend to them, even though they tried to kill him. Or it could refer to his claims of integrity in contrast to what the wicked rulers had said about him (for example, as in the episode of David and Saul in the cave in 2 Sam. 24).

In the meantime, he wants to be separate from them, but not offensive to them (his prayer for God to guard his words), so that in their downfall he will say the right thing. He will not delight in their pleasantries, but desires to be pleasant to them. He wants his words to be moderate and well-chosen, so that when they hear them (learn of them) they will respond correctly. So the rebuke of a righteous person will be vital for him to hold this balance in what he says.

Verse 7 most likely describes the bitter circumstances of the wicked, although some commentators have taken the view that the psalmist is describing his own plight and that of the entire nation. Leupold[24] and Delitzsch[25] take the view that it describes the nation's bitter lot. Their bones are seen as seed scattered over freshly ploughed soil. But this idea is then taken further to mean that it is not the end of their life, for it is essential that seeds be sown and "die" as it were before new life comes from them. Taking the references to the bones to be the suffering righteous is one thing (and harmonizes literally with "our bones" in the Masoretic Text); but extending the imagery to such lengths is truly forced.

---

24. *Exposition of the Psalms*, p. 957.
25. *Psalms*, III:366.

The first interpretation is better, i.e., that it refers to the devastation to come on the leaders of the wicked. The imagery of making furrows in the earth suggests that like seeds their bones will be scattered in the furrows (see the similar descriptions for the destruction of the Edomites in 2 Chronicles 25:12). Some texts change the wording to say "their bones," to clarify it refers to the wicked. But the same clarification can be achieved by adding "*They will say*" to the verse. The idea of bones being scattered at the entrance to the graves defiles burial rites of the time. There will be devastation without proper respect for the dead in burial.

IV. The righteous confidently pray for deliverance from the traps of the wicked by means of the wicked being destroyed in their own traps (8–10).

A. *They affirm their confidence in the LORD (8a–b).*

In verse 8a-b, the psalmist reiterates his confidence in the LORD. Westermann would call this section their confession of trust.[26] He affirms that his eyes are on Yahweh, the Lord, meaning that his faith is unwavering as he follows God's righteous guidance. "In you" is also featured prominently as the focus of his trust (a present perfect, "I have found refuge," חָסָה; s.v. Ps. 7:1).

B. *They pray to be preserved from the plans of the wicked (8c–10).*

The last colon of verse 8 begins the petition proper: "do not end my life." The verb (עָרָה) "to pour out" the life is used for physical death in Isaiah 53:12. Life can be poured out when the blood is shed. He wants to be preserved in his present life.

Then, in verse 9 one imperative is used with two objects: "protect me" from the power of the traps and from the snares of the evildoers. The enemies are here portrayed as hunters laying traps to destroy the psalmist (see 7:15). The trap (פַּח) was set either along the path or in the ground. The word may refer to a

---

26. *The Praise of God in the Psalms*, p. 74.

trap stick; as soon as the prey dislodged the stick the trap would fly up and enclose the animal in the net or capture its foot in the trap. The word presents the trap as figuratively referring to the plans the enemies set in motion to catch and destroy him. The word "snares" (מֹקְשׁוֹת) then focuses on the bait in the trap. It too is used figuratively (implied comparisons) for the evil allurements that the enemy plans to use to destroy the psalmist and other righteous servants of the LORD—perhaps the "delicacies" offered to him.

The last verse turns the prayer for protection into a prayer for retaliation, so that the wicked receive their own planned destruction. It is a prayer for their scheme to backfire on them, i.e., that the wicked will fall by their own plans for him. The fate of Haman in the book of Esther provides a good example of how people's wicked plans can be turned back on them. The psalmist prays for this to happen while he passes by safely, i.e., all alone (NEB: "I escape in one piece"). Kidner observes that this last line "has a buoyancy worthy of the man who has slipped through a net with the help of God, and is sure that his journey is by no means over."[27]

MESSAGE AND APPLICATION

What makes this psalm different than other prayers to be delivered from the wicked enemies is the emphasis on the integrity of the believer. The summary expository idea should focus on this distinct emphasis: *When believers pray for the LORD to defend them from the schemes of the wicked to bring them down, they must also pray that the LORD will help them maintain their integrity so that even their enemies will have to acknowledge their righteousness.* David himself provides a good example for this integrity: given the chance to kill Saul in the cave, David refuses and spares the life of his enemy, prompting the king to acknowledge that David was more righteous than he (1 Sam. 24).

This prayer includes the petition that God prevent the psalmist from saying the wrong things or from being caught up in the allurements of the wicked. In other words, the psalmist

---

27. *The Psalms*, p. 472.

A Righteous Prayer for Protection from a Sanctified Believer

wants to remain righteous in his dealings with these people, so that when God answers his prayer and they are thrown down they will see that he handled himself appropriately. There is nothing to be gained by responding to the wicked with rash and inappropriate words, for that would lower the conflict to the level of the world. Similarly the apostle Paul was careful to renounce the hidden things of shame when dealing with unbelievers who are blind to the truth (2 Cor. 4). The integrity of the righteous may be sufficient to draw people to the faith; but if they do not believe, they will know the evil was all on their side. They will know that they were the ones laying the plots to destroy the righteous. It is hard for the righteous to deal with overtly wicked people with such grace, but it is what the LORD wants.

PSALM 142
No One Cares, except the LORD

INTRODUCTION

Text and Textual Variants

> A Contemplative Poem, of David,
>   when he was in the cave. A Prayer.
>
> 1 With my voice I cry[1] unto the LORD;
>   with my voice I plead to the LORD for mercy.
> 2 I pour out my complaint before him;
>   before him I tell my trouble.
>
> 3 When my spirit grows[2] faint within me,
>   then you know my way.[3]
>   In the path where I walk

---

1. The verbs in this verse are imperfect tenses; the Greek version translated them with the past tense, e.g., "I cried" (ἐκέκραξα).
2. The infinitive "grows faint" and the following verb "you know" (a perfect tense) could be put into the past tense translation as the Greek version did.
3. Several versions have the plural.

men have hidden a trap for me.
4 Look[4] to my right and see;
that no one takes notice[5] of for me.
Refuge has failed me;[6]
no one cares[7] for my life.

5 I cry to you, O LORD;
I say, "You are my refuge,[8]
my portion in the land of the living."
6 Pay attention to my loud cry,
for I have been brought very low;
deliver me from those who pursue me,
for they are too strong for me.
7 Bring me out from my prison,
so *that* I may praise your name.[9]
Then the righteous will gather about me[10]
because you will have dealt bountifully with me.[11]

Composition and Context

The superscription attributes the psalm to David when he was

---

4. The MT has imperatives: הַבֵּיט and רְאֵה. The Greek version translates these as "I would look" (κατενόουν) and "I would observe" (ἐπέβλεπον), as also the Dead Sea Scroll (*11QPs*ᵃ). The first could be interpreted as an infinitive absolute and made a finite verb, but the second would have to be changed to the infinitive absolute form, which the editors of BHS propose.
5. The form is the participle מַכִּיר; the Greek versions translates it "who recognized me" (ὁ ἐπιγινώσκων με). The idea of "taking notice" has a good sense, i.e., to be concerned for someone, as in Ruth 2.
6. The MT has אָבַד, "perished." The Greek version reads "escape vanished from me."
7. MT has דּוֹרֵשׁ, "seeks" in the sense of looking for him to rescue him in this context. The Greek version has the reading "sought out," ὁ ἐκζητῶν.
8. The Greek version interprets with "hope," ἐλπίς.
9. The Greek adds, "O Lord."
10. The MT has the *hiphil* verb יַכְתִּרוּ, which here has the idea of "surround"; this translation forms a good contrast to the lament concerning his isolation and apparent abandonment. The Greek version has "are waiting for me" (ἐμὲ ὑπομενοῦσιν), perhaps for יְכַתְּרוּ, the *piel*. For the form בִּי, "about me," a few manuscripts have כִּי.
11. The MT has כִּי תִגְמֹל עָלָי, "for you will (have dealt/deal) bountifully with me." The Greek version has "until (ἕως = עַד) you requite me (οὗ ἀνταποδῷς).

866

in the cave. He was in at least two caves, Adullam (1 Sam. 22:1, 4) and En Gedi (1 Sam. 24:1–21); the reference could be to either, but most likely Adullam because of the desperate tone of this psalm. It would then be the last of eight psalms that reflect David's flight from Saul.[12]

If the superscription is correct, then a psalm written by David has been placed with later psalms in the fifth section of the collection of psalms. There is no compelling reason to reject this view. But many commentators conclude that the composition is later than David, most likely exilic; but they do not provide very good reasons for this view. As Perowne says, we are left with a choice of two conclusions: either David wrote it, or someone later wrote it in imitation of David's manner.

The psalm is clearly the lament of an individual. The old view that it was the lament of Israel in exile has been rightly abandoned. The psalm has all the aspects of an individual lament; and besides, it anticipates how the "the righteous," the people, will rejoice when the psalmist is delivered. The occasion for the psalm has also been given a different interpretation than the superscription indicates. Taking the use of the word "prison" in verse 7 literally, some have classified this as the prisoner's prayer, and speculated on the reason for the imprisonment. But "prison" may just as easily be taken figuratively of the distress of the psalmist. Of course the psalm may have been used afterwards by people in prison, but that is another matter.

There is no major problem in acknowledging the original composition to be David's, while allowing that it was adapted down through history for similar situations. It is less convincing that the superscription was only a way of noting the value of the psalm. Bruce says that the "heading provides valuable evidence for a particular exposition" and adds that this has a proper place in the history of biblical interpretation.[13] This would also be true if the superscription was an historically reliable witness. Eaton

---

12. Perowne, *Psalms,* II:456.
13. F. F. Bruce, "The Earliest Old Testament Interpretation," *OTS* 17 (1972):37–52. See also M. Gertner, "Terms of Scriptural Interpretation: A Study in Hebrew Semantics," *BSOAS* 25 (1962):1–27.

has argued for a pre-exilic date of the psalm by classifying the work as a royal psalm, but clear royal-psalm motifs are lacking.[14]

Exegetical Analysis

Summary

Because he is utterly helpless before his enemies—there is no one else who cares for his life and he cannot save himself—the psalmist must depend completely on the LORD for his deliverance.

Outline

   I. The psalmist addresses the congregation: He cries aloud to the LORD from his trouble (1–2).
      A. He cries aloud to the LORD for mercy (1).
      B. He makes his complaint known to the LORD (2).
  II. The psalmist addresses the LORD: Even though he is overwhelmed by the attempts of his enemies to destroy him and by the absence of people who care for him, he expresses his confidence in the care of the LORD who knows his way (3–5).
      A. Lament: David laments that he is overwhelmed by the fact that his foes seek to kill him and there is no one who cares (3–4).
         1. He acknowledges that even though his spirit is overwhelmed within him the LORD knows his way (3a).
         2. He explains that his foes have set a trap for him (3b).
         3. He laments that there is no one who cares for him, challenging God to see for himself that there is no one to help and no place to go (4).
      B. Confidence: David cries out to God with confidence that he is his protection and provision for life (5).
 III. Petition: David petitions the LORD to deliver him so that he might offer praise for what is about to be accomplished (6–7a).

---

14. Eaton, *Kingship,* p. 85.

A. Petition: He pleads with the LORD to deliver him because he is helpless (6).
B. Motivation: He prays to be set free from his dilemma so that he might praise the LORD (7a).
C. Anticipation: He fully expects that the righteous will gather around him to hear of God's bountiful provision (7b).

COMMENTARY IN EXPOSITORY FORM

I. Bold and urgent cries for the LORD's mercy reflect times of great trouble for believers (1–2).

The first two verses of the lament record the psalmist's initial cry to the LORD. Everything in these verses fit well with the desperation and urgency of the moment. It is still true that the seriousness of the dilemma will be reflected in the way the prayer is expressed.

In the first verse we have standard verbs for laments: the general expression "I cry out" (the progressive imperfect of זָעַק signifying that the crying out is going on), and then a parallel and more specific verb, "I plead for mercy" (the imperfect אֶתְחַנָּן from חָנַן; s.v. Ps. 4:1). What he wants, the passage will show, is divine intervention to deliver him from his enemies. And so "mercy" may be understood with the connotation of aid or deliverance—what the mercy will mean to him.

But in both halves of the verse the expression *"with* my voice" (קוֹלִי, an adverbial accusative) is used. It means that he is crying aloud for God to help him. Crying out loud gives relief to pent up feelings and expresses the intensity of the distress.[15] Technically this is not part of the prayer because it is not addressed to God; rather, it may indicate a corporate concern by the psalmist, a kind of instruction for the benefit of others.[16] The psalmist will not shrink into silence, but perseveres in his prayer even more intensely than before.

In the second verse the introductory description of his

---

15. Kirkpatrick, *Psalms,* p. 801.
16. See Broyles, *Psalms,* p. 494; and Anderson, *Psalms 73–150,* p. 923.

prayer continues, and here it is possible that we have a hint that the petition might have been made in a cultic setting. Twice we have "before him" (לְפָנָיו), which could mean the prayer was in the house of the LORD, although the focus of the prayer in this manner need not mean the one praying was there (see Jonah 2). The psalmist is pouring out his complaint, a verb that also stresses the flow of his cry for help. Here the prayer is described as "my complaint" (שִׂיחִי, s.v. Ps. 119:15) in the first colon, and "my trouble" (צָרָתִי, s.v. Ps. 120:1) in the second. The first describes the nature of the prayer—a lament; the second relates the need for the prayer—trouble. The line stresses these two words by their close proximity in the chiastic arrangement: "I pour out / before him / my complaint // my trouble / before him / I tell."

II. In times of overwhelming opposition when no one seems to care believers should rehearse their confidence that the LORD knows and cares for them (3–5).

A. Believers may feel overwhelmed when enemies try to destroy them and no one seems to care (3–4).

In the next two verses we have the lament proper. But mingled with the expressions of lament are words of confidence that keep things in perspective. This is a good model for believers to follow rather than focusing only on the dilemma. Verse 3 begins with the temporal clause, "When my spirit grows faint within me." The verb of the clause (the infinitive with a preposition: בְּהִתְעַטֵּף) is a forceful term; it has a sense of being dark, here "darkens itself," and so can be translated "overwhelmed," perhaps with the connotation of spiritual and physical depression (see also Jon. 2:7; Pss. 77:3 and 143:4). But the line takes a turn in the second colon; rather than saying "when I am overwhelmed . . . I cry out," or the like, he says "then you, you know my way (נְתִיבָתִי)." The pronoun is not normally necessary; but here it strengthens the idea and makes the contrast with the first colon more noticeable: "You, are the one who knows" is a useful paraphrase. He is confident that the LORD knows (the perfect tense indicating the constant divine awareness) all about him, even the way of trouble he is experiencing. But the fact that God knows and cares for him at all times does not mean that prayer is unnecessary—it encourages him to pray all the more for guidance and deliverance.

The trouble that the psalmist was in is now made clear: "In the path (now אֹרַח) where I walk *men* have hidden a trap for me." Some enemies have set a trap for him as he goes about his activities. The trap is a figure of speech (an implied comparison); what it represents is unclear, but it certainly was designed to defeat or destroy him. It may include some false accusation or slander about the way he was living (see Pss. 38:13 [12]; 140:2–6 [1–5]). The "path" here refers to his daily concourse; but God knows his way, his course in life.

B. Believers should express their confidence in the LORD's care because he knows the way through trouble (4).

The urgency of the prayer is further intensified as the psalmist tells God to look and see for himself that no one is there to help him. The language is rather bold; it is the way humans would express their frustration and anxiety (and so it is anthropomorphic, as indeed all prayer is when we ask God to hear, listen, pay attention, or as here, look). The point the psalmist wants to make in his lament is that he is alone and needs help. So he calls on the LORD to "Look (הַבֵּיט from נָבַט, "to look intently and closely") to my right and see" (וּרְאֵה, expressing the result of the looking). What he wants God to see is "that no one is taking notice" of him. The participle (מַכִּיר, from נָכַר; s.v. Ps. 144:7) basically means "to take notice, to recognize as a friend." The connotation would be that there is no one who is concerned about him. His narrowing God's search to his right hand is significant, because the defender would be at the right hand. But there was no one.

And so he can only conclude that he is without hope for help from anyone—he has nowhere to go. "Refuge has perished (אָבַד)"—wherever he had found safety and security in the past, wherever he had found such "refuge" (מָנוֹס), no longer was available. People who used to help him and places he used to go for safety had all vanished, and he was left without hope. What he means specifically by "refuge" is probably captured in the second colon of the verse: "there is no one caring for my life." The participle in this expression (דּוֹרֵשׁ) literally means "seeking." The seeking could be good or evil; here it would have a good sense: to seek with care, to care for, to regard (Jer. 30:14, 17; see also Deut. 11:12). There is no one caring for him so he has no one to turn to for help—all refuge is gone.

III. When believers have nothing left of their own strength then they know that the LORD will deliver them and receive all the glory (5–7).

A. *People turn more confidently to the LORD when they are brought low and have nothing left (5–6).*

1. *Confidence: The LORD cares.*

Quickly the weakening psalmist turns from his lament to appeal to the LORD for deliverance. But his new cry to the LORD begins with confidence. "I cry (זָעַק again, but now in the perfect tense to express instantaneous action) to you, O LORD." Now the cry is directed to the LORD, rather than telling others that he cries to the LORD (v. 1). And what he expresses first is confidence: "You are my refuge." Now the word used is different (מַחְסִי), a place of taking refuge (s.v. Ps. 7:1). The reference might be to the sanctuary where he could seek the LORD's help (see. Ps. 63:1). Or, it may simply be a description of divine intervention. There was no one around him who could help him find safety and security—but there was always the LORD. This metaphor appears in a number of psalms as an expression of trust as well as confidence. Human help may fail, but God is always there—he knows the path of the psalmist, and he is his refuge.

The second metaphor is "my portion in the land of the living." The word "portion" reminds the reader of the land inheritance given to the families of Israel. And so what he has received as his portion is the LORD—his presence, his protection, his promises (see Ps. 73:26).

No One Cares, except the LORD

2. Prayer: The LORD will deliver.

And so with these images in his mind, and because people to whom he might turn are not there, and places to which he might flee are not available, he prays urgently to the only refuge, the LORD. The prayer is again bold and urgent: "Pay attention (הַקְשִׁיבָה from קָשַׁב) to my loud cry (רִנָּתִי; s.v. Ps. 33:1).[17] Not only was he crying out loud, he apparently was shouting, judging from the meaning of this word. Things were getting desperate: "I have been brought very low" (דַלּוֹתִי). The verb is metaphorical of a distress that has taken everything out of him.

Not only is the prayer urgent because he is low, but also his enemies are strong: "deliver me (הַצִּילֵנִי; s.v. Ps. 22:20) "from those who pursue me, for they are too strong for me." He had not the strength to fight them; there were no other people around to care for him—only the LORD was able to deliver him. The tone of the psalm indicates that the need was urgent.

B. Their prays will be filled with vows of praise because only the LORD can set them free (7a).

The prayer continues in verse 7, but now it is expressed with a different image: "Bring me out from my prison." Most likely "prison" is used figuratively, an implied comparison with the difficulty he faced (see Ps.143:11). He was trapped by his enemies who pursued him, there was no place to turn for help, and he had not the strength to resist. It is as if he was in prison waiting to die.

But the prayer is expressed with a new purpose as well: "so that I may praise your name." The motivation for God to act is that praise will be given to him in the sanctuary. The infinitive (לְהוֹדוֹת; s.v. Ps. 6:5) "to acknowledge," indicates a public acknowledgment of who the LORD is and what he has done (as "name" implies, for it figuratively refers to the person and the works of the LORD; s.v. Ps. 20:1). The praise will be given in the assembly of the believers to glorify God and to strengthen their faith. When God delivers the psalmist, he will receive the glory

---

17. See N. E. Wagner, "רִנָּה in the Psalter," *VT* 10 (1960):435–41.

and the praise; therefore, if God wants this to happen, he must deliver the troubled psalmist.

C. They anticipate sharing the account of their deliverance with the congregation (7b).

Finally, with this great confidence in the LORD, the psalmist anticipates the effect his deliverance will have on the congregation. The righteous will gather around him. The verb used here (יַכְתִּרוּ) means "to surround, to circle triumphantly" (the related noun is "crown"); it is elsewhere used in a hostile sense, but here it has a favorable connotation. When he is delivered and appears in the sanctuary to praise the LORD, the believers, the righteous, will gather around him, perhaps to share in his happiness and his praise. There were righteous people in the land after all; perhaps he was not so isolated as he thought, or perhaps they did not wish to get involved in his struggle but were happy to celebrate the outcome. Whatever the situation was, God's deliverance was proof of his integrity. They would all see that. And they would see that the fervent prayers of the righteous are honored by the LORD.

What they will see is that the LORD "will have dealt bountifully with him." The verb is a simple imperfect, but has the sense of a future perfect because this is a lament and the deliverance and the provision of life and freedom have not yet materialized. The verb "deal bountifully" (גָּמַל) conveys the sense of bringing abundant provision and good gifts. God's power and God's wonderful provisions will be very much on display in the sanctuary.

MESSAGE AND APPLICATION

When our Lord was on earth he warned his disciples (and us) that the world would hate them and persecute them because they hated him and sought to destroy him. If believers are blessed with times of peace and safety, they should be thankful, because it may not always be so, and in many places it is not so. Times of persecution are very painful times in which the suffering saints feel overwhelmed and very much abandoned and alone. And so in anticipation of such threats they must build a strong faith that will overcome the world: *the faithful must depend on the LORD completely when they are in grave difficulties because there is no one else who truly cares for them.* We see this in the suffering of the Savior: in his darkest hour his disciples fled and he was left alone. Believers would hope for better care and help from other believers, but even then they will have to acknowledge that no one cares for them like the Lord; and even if believers did care, they might not be able to deliver them from the wicked. The LORD is the psalmist's refuge and portion in the land of living; and so he cries to him to take notice of his plight and deliver him. And when the LORD delivers him from almost certain death, the righteous at least will gather to hear his praise. Believers today must develop a strong faith in the Lord, because in times of distress he is the one they must turn to for help.

PSALM 143

Deliverance and Guidance

INTRODUCTION

Text and Textual Variants

A Psalm of David

1 O LORD, hear my prayer,
  give ear to my supplications.
 In your faithfulness[1] answer me,
  and in your righteousness.
2 And do not enter into judgment with your servant,
  for before you no one living is righteous.[2]

3 For *my* enemy pursues me;
  he crushes me to the earth,

---

1. The Syriac reads "your word" (< אִמְרָה) instead of "your faithfulness." Also, the Greek translation makes a break in the clauses here, yielding: "give ear to my supplications in your faithfulness, and in your righteousness answer me."
2. Allen suggests taking the verb with a modal nuance: "no one can be right" (*Psalms 101–150,* p. 352).

he makes me dwell in darkness
    like those who have long been dead.
4 And *so* my spirit[3] is overwhelmed within me;
    my heart within me is distressed.
5 I remember the days of old;[4]
    I[5] meditate on all that you have done,
        on the work[6] of your hands do I muse.
6 I spread forth my hands unto you;
    my soul *thirsts* for you like[7] a thirsty land. S*elah*

7 Make haste to answer me, O LORD,
    for my spirit fails;
   do not hide your face from me,
    lest I become like those who go down to the pit.
8 Cause me to hear your loyal love in the morning,
    for in you I trust;
   Cause me to know[8] the way in which I should walk,
    for to you I lift my soul.
9 Deliver me from my enemies, O LORD,
    in you I find protection.[9]
10 Teach me to do your will, for you are my God;
    let your good Spirit[10] lead me on level ground.
11 For your name's sake, O LORD, revive me;[11]

---

3. A few manuscripts have נַפְשִׁי instead of רוּחִי.
4. The Syriac has "I have remembered you, O LORD."
5. A few manuscripts and the versions have "and."
6. The Greek version and a few manuscripts have the plural.
7. Many manuscripts have "in" instead.
8. The Greek version adds "O LORD."
9. The MT has כִּסִּתִי, which would be "I cover" or "I have covered." The difficulty of the word in the line is attested to by the varying attempts to resolve it. One suggestion is that the word should be נַסְתִּי, "I fled"; this is probably behind the Greek translation "I fled to you for refuge" (ὅτι πρὸς σὲ κατέφυγον). One manuscript has הָסִיתִי, "I have taken refuge." Allen suggests that the simplest solution is a slight repointing of the verb to the passive voice, כֻּסֵּתִי, "I am covered" and so protected (*Psalms*, p. 352).
10. The syntax could be explained to mean: "lead me . . . by your good Spirit," taking "your good Spirit" as an accusative of means. Or, it could be read as a separate noun clause: "Your Spirit is good; lead me . . . ."
11. For MT's תְּחַיֵּנִי the Syriac reads "comfort me" (= תְּנַחֲמֵנִי).

>   in your righteousness bring my life out of trouble.
> 12 And in your loyal love cut off my enemies
>   and destroy all those who afflict my life
>   for I am your servant.

Composition and Context

This psalm is one of the seven penitential psalms because of its emphasis on grace and favor. There is no expressed confession of sin, but the fact that the psalmist acknowledges that no one is righteous before the LORD and that everyone needs divine guidance to live righteously in this world forms an implicit confession.[12] The psalm resembles an individual lament; it begins with a prayer for God's righteousness (1–2), then records a lament proper (3–6), then a petition (7–11), and finally a prayer for God's righteousness. It is easier to analyze the structure in two parts: verses 1–6 set forth the basic lament motifs of petition, lament and avowal, and then verses 7–12 are arranged with five confessions of trust interspersed with petitions.

There does not seem to be sufficient evidence for dating the psalm either early or late. Many commentators nevertheless accept a late post-exilic date on the basis that the psalm makes numerous allusions to other psalms. But it is difficult to date a psalm by allusions to other psalms that may also be difficult to date with certainty.

Exegetical Analysis

Summary

Recognizing that no living person is righteous, and feeling overwhelmed in his spirit by the oppression of the wicked, the psalmist prays for deliverance and guidance from the LORD, remembering his great ways.

---

12. Anderson, *Psalms 73–150*, p. 925.

PSALM 143

Outline

I. Acknowledging that no one is righteous before God and deserving of his help, but also keeping in mind the ways of the LORD with his people, the psalmist pleads with the LORD to deliver him in righteousness from his enemies who have overwhelmed him (1–6).
   A. He pleads with the LORD to answer in righteousness even though he knows that no living person is righteous (1–2).
      1. The prayer is for God to respond in faithfulness and in righteousness (1).
      2. The appeal acknowledges that none are righteous and that entering into judgment with God would be the result were it not for grace (2).
   B. He rehearses his lamentable situation to the LORD: the enemy has overwhelmed him (3–4).
      1. The enemy has attacked and driven him out (3).
      2. His spirit was overwhelmed because of this (4).
   C. He builds his confidence for the appeal by remembering what the LORD did in the past and then makes his desperate appeal (5–6).
      1. He remembers the days of old and the ways of God (5).
      2. He spreads his hands in urgent prayer for the LORD to meet his desperate need (6).
II. Knowing that his needs go beyond the immediate crisis, the psalmist appeals to the LORD for deliverance and guidance because he trusts in him (7–12).
   A. He prays for quick deliverance lest he should join the dead in the pit (7).
   B. He prays for guidance and deliverance (8–12).
      1. He wants the loyal love of the LORD to lead him (8).
      2. He wants to be delivered from his enemies (9).
      3. He wants to be taught the will of God (10).
      4. He wants to be revived from his physical condition (11).
      5. He wants the enemies to be cut off since he is the servant of the LORD (12).

COMMENTARY IN EXPOSITORY FORM

I. Even though we know that none are righteous we may still pray with confidence for God's deliverance in times of trouble because of his faithfulness and righteousness (1–6).

A. We may plead with the LORD to answer in righteousness even though we know that we are all unrighteous (1–2).

The psalmist employs many liturgical expressions in his opening cry to God. It is an intense appeal to God to answer the prayers for God's gracious provisions (תַּחֲנוּנַי; s.v. Ps. 4:1). He desires the LORD to answer him "in faithfulness" (אֱמֻנָה; s.v. Ps. 15:2) and "in righteousness" (צְדָקָה; s.v. Ps. 1:5). These words should be linked to the covenant: he is expecting God to act in faithfulness to the covenant by making things right. In answering the prayer God will show himself trustworthy and righteous. VanGemeren comments, "The ground for answered prayer is the LORD's commitment to his people."[13]

Because his prayer is an appeal for gracious intervention, he also prays, "Do not enter into judgment with your servant." VanGemeren explains that if that were to happen, God could find him guilty and condemn him to remain in his troubles. The reason he pleads for God's grace is his awareness of his own sinfulness. He does not protest innocence in this psalm; he is guilty. If he is not innocent, then the appeal for gracious intervention is also urgent.[14] He desires gracious intervention, not a legal decision.

B. We can and must pour out our troubles to the LORD when we feel overwhelmed in our spirits (3–4).

Here we have the lament proper, beginning with the "they"

---

13. *Psalms,* p. 977.
14. See L. C. Allen, "The Old Testament in Romans I-VIII," *VT* 3 (1964):11–12. See also H. McKeating, "Divine Forgiveness in the Psalms," *SJT* 18 (1965):69–83, and R. B. Hays, "Psalm 143 and the Logic of Romans 3," *JBL* 99 (1980):107–19.

portion, what the enemies have done. First, the enemy pursues (רָדַף) him and crushes (דִּכָּא) his life. The verbs may be taken as characteristic perfects, reporting activities that began in the past and were still going on at the moment. In other words, the enemy has been hunting him down and trying to destroy his life. The effect is that his life is in darkness, like those who have been dead a long time (כְּמֵתֵי עוֹלָם). "Darkness" in this context describes a *she'ol*-like condition, a description of the estate of the dead. His existence is like that—there is no hope, no clear way out, and no future. He was becoming like those long dead—lifeless and easily forgotten.

As a result his spirit was overwhelmed (וַתִּתְעַטֵּף)—he was fading away to death (see Pss. 61:12; 77:3; 142:3; and Jon. 2:8). And his heart was distressed (יִשְׁתּוֹמֵם). This word occurs only here, but means something like "driven to numbness." The Greek translation used "troubled," an adequate interpretation although weak. The point of the verse is that he was so overwhelmed he was at the point of despair—he was losing heart, i.e., his will to resist. The psalmist feels the overwhelming sense of helplessness under the pressure from his enemies. His suffering is so intense he almost despairs of living. But he does not give up; he intensifies his prayer for divine intervention.

C. We need to build confidence by remembering how the LORD helped his people (5–6).

While the psalmist's spirit was failing under the pressure from his enemies, he renewed his confidence and regained his hope by meditating on the things that the LORD had done for his needy people down through the ages. He uses three verbs for meditation: "I remember" (זָכַרְתִּי; s.v. Ps. 6:5), "I meditate" (הָגִיתִי; s.v. Ps. 2:1), and "I muse" (אֲשׂוֹחֵחַ; s.v. Ps. 119:15). All these words indicate that he was constantly rehearsing and pondering what God had done, beginning in antiquity. The "days of old" stretch back to the very beginning; and the "works" refer to his care for people, especially for his nation.

As a result of pondering all these things, the psalmist is strengthened in his spirit to pray more intensely: "I spread out my hands (palms) to you." The posture is that of kneeling down and then bowing to the ground with hands spread out on the ground before him. Such a posture signifies the intensity of the prayer. And the reason for its intensity is the deep seated need he has: "my soul *thirsts* for you like a thirsty land." The simile provides the picture of something very needy if life is to continue—water to a thirsty land, deliverance and renewal for the sufferer (see Pss. 42:1–2, 63:1).

II. Because our needs are many and often urgent we must pray for the LORD to preserve our lives and guide us in his ways (7–12).

A. We will appeal to God to deliver us quickly when we are in life-threatening situations (7).

The second half of the psalm is a series of petitions for deliverance and guidance that include numerous expressions of the psalmist's faith. The first petition is the basic prayer of the psalm; it may form something of a summary statement. The general petition here is for God to answer quickly with his saving grace. The literal rendering of the first two imperatives would be "make haste, answer me" (מַהֵר עֲנֵנִי), but if taken as a verbal hendiadys, the first word becomes an adverb: "answer me quickly." And the answer will come by God's grace, expressed by the appeal for God not to hide his face from him. For the LORD to hide his face would mean that he would withhold favor (see Ps. 30:7; 27:9, and 102:2); corresponding to this, seeking God's face means to seek his favor. The idea of God's hiding his face (an anthropomorphism) presents a very human picture; it would be as if the LORD was not even showing an interest in helping the suppliant. If that were to happen, then fear and dismay would follow—it would be like being cast off and left to die. So the negative petition here carries forward the positive need expressed in the word "supplications," i.e., appeals for grace.

The reasons for the urgent answer repeat what has been said in the previous verses: 1) his spirit fails (כָּלְתָה, comes to an end; s.v. Ps. 90:7), and he is in danger of dying—he will become like those who are going down to the pit, meaning the grave. He is already among the dying—he just has not breathed his last.

The Old Testament believer knew he would be with God forever, but he also wanted to tell others that God answers prayer. If he died and went to be with the LORD he could not do this.

B. We must pray for guidance as well as deliverance (8–12).

The petition in verse 8 is expressed more positively. "Cause me to hear your loyal love in the morning." How does one "hear" God's love? The verb "to hear" (s.v. Ps. 45:10) carries the force of responding to something said or done. God's love will cause him to be delivered from his plight, i.e., his whole being will respond to God's love (for "loyal love," s.v. Ps. 23:6). The image of the morning signifies a new beginning, a new day dawning, as opposed to the dark night that he is now enduring (compare Ps. 130:6). He prays this because he trusts (בָּטַחְתִּי; s.v. Ps. 4:5) in the LORD—he does not simply believe in the LORD, he casts himself on him for deliverance.

And then the second petition of the verse is for guidance: "Cause me to know the way in which I should walk." The immediate concern is how he should conduct his affairs in the midst of this crisis—he simply does not know how to deal with it; but the petition is broad enough to mean all his decisions and actions throughout his entire life. The motivation for this is parallel to the expression of trust above: "for to you I lift up my soul." His trusting is displayed in his praying. He is totally committed to trusting the LORD, so along with deliverance from the current crisis, he wants guidance. How will God show him guidance? He might reveal it to him through his meditation on God's word (see Pss. 119 and 63:6–8), or through instruction from priests or prophets, or through a specific direction from the LORD.

Verse 9 reiterates the petition for deliverance: "Deliver me (הַצִּילֵנִי; s.v. Ps. 22:20) from my enemies." The reason for this appeal is another expression of trust, but its precise meaning is not clear. Different translations have been proposed: "I hide myself," "I cover myself," "I take shelter," "I am covered" or "protected." At least we can say that he is secure in his faith.

This is followed by another appeal for guidance (v. 10): "Teach me to do your will." The will of God (רְצוֹן; s.v. Ps. 30:5) means what is pleasing or acceptable to God—he wants to learn how to live so that his life pleases God. First, it would please God for him to avoid sin and its devastating results; and secondly, it would also mean living a life of positive righteousness. And this appeal is appropriately based on the covenant relationship he has with the LORD and his loyalty to it: "you are my God."

The third colon of the verse is a request for God's "good Spirit", the Holy Spirit, to lead him "on level ground." This last expression may mean "into a land of uprightness," unless it is taken figuratively for a secure and stable life. The leading by the "good Spirit" probably refers to manifestations of the presence of the LORD, guiding him in the right way.[15]

The last two verses complete this series of petitions, but now using imperfect tenses in the petition to God. The first is "revive me" (תְּחַיֵּנִי), an appeal made urgent by his failing spirit within him. The way God would do that would be by bringing him out (תּוֹצִיא) from his trouble (צָרָה; s.v. Ps. 120:1). And God should do it for his name's sake (s.v. Ps. 20:1), i.e., for the sake of his reputation as a God who cares for his covenant people. In this the nature of God would be seen in his goodness and readiness to help his people.[16] The answer to the prayer should also be "in righteousness" (s.v. Ps. 1:5). The word refers to God's faithful keeping of the covenant. God always does what is right; and that means he will be keeping his covenant promises by delivering his servant.

Finally, verse 12 reiterates the motif of God's loyal love: "and in your loyal love cut off my enemies." In delivering his people the LORD often must destroy (< צָמַת, "to cut off") those who are trying to destroy the people of God and therefore the covenant. So the prayer is that those who afflict his life (צֹרְרֵי נַפְשִׁי; s.v. Ps. 120:1) be destroyed (< אָבַד). They had to be stopped, once and for all.

He makes this appeal with a clear statement of his faith and loyalty—"I am your servant" (s.v. Ps. 134:1). To be a servant of the LORD is to be in a covenant relationship with the LORD and

---

15. See further Kraus, *Psalms 60–150,* p. 538; see also Nehemiah 9:20 and Psalm 51:11–12.
16. Kraus, *Psalms 60-150*, p. 538.

remain loyal to him. Servants do not always live up to their commitments, but they try to live faithfully, with God's help.

MESSAGE AND APPLICATION

So in this passage we have a series of petitions for deliverance and guidance accompanied by reasons for them, either descriptions of the problem or statements of faith and commitment:

Answer me quickly	because	my spirit fails
Show me favor	lest	I go down to the pit
Reveal your love	because	I trust in you
Teach me the way	because	I lift my soul to you
Deliver me	because	I have protection in you
Teach me your will	because	you are my God
Let your good Spirit guide me in a land of uprightness[17]		
Revive me		for your name's sake
Deliver me		in your righteousness
Destroy my enemies	because	I am your servant

Faith in the grace and love of God is the basis of prayer for protection and guidance in this wicked world.

Several great doctrines of the Bible come to mind by the short statements of faith and commitment by the suffering psalmist. As with so many biblical teachings, they will find their fullest expression in the New Testament, in passages such as Galatians 2:16 and Romans 3:20. Like the psalmist, the New Testament believer will confess trust in the LORD when praying, and that confession will include more revelation concerning God's grace, love, and righteousness. And as with the psalmist, our prayer may be for deliverance from some wicked oppression, but it will be prayed with greater understanding, for we are to also pray for our enemies. Our confidence is based on the sure revelation that

---

17. If we were trying to stay with the pattern, this verse could be translated, your Spirit is good, let him lead me . . . ." In the chart: Let him lead me; with the reason, your Spirit is good. But there is a change in the pattern here for this line uses a jussive and not the imperatives, and the following lines use the imperfect tense.

complete deliverance will come with the coming of the Lord. So until then, we need guidance to live the way the LORD wants us to live. Jesus instructed his disciples to learn from him, and so Christians have clearer instructions and greater provisions for living in this wicked world than the Old Testament believer had. And as an essential part of the new covenant, the Lord sent the Holy Spirit to lead us into all righteousness (John 16:8–15 and Rom. 8.14).

Many Christians will never face such terrifying persecution in their lives, but around the world the persecuted Church knows exactly the suffering and despair of the psalmist. Their cries to God do not betray a weak faith; on the contrary, they represent faith and hope in the only one who can deliver. The full revelation of the new covenant inspires greater confidence and trust, but it does not immediately end the overwhelming suffering that many must endure.

PSALM 144

A Prayer for Peace and Prosperity

INTRODUCTION

Text and Textual Variants

By David

1 Blessed be the LORD, my rock,[1]
   who trains my hands for battle,
   my[2] fingers for war;
2 My loyal love and my fortress,
   my stronghold[3] and my deliverer,[4]
   my shield, and he in whom I take refuge,
     who subdues my people[5] under me.[6]

---

1. The Greek version interprets with "my God"; a few manuscripts and the Syriac do not have "my rock."
2. Some manuscripts and versions have the conjunction.
3. The Greek translation uses "helper," ἀντιλήμπτωρ, here.
4. The MT has וּמְפַלְטִי לִי; a few manuscripts and the Greek translation do not retain לִי.
5. For "my people," עַמִּי, the majority of the manuscripts and the versions have "peoples" in line with Psalm 18:48.
6. Instead of "under me," a few manuscripts have "under him."

PSALM 144

3 O LORD, what is man that you take knowledge of him,
    the son[7] of man that you take account of him?
4 Man is like a breath;
    his days are like a fleeting[8] shadow.
5 Part[9] your[10] heavens, O LORD, and come down;
    touch the mountains, so that they smoke.
6 Flash forth lightning and scatter them;[11]
    send your arrows and rout them.
7 Stretch forth your hands[12] from on high;
    deliver me and rescue me
        from many waters,
        from the hand of foreigners[13]
8 whose mouth has spoken lies,
    whose right hand is a right hand of deceit.[14]
9 O God, a new song I will sing to you;
    on the ten-stringed lyre I will sing praises to you,
10 to you who gives victory to kings,
    who delivers David, his servant, from the cruel sword.
11 Deliver me and rescue me
    from the hand of foreigners
        whose mouth has spoken lies,
        whose right hand is a right hand of deceit.
12 Then our[15] sons in their youth

---

7. Many manuscripts and the Syriac have a conjunction, "and the son of."
8. The participle in the MT is singular, modifying shadow; but in the Greek and Syriac versions it is plural in harmony with days: "his days are passing like a shadow."
9. הַט in the MT; the Greek version has κλῖνον, "tilt, bow."
10. Instead of "your heavens" in the MT, a couple of manuscripts and some versions simply have "heavens" (see Ps. 18:10).
11. Some translations clarify the pronoun with "the enemies."
12. The MT has the plural, "your hands"; but most manuscripts and the versions have the singular.
13. MT has בְּנֵי נֵכָר, "sons of a stranger" or "foreigner," so "foreign sons"; the Greek version has "strange sons" ("sons of strangers").
14. Here and in verse 11 the Greek makes a general translation of "hand of deceit" as "hand of iniquity."
15. The Greek version translated אֲשֶׁר as "who," and read the line: "whose sons are like young plants . . . ." The Greek version (and usually the Syriac) have "their" instead of "our" in verses 12–14.

A Prayer for Peace and Prosperity

w*ill be* like flourishing plants,
and our daughters like corner pillars,
sculptured to grace a palace;
13 our[16] barns will be filled
w*ith every kind of* provision.[17]
our sheep will increase by thousands,
by tens of thousands in our fields;[18]
14 our oxen will be well-laden;
there will be no breach *in our*[19] *walls*,
*a*nd no going out *into captivity*,
and no cry *of distress* in our streets.
15 Blessed are the people of whom this is true;[20]
blessed are the people whose God is the LORD.

Composition and Context

Peace and prosperity seem to remain elusive dreams. Those who believe in the LORD know that such things are not only assured in the world to come, but are to a certain extent possible now. But the biblical history is a record of invasion and warfare in the promised land, and with that there was little chance for the land to flourish over long periods of time. Occasionally a king was able to unify the people and stave off invasions so that the people could enjoy a season of peace and prosperity. But that took more than a powerful military leader, for only God could grant them that (see Ps. 72). These are some of the themes that form the substance of Psalm 144, the final royal psalm in the collection.

The psalm is attributed to David, and even though this is generally rejected by commentators, it is not impossible that the greater part of it is Davidic, for the psalm uses earlier works such as Psalm 18. The first part of the passage, verses 1–11, can be called a royal psalm; but the last part is different and may have been

---

16. The Greek (and Syriac) have "their barns."
17. MT has מִזַּן אֶל־זַן; the Greek version ἐκ τούτου εἰς τοῦτο, "(bursting) from side to side."
18. The Greek version has "(multiplying) in their issue" (or, "in their pathways").
19. Greek and Syriac have "their" in these verses instead of "our."
20. Greek has, "They counted happy the people to whom these things fall."

appended in the final compilation. Allen allows that the first part might be pre-exilic, but not the latter part.[21] This would mean that the nation never lost sight of the promises for the Davidic dynasty; by bringing forward material appropriate for a royal psalm and joining it with the new hope for peace and prosperity and placing it all in Book V, the psalmist clearly saw those promises as relevant and foundational for the future of the nation. The renewed hope for peace and prosperity was strengthened by recalling how God saved David. And for the generation that endured exile because of their great sins, the idea that God would actually think of them as he renewed their destiny must have been truly amazing.

The literary classification of this psalm has been debated because it does not fit normal patterns, largely because so many lines are taken from other psalms. One approach is to follow Gunkel and classify it as a lament—perhaps a prayer as the king goes into battle. Verses 5–8 (and 11) definitely form a section of petition, and verses 9 and 10 a vow of praise. The last part of the psalm, verses 12–15, may be interpreted as the desired result of God's answering the prayer and delivering the people. But it is difficult to fit the first four verses into a lament pattern. Another possibility is to follow Westermann and take the psalm as a declarative praise. Accordingly, verse 9 is the shout of praise, and verse 10 the report of God's act. The petition section in the middle of the psalm (vv. 5–8) then becomes the psalmist's recollection of what his petition was. On the whole, however, it is easier to see the psalm as a lament, even though it does not fully follow the pattern. The psalmist rehearses how God has delivered him in the past, and then makes his petition. There is just no strong lament section that tells of his plight. Perhaps instead of classifying it as a standard lament, it may be better to call it a prayer or perhaps a meditation on the prayer of the king and the following blessings from God.

The argument of the psalm may be traced in three sections. The first section (vv. 1–2) is an acknowledgment of God's protection and support in previous conflicts. The second (vv. 3–11) includes the prayer itself (vv. 5–8, 11). But before making the petition the psalmist marvels that God should take any notice at all of frail and faltering humans. God is majestic and powerful,

---

21. *Psalms 101–150,* p. 362.

A Prayer for Peace and Prosperity

and people are frail as dust, but God delights in focusing his attention on them. The prayer is for God once again to intervene and deliver his people; and the petition proper appears in the form of a refrain in the psalm, which gives to it an added power. What is interesting is that all the lines in this section of the psalm can be found in earlier Davidic psalms. They have been brought together to compose this royal petition for victory.

The final lines (12–15) are new; they express the results that will come when God delivers his people. Because God has saved his servant in battle before, the faithful can be confident that he will do it again; and when God does deliver them, they will enjoy a time of peace and prosperity under the blessing of God. It seems that the last section of the psalm, although a little unusual and difficult to connect to the overall message of the psalm, expresses the point that the psalmist wanted to put across because it is the new material and is based on the first part.

Exegetical Analysis

Summary

After praising God for past victories, the royal psalmist prays for divine intervention in battle, marveling that God takes notice of people who are frail and perishing, and anticipating that when God gives victory to his people they will experience peace and prosperity.

Outline

I. The psalmist blesses God for who he is and for past victories (1–2).
   A. He blesses the LORD who enables him to fight (1).
   B. He blesses the LORD as his faithful defender and deliverer because he has subdued people under him (2).
II. The psalmist, marveling that God takes note of man, confidently prays for divine intervention in the battle (3–11).
   A. He marvels that God even takes note of mortal man (3–4).
   B. He prays for divine intervention in the battle (5–8).

1. He desires that the LORD come with glorious power (5).
   2. He desires that the LORD use nature to scatter the enemy (6).
   3. He longs for the LORD to deliver him from evil enemies (7–8).
   C. He expresses his confidence in the LORD by voicing his vow of praise (9–10).
   1. He vows to praise God with music (9).
   2. He will praise God because God gives salvation to the king (10).
   D. He reiterates the refrain of his petition for deliverance from the enemy (11).
III. The psalmist is confident that the nation will experience peace and prosperity when the LORD delivers his anointed king in battle (12–15).
   A. He anticipates the peace and prosperity to come (12–14).
   1. The subjects of the king will flourish (12).
   2. The nation will prosper economically (13–14a).
   3. The people will be blessed with peace (14b).
   B. He explains that the nation will be blessed because of the LORD (15).

COMMENTARY IN EXPOSITORY FORM

I. The righteous must praise the LORD for the way he has protected and delivered them in the past (1–2).

A. Praise is due the LORD who enables his people to have victory in times of trouble (1).

It is difficult to summarize these first verses because of the many images, nine of them in all. But these images, all having to do with protection and deliverance, are expressed in a very personal way as the psalmist refers to himself eleven times. The royal psalmist is acknowledging how much the LORD has done for him personally.

He not only declares divine intervention in the past, but also expresses hope for the future. The key idea running through the images is that the LORD is David's faithful, strong deliverer.

A Prayer for Peace and Prosperity

The language is very similar to, if not borrowed from, Psalm 18, a thanksgiving song of David.

The psalm begins with the metaphor of the rock ("my rock" is in apposition), expressing the belief that the LORD is strong, solid, and immovable (see Ps. 18:1–2). The expression of praise, "blessed [be] the LORD, my rock," uses the term for praise (בָּרוּךְ; s.v. Ps. 5:12) that emphasizes the enrichment that words of praise will bring to God and his reputation in the world.[22]

The praise is qualified by two parallel lines that form a relative clause. The clause begins with the statement that the LORD trains him. The text uses the participle (מְלַמֵּד) and the article with the function of an attributive adjective: it is the LORD "who trains" his hands for battle, and his fingers for war. God enabled David to learn how to be a warrior and win victories on the battlefield. The emphasis on "hands" and "fingers" is a figurative way (synecdoche) of focusing on his complete involvement in battle. The teaching probably refers to a combination of past experiences of divine intervention showing David how God fights for his people as well as divine instructions for David to follow when in battle (Ps. 18:34).

B. The LORD is to be acknowledged as the one who defends and protects his own (2).

The second verse continues with familiar figures. The first half of the verse contains four: loyal love, stronghold, high tower, and deliverer. The first gives the basis (a metonymy of cause), and the fourth the result (a metonymy of effect). The second and third images in the line stress the idea of protection. The first expression is that the Lord is "his loyal love" (חֶסֶד, s.v. Ps. 23:6). This is a poetic way of saying that the LORD has continuously acted on his behalf because of his faithful covenant love. The LORD is also his fortress or "stronghold" (מְצוּדָה), a noun that refers to a strong or impregnable place of safety. Parallel to this is the figure of the "high tower" (מִשְׂגָּב), a word that comes from the verb "to be high." It also stresses a secure place of safety. The fourth expression in the first half

---

22. For the word see also Claus Westermann, *Blessing in the Bible and in the Life of the Church* (Philadelphia: Fortress Press, 1978).

of the verse is "my deliverer" (מְפַלְטִי; s.v. Ps. 37:20), one who makes the way of escape.

The second half of the verse uses a metaphor, "my shield," and then two verbal descriptions, "the one in whom I take refuge" and "the one who subdues." "My shield" (מָגִנִּי) affirms that the LORD is the one who protects him from injury and harm in battle. The reason that God protects him, of course, is that he has taken refuge in him. The verb "to take refuge" (חָסָה; s.v. Ps. 7:1) compares the idea of taking refuge, such as in a storm or in a battle, to the simple idea of trusting in the LORD.

The last expression has a textual difficulty. It either says that the LORD has subdued "peoples" (עַמִּים i.e., his enemies) under him," or what the Hebrew Bible has here, "my people (עַמִּי) under me." Psalm 18:39 uses the expression "peoples" instead of "my people" that we find in the text here, and so many have thought that it should be "peoples" here as well. This would mean God gave him victory in war, and that would fit the psalm nicely. But there is no real reason to make the line conform to that psalm, even if some of the material was borrowed from it. The psalm may seem a little unusual to be saying that God has subdued "my people under me." But it would mean either that God gave him his kingdom, or put down his enemies. The fact is that the nation had to submit to its king if there was going to be any success. So the king would be saying the authority he holds came from God.

Thus, with a string of descriptions the royal psalmist has portrayed the Lord as the one who defends him, protects him, keeps him safe, delivers him, and gives him the people who are under him. All of these ideas required faith on David's part to be effectual, and so the one expression of taking refuge is representative of the underlying faith in each of them.

II. Even though they may feel insignificant, the righteous can pray with confidence to the LORD who takes note of them to deliver them in their time of need (3–11).

A. Believers marvel that God even takes note of humans (3–4).

In contrast to the first stanza which acknowledged that God

is everything, this little section forms an expression of amazement that God should take notice of them let alone answer their prayers. "What is man that you take knowledge of him, or the son of man, that you take account of him?" The words are taken from Psalm 8:5 where the psalmist marvels how God condescends to help humans. It is a rhetorical question (erotesis) designed to make the point that humans seem too insignificant for God to consider, but he does nonetheless.

The two verbs in the line are specific. The first is the common verb "to know" (יָדַע; s.v. Ps. 67:2; the form has the *waw* consecutive for sequence), which although straightforward in translation has an emphasis on personal, experiential knowledge. The idea that God should "know" or take knowledge of mortals in this way is astounding. But the second verb takes the idea further; "to take account, think, reckon" (חָשַׁב; s.v. Ps. 32:2) adds the sense of devising a plan. God actually thinks about all human beings with specific plans and intentions.

The marvel is intensified by the use of the words for "humans" in the verse. The first is the normal word "man" (אָדָם), the word for mankind that is related to the "earth" (אֲדָמָה), signifying the earthiness of mankind. The other word (אֱנוֹשׁ) may add the sense of simplicity or frailty. So the choice of these words underscores the point of the verse, that this sovereign God of the universe should even bother to think about mere mortals, let alone intervene in their lives to deliver and defend them. This is the amazing thing.

The next verse develops the idea even more by focusing on how fleeting life is. Mortals are not just earthbound and insignificant in the universe, but their life is brief, like a fleeting breath or a wisp of air. The human being is like a breath that passes away (עוֹבֵר) quickly, whose days are like a passing shadow (see also 39:6, 11; 62:10; 102:12 and 109:23). The word "days" represents the whole life (a synecdoche), although it may include what was done on those days (so then a metonymy of subject). The participle modifies "shadow" as moving away. The image (simile) of the passing shadow fits the swift passing of time as well as the image of man as a breath.

So David had all the more reason to praise God, for without God he was nothing, a mere mortal passing quickly away. But because God has delivered him time and time again, his insignificance notwithstanding, he was confident to petition him again.

B. Believers are confident that God is willing and able to deliver them from their deceitful enemies (5–8).

This is the petition proper of the psalm. It is cast in highly poetic language that calls for divine intervention with the phenomena of nature, reminiscent of Mount Sinai. Basically, with a few changes, this section is from Psalm 18 where David celebrated the deeds of God.

The prayer begins with, "Part your heavens, O LORD, and come down" (v. 5). The request is for a spectacular intervention from heaven. The image of the LORD parting (הַט) the heavens and coming down means that he will act in human affairs. The appeal also asks that he touch the mountains so that they smoke. The picture is that of dense, low hanging clouds obscuring the hills and the mountains, mingling heaven and earth as it were. The imagery signifies divine judgment on the earth. In the verse the psalmist uses an imperative ("part") followed by an imperfect ("and come down" or "that you may come down"), and the same again in the second half of the verse, an imperative ("touch") and an imperfect ("that they may smoke").

The picture is figurative, describing divine intervention for judgment in terms of God's coming down, as at Sinai. The Bible uses these descriptions for divine intervention, especially when the elements of nature are involved in God's judgment on the enemies (see Judges 5:20–21 for example). The psalmist was praying for some immediate deliverance. But the final answer to this prayer will undoubtedly be at the second coming of the Lord, when he does actually come down and destroy the wicked. So here is another case of a messianic interpretation that uses a type to point to the time when the poetic language will become historically literal.

Verse six changes the picture with the request that God send lightning flashes. The images from nature are used to describe the intervention. God should flash lightning (בְּרוֹק בָּרָק) and scatter (וּתְפִיצֵם) them—the enemy. Then, the second line of the verse calls for God to send ((שְׁלַח) his arrows. It is unlikely that literal arrows are meant; the clause may provide an emblem for

898

A Prayer for Peace and Prosperity

the lightning flashes—they are like arrows that God is shooting. Or, the arrows may represent by implied comparison something else, perhaps the word of the Lord that may be compared to a sharp arrow. The former makes better sense in the passage if the context is anticipating that God will intervene using forces of nature (see Ps. 97).

In verse 7, the petition is for God to stretch out (שָׁלַח again) his right hand and deliver him. Here the Hebrew text has a plural, "your hands," which is an unusual but not impossible reading. If left to stand it would simply be part of the intensification used for the LORD and his power; at any rate, the image of the hand, an anthropomorphism, represents the powerful strength of the LORD.

Finally, the second part of verse seven gets away from the figures to express the prayer in plain terms: "Rescue me (פְּצֵנִי) and deliver me" (וְהַצִּילֵנִי; s.v. Ps. 22:20). Since the request is repeated in verse 11, it serves in the psalm as a refrain. The first word (פָּצָה) is vivid; it means "to open wide." It may be related to the Aramaic idea "to set free, snatch away"; a link to Arabic "rid me" of my enemies is also possible. Whatever the etymology, the point is that he wants God to deliver him from his enemies.

The crisis he was facing is first described as "many waters" (see Ps. 69:1, 14). "Water" is an implied comparison for the idea of deep trouble or chaos. Isaiah 8:7–8 describes the Assyrian invasion in terms of a great flood from the Euphrates River (see also Ps. 32:6). The parallelism here in Psalm 144 lets us know that the waters mean enemies.

Verses 7c and 8 then describe the enemies that David faced. First, they were foreigners ("sons of a foreigner," בְּנֵי נֵכָר),[23] and

---

23. The word נֵכָר means "that which is foreign, foreignness." The supposed root for the word has diverse meanings in the cognates, from foreign, strange, to change and enmity. But in the Hebrew text the noun retains the idea of "foreign." One main usage is to refer to pagan gods, "foreign gods" (Josh. 24:20; and Mal. 2:11 which refers to women who are pagans as "daughters of a foreign god." A second use is to refer to foreigners. Genesis 17:2 includes in the laws of circumcision foreigners bought or born in the camp. Foreigners were excluded from the sanctuary proper according to Ezekiel 44:7. But in the prophetic oracles, they would work for Israel (Isa. 60:10 and 61:5).

he needed deliverance from them (literally, "their hand" which signifies power). Apparently non-Israelite forces were harassing the land. Second, to make matters worse, they were people who could not be trusted, whose word was just no good: "Whose mouth speaks falsehood (שָׁוְא; s.v. Ps. 127:1) and whose right hand is a right hand of deceit" (שֶׁקֶר).[24] These two words, "falsehood" and "deceit," together stress how untrustworthy the enemies were—what they said with their mouth was false, meaning they spoke to a false purpose; and what they did with their hand, i.e., their power, went against what they said. Their deeds proved their words were false.

C. God will be praised when he sets his people free from their enemies (9–11).

In verse 9 David makes a vow to praise the LORD. This section fits the vow of praise in a lament psalm. He uses cohortatives (אָשִׁירָה; s.v. Ps. 33:3; and אֲזַמְּרָה; s.v. Ps. 33:2) to express his resolve to sing praises: "I will sing a new song to you, O God; upon a harp

---

Related is the adjective נָכְרִי, "foreign, alien." The most famous use is in 1 Kings 11:1, 8 when Solomon loved many foreign women—and they brought pagan religion into Israel. The Israelites were forbidden to marry foreign women for this very danger. But Boaz marries Ruth, who is a foreigner, because she is a Yahwist at heart (Ruth 2:10).

24. שֶׁקֶר is a noun that means "deception, disappointment, falsehood." The first category of meaning is deception, what deceives or disappoints. And so we read that it is useless to trust in a horse for battle (Ps. 33:17). Also, false gods are disappointing (Jer. 10:14) as the devoteee would feel betrayed.

A second category would be deceit or fraud. Proverbs 20:17 speaks of the effects of food that is obtained by fraud—it is sweet at first, then like gravel. It does not satisfy.

A third category is falsehood that is harmful to others. The Law prohibited false witness (Exod. 20:16; Deut. 19:18. Zechariah 8:17 speaks of false oaths. These things would destroy society; and so a lying tongue (in general) is among the things the LORD hates (Prov. 6:17).

But perhaps the most serious crime is reflected in the fourth category, falsity. Here we encounter false, or self-deceived, prophets (Jer. 23:25) who prophesy lies.

There is a denominative verb that is related to this noun, meaning "deal falsely." For example, it is used in Genesis 21:23 in the treaty of Beersheba, ensuring the parties would not deal falsely.

A Prayer for Peace and Prosperity

of ten strings I will sing praises to you" (see Pss. 40:3; 33:2, 3). What a contrast this is to the wicked that he must face! Whereas they open their mouth and speak lies, he will praise God; whereas they raise their hands in vain to make promises they would not keep, he uses his hand to play music to God.

That the psalmist vows to sing a "new song" (שִׁיר חָדָשׁ) means that he will sing a song of praise for a "new" answer to prayer. A new favor from God will inspire a new praise. Thus, the "new song" implies the cause for the new song, the new deliverance (and so is a metonymy of effect).

The anticipated focus of this praise will be the LORD "who gives salvation (תְּשׁוּעָה; s.v. Ps. 3:2) to kings, who delivers (הַפּוֹצֶה) David his servant from the cruel or deadly (רָעָה; s.v. Ps. 10:15) sword" (v. 10; see Ps. 18:50; Ps. 140:7; and 2 Sam. 18:7). The sword is figurative for those who wield the sword (a metonymy of adjunct); and it is cruel, literally evil, because it inflicts pain and death. This is the heart of the message of the psalm; it is the anticipated result of the prayer for divine intervention and therefore the focus of the praise.

Verse 10 begins with the participle and an article, which should be translated as a relative clause, "who gives...." It could also be translated, "He is the one who gives," but the former is the more natural way to interpret it, connecting it to the pronoun in the last verse: "to you, who gives." And what God gives is salvation or victory to kings (and their people). The details of this are in the parallel expression of delivering David from the sword. The clear meaning is that David knows that God will deliver him from harm on the battlefield from those who wield the cruel sword, i.e., the deceitful enemies mentioned before; thus, verse 11 repeats the refrain of his petition.

III. When the LORD gives victory to his anointed in conflicts his people will enjoy peace and prosperity (12–15).

The rest of the psalm describes the result of the deliverance for which the king prays. The connection between verses 12–15 and all that went before it hangs on the interpretation of the pronoun (אֲשֶׁר) that is commonly a relative pronoun "who, which." However, the word can have a good number of meanings in Hebrew, including introducing a result clause, "so that" or "then," which fit very well here. But some other translations give it a different rendering. The NIV simply has "then" which probably reflects the same interpretation that what follows is the result of the petition. The NASV disregarded it and made the line a petition, "Let our sons in their youth be." Others have taken it as a relative, "who makes our sons . . ." (see the Greek version). And another possibility is that it is an asseverative, "surely," which also looks to the result of the deliverance. What follows is a description of the peace and prosperity that the king anticipates will come to his nation when God delivers him from his enemies in battle. It describes the people's blessed state expressed in verse 15.

A. Peace and prosperity will come (12–14).

Verse 12 focuses on the subjects of the king, referred to here as sons and daughters to indicate the extending benefits of peace and prosperity to future generations. He first anticipates "that our sons *will be* like plants . . . ." The figure of a plant (a simile) describes the people as they settle into the land and flourish, putting down their roots as it were. The word "plants" is modified by the participle "brought up" ("grown big, well-nurtured," מְגֻדָּלִים; s.v. Ps. 34:3), indicating that they would mature and become strong.

Parallel to this is the image for the daughters. They will be like (simile) corner-pieces hewn for the pattern of the palace. The image is that of polished gracefulness, such as sculptured forms or edges in the palace.[25] There is a problem with the translation "hewn" (מְחֻטָּבוֹת) because the idea does not fit. Delitzsch translates it "our daughters are as corners adorned in varied colors after the architecture of the palace."[26] Whatever translation is accepted, the point of the verse is that they will be flourishing in full vigor and wondrous beauty into the next generations. There

---

25. See Perowne, *Psalms*, II:467.
26. *Psalms*, III:384.

A Prayer for Peace and Prosperity

will be time to cultivate these qualities of life because the war will be over.

The next thing mentioned is the harvest (v. 13): the barns (or storehouses, the only occurrence of the word) will be filled with every kind (literally "from kind to kind") of produce. The parallel line describes another blessing of God: the sheep will bring forth by the thousands (מַאֲלִיפוֹת), multiplying by the tens of thousands (מְרֻבָּבוֹת) in the fields outside (חוּצוֹת). The first word is "thousand," put here in the causative conjugation (*hiphil*), yielding the meaning "bring forth thousands," and the word "myriad" or "ten thousand" likewise is put in a causative (denominative) form of the word, meaning "multiplied by ten thousands." When God gives peace to the nation, he will also bless the nation with prosperity in field and fold.

The interpretation of verse 14 is difficult, because it is cryptic. The first colon seems to fit with what has been said in verse 13: "our oxen will be well-laden (draw heavy loads)." But the meaning "our oxen" (אַלּוּפֵינוּ) is disputed; it could mean "our princes" or "chieftains." If the line is referring to chieftains, it might say, "our chieftains will be firmly established." But this section of the psalm seems focused on material prosperity. The second word means "to bear a heavy load" (it is the passive of סָבַל). Does it mean the cattle are loaded down with goods, or that they are pregnant? The former makes the best sense in the context. The idea of pregnancy could work, depending on how the rest of verse 14 is interpreted.

The remainder of the verse focuses on peace: "there will be no breaching (פֶּרֶץ), there will be no going out (יוֹצֵאת), and no crying out (צְוָחָה) in our streets." If this is also referring to a time of peace, then it could mean no army would break through (see Neh. 6:1), no one would be led out into captivity (Amos 4:3), and no cries of lamentation would be heard in the streets (Jer. 14:2) because there will be no reason for lament.[27]

---

27. It is also possible to take this verse as referring to the cattle, i.e., that they will bear "without mishap and without loss." But the last expression, that there be no outcry in the streets, seems to have no meaning if these expressions are taken to refer to mishaps with the animals. So the latter part of verse 14 refers to peace in the cities.

B. The blessing comes from the LORD (15).

The psalmist concludes his detailed prayer and meditation with an acknowledgment of God's blessing on the nation "Blessed are the people of whom this is true; blessed are the people whose God is the LORD." He introduces both of these clauses with the word "blessed" (אַשְׁרֵי; s.v. Ps. 1:1). The word describes the joyful condition of those who are right with God and enjoying the benefits of that relationship.

The first statement is simply a confirmation that all of the things described in this psalm are evidence of that happy estate. The unusual wording (שֶׁכָּכָה לּוֹ, "who like you to him") could be translated: "(How blessed are the people) *who are so situated*." And their blessing is that they have the LORD as their God. But what does it mean when it refers to a people whose God is the LORD? The whole nation of Israel would have claimed that down through their history. But such a claim has to be an expression of an active faith that trusts in him for victory, security, peace and prosperity. And the blessing is for the nation whose God is the LORD. It would be unlikely that God's blessing would only be granted if every single member of the society was a true believer and living obediently. So what is meant is the nation as a whole, the great majority. Nevertheless, in the future fulfillment in the Messianic age everyone will serve the LORD and enjoy his full blessings.

If the country is led by a devout, believing king, and the nation as a whole seeks to live faithfully before the LORD, then people can expect the blessing of peace and prosperity.

MESSAGE AND APPLICATION

As a piece of the royal liturgy this prayer would have found usefulness in many settings since the nation was so frequently at war. The psalm has been pasted together from a number of passages in the book of Psalms, drawing on some rather profound spiritual reflections. As a result, when the king prayed this prayer before battle, he would be reminded of the spiritual prerequisites for God's answer to his prayer. On the one hand he would be confident in the LORD in whom he trusted; but on the other hand he would be amazed that the LORD would take notice of him.

This was not just the prayer and praise of a righteous man who happened to be the king; it was the prayer and praise that was written to become part of the royal ideology. This psalm was deposited in the sanctuary to be used by any king who found himself in the same position and wanted to ensure the peace and prosperity for his people. Its message was to be remembered in every generation: *The people of God will enjoy lasting peace and prosperity when God gives their king victory in battle.* Whenever they remembered this truth, they were to seek the LORD's intervention through confident prayers.

It is a challenge to make an application of a psalm like this to modern believers, because they do not form a specific nation in a specific land. However, the application may be made in general terms for today, and more specific terms for the age to come. The point in the Bible is that God blesses righteousness in any nation, and in any individual. But the true people of God today are believers from every country (1 Pet. 2); and their king is a righteous king, the Davidic king *par excellence.* When he fights on our behalf to put down our enemies, the blessing of heaven is upon him. At the present time the victories are more spiritual than physical, and the victories he gains provide us with peace and provisions for this life. Then, at the second coming, when he comes with the clouds he will put down all enemies once and for all, and bring in an age of peace and prosperity that the world has never seen. Every victory over the world today demonstrates his power and his love and anticipates the final victory.

The task of all who are subjects of this divine King is to follow him with absolute allegiance and trust, and to make sure that their lives demonstrate that he is their God. They can then look with confidence to him for the peace he has promised, and the fulfillment of the eternal blessings he has stored up for them in glory.

PSALM 145

Praise for the Kingdom of the LORD, Its Greatness and Its Grace

INTRODUCTION

Text and Textual Variants

A Praise. Of David.

א 1 I will exalt you, my God the King;
      and I will bless your name for ever and ever.
ב 2 On every day I will bless you
      and praise your name for ever and ever.

ג 3 Great is the LORD and greatly *to be* praised;
      and concerning his greatness which is unsearchable.
ד 4 Generation to generation will praise your works;
      they will tell of your mighty acts.[1]

---

1. The major versions have the singular.

PSALM 145

ה 5 They will speak[2] of the glorious splendor of your majesty,
    while I will meditate[3] on your wonderful works.
ו 6 They will tell of the power of your awesome works,
    while I will proclaim[4] your great deeds.[5]
ז 7 They will celebrate the memory of your abundant goodness
    and joyfully sing of your righteousness.[6]

ח 8 The LORD is gracious and compassionate,
    slow to anger and rich in loyal love.
ט 9 The LORD is good to all;[7]
    and his compassion is upon all his works.
י 10 All your works will praise you, O LORD;
    those who receive your love will bless you.
כ 11 They will tell of the glory of your kingdom
    and speak of your might,[8]
ל 12 to make known to the sons of man his mighty works[9]
    and the glorious splendor of his[10] kingdom.
מ 13a Your kingdom is an everlasting kingdom,
    and your dominion endures throughout all generations.

---

2. The form in the MT is וְדִבְרֵי, "and the words of"; this would work well enough if taken with 5b. The Greek version interpreted it as a verb, "they will speak," λαλήσουσιν (= יְדַבְּרוּ). Most versions change the form to agree with the Greek; the MT is a more difficult reading, but perhaps too difficult.
3. The 1st person form of the verb, אָשִׂיחָה, is unexpected; we would expect "they will meditate / contemplate." The Greek (and the Syriac) have a 3rd plural to match the first colon: διηγήσονσαι (= יָשִׂיחוּ).
4. Here too for the 1st person form in the MT, אֲסַפְּרֶנָּה, the Greek (and Targum) have a 3rd plural verb.
5. The K<i>ethiv</i> reading is וּגְדוּלֹתָיךָ, the plural form; the Q<i>ᵉre'</i>, which is followed by most manuscripts and the major versions, is וּגְדוּלָתְךָ, the singular. But the plural fits the context the best.
6. Jerome and Symmachus have a plural.
7. "To all" is not in the Syriac version.
8. Jerome has the plural.
9. The Greek and Syriac have the singular.
10. The Greek and Syriac have "your."

Praise for the Kingdom of the LORD, Its Greatness and Its Grace

נ 13b The LORD is faithful to all his promises
       and loving toward all he has made.[11]
ס 14   The LORD upholds all those who fall
       and lifts up all who are bent down.
ע 15   The eyes of all look to you,
       and you give them[12] their food in its time.
פ 16   You open your hand[13]
       and satisfy the desires of every living thing.

צ 17   The LORD is righteous in all his ways
       and loving toward all he has made.
ק 18   The LORD is near to all who call on him,
       to all who call on him in truth.
ר 19   He fulfills the desires of those who fear him;
       he hears their cry and saves them.
ש 20   The LORD watches over all who love[14] him,
       but all the wicked he will destroy.
ת 21   My mouth will speak in praise of the LORD.
       Let all flesh bless his holy name
           For ever and ever.

Composition and Context

This is the only psalm that is called "Praise" (תְּהִלָּה [*tᵉhillāh*]),

---

11. This verse numbered 13b was apparently omitted in the Hebrew text. The verse is in the Qumran manuscript, the Greek and Syriac versions, and one manuscript by Kennicott. Most modern translations include it and thereby fill out the acrostic pattern. However, missing lines in acrostic psalms is not unusual, especially in Davidic psalms such as 25, 34, and 37. See further B. Lindars, "The Structure of Psalm cxlv," *VT* 29 (1979):23–30; R. Kimelman, "Psalm 145: Theme, Structure and Impact," *JBL* 113 (1994):37–58; and J. Chinitz, "Psalm 145: Its Two Faces," *JBQ* 24 (1996):229–32.
12. "To them" makes the line metrically difficult; it is not in the Greek version. See Ps. 104:27.
13. "Your hand" in the Hebrew is אֶת יָדֶךָ. Instead of the sign of the accusative the pronoun אַתָּה is represented in the Greek and Syriac as well as Qumran. The pronoun was apparently read before the sign of the accusative which was lost due to the similarity. The noun is in the plural in most manuscripts and several versions.
14. The ancient versions and Qumran have "fear" instead of "love."

909

even though the Hebrew title for the book is "Praises" (תְּהִלִּים [t*e*hillîm]). It is also the last psalm in the Psalter that is attributed to David; and it is the last of the eight alphabetic (acrostic) psalms, five of which are Davidic. Here the acrostic arrangement in the Hebrew Bible is incomplete; a verse beginning with an "n" is not in the text. However, there is a verse in one Hebrew manuscript, the Qumran scroll and the Greek and Syriac versions; most versions, therefore, restore it for the full acrostic order.[15]

In addition to these features, the psalm is also a unique type of hymn, occasionally referred to as an imperatival hymn because it prefaces the descriptions of God's greatness and grace with calls to praise.[16] Even these calls to praise form indirect praises as they reflect on the greatness of the LORD as the subject matter for the praise. And that greatness describes the kingdom of the LORD, not only for its unsearchable greatness and majesty, but also for its uniqueness in the ancient world of kingdoms in that the LORD condescends to meet the needs of all his creation, but especially those with whom he has a covenant.

Most commentators place the psalm in the post-exilic period for the familiar reasons that the language seems to be late, not early, that it uses other late psalms frequently, that it follows an acrostic pattern, and that it has the later emphasis on kingship.[17] The superscription is explained as having a homiletical purpose, namely to link this passage with Psalm 30 because of similar language.[18] These explanations do not convince everyone that the psalm could not have been an earlier composition adapted to be the introductory psalm of the doxology of the Psalter. Nevertheless, the message is a timeless one and came to be repeated by devout Jews in their morning and evening prayer services. Moreover, the Talmud has the saying that those who repeat it three times have a share in the world to come (*b. Ber.* 4b).

The structure of the psalm is relatively uncomplicated, although there have been numerous attempts to understand

---

15. The Qumran scroll's version of the psalm was clearly written for later cultic use because between every verse it has the refrain, "Blessed be the LORD and blessed is his name forever."
16. Allen, *Psalms 101–150*, p. 368.
17. See, for example, Anderson, *Psalms 73–150*, p. 936.
18. Allen, *Psalms 101–150*, p. 371.

the precise arrangement of the sections. It seems to have two main parts, the first praising God for his kingdom (vv. 1–9), and the second praising him for his care for his creation (10–21). However, further analysis of the structure varies among commentators. Anderson[19] arranges it according to sections of calls (vv. 1–2, vv. 4–7, and vv. 10–12), interspersed with descriptions of the LORD (v. 3, vv. 8–9, and vv. 13–20). I have followed this somewhat, taking verses 1–9 as the first part, with the pattern of a resolve to praise (1–2), the praise (3), a report of the praise of the people (4–7), and the praise (8–9). But I have kept verses 10–13a as a separate point because it is about the central theme of the psalm. The last part praises the LORD for his grace and goodness to all his creation (13b–20) and ends with a call to praise (v. 21).[20]

Exegetical Analysis

Summary

Understanding how gracious and righteous the LORD is, the psalmist praises him for his mighty acts which are passed from one generation to another, for his glorious everlasting kingdom which will be praised, and for the manner in which he responds to those who love him.

Outline

I. The psalmist vows to praise the LORD everyday because of his great and marvelous acts which one generation lauds to another and his grace and goodness to all his creatures (1–9).

   A. He will praise God his King everyday for his greatness (1–3).

---

19. Anderson, *Psalms 73–150*, p. 936.
20. For more detailed study of the structure see Adele Berlin, "The Rhetoric of Psalm 145," in *Biblical and Related Studies Presented to Samuel Iwry*, edited by Ann Kort and Scott Morschauer (Winona Lake, IN: Eisenbrauns, 1985), pp. 17–22; Jonathan Magonet, "Some Concentric Structures in Psalms," *HeyJ* 23 (1982):365–69; as well as the previously mentioned articles.

    1. Resolve: He will bless and extol God his King every day (1–2).
    2. Reason: His greatness is unsearchable (3).
  B. The people will praise the LORD from generation to generation for his marvelous works (4–7).
    1. One generation lauds the marvelous works to another and speaks of his glory (4–5a).
    2. He will meditate on those wonderful works (5b).
    3. People will speak and sing of God's awesome works, goodness and righteousness (6a, 7).
    4. He will proclaim his great deeds (6b).
  C. The LORD is to be praised for his covenant faithfulness revealed in his attributes (8–9).
    1. The LORD is gracious and merciful, slow to anger and full of loyal love (8).
    2. The LORD is good and merciful to all (9).
II. The psalmist tells how all creation will praise the LORD's power and glory seen in his everlasting kingdom (10–13a).
  A. All of God's works and especially his saints will praise him (10).
  B. They will praise the LORD for his everlasting kingdom (11–13a).
    1. People will speak of his power and glory (11–12).
    2. His kingdom is an everlasting kingdom (13a).
III. The psalmist extols the praiseworthy loving care and righteousness of the LORD to his creation, but especially to those who call on him (13b–21).
  A. He tells how the LORD is faithful and loving to all he has made (13b–16):
    1. Summary: The LORD is faithful and loving to all he has made (13b).
    2. Specific Samples: The LORD upholds the fallen, provides food for his creation, and satisfies the desires of every living thing (14–16).
  B. He tells how the LORD is righteous and loving to his people (17–20).
    1. Summary: The LORD is righteous and loving to all (17).

Praise for the Kingdom of the LORD, Its Greatness and Its Grace

    2. Specific Samples: The LORD is near to those who call on him, fulfilling their desires, saving them, and watching over them (18–20).

  C. All flesh should join him in praising the LORD and bless his holy name (21).

COMMENTARY IN EXPOSITORY FORM

I. The faithful praise the LORD from generation to generation for his mighty works and his loving care (1–9).

A. *Devout believers praise the LORD their king every day for his greatness (1–3).*

The psalmist, probably speaking on behalf of the congregation, resolves to exalt and praise his "God and King." These two words alone would call for praise; but the psalmist will develop their meanings more specifically in the following verses. Here he will "exalt" God (רוּם; s.v. Ps. 46:10), "bless him" (בָּרַךְ; s.v. Ps. 5:12), and "praise" his name (הָלַל; s.v. Ps. 33:1). Because he will praise the everlasting God and King his praise will necessarily be unending—he will praise the name of the LORD for ever and ever. All believers know that praise must not cease, and will never cease. The psalmist may not have meant that his praise would extend into the life to come; but the Bible makes that point clearly.

Verse 3 provides the opening reason for praising the LORD—he is great (גָּדוֹל; s.v. Ps. 34:3) and greatly to be praised (meaning that because he is completely praiseworthy he is given great praise). The psalm will probe the greatness of the LORD; but at this point it reminds people that no one can fully discover (חֵקֶר; s.v. Ps. 139:1) his greatness. Anderson paraphrases this by saying the full extent of God's greatness and power is beyond human comprehension.[21]

B. *Their praise for the LORD's greatness is passed down from generation to generation (4–7).*

Praise helps preserve the faith as it is passed down from one

---

21. *Psalms 73–150*, p. 936.

generation to the next. And this is the point made in the next four verses. The knowledge of the LORD is preserved largely through instruction, but the living faith through continued proclamation. Each generation will testify to God's mighty works, his glorious majesty, and the might of his awe-inspiring deeds. The descriptions used here are found frequently in the Psalter, but the piling up of them is almost overpowering:

First it is simply "your works," מַעֲשֶׂיךָ; then it is "your mighty acts," גְּבוּרֹתֶיךָ (s.v. Ps. 45:3); then it increases to "the glorious splendor of your majesty," הֲדַר כְּבוֹד הוֹדֶךָ (s.v. Ps. 19:1; Ps. 96:6); it changes to "your wonderful works," נִפְלְאוֹתֶיךָ (s.v. Ps. 139:5); then "the power of your awesome deeds," עֱזוּז נוֹרְאֹתֶיךָ (s.v. Ps. 29:1 and Ps. 2:11); "your great deeds," גְּדוּלֹּתֶיךָ (s.v. Ps. 34:3); "the fame of your abundant goodness," זֵכֶר רַב־טוּבְךָ (s.v. Ps. 6:5 and Ps. 34:8); and finally "your righteousness," צִדְקָתְךָ, signifying the cause for these works (s.v. Ps. 1:5).

And according to verse 7, their praise will be enthusiastic: they will "pour forth" the fame of his abundant goodness. These are all general descriptions; individual praise would necessarily elaborate on them with specific personal experience that could only be described with these terms. And that is what the psalmist will proceed to do in this composition.

It is also interesting to note that in verses 5 and 6 in the first half of each verse the psalmist states that the people will praise, and in the second half he says he will meditate on and proclaim these same wonders (unless we change the text). Because he is speaking on behalf of the people, the people may be following his lead: they will praise while he praises, and then they will continue to praise from one generation to the next.

C. The LORD is to be praised for his covenant faithfulness (8–9).

In these two verses the psalmist focuses his attention on the wonderful and gracious works of God that are gracious. The list is similar to Psalm 103:8 and probably represents a liturgical formula. It is drawn from Exodus 34:6. God is gracious (חַנּוּן; s.v. Ps. 4:1), compassionate (רַחוּם; s.v. Ps. 25:6), slow to anger (אֶרֶךְ אַפַּיִם; s.v. Ps. 30:5), and great in loyal love (חֶסֶד; s.v. Ps. 23:6).

Praise for the Kingdom of the LORD, Its Greatness and Its Grace

These attributes were revealed to Moses after the great sin of the golden calf, when people needed confirmation of God's grace and love. Here it is applied in general to God's loving care of his people; verse 9 expands the application to say that the LORD is good to all and his compassion is upon everything he has made.

II. The faithful praise the LORD for his everlasting kingdom (10–13a).

A. All God's works, especially his saints, will praise the LORD (10).

This central section carries the motif of the LORD's kingship further with similar descriptions of his greatness. The psalmist begins with a general statement that everything God made will praise him (for יָדָה, s.v. Ps. 6:5), particularly those who receive his love, that is, the beloved (חֲסִידִים; s.v. Ps. 23:6) will bless him.[22] The verbs in this section could be interpreted as prayers (jussives) and so read "Let all your works praise you," etc. But since the psalmist is lauding the everlasting kingdom of the LORD, and since he has spoken of how the praise will be handed down, this section may simply anticipate increasing praise throughout all creation.

B. They tell of his power and glory and his everlasting kingdom (11–13a).

The emphasis here is on the LORD as ruler. He repeats many of the words used above for the praise of the people: the LORD's kingdom is glorious, powerful, and majestic. Now however he adds "everlasting"; literally, it is "a kingdom of all ages" (כָּל־עֹלָמִים; s.v. Ps. 61:4). The word "everlasting" (or "ages") includes all time from the remotest past to the distant future.[23] The language used here is similar to the words of the Babylonian king who finally extolled the sovereign greatness of the LORD (Dan.

---

22. The usage of "beloved" parallels in many ways what the New Testament means by "saints," people who have received the love of God and in response also practice covenant love.
23. Anderson, *Psalms 73–150*, pp. 938–39.

4:3). Even with the additional revelation in the New Testament it is difficult to imagine what a kingdom of all ages fully means. But understand it all or not, the righteous will proclaim the glory of God's kingdom so that everyone might know of his mighty acts and the glory of the splendor of his kingdom. It is the mighty acts that make the kingdom so great.

III. The faithful praise the LORD and call on everyone to bless his name because in his love he responds to his people to save and protect them (17–21).

A. *The LORD is faithful and loving to all that he has made (13b–16).*

The kingdom of God is truly great. What sets it apart from all earthly kingdoms is that it is eternal and that its greatness is its grace. Perowne writes, "Where is the cosmic excellence of the kingdom seen? Not in symbols of earthly pride and power, but in gracious condescension to the fallen and the crushed, in a gracious care which provides for the wants of every living thing."[24] The greatness is seen in the condescension of the king to meet the needs of his creation; or, to put it another way, the marvel of his divine condescension lies in his magnificence and eternal dominion.[25]

Verse 13b introduces this section by declaring that the LORD is faithful in all his words and loving to all he has made. The section will focus on the fidelity of the king—he keeps his promises. In this way he extends his love to all he made by meeting the needs of every living creature. Here is God the faithful provider.

The initial sample of his care is in helping those who have fallen or bent low (v. 14). The expressions describe people who are beaten down, perhaps by oppression or illness. They are weakened and depressed. But the LORD intervenes in numerous ways to restore them. He is their king for sure, but he is also their God; he can deliver people from any and every difficulty. Moreover, he provides food for all his creation so that their needs

---

[24]. *Psalms,* II:471.
[25]. VanGemeren, *Psalms,* p. 990.

Praise for the Kingdom of the LORD, Its Greatness and Its Grace

will be satisfied (verses 15 and 16 are drawn from Ps. 104:27, 28; also compare Job 38:39–41).

B. The LORD responds to those who call on him, satisfying their desires, saving them, and watching over them (17–20).

The provision of care from this divine king now is directed to the saints. The section is introduced with the declaration that the LORD is righteous in all his ways and loving to all he made. His loving care for all creation is the natural outworking of his righteousness—everything he does is right because it flows from his character. If he is good to creation in general, how much more to his covenant people. And so within the covenant his righteousness will be most clearly displayed, for he has bound himself to those who trust in him.

Verse 18 says the LORD is near to those who call on him in truth (i.e., faithfully). To be near means that he answers their prayers and helps them (recall in Ps. 22 that unanswered prayer was explained as God's being far off). Those who call on him are the believers who pray for help, appealing to his covenant promises and basing their confidence on his revealed nature. They are committed believers because they fear the LORD. They are not strangers to the covenant who in a moment of panic try calling on God. No, they believe in him, they fear him, they love him, and they cry out to him for help. And the LORD responds to their faith with faithfulness: he hears their cries and saves them (for יָשַׁע, s.v. Ps. 3:2).

In general the LORD watches over (שׁוֹמֵר; s.v. Ps. 12:7) those who love him, that is all who are faithful to the covenant (for אָהֵב and its significance for covenant loyalty, s.v. Ps. 11:7). But the loving care does not extend to the wicked whom he will destroy (see Ps. 1:6). From the divine king comes amazing acts of grace and care; but if people refuse to trust and obey, they will have no share in his kingdom, now or in the ages to come.

C. All flesh should join in praise of his holy name (21).

The psalmist concludes were he began with a declaration that he will praise the LORD: "my mouth will speak in praise of the LORD." This is the natural and expected response to anyone's contemplation of the greatness and goodness of God. Moreover, in his praise he also desires that all flesh, everyone, will bless his holy name forever. Because the LORD's reign is universal, all flesh must praise him.

MESSAGE AND APPLICATION

The message of this praise psalm, and the others to follow in the grand doxology, have a very clear application: Praise the LORD, now and always, faithfully and enthusiastically. And although each of these psalms offer similar reasons for the praise, they each have their own emphases. An expository idea for Psalm 145 could be stated this way: *Believers must praise the LORD now and forever for the greatness of his everlasting kingdom and for the gracious ways he responds to those who love him.*

There are many passages that can be correlated to the message of this psalm easily. The ways of the LORD are beyond our knowledge (Rom. 11:13–6), but he has revealed his sovereign kingdom to us by and through the Messiah (Dan. 7:14). It is an everlasting kingdom that will come in its full glory at the end of the age (Rev. 19:6; Phil. 2:9–11). But its greatness will extend to his condescension to care for his creation and to deliver those who trust in him and bring them into his eternal kingdom (Rev. 19:7). At his appearance kings will be dumbfounded, for this one who emptied himself to redeem people will be high and lifted up above everyone (Isa. 52:13–53:12). What the psalmist writes about from his knowledge and experience will ultimately be revealed in a splendor and glory that is for now beyond comprehension. And praise offered now will become far more glorious in the world to come.

PSALM 146
Praise for the Faithfulness of the Sovereign Creator

INTRODUCTION

Text and Textual Variants[1]

Praise the LORD![2]

1 Praise the LORD, O my soul.
2 I will praise the LORD all my life;
   I will sing praise to my God as long as I live.[3]

3 Do not put your trust in princes,
   in mortal man,[4] who has no salvation.
4 When[5] his spirit leaves, he returns to his ground;

---

1. The Greek has a superscription reading "Of Haggai and Zechariah." The close links between some verses in this psalm to passages in those prophets may lie behind the association (e.g., vv. 6–7 and Zech. 4:6).
2. This prologue is not in some manuscripts.
3. The Greek reads "while I have being," ἕως ὑπάρχω.
4. The text has "a son of man," בֶּן־אָדָם.
5. The subordination of the clause is based on the simple juxtaposition of the two clauses in the colon.

      on that very day his plans perish.
5 Blessed is *the one* whose help is[6] the God of Jacob;
      his hope is in the LORD his God,
6 the maker of heaven and earth,
      the sea, and everything in them.[7]

      H*e* preserves[8] faithfulness forever:
7 *he* maintains justice for the oppressed
      and gives food to the hungry.
    The LORD sets prisoners free;
8 the LORD gives sight[9] to the blind,
      the LORD lifts up those who are bent down.
        The LORD loves the righteous.
9 The LORD watches[10] over the alien
      and sustains the fatherless and the widow;
    but the way of the wicked he turns away.
10 The LORD reigns forever,
      your God, O Zion, for all generations.

    Praise the LORD!

Composition and Context

Here we have a hymn that celebrates the faithfulness and the justice of the sovereign LORD. The psalmist, speaking on behalf of the congregation, has compiled a number of traditional statements about the LORD—he alone can save, he is the creator, he is faithful, he administers justice in the earth, and he reigns

---

6. The preposition בְּ is a *beth of essence* here: "... who the God of Jacob is his help." Some suggest that the letter בְּ should be deleted due to dittography with "Jacob."
7. There are different ways to make the break here to the next clause. VanGemeren suggests: " ... the sea and everything in them—is he who remains faithful" (*Psalms,* p. 994).
8. The form is the participle with the article: "who guards."
9. The Greek translation says "wisdom" or "skill," σοφοί, perhaps understanding "the blind" figuratively.
10. The Greek version reads "converts," τοὺς προσηλύτους.

forever—and has reaffirmed them for a new audience.[11] The exposition of the psalm is facilitated by the straightforward listing of the gracious things that the LORD does.

The work is generally taken to be post-exilic, primarily because of a few later words and constructions in it. But Anderson points out that though it may be post-exilic in origin it still depends on earlier psalms and traditions.[12]

The structure is a little difficult for a short work. There is a prologue and epilogue—"Praise the LORD." The first two verses record the psalmist's commitment to praise the LORD (vv. 1–2); and there is an acclamation of the LORD's kingship at the end (v. 10). In between are two strophes supplying the reasons for the praise: verses 3–6a declare that the faithful hope in the LORD for salvation because he is the creator of all things; and verses 6b–9 rehearse specific ways the LORD helps his people.

Exegetical Analysis

Summary

The psalmist commits himself to praise the LORD who alone is trustworthy because as the sovereign creator he is able to help those who trust in him; and because he is faithful he will meet their needs.

Outline

Prologue: "Praise the LORD!"

I. The psalmist resolves to praise the LORD all his life.
   A. He exhorts himself to praise the LORD (1b).
   B. He resolves to praise the LORD all of his life (2).
II. The psalmist declares that those who put their faith and hope in the sovereign Lord of creation are truly blessed, but warns them of the futility of trusting mere mortals (3–6a).

---

11. Allen, *Psalms 101–150,* p. 379. See further J. S. Kselman, "Psalm 146 in Its Context," *CBQ* 50 (1988):586–99.
12. *Psalms 73–150,* p. 940.

A. He warns people not to put their trust in humans who have no power to save themselves or others (3–4).
   B. He declares that those who put their faith and hope in the sovereign Lord of all creation are blessed (5–6a).
III. The psalmist delineates the different ways that the LORD is faithful and just in his dealings with the many afflictions and troubles his people encounter (6b–9).
   A. Summary statement: The LORD is faithful (6b).
   B. Samples (7b–9):
      1. The LORD helps the oppressed and the needy (7).
         a. He maintains justice for the oppressed (7a).
         b. He provides food for the hungry (7b).
         c. He sets prisoners free (7c).
      2. The LORD helps those who suffer physically (8).
         a. He gives sight to the blind (8a).
         b. He lifts up the bent down (8b).
      3. The LORD champions righteousness (8).
         a. He loves the righteous (8c).
         b. He watches over the alien (9a).
         c. He sustains the widow and orphan (9b).
         d. He diverts the way of the wicked (9c).
IV. The psalmist declares that the LORD their God will reign forever (10).

Epilogue: "Praise the LORD!"

COMMENTARY IN EXPOSITORY FORM

I. Believers must commit themselves to a life of praise (1b–2).

After the prologue, "Praise the LORD," which is a call for all to praise, the psalmist exhorts himself to offer praise: "Praise the LORD, O my soul." By addressing this call to his soul (נַפְשִׁי; s.v. Ps. 11:5), he was calling for wholehearted praise from his entire being. Then, as if in obedience to this call, he commits himself to a life-time of praise: "I will praise" (אֲהַלְלָה; s.v. Ps. 33:1) and "I will sing praise" (אֲזַמְּרָה; s.v. Ps. 33:2). The forms emphasize his determination to praise the LORD for his entire lifetime (as long as he exists; compare Ps. 104:33). Kidner explains that by using these cohortatives he puts the matter on a broader base than the mood of the moment.[13] Believers today should consider making such a commitment.

II. Their praise is an expression of their faith and hope in the LORD, the sovereign creator of the world, and not in mere mortals (3–6a).

In this section we are reminded of the help and hope we have in the LORD that makes him praiseworthy. To get to this point the psalmist begins with a warning not to trust (אַל־תִּבְטְחוּ; s.v. Ps. 4:5) in princes or in mere mortals in general (compare Ps. 118:9). The "princes" (נְדִיבִים) were powerful men of influence, but in reality they were mere mortals, literally "son of man" (בֶּן־אָדָם). The warning might indicate that there were people in Zion who advocated alliances with foreign powers for deliverance from danger. But mere humans cannot be looked to for security, whether they are powerful or not. The point is that mortals have no salvation in and of themselves (תְּשׁוּעָה; s.v. Ps. 3:2), meaning they cannot save themselves and therefore cannot save others. How could a man save anyone if he could die at any moment: "When his spirit departs from him, he returns to his ground." The word play here between "man" (אָדָם) and "ground" or "earth" (אֲדָמָה) draws greater attention to immortality (Gen. 2:7 and 3:19; see also Eccl. 12:7)—he goes to his earth because he is earthy. Obviously, this description of the frailty of humans stands in strong contrast to the LORD who is the creator of all things and reigns forever as king. He can be trusted, he must be trusted, for salvation because he alone is able to save.

The verse develops the theme of human morality further by observing that when a man dies his plans perish with him. The word for "his plans" is a rare word (עֶשְׁתֹּנֹתָיו from עֶשֶׁת). It is called an Aramaism (a word more common in Aramaic than Hebrew), which usually means it is a late word. That it occurs more frequently in Aramaic does not necessarily mean it is a late word, only that it occurs more frequently in Aramaic than Hebrew. But

---

13. *Palms 73–150*, p. 483.

in fact, this word is found in an eighth-century Sefire inscription, and the related verb is used once in the Hebrew Bible, in Jonah 1:6.[14] The word has the sense of "his thinking": so whatever he was planning to do, whether good or evil, perishes when he breathes his last.

The positive contrast comes next in verses 5 and 6. It is announced in the form of a blessing (אַשְׁרֵי; s.v. Ps. 1:1): "Blessed is the one whose help (עֶזְרוֹ; s.v. Ps. 46:1) is the God of Jacob" (Ps. 46:7, 11). There is inner joy and comfort in knowing that help is coming from the sovereign Lord of creation and not from mere humans (see Ps. 121:1–2). The writer may have had Psalm 46 in mind here. The identification of the LORD as the God of Jacob probably refers to the way the LORD helped the patriarch even though he deserved no help. With that in mind, the name "Jacob" probably is a designation for the people of Israel in general, who like their ancestor needed and found great help in their God.

Because the LORD is their help he is also their hope.[15] Believers in all ages who hope in the LORD, knowing that he is fully able to deliver them because he is the maker of all things—the heavens and the earth, the sea and everything in them. He has all the power to meet the needs of his people, and delights in doing so.

III. The LORD demonstrates his everlasting faithfulness by meeting the needs of his people (6b–9).

A. *The LORD remains faithful forever (6b).*

The last colon of verse 6 is more connected to this third section of the psalm than to the second: it announces that the LORD "is the one who preserves faithfulness forever." The participle with the article (הַשֹּׁמֵר; s.v. Ps. 12:7) emphasizes that he is the one who naturally guards or maintains faithfulness. And preserving "faithfulness" implies that he himself is faithful. The word "faithfulness" is the simple word "truth" (אֱמֶת; s.v. Ps. 15:2), which refers to something that is reliable and trustworthy; and

---

14. See Anderson, *Psalms 73–150,* p. 941; and Dahood, *Psalms,* III:341.
15. שִׂבְרוֹ is another Aramaic word, found also in Ps. 119:116.

so it often carries the meaning of faithfulness. And this the LORD maintains "forever" (לְעוֹלָם; s.v. Ps. 61:4). As Anderson explains it, the commitment of the LORD is unchangeable.[16] This is why it is essential to come to faith in him and look forward in hope in him. Because he is forever faithful, the salvation he gives is eternal, and he is always ready to help those who pray to him for help.

B. The LORD demonstrates his faithfulness by meeting the needs of his people (7–9).

The next few verses list things the LORD does that show him to be faithful. It is not automatic; he does not always do these things; but he can be trusted to do them because he has done them again and again. There is nothing in the following list that is new; the descriptions are the fundamental works of God for his people. Those who know the Bible will be familiar with them, not only from what is recorded in the Old Testament, but also from the claims of Jesus to be fulfilling these mighty works (e.g., Luke 4, from Isaiah 61).

The first few refer to justice. He maintains (does) justice for the oppressed (7a), he gives food to the hungry (7b), and he sets the prisoner free (7c). God's justice, the decisions he makes (מִשְׁפָּט; s.v. Ps. 9:4), always seeks to correct the wrongs in the world. He may intervene directly, but he often chooses to use his covenant people as the agents, especially in championing justice for those who are oppressed and for feeding the hungry. Next we are told he sets the prisoners free. The word "prisoners" could be literal (as those set free from captivity according to Isaiah 61), but it may also be figurative of people who need deliverance from any bondage (see Ps. 68:6; 107:10–16). Justice, food, and freedom are things the LORD can provide; therefore, they are things for which believers pray, and then praise.

The next two concern physical needs. First, the LORD gives sight to the blind (8a). The text simply says "he opens the blind" without mentioning the eyes. Here too blindness could be literal, but it is also used figuratively for spiritual blindness. The

---

16. *Psalms 73–150*, p. 942.

Targum translates this with "the LORD (is the one who) opens the eyes of strangers who may be compared to the blind." And in Jesus's ministry healing someone who was blind might also resolve spiritual blindness as well (see John 9:35–41). Second, he also lifts up people who are bent down, perhaps with oppression or discouragement or weakness (8b; the line comes from Ps. 145:14; see also Isa. 58:5).

The last four statements are reminders of the standard acts of righteousness. They are introduced with the summary that the LORD loves the righteous, that is, true believers, members of the covenant (s.v. Ps. 1:5). They, in return, must love the LORD their God (Deut. 6:4–5), whose love for them is demonstrated by doing righteous acts in faithfulness to the covenant (s.v. Ps. 11:7). Accordingly, we read that he watches over the alien (or the sojourner) in the land (9a), and sustains the fatherless and the widow (9b). The widow, the orphan, and the stranger in the land were major concerns for Israel; they were the ones who had the most difficult lot in life because they had no resources of their own and were easily mistreated or cast out. When the LORD cared for them, it became the standard of righteousness and a test for the righteousness of Israel.

Finally in contrast to these provisions for needy people the LORD rejects the way of the wicked. The verb (יְעַוֵּת) means "to be bent, crooked," and in this form it has the idea that the LORD makes their way, their life and their work, crooked—he diverts it so it cannot come to its intended end.

In this section (vv. 7b–9) the holy name Yahweh ("the LORD") is used five times, and in the clauses where it is found it is always the first word of the clause. Such an intentional focus on the personal name of the covenant God would remind people that his faithfulness to meet their needs is a central part of the covenant.

IV. The LORD God reigns forever (10).

The proclamation that the LORD reigns forever and ever closes the psalm. The verb is an imperfect tense, which may be given an English present tense translation. But since the verse says this reign will be forever, some translators find the future tense more fitting. The English present tense indicates that he is now reigning; and "forever" extends his reign into the distant future. What the psalmist is saying to the people (referred to figuratively as Zion) is that the LORD, "your God," always reigns, now and forever.[17] This means that all the things he now does as king he will continue to do as long as he needs to—and even greater things in the coming kingdom. It also means that the psalmist's resolve to praise as long as he exists means that it will be an eternity of praise. Who in the world would reject the sovereign Lord of creation and put their trust in people, no matter how powerful? No wonder the psalmist calls such a person a fool (Ps. 14:1).

MESSAGE AND APPLICATION

The expository idea of this psalm may be stated as follows: *Believers must commit themselves to praise the LORD because as the sovereign creator he alone is able to help them in all their needs, and because as the creator he is faithful to do it.* And the counterpoint of this is: *It is folly to rely on humans who are weak and transitory when God is able and willing to meet all our needs.* The primary application is for people to praise the LORD all their life, as Hezekiah vowed to do when restored to health (Isa. 38). The content of their praise may still focus on the power of the creator and the faithfulness of the LORD to his covenant people.

But the most practical application comes from this latter emphasis on God's faithfulness to the righteous whom he loves. The righteous, therefore, should demonstrate their love for him by emulating his faithfulness to the covenant, championing justice, feeding the hungry, bringing relief to those in bondage, and taking care of the stranger, the widow and the orphan. It remains true in the New Testament that God most often meets these needs through the ministry of his servants.

---

17. See further B. V. Malchow, "God or King in Psalm 146," *The Bible Today*, 89 (1977):1166–70.

PSALM 147

God's Gracious Restoration, Sovereign Rule, and Powerful Word

INTRODUCTION

Text and Textual Variants[1]

1 "Praise the LORD!"

   How good *it is* to sing praises to our God,
      how pleasant *and* fitting *it is* to praise him![2]

2 The LORD builds up Jerusalem;
      he[3] gathers the exiles of Israel.
3 He heals the brokenhearted
      and binds up their wounds.[4]

4 He determines the number of the stars;
      to[5] all of them he calls names.

---

1. The Greek version adds "Of Haggai and Zachariah."
2. The Greek version renders the words differently: "Praise the LORD, for a psalm is good; may praise be fitting for our God." In the first colon the infinitive זַמְּרָה, "to praise," was taken as the imperative זַמְּרוּ, and נָאוָה in the second colon was omitted.
3. The Greek and Syriac have a conjunction here.
4. This is interpreted as "fractures" in the Greek, συντρίμματα.
5. The Greek and Syriac have a conjunction here.

PSALM 147

5 Great is our Lord and mighty in power;
   his[6] understanding has no limit.
6 The LORD sustains the humble
   but casts the wicked to the ground.

7 Sing[7] to the LORD with thanksgiving;
   make music to our God upon the harp.

8 He covers the sky with clouds;
   he supplies the earth with rain
   and makes grass grow on the hills.[8]
9 He provides food for the cattle
   and[9] for the young ravens when they call.[10]

10 He does not desire the strength of the horse,
   nor take delight in the legs of a man;
11 The LORD delights in those who fear him,
   who put their hope in his unfailing love.

12 [11]Extol the LORD, O Jerusalem;
   praise your God, O Zion,
13 for he strengthens the bars of your gates
   and blesses your sons within you.

---

6. One manuscript, the Greek and the Syriac have a conjunction here.
7. The MT has the imperative form עֲנוּ from עָנָה, "to sing" (perhaps antiphonally if connected to "answer"). The Greek versions reads "Lead off," ἐξάρξατε.
8. Greek manuscripts add a colon, "and plants for the service of man," καὶ χλόην τῇ δουλείᾳ τῶν ἀνθρώπων. It provides a fourth colon to form a nicely balanced line; but the line makes the same point with the three cola present.
9. The conjunction is in one manuscript, the Greek, and the Syriac.
10. Some commentators suggest translating this verb as "(that which) they gather." But Job 38:41 supports the idea of the ravens crying out. The poetry interprets the crying of the bird as prayer.
11. The rest of the psalm is a separate psalm in the Greek and Vulgate. It is introduced here by Ἀλληλουια with "Of Haggai and Zachariah," as was the beginning of Psalm 147. The numbering of the Psalms has differed from the Hebrew in the Greek and Latin versions from Psalm 10 until here; now the numbering is the same through the end of the Psalter.

God's Gracious Restoration, Sovereign Rule, and Powerful Word

14 He gives to your borders peace
     and satisfies you with the finest wheat.

15 He sends his oracle to the earth;
     his word runs swiftly.
16 He gives snow like wool;
     he scatters the frost like ashes.
17 He hurls down his hail like pebbles.
     Who can withstand[12] his icy blast?
18 He sends his word[13] and melts them;
     he stirs up his breezes,[14] and the waters flow.
19 He has revealed his word to Jacob,
     his laws and decrees to Israel.
20 He has not done so for any other nation;
     they do not know[15] his laws.

"Praise the LORD!"

---

12. The insertion of a rhetorical question at this point seems out of place, and so there have been attempts to rework the expression. One proposal is rather simple: the word "who" (מִי) is taken to be an abbreviation of "water" (מַיִם) and the clause read as "water stands frozen" (icy blast). Allen points out that this would fit the context well since the ideas in verses 16 and 17 are reversed in verse 18, and that there is support for it Job 37:10 (*Psalms 101–150*, p. 382). This may be the original idea, even though the psalm does include changes of subjects in the second colon (v. 15, and perhaps here and in v. 20 if the MT stands).

13. There is a *K*ᵉ*thiv-Q*ᵉ*re'* reading here. *Q* has the word as plural, דְּבָרָיו, "his words"; it has the support of most manuscripts. The *K* reading is singular, דְּבָרוֹ, "his word"; it is the reading in the Greek, Aquila, Symmachus and the Syriac.

14. For the MT's יַשֵּׁב רוּחוֹ, "he stirs up his wind / breezes"; the Greek version has "he will blow with his breath," πνεύσει τὸ πνεῦμα αὐτοῦ.

15. The MT has בַּל־יְדָעוּם, "they do not know them." The verb is taken to be the causative *hiphil* in the Greek, Syriac and Targum; the Greek has οὐκ ἐδήλωσεν αὐτοῖς, "he did not explain to them," which would represent a form יוֹדִיעֵם, perhaps written defectively (without the *waw* or *yod*, יֹדְעֵם). Qumran has a form (הוֹדִיעָם) that follows the Greek version in meaning. Those who accept this variant reading note that it keeps the LORD as the subject in both halves of the verse. But this may indicate it was a secondary reading.

PSALM 147

Composition and Context

This palm is a hymn that celebrates the LORD's sovereign rule over his creation and his loving are for his covenant people. The psalm mixes the two motifs throughout: God's dominion over creation (in verses 4, 8–9, 14b and 15–18) and his covenant faithfulness (in verses 2, 13, and 19, and more generally in 3, 6, and 13–14). It had a cultic setting, but is difficult to be more specific than that. Anderson, among others, suggests it was for the feast of Tabernacles because of the emphasis on rain, the next harvest, and the law.[16]

The hymn is made up of three parts, the third being the longest. Some scholars have suggested that there were originally three separate psalms that have been combined. But Allen, however, demonstrates that there are enough features to support its original unity; for example, "Jerusalem" begins the first and third stanzas; each of the three stanzas use "God" with the possessive pronoun; all three stanzas end with antithetical statements (vv. 6, 10–11, and 19–20); and there are numerous vocabulary links between the three.[17] The psalm also shows movement in the description of the LORD's rule from the stars in verse 4, to the heavenly and earthly phenomena beneficial to life in verses 8 and 9, and finally to specific provisions for his people in verses 14–18.

Psalm 147 draws frequently on other passages, such as Psalm 33, Psalm 104, Isaiah 40–66, Job 37–39, and Deuteronomy 4. Kidner points out that at times the psalmist takes up the rhetorical questions of Isaiah 40, and at other times the LORD's questioning of Job, turning them into praise.[18] The flow of the hymn is natural, declaring that the sovereign God of all creation is the faithful Lord of the covenant.

It is also difficult to determine the occasion for the composition. Most scholars put it in the post-exilic period because of its literary references. The mention of building (or rebuilding) Jerusalem and its gates suggests the time of Nehemiah, a celebration at the completion of the building of the walls and gates

---

16. *Psalms 73–150*, p. 944.
17. *Psalms 60–150*, p. 383–85.
18. *Psalms 73–150*, p. 485.

(Neh. 12:27–43). Hengstenberg mentions that Psalms 147–150 were all written for this same event, but Anderson cautions that "building" Jerusalem could be a general reference to the LORD's constant building up of the city.[19] The restoration period after the exile however fits very well.

Psalm 147 is divided into two psalms in the Greek and Latin versions, first verses 1–11 and then verses 12–20. There is some debate about which version to follow: the Greek and Latin with two psalms, or the Hebrew with one. Expositors need to be aware of this when using commentaries that follow the Greek and Latin division.

Exegetical Analysis

Summary

The psalmist summons the people of Jerusalem to praise the LORD because he restores his people, controls his creation, sustains life, especially of those who trust in him, and reveals his will to his covenant people and not to the nations.

Outline

Prologue: "Praise the LORD"

I. The first cycle of praise: Praise for the LORD is appropriate because he restores his people and displays his greatness in creation (1b–6).
   A. Call to praise: It is fitting and pleasing to praise God (1b).
   B. Cause for praise: He restores his people and controls creation (2–6).
      1. He builds up Jerusalem and heals his oppressed people (2–3).
      2. He controls his creation with power and understanding (4–5).
      3. He exalts the lowly, but abases the wicked (6).

---

19. *Psalms 73–150,* p. 485.

II. The second cycle of praise: Praise must be given to the LORD because he makes provisions in nature for life and delights in those who trust in his love (7–11).
  A. Call to praise: Sing praises to the LORD with musical accompaniment (7).
  B. Cause for praise: He provides for his creation and delights in those who put their trust in his love (8–11).
    1. His greatness and grace are seen in the way he sustains life (8–9).
    2. In his sovereign grace he delights in those who trust in his unfailing love (10–11).
III. The third cycle of praise: Praise is to be given to the LORD because he sustains creation by his powerful word and reveals his will to his people in his word (12–20).
  A. Call to praise: His people are to praise him (12).
  B. Cause for praise: His powerful word sustains creation and is given exclusively to Israel (13–20)
    1. He preserves his people in their place (13–14).
    2. He sustains nature by his decree (15–18).
    3. He reveals himself to his people in his word (19–20).

Epilogue: "Praise the LORD"

COMMENTARY IN EXPOSITORY FORM

I. Praising the LORD is appropriate because he restores his people and controls creation (1–6).

A. It is right to praise our God (1b).

"Praise the LORD" (הַלְלוּ־יָהּ) is both the prologue and the epilogue; this call for praise forms the framework for each of Psalms 146–150, the grand doxology to the Psalter.

Verse 1b announces the appropriateness of praise. The first word (כִּי) is emphatic and not causal because the call to praise stands outside the psalm proper. It may be translated as "Surely" or "How."

The first colon uses the infinitive (זַמְּרָה; s.v. Ps. 33:2) as the subject: "How good it is to sing praises to our God." The second colon is normally translated: "how pleasant *and* fitting is praise."

God's Gracious Restoration, Sovereign Rule, and Powerful Word

The second colon forms a close parallel, so that "fitting praise" (נָאוָה תְהִלָּה) is parallel to the infinitive and is to be translated "*to make* a fitting praise is pleasant"; the word "pleasant" (נָעִים; s.v. Ps. 133:1) parallels "good" (טוֹב; s.v. Ps. 34:8). The verse begins the psalm by declaring that praising God ("our God" for believers) is not just appropriate and right, but also delightful and fulfilling.

B. He must be praised because he restores his people and controls his creation (2–6).

1. He restores his people (2–3).

After reminding the faithful how appropriate and pleasant praise is, the psalmist now lays out several reasons for the praise. This is what makes praise far superior to hollow celebration. Verses 2 and 3 recounts how the LORD restores his people, first in building Jerusalem and then by healing people. The statement that the LORD builds Jerusalem could refer to the work of Nehemiah, but it could be the continued building of the city because the verb is a participle (בּוֹנֵה). The parallel colon supports the connection to the restoration by affirming that the LORD regathers the "outcasts" of Israel. This word (נִדְחֵי), often interpreted to mean "exiles," describes people who are driven away or cast out (see Isa. 11:12; 56:8). The next verse provides a parallel description of them as "broken-hearted" (שְׁבוּרֵי לֵב; for "heart" see Ps. 11:1), a term used for exiles in Isaiah 61:1; it describes them as people whose spirit has been broken by oppression. But the LORD gathers them and heals them (for רָפָא, s.v. Ps. 30:2). This healing is specified with a figure of speech, a human description of medical attention: "he binds their wounds." Not only does the LORD deliver them from their trouble but also he restores them to full health (see also Isa. 57:18–19; Jer. 30:17). If these clauses refer to the restoration after the exile, and they surely seem to, then this rebuilding was in accord with the words of Jeremiah 31:38–40 and therefore the very early beginning of the eschatological message of Isaiah 61.

2. He controls creation (4–5).

The focus of the psalm now is on creation. In so many psalms creation and redemption or restoration are given as the reasons for praise; these works of God with all their marvelous details are enough to inspire worship forever. In verse 4 we read that God counts (מוֹנֶה) the stars and names them. The LORD knows the number of the stars—and this sets him apart from human beings for whom this is impossible (Isa. 40:26, and Gen. 15:5). Giving them names affirms that he is both creator and Lord—they are under his dominion.[20] Perowne calls attention to the significance of this as a revelation of his intimate care and knowledge of his creation, much like a shepherd and his sheep (see John 10:3), as well as an implied connection with the previous verses to indicate that if God knows the stars this well, how much more his people (II:476).

All of this prompts the psalmist to declare the greatness (see Ps. 145:3) and power of God ("abundant in power"). Here he is referred to as "our Lord" (אֲדוֹנֵינוּ): the idea of the LORD's dominion over creation is not lost on the faithful—he is our master, our sovereign Lord, both by creation and redemption. The second half of the verse adds to the acclaim by saying his understanding (תְּבוּנָה; s.v. Ps. 49:1) is infinite. The statement forms a play on verse 4: there is no number to his understanding for he numbers all the stars. It was by this infinite wisdom that the world was created. For that the LORD is worthy to be praise—and obeyed.

3. He exalts the humble (6).

God uses his power and understanding to sustain (עוּד) the lowly, meaning people who have been afflicted by oppression (Ps. 146:9). This vindication is at the expense of the oppressors whom he casts down to the ground. It is not simply justice at work, but the divine justice of the creator whose rule corrects man's anarchy and disorder.[21]

---

20. There is probably a subtle polemic here against the religions of the ancient Near East. In them the stars were considered deities that determined the destiny of life on earth; but in the Bible they are the creation of God and under his sovereign control.
21. Perowne, *Psalms 73–150*, II:476.

II. People must praise the LORD because he sustains life and delights in believers (7–11).

A. Believers should praise the LORD with musical accompaniment (7).

This section has a clear call to praise followed by two causes, God's provision for nature and his delight in believers. It is something of a fresh burst of praise, amplifying the two motifs of the LORD's relation to creation and his covenant people. The verb "sing" is not the common word for singing (עָנָה, and not שִׁיר). If it is related to the verb "to answer," then it would indicate antiphonal singing; but it may be a separate word altogether. The call now is for praise to be given to God ("our God" again) with musical instruments.

B. Believers must praise the LORD because he sustains life and takes delight in those who trust in him (8–11).

1. The LORD provides for life on earth (8–9).

The LORD is sovereign over his creation (compare Ps. 104:13–14). First, he brings the clouds overhead and causes the rain to fall and makes the grass grow. Second, this provides food for animals (literally "beasts," but referring to animals in general). He singles out the young ravens in particular, perhaps because ravens were known to abandon their young, leaving the young destitute and defenseless; their calling is perceived as an equivalent to prayer (see also Ps. 104:21, Job 38:41, and also Luke 12:24). The psalm reminds us of the amazing extent of God's dominion—he is concerned with all the stars, as well as with the birds.

2. The LORD delights in believers (10–11).

Negatively, God takes no delight in the natural abilities of his creatures. The background of these verses may be warfare. A horse was a powerful animal in war, depended on by ancient armies; but in God's estimation it was a vain thing (Ps. 33:17). Warriors appeared to gain the victories, but in God's estimation dependence on human means was vanity (see Zech. 4:6). Powerful horses and men are part of God's wonderful creation; but they were trusted as the means of conquest. Not so with God. What pleases the LORD is faith, not self-sufficiency. Those who fear (s.v. Ps. 2:11) the LORD and put their hope (s.v. Ps. 31:24) in his loyal love (s.v. Ps. 23:6) are faithful members of the covenant. They may use their strength in battle, but they must not trust in it (Ps. 20:7).

III. The people Of God must praise him because he sustains creation by his word and reveals his word to his people (12–20).

A. *The people of God must praise him (12).*

The third section also begins with a call to praise, which is now addressed to Jerusalem and to Zion, meaning the people who live and worship there (metonymies of subject). He addresses the people this way because he will quickly focus on the strengthening of the city and securing of the borders, as well as the promise of his presence among them. Now the call is to the people to praise "your God" (both שָׁבַח and הָלַל in Ps. 117) "your God."

B. *He must be praised because he preserves his people (13–14).*

God's dealings with his covenant people provides unlimited reasons for praising him. Here he focuses on security and provision. Strengthening the bars of the gates is probably a reference to the rebuilding of Jerusalem, although it may not be limited to that occasion. The description signifies God's provision of security; the effect is that within the gates he blesses his people. Israel is addressed as "your sons" (O Jerusalem) to underscore their covenant relation to the holy city (see Isa. 54). Not only does he strengthen the gates, but he also gives peace and prosperity to the land. The word "borders" is used to signify what is within the borders, the promised land (see further Isaiah 60:17–18). Once again eschatology is drawn into the hymn, for Israel was experiencing a partial fulfillment of the eschatological promises.

C. He must be praised for his word (15–20).

1. He sustains nature by his word (15–18).

The rest of the psalm offers praise for the powerful word of the LORD—all of his works in creation and in covenant are accomplished by his decrees. He sends his word (or oracle, אִמְרָה; s.v. Ps. 119:11) and the word (דָּבָר) runs swiftly, as if it is a messenger hastening to carry out his will. That it runs swiftly means that it efficiently and instantly attains its goal. God created everything by his powerful word; but he did not leave creation to run its course. He carries it along on its course by his spoken word (see Heb. 1:3). The entire order of creation continues and functions by divine decree. These verses specify the all-encompassing sovereignty of God in nature: in verses 16 and 17 we read that he gives the snow, scatters the frost, and hurls down hail and ice, all part of the creative command. These things are then reversed in verse 18: by his word he melts them, and causes them to flow again as water. We may explain these things today with their immediate causes, but what remains to be acknowledged is the ultimate cause, God.

2. He reveals his word to his people exclusively (19–20).

The climax of creation came with the forming of human beings; and so ultimately God entrusted them with his word. But because people rejected the creator and his word, he gave it to his covenant people to make them distinct from the nations. Here the grace of God is at work; here is great cause for praise. God declares (מַגִּיד; s.v. Ps. 75:9) his word to Jacob, his laws and decrees to Israel. The divine word came to the world first through Israel; and it was to have the same effect on them as it had on nature—they were to respond immediately with obedience and praise. God did not do this for other nations; they may have had their holy writings, which in many points were similar to the law in Israel, but through them they had nothing that would lead them to worship and serve the true God. Israel was to be the swift witness now, by living in accordance with the will of God and taking his word to the nations (Isa. 49:6). This was the greatest blessing for people, to receive divine revelation and the calling to proclaim it. Paul will make this clear when he asks rhetorically about the advantage of Israel: "much in every way. First because that to them were committed the oracles of God" (Rom. 3:1–2). He would also explain that this same trust has been given to the people of the new covenant.

MESSAGE AND APPLICATION

God is to be praised for his powerful word, by which he created and sustains all life, redeems and cares for those who trust in him, and reveals his will to his covenant people. Because the LORD is the sovereign and eternal God, there should be no end to praise.

Jaki points out that "The perspective of seeing God at work everywhere is even more needed if one is to absorb and savor the message of the second half of the psalm."[22] Meditation on the great works of the LORD, creation and redemption, are foundational to our praise; he created and sustains everything by his powerful word, and he also redeems people by his word. His redemption does not find completion in the act of deliverance, for he provides for all the needs of his people. But with his redemption he entrusts his word to his covenant people, and not to the nations of the world. All of us who have been redeemed are entrusted with the word of God. This is not only a reason for praise, but a solemn responsibility to carry the message of God to people who remain alienated from him. Knowing what God has done with his word should expand our vision of what he can do through our ministry of his word.

---

22. *Praying the Psalms*, p. 253.

PSALM 148

Praise in the Heavens and on Earth

INTRODUCTION

Text and Textual Variants[1]

1 "Praise the LORD!"

    Praise the LORD from the heavens,
        praise him in the heights above.
2 Praise him, all his angels,
        praise him, all his heavenly hosts.[2]
3 Praise him, sun and moon,
        praise him, all you shining stars.[3]

---

1. The Greek version has a superscription attributing this composition to Haggai and Zachariah.
2. The form in the text is צְבָאָו. The *Qᵉreʾ* would be צְבָאָיו, "his hosts," which is the reading in most manuscripts. The *Kᵉthiv* would be the singular form, צְבָאוֹ, which has the most support.
3. The text literally reads "stars of light." The Greek translation has "the stars and the light," τὰ ἄστρα καὶ φῶς, perhaps confusing the י on כּוֹכְבֵי, "stars of" with a conjunction ו.

PSALM 148

4 Praise him, you highest heavens
    and you waters above the skies.
5 Let them praise the name of the LORD,[4]
    for he commanded and they were created.
6 He established them for ever and ever,
    making a ruling that will never pass away.

7 Praise the LORD from the earth,
    you great sea creatures and all ocean deeps,
8 lightning and hail, snow and clouds,[5]
    stormy winds that act on his word,
9 you mountains, and all hills,
    fruit trees, and all cedars,
10 wild animals, and all cattle,
    small creatures, and winged birds,
11 kings of the earth and all peoples,
    you princes and all judges on earth,
12 young men and also maidens,
    old men with the young.

13 Let them praise the name of the LORD
    for his name alone is exalted on high;
        his splendor[6] is above *the* earth and *the* heavens.
14 He has raised up[7] for his people a horn,
    the praise of all his saints,
        the people of Israel, a people close to him.[8]

"Praise the LORD!"

---

4. Between the two cola of verse 5 the Greek translation added "he spoke and it came to be." This was influenced by Psalm 33:9.
5. The word קִיטוֹר may mean "mist" here. The Greek version used χρύσταλλος, "ice."
6. The MT has הוֹדוֹ, "his splendor"; the Greek translation reads "his being acknowledged," ἡ ἐξομολόγησις αὐτοῦ, most likely taking the word to be from הוֹדָה, יָדָה in the *hiphil* stem.
7. For וַיָּרֶם the Greek has "he will raise up."
8. The Hebrew has עַם־קְרֹבוֹ; the Greek version translated it "(a people who) draw near to him," ἐγγίζοντι αὐτῷ.

Praise in the Heavens and on Earth

Composition and Context

The great doxology of the Psalter continues with this hymn calling for praise to be given to the LORD for his marvelous creation. *Hall^elû-Yāh* begins and ends the psalm (vv. 1a and 14b). The content of the psalm is laid out in two main sections, a call for heaven and everything in it to praise the LORD (1b–6), and a call for earth and everything on it to praise the LORD (7–14a). The focus of the psalm descends from the heavenly host to earth and finally to mankind and then specifically to Israel.[9] This movement suggests that the praise on earth, in Israel especially, should echo the worship in heaven.[10] The call for praise therefore unites all creation, addressing both rational and irrational elements. The pattern is as follows: praise from heaven (1), angels (2), and heavenly phenomena (3–6); then praise from earth (7), earthly phenomena (8–10), and people, especially Israel (11–14). This generally follows the order of creation with the formation of the heavenly hosts (angels singing for joy, Job 38:4–7), then the formation of everything in the earth, climaxing with humans as the crown of creation. It is a comprehensive view of the relation of all creation to the creator. It is not a complete description of every aspect of creation; the creatures listed however encompass all of creation, as in Job 38–42,[11] and are marvelous examples of it. They prompt the reader to think of all related aspects as well; and the believer's natural response to it all is endless praise.

There is no clear indication concerning the occasion for the writing of this psalm. Creation psalms could come from various times in Israel's history. Kirkpatrick suggests that the end of the psalm that mentions raising a horn for Israel hints at Israel's restoration after the exile, and that was evidently the motive for all things to praise the LORD.[12] The idea of renewing strength for Israel could fit other times as well.

The parts reflect the basic hymnic structure. There are the calls for praise (1–4 and 7–12) and the causes for praise (5–6 and 13–14). The call for praise seems to be a formal aspect of

---

9. Kidner, *Psalms 73–150,* p. 487.
10. VanGemeren, *Psalms,* p. 1002.
11. Anderson, *Psalms 73–150,* p. 949.
12. *Psalms,* p. 825.

the hymn; but as Anderson notes, the extended call for praise throughout this psalm is in itself an implicit glorification of God—the enumeration displays his glory.[13] The causes given for praise move from the general to the specific: in verse 5 the celestial bodies are the focus, and in verse 6 the word of God the reason; in verse 13 humans are the focus, and in verse 14 God's gracious dealings are the focus.

Exegetical Analysis

Summary

The psalmist calls all of heaven and its hosts to praise the LORD because he has established them by decree, and all of the earth and its hosts to praise his glorious name for he has lifted up the horn of his people Israel.

Outline

Prologue: "Praise the LORD!" (1a)

I. The psalmist calls all of heaven and its hosts to praise the LORD because he has established them by decree (1b–6).
 A. Call to praise: He summons all heavenly hosts to praise (1b–4).
  1. Heaven should praise from the heights (1b).
  2. Angelic hosts should praise (2).
  3. Heavenly hosts should praise (3).
  4. Elements of nature in the heavens should praise (4).
 B. Cause for praise: He has established them by decree (5–6).
  1. The LORD created all things by command (5).
  2. The LORD made a decree that will not pass away (6).
II. The psalmist calls all the earth and its hosts to praise the LORD because he has exalted the horn of his people (7–14).
 A. Call to praise: He summons all earthly hosts to praise the LORD (7–12).
  1. Sea creatures of the deep should praise (7).

---

13. *Psalms 73–150*, p. 948

2. Elements of nature fulfill his word (8).
3. Mountains and hills and trees also show his praise (9).
4. All animal life should fulfill his glory (10).
5. Rulers of the people should praise (11).
6. All mankind should praise the LORD (12).
B. Cause for praise: His name is glorious and he has exalted the horn of Israel (13–14a).
1. The LORD's name is glorious above the heaven and the earth (13).
2. He has lifted up the horn of his people Israel (14a).

Epilogue: "Praise the LORD" (14b).

COMMENTARY IN EXPOSITORY FORM

I. All of heaven and its hosts should praise the LORD because he established them by his word (1–6).

A. *All of heaven and its hosts should praise the LORD (1–4).*

After the prologue to set the tone for the psalm, the call is issued for praise to be given "from the heavens" and "in the heights above" (בַּמְּרוֹמִים). In the sequence of the psalm, and in the history of creation, praise is initiated there. The heavens above provide the setting for the praise, and the different parts in the heavens offer the praise. Within that arena the angels form the articulate singers, as people will be in the earthly arena.

The angels (מַלְאָכָיו, "his angels" or "his messengers") in verse 2 are also called "his hosts" (צְבָאָיו), a term that often refers to the sun, moon and stars, but in this context refers to the various orders of angels (see 1 Kings 22:19). The angels surround the throne of God and proclaim his glory unceasingly (e.g., Job 38, Isa. 6, Rev. 4, 5). These are the angelic hosts who also wait to do his bidding (see Ps. 91:11; 103:20–21).

In verses 3 and 4 the psalmist calls on the elements of the heavens to praise—sun, moon, stars, as well as highest heaven and waters above the skies. These are inanimate things and do not express verbal praise; so calling for them to praise is a personification, such as that used in Psalm 19. The nature of each element reveals the glory of God. Allen offers the analogy that a fine piece of craftsmanship brings glory to the one who made it.[14] Each part of creation tells of the sovereign power and glory of the creator.

The expression "highest heavens" is literally "heavens of heavens," a construction to signify the superlative degree. The psalmist was not likely to be thinking of later understandings of the levels of "heaven" (as in 2 Cor. 12:2), only that there should be no limit to the extent of praise. And in our modern knowledge of space, we cannot even imagine the extent of the highest heavens in God's creation.

And the reference to the "waters above the skies" reflects the ideas of Genesis 1:7, 7:11 and 8:2. The firmament, or atmosphere perhaps, was created to divide the waters above from the waters below. The waters above were understood to be the source of rain. The language is then poetic for the rain clouds in the skies, a wonder of creation that makes life possible on earth.

B. They should praise him because he established them by his word (5–6).

This call for praise is now provided with the reason for it—the word of the LORD. The ancient world had their gross explanations of how creation came about, but the truth is not cluttered by mythological ideas. In a clear, direct command, the sovereign Lord created everything that exists. All of the heavenly elements are to praise the name of the LORD, reflect his power and glory (for "name" s.v. Ps. 20:1), because they were created (וְנִבְרָאוּ; s.v. Ps. 51:10) by his command (צִוָּה; s.v. Ps. 119:6). Here is absolute power: one God creating everything by his command; and that divine word also fixed the order of creation, for verse 6 says that "he established them" (וַיַּעֲמִידֵם). The word literally means "and he caused them to stand": what he created found its fixed place in creation—as "and it was so" signifies in Genesis 1. This verb also has the connotation of standing ready to do God's will—all of creation is at his service.

---

14. *Psalms 101–150,* p. 393.

The creative act established them forever; but the word behind it is God's decree (חֹק; s.v. Ps. 119:5). This term often refers to a binding law or statute, but it can also have the sense of a boundary or established limit. The idea that "he gave them a boundary" by decree forms a good parallel with his setting them in place. The two verses not only focus on the power of God's word to create all things but also to maintain them in their course and functions.

II. All of the earth and its hosts should praise the LORD because his name is glorious and he has exalted the horn of Israel (7–14).

A. All earthly hosts should praise the LORD (7–12).

Now the attention turns to the earth below; it too will join the heavenly choir, now and in the ages to come. The psalmist introduces the section by calling for praise from the earth (7a), but then immediately sets about to list elements in the earthly sphere that are representative of creation. He begins with the great sea creatures (תַּנִּינִים) mentioned in Genesis 1:21 (see also Ps. 74:13) and the "deeps" (תְּהֹמוֹת). Starting with these may sound a polemical note to the section, for these were objects of veneration and worship to the pagans. But the truth is that the sea creatures are merely animals, and the deep is the ocean, not a spiritual force. The mention of "deeps" here provides a balance to "highest heavens" in the previous section—there is no limit to the extent of creation that speaks of God's glory.

In the next few verses the psalmist lists lightning, hail, snow, mists and stormy winds that function according to his word—all of nature functions by divine decree. The mountains and hills, fruit and trees, beasts and cattle and birds—all of them were made by the LORD and reflect his glory by their existence and activity.

But in verses 11 and 12 the psalm focuses on the articulate members of the arena of the earth, and the focus is all-encompassing. In the heavens it was the angels who sang praises to the LORD; on earth it is human beings of all kinds. The order of the psalm is instructive: the angels were the first to praise even at the time of creation, but mankind is the crowning point of all creation. So the psalmist here calls kings and peoples alike to praise him, princes and judges (or rulers in general). Those who are great, who have power in their position and in their decrees, can only acknowledge they have no power at all unless it was given to them from above. Those called "peoples" probably refers to the kingdoms and clans that were governed by these leaders. And in verse 12 the call is for young men and maidens, elders and youth. All of humanity must praise the LORD for his marvelous creation.

B. They should praise because he is glorious and he has exalted a horn for Israel (13–14).

In the last two verses the psalmist provides the reason for the praise. Verse 13 reiterates the call for praise, now as in verse 5 with the jussive and not the imperative: "Let them praise." The primary reason is that the name of the LORD, i.e., the LORD himself in all his glory, alone is highly exalted (נִשְׂגָּב, a term that signifies that something is unattainably high (see Ps. 139:5). No one is higher in position or power. In fact, his splendor (הוֹדוֹ; s.v. Ps. 96:6) is above earth and heaven, meaning everything this psalm has listed in earth and heaven—and more. The LORD is over it all, because he made it all and sustains it all by his word.

Verse 14 narrows the cause for praise to what God has done for Israel: he has raised a horn for Israel. The word "horn" refers to power (a figure drawn from the animal world). In many places it refers to kings who had power (see Ps. 78:6 and 132:17). But here there is no internal support for the meaning of raising up a king, or ultimately the Messiah. Rather, it likely refers to the LORD's giving renewed strength and courage to Israel;[15] and this renewal of Israel is said to be "the praise of all his saints" (חֲסִידָיו, the beloved, true believers who received his love; s.v. Ps. 23:6). In apposition to this word "beloved" is the expression "the people of (sons of) Israel, the people close to him." These expressions describe Israel as the beloved people of God who have a special relationship to him. They of all people should praise the

---

15. Anderson, *Psalms 73–150*. p. 950.

LORD for renewing their strength and making in them the main source of praise. Moreover, the implication is that the praise of God is the purpose of God's loving intentions for Israel, as it is for all who are redeemed. Kirkpatrick explains that if human beings are the crowning point of creation and Israel is the LORD's special servant for revelation and redemption, then all of creation should rejoice when Israel is renewed and restored.[16]

MESSAGE AND APPLICATION

The message and application of this psalm is straightforward, like the other psalms in this grand doxology to the collection: *Everything in the heavens above and everything on earth below must display the glory of God and praise him forever, especially for his redemption and renewal of his people.* The psalm brings forward the creation hymns that display God's glory in creation, first in the heavens and then on the earth. The listing of aspects of creation prompt the worshiper to think of the details and other aspects of each category, for praise is endless when we consider the works of his hands. But the psalm culminates in the greatest reason for praise, the greatness demonstrated in his grace—he has redeemed and restored his people, and they in all creation are close to him. This psalm, indeed all these final psalms, have a number of parallels with the great hymns in heaven recorded in Revelation 4 and 5, particularly in the major causes for praise: creation and redemption.

---

16. *Psalms*, p. 825.

PSALM 149

A Hymn of Triumph for the Final Victory

INTRODUCTION

Text and Textual Variants

Praise the LORD!

1 Sing to the LORD a new song,
　　his praise in *the* assembly of the beloved.[1]
2 Let Israel rejoice in its maker,[2]
　　let[3] the people[4] of Zion exult in their king.

---

1. The MT has חֲסִידִים, "beloved," covenant members who were beneficiaries of God's covenant love; one manuscript has קְדוֹשִׁים, "saints," instead. Translations today use either "saints," or "the devout," or even "recipients of divine love" (Allen, *Psalms 101–150,* p. 396).
2. The form in the text is the plural participle with a suffix, בְּעֹשָׂיו, "in its maker(s)"; it is in the plural to express divine majesty and not as a numerical plural. The Greek and Syriac versions simply made it singular as do modern translations.
3. The Greek and Syriac versions have a conjunction with the second colon.
4. The Hebrew text has "sons of Zion," meaning all who live there.

3 Let them praise his name with dance;
  with tambourine and harp let them sing praises to him,
4 because the LORD takes delight in his people,
  and he will honor[5] the lowly with saving victory.[6]
5 Let the devout exult in *this* glory
  and[7] rejoice on their beds.[8]
6 May the exaltations of God be in their mouth,
  and a two-edged sword[9] in their hand
7 to exact vengeance on the nations,
  punishment[10] on *the* peoples;
8 to bind their kings with fetters
  and their nobles with iron manacles;
9 to execute the judgment written against them.
  It is an honor[11] for all his beloved.

Praise the LORD![12]

Composition and Context

The psalm is a hymn that celebrates a victory—but what victory? It is perhaps praise for a past, probably recent, victory. A fairly common view is to place the work in the time of Nehemiah. Perowne links it to the restoration from the exile, suggesting that the "burning sense of wrong, the purpose of terrible revenge," which was the feeling people had at the end of the captivity, was

---

5. The Greek version interprets the word יְפָאֵר with "exalts," ὑψώσει. The Greek and Syriac also have a conjunction.
6. The text simply has "salvation"; this translation clarifies the word within the context.
7. The conjunction is in the versions but not the Hebrew.
8. The word in the text is מִשְׁכְּבוֹתָם, either "their beds" or "their couches," as the word is connected to the verb "to lie down." But some commentaries suggest either changing the text slightly (to מִשְׁפְּחוֹתָם, "their families") or proposing different meanings (see the discussion below).
9. The form in the Greek translation is plural.
10. A few Hebrew manuscripts and one Syriac manuscript add the conjunction to the second colon.
11. The MT has הָדָר הוּא; "it *is* an honor"; the Greek version renders this δόξα αὕτη ἐστίν, "this glory is."
12. In the Greek, Syriac and Jerome this expression begins Psalm 150.

now changed to hope for a series of victories over the nations. In other words, the old martial spirit was revived at the start of a new era.[13] Some scholars suggest the psalm is a cultic ritual drama and not necessarily linked to an immediate victory. Anderson explains that "the conventionalized representation of past events" had significance in the present and for the future.[14] There is no doubt some truth to this, but all the psalms might be put to similar use. A number of commentators interpret it as a hymn with an eschatological focus, similar in several aspects to eschatological psalms (Pss. 93 and 96–99); this fits the material best. The hymn celebrated a recent saving victory, perhaps the deliverance from exile; but it replaces the normally expected existing cause for praise with a section of future hope (vv. 7–9b). The experienced victory is then a sign of things to come.[15] Kidner says with this psalm we are singing of no less than God's advent in the future.[16]

It is difficult to be certain of the historical setting for this psalm. The language and the apocalyptic tone are taken as evidence of a post-exilic date.[17] The links to Isaiah would suggest a post-exilic time, if one assumes the Isaianic material is late. The psalm may be post-exilic, but not all the evidence is compelling.

The structure of the psalm is uncomplicated. It works well to divide it into two parts: verses 1–4 celebrate God's saving victory of Israel, and verses 5–9 calls for praise to be given to God for the future victory that will vindicate Israel.

Exegetical Analysis

Summary

The psalmist invokes the assembled worshipers to sing and

---

13. *Psalms,* II:483.
14. *Psalms 73–150,* p. 951–2.
15. So VanGemeren, *Psalms,* p. 1005, and Allen, p. 397. Allen clarifies that in the section that looks ahead to the future (vv. 7–9) there are numerous similarities with the words and ideas in Isaiah 61, and that the expectation of the nations' submission or destruction finds a parallel in Isaiah 60:12, 14. For further discussion, see A. R. Ceresko, "Psalm 149: Poetry, Themes (Exodus and Conquest), and Social Function," *Bib* 67 (1986):179–94.
16. *Psalms 73–150,* p. 489.
17. Anderson, *Psalms 73–150,* p. 952.

shout praises to the LORD who gives salvation to his people and anticipates their praise when the LORD will bring honor to his people by finally destroying the oppressing nations.

Outline

Prologue: "Praise the LORD!" (1a)

I. Celebration for Victory: The psalmist calls the faithful to praise the LORD because he takes delight in them and brings them victory (1b–4).
   A. They should sing a new song in the assembly of the devout and praise with dance and musical instruments (1b–3).
   B. They should praise the LORD because he delights in them and gives them victory (4).
II. Anticipation of the final Victory: The psalmist calls the faithful to praise the LORD in anticipation of the final victory over his enemies (5–9b).
   A. He prepares the people to rejoice when they live in safety (5).
   B. He calls the people to praise the LORD for the victory over the wicked (6–9).
      1. They are to sing high praises to the LORD (6a).
      2. They are to exult when the LORD's decreed vengeance is carried out on their oppressing enemies (6b–9a).
   C. This is the honor of all the beloved (9b).

Epilogue: "Praise the LORD!" (9c).

COMMENTARY IN EXPOSITORY FORM

I. The faithful are to sing a new song in the assembly because the LORD takes delight in delivering them (1b–4).

The first part of the psalm includes three verses calling for praise and a fourth giving the reason for it. The call is to sing a new song, which means a song celebrating a new experience with new joys and new hopes (see also Pss. 33:3 and 96:1; it is a metonymy of effect, the cause being the LORD's recent intervention). The praise is to be given in the midst of the congregation in the sanctuary. It is an "assembly of the beloved." This word rendered "beloved" (חֲסִידִים ; s.v. Ps. 23:6) is difficult to translate. It basically means those who are recipients of the covenant love of the LORD; but it has been translated as "the saints," "the faithful," or "the devout," because they are the true believers and faithful worshipers. It basically refers to the faithful worshiping community.[18] Then, in verse 2, the devout are also "Israel," which is qualified by the epithet "the sons of Zion," meaning the true worshipers of the LORD. This would indicate that "Israel" here means the congregation worshiping on Mount Zion.

They are called to rejoice in their maker. This description of God is more likely a reference to the LORD's formation of the nation of Israel than the creation of mankind in general, because the parallel colon refers to him as their king. Calling the LORD their king does not necessarily imply that there was no human monarch at the time; Isaiah 6 envisions the LORD sitting enthroned as king even though the Davidic monarchy was in existence, albeit in transition. That God is Israel's king means they have nothing to fear— human kings cannot thwart the sovereign authority of the LORD. So praise must be given to the name of the LORD (s.v. Ps. 20:1), and given with enthusiasm, expressed with dancing and musical instruments, such as the tambourine and the harp (or lyre).[19]

The psalmist provides a simple statement expressing the reason for the praise (v. 4). He declares that the LORD delights in his people (see Isa. 54:7–8). The use of a participle indicates that this is a constant delight that will be true in the future as well, which is made clear by the use of the imperfect tense in the second colon.[20] Because God delights in his people he will give them salvation, i.e., saving victory, as he has done in the past. The text says that he will "honor the lowly with salvation."

---

18. VanGemeren suggests that it is a designation of the Godly people within the larger covenant fellowship, equal to the "assembly of the righteous" (p. 1006). This would be difficult to support; but most likely the people in the assembly of worshipers are faithful believers.
19. For bibliography on the musical instruments mentioned in these texts, see footnote 21 in the exposition of Psalm 150.
20. Kraus, *Psalms 60–150*, p. 399.

The verb includes the meanings of "glorify" or "beautify" (יְפָאֵר; see also Isa. 55:7, 8; and Isa. 60:7, 9, 13). The recipients of this glorious victory are "the lowly," which in the parallelism refers to the people of God, those who trust in him and not in their own abilities. To honor his people with victory over the enemies would require warfare, and in the eschatological anticipation of this and other psalms like it, a war to end all warfare.

II. The faithful are to exalt the LORD with praise when he judges the wicked in accordance with the written decree (5–9).

A. *They expect to sing praises to him as they live in safety (5).*

In verse 5 the psalmist prays that the people will praise in times of peace and safety. Some commentators take the verbs here as future, but in the flow of this context they are better taken as jussives, "Let the devout exult in *this* glory, and rejoice on their beds." It is therefore a prayer for this to happen; but the prayer that praise be given implies a reason for the praise—let them enjoy victory so that they may praise.

Their praise is to be on their "beds" (or "couches). The text would simply mean that when the people of God lie down to rest they should sing praises to him for victory. This indicates they will be able to lie down at night without fear. It is possible the word "beds" might refer to couches at meals, perhaps reclining at a festal meal. Less likely is the idea that it refers to something like a prayer mat, so that when they prostrate themselves in worship they will exult in the LORD. The word "bed" is connected to the verb "to lie down," and to obtain an idea of kneeling or prostrating oneself before God is forced. The fact is that there is no textual problem with the word and while it might present a difficulty in the parallelism, it makes sense enough to retain it.

B. *They are to exalt him with praise when he vindicates them by judging the wicked according to the written decree (6–9).*

This praise is connected to the future victory of God. The parallelism of verse 6 includes ideas that come from Israel's experience: the psalmist wishes for the exaltations of God to be in their mouths and a two-edged sword in their hands.[21] What is reflected is the spirit of the people in the land faced with opposition (compare Neh. 4:17[11], where the people did their work armed). The exaltations (רוֹמְמ; s.v. Ps. 46:10) are in their mouths, literally, their throats. "Throats" is an instrument of speech, so that what is being said is intended. The use of "throats" rather than "mouths" in the Hebrew would convey a loud utterance.[22]

This is paralleled with the idea of the two-edged sword (literally, a "sword with two mouths") in their hands—it would be a sharp, "devouring" sword. The appeal of the line is for the people not only to praise soundly but also to be vigilant for the battle to come. Commentators who follow a more cultic approach for this psalm do not think this is a reference to being armed for battle, but part of the cultic ceremony in which the drama re-enacts past victories. They suggest that the expression is a reference to a sword-dance in the celebration. If this were the intended meaning, it is difficult to see it in the simple reference to having a two-edged sword in hand. The verse leads into the next section.

The next three verses begin with infinitives; a simple reading would imply that the people have a sword in their hand to execute the LORD's vengeance on the nations. But in these lines we have to determine who is the subject of the infinitives, Israel or the LORD? It is certainly true that the LORD used Israel to carry out his judgment on the nations. Throughout their history the Israelites had to be ready for war when he destroyed their enemies. But in this case the descriptions of the actions to come indicate it is the LORD who will take vengeance on the nations, inflict punishment on the peoples of the world, and utterly defeat them by binding their leaders (see Deut. 7:23–24). In the eschatological psalms these are the things that the LORD will do when he comes to judge the world. The language fits the prophetic descriptions of the final victory when Israel will have to prepare for war against all the nations—but the LORD will come with his holy angels to destroy the oppressing enemies of his

---

21. See W. S. Prinsloo, "Psalm 149: Praise Yahweh with Tambourine and Two-edged Sword," *ZAW* 109 (1997):395–407.
22. Perowne, *Psalms*, II:485.

people. The ideas may be illustrated from the historical account of Jehoshaphat's war against the Moabites and Ammonites in 2 Chronicles 20. The king who had prepared for battle prayed for victory; and a message came from the Spirit through a Levite that the people need not fear because they would not have to fight—the battle was not theirs but God's. So as they marched forth to the battle Jehoshaphat put the singers at the head of the army to praise the LORD: "Give thanks to the LORD for his loyal love endures forever." The LORD confused the enemies so that they were destroyed, leaving only the dead for Jehoshaphat to discover. They returned to the sanctuary with great praise.

The judgment described in the psalm is one that is planned by God. Verse 9a says it is "to execute the judgment written against them." The reference to the written judgment could be an allusion to heavenly books recording their deeds, or to texts reporting holy wars; the language used in these verses, however, suggest prophecies foretelling the day of judgment (see Isa. 65:6, which describes coming judgment as written). If the judgment written has this sense, then it will surely be fulfilled; and if it is the LORD who executes this judgment, it will not be marred by human flaws, such as self aggrandizement or personal vendetta. It will be just.

The final line announces that this "is an honor for all the beloved." The psalm has already announced that the LORD delights in honoring his people with saving victory; and now it concludes that the final victory is an honor (now הָדָר; s.v. Ps. 96:6). The final victory will be the most spectacular glory for the beloved people of God.

MESSAGE AND APPLICATION

Psalm 149 encourages believers to praise the LORD for his saving help, not simply in their experience, but in the dawning of a new era when justice will be done. They are encouraged to anticipate the final victory with faith in the LORD's sovereignty and his prophetic word. The faith and the hope in this hymn are renewed in the hymn in Luke 1:67–79; and they are carried forward in the apostolic writings as well (see I Thess. 1:4–12; Rev. 19:1–8).

The message could be drawn together in this way: *Believers should sing and shout to the LORD who honors them with salvation, both now and at the end of the age when he will vindicate them in the final victory.* The language of judgment often troubles people when they read the descriptions about taking vengeance and destroying the wicked, and in particular when the righteous seem to take some part in it by having a sword in their hands. Expositors often try to soften the impact by drawing on the analogies in the New Testament. It is true that the church is fighting a spiritual warfare, and the enemies are not flesh and blood; their sword is the word of God; and their victory is taking thoughts into captivity (see 2 Cor. 10:5; Eph. 6:12; Heb. 4:12). All of this is true for the present to be sure. But the primary view of the psalm is eschatological: it is a hymn of praise for the retribution that will overtake the enemies of God. And that victory will be with a war that will be used by God to vindicate his people through judgment on the wicked. The psalm calls for praise in anticipation of God's crowning glory for his people, ultimate victory in the LORD.

PSALM 150

Let Everything Praise the LORD

INTRODUCTION

Text and Textual Variants

1 Praise the LORD![1]

   Praise God[2] in his sanctuary,[3]
     praise him in his powerful firmament.
2 Praise him for his mighty acts,[4]
     praise him according to[5] the abundance of his greatness.
3 Praise him with the sound of the horn,
     praise him with lyre and harp.

---

1. A few manuscripts and the Syriac version do not have this initial clause.
2. Instead of אֵל, "God," the Syriac (and Jerome) have the abbreviation of the name, יָהּ, "*Yāh*."
3. The word rendered "sactuary" or "holy place" in the MT may specifically mean "in his holiness" or "sanctity." The Greek version has plural ἐν τοῖς ἁγίοις ἀυτοῦ, "in his holy places" or "among his saints."
4. The Syriac has the singular.
5. A few manuscripts and the Syriac have "with" (בְּרֹב) instead of "according to" (כְּרֹב).

4 Praise him with tambourine and dance,⁶
   praise him with strings and flute.
5 Praise him with clear sounding cymbals.
   praise him with loud clashing cymbals.⁷
6 Let everything that has breath praise the LORD!⁸
   Praise the LORD!⁹

Composition and Context

Psalm 150 is a series of calls to praise the LORD, not just in one part but in the entire psalm. It is an appropriate conclusion to Psalms 146–150, the grand doxology of the collection. Each of the books in the present arrangement of the Psalter end with doxologies; Book V ends with this elaborate doxology, because it brings to a conclusion the entire collection of psalms.

It is impossible to say with certainty when and why this last psalm was written. One view is that the psalm was written especially for this conclusion, and like the other psalms in this grand doxology, was written well into the second temple period.[10] There is nothing in the psalm that could not have been written in an earlier period. Goldingay suggests that the use of the "ram's horn" in the psalm may be evidence of a pre-exilic composition.[11] It is possible that the psalm was not originally intended for this conclusion, but had been written earlier and was found to be an appropriate conclusion to the collection.[12] It is clear that the psalm formed part of the liturgy for temple worship; and in that use it focused on the meaning of the whole Psalter, the praise of God.[13] Here we find the purpose and the outcome of the psalms.

Between the prologue and epilogue the psalm can be

---

6. For וּמָחוֹל a few manuscripts have וּבְמָחוֹל, "and with dance"
7. Allen renders these two parallel expressions as "cymbals of attention" and "cymbals of acclamation" (*Psalms 101–150*, p. 402).
8. The holy name is the abbreviated: יָהּ.
9. This last clause is not in some manuscripts of the versions.
10. Clifford, *Psalms 73–150*, p. 319.
11. *Psalms 90–150*, p. 747.
12. Allen, *Psalms 101–150*, p. 323.
13. Weiser, *Psalms*, p. 841.

divided into three parts. Verses 1b and 2 form the introduction to the psalm because of the pattern: each colon has an imperative followed by a prepositional phrase and a noun with a third masculine singular suffix. Verse 1a calls for praise within God's sanctuary, and verse 2 calls for praise for his great acts. Then, verses 3–5 call for the praise to be with musical instruments and dance. And finally, a verb change in verse 6a signals the climax of the psalm: there was a series of imperatives throughout the passage, but in verse 6a the verb is a jussive (the same pattern found in Psalm 148): "Let everything that has breath praise the LORD." The end of this sentence is the abbreviation of the holy name, *Yah;* it balances the use of the title "God" in the beginning of verse 1b to form an inclusio. The psalm then calls for universal and elaborate praise for the LORD God for his greatness.

Exegetical Analysis

Summary

Because of the excellence of God's works, the psalmist calls for praise to be given to him in the sanctuary with all kinds of musical expression—in short, everything that has breath should praise the LORD.

Outline

Prologue: "Praise the LORD!" (1a)

I. The psalmist calls for praise to be given to God in his sanctuary for his great and mighty acts (1b–2).
   A. People should praise God in his sanctuary, the place of his power (1b).
   B. People should praise God for his excellence in the things he does (2).
II. The psalmist calls for praise to be given to God with all kinds of musical expression (3–5).
   A. Praise is to be given to him with horn, lute and harp (3).
   B. Praise is to be given to him with timbrel and dance (4a).
   C. Praise is to be given to him with strings and pipe (4b).

D. Praise is to be given to him with clear and loud cymbals (5).
III. The psalmist finally calls for everything that has breath to praise the LORD (6a).

Epilogue: "Praise the LORD!" (6b).

COMMENTARY IN EXPOSITORY FORM

Prologue: "Praise the LORD!" (1a).

This final psalm also begins with the prologue calling people to "praise the LORD" (הַלְלוּ־יָהּ). This expression is often used as an exclamation; but it is the plural imperative form joined to the abbreviation of the holy name. The expression summarizes the message of the book of Psalms succinctly. In fact, this summary point is emphatically made as the verb "praise" (most often הַלְלוּ) occurs thirteen times in the psalm. The name "*Yah*" (יָהּ) is the abbreviated form of the personal, covenant name of God, *Yahweh*. The collection of psalms has described in so many ways the person and works of the LORD (often by delineating specific attributes or acts, but frequently by summarizing them with things like "the name of the LORD"), so that this final psalm need say little more than to invite praise for all of that with the simple expression, "praise *Yah*." This particular word for "praise" (הָלַל; s.v. Ps. 33:1) essentially means to give a glowing, spontaneous description of who the LORD is and what he has done. Devout believers will not see this call as a fixed duty, for praise will already be on their lips from their reflections in the psalms; rather, this will be seen as the call in worship for them to express their greatest praise, using all manner of expression and all means of musical accompaniment. The psalm is, after all, part of the great doxology.

I. The LORD is to be praised in his sanctuary (1b).

The first verse calls for praise to be given to God, the imperative stressing the necessity and the immediacy of the call. Here the focus of the praise is to be "God" (אֵל), the title being used to stress his powerful sovereignty; and this praise is to be given "in his sanctuary" (בְּקָדְשׁוֹ; s.v. Ps. 22:4). This prepositional phrase has been given several different interpretations. It can be taken to mean the holy place, the sanctuary. It is not clear however whether this would be the earthly sanctuary or the heavenly reality behind it.[14] Both are identified as the dwelling place of the LORD; and both are filled with praise for God. In favor of the view that it is primarily the heavenly sanctuary is the parallelism with "firmament." VanGemeren takes the view that the sanctuary refers to the heavenly sanctuary where the angels are called to praise, and the firmament refers to the heavenly bodies above the skies.[15] Verses 1 and 2 would then be a very general call for praise, and verses 3–6 the specific earthly call.

However, the entire focus of the psalm is for humans to praise God with all human means, clearly a focus on the earthly sanctuary; and angels are not addressed, as they were in Psalm 148. Another approach is to take the language as deliberately ambiguous, including both the heavenly and earthly sanctuaries in the expression.[16] The two are in fact intertwined in Scripture. A less convincing view is to take the expression to mean "in his holiness" to stress that the praise should focus on his holy nature, for there is no one like him in existence, anywhere, ever. But the parallelism with "firmament" suggests a location for the phrase.[17]

Perowne observes the primary meaning is likely the earthly sanctuary because the psalm is a liturgical anthem for the worship in Israel and because it calls for all kinds of earthly instruments to be used in the praise.[18] But one cannot rule out the idea that the first verse at least includes the heavenly sanctuary in the expression.

The parallel line is, "praise him in his powerful firmament" (literally, "in the firmament of his power"; בִּרְקִיעַ עֻזּוֹ). This half of

---

14. See H. P. Mathys, "Psalm cl," *VT* 50 (2000):328–344.
15. *Psalms,* p. 1009.
16. Eaton, *Psalms,* p. 316.
17. Briggs notes that there is no reference to heavenly beings in the passage and so the parallelism with "firmament" does not clarify the location of the sanctuary (*Psalms,* II:544).
18. *Psalms,* II:456.

the verse refers to the heavenly arena, for the word "firmament" refers to the heavens or skies above. The call would be for the heavenly hosts in the firmament to praise God, whether angelic beings or nature. The verse may then be all inclusive for earth and heaven, calling for praise both in the earthly sanctuary (1a) and in the heavens (1b). The word "firmament" is qualified with the genitive "his power" (for the word, s.v. Ps. 29:1).[19] It may be used as an attributive here, "his mighty firmament," or specification, "in the firmament where his power is displayed" ("power" being a metonymy of cause). The latter interpretation is more convincing (see Ps. 19:1; 68:34).[20]

B. The LORD is to be praised for all his marvelous works (2).

The call now turns to the substance of this praise in two general terms. The first is "his mighty acts" (גְּבוּרֹתָיו; s.v. Ps. 45:3 and 117:2); and the second is "the abundance of his greatness" (רֹב גֻּדְלוֹ; for "greatness, s.v. Ps. 34:3). The praise will declare God's power and greatness as displayed through his marvelous works—creation, redemption, judgment, deliverance, healing, forgiveness, to name but a few that the Psalter has proclaimed. Such praise necessarily includes the acknowledgment, voiced or not, that the people praising are totally dependent on the LORD. After all, God made them, redeemed them, protects them, and leads them in the everlasting way.

II. The LORD is to be praised by all means (3–5).

The call to praise in the first two verses introduced the theme of the psalm with the familiar expression; it normally would signify praise given by the human voice, and this would anticipate the emphasis of verse 6. Now in verses 3–5 the psalmist calls for

---

19. Psalm 29 calls for praise for the power of the LORD, and there the call is directed to the "sons of the mighty" in the LORD's holy temple, most likely referring to angels to praise him in the heavenly sanctuary.
20. Dahood interprets the word "strength" as "stronghold," and renders the expression as "in his firmament, his stronghold" (*Psalms,* III:360).

this praise to be given to God with all kinds of instruments and rejoicing. But the repetition of the command to praise the LORD in every colon of the section is a constant reminder that the celebration is to be directed to him.

According to verse 3 the praise should be with blowing the horn (שׁוֹפָר, referring probably to the ram's horn but later also to the trumpet). Such an instrument would sound the initial blast, appropriate to summon the people. The parallel colon adds "with lyre (נֵבֶל) and harp (כִּנּוֹר)," softer sounding instruments frequently referred to in the collection for accompanying the singing of psalms. The two words refer to very similar instruments, perhaps to the same instrument.[21]

Additional instruments are listed in verse 4: timbrel (תֹף), strings (מִנִּים), and pipe (עוּגָב)–a percussion instrument, stringed instrument, and wind instrument. The timbrel is a tambourine, or hand-drum; and the pipe is a shepherd's flute, an instrument used in secular settings; these three instruments are not mentioned elsewhere in conjunction with sanctuary worship. These accompany the "dance" (מָחוֹל) in the call to praise with celebration. This is clearly not a reference to secular or sensual dance, but a spontaneous celebration of the LORD.[22] The word indicates the dancing was whirling or turning, perhaps dancing in circles (for use in the sanctuary see Ps. 87:7).

Verse 5 brings in the clashing sound of cymbals, as if to highlight vividly the words and the sounds of praise being given to God. The first colon uses "clear cymbals," i.e., "sounding

---

21. On the subject of the instruments and music in general, see Joachim Braun, *Music in Ancient Israel/Palestine* (Grand Rapids: Eerdmans, 2002); J. H. Eaton, "Music's Place in Worship," *OTS* 23 (1984):85–107; I. H. Jones, "Musical Instruments in the Bible, Part I," *BT* 37 (1986):101–116; and Edo Šulj, "Musical Instruments in Psalm 150," in *The Interpretation of the Bible,* edited by Jože Krašovec (Sheffield: Sheffield Academic Press. 1998), pp. 1117–30.
22. For dancing to be in praise of the LORD it had to be inspired by some great or gracious act of God (and so a natural and spontaneous response), it had to communicate that God was the focus of the praise (and so not a performance or entertainment), and it had to be consonant with purity and righteousness (not distracting or suggestive, and not mixing the sexes). Worshipers witnessing the dance would be caught up in praising the LORD (Ross, *Recalling the Hope of Glory,* p. 163).

cymbals" (צִלְצְלֵי־שָׁמַע), and the parallel colon "loud clashing cymbals" (צִלְצְלֵי תְרוּעָה). The first may refer to smaller instruments that had a clear sound, and the latter to larger cymbals that had a deeper and louder sound.

III. The LORD is to be praised by everything that has breath (6).

The sixth verse provides the concluding statement, not only for Psalm 150, but also for the entire book: "Let everything that has breath praise *Yah*." The word "breath" (נְשָׁמָה) is critical to this psalm; it is a term that is essentially a provision from God for human life.[23] In addition to describing the breath of life, i.e., that which make the human a living being (see Gen. 2:7), the word is used in different places in Scripture to indicate that when God imparted breath to humans they received the capacity for spiritual understanding (Job 34:8) and for distinguishing between what is right and wrong (Prov. 20:22), aspects necessary to the praise of God. Every person, not just Israel, must praise the LORD. Here then is the glory of creation. God gave humans breath, and so they owe their breath to him, making praise the primary reason they have it.[24] The call is for the breath to be used in this way.

---

23. The word is probably related to a verb "to pant," more common in the cognates than in the Bible (Isa. 42:14, for strong breathing). The noun is simply translated "breath"; but it has three categories of meaning. First, it is used of God's breath, for giving life to man (Gen. 2:7), for kindling a flame of wrath (Isa. 30:33), sending a destroying wind (2 Sam. 22:16), or cold wind to produce ice (Job 37:10). Second, it refers to the breath of human beings as breathed in by God (Isa. 2:22) which has the characteristics listed above in the commentary: life, spiritual understanding, and a functioning conscience, all of which make biblical praise possible. Third, it refers to living beings in general and so is parallel to נֶפֶשׁ, "life, soul." Almost always does it refer to humans, and very rarely to lower creatures; but some of the references that seem to refer to animal life may be explained more generally (such as Gen. 7:22 referring to all human life). See T. C. Mitchell, "The Old Testament Usage of *Nešamâ*," *VT* 11 (1961):177–87.
24. Clifford, *Psalms 73–150,* p. 320.

Let Everything Praise the LORD

MESSAGE AND APPLICATION

The repeated call to praise states the obvious message of the psalm. We may state the expository idea to capture this: *Everyone must praise the LORD in his sanctuary, using whatever means they have to enhance their celebration of his greatness.* The contents of the psalm specify who is to be praised, where he is to be praised, why he is to be praised, and with what means he is to be praised. The musical instruments and the dancing, all part of the Israelite culture, were to be put to use in the praise of God, even if they were not officially designated for temple service. The instruments represent the major types of musical instruments: percussion, strings, and winds. Over the centuries a greater number of instruments have been developed within these various categories, and it is natural and appropriate that they all should be put to use in their highest service. To do that would mean their use must be clearly directed to the glory of God and must not be readily confused with secular or pagan sounds and expressions. So the application is easy, for the psalm states it repeatedly: praise the LORD; and the New Testament reiterates this point, especially in the numerous acclamations, doxologies and praises in heaven and on earth recorded throughout the book of Revelation. Even now, as the apostle Paul reminds us in his letter to the Ephesians, we were chosen and redeemed for the praise of his glory (1:12).

Index of Hebrew Word Studies

א

אָבִיר	*mighty, valiant*	78:25
אַדִּיר	*majestic*	8:1
אָהֵב	*love*	11:7
אָוֶן	*trouble, sorrow, wickedness*	28:3
אָלַף	*learn, be familiar with*	55:13
אִמְרָה	*saying, word, utterance*	119:11
אֱמֶת, אָמַן	*believe, truth (faithful)*	15:2
אַף	*anger, nose, face*	30:5
אָשֵׁם, אָשָׁם	*be guilty, guilt*	34:22

ב

בָּגַד	*deal treacherously*	78:57
בָּהַל	*be terrified >terrify*	83:15
בּוֹשׁ	*be ashamed > put to shame*	31:1
בָּזָה	*despise*	22:6
בָּחַן	*test, examine, prove*	139:23
בָּטַח	*trust*	4:5
בִּין	*discern, understand*	49:3
בְּלִיַּעַל	*worthlessness, wicked*	18:5
בָּקַשׁ	*seek*	83:16

בָּרָא	create, shape anew	51:10
בָּרַךְ	bless, enrich	5:12

ג

גָּאָה	rise up in > majesty	93:1
גָּאַל	redeem, act as kinsman	19:14
גָּבַר	be strong, mighty, >prevail	117:2
גִּבּוֹר	mighty, strong	45:3
גָּדַל	be great > strong	34:3
גִּיל	rejoice	13:6
גּוֹי	nation	43:1
גָּלַל	roll, roll away, > trust	22:8
גָּעַר	rebuke, restrain	76:6

ד

דָּבַר	word, speech	119:9
דִּין	judge, govern, do justice	140:12
דַּעַת	knowledge	67:2
דָּשֵׁן	be fat > make fat, accept	20:3

ה

הָגָה	meditate, utter, devise	2:1
הָדָר	honor, adornment	96:6
הוֹד	glory, splendor, majesty	96:6
הֵיכָל	temple	5:7
הָלַל	praise	33:1

ז

זֵדִים	the arrogant, presumptuous	119:21
זָכָה	be clean, free, pure	51:4
זָכַר	remember, ponder	6:5
זָמַר	sing praises, play music	33:2
זָנַח	spurn, cast off, reject	43:2

ח

חָוָה	bow down, worship	95:6
חוּס	have pity, spare	72:12
חָזַק	be strong, firm > strengthen	27:14
חָטָא	sin, miss the mark	51:2

Index of Hebrew Word Studies

חַיִל	pomp, wealth, power	49:6
חָכְמָה	wisdom, skill	19:7, 49:3
חָלָה	mollify, appease, entreat	119:58
חָלַל	be profane > pollute, defile	74:7
חָמָס	treat violently > violence	58:2
חֵן, חָנַן	be gracious, grace	4:1
חֶסֶד	loyal love	23:6
חָסָה	take refuge	7:1
חֹק	statute, decree	119:5
חָרָה	be hot, angry > fret	37:1
חֶרְפָּה	taunt, reproach, scorn	22:6
חָשַׁב	think, account, reckon	32:2

ט

טָהַר	clean, pure	51:2
טוֹב	good, goodness, pleasing	34:8

י

יָדָה	acknowledge, praise	6:5
יָדַע	know	67:2
יָחַל	wait, hope	31:24
יָכַח	correct, rebuke, reprove	38:1
יָסַד	be established > establish	87:1
יָסַר	discipline, admonish	6:1
יָצַר	plan, form, fashion	33:15
יָרֵא	fear, reverence	2:11
יָשַׁע	save, deliver,	3:2
יָשָׁר	be straight > upright	67:4
מִישׁוֹר, equitable		67:4

כ

כָּבוֹד	glory, honor	19:1
כּוּן	be established, firm	93:1
כָּלָה	be finished, complete	90:7
כִּפֶּר	atone, ransom, propitiate	49:7

ל

לֵב	heart, mind	111:1
לִיץ	scorn	119:51

Index of Hebrew Word Studies

מ

מוּט	slip, totter, shake	62:2
מוּל	circumcise, cut to pieces	118:10
מְזִמָּה	purpose, thought, device	10:2
מָלַט	slip away, escape, deliver	41:1
מִרְמָה	deceit, guile, treachery	5:7
מִצְוָה	commandment	119:6
מָשַׁח	anoint	132:10
מָשַׁל	rule, have dominion	66:7
מָשָׁל	proverb, by-word	49:3

נ

נָבָל	foolishness, senseless	14:1
נָגַד	be conspicuous > tell	75:9
נְדָבָה	freewill offering, free	110:3
נוּחַ	rest	95:11
נָחָה	lead, guide	23:3
נָחַם	comfort, be sorry	119:76
נֵכָר	strange, foreign	144:7
נָסָה	test, try	26:2
נָעִים	pleasant	133:1
נֶפֶשׁ	life, soul	11:5
נָצַל	plunder > deliver	22:20
נָצַר	guard, store up, treasure	119:2
נָקִי	clean, free, innocent	19:13
נָקַם	take revenge, avenge	18:48
נָשָׂא	lift up, take away, forgive	24:7
נְשָׁמָה	breath	150:6

ס

| סָלַח | forgive | 130:4 |
| סָמַךְ | lean, sustain | 51:12 |

ע

עָבַד	serve, work	134:1
עֵדוּת	statute, testimony	119:2
עַוְלָה	iniquity, injustice, wrong	43:1
עוֹלָם	ever, eternity, antiquity	61:4
עָוֹן	iniquity, guilt, punishment	32:5

Index of Hebrew Word Studies

עֹז	strength, might	29:1
עָזַר	help	46:1
עָנִי	poor, afflicted, humble	9:12

פ

פָּאַר	be beautiful	96:6
פָּדָה	ransom	25:22
פָּחַד	fear, terror, dread	119:120
פָּלָא	be wonderful, wonderful	139:5
פָּלַט	escape, deliver	37:20
פָּלַל	intervene, interpose > pray	5:2
פָּקַד	visit, appoint, attend to, care	8:4
פָּשַׁע	transgress > transgression	51:1

צ

צָבָא	army [host], warfare	24:10
צַדִּיק	righteous, just	1:5
צִוָּה	lay charge, order, command	119:6
צָלַח	prosper, advance	45:4
צָרָה	bind, restrict > distress	120:1

ק

קָדוֹשׁ	holy, sacred	22:3
קָוָה	wait, hope	25:3
קוּם	arise, rise up, stand	3:1
קָלַל	be light > curse, treat lightly	109:28
קָנָא	jealous, zealous	37:1

ר

רָדָה	rule	110:2
רוּם	be high > exalt	46:10
רוּעַ	raise a shout, give a blast	100:1
רָחַם	have compassion, love	25:6
רִיב	strive, contend, plead a case	95:8
רָנַן	give a ringing cry, cry aloud	33:1
רַע	evil, distress, misery	10:15
רָפָא	heal	30:2
רָצָה	favor > acceptance	30:5
רָשָׁע	ungodly, wicked, guilty	1:1

שׂ

שִׂיחַ	meditate, muse, complain	119:15
שָׂכַל	have insight, deal wisely	36:4
שָׂמַח	rejoice, be glad	48:11
שָׂנֵא	hate > reject	139:21
שַׂרְעַפִּים	disquieting thoughts (שָׂעַף)	94:19

שׁ

שְׁאוֹל	she'ol, hell, grave, death	6:5
שָׁבַע	swear	90:14
שָׁבַת	cease, rest > cause to end	46:9
שָׁוְא	vanity, emptiness, vain	127:1
שׁוּב	turn back, return > repent	126:1
שָׁחַת	be ruined > ruin, spoil	14:1
שִׁיר	sing, song	33:3
שָׁכַח	forget	103:2
שָׁלַם	be whole > repay, complete	38:3
שֵׁם	name, nature	20:1
שָׁמַע	hear, obey	45:10
שָׁמַר	keep, guard, watch	12:7
שָׁעַע	sport, take delight in	119:16
שָׁפַט	judge, govern, vindicate	9:4
שֶׁקֶר	falsehood, deception	144:8

ת

תָּעַב	do abominably תּוֹעֵבָה, abomination	14:1
תּוֹרָה	direction instruction, law	1:2
תָּמִים	complete, sound, blameless, having integrity	7:8

Selected Bibliography for the Exposition of the Psalms

Introductory Works

Anderson, Bernhard H., with Bishop, Steven. *Out of the Depths: The Psalms Speak for Us Today.* Philadelphia: Westminster John Knox Press, 2000.

Bellinger, W. H. Jr. *Psalms.* Peabody, MA: Hendrickson Publishers, 1990.

Breuggemann, Walter. *The Message of the Psalms.* Minneapolis, MN: Augsburg, 1984.

Bullock, Hassell C. *Encountering the Book of Psalms.* Grand Rapids: Baker, 2001.

Clines, D. J. A. "Psalm Research Since 1955: I. The Psalms and the Cult." *TynB* 18 (1967):103–125; "II. The Literary Genres." *TynB* 20 (1969):105–25.

Cole, Robert L. *The Shape and Message of Book III (Psalms 73–89).* Sheffield: Sheffield Academic Press, 2000.

Crenshaw, James L. *The Psalms, An Introduction.* Grand Rapids: Eerdmans, 2001.

Crim, Keith R. *The Royal Psalms.* Richmond, Virginia: John Knox Press, 1962.

Drijvers, Pius. *The Psalms, Their Structure and Meaning.* New York: Herder and Herder, 1965.

Eaton, J. H. *Kingship and the Psalms.* London: SCM, 1976.

Estes, Daniel J. *Handbook on the Wisdom Books and Psalms.* Grand Rapids: Baker, 2005.

Flint, Peter W. Miller, Patrick D., Jr., Brunell, Aaron, and Roberts, Ryan, editors. *The Book of Psalms: Composition* and *Reception.* Leiden: Brill, 2005.

Futato, Mark D. *Interpreting the Psalms: An Exegetical Handbook.* Grand Rapids: Kregel, 2007.

Goulder, Michael. *The Psalms of the Sons of Korah.* JSOT Supplement 20. Sheffield: ISOT Press, 1982. Pp. 37–50. (Ps. 84).

Gunkel, Hermann. *The Psalms: A Form Critical Introduction.* Philadelphia: Fortress Press, 1967.

Hayes, J. H. *Understanding the Psalms.* Valley Forge, PA: Judson Press, 1976.

Holladay, William L. *The Psalms through Three Thousand Years, Prayerbook of a Cloud of Witnesses.* Minneapolis: Fortress Press, 1993

Howard, David M., Jr. *The Structure of Psalms 93–100.* Winona Lake, IN: Eisenbrauns, 1997.

Keet, C. C. *A Study of the Psalms of Ascents. A Critical and Exegetical Commentary upon Psalms 120–134.* London, 1969.

Kim, Jinkyu. "The Strategic Arrangement of Royal Psalms in Books IV-V." *WTJ* 70 (2008):143–57.

Kraus, Hans-Joachim. *Theology of the Psalms.* Translated by Keith Crim. Minneapolis: Augsburg Publishing House, 1986.

Mays, James Luther. *The Lord Reigns: A Theological Handbook to the Psalms.* Louisville: Westminster John Knox, 1994.

McCann, J. C., Jr., ed. *The Shape and Shaping of the Psalter.* Sheffield: Sheffield Academic, 1993.

_____. *A Theological Introduction to the Book of Psalms: The Psalms as Torah.* Nashville: Abingdon, 1993

Mowinckel, Sigmund. *The Psalms in Israel's Worship.* 2 Volumes. Translated by D. R. Ap-Thomas. New York: Abingdon Press, 1967.

Sabourin, Leopold. *The Psalms: Their Origin and Meaning.* New York: Alba House, 1974.

Sanders, J. A. *The Psalm Scroll of Qumran Cave 11.* Oxford: At the Clarendon Press, 1965.

Sarna, Nahum M. *The Psalms: Their Origin and Meaning.* New York: Schocken Press, 1993.

Seybold, K. *Introducing the Psalms.* Edinburgh: T. & T. Clark, 1981.

Westermann, Claus. *The Praise of God in the Psalms.* Translated by Keith R. Crim. Richmond, Virginia: John Knox Press, 1965.

_____. *Praise and Lament in the Psalms.* Translated by Keith R. Crim and Richard N. Soulen. Atlanta: John Knox Press, 1981.

Wevers, J. W. "A Study in the Form Criticism of Individual Complaint Psalms." *VT* 6 (1956):80–86.

Whitelocke, L. T. *The rîb Pattern and the Concept of Judgment in the Book of Psalms.* Dissertation: Boston University Graduate School, 1968. DissAbstr 29 (1968f), 1950f-A.

Wilson, Gerald H. *The Editing of the Hebrew Psalter.* Chico: CA: Scholars Press, 1985.

_____. "Editorial Decision in the Hebrew Psalter." *VT* 34 (1984):342–43.

_____. "The Shape of the Book of Psalms." *Int* 46 (1992):129–42.

_____. "Shaping the Psalter: A Consideration of Editorial Linkage in the Book of Psalms." In *The Shape and Shaping of the Psalter.* Ed. by J. C. McCann, Jr. Pp. 72–82. Sheffield: Sheffield Academic, 1993.

_____. "The Use of Royal Psalms at the 'Seams' of the Hebrew Psalter." *JSOT* 35 (1986):85–94.

Commentaries

Allen, Leslie C. *Psalms 101–150.* Word Biblical Commentary. Waco, TX: Word, 1983.

Anderson, J. A. *The Psalms Translated and Explained.* Grand Rapids: Baker Books, 1977 reprint of the 1873 edition.

Anderson, A. A. *The Book of Psalms.* New Century Bible. 2 Volumes. London: Marshall, Morgan & Scott, 1972.

Braude, William B., editor. *The Midrash on the Psalms.* London: The Soncino Press, nd.

Selected Bibliography for the Exposition of the Psalms

Briggs, Charles A. and Briggs, E. G. *A Critical and Exegetical Commentary on the Psalms.* The International Critical Commentary. 2 Volumes. Edinburgh: T. & T. Clark, 1903.

Broyles, Craig C. *Psalms.* New International Commentary. Peabody, MA: Hendrickson, 1999.

Buttenwiesser, Moses. *The Psalms.* Chicago: University of Chicago Press, 1938.

Calvin, John. *Commentary on the Book of Psalms.* Translated by James Anderson. 3 Volumes. Grand Rapids: Eerdmans, 1963 reprint.

Clifford, Richard J. *Psalms.* 2 Volumes. Nashville: Abingdon, 2002, 2003.

Cohen, A. *The Psalms.* Soncino Books of the Bible. London: The Soncino Press, 1945.

Craigie, Peter C. *Psalms 1–50.* Word Biblical Commentary. Waco, TX: Word, 1983.

Dahood, Mitchell. *Psalms.* The Anchor Bible. 3 Volumes. Garden City, NY: Doubleday, 1965.

Delitzsch, Franz. *Biblical Commentary on the Psalms.* 3 Volumes. Translated by David Eaton. Grand Rapids: Wm. B. Eerdmans Publishing Co., reprint.

Eaton, John. *Psalms.* London: SCM Press, 1967.

Gerstenberger, Eberhard S. *Psalms and Lamentations.* 2 Volumes. Grand Rapids: Eerdmans, 1988, 2001.

Goldingay, John. *Psalms.* 3 Volumes. Grand Rapids: Baker Book House, 2006, 2007, 2008.

Goulder, Michael D. *The Psalms of the Sons of Korah.* Sheffield: JSOT, 1982.

Gunkel, Hermann. *Die Psalmen.* Goettingen: Vandenhoeck und Ruprecht, 1926.

Hengstenberg, E. W. *Commentary on the Psalms.* 3 Volumes. Cherry Hill, NJ: Mack, nd.

Hossfeld, Frank-Lothar, and Erich Zenger. *Psalms 3. A Commentary on Psalms 101–150.* Translated by Linda M. Maloney. Minneapolis: Fortress Press, 2011.

Jacquet, L. *Les Psaumes et le couer de l'homme. Etude textuelle, litteraire et doctrinale.* 3 Volumes. Gembloux: Duculot, 1975.

Selected Bibliography for the Exposition of the Psalms

Keet, Cuthbert C. *A Study of the Psalms of Ascent: A Critical and Exegetical Commentary on Psalms cxx–cxxxiv."* London: Mitre Press, 1969.

Kidner, Derek. *Psalms 1–72, Psalms 73–150.* 2 Volumes. London: InterVarsity Press, 1975.

Kirkpatrick, A. F. *The Book of Psalms.* The Cambridge Bible for Schools and Colleges. 3 Volumes. Cambridge: At the University Press, 1906. Reprinted in one volume by Baker Book House.

Kraus, Hans-Joachim. *Psalms 1–59, Psalms 60–150.* 2 Volumes. Translated by Hilton C. Oswald. Minneapolis: Augsburg Publishing House, 1988.

Leupold, H. C. *Exposition of the Psalms.* Grand Rapids: Baker Book House, 1969.

Mays, James L. *Psalms.* Interpretation. Louisville: Knox, 1994.

McCann, J. Clinton. "The Book of Psalms," in *The New Interpreter's Bible,* Volume 4. Edited by Leander E. Keck. Nashville: Abingdon, 1996, Pp. 639–1280.

Moll, Carl Bernhard. *The Psalms.* Lange's Commentary on the Holy Scriptures. Edited by John Peter Lange. Grand Rapids: Zondervan Publishing House reprint of the 1869 edition.

Oesterley, W. O. E. *The Psalms.* London: S.P.C.K., 1962.

Perowne, J. J. Stewart. *The Book of Psalms.* 2 Volumes. Grand Rapids: Zondervan Publishing House, reprint of 1878 edition.

Rogerson, J. W. and McKay, J. W. *Psalms.* 3 Volumes. The Cambridge Bible Commentary. Cambridge: Cambridge University Press, 1977.

Tate, Marvin E. *Psalms 51–100.* Waco: Word, 1990.

Terrien, Samuel. *The Psalms.* Grand Rapids: Eerdmans, 2002.

VanGemeren, Willem. *Psalms.* The Expositor's Bible Commentary. Grand Rapids: Zondervan, 2008.

Weiser, Artur. *The Psalms: A Commentary.* Old Testament Library. Translated by Herbert Hartwell. Philadelphia: The Westminster Press, 1962.

Wilson, Gerald H. *Psalms 1–72.* NIV Application Commentary. Grand Rapids: Zondervan, 2002.

The Psalms as Poetry

Alden, Robert. "Chiastic Psalms." *JETS* 17 (1974):11–18; 19 (1976):191–200; 21 (1978):199–210.

Alonso-Schökel, Luis. *Estudios de Poetica Hebrea*. Barcelona: Juan Flors, 1963.

_____. "Hermeneutics in the Light of Language and Literature." *CBQ* 25 (1963):371–386.

Alter, Robert. *The Art of Biblical Poetry*. New York: Basic Books, 1985.

Berlin, Adele. *The Dynamics of Biblical Parallelism*. Bloomington: Indiana University Press, 1985.

Blenkinsopp, J. "Stylistics of Old Testament Poetry." *Bib* 44 (1963):352–358.

Boling, R. G. "Synonymous Parallelism in the Psalms." *JSS* 5 (1960):221–255.

Bouzard, Walter C., Jr. *We Have Heard with Our Ears, O God: Sources of the Communal Laments in the Psalms*. Atlanta: Scholars Press, 1997.

Bright, John. *Jeremiah*. The Anchor Bible. Garden City, NY: Doubleday and Company, 1965. Pp. cxxvi-cxxxviii.

Broyles, C. *The Conflict of Faith and Experience, A Form Critical and Theological Study of Selected Lament Psalms*. Sheffield: Academic Press, 1989.

Bywater, Ingram. *Aristotle on the Art of Poetry*. Oxford: At the Clarendon Press, 1909.

Bullinger, E. W. *Figures of Speech Used in the Bible*. Grand Rapids: Baker Book House, reprint of 1898 edition.

Caird, G. B. *The Language and Imagery of the Bible*. Philadelphia: Westminster, 1980.

Casanowicz, Immanuel M. *Paronomasia in the Old Testament*. Boston: Norwood Press, 1894.

Creach, Jerome F. D. *Yahweh as Refuge and the Editing of the Hebrew Psalter*. *JSOT* Supplement 217. Sheffield: Sheffield Academic Press, 1996.

Cross, F. M., and Freedman, D. N. *Studies in Ancient Yahwistic Poetry*. Missoula, Montana: Scholars Press, 1975.

Driver, G. R. "Poetic Diction." *VT* Supplement 1 (1953):26–39.

Empsom, W. *Seven Types of Ambiguity*. London: Chatto and Windus, 1947.

Selected Bibliography for the Exposition of the Psalms

Engnell, Ivan. "The Figurative Language of the Old Testament." In *Critical Essays of the Old Testament*. Edited by John T. Willis. London: S.P.C.K., 1970.

Gevirtz, Stanley. "On Canaanite Rhetoric: The Evidence of the Amarna Letters from Tyre." *Orientalia* ns 42 (1973):162–177.

_____. "Of Patriarchs and Puns: Joseph at the Fountain, Jacob at the Ford." *HUCA* 46 (1975):33–54.

_____. *Patterns in the Early Poetry of Israel*. Chicago: University of Chicago Press, 1963.

Glueck, J. J. "The Figures of Inversion in the Book of Proverbs." *Semitics* 5 (1976):25.

_____. "Paronomasia in Biblical Literature." *Semitics* 1 (1970):50–78.

Good, Edwin. *Irony in the Old Testament*. London: S.P.C.K., 1965.

Herder, Johann Gottfried von. *The Spirit of Hebrew Poetry*. Burlington, England: Edward Smith, 1833.

Honeyman, A. M. "*Merismus* in Biblical Literature." *JBL* 85 (1966):401–435.

Jackson, Jared J., and Kessler, Martin. *Rhetorical Criticism*. Essays in Honor of James Muilenberg. Pittsburgh: The Pickwick Press, 1974.

Keel, Othmar. *The Symbolism of the Biblical World. Ancient Near Eastern Iconography and the Book of Psalms*. Translated by Timothy J. Hallett. New York: Seabury Press, 1978.

Kessler, M. "*Inclusio* in the Hebrew Bible." *Semitics* 6 (1978):4.

Kikawada, Isaac M. "Some Proposals for the Definition of Rhetorical Criticism." *Semitics* 5 (1977): 67–91.

Kugal, James L. *The Idea of Biblical Poetry*. London: Longman Group Ltd., 1969

Lewis, C. S. *Reflections on the Psalms*. A Harvest Book. New York: Harcourt, Brace and World, Inc., 1958.

Longman, Tremper, III. *Literary Approaches to Biblical Interpretation*. Grand Rapids: Zondervan, 1987.

Lowth, Robert. *Lectures on the Sacred Poetry of the Hebrews*. Translated by G. Gregory. Andover: Codman Press, 1829.

Muilenberg, James. "Form Criticism and Beyond." *JBL* 81 (1969):1–18.

———. "A Study in Hebrew Rhetoric: Repetition and Style." *VT* Supplement 1 (1953):97–111.
Payne, D. F. "Old Testament Exegesis and the Problem of Ambiguity." *ASTI* 5 (1967):48–68.
Perdue, Leo. *Wisdom and Cult.* Missoula, MT: Scholars Press, 1977.
Preminger, A., Warnke, F. J., and Hardison, O. B. *Princeton Encyclopedia of Poetry and Poetics.* Revised Edition. Princeton: Princeton University Press, 1975.
Rankin, O. S. "Alliteration in Hebrew Poetry." *JTS* 31 (1930):285–300.
Robinson, Theodore H. "Hebrew Poetic Form: The English Tradition." *VT* Supplement 1 (1953):128–149.
———. *The Poetry of the Old Testament.* London: Duckworth, 1947.
Ryken, Leland. *How To Read the Bible as Literature.* Grand Rapids: Zondervan, 1984.
Saydon, P. P. "Assonance in Hebrew as a Means of Expressing Emphasis." *Bib* 36 (1955):36–50; 287–304.
Shepherd, John. "The Place of the Imprecatory Psalms in the Canon of Scripture." *Churchman* 111 (1997):27–43, 110–26.
Slotki, Israel W. "Antiphony in Ancient Hebrew Poetry." *JQR* 26 (1935):199–219.
Waltke, Bruce K. "Superscripts, Postscripts, or Both." *JBL* 110 (1991):583–96.
Watters, William R. *Formula Criticism and the Poetry of the Old Testament.* Berlin and New York: Walter de Gruyter, 1976.
Wieder, Laurance, editor. *The Poet's Book of Psalms. The Complete Psalter as Rendered by Twenty-Five Poets from the Sixteenth to the Twentieth Centuries.* Oxford: Oxford University Press, 1995.
Wright, Addison G. "The Literary Genre Midrash." *CBQ* 28 (1966):105–138, 417–457.

Additional Resources

Aharoni, Yohanan. *The Land of the Bible: A Historical Geography.* Philadelphia: Westminster, 1979.
Aharoni, Yohanan, and Michael Avi-Yonah. *The Macmillan Bible Atlas.* New York: Macmillan, 1993.

Beckwith, Roger T. "The Early History of the Psalter." *TynB* 46 (1995):1–27.

Bonhoeffer, Dietrich, *Meditating on the Word*. Minneapolis: Augsburg, nd.

_____. *Psalms, The Prayer Book of the Bible*. Minneapolis: Augsburg, 1970.

Botterweck, G. Johannes, Ringgren. Helmer, and Fabry, Heinz-Josef, editors. *Theological Dictionary of the Old Testament*. 15 Volumes. Translated by John T. Willis, Geoffrey W. Bromiley, and David E. Green. Grand Rapids : Eerdmans, 1978.

Borowski, Oded. *Agriculture in Iron Age Israel*. Winona Lake, IN: Eisenbrauns, 2002.

Braun, Joachim. *Music in Ancient Israel/Palestine*. Grand Rapids: Eerdmans, 2002.

Bruce, F. F. "The Earliest Old Testament Interpretation," *OTS* 17 (1972):37–52.

Childs, Brevard S. *Memory and Tradition in Israel*. Naperville, IL: Allenson, 1962.

Chisholm, Robert B., Jr. *From Exegesis to Exposition. A Practical Guide to Using Biblical Hebrew*. Grand Rapids: Baker Books, 1998.

Creach, Jerome F. D. *The Destiny of the Righteous in the Psalms*. St. Louis: Chalice, 2008.

Crow, Loren S. *The Songs of Ascent (Psalms 120–134): Their Place in Israelite History and Religion*. Atlanta: Scholars Press, 1996.

Curtis, Edward M. "Ancient Psalms and Modern Worship." *BibSac* 154 (1997):285–96.

Dalglish, Edward R. *Psalm Fifty-One in the Light of Ancient Near Eastern Patternism*. Leiden: E. J. Brill, 1962.

Davies, G. Henton. "The Ark in the Psalms." In *Promise and Fulfillment: Essays Presented to Professor S. H. Hooke*. Ed. by F. F. Bruce. Edinburgh: T. & T. Clark, 1963. Pp. 51–61.

Day, John. *God's Conflict with the Dragon and the Sea: Echoes of Canaanite Myth in the Old Testament*. Cambridge: Cambridge University Press, 1985.

Day, John N. *Crying for Justice. What the Psalms Teach Us about Mercy and Vengeance in an Age of Terrorism*. Grand Rapids: Kregel, 2005.

Dell, Katharine J. "The Use of Animal Imagery in the Psalms and Wisdom Literature of Ancient Israel." *SJT* 53 (2000):275–91.

DePinto, B. "The Torah and the Psalms." *JBL* 86 (1967):154–74.

De Vaux, Roland. *Ancient Israel.* 2 Volumes. New York: McGraw-Hill, 1965

Eichrodt, W. *Theology of the Old Testament.* 2 Volumes. Translated by J. A. Baker. Philadelphia: Westminster, 1961, 1967.

Engnell, Ivan. *Studies in Divine Kingship in the Ancient Near East.* Oxford: Basil Blackwell, 1967 reprint of 1943 Uppsala edition.

Fensham, F. C. "Widow, Orphan, and the Poor in Ancient Near Eastern Legal and Wisdom Literature." *JNES* 21 (1962):129–139.

Field, Fredericus. *Origenis Hexaplorum.* 2 Volumes. Oxonii: E. Typographea Clarendoniano, 1875.

Finkelstein, L. "The Origin of the Hallel (Pss. 113–118)." *HUCA* 23 (1950):319–337.

Fisher, L. R., editor. *Ras Shamra Parallels. The Texts from Ugarit and the Hebrew Bible.* 2 Volumes. Rome: Analecta orientalia, 1972. See especially "Literary Phrases" by Schoors, pp. 1–70; "Ugaritic-Hebrew Parallel Pairs" by Dahood and Penar, pp. 383–452; and "Flora, Fauna, and Minerals" by Sasson.

Flint, Peter W. *The Dead Sea Psalms Scrolls & the Book of Psalms.* Leiden: Brill, 1997.

Gertner, M. "Terms of Scriptural Interpretation: A Study in Hebrew Semantics," *BSOAS* 25 (1962):1–27.

Gillingham, Susan E. *The Poems and the Psalms of the Hebrew Bible.* Oxford: Oxford University Press, 1994.

———. "Studies of the Psalms: Retrospect and Prospect." *ExT* 119 (2008):209–216.

Habel, Norman C. *Yahweh versus Baal, A Conflict of Religious Cultures: A Study in the Relevance of Ugaritic materials for the Early Faith of Israel.* New York: Bookman Association, 1964. Pp. 52–71. (Ps. 93)

Hardin, J. M. *Psalterium iuxta Hebraeos Hieronymi.* London: S.P.C.K., 1922.

Hareuveni, Nogah. *Desert and Shepherd in Our Biblical Heritage.* Translated by Helen Frenkley. Neot Kedumim, Israel, 1991.

Harmon, A. M. "Aspects of Paul's Use of the Psalms." *WJT* 32 (1969):1–23.

Hilber, John W. *Cultic Prophecy in the Psalms*. New York: Walter de Gruyter, 2005.

Holladay, W. L. *The Root ŠUBH in the Old Testament with Particular Reference to Its Usage in Covenantal Contexts*. Leiden: Brill, 1958.

Howard, David M. "Recent Trends in Psalms Study." In *The Face of Old Testament Studies: A Survey of Contemporary Approaches*. Ed. by David W. Baker and Bill T. Arnold. Grand Rapids: Baker Books, 1999.

Hooke, S. H., editor. *Myth and Ritual. Essays on the Myth and Ritual of the Hebrews in Relation to the Cultic Pattern of the ANE*. Oxford: Clarendon Press, 1933.

Human, Dirk J., and Vos, Cas J. A., eds. *Psalms and Liturgy*. London: T. & T. Clark, 2004.

Hvidberg, F. F. *Weeping and Laughing in the Old Testament*. Leiden: E. J. Brill, 1962.

Jaki, Stanley L. *Praying the Psalms, A Commentary*. Grand Rapids: Eerdmans, 2001.

Jenni, Ernst, and Westermann, Claus, editors. *Theological Lexicon of the Old Testament*. 3 Volumes. Translated by Mark E. Biddle. Peabody, MA: Hendrickson Publisher, Inc., 1997 (German edition, 1976).

Johnson, A. R. *The Cultic Prophet and Israel's Psalmody*. Cardiff: University of Wales Press, 1962.

Knight, Jack C. and Sinclair, Lawrence A., eds. *The Psalms and other Studies in the Old Testament,* FS for Joseph I. Hunt. Nashotah, WI: Nashotah House, 1990.

Kohlenberger, John R. III, editor. *The Comparative Psalter: Hebrew-Greek-English*. Oxford: Oxford University Press, 2007.

Kraus, Hans-Joachim. *Worship in Israel*. Oxford: Clarendon Press, 1966.

Lamb, John A. *The Psalms in Christian Worship*. London: Faith Press, 1962.

Laney, J. Carl. "A Fresh Look at the Imprecatory Psalms." *BibSac* 138 (1981):35–45.

Levenson, Jon D. *Sinai and Zion: An Entry into the Jewish Bible.* Minneapolis, MN: Winston Press, 1985.

Lewalski, Barbara. *Protestant Poetics and the Seventeenth Century Religious Lyric.* Princeton: Princeton University Press, 1979.

Lipinski, E. "Yahweh malak." *Bib* 44 (1963):405–460.

Mays, James L. *The Lord Reigns: A Theological Handbook to the Psalms.* Louisville: Westminster John Knox, 1994.

McCann Jr., J. Clinton. *A Theological Introduction to the Book of Psalms: Psalms as Torah.* Nashville: Abingdon, 1993.

McConville, Gordon. "The Psalms: Introduction and Theology." *Evangel* 11 (1993):43–54.

McKeating, H. "Divine Forgiveness in the Psalms." *SJT* 18 (1965):69–83.

McKenzie, J. L. "Royal Messianism." *CBQ* 19 (1957):25–52.

Merton, Thomas. *Praying the Psalms.* Collegeville, MN: Liturgical Press, 1956.

Mettinger, T. N. D. *King and Messiah, The Civil and Sacral Legitimization of the Israelite Kings.* Lund: C. W. K. Gleerup, 1976. (Ps. 110)

Meyers, Carol L. "The Drum-Dance-Song Ensemble: Women's Performance in Biblical Israel." In *Rediscovering the Muses: Women's Musical Tradition.* Ed. by Kimberly Marshall. Boston: Northeastern University Press, 1993. Pp. 49–67.

Miller, Patrick D. *They Cried to the LORD: The Form and Theology of Biblical Prayer.* Minneapolis: Fortress, 1994.

———. *The Way of the LORD: Essays in Old Testament Theology.* Grand Rapids: Eerdmans, 2007.

Moreton, M. J. "The Sacrifice of Praise." *Church Quarterly Review* 165 (1964):481–494.

Morgenstern, J. "The Cultic Setting of the Enthronement Psalms." *HUCA* 35 (1964):1–42.

Pietersma, Albert, and Wright, Benjamin C. Editors. *A New English Translation of the Septuagint.* Oxford: Oxford University Press, 2007.

Pritchard, James. *Ancient Near Eastern Texts Relating to the Old Testament.* Princeton: Princeton University Press, 1969.

Rabinowitz, L. J. "The Psalms in Jewish Liturgy." *Historia Judaica* 6 (1944):109–122 (cf. *CBQ* 1945).

Ringgren, Helmer. *Religions of the Ancient Near East.* Philadelphia: Westminster, 1973.

Rosenbloom, Joseph R. *Conversion to Judaism, From the Biblical Period to the Present.* New York: KTAV Pub. Inc., 1979.

Ross, Allen P. *Recalling the Hope of Glory.* Grand Rapids: Kregel, 2006.

_____. "The Theology of the Psalms: Our Living Hope." *BibV* 4 (1970):126–135.

Ross, J. P. "*Yahweh Ṣebā'ôt* in Samuel and Psalms." *VT* 17 (1967):76–92.

Rowley, H. H. *Worship in Israel.* London: SCM Press, Ltd., 1967.

Sellers, Ovid R. "Musical Instruments of Israel." In *Biblical Archaeologist Reader, 1.* Ed. by George Ernest Wright and David Noel Freedman. New York: Doubleday, 1961. Pp. 81–94.

Sire, James W. *Learning to Pray through the Psalms.* Downers Grove, IL: InterVarsity, 2005.

Smick, Elmer B. "Mythopoetic Language in the Psalter." *WTJ* 44 (1982):88–98.

Snaith, N. H. "Selah." *VT* 2 (1952):42–56.

_____. *The Seven Psalms.* London: Epworth Press, 1964.

Stackhouse, Rochelle A. *The Language of the Psalms in Worship: American Revisions of Watts' Psalter.* Lanham, MD: Scarecrow Press, 1997.

Stec, David M. *The Targums of Psalms.* Collegeville, MN: Liturgical Press, 2004.

Suring, Margrit L. *The Horn-Motif in the Hebrew Bible and Related Ancient Near Eastern Literature and Iconography. AUSS DDS 4.* Berrien Springs, MI: Andrews University Press, 1980.

Terrien, S. *The Elusive Presence.* San Francisco: Harper & Row, 1978.

Thomas, D. Winton. *Text of the Revised Psalter.* London: SPCK, 1963.

VanGemeren, Willem, editor. *The New International Dictionary of Old Testament Theology and Exegesis,* 5 Volumes. Grand Rapids: Zondervan Publishing Company, 1999.

Viviers, Hendrek. "The Coherence of the *maʿălôt* Psalms (Pss 120–134)." *ZAW* 106 (1994):275–89.

Wallace, Howard N. "King and Community: Joining with David in Prayer." In *Psalms and Prayers*. Edited by Bob Becking and Eric Peels. Leiden: E. J. Brill, 2007.

Waltke, Bruce K., and Houston, James M. *The Psalms as Christian Worship: A Historical Commentary*. Grand Rapids: Eerdmans, 2010.

Walton, John H. *Ancient Israelite Literature in Its Cultural Context: A Survey of Parallels Between Biblical and Ancient Near Eastern Texts*. Grand Rapids: Zondervan, 1989.

Watts, John D. W. "A History of the Use and Interpretation of the Psalms." In *An Introduction to Wisdom Literature and the Psalms*. Edited by H. Wayne Ballard and W. Dennis Tucker. Macon, GA: Mercer University Press, 2000. Pp. 21–35.

Weiss, Meier. *The Bible from Within: The Method of Total Interpretation*. Jerusalem: Magnes Press, 1984.

Wells, C. Richard, and Van Neste, Ray, eds. *Forgotten Songs: Reclaiming the Psalms for Christian Worship*. Nashville: B&H Academic, 2012.

Wenham, Gordon J. *Psalms as Torah: Reading Biblical Song Ethically*. Studies in Theological Interpretation. Grand Rapids: Baker Academic, 2012.

Westermann, Claus. *The Living Psalms*. Translated by J. R. Porter. Grand Rapids: Eerdmans, 1989 (original date, 1984).

Wieder, Laurance. Editor. *The Poets' Book of Psalms*. Oxford: Oxford University Press, 1995.

Wilson, Gerald H. *The Editing of the Hebrew Psalter*. Society of Biblical Literature Dissertation Series 76. Chico, CA: Scholars Press, 1985.

Wolff, Hans Walter. *Anthropology of the Old Testament*. Philadelphia: Fortress Press, 1974.

Wright, G. E. *The Old Testament Against Its Environment*. London: SCM Press, Ltd., 1950.

Yadin, Yigael. *The Art of Warfare in Biblical Lands*. New York: McGraw-Hill, 1963.

Zenger, Erich. *A God of Vengeance. Understanding the Psalms of Divine Wrath*. Philadelphia: Westminster John Knox, 1995.

Specific Studies for Individual Psalms or Motifs

Ackerman, J. S. "An Exegetical Study of Psalm 82." Dissertation, Harvard, 1966.

Ackroyd, Peter R. "Some Notes on the Psalms." *JTS* 17 (1966):392–99. (Pss. 29, 96)

Albright, W. F. "A Catalogue of Early Hebrew Lyric Poems (Psalm LXVIII)." *HUCA* 23 (1950):1–39.

Allen, Leslie C. "Faith on Trial: An Analysis of Psalm 139," *Vox evangelica* 10 (1977):5–23.

_____. "Psalm 73: An Analysis." *TynB* 33 (1982):93–118.

_____. "The Old Testament in Romans I-VIII," *VT* 3 (1964):11–12. (Ps. 143)

_____. "Structure and Meaning in Psalm 50." *Vox evangelica* 14 (1984):17–37.

_____. "The Value of Rhetorical Criticism in Psalm 69." *JBL* 105 (1986):577–98.

Alonso-Shökel, Luis. "The Poetic Structure of Psalms 42–43." *JSOT* 1 (1976):4–11.

Althann, Robert. "The Psalms of Vengeance against Their Ancient Near Eastern Background." *JNSL* 18 (1992):1–11.

_____. "Atonement and Reconciliation in Psalms 3, 6, and 83." *JNSL* 25 (1999):75–82.

_____. "Psalm 58:10 in the Light of Ebla." *Bib* 64 (1983):122–24.

Anderson, G. W. "Enemies and Evildoers in the Book of Psalms." *BJRL* 48 (1965):18–29. (Pss. 5, 28)

_____. "A Note on Psalm i 1," *VT* 24 (1974):231–34.

Ap-Thomas, D. R. "Some Aspects of the Root ḤNN in the Old Testament." *JSS* 2 (1957):128–48. (Ps. 4)

Arbez, E. P. "A Study of Psalm 1." *CBQ* 7 (1945):398–404.

Armerding, C. E. "Were David's Sons Really Priests?" In *Current Issues in Biblical and Patristic Interpretation.* Ed. by G. F. Hawthorne. Grand Rapids: Eerdmans, 1975. Pp. 75–86. (Ps. 110)

Auffret, Pierre. *The Literary Structure of Psalm 2.* JSOT Supplement 3. Sheffield: Sheffield Academic, 1977.

_____. "Note on the Literary Structure of Psalm 134." *JSOT* 45 (1989):87–9.

_____. "YHWH, *qui sejournera en ta tente?*" *VT* 50 (2000):143–51. (Ps. 15)

Barentsen, Jack. "Restoration and Its Blessing." *GTJ* 5 (1984):247–69. (Pss. 32, 51)

Barker, David G. "The LORD Watches Over You." *BibSac* 152 (1995):163–81. (Ps. 121)

Barré, Michael L. "The Formulaic Pair טוב (ו) חסד in the Psalter." *ZAW* 98 (1986):100–105.

_____. "Hearts, Beds, and Repentance in Psalm 4:5 and Hosea 7:14." *Bib* 76 (1995):53–62.

_____. "Psalm 116: Its Structure and Its Enigmas." *JBL* 109 (1990):61–78.

_____. "Recovering the Literary Structure of Psalm xv." *VT* 34 (1984):207–11.

_____. "The Seven Epithets of Zion in Ps. 48:2–3." *Bib* 69 (1988):557–63.

_____. "The Shifting Focus of Psalm 101," in *The Book of Psalms*, ed. by Peter W. Flint and Patrick D. Miller. Leiden: Brill, 2005. Pp. 206–223.

_____. "'Walking About' as a *Topos* of Depression in Ancient Near Eastern Literature and the Bible." *JNES* 60 (2001):171–87. (Pss. 42, 43).

_____ and Kselman, John S. "New Exodus, Covenant and Restoration in Psalm 23." In *The Word Shall Go Forth*. Ed. by Carol F. Meyers and M. O'Connor. Winona Lake, IN: Eisenbrauns, 1983. Pp. 97–127.

Bazak, J. "The Geometric-Figurative Sequence of Psalm cxxxvi," *VT* 35 (1985):129–38.

Bee, R. E. "The Textual Analysis of Psalm 132." *JSOT* 6 (1978):68–70.

Begg, C. T. "The Covenantal Dove in Psalm lxxiv 19–20." *VT* 37 (1987):78–81.

Bellinger, W. H. "The Interpretation of Psalm 11." *EvQ* 56 (1984):95–101.

_____. "Psalm 26." *VT* 43 (1993):452–61.

_____. "Psalms of the Falsely Accused: A Reassessment." *SBL Seminar Papers* 25 (1986):463–69. (Ps. 7)

Bennett, Robert A. "Wisdom Motifs in Psalm 14 = 53–*nābāl* and '*ēṣāh*." *BASOR* 220 (1975):15–21.

Berlin, Adele. "On the Interpretation of Psalm 133." In *Directions in Biblical Hebrew Poetry, JSOT* Supplement 40. Ed. by

Elaine R. Follis. Sheffield: Sheffield Academic Press, 1987). Pp. 141–147.

———. "Psalm 118:24." *JBL* 96 (1977):567–68.

———. "The Rhetoric of Psalm 145." In *Biblical and Related Studies Presented to Samuel Iwry*. Edited by Ann Kort and Scott Morshauer. Winona Lake, IN: Eisenbrauns, 1985. Pp. 17–22.

Beuken, W "Psalm 39: Some Aspects of the Old Testament Understanding of Prayer." *Heythrop Journal* 19 (1978):1–11.

———. "Psalm XLVII: Structure and Drama." In *Remembering the Way*. Ed. by A. Albrektson. Leiden: E. J. Brill, 1981. Pp. 38–54. (*OTS* 21).

Blakeney, E. H. "Psalm 121:1–2." *ExT* 56 (1944, 1945): 111.

Boers, H. W. "Psalm 16 and the Historical origin of the Christian Faith." *ZNW* 60 (1969):105–10.

Boling, R. G. "Synonymous Parallelism in the Psalms." *JSS* 5 (1960):221–255.

Booij, Thijs. "The Background of the Oracle in Psalm 81." *Bib* 65 (1984):465–75.

———. "The Hebrew Text of Psalm xcii 11." *VT* 38 (1988):210–13.

———. "Psalm 90:5–6: Junction of Two Traditional Motifs," *Bib* 68 (1987):393–96.

———. "Psalm ci 2. *VT* 38 (1988):458–62.

———. "Psalm 104:13b: The Earth Is Satisfied with the Fruit of Your Works." *Bib* 70 (1989):409–12.

———. "Psalm 109:6–19 as a Quotation: A Review of the Evidence." In *Give Ear To My Words: Psalms and Other Poetry in and around the Hebrew Bible*. FS for N. A. Van Uchelin. Ed. by J. Dyk. Amsterdam: Societas Hebraica Amstelodamensis, 1996. Pp. 91–106.

———. "Psalm cxxii 4." *VT* 51 (2001):262–6.

———. "Psalm 127, 2b." *Bib* 81 (2000):262–68.

———. "Psalm 133." *Bib* 83 (2002):258–67.

———. "The Role of Darkness in Psalm cv 28." *VT* 39 (1989):209–14.

———. "Royal Words in Psalm lxxxiv 11." *VT* 36 (1986):117–20.

———. "Rule in the Midst of Your Foes." *VT* 41 (1991):396–407.

_____. "Some Observations on Psalm lxxxvii." *VT* 37 (1987):16–25.

Bos, J. W. H. "Oh, When the Saints: A Consideration of the Meaning of Psalm 50." *JSOT* 24 (1982):65–77.

Bowker, J. W. "Psalm 110." *VT* 17 (1967):31–41.

Bracke, John M. "*Šûb šebût:* A Reappraisal." *ZAW* 97 (1985):233–44. (Pss. 14, 126)

Brekelmans, C. "Psalm 132: Unity and Structure." *Bijdr* 44 (1983):262–65.

Brooke, G. J. "Psalms 105 and 106 at Qumran." *RevQ* 14 (1989–90):267–92.

Broyles, C. *The Conflict of Faith and Experience, A Form Critical and Theological Study of Selected Lament Psalms.* JSOT Supplement 52. Sheffield: Academic Press, 1989. Pp. 139–44. (Ps. 44)

Brown, W. P. "A Royal Performance: Critical Notes on Psalm 110:3a-b." *JBL* 117 (1998):93–96.

Bruce, F. F. "The Earliest Old Testament Interpretation." *OTS* 17 (1972):37–52.

Brueggemann, W. *Israel's Praise: Doxology against Idolatry and Ideology.* Philadelphia: Fortress Press, 1988. (Ps. 93)

_____. "Psalm 100." *Int* 39 (1985):65–9.

Brongers, H. A. "Psalms 1–2 as a Coronation Liturgy." *Bib* 52 (1971):321–336.

Buber, M. "The Heart Determines: Psalm 73." In *Theodicy in the Old Testament.* Ed. by James L. Crenshaw. Philadelphia: Fortress Press, 1983. Pp. 109–18.

Buchanan, G. W. "The Courts of the Lord." *VT* 16 (1966):231–32.

Bullough, Sebastian. "The Question of Meter in Psalm i." *VT* 17 (1967):42–49.

Buss, M. J. "Psalms of Asaph and Korah." *JBL* 82 (1963):382–92. (Pss. 50, 83)

Cahill, M. "Not a Cornerstone! Translating Ps 118, 22 in the Jewish and Christian Scriptures." *RB* 106 (1999):345–57.

Campbell, A. F. "Psalm 78: A Contribution to the Theology of Tenth Century Israel." *CBQ* 41 (1979):51–79.

Carroll, R. P. "Psalm lxxviii: Vestiges of a Tribal Palestine." *VT* 21 (1971):133–50.

Cassuto, U. "Psalm LXVIII." In *Biblical and Oriental Studies,* Vol 1. Translated by Israel Abrahams. Jerusalem: Magnes Press, 1973. Pp. 241–284.

Cazelles, H. "La question du *lamed auctoris.*" *RB* 56 (1949):93–101.

Ceresko, Anthony R. "The ABC's of Wisdom in Psalm xxxiv." *VT* 35 (1985):99–104.

———. "The Chiastic Word Pattern in Hebrew." *CBQ* 38 (1976):303–11.

———. "A Note on Psalm 63: A Psalm of Vigil." *ZAW* 92 (1980):435–36.

———. "A Poetic Analysis of Psalm 105, with Attention to Its Use of Irony." *Bib* 64 (1983):20–46.

———. "Psalm 121: Prayer of a Warrior?" *Bib* 70 (1989):496–510.

———. "Psalm 149: Poetry, Themes (Exodus and Conquest), and Social Function." *Bib* 67 (1986):179–94.

Charlesworth, James H. "Prolegomenon to a New Study of the Jewish Background of the Hymns and Prayers in the New Testament." *JJS* 1–2 (1982):265–85.

Childs, B. S. "Analysis of a Canonical Formula: 'It Shall Be Recorded for a Future Generation.'" In *Die Hebraische Bibel und ihre zweifache Nachgeschichte,* FS for R. Rendtorff. Ed., by E. Blum, et al. Neukirchen-Vluyn: Neukirchen Verlag, 1990. Pp. 357–64.

———. "Deuteronomic Formulae of the Exodus Traditions," *VT* Supplement 16 (Leiden: Brill, 1967): pp. 30–39.

———. "Psalm 8 in the Context of the Christian Canon." *Int* 23 (1969):20–31.

Chinitz, J. "Psalm 145: Its Two Faces." *JBQ* 24 (1996):229–32.

Clifford, Richard J. *The Cosmic Mountain in Canaan and the Old Testament.* HSM 4 Cambridge: Harvard University Press, 1972. Pp. 142–44. (Ps. 48).

———. "Psalm 89: A Lament Over the Davidic Ruler's Continued Failure." *HTR* 73 (1980):35–47.

———. "Style and Purpose in Psalm 105." *Bib* 60 (1979):420–27.

———. "What Does the Psalmist Ask for in Psalm 39:5 and 90:12?" *JBL* 119 (2000):59–66.

Clines, D. J. A. "The Evidence for an Autumnal Year in Pre-Exilic Israel Reconsidered." *JBL* 93(1974):22–40.

Coetzee, J. H. "The Functioning of Elements in Tension in Psalm 44." *Theologica Evangelica* 21 (1988):2–5.

Cogan, M. "A Technical Term for Exposure." *JNES* 27 (1968):133–35. (Ps. 71)

Cohen, M. "'AŠŠŪRÊNÛ 'ATTÁ SEBĀBÛNÎ (Q. SEBABÛNÛ) (PSAUME XVII IIA)." *VT* 41 (1991):137–44. (Ps. 17)

Cole, Robert. "An Integrated Reading of Psalms 1 and 2." *JSOT* 98 (2002):75–88.

Condon, K. "The Biblical Doctrine of Original Sin." *ITQ* 34 (1967):20–36.

Cooke, Gerald. "The Israelite King as Son of God." *ZAW* 73 (1960):202–25. (Ps. 2)

Coppens, J. "Les paralleles du Psautier avec les textes de Ras Shamra." *Le Museon* 59 (1946):113–42.

―――. "Les Psaumes 6 et 41 dependent-ils au livre de Jeremie." *HUCA* 32 (1961):217–226.

Costacurta, B. "L'aggressione contri Dio: Studio del Salmo 83." *Bib* 64 (1983):518–41.

Craigie, P. C. "The Comparison of Hebrew Poetry: Psalm 104 in the Light of Egyptian and Ugaritic Poetry." *Sem* 4 (1974):10–21.

―――. "Parallel Word Pairs in Ugaritic Poetry: A Critical Appraisal of Their Relevance for Psalm 29." *UF* 11 (1979):135–40.

―――. "Psalm xxix in the Hebrew Poetic Tradition." *VT* 22 (1972):143–54.

Creach, Jerome F. D. "Like a Tree Planted by the Temple Stream: The Portrait of the Righteous in Psalm 1:3." *CBQ* 61 (1999):34–46.

―――. "Psalm 121." *Int* 50 (1996):47–51.

Crenshaw, James L. "Knowing Whose You Are: Psalm 24." In *The Psalms: An Introduction*. Grand Rapids: Eerdmans, 2001. Pp. 155–67.

―――. "5. Standing Near the Flame: Psalm 73." In *A Whirlpool of Torment*. Philadelphia: Fortress Press, 1984.

Cross, F. M. Jr. "Notes on a Canaanite Psalm in the Old Testament." *BASOR* 117 (1949):19–21. (Ps. 29)

―――. "Notes on Psalm 93: A Fragment of a Liturgical Psalm." In *A God So Near: Essays on Old Testament Theology in*

Honor of Patrick D. Miller. Ed. by Brent A. Strawn and Nancy R. Bowen. Winona Lake, IN: Eisenbrauns, 2003. Pp. 73–78.

_____, and Freedman, D. N. "A Royal Song of Thanksgiving: II Samuel 22 = Psalm 18." *JBL* 72 (1953):15–34.

Crow, L. D. "The Rhetoric of Psalm 44." *ZAW* 104 (1992):384–401.

Culley, R. C. "Psalm 102, A Complaint with a Difference." *Semeia* 62 (1993):19–35.

Dahood, M. "The Four Cardinal Points in Psalm 75, 7 and Joel 2, 20." *Bib* 52 (1971):357.

_____. "The Language and Date of Psalm 48." *CBQ* 16 (1954):15–19.

_____. "Philological Observations on Five Biblical Texts." *Bib* 63 (1982):390–94. (Ps. 55)

_____. "A Sea of Troubles: Notes on Psalms 55:3–4 and 140:10–11." *CBQ* 41 (1979):504–7.

Dalglish, Edward R. *Psalm Fifty-One in the Light of Ancient Near Eastern Patternism.* Leiden: E. J. Brill, 1962.

Darby, J. H. "Psalm 44 [45]: The King and His Bride." *Irish Ecclesiastical Record* 91 (1959):249–55.

Davidson, R. "Some Aspects of the Theological Significance of Doubt in the Old Testament." *ASTI* 17 (1970):44–46. (Ps. 73)

Davies, G. Henton. "The Ark in the Psalms." *ASTI* 14 (1966–67):30–47.

_____. "Psalm 95." *ZAW* 85 (1973):183–198

Day, John N. *Crying for Justice, What the Psalms Teach Us about Mercy and Vengeance in an Age of Terrorism.* Grand Rapids: Kregel, 2005. Pp. 62–72. (Ps. 137)

_____. "Echoes of Baal's Seven Thunders and Lightnings in Psalm xxix." *VT* 29 (1979):143–51.

DeBoer, P. A. H. "Psalm cxxxi 2." *VT* 16 (1966):287–92.

_____. "Vive le roi!" *VT* 5 (1955):225–31.

Denton, Robert C. "An Exposition of an Old Testament Passage." *JBR* 15 (1947):158–61. (Ps. 130)

DePinto, B. "The Torah and the Psalms." *JBL* 86 (1967):154–74.

Dion, P. E. "YHWH as Storm-god and Sun-god: The Double Legacy of Egypt and Canaan as Reflected in Psalm 104." *ZAW* 103 (1991):43–71.

_____. "Psalm 103: A Meditation on the Ways of the LORD." *Eglise et théologie* 21 (1990):13–31.

Driver, G. R. "Reflections on Recent Articles. 2. Hebr. *môqēš* 'Striker.'" *JBL* 73 (1954):131–6.
———. "Studies in the Vocabulary of the Old Testament. I." *JTS* 31 (1930):274–84. (Ps. 129)
———. "Studies in the Vocabulary of the Old Testament. V." *JTS* 34 (1933):41–4. (Ps. 58)
———. "Thou Tellest My Wanderings." *JTS* 21 (1970):402–3.
———. "Will he not . . .?" *JSS* 13 (1968):37. (Ps. 121)
Durham, J. "The King as 'Messiah' in the Psalms." *Review and Expositor* 81 (1984):425–36.
Durlesser, James R. "A Rhetorical Critical Study of Psalms 19, 42, and 43." *Studia Biblica et Theologica* 10 (1980):179–97.
Eaton, John H. "Hard Sayings: Psalm 4:6–7." *Theology* 67 (1964):355–7.
———. "Music's Place in Worship." *OTS* 23 (1984):85–107. (Ps. 150)
———. "Some Questions of Philology and Exegesis in the Psalms." *JTS* 19 (1968):603–9. (Pss. 18, 93)
Eddleman, H. Leo. "Word Pictures of the Word: An Exposition of Psalm 19." *Review and Expositor* 49 (1952):413–24.
Eitan, I. "An Identification of *tiškaḥ yᵉmīnī*," Ps. 137:5." *JBL* 47 (1928):193–95.
Eissfeldt, O. "Psalm 76." *ThLZ* (1957): pp. 801–8.
Emerton, John A. "A Consideration of Some Alleged Meanings of ידע in Hebrew," *JSS* 15 (1970):145–80.
———. "The Etymology of *Hištaḥăwāh*." *OTS* 20 (1977):41–55.
———. "A Further Consideration of D. W. Thomas's Theories about *yada'*," *VT* 41 (1991):145–63.
———. "How Does the LORD Regard the Deaths of His Saints in Psalm cxvi 15?" *JTS* 34 (1983):146–156.
———. "The Interpretation of Psalm lxxxii in John x." *JTS* 11 (1960):329–34.
———. "The Meaning of *šēnā'* in Ps cxxvii 2." *VT* 24 (1974):15–31.
———. "Melchizedek and the Gods: Fresh Evidence for the Jewish Background of John 10:34–36." *JTS* 17 (1966):399ff.
———. "The 'Mountain of God' in Psalm 68:16." In *History and Traditions in Early Israel: Studies Presented to Eduard*

Nielsen. Ed. by A Lemaire and B. Otzen. *VT* Supplement 50 (1993):24–37.

_____. "A Neglected Solution of a Problem in Psalm lxxvi 11." *VT* 24 (1974):136–46.

_____. "Notes on Three Passages in Psalms Book III." *JTS* 14 (1963):374–381. (Ps. 74)

_____. "Notes on Three Passages in Psalms Book III." *JTS* 14 (1963):374–81.

_____. "Sheol and the Sons of Belial." *VT* 37 (1987): 214–18.

_____. "Spring and Torrent in Psalm 74:15." *VT* Supplement 15 (1966):122–33.

_____. "The Syntactical Problem of Psalm XLV, 7." *JSS* 13 (1968):58–63.

_____. "The Text of Psalm lxxvii 11." *VT* 44 (1994): 183–94

_____. "The Translation of Psalm 74:4." *JTS* 27 (1976):391–2.

_____. "The Translation of the Verbs in the Imperfect in Psalm ii. 9." *JTS* 29 (1978):499–503.

Estes, Daniel J. "Like Arrows in the Hand of a Warrior." *VT* 41 (1991):304–11. (Ps. 127)

Feinberg, C. L. "Old One Hundredth Psalm." *BibSac* 104 (1947):43–66.

_____. "Parallels to the Psalms in Near Eastern Literature." *BibSac* 104 (1947):290–97.

Fensham, F. C. "Psalm 68:23 in the Light of Recently Discovered Ugaritic Tablets." *JNES* 19 (1960):292.

_____. "Neh. 9 and Pss. 105, 106, 135, and 136: Post-Exilic Historical Traditions in Poetic Form." *JNSL* 9 (1981):35–51.

_____. "Ugaritic and the Translator of the Old Testament." *Bible Translator* 18 (1967):71–74.

_____. "Widow, Orphan, and the Poor in Ancient Near Eastern Legal and Wisdom Literature." *JNES* 21 (1962):129–139.

Finesinger, S. B. "Musical Instruments in the Old Testament." *HUCA* 3 (1926):21–76.

_____. "The Shofar." *HUCA* 8–9 (1931–32):193–228.

Finkelstein, L. "The Origin of the Hallel (Pss. 113–118)." *HUCA* 23 (1950):319–37.

Fox, Michael. "*ṬOB* as Covenant Terminology." *BASOR* 209 (1973):41–2. (Ps. 23)

Freedman, David Noel. "Acrostic Psalms in the Hebrew Bible: Alphabetic and Otherwise." *CBQ* 47 (1985):624–42. (Ps. 94)

_____. "Psalm 113 and the Song of Hannah." In *Pottery, Poetry, an Prophecies, Studies in Early Hebrew Poetry*. Winona Lake, IN: Eisenbrauns, 1980. Pp. 243–61.

_____. *Psalm 119, The Exaltation of Torah*. Winona Lake, IN: Eisenbrauns, 1999.

_____. "The Structure of Psalm 137." In *Near Eastern Studies*. FS for W. F. Albright. Ed. by H. Goedicke. Baltimore: Johns Hopkins, 1971. Pp. 187–205.

_____. "Who Asks (or Tells) God to Repent?" *Bible Review* 1 (1985):56–9.

Fretheim, T. E. "Psalm 132: A Form Critical Study." *JBL* 86 (1967):289–300.

Frost, S. B. "The Christian Interpretation of the Psalms." *CJT* 5 (1959):25–34.

_____. "Psalm 118: An Exposition." *CJT* 7 (1961):155–66.

_____. "Psalm 22: An Exposition." *CJT* 8 (1962):102–15.

Gaiser, Frederick J. "'It Shall Not Reach You': Talisman or Vocation? Reading Psalm 91 in Time of War." *WW* 25 (2005):191–202.

Gaster, Th. H. "Psalm 29." *JQR* 37 (1946,7):55–65.

_____. "Psalm 45." *JBL* 74 (1955):239–51.

_____. "Short Notes." *VT* 4 (1954):73–79 (Ps. 41)

Geller, S. A. "The Language of Imagery in Psalm 114." FS for W. L. Moran. Ed. by T. Abusch, et al. HSS 37. Atlanta: Scholars Press, 1990. Pp. 179–94.

Gelston, A. "A Note on *YHWH MLK*." *VT* 16 (1966):507–12.

_____. "A Sidelight on the 'Son of Man'." *SJT* 22 (1969):189–96.

Gemser, B. "The *rîb*–or Controversy-Pattern in Hebrew Mentality." *VT* Supplement 3 (1955):122–25. (Ps. 95)

Gertner, M. "Terms of Scriptural Interpretation: A Study in Hebrew Semantics." *BSOAS* 25 (1962):1–27.

Girard, Marc. "The Literary Structure of Psalm 95." *Theology Digest* 30 (1982):55–58.

Glass, Jonathan T. "Some Observations on Psalm 19." In *The Listening Heart*, FS for Roland E. Murphy. Ed. by Kenneth G. Hoglund, et al. *JSOT* Supplement 58 (1987):147–59.

Glenn, Donald R. "Psalm 8 and Hebrews 2: A Case Study in Biblical Hermeneutics and Biblical Theology." In *Walvoord: A Tribute.* Ed. by Donald K. Campbell. Chicago: Moody Press, 1982. Pp. 39–52.

Goldingay, J. "Repetition and Variations in the Psalms." *JQR* 68 (1977):148–9. (Ps. 59)

Goodwin, E. W. "A Rare Spelling, or a Rare Root in Ps. lxviii 10?" *VT* 14 (1964):490–91.

Gordis, Robert. "Psalm 9–10—A Textual and Exegetical Study." *JQR* 48 (1957):104–22.

Gordon, Cyrus H. "The Wine-Dark Sea." *JNES* 37 (1978):51–2. (Ps. 48)

Gordon, Robert P. "How Did Psalm 48 Happen?" In *Holy Land, Holy City.* Carlisle, UK: Paternoster, 2004. Pp. 35–45.

Goulder, Michael. "Psalm 8 and the Son of Man." *NTS* 48 (2002):18–29.

Graber, P. L. "The Structural Meaning of Psalm 113." *Occasional Papers in Translation and Text Linguistics* 4 (1990):340–52.

Gray, John. "Canaanite Kingship in Theory and Practice." *VT* 2 (1952):193–220.

_____. "A Cantata of the Autumn Festival: Psalm LXVIII." *JSS* 22 (1977):2–26.

_____. "The Kingship of God in the Prophets and the Psalms." *VT* 11 (1961):1–29

Greenberg, Moshe, "Two New Hunting Terms in Psalm 140:12." *HAR* 1 (1977):149–53.

Grelot, P. "*HOFŠĪ* [Ps lxxxviii 6]." *VT* 14 (1964):256–63.

Gruenthaner, M. "The Future Life in the Psalms." *CBQ* 2 (1940):57–63

Guillaume, A. "The Meaning of *tôlēl* in Psalm 137:3." *JBL* 75 (1956):143–4.

_____. "A Note on Psalm 109:10." *JTS* 14 (1963):92–93.

Gunnel, Andre. "'Walk,' 'Stand,' and 'Sit' in Psalm i 1–2." *VT* 32 (1982):327.

Habel, Norman C. "'Yahweh, Maker of Heaven and Earth': A Study in Tradition Criticism." *JBL* 91 (1972):321–37. (Ps. 136)

Haran, M. "The Ark and the Cherubim: Their Symbolic Significance in Biblical Ritual." *IEJ* 9 (1959):30–38; 89–94.

Hardy, E. R. "The Date of Psalm 110." *JBL* 64 (1945):385–90.
Harmon, Allen M. "Aspects of Paul's Use of the Psalms." *WJT* 32 (1969):1–23.
_____. "The Setting and Interpretation of Psalm 126." *RTR* 44 (1985):74–80.
Harrelson, Walter. "On God's Care for the Earth: Psalm 104." *CTM* 2 (1975):19–22.
_____. "Psalm 19." In *Worship and the Hebrew Bible,* FS for John T. Willis. Ed. by M. Patrick Graham, et al. *JSOT* Supplement 284 (Sheffield: *JSOT*, 1999):142–7.
Harris, Murray J. "The Translation of Elohim in Psalm 45:7–8." *TynB* 35 (1984):65–89.
Hay, David M. *Glory at the Right Hand: Psalm 110 in Early Christianity.* Nashville: Abingdon, 1973.
Hays, R. B. "Psalm 143 and the Logic of Romans 3." *JBL* 99 (1980):107–19.
Heidel, Alexander. *The Gilgamesh Epic and Old Testament Parallels.* Chicago: University of Chicago Press, 1946. Chapter 3: "Death and Afterlife," pp. 137–223. (Ps. 6)
Heinemann, H. "The Date of Psalm 80." *JQR* 40 (1949/50):297–302.
Hilber, John W. *Cultic Prophecy in the Psalms.* Berlin: Walter de Gruyter, 2005. (Ps. 60)
Hill, David. "'Son of Man' in Psalm 80 v. 17." *NovT* 15 (1973):261–69.
Hillers, D. R. "Ritual Procession of the Ark and Psalm 132." *CBQ* 30 (1968):48–55.
Holman, J. C. M. "Analysis of the Text of Psalm 139." *BZ* 14 (1970):37–71.
_____. "The Structure of Psalm cxxxix." *VT* 21 (1971):298–310.
Holm-Nielsen, S. "The Exodus Tradition in Psalm 105." *ASTI* 11 (1978):22–30.
Honeyman, A. M. "The Evidence for Regnal Names Among the Hebrews." *JBL* 67 (1948):13–25.
Hooke, S. H., editor. *Myth and Ritual. Essays on the Myth and Ritual of the Hebrews in Relation to the Cultic Pattern of the ANE.* Oxford: Clarendon Press, 1933.
Houk, Cornelius B. "Psalm 132, Literary Integrity and Syllable-Word Structures." *JSOT* 6 (1978):41–48.

Hubbard, R. L., Jr. *Dynamics and Legal Language in Conflict Psalms.* Dissertation, Claremont Graduate School, 1980. Ann Arbor: UMI, 1984.
Hubbard, R. L. "Dynamistic and Legal Processes in Psalm 7." *ZAW* 94 (1982):268–79.
Huffmon, Herbert B. "The Treaty Background of Hebrew *YADA'*." *BASOR* 181 (1961):31–3. (Ps. 37)
Human, D. J. "Psalm 44: 'Why Do You Hide Your Face, O God?'" *Skriff en kerk* 19 1998):566–83.
Hurowitz, Victor A. "Additional Elements of Alphabetical Thinking in Psalm xxxiv." *VT* 52 (2002):326–33.
Hutton, R. R. "Cush the Benjaminite and Psalm Midrash." *HAR* 10 (1986):123–37.
Huweiler, Elizabeth F. "Patterns and Problems of Psalm 132." In *The Listening Heart, Festschrift* for R. E. Murphy. *JSOT* Supplement 8. Ed. by K. G. Hoglund, et al. Sheffield: Sheffield Academic Press, 1987. Pp. 199–215.
Hvidberg, F. F. *Weeping and Laughing in the Old Testament.* Leiden: E. J. Brill, 1962. (Ps. 126)
Iwry, A. "Notes on Psalm 68." *JBL* 71 (1942):161–65.
Janecko, B. "Ecology, Nature, Psalms." In *The Psalms and Other Studies in the Old Testament."* FS for J. I. Hunt. Edited by J. C. Knight and I. A. Sinclair. Nashotah, WI: Nashotah House Seminary, 1990. Pp. 96–108.
Janzen, J. G. "Another Look at Psalm xii 6." *VT* 54 (2004):157–64.
Janzen, Waldemar. "'Ašrê' in the Old Testament." *HTR* 58 (1965):215–226.
Jarick, J. "The Four Corners of Psalm 107." *CBQ* 59 (1997): 270–87.
Jefferson, Helen G. "The Date of Psalm lxvii." *VT* 12 (1962):201–5.
_____. "Psalm lxxvii." *VT* 13 (1963):87–91.
_____. "Psalm 93." *JBL* 71 (1952):155–160.
_____. "Is Psalm 110 Canaanite?" *JBL* 73 (1954):152–56.
Jenson, R. W. "Psalm 32." *Int* 32 (1979):172–76.
Jinkins, Michael. "The Virtues of the Righteous in Psalm 37." In *Psalms and Practice.* Ed. by S. B. Reid. Collegeville, MN: Liturgical Press, 2001. Pp. 154–201.
Joffe, Laura. "The Elohistic Psalter." *SJOT* 15 (2001):142–66. (Ps. 42)

Johnson, A. R. "The Psalms." In *The Old Testament and Modern Study.* Ed. by H. H. Rowley. Oxford: Clarendon Press, 1951.

Johnston, W. "YD' II, 'Be Humbled, Humiliated'?" *VT* 41 (1991):49–62145–63.

Jones, G. H. "The Decree of Yahweh."*VT* 15 (1965):335–44. (Ps. 2)

Jones, I. H. "Musical Instruments in the Bible, Part I." *BT* 37 (1986):101–16.

Kaiser, Walter C. "The Promise Theme and the Theology of Rest." *BibSac* 130 (1973):135–150. (Ps. 95)

_____. "The Promise to David in Psalm 16." *JETS* 23 (1980):219–29.

Kapelrud, A. S. "Scandinavian Research in the Psalms after Mowinckel." *ASTI* 4 (1965):148–162.

Keel, Othmar. "Kultische Brüderlichkeit-Psalm 133.*" Freiburger Zeitschrift für Theologie und Philosophie* 23 (1976):68–80.

Kelly, S. L. "The Zion-Victory Songs: Psalms 46, 48, and 76. Vanderbilt Dissertation, 1968.

Kenik, Helen Ann. "Code of Conduct for a King," *JBL* 95(1976):391–403. (Ps. 101)

Kilgallen, J. J. "The Use of Psalm 16:8–11 in Peter's Pentecost Speech." *ExT* 113 (2001):47–50.

Kim, Jinkyu. "The Strategic Arrangement of Royal Psalms in Books IV-V." *WTJ* 70 (2008):143–57.

Kimelman, R. "Psalm 145: Theme, Structure and Impact." *JBL* 113 (1994):37–58.

Kissane, E. J. "The Interpretation of Psalm 110."*Irish Theological Quarterly* 21 (1954):103–14.

Kleber, A. "Ps. 2:9 in the Light of an Ancient Oriental Ceremony." *CBQ* 5 (1943):63–67.

Knight, Leonard C. "I Will Show Him My Salvation." *ResQ* 43 (2001):280–92. (Ps.91)

Kselman, John S. "A Note on Psalm 4:5." *Bib* 68 (1987):103–5.

_____. "A Note on Psalm 51:6." *CBQ* 39 (1977):251–53.

_____. "A Note on Psalm 85:9–10." *CBQ* 46 (1984):23–27.

_____. "Psalm 3: A Structural and Literary Study." *CBQ* 49 (1987):572- 580.

_____. "Psalm 72: Some Observations on Structure." *BASOR* 220 (1975):77–81.

Selected Bibliography for the Exposition of the Psalms

_____. "Psalm 77 and the Book of Exodus." *JANES* 15 (1963):51–58.
_____. "Psalm 101." *JSOT* 33 (1985):45–62.
_____. "Psalm 146 in Context." *CBQ* 50 (1988):586–99.
Kuntz, J. Kenneth. "The Canonical Wisdom Psalms of Ancient Israel—Their Rhetorical, Thematic, and Formal Dimensions." In *Rhetorical Criticism*. Ed. by Jared J. Jackson and Martin Kessler. Pittsburgh: Pickwick Press, 1974. Pp. 186–222.
_____. "Psalm 18: A Rhetorical-Critical Analysis." *JSOT* 26 (1983):3–31.
_____. "The Retribution Motif in Psalmic Wisdom," *ZAW* 89 (1977):223–33. (Ps. 112)
Kwakkel, G. "'According to My Righteousness': Upright Behavior as Grounds for Deliverance in Psalms 7, 17, 18, 26, and 44." *OTS* 46. Leiden: E. J. Brill, 2002.
Laato, Antti, "Psalm 132 and the Development of the Jerusalemite/Israelite Royal Ideology." *CBQ* 54 (1992):49–66.
_____. "Psalm 132." *CBQ* 61 (1999):24–33.
Lakatos, E. "Psalm 44." *RB* 76 (1955):40–42.
Laney, J. Carl, Jr. "A Fresh Look at the Imprecatory Psalms." *BibSac* 138 (1981):35–45.
Lange, H. D. "The Relation between Psalm and the Passion Narrative." *CTM* 43 (1972):610–21.
Levenson, J. D. "A Technical Meaning for N'M in the Hebrew Bible." *VT* 35 (1985):61–7.
Leveen, Jacob. "The Textual Problems of Psalm vii." *VT* 16 (1966):439–45.
_____. "The Textual Problems of Psalm xvii." *VT* 11 (1961):48–84.
Lewis, J. O. "An Asseverative לא in Psalm 100:3?" *JBL* 86 (1967):216.
Liebreich, Leon J. "Psalms 34 and 145 in the Light of their Key Words." *HUCA* 27 (1956):181–92.
_____. "The Songs of Ascents and the Priestly Blessing." *JBL* 74 (1955):33–36.
Limberg, J. "The Root *ryb* and the Prophetic Lawsuit Speeches." *JBL* 88 (1969):291–304.
Lindars, B. "The Structure of Psalm cxlv." *VT* 29 (1979):23–30.

Lipinski, E. "Judges 5, 4–5 et Psaume 68, 8–11." *Bib* 48 (1967):185–206.

———. *"Yahweh malak." Bib* 44 (1963):405–60.

Loader, J. A. "A Structural Analysis of Psalms 113." *Die Ou Testamentiese Werkgemeenskap Suid-Afrika* 19 (1977):64–68.

Logan, Norman A. "The Old Testament and a Future Life." *SJT* 6 (1953):165–172. (Ps. 16)

Longman, T., III. "Psalm 98: A Divine Victory Song." *JETS* 27 (1984):267–74.

Loewenstamm, S. E. *"Balloti bešaman ra'anān." UF* 10 (1978):211–13. (Ps. 92)

———. "The LORD Is My Strength and My Glory." *VT* 19 (1969):464–70. (Ps. 118)

———. "The Number of Plagues in Psalm 105." *Bib* 52 (1971):34–38.

Luke, K. "The Setting of Psalm 115." *ITQ* 34 (1967):347–57.

———. "Under the Shadow of the Almighty." *ITQ* 3 (1972):187–93. (Ps. 91)

Lundbom, Jack R. "Psalm 23: Song of Passage." *Int* 40 (1986):6–16.

Luria, B. Z. "Psalms from Ephraim." *Beth Mikra* 23 (1978):151–60. (Ps. 81).

Macintosh, A. A. "A Consideration of Hebrew *gʻr*." *VT* 19 (1969):471–79.

———. "A Consideration of the Problems Presented by Psalm II. 11, 12." *JTS* 27 (1976):1–14.

———. "A Consideration of Psalm vii. 12f." *JTS* 33 (1982):481–90.

———. "Psalms xci 4 and the Root סהר." *VT* 23 (1973):56–62.

Magne, J. "Répétitions de mots et exégèse dans quelques Psaumes et la Pater." *Bib* 9 (1958):177-97.

Magonet, Jonathan. "Some Concentric Structures in Psalms." *HeyJ* 23 (1982):365–69.

Malchow, B. V. "God or King in Psalm 146." *BiTod* 89 (1977):1166–70.

March, W. E. "A Note on the Text of Psalm xii 9." *VT* 21 (1971):610–12.

Marrs, Rick R. "A Cry from the Depths." *ZAW* 100 (1988):81–90.

———. "Psalm 122: 3, 4." *Bib* 68 (1987):106–9.

Martin, Chalmers. "The Imprecations in the Psalms." *PTR* 1 (1903):537–53.
Massouh, Samir. "Psalm 95." *Trinity Journal* 4 (1983):84–88.
Mathys, H. P. "Psalm cl." *VT* 50 (2000):328–44.
Mays, James L. "Worship, World, and Power: An Interpretation of Psalm 100." *Int* 23 (1969):315–30.
_____. "The Place of the Torah Psalms in the Psalter." *JBL* 106 (1987):3–12.
_____. "Psalm 13." *Int* 34 (1980):279–83.
_____. "There the Blessing: An Exposition of Psalm 133." In *A God So Near: Essays on Old Testament Theology in Honor of Patrick D. Miller.* Ed. by Brent A. Strawn and Nancy R. Bowen. Winona Lake, IN: Eisenbrauns, 2003. Pp. 79–90.
McCarthy, D. J. "'Creation' Motifs in Ancient Hebrew Poetry." *CBQ* 29 (1967):395–406.
McKay, John W. "My Glory–A Mantle of Praise." *SJT* 31 (1978):167–72 (Pss. 7, 16)
_____. "Psalms of Vigil." *ZAW* 91 (1979):229–47. (Pss. 5, 63)
McKeating, H. "Divine Forgiveness in the Psalms." *SJT* 18 (1965):69–83. (Ps. 130, 143)
McKenzie, J. L. "Royal Messianism." *CBQ* 19 (1957):25–52.
Mejia, J. "Some Observations on Psalm 107." *BTB* 5 (1975):56–66.
Menken, M. J. J. "The Translation of Psalm 41:10 and John 13:18." *JSNT* 40 (1990):61–79.
Merrill, A. L. "Psalm xxiii and the Jerusalem Tradition." *VT* 15 (1965):354–60.
Meye, R. "Psalm 107 as Horizon for Interpreting the Miracle Stories of Mark 4:35–8:26." In *Unity and Diversity in New Testament Theology.* FS for G. E. Ladd. Ed. by R. Guelich. Grand Rapids: Eerdmans, 1978. Pp. 1–13.
Milgrom, Jacob. "The Cultic שגגה and Its Influence in Psalms and Job." *JQR* 58 (1967–68):115–25. (Ps. 19)
Miller, Patrick D. "Poetic Ambiguity and Balance in Psalm xv." *VT* 29 (1979):416–24.
_____. "Psalm 127– The House that Yahweh Builds." *JSOT* 22 (1982):119–32.
_____. "Psalm 136:1–9, 23–26." *Int* 49 (1995):390–93.
_____. "The Ruler in Zion and the Hope of the Poor: Psalms 9–10 in the Context of the Psalter." In *David and Zion,*

Biblical Studies in Honor of J. J. M. Roberts. Ed. by B. F. Batto and K. L. Roberts. Winona Lake: Eisenbrauns, 2004. Pp. 187–98.
_____. "Trouble and Woe: Interpreting the Biblical Laments." *Int* 37 (1983):32–45.
_____. "*Yāpîaḥ* in Psalm xii 6." *VT* 29 (1979):495–501.
_____. "When the Gods Meet: Psalm 82 and the Issue of Justice." *Journal for Preachers* 9 (1986):2–5.
Mitchell, Christopher Wright. *The Meaning of BRK, "To Bless," in the Old Testament.* SBL Dissertation Series 95. Atlanta: Scholars Press, 1987.
Mitchell, T. C. "The Old Testament Usage of *Nešāmâ*." *VT* 11 (1961):177–87.
Morag, S. "Light is Sown (Ps. 97)." *Tarbiz* 33 (1963):140–48.
Moran, W. L. "A Note on the Treaty Terminology of the Sefire Stela." *JNES* 22 (1963):173–76. (Ps. 73)
Moreton, M. J. "The Sacrifice of Praise." *Church Quarterly Review* 165 (1964):481–494.
Morgenstern, Julian. "The Cultic Setting of the 'Enthronement Psalms'." *HUCA* 35 (1964):1–42. (Ps. 47)
_____. "'The Gates of Righteousness." *HUCA* 6 (1929):1–37. (Pss. 24, 118)
_____. "The Mythical Background of Psalm 82." *HUCA* 14 (1939):29–126.
_____. "Psalm 48." *HUCA* 16 (1941):1–95.
_____. "Psalm 8 and 19A." *HUCA* 19 (1945–46):491–523.
_____. "Psalm 11." *JBL* 69 (1950):221–31.
_____. "Psalm 23." *JBL* 65 (1946):13–24.
_____. "Psalm 121." *JBL* 58 (1939):311–23.
_____. "The Cultic Setting of the Enthronement Psalms." *HUCA* 35 (1964):1–42.
Mosca, Paul G. "Psalm 26: Poetic Structure and the Form-Critical Task.' *CBQ* 47 (1985):21–37.
Mowinckel, Sigmund. "Psalms and Wisdom." *VT* Supplement 3 (1955):204–24.
_____. "Traditionalism and Personality in the Psalms." *HUCA* 22 (1950):205–31.
_____. "The Verb *śiᵃḥ* and the Nouns *śiᵃḥ, siḥa*." *ST* 15 (1961):1–10.

Muilenberg, J. "Psalm 47." *JBL* 63 (1944):235–56.
Mulder, Jan S. *Studies on Psalm 45.* Nijmegen, The Netherlands, 1972.
Mullen, E. T., Jr. *The Assembly of the Gods: The Divine Council in Canaanite and Early Hebrew Literature,* HSM 24. Chico, CA: Scholars Press, 1980. Pp. 226–44. (Ps. 82)
Murtonen, A. "The Use and meaning of the Words *Lᵉbārēk* and *Bᵉrākāh* in the Old Testament." *VT* 9 (1959):166–68. (Ps. 5)
Nel, P. J. "Psalm 110 and the Melchizedek Tradition." *JNSL* 22 (1996):1–14.
Neuberg, Frank J. "An Unrecognized Meaning of Hebrew *dôr.*" *JNES* 9 (1950):215–17.
Neusner, Jacob. "The Eighty-Ninth Psalm: Paradigm of Israel's Faith." *Judaism* 8 (1959):226–33.
Neyrey, J. H. "I Said: 'You Are Gods': Ps. 82:6 and John 10." *JBL* 108 (1989):647–63.
Niehaus, Jeffrey. "The Use of *lûlê* in Psalm 27." *JBL* 98 (1979):88, 9.
Norin, S. "Zusammenhang und Datierung." *ASTI* 11 (1978):90–95. (133)
North, C. R. "אעלזה אחלקה שכם, (Psa lx 8 // Ps cviii 8)." *VT* 17 (1967):242, 3. (Ps. 60)
O'Callaghan, R. T. "Echoes of Canaanite Literature in the Psalms." *VT* 4 (1954):164–176.
Ogden, Graham S. "Joel 4 and Prophetic Responses to National Laments." *JSOT* 26 1983):97–106.
————. "Prophetic Oracles Against Foreign Nations and the Psalms of Communal Lament: The Relationship of Psalm 137 to Jeremiah 49:7–22 and Obadiah," *JSOT* 24 (1982):58–97.
————. "Psalm 60, Irs Rhetoric, Form, and Function." *JSOT* 31 (1985):83–94. (Pss. 60,137)
Ollenburger, B. C. *Zion the City of the Great King.* JSOT Supplement 41. Sheffield: *JSOT*, 1987. Pp. 25–33. (Ps. 93)
Olofsson, S. "The Crux Interpretum in Ps 2,12." *SJOT* 9 (1995):185–99.
Oosterhoff, B. J. "Het Loven van God in Psalm 118." In *Leven en Geloven.* Ed. by M. H. Van Es, et al. Amsterdam: Ton Bolland, 1975. Pp. 175–90.

Owen, John. "A practical Exposition upon Psalm cxxx." In *The Works of John Owen*. Edinburgh: T. & T. Clark, 1862 reprint. 6:325–648.
Palmer, M. "The Cardinal Points in Psalm 48." *Bib* 46 (1965):357–8.
Pardee, D. "*YPH* 'Witness' in Hebrew and Ugaritic." *VT* 28 (1979):204–13.
Parker, N. H. "Psalm 103: God Is Love. He Will Have Mercy and Abundantly Pardon." *CJT* 1 (1955):191–196.
Parunak, H. Van Dyke. "A Semantic Survey of NḤM." *Bib* 6 (1975):48–87.
Patterson, Richard D. "Psalm 22." *JETS* 47 (2004):213–33.
Paul, Shalom M. "Psalm xxvii 10 and the Babylonian Theodicy." *VT* 32 (1982):489–92.
_____. "Psalm 72:5–A Traditional Blessing for the Long Life of the King." *JNES* 31 (1972):351–54.
Perdue, Leo G. "The Riddles of Psalm 49." *JBL* 93 (1974):533–42.
Pettey, Richard J. "Psalm 130." In *The Psalter and Other Studies in the Old Testament. FS* for Joseph I. Hunt. Ed. by Jack C. Knight and Lawrence A Sinclair. Nashotah, WI: Nashotah House, 1990. Pp. 45–53.
Pinto, B. De. "The Torah and the Psalms." *JBL* 86 (1967):154–74.
Pitkin, Barbara. "Psalm 8:1–2." *Int* 55 (2001):177–80.
Pleins, T. D. "Death and Endurance: Reassessing the Literary Structure and Theology of Psalm 49." *JSOT* 69 (1996):19–27.
Ploeg, J. v. d. "Psalm XIX and Some of Its Problems." *Jaarsbericht v. h. Vooraziatisch-Egyptisch Genootschop 'Ex Oriente Lux'* 17 (1963):192–201.
Porter, J. R. "The Interpretation of 2 Samuel vi and Psalm cxxxii." *JTS* 5 (1954):161–73.
Porúbčan, S. "Psalm cxxx 5–6." *VT* 9 (1959):322–23.
Prasad, J. "Psalm 47: A Case Study in Poetic Techniques in the Psalms." *Bible Bhashyam* 29 (2003):5–25.
Prinsloo, W. S. "Psalm 149: Praise Yahweh with Tambourine and Two-Edged Sword." *ZAW* 109 (1997):385–407.
Rabinowitz, L. J. "The Psalms in Jewish Liturgy." *Historia Judaica* 6 (1944):109–122 (*CBQ* 1945, 353).
Reif, S. "Ibn Ezra on Psalm i 1–2." *VT* 34 (1984):232–36.

Reumann, John H. "Psalm 22 at the Cross: Lament and Thanksgiving for Jesus Christ." *Int* 28 (1974):39–58.

Reynolds, Carol Bechtel. "Psalm 125." *Int* 48 (1994):272–75.

Rice, Gene. "The Integrity of the Text of Psalm 139:20b." *CBQ* 46 (1984):28–30.

Ridderbos, H. "Psalm 51:5–6." In *Studia Biblica et Semitica* (1966):299–312.

―――――. "The Psalms: Style, Figures and Structure." *OTS* 13 (1963):43–76. (Pss. 22, 25, 44)

―――――. "The Structure of Psalm 40." *OTS* 14 (1965):296–304.

Ridderbos, J. "Jahwah Malak." *VT* 4 (1954):87–89. (Ps. 93)

Riding, C. B. "Psalm 95:1–7c as a Large Chiasm." *ZAW* 88 (1976):418.

Ringgren, Helmer. "Behold Your King Comes," *VT* 24 (1974):207–11. (Ps. 96)

―――――. "Enthronement Festival or Covenant Renewal?" *Biblical Research* 7 (1962):45–48.

―――――. "Psalm 2 and *Belit's* Oracle for Ashurbanipal." In *The Word of the Lord Shall Go Forth*. FS for David Noel Freedman. Ed. by C. L. Meyers and M. O'Connor. Winona Lake: Eisenbrauns, 1983. Pp. 91–95.

Rios, R. "A Call to Worship (Ps. 94, Vulgate)." *Scripture* 1 (1946):74–77.

―――――. "Thirst for God (Pss. 41, 42, Vulgate)." *Scripture* 2 (1947):34–38.

Roberts, J. J. M. "The Davidic Origin of the Zion Tradition." *JBL* 92 (1973):329–44. (Ps. 48)

―――――. "Of Sages, Prophets, and Time Limits: A Note on Psalm 74:9." *CBQ* 39 (1977):474–81.

―――――. "The Religio-Political Setting of Psalm 47." *BASOR* 220 (1975):129–32.

―――――. "The Young Lions of Psalm 34,11." *Bib* 54 (1973):165–7.

Robinson, A. "A Possible Solution of Psalm 74:5." *ZAW* 89 (1977):120, 21.

Robinson, A. "Zion and Saphon in Psalm xlviii 3." *VT* 24 (1974):118–23.

Robinson, B. P. "Form and Meaning in Psalm 131." *Bib* 79 (1998):180–97.

Robinson, T. H. "Notes on Psalm xxxiv. 21." *ExT* 52 (1940, 41):117.

Rosenbaum, Stanley N. "New Evidence for Reading *ge'im* in Place of *goyim* in Psalms 9 and 10." *HUCA* 45 (1975):65–70.
Rosenberg, R. A. "Yahweh Becomes King." *JBL* 85 (1966):297–307.
Ross, Allen P. "Anything In My Name." *BibV* 4 (1970):95–103. (Ps. 20)
_____. "Name." In *NIDOTTE*. Ed. by W. VanGemeren. Grand Rapids: Zondervan. (Ps. 20)
_____. "The 'Thou' Sections of Laments, The Bold and Earnest Prayers of the Psalmists." In *The Psalms, Language for All Seasons of the Soul*. Ed. by Andrew J. Schmutzer and David M. Howard, Jr. Chicago: Moody Press, 2013. Pp. 135–150.
Ross, James P. "Psalm 73." In *Israelite Wisdom*. Ed. by J. G. Gammie, et al. Missoula: Scholars Press, 1978. Pp. 161–175.
_____. "Yahweh Ṣebā'ôt in Samuel and Psalms." *VT* 17 (1967):76–92.
Rowley, H. H. "The Structure of Psalm 42/43." *Bib* 21 (1940):45–55.
_____. "The Text and Structure of Psalm 2." *JTS* 42 (1941):143.
_____. "Melchizedek and Zadok (Gen. 14 and Ps. 110)." FS for A. Bertholet. Tübingen, 1950.
Ruppert, L. *"Zur Frage der Einheitlichkeit von Psalm 114."* In *Altes Testament: Forschung und Wirkung*. FS für H. Graf Reventlow. Ed. by P. Mommer and W. Thiel. Frankfurt am Main: Long, 1994. Pp. 81–94.
Sabottka, Liudger. "Rēʿeykā in Psalm 139:17." *Bib* 63 (1982):558–59.
Sanders, J. A. "The Scroll of Psalms (11QPsa) from Cave 11." *BASOR* 165 (1962):11–15.
_____. "Psalm 151 in 11QPsa." *ZAW* 75 (1963):73–86.
Sarna, N. M. "The Psalm for the Sabbath Day (Ps. 92)." *JBL* 81 (1962):155–168.
_____. "Psalm XIX and the Near Eastern Sun-God Literature." *Fourth World Congress of Jewish Studies* 1 (1967):171–75.
Schedl, C. "*Hesed* in Psalm 52 (51)." *BZ* (1961):259–60.
Schenkel, J. D. "An Interpretation of Ps. 93:5." *Bib* 46 (1965):401–16.
Schmidt, W. H. "Gott und Mensch in Ps. 130. Formgeschichtliche Erwägungen." *ThZ* 22 (1966):241–53.
Schmutzer, Andrew J. and Howard, David M. Jr. *The Psalms, Language for All Seasons of the Soul*. Chicago: Moody, 2013.

Schroeder, Christopher. "Psalm 3." *Bib* 81 (2000):243–51.
Seitz, C. R. "The Divine Council: Temporal Transition and New Prophecy in the Book of Isaiah." *JBL* 109 (1990):229–47. (Ps. 82)
Shafer, B. E. "The Root *bhr* and Pre-exilic Concepts of Chosenness in the Hebrew Bible." *ZAW* 89 (1977):20–42. (Ps. 135)
Sharrock, Graeme E. "Psalm 74: A Literary-Structural Analysis." *AUSS* 21 (1938):211–23.
Shepherd, John. "The Place of Imprecatory Psalms in the Canon of Scripture." *Churchman* 111 (1997):27–47, 110–26.
Shoemaker, H. Stephen. "Psalm 131." *RevExp* 85 (1988):89–94.
Skehan, P. W. "Strophic Structure in Psalm 72 (71)." *Bib* 40 (1959):302–8.
Šulj, Edo. "Musical Instruments in Psalm 150." In *The Interpretation of the Bible*. Ed. by Jože Krašovec. *JSOT* Supplement 289. Sheffield: Sheffield Academic Press, 1998. Pp. 1117–30.
Slotki, I. W. "Omnipresence, Condescension and Omniscience in Psalm 113:5–6." *JTS* 32 (1931):367–370.
_____. "Psalm 49:13, 21 (AV 12, 20)." *VT* 28 (1978):361–62.
Smick, E. B. "Mythological Language in the Psalms." *WTJ* 44 (1982):88–98. (Pss. 74, 82)
Smith Mark S. "The Invocation of Deceased Ancestors." *JBL* 112 (1993):105–7. (Ps. 49)
_____. "Psalm 8:2b–3." *CBQ* 59 (1997):637–41.
_____. "'Seeing God' in the Psalms: The Background to the Beatific Vision in the Hebrew Bible." *CBQ* 50 (1988):171–83. (Pss. 42, 43)
_____. "Setting and Rhetoric in Psalm 23." *JSOT* 41 (1988):61–66.
Snaith, H. *Hymns of the Temple (Pss. 42/43; 44; 46; 50–73)*. 1951 London: SCM Press, Ltd., 1951.
_____. "The Meaning of Hebrew אַף." *VT* 14 (1964):221–25.
_____. "Selah." *VT* 2 (1952):42–56.
Sonne, Isaiah. "Psalm 11." *JBL* 68 (1949):241–45.
_____. "The Second Psalm." *HUCA* 19 (1945):43–55.
Spangenberg, I. J. J. "Psalm 49 and the Book of Qoheleth." *Strif en kerk* 18 (1997):328–44.

Selected Bibliography for the Exposition of the Psalms

Spero, S. "Psalm 50: Prophetic Speech and God's Performative Utterances." In *Prophets and Paradigms.* Ed. by S. B. Reid. Sheffield: Sheffield Academic Press, 1996. Pp. 217–30.

Speiser, E. A. "'People' and 'Nation' of Israel." *JBL* 79 (1960):157–63.

_____. "The Stem *PLL* in Hebrew." *JBL* 82 (1963):301–6.

Steyl, C. "The Construct Noun, *Ešet,* in Ps. 58,9." *JNSL* 11 (1983):133–34.

Strugnell, John. "A Note on Ps. cxxvi.i." *JTS* 7 (1956):239–43.

Tate, Marvin. "An Exposition of Psalm 8." *Perspectives in Religious Studies* 28 (2001):343–59.

_____. "Psalm 88." *RevExp* 87 (1990):91–95.

Thierry, G. J. "Remarks on Various passages of the Psalms." *OTS* 13 (1963):77–82. (Ps. 7)

Thomas, D. W. "נצב in Psalm XXXIX 6." In *Studies in the Bible. FS* for M. H. Segal. *Publication of the Israel Society for Biblical Research* 17 (1964):10–16.

_____. "Hebrew עֱנִי, 'Captivity'." *JTS* 16 (1965):444–5. (Ps. 109)

_____. "The Meaning of זיו in Psalm lxxx. 14." *ExT* (1965):385.

_____. "A Note on זְרַמְתָּם שֵׁנָה יִהְיוּ in Psalm 90:5," *VT* 18 (1968):267–68.

_____. "The Root ידע in Hebrew. 2," *JTS* 36 (1935):409–412.

_____. "Some Observations on the Hebrew Word רַעֲנָן." In *Hebraische Wortforschung.* FS for Walter Baumgartner. *VT* Supplement 16. Leiden: E. J. Brill (1967). Pp. 387–97. (Ps. 92)

_____. "Some Rabbinic Evidence for a Hebrew Root ידע = (Arabic) *wd'*," *JQR* NS 37 (1946, 47):177–78.

Thomas, M. E. "Psalms 1 and 112 as a Paradigm for the Comparison of Wisdom Motifs in the Psalms," *JETS* 29 (1986):15–24.

Thompson, Thomas L. "From the Mouth of Babes, Strength: Psalm 8 and the Book of Isaiah." *SJOT* 16 (2002):226–45

Tigay, J. H. "Divine Creation of the King in Psalm 2:6." *Eretz-Israel* 23 (2003):246–51.

_____. "Psalm 7:5 and Ancient Near Eastern Treaties." *JBL* 89 (1970):176–86.

Torrance, T. F. "The Last of the Hallel Psalms." *EvTh* 28 (1956):101–108.
Treves, M. "The Date of Psalm 24." *VT* 10 (1960):428–37.
Tromp, N. "The Text of Psalm cxxx 5–6." *VT* 39 (1989):100–103.
Trull, G. V. "An Exegesis of Psalm 16:10." *BibSac* 161 (2004):304–21.
_____. "Views on Peter's Use of Psalm 16:8–11 in Acts 2:25–32." *BibSac* 161 (2004):194- 204.
Tsevat, Matitiahu. "God and the Gods in the Assembly." *HUCA* 40 (1969):123–37.
_____. "God and the Gods in the Assembly: An Interpretation of Psalm 82." In *The Meaning of the Book of Job and Other Studies*. New York: KTAV, 1986. Pp. 131–148.
_____. "Psalm XC 5–6." *VT* 35 (1985):115–17.
Tsumura, David Toshio. "The Literary Structure of Psalm 46,2–8." *AJBI* 6 (1980):29–55.
Tur-Sinai [Torczyner], H. H. "The Literary Character of the Book of Psalms." *OTS* 8 (1950):263–281.
VanGemeren, Willem A. "Psalm 131:2–*kegāmul:* The Problem of Meaning and Metaphor." *Hebrew Studies* 23 (1982):51–57.
Van der Ploeg, J. P. M. "Psalm 19 and Some of its Problems." *JEOL* 17 (1964):193–201.
_____. "Psalm cxxxiii and its Main Problems." In *Loven en geloven, FS* for N. H. Ridderbos. Amsterdam: Ton Bolland, 1975. Pp. 191–200.
Van der Wal, A. J. O. "The Structure of Psalm cxxix." *VT* 28 (1988):364–67.
Van Zijl, P. J. "A Discussion of the Root *ga'ar* (Rebuke)." In *Biblical Essays*. Edited by A. H. Van Zyl. Potchefstroom: Pro Rege-Pers, 1969. Pp. 56–63.
Van Zyl, A. H. "Psalm 19." *Biblical Essays 1966* (1967):142–58.
_____. "The Unity of Psalm 27." In *De Fructu Oris Sui. FS* for A. Van Selms. Ed. by I. H Eybers, et al. Leiden: E. J. Brill, 1971. Pp. 233–51.
Vawter, B. "Post-exilic Prayer and Hope." *CBQ* 37 (1975):460–70. (Ps. 90)
Vogels, Walter. "A Structural Analysis if Ps 1." *Bib* 60 (1979):410–16.
Victor, P. "Note on Psalm LXXX.13." *ExT* 76 (1965):294–95.

Vogt, E. "The 'Place in Life' of Psalm 23." *Bib* 34 (1953):195–211.
Volz, P. "Psalm 49." *ZAW* 55 (1937):235–65.
Wagner, N. E. "רִנָּה in the Psalter." *VT* 10 (1960):435–41. (Ps. 142)
Wahl, Harold Martin. "Psalm 90, 12." *ZAW* 106 (1994):116–23.
Waltke, B. K. "Responding to an Unethical Society." *Stimulus* 1 (1993):13–18.
Wanke, D. *Die Zionstheologie der Korachiten. Beiheft fur ZAW* 97 (1966):23–31.
Ward, J. M. "The Literary Form and the Liturgical Background of Psalm lxxxix." *VT* 11 (1961):321–39.
Ward, Martin J. "Psalm 109: David's Psalm of Vengeance." *AUSS* 18 (1980):163–168.
Watson, Wilfred G. E. "The Hidden Simile in Psalm 133." *Bib* 60 (1979):108–9.
Watts, J. D. W. "*Yahweh Malak* Psalms." *ThZ* 21 (1965):341–48. (93)
Watts, J. W. "Psalm 2 in the Context of Biblical Theology." *HBT* 12 (1990):73–97.
Weir, J. E. "The Perfect Way," *EvQ* 53 (1981):54–59.
Weir, T. H. "Psalm 121:1." *ExT* 27 (1915–16):90–91.
Wenham, J. W. "Large Numbers in the Old Testament." *TynB* 17 (1967):19–53. (Ps. 50)
Wernberg-Moller, P. "Two Difficult Passages in the Old Testament." *ZAW* 69 (1957):69–73. (Ps. 12)
Werner, Eric. "Musical Instruments." In *IDB* 3:474–5. (Ps. 33)
Westermann, C. "Psalm 90: A Thousand Years Are But As Yesterday." In *Living the Psalms*. Translated by J. R. Porter. Grand Rapids: Eerdmans, 1989. Pp. 156–65.
_____. "Struktur und Geschichte der Klage im Alten Testament." *ZAW* 66 (1954):44–80.
Whitley, C. F. "Psalm 99:8." *ZAW* 85 (1973):227–30.
_____. "Some Remarks on *lu* and *lo*." *ZAW* 87 (1975):212–4. (Ps. 100)
_____. "Textual and Exegetical Observations on Ps 45,4–7." *ZAW* 98 (1986):277–82.
_____. "The Text of Psalm 90, 5." *Bib* 63 (1982): 267–68.
Wildberger, H. "Die Thronenamen des Messias, Jes. 9, 5b." *ThZ* 16 (1960):285–97.

Whybray, R. N. "'Their Wrongdoings'" in Psalm 98:8." *ZAW* 81 (1969):237–39.

Wilfall, W. "The Foreign Nations: Israel's 'Nine Bows'." *Bulletin of Egyptological Seminar* 3 (1981):113–24.

Willesen, F. "The Cultic Situation of Psalm lxxiv." *VT* 2 (1952):289–306.

Williams, W. G. "Liturgical Problems in Enthronement Psalms." *JBR* 25 (1957):118–122.

Willis, John T. "An Attempt to Decipher Psalm 121:1b." *CBQ* 52 (1990):241–51.

———. "The Song of Hannah and Psalm 113." *CBQ* 35 (1975):139–54.

———. "Psalm 121 as a Wisdom Poem." *HAR* 11 (1987):435–51.

Willis, T. M. "So Great Is His Steadfast Love: A Rhetorical Analysis of Psalm 103." *Bib* 72 (1991):525–37.

Wolff, Hans Walter. "Der Aufruf zur Volksklage." *ZAW* 76 (1964):48–56.

———. "Psalm 1," *EvTh* 9 (1949, 50):385–94.

———. "Psalm 110:4." In *Herr, tue meine Lippen auf.* Edited by C. Eicholz. 2nd Edition. 5 Volumes. Wuppertal-Barmen: Müller, 1961. 5:310–23.

Wolverton, W. I. "The Psalmist's Belief in God's Presence." *CJT* 9 (1963):82–94. (Ps. 139)

———. "The Meaning of the Psalms." *ATR* 47 (1965):16–33.

Woudstra, Marten H. *The Ark of the Covenant from Conquest to Kingship.* Philadelphia: Presbyterian and Reformed Publishing Company, 1965. (Ps. 63)

Wright, D. P. "Ritual Analogy in Psalm 109." *JBL* 113 (1994):385–404.

Würthwein, E. "Erwägungen zu Psalm 73." *FS* for A. Bertholet. Tübingen, 1950. Pp. 532–49.

———. "Erwägungen zu Psalm 139." *VT* 7 (1957):165–182.

Yadin, Yigael. "New Gleanings on Resheph from Ugarit." In *Biblical and Related Studies Presented to Samuel Iwry.* Ed. by Ann Kort and Scott Morschauer. Winona lake, IN: Eisenbrauns, 1985. (Ps. 57)

Yaron, Reuven. "The Meaning of *zānaḥ*." *VT* 13 (1963):237–39. (Ps. 44)

Selected Bibliography for the Exposition of the Psalms

Young, E. J. *A Study of the Omnipresence of God.* London: Banner of Truth Trust, 1965. (Ps. 139).

Youngblood, R. "A New Look at Three Old Testament Roots for 'Sin.'" In *Biblical and Near Eastern Studies. FS* for W. S. LaSor. Ed. by G. A. Tuttle. Grand Rapids: Eerdmans, 1 978. (Ps. 51)

Zevit, Ziony. "Psalms at the Poetic Precipice." *HAR* 10 (1986):351–66. (Ps. 134)

Zimmerli, W. "Knowledge of God according to the Book of Ezekiel." In *I Am Yahweh.* Translated by D. W. Stott. Atlanta: John Knox Press, 1954/1982). (Ps. 100)

Zink, J. K. "Uncleanness and Sin. A Study of Job xiv 4 and Psalm li 7." *VT* 17 (1967):354–61.